Germany

24th Edition

by Christopher N. Anderson &
Caroline Sieg

WILEY

John Wiley & Sons, Inc.

Published by:

JOHN WILEY & SONS, INC.

111 River St.

Hoboken, NJ 07030-5774

ISBN 978-1-118-02743-1 (paper); ISBN 978-1-118-16903-2 (ebk); ISBN 978-1-118-16904-9 (ebk); ISBN 978-1-118-16905-6 (ebk)

Editor: Ian Skinnari
Production Editor: Lindsay Beineke
Cartographer: Elizabeth Puhl
Photo Editor: Richard Fox
Production by Wiley Indianapolis Composition Services
Front Cover Photo: Vineyard in the Rheingau region ©Mick Rock / Cephas Picture Library / Alamy
Back Cover Photo: Cyclists in front of the Brandenburg Gate, Berlin ©Lucas Vallecillos / AGE Fotostock, Inc.

CONTENTS

List of Maps viii

1 THE BEST OF GERMANY 1

The Best Experiences 1

The Best Museums 3

The Best Castles & Palaces 4

The Best Cathedrals 5

The Most charming Small
    Villages 6

The Best Driving Tours 7

The Best Walks 7

The Best Biking 8

The Best Spas 8

The Best Luxury Hotels 9

The Best Small Inns & Hotels 10

The Best Restaurants 10

The Best Beer Halls & Taverns 11

The Best Shopping 12

2 GERMANY IN DEPTH 13

Germany Today 13

Looking Back: German History 14

LIFE IS A CABARET 18

Art & Architecture 23

Germany in Pop Culture 30

GERMAN LITERATURE: FROM GUTENBERG TO
    GRASS 30

MEN (AND WOMEN) OF NOTE: GERMANY'S
    RICH MUSICAL HISTORY 32

BEYOND BAROQUE: THE MODERN GERMAN
    MUSIC SCENE 35

Eating & Drinking 37

THE BEST OF THE WURST 38

O'ZAPFSTISL ("THE BARREL IS TAPPED") 40

When to Go 41

CALENDAR OF EVENTS 41

Responsible Travel 43

Tours 44

3 SUGGESTED GERMANY ITINERARIES 47

The Regions in Brief 47

HIGHLIGHTS OF GERMANY IN 1 WEEK 51

The Rhineland & Northern Germany
    in 1 Week 55

SOUTHERN GERMANY IN 1 WEEK 56

Germany for Families 58

The Fairy-Tale Road 61

4 BERLIN 65

Essentials 66

BERLIN TODAY & TOMORROW 67

NEIGHBORHOODS IN BRIEF 69

SAFARI TOURS IN THAT SARDINE CAN
    ON WHEELS 75

FAST FACTS: BERLIN 76

Exploring Berlin 78

ART COLLECTIONS & WORLD WAR II 78

A DAY IN CHARLOTTENBURG 82

FROMMER'S FAVORITE BERLIN
EXPERIENCES 88

MARKER IDENTIFIES HITLER'S BUNKER 94

REMEMBERING THE BERLIN WALL 96

THE HISTORIC NIKOLAI QUARTER 97

ARCHITECTURE BEYOND THE MAIN
SIGHTS 99

FUN FOR KIDS 102

Where to Eat 103

Shopping 116

TREASURES IN THE BARN DISTRICT 118

CALLING ALL CERAMICS LOVERS 121

Entertainment & Nightlife 123

Where to Stay 133

A Side Trip: Potsdam & Its
Palaces 147

5 SAXONY & THURINGIA 154

Weimar 154

STATE-OF-THE-ART CHINA: MEISSEN
PORCELAIN 160

THE THURINGIAN FOREST: GERMANY'S
GREEN HEART 164

Leipzig 169

SINGING THROUGH THE CENTURIES: THE ST.
THOMAS BOYS' CHOIR 173

Dresden 184

Meissen 197

6 FRANCONIA & THE GERMAN DANUBE 200

Bayreuth 201

Bamberg 206

Nürnberg (Nuremberg) 211

CANAL & RIVERBOAT TOURS 214

Regensburg 221

Passau 226

CRUISING THE DANUBE 229

Ulm 230

7 THE ROMANTIC ROAD 235

Würzburg 236

A Detour to Miltenberg &
Amorbach 242

Weikersheim 245

Creglingen 246

Rothenburg ob der Tauber 247

Dinkelsbühl 253

Nördlingen 255

Donauwörth 257

Augsburg 259

Füssen 264

Neuschwanstein &
Hohenschwangau 267

THE FAIRY-TALE KING 268

8 MUNICH 273

Essentials 274

NEIGHBORHOODS IN BRIEF 278

FAST FACTS: MUNICH 281

Exploring Munich 283

FROMMER'S FAVORITE MUNICH
EXPERIENCES 287

Where to Eat 300

FAMILY-FRIENDLY RESTAURANTS 306

BEER GARDENS, CELLARS & TAVERNS 312

Shopping 314

Entertainment & Nightlife 316

Where to Stay 323

Side Trips from Munich 329

BEFORE HITLER, A BELOVED ARTISTS'
COLONY 330

9 THE BAVARIAN ALPS 331

Berchtesgaden 333
Bad Reichenhall 340
Chiemsee 342
Mittenwald 345

Garmisch-Partenkirchen 347
HIKING IN THE BAVARIAN ALPS 348
Oberammergau 354
SHOPPING FOR WOODCARVINGS 355

10 LAKE CONSTANCE (BODENSEE) 360

Lindau 361
Friedrichshafen 365
REBIRTH OF THE ZEPPELIN 367
Meersburg 368

Konstanz (Constance) 372
Reichenau 375
Überlingen 377
Ravensburg 379

11 THE BLACK FOREST (SCHWARZWALD) 383

Freiburg im Breisgau 384
AN EXCURSION TO THE UPPER
    BLACK FOREST 387
Titisee 390
Triberg 392
WUNDERHIKING IN THE BLACK FOREST 393

Freudenstadt 395
Calw 398
Pforzheim 400
MEDIEVAL EXCURSION FROM
    PFORZHEIM 401
Baden-Baden 402

12 HEIDELBERG, STUTTGART & THE NECKAR VALLEY 410

Heidelberg 410
Hirschhorn, Eberbach &
    Heilbronn 423
Stuttgart 426

Tübingen 435
Schwäbisch Hall 438

13 FRANKFURT 440

Essentials 441
FAST FACTS: FRANKFURT 445
Exploring Frankfurt 446
FRANKFURT'S TOWERS 448
Where to Eat 452

Shopping 457
Entertainment & Nightlife 459
Where to Stay 463
Side Trips from Frankfurt 469

14 THE RHINELAND 479

Speyer 479
WATCH ON THE RHINE 480
CRUISING THE MYTHICALLY RICH RIVERS OF GERMANY 482
Worms 484
Mainz 489
The Rheingau 494
Koblenz 497

Bonn 500
Bad Godesberg 505
Aachen (Aix-la-Chapelle) 506
Cologne (Köln) 510
BEER TAVERNS 518
Düsseldorf 525

15 THE MOSEL VALLEY 535

Cochem 535
Beilstein 539
Zell an der Mosel 539
Traben-Trarbach 541

Bernkastel-Kues 542
THE TASTE OF THE GRAPE & AN OVERNIGHT TOO 544
Trier 545

16 THE FAIRY-TALE ROAD 552

Hanau 552
Gelnhausen 555
Steinau an der Strasse 556
Fulda 557
Marburg 559
Kassel 561
GERMAN LEGENDS & THE BROTHERS GRIMM 564
Hann. Münden 565
Höxter 567

Bodenwerder 569
Hameln 570
Hannover 572
Bremen 578
Lüneburg 588
THE LÜNEBURG HEATH 589
Celle 591
Goslar 593
Göttingen 596

17 HAMBURG 600

Essentials 600
NEIGHBORHOODS IN BRIEF 602
FAST FACTS: HAMBURG 603
Exploring Hamburg 604
FAMILY-FRIENDLY ACTIVITIES 608
Where to Eat 608

Shopping 612
Entertainment & Nightlife 614
THE REEPERBAHN: A WALK ON THE WILD SIDE 617
Where to Stay 620

18 SCHLESWIG-HOLSTEIN 630

Lübeck 630

Kiel 637

Schleswig 640

The Island of Sylt 642

A DISAPPEARING PLAYGROUND 645

19 PLANNING YOUR TRIP TO GERMANY 648

Getting There 648

GETTING THROUGH THE AIRPORT 650

Getting Around 651

Tips on Accommodations 654

Fast Facts: Germany 658

20 USEFUL TERMS & PHRASES 669

Getting There & Getting
Around 669

General Terms 670

Menu Terms 672

Index 675

LIST OF MAPS

Germany's Historic Borders   15

The Berlin Wall   21

Suggested Germany Itineraries   53

Berlin Neighborhoods   70

Charlottenburg Attractions   79

Berlin-Mitte Attractions   81

Tiergarten Area Attractions   85

Berlin-Mitte Restaurants & Hotels   105

Western Berlin Restaurants & Hotels   106

Potsdam   149

Sanssouci Palace   151

Saxony & Thuringia   155

Weimar   157

Leipzig   171

Dresden   185

Franconia & the German Danube   203

Nürnberg   213

Würzburg   237

Rothenburg ob der Tauber   249

Augsburg   261

Füssen & the Royal Castles   269

Neuschwanstein   271

Munich Neighborhoods   276

Munich U-Bahn & S-Bahn   279

Central Munich Attractions   284

Residenz   289

Alte Pinakothek   291

Deutsches Museum   297

Central Munich Restaurants & Hotels   302

The Bavarian Alps   335

Lake Constance   363

The Black Forest   385

The Neckar Valley   411

Heidelberg   413

Stuttgart   427

Frankfurt   442

The Rhineland   481

Cologne (Köln)   511

Düsseldorf   527

The Mosel Valley   537

The Fairy-Tale Road   553

Bremen   579

What to See & Do in the Altstadt   605

Where to Stay & Eat in Hamburg   622

Schleswig-Holstein   631

ABOUT THE AUTHORS

Ever since packing his bag and leaving North Carolina, **Christopher N. Anderson** (chapters 6, 7, 8, 9, 10, 11, 12, 13, 15) has accumulated over thirteen years of traveling and writing experience. From crossing Siberia and sailing the Caribbean, to teaching English in Russia, Brazil, Switzerland, Austria and France, his diverse experiences have provided excellent fodder for his writing, featured in publications such as the *Vienna Review, Frommer's* and *Yanks Abroad*. In addition to his traveling exploits, he has earned a Master's in International Relations and speaks fluent French and German along with conversational Italian, Portuguese, Spanish, and Russian. More recently, he covered and reported live from the FIFA World Cup in South Africa.

Half-Swiss, half-American, **Caroline Sieg**'s (chapters 2, 4, 5, 14, 16, 17, 18, 19) relationship with Germany began with childhood trips to Munich to visit her Polish-German aunt. Later, she visited Berlin for the first time in 1989—two weeks after the Berlin Wall fell—and obtained her own piece of the wall. Later, she lived in Berlin and explored the often-overlooked northern part of the country. These days, she hangs her hat in London, but visits Germany as often as possible to indulge in *Kaffee und Kuchen* (coffee and cake), sniff out the best *currywurst* and explore the latest gallery opening.

HOW TO CONTACT US

In researching this book, we discovered many wonderful places—hotels, restaurants, shops, and more. We're sure you'll find others. Please tell us about them, so we can share the information with your fellow travelers in upcoming editions. If you were disappointed with a recommendation, we'd love to know that, too. Please write to:

Frommer's Germany, 24th Edition
John Wiley & Sons, Inc. • 111 River St. • Hoboken, NJ 07030-5774
frommersfeedback@wiley.com

ADVISORY & DISCLAIMER

Travel information can change quickly and unexpectedly, and we strongly advise you to confirm important details locally before traveling, including information on visas, health and safety, traffic and transport, accommodations, shopping and eating out. We also encourage you to stay alert while traveling and to remain aware of your surroundings. Avoid civil disturbances, and keep a close eye on cameras, purses, wallets, and other valuables.

While we have endeavored to ensure that the information contained within this guide is accurate and up-to-date at the time of publication, we make no representations or warranties with respect to the accuracy or completeness of the contents of this work and specifically disclaim all warranties, including without limitation warranties of fitness for a particular purpose. We accept no responsibility or liability for any inaccuracy or errors or omissions, or for any inconvenience, loss, damage, costs, or expenses of any nature whatsoever incurred or suffered by anyone as a result of any advice or information contained in this guide.

The inclusion of a company, organization, or website in this guide as a service provider and/or potential source of further information does not mean that we endorse them or the information they provide. Be aware that information provided through some websites may be unreliable and can change without notice. Neither the publisher nor author shall be liable for any damages arising herefrom.

FROMMER'S STAR RATINGS, ICONS & ABBREVIATIONS

Every hotel, restaurant, and attraction listing in this guide has been ranked for quality, value, service, amenities, and special features using a **star-rating system.** In country, state, and regional guides, we also rate towns and regions to help you narrow down your choices and budget your time accordingly. Hotels and restaurants are rated on a scale of zero (recommended) to three stars (exceptional). Attractions, shopping, nightlife, towns, and regions are rated according to the following scale: zero stars (recommended), one star (highly recommended), two stars (very highly recommended), and three stars (must-see).

In addition to the star-rating system, we also use **seven feature icons** that point you to the great deals, in-the-know advice, and unique experiences that separate travelers from tourists. Throughout the book, look for:

special finds—those places only insiders know about

fun facts—details that make travelers more informed and their trips more fun

kids—best bets for kids and advice for the whole family

special moments—those experiences that memories are made of

overrated—places or experiences not worth your time or money

insider tips—great ways to save time and money

great values—where to get the best deals

The following abbreviations are used for credit cards:

AE	American Express	DISC	Discover	V	Visa
DC	Diners Club	MC	MasterCard		

TRAVEL RESOURCES AT FROMMERS.COM

Frommer's travel resources don't end with this guide. Frommer's website, www.frommers.com, has travel information on more than 4,000 destinations. We update features regularly, giving you access to the most current trip-planning information and the best airfare, lodging, and car-rental bargains. You can also listen to podcasts, connect with other Frommers.com members through our active-reader forums, share your travel photos, read blogs from guidebook editors and fellow travelers, and much more.

THE BEST OF GERMANY

In this chapter, you'll find our carefully compiled lists of the best that Germany has to offer, from castles and cathedrals to spas, restaurants, and sightseeing—and nearly everything else you'll want to see and do.

THE best EXPERIENCES

o **Exploring the New Berlin:** Anyone who lived through the fear of the Cold War can't help but shudder at the memory of the Berlin Wall. Since reunification, civic planners, with almost manic enthusiasm, have demolished large sections of what once stood as a scar across the face of a defeated nation. The architectural changes and urban developments that constantly update the cityscape around Berlin's Friedrichstrasse and Potsdamer Platz can be confusing. But regardless of which renewal program is churning up rubble at the time of your visit, a pilgrimage through what used to be the most bitterly contested urban turf in Europe can't help but provoke powerful emotions. See chapter 4.

o **Spending a Midsummer's Night in a Biergarten:** When the temperature rises, head for the unpretentious cheer of the nearest *Biergarten* (everybody in Germany seems to have a favorite, so we're not even going to try to name the "best"). These watering holes, which often feature trellises, climbing vines, Chinese lanterns, and arbors, offer low-cost fun on soft summer nights. You can order platters of hearty food with your beer or bring your own picnic.

o **Cruising the Elbe, the Danube, and the Rhine:** This trio of rivers, along with their tributaries, dominated German commerce for hundreds of years. Today, an armada of tugboats, barges, and cruise ships still plies the muddy waters beside riverbanks lined with the historic majesty (and sometimes the industrial might) of central Europe. Cruises begin and end at large cities of historic interest and last anywhere from 6 hours to 7 days. See "A Cruise on the Elbe" in chapter 5, "Cruising the Danube" in chapter 6, and "Cruising the Mythically Rich Rivers of Germany" in chapter 14.

o **Boating on the Königssee:** A "King's Lake" must surely be the best, and the natural beauty surrounding this body of cold, dark water doesn't disappoint. The quiet boat ride using electric motors will allow you to hear the echoes off the forest-covered mountainsides, as you discover baroque chapels and isolated hamlets along the shore. It might just make a Romantic poet out of you. See p. 337.

o **Hiking in the Bavarian Alps:** If you're heeding the call to climb every mountain, then the Bavarian Alps are the place to be in summer. Germany's excellent network of trails, guides, and huts will allow you to discover the wealth of wildlife and stunning scenery. Two of the countless highlights include the 1,240m (4,070-ft.) Eckbauer south of Partenkirchen, and the southeastern "ear lobe" of Berchtesgaden National Park. See chapter 9.

o **Ascending the Zugspitze:** If the gentle inclines of the Harz Mountains or the Thuringian forests aren't dramatic enough for you, ride the cable car from Garmisch-Partenkirchen to the top of Germany's tallest mountain, 2,960m (9,700 ft.) above sea level. The view from the top is suitably panoramic, and you'll find an appealing aura of German-ness that comes from the many climbers and trekkers who fan out across the hiking trails. See p. 349.

o **Experiencing a German Spa:** In Germany, the question isn't whether to visit a spa, but rather which spa to visit. Each resort has its virtues and historical associations, and can supply a list of the health benefits associated with its awful-tasting waters. Regardless of your choice, you'll emerge from your treatment with a more relaxed attitude and a greater appreciation of German efficiency and sensuality. The most famous spas are in Baden-Baden. See p. 402.

o **Motoring along the Neckar:** The Neckar River meanders through about 80km (50 miles) of some of Germany's most famous vineyards. But the real appeal of the winding road along the water is the medieval castles scattered along the way. Highlights en route include Heidelberg, Neckarsteinach, Hirschhorn, Eberbach, Zwingenberg, and Burg Hornberg. Don't forget to stop en route for samplings of the local wines. See chapter 12.

o **Spending Harvest Time in the German Vineyards:** Springtime in Germany brings the promise of bounty to the legendary vineyards of the Rhine and Mosel valleys, but the autumn harvest is truly the time to visit. Between late August and mid-October, the banks of the rivers turn gold and russet, and armies of workers gather buckets of grapes from rows of carefully pruned vines. Most of the medieval villages and historic castles scattered between Koblenz and Trier are associated with estates where you can sample the wines. See chapters 14 and 15.

o **Touring the Fairy-Tale Road (Märchenstrasse):** This is one of the newer marketing ideas of the German tourist authorities, but considering its appeal, you'll wonder why they didn't think of it earlier. From the town of Hanau (a 30-min. drive northeast of Frankfurt), the route zigzags northward along the Weser River for about 600km (370 miles), through some of Germany's most evocative folkloric architecture, ending in Bremen. Scores of well-marked detours pepper the way. Required reading for the trip is a collection of the fairy tales of the Brothers Grimm and the Nibelungen legends. Don't overlook the psychological implications of Goldilocks, the Big Bad Wolf, and the Pied Piper of Hameln. See chapters 3 and 16.

o **Lounging on the Island of Sylt:** Don't expect a lush or verdant island—the climate is temperamental, the setting is savage, the winds blow cold from the north even in summer, and the grasses that manage to survive in the sandy dunes are as weathered and sturdy as the soldiers in a Prussian regiment. Why is it wonderful? Here, the no-nonsense residents of north Germany can preen, flutter, and show off to each other, far from the strictures of their workplaces and the hardworking grind of their everyday lives. See p. 642.

THE best MUSEUMS

Financial prosperity, artistic flair, and academic curiosity have helped the Germans develop some of the finest museums anywhere.

o **Neues Museum,** Berlin: Left in ruins for decades after World War II, this museum today houses one of the greatest Egyptian museums in the world, filled with plunder from ancient Egypt. It is home to the celebrated bust of Queen Nefertiti, and its Papyrus Collection is also one of the finest in the world. See p. 97.

o **Bode-Museum,** Berlin: One of the greatest museums of Germany, the Bode reopened in 2008 to great acclaim. It houses a vast array of museums including a collection of late ancient and Byzantine art. The Picture Gallery is one of the grandest in Germany, and it is particularly strong in masterpieces from the Dutch and German schools of the 15th and 16th centuries. See p. 97.

o **Gemäldegalerie,** Berlin: This is one of Europe's leading art museums, with a celebrated collection of works from the 13th to the 18th century. The cavalcade of major European masters ranges from Botticelli and Bruegel to Vermeer and Velázquez. Divided during the Cold War, the collection has been reunited in one home since 1998. The lighting and displays are better than ever. See p. 84.

o **Pergamonmuseum,** Berlin: Built in 1930 on an island in the Spree, this museum contains entirely reconstructed temples from ancient Assyria, Greece, Rome, and Sumer. Don't miss the sprawling exhibitions devoted to the ancient art of the Islamic world and the Far East. See p. 98.

o **Zwinger,** Dresden: A vast rectangular esplanade flanked with pavilions, heroic statues, formal gardens, and galleries, this museum was designed for August the Strong (elector of Saxony and king of Poland), by his favorite architect, Pöppelmann (1662–1736). The destruction of the Zwinger (in the final days of World War II), one of Dresden's most beautiful buildings, was a great loss, though its postwar reconstruction was a triumph for the East German government. Among the treasures amassed inside are paintings, 18th-century Dresden porcelain, and an ornamental collection of antique weapons. See p. 188.

o **Deutsches Museum,** Munich: Since 1925, this Louvre of science and technology has led the way in documenting humanity's innovation. Thoroughly fascinating and amusingly hands-on, its historical exhibits will surely keep you entertained for hours. See p. 295.

o **Alte Pinakothek,** Munich: This outstanding collection of paintings spanning the 15th to 18th centuries rivals its counterparts in Cologne and Berlin. Its Rubens are gems, and Dürer fans may have to be subdued by the guards. The 19th-century hall provides just the right dosage of art for a few hours. See p. 290.

o **Dachau Concentration Camp Memorial Site,** Dachau, near Munich: Heinrich Himmler first organized Dachau as a concentration camp for enemies of the Reich in 1933. An escaped inmate, Joseph Rovan, described it as "implacable, perverted, an organization that was totally murderous, a marvelous machine for the debasement and dehumanizing of man." Today, it's one of the most poignant museums in the world. See p. 329.

o **Lenbachhaus,** Munich: Housed in the former villa of portrait painter Franz von Lenbach, this museum has a stunning and internationally renowned collection of modern art. In addition to works from the Blaue Reiter (Blue Rider) group, including Kandinsky, a rich collection of Gothic artwork is an added treat. See p. 292.

o **Gutenberg Museum,** Mainz: This museum is one of the most comprehensive tributes to printing and publishing anywhere in the world. The bulky presses, on which Johannes Gutenberg used movable type (42 lines per page), and two of the earliest Bibles ever printed are the primary displays here. There's also a historical rundown on the science and technologies that have dominated the printing industry ever since. See p. 490.

o **Museum Ludwig,** Cologne: This is the home of one of the world's largest collections of the works of Pablo Picasso, equaled only by the Picasso museums of Barcelona and Paris. The museum's collection was beefed up when Irene Ludwig, widow of the late German art patron Peter Ludwig, donated 774 works of Picasso to the museum. See p. 514.

o **Wallraf-Richartz Museum/Foundation Corboud,** Cologne: The oldest museum in Cologne presents one of Germany's grandest collections of art, covering the 14th to the 19th century. The collection of Gothic works alone is one of the finest in Europe, and the galleries are a virtual encyclopedia of art, from Flemish old masters to the French Impressionists. See p. 515.

o **Kunsthalle,** Hamburg: The leading art museum in northern Germany, the Kunsthalle is one of the most important in Europe, with some 3,000 paintings in its treasure-trove, along with some 400 sculptures. Some of its rare treasures date from the 14th century, including works by Bertram, the leading German master of the time. One section of the gallery also displays modern works, including pieces by such artists as Andy Warhol, Joseph Beuys, and Picasso. See p. 606.

THE best CASTLES & PALACES

During the Middle Ages, Germany was divided into many intensely competitive feudal states and principalities. This unstable atmosphere encouraged the construction of fortified castles. As hostilities died down, architects began to design for comfort, style, and prestige, adding large windows, gilded stucco and plaster, frescoes, and formal gardens. As a result, Germany is full of all kinds and styles of *Burg* and *Schloss* (various names for castles and palaces).

o **Sanssouci Palace,** Potsdam: Friedrich the Great's retreat, where he came to read, listen to music, and generally renew his allegiance to the principles of the Enlightenment, is Germany's most successful blend of landscape and architecture. The more than 120 hectares (300 acres) of intricately landscaped gardens have enough pavilions, fountains, orangeries, and heroic statues to keep a visitor intrigued for days. The palace itself is an architectural highlight, approached by a terraced staircase of sublime beauty. See p. 148.

o **Schloss Wartburg,** Eisenach: Built between the 11th and 16th centuries, this was the headquarters of the Landgraves of Thuringia, a center of patronage for the *Minnesinger* (troubadours) of Germany, and a place of refuge for Martin Luther, who completed his translation of the Bible within its massive walls. Wagner used it as inspiration for the setting of *Tannhäuser,* and Johann Sebastian Bach and Goethe both visited. Today, from its position on a rocky hilltop, it's a regional museum. See p. 168.

o **Residenz,** Würzburg: Built between 1720 and 1744 as the official residence of the powerful bishops of Würzburg, this is one of the most massive baroque palaces in Germany. It combines a *Hofkirche* (chapel) with gardens, a gallery of paintings, frescoes by Tiepolo, and enough decoration to satisfy the most demanding taste for ornamentation. Also within its showrooms are a worthy collection of ancient Greek and Roman artifacts and valuable paintings from the 14th to the 19th century. See p. 238.

○ **Neuschwanstein,** near Füssen: Love it or hate it, this fairy-tale castle is actually a phenomenon worth seeing. Enter the romantic world of "Mad" King Ludwig II and his theater set designer, a world that further inspired the folks at Disneyland, or marvel at the tourist circus surrounding the 19th-century fantasy. Either way, the outstanding mountain scenery alone is worth the trip. See p. 267.

○ **Hohenschwangau Castle,** near Füssen: Watching its bombastic younger brother from the opposite hill, this lesser-known residence built on 12th-century ruins merits just as much a visit. Finished in 1836, the eventual king Maximilian II lived here with his family, which included the young Ludwig II. See p. 267.

○ **Schloss Nymphenburg,** Munich: This summer palace constructed between 1664 and 1674 features fine interiors on a modest scale that will leave you with enough energy to enjoy the splendid gardens and pavilions. An ideal place to experience the former glory of the long-lost Bavarian kingdom. See p. 296.

○ **Schloss Linderhof,** near Oberammergau: This palace was built in the 1870s as a teenage indulgence by Ludwig II. Its architects created a whimsically eclectic fantasy, inspired by Italian baroque architecture. In the surrounding park, Moorish pavilions and Mediterranean cascades appear against Alpine vistas in combinations that are as startling as they are charming. See p. 358.

○ **Altes Schloss,** Meersburg: Legend has it that this palace's cornerstone was laid in 628 by Dagobert, king of the Franks. The palace remained a Catholic stronghold even during the Protestant Reformation, housing bishops who appreciated its 3m-thick (10-ft.) walls as a bulwark against the rising tempest around them. In the early 1800s, when its owners threatened to tear the palace down, a German Romantic, Baron Joseph von Lassberg, bought it and transformed it into a refuge for writers, poets, and painters. Although it remains mostly a private residence, you can visit many parts of the palace. See p. 369.

○ **Heidelberg Castle,** Heidelberg: This castle originated as a Gothic-Renaissance masterpiece in the 1500s and was massively expanded as rival rulers competed for control of the Rhineland. After the French sacked and burned the town and the castle in 1689, it never regained its original glory. Today, the ruins brood in dignified severity from a position on a rocky hilltop high above the student revelry and taverns of the folkloric city below. See p. 414.

○ **Burg Eltz,** Moselkern, near Cochem: Its multiple turrets and towers, which rise amid a thick forest near the Mosel River, evoke the chivalry and poetry of the Middle Ages. This is one of the best-preserved medieval castles in Germany. See p. 538.

THE best CATHEDRALS

○ **Kaiserdom (Imperial Cathedral),** Speyer: Partly because of their age, Romanesque churches are the most impressive symbols of early medieval Germany. This massive church, from 1030, has four bell towers; a cornerstone laid by one of Germany's earliest kings, Konrad II; and an undeniable sense of the (anonymous) architect's aesthetic links with the traditions of ancient Rome. See p. 480.

○ **Dom St. Peter,** Worms: This church is a grand example of High Romanesque style, its oldest section dating from 1132. The Diet of Worms, held here in 1521, condemned the beliefs of the young Martin Luther and banished him to the far boundaries of the Holy Roman Empire. See p. 485.

o **Kölner Dom,** Cologne: Based on French Gothic models in Paris and Amiens, this cathedral was envisioned as one of the largest religious buildings in Christendom. It required 600 years to finish—work stopped for about 300 years (1560–1842), until the neo-Gothic fervor of the Romantic age fueled its completion. In 1880, it was inaugurated with appropriate pomp and circumstance in the presence of the German kaiser. Today, its vast russet-colored bulk towers are instantly recognizable from miles away. See p. 513.

o **Dom (Cathedral),** Aachen: Its size and the stonework dating from 1414 are deeply impressive, but even more so is the cathedral's association with the earliest of German emperors, Charlemagne. He was crowned in an older building on this site in A.D. 800. The cathedral's treasury contains gem-encrusted Christian artifacts from the 10th century, with heft and barbaric glitter that evoke pre-Christian Germania. See p. 507.

THE most charming SMALL VILLAGES

o **Quedlinburg:** Spared in part from the ravages of World War II, this town in the Harz mountains still evokes the Middle Ages with its 1,600 half-timbered buildings, more than any other town in the country. Named a UNESCO World Heritage Site, Quedlinburg is a gem of yesterday and was an imperial residence for 2 centuries. Wander the cobblestone streets of the Altstadt (Old Town) for a journey back in time. See p. 182.

o **Meissen:** Some 25km (16 miles) north of Dresden, this is a romantic little town built along the banks of the River Elbe. It's celebrated for its porcelain, which carries a trademark of two crossed blue swords and is valued by collectors the world over. Even without its porcelain factory, the town merits a visit for its quiet charm, its old buildings, and its 15th-century castle. See p. 197.

o **Rothenburg:** If you have time for only one stop along the Romantic Road, make it Rothenburg ob der Tauber, which may be your only chance in life to see a still-intact medieval walled city. Rothenburg exists in a time capsule, though 40% of the town was destroyed during World War II. Luckily, locals quickly rebuilt their Altstadt in its former style to reclaim their glorious architectural past. See p. 247.

o **Dinkelsbühl:** If you have time for a second stop along the Romantic Road, try Dinkelsbühl. Though not as grand as the more celebrated Rothenburg, it has far fewer tourists and therefore retains more old-time charm. See p. 253.

o **Mittenwald:** This town has long been celebrated as the most beautiful in the Bavarian Alps, with magnificently decorated houses, painted facades and ornately carved gables. In the mid–17th century, it was known as "the Village of a Thousand Violins" because of the stringed instruments made here. See p. 345.

o **Lindau:** Dating from the 9th century, this former free imperial town of the Holy Roman Empire is like a fantasy of what a charming Bavarian lakeside village should look like, if only in the movies. But this garden "city," under landmark protection, is for real. Lindau is enveloped by aquamarine waters, and one part of it is known as the Gartenstadt because of its luxuriant flowers and shrubs. See p. 361.

- **Rüdesheim:** The Rhine Valley's most popular wine town is set along the edge of the mighty river. Rüdesheim is known for its half-timbered buildings and its Drosselgasse (Thrush Lane), a narrow cobblestone lane stretching for 180m (600 ft.) and lined with wine taverns and cozy restaurants. See p. 495.

- **Cochem:** If you're seeking an idyllic medieval riverside town during your "grape tour" of the Mosel River valley, make it Cochem, famous for its towering castle, dating from 1027. On the left bank of the Mosel, Cochem lies in a picture-postcard setting of vineyards. Little inns serving a regional cuisine along with plenty of Mosel wine make Cochem a highly desirable overnight stop and a nice alternative to the more commercial centers found along the nearby Rhine. See p. 535.

THE best DRIVING TOURS

The appeal of the open road is a prominent part of German culture. Some of the best drives include the following:

- **The Romantic Road:** This well-traveled 350km (220 mile) route, which stretches between Würzburg and Füssen at the foot of the Bavarian Alps, is dotted with lovely medieval towns. See chapter 7.

- **The Fairy-Tale Road:** The colorful characters of the Brothers Grimm live again along this 595km (370-mile) stretch, beginning in the little town of Hanau and stretching all the way north to Bremen. This is one of the great motor trips of Germany for those who thrilled to those nursery-room favorites. See "The Fairy-Tale Road" in chapter 3 for an abbreviated route. For the complete route, see chapter 16.

- **Alpine Road:** Scenic majesty and architectural charm combine for an unforgettable experience on this 480km (300-mile) road through the foothills of the Bavarian Alps. See "Exploring the Region by Car" on p. 332.

- **Upper Black Forest:** Fairy tales always seem more believable when you're in the Black Forest, and the twisting secondary roads that connect Freiburg with Lake Titisee pass through lots of charming scenery and architecture. See the box "An Excursion to the Upper Black Forest" on p. 387.

- **Mosel Valley:** The road along this Rhine tributary passes by some of the country's most famous vineyards. At least a half-dozen of the cities en route are worth visiting as well. See chapter 15.

THE best WALKS

- **The Royal Castle Walk:** For one of the grandest panoramas in all of the Alps (in any country), hike up to the Marienbrücke, the bridge that spans the Pöllat Gorge behind Neuschwanstein Castle. From there, if you're up to it, you can continue uphill for about an hour for an amazing view of "Mad" King Ludwig's fantasy castle. See "Neuschwanstein & Hohenschwangau" in chapter 7.

- **Partnachklamm:** One of the most dramatic walks in all of the Bavarian Alps starts from the great winter sports resort of Garmisch-Partenkirchen. A signposted trail leads to the dramatic Partnachklamm Gorge. Carved from solid rock, the route passes two panoramic bottlenecks amid the thunder of falling water and clouds of spray. See "Hiking in the Bavarian Alps" in chapter 9.

- **Mainau Island:** A walk across the footbridge to Mainau, in Lake Constance, is like a visit to a tropical country. Mainau is filled with exotic plants collected by the

Baden princes and members of the Royal House of Sweden. Tropical brushwood and other botanical wonders still thrive in this mild climate. You'll hardly believe you're in Germany. See p. 373.

o **Cochem:** Reichsburg Cochem (Cochem Castle), which towers over the little town of the same name, can be reached on foot in about 15 minutes from the town's Marktplatz. Although hardly an Alpine climb, this walk is one of the most rewarding you'll find in Germany, with panoramas in all directions. See p. 535.

THE best BIKING

o **Munich by Bike:** You see so many locals riding bikes that you might think Munich is the biking capital of Germany. If you'd like to join the fun, pick up a copy of the pamphlet *Rad-Touren für unsere Gäste (Bike-Riding for Our Guests)* at the tourist office. It outlines itineraries for touring Munich by bike. See p. 273.

o **Lake Constance:** Rent a bike at the train station in the former imperial town of Lindau, and set out in any direction to enjoy the views of this beautiful lake. The Lindau tourist office will provide a map and suggestions for the best routes to follow. See p. 360.

o **The Neckar Valley Cycle Path:** This signposted path allows you to follow the source of the Neckar, beginning in Villingen-Schwenningen and going all the way to the confluence of the Rhine at Mannheim. Instead of going the entire way, many visitors prefer to pick up a bicycle in Heidelberg and cycle along the riverbanks until they find a good spot for a picnic. See "Exploring on Two Wheels" on p. 412.

o **Lüneburg Heath:** This wild heath in northern Germany is one of the country's major natural attractions. (Some of Germany's greatest poets have waxed rhapsodic about this shrub-covered land.) Rent a bike, pick up a map at the Lüneburg tourist office, and set out on your adventure. See "The Lüneburg Heath" on p. 589.

THE best SPAS

o **Bad Reichenhall:** Many spa lovers head for this remote corner of Bavaria to "take the waters." Europe's largest saline source was first tapped in pre-Christian times and the place has a definite 19th-century aura. And though some of the hotels in the town are better than others, all have equal access to the spa and lie about a 5-minute walk away. See "Bad Reichenhall" in chapter 9.

o **Baden-Baden:** There's no better spa in all of Germany, and certainly none more fashionable or famous—it's also site of the country's most celebrated casino. Baden-Baden's spa's been going strong since the leisure class of the 19th century discovered its healing waters, although the Roman legions of Emperor Caracalla had discovered the springs long before that. As at Bad Reichenhall, all hotels, no matter the price range, have equal access to the spa. See "Baden-Baden" in chapter 11.

o **Wiesbaden:** One of Germany's oldest cities, Wiesbaden attracted Roman legions to its hot springs, and lures today's fashionable traveler as well. It's not as chic as Baden-Baden, but Wiesbaden has one of Germany's most elegant casinos and concert halls, along with two gourmet restaurants. In summer, the beer garden at the Kurhaus is one of the liveliest along the Rhine. See "Side Trips from Frankfurt" in chapter 13.

- **Bad Homburg:** Bad Homburg lies at the foot of the Taunus Hills in a setting of medieval castles and luxuriant forests. There are more than 31 fountains in the town's Kurpark. The Bad Homburg Palace was once the summer residence of Prussian kings. See "Side Trips from Frankfurt" in chapter 13.

THE best LUXURY HOTELS

German efficiency and cleanliness are legendary, so it's not surprising that you can choose from a great number of well-managed hotels.

- **Grand Hotel Esplanade,** Berlin (www.esplanade.de; ✆ 866/597-8341 in the U.S., or 030/254788255): This strikingly contemporary hotel near several foreign embassies is one of the most prestigious in the German capital. With its collection of modern art, its spacious, cheerfully decorated rooms, and its first-class service, it is a prime address for the luxury minded. See p. 135.
- **The Regent,** Berlin (www.theregentberlin.com; ✆ 888/201-1806 in the U.S., or 030/20338): One of Germany's great luxury hotels, the Regent is all about opulence, superb service, and comfort. It's discreet, tasteful, reliable, and a brilliant addition to the roster of luxury leaders in Germany's capital. See p. 142.
- **Hotel Elephant,** Weimar (www.starwoodhotels.com; ✆ 03643/8020): This is one of Germany's most interesting hotels because of its age (over 300 years), its name, its 50-year survival in Germany's eastern zone, and its associations with such luminaries as Schiller, Liszt, and Goethe. Today, it's a cost-conscious treasure chest of German history. See p. 162.
- **Eisenhut,** Rothenburg ob der Tauber (www.eisenhut.com; ✆ 09861/7050): This hotel's 16th-century walls and valuable collection of antiques enhance the appeal of the most authentic Renaissance town in Germany. See p. 252.
- **Hotel Vier Jahreszeiten Kempinski München,** Munich (www.kempinski.com; ✆ 800/426-3135 in the U.S., or 089/21250): Munich's most prestigious choice offers elegance and luxury. The wealthy and titled have checked in here for more than a century, enjoying the ambience, the antiques, the style, and the grace. See p. 324.
- **Bayerischer Hof & Palais Montgelas,** Munich (www.bayerischerhof.de; ✆ 089/21200): This deluxe hotel and 17th-century Bavarian palace together form Munich's answer to New York's Waldorf-Astoria. This is the only hotel in Munich to provide serious competition for the Kempinski Hotel. See p. 323.
- **Der Kleine Prinz,** Baden-Baden (www.derkleineprinz.de; ✆ 07221/346600): This hotel's director once helped manage the New York Hilton and the Waldorf-Astoria. Today, he and his wife run a century-old pair of neobaroque houses in the heart of Germany's most elegant resort, Baden-Baden. Inspired by Saint-Exupéry's *The Little Prince* this stands as one of the most romantic of Germany's many romantic hotels. See p. 407.
- **Krone Assmannshausen,** Rüdesheim-Assmannshausen (www.hotel-krone.com; ✆ 06722/4030): Sprawling along the banks of the Rhine in an oversize, grange-like, gingerbread-laden fantasy, this hotel has witnessed the arrival of many important Germans (including Goethe) in its 400 years. It also contains one of the best traditional restaurants in town. See p. 496.
- **Fürstenhof Celle,** Celle (www1.fuerstenhof.de; ✆ 05141/2010): This 17th-century manor, enlarged with half-timbered wings, stands out even in a town legendary for its medieval and Renaissance buildings. There's a cozy bar in the medieval cellar and one of the best dining rooms in Lower Saxony. See p. 592.

o **Fairmont Hotel Vier Jahreszeiten,** Hamburg (www.fairmont.com/hamburg; ℂ 888/425-8227 in the U.S. and Canada, or 040/34940): Its dignified interior is as opulent as its 19th-century facade. This hotel's appeal is correctly aristocratic, but it has a touch of the saltwater zestiness that makes Hamburg a great city. See p. 626.

THE best SMALL INNS & HOTELS

o **Art'otel,** Berlin (www.artotels.com; ℂ 030/884470): This hotel in the heart of Berlin is chic, discreet, and unique. The swirling action of the Ku'Damm lies right outside the door, but inside, the decor is soothing and serene, the work of some of the Continent's top designers. See p. 139.

o **Altstadt-Hotel,** Passau (www.altstadt-hotel.de; ℂ 0851/3370): This inexpensive hotel stands at the convergence of three rivers—the Danube, the Ilz, and the Inn. But the hotel offers more than river views—it's comfortably and traditionally furnished, and its regional cuisine and convivial pub attract the locals. See p. 229.

o **Gästehaus Englischer Garten,** Munich (www.hotelenglischergarten.de; ℂ 089/3839410): This is an oasis of charm and tranquillity, close to the Englischer Garten, where buffed Munich lies out nude in the sun. The furnishings are in an old-fashioned Bavarian style, but the comfort level is first-rate. See p. 328.

o **Parkhotel Atlantic Schlosshotel,** Heidelberg (www.parkhotel-atlantic.de; ℂ 06221/60420): This 24-room inn is on the wooded outskirts of Heidelberg, near the famous castle. Every room is comfortable and convenient, and in the afternoon you can go for long walks along the woodland trails surrounding the property. See p. 421.

o **Antik-Hotel Bristol,** Cologne (www.antik-hotel-bristol.de; ℂ 0221/120195): In the heart of this cathedral city along the Rhine, this unique hotel is filled with antiques, both country rustic and town-house elegant, making the atmosphere both authentic and inviting. See p. 523.

THE best RESTAURANTS

o **Die Quadriga,** Berlin (ℂ 030/214050; www.brandenburger-hof.com): Critics hail this gastronomic wonder in the Hotel Brandenburger Hof as Berlin's finest dining choice. Celebrated for its modern Continental cuisine, it's where the president of Germany takes his favorite guests when he wants to "show off." While seated in a 1904 chair designed by Frank Lloyd Wright, you can enjoy food that is, in a word, sublime. See p. 104.

o **Essigbrätlein,** Nürnberg (ℂ 0911/225131): Food critics single this out as the best dining spot in Nürnberg, and we heartily agree. Its upscale Franconian and Continental cuisine is reason enough to visit the city. See p. 217.

o **Weinhaus Zum Stachel,** Würzburg (ℂ 0931/52770; www.weinhaus-stachel.de): This is the oldest (ca. 1413) wine house in a town loaded with them. Food is good, portions are copious, the wine flows, and everyone has a wonderful time. This is old-time Deutschland at its most appealing. See p. 239.

o **Tantris,** Munich (ℂ 089/3619590; www.tantris.de): Savvy German food critics have honored Tantris's Hans Haas as the country's top chef. He definitely serves some of the finest and most innovative food in Bavaria. See p. 311.

- **Hanse Stube,** Cologne (© 0221/2701; www.excelsiorhotelernst.com): Located in a landmark hotel, this restaurant lies on the same square as the fabled Rhineland cathedral. French cuisine in Cologne doesn't get any better than this—the chefs have a prodigious talent for preparing food using only the finest and freshest ingredients. See p. 516.

- **Victorian Restaurant,** Düsseldorf (© 0211/865500; www.restaurant-victorian. de): Regulars know what a treasure they have in this restaurant: Market-fresh ingredients and a steady hand in the kitchen produce award-winning traditional and modern food. See p. 530.

- **Waldhotel Sonnora,** outside Bernkastel-Kues (© 06578/406; www.hotel-sonnora.de): In the Mosel Valley, the Waldhotel Sonnora is one of the most justifiably acclaimed restaurants in the country. Be sure to make a reservation as far in advance as possible and prepare yourself for a gastronomic adventure in Continental cuisine. Herr Thieltges, the chef, told us, "We don't just serve dishes—rather, culinary masterpieces." We agree. See p. 543.

- **Fischereihafen Restaurant,** Altona, near Hamburg (© 040/381816; www. fischereihafenrestaurant.de): Patrons from Tina Turner to Helmut Kohl have pronounced the food here delightful. From a window seat, you can overlook the boats that might have hauled in your sole, eel, turbot, herring, or flounder from the seas that day. See p. 609.

THE best BEER HALLS & TAVERNS

- **Auerbachs Keller,** Leipzig (© 0341/216100; auerbachs-keller-leipzig.de): The most famous tavern in eastern Germany, this is where Goethe staged the debate between Faust and Mephistopheles. The tavern dates from 1530 and has a series of murals evoking the Faust legend. See p. 174.

- **Augustiner Bräustuben,** Munich (© 089/5022569; www.braeustuben.de): Although many raid the famous Hofbräuhaus (see below), this authentic tavern at the backdoor of the Augustiner brewery combines the Bavarian camaraderie and flavorful fare without the tourist circus. It occupies the former horse stalls, but don't fret—the odor has long since dissipated. Best of all, they fill the massive *Mass* glasses for one of the lowest prices in town.

- **Hofbräuhaus,** Munich (© 089/221676; www.hofbraeuhaus.de): Needing no introduction, the Hofbräuhaus can stake the claim as the world's most famous beer hall, packing in up to 4,500 beer drinkers on any given night. Music from live bands and huge mugs of beer served at wooden tables combine to produce the best of Bavarian nighttime fun. See p. 313.

- **Zum Roten Ochsen,** Heidelberg (© 06221/20977; www.roterochsen.de): Over the years, "The Red Ox" has drawn beer drinkers from Mark Twain to Bismarck. Students have been getting plastered here since 1703, and the tradition continues to this day. See p. 419.

- **Ratskeller,** Bremen (© 0421/321676; ratskeller-bremen.de): This is one of the most celebrated Ratskellers in Germany. A tradition for decades, it serves top-notch German and international food and some of the best suds along the Rhineland, as well as one of the longest lists of vintage wines from the country's vineyards. See p. 583.

THE best SHOPPING

The best way to approach shopping here is to make it a part of your overall experience and not an end unto itself. Though Berlin and Munich are the major shopping centers in Germany, the rest of the country is okay—neither a shopper's mecca nor the bargain basement of Europe. Still, you can find some good buys here.

o **Porcelain:** For centuries, Germany has been known for the quality of its porcelain. Names such as KPM, Rosenthal, and Meissen are household words. KPM, for example, has been a Berlin tradition for more than 2 centuries.

o **Handicrafts:** In the Bavarian Alps, woodcarvers still carry on their time-honored tradition. The best place to purchase woodcarvings is in the Alpine village of Oberammergau. See "Shopping for Woodcarvings" in chapter 9.

o **Timepieces:** Corny though they may be, carved Black Forest cuckoo clocks remain an enduring favorite. See chapter 11.

o **Cutlery:** WMF (Württembergische-Metalwaren-Fabrik) and J. A. Henckels are two of the country's premier producers of fine cutlery. Their knives are expensive, but longtime users say they last forever. Both WMF and Henckels stores are found all over Germany.

GERMANY IN DEPTH

A unified, wealthy, industrial yet beautiful Germany awaits you and promises some of the most intriguing travel experiences in Europe.

Many of its treasures were lost in World War II, but much remains and has been restored. Natural scenery, particularly in the Black Forest, the Mosel Valley, the Harz Mountains, and the Bavarian Alps, is a potent lure.

For those who want to see history in the making, we'd recommend visiting Potsdam, Leipzig, Dresden, Meissen, and Weimar, all centers of East Germany before German unification in October 1990. Keep in mind, however, that although political developments have been fast paced, the infrastructure of the five new states cannot change overnight, and living standards there are still different from those in (the former) West Germany.

Germany is one of the most modern and, at the same time, the most traditional of countries. Its advanced technology and industry are the envy of the rest of the world. Here you'll likely meet people of learning and sophistication, boasting a long cultural heritage and devotion to music and the arts.

This guide is meant to help you decide where to go in Germany and how best to enjoy its charms, but ultimately the most gratifying rewards will be your own serendipitous discoveries—drinking beer in a yard shaded by chestnut trees, picnicking in a Bavarian meadow, or spending time chatting with a winemaker in the Mosel Valley. You will surely remember experiences like these for years to come.

GERMANY TODAY

In late September 2009, Chancellor Angela Merkel swept to reelection, making her one of the longest-serving leaders among Europe's major powers. Her Christian Democrats formed a new center-right government, triumphing over Social Democrats, who fared badly in the election.

In a union with the probusiness Free Democrats, Merkel strengthened her hand in Germany, and in the next year or so may begin to enact the kind of liberalizing economic plans she proposed when she first ran for chancellor.

Her victory was muted by Germany's rising budget deficits as a result of the global economic crisis.

As an example of the changing times, Ms. Merkel, Germany's first female chancellor, is joined by the first openly gay vice-chancellor and foreign minister, Guido Westerwelle, who shepherded his Free Democrats to their strongest showing ever. All this occurring in a country that a few decades ago sent homosexuals to the concentration camps and the gas chambers, along with Jews and Gypsies.

It is still ranked low on the threat of terrorism in spite of memories of the 1972 Munich Massacre at the Olympic Games, in which 11 Jewish athletes were killed.

Germany has about 84 million citizens, making it the most densely populated of the nations in the E.U. The capital, Berlin, has the largest population, with some 3.5 million residents, trailed by Hamburg and Munich.

Germany today remains split between Protestantism and Catholicism, and it is not homogeneous, as each year it greets an influx of non-German immigrants.

Turks form the largest group of immigrants (2.3 million), followed by Sorbs (about 60,000) and even some 50,000 Dane, who live in Schleswig-Holstein near the Danish border.

In spite of a gloomy economy, Germany still remains the third-largest economy in the world, with exports counting for 40% of its GDP.

Although East and West Germany long ago united as the Berlin Wall came tumbling down, conflicts remain. Westerners often express resentment at having to spend so many of their euros on propping up the less affluent Easterners, who lived for so long under Communist rule.

The *Ossis*, as Easterners are known in Germany, often claim that they feel like poor cousins come to live with a far more affluent family, the *Wessis* (those from the former West Germany).

The friends you're likely to meet in Germany (and you're likely to meet many) will probably be well educated and will possess linguistic skills (almost certainly including English) that, by the standards of the rest of the world, particularly the United States, are astonishing. Many younger Germans are likely to be guided by a sense of idealism, even zeal, for ecological and other causes.

Germans, like Americans, are worried about job security. The greatest fear sweeping across Germany today is of "job hemorrhage." German companies are finding that more and more of their manufacturing plants and jobs can be farmed out to other locations, including, ironically enough, Alabama and South Carolina, where wages and benefits for workers at a BMW plant are about 30% less than in Germany. In the Czech Republic, just across the border, wages are equivalent to 10% of those paid in Germany, for workers nearly as well qualified.

But in spite of its problems, a modern Germany, centered around Berlin, continues to remain at the epicenter of European culture and a continuing powerhouse in the E.U.

LOOKING BACK: GERMAN HISTORY

Early Days

"A large build, very strong in the attack, but not suitable to the same extent for heavy work" was how Tacitus, the Roman historian, described the Teutons in A.D. 60. The Romans had been trying to push the borders of their empire up to the Rhineland, with mixed success, since 9 B.C., but the Teutonic tribes fought back ferociously. The first recognized German national hero was Arminius, who led his tribe (the Cherusci) in defeating three Roman legions near modern-day Bielefeld in A.D. 9.

Germany's Historic Borders

**The German Empire
1871-1918**

‑‑‑‑‑‑ Present-day borders

**Border Changes in
the 20th Century**

After World War I: 1919–1937

After World War II: 1945-1989
West Germany
East Germany
‑‑‑‑‑ Present-day borders

After the deterioration of the Roman Empire, the Franks ruled much of what we now know as Germany. In 800, a Frankish king, Charlemagne, extended the Carolingian Empire from the Pyrenees to Saxony and Bavaria. His rule marks the high point of cultural and political development of that period. He divided the empire into counties, each with an administrator directly responsible to him, and promoted education, scholarship, and the revival of Greek and Roman culture.

The Holy Roman Empire

After Charlemagne's death, the Carolingian Empire fell apart. In 843, the Treaty of Verdun granted the empire's eastern territory to Louis the German, marking the beginning of German history.

In 962, the pope recognized Otto I as emperor of what was later called the Holy Roman Empire. This new political entity was formed both to impose unity on the European political world and to create a bulwark against the invasion of non-Christian tribes. It claimed direct links to the grandeur of ancient Rome and to the more contemporary might of the church.

Unity, however, did not prevail. The empire splintered into a bickering alliance of dukedoms, bishoprics, and principalities. The emperor's authority was often dependent on German nobles and the pope. A capital city that could have served as a center of power was never established—the monarch simply moved from one city to another, mustering an army and collecting revenue wherever he could—so the possibilities for dynastic intrigues were endless. In subsequent jockeying, the church itself was a voracious competitor for power. This power struggle broke out into open conflict in 1076, when Pope Gregory VII excommunicated the emperor, Henry IV, who was forced to stand barefoot in the snow outside Canossa, humiliated, awaiting a repeal.

To strengthen their position as the Holy Roman Empire declined, the emperors turned to alliances with the wealthy, independent trading ports to the north and east, under the federation of the Hanseatic League. Such German cities as Hamburg, Lübeck, and Bremen grew in both economic and political power. Eventually the league controlled trade as far as Novgorod in Russia.

The Reformation & the Religious Wars

When an Augustinian monk, Martin Luther, nailed his theological and political complaints to a church door in Wittenberg in 1517, he set off a political and religious wildfire that spread across the landscape of Europe. The fragmented political situation in Germany played into Luther's hands: For every prince who condemned him, he found one to protect him. Luther's Reformation fanned the flames of Germany's political factions. A new conflict between Catholics and Protestants set the stage for the devastation of the Thirty Years' War (1618–48), which entrenched the divided sensibilities of the splintered nation.

The only powerful German state to emerge from these conflicts was Prussia, a tiny northeast kingdom on the Baltic Sea. The rise of Prussian power continued through the 18th century until, led by a soldier and patron of the Enlightenment, Friedrich (Frederick) the Great, Prussia became a major kingdom, with Berlin as its capital.

Napoleon Arrives

After the French Revolution, Napoleon and his new political ideas swept across Europe. The left bank of the Rhine came under French control. Under these pressures, the Holy Roman Empire officially came to an end in 1806. Around the same time, Napoleon's armies invaded Prussia, making it, for a brief time, a part of the French Empire. But Napoleon was defeated at Leipzig in 1813; 2 years later, Britain and Prussia crushed him at the Battle of Waterloo.

Bismarck & Prussia

The Congress of Vienna (1814–15) redrew the map of Germany after Napoleon's defeat, giving more territory to Prussia but making Austria the leader in a German Confederation. During this time, there was a rising spirit of nationalism, exploited to good effect by Prince Otto von Bismarck when he became Prussia's prime minister in 1862. Prussia triumphed in the Austro-Prussian War of 1866, and after the subsequent Franco-Prussian War (1870–71), when Prussia laid siege to Paris, Bismarck succeeded in his goal of unification. Wilhelm I was made emperor of all Germany in 1871, and a strong, unified Germany at last took shape. Under Bismarck's leadership, Germany adopted an advanced social welfare system and brought its military and industrial production, as well as technical and scientific achievements, to new heights.

World War I

By 1907, Europe was divided into two camps: the Triple Alliance (Germany, Austria-Hungary, and Italy) and the Triple Entente (France, Great Britain, and Russia). The match that ignited the powder keg was struck at Sarajevo in 1914, with the assassination of Archduke Franz Ferdinand, heir to the Austro-Hungarian Empire. The subsequent German invasion of France launched the bloodiest war the world had ever seen. A new and particularly demoralizing form of battle, "trench warfare," produced staggering casualties. On August 8, 1918, the Allies penetrated German lines, and the German high command realized the situation was hopeless.

To get more favorable treatment from the Allies, the Germans voluntarily declared a parliamentary democracy, ending the reign of the kaiser. Despite that concession, in 1918 Germany was forced to sign the humiliating Treaty of Versailles, which demanded the surrender of strategic territories, including Alsace-Lorraine, just west of the Rhine. The Allies—especially the French—also demanded huge monetary reparations.

Weimar Republic

In 1919, the National Assembly met in Weimar to draw up a new constitution, hailed at the time as the most progressive in the world. But in defeated and humiliated postwar Germany, extremists from both the left and the right launched savage attacks against the inexperienced and idealistic government. Enormous payments demanded by the Allies crippled the German economy. When Germany couldn't make reparations, France retaliated by occupying the Ruhr, one of Germany's most valuable industrial resources. Inflation destroyed what was left of the German economy.

The Prussians

Take, for instance, the Prussians: they are saints when compared with the French. They have every sort of excellence; they are honest, sober, hardworking, well instructed, brave, good sons, husbands, and fathers and yet . . . all with whom I have been thrown were proud as Scotchmen, cold as New Englanders, and touchy as only Prussians can be.
—Henry Labouchere, 1871

LIFE IS A cabaret

by George McDonald

Cabaret existed in Germany long before World War I, and even in its early days it strained against the boundaries of censorship and the prevailing moral climate. But the form really came into its own during the years that followed defeat in the war. During the 1920s and 30s, the chaos of the Weimar Republic, hyperinflation and economic meltdown, street battles between militias of right and left, and the steady rise of the anti-Semitic Nazi Party formed the backdrop to a collapse of traditional values. Live it up while you can and spend money while you have it was the new morality. Cabaret provided entertainment with a satirical and political bent that suited the mood and circumstances of the times, influenced by cutting-edge artistic and social movements such as Dadaism, social expressionism, and *Neue Sachlichkeit* (new objectivity).

Berlin between the wars generally gets the historical kudos when it comes to cabaret, but in fact the capital was a long way behind pre-war Munich in taking to the genre. German *Kabarett* emerged as different from original French form in that it was nearly always a vehicle for political satire. In clubs like Die Elf Scharfrichter (The Eleven Executioners), founded in 1901 in the Schwabing district, Munich's bohemians, socialists, progressives, and avant-gardistes of all stripes got together to gripe and poke fun at the smug, stultifyingly bourgeois society in which they lived.

Life in between-the-wars Berlin inspired writers like, among others, Christopher Isherwood, who lived in the city from 1929 to 1933. He wrote *The Berlin Stories* (1946), comprising two novellas—*Good-Bye to Berlin* and *Mr. Norris Changes Trains*—based in part on his experiences. The first of the two stories became the source of the stage and film versions of *Cabaret*.

"Old chums" and many more fans are still rolling up to the louche cabaret depicted in the modern Broadway show *Cabaret,* first performed in 1966 and revived at regular intervals ever since, and in the Hollywood movie based on the show, *Cabaret* (1972), directed by Bob Fosse and starring Liza Minnelli and Joel Grey.

The Rise of Nazism

This was just the right climate for the rise of Adolf Hitler and the Nazi Party. The Nazis believed in the superiority of the Aryan race and blamed non-Aryans, particularly Jews, for Germany's woes. At first Hitler's anti-Semitic, nationalist ideas failed to gain popular support, even with right-wingers. Nazi membership in the Reichstag (parliament) dropped from 25 in 1925 to only a dozen following the elections of 1928.

In 1932, Hitler lost the electoral race for president against the compromise candidate of the democratic parties, war hero Paul von Hindenburg. Nevertheless, Hitler's power increased, and on January 30, 1933, Hindenburg submitted to right-wing pressure and appointed Hitler chancellor. Upon Hindenburg's death in 1934, Hitler declared himself *Führer* (leader) of the Third Reich, a new German empire. Protected by hastily drafted laws and regulations, he made his power absolute.

On June 30, 1934, Hitler disposed of any opposing elements in his own party in the "Night of Long Knives," when hundreds were massacred, including Ernst Röhm,

Famous Period Cabarets

Die Katakombe Comedian Werner Finck (1902–78) found "The Catacombs" on Bellevuestrasse, just off Potsdamer Platz, in Berlin in 1929. His subtle jibes at Brownshirts, the Gestapo, and other "pillars" of the Nazi establishment made him popular—and brought secret policemen into the audience to "take notes." Nazi propaganda minister Joseph Goebbels ordered the cabaret closed in 1935, and Finck spent 6 weeks in a concentration camp before enlisting in the German army.

Kabarett der Komiker Better known as Kadeko, the Cabaret of Comics took a less risky approach than Die Katakombe in its choice of material. A well-known Kadeko *Conferencier* (Master of Ceremonies), Fritz Grunbaum, frequently employed his acid wit on his own audiences, ribbing them for, among other things, their disgusting eating habits.

Wien-München From 1915 to 1916, the "Vienna-Munich" cabaret in Munich had as its director the comic actor Karl Valentin, who has been dubbed "the German Chaplin." In the 1930s, Valentin made two failed attempts to get his

Panoptikum für Gruseliges und Nonsens (Panopticon for Horror and Nonsense) exhibit in Munich off the ground.

Living the Revival

Popular among visitors to Berlin, Munich, Frankfurt, Dresden, and other German towns is the kind of nightspot depicted in the musical *Cabaret*, with floor-show patter and acts that satirize the political and social scene, though the satire is less biting than it was during the time of the Weimar Republic. Some of today's cabaret shows may remind you of Broadway blockbusters, without much of the intimacy of the smoky, trenchant cellar revues of the 1920s and early 1930s.

Playlist

- *Berlin;* Marlene Dietrich.
- *Berlin Cabaret Songs;* Ute Lemper, Mischa Spoliansky.
- *Kurt Weill's The Seven Deadly Sins & Berlin Theatre Songs;* Lotte Lenya.
- *Songs of the Berlin Cabaret 1920–29;* Friedrich Hollaender, Jody Karin Appelbaum, Marc-André Hamelin.

chief of his notorious Brownshirts. Heinrich Himmler's black-shirted *Schutzstaffel* (SS) became a powerful political force. Surrounded by adoring fans (or, at best, passive witnesses), Hitler now viewed his empire as a worthy successor to those of Charlemagne and Bismarck.

In 1936, Hitler remilitarized the Rhineland and signed agreements with Japan and fascist Italy, forming the Axis alliance. In 1938, he enforced the *Anschluss* (annexation) of Austria and marched triumphantly into the country of his birth, and he occupied the German-speaking Sudetenland in Czechoslovakia, an act that other western powers could not summon the will to oppose.

The horrors of unchecked Nazi rule lasted until 1945. The Gestapo, or secret police, launched one of the most notorious reigns of terror in history. Anyone whom the Nazis considered enemies or simply undesirables—which included Communists, Social Democrats, homosexuals, political dissidents, Gypsies, and many others—was persecuted. Jews were disenfranchised, terrorized, and forced into ghettos and concentration camps.

World War II

In late August 1939, Hitler signed a nonaggression pact with the Soviet Union that gave him free rein to launch an invasion of Poland, which he did on September 1. France and Britain, honoring their agreements with Poland, declared war on Germany. Germany scored early victories, and in one of the most stunning campaigns of the 20th century, invaded and occupied France in June 1940. In 1941, Hitler turned on the Soviet Union.

Meeting in the Berlin suburb of Wannsee in 1942, the Nazi leadership formulated the implementation of the "final solution" to the "Jewish question," the systematic extermination of millions of Jews. The mass murders of homosexuals, Gypsies, Communists, Slavs, and other "undesirables" were less systematic but also numbered in the millions.

Following Japan's attack on Pearl Harbor, Germany declared war on the United States on December 11, 1941. But after defeats in north Africa in 1942 and at Stalingrad in 1943, the recurrent theme became one of Nazi retreat. The D-day landings along the coast of Normandy on June 6, 1944, began the steady advance of the Allied armies from the west, while Soviet armies relentlessly marched toward Berlin from the east. Hitler committed suicide in Berlin in April 1945. His country, along with much of Europe, lay in ruins.

Division of Germany

At war's end, Germany and its capital were divided. The nation shrank in size, losing long-held territories (among them East Prussia and Upper Silesia). The United States, Great Britain, France, and the Soviet Union divided the country into four zones of occupation. Berlin, in the heart of the Soviet district, was also divided among the four powers. In the late 1940s, the Soviet Union tried to cut off Allied access to Berlin, but a massive U.S.-sponsored airlift into the city thwarted the effort. In 1949, the Soviets established the German Democratic Republic (GDR). In response, the Federal Republic of Germany was established in the American, British, and French zones. In 1961, the GDR sealed off its borders and erected the Berlin Wall, a stark symbol of the Cold War.

Throughout the 1960s, the financial world buzzed with the talk of an economic miracle in Germany. Led by Ludwig Erhard, the economist, this miracle was called *Wirtschaftswunder,* and it saw West Germany rise to become the fourth-largest economy in the world.

This era of prosperity also saw the rise of a young German leader, Willy Brandt. Along with his Social-Liberal Coalition, Brandt, as chancellor, brought about long-overdue reform, an overhaul of education, and much improvement in industrial relations. His controversial *Ostpolitik* (Eastern Policy) improved relations with Soviet-dominated East Germany and other Communist countries to the east of Germany. His efforts in normalizing relations with the GDR brought Brandt the Nobel Prize of 1971.

The 1972 Summer Olympic Games were meant to show the entire world the bold new face of a radically rebuilt Munich. However, the terrorist attack on and murder of 11 Israeli athletes revived memories of the recent past.

Helmut Schmidt became chancellor in 1974, as West Germany continued to amaze the world with its economic muscle. Problems such as mounting unemployment remained, however, and in 1982, Helmut Kohl became the new German leader,

The Berlin Wall

pursuing welfare cuts, a tight-fisted money policy, and military cooperation with the U.S. The Kohl era saw the Green Party rise as a political force, with its goals of disarmament and protecting a fragile environment.

Fall of the Wall & Unification

The year 1989 was one of change and turmoil. In the wake of the collapse of Communist power across eastern Europe, the Berlin Wall also fell. The following year was perhaps the most significant in postwar German history. The two German nations announced economic unification in July, followed by total unification—with its thousands of inherent problems and headaches—on October 3, 1990. In 1991, Parliament voted to quit Bonn, seat of the West German government, and reestablish the once-mighty capital of Berlin.

After the first heady period of reunification, disillusionment set in, especially in eastern Germany, which was riddled with unemployment and unrealized expectations. Resentment against immigrant workers led to some violent neo-Nazi marches, bombings, and physical assaults. However, most Germans rose up to condemn the ultrarightists and the sporadic violence.

Psychological and emotional differences between the two zones were almost overwhelming, as were the vast disparities in industrial development. As the influential newspaper *Frankfurter Rundschau* editorialized, "The terms of east and west are not so much geographical expressions as they are descriptions of states of mind."

Modern Germany

As the 21st century began, Germany, despite the enormous costs of reunification, remained an economic powerhouse in Europe. As a member of the European Union (E.U.), NATO, and the G8 group of the world's industrial powers, Germany's influence extends throughout Europe and across the globe.

Moving deeper into the 21st century, Berlin has become the center of the Continent. Of the three major European powers, including France and Great Britain, Germany appears to be the most dynamic. In fact, of all E.U. members, Germany most actively pursued the abandonment of national currencies, such as its own historic deutsche mark, and the adoption of the euro as the standard unit of currency for all E.U. countries. Other countries, such as Great Britain, though a member of the E.U., still hold back. German economists continue to hope that the adoption of a single currency for Europe will lead to prosperity for all in a future "United States of Europe."

Homosexuals, once persecuted by the Nazis and sent to death camps along with Jews and Gypsies, moved significantly forward in postmillennium Germany. In 2001, in spite of fierce opposition from some conservatives, same-sex partners won legal status in Germany. The law, announced in Germany's unofficial gay capital of Berlin, allows gay couples to register their unions at government offices and requires a court decision for divorce. Same-sex couples also receive the inheritance and health-insurance rights given married spouses.

In the aftermath of World War II, Germany had become an economic giant but remained a military midget. Because of its aggression in Hitler's war, Germany appeared reluctant to make a strong show of military force anywhere in the world. But in 2001, Chancellor Gerhard Schröder announced a major change in military policy in which Germany would pursue a "more muscular policy." He pronounced as "irrevocably passed" the day when Germany would be economically powerful but militarily passive. Schröder stated that now that Germany was reunited, it had to take on more responsibilities in the international community. As proof of his stated goal, Germany sent troops to aid the United States in its military strikes against terrorist bases in Taliban-controlled Afghanistan following the terrorist attacks against the United States on September 11, 2001.

But support for U.S. policies abruptly ended in 2003, when Chancellor Schröder took a stance against America's war with Iraq. While this course proved politically rewarding in Germany, where most voters opposed U.S. involvement, it created a sharp rift with Washington, D.C., and irritated President George W. Bush. Schröder's opposition to the war led to the lowest point in German-American relations since World War II. Since then, relations have been more cordial. In 2004 Schröder and Bush issued a joint statement on "The German-American Alliance for the 21st Century." Schröder also attended the funeral of President Reagan as well as the 60th anniversary of the commemoration of the Allied D-day invasion of Normandy.

In a surprise development in 2005, conservative Angela Merkel became the first woman to govern modern Germany and the country's first leader to grow up under communism in the Soviet-occupied East. Her conservatives finished just 1 percentage point ahead of Chancellor Gerhard Schröder's center-left Social Democrats, with neither party getting a majority.

Merkel campaigned on pledges to shake up Germany's highly regulated labor market and get the stagnant economy going again. She also promised to reinvigorate relations with the U.S. Merkel faced massive problems, including unemployment. Like the United States, the German economy remained strong but there were horrendous problems, including an economic slowdown. The financial burden of reunification has exerted a terrible price on Germany.

The new "First Man" of Germany, Merkel's husband is mild-mannered chemistry professor Joachim Sauer, who likes to cook for friends and watch old Dustin Hoffman movies.

Although Germany in 2006 and early 2007 didn't do anything earthshaking enough to discuss here, a significant historical event occurred in Luxembourg. An agreement was reached to open up millions of Nazi secret archives locked away since World War II. The vast archive has been hidden for decades in the German town of Bad Arolsen, but will in time become available to researchers.

An 11-nation International Commission has overseen the archives since the war. The files are available to Holocaust survivors and families of victims whose fate may not be clear. The files contain most of what the Nazis recorded on their death camps, including the prisoners held there, not only Jews but Gypsies and gay people, including "patients" subjected to cruel medical experiments.

In the fall of 2009, Chancellor Angela Merkel swept to victory with her conservative Christian Democrats in an alliance with the probusiness Free Democrats. Since then, her popularity has declined as Germany's economy suffered under the global economic crisis. The nation as a whole is on the gloomy side, since the country's money formed a significant part of the bailout for Greece in 2010.

ART & ARCHITECTURE

Germany's art ranges from medieval carved wood statues to Dürer prints to expressionist paintings, its architecture from Gothic cathedrals and riotous baroque chapels to neoclassical temples and Bauhaus buildings. This overview should help you make sense of it all.

German Art

ROMANESQUE (11TH–12TH C.)

Artistic expression in early medieval Germany was largely church related. Because Mass was said in Latin, the illiterate masses had to learn Bible lessons via **bas reliefs** (sculptures that project slightly from a flat surface) and **wall paintings,** which told key tales to inspire faith in God and fear of sin.

The best examples of this period include scraps of surviving Romanesque sculpture on the 11th-century, carved wood doors at **Cologne's St. Maria im Kapitol** (p. 515), **Augsburg's Dom St. Maria** (p. 259), and the intricate *The Shrine of the Magi* reliquary (1182–1220) in **Kölner Dom** (**Cologne Cathedral;** p. 513).

GOTHIC (13TH–15TH C.)

Late medieval German art continued to be largely ecclesiastical, including **stained glass, church facades,** and massive **wooden altarpieces** festooned with **statues** and **carvings.** In Gothic **painting** and **sculpture,** figures tended to be more natural looking than in the Romanesque, but remained highly stylized.

The best examples and artists include **stained glass** in **Ulm Münster, Rothenburg's St. Jakobskirche,** and **Cologne's St. Gereon's Sacristy** (p. 232, 250, and 515). **Stephan Lochner** (active 1400–51) was the premier artist of the School of Cologne, where he painted the **Cologne Cathedral's** *Altar of the City Patrons* (ca. 1440; p. 513) and the **Wallraf-Richartz Museum's** *Madonna in the Rose Garden* (1450; p. 515). **Bamberger Reiter** is an anonymous equestrian statue in Bamberg's Kaiserdom, a masterpiece of 13th-century sculpture (p. 207). **Tilman Riemenschneider** (1460–1531) was Germany's genius Gothic woodcarver of languid figures draped in flowing, folded robes. Some of his best works remain in **Würzburg,** including statues in the **Mainfränkisches Museum** (p. 238).

RENAISSANCE (LATE 15TH TO 16TH C.)

The German Renaissance masters, striving for greater naturalism, included the greatest of them all, Albrecht Dürer (1471–1528). A genius painter, superb illustrator, and one of the greatest draftsmen ever, Dürer was the most important Renaissance artist outside Italy. His art matched the scientific and geometric precepts of the Florentine Renaissance with a command of color learned in Venice, a Flemish eye for meticulous detail, and the emotional sensibility of the German Gothic. He was the first to paint stand-alone self-portraits (including one in **Munich's Alte Pinakothek;** p. 290), as well as watercolors and gouaches for their own sake rather than merely as sketches. His paintings grace **Berlin's Gemäldegalerie** (p. 84) and the **Germanisches Nationalmuseum** (p. 215) in his native **Nürnberg.**

Lucas Cranach the Elder (1472–1553) melded Renaissance sensibilities with a still somewhat primitive, medieval look. As a young artist in Vienna, he helped popularize landscape painting as a member of the Danube School (*Rest on the Flight into Egypt* [1504] in **Berlin's Gemäldegalerie;** p. 84) and invented the full-length portrait (*Duke of Saxony* [1514] and *The Duchess* [1514] in **Dresden's Gemäldegalerie Alte Meister,** in the Zwinger complex; p. 188). **Hans Holbein the Younger** (1497–1543) was second only to Dürer in the German Renaissance, and one of the greatest portraitists ever. Germany preserves precious little of his work, but you can see the *Portrait of Georg Gisze* (1532) in **Berlin's Gemäldegalerie** (p. 84) and a Nativity in the **Freiburg Cathedral** (p. 384).

BAROQUE & ROCOCO (16TH–18TH C.)

The **baroque** is more theatrical and decorative than the Renaissance, mixing a kind of superrealism based on the use of peasant models and the exaggerated chiaroscuro ("light and dark") of Italy's Caravaggio with compositional complexity and explosions of dynamic fury, movement, color, and figures. **Rococo** is this later baroque art gone awry, frothy and chaotic. Artists from this period include **Andreas Schlüter** (1660–1714), whose sculptures can now be found at Berlin's **Schloss Charlottenburg** (p. 80). **Balthazar Permoser** (1651–1732) was court sculptor at Dresden. His stone pulpit stands in **Katholische Hofkirche** (p. 187), his sculptures in the **Zwinger** (p. 188).

ROMANTIC (19TH C.)

The paintings of the Romantics were heroic, historic, dramatic, and beautiful in contrast to the classically minded Renaissance artists or the overly exuberant baroque artists. **Adam Elsheimer** (1578–1610) created tiny paintings that bridged the gap from late Renaissance Mannerism (a style characterized by twisting figures in exaggerated positions), through baroque, to proto-Romantic. His *Flight into Egypt* (1609) resides in **Munich's Alte Pinakothek** (p. 290). **Caspar David Friedrich** (1774–1840) was the greatest of the German Romantics. **Dresden's Gemäldegalerie Alte Meister** in the Zwinger complex (p. 188) houses his famous *Cross in the Mountains* (1808).

EARLY 20TH CENTURY

Until Hitler, Germany was one of Europe's hotbeds of artistic activity. But the Nazis outlawed and confiscated what they called "degenerate" modern art. Almost all the artists listed below are represented at **Cologne's Museum Ludwig** (p. 514), save Höch and Grosz, whom you can find at **Berlin's Neue Nationalgalerie** (p. 87). At least one artist from every movement is at **Stuttgart's Staatsgalerie** (p. 430), and there are also good modern collections at **Düsseldorf's Kunstsammlung Nordrhein-Westfalen** (p. 529) and **Dresden's Albertinum** (p. 188). **Munich's Pinakothek der Moderne** (p. 293) is strong on expressionist artists.

The major artists and movements of the early 20th century include **expressionism,** which abandoned realism and embraced, to varying degrees, exaggeration, visible artistry (thick paint, obvious brush strokes, and strong colors) and, most important, abstraction—all to try to "express" the emotions or philosophy of the artist himself. Pure expressionism fell into two main groups, especially **Die Brücke,** founded in 1905 Dresden, which sought inspiration in folk art, medieval examples, and "unspoiled" landscapes. Its greatest members were **Ernst Kirchner** (1880–1938) and **Karl Schmidt-Rottluff** (1884–1976), though Impressionist **Emil Nolde** (1867–1956) also later joined for a while. They have their own **Brücke Museum** in Berlin (p. 98). The second movement was **Der Blaue Reiter** group, set up in Munich in 1911 by Russian-born **Wassily Kandinsky** (1866–1944), **Franz Marc** (1880–1916), and **August Macke** (1887–1914) to oppose the cultural insularity and antimodern stance of Die Brücke. The "Blue Riders" embraced international elements, modern abstraction techniques, and bright, vibrant color schemes to seek an emotional, visceral intensity in their work. Determined critics of the horrors of World War I, **Dadaists** were by turns abstract, nihilistic (inviting gallery visitors to help destroy the art), and just generally anti-art (many made random collages of found materials). Its proponents included **Hannah Höch** (1889–1978), who collaged photographs and magazine cutouts to make social statements; **George Grosz** (1893–1959), who was more strictly a painter, and later moved on to the Neue

Church floor plan

Sachlichkeit movement (below); and **Kurt Schwitters** (1887–1948), who eventually started his own splinter group called "Merz," which experimented with abstract and Russian constructivist elements.

Both **Max Ernst** (1891–1976) and Alsatian **Jean "Hans" Arp** (1887–1966) started as Blaue Reiter expressionists and, after their Dada collage period, ended up in Paris as surrealists (Ernst as a painter, Arp as a sculptor and painter of amorphous shapes).

Neue Sachlichkeit (New Objectivity) was a 1920s Berlin movement opposed to the abstraction of the expressionists. Their caricature-filled art was painted in harsh colors and focused on even harsher subjects such as sex and violence. Proponents included **Otto Dix** (1891–1969), who started as an expressionist but quickly became one of the most scathing and disturbing New Objectivity painters; **George Grosz** (see above); and **Max Beckmann** (1884–1950), who also was originally an expressionist.

POST-WORLD WAR II ART

Germany hasn't had any one style or school to define its art since World War II, though terms such as neoexpressionism (an antiabstract, antiminimalist, anticonceptual trend that grounds itself more in tradition and figurative art) are often bandied about. There have been, however, several important artists. All three listed below are represented in **Stuttgart's Staatsgalerie** (p. 430) and **Bonn's Kunstmuseum** (p. 502). Notable post–World War II artists include **Josef Beuys** (1921–86), an iconoclast and nonconformist who made constructivist sculpture from trash; **Anselm Kiefer** (b. 1945), who made a return to huge, mixed-media figurative art, often with a strong historical bent; and **Georg Baselitz** (b. 1938), a figurative painter—and a sculptor, since the 1980s—a neoexpressionist with a penchant for portraying people upside down.

Dom, Mainz

Architecture
ROMANESQUE (10TH–13TH C.)

Romanesque architects concentrated on building large churches with wide aisles to accommodate the masses. Identifiable features include rounded arches, thick walls, small windows, huge piers, tall towers, dual chancels, and blind arcades.

The best examples include **Mainz's Dom** (p. 490), which looks more like a castle fortress than a church; **Worms's Dom St. Peter** (p. 485), with a dual-chancel arrangement and two imposing facades; and **Speyer's Kaiserdom** (p. 480), the largest cathedral in Germany, a four-towered Romanesque basilica with dwarf galleries and blind arcades.

GOTHIC (13TH–16TH C.)

Ceilings began to soar with Gothic architects, walls became thinner, and windows—often stained glass—proliferated. On the exterior, graceful buttresses and soaring spires rose over a town. Pointed arches, it was discovered, carried more weight than rounded ones. Other features included cross vaulting, a facade flanked by two towers, flying buttresses, spires, gargoyles, and delicate tracery.

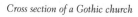

Cross vault

The best examples of Gothic include **Cologne Cathedral** (p. 513), Germany's finest, at once massive and graceful; **Freiburg Cathedral** (p. 384), built almost entirely during the Middle Ages; and **Ulm Münster** (p. 232), second in size only to Cologne's cathedral. Ulm's Münster sports the world's tallest spire—though it did take 500 years to complete. The best-preserved town centers with Gothic-style houses and buildings include **Rothenburg ob der Tauber, Goslar, Regensburg,** and **Tübingen** (p. 247, 593, 221, and 435).

Flying Buttress

RENAISSANCE (LATE 15TH THROUGH MID-17TH C.)

Germany was so busy with the Reformation that the country had little time for the Renaissance, which really had an effect only in southern Germany (transalpine influences from Italy) and a few isolated examples in the far north (influences from Flemish and Dutch neighbors). Other

Cross section of a Gothic church

than a close eye to the Renaissance ideals of proportion, symmetry, and the classical orders (distinguished by the use of three column capitals: Corinthian, Ionic, and Doric), little specifically identifies Italianate Renaissance buildings.

Weser Renaissance was a late-16th- and early-17th-century style prevalent in Lower Saxony, distinguishable on houses by pinnacled gables (the triangular upper portion of a wall at the end of a pitched roof), heavy scrollwork, elaborate dormers (an upright window projecting from a sloping roof), rounded pediments (a low-pitched feature above a window, door, or pavilion), and decorative stone bands.

Celle is the best preserved town center in the Weser Renaissance style, including its moated **Herzog-schloss** (p. 591). The Pied Piper town of **Hameln** has several fine Weser Renaissance houses, including the **Rattenfängerhaus, Hochzeitshaus,** and **Dempterscheshaus** (p. 571). The only solidly Renaissance church in Germany is **Michael-skirche** in Munich, built 1583 to 1597 by Jesuits to resemble their church in Rome (see chapter 8).

BAROQUE & ROCOCO (17TH–18TH C.)

With a seamless meshing of architecture and art, the German baroque flourished in the south and in Lower Saxony. Germany's brand of over-the-top,

Cologne Cathedral

Cornice
Modillion
Entablature
Frieze
Architrave
Capital
Shaft
Base

Corinthian Order

Ionic Order

Doric Order

Classical orders

baroque chaos worked better perhaps than in any other country. Whereas **rococo** is usually used as a derogatory term for the baroque gone awry into the grotesque, in Germany the rococo actually succeeds (sometimes). Baroque lines follow a complex geometry and interplay of concave and convex surfaces. The overall effect is to lighten the appearance of structures and add movement of line and vibrancy to the static look of the Renaissance.

The best example of a baroque palace is the **Residenz in Würzburg** (1720–44; p. 238), designed by Balthasar Neumann, including a monumental staircase under the world's largest ceiling fresco by the Italian master Tiepolo. Friedrich the Great's **Sanssouci Palace** at **Potsdam** (1744–1860) is one of Europe's best examples of the rococo (p. 148).

Jean François de Cuvilliés (1698–1767), a French dwarf, was originally the elector of Bavaria's court jester until his talent for architecture was recognized. After schooling in France, he returned to **Munich** to craft its greatest rococo monuments, including the jewel box of the **Residenz's Altes Residenztheater** (p. 317), which now bears his name, and the facade of the baroque **Theatinerkirche** (p. 290). His masterpiece is **Schloss Nymphenburg's Amalienburg** hunting lodge (p. 296), which became a model for palaces across Europe.

NEOCLASSICISM & ROMANTIC (MID–18TH THROUGH 19TH C.)

As a backlash against the excesses of the baroque and rococo, by the middle of the 18th century architects began turning to the austere simplicity and grandeur of the classical age and inaugurated the **neoclassical** style. Their work was inspired by the rediscovery of Pompeii and other ancient sites. However, many of their interiors continued to be rococo, though more muted than before. The sterility of German neoclassicism didn't last long, however, and the 19th century left the increasing nationalist German society looking into its own past for inspiration, kicking off the neo-Gothic **Romantic Movement.**

Amalienburg, Schloss Nymphenburg

The Prussians remade Berlin in a neoclassical image, starting with the **Brandenburger Tor** (p. 89) and moving on to the buildings of Karl Friedrich Schinkel

(1781–1841), among which **Altes Museum, Schloss Charlotten-hof,** and **Nikolaikirche** are his best (p. 96, 150, and 97). There's a museum devoted to him called the **Friedrichswerdersche Kirche–Schinkelmuseum** (p. 91). In Munich, Ludwig I had Leo von Klenze lay out neoclassical structures across his "new Athens," including those surrounding **Königsplatz** (p. 290) and the nearby **Alte and Neue pinakotheks** (p. 290 and 293). Caught up in Wagner's dramatic operas set in the heroic Middle Ages, "Mad" King Ludwig II was the ultimate Romantic, building for himself a series of faux medieval fairy-tale castles, including **Herrenchiemsee's Neues Schloss** (p. 343) and the incomparable fantasy of **Neuschwanstein Castle** (p. 267), a festival of banner-fluttering towers and battlements right out of a Brothers Grimm folk tale, its entire setting chosen solely for its picture-postcard perfection.

Neuschwanstein

20TH-CENTURY ARCHITECTURE

Germany's take on the early-20th-century Art Nouveau movement was called *Jugendstil*. The **Bauhaus** was a 1920s avant-garde school of architecture led by **Walter Gropius** (1883–1969) that combined industrial-age architecture with art and craft to create functional buildings and furnishings. Among its chief designers and institute teachers were Marcel Breuer, Wassily Kandinsky, Oskar Schlemmer, and Paul Klee. The Nazis closed the school in 1933, though it was reborn in Chicago. *Jugendstil* houses and hotels exist across Germany, but the movement took its name from *Jugend* magazine published in the **Schwabing district of Munich,** where many buildings in the style survive. Munich is also home to the **Jugendstil Museum** in the Stuck-Villa, a hybrid neoclassical/*Jugendstil* structure. Bauhaus structures, too, pepper Germany in unobtrusive ways, often in city outskirts. One fine example is Berlin's **Die Siemensstadt,** the first modern housing complex, built with long "slab" blocks by Walter Gropius. Berlin also has the **Bauhaus-Archiv Museum für Gestaltung** (p. 83), devoted to Bauhaus drawings, photographs, and some design examples.

Siemensstadt

GERMANY IN POP CULTURE

Books

BIOGRAPHY

- Taylor, A. J. P. *Bismarck: The Man and the Statesman* (1967). This is the story of the "Iron Chancellor," who was instrumental in unifying the German states into the German Empire.
- Trevor-Roper, Hugh. *The Last Days of Hitler* (1986). This is an insightful reconstruction of the twilight of the Third Reich.

GERMAN literature: FROM GUTENBERG TO GRASS

Even before Gutenberg invented the first printing press in the Western world in the 15th century, German literature—both oral and written—was being produced. The first written literary work known is *The Lay of Hildebrand*, a narrative poem handed down by ancient storytellers and copied by monks at the Benedictine Abbey at Fulda. Such tales of valor, love, sorrow, and death were strong in oral tradition, with the Rhine valley giving rise to many legends and songs through the centuries, Lohengrin, Roland, the Lorelei, and the Nibelungen being among the subjects.

The age of chivalry gave birth to lyric poetry in Germany. Like the troubadours in France, *Minnesingers* of the Holy Roman Empire roamed the land singing songs of love and derring-do inspired by the Crusades. One of these, **Walter von der Vogelweide,** a knight of the late 12th and early 13th centuries, is seen as the father of lyric poetry in Germany. Another early-13th-century poet of note was **Wolfram von Eschenbach,** whose epic, *Parsifal,* glorifies chivalry and religious devotion. By the 16th century, another "hero" had joined German folklore and literature—Til Eulenspiegel, a clownish fellow whose life around 1300 became the subject of story and song.

From the time of the Reformation (16th c.), **Martin Luther**'s influence can be traced in many fields of the German life of the mind and spirit. His translation of the Bible into modern German was hailed as the first great literary work in the language. A Luther contemporary, **Hans Sachs,** a *Meistersinger* (a "master singer" who carried on the traditions of the earlier Minnesingers), was a prolific author of stories, poems, plays, and songs.

Publications of a picaresque novel, *Simplicissimus,* by **Grimmelshausen** (17th c.), marked the start of production of long prose narratives in the country. The Age of Enlightenment in German literature dawned in the late 17th century, inaugurated by **Klopstock** in his epic, *Der Messias,* and his *Odes,* and it continued into the 18th century. Rationalization was the watchword in this Enlightenment period, or *Aufklärung*. Much writing was in the form of philosophical treatises (for example, the works of **Leibniz** and **Kant**). Also in this era, the principles of German drama were laid out by **Lessing.**

As a reaction to rationalization, a literary movement known as *Sturm und Drang* was born in the 18th century, marked especially by poetry and drama extolling both sentiment and grand passions and rejecting previous social, political, moral, and literary authority.

In this time, when ideas of storm and stress dominated the literati, **Johann Wolfgang von Goethe** arrived on the scene, a giant of letters. Dramatist, novelist, philosopher, and Germany's greatest poet, Goethe followed the pattern of the times in youth and early manhood (the *Urfaust*

FICTION

○ Goethe, Johann Wolfgang von. *The Sorrows of Young Werther* (1990). This is required reading for every German schoolchild. Goethe explored the theme of suicide in this early epistolary novella.

○ Grass, Günter. *Dog Years* (1989), *The Tin Drum* (1990), and *The Flounder* (1989). Grass's works deal with the German psyche coming to terms with the dreadful legacy of Nazism and World War II.

○ Isherwood, Christopher. *The Berlin Stories* (1954). Isherwood lived in Berlin from 1929 to 1933. His most famous story was "Good-Bye to Berlin," which became the source of the stage and film versions of *Cabaret*.

or *Early Faust, Egmont,* and *The Sorrows of Young Werther*). However, he soon became disenchanted with *Sturm und Drang,* turning in midlife after a stay in Italy to a classical mode (*Nausikaa*). During this period, he reworked *Faust* so that the final product begins with storm and stress and then levels off into tranquil classicism. It was after his sojourn in Italy that he also produced *Wilhelm Meisters Lehrjahre,* a novel that served for decades as the prototype of the best German fiction.

Another literary immortal, **Johann Friedrich Schiller,** playwright and poet, a contemporary and friend of Goethe, also turned away from *Sturm und Drang* after presentation of *Don Carlos,* a powerful historical drama honoring liberty. Similar dramas were *Wallenstein* and *Wilhelm Tell.* Schiller's outlook placed his interests in the fields of history and philosophy.

Besides these two masters of the literary world, which soon moved on from classicism to romanticism to historical romanticism, such names of world note as the brothers **Jakob and Wilhelm Grimm,** famous for their collection of fairy tales, folk tales, and myths, and **Heinrich Heine** appeared. Many of the works of Heine, second only to Goethe as Germany's greatest poet, have become folk songs.

A poet who became known for his work in the first quarter of the 20th century was **Rainer Maria Rilke.** Another German, the novelist **Erich Maria Remarque** (*All Quiet on the Western Front*), moved to the United States to escape the political conditions of his homeland. **Franz Kafka** became known for his novels of the absurd. **Bertolt Brecht** (*The Threepenny Opera* and *Mother Courage*) chose to live in East Germany after World War II.

In 1959 **Gunther Grass** burst onto the scene with his extraordinary first novel, *Blechtrommel (The Tin Drum)*. He became a spokesman for the German generation that grew up in the Nazi era and received the Nobel Prize in literature in 1999 as a poet, novelist, and playwright.

Other Germans who won the Nobel Prize for literature:

○ **Theodor Mommsen,** 1902, philosopher
○ **Paul J. L. Heyse,** 1910, novelist, dramatist, and poet
○ **Gerhart J. R. Hauptmann,** 1912, dramatist
○ **Thomas Mann,** 1929, novelist
○ **Hermann Hesse,** 1946, novelist
○ **Heinrich Böll,** 1972, novelist

The influence of German thought on the Western mind has been powerful, from as far back as the 13th century when **Albertus Magnus** became known as a scholastic philosopher, naturalist, and theologian. Through the centuries, other notable philosophers have been **Kant, Moses Mendelssohn, Schopenhauer, Hegel, Marx, Engels,** and **Nietzsche** (*Thus Spake Zarathustra*).

- Mann, Thomas. *The Magic Mountain* (1969). This is Mann's most celebrated masterpiece.
- Remarque, Erich Maria. *All Quiet on the Western Front* (1987). This is a classic novel of World War I.

FOLKLORE & LEGENDS

- Grimm, Jacob, and Wilhelm Grimm. *Complete Grimm Tales*. This is the world's most famous collection of folk tales, with a cast of characters that includes everybody from Little Red Riding Hood to Tom Thumb.
- *The Nibelungenlied*. Every school kid in Germany reads this great epic poem, which details the exploits of Siegfried and Kriemhild and the fall of the Burgundians. *The Nibelungenlied* is characterized by the violence of its emotions and its uncompromising emphasis on vengeance.

MEN (AND WOMEN) OF NOTE: GERMANY'S RICH
musical history

by Donald Olson

Some of the greatest works of Western music have been written by German composers. The roster includes Bach, Handel, Beethoven, Brahms, Mendelssohn, Schumann, and Wagner, as well as 20th-century greats Alban Berg and Kurt Weill. The country's rich musical history dates back to 12th-century *Minnesängers* (troubadours) and religious chants. Over the centuries, Germany's musical traditions were fostered in convents, monasteries and churches where composers were hired to write sacred songs, cantatas and oratorios. Eventually, as opera houses and concert halls became a fixture in German cities, a wider public clamored for musical performances. Classical music remains an important part of German culture today and can be enjoyed in concert halls and opera houses throughout the country.

Hildegard of Bingen (1098-1179) Known as Saint Hildegard, this Benedictine abbess was revered in her day as an author, visionary, herbalist, poet, and composer. Over 70 of her compositions have survived, one of the largest repertoires among medieval composers.

Hildegard's music is monophonic, consisting of only one melodic line, but her soaring melodies go well beyond the range of medieval chant.

Johann Sebastian Bach (1685-1750)
After stints as a violinist, an organist, and a Kapellmeister, Bach arrived in Leipzig in 1723 and stayed for the rest of his life, writing more than 200 cantatas, the *Passion According to St. Matthew,* and the Mass in B Minor. He was prolific in other ways as well, fathering 17 children. Every June, Leipzig celebrates Bach's musical legacy with the famous **Bachfest** (www.bach-leipzig.de), during which Bach's works are performed in the Thomaskirche, where he is buried.

Ludwig van Beethoven (1770-1827)
Beethoven brought emotional depth and new tone colors to music in the transitional period between the Classical (Bach) and Romantic (Brahms) eras. He began his career by composing and performing piano concertos, and he continued to compose (9 symphonies, the opera *Fidelio*) even when his hearing began to deteriorate in the late 1790s. By the time his monumental Ninth Symphony was premiered in 1824,

HISTORY

- Beevor, Antony. *The Fall of Berlin 1945* (2002). This is one of the most vivid accounts ever written of the Red Army's assault on Berlin.

- Large, David Clay. *Berlin* (2000). In this controversial and caustic survey of Berlin since 1871, the author claims that "no other place has so dramatically encapsulated the highs and lows of our modern human experience" as Berlin.

- Schneider, Peter. *The German Comedy: Scenes of Life after the Wall,* translated by Leigh Hafrey and Philip Boehm (1992). Comic absurdities surrounding the collapse of the Wall fill this book, but Schneider (author of *The Wall Jumper*) also explores resurgent anti-Semitism and how West Germans are coping with the flood of refugees from the former East Germany.

- Shirer, William L. *The Rise and Fall of the Third Reich: A History of Nazi Germany* (1959–60). This story has never been told better—the complete saga of Hitler's empire from beginning to end.

Beethoven was so deaf that he had to be turned around to see the tumultuous applause of the audience. Music lovers can visit his birthplace, the Beethoven House Museum, in Bonn.

Johannes Brahms (1833-1897) Like Beethoven, Brahms was a composer and virtuoso pianist who performed many of his own works. He composed for piano, chamber ensembles, symphony orchestra, and for voice and chorus. The structure of Brahms's music is rooted in the traditions of Baroque and Classical composition, but he developed musical themes in a way pioneered by Beethoven, creating bold new harmonies and melodies. Brahms's glory years as a composer were between 1868, when he premiered *A German Requiem*, his largest choral work, and 1885, by which time he had composed his four symphonies and the Piano Concerto No. 2. In 1889, Brahms made an experimental recording of his first Hungarian dance on the piano, the earliest recording made by a major composer.

Richard Wagner (1813-1883) Known primarily for his operas, Wagner pioneered advances in musical language that greatly influenced the development of European classical music. His life was tumultuous, requiring periodic flights to escape creditors. It was while in exile from Germany that Wagner completed his four-act *Ring* cyle, the opera *Tristan and Isolde*, and developed his revolutionary vision of operas as *Gesamtkunstwerk*, or "total artwork", a fusion of music, song, dance, poetry, visual arts, and stagecraft. His fortunes brightened when Ludwig II, king of Bavaria, became Wagner's patron., Wagner built the **Festspielhaus** in Bayreuth, a theater where his operas—and only his—would be performed. He is buried in the garden at Villa Wahnfriend in Bayreuth.

Kurt Weill (1900-1950) Although he was classically trained and had some success with his works for the concert hall, it was Weill's musical-theatre songs that became popular in Germany in the late 1920s and early 1930s. His best-known work, *The Threepenny Opera*, was written in 1928 in collaboration with the German playwright Bertolt Brecht contained his most famous song, "Mack the Knife." As a prominent Jewish composer, Weill became a target of the Nazis and was forced to flee Germany in 1933.

o Taylor, Frederick. *Dresden: Tuesday, February 13, 1945* (2004). This book takes a new look at the destruction of Dresden by Allied bombings, which was more famously brought home in Kurt Vonnegut's 1969 novel *Slaughterhouse Five*. A British historian, Taylor debunks the theory that Dresden contributed little toward the Nazi war effort, but was "one of the foremost industrial locations of the Reich."

TRAVEL

o Twain, Mark. *A Tramp Abroad* (1989). The American humorist's travels through Germany are comically detailed here. Read also his comments on "The Awful German Language."

Music

Music is an important and pervasive facet of German life. German disunity over the centuries actually helped foster German music. The many small principalities and bishoprics that split up the German-speaking world meant that there were many courts to offer opportunities to musicians, both composers and instrumentalists. As a result, the German-speaking nations produced more composers of indisputable greatness than any other.

Today, the musical scene in Germany is as vibrant as ever. Every major city has an opera house and an orchestra, many of them world renowned. New composers are encouraged, and productions are often at the cutting edge.

A HISTORY OF GERMAN MUSIC

BAROQUE MUSIC   The greatest composer of the baroque era was **Johann Sebastian Bach** (1685–1750), who was a supreme master of all musical forms of his time. Bach produced many church cantatas, especially for St. Thomas Church in Leipzig (see chapter 5), where he served as cantor. His compositions were technically outstanding, vigorous, and profound. Little of his music was published during his lifetime, but after his death, his influence steadily grew, especially that of his organ works. The musical tradition in his large family was maintained by two of his talented sons, Carl Philipp Emanuel Bach (1714–88) and Johann Christian Bach (1735–82). The Brandenburg Concertos are highly recommended.

Bach's contemporary **George Frideric Handel** (1685–1759) was another great composer. He first rose to prominence as musician of the court of Hannover, a post that he left to become composer at the court of St. James of England. He was a leading composer of operas and instrumental music for the court. Listen to his oratorio, *Messiah*.

THE CLASSICAL PERIOD   **Wolfgang Amadeus Mozart** (1756–91), although an Austrian, cannot be omitted from any discussion of German music. His operas, with their contemporary themes and lively musical characterizations, paved the way for later composers. **Franz Joseph Haydn** (1732–1809), another Austrian, also exerted great influence on German music, especially instrumental music. Listen to Mozart's *The Marriage of Figaro* and *Don Giovanni* and Haydn's "Drum Roll" Symphony no. 103.

THE 19TH CENTURY & ROMANTICISM   The 19th century was rich in musical genius. **Ludwig van Beethoven** (1770–1827) ushered in romanticism. His works included symphonies, piano concertos, piano sonatas, quartets, and many others. He greatly expanded and developed the orchestra. Tragically, he completely lost his hearing in 1819. However, the chamber music he wrote after this event shows an even greater depth and complexity than his previous compositions. Listen to symphonies no. 5 and no. 9.

Other great composers of the era include **Franz Schubert** (1797–1828), **Felix Mendelssohn** (1809–47), **Robert Schumann** (1810–56), and **Johannes Brahms** (1833–97). Listen to Schubert's *Lieder*, Mendelssohn's "Overture" to *A Midsummer Night's Dream*, Schumann's Symphony no. 3, and Brahms's *German Requiem*.

The giant of the 19th-century opera world was **Richard Wagner** (1813–83). His theories of musical drama exerted a tremendous influence on everyone who followed him, even his detractors. His influence can best be heard in the music of the later Romantic composer **Richard Strauss** (1864–1949), whose operas carry Wagner's ideas of character development to greater psychological depth. Listen to Wagner's *The Ring of the Nibelungs* and Strauss's *Salome*.

THE 20TH CENTURY Musical experimentation flourished in early-20th-century Germany. Austrian-born **Arnold Schönberg** (1874–1951) developed the 12-tone

BEYOND BAROQUE: THE MODERN GERMAN music SCENE

Modern German music tastes are heavily influenced by the American or British pop worlds, but many German musicians have created their own Teutonic sounds, notably the amusingly named "Krautrock." Kraut, of course, was originally an ethnic slur used by American GIs to refer to Nazi soldiers. One critic defined Krautrock "as a mix of Anglo-American post-psychedelic jamming and moody progressive rock." Its stars were the band **Can,** often compared to the Velvet Underground, and the band **Faust,** which became one of the first acts to sign with Richard Branson's Virgin Records.

Crossing international boundaries is the German industrial metal band **Rammstein,** which nonetheless performs almost exclusively in German. The group is known for its rock hit "Du Hast." Rammstein is also controversial—a liquid-ejecting dildo earned them a night in a Massachusetts jail. Rammstein band members much admire the music of **Nina Hagen,** who often leads protests concerning issues such as the war in Iraq. She headlined the Drop Dead Festival in New York City in 2005.

Neue Deutsche Welle (New German wave) was a form of punk rock and new wave music that rose in the mid-'70s. Out of this movement came a German band from Berlin, **Wir Sind Helden (We Are Heroes),** which has achieved great success, including sold-out concerts in London, with non-English lyrics.

Punk music became popular in the 1970s in the wake of the success of British bands like the Sex Pistols, who developed a devoted following in West Germany. After reunification, many punk bands such as **Slime** rose to rant against politicians who ignore the dangers of neo-Nazis in Germany. The late '70s also saw the rise of Goth rock, with strong ties to the English punk rock scene. Since the turn of the millennium, Goth rock has declined in popularity but still flourishes in pockets.

German hip-hop entered the mainstream only in the early '90s, bringing with it graffiti and break dancing. The controversial and mysterious Berlin rapper **Sido** released *Maske,* a debut album in 2004, which was hailed as the first real German hip-hop music. His most recent releases are the 2008 album *Ich und meine Maske (Me and My Mask)* and the 2009 album *Aggro Berlin.*

system of musical structure. **Kurt Weill** (1900–50) and **Paul Hindemith** (1895–1963) tried to reach a more popular audience. During the Nazi era, many composers fled Germany. Others, like **Hans Pfitzner** (1869–1949) and Strauss, remained in an uneasy relationship with the Nazis. Listen to Schönberg's *Five Pieces for Orchestra*, Weill's *Three-penny Opera,* and Hindemith's *Mathis der Maler.* The music of Pfitzner is still heard in such operas as *Palestrina* from 1917 and *Das Herz* from 1931. The compositions of Strauss are among the most frequently played around the globe, especially his operas such as *Salome* (1905) and *Elektra* (1909).

More recently, major composers such as **Karlheinz Stockhausen** (1928–2007) and **Hans Werner Henze** (b. 1926) have brought the traditions of Germany's musical past into the present. Listen to Stockhausen's *Gesang der Jünglinge (Song of the Youths).* Henze has won cultural awards around the world for such compositions as *The English Cat* in 1980 and *La Cubana* in 1973.

Film

German cinema came into its own in the aftermath of World War I, although it actually began in 1895, when the brothers Skladanowsky presented their Bioscop in the Wintergarten at Berlin. Early German film not only has earned a place in cinema history, but also has been enormously influential in both Europe and the United States. *Das Cabinet des Dr. Caligari (The Cabinet of Dr. Caligari)*, directed by Dr. Robert Wiene and released in Berlin in 1920, was hailed as "the first work of art on the screen." After viewing the film, the French coined the term *Caligarisme* to describe the "all upside-down" postwar world.

The 1920s saw the production of many notable German films, such as Fritz Lang's *Dr. Mabuse, der Spieler (Dr. Mabuse, the Gambler),* a 1922 screen version of a novel by Norbert Jacques. In 1924, Lang achieved great popular success with his two *Nibelungen* films, which became classics. The influence of Lang's science fiction film *Metropolis* (1927) can still be seen today, and his *Spione (The Spy)* became the forerunner of the Hitchcock thrillers. Carl Mayer achieved renown for his scripts, which were called "screen poems." These include the expressionist 1920 film *Genuine* and 1924s *Der Letzte Mann (The Last Laugh).* Mayer is said to have "unchained" the camera.

In the late 1920s, Hollywood began drawing away Germany's brightest stars, including directors Ernst Lubitsch and F. W. Murnau (*Faust,* 1926) and stars such as Conrad Veidt and Emil Jannings. As the worldwide recession hit Germany, film production suffered further. The most notable film to come out of this troubled period was *Der Blaue Engel (The Blue Angel),* released in 1930. It starred Emil Jannings and brought world acclaim to its female lead, Marlene Dietrich, who later found even greater glory in Hollywood.

When the Nazis came to power, German films became propaganda tools. Nazi films reached the zenith of their power in Leni Riefenstahl's 1934 *Triumph des Willens (Triumph of the Will),* acclaimed for its cinematic techniques in spite of its glorification of Nazism. She went on to make *Olympia,* her classic account of the 1936 Berlin Olympics. Her innovative camera angles and close-ups of the athletes in action were brilliant, and the films won her both praise and condemnation.

In the first decades after World War II, the German film industry was not very creative. By the 1970s, however, a group of talented directors was emerging, including Rainer Werner Fassbinder, Werner Herzog, Wim Wenders, and Volker Schlöndorff.

Currently, there are few screen giants in Germany. The Berlin Film Festival often honors golden oldies, such as *Pandora's Box,* by G. W. Pabst, starring American Louise

Brooks. Many Pabst films have been restored and reconstructed. Pabst's critical treatment of social issues earned him the sobriquet "The Red Pabst" during the Weimar Republic. Franz Seitz is often honored for producing some 80 films during his career, including 1979's *The Tin Drum*.

The 1981 story of a doomed Nazi submarine, *Das Boot (The Boat)* still holds the record for the most Academy Award nominations for a German film, a total of six. The 1990 film *Das schreckliche Mädchen (The Nasty Girl)* tells the often shocking story of what a Bavarian high-school student uncovers when she sets out to investigate the Nazi past of her hometown. Michael Verhoeven's picture was nominated for an Oscar as best foreign film. The movie is said to have been based on true-life experiences of a young woman. The German hometown in the film is actually Passau, covered later in this guide. Hitler once resided in Passau.

In 2006, *Das Leben der Anderen (The Lives of Others)* won an Academy Award as best foreign-language film. The film documented how Stasi (the East German secret police) spied on the lives of its citizens. In 2007, *Die Fälscher (The Counterfeiters)* also won an Oscar as best foreign-language film. Shot in Berlin, this Austro-German production told the story of how forgers were assigned the job of producing massive amounts of fake U.S. dollars and British pounds in an effort by the Nazi regime to weaken the Allied economy.

Modern films continue to offer us a glimpse of contemporary German life and culture as well. Most of these are available in the U.S. either dubbed or translated into English. Tom Tykwer's *Lola Rennt* (1998) remains one of our favorites. It was called *Run Lola Run* in its English release. Starring Franka Potenta as Lola, the film has been called iconic of a reunified Germany. The plot involves a young woman who has 20 minutes to find and bring 100,000 German marks to her boyfriend before he robs a supermarket. The action is riveting, the soundtrack dynamic.

In *Der Krieger und die Kaiserin (The Princess and the Warrior)*, director Tykwer is reunited with Potenta. First released in 2000, the film follows the travails of Sissi, who works in a psychiatric hospital. She becomes involved with a tormented ex-soldier who stages a bank robbery. A near-death experience throws Sissi's life into chaos.

One of the freshest post-reunification films is Wolfgang Becker's 2003 comedy *Goodbye, Lenin!*, set in East Germany in 1989. A young man, to protect his fragile mother from a fatal shock after a long coma, tries to prevent her from learning that her beloved East Germany has disappeared.

EATING & DRINKING

Though traditional dishes like dumplings, *Wurst* (sausages), pastries, and beer may make Germany seem the worst possible place to eat healthfully, in reality, restaurants are offering foreign foods and *neue Küche* (modern cuisine). Chefs trained in Switzerland, France, or Italy return to Germany to open Continental restaurants, and Italians and Turks, many of whom originally came to Germany as "guest workers," own restaurants featuring their own culinary traditions.

Regional Specialties

○ **Bavaria & Franconia:** In southern Germany, you can feast on such hearty fare as *Leberkäs* (a chilled mold of minced pork, beef, and liver), *Knödel* (dumplings or soaked bread), *Haxen* (pork or veal trotters, most often consumed with *Sauerkraut*), *Rostbratwürste* (small finger sausages), and *Leberknödel* (large liver dumplings in a clear broth). *Schweinwurst mit Kraut* (pork sausages with *Sauerkraut*) is another unforgettable local dish.

o **Lower Saxony & Schleswig-Holstein:** Here in northwest Germany, with its maritime tradition, a typical local dish is *Aalsuppe*—sweet-and-sour eel soup flavored with bacon, vegetables, and sometimes even pears and prunes (or perhaps other fruits). The sailor's favorite is *Labskaus,* a ground-together medley of pork, salt herring, and beef, along with potatoes and beets. The traditional topping is a fried egg and a side dish of cucumbers. *Bruntes Huhn* is salt beef on a bed of diced vegetables, a robust winter favorite. *Rollmops,* pickled herring rolled in sour cream, is another local specialty, as is *Finkenwerder Scholle* (plaice) and oysters, raw or baked with cheese.

o **Berlin:** During those cold nights in old Prussia, Berliners took comfort in their soups, notably *Kohlsuppe* (cabbage soup) and *Erbsensuppe* (pea soup), along with dark bread, especially Westphalia pumpernickel. *Hase im Topf* is a delicious rabbit pâté. Other favorites are *Bratwurst,* a pork sausage, and *Regensburger Wurst,* a spicy pork sausage. For dessert, Berliners like *Kugelhupf,* a marvelous coffeecake, and *Käsekuchen,* or cheesecake. But probably the most typical Berlin delicacy is *Eisbein* (pigs' knuckles).

o **Hassen & Westphalia:** Famed for its hams, this region eats food guaranteed to put hair on your chest. Sample their *Sulperknochen,* made from the pigs' trotters (feet), ears, and tail, and served traditionally with pea pudding and pickled cabbage. Try *Tüttchen,* a ragout of herb-flavored calves' heads and calves' brains, or settle for *Pickert,* sweet-potato cakes flavored with raisins.

o **Baden-Württemberg:** In the southern region around Stuttgart, begin with such dishes as *Schneckensuppe* (snail soup), *Spätzle* (egg-based pasta), or perhaps *Maultaschen* (ravioli stuffed with ground meat, spinach, and calves' brains). A dish beloved in the area and widely consumed is *Geschnetzeltes* (slices of veal in a cream sauce). The favorite local dish in Stuttgart itself is *Gaisburger Marsch,* a beef stew. Another commonly served dish is *Rostbraten,* braised beef, invariably accompanied by *Sauerkraut* or *Linsen mit Saiten,* lentil stew cooked with sausages.

o **Saxony & Thuringia:** In eastern Germany, you can feast on everything from *Linsensuppe mit Thüringer Rotwurst* (lentil soup with Thuringian sausages) to *Rinderzunge in Rosinen-Sauce* (calves' tongues in grape sauce). *Kartoffelsuppe* (potato soup) remains a favorite of the district, as does a baked appetizer, *Quarkkeulchen,* made from curd, boiled potatoes, flour, sugar, and raisins, topped with cinnamon and

THE BEST OF THE wurst

The German love affair with **Wurst** (sausage) dates from the dawn of history. Every region of Germany has its own specialty, but the overall favorite seems to be *Bratwurst* from Nürnberg, made of seasoned and spiced pork. Germans often take their *Wurst* with a bun and a dab of mustard. **Weisswurst** (white sausage) is a medley of veal, calves' brains, and spleen. **Bauernwurst** (farmer's sausage) and **Knockwurst** are variations of the *Frankfurter,* which originated (naturally) in Frankfurt. (Oddly enough, small *Frankfurters,* which are called wieners or Vienna sausages in the United States and **Wienerwurst** in Germany, are known as *Frankfurters* in Austria.) **Leberwurst** (made from liver) is a specialty of Hesse. **Rinderwurst** and **Blutwurst** (beef sausage and blood sausage) are Westphalian specialties and are often eaten with *Steinhäger* (corn brandy).

served with applesauce. Each city in the district also has its own popular local dishes. Leipzig, for example, has its *Leipziger Allerlei,* a blend of carrots, peas, asparagus, cauliflower, mushrooms, crayfish, oxtails, bits of veal, and dumplings.

○ **Rhineland:** The Rhineland features dishes that have made Germans the subject of good-natured ridicule, especially in neighboring France. For example, there's *Saumagen,* stuffed pork belly with pickled cabbage. Also beloved is *Schweinepfeffer,* a highly seasoned and spicy pork ragout that's thickened with pig blood. After that feast, it's on to *Hämchen,* pork trotters with pickled cabbage and potatoes, or else *Sauerbraten,* beef marinated in wine vinegar and spices. Postwar Chancellor Konrad Adenauer was a Rhinelander, and one of his favorite foods was *Reibekuchen,* small potato pancakes with a blueberry sauce or applesauce. Taverns along the Rhine fill up when *Federweisser,* partially fermented new wine, comes in. They drink it while devouring onion tarts.

Beer & Wine

BEER   For variety and quality, German beer is unequaled. The world's oldest brewery is in Bavaria, but other regions in Germany have proud beer-making traditions. **Export beers** and the rather more bitter **Pils,** the most popular type of beer, are also produced in Berlin, Hamburg, the Ruhr, Hesse, and Stuttgart. **Altbier,** a very early product of the brewer's art, can be found today all over Germany.

In Germany, if you go into a beer hall and ask the bartender for *ein Bier,* you'll probably get the standard stock beer, **Vollbier,** which is 4% alcohol. More potent is **Export** at 5% or **Bockbier** at 6%. Connoisseurs specify the type of beer they want and often the brewery. The following is a bit of beer vocabulary. When the malt has been darkly roasted and fermented for much longer, it becomes **dunkles Bier,** or dark beer. **Doppelbock** is an extra-dark beer with a 6% alcoholic content. **Helles Bier** is light and brewed from malt dried and baked by the local brewery, or *Brauerei.* Many Germans, especially the citizens of Bamberg, like their beer "smoked." If that appeals to you, request **Rauchbier.** In nearby Bayreuth, Richard Wagner's old hometown, locals prefer a "steam beer" known as **Dampfbier.** The denizens of Düsseldorf and Frankfurt can often be heard requesting **Alt,** a brown, barley-malt brew. **Kölsch** is a light beer drunk mainly in Cologne in tall fluted glasses. **Hefeweizen** is a yeasty wheat beer consumed often with a squeeze of lemon. **Berliner Weisse** is made from wheat, like a Bavarian white beer, but with a dash of raspberry or woodruff syrup. Dark and sweet, **malt beer** has hardly any alcohol, whereas **Starkbier** is a powerful beer served when the barrels are opened after the post-Lenten celebrations in March. It has the highest alcohol content of them all. Finally, **Pils,** or pilsner, beers are light and contain more hops. Dortmund has earned a reputation in this field.

WINE   Germany has produced delightful wines for centuries, but sometime in the 1970s, German wine became the butt of jokes. The postwar German economic miracle had led to a boom in wine production. Many new vineyards sprang up suddenly, and quality was not always their first priority. Cheap, cloyingly sweet table wines flooded the market. One label in particular, Liebfraumilch, began to sully the reputation of the entire industry; the mere mention of its name to anyone in the know met with a knowing titter or contemptuous sneer. Today, however, German viticulture has many smaller producers producing excellent wines.

Good German wine is renowned for its natural lightness and its delicate balance of sweetness and acidity. Most vineyards flourish on steep hillsides, protected from harsh winds by wooded neighboring hills, especially on the banks of the Rhine and

💬 o'zapfstisl ("THE BARREL IS TAPPED")

The oldest brewery in the world is at Weihenstephan, a former Benedictine monastery 30km (19 miles) northeast of Munich in Old Bavaria. It dates from the year 1040, although there is evidence that a hop garden already existed near the grounds of the monastery in A.D. 768. The monks here brought beer to the masses in Europe. Even today, the oldest brewery within Munich itself, **Augustiner,** reflects brewing's monastic heritage.

Over the centuries, monks brewed a strong beer for consumption during the fasting period of Lent, during which they were technically supposed to drink only water. The story goes that the pope heard about this custom and ordered that the beer be transported to Rome for him to sample. When the pope finally tasted the beer after its long journey (it didn't have preservatives back then), he decided it tasted foul and decreed that the beer was strong enough punishment for the Bavarian monks to drink it during Lent. Today, all Munich breweries brew this strong beer during Lent; *Salvator* and *Triumphator* are the best-known brands. *Ator* in German means a strong beer. By long-standing tradition, the names of German *Doppelbock Bier* (a type of strong beer) end with an "-ator" suffix.

Mosel rivers and their tributaries. The vineyards profit from the warmth reflected off the sunlit water. The slow maturing of the grapes gives German wines their typical fresh, fruity acidity.

Germany does produce red wine, but as a rule it's better to stick to white or perhaps a rosé. **Trocken (dry)** or **halbtrocken (semidry)** are often given on the labels; look for them if you want to escape anything sweet. This avoidance, however, should not extend to the dessert wines, which resemble nectar.

The overload of information on a German wine label is often puzzling to foreigners, but it's not really that hard to decipher. First of all, the grape variety should be indicated. Legally, German wines are only required to contain 85% of the declared variety. The classic is **Riesling,** which can range widely in taste from fruity to spicy. Other grapes include **Weissburgunder,** used to make dry wines, often with an aroma of melon or pear, and **Scheurebe,** which produces delicious, high-quality wine with the aroma of red currant. No grape reference on the label often means a poorly blended, inferior-quality wine.

"Vintage" refers to when the grapes were grown (not harvested). The question of origin is also something to keep an eye on. It's best if the label gives a single vineyard, but these can be distinguished from the less specific vineyard zones only if you are in the know or can consult a pocket guide, such as Johnson's.

Next, check for the level of ripeness. German law distinguishes between **Tafelwein (table wine)** and **Qualitätswein (quality wine).** QbA (Qualitätswein bestimmter Anbaugebiete) on a bottle means the wine is made from the approved grape varieties, which will give it the particular and traditional taste of its region. **QmP** refers to **Qualitätswein mit Prädikat** (wine with distinction) and carries one of six special attributes. These, in order of ascending price, are *Kabinett, Spätlese, Auslese, Beerenauslese* (BA), *Eiswein,* and the exclusive *Trockenbeerenauslese* (TBA).

As a classification, **Kabinett** was first used by Eberbach Abbey in 1712 to denote quality. This wine is especially good as an aperitif with light snacks or veal. The mildly sweet and fruity *Auslese* from the Mosel-Saar-Ruwer region and the rich *Spätlese* are well suited to richer dishes such as duck, smoked fowl, and oysters. Those *trocken* and *halbtrocken* Rieslings from the Rheingau and Mosel-Saar-Ruwer are perfect with pork, sausages, and *Sauerkraut*, as well as with mild cheeses. A fuller-bodied Riesling *Spätlese* and *Auslese Trocken* from Rheingau or Pfalz goes excellently with wild boar and lobster. The rarest vintages, those sweet wines carrying the BA and TBA designations, are best left for anything oily or pungent in flavor, such as goose-liver pâté or rich cheeses. They are also wonderful with desserts.

Many foreign visitors tour one of the winegrowing districts. Since reunification, a number of wine districts have emerged in eastern Germany; however, the traditional German wine country, stretching from the middle Rhine at Bonn down to Lake Constance on the Swiss border, is still the most charming, with its classic scenery of imposing castle ruins, elegant spas, and Brothers Grimm villages replete with spires and black-and-white gabled houses.

WHEN TO GO

The most popular tourist months are May to October, although winter travel to Germany is becoming increasingly popular, especially to the ski areas in the Bavarian Alps. Germany's climate varies widely. In the north, winters tend to be cold and rainy; summers are most agreeable. In the south and in the Alps, it can be very cold in the winter, especially in January, and very warm in summer, but with cool, rainy days even in July and August. Spring and fall are often stretched out—in fact, we've enjoyed many a Bavarian-style "Indian summer" until late in October.

Berlin's Average Daytime Temperature & Rainfall (in.)

	JAN	FEB	MAR	APR	MAY	JUNE	JULY	AUG	SEPT	OCT	NOV	DEC
TEMP. (°F)	30	32	40	48	53	60	64	62	56	49	40	34
TEMP. (°C)	-1	0	4	9	12	16	18	17	13	9	4	1
RAINFALL	2.2	1.6	1.2	1.6	2.3	2.9	3.2	2.7	2.2	1.6	2.4	1.9

Frankfurt's Average Daytime Temperature & Rainfall (in.)

	JAN	FEB	MAR	APR	MAY	JUNE	JULY	AUG	SEPT	OCT	NOV	DEC
TEMP. (°F)	34	36	42	49	57	63	66	66	58	50	41	35
TEMP. (°C)	1	2	6	9	14	17	19	19	14	10	5	2
RAINFALL	6.5	5.1	5.6	5.7	5.9	5.5	5	5.1	4.2	4.8	6.5	6

HOLIDAYS

Public holidays are January 1 (New Year's Day), Easter (Good Friday and Easter Monday), May 1 (Labor Day), Ascension Day (10 days before Pentecost/Whitsunday, the seventh Sun after Easter), Whitmonday (day after Pentecost/Whitsunday), October 3 (Day of German Unity), November 17 (Day of Prayer and Repentance), and December 25 and 26 (Christmas). In addition, the following holidays are observed in some German states: January 6 (Epiphany), Corpus Christi (10 days after Pentecost), August 15 (Assumption), and November 1 (All Saints' Day).

Calendar of Events

All dates and events are subject to change. Contact the German National Tourist Board (www.germany-tourism.de) for more information. The board publishes a free calendar of forthcoming events three times a year, in April, October, and January; the first two are biannual calendars and the last is a yearly preview. They give the dates of trade fairs and exhibitions, theatrical and musical performances, local folk festivals, sporting events, conferences, and congresses throughout Germany.

For an exhaustive list of events beyond those listed here, check http://events.frommers.com, where you'll find a searchable, up-to-the-minute roster of what's happening in cities all over the world.

JANUARY

New Year's Day International Ski Jumping, Garmisch-Partenkirchen. This is one of Europe's major winter sporting events. For more information, contact the tourist bureau on Richard-Strauss-Platz (✆ 08821/180700; www.gapa.de). January 1.

FEBRUARY

International Film Festival, Berlin (at various theaters; announced in local newspapers). Stars, would-be stars, directors, and almost anyone with a film to peddle show up at this well-attended festival. It lasts for 10 days and is a showcase for the work of international film directors as well as the latest German films. Tickets can be purchased at any box office. Contact the **Berlin International Film Festival** (✆ 030/259200; www.berlinale.de) for more information. Early February.

Ambiente. This is one of the principal consumer goods trade fairs of Europe. Its origins go back centuries. For information, call ✆ 069/75750 (http://ambiente.messefrankfurt.com). Mid-February.

Fasching. Carnival festivals take place throughout Germany, reaching their peak on the Tuesday (Mardi Gras) before Ash Wednesday. Particularly famous carnivals take place in Bonn, Cologne, Düsseldorf, and especially Munich.

MARCH

Spring Fairs. Highlights throughout Germany, especially in Augsburg, Münster, Nürnberg, Hamburg, and Stuttgart. Dates vary from year to year.

APRIL

Walpurgis Festivals. Celebrated in the Harz Mountains. Festivities occur on the night of April 30.

MAY

Hamburg Summer. An entire series of cultural events, including concerts, plays, festivals, and special exhibitions throughout May, June, and July. For information, contact the **Hamburg Tourist Bureau,** in Hauptbahnhof (✆ 040/30051300; www.hamburg-tourism.de).

International **May Theatre Festival,** Wiesbaden. This city near Frankfurt hosts a premier cultural event—a series of artistic celebrations lasting 1 month. For information, contact the **Wiesbaden Tourist Office,** Marktstrasse 6 (✆ 0611/1729780; www.wiesbaden.de).

JUNE

Floodlighting **of the Castle,** Heidelberg. Fireworks enliven the display in this storied university city. For more information, contact the **Heidelberg Tourist Bureau,** Willy-Brandt-Platz 1 (✆ 06221/14220; www.heidelberg-marketing.de). June, July, and September.

Mozart Festival, Würzburg. Mozart fans flock to this major cultural event in the baroque city of Würzburg. For more information, contact **Tourismus Zentrale,** Falkenhaus am Markt Centrum (✆ 0931/372336; www.wuerzburg.de or www.mozartfest-wuerzburg.de). Early June to early July.

JULY

See **Floodlighting of the Castle,** Heidelberg, under June, above.

Freiburg Wine Tasting. Local residents and visitors enjoy the first vintages from grapes grown in the Black Forest district. For more information, contact the **Freiburg Tourist Board,** Rathausplatz 2–4 (✆ 0761/3881880; www.freiburg.de). Early July.

Richard Wagner Festival, Bayreuth. One of Europe's two or three major opera events, this festival takes place in the composer's Festspielhaus in the capital of upper Franconia. Note that opera tickets often must be booked years in advance. For information, contact Festival Administration, **Bayreuther Festspiele,** Kartenbüro, Postfach 100262 (✆ 0921/78780; www.bayreuther-festspiele.de). Late July to late August.

AUGUST

Red Wine Festival, Rüdesheim/Assmannshausen. This is held in Assmannshausen, the Rhine village most famous for red wines. For exact dates, contact the **Rüdesheim Tourist Bureau,** Geisenheimer Strasse 22 (✆ 06722/906150; www.ruedesheim.de). Late August.

Musikfest Berlin (✆ 030/254890; www.berlinerfestspiele.de) takes place for a little more than 2 weeks. During the festival, Berlin plays host to orchestras, ensembles, conductors, and soloists from around the world. The festival is organized in conjunction with the Stiftung Berliner Philharmoniker. Late August to mid-September.

SEPTEMBER

See **Floodlighting of the Castle,** Heidelberg, under June, above.

Oktoberfest, Munich. Much of Germany's most famous festival takes place in September, not October. Millions show up, and hotels are packed. Most activities are at Theresienwiese, where local breweries sponsor gigantic tents that can hold up to 6,000 beer drinkers. Contact the **Munich Tourist Bureau** (✆ 089/23396500; www.muenchen.de) for particulars or just show up. Reserve hotel rooms well in advance. Mid-September to mid-October.

OCTOBER

Frankfurt Book Fair. A major international event for publishers, book dealers, agents, and authors. For more information call ✆ 069/21020 (www.frankfurt-book-fair.com) or contact the **Frankfurt Tourist Office** (✆ 069/21238800; www.frankfurt-tourismus.de). Mid-October.

Spielzeit'europa. Schaperstrasse 24, Berlin (✆ 030/254890; www.berlinerfestspiele.de), is a 4-month season of theater and dance performances at Festspiele. October to January.

NOVEMBER

Jazz-Fest Berlin. This annual festival, staged at the Philharmonie, attracts some of the world's finest jazz artists, ranging from traditional to experimental. Contact the **Berlin Festspiele Ticket Office** (✆ 030/254890; www.berlinerfestspiele.de) for more information. Early November.

Winter Dom, Hamburg. An annual amusement fair (sometimes called Hamburg Dom) at the Heiligengeistfeld. For more information, contact the **Hamburg Tourist Bureau,** in Hauptbahnhof (✆ 040/30051300; www.hamburg-tourism.de). Early November to early December.

DECEMBER

Christmas Fair, Mainz. Mainz stages its Christmas fair on the Rhine for the 4 weeks preceding Christmas. For more information, contact the **Mainz Tourist Bureau,** Brueckenturm am Rathaus (✆ 06131/286210; www.mainz.de). December. (Other German towns hold Christmas fairs in Nov.)

RESPONSIBLE TRAVEL

Germans, with some justification, consider themselves in the avant-garde of green travel. Although they suffered one of history's most devastating attacks on their environment (World War II), in the postwar years they became a front-runner in preserving their environment and protecting nature.

"Germans are known for recycling and reusing their natural resources," said Berlin activist Hans Welder.

In Germany, more and more systems are going into place to generate energy from wind and solar power.

Germans didn't exactly invent walking or hiking across their countryside, but you would think so when you notice the numbers of citizens who prefer this form of exploration. It's a way to stay in good health, enjoy nature, and avoid harming the environment, all at the same time.

Trails in Germany are often signposted, cutting through all areas of the country, from tidal shores to low mountain regions, with tours offered to some of the more difficult-to-reach points along mountaintops.

The outdoor enthusiast might want to concentrate on Germany's national parks, 14 in all, with the heaviest concentration in Bavaria and in old East Germany. Our favorite of these biosphere reserves is the **Bavarian Forest National Park** in the south and the **Harz National Park** in Lower Saxony and Saxony-Anhalt.

We applaud the German effort to reintroduce wildlife that was once native to these parks. The last lynx in the Harz Mountains was shot in 1818. But the animal was reintroduced in 1999, and wild lynxes began to give birth in 2002. However, other attempts have failed, including an attempt to return the capercaillie to its former native habitat.

For general data about the parks of Germany, consult **Nationalpark Service, Informationshaus,** 17192 Federow, Germany (© **039/91668849;** www.national park-service.de). The national parks are free, but camping at designated areas ranges from 5€ to 10€ per night. Some parks have huts that are basic but better than a tent, and this form of accommodations costs from 10€ to 20€ per person. Park rangers crack down on those who harm the environment.

If you're interested in camping, check the Great Outdoor Recreation Page (www. gorp.com) before you go. It has some fine data not only on camping but also on ways to enjoy the landscapes of Germany.

Many organizations are devoted to eco-tourism today, including **Biosphefere Expedition,** P.O. Box 917750, Longwood, FL 32791 (© **800/407-5761;** www. biosphere-expeditions.org). This group sets up ecofriendly tours to the Bavarian Alps, for example. **Earthwatch,** 3 Clocktower Place, Ste. 1000, P.O. Box 75, Maynard, MA 01754 (© **800/776-0188;** www.earthwatch.org), often includes Germany in its 1- to 3-week jaunts to promote conservation of natural resources.

An unusual offering for the true green visitor is provided by **Willing Workers on Organic Farms,** Postfach 210259, 01263 Dresden (www.wwoof.de). Charging a membership of 20€, the organization's name says it all—participants get free room and board at a variety of organic farms throughout the country, but they must be willing to work for their supper.

One of the best ways for the green traveler in Germany is to take a tour from one bio hotel to another. These jaunts take you to the most scenic parts of the country, ranging from Lüneburg in the north to the Bavarian Forest in the south. For information and a list of these places to stay, check www.biohotels.info.

Increasingly popular is spending a vacation on a German farm, a welcome alternative for families with children. Sometimes guests can help with the activities, such as feeding the cows or helping with the harvest. Some lodgings are no longer working farms but have been turned into tranquil guesthouses with typical regional charm. Find out more about this type of holiday by searching www.landtourismus.de.

In addition to the resources for Germany listed above, see frommers.com/planning for more tips on responsible travel.

TOURS

Germany is one of the great outdoor destinations of Europe. From its mountains to its beaches, from its rivers to its castles, there is much to see and explore. It has summer attractions galore, plus skiing on its Alpine slopes in winter. Here is but a sampling of the offerings that await you.

Biking

In Germany you can bike through green valleys and past rivers while enjoying rural landscapes and villages. **Allgemeiner Deutscher Fahrrad-Club,** P.O. Box 107747, 28077 Bremen (© **0421/346290;** www.adfc.de), offers complete information on biking in Germany.

For over 20 years, **Classic Adventures,** P.O. Box 143, Hamlin, NY 14464 (© **800/777-8090;** fax 585/964-7297; www.classicadventures.com), has offered bike tours of such areas as the Romantic Road. **Euro-Bike and Walking Tours** has teamed with **Austin-Lehman Adventures** to offer some of the best biking and walking tours in Germany. The company's trips in Bavaria are particularly notable. For more information, check out www.austinlehman.com. You can also call **800/575-1540** in the United States and Canada, or else write to P.O. Box 81025, Billings, MT 59108.

Dozens of companies in Britain offer guided cycling tours. One of the best is the **Cyclists Touring Club,** Parklands, Railton Road, Guildford, Surrey GUZ 9JX (© **0870/873-0060;** www.ctc.org.uk). It charges £36 a year for membership.

Cruises

The most popular cruises in Germany are along the Rhine. For more details, see chapter 15.

Jody Lexow Yacht Charters rents hotel barges (including crew, food, and beverages) and smaller self-drive craft for touring the canals and rivers of Germany. For additional information, contact the agency at 26 Coddington Wharf, Newport, RI 02840 (© **800/662-2628;** www.jodylexowyachtcharters.com).

Canal barge cruises are the way to see a rarely viewed part of Germany. The best such packages are available through **European Barging,** 25132 Oakhurst Dr., No. 130, Spring, TX 77386 (© **888/869-7907;** www.europeanbarging.com). German itineraries focus on Berlin and the Mecklenburg lakes, and the "Mosel Cruise," from Trier to Koblenz.

Escorted General-Interest Tours

Escorted tours are structured group tours with a group leader. The price usually includes everything from airfare to hotels, meals, admission costs, and local transportation.

Many people derive a sense of ease and security from escorted trips. Escorted tours—whether by bus, motorcoach, train, or boat—let travelers sit back and enjoy the trip without having to spend lots of time behind the wheel or worrying about details. You know your costs upfront, and there are few surprises. Escorted tours can take you to the maximum number of sights in the minimum amount of time with the least amount of hassle—you don't have to sweat over the plotting and planning of a vacation schedule. Escorted tours are particularly convenient for people with limited mobility. They can also be a great way to meet people.

On the downside, an escorted tour often requires a big deposit upfront, and lodging and dining choices are predetermined. You'll have few opportunities for serendipitous interactions with locals. The tours can be jampacked with activities, leaving little room for individual sightseeing, whim, or adventure—plus they often focus only on the heavily touristed sites, so you miss out on lesser known gems.

Brendan Vacations (© **800/421-8446;** www.brendanvacations.com) has a selection of 8- to 15-day tours. Accommodations are at the better hotels, and rates include everything except airfare. **Collette Vacations** (© **800/340-5158;**

www.collettevacations.com) has an "Alpine Countries" tour that covers southern Germany, Austria, and Switzerland. **Globus & Cosmos Tours** (© 800/338-7092; www.globusandcosmos.com) offers 9- to 16-day escorted tours of various parts of Germany. It also has a budget branch that offers tours at lower rates. **Maupintour** (© 800/255-4266; www.maupintour.com) has a selection of upscale tours, such as a Rhine River tour of Berlin, Dresden, Meissen, Nürnberg, and Heidelberg. Its most popular tour is a 14-day trip that takes in such cities as Dresden, Berlin, Rothenburg, Munich, Meissen, Baden-Baden, and Potsdam, including a Rhine River cruise past the Lorelei Rock.

Abercrombie & Kent (© 800/554-7016; www.abercrombiekent.com) provides customized group tours to various areas of Germany.

Golf

Most German golf courses welcome visiting players who are members of courses at home. Weekday greens fees are usually around 50€, rising to as much as 90€ on Saturday and Sunday. For information about the various golf courses, write to the **Deutscher Golf/Verband,** Viktoriastrasse 16, 65189 Wiesbaden (© 0611/990200; www.golf.de/dgv).

The Swabian region of Allgäu has several good courses. **Golf Club Oberstaufen und Steibis** (© 08386/8529; www.golf-oberstaufen.de), at Oberstaufen, is an 18-hole course close to a forest and nature park. Ofterschwang, a small, peaceful resort on the scenically beautiful Tiefenberger Moor, has **Golf Club Sonnenalp** (© 08321/272181; www.golfresort-sonnenalp.de). A good 18-hole course is found at **Golf Bodensee** (© 08389/89190; www.gcbw.de) on Lake Constance in southern Germany. Farther north, the city of Augsburg has an 18-hole course at **Golf Augsburg** (© 08234/5621; www.golfclub-augsburg.de).

Hiking & Mountain Climbing

These sports are popular in the German uplands. It's estimated that Germany has more than 80,000 marked hiking and mountain-walking tracks. The **Deutschen Wanderverband,** Wilhelmshöher Alle 157–159, 34121 Kassel (© 0561/938730; www.wanderverband.de), services the trails and offers details about trails, shelters, huts, and addresses of hiking associations in various regions. The **Deutscher Alpenverein (DAV),** Von-Kahr-Strasse 2–4, 80997 Munich (© 089/140030; www.alpenverein.de), owns and operates 50 huts in and around the Alps that are open to all mountaineers. This association also maintains a 15,000km (9,300-mile) network of Alpine trails.

The best **Alpine hiking** is in the Bavarian Alps, especially the 1,240m (4,070-ft.) Eckbauer, on the southern fringe of Partenkirchen. The tourist office will supply hiking maps and details (see chapter 10). Another great place for hiking is **Berchtesgaden National Park,** Franziskanerplatz 7, Berchtesgaden (© 08652/64343; www.nationalpark-berchtesgaden.bayern.de), bordering the Austrian province of Salzburg (p. 331). This park offers the best-organized hikes and will hook you up with various groups offering hikes.

SUGGESTED GERMANY ITINERARIES

Germany has so much enchantment off the beaten path that it's easy to get lost here. In fact, one of the joys of travel is wandering about at leisure, making new discoveries of your own.

If you're a time-pressed traveler, however, you may find one of these two itineraries most helpful: **The Rhineland & Northern Germany in 1 Week** or **Southern Germany in 1 Week.** If have 2 weeks to spend in Germany, you can combine the two regional tours. If you've been to Germany before, you might want to focus on less visited parts of the country—perhaps a drive along the Fairy-Tale Road.

Germany ranks with France and England in offering Europe's fastest and best-maintained highway systems (autobahns), and it has one of the most efficient public transportation systems in the world, especially in its national train system.

The itineraries that follow take you to major attractions and charming towns. The pace may be a bit breathless for some visitors, so skip a town or sight occasionally to have some chill-out time—after all, you're on vacation.

THE REGIONS IN BRIEF

Germany lies in the heart of Europe, bordered by Switzerland and Austria to the south; France, Luxembourg, Belgium, and the Netherlands to the west; Denmark to the north; and Poland and the Czech Republic to the east. The country encompasses 356,216 sq. km (137,535 sq. miles) and has a population of about 80 million.

Berlin & Potsdam

Berlin has once again taken its place as Germany's capital and cultural center. It beckons visitors with glorious museums, wonderful cultural offerings, and cutting-edge nightlife. Southwest of Berlin is Potsdam, with its famous palace and elegant gardens and parks, set in an idyllic landscape along the Havel River. See chapter 4.

Thuringia

Long a tourist mecca for workers from the Eastern Bloc countries, Thuringia, with its untouched villages, churches, and medieval fortress ruins, is now being discovered by westerners. If your idea of East Germany is grim industrial cities and cheap housing projects, be prepared for a surprise. Here you can still see the small towns once known to Luther, Bach, and Wagner. The region's densely forested mountains are prime hiking country. The cultural center, with many attractions, is the city of Weimar, once the bastion of such greats as Walter Gropius, Mies van der Rohe, Liszt, Goethe, and Schiller. See chapter 5.

Saxony: Leipzig & Dresden

Known for its annual trade fair that draws participants from around the world, Leipzig is the most important industrial center in the east after Berlin. But this city, once the home of Bach, is also a cultural treasure, with museums, old churches, and *Thomanerchor* (the famous boys' choir). For those who find Berlin too overwhelming, Leipzig is an excellent alternative. See chapter 5.

However, if it's a choice between Leipzig and Dresden, make it Dresden, still one of the most beautiful cities in Germany, though 80% of its center was destroyed in an infamous 1945 Allied air raid. Today, Dresden is bouncing back fast, particularly in light of the reopening of the Frauenkirche in 2005. See chapter 5.

Franconia & the German Danube

Some of Germany's greatest medieval and Renaissance treasures came from this region, which gave the world such artists as Albrecht Dürer and Lucas Cranach the Elder. Come here to visit some of the most beautiful and historical towns in Germany, notably Regensburg, Bamberg, Nürnberg, and Bayreuth, where Wagner built his theater and created Festspiele, the famous opera festival. Though tourists often pass it by, Regensburg, about 100km (60 miles) southeast of Nürnberg, is well worth a visit. It suffered no major bombings in World War II and so remains one of the best-preserved cities in Germany. Nürnberg, although it holds much interest today with its many preserved art treasures, was heavily bombed and had to be virtually rebuilt. The Danube, which flows through this region, isn't blue and doesn't have the allure, dramatic scenery, or castles of the Rhine, but it's worth exploring for its own quiet charm. See chapter 6.

The Romantic Road

One of the most scenically beautiful (but overrun) attractions in Germany, the *Romantische Strasse* winds south from Würzburg to the little town of Füssen at the foot of the Bavarian Alps. Don't miss Würzburg, Germany's baroque city on the banks of the Main River. This glorious old city is overlooked by a fortified castle. Along the way, Rothenburg ob der Tauber is one of the most splendidly preserved medieval towns in Europe. The road comes to an end at "Mad" King Ludwig's most fantastic creation: Neuschwanstein Castle. The Romantic Road, originally a bit of PR hype to promote the area, was launched in 1950. It was such a success that the road is now clogged with traffic in summer, so the trip is best made in spring or autumn, before the tour buses arrive. (For an admittedly less scenic, but still charming, "romantic road," try the Fairy-Tale Road in Lower Saxony and North Hesse; see below.) The region of the Romantic Road is known for its folk traditions, old-world charm, and unspoiled medieval towns still surrounded by their original walls. Despite its drawbacks, the road remains one of the most beautiful and interesting trails in Europe. See chapter 7.

Munich & the Bavarian Alps

Rebuilt from the rubble of World War II, Munich is one of the most visited cities of Europe and probably the best place in Germany for old-fashioned fun. It should be included even on the briefest of itineraries. As chic and cosmopolitan as Frankfurt or Berlin, Munich is also kitschy in the best sense of Bavarian tradition. A night at the Hofbräuhaus or Augustiner Bierstuben with its liter mugs and oom-pah bands, will get you into the spirit of Munich life. After strolling through the Englischer Garten and having a glass of Bavarian wine in Schwabing (the legendary artists' district), you can tackle Munich's vast array of museums and palaces. Save time for the Deutsches Museum, the largest technological museum in the world. Munich also lies at the gateway to the Bavarian Alps. Shimmering Alpine lakes, half-timbered houses frescoed with paintings, and picture-postcard towns like Mittenwald and Oberammergau are all here, plus hiking, nature, wildlife, and Alpine-ski trails in winter. See chapters 8 and 9.

Lake Constance (Bodensee)

The 260km (160-mile) coastline of the Bodensee is shared with Austria and Switzerland, but Germany got the best part, the lake's beautiful northern rim. A boat trip on the Bodensee, while not comparable to a Rhine cruise, is a major attraction. The tour takes in castles and towns built on islands near the shoreline. The best place to be based is Lindau, at the southeastern part, near the Austrian border. Reached by a causeway, this island town has the most luxuriant flowers and shrubs of any resort along the lake. But Konstanz, the largest city on the lake, also merits a visit because it's one of the best-preserved major medieval cities in Germany. See chapter 10.

The Black Forest (Schwarzwald)

This dense fir forest, filled with beauty, charm, and myth, actually receives more sunshine than most other forests in Germany. The major center of the region is Freiburg, but the most visited city is the elegant Baden-Baden resort. Black Forest cake and smoked ham may be reason enough to visit the area, but other draws include casino gambling, great spas, hiking, bicycling, and cross-country skiing. Freiburg im Breisgau remains one of the most beautiful and historic towns in Germany and makes the best center for exploring the region. If you want a Black Forest cuckoo clock—just as good as those sold in Switzerland—head for Triberg. See chapter 11.

Heidelberg & the Neckar Valley

Except for the Bavarian Alps, there is no more tranquil and scenic part of Germany than the Neckar Valley. The area's Burgenstrasse (Castle Road) has more castles than any comparable stretch along the mighty Rhine, and the Neckar River Valley is just as romantically charming as the more overrun Romantic Road. Allow time to take detours into hidden side valleys to see sleepy little towns, most often with a protective castle hovering over them. Heidelberg, the apotheosis of romantic Germany, needs no selling. This famous medieval university town, with its historic castle, perfectly captures the spirit of south Germany and has attracted poets and composers over the decades. Goethe and hard-to-impress Mark Twain both fell in love here—Goethe with a woman of striking beauty, and the more cynical Twain with Heidelberg itself. Unfortunately, Heidelberg suffers from overcrowding, especially in July and August, when tourists descend by the bus load. See chapter 12.

Stuttgart & Tübingen

The capital of the state of Baden-Württemberg, Stuttgart is an industrial giant, headquarters of both Mercedes and Porsche. It's also a city of world-class museums and home to the acclaimed Stuttgart Ballet and Stuttgart State Opera. Its setting, surrounded by green hills with vineyards and orchards, is attractive, but the town isn't a serious contender for visitors when compared to Berlin or Munich. If you can give Stuttgart a day, fine. If not, head at once to nearby Tübingen, the ancient university city on the upper Neckar that has been compared favorably to Heidelberg. It doesn't have Heidelberg's grandeur (or its hordes of visitors), but we prefer its youthful air, its tranquillity, and the quiet beauty of its half-timbered houses and alleyways. Don't worry about rushing around to see a lot of attractions—just soak up the old-time atmosphere. See chapter 12.

Frankfurt

Frankfurt is vibrant, dynamic, and flashy, earning it the dubious distinction of the most Americanized city in Germany, maybe in Europe. Come here for the glitz and excitement of a major world player on the financial scene and its thriving, modern, and international feeling, not for Romantic Road architecture. Our recommendation is to treat it as a center worthy of at least 2 days of your time (it has any number of attractions), rather than as a transit hub. For many visitors, Frankfurt is their introduction to Germany, in the way that New York is the entry to America for thousands. Like New York, Frankfurt is hardly typical of the country in which it sits, but that doesn't mean you can't have a good time here. It's very civilized and filled with artistic treasures—in fact, the metropolis spends more per year on the arts than any other city in Europe. When not attending the ballet, a Frankfurter may be found slugging down a few jugs of apple wine in the open-air taverns of Sachsenhausen on the city's Left Bank. See chapter 13.

The Rhineland

After the Rhine's beginnings, in the mountains of Switzerland, as a narrow stream, this mighty river of legend flows for some 1,370km (850 miles) through one of the most picturesque and industrialized regions of Europe. For 2,000 years, it has been a major trade route. Bonn, Cologne, Düsseldorf, and Koblenz all lie on its banks. For most visitors, the number-one attraction is a romantic cruise down the Rhine, through gorges and past ancient castles, vineyards, and the fabled Lorelei. The most panoramic stretch is between Rüdesheim and Koblenz. Start your Rhine cruise at Rüdesheim, Germany's favorite wine village, about 72km (45 miles) west of Frankfurt. If you have time for only one Rhineland city, make it Cologne rather than the more commercialized Düsseldorf. Cologne is dominated by its famous cathedral, the largest in Germany, but this ancient city is also filled with dozens of other attractions, including restored Romanesque churches, striking Roman ruins, and the best modern-art galleries in the country. See chapter 14.

The Mosel Valley

Known as La Moselle in nearby France, the Mosel River weaves a snakelike path through the mountains west of the Rhineland. It doesn't have the Rhine's dramatic scenery, but we somehow prefer it, with its vineyards, castles, and fortresses that attract far fewer visitors. The swift-moving Rhine is filled with commercial traffic, but the Mosel is slow-moving, tranquil, and inviting, dotted with sleepy wine towns where you can sample some of the world's greatest vintages. Trains rumble all night along the Rhine, but not on the Mosel. (The inevitable tour buses do get through, however.) The best time to visit is during the annual fall grape harvest, centering in Cochem or Bernkastel-Kues. We've saved the best of this area for last: Near the Luxembourg border lies Trier, one of Europe's most fascinating antiques and the oldest city in Germany; it existed 1,300 years before Rome. Trier is a virtual theme park of Roman culture and architecture. See chapter 15.

Lower Saxony & North Hesse: The Fairy-Tale Road

Hansel and Gretel, Rumpelstiltskin, the Pied Piper, and even Cinderella list their addresses as "the Fairy-Tale Road." Frankly, the Fairy-Tale Road isn't as architecturally splendid as the Romantic Road, but it's also not as crowded, and it does have a wealth of treasures for visitors interested in German lore and legend or lovers of the tales of the Brothers Grimm, who lived and worked here. The road begins at Hanau, just east of Frankfurt, and stretches for 600km (370 miles) north, coming to an end in Bremen. The trail passes through colorful towns with half-timbered buildings and past plenty of castles. Naturally, it's haunted by witches, goblins, and memories of the Pied Piper of Hameln. See chapter 16.

Hamburg

The port city of Hamburg is exhilarating. The Germans often go to Frankfurt "for the banking," but to Hamburg "to have a good time." This Hanseatic city along the Elbe River has been beautifully rebuilt after the devastation caused by bombers in World War II, especially the night of July 28, 1943. A city of lakes, parks, and tree-lined canals, it is more famous for the tall tales of its red-light district. But these steamy after-dark diversions are only a small part of what Hamburg is. Restored architectural masterpieces and historic churches give this industrial city of two million prestige and allure. The world press may still call Hamburg Germany's "capital of lust" because of its sex clubs, but the city is also concerned with its environment, historical preservation, and art and intellectual pursuits. If you can, spend at least 2 days here. See chapter 17.

Schleswig-Holstein

This northwestern corridor of Germany, sandwiched between the North Sea and the Baltic, evokes bucolic Denmark, to which it was linked before Bismarck's defeat of that Scandinavian country in 1867.

Germany's northernmost province is one of our favorites because of its offshore vacation islands and the chance it offers to escape from the industrialization of northern Germany into acres upon acres of rolling green fields used for agriculture. Large areas are still forested, and there is enough moorland to delight a native of Yorkshire, England. Most interesting historically is the ancient merchant city of Lübeck, former capital of the Hanseatic League and the hometown of Thomas Mann, the great German writer. Although heavily restored after World War II, Lübeck is loaded with attractions, and its Altstadt (Old Town) has been designated a UNESCO World Heritage Site. The province is also home to Germany's most sophisticated seaside resort and its northernmost point, the island of Sylt, famed for its cosmopolitan atmosphere, its celebrities, and its climate of iodine-rich air and lots of rain. The port city of Kiel is short on charm because it was severely bombed in World War II, but the ancient stronghold of Schleswig invites wandering, exploring, and dreaming of the golden age of the Vikings. See chapter 19.

HIGHLIGHTS OF GERMANY IN 1 WEEK

There is no way you can really see Germany in 1 week. But you can have a memorable vacation in Berlin and Munich and see some highlights of Germany, if you budget your time carefully.

Days 1 & 2: Arrive in Berlin ★★★

Take a flight that arrives in Berlin as early as possible on **Day 1.** After unpacking at your hotel, set out to visit the **Brandenburg Gate** (p. 89), symbol of Berlin, and then walk down **Unter den Linden** (the main drag of Berlin), stopping for a German pastry and a coffee at one of the cafes that line the edges of this boulevard.

Spend the rest of the morning at the **Gemäldegalerie** (p. 84) museum, viewing some of the great masterpieces of early German artists as well as an array of international painters (especially rich in the Italian department). If the weather's fair, take a boat tour of the Spree (the main river of Berlin) and have lunch in a typical tavern. In the afternoon, climb the dome of the **Reichstag** (p. 95), the German Parliament building.

In what's left of your afternoon, visit what used to be called East Berlin, taking in the beautiful neoclassical square, **Gendarmenmarkt,** and exploring the rebuilt **Nikolaiviertel** (**Nikolai Quarter;** p. 97). After a rest back at your hotel, take in some of Berlin's fabled nightlife.

On **Day 2,** begin your morning with a tour of **Schloss Charlottenburg** (p. 80), one of the great baroque palaces of Germany. Allow at least 1½ hours for a tour. Nearby you can visit **Die Sammlung Berggruen** (p. 80), with its Picasso collection, if time remains. End your morning with a stroll through Charlottenburg's beautiful formal gardens.

After lunch in a typical Berlin restaurant, head for the **Bode-Museum** (p. 97), which displays the city's famous Egyptian collection. The collection has been returned to its original home, which it hasn't occupied since the start of World War II in 1939. The most celebrated bust of Queen Nefertiti, dating from 1360 B.C., can be viewed here in a home all her own.

While on Museumsinsel, head for the **Pergamon Museum** (p. 98), with its Greek and Roman antiquities. The Pergamon Altar is the highlight of this collection, as is the colossal blue Ishtar Gate that once stood in Babylon in 575 B.C.

Spend the rest of the day going for a refreshing stroll through Berlin's **Tiergarten** (p. 102), the most famous park in Berlin. That evening, take in a cultural presentation at one of Berlin's famous opera houses, perhaps a performance of one of its symphony orchestras. Not into classical music? Then head for the cabaret.

Day 3: A Side Trip to Potsdam ★★★

While still based at a hotel in Berlin, take the S-Bahn to the baroque town of **Potsdam,** on the Havel River. While at Germany's answer to Versailles, you can wander for hours, exploring the palaces and gardens of **Sanssouci** (p. 148), which was the former palace of Friedrich (Frederick) the Great. After lunch, you can also tour **Schloss Cecilienhof** (p. 150), the former country house of Kaiser Wilhelm II and site of the 1945 Potsdam Conference that included Truman, Stalin, and Churchill.

Return to Berlin by fast train in the afternoon for a final look at Germany's unified capital. Before the day completely fades, pay a visit to the **Kaiser Wilhelm Memorial Church,** in western Berlin (p. 84), and stroll down the **Kurfürstendamm** (known as Ku'Damm), the most famous boulevard in western Berlin.

Suggested Germany Itineraries

★ **Highlights of Germany in 1 Week**
Days 1–2: Berlin
Day 3: Potsdam
Day 4: Nürnberg
Days 5–6: Munich
Day 7: Ludwig's Castles

N The Rhineland & Northern Germany in 1 Week
Days 1–3: Cologne
Days 4–5: Bremen or Hamburg
Days 6–7: Berlin

S Southern Germany in 1 Week
Days 1–2: Munich
Day 3: Ludwig's Castles
Day 4: Rothenburg ob der Tauber
Day 5: Würzburg
Day 6: Heidelberg
Day 7: Frankfurt

Germany For Families
Days 1–2: Berlin
Days 3–4: Munich
Day 5: Ludwig's Castles
Day 6: Rothenburg
Day 7: Heidelberg

The Fairy-Tale Road
Day 1: Frankfurt
Day 2: Hanau, Gelnhausen, Fulda
Day 3: Lauterbach, Alsfeld, Neustadt, Homburg, Kassel
Day 4: Münden, Göttingen
Day 5: Sababurg, Bad Karlshafen, Höxter, Bodenwerder
Day 6: Hameln
Day 7: Bremen

For something truly typical and evocative, have a mug of beer and regional food in a *Kneipe* (the Berlin equivalent of a London pub). Try **Lutter und Wegner 1811** (p. 129).

Day 4: Nürnberg ★★

In 6 hours, you can take a train from Berlin to Nürnberg, deep in the heart of Franconia. This ancient city, heavily bombed in World War II, makes an ideal stopover on the way to Munich. After checking into a hotel and enjoying a lunch of Nürnberg-style *Bratwurst* (finger-size sausages), head in the afternoon for the **Germanisches Nationalmuseum** (p. 215), the city's premier attraction. The National Museum is strong on the works of native son Albrecht Dürer, whose paintings are reason enough for a visit.

If time remains, visit the **Kaiserburg** (p. 215) on a hilltop at the northern edge of the Altstadt (Old City). Until 1571, it was the official residence of German kings and emperors. You might also get a look at **St.-Lorenz-Kirche** (p. 216), across the Pegnitz River, dating from 1270. It's the most appealing of Nürnberg's churches.

Days 5 & 6: Munich ★★★

Take an early-morning train to Munich (trip time: 2 hr.) so you can more or less get in a full day of sightseeing. For orientation purposes, walk over to the main square of Munich, **Marienplatz** (p. 283), where, three times during the day, you can witness a miniature "tournament" on its **Glockenspiel,** the city's clock tower. Climb or take an elevator to the top of the Rathaus tower here. This is the old city hall building, and from its peak, you'll have a panoramic sweep of the Munich skyline.

While you're in the area, stop at **Frauenkirche** (p. 286), Munich's largest church, rebuilt in the Gothic style. For lunch that day, dine at **Viktualienmarkt,** Munich's most famous open-air market and one of the greatest such food markets in Europe.

After lunch, spend 2 hours at **Alte Pinakothek** (p. 290), one of the world's greatest art museums, especially strong in European artists from the 14th to the 18th century.

To cap your afternoon, stroll through the beautiful **Englischer Garten** (p. 299), and don't be surprised to meet some local residents in the nude. For your night fun, follow the oom-pah sounds to the **Hofbräuhaus** (p. 313), the world's most famous beer hall.

On **Day 6,** visit the **Deutsches Museum** (p. 295) in the morning. This German Museum of Masterpieces of Science and Technology is the largest technological museum in the world. It even shelters the first automobile (a Benz from 1886). Allow at least 2 hours for a visit. After lunch, plan on spending the afternoon at **Schloss Nymphenburg** (p. 296), the summer palace of the Wittelsbach dynasty. Allow at least 2½ hours, with time reserved for a stroll through the famous Nymphenburg gardens or park. One of the highlights here is an array of ornate sleighs and coaches once used by "Mad" King Ludwig of Bavaria.

After a return to town, consider attending a cultural performance at the **Cuvilliés Theater** (p. 317), the most beautiful rococo theater in the world.

Day 7: Ludwig's Castles ★★★

It's easier and more luxurious to rent a car in Munich and drive to Germany's two most famous castles at **Neuschwanstein** (p. 267) and **Hohenschwangau**

(p. 267). You can also travel by train to Füssen, 119km (74 miles) southwest of Munich, where you can then take the bus to Neuschwanstein, a distance of 7km (4 miles) east of Füssen. However, you'll spend so much time in travel that you'll have time to visit only one castle that day.

If you're that rushed, make it Neuschwanstein, as it's the true fairy-tale castle of King Ludwig. Hohenschwangau is not as glamorous or as spectacular. Tours of Neuschwanstein take an hour. But because of the rush of visitors to the area, there are often long delays in summer. After your castle tour, return to Munich and travel back to Berlin by train.

THE RHINELAND & NORTHERN GERMANY IN 1 WEEK

This spin takes you from Cologne, the cathedral city in the heart of the Rhineland, up to the best of Northern Germany. After Cologne, choose from spending a few days in tranquil, compact Bremen (a fine break from the larger cities on this trip) or hit the sleek Hanseatic port city of Hamburg and meander its endless waterways. Whatever you decide, end the tour in Berlin, Germany's most fascinating and edgy city.

Days 1, 2 & 3: The Cathedral City of Cologne ★★★

You'll likely arrive in the afternoon, so check into your hotel and, time-willing, take a short stroll to get a feel for your immediate neighborhood—**Cologne** (p. 510) is friendly and fun, and you'll quickly soak up the vibe. Later that night hit one of the city's famous old beer taverns for drinks and dinner, a favorite being **Früh am Dom** (p. 517).

On **Day 2,** launch your stay with an exploration of the highlights of the city. Head straight to Cologne's major attraction, the **Kölner Dom** (**Cologne Cathedral;** p. 513), followed by a visit to **Museum Ludwig** (p. 514), which boats one of the world's largest collections of the works of Pablo Picasso, among other attractions.

On the morning of **Day 3,** visit Cologne's oldest museum, **Wallraf-Richartz Museum/Foundation Corboud** (p. 515), with its amazing exhibition of Gothic works

After a Rhineland lunch, continue sightseeing at the **Museum Schnütgen** (p. 515), which contains Cologne's best collection of religious art and sculpture.

Spend the afternoon strolling through the old city and shopping—perhaps picking up a bottle of the famous Eau de Cologne. Consider an evening performance of the **Kölner Philharmonie** (p. 519).

Days 4 & 5: Bremen ★★★ or Hamburg ★★★

If you opt to head to the port of **Bremen** (p. 578) after Cologne, you'll find trains leave roughly every hour and take 3 hours—plan to arrive in early midafternoon.

Spend the afternoon exploring Bremen's many attractions. Begin at the **Marktplatz** (p. 580), the heart of town and the main square, with its towering statue of Roland, the port's protector. Next, be sure to take a stroll along the medieval alley **Böttcherstrasse** (p. 582), which runs from Marktplatz to the West River.

Continue to wander at leisure, taking in such attractions as the **Schötting** (p. 580), a 16th-century guild hall, and the **Haus der Bürgerschaft** (p. 581), home of Bremen's Parliament. The town's cathedral is **Dom St. Petri** (p. 581). Check out the **Rathaus (Town Hall;** p. 581), take in some shopping, and walk the rampart promenade, **Wallanlagen** (p. 582).

That evening, head to the **Schnoor** (p. 582), a restored old quarter of town with an artsy feel. It's chock-full of cozy restaurants.

Your other option after Cologne is **Hamburg** (p. 600). Trains leave Cologne every hour and take roughly 4 hours. Take a morning train and check into your hotel. Then, head straight to the harbor and hop on a **boat tour** (p. 604) that takes you along the Inner and Outer Alster, the main waterway running through Hamburg. It's a sublime way to enjoy the city and you'll immediately understand how much water is a part of this city.

In the evening, feast on northern German cuisine at the **Old Commercial Room** (p. 611), one of Hamburg's most historic restaurants and a fantastic place to enjoy local seafood.

The next day, visit **Hauptkirche St. Michaelis** (p. 604), a gorgeous baroque church, and wander around the Altstadt (Old Town). This is the last day of your tour, but if you have time for one more sight, be sure to visit the **Kunsthalle** (p. 606), northern Germany's finest art museum.

Days 6 & 7: Berlin ★★★

For your last stop, head to Berlin (p. 65). From Hamburg, trains leave every 30 minutes and take roughly 70 to 80 minutes; from Bremen, trains leave every 30 minutes and take roughly 3 to 4 hours (change in Hamburg). Follow the itinerary for Days 1 and 2 in the Germany Highlights tour on p. 51.

SOUTHERN GERMANY IN 1 WEEK

If you arrive in Munich, you'll be plopped into the middle of the action, with many prime sites a short train ride or drive away. An arrival in Frankfurt is also a perfectly fine way to start your trip—Frankfurt and Munich are just a tad over 3 hours from each other by train. Whether you fly into Munich or Frankfurt, this itinerary will show you the best of Bavaria and Baden-Würtemberg. Outside the cities, the main stops lie mostly along the Romantic Road, including **Rothenburg ob der Tauber** and **Würzburg.** Rounding northwest, you'll stay in historic Heidelberg for a night before continuing on and experiencing the modern heart of Frankfurt.

Days 1 & 2: Arrival in Munich, the Heart of Bavaria ★★

Try to arrange a flight that arrives in **Munich** (p. 273) early, and check into your hotel right away. If necessary, plan your two days around the weather. When pleasant, enjoy the outside sights like the **Nymphenburg Palace** and the **Englischer Garten.** Also, be sure to take a stroll around the **Old Town** (p. 275) and relax in a Biergarten. If the weather is uncooperative, the museums and churches will provide plenty to see before hunkering down in a Bierkeller for an afternoon drink or dinner.

To get oriented on **Day 1,** your first stop should be **Marienplatz** (p. 283), where the **Neues Rathaus** displays it famous **Glockenspiel** show at 11am and noon. Swing by the nearby **Frauenkirche** (p. 286), the city's symbol, and then head over to **Peterskirche** (p. 286), where a climb up the old tower offers a wide panorama of the city—and possibly the Alps you will soon visit. For lunch grab a bite to eat at the adjacent **Viktualienmarkt** (p. 286).

From there, fight off jet-lag with a walk via the old **Isartor** (p. 286) to the **Deutsches Museum** (p. 295), where the hands-on activities—and kids playing them—will surely stave off fatigue and boredom. Cap off your day at the **Englischer Garten** (p. 299) and get a good spot on the **Monopteros** rotunda on the hill for the sunset behind the spires of the city. For evening entertainment and hearty Bavarian fare, join the rowdy crowd at the famous **Hofbräuhaus** (p. 313), the local favorite **Augustiner Bräustuben** (p. 312), or any Bierkeller listed on p. 312.

Day 2 can start with a stroll around the stately **Odeonplatz, Ludwigstrasse,** and **Briennerstrasse.** When it opens at 10am, devote 2 hours to the **Alte Pinakothek** (p. 290), one of Germany's premier painting galleries from the 13th to 18th century.

Weather permitting, spend the afternoon at the **Schloss Nymphenburg** (p. 296), the summertime playground of the Wittelsbach royalty. The **palace** itself is worth a look, as are the exuberant sleighs and coaches in the **Marstallmuseum.** Although the pavilion interiors are not must-sees, a stroll around the gardens and ponds is a highlight.

Sample some of Munich's modern cuisine for dinner, before enjoying a show at the **Cuvilliés Theater** (p. 317), or any other venue listed on page p. 317.

Day 3: Ludwig's Castles ★★★

Driving through the Bavarian countryside to the mountains is an unforgettable experience (it's also quicker and more convenient than public transportation). **Neuschwanstein** (p. 267) and **Hohenschwangau** (p. 267) are the main draws, but the natural beauty alone is worth the trip. You can also travel by train to Füssen, 119km (74 miles) southwest of Munich, where you can then take the bus east to Neuschwanstein, a distance of 7km (4 miles). However, you'll spend so much time in travel that you'll have time to visit only one castle that day.

If you're pressed for time on **Day 3,** see only Neuschwanstein, as it's the true fairy-tale castle of King Ludwig II; Hohenschwangau is not as glamorous or as spectacular. Allow time for a long wait in summer, in addition to the hour-long tour. If you end up with extra time, consider spending the night further up the Romantic Road in **Augsburg.**

Day 4: Rothenburg ob der Tauber ★★★

If you aren't there already, spend the morning of **Day 4** in **Augsburg** (p. 259), just over 100km (62 miles) north of Füssen. Once you can park the car, take in the central pedestrian area with the Rathaus and its golden chamber. Stroll up to the **Dom St. Maria** with the oldest stained glass in the world, then over through the **Fuggerei** (p. 260). If there's time, the **churches of St. Ulrich and St. Afra** are worth a look, but the Romantic Road is calling.

Rothenburg ob der Tauber (p. 247) is some 175km (109 miles) north of Augsburg. On the leisurely drive up there, you can stop for coffee at the picturesque towns of **Nördlingen** (p. 255) and **Dinkelsbühl** (p. 253), but make sure you're in Rothenburg ob der Tauber by dinner. At 8pm, meet the night watchman at the Marktplatz for a tour in English, as he leads you through the old lanes and annals of history in this unforgettable medieval town.

Day 5: Wrap Up the Romantic Road in Würzburg ★★

Spend the morning seeing the sights of Rothenburg, beginning with the splendid altars in the **St. Jakobskirche** (p. 250). You can explore any section of this town and never cease to be amazed at the preservation of its medieval core. Before you leave, be sure to walk along the **ramparts,** ideally in the south and eastern sections.

By midday, hop in the car and follow the meandering Tauber river past other picturesque towns like **Creglingen, Weikersheim,** and **Bad Mergentheim.** Finally, unwind and stretch your legs in **Würzburg** (p. 236), the northern bookend of the Romantic Road.

The sights of Würzburg include the pinnacle of German Baroque embodied in the **Residenz** (p. 238), the **Dom St. Kilian** (p. 237) dedicated to the 7th-century Irish saint, and the mighty **Festung Marienberg** (p. 238) on the opposite hill, which also contains one of Germany's oldest churches, the **Marienkirche.** This last site may need to be saved for the next morning.

Alternatively, **Day 5** could also be spent in **Nürnberg** (p. 211) or **Bamberg** (p. 206), as all three of these towns are worthy in their own right.

Day 6: The University City of Heidelberg ★★★

On **Day 6,** Leave Würzburg early in the morning and head west for an overnight stopover in the city of **Heidelberg** (p. 410). Called "everybody's favorite town" in Germany, Heidelberg, on the Neckar River, can be explored in a day if you move fast enough. Check into a hotel in the Altstadt (Old Town) for atmosphere and wander its cobblestone streets at your leisure.

If you arrive early enough, spend at least 2 hours exploring **Heidelberg Castle** (p. 414), taking in the panoramic view of the town and its surrounding river valley. Follow this with a **boat ride on the Neckar** (p. 415) and a visit to the **Kurpfälzisches Museum** (p. 415).

Cap your evening by spending it in one of the fabled and historic student drinking clubs, our favorite being **Zum Roten Ochsen** (p. 419).

Day 7: Frankfurt ★★★: Your Exit from Southern Germany

After checking out of your hotel in Heidelberg, head up the road to Frankfurt in time to check into a hotel and enjoy lunch with the business crowd in the financial district. Spend the afternoon wandering its rebuilt **Altstadt** (p. 446) and visiting the **Goethe Haus** (p. 447). For an unforgettable view, ride up the **Main Tower elevator** (p. 448). If there's time, walk along the Main river and visit one of Germany's greatest art galleries, the **Städel Museum** (p. 448), with its collection of European old masters.

End your night with dinner in the restaurant of your choice. In the morning you can take the train, or else fly out of Frankfurt, perhaps after promising yourself another trip to Germany in the future.

GERMANY FOR FAMILIES

Germany offers many attractions that kids enjoy. And if pacing yourself with enough museum time is a concern, rest easy: Many museums in Germany, especially in Munich, have exhibitions that fascinate children of all ages.

Our suggestion is to spend 1 week in Germany as follows: 2 days in **Berlin,** 2 days in **Munich,** and the final 3 days visiting towns and castles that your kids will swear were created by Walt Disney himself—namely, **Ludwig's fairy-tale castles** in Bavaria; **Rothenburg,** a medieval city along the Romantic Road that looks like a stage setting; and, finally, everybody's favorite German town, **Heidelberg,** with its famous castle and other attractions.

Days 1 & 2: Berlin ★★★: Your Gateway to Germany

On **Day 1,** arrive as early as possible to get in a full day of sightseeing, as time is rushed. Before launching any specific sightseeing, take yourself and your kids to the **Brandenburger Tor** (p. 89), a gate that is the very symbol of Berlin. After a look around, head down Berlin's major boulevard, the famous **Unter den Linden** (see the "Frommer's Favorite Berlin Experiences" box on p. 88), filled with great Prussian architecture and world-class museums.

Unter den Linden turns into Karl-Liebknecht-Strasse, leading into **Alexanderplatz,** the heart of old East Berlin in the Cold War days (p. 88). You can take your kids for an elevator ride on the **Fernsehturm** (**TV Tower;** p. 88), the second-highest structure in Europe, for a view of the united city.

Before lunch, pay a visit to the **Pergamon Museum** on Museumsinsel (p. 98), where your kids are likely to be awed by such famous displays as the Pergamon Altar.

Secure the makings of a picnic lunch and head for the 167-hectare (413-acre) **Tiergarten** (p. 102), the former hunting grounds of Prussian rulers.

After lunch, hop over to see the multimedia extravaganza, **The Story of Berlin** (p. 87), telling in pictures and films the saga of the 8 centuries of the city's turbulent history. Allow 2 hours for a visit.

To cap the afternoon, take your brood on a boat tour of the **River Spree** (p. 75) that cuts across the once-divided city. Have dinner that night in a typical Berlin restaurant.

On **Day 2,** visit the **Reichstag** (p. 95) for a climb up its dramatic dome. Arrive before 8:30am to beat the crowds. After your assault on this monument, head for the **Zoologischer Garten Berlin** (p. 103), Germany's oldest zoo, housing some 13,000 animals, many of them quite rare and all in open natural habitats. You can also visit the adjoining aquarium.

After lunch, take an afternoon visit to **Potsdam** on the Havel River. Potsdam is only 24km (15 miles) southwest of Berlin. It's reached by frequent trains, taking 23 minutes from the Bahnhof Zoo. You can spend the rest of the day exploring **Sanssouci Palace** (p. 148) and its adjacent gardens. There is something here for everyone to see, even kids who bore easily. Head back to Berlin on the train for your final night before taking an early-morning flight to Munich.

Days 3 & 4: Munich ★★★: Gateway to Bavaria

On **Day 3,** head for the **Marienplatz** (p. 283) in the center of Munich, where if you arrive at the right hour you can treat your kids to a miniature tournament staged with enameled copper figures on the town's clock tower, **Glockenspiel.** Later, head for the **Deutsches Museum** (p. 295), the German Museum of Masterpieces of Science and Technology, on an island in the Isar River. The largest technological museum in the world is a very hands-on museum with buttons to push, levers to crank, and gears to turn—kids will love it. Allow 2 hours for a visit and plan to have lunch on-site at the museum's affordable restaurant.

In the afternoon, plan a family visit to **Schloss Nymphenburg** (p. 296), the summer palace of the Wittelsbachs. Children delight in the fantasy coaches and sleighs of Ludwig II and enjoy walks through the 200-hectare (500-acre) park. Return to Munich for the night.

In the morning of **Day 4,** take the kids to the **Bavaria Film Studio** (p. 300), Europe's largest filmmaking center. Children love the "Bavaria Action Show" with its simulated fistfights and fire stunts. Allow 1½ hours for a tour.

Follow this with a visit to the fabled royal **Residenz** (p. 288), where the Wittelsbachs lived from 1385 to 1918. Some very young children might be a bit bored with these stately halls, but as an adult you wouldn't want to visit Munich without seeing it.

After a stroll through the **Englischer Garten** (p. 299), treat yourself and your kids to a lunch of *Weisswurste,* those little white sausages for which Munich is known. A good spot to sample them is the **Ratskeller** (p. 306).

In the afternoon, visit **Münchner Stadtmuseum** (p. 287), where children are entertained by an array of carousel animals, marionettes, and hand puppets from around the world. That can be followed with a visit to the **Hellabrunn Zoo** (p. 299) in Tierpark Hellabrunn, lying 6km (4 miles) south of Munich and reached by U-Bahn to Thalkirchen. Hundreds of animals roam here in their natural habitat.

To cap your visit to Munich, take the entire family to **Zum Alten Markt** (p. 308), a moderately priced restaurant on a small square off Munich's largest outdoor food market. In summer, tables are set outside, and it makes for a festive evening as you bid farewell to Munich.

Day 5: Ludwig's Castles ★★★

On **Day 5,** rent a car in Munich and set out south, deep into Bavaria, to explore the fairy-tale castles of "Mad" King Ludwig: **Neuschwanstein** (a must) and **Hohenschwangau** (if time remains). Kids find that Neuschwanstein evokes a Disney architectural fantasy and delight in touring its lofty precincts, especially when it's reached by horse-drawn carriage. In the afternoon, the 12th-century Hohenschwangau can also be explored. This is where Ludwig spent a "joyless" childhood. You can return to Munich for the night or else find lodgings in **Füssen** (coverage begins on p. 264).

Day 6: Rothenburg ★★★

The next morning, **Day 6,** from your base in either Munich or Füssen, drive north or northwest, respectively, to Rothenburg ob der Tauber, the most glorious stopover along the Germany's Romantic Road. This is the best-preserved medieval city in Europe. With your kids in tow, you can wander for hours along its ancient streets, stopping in at the **Kriminalmuseum** (p. 248) or visiting the picture-book **Rathaus** (**Town Hall;** p. 249). Rothenburg is encircled by ramparts, and kids delight in walking along them, taking in the medieval tower gates. At some point along the way, stop at one of the kiosks selling *Schneeballen* (snowballs). These are round pastries covered with sugar that are sold all over town as a local specialty. Spend the night in Rothenburg.

Day 7: Heidelberg ★★★

On **Day 7,** journey west to the city of Heidelberg. You can arrive in time to tour the **Altstadt (Old Town),** beginning at **Marktplatz,** the main market square. Allow at least 1½ hours to walk about the ancient streets, and count yourself lucky if you're here on one of the market days (either Wed or Sat), as the entire city is more festive then.

After a lunch in one of Altstadt's student taverns, head up the hill to **Heidelberg Castle** (p. 414) for its stunning views and exploration, allowing about 2 hours for the entire jaunt. In the remaining part of the afternoon, take a **boat ride on the Neckar River** (p. 415). Overnight in Heidelberg.

You can drive to such transportation hubs as Munich in the east or Frankfurt in the north for your return flight.

THE FAIRY-TALE ROAD

To tour the Märchenstrasse is to take a trip through the land immortalized by the Brothers Grimm. In the gnarled forests and half-timbered cottages, you can still conjure up wicked witches, along with fairies, wizards, dwarfs, and goblins. The Grimm brothers were the earliest scholars of their country's folklore; they traveled to far-flung corners of Germany in the early 19th century to record the tales they heard. Their compendium, *Kinder- und Hausmärchen (Grimm's Fairy Tales),* is the world's second-most frequently translated book, after the Bible.

Today, you can follow the Fairy-Tale Road, a 595km (370-mile) route from Hanau, near Frankfurt, where the Brothers Grimm were born, to Bremen, where the "Bremen Town Musicians" lived. The route goes through some of the prettiest medieval villages in the country. To complete this tour, it's best to rent a car in Frankfurt, as the local public transportation is not adequate for what we've outlined. If you'd like to explore the Fairy-Tale Road in more depth, see chapter 16.

Day 1: Arrive in Frankfurt ★★★

Take a flight that arrives in Frankfurt as early as possible on **Day 1.** Check into your hotel and enjoy a coffee and a German pastry at a local cafe.

Although Frankfurt was heavily bombed in World War II, there is a lot of the old here—though mostly rebuilt. Head for the **Römerberg,** the heart of the old city where Charlemagne once erected his fort. Visit the **Römer** (p. 448), with its Imperial Hall, exhibiting a portrait gallery of German emperors. Nearby is the **Goethe Haus** (p. 447), former home of Germany's most famous writer.

Later you can follow in the footsteps of Goethe and wander for at least 2 hours in the **Altstadt (Old Town).**

For lunch, we'd recommend **Kameha Suite** (p. 453), a neoclassical villa that is a bar, cafe, and restaurant during the day.

In the afternoon, see the impressive array of European paintings from various schools in the **Städel Museum** (p. 448). If time remains, explore the **Liebieghaus** (p. 447), one of the great sculpture galleries of Europe.

Day 2: From Hanau to Fulda ★

In your rented car, leave Frankfurt in the morning and drive to the town of **Hanau** (p. 552), 20km (12 miles) east of Frankfurt, on the River Main. It was in Hanau that Jakob (1785–1863) and Wilhelm (1786–1859) Grimm were born.

Appropriately, the Fairy-Tale Road starts at a monument to the storytelling brothers at Neustadter Marktplatz. The memorial, erected in 1898, is about all that will interest you in this traffic-clogged suburb of Frankfurt. Hanau was heavily bombed in World War II.

From Hanau, go along B43 about 20km (12 miles) northeast to **Gelnhausen** (p. 555), where the remains of the imperial palace evoke memories of the emperor, Friedrich Barbarossa, and his lover, the beautiful Gela. Barbarossa constructed the castle here on an island in the 12th century.

Continue another 30km (19 miles) to **Steinau an der Strasse** (p. 556), where the Brothers Grimm spent their carefree youth. Visit the Amtshaus, the Renaissance palace, and see a performance at the fairy-tale puppet theater. Performances are held most Saturdays and Sundays at 3pm, though shows are not always guaranteed. Half-timbered buildings line cobblestone streets, and the surrounding woods might have been the home of Snow White. In the center of the main square is a memorial fountain honoring the brothers.

Continue north another 32km (20 miles) on B40, following the signs to **Fulda** (p. 557), noted for its baroque architecture, as exemplified by the bishops' palace on Schlossstrasse, overlooking the city. The prince-bishops were guardians of the tomb of St. Boniface, the apostle of Germany. Fulda's cathedral dates from 1704, and pilgrims still worship at the tomb of St. Boniface, in a crypt beneath the main altar. Consider staying overnight in Fulda.

Day 3: Lauterbach ★ to Kassel

Leave Fulda in the morning and take B254 into the Vogelsberg Mountains, going via Grossenlüder to **Lauterbach,** 24km (15 miles) northeast of Fulda. (In one of the Grimms' tales, the Little Scalawag loses his sock in Lauterbach.) The town is known for its medieval half-timbered houses and its two castles, Eisenbach and Riedesel. After your visit, follow Rte. 254 northwest to **Alsfeld,** a town of half-timbered houses and cobblestone streets. Its 1512 Altes Rathaus (Old Town Hall) is a showpiece.

Follow the route along the Schwalm River, which the Germans call *Rotkäppchenland,* or Little Red Riding Hood country. Signs point to **Neustadt,** with its circular tower, from which Rapunzel might have let down her golden tresses. Continue north through Schwalmstadt for 29km (18 miles) to **Homberg.**

From Homberg, follow the signs for 39km (24 miles) north to **Kassel** (p. 561), where you'll want to spend the night. The Waldeck region and the Reinhards Forest around Kassel were the birthplace of many legends about witches, sleeping princesses, strange beasts, and magic spells. These tales had a profound influence on the Grimm brothers, who lived in Kassel from 1798 to 1830. The **Brüder Grimm Museum** (p. 562), at Brüder Grimm Platz 4A, contains letters, portraits, and mementos.

Day 4: Münden ★ to Göttingen

Leaving Kassel, go along B3 for some 15km (10 miles) north to **Münden** (p. 565; known more properly as Hann. Münden). The Fulda and Werra rivers meet here. In the town center are some 700 half-timbered houses built in many styles. Also in Münden is the tombstone of the much-maligned Doctor Eisenbart (a Grimm character), who is remembered every year at a folk festival.

From Münden you can detour from the Fairy-Tale Road, taking the E45 Autobahn to **Göttingen** (coverage begins on p. 596). This is an ideal place to spend the night.

One of the great university centers of Germany, Göttingen is imbued with a lively student life and retains a certain air of medieval romanticism. You can spend hours wandering its narrow streets and looking at its enchanting half-timbered houses, evocative of a story by the Brothers Grimm.

Start your voyage of discovery in its **Marktplatz** (market square), with a statue of the little goose-girl, "the most kissed statue in the world." You can visit the Altes Rathaus (Old Town Hall) on the square and later spend an hour wandering through the **Stadtisches Museum** (p. 597), with its fascinating look at the history and culture of Lower Saxony. Visit one of the student taverns after dark, perhaps dining at the **Ratskeller** (p. 597), the cellar tavern of the town hall.

Day 5: Sababurg to Bodenwerder

Return to the Fairy-Tale Road by going back to Münden and then heading north on Rte. 80. About 10km (6 miles) north of Münden, in the village of Veckerhagen, go left and follow the signs to **Sababurg** (p. 566).

Right outside the village of Sababurg lies **Dornröschenschloss Sababurg,** Hofgeismar (p. 567), a park and castle said to be the setting of the Sleeping Beauty legend. You'll almost start to believe the tale when you see the Italianate turrets of the castle. The park is said to be the oldest zoological garden in the world.

After viewing the castle, take the road back to the Weser Valley village of Oberweser and make a left turn onto B80 heading north. After some 13km (8 miles), you reach the spa of **Bad Karlshafen,** a resort noted for its baroque buildings.

Continue north on Rte. 80 (which becomes Rte. 83) to **Höxter** (p. 567), the easternmost town in Westphalia. Among its many Renaissance and baroque buildings, the town's most visited attraction is **Dechanei (the Deanery).** You can take Corveyer Allee from Höxter for about 3km (2 miles) to **Corvey,** one of the oldest Benedictine abbeys in Germany, planned by Charlemagne and constructed by his son, Ludwig the Pious, in 822.

Follow the Weser River north for some 30km (20 miles) to the town of **Bodenwerder** (p. 569), the birthplace of Lügenbaron von Münchhausen, one of the most colorful characters who ever lived along the Fairy-Tale Road.

The baron grew up in a building that today is the Rathaus. Here you can visit the memento-filled **Münchhausen-Erinnerungszimmer** (**Münchhausen Memorial Room;** p. 569).

Day 6: Hameln ★ of Pied Piper Fame

After a night in Bodenwerder, head northwest on Rte. 83 for **Hameln** (coverage begins on p. 570).

Immortalized by the Brothers Grimm, and even Goethe and Robert Browning, this is the setting for the famous Pied Piper folk tale. Pied Piper, of course, was the world's most famous rat catcher, luring the town's children away, never to be heard from again. It's a romantic old town that invites a day's exploration. Rat figures in every conceivable form are for sale in the local shops. Explore its Gothic **Münsterkirch** (p. 571), or church, and take in such attractions as the **Rattenfängerhaus (Rat-Catcher's House),** where you can also order lunch (p. 571). Shop for souvenirs and absorb the atmosphere, overnighting in one of the town's inns.

Day 7: Bremen ★★, the Final Stopover

After a night in Hameln, take Rte. 83 northwest to the A30 Autobahn and continue west beyond Osnabrück until you connect with the E37 Autobahn heading northwest to the port of **Bremen** (coverage begins on p. 578).

In this "ancient town by the gray river," you can spend the day exploring its many attractions. Begin at the **Marktplatz** (p. 580), the heart of town and the main square, with its towering statue of Roland, the port's protector.

Wander at leisure, taking in such attractions as the **Schötting,** a 16th-century guild hall, and the **Haus der Bürgerschaft,** home of Bremen's Parliament. The town's cathedral is **Dom St. Petri.** You can also visit its **Focke-Museum,** one of the best regional museums of Germany. Call on its **Rathaus (Town Hall),** take in some shopping, and walk the rampart promenade, **Wallanlagen.** (Coverage of all these attractions begins on p. 580.) Overnight in Bremen. The following morning return to Frankfurt for your flight home.

BERLIN

Ask Berliners what they love about the German capital and some will talk about the joys of post-Communist freedom, others about Kreuzberg's throbbing nightlife, others about Friedrichshain's exciting young designers.

Berlin can fill you with wonder, contemplating the future in the crystalline Reichstag and high-rise Potsdamer Platz, and with horror, revisiting the past at the Jewish Museum and remnants of the Berlin Wall. The nostalgic, the party lover, the trendsetter, today's Berlin is one city, many characters—different every time you look but never looked at indifferently.

4

THINGS TO DO   Berlin is a monster-size capital, eight times the size of Paris. Plan wisely. First, head up to Norman Foster's panoramic glass-domed **Reichstag** (German Parliament), and join photographers for the obligatory twilight snapshot of the glowing **Brandenburg Gate.** You can spend days roaming **Tiergarten** park's lake-dotted woodlands and UNESCO-listed **Museum Island's** galleries, where Egypt's Queen Nefertiti hides. Trace Berlin's turbulent past at the Libeskind-designed **Jewish Museum** and walk the artiest stretch of Wall at the **East Side Gallery.**

SHOPPING   Individuality defines free-spirited Berlin. Go beyond the big-name designers on stately **Kurfürstendamm** to its quieter specialty stores, like **L. & M. Lee** with its German-made porcelain and glass. Poke around hip **Prenzlauer Berg** and **Kreuzberg** for urban, young designers and quirky boutique shopping. The **Hackesche Höfe's** Art Nouveau courtyards make for a leisurely stop, with their upscale shops and people-watching cafes.

NIGHTLIFE & ENTERTAINMENT   The fall of the Wall was *the* party of the 20th century, and even today Berlin still hasn't run out of steam. Glitzy 1920s cabaret lives on along **Friedrichstrasse,** while classical music rings out of **Mitte's** lavish concert halls like the neoclassical **Staatsoper.** Canal-side bars with alternative attitudes and industrial-style techno clubs draw revelers to **Kreuzberg** and **Friedrichshain.** Summer evenings are best spent chatting and sipping foamy wheat beer under chestnut trees in Prenzlauer Berg's **Prater Garten** beer garden.

RESTAURANTS & DINING   Down-to-earth and sociable, Berliners love lazy brunches in **Prenzlauer Berg's** bohemian cafes and fun street food. Join the queue in muticultural **Kreuzberg** for mustard-slathered *Currywurst* (curried sausage), pan-fresh falafel and shawarma. Foodies dine at **Mitte's** Michelin-starred restaurants and enjoy French food by candlelight in **Charlottenburg's** intimate bistros. For a real taste of Berlin, feast (as Napoleon once did) on fat pork knuckles with lashings of sauerkraut at the wood-paneled 17th-century tavern **Zur Letzten Instanz.**

ESSENTIALS

Getting There

BY PLANE   At press time Berlin still contained two international airports Tegel and Schönefeld.

Tegel Airport, north of the city and formerly Berlin's busiest, is slated to close sometime in 2012 when Schönefeld southeast of the center is fully expanded and officially turns into the new **Berlin Brandenburg International Airport**. For information about either, as well as the status of the new airport, go to www.berlin-airport.de. Most international flights will arrive at the new BBI, which will have a rail station under the main terminal. It will take only 20 minutes for the airport shuttle to travel the 20km (12-mile) stretch of track in Berlin's center.

Lufthansa (✆ **800/645-3880;** www.lufthansa-usa.com) routes transatlantic passengers from North American cities through the airline's hubs at Frankfurt and Munich.

Delta (✆ **800/221-1212;** www.delta.com) has flights to Berlin in the evening from New York's JFK airport. However, daily flights, depending on the season or on business, are not always a sure thing, so you'll need to check with a travel agent or the airline itself.

The best and most convenient service into Berlin is available aboard **British Airways** (✆ **800/247-9297;** www.ba.com), which efficiently funnels dozens of daily flights from North America to Germany, including five a day into Berlin, through its vast terminals at London-Heathrow. Connections to Berlin are available from at least 40 gateways in the U.S. and Canada, more than those offered by any other airline. Frequent transatlantic price wars keep fares to Berlin aboard BA lower than you may have thought, especially in the off season. Stopovers in London can be arranged at minimal cost, and deeply discounted hotel packages are available in either Berlin or London, at rates that are significantly less than what you'd have paid if you'd arranged them yourself. And if you opt for passage in business class (BA calls it "Club Class"), you'll ride on the most comfortable, and one of the largest, airline seats in the industry, in a configuration that can be transformed into something approaching a bed.

BY TRAIN   As Berlin strengthens its role as Germany's capital, increasing numbers of trains are speeding their way into town. All points of the country, especially Frankfurt, Munich, and Bonn, maintain excellent rail connections, with high-tech, high-speed improvements being made to the country's railway system virtually all the time. One major improvement is that Berlin and the great port of Hamburg are now 15 minutes closer, thanks to high-speed (250kmph/155 mph) InterCity Express service (the trip is now 2 hr., 8 min.). Since reunification, Berlin has improved the facilities of railway stations in both the western zone (Bahnhof Zoologischer Garten) and eastern zone (Berlin Ostbahnhof), installing improved S-Bahn links to interconnect them. The station you'll use depends on the destination or origin of your train, or the location of your hotel within the city. Some trains, but not all, make arrivals and departures from both stations. A third station, Berlin Lichtenberg, within the city's eastern half, is used for trains pulling in from small towns. For information about any railway station, call ✆ **01805/996633** or visit www.bahn.de. **Lehrter Hauptbahnhof** (known better as **Berlin Hauptbahnhof**), is the main train station, situated about a 10- to 15-minute walk from the Reichstag. It incorporates the lines that lead to the three other railway stations mentioned above, eliminating the need for cross-town commutes among the city's railway stations.

berlin TODAY & TOMORROW

Berlin is living up to its reputation as a dynamic, exciting hub of activity as never before. The city's nightlife is among Europe's best and wildest. And since the German government relocated here from Bonn, Berlin is bidding to become the reborn capital not only of Germany, but of all Europe.

As befits a capital, the city has undergone a major face-lift in the past 20 years. More than $150 billion was invested into new streets, buildings, and railways. The former East Berlin is restored and gentrified, particularly in the **Mitte (central)** district. Here, luxury hotels and shopping arcades compete with the glitter—and litter—of the **Ku'Damm** (short for Kurfürstendamm, a wide boulevard at the center of activity in the western part of Berlin). The Hotel Adlon (p. 141), overlooking the Brandenburg Gate, is particularly notable, evoking the restoration of Unter den Linden and the return to some of its prewar glory; Adlon, at one time, was the most important hotel not only in Berlin, but in all of Germany. **Prenzlauer Berg,** a blue-collar eastern neighborhood that escaped the worst of the wartime bombing, is now a chic district of cafes and boutiques. The downside of all this for Berliners has been the sharp increase in real estate prices.

Many of Berlin's famous buildings were also restored. The rebuilt **Reichstag** (p. 95) has a glittering glass dome; upon the building stands not the old glowering imperial hunter, but the national symbol, the eagle (locals refer affectionately to the statue as "the fat hen"). The **Oranienburger Strasse Synagogue** (commonly known as Neue Synagoge Berlin–Centrum Judaicum/The New Synagogue; p. 94), wrecked on Kristallnacht and finished off by Allied bombers, has been rebuilt to its previous splendor. Likewise, **Berliner Dom** (**Berlin Cathedral;** p. 89) and the five state museums on **Museumsinsel** (**Museum Island;** p. 95) have been returned to their original glory.

Visitors unfortunately often overlook Berlin's **natural attractions.** Few metropolitan areas are blessed with as many gardens, lakes, woodlands, and parks—all of which cover an amazing one-third of the city. First-time visitors are often surprised to learn that small farms with fields and meadows still exist within the city limits.

BY BUS (COACH)   Regularly scheduled buses operate from 250 German and continental cities, including Frankfurt, Hamburg, and Munich. Long-distance bus companies servicing Berlin include **Berlin Linien Bus** (✆ **030/8619331;** www.berlinlinienbus.de).

Arrivals and departures are at the **ZOB Omnibusbahnhof am Funkturm,** Masurenalle, Charlottenburg. Taxis and bus connections are available at the station and at the U-Bahn, at the nearby Kaiserdamm station.

BY CAR   From Frankfurt, take the E451 north until it connects with the E40 going northeast. Follow this autobahn past Jena and then head north on the E51 into Berlin. From Nürnberg, also take the E51 into Berlin. From Dresden, take the E55 north to Berlin. Expect heavy traffic on the autobahns on weekends and sunny days when everybody is out touring.

Visitor Information

For visitor information, head for **Berlin Hauptbahnhof** (the central rail station), open daily 8am to 10pm. There's another tourist office at Neues Krarnzler Eck, along the Kurfürstendamm, the popular shopping boulevard, open Monday to Saturday 10am to 8pm, Sunday 10am to 6pm. Another office is at the south wing of the Brandenburg Gate, open daily 10am to 6pm. The central phone number for all tourist information is ℂ **030/250025** (www.visitberlin.de). The staff will make hotel reservations for you and book tickets for major events and sightseeing tours.

City Layout

Berlin is one of the largest and most complex cities in Europe. Because it's so spread out, you'll need to depend on public transportation. No visitor should try to explore more than two neighborhoods a day, even superficially.

The center of activity in the western part of Berlin is the 4km-long (2½-mile) **Kurfürstendamm,** called the Ku'Damm by Berliners, who seem to have a habit of irreverently renaming every street and building in the city. Along this wide boulevard you'll find the best hotels, restaurants, theaters, cafes, nightclubs, shops, and department stores. It's the most elegant and fashionable spot in Berlin, but, like much of the city, it combines chic with sleaze in places. Walkers can stop off at one of the popular cafes lining the boulevard.

From the Ku'Damm, you can take Hardenbergstrasse, which crosses Bismarckstrasse and becomes Otto-Suhr-Allee, which will lead to the **Schloss Charlottenburg** area and its museums, a major sightseeing area. The **Dahlem Museums** are in the southwest of the city, often reached by going along Hohenzollerndamm.

The huge **Tiergarten** is the city's largest park. Running through it is **Strasse des 17 Juni,** which leads to the famed **Brandenburg Gate** (just south of the Reichstag). On the southwestern fringe of the Tiergarten is the **Berlin Zoo.**

The Brandenburg Gate is the start of eastern Berlin's most celebrated street, **Unter den Linden,** the cultural heart of Berlin before World War II. It runs from west to east, leading to **Museumsinsel (Museum Island),** where the most outstanding museums of eastern Berlin, including the Pergamonmuseum, are situated.

Unter den Linden crosses another major artery, **Friedrichstrasse.** If you continue south along Friedrichstrasse, you'll reach the former location of **Checkpoint Charlie,** a famous border site of the Cold War days. No longer a checkpoint, it now has a little museum devoted to memories of the Berlin Wall.

Unter den Linden continues east until it reaches **Alexanderplatz,** the center of eastern Berlin, with its towering television tower, or **Fernsehturm.** A short walk away is the restored **Nikolaiviertel (Nikolai Quarter),** a neighborhood of bars, restaurants, and shops that evoke life in the prewar days.

📎 Finding an Address

As for the numbering of streets in Berlin, keep in mind that the city sometimes assists you by posting the range of numbers that appears within any particular block, at least within major arteries such as the Kurfürstendamm. These numbers appear on the street signs themselves, which is a great help in finding a particular number on long boulevards. You won't find these numbers on street signs of smaller streets, however. Although some streets are numbered with the odds on one side and the evens on the other, many (including the Ku'Damm) are numbered consecutively up one side of the street and back down the other.

MAPS Good maps of Berlin can be purchased at bookstores or news kiosks, such as the Europa Press Center (a magazine and newspaper store in the Europa Center). One of the best maps is the **Falk map,** which offers full-color detail and comprehensive indexes (consequently, it's sometimes awkward to unfold and refold). Be sure to obtain an up-to-date map showing the most recent changes.

Neighborhoods in Brief

Visitors who knew Berlin during the Cold War are amazed at the way traffic now zips between sectors that once were rigidly segregated by border guards. Today, your taxi will blithely drive beneath the Brandenburg Gate or along the Friedrichstrasse, without regard to barriers that once used to be virtually impenetrable. Below are some names you're likely to hear as you navigate your way through the reunited city.

IN THE FORMER WESTERN ZONE

Charlottenburg Despite being renamed by Berlin wits as Klamottenburg (Ragsville) after the bombings of World War II, this is still the wealthiest and most densely commercialized district of western Berlin. Its centerpiece is Charlottenburg Palace. One of the most interesting subdivisions of Charlottenburg is the neighborhood around **Savignyplatz,** a tree-lined square a short walk north of the western zone's most visible boulevard, Kurfürstendamm. Lining its edges and the streets nearby are a profusion of bars, shops, and restaurants; an engaging aura of permissiveness; and an awareness that this is the bastion of the city's prosperous bourgeoisie.

Dahlem Now the university district, Dahlem was originally established as an independent village to the southwest of Berlin's center.

Ku'Damm In the 1950s and 1960s, during the early stages of the Cold War, the Ku'Damm emerged as a rough-and-tumble boomtown, bristling with boxy-looking new construction and permeated with a maverick sense of parvenu novelty. Since reunification, when vast neighborhoods within Mitte opened for real estate speculation and instant gentrification, the Ku'Damm has reinvented itself as a bastion of capitalistic and corporate conservatism, with a distinct sense of old and established money that's waiting for public perceptions to grow bored with the novelties that have been associated with the opening of the former East Berlin. The poignancies of the Weimar Republic and the Cold War are not lost, however, even upon the corporate sponsors of the big-money real estate ventures that line the Ku'Damm. If you look at the Hochhaus entrance of the Europa Center, on the Tauentzienstrasse side, whose glossy chrome-trimmed interior decor may remind you of an airport waiting lounge, you'll find a plaque honoring the long-ago site of the private home of Weimar statesman Gustav Stresemann, which used to stand at 12A Tauentzienstrasse. Immediately adjacent to that plaque is an artfully graffitied chunk of the former Berlin Wall, encased in Plexiglas like an irreplaceable work of ancient archaeology. It is dedicated to the people who lost their lives trying to escape over the Wall during the peak of the Cold War.

Grunewald Many newcomers are surprised by the sheer sprawl of Grunewald's 49 sq. km (19 sq. miles) of verdant forest. The area serves as a green lung for the urbanites of Berlin. It lies southwest of the city center.

Hansaviertel This neighborhood, northwest of Tiergarten park, contains a series of residential buildings designed by different architects (including Le Corbusier, Walter Gropius, and Alvar Aalto).

Kreuzberg Originally built during the 19th century to house the workers of a rapidly industrializing Prussia, this has traditionally been the poorest and most overcrowded of Berlin's districts. Today, at least 35% of its population is composed of guest workers from Turkey, Greece, and the former Yugoslavia. Prior to reunification, the district evolved into the headquarters for the city's artistic counterculture. Since reunification,

Berlin Neighborhoods

See "Charlottenburg Attractions" map

Kurt-Schumacher-Damm

Goerdeler Damm

Westhafenkanal

Siemensstrasse

Quitzowstrasse

Putlitzstrasse

Perleberger Strasse

MOABIT

Max-Dohrn-Strasse

Sickingenstr.

Beusselstrasse

Olbersstrasse

Tegeler Weg

Gaussstr.

Schlossgarten

Kaiserin- Augusta- Allee

Turmstrasse

Stromstr.

Mierendorffstrasse

Levetzowstrasse

Lessingstrasse

Schloss Charlottenburg

Spree

Otto- Suhr- Allee

Kaiser- Friedrich- Str.

Cauerstr.

Franklinstr.

Marchstrasse

Bachstrasse

BELLEVUE S

HANSA-VIERTEL

TIERGARTEN S

Strasse des

Spandauer Damm

Wilmersdorfer Str.

Bismarckstr.

str.

Hardenbergstr.

Spandau ←

Kaiserdamm

CHARLOTTENBURG

ZOOLOGISCHER GARTEN S

ZOO BERLIN

Kantstrasse

Kantstrasse

Savignyplatz

Breitscheidplatz

Budapester Strasse

Europa Center

eue

CHARLOTTENBURG S

Lewishamstr.

Leibniz

SAVIGNYPLATZ

Tauentzienstr.

Wittenbergplatz

Kleiststr.

WESTKREUZ S

Kurfürstendamm

Lietzenburger

Strasse

Uhlandstr.

See "Tiergarten Area Attractions" map

HALENSEE S

Brandenburgische Strasse

Konstanzer Strasse

Hohenzollerndamm

Hohenstaufenstr.

Rudolfstädter

Friedrichsruher Strasse

Fehrbelliner Platz

Bundesallee

See "Western Berlin Restaurants & Hotels" map

HOHENZOLLERNDAMM S

Hohenzollerndamm Strasse

WILMERSDORF

SCHÖNEBERG

Grunewald ←

Hohenzollerndamm

Hauptstrasse

Hundekehlestr.

Mecklenburgische Strasse

SCHÖNEBERG S

Breite Strasse

FRIEDENAU

↙ *Dahlem*

however, the fast-changing neighborhoods within Mitte, especially Hackesche Höfe (see below), have offered stiff competition.

Schöneberg Like Kreuzberg, it was originally an independent suburb of workers' housing, but after the war it was rebuilt as a solidly middle-class neighborhood that also happens to include the densest concentration of gay bars and clubs (btw. Nollendorfplatz and Victoria-Luise-Platz).

Spandau Set near the junction of the Spree and Havel rivers, about 10km (6 miles) northwest of the city center, Spandau boasts a history of medieval grandeur. Though it merged with Berlin in 1920, its Altstadt (Old City) is still intact. The legendary Spandau prison was demolished in the early 1990s.

Tiergarten Tiergarten (which means "Animal Garden") refers to both a massive urban park and, to the park's north, a residential district. The park was originally intended as a backdrop to the grand avenues laid out by the German kaisers. The neighborhood contains the Brandenburg Gate, the German Reichstag (Parliament), the Berlin Zoo, and some of the city's grandest museums.

IN THE FORMER EASTERN ZONE

Alexanderplatz The former East German regime threw up lots of ugly modern buildings and defined Alexanderplatz as the centerpiece of its government. Today, the large and sterile-looking square is dominated by the tallest structure in Berlin, the Sputnik-inspired TV Tower.

Hackesche Höfe A warren of brick-sided factories during the 19th century, it's evolving into one of the city's most visible counterculture strongholds. Part of this derives from the fact that it wasn't too badly mangled by the former East German regime. Another factor in its renaissance involves a thirst by cutting-edge, youthful Berliners to recolonize what used to be the heart of the GDR. You'll sense the rising real-estate values and combined aspects of Paris's Latin Quarter and New York's Greenwich Village.

Mitte (Center) Closed to capitalist investment for nearly 50 years, this monumental district in the heart of Berlin is the one that's on every speculator's mind these days. It was originally conceived as the architectural centerpiece by the Prussian kaisers. Its fortunes declined dramatically as the Communist regime infused it with starkly angular monuments and architecturally banal buildings. Although some of Mitte's grand structures were destroyed by wartime bombings, unification has exposed its remaining artistic and architectural treasures. The district's most famous boulevard is Unter den Linden. Famous squares within the district include Pariser Platz (the monumental square adjacent to the Brandenburg Gate), Potsdamer Platz (see below), and Alexanderplatz (see above).

Museumsinsel (Museum Island) This island in the Spree River hosts a complex of museums housed in neoclassical buildings that always seem to be under renovation. Its most famous museum, the Pergamon, contains magnificent reconstructions of ancient temples.

Nikolaiviertel Near the Alexanderplatz, the Nikolaiviertel is the most perfectly restored medieval neighborhood in Berlin, a triumph of the restoration skills of the former East German regime.

Potsdamer Platz Before World War II, this was the thriving heart of Berlin. Blasted into rubble by wartime bombings, it was bulldozed into a no man's land when the Wall went up on its western edge. After reunification, it was transformed into the biggest building site in Europe, out of which emerged a glittering, hypermodern square dominated by such corporate giants as Daimler-Chrysler. It's often cited as a symbol of the corporate culture of a reunited Germany.

Prenzlauerberg This former working-class neighborhood northeast of Berlin-Mitte morphed into the center of creativity in the 1990s. While it has mellowed out a bit, it is still one of Berlin's hottest quarters and boasts a thriving nightlife, particularly along and around Kollwitzplatz and Kastanienallee. Trendy clothing boutiques and art galleries share sidewalks with hip restaurants and bars, and the area has a fairly prominent gay and lesbian scene. In clement weather, people-watching, with a Pilsener, at one of Prenzlauerberg's many sidewalk cafes and restaurants is an entertaining way to spend an afternoon, and it won't take long to comprehend why this is one of the most popular (and expensive) places for 20- and 30-somethings to live in Berlin.

Getting Around

BY PUBLIC TRANSPORTATION

The Berlin transport system consists of buses, trams, and U-Bahn (underground) and S-Bahn (elevated) trains. The network is run by the **BVG,** or Public Transport Company Berlin-Brandenburg. Public transportation throughout the city operates from about 4:30am to 1:30am daily (except for 68 night buses and trams, and U-Bahn lines U-9 and U-12). For information about public transport, call © **030/19449,** or visit www.bvg.de. For a plan of Berlin's **U-Bahn and S-Bahn system,** see the inside front cover of this guide.

The BVG *Einzelfahrschein* (**standard ticket**) costs 2.10€ to 2.80€ and is valid for 2 hours of transportation in all directions, on all forms of public transport, transfers included. A 24-hour ticket for the entire city costs 6.10€ to 6.50€. Only standard tickets are sold on buses.

Tram tickets must be purchased in advance. All tickets should be kept until the end of the journey; otherwise, you'll be liable for a fine of 40€. Unless you buy a day pass, don't forget to time-punch your ticket into one of the small red boxes prominently posted at the entrance to city buses and underground stations. Standard tickets, valid for all public transport within the city of Berlin, are available at all BVG and S-Bahn and U-Bahn ticket counters.

If you're going to be in Berlin for 3 days, you can purchase a 26€ **Berlin-Potsdam Welcome Card,** which entitles holders to 72 free hours on public transportation in Berlin and Brandenburg. You'll also get free admission or a price reduction of up to 50% on sightseeing tours, museums, and other attractions, and a 25% reduction at 10 theaters as well. The card is sold at many hotels, visitor information centers, and public-transportation sales points. It's valid for one adult and three children 13 and under.

Two **excursion bus lines** make some beautiful scenic spots accessible. Bus no. 218 operates from the Theodor-Heuss-Platz U-Bahn station (near the radio tower) via Schildhorn, Grunewald Tower, and Wannsee Beach to the Wannsee S-Bahn station, and bus no. 218 runs from the Wannsee S-Bahn station to Pfaueninsel.

BY TAXI

Taxis cruise restlessly along the major boulevards, indicating their availability by an illuminated roof light. The meter begins ticking at 3.20€. Within the city center, each kilometer costs around 2€, depending on the time of day. Prolonged taxi rides that you arrange to distant suburbs are factored at a per-kilometer rate of 1.30€. Staff members at hotels and restaurants can easily summon a cab for you, in some cases simply by throwing a switch on their phone. Otherwise, dial © **030/202020.**

BY CAR

U.S. companies have outlets in Berlin. If possible, you should make reservations in advance. You'll find **Hertz** at Berlin-Tegel Airport (℗ **030/41704674;** www.hertz. com) and at Friedrichstrasse 50–55 (℗ **030/2424440**). **Avis** is also at Berlin-Tegel (℗ **030/41013148;** www.avis.com) and at Budapesterstrasse 41 (℗ **030/2309370**).

If you can, avoid driving in Berlin, though. Traffic is heavy, and parking is difficult to come by. Use the excellent public transportation instead.

PARKING If you're driving into Berlin, chances are that you'll want to safely store your car once you arrive. Many hotels offer parking facilities; otherwise, you'll find parking garages that remain open throughout the day and night. Those located near the Ku'Damm and the Europa Center include the **Parkhaus Metropol,** Joachimstaler Strasse 14–19; **Parkhaus Los-Angeles-Platz,** Augsburger Strasse 30; **Parkhaus Europa Center,** Nürnberger Strasse 5–7; and **Parkhaus am Zoo,** Budapesterstrasse 38. Charges start at 3€ per hour.

CITY DRIVING One problem that often infuriates drivers in Berlin is that it's almost impossible to turn left on major avenues (except at major intersections in the east) because of the positioning of metal barriers and tram lines. Oversize signs tell you to drive straight on. Drivers have to make a right-hand turn, swing around the block, and then proceed straight across the tram lines wherever a traffic light will allow.

In 2010, vehicles with high emissions of noxious substances were banned from the inner city of Berlin. Drivers must display an emission control sticker, called a Euro Class 4 green sticker, or else they will be banned. Cars not having this sticker will face a fine of 40€.

BY BICYCLE

Berlin marks biking trails along major streets, especially in the leafy neighborhoods of the former West Berlin. A bike is also ideal for exploring old East Berlin, a city still in redevelopment. One of the best companies for rentals is **Fahrradstation,** Auguststrasse 29A (℗ **030/22508070;** www.fahrradstation.com; S-Bahn: Hackescher Markt), open Monday to Friday 10am to 7:30pm, and Saturday 10am to 6pm. A 24-hour rental costs 15€ to 30€.

Organized Tours

WALKING TOURS

For an excellent introduction to Berlin and its history, try one of the walking tours offered by **Berlin Walks** (℗ **030/3019194;** www.berlinwalks.de). **"Discover Berlin"** is a 4-hour introductory tour that takes you past the New Synagogue, the Reichstag, and the Brandenburg Gate, among other major sites. It starts daily at 10am and 1:30pm (in winter at 10am only). **"Infamous Third Reich Sites"** focuses on the sites of major Nazi buildings in central Berlin, such as Goebbels' Propaganda Ministry and Hitler's New Reichschancellery. The Third Reich tour starts Tuesday and Thursday at 10am, Saturday at 10:30am, and Sunday at 10am. Tours are less frequent in the off season; call for times. **"Jewish Life in Berlin"** takes you through the prewar Jewish community; sights include the Old Cemetery and the former Boys' School. The tour starts April to October Monday at 10am. One of the most intriguing tours is **"Berlin—Nest of Spies,"** which takes you to some of the most infamous sites associated with both the Nazis and the Communist takeover of East Germany. Lasting 4 hours, this tour is conducted April to October only on Saturday at 10am. For all tours, reservations are unnecessary—simply meet the guide, who will

safari TOURS IN THAT SARDINE CAN ON WHEELS

A trend devoted to Communist kitsch is sweeping this once-divided capital. Germans call it Ostalgie, meaning nostalgia for the East during the Cold War. They celebrate it as Americans do the '50s. Years after the fall of the so-called German Democratic Republic, East Berlin is making a comeback. One social critic called it "a profound longing for a golden time that never was." Some Berlin entrepreneurs are even offering self-guided "safari tours" in the Trabi, that "sardine can on wheels," built in East German factories between 1955 and 1991. The car was constructed mostly of plastic. The "Trabi Safari" starts at BallonGarten, on Wilhelmstrasse, corner Zimmerstrasse (close to Checkpoint Charlie), costing from 30€ to 50€ per passenger for a tour that lasts 1½ hours. You're taken to the famous Cold War sites of East Berlin, most of which are off the beaten path. For reservations, call ⓒ **030/27592273** or visit www.trabi-safari.de.

be wearing a Berlin Walks badge, outside the main entrance to Hackescher Markt station. Tours (in English) last from 2½ to 6 hours, and cost 12€ for those 26 and over, 10€ for those 14 to 25, and free for children 13 and under (with an adult). Berlin Walks also offers a tour to Potsdam, starting every Sunday at 10am from May to September. **"Discover Potsdam"** lasts 5 to 6 hours, and costs 15€ for those 26 and over, 12€ for those 14 to 25, and free for children 13 and under.

BUS TOURS

Berlin is a sprawling metropolis with interesting neighborhoods that are often separated by extended areas of parks, monumental boulevards, and Cold War wastelands. Because of these factors, organized bus tours can be the best way to navigate the city.

Some of the best are operated by **Severin+Kühn,** Kurfürstendamm 216 (ⓒ **030/8804190;** www.severin-kuehn-berlin.de; U-Bahn: Kurfürstendamm), located on the second floor of a building across from the Kempinski Hotel. This agency offers a half-dozen tours of Berlin and its environs. Their 2-hour **"Berlin Classic Live Tour"** departs April to October daily at 10am. Tickets cost 20€ per person. The tour passes 14 important stops in Berlin, including the Europa Center, the Brandenburg Gate, and Potsdamer Platz; provides taped audio commentary in eight languages; and offers the option of getting on and off the bus at any point during the hour. Retain your ticket stub to reboard the bus.

One of the more intriguing tours visits Potsdam, site of the famed World War II conference and of Sanssouci Palace, former residence of Friedrich the Great. The price is 39€ per person. Departures are Tuesday, Thursday, Saturday, and Sunday at 10am; May and October, there are additional departures Friday to Sunday at 2:15pm.

BOAT TOURS

It may not be the obvious choice for transportation in Berlin, but a boat ride can offer visitors a good change of pace. The networks of canals that bisect the plains of what used to be known as Prussia were an engineering marvel when they were completed in the 19th century. Today, transport through the lakes, locks, and canals around Berlin retains its nostalgic allure and affords unusual vistas that aren't available from the windows of more conventional modes of transport. Berliners boast that their city has more bridges than Venice. Local waterways include the Spree and Havel rivers—ranging in size from narrow channels to large lakes—as well as many canals. You can take short tours that offer close-up views of the city or daylong adventures along the Spree and Havel; the latter often turn into beer-drinking fests.

The city's best-known boat operator is **Stern und Kreisschiffahrt,** Pushkinallee 15 (*℃* **030/5363600;** www.sternundkreis.de). Since Germany's reunification, this company has absorbed the piers and ferryboats of several of its former East German counterparts. The resulting entity is ready and able to take you on waterborne cruises that incorporate sights that were once restricted to Berlin's eastern zone.

The most popular of the cruises, **"Historische Stadtfahrt,"** takes you for a 1-hour ride along the banks of the Spree, the river that helped build Berlin. Departing at 30-minute intervals March to October daily between 10:30am and 5pm, they take in river-fronting views of the city's central core, beginning at a point in the Nikolaiviertel, close to Berlin's imposing 19th-century cathedral, on the Am Palast Ufer (U-Bahn: Nikolaiviertel).

More comprehensive are the **4-hour tours along the River Spree** and some of its canals. Originating at the Treptow quays (S-Bahn: Treptow Park), they depart late March to October daily at 9:45am and again at 2pm. These trips offer good views of the exteriors of the Reichstag, the Pergamonmuseum, the Königliche Bibliothek (Royal Library), and the monumental heart of what used to be known as East Berlin.

Tours depart from the Jannowitz Brücke (U-Bahn: Jannowitz Brücke). Reservations are usually necessary for all boat rides described above. Rides operate only from late March to late October, depending on the tour, although there might be a special river tour offered around Christmas if demand warrants. Tours lasting 1 hour cost 9€ per person; tours lasting 4 hours cost 18€ per person. Students and children between the ages of 6 and 15 receive discounts of 50%, and children 5 and under ride for free. Prices and actual itineraries change seasonally; call for more details.

[Fast FACTS] BERLIN

Business Hours Most **banks** are open Monday to Friday 9am to either 1 or 3pm. Most other **businesses** and **stores** are open Monday to Friday 9 or 10am to either 6 or 6:30pm and Saturday 9am to 4pm. Some stores close late on Thursday (usually 8:30pm).

Currency Exchange You can exchange money at all airports, major department stores, and any bank.

Dentists & Doctors The tourist office (see "Visitor Information," earlier in this chapter) keeps a list of English-speaking dentists

and doctors in Berlin. In case of a medical emergency, call *℃* **030/310031.** For a dental emergency, call *℃* **030/89004333.**

Drugstores If you need a pharmacy (Apotheke) at night, go to one on any corner. There you'll find a sign in the window giving the address of the nearest drugstore open at night; such posting is required by law. A central pharmacy is **Alex-AApotheke,** Grunerstrasse 20 (*℃* **030/27581640;** U-Bahn: Alexanderplatz). It's open Monday to Friday 9am to 10pm and Saturday 10am to 10pm.

Embassies & Consulates See chapter 19.

Emergencies To call the police, dial *℃* **110.** To report a fire or to summon an ambulance, dial *℃* **112.**

Hospitals Hotel employees are usually familiar with the locations of the nearest hospital emergency room. In an emergency, call *℃* **112** for an ambulance.

Hot Lines If you're the victim of rape or sexual assault, call **LARA,** Tempelhoferufer 14 (*℃* **030/ 2168888;** www.lara-berlin. de). For problems relating to drug use or drug addiction, call the drug help line at ☏ **030/19237.** Gays seeking legal or health-related advice should call **Maneo** (☏ **030/2163336**). Gays can also call **Mann-o-Meter** (☏ **030/2168008;** www.mann-o-meter.de) for information about anything to do with gay life or gay events in Berlin or the rest of Germany. All of the above are staffed with some English speakers.

Internet Access Try Netlounge, Auguststrasse 89 (☏ **030/24342597;** www.netlounge-berlin.de), open daily noon to midnight. It charges 2.50€ per hour. Take the U-Bahn to Oranienburger Strasse. If you have your own device, a large number of cafes and casual restaurants offer free Wi-Fi when you purchase a beverage—look for the universal Wi-Fi symbol or ask if there is access.

Laundry & Dry Cleaning Deluxe and first-class hotels offer laundry service, but prices tend to be high. You'll find laundromats *(Wascherei)* and dry cleaning outlets *(Reiningung)* all over town. Ask at your hotel for options.

Lost Property For items lost on the bus or U-Bahn, go to **BVG Fündbüro,** Potsdamerstrasse 180–182 (☏ **030/19449;** U-Bahn: Kleistpark); it's open Monday to Thursday 9am to 6pm and Friday 9am to 2pm. For items lost on the S-Bahn, go to **S-Bahn Berlin GmbH,** Invalidenstrasse 19 (☏ **030/29743333;**

www.s-bahn-berlin.de; U-Bahn: Friedrichstrasse), Monday, Wednesday, or Thursday 10am to 4pm, Tuesday 10am to 6pm, or Friday 8am to noon. The general lost-property office, **Zentrales Fündbüro,** is at Platz der Luftbrücke 6 (☏ **030/75603101;** U-Bahn: Platz der Luft-brücke). Hours are Monday and Tuesday 8am to 3pm, Thursday 1 to 6pm, and Friday 8am to noon.

Post Office You'll find post offices scattered throughout Berlin, with particularly large branches positioned at Bahnhof Zoo, Hardenbergplatz (U-Bahn: Zoologischer Garten), Tegel and Schönefeld airports, the Hauptbahnhof (main railway station), and in the town center at Joachimstalerstrasse 10. With a limited number of exceptions, most post offices in Germany are open Monday to Friday from 8am to 6pm and Saturday from 8am to 1pm. None of them receives direct telephone calls from the public, but if you're interested in postal rates and procedures, call ☏ **0180/23333,** or click on www.deutsche post.de. Unlike the old days, German post offices no longer offer the use of pay telephones for long-distance calls and no longer send international telegrams. (A limited number, however, offer telegram service for destinations within Germany.) When you enter a German post office, know in advance that the yellow-painted windows are for issues about the

mail and that the blue-painted windows are for issues associated with money orders and banking rituals. If you just want to buy a stamp for mailing a letter, it's usually more convenient to buy it at any of thousands of small stores, newsstands, or tobacco shops throughout the country that stock them.

Safety One unfortunate side effect of reunification has been an increase in muggings, bank robberies, hate crimes, and car break-ins. Residents of Berlin sometimes feel unsafe at night, especially in the dimly lit streets of Kreuzberg. Nonetheless, Berlin is still much safer than most large American cities. In case of a robbery or an attack, report the problem immediately to the police. You'll need a police report for any insurance claims.

Taxis See "Getting Around," earlier.

Toilets A restroom is called a *Toilette* and is often labeled WC, with either F (for *Frauen,* "women") or H (for *Herren,* "men"). Public facilities are found throughout Berlin and at all terminals, including the Europa Center on Tauentzien-strasse. It's customary to tip attendants at least 1€.

Water The tap water in Berlin, as in all German cities, is safe to drink. However, most Berliners prefer to ask for bottled water, either carbonated or noncarbonated.

EXPLORING BERLIN
Sightseeing Suggestions for First-Time Visitors

IF YOU HAVE 1 DAY Get up early and visit the **Brandenburg Gate,** symbol of Berlin, and then walk down **Unter den Linden** and have coffee and a pastry at one of the cafes along the edges off this boulevard. Visit the **Gemäldegalerie** to see some of the world's greatest masterpieces. Afterward, go explore **Schloss Charlottenburg,** one of the finest examples of baroque architecture in Germany. In the evening, walk along the Kurfürstendamm, visit the **Kaiser Wilhelm Memorial Church,** and dine in a local restaurant.

IF YOU HAVE 2 DAYS On Day 2, visit the **Pergamonmuseum** on Museum Island; be sure to see the Pergamon Altar. You can also visit the **Neues Museum** to gaze upon the celebrated bust of Queen Nefertiti. Explore the **National Gallery** and the **Jewish Museum,** and then head for Alexanderplatz. Take the elevator up for a view from its TV Tower.

IF YOU HAVE 3 DAYS On Day 3, go to **Potsdam** (see "A Side Trip: Potsdam & Its Palaces," later in this chapter).

IF YOU HAVE 4 OR 5 DAYS On Day 4, take a walk through the restored Nikolai Quarter. In the afternoon return to Charlottenburg Palace and explore the **Historical Apartments,** and in the evening visit the **Europa Center** for drinks and dinner. On Day 5, see some of the sights you might have missed. Take some walks through Berlin and stop at the Cold War's **Checkpoint Charlie,** with its museum. If time remains, visit the **Berlin Zoo,** stroll through the **Tiergarten,** and attend a cabaret in the evening.

Charlottenburg

Bröhan Museum MUSEUM This wonderful museum specializes in decorative objects of the *Jugendstil* (Art Nouveau) and Art Deco periods (1889–1939), with exquisite vases, glass, furniture, silver, paintings of artists belonging to the Berlin Secession, and other works of art, arranged in drawing room fashion, including an outstanding porcelain collection.

Schlossstrasse 1a. (*) **030/32690600.** www.broehan-museum.de. Admission 6€ adults, 4€ students, free for children 12 and under. Tues–Sun 10am–6pm. U-Bahn: Sophie-Charlotte-Platz. Bus: 109 or 309 to Schloss Charlottenburg.

art collections & WORLD WAR II

The great art collections of old Berlin suffered during and after World War II. Although many paintings were saved by being stored in salt mines, many larger works were destroyed by fire. Part of the surviving art stayed in the east, including a wealth of ancient treasures that remind us of the leading role played by German archaeologists during the 19th and early 20th centuries. The paintings that turned up in the west, and were passed from nation to nation in the late 1940s, have nearly all been returned to Berlin.

Charlottenburg Attractions

Belvedere **1**
Bröhan Museum **6**
Die Sammlung Berggruen:
  Picasso und Seine Zeit **5**
Mausoleum **2**
Olympiastadion **7**
Schinkel Pavilion **4**
Schloss Charlottenburg **3**

Post office
S-Bahn
U-Bahn

0   1/4 mi
0   0.25 km

Die Sammlung Berggruen: Picasso und Seine Zeit (The Berggruen Collection: Picasso and His Era) ★ 👤 MUSEUM One of the most unusual private museums in Berlin has accumulated the awesome collection of respected art and antiques dealer Heinz Berggruen. A native of Berlin who fled the Nazis in 1936, he later established antiques dealerships in Paris and California before returning, with his collection, to his native home in 1996. The setting is a renovated former army barracks designed by noted architect August Stüler in 1859. Although most of the collection is devoted to Picasso, there are also works by Cézanne, Braque, Klee, and van Gogh. Some 60 or more works in all, the Picasso collection alone is worth the trip, ranging from his teenage efforts to all of his major periods.

Schlossstrasse 1. ⓒ **030/3269580.** www.smb.museum. Admission 8€ adults, 4€ students and children. Tues–Sun 10am–6pm. U-Bahn: Richard-Wagner-Platz, followed by a 10-min. walk. Bus: 129, 145, or 210.

Olympiastadion PARK Built in 1936 by Werner March for the XI Summer Olympic Games, the Olympiastadion, which seats 100,000 people, was the first in Europe to supply all the facilities necessary for modern sports. Hitler expected to see his "master race" run off with all the medals in the 1936 Olympics, but his hopes were dashed when an African American, Jesse Owens, took four golds for the U.S. team.

The stadium area covers a total of 136 hectares (336 acres), but the main attraction is the arena. The playing field in its center lies 14m (46 ft.) below ground level. For a panoramic view of Berlin, take the elevator to the top of the 80m (262-ft.) platform, where the Olympic bell hangs. Sporting or cultural events are still presented here about once a week during spring, summer, and autumn. For ticket sales and information for sporting events within the stadium, call the **Herta-Berlin Soccer Club (Herta-BSC)** at ⓒ **030/3009280.** For information about the occasional live concerts, call **Conzert Concept** at ⓒ **030/810750.**

Olympischer Platz 3. ⓒ **030/30688100.** www.olympiastadion-berlin.de. Admission 4€ adults, 3€ children 5 and under. Mar–Oct daily 10am–7pm; Nov–Feb daily 9am–4pm. U-Bahn: Olympia-Stadion.

Schloss Charlottenburg ★★ HISTORIC BUILDING Schloss Charlottenburg, one of the finest examples of baroque architecture in Germany, was built by Sophie Charlotte. This beautiful and intelligent woman, a patron of philosophy and the arts, was the wife of Friedrich III, elector of Brandenburg, who, on January 18, 1701, crowned himself Friedrich I, "King in Prussia." He dared not call himself "King of Prussia" because some parts of Prussia were still dominated by Poland. He nearly bankrupted the state with his extravagant ways.

Alte Nationalgalerie **20**
Altes Museum **19**
Aqua Dom & Sea Life
  Berlin **27**
Berliner Dom **18**
Berlinische Galerie **13**
Berlin Wall Memorial **2**
Bode-Museum **23**
Brandenburger Tor **4**
Dalí Museum **9**
DDR Museum **26**
Deutsche Guggenheim
  Berlin **14**
Deutsches Historisches
  Museum **17**
Deutsche Staatsoper **31**
East Side Gallery **1**
Fernsehturm **29**
Friedrichswerdersche
  Kirche **16**
Hackesche Höfe **25**
Hitler's Bunker **8**
Jüdisches Museum
  Berlin **13**
Kennedy Museum **5**
Madame Tussauds
  Berlin **6**
Marienkirche **28**
Märkisches Museum **32**
Martin-Gropius-Bau **10**
Memorial to the Murdered
  Jews of Europe **7**
Museum für Naturkunde **1**
Museum Haus am
  Checkpoint Charlie **12**
Neues Museum **21**

Neue Synagoge Berlin–
  Centrum Judaicum **24**
Nikolaikirche **30**
Pergamonmuseum **22**
Reichstag **3**
Topography of Terror **11**

A DAY IN charlottenburg

Charlottenburg—which lies just west of the Tiergarten—contains enough attractions to easily fill an entire day; the area contains several museums as well as the royal apartments. After seeing the main sights, you can enjoy a ramble through **Schlossgarten Charlottenburg.** These formal gardens look much as they did in the 18th century. A grove of cypresses leads to a lake with swans and other waterfowl.

North of the palace stands the **Mausoleum,** which holds the tombs of King Friedrich Wilhelm II and Queen Luise—sculpted by Rauch—as well as several other interesting funerary monuments of the Prussian royal family.

The residence was begun as a summer palace but got out of hand, eventually growing into the massive structure you see today. When you pass through the heavy iron gates and enter the courtyard, you'll immediately encounter a baroque equestrian statue of Friedrich I himself, by Andreas Schlüter. The main entrance to the palace is directly behind, marked by the 48m (157-ft.) cupola capped by a gilded statue of Fortune. Inside, you'll find a columned rotunda with stucco reliefs depicting the virtues of Prussian princes in mythological terms. From this vestibule, you can take guided tours of the Historical Apartments. English translations of the guide's lecture are sold at the ticket counter.

The main wing of the palace contains the apartments of Friedrich and his "philosopher queen." Of special interest in this section is the **Reception Chamber.** This large room is decorated with frieze panels, vaulted ceilings, and mirror-paneled niches. The tapestries on the walls (1730) are based on Plutarch's *Lives;* included are such classical scenes as Pericles in battle and the sacrifice of Theseus on Delos. At the far end of the west wing is the **Porcelain Chamber,** containing a fine collection of Chinese porcelain.

The Knobelsdorff-Flügel Wing, built from 1740 to 1746, contains the apartments of Friedrich the Great. Today, these rooms serve as a museum of paintings, many of which were collected or commissioned by the king—the finest are on the upper floor. Works by Watteau include *The Trade Sign of the Art Dealer Gersaint,* purchased by Friedrich in 1745 for the palace's music hall. Also note the decoration on the walls and ceilings.

At the far eastern end of the Schloss is the **Schinkel Pavillon,** a summer house in the Italian style. Karl Friedrich Schinkel, the leading architect of the day, constructed this villa in 1825. Today, it holds a small but noteworthy museum, containing paintings, drawings, and sketches from the early 1800s. Some of the sketches are by Schinkel himself, who was both an architect and an artist.

At the far end of Schlossgarten Charlottenburg is the **Belvedere,** close to the Spree River. This former royal teahouse contains exquisite Berlin porcelain, much of it from the 1700s.

Luisenplatz. ✆ **030/32091275.** www.spsg.de. Combined ticket for all buildings and historical rooms 12€ adults, 9€ students and children 13 and under. Palace Tues–Fri 9am–4pm; Sat–Sun 10am–4pm; museum Tues–Fri 10am–6pm; gardens (free admission) daily 6:30am–8pm (Nov–Feb until 6pm). U-Bahn: Richard-Wagner-Platz. Bus: 145 or 204.

Around the Tiergarten

Bauhaus-Archiv Museum für Gestaltung (Bauhaus Design Museum)
MUSEUM   The Bauhaus Museum houses a permanent exhibition of photos and architectural designs relating to the Bauhaus school. Even if you're not a student of architecture, this museum is fascinating; it will bring you closer to the ideas and concepts that inspired modern design.

Klingelhöferstrasse 14. (✆ **030/2540020.** www.bauhaus.de. Admission Sat–Mon 7€ adults, 4€ children 11 and under; Wed–Fri 6€ adults, 3€ children 11 and under. Daily 10am–6pm (Thurs until 10pm). U-Bahn: Nollendorfplatz.

Erotik-Museum MUSEUM   This "museum" lies on the corner of the seediest-looking block in Berlin. You start out on the third floor and work your way down. Believe it or not, this is now Berlin's fifth-most visited museum. The museum shelters some 5,000 sexual artifacts from around the world, including many Indian and Asian miniatures of erotic positions, even large carved phalli from Bali, along with such relics as African fertility masks. Life-size dioramas explore such topics as S&M and fetishism. There are some Chinese wedding tiles from the 18th and 19th centuries that were supposed to provide sexual education to a newly married couple. The museum in its exhibits also honors the "queen of the Rubber Willy" herself, Beate Uhse, a household name in Germany until her death in 2001. Her life is documented from her Luftwaffe days to pictures of her at the helm of a large speedboat. This septuagenarian opened the world's first shop devoted to "marital hygiene," ultimately championing the right to sell contraceptives, and headed the world's largest sex-related merchandising business. Downstairs are video cabins filled with middle-aged men in raincoats and a "sex superstore."

Holocaust Memorial

Although it's colloquially referred to as the **Holocaust Memorial,** you might call it "concrete memory." A few hundred yards from Checkpoint Charlie, the **Memorial to the Murdered Jews of Europe (Stiftung Denkmal für die ermordeten Juden Europas)** now occupies a vast site in the center of Berlin, with 2,711 gravestone-like columns. Located in the former East Berlin, just south of the Brandenburg Gate, the memorial was opened on May 10, 2005, 2 days after the 60th anniversary of V-E Day, signaling the ending of World War II in Europe. The official address is Stresemannstrasse 90 (✆ **030/26394336;** www.stiftung-denkmal.de). The memorial lies at the edge of the Grosser Tiergarten between Ebertstrasse and Wilhelmstrasse. Take the S-Bahn to Unter den Linden. Admission is free.

Peter Eisenman was the architect who designed the controversial site, filled with claustrophobic pathways through the slabs, some of which are 4.5m (15 ft.) long. The American architect deliberately placed many of the dark gray slabs, with their knife-sharp edges, off-kilter, evoking tombstones in an unkempt graveyard. Wandering through the memorial is like getting lost in a maze. James Young, a professor at the University of Massachusetts, called it "the Venus flytrap of Holocaust memorials."

Under heavy guard, the memorial is open 24 hours a day. Underneath the monument are four large rooms containing exhibits that document Nazi crimes against humanity.

Joachimstaler Strasse 4. ℗ **030/8860666.** www.erotikmuseum.de. Admission 10€ before noon, 14€ after noon. No children 17 or under. Mon–Sat 9am–midnight; Sun 11am–midnight. U-Bahn or S-Bahn: Zoologischer Garten.

Filmmuseum Berlin ★ MUSEUM   A thematic and chronological tour through the saga of the much-troubled German cinema is on show here. The link between Berlin and Hollywood is one of the main focuses of the collection, which is supplemented with special exhibitions. Currently, the museum also owns some 9,000 German and foreign films, both silents and talkies. The collection here includes a million stills of scenes, portraits, and productions, along with 30,000 screenplays, 20,000 posters, and 60,000 film programs. Germany's only world-class star, Marlene Dietrich, comes alive again in one wing. Berlin acquired part of her extensive estate of memorabilia in 1993. On display are such costumes as her famous "naked" pearl dress, which gave the illusion of transparency, and the swan's-down coat designed by Jean Louis. Photos, costumes, props, letters, and documents recall the remarkable life of this diva, who startled the world with her performance in Josef von Sternberg's *Der Blaue Engel* in 1930. Highlights of other films include props from *Das Cabinet des Dr. Caligari*, the most famous German film of the Weimar Republic. One room is devoted to the controversial Leni Riefenstahl, the star director of the fascist era, whose key films *Triumph des Willens* and *Olympia* established her as one of the world's major filmmakers and the leading exponent of Nazi propaganda.

Potsdamer Strasse 2. ℗ **030/30090372.** www.filmmuseum-berlin.de. Admission 6€ adults; 4.50€ students, seniors, and children 15 and under. Tues–Sun 10am–6pm (Thurs until 8pm). U-Bahn or S-Bahn: Potsdamer Platz.

Gemäldegalerie (Portrait Gallery) ★★★ MUSEUM   This is one of Germany's greatest art museums. Several rooms are devoted to early German masters, with panels from altarpieces dating from the 13th to the 15th century. Note the panel, *The Virgin Enthroned with Child* (1350), surrounded by angels that resemble the demons in the works of Hieronymus Bosch. Eight paintings make up the Dürer collection, including several portraits.

Most of the great European masters are represented. The Italian collection contains five Raphael Madonnas, along with works by Titian (*The Girl with a Bowl of Fruit*), Fra Filippo Lippi, Botticelli, and Correggio (*Leda with the Swan*). There are early Netherlandish paintings from the 15th and 16th centuries (van Eyck, van der Weyden, Bosch, and Bruegel) as well. Several galleries are devoted to 17th-century Flemish and Dutch masters, with no fewer than 15 works by Rembrandt, such as his famous *Head of Christ. The Man with the Golden Helmet,* long famous as a priceless Rembrandt, was proven in 1986 to be by another hand. This remarkable painting is now accepted as a fine independent original.

Stauffenbergstrasse (entrance is at Mattäiskirchplatz 4). ℗ **030/20905555.** www.smb.spk-berlin.de/gg. Admission 8€ adults, 4€ students, free for children 16 and under. Tues–Sun 10am–6pm (Thurs until 10pm). U-Bahn: Potsdamer Platz. Bus: 200 or 347.

Kaiser-Wilhelm Gedächtniskirche (Kaiser Wilhelm Memorial Church) CHURCH   There is no more evocative site in the western sector of Berlin to remind us of the horrors of war. The massive red-sandstone church that originally stood here was dedicated in 1895 as a memorial to Kaiser Wilhelm II. In 1945, during the closing months of World War II, a bomb dropped by an Allied plane blasted it to pieces, leaving only a few gutted walls and the shell of the neo-Romanesque bell tower. After the war, West Berliners decided to leave the artfully evocative ruins as a reminder of

Aquarium **11**
Bauhaus-Archiv Museum
   für Gestaltung **8**
Erotik-Museum **13**
Europa Center **10**
Filmmuseum Berlin **3**
Gemäldegalerie **6**
Kaiser Wilhelm
   Gedächtniskirche **14**
Käthe-Kollwitz-Museum **15**
Kongresshalle **2**
Kunstgewerbemuseum **5**
Museum für Gegenwart
   Hamburger Bahnhof **1**
Neue Nationalgalerie **7**
Philharmonie **4**
Schöneberg Rathaus **9**
The Story of Berlin **16**
Zoologischer Garten **12**

⊠ Post office
Ⓢ S-Bahn
Ⓤ U-Bahn
ⓘ Information
✝ ⬛ Church

4

BERLIN | Exploring Berlin

the era's suffering and devastation. In 1961, directly at the base of the ruined building, they erected a small-scale modern church designed by Egon Eierman. Always irreverent, Berliners, noting the avant-garde architecture and geometric design of the new church, nicknamed it "the lipstick and powder box." Its octagonal hall is lit solely by thousands of colored glass windows set into a honeycomb framework. On its premises, you can visit a small museum with exhibitions and photographs documenting the history of the original church and the destructive ravages of war. The new church can hold up to 1,200 worshipers, and 10-minute religious services—conceived for office workers heading home—are held there every day at 5:30 and 6pm. Between June and August, English-language services are conducted daily at 9am, and free organ concerts are presented here every Saturday year-round at 6pm.

Breitscheidplatz. ✆ **030/2185023.** www.gedaechtniskirche-berlin.de. Free admission. Ruined church Mon–Sat 10am–4pm; new church daily 9am–6pm. U-Bahn: Zoologischer Garten or Kurfürstendamm.

Käthe-Kollwitz-Museum ★ MUSEUM

This museum has been called a personalized revolt against the agonies of war. Many works express the sorrow of wartime separation of mother and child, inspired in part by the artist's loss of a son in World War I and a grandson during World War II. Berlin-born Käthe Kollwitz (1867–1945) was an ardent pacifist and socialist whose works were banned by the Nazis. The first woman ever elected to the Prussian Academy of the Arts, she resigned her position in 1933 to protest Hitler's rise to power. Her husband, Karl Kollwitz, was a physician who chose to practice among the poor on a working-class street (now called Kollwitzstrasse). In 1943, Allied bombing drove Käthe to the countryside near Dresden, where she died in 1945 while a guest of the former royal family of Saxony in its castle at Moritzburg.

The lower floors of the museum are devoted to woodcuts and lithographs, the upper floors to particularly poignant sculptures. *Note:* The collection is closed twice a year for special exhibits.

Fasanenstrasse 24. ✆ **030/8825210.** www.kaethe-kollwitz.de. Admission 6€ adults, 3€ students and children. Daily 11am–6pm. U-Bahn: Kurfürstendamm or Uhlandstrasse. Bus: 109, 110, 204, or 249.

Kunstgewerbemuseum (Museum of Applied Arts) MUSEUM

This museum displays applied arts and crafts from the Middle Ages through the 20th century. Its outstanding exhibition is the Guelph Treasure, a collection of medieval church articles in gold and silver. The basement rooms show contemporary design from the Bauhaus school to Charles Eames and Memphis. Venetian glass, Italian majolica, German Renaissance goldsmiths' work, and 18th-century porcelain figurines are also displayed. Notable are such Art Nouveau works as a translucent opal-and-enamel box by Eugène Feuillâtre. A cafeteria inside is open from 10am to 4:30pm.

Mattäiskirchplatz (opposite the Philharmonie), Tiergartenstrasse 6. ✆ **030/2662902.** www.smb.spk-berlin.de. Admission 8€ adults, 4€ students, free for children 16 and under. Tues–Fri 10am–6pm; Sat-Sun 11am–6pm. U-Bahn: Potsdamer Platz. Bus: 129 from Ku'Damm to Potsdamer Brücke.

Museum für Gegenwart Hamburger Bahnhof MUSEUM

This Museum of Contemporary Art opened in 1996 north of the Spree River in the old Hamburger Bahnhof, the oldest train station in Berlin. The structure was the terminus of the 290km (180-mile) train run from Hamburg. Today, the 19th-century station no longer receives trains but is a premier storehouse of postwar art, a sort of Musée d'Orsay of Berlin. Traces of its former function are still evident, including the high roof designed for steam engines. The modern art on display is some of the finest in Germany; the nucleus of the collection was donated by the Berlin collector Erich Marx (no relation to Karl). You can view everything from Andy Warhol's now-legendary *Mao* to an audio-visual Joseph Beuys archive. The museum houses one of the best collections of the work of Cy Twombly in the world because the curator, Heiner Bastian, was once his assistant. Other works are by Rauschenberg, Lichtenstein, and Dan Flavin. Beuys is also represented by 450 drawings.

Invalidenstrasse 50–51. ℂ **030/39873411.** www.hamburgerbahnhof.de. Admission 8€ adults, 4€ students, free for children 16 and under. Tues–Fri and Sun 10am–6pm; Sat 11am–8pm. U-Bahn: Zinnowitzer Strasse; S-Bahn: Lehrter Bahnhof. Bus: 123, 147, 240, or 245.

Neue Nationalgalerie (New National Gallery) ★ MUSEUM   In its modern glass-and-steel home designed by Ludwig Mies van der Rohe (1886–1969), the Neue Nationalgalerie is a sequel of sorts to the art at Dahlem. It contains a continually growing collection of modern European and American art. You'll find works of 19th-century artists, with a concentration on French Impressionists. German art starts with Adolph von Menzel's paintings from about 1850. The 20th-century collection includes works by Max Beckmann and Edvard Munch and E. L. Kirchner's *Brandenburger Tor* (1929), as well as paintings by Bacon, Picasso, Ernst, Klee, and American artists such as Barnett Newman. There's food service in the cafe on the ground floor, open 10:30am to 5:45pm when the museum is open.

Potsdamerstrasse 50 (just south of the Tiergarten). ℂ **030/2662651.** www.neue-nationalgalerie.de. Admission 10€ adults, 5€ students, free for children 16 and under. Tues–Sun 10am–6pm (Thurs until 10pm). S-Bahn: Potsdamer Platz; U-Bahn: Mendelssohn-Bartholdy-Park.

Schöneberg Rathaus HISTORIC BUILDING   This former political and administrative center of West Berlin is of special interest to Americans. It was the scene of John F. Kennedy's memorable (if grammatically shaky) *"Ich bin ein Berliner"* speech on June 26, 1963. Berliners have renamed the square around the building the John-F.-Kennedy-Platz. From the 72m (236-ft.) tower, a Liberty Bell replica is rung every day at noon. Most visitors come here to climb the tower for a panoramic view of Berlin. This Freedom Bell, a gift from the American people in 1950, symbolized U.S. support for the West Berliners during the Cold War. The document chamber contains a testimonial bearing the signatures of 17 million Americans who gave their moral support to the struggle.

John-F.-Kennedy-Platz. ℂ **030/75600.** Free admission. Rathaus daily 10am–6pm; tower daily 10am–5pm. Tower closed Nov–Mar. U-Bahn: Rathaus Schöneberg.

The Story of Berlin MUSEUM   This multimedia extravaganza portrays 8 centuries of the city's history through photos, films, sounds, and colorful displays. Beginning with the founding of Berlin in 1237, it chronicles the plague, the Thirty Years' War, Friedrich the Great's reign, military life, the Industrial Revolution and the working poor, the Golden 1920s, World War II, divided Berlin during the Cold War, and the fall of the Wall. Lights flash in a media blitz as you enter the display on the fall of the Wall, making you feel like one of the first East Berliners to wonderingly cross to the West. Conclude your tour on the 14th floor with a panoramic view over today's Berlin. Allow at least 2 hours to see the museum. Though the displays are a bit jarring and the historical information is too jumbled to be truly educational, the museum does leave a lasting impression.

Ku'Damm-Karree, Kurfürstendamm 207-208 (at the corner of Uhlandstrasse). ℂ **030/88720100.** www.story-of-berlin.de. Admission 10€ adults, 8€ students, 5€ children 6–13, 23€ family ticket. Daily 10am–8pm (you must enter by 6pm). U-Bahn: Uhlandstrasse.

4

FROMMER'S favorite BERLIN EXPERIENCES

Strolling Along Unter den Linden and the Kurfürstendamm. You can't know Berlin until you've strolled the Ku'Damm, that glossy, store-lined showcase of Western capitalism, or Unter den Linden, the Prussian centerpiece of the Berlin-Mitte district.

***Kneipen* Crawling.** This is the Berlin version of pub crawling. Whether you want breakfast or a beer at 4am, there's always a *Kneipe* waiting for you, no matter what neighborhood you're in.

Looking for a Touch of Culture. The baton of the late Herbert von Karajan is no longer raised, but the Berlin Philharmonic is still one of the world's leading orchestras.

Wandering the Nikolai Quarter. A symbol of Berlin's desire to bounce back after war damage, this charming 16th-century neighborhood has been completely rebuilt. Period taverns and churches make it ideal for a leisurely stroll down narrow streets illuminated by gas lanterns.

Picnicking in the Tiergarten. What better place for a picnic than the former hunting grounds of the Prussian electors? Wander through this 167-hectare (413-acre) park until you find the ideal spot, but first stop off at Kaufhaus des Westens (KaDeWe; p. 120), a sixth-floor food emporium at Wittenbergplatz, 20 minutes away, for the makings of a memorable meal.

Café-Hopping in Prenzlauer Berg. One of the first neighborhoods in Berlin's former East to gentrify and become popular, this trendy neighborhood is chock-full of prime spots to people-watch and relax Berlin style.

Berlin-Mitte

EXPLORING BERLIN-MITTE

It's hard to know where to begin in Berlin-Mitte: this area is chock-full of sights, including the **Museumsinsel** (Museum Island; p. 95), home cluster of the capital's top five museums. The area is also huge—so don't let that map fool you. Meandering from one end to the next would take you all day. But meander you should—in fact, the best street for strolling in eastern Berlin is the famous **Unter den Linden,** beginning at Brandenburg Gate.

Alexanderplatz, named for Russian Czar Alexander I, was the center of activity in the old East Berlin. This square has brightened considerably since reunification, though aesthetically speaking it's got a long way to go. Neon lights and bright murals now coexist alongside the dull and fading GDR-era structures, while street musicians and small markets give the area new life.

The massive 368m (1,207-ft.) **Fernsehturm (TV Tower;** © **030/2423333;** www.berlinerfernsehturm.de) on Alexanderplatz is the highest structure in Germany. It's worthwhile to take the 40-second elevator ride to the observation platform, 204m (669 ft.) above the city. From this isolated vantage, you can clearly distinguish most landmarks, and on the floor above, you can enjoy cake and coffee in the revolving Tele-Café. The elevator to the top costs 10€ for adults and 5.50€ students and children. The tower is open daily March to October 9am to midnight and November to February daily 10am to midnight.

At the foot of the Fernsehturm stands Berlin's second-oldest church, the brick Gothic **Marienkirche (St. Mary's Church),** Karl-Liebknecht-Strasse 8 (© **030/2424467**), dating from the 15th century. Inside you can see the painting

Der Totentanz (The Dance of Death), painted in 1475 and then discovered in 1860 beneath a layer of whitewash in the church's entrance hall. Also worth seeing is the marble baroque pulpit carved by Andreas Schlüter (1703). The cross on the top of the church annoyed the Communist rulers of the former East Germany—its golden form was always reflected in the windows of the Fernsehturm. The church is open Monday to Thursday 10am to noon and 1 to 6pm, Friday to Sunday noon to 4pm.

At Rosenthaler Strasse 40–41, the trendy rebuilt **Hackesche Höfe** has risen from the ashes of World War II to become a chic place for dining, drinking, going to the theater, or patronizing fashionable boutiques and art galleries. Originally these Hacke warehouses were constructed beginning in 1905 as shining examples of Berlin's take on Art Nouveau industrial architecture. Heavily damaged in Allied bombing raids, all nine interconnecting courtyards are new again, with shiny white tiles interspersed with Moorish mosaic designs. Also at this location are a theater and a movie house.

Berliner Dom CHURCH   The cathedral of Berlin took some devastating hits in the British bombardments of 1940, but it was restored to some of its former glory in the postwar decades, reopening in 1993. Unlike many European capitals where the cathedral is among the top two or three attractions, here you can safely miss Berlin's Dom without feeling cultural deprivation. That said, the best way to get an overview of this 19th-century cathedral is from the **Dome Gallery ★**, reached after climbing 270 steps. From here, you get a good glimpse of the Dom's ceiling and the rest of its much-restored neo-classist interior. Its most notable features include a wall altar with the Twelve Apostles by Karl Friedrich Schinkel and the magnificent Sauer organ containing 7,000 pipes.

The stained-glass windows are especially stunning, depicting such scenes as the Resurrection, as symbolized by an angel holding a palm branch. The tombstones of Prussian royals are displayed in the crypt, the most impressive tombs being those of Friedrich I and his queen, Sophie Charlotte. *Tip:* The best time to visit is during one of the organ concerts, conducted year-round, usually on Saturday at 6pm. An announcement is printed within the church listing hours of all ecclesiastical and musical events.

In the Lustgarten, Museumsinsel. (C) **030/20269136.** www.berliner-dom.de. Admission 5€ adults, 3€ students and seniors, free for children 13 and under. Mon–Sat 9am–8pm; Sun noon–8pm (until 7pm in winter). S-Bahn: Alexanderplatz or Hackescher Markt.

Berlinische Galerie MUSEUM   Modern art, photography, and architectural models from 1870 to the present day are sheltered under one roof here in a museum that displays everything from the satirical portraits of George Grosz to the works of Dadaists. The collection of fine art alone comprises some 5,000 works, mostly paintings, including everything from the Berlin Secession movement to abstract expressionism. Since reunification, a number of works were acquired from artists in eastern Berlin. The Collection of Graphic Art offers some 15,000 works, including the complete printed graphic works of Otto Dix. The Photographic Collection ranges from early daguerreotypes to 21st-century works. Some 300,000 plans and drawings, plus some 2,500 architectural models, form the Architecture Collection.

Alte Jakobstrasse 124–128. (C) **030/78902600.** Admission 6€. Wed–Mon 10am–6pm. U-Bahn: Kochstrasse.

Brandenburger Tor (Brandenburg Gate) ★★ MONUMENT   This triumphal arch—now restored—stands in the very heart of Berlin and once was the symbol of the divided city. In the heyday of East Germany, the structure was integrated into the Berlin Wall, which followed a north-south axis as it made its wicked way to the Potsdamer Platz. Six Doric columns hold up an entablature that was inspired by the Propylaea of the Parthenon at Athens. Surrounded by the famous and much-photographed Quadriga of Gottfried Schadow from 1793, the gate was designed by Carl Gotthard Langhans in 1789. Napoleon liked the original Quadriga so much he ordered them taken down and shipped to Paris, but they were returned to Berlin in 1814. In Berlin's heyday before World War II, the gate marked the grand western extremity of the "main street," Unter den Linden. In the Room of Silence, built into one of the guardhouses, visitors still gather to meditate and reflect on Germany's past.

Unter den Linden. Free admission. Room of Silence daily 10am–6pm. S-Bahn: Unter den Linden. Bus: 100.

Dalí Museum MUSEUM   Famous for his images of burning giraffes and running clocks, Salvador Dalí, the surrealist artist, now has a museum in Berlin. The museum offers a representative overview of this eccentric, controversial, and versatile Catalan, including more than 400 portfolios, illustrated books, sculptures, coins, and three-dimensional installations. Dalí's works are supplemented by an alternating selection from more than 3,000 works concerning the artist. "Dalí scouts on site" are actually guides who stand by to help visitors understand the artworks if they appear confused.

Leipziger Platz 7. ✆ **01805/103323** ticket hot line. Admission 11€, free for children 6 and under. Mon-Sat noon–8pm; Sun 10am–8pm. U-Bahn: Potsdamer Platz.

DDR Museum MUSEUM   This museum admirably sets out to showcase what daily life was like for the citizens of the now-defunct German Democratic Republic. Visitors are encouraged to open drawers and cupboards and touch almost everything. Here's your chance to drive the famous Trabi and to handle other once utilitarian, but now historic, artifacts of the Communist-held East Germany.

Karl-Liebknecht-Strasse 1. ✆ **030/847123731**. www.ddr-museum.de. Admission 5.50€ adults, 3.50€ students. Sat 10am–10pm; Sun–Fri 10am–8pm. S-Bahn or U-Bahn: Alexander-Platz.

Deutsche Guggenheim Berlin ★ MUSEUM   This state-of-the-art museum is devoted to modern and contemporary art. The exhibition space is on the ground floor of the Berlin branch of Deutsche Bank. The Guggenheim Foundation presents several exhibitions at this site annually and also displays newly commissioned works created specifically for this space by world-renowned artists. The bank supports young artists from the German-speaking world by purchasing their works and displaying them throughout the company's offices and public spaces. Exhibitions have ranged from the most avant-garde of modern artists to Picasso, Cézanne, and Andy Warhol.

⦿ Night of Shame

Best visited at night, as it is more evocative then, **Bebelplatz** is a square along Unter den Linden, in Berlin-Mitte, approached just before you reach Staatsoper. Located here is an eloquent memorial to the notorious Nazi book burning that took place on the night of May 10, 1933. Through a window set in the pavement, you can look below to a small library lined with empty bookshelves. Some 25,000 books were burned, all by authors considered enemies of the Third Reich. Nearby is a plaque with the prophetic words of the poet Heinrich Heine. In 1820 he wrote, "Where books are burned, in the end people will burn."

Unter den Linden 13–15 (at the intersection with Charlottenstrasse). ✆**030/2020930.** www.deutsche-guggenheim.de. Admission 4€ adults, 3€ children, free Mon. Daily 10am–8pm (Thurs until 10pm). S-Bahn: Unter den Linden.

Deutsches Historisches Museum MUSEUM   From the Neanderthals to the Nazis and beyond, the entire saga of German history is presented. The collection includes extensive posters and documents of the history of the workers' movement as well as a few remains from the former *Zeughaus* (arsenal) collection, which, before World War II, had been the largest collection of militaria from the history of Brandenburg and Prussia. The museum also owns tons of the old GDR Communist art (naturally all the workers are depicted with smiling faces). There is a permanent exhibition on German history in the main building, with temporary exhibitions in an annex. The museum has added a new wing designed by famous architect I. M. Pei. A transparent glass wall bridges the gap between the new wing and the original structure, an 18th-century arsenal for the Prussian army. The stunningly modern new wing offers 2,700 sq. m (29,000 sq. ft.) of space, which will be used for some of the city's most fascinating traveling exhibits.

Unter den Linden 2. ✆**030/203040.** www.dhm.de. Admission 5€. Daily 10am–6pm. U-Bahn: Franzö-sische Strasse.

Friedrichswerdersche Kirche–Schinkelmuseum MUSEUM   This annex of the Nationalgalerie is located in the deconsecrated Friedrichswerdersche Kirche, which was designed in 1828 by Karl Friedrich Schinkel (1781–1841). It lies close to Unter den Linden, not far from the State Opera House. The twin Gothic portals of the old church shelter a bronze of St. Michael slaying a dragon. Inside, the museum is devoted to the memory of Schinkel, who designed many of Berlin's great palaces, churches, and monuments. Memorabilia and documents record his great accomplishments. There are also exhibitions of neoclassical sculptures, portraits, and tombs by Johann Gottfried Schadow, Christian Daniel Rauch, Friedrich Tieck, and Berthel Thorvaldsen, the Danish sculptor.

Werderscher Markt. ✆**030/2081323.** Free admission. Daily 10am–6pm. U-Bahn: Hausvogteiplatz.

Jüdisches Museum Berlin (Jewish Museum Berlin) ★★MUSEUM   Europe's largest Jewish Museum presents the panorama of German-Jewish history, its cultural achievements, and its horror. The history of German Jewry is portrayed through objects, works of art, and documentation. The most talked-about museum in Berlin, the Jewish Museum is housed in a building that is one of the most spectacular in the entire city. Called "the silver lightning bolt," it was designed by architect Daniel Libeskind. To some viewers, the building plan and the scarring in the zinc-plated facade suggest a shattered Star of David. Oddly shaped windows are haphazardly embedded in the building's exterior.

Inside, the spaces are designed to make the visitor uneasy and disoriented, simulating the feeling of those who were exiled. A vast hollow cuts through the museum to mark what is gone. When the exhibits reach the rise of the Third Reich, the hall's walls, ceiling, and floor close in as the visitor proceeds. A chillingly hollow Holocaust Void, a dark, windowless chamber, evokes much that was lost.

The exhibits concentrate on three themes: Judaism and Jewish life, the devastating effects of the Holocaust, and the post–World War II rebuilding of Jewish life in Germany.

The roots of this museum were in an older museum opened in 1933 shortly before Hitler's rise to power. That collection of art and Judaica was shut down by the Gestapo in 1938, and all of its holdings were confiscated.

The on-site Liebermanns Restaurant features a world cuisine, with an emphasis on Jewish recipes—all strictly kosher.

Lindenstrasse 9-14. ✆ **030/25993300.** www.juedisches-museum-berlin.de. Admission 5€, free for children 6 and under, 10€ family ticket for 2 adults and up to 4 children. Daily 10am–8pm (Mon until 10pm). U-Bahn: Hallesches Tor or Kochstrasse. Bus: M29, M41, or 265.

Kennedy Museum MUSEUM   John F. Kennedy's famous *"Ich bin ein Berliner"* speech inspired this museum near the Brandenburg Gate and the Reichstag. The museum documents this beloved president and his iconic family, with such artifacts ranging from the president's black Hermès attaché case to Jackie Kennedy's signature pillbox hat. Naturally, there are artifacts from Kennedy's historic visit to Berlin in June

Modern Art in a World War II Bunker

Collector Christian Boros, who owns a vast collection of contemporary art, operates a unique gallery in a converted World War II 1942 air raid bunker in Berlin's Mitte district. The former State Railway Bunker was constructed to protect up to 2,000 passengers from the Berlin-Friedrichstrasse Railway station and local citizens during Allied air raids. After the Nazi collapse, Russia's Red Army took over the bunker and turned it into a prison; from the 1950s, it was used for fruit and vegetable storage.

Boros bought the bunker in 2003 and spent the next five years converting its interior into a dramatic exhibit space to display paintings, including some 500 works in all, with such world-class names as Damian Hirst, Olafur Eliasson, Elilzabeth Peyton, Wolfgang Tillmans, and Anselm Reyle. The rooftop has been converted into a kind of penthouse with a garden. The bunker's monumental character has been retained, and the markings of war are still visible on both the exterior and the interior. The Boros Collection can be viewed only on Saturday and Sunday, costing 10€ per person. Reservations for tours are available only on the Web at www.sammlung-boros.de.

The bunker lies on the corner of Albrechtstrasse and Reinhardtstrasse in Berlin Mitte (U-Bahn: Oranienburger Tor).

1963. The museum's collection includes one of the most comprehensive compilations of Kennedy photographs and both private and official documents.

Pariser Platz 4A. © **030/31007788.** www.thekennedys.de. Admission 7€ adults, 3.50€ students, free for children 16 and under. Daily 10am–6pm. S-Bahn: Unter den Linden. Bus: 100 or 200.

Madame Tussauds Berlin MUSEUM The opening of this museum marked the eighth such museum in the world, the most famous being in London. Lifelike wax figures include Hollywood A-listers (naturally Marlene Dietrich), sports stars, icons of contemporary culture, and historic figures. You can try on Bismarck's helmet or see John F. Kennedy's famous *"Ich bin ein Berliner"* speech. In the Culture Zone, visitors play with Beethoven on an interactive piano or test their genius with an IQ test with Einstein. You can even relax on Sigmund Freud's sofa. In the sports section, you can jump on court with Boris Becker.

The most controversial exhibit is of Hitler himself. The museum received large protests about exhibiting a likeness of the Nazi dictator. The museum countered that it could not depict the history of Berlin without including the dictator who led to the city's destruction in 1945. The likeness of Hitler is displayed behind glass, preventing visitors from having their pictures taken with it, and the showcase is monitored by video cameras.

Unter den Linden 74. © **0180/5545800.** www.madametussauds.com/berlin. Admission 19€ adults, 14€ children 16 and under. Daily 10am–6m. S-Bahn: Unter den Linden.

Märkisches Museum MUSEUM The full cultural history of Berlin is displayed in one of the most prominent buildings on the banks of the Spree; 42 rooms contain collections of artifacts from excavations, plus such art treasures as Slav silver and Bronze Age finds. You can learn about Berlin's theaters and literature, the arts in Berlin and Brandenburg, and the life and work of Berlin artisans. Most visitors like the array of mechanical musical instruments that can be played Sunday at 3pm, for an extra 1€.

Am Källnischen Park 5. © **030/308660.** Admission 5€ adults, 3€ children. Tues–Sun 9am–5pm. U-Bahn: Märkisches Museum. Bus: 147, 240, or 265.

Martin-Gropius-Bau MUSEUM This museum is dedicated to architect Martin Gropius, who was the uncle of the far more famous Walter Gropius of the Bauhaus movement. Martin Gropius designed the building in the Renaissance style, and it was originally an arts-and-crafts museum. Since reunification, the building has become one of the most beautiful exhibition halls in Berlin. Today it is a venue for changing exhibitions of art and culture, ranging from Aztec sculptures from Mexico to set designs for the films of Stanley Kubrick, including *A Clockwork Orange.*

Niederkirchnerstrasse 7. © **030/254860.** Admission varies with the event. Wed–Mon 10am–8pm. U-Bahn: Kochstrasse or Potsdamer Platz.

Museum für Naturkunde ★★ MUSEUM Five new halls were designed and constructed in 2007 in this natural history museum, which was inaugurated in 1889 by Emperor Wilhelm II. In a modern exhibit hall, the most stunning attraction is the **Brachiosaurus Brancai ★★★**, the world's tallest mounted dinosaur skeleton, a beast that lived some 150 million years ago and was discovered in Tanzania in 1909. The reptile's bones are presented in accordance with the latest scientific findings.

The exhibition features a total of seven dinosaurs "running" as a group. Adjoining halls feature a scientific Jurassic Park filled with prehistoric reptiles. An original fossil

MARKER IDENTIFIES hitler's bunker

For the first time since World War II, the notorious bunker of the Third Reich was marked publicly in 2006. The Führer Bunker, as it is called, was where Hitler staged his last stand, committing suicide on April 30, 1945, as Soviet troops encircled the bunker. Stalin had issued orders to bring Hitler to Moscow alive.

"History can be good or bad, but even if it's about a devil, people must be informed of history," said former SS Staff Sgt. Rochus Misch, a Hitler bodyguard who lived in the bunker with him and attended the unveiling of the marker in June 2006.

For decades, Berlin officials refused to mark the site, fearing it would become a place of pilgrimage for neo-Nazis. Misch dispelled the widely circulated myth that the bunker had 12 floors and an underground highway that Hitler used to cruise beneath the city. The bunker was constructed in 1935 and was fortified by walls 4.2m (14 ft.) thick. The bunker is not intact under the parking lot that covers it. Soviet soldiers blew up most of the bunker in the 1980s, and the foundation and walls were filled with rubble. The marker bears graphics, photographs, and a chronology of events in both German and English. The location of the bunker is at the corner of In den Ministergarten and Gertrude Kolmar Strasse near the Potsdamer Platz.

of the ancient bird Archaeopteryx went on display for the first time in 2007. You can also see the biggest collection of **meteorites** ★ in Germany, including the gigantic iron meteorite found in Namibia. Large dioramas depict the fauna of the Bavarian Alps and an Icelandic bird colony from 1918 (one of the first of its kind ever designed). Part of Berlin's Humboldt University, the museum owns 25 million objects and exhibits, and is one of the most significant institutions of its type in the world.

Invalidenstrasse 43. ✆ **030/20938591.** www.naturkundemuseum-berlin.de. Admission 6€ adults, 4€ children 14 and under. Tues–Fri 9:30am–6pm; Sat–Sun 10am–6pm. Tram: 6, 8, or 12.

Museum Haus am Checkpoint Charlie MUSEUM   Exhibits in this small building evoke the tragic events connected with the former Berlin Wall. You can see some of the instruments of escape used by East Germans, including chairlifts, false passports, hot-air balloons, and even a minisub. Photos document the construction of the Wall, the establishment of escape tunnels, and the postwar history of both parts of Berlin from 1945 to today, including the airlift of 1948 to 1949. One of the most moving exhibits is the display on the staircase of drawings by schoolchildren who, in 1961 to 1962, were asked to depict both halves of Germany in one picture. Close to Checkpoint Charlie, and straddling the two sides of Friedrichstrasse, is a memorial of large wooden crosses, some 1,000 in all, which commemorate would-be escapees shot or killed near the Wall from 1961 to 1989.

Friedrichstrasse 43–45. ✆ **030/2537250.** www.mauermuseum.de. Admission 13€ adults, 9.50€ students, free for children 16 and under. Daily 9am–10pm. U-Bahn: Kochstrasse or Stadtmitte. Bus: 129.

Neue Synagoge Berlin–Centrum Judaicum (The New Synagogue) SYNAGOGUE   Originally consecrated on Rosh Hashana in 1866 and capped with what's remembered as one of the most spectacular domes in Berlin, this synagogue was vandalized in 1938 during *Kristallnacht,* torched by Berliners in 1944, blasted by Allied bombs in 1945, and finally, after about a decade of further deterioration, demolished by the Communist East Germans in the 1950s. During its heyday, with

3,200 seats and a design inspired by the Moorish architecture of the Alhambra in Granada, Spain, it was the largest synagogue in Germany. In recent times, it was partially rebuilt, and capped with a gilded dome that's visible for many surrounding blocks. Inside, there's a replica, using some of the original carvings, of some of the original synagogue's entrance vestibules and anterooms, within which are exhibitions detailing the events that transpired in this building since its original construction. The bulk of the synagogue was never rebuilt. In its place is a gravel-covered plot of land where markers indicate the original layout of the building. If you visit, you'll gain a disturbing and unnerving insight into the destruction of a way of life that used to be and a sense of the passion with which Berlin's Jewish and German communities commemorate the memory of their murdered kinfolk.

Oranienburgerstrasse 28–30. © **030/88028300.** www.cjudaicum.de. Admission 3€ adults, 2€ students and children 13 and under. Apr–Sept Sun–Mon 10am–8pm, Tues–Thurs 10am–6pm, Fri 10am–5pm; Mar and Oct Sun–Mon 10am–8pm, Tues–Thurs 10am–6pm, Fri 10am–2pm; Nov–Feb Sun–Thurs 10am–6pm, Fri 10am–2pm. Guided tours in German Sun 2 and 4pm (year-round), Wed 4pm (Mar–Oct only); call to request tours in English (not always available). Last entrance 30 min. before closing. S-Bahn: Oranienburgerstrasse or Hackescher Markt.

Reichstag (Parliament) ★ GOVERNMENT BUILDING   The night of February 17, 1933, was a date that lives in infamy in German history. On that night, a fire broke out in the seat of the German house of parliament, the Reichstag. Historians still debate whether it was set by the Nazis, but in any event, the German Communist Party was blamed. That was all the excuse Hitler's troops needed to begin mass arrests of "dissidents and enemies of the lawful government." Because of this mysterious fire, democracy came to an end in Germany. The Reichstag was in for even greater punishment as it faced massive Allied bombardment in World War II.

Today, the Reichstag is back and is once again the home of the country's parliament in the wake of the collapse of the Berlin Wall and subsequent reunification in 1990. The building still evokes the neo-Renaissance style it had when it opened in 1894. It's crowned by a new glass dome designed by Sir Norman Foster, the famous English architect. You can go through the west gate for an elevator ride up to the dome, where a sweeping vista of Berlin opens before you. There's both an observation platform and a rooftop restaurant (but the view is better than the food).

Platz der Republik 1. © **030/22732152.** Free admission. Daily 8am–midnight (last entrance 10pm). S-Bahn: Unter den Linden. Bus: 100.

Topography of Terror WWII SITE   Located on the grounds of Hitler's SS and the Gestapo Headquarters, this center provides historical information on National Socialism and its heinous crimes. It's a site of "remembrance and learning," with a documentation center that opened in 2010, 65 years after the end of World War II. From this site between 1933 and 1945, the Nazi regime orchestrated the genocide of European Jews and the systematic persecution of political opponents. The site is a modern concrete and glass building in the form of a transparent cube. There are four exhibition halls for temporary and permanent exhibitions of the Nazi regime.

Niederkirchnerstrasse 8. © **030/2545099-50.** Free admission. May–Sept daily 10am–8pm; Oct–Apr daily 10am–6pm. U-Bahn: Potsdamer Platz.

MUSEUMSINSEL (MUSEUM ISLAND)

Alte Nationalgalerie ★ MUSEUM   This museum is known for its collection of 19th-century German and French Impressionists. The museum also has the world's largest collection of the works of one of the best known of all Berlin artists, Adolph

REMEMBERING THE berlin wall

While Berliners won't forget the **Berlin Wall** anytime soon, the majority of it was torn down in the early '90s. But there are still a few places to see remnants of the Wall.

The **East Side Gallery** (U-Bahn: Warschauerstrasse Strasse), a 1.2km (¾-mile) section of the wall along the Spree River southeast of Alexanderplatz, is the longest and best preserved section left standing. It was painted by artists in the 1990s and the feel is more like an outdoor art gallery.

The government created a memorial center and reconstructed a partial stretch of the Wall at Bernauer Strasse and Ackerstrasse (**Berlin Wall Memorial/Berliner Mauer Dokumentationszentrum;** www. berliner-mauer-dokumentationszentrum. de; Bernauer Strasse 111; free admission; open 10am–6pm Tues–Sun Apr–Oct, to 5pm Nov–Mar; U-Bahn: Bernauer Strasse), at a cost of over a million euros. The 70m-long (230-ft.) memorial consists of two walls that include some of the fragments of the original wall (those fragments not bulldozed away or carried off by souvenir hunters). The memorial is mostly made of mirrorlike stainless steel. Slits allow visitors to peer through. Across from the wall is a memorial building with newspaper clippings and stations where you can see photos of the area pre-1989 and listen to eyewitness testimonies of what it was like when the wall stood. Part of the memorial is the **Chapel of Reconciliation (Kapelle der Versöhnung),** a contemporary wood, round building set on the site of the former church which was blown up in 1985 in order to widen the border strip at this spot. A 20-minute service (in German), held to remember those who perished trying to flee to the west, takes place in the church every Tuesday through Friday at 12pm.

von Menzel (1815–1905). We especially like his *Das Balkonzimmer*. Other paintings include a galaxy of art representing the romantic and classical movements as well as the Biedermeier era, the latter especially well represented by Caspar David Friedrich and Schinkel. Allow at least an hour and a half to take in canvases by everybody from Pissarro to Cézanne, from Delacroix to Degas, and from van Gogh to Monet. We are especially fond of the works of Max Liebermann and Max Beckmann. The collection would have been far greater than it is had not the Nazis either sold or destroyed so many early-20th-century works they viewed as "degenerate."

Bodestrasse 1–3. ✆ **030/20905577.** www.smb.museum.de. Admission 8€ adults, 4€ students, free for children 16 and under. Tues–Sun 10am–6pm (Thurs until 10pm). S-Bahn: Hackescher Markt. Tram: 3, 4, 5, 12, 13, 15, or 53. Bus: 100, 157, or 378.

Altes Museum MUSEUM   Karl Friedrich Schinkel, the city's greatest architect, designed this structure, which resembles a Greek Corinthian temple, in 1822. On its main floor is the **Antikensammlung (Museum of Antiquities),** a collection of Greek and Roman antique decorative art. Some of the finest Greek vases of the black-and-red-figures style, from the 6th to the 4th century B.C., are here. The best-known vase is a large Athenian amphora (wine jar) found in Vulci, Etruria. It dates from 490 B.C. and shows a satyr with a lyre and the god Hermes. One of several excellent bronze statuettes, the Zeus of Dodone (470 B.C.) shows the god about to cast a bolt of lightning. You can also see a rare portrait of Cleopatra (from Alexandria). In the Brandenburg-Prussian art collection is an exceptional bronze statue of the goddess Luna descending through an "arch of the sky." The Prussians called it "the pearl of the collection."

Museumsinsel am Lustgarten. (℃ **030/20905555.** www.smb.museum. Admission 8€ adults, 4€ students, free for children 16 and under. Tues–Sun 10am–6pm (Thurs until 10pm). S-bahn: Hackescher Markt. Bus: 100 to Lustgarten, 147, 157, or 358.

Bode-Museum ★★★ MUSEUM   One of the great museums of Germany, long closed for restoration, is now open with enlarged exhibits, better lighting, and more viewer-friendly exhibitions. It contains a vast array of museums, including the Museum of Late Ancient and Byzantine Art, the Sculpture Collection, the Picture Gallery (highly recommended), the Museum of Prehistory, the Children's Gallery, and the extensive Cabinet of Coins and Medals.

The Museum of Late Ancient and Byzantine Art has displays of early Christian sarcophagi, Coptic and Byzantine sculpture, icons, and even gravestones dating from the 3rd to the 18th century. The rich Sculpture Collection exhibits magnificent pieces from ancient churches and monasteries, including a sandstone pulpit support by Anton Pilgram (1490) carved in the shape of a medieval craftsman.

The Picture Gallery is devoted in part to masterpieces from the Dutch and German schools of the 15th and 16th centuries, as well as great works by Italian, Flemish, Dutch, French, and British painters of the 14th to the 18th century.

Monbijoubrücke, Bodestrasse 1–3. (℃ **030/20905577.** www.smb.museum. Admission 8€ adults, 4€ students and children. Daily 10am–6pm; Thurs 10am–10pm. U-Bahn: Friedrichstrasse.

Neues Museum ★★★ MUSEUM   When the doors of this museum opened in 2009, it was the first time in 70 years that all five museums on Museum Island could be visited. Severely damaged in World War II, it was left in ruins for decades. The museum now contains the collections of the **Egyptian Museum ★★★** and the Papyrus Collection, as well as a part of the collection of the Museum of Prehistory and Early History and the Antiquities Collection.

The famous artifact of Berlin is the bust of **Queen Nefertiti ★★★**, which rests in the North Cupola. She gazes through the Niobe Room, the Bacchus Room, and the Roman Room into the South Cupola. Here, her gaze is returned by two monumental statues that stood in the Egyptian city of Alexandra during the late Roman Empire.

THE HISTORIC nikolai quarter

The historic **Nikolaiviertel** (U-Bahn: Klosterstrasse) was restored in time for the city's 750th anniversary in 1987. Here, on the banks of the Spree River, is where Berlin was born. Many of the medieval and baroque buildings in the neighborhood were completely and authentically reconstructed after World War II. Subsequently, some of the city's old flavor has been recaptured here.

The area is named for the **Nikolaikirche (Church of St. Nicholas),** Nikolaikirchplatz, off Spandauerstrasse ((℃ **030/24724529**). The church, the oldest in Berlin, was originally constructed in the 14th century on the remains of a 13th-century Romanesque church. The restored building now displays the finds of postwar archaeological digs; during the reconstruction, 800-year-old skeletons were found. It's open daily from 10am to 6pm. Admission to the church and tower is free.

The Egyptian collection ranges from the huge sphinx of Hatsheput (1490 B.C.) to fragments of reliefs from Egyptian temples. Of special interest is the **Burial Cult Room ★★**, where coffins, mummies, and grave objects are displayed along with life-size X-ray photographs of the mummies of humans and animals.

The **Papyrus Collection ★★** displays about 25,000 documents of papyrus, ostraca, parchment, limestone, wax, and wood in eight different languages.

Museumsinsel. © **030/266424242.** www.neues-museum.de. Admission 10€ adults, 5€ students and children. Sun–Wed 10am–6pm; Fri–Sat 10am–8pm. U-Bahn: Friedrichstrasse.

Pergamonmuseum ★★★ MUSEUM   Pergamonmuseum houses several departments, but if you have time for only one exhibit, go to the **Department of Greek and Roman Antiquities,** housed in the north and east wings of the museum, and enter the central hall to see the **Pergamon Altar ★★★** (180–160 B.C.), which is so large that it has a huge room all to itself. Some 27 steps lead from the museum floor up to the colonnade. Most fascinating is the frieze around the base. It shows the struggle of the Olympian gods against the Titans and is strikingly alive, with figures that project as much as a foot from the background. If you explore further, you'll find a statue of a goddess holding a pomegranate (575 B.C.), found in southern Attica, where it had been buried for 2,000 years. It was so well preserved that flecks of the original paint are still visible on her garments. Many visitors come here to see the fabled **Market Gate of Miletus ★★★**, a Roman gate built around A.D. 120 in the Aegean coastal city of Miletus (now part of Turkey). Regrettably, it is in restoration until 2015. Nonetheless, museum officials have put up a transparent wall that contains the dust and noise but still allows visitors to view this world-class attraction.

The **Near East Department ★**, in the south wing, contains one of the largest collections anywhere of antiquities from ancient Babylonia, Persia, and Assyria. Among the exhibits is the Processional Way of Babylon with the **Ishtar Gate ★★★**, dating from 575 B.C. You can also visit the throne room of Nebuchadnezzar. Cuneiform clay tablets document a civilization that created ceramics, glass, and metal objects while Europe was still overrun with primitive tribes. The museum's upper level is devoted to **Islamic Art.** Of special interest are the miniatures, carpets, and woodcarvings.

Bodestrasse 1-3. © **030/20905577.** www.smb.museum. Admission 10€ adults, 5€ students, free for children 16 and under. Daily 10am–6pm (Thurs until 10pm). U-Bahn or S-Bahn: Friedrichstrasse. Tram: 1, 2, 3, 4, 5, 13, 15, or 53.

Sights in the Environs

Brücke Museum ★★ MUSEUM   Some of our all-time favorite German artists, especially Ernst Kirchner (1880–1938), have a museum devoted to their work. The

---

📷 In Memory of . . .

At the corner of Lewetzov and Jagow streets is a **Jewish War Memorial** to the many Berliners who were deported—mostly to their deaths—from 1941 until the end of the war in 1945. The memorial is a life-size sculpture of a freight car with victims being dragged into it. Behind it is a 15m (50-ft.) structure listing the dates of the various death trains and the number of prisoners shipped out. The memorial stands on the site of a former synagogue destroyed by the Nazis.

architecture BEYOND THE MAIN SIGHTS

Just north of the Tiergarten is the **Hansaviertel,** or Hansa Quarter (U-Bahn: Hansaplatz). The architecture of this area was an outgrowth of the great INTERBAU 1957 (International Builder's Exhibition), when architects from 22 nations designed buildings for the totally destroyed quarter. The diversity here is exhilarating: Fifty architects took part, including Gropius, Niemeyer, and Duttman.

Le Corbusier also submitted a design for an apartment house for INTERBAU 1957, but the structure was so gigantic that it had to be built near the **Olympic Stadium** (U-Bahn: Olympia-Stadion). The **Corbusier House,** called *Strahlende Stadt* (radiant city), is one of Europe's largest housing complexes—its 530 apartments can house up to 1,400 people. Typical of the architect's style, this tremendous building rests on stilts.

The architects of rebuilt Berlin were also encouraged to design centers for the performing arts. One of the most controversial projects was the **Kongresshalle (Congress Hall),** on John-Foster-Dulles-Allee, in the Tiergarten, just west of Brandenburg Gate (S-Bahn: Unter den Linden). This building was conceived as the American contribution to INTERBAU 1957. The reinforced concrete structure has an 18m-high (60-ft.) vaulted ceiling that reminds some viewers of an oversize

flying saucer. Berliners immediately christened it the "Pregnant Oyster." The building today is used mainly for conventions. More successful was the **Philharmonie,** new home of the Berlin Philharmonic, at Matthäikirchstrasse, and its adjacent chamber music hall, next to the Tiergarten. The tentlike roof arches up in a bold curve, and the gold-colored facade glitters.

One of the city's tallest buildings sits in the midst of the city's busiest area. The 22-story **Europa Center,** just across the plaza from the Kaiser Wilhelm Memorial Church at Breitscheidplatz (U-Bahn: Kurfürstendamm), is the largest self-contained shopping center and entertainment complex in Europe. This town-within-a-town opened in 1965 on the site of the legendary Romanisches Café, once a gathering place for actors, writers, and artists in the flamboyant 1920s. Berliners dubbed it "Pepper's Manhattan," after its owner, K. H. Pepper. In addition to three levels of shops, restaurants, nightclubs, bars, and cinemas, it contains dozens of offices, a parking garage, and an observation roof. At the Tauentzienstrasse entrance, you can find two pieces of the former Berlin Wall. The building is open daily 9am to midnight (to 10pm in winter). Admission to the observation roof is 4€.

art movement, Die Brücke, originated in Dresden in 1905 and rejected the emerging modern trends of the 20th century, turning once again to landscapes, folk art, and other retrograde sources for inspiration. This school was an influential predecessor to 20th-century expressionism. Although exhibits change, this museum presents an extensive collection of these expressionist works, including art by Max Kaus, Walter Gramatte, Otto Herbig, and Anton Kerschbaumer. Today, the Brücke Museum owns around 400 paintings and sculptures of the era, along with thousands of prints, watercolors, and drawings, although not all the treasure-trove can be displayed at the same time.

Bussardsteig 9. ✆ **030/8312029.** www.bruecke-museum.de. Admission 4€ adults, 3€ children 5-13. Wed–Mon 11am–5pm. U-Bahn to Fehrbelliner Platz, then bus 115.

Haus der Wannsee-Konferenz WWII SITE   This was the site of one of the most notorious conferences in history: a meeting of Nazi bureaucrats and SS officials to plan the annihilation of European Jewry. The minutes of the Wannsee Conference were kept by Adolf Eichmann, the sallow-faced SS functionary who later mapped out transport logistics for sending millions of Jews to their deaths.

The villa is now a memorial to the Holocaust. It includes a selection of photographs of men, women, and children who were sent to concentration camps. This exhibit is not for the squeamish. Nearly all the pictures on display are official Nazi photographs, including some of Nazi medical experiments. As noted at the trials at Nürnberg, "No government in history ever did a better job of photographing and documenting its crimes against humanity."

Am Grossen Wannsee 56-58. © **030/8050010.** www.ghwk.de. Free admission. Daily 10am–6pm. S-Bahn: Wannsee, then bus 114.

Jüdischer Friedhof (Jewish Cemetery) CEMETERY   This famous Jewish cemetery was opened in 1880. It contains 110,000 graves of Jewish residents of Berlin. Many distinguished artists, musicians, scientists, and religious leaders are buried here. Some tombs are of Jewish soldiers who fought for Germany in World War I. A memorial honors Jewish victims murdered during the Nazi era. You may have a hard time finding the cemetery on your own, so we recommend a taxi.

Herbert-Baumstrasse 31, Weissensee (a suburb east of Berlin). © **030/9253330.** www.berlin-juedisch. de. Free admission. Apr–Oct Sun–Wed 8am–5pm, Fri 8am–3pm; Nov–Mar Sun–Thurs 8am–4pm, Fri 8am–3pm. Tram: 2,12, 23, or 24, or taxi.

Museen Dahlem ★★ MUSEUM   After extensive reorganizing, this complex of museums, occupying one mammoth structure in the heart of Dahlem's Freie Universität, contains institutions devoted to everything from ethnological collections to Far Eastern art.

Occupying most of the main building is the **Ethnologisches Museum ★★★**, which is the one to visit if you have to skip the rest. This is the greatest ethnological collection on earth, totaling some 500,000 artifacts from all continents, even prehistoric America. Many of the figures are ritualistic masks and are grotesquely beautiful. The Incan, Mayan, and Aztec stone sculptures alone equal the collections of some of the finest museums of Mexico. The best part is the collection of authentic boats from the South Pacific. The museum displays an intriguing assemblage of pre-Columbian relics, including gold objects and antiquities from Peru. The museum's Department of Music allows visitors to hear folk music recordings from around the globe.

In the same complex is the **Museum für Asiatische Kunst (Museum for Asian Art),** which now includes both the Far Eastern collection and the Museum of Indian Art. **Museum für Ostasiatische Kunst (Museum for Far Eastern Art) ★★** is a gem of a museum devoted primarily to Japan, Korea, and China, with artifacts dating back to as far as 3000 B.C. Launched in 1906 as the first Far Eastern museum of art in Germany, this museum is one of Europe's finest in presenting an overview of some of the most exquisite ecclesiastical and decorative art from the Far East. It is the equal of or better than similar collections in Paris. In essence, the museum represents the loot acquired during a massive "shopping expedition" the Germans took to Asia, where they even managed to garner the 17th-century imperial throne of China, all lacquered and inlaid with mother-of-pearl. The Japanese woodblock prints, each more exquisite than the next, are reason enough to visit.

Germany's greatest collection of Indian art is on exhibit in the same building at the **Museum für Indische Kunst (Museum for Indian Art),** covering a span of

40 centuries. It's an international parade of some of the finest art and artifacts from the world of Buddhism, representing collections from such lands as Burma, Thailand, Indonesia, Nepal, and Tibet.

Outside the Dahlem museum complex, and only a 5-minute walk away, **Museum Europäischer Kulturen (Museum of European Culture)** is devoted to the German people themselves—not the aristocrats but the middle class and the peasant stock who built the country. It is a true "museum of the people." The exhibits go back 4 centuries, tracing how artisans and homemakers lived and worked. Household items are displayed along with primitive industrial equipment such as a utensil for turning flax into linen. Furnishings, clothing, pottery, and even items used in religious observances are shown, along with some fun and whimsical exhibits, including depictions of pop culture from the 1950s to the 1980s.

Lansstrasse 8. ℭ **030/8301438.** www.smb.museum. Admission 6€ adults, free for students and children 16 and under. Tues–Fri 10am–6pm; Sat–Sun 11am–6pm. U-Bahn: Dahlem-Dorf.

Sachsenhausen Gedenkstätte (Sachsenhausen Memorial & Museum)

WWII SITE   Just north of Berlin, Sachsenhausen was one of the most notorious death camps of the Nazi empire and was liberated by Allied troops in 1945. The freedom was short-lived. The Soviet secret police turned it into a prison camp, and the misery and death continued for another 5 years.

The largest prison camp in East Germany, Sachsenhausen was home to some 12,000 inmates from 1945 to 1950, when the prison was shut down. Mass graves of the former prisoners were discovered here only in 1990. A museum has opened on the site documenting the tragic history of two totalitarian regimes, the Nazi and Soviet enslavements. Exhibits show that, during World War II, Sachsenhausen was the administrative headquarters for all the concentration camps, winning the praise of the dreaded SS chief, Heinrich Himmler.

The SS learned its methods of mass killing at this camp. Most of the 30,000 or so victims of the Nazi regime were prisoners of war and included Stalin's oldest son. The Soviet prisoners included 6,000 Nazi officers and other functionaries. After the war, Russian soldiers who contracted sexually transmitted diseases from German women were also sent here.

Strasse der Nationen 22, Oranienburg (35km/22 miles north of Berlin). ℭ **03301/2000.** www.stiftung-bg.de. Free admission. Mar 15–Oct 14 daily 8:30am–6pm; Oct 15–Mar 14 daily 8:30am–4:30pm. Take S-Bahn 1 from Friedrichstrasse to Oranienburg, the last stop; from there, it's a 25-min. walk (it's signposted).

Schloss Schönhausen ★ HISTORIC BUILDING   One of Germany's most

historic palaces showcases years of Prussian history. In the Berlin-Pankow district, the *Schloss* dates from the 1660s, when it was the residence of Sophie Dorothea zu Dohna. Queen Elisabeth Christine, wife of Frederick the Great, used the palace as a summer residence from 1740 to 1797. Some of the living rooms have been faithfully reconstructed on the ground floor. From 1949 to 1960, Schönahsen was the seat of the first president of the DDR, and from 1964 to 1990, it was the residence for official guests of East Germany. On the upper floor, visitors can view the office of Welhelm Pieck and an exclusive suite reserved for visiting VIPs, including Fidel Castro and Indira Gandhi. The palace is one of the very few mammoth Berlin buildings that was not bombed in World War II.

Tschaikowskistrasse 1 (Berlin-Pankow). ℭ **0331/9694200.** www.spsg.de. Admission 6€. Tues–Sun 10am–5pm. U-Bahn: Pankow (a 10-block walk).

Spandau Zitadelle (Spandau Citadel) HISTORIC BUILDING   This citadel stands at the confluence of the Spree and Havel rivers in northwestern Berlin. The Hohenzollern electors of Brandenburg used it as a summer residence, and, in time, it became the chief military center of Prussia. The citadel has been besieged by everybody from the French to the Prussians. The Juliusturm (Julius Tower) and the Palas, constructed in the 13th to the 15th century, are the oldest buildings in Berlin still standing. The main building, accessible by footbridge, houses a local-history museum.

Am Juliusturm. ✆ **030/3549440.** www.zitadelle-spandau.de. Admission 4.50€ adults, 2.50€ students. Tues–Fri 9am–5pm; Sat–Sun 10am–5pm. U-Bahn: Zitadelle.

Berlin's Parks & Zoo

The huge **Botanischer Garten (Botanical Garden),** Königin-Luise-Strasse 6–8 (✆ **030/83850100;** www.bgbm.org/bgbm; S-Bahn: Botanischer Garten or Rathaus Steglitz), near the Dahlem Museums, has vast collections of European and exotic plants. The big palm house is one of the largest in the world. A large arboretum is here, as well as several special collections such as a garden for blind visitors and another with water plants. Admission is 6€ for adults, 3€ for children 6 to 14, and free for children 5 and under. The gardens are open daily April and August 9am to 8pm; May, June, and July 9am to 9pm; September 9am to 7pm; March and October 9am to 6pm; February 9am to 5pm; and November to January 9am to 4pm. The museum is open year-round daily from 10am to 6pm.

   Tiergarten ★ is the largest green space in central Berlin, covering 2.5 sq. km (just under 1 sq. mile), with more than 23km (14 miles) of meandering walkways. It was originally laid out as a private park for the electors of Prussia by a leading landscape architect of the day, Peter Josef Lenné. The park was devastated during World War II, and the trees that remained were chopped down for fuel, as Berliners shivered through the winter of 1945 and 1946. Beginning in 1955, trees were replanted, and walkways, canals, ponds, and flower beds were restored to their original patterns. The park is popular with joggers and (sometimes nude) sunbathers. Inside the park is the Berlin Zoo (see below).

   Among the park's monuments is the **Siegessäule (Victory Column),** a golden goddess of victory perched atop a soaring red-granite pedestal. The monument stands in the center of the wide boulevard (Strasse des 17 Juni) that neatly bisects the park.

☺ FUN FOR kids

Children love the **Berlin Zoo-Aquarium** (see below). Its most famous residents, the giant pandas, are perennial favorites. The zoo also has playgrounds and a children's section, where the animals welcome a cuddle. Another place to take the kids is **Grips-Theater,** Altonaerstrasse 22 (✆ **030/39747477;** www.grips-theater. de; U-Bahn: Hansaplatz), known for its bright, breezy productions. Children are sure to enjoy the music and dancing (if not the simple German-language dialogue). Tickets cost 6€ to 18€. Call for current productions. Most performances begin at 7:30pm, although there are some matinees as well, depending on the production. The theater is closed from late June to mid-August.

A 48m-high (157-ft.) observation platform can be reached by a climb up a 285-step spiral staircase (there's no elevator).

Zoologischer Garten Berlin (Berlin Zoo-Aquarium) ★, Hardenbergplatz 8 (© **030/254010;** www.zoo-berlin.de; U-Bahn/S-Bahn: Zoologischer Garten), founded in 1844, is Germany's oldest zoo. It occupies almost the entire southwest corner of the Tiergarten. Until World War II, the zoo boasted thousands of animals— many were familiar to Berliners by nickname. By the end of 1945, however, only 91 had survived. Today, more than 13,000 animals live here, many of them in large, open natural habitats. The most valuable residents are the giant pandas. The zoo also has Europe's most modern birdhouse, with more than 550 species.

The aquarium is as impressive as the adjacent zoo, with more than 9,000 species of fish, reptiles, amphibians, insects, and other creatures. Crocodiles, Komodo dragons, and tuataras inhabit the terrarium within. You can walk on a bridge over the reptile pit. There's also a large collection of snakes, lizards, and turtles. The glass-roofed "hippoquarium" is yet another attraction.

Individual admission to either the zoo or the aquarium is 12€ for adults, 9€ for seniors and students, and 6€ for children 5 to 15. A combined ticket costs 18€ for adults, 14€ for seniors and students, and 9€ for children 5 to 15. The zoo is open daily 9am to 5pm January 1 to March 20 and October 26 to December 31; March 21 to September 14 daily 9am to 7pm; September 15 to October 25 daily 9am to 6pm.

AquaDom & Sea Life Berlin, Spandauer Strasse 3 (© **030/992800;** www. sealife.de; U-Bahn: Hackescher Markt), is hardly the greatest aquarium in Europe, but it has some unique features. The tanks begin on the River Spree and then flow into the Wannsee, a Berlin lake, before heading to the ocean. Thus, you go from freshwater to saltwater. Along the way you meet some 4,000 marine creatures from the octopus to the hound shark, even sea horses. After a Sea Life visit, you can go to the AquaDom to view the largest free-standing aquarium in the world. It's home to a vast collection of rainbow-hued tropical fish. At the end of your visit, you take a dramatic glass elevator through a silo-shaped "fish tank" to the exit. Admission is 17€ for adults, 12€ for children 3 to 14, and free for children 2 and under. It's open April to September daily 10am to 7pm, October to March daily 10am to 6pm.

WHERE TO EAT

If it's true that optimism and appetite go hand in hand, Berliners must be among the most optimistic people in Europe. But just because Berliners like to eat doesn't mean that they like to spend a lot on food. Locals know that you can often have a memorable dinner here in an unheralded wine restaurant or sidewalk cafe.

Examples of typical dishes are the Berliner *Schlachteplatte* (cold plate), pigs' feet cooked with *Sauerkraut* and pea purée, and *Eisbein* (pickled knuckle of pork with *Sauerkraut*). Venison, wildfowl, and wild boar also appear frequently, as do carp and trout, along with an infinite variety of sausages.

But Berlin does not limit itself to traditional cuisine. A new wave of restaurants has swept across the city, from east to west. More and more are going ethnic, serving everything from Indonesian or French to Thai or Japanese. Eastern European wines are now almost as popular as those from Germany itself.

Note: If a restaurant bill says *Bedienung*, then a service charge has already been added, so just round up to the nearest euro.

On or Near the Kurfürstendamm

VERY EXPENSIVE

Die Quadriga ★★★ MODERN CONTINENTAL   This is the kind of place so hushed, so "correct," and so seamlessly upscale that even when the president of Germany shows up (as he does in an informal and unofficial capacity), it barely makes a ripple in the smooth and well-rehearsed service rituals. The setting is a cherry-paneled room on the lobby level of a hotel (the Brandenburger Hof) that's a long urban trek from the restaurant's namesake, the four-horsed statue atop the Brandenburg Gate, in faraway Berlin-Mitte. Meals are served atop snowy linen to no more than 28 clients at a time, each seated on a chair designed in 1904 by Frank Lloyd Wright. Wines are available by the bottle or by the glass, and menu items vary with the season and the inspiration of the chef. The best examples might include arctic codfish flavored with lemon thyme and served with a potato risotto; foie gras accompanied by Riesling grapes and Périgord truffles; grilled sole with cauliflower; and saddle of venison stuffed with walnuts, black pudding, and pine nuts.

In the Hotel Brandenburger Hof, Eislebener Strasse 14. ⓒ **030/214050.** Reservations required well in advance. Main courses 30€–39€. AE, MC, V. Tues–Sat 7–10:30pm. Closed 2 weeks in Jan and 2 weeks in Aug. U-Bahn: Kurfürstendamm or Augsburgerstrasse.

Hugos ★★★ MEDITERRANEAN   In the Hotel InterContinental Berlin, this is the hot, chic restaurant of a united capital. *Der Feinschmecker,* Germany's leading magazine for traveling, eating, and drinking in style, named it Restaurant of the Year for 2005. Today it seems to be even better than it was when it earned that designation. Choice delicacies are created daily by Thomas Kammeier, one of Berlin's leading masters of the kitchen. You get not only superb food, but a panoramic view from your dining table as well. Backed up by an exquisite, albeit expensive, wine list, this Michelin-starred restaurant is filled with nuanced, market-fresh cuisine.

Appetizers range from simple to complex, but each is delicious, as exemplified by glazed foie gras with mango or a risotto with Périgord truffles and quail-egg croutons. For a main dish, try the codfish with chicory salad, fresh oranges, and virgin olive oil, or else the shoulder of beef with Périgord truffles.

In the Hotel InterContinental Berlin, Budapesterstrasse 2. ⓒ **030/26021263.** www.hugos-restaurant. de. Reservations required. Main courses 28€–55€; fixed-price menus 90€–130€. AE, DC, MC, V. Mon–Sat 6–11:30pm. Closed July 17–Aug 18. U-Bahn or S-Bahn: Zoologischer Garten.

EXPENSIVE

Paris Bar ★ FRENCH   This French bistro has been a local favorite since it cheered up the postwar years in dismal bombed-out Berlin. It's crowded with elbow-to-elbow tables like a Montmartre tourist trap but is a genuinely pleasing little place on the see-and-be-seen circuit, close to the Theater des Westens. The food is invariably fresh and well prepared, but not particularly innovative.

Kantstrasse 152. ⓒ **030/3138052.** Reservations recommended. Main courses 13€–32€. AE, MC, V. Daily noon–2am. U-Bahn: Uhlandstrasse.

MODERATE

Arlecchino ★ ITALIAN   One of the best Italian restaurants in Berlin not only serves a good cuisine but also is one of the most affordable restaurants in its neighborhood. It attracts homesick Italian expats as well as serious Berlin foodies. The cooks are definitely from the sunny Mediterranean, as reflected by their succulent pastas, which are homemade and served fresh daily. In fact, you can easily fill up on a platter

Berlin-Mitte Restaurants & Hotels

RESTAURANTS ◆
Aigner **18**
Burgermeister **34**
Dressler **23**
FACIL **12**
Fischers Fritz **21**

FraRosa **27**
Ganymed **6**
Guy **17**
Lorenz Adlon **10**
Malatesta **16**
Margaux **9**

Pasternak **31**
Remake **25**
Restaurant VAU **19**
Ristorante Sale
e Tabacchi **14**
Rutz **4**

StäV **7**
Vox **13**
Zur Letzten
Instanz **32**

HOTELS ■
Alexander Plaza **28**
Arcotel Velvet **2**
Arte Luise Kunsthotel **8**
Berlin Hilton **15**
Circus Hotel **26**
Grand Hyatt Berlin **13**
Hotel Adlon **10**
Hotel de Rome **20**
Hotel Honigmond **3**
Hotel Luisenhof **33**
Hotel MitArt **1**
Lux 11 **29**
The Mandala Hotel **12**
Maritim Pro Arte **24**
Meliá Berlin **5**
Myer's Hotel Berlin **30**
The Regent **21**
The Ritz-Carlton **11**
Westin Grand Hotel **22**

Western Berlin Restaurants & Hotels

HOTELS ■
Alexandra Hotel-Pension **11**
Ambassador Berlin **35**
Arco Hotel **37**
Art'otel **28**
Art Nouveau **10**
Askanischer Hof **12**
Bleibtreu Hotel **14**

Bogota **13**
Brandenburger Hof/
 Relais & Châteaux **29**
Concorde Berlin **27**
Ellington Hotel **36**
Grand Hotel Esplanade **38**
Hecker's Hotel **21**
Hollywood Media Hotel **15**

Hotel Domus **18**
Hotel-Pension Bregenz **9**
Hotel-Pension Funk **20**
Kempenski Hotel Bristol **22**
Kronprinz Berlin **5**
Ku'Damm 101 **6**
Mövenpick Hotel Berlin **39**
Palace Berlin **33**

Legend:
- ⊠ Post Office
- Ⓢ S-Bahn
- Ⓤ U-Bahn
- 🚉 Train station

Pension München 19
Pension Nürnberger Eck 30
Propeller Island
  City Lodge 8
Savoy 24
Schlosshotel im Grunewald 7
Steigenberger Berlin 31
Villa Kastania 2

RESTAURANTS ◆
Alt-Luxemburg 3
Ana e Bruno 1
Arlecchino 25
Daitokai 32
Die Quadriga 29
First Floor 33
Funkturm Restaurant 4
Hard Rock Café 26

Hugos 34
Kaefer's Restaurant
  Dachgarten 40
Lubitsch 17
Marjellchen 16
Paris Bar 23
Paris-Moskau 39
Vivaldi 7

Hamburg
Berlin ★
GERMANY
• Frankfurt
  am Main
• Munich

of one of these pastas, including penne with bacon and fresh tomatoes or tagliatelle with salmon. Another worthy pasta dish is fettuccine with spinach and mushrooms. Excellent wines also appear on the *carte*—you can, for example, order a fine wine by the glass or a full liter. The staff speaks English and is both friendly and competent.

Meinekestrasse 25. ℰ **030/8812563.** Reservations recommended. Main courses 12€–26€. MC, V. Daily noon–10pm. U-Bahn: Uhlandstrasse.

Kaefer's Restaurant Dachgarten CONTINENTAL   When a team of cutting-edge architects redesigned the most famous building in Berlin, the Reichstag (Parliament House), they added a restaurant on the uppermost floor, just behind the soaring dome that has inspired so many photographs. The setting is metallic looking and edgy. Lines to get in can be overwhelming, mingling sightseers and diners in the same queues, so here's our advice on how to short-circuit the potential wait: Phone in advance for a dining reservation and note the reservation number an attendant will give you. Head for the Reichstag's entrance, on the building's west side, facing the Platz der Republik, give the attendant your number, and then ride an elevator directly to the restaurant, avoiding the lines of sightseers coming just to admire the building's dome.

Included in the price of your meal will be a close-up view of the dome and the rest of the building's interior. Frankly, a visit here for breakfast may be your best bet, when there's a businesslike aura that's consistent with this building's august role as a Teutonic icon. Views sweep from the dining room out over what used to be known as East Berlin. The lunch menu is more "Berliner" than the Continental/Asian evening menu. Some of the more tempting main-dish specialties include filet of beef stuffed with foie gras, wrapped in bacon, and served in a shallot sauce; filet of veal under a shrimp crust; sautéed breast of duck with an apricot flavoring; and pan-fried filet of cod seasoned with fresh tarragon and served with German caviar.

In the Reichstag, Platz der Republik. ℰ **030/22629900.** www.feinkost-kaefer.de. Reservations necessary. Main courses 25€–30€. AE, DC, MC, V. Daily 9am–4:30pm and 6:30–9:30pm (last food order). S-Bahn: Unter den Linden.

Marjellchen ★ EAST PRUSSIAN   This is the only restaurant in Berlin specializing in the cuisine of Germany's long-lost provinces of East Prussia, Pomerania, and Silesia. Ramona Azzaro, whose East Prussian mother taught her many of the region's famous recipes, is the creative force. Amid a Bismarckian ambience of vested waiters and oil lamps, you can enjoy a savory version of red-beet soup with strips of beef, East Prussian potato soup with shrimp and bacon, *Falscher Gänsebraten* (pork spareribs stuffed with prunes and bread crumbs "as if the cook had prepared a goose"), marinated elk, and roast filet of hare with a cherry sauce, served with braised cabbage and potato dumplings. This is the type of food Goethe and Schiller liked. Of course, Marjellchen isn't the place to go if you want to keep tabs on your cholesterol intake.

Mommsenstrasse 9. ℰ **030/8832676.** www.marjellchen-berlin.de. Reservations required. Main courses 11€–24€. AE, DC, MC, V. Daily 5pm–midnight. Closed Dec 23, 24, and 31. U-Bahn: Adenauerplatz or Uhlandstrasse. Bus: 109, 119, or 129.

INEXPENSIVE

Lubitsch CONTINENTAL/GERMAN/MEDITERRANEAN   Lubitsch is deeply entrenched in the consciousness of many local residents, and it's considered, in some quarters, to have a degree of conservative chic. Menu items include lots of cafe drinks, with glasses of wine priced at 4.50€ to 7€ and steaming pots of afternoon tea. If you drop in for a meal, expect platters of chicken curry salad with roasted potatoes,

Berlin-style potato soup, braised chicken with salad and fresh vegetables, a roulade of suckling pig, and Nürnberger-style *Wursts*. Count on a not-so-friendly staff, a black-and-white decor with Thonet-style chairs, and a somewhat arrogant environment that, despite its drawbacks, is very Berliner.

Bleibtreustrasse 47. ℰ **030/8823756.** www.restaurant-lubitsch.de. Reservations not necessary. Main courses lunch 8€–10€, dinner 14€–22€. AE, DC, MC, V. Mon–Sat 10am–midnight; Sun 6pm–1am. U-Bahn: Kurfürstendamm.

Near the Memorial Church & Zoo
VERY EXPENSIVE
First Floor ★★ REGIONAL GERMAN/FRENCH   This is the showcase restaurant within one of the most spectacular hotels ever built near the Tiergarten. Set one floor above street level, it features a perfectly orchestrated service and setting that revolve around the cuisine of a master chef. Winning praise is the seasonal menu with such dishes as a filet of sole with mussels and fennel, or a saddle of venison veal in a spicy crust. Starters may include champagne cabbage soup with crab and celery mousse and biscuit with spring vegetables..

In the Palace Berlin, Budapesterstrasse 42. ℰ **030/25021020.** www.firstfloor.palace.de. Reservations recommended. Main courses 38€–42€; 3-course fixed-price menu 45€, 4 courses 92€, 5-course fish menu 112€. AE, DC, MC, V. Mon–Fri noon–3pm; daily 6:30–11pm. Closed July 18–Aug 15. U-Bahn: Zoologischer Garten.

Near the Tiergarten
EXPENSIVE
Paris-Moskau INTERNATIONAL   The grand days of the 19th century are alive and well at this restaurant in the beautiful Tiergarten area, where good dining spots are scarce. Menu items are both classic and cutting edge. The fresh tomato soup is excellent. Some dishes—such as grilled filet of beef in mushroom sauce—are mundane, but other, lighter dishes with delicate seasonings are delightful. We recommend the grilled North Sea salmon with herbs accompanied by basil-flavored noodles. The chef should market his recipe for saffron sauce, which accompanies several dishes. You'll receive attentive service from the formally dressed staff.

Alt-Moabit 141. ℰ **030/3942081.** www.paris-moskau.de. Reservations recommended. Main courses 21€–29€; fixed-price menus 56€–72€. AE, DC, MC, V. Daily 6–11:30pm. S-Bahn: Anhalter Bahnhof.

In Greater Charlottenburg
VERY EXPENSIVE
Alt-Luxemburg ★★ CONTINENTAL/FRENCH/GERMAN   Karl Wannemacher is one of the most outstanding chefs in eastern Germany. Known for his quality market-fresh ingredients, he prepares a seductively sensual plate. Everything shows his flawless technique, from the filet of turbot with baby leeks and a sweet vinegar sauce to the roast scallops in a balsamic sauce with silver beets. Other delectably flavored dishes include an olive-crusted saddle of Irish lamb or a filet of veal with shiitake mushrooms and polenta. Featured desserts include a chocolate bar with a piña colada parfait and pineapple. Alt-Luxemburg offers a finely balanced wine list, and service is both unpretentious and gracious.

Windscheidstrasse 31. ℰ **030/3238730.** www.alt-luxemburg.de. Reservations required. Main courses 26€–32€; fixed-price 4-course menu 48€. AE, DC, MC, V. Mon–Sat 5–11pm. U-Bahn: Sophie-Charlottenplatz.

EXPENSIVE

Ana e Bruno ★ ITALIAN   This is one of Berlin's most charming Italian restaurants, turning out a delectable cuisine that takes full advantage of the freshest ingredients and produce in any season. *Nuova cucina* is emphasized here more strongly than traditional Italian classics, and the chefs like to experiment. The combinations of food yield delicious and harmonious medleys. Expect such dishes as homemade pasta with Norcia truffles and goose-liver sauce, or venison in a radish sauce with chestnuts and a quince purée. You might also go for the wild halibut with duck liver and a Marsala jus, or else marinated lobster with couscous. Regular customers and gourmets keen on experimenting always seem satisfied with the results. A large wine selection, mostly reasonable in price, complements the menu.

Sophie-Charlotten-Strasse 101. © **030/3257110.** www.ana-e-bruno.de. Reservations recommended. Main courses 17€–35€; fixed-price menus 65€–95€. AE, MC, V. Daily 5–10:30pm. S-Bahn: Westend.

MODERATE

Funkturm Restaurant ☺ INTERNATIONAL   This restaurant at the radio tower's 52m (170-ft.) midway point provides both good food and sweeping, high-altitude views. Inside the restaurant's metallic, glossy interior, every table sits near a window, which is entertaining for kids. Some of the best items on the menu include grilled lamb with a fresh herb sauce, or else honey flavored rib-eye of beef, or even leg of lamb cooked with fresh rosemary and served with a maple syrup dressing.

You can take the elevator to the observation platform Monday 10am to 8pm, Tuesday to Sunday 10am to 11pm. The cost is 4.50€, 2.50€ for kids 12 and under. For information about the tower and its upper-tier observation platform, call © **030/ 30382996.**

Messedamm 22. © **030/30382900.** Reservations not necessary. Main courses 15€–25€. AE, DC, MC, V. Wed–Sun 11:30am–11pm; Tues 6:30–11pm. U-Bahn: Kaiserdamm.

In Grunewald

EXPENSIVE

Vivaldi ★ FRENCH   This restaurant is the culinary showcase of one of the most unusual small hotels in Berlin, a neo-Renaissance palace built in 1912 by an advisor to Kaiser Wilhelm II. Vivaldi serves, with panache, some of the most elegant hotel food in Berlin, within a paneled and antiques-strewn setting that's as grand as anything you're likely to find in Europe. Most diners opt for one of two fixed-price menus, each with its own regional theme, which offer the choice of three to six courses (60€–110€). There's also a limited a la carte list. Your best bet is to look for the day's suggestion. Two specialties we especially like are the Brandenburg duck with creamy potatoes or the roast halibut with lobster sauce, spinach, and a cauliflower purée. You can also count on the sauté of Bresse rabbit with morels. The chefs take special care with their roast suckling pig with truffled vegetables and a lavender sauce.

In the Schlosshotel im Grunewald, Brahmsstrasse 10. © **030/895840.** Reservations recommended. Main courses 28€–49€. AE, DC, MC, V. Tues–Sat noon–2pm and 6–10pm. S-Bahn: Grunewald.

In Berlin-Mitte

VERY EXPENSIVE

Fischers Fritz ★★ FRENCH/SEAFOOD   In the Regent hotel, this is the domain of chef de cuisine Christian Lohse. Fischers Fritz is the two-star Michelin restaurant in Berlin. In elegant surroundings, the cuisine is both subtle and sophisticated, and the chef cooks with the ardent lyricism of a culinary troubadour. Need convincing? Try such starters as terrine of foie gras and smoked eel with eggplant jam. The fish and seafood dishes are perhaps the finest in Berlin, featuring wild sea bass in a salt crust with seasonal vegetables or a suprême of Atlantic turbot with white asparagus and morels. Another tantalizing main dish is chargrilled Bresse pigeon with green asparagus and fresh mushrooms.

Charlottenstrasse 49. (C) **030/20336363.** www.fischersfritzberlin.com. Reservations required. Main courses 28€–78€; fixed-price menus 110€, 130€, and 150€. AE, DC, MC, V. Daily noon–2pm and 6:30–10:30pm. U-Bahn: Französische Strasse.

EXPENSIVE

FACIL ★★★ CONTINENTAL At tremendous expense, in the infrastructure of the Mandala Hotel (p. 143), a crane lifted a vast tonnage of glass, steel, and garden supplies to the hotel's fifth-floor terrace. Don't expect a view of the city skyline, as you'll probably get something even better: a verdant oasis of Zen-like calm smack in the middle of one of Berlin's most frenetic neighborhoods. A glass roof, tightly closed for midwinter views of the falling rain and snow, opens dramatically during clement weather for a view of the moon and stars. All this is available to only about 50 diners placed at 14 tables. Service from the well-trained staff is formal, alert, and attentive.

A medley of extremely sophisticated menu items changes with the seasons and the inspiration of the chef, but may include such starters as lukewarm octopus with clams or gnocchi with Cèpes (flap mushrooms). The freshest of fish is shipped in, and the chef grabs the best of the catch, fashioning the bounty into Atlantic turbot with fresh fennel and an anchovy sauce or else sea bass with bouillabaisse salad. Meat and poultry dishes also use quality ingredients, and our favorites are the black feather fowl with kohlrabi and dumplings or the lobster with roasted vegetables.

In the Mandala Hotel, Potsdamer Strasse 3. (C) **030/590051234.** www.facil.de. Reservations recommended. Main courses 16€–55€; fixed-price menus 70€–140€. AE, DC, MC, V. Mon–Fri noon–3pm and 7–11pm. Closed Jan 1–17 and July 24–Aug 8. U-Bahn: Potsdamer Platz.

Guy ★ INTERNATIONAL At this top-notch restaurant, anticipate a strong sense of gastronomy as theater. Proceed to any of three separate balconies, each supporting at least one row of artfully decorated tables. The effect can be compared to the balconies and private boxes of an old-fashioned opera house. The cuisine is very haute, even to the point of seeming experimental. Offerings change monthly but might include wild salmon confit with a beetroot polenta, or fresh trout cooked in buttermilk and served with a sauce of fresh fennel and lemon. Baked crayfish appears with caramelized fennel and an orange sauce or you can order a carpaccio of venison with foie gras and lime vinaigrette.

Jägerstrasse 59-60. (C) **030/20942600.** www.guy-restaurant.de. Reservations recommended. Main courses 28€–32€; fixed-price lunches 17€–22€. AE, MC, V. Mon–Fri noon–3pm and 6pm–1am; Sat 6pm–1am. U-Bahn: Stadtmitte or Französische Strasse.

Margaux ★★★ CONTINENTAL Chef Michael Hoffmann will dazzle your palate with his seductive, inventive dishes and his brilliant wine cellar. Several food magazines have named this the best gourmet restaurant in Berlin. Only a few steps from the Brandenburg Gate, the restaurant has a stunning, modern interior, designed by the noted architect Johanne Nalbach. The exceptional food, such as the steamed char served with ravioli stuffed with pulverized *tête de veau* or the pigeon stuffed with olives and served with a wine and thyme jus, is made from only the highest-quality ingredients. One delectable specialty is pink shrimp with steamed vegetables, candied lemon, and green apple jam.

Unter den Linden 78. ℂ **030/22652611.** www.margaux-berlin.de. Reservations required. Main courses 36€–42€; fixed-price menus 95€–165€. AE, DC, MC, V. Mon–Sat 7–10:30pm. S-Bahn: Unter den Linden.

Remake ★★ INTERNATIONAL   Wait till you try Cristiano Reinzner's licorice-scented scallops mated with a cherry sorbet. A horrible combination, you say, until you taste this talented chef's experimental dishes prepared with culinary flair learned at the futurist cooking school of El Bulli, in Spain (hailed as that country's best). Scallops might also appear in a pumpkin and passion fruit sauce. Another divine creation is the chef's quail breast with bitter chocolate foam and berry reduction. If not that, perhaps you'll go for the saddle of lamb with braised bananas and vanilla-scented tomatoes, or the homemade tortellini with a stuffing of goat cheese and olives, the dish bound with a caramelized walnut and sage butter. The chic restaurant lies off Oranienburgerstrasse, in the Mitte district, in a series of small rooms with exposed brick and "spider" chandeliers hanging over tiled floors.

Grosse Hamburger Strasse 32. ℂ **030/20054102.** www.restaurant-remake.de. Reservations required. Main courses 20€–30€; fixed-price menus 62€–72€. AE, MC, V. Mon–Sat 7–11pm. U-Bahn: Weinmeister Strasse.

Restaurant VAU ★★ INTERNATIONAL   This restaurant serves fabulous cuisine, celebrating the bounty of Germany. You shouldn't pass up the chance to sample the crispy pikeperch with savoy cabbage and bacon or the roast bison with black radishes, or even the roast scallops with quail eggs, goat cheese, and Swiss chard. VAU hits a culinary stride with such delights as marinated lobster in yellow turnip and truffles from Périgord, or confit of breast of veal. One of the chef's most imaginative dishes is fresh lobster served with beetroot, goat cheese, chili peppers, and crushed peanuts.

Jägerstrasse 54–55 (near the Four Seasons Hotel and the Gendarmenmarkt). ℂ **030/2029730.** www.vau-berlin.de. Reservations recommended. All courses 38€; fixed-price menus 100€–120€. AE, DC, MC, V. Mon–Sat noon–2:30pm and 7–10:30pm. U-Bahn: Hausvogteiplatz.

Rutz ★ GERMAN/CONTINENTAL   This restaurant and wine bar is definitely for the sophisticated palate. Marco Müller makes what many foodies have described as the best burger in Berlin. It consists of stuffed pig stomach, cabbage, and goose liver. Of course, if you prefer classic German food, you'll find it here, including spicy veal goulash soup or roast black pudding. But most diners, especially the young ones, prefer the more experimental dishes, including breast and confit of wild pigeon with black leaf kale and a spring onion cannelloni, with cherries, or else grilled octopus with an artichoke bean ragout, fresh rosemary, and balsamic-marinated figs. Wines are served by the glass for each course. Finish with a spectacular dessert such as a semiliquid chocolate soufflé with aloe vera, fresh orange, papaya, and saffron mascarpone ice cream.

Chausseestrasse 8. ℂ **030/24628760.** www.rutz-weinbar.de. Reservations required. Main courses 36€–42€. AE, MC, V. Mon–Sat 6:30–10:30pm. U-Bahn: Oranienburger Tor.

Vox ★ INTERNATIONAL/SUSHI   This is one of the most exciting and creative restaurants in Berlin, far outshining any competition within the vast architectural complex at Potsdamer Platz. One of Switzerland's best design teams created the minimalist decor, with lots of visual emphasis on a mostly stainless-steel, open-to-view kitchen. Here a team of uniformed chefs concocts artfully presented platters of braised goose liver with apple-flavored vinaigrette; filet of lamb cooked in a wood-burning oven with goat cheese, pepper oil, and Mediterranean vegetables; rotisserie-cooked breast of Barbary duck with mango chutney; and roasted sturgeon on a frothy sauce of white rosemary. The culinary philosophy here combines Mediterranean with Asian cuisines in ways you may not expect. One corner of the restaurant features the best sushi bar in Berlin. The venue is enhanced by an attentive and very hip staff, some of whom shuttle between the restaurant and a stylish cocktail lounge that features jazz and blues every night, beginning at 10pm. During clement weather, tables spill out onto the terrace, beneath verdant rows of linden trees.

In the Grand Hyatt Berlin, Marlene-Dietrich-Platz 2. © **030/25531772.** www.vox-restaurant.de. Reservations recommended. Main courses lunch 11€–20€, dinner 21€–35€; platters of sushi 12€–31€. AE, DC, MC, V. Restaurant Mon–Fri noon–2:30pm; daily 6:30pm–midnight. Bar daily 6pm–2am. U-Bahn: Potsdamer Platz.

MODERATE

Aigner REGIONAL/AUSTRIAN   Habsburg Austria lives on here. In the late 1990s, the Dorint chain bought the furnishings from one of Vienna's oldest cafes, the Aigner, and moved them into the ground floor of one of Berlin's most modern hotels. The result is a black-and-white *Jugendstil* setting replete with Thonet chairs. There's a lot of ambience here, thanks partly to a location that overlooks the Gendarmenmarkt; the staff provides old-fashioned service with a modern flair. The restaurant's signature dish is *Tafelspitz*, the boiled-beef-with-horseradish dish. It's served in a big brass kettle with both haunch and shoulder of beef, with lots of soup, vegetables, savoy cabbage, crème fraîche, and apple-flavored horseradish. Other good choices include saddle of deer roasted with coffee beans; braised shoulder of lamb and pink filet of lamb with roasted artichokes; or veal dumplings with beetroot and mashed chive-studded potatoes.

In the Sofitel Berlin am Gendarmenmarkt, Charlottenstrasse 50–52. © **030/203751850.** www.aigner-gendarmenmarkt.de. Reservations recommended. Main courses 15€ 32€. AE, DC, MC, V. Daily noon–11:30pm. U-Bahn: Französichestrasse.

Ganymed FRENCH   There's nothing trendy or immediately fashionable about this restaurant, which occupied these premises beginning in 1929 and stalwartly continued doing business within East Berlin throughout the Cold War. The setting includes two formal dining rooms, one with an ornate plaster ceiling of great beauty, the other a more modern, big-windowed affair that overlooks the Spree. Food arrives in worthy portions, with plenty of flavor. Many Berlin restaurants have abandoned soups altogether, but the chefs here continue to turn out that old Berlin favorite, green-pea soup, although the ginger-flavored carrot soup is more up-to-date. You might be tempted by one of the carefully crafted main courses such as braised veal cheeks with root vegetables or saddle of lamb stuffed with oyster mushrooms and served under a pistachio crust. Sometimes a whole lobster from Nantes is served grilled.

Schiffbauerdamm 5. © **030/28599046.** www.ganymed-brasserie.de. Reservations recommended. Main courses 16€–57€. AE, DC, MC, V. Daily noon–midnight. U-Bahn: Friedrichstrasse.

Malatesta ITALIAN   Flavorful Italian food, served within an all-black-and-white venue whose rectilinear simplicity might remind you of a spartan version of a sushi bar, is the heartbeat of this likable Italian restaurant. The aura is high style rather than cozy, with an emphasis on the kind of offhanded hip you might have expected in Milan or Rome. The menu reflects whatever is fresh and succulent at the time, with dishes crafted anew almost every day. Some enduring specialties include sea bass cooked under a parsley and olive crust; grilled turbot flavored with orange and fresh thyme; or spaghetti with clams spiced with hot chili peppers. Specialties from throughout Italy are the draw here, with no particular emphasis on northern, southern, or central Italian cuisine over any of the country's other regions.

Charlottenstrasse 59. © **030/20945071.** www.ristorante-malatesta.de. Reservations recommended. Main courses 17€–25€. AE, MC, V. Mon–Sat 12:30pm–1:30am. U-Bahn: Stadtmitte.

Zur Letzten Instanz GERMAN   Reputedly, this is Berlin's oldest restaurant, dating from 1525. Zur Letzten Instanz has supposedly been frequented by everybody from Napoleon to Beethoven. Prisoners used to stop off here for one last beer before going to jail. The place is located on two floors of a baroque building just outside the crumbling brick wall that once ringed medieval Berlin. Double doors open on a series of small woodsy rooms, one with a bar and ceramic *Kachelofen* (stove). At the back, a circular staircase leads to another series of rooms, where every evening at 6pm, food and wine (no beer) are served. The menu is old-fashioned, mainly limited to good, hearty fare in the best of the Grandmother Berlin tradition of staples.

Waisenstrasse 14–16 (near the Alexanderplatz). © **030/2425528.** www.zurletzteninstanz.de. Reservations recommended. Main courses 12€–20€. AE, DC, MC, V. Mon–Sat noon–1am. U-Bahn: Klosterstrasse.

INEXPENSIVE

Burgermeister HAMBURGERS   Berliners claim their beloved Burgermeister, under the arches of the U-Bahn station at Schlesisches Tor, makes the best burgers in Berlin. Of course, among burger aficionados, that's debatable. From chili cheeseburgers (a greasy delight) to barbecue burgers like they serve in the American South, this place keeps its fast-order cooks grilling until late at night. When it gets crowded, you have to take a number and wait in line with the hungry masses. Burgermeister wins praises for its "special sauces."

Oberbaumstrasse 8. © **030/22436493.** Reservations: take a number. Hamburgers 4.50€–9€. No credit cards. Mon–Thurs 11am–2am; Fri–Sat 11am–4am; Sun 3pm–2am. U-Bahn: Schlesisches Tor.

Curry 36 BRATWURST   As a former mayor of Berlin once said, "You haven't been to Berlin until you've sampled our most famous street food." Basically, it's Currywurst, which is Bratwurst sausage covered in ketchup and seasoned with curry powder. Traditionally, it's served with mayonnaise-topped fries. The most famous Currywurst Imbiss in Berlin is Curry 36. That same mayor told us that the treat (that's debatable) was served to President John F. Kennedy during his visit to the city. After downing it, Kennedy said, "Now I am a true Berliner, but I don't have to eat it ever again, do I?"

36 Mehringdamm. © **030/2517368.** Reservations not needed. Bratwurst 2€–7.50€. No credit cards. Mon–Fri 9am–4pm; Sat 10am–4pm; Sun 11am–3pm.

Dressler CONTINENTAL   No other bistro along Unter den Linden re-creates Berlin's prewar decor and style as successfully. Designed to resemble an arts-conscious bistro of the sort that might have entertained tuxedo-clad clients in the 1920s, it's set behind a wine-colored facade and outfitted with leather banquettes, black-and-white tile floors, mirrors, and film memorabilia from the great days of early German cinema. Waiters scurry around in vests and aprons, carrying trays of everything from caviar to strudel, as well as three kinds of oysters and hefty portions of lobster salad. You can always drop in to ogle the racks of elegant pastries, consuming them with steaming pots of tea or coffee. Otherwise, more substantial menu items include turbot with champagne vinaigrette, pheasant breast with Riesling sauce, local salmon trout with white-wine sauce and braised endive, stuffed breast of veal, and calves' livers with apples.

Unter den Linden 39. © **030/2044422.** www.restaurant-dressler.de. Reservations recommended. Main courses 15€–28€. AE, DC, MC, V. Daily 8am–midnight. S-Bahn: Unter den Linden.

FraRosa 🌶 FUSION   This popular haunt of Berlin youth has a startling pay-what-you-want policy. Needless to say, its 15 tables fill up quickly every evening. As you enter, the bartender asks you to put 2€ into the piggy bank. That's for the rental of a wineglass. After that, you can drink what you want. The decor is an electric set of mismatched pieces and flea market accessories set against a backdrop of paint-chipped walls and frescolike murals inspired by Toulouse-Lautrec. The food is reasonably good, not spectacular; the chef calls it "con-fusion." After you dine and drink what you want, you discuss with the waiter what you think is a fair price to pay and then scurry out (that is, if you left too little).

Zionskirchstrasse 40. ℘**030/65706756.** Reservations recommended. Suggested donation 40€ for 2; glass rental 2€. No credit cards. Daily noon–4pm and 8pm–midnight. U-Bahn: Senefelder-Platz.

Hartmanns ★ GERMAN/MEDITERRANEAN   Chef Stefan Hartmann is arguably the best chef in Kreuzberg, at least among his many fans. This talented chef turns out dishes that are inspired, and many of his specialties given Mediterranean flavors. His market-fresh menu is wisely limited so that all ingredients are shopped for on any day. Among starters, we recommend, if featured, smoked duck liver terrine with mango and shiitake mushrooms or else codfish with a mussel jus, perhaps seared foie gras and caramelized apples. For a main course, he carefully crafts such delights as roast lamb with artichokes and arugula or pikeperch in a laurel jus. He truly shines on his fixed-price menus that range from 45€ to 74€.

Fichtestrasse 31. ℘ **030/61201003.** Reservations required. Main courses 28€; fixed-price menus 45€–74€. AE, DC, MC, V. Mon–Fri noon–2:30pm; Mon–Sat 6pm–midnight. U-Bahn: Kottbusser Tor.

Ristorante Sale e Tabacchi ★ ITALIAN   This elegant restaurant, cafe, and bar—called "Salt and Tobacco" in English—is popular with an artsy crowd from the nearby Kreuzberg galleries. The restaurant has large windows in its bar and cafe up front facing the street. In the rear is a high-ceilinged dining room opening onto a Mediterranean courtyard. The establishment is in the Rudi-Dutschke Haus, and is owned by the leftist newspaper *Tageszeitung.*

The restaurant serves Italian specialties that are a delight to the palate, including *zuppa di pesca* (fish soup). This might be followed by some of Berlin's best antipasti, including shellfish or perhaps zucchini stuffed with ricotta and served with a tomato cream sauce. Succulent pastas and freshly made salads are also on the menu.

Rudi-Dutschke-Strasse 23. ℘ **030/1521155.** www.sale-e-tabacchi.de. Reservations recommended. Main courses 10€–28€. MC, V. Daily 10am–2am. U-Bahn: Kochstrasse.

StäV ★ 🎁 RHENISH   For years, this upscale tavern entertained the politicians and journalists whose business involved the day-to-day running of the German government from Germany's former capital of Bonn. Although its owners at first opposed the reinauguration of Berlin as the German capital, when the switch was made, they valiantly pulled out of the Rhineland and followed their clientele to new digs, within a 5-minute walk of the Brandenburg Gate, near the Friedrichstrasse Bahnhof. The most visible beer served is *Kölsch,* a brew more closely associated with the Rhineland than any other beer. Rhenish food items include a mass of apples, onions, and blood sausage known as *Himmel und Ärd* ("heaven and hell"); braised beef with pumpernickel and raisin sauce; and Rhineland *Sauerbraten* with noodles. Other items, many influenced by the culinary traditions of Berlin, include pickled pork in aspic jelly with a rémoulade sauce or boiled pork knuckle on a bed of sauerkraut.

Schiffbauerdamm 8. ℘ **030/2823965.** www.staev.de. Reservations recommended. Main courses 8.50€–16€. AE, DC, MC, V. Daily 10am–1am. U-Bahn: Friedrichstrasse.

In Kreuzberg

EXPENSIVE

Horváth ★★ INTERNATIONAL   One of the hot dining tickets of Berlin is this restaurant opened on the site of that former celebrity favorite Exil, where David Bowie partied and Andy Warhol painted. In the Kreuzberg district, it is installed in a 19th-century front room, a showcase for the savory viands of Chef Wolfgang Müller. Celebrities, including the mayor of Berlin, continue to frequent these airy, hyper-avant-garde dining rooms, enjoying dishes that are inspired by recipes from Bavaria to Bangkok. Over chilled elderberry soup, you can decide on your next course—perhaps stuffed shoulder of veal with artichoke hearts, olives, pine nuts, and a mushroom-flavored risotto. Finish off with, perhaps, the passion fruit tart with marinated fruit and a coconut-flavored lime sauce.

Paul-Lincke-Ufer 44/A. ℂ **030/61289992.** www.restaurant-horvath.de. Reservations recommended. Main courses 13€–17€; fixed-price menus 45€ for 5 courses, 59€ for 7 courses, 73€ for 10 courses. No credit cards. Tues–Sun 6pm–midnight. U-Bahn: Kottbusser Tor.

In Prenzlauer

MODERATE

Pasternak ★ 🍴 RUSSIAN   Its setting, a pink-walled dining room within a distinguished-looking 150-year-old building adjacent to a synagogue in what used to be the eastern zone, evokes nostalgia in many of its patrons. Menu items read like what the characters in a Dostoevsky novel might have ordered: borscht, blinis, chicken Kiev, pork skewers with pomegranate and walnut sauce, *Taig Taschen* (Russian-style ravioli stuffed with spinach and cheese), beef stroganoff, and Russian-style hot apple tart. Expect generous portions, an evocative setting, and the kind of clients who don't necessarily remember the former Russian regime in Berlin with any particular distaste. You might get the vague suspicion that some, in fact, might even miss it.

Knaackstrasse 22–24, Prenzlauer Berg. ℂ **030/4413399.** www.restaurant-pasternak.de. Reservations recommended. Main courses 10€–38€. AE, MC, V. Daily 11am–1am. U-Bahn: Senefelderplatz.

SHOPPING

The **Ku'Damm (Kurfürstendamm)** is the Fifth Avenue of Berlin. It's filled with quality stores but also has outlets hustling cheap souvenirs and T-shirts. Although Berliners themselves shop on the Ku'Damm, many prefer the specialty stores on the side streets, especially between **Breitscheidplatz** and **Olivaer Platz.** You may also want to check out **Am Zoo** and **Kantstrasse.**

Another major shopping street is the **Tauentzienstrasse** and the streets that intersect it: **Marburger, Ranke,** and **Nürnberger.** This area offers a wide array of stores,

---

💬 *Berlin* in Berlin

Midway along the Tauentzienstrasse, near the Kaiser Wilhelm Memorial Church, is the imposing sculpture *Berlin,* commissioned to celebrate the city's 750th anniversary. Unveiled in 1987, its broken-chain motif symbolized the broken link between East and West Berlin. Today, it serves as a striking reminder of the city's painful past.

many specializing in German fashions for women. Stores here are often cheaper than on the Ku'Damm. Also on Tauentzienstrasse (near the Ku'Damm) is Berlin's major indoor shopping center, the **Europa Center** (✆ **030/26497940**), with around 75 shops, as well as restaurants and cafes. At the end of this street lies the **KaDeWe,** the classiest department store in Berlin and the biggest in continental Europe.

A new, upmarket version of the Europa Center is the **Uhland-Passage,** at Uhlandstrasse 170, which has some of the best boutiques and big-name stores in Berlin. Shoppers interested in quality at any price should head to **Kempinski Plaza,** Uhlandstrasse 181–183, a pocket of posh, with some of the most exclusive boutiques in the city. Haute-couture women's clothing is a special feature here. More trendy and avant-garde boutiques are found along **Bleibtreustrasse.**

If you're looking for serious bargains, head to **Wilmersdorferstrasse,** with a vast number of discount stores, although some of the merchandise is second rate. Try to avoid Saturday morning, when it's often impossibly overcrowded.

In eastern Berlin, not that long ago, you couldn't find much to buy except a few souvenirs. All that has changed now. The main street, **Friedrichstrasse,** offers some of Berlin's most elegant shopping. Upmarket boutiques—selling everything from quality women's fashions to Meissen porcelain—are found along **Unter den Linden.** The cheaper stores in eastern Berlin are around the rather bleak-looking **Alexanderplatz.** Many specialty and clothing shops are found in the **Nikolai Quarter.** The largest shopping mall in eastern Berlin, with outlets offering a little bit of everything, is at the **Berliner Markthalle,** at the corner of Rosa-Luxemburg-Strasse and Karl-Liebknecht-Strasse.

Most stores in Berlin are open Monday to Friday 9 or 10am to 6 or 6:30pm. Many stay open late on Thursday evenings, often to 8:30pm. Saturday hours are usually 9 or 10am to 2pm.

Antiques

Harmel's   Most of Harmel's inventory was gathered in England and France, a commentary on the relative scarcity of genuine German antiques because of wartime bombing. The carefully chosen collection stresses furniture, jewelry, and accessories from the Victorian and Edwardian eras. Damaschkestrasse 24. ✆ **030/3242292.** U-Bahn: Adenauerplatz.

L. & M. Lee ★   This is one of several sophisticated antiques stores on the Kurfürstendamm's eastern end. The inventory includes mostly German-made porcelain, silver, and glass from the early 20th century, and an assortment of 19th-century pieces from other European countries. Kurfürstendamm 32. ✆ **030/8817333.** www.lampen-lee-berlin.de. U-Bahn: Uhlandstrasse.

Art Galleries

Arndt & Partner Berlin   Among the first art galleries to establish itself after the collapse of the Berlin Wall, Arndt & Partner has focused on the discovery of new artists and the emergence of new trends since its inception. The gallery houses the works of today's emerging artists, and of established ones as well. In 2006, the gallery received upgrades, with the addition of a second floor, allowing for larger exhibitions and museum-size installations, and a lounge where film artists can share their work with the viewing public. Zimmerstrasse 90–91. ✆ **030/2808123.** www.arndt-partner.de. U-Bahn: Kochstrasse.

Galerie Brusberg ★   One of Germany's most visible and influential art galleries, Galerie Brusberg was established in 1958 by Dieter Brusberg. The gallery has handled the work of Salvador Dalí, Paul Delvaux, Henri Laurens, Pablo Picasso, and René Magritte, plus German artists Altenbourg, Antes, Ernst, and Klapheck. Long before unification, it promoted painters of the old Eastern Bloc, notably Bernhard Heisig, Harald Metzkes, and Werner Töbke. No one will mind if you drop in just for a look. Kurfürstendamm 213. ✆ **030/8827682.** www.brusberg-berlin.de. U-Bahn: Uhlandstrasse.

Galerie Pels-Leusden and Villa Grisebach Auktionen ★   This building, constructed in the 1880s by architect Hans Grisebach as his private home, is a historic monument in its own right. Two floors are devoted to 19th- and 20th-century art, mainly German. Prices begin at around 100€ for the least expensive lithograph and go much higher. The building also functions as headquarters and display area for an auction house. Sales are held every spring and fall. Fasanenstrasse 25. ✆ **030/8859150.** U-Bahn: Uhlandstrasse.

Galerie Thomas Schulte ★   Established in 1991 in the wake of the reunification of Berlin, this quickly became one of Germany's leading international galleries. Focusing on contemporary conceptual art since 1960, the gallery displays the works of well-known artists such as Robert Mapplethorpe, Richard Deacon, and Rebecca Horn. The gallery, located on the first floor, welcomes visitors Tuesday through Saturday, noon to 6pm. Charlottenstrasse 24. ✆ **030/20608990.** www.galeriethomasschulte.de. U-Bahn: Stadtmitte.

KW Institute for Contemporary Art ★   Located on the site of what was once a margarine factory, this building has been transformed into one of the city's major centers of contemporary art. The institute houses no permanent collection of its own, and is instead considered a testing ground for emerging artists, with five floors of

🎁 treasures IN THE BARN DISTRICT

The heart of Berlin's fashion and art revival is the **Scheuenviertel**, or "Barn District" (S-Bahn: Hackescher Markt). The name comes from a period in the 17th century when hay barns were built far from the city center for fear of fires. In time, the city's growth overtook the area, and it became Berlin's Jewish quarter. For some reason, many of its oldest buildings survived World War II bombing assaults.

The remains of a grand 1909 shopping arcade—which occupies most of the block formed by Oranienburger, Rosenthaler, Grosse Hamburger Strasse, and Sophienstrasse—have been turned into a series of galleries, studios, and theaters. Worth a visit is **Tacheles,** Oranienburger Strasse 54–56 (✆ **030/2826185;** www.tacheles.de; S-Bahn: Hackescher Markt), or "Talking Turkey" in Yiddish. It's an alternative arts center.

The more prestigious galleries are found along Auguststrasse. **Galerie Wohnmaschine,** Invalidenstrasse 50–51 (✆ **030/30872015;** www.wohnmaschine.de; S-Bahn: Lehrter Bahnhof), opened in 1988. Some of the best artists in the city are on exhibit here, most of them of a conceptual or minimalist bent.

Johanna Petzoldt, Sophienstrasse 9 (✆ **030/2826754;** www.petzoldt.org; U-Bahn: Weinmeisterstrasse), sells handicrafts from the old Erzebirge region, including wooden toys and assorted curiosities, such as scenes fitted into a matchbox.

exhibition space and six artists' studios. The courtyard on the grounds, which once lay in ruins, has been refurbished to provide an airy space for visitors to stroll or sit and chat. Check out the Café Bravo Pavilion, which is an art exhibit in itself. Auguststrasse 69. © **030/2434590.** www.kw-berlin.de. U-Bahn: Weinmeister Strasse.

Bookshops

This literate and culture-conscious city boasts lots of bookshops catering to a multilingual clientele. An outfit richly stocked with works from German publishing houses is **Literaturhaus Berlin,** Fasanenstrasse 23 (© **030/8872860;** www.literaturhaus-berlin.de; U-Bahn: Uhlandstrasse). The leading gay bookstore of Berlin, containing both erotica and upscale literature in several languages, is **Prinz Eisenherz,** Lietzenburgerstrasse 9A (© **030/3139936;** www.prinz-eisenherz.com; S-Bahn: Wartenberg). Since its opening in 1999, **Pro qm,** Almstadtstrasse 48–50 (© **030/24728520;** www.pro-qm.de; U-Bahn: Rosa-Luxemburg-Platz), has been known as one of Berlin's best bookstores for publications on art, architecture and design, and pop culture. As a testament to its success, the shop has relocated to a new spacious building. This new structure was designed by architects not only to accommodate a larger inventory, but primarily to facilitate discussion and movement among patrons.

China & Porcelain

KPM ★★★ This prestigious emporium was founded in 1763, when Friedrich the Great invested his personal funds in a lackluster porcelain factory, elevated it to royal status, and gave it a new name: **Königliche Porzellan-Manufaktur (Royal Porcelain Factory).** It was Prussia's answer to Meissen, in Saxony. Since then, the factory has become world famous for its artistry and delicacy. Each exquisite, hand-painted, hand-decorated item is carefully packed for shipment to virtually anywhere in the world. Patterns, for the most part, are based on traditional 18th- and 19th-century designs. All objects carry a distinctive official signature, an imperial orb, and the letters KPM. There's also an array of high-quality trinkets for visitors.

You can visit the **factory** itself at Wegelystrasse 1 (© **030/390090;** U-Bahn: Tiergarten). Guided tours let you look at the craftsmanship of the employees, and you can buy pieces here. Tours are provided once a day from Monday to Thursday at 10am. The charge is 8€, which is applied to any purchase. Children 15 and under are prohibited, as are video cameras and photography. Kurfürstendamm 27 (in the Kempinski Hotel Bristol). © **030/88627961.** http://en.kpm-berlin.com. U-Bahn: Kurfürstendamm.

Commie Relics

Mondos Arts As the memories of Berlin's division fade, nostalgia for the era of Soviet rule is popping up in this ever-evolving city. This tiny shop is chock-full of relics from the Eastern Bloc period and kitschy items commemorating the old days—good or bad—of communism. There is an eclectic variety of unique items to choose from here, from items emblazoned with the images of Marx, Lenin, and Rosa Luxemburg, to bottles of Soviet-era beer. Ampelmännchen, the ubiquitous red-and-green man on eastern traffic crossings, serves as the store's unofficial mascot, with the symbol adorning all sorts of items. There's a wide variety of DVDs to choose from, including the propaganda-tinged films of East Berlin. Schreinerstrasse 6. © **030/42010778.** U-Bahn: Samariter Strasse.

Department Stores

Corner Berlin ★ 📖 This creation of a former movie producer and a former cosmetics executive is not really a department store, not really a boutique. "It's what it is," one of the owners enigmatically proclaimed. That means you can expect a little of everything: fashion accessories, jewelry, beauty products, gifts, electronics, art, vintage furniture, food, drink, books, and magazines. Almost every item on display is made exclusively in Germany. Französische Strasse 40. ✆ **030/20670940.** www.thecorner berlin.de. U-Bahn: Französische Strasse.

Departmentstore Quartier 206 Located in the center of Berlin, this exclusive shopping center is not just about the merchandise. Housed in a building designed by the renowned architect I. M. Pei's firm, this Art Deco–style glass-and-marble structure contains 8,000 sq. m (86,000 sq. ft.) of retail space. Shopping here is top-notch, and you'll find such luxury brands as Louis Vuitton, Gucci, and Yves Saint Laurent. Friedrichstrasse 71. ✆ **030/20946800.** www.quartier206.com. U-Bahn: Stadtmitte.

Galeries Lafayette ★ Paris in Berlin is found at this modern department store, right off Friedrichstrasse, designed by Jean Nouvel with a spectacular interior. The opening of this store has made Friedrichstrasse, the "street of spies" in the Cold War era, one of the most fashionable shopping areas in eastern Europe. Its French food department evokes what is meant by "died and gone to heaven." Französische Strasse 23. ✆ **030/209480.** www.galeries-lafayette.de. U-Bahn: Französische Strasse.

Kaufhaus des Westens (KaDeWe) ★★★ This huge luxury department store, known popularly as KaDeWe (pronounced *Kah*-Day-Vay), was established nearly a century ago. It's best known for its sixth-floor food department, where more than 1,000 varieties of German sausages are displayed along with delicacies from all over the world. Even the most jaded epicure should find delight here with its wide range of sausages and the tastiest herring sandwiches in Berlin. Sit-down counters are available. After fortifying yourself here, you can explore the six floors of merchandise. KaDeWe is more than a department store—one shopper called it a "collection of first-class specialty shops." Tauentzienstrasse 21. ✆ **030/21210.** www.kadewe.de. U-Bahn: Wittenbergplatz.

Wertheim This centrally located store is good for travel aids and general basics. It sells perfumes, clothing for the entire family, jewelry, electrical devices, household goods, photography supplies, and souvenirs. It also has a shoe-repair section. Shoppers can fuel up at a large restaurant with a grand view over half the city. Kurfürstendamm 231. ✆ **030/880030.** www.karstadt.de. U-Bahn: Kurfürstendamm.

Design

Bauhaus Archive The shop at the landmark Bauhaus Archive Museum of Design offers a stunning variety of items in contemporary styles, some designed by artists of the Bauhaus movement. More than 250 items, which incorporate not only design, but also utility, are available for the home and office. Profits from the shop support the Bauhaus Archive in its quest to both sustain its current collections and obtain new acquisitions. Klingelhöferstrasse 14. ✆ **030/2540020.** www.bauhaus.de. U-Bahn: Nollendorfplatz.

Fashion

Bleibgrün It's small, it's fashionable, and it's sought after by well-dressed and well-heeled women from Berlin and its suburbs. And best of all, the staff is charming and helpful. Come here for access to things that are terribly chic and contemporary, including dresses by Jean-Paul Gaultier, Paul Smith, Marithé François Girbaud, and a handful of other currently fashionable trendsetters. Bleibtreustrasse 29–30. © **030/ 8821689.** www.bleibgruen.de. S-Bahn: Savignyplatz.

Sonia Rykiel This stylish showcase is the only shop in Germany devoted exclusively to Ms. Rykiel, the successful French fashion mogul. She designed the store's interior herself. Beware—even a Sonia Rykiel T-shirt is expensive. There are a children's shop and a women's shop. Kurfürstendamm 186. © **030/8821774.** www.soniarykiel.com. U-Bahn: Adenauerplatz.

Triebel This elegant store offers everything you may need for a weekend retreat at a private hunting lodge, such as clothing, shoes, boots, and sporting equipment. If you dream of looking like the lord of a Bavarian manor in a loden coat and feather-trimmed hat, or if you've been invited on a fox hunt, come here first. The inventory also includes a selection of hunting rifles and shooting equipment. Schönwalder Strasse 12, Spandau. © **030/3355001.** www.triebel.de. U-Bahn: Rathaus Spandau. S-Bahn: Spandau.

Werner Scherer ★ The arrival of this upscale menswear emporium symbolized to some extent the rebirth of the Unter den Linden as a glamorous shopping destination. Set on the street level of the Hotel Adlon, it's the showplace of Munich-based designer Werner Scherer, who makes the kinds of clothes that millionaires love to buy. Expect access to the best-made shirts we've ever seen, silk neckties, and curiosities that include bomber jackets crafted from a mixture of silk and linen, and buttery-soft black leather coats. Despite its high prices, the shop does a roaring business with the glam crowd, many of whom wouldn't consider buying their shirts anywhere else. Unter den Linden 77. © **030/22679893.** www.werner-scherer.de. S-Bahn: Unter den Linden.

Jewelry

Treykorn ★ 👔 This outlet displays the most avant-garde jewelry in Berlin. Owners Andreas and Sabine Treykorn provide a showcase for more than three dozen of the boldest and often most controversial jewelry artisans in the city. Although some pieces sell in the thousands, there are many selections in a more affordable price range. Savignyplatz 13-Passage. © **030/31802354.** www.treykorn.de. S-Bahn: Savignyplatz.

Markets

Berliner Trödelmarkt This flea market is near the corner of the Bachstrasse and the Strasse des 17 Juni, at the western edge of the Tiergarten, adjacent to the Tiergarten

---

🎁 CALLING ALL ceramics LOVERS

As ceramics lovers learn more about the late Hedwig Bollhagen, a great ceramics artist who died in 2001, they are making their way to her **Ceramics Studio** in the little village of Marwitz outside Berlin. The location is at Hedwig-Bollhagen Strasse 4 (© **03304/39800**), reached on the A111 Autobahn toward Hamburg. The unmistakable and brightly colored geometric patterns of her tableware, with its HB monogram, are appearing in more and more collections around the world. Under the East German Communists, her Bollhagen ceramics were unavailable in the West for decades. The workshop here is open Wednesday 9am to 5pm and Saturday 10am to 2pm. You can purchase seconds at prices beginning at 10€. Free tours in German are offered the last Wednesday of every month at 1pm.

S-Bahn station. It's the favorite weekend shopping spot of countless Berliners, who come here to find an appropriate piece of nostalgia, a battered semi-antique, or used clothing. The market is held every Saturday and Sunday 10am to 5pm. Strasse des 17 Juni. ✆ **030/26550096.** www.berliner-troedelmarkt.de. S-Bahn: Tiergarten.

Military Figures

Berliner Zinnfiguren   A mecca for collectors since 1934, this shop carries an impressive inventory of German-language books on military history and more than 10,000 different pewter figurines of soldiers from many different imperial armies, including the Franco-Prussian War of 1870. Also included are hand-painted models of Roman and ancient Greek foot soldiers. Flat, hand-painted pewter figures are sold only in sets of 12 or more. Knesebeckstrasse 88. ✆ **030/3157000.** www.zinnfigur.com. S-Bahn: Savignyplatz.

Music

Bauer & Hieber   Most of the professional musicians of Berlin have a working familiarity with this well-established store, as it's been selling musical instruments and sheet music since 1910. Regardless of how esoteric your tastes, you're likely to find the score to whatever it is that interests you—sometimes in used folios that have some historical interest in their own right. You can also find a good selection of CDs. Uhlandstrasse 38. ✆ **030/8827395.** U-Bahn: Uhlandstrasse.

Perfume

Harry Lehmann   This is the kind of shop where German mothers and grandmothers might have bought their perfume between the two world wars. Don't expect a standardized list of the big names you'd find at a duty-free airport shop. Most scents are family recipes, distilled from flowers, grasses, and leaves. The reasonable prices may surprise you—10 grams (1/3 oz.) for as little as 5€. Coming here is a cheap and amusing way to experience the scents of a Prussian spring. Kantstrasse 106. ✆ **030/3243582.** U-Bahn: Wilmersdorferstrasse.

Punk Memorabilia

Kaufhaus Schrill   Few stores mingle junkiness and kitsch with such artful abandon. Stock here would gladden any punk rocker's heart, especially if he or she were on the lookout for Elvis-era memorabilia, hair barrettes that glow in the dark, and jewelry that may appeal to Courtney Love for her date with a group of bikers. Don't expect anything tasteful—that isn't its style. Partly because of that, and partly because the place evokes a vivid sense of the long-ago rebelliousness of the '60s, the place is something of an icon for counterculture youth. Bleibtreustrasse 46. ✆ **030/8824048.** www.gallery-schrill.de. S-Bahn: Savignyplatz.

Sculpture

Gipsformerei der Staatlichen Museen Preussischer Kulturbesitz (Plasterworks of the State Museums of Prussia) ★ 🛍   This company has duplicated the world's great sculptures as plaster casts since 1819. Today, there's an inventory of more than 6,500 of them, everything from busts of Queen Nefertiti to a faithful reproduction of the Farnese Bull. Objects can be crated and shipped around the world. Sophie-Charlotten-Strasse 17. ✆ **030/3267690.** S-Bahn: Westend.

Shoes

Trippen   Founded on the concept that economic success does not need to come at the cost of social responsibility, Trippen produces shoes that are both environmentally friendly and trendy. The creative team behind the company constantly strives to produce artistic and stylish designs, but not at the expense of the environment. As a means of challenging the disposable nature of the fashion industry, Trippen continues to sell its previous collections, even while putting out new designs each season. Rosenthaler Strasse 40–41. ✆ **030/28391337.** www.trippen.com. U-Bahn: Weinmeisterstrasse.

Shopping Arcades

One of the many surprising aspects of the rebuilt and redesigned Potsdamer Platz is the **Potsdamer Platz Arkaden** (✆ **030/2559270;** www.potsdamer-platz-arkaden. de; U-Bahn/S-Bahn: Potsdamer Platz), one of the most comprehensive shopping malls in Berlin. In a deliberate rejoinder to more outdated Ku'Damm malls, such as the Europa Center, it contains more than 100 shops scattered over three levels.

ENTERTAINMENT & NIGHTLIFE

Nightlife

In Berlin, "nightlife" runs round-the-clock, and there's plenty to do at any time. Berlin has a monthly English-language newspaper, *The Ex-Berliner,* providing a witty, informative guide to the city's culture and entertainment. This magazine is available at newsstands and tourist offices. Tourist offices also distribute a free magazine called *New Berlin* providing tips and recommendations to visitors. The German-language *Berlin Programm* is available at newsstands. The most detailed listings are found in *zitty,* a biweekly publication in German.

THE PERFORMING ARTS
Opera & Classical Music

Berliner Philharmonisches Orchester (Berlin Philharmonic Orchestra) ★★★
The Berlin Philharmonic is one of the world's premier orchestras. Its home, the **Philharmonie** in the Kulturforum, is a significant piece of modern architecture; you may want to visit even if you do not attend a performance. None of the 2,218 seats are more than 30m (100 ft.) from the rostrum. The box office is open Monday to Friday 3 to 6pm and Saturday and Sunday 11am to 2pm. You can place orders by phone at ✆ **030/25488999.** If you're staying in a first-class or deluxe hotel, you can usually get the concierge to obtain seats for you. Herbert-von-Karajan-Strasse 1. ✆ **030/254880.** www.berlin-philharmonic.com. Tickets 14€–85€; special concerts 53€–138€. U-Bahn: Potsdamer Platz.

Deutsche Oper Berlin ★   This opera company performs in Charlottenburg in one of the world's great opera houses, a notable example of modern theater architecture that seats 1,885. The company tackles Puccini favorites, Janáček rarities, or modern works, and has a complete Wagner repertoire. A ballet company performs once a week. Concerts, including *Lieder* evenings, are also presented on the opera stage. Bismarckstrasse 35. ✆ **030/34384343.** www.deutscheoperberlin.de. Tickets 12€–120€. U-Bahn: Deutsche Oper. S-Bahn: Charlottenburg.

Komische Oper Berlin   The Komische Opera has become one of the most highly regarded theater ensembles in Europe, presenting many avant-garde opera productions as well as ballet and musical theater. The box office is open Monday to Saturday 11am to 7pm and Sunday 1pm until 1½ hours before the performance. Behrenstrasse 55-57. ☎ **030/202600.** www.komische-oper-berlin.de. Tickets 8€–93€. U-Bahn: Französische Strasse. S-Bahn: Friedrichstrasse or Unter den Linden.

Konzerthaus Berlin   This 1821 building was created by Friedrich Schinkel. It offers two venues for classical concerts: the Grosser Konzertsaal for orchestra and the Kammermusiksaal for chamber music. Its organ recitals are considered the finest in Germany. Performances are often daring and innovative. The Deutsches Sinfonie-Orchester is also based here. In the Schauspielhaus, Gendarmenmarkt. ☎ **030/203092101.** www.konzerthaus.de. Tickets 10€–99€. U-Bahn: Französische Strasse.

Theater

Berlin has long been known for its theater. Even if you don't understand German, you may enjoy a production of a familiar play or musical.

Perhaps the most famous theater is the **Berliner Ensemble,** Am Bertolt-Brecht-Platz 1 (☎ **030/28408155;** www.berliner-ensemble.de; U-Bahn/S-Bahn: Friedrich-strasse), founded by the late playwright Bertolt Brecht. His wife, Helene Weigel, played an important role in the theater's founding and was the ensemble's longtime director. Works by Brecht and other playwrights are presented here. Seats are reasonably priced, ranging from 6€ to 40€.

The most important German-language theater in the country is **Schaubühne am Lehniner Platz,** Kurfürstendamm 153 (☎ **030/890023;** www.schaubuehne.de; U-Bahn: Adenauerplatz), at the east end of the Ku'Damm, near Lehniner Platz. There are three different stages here. Tickets range from 10€ to 38€.

Theater des Westens, located between the Berlin Zoo and the Ku'Damm at Kantstrasse 12 (☎ **030/319030;** U-Bahn/S-Bahn: Zoologischer Garten), specializes in plays, musical comedies, and the German equivalent of Broadway extravaganzas. The theater was built in 1896. Performances are held Tuesday to Saturday at 8pm and Sunday at 7pm. Saturday matinees are occasionally available. Ticket prices range from 20€ to 110€.

THE CLUB & MUSIC SCENE
Cabaret

Very popular among visitors to Berlin is the kind of nightspot depicted in the musical *Cabaret,* with floor-show patter and acts that make fun of the political and social scene. Cabaret life in between-the-wars Berlin inspired writers such as Christopher Isherwood, among many others. These emporiums of schmaltz have been reborn in the former East Berlin—though the satire may be a bit less biting than it was during the Weimar Republic. Today's cabaret shows may remind you of Broadway blockbusters, without much of the intimacy of the smoky and trenchant cellar revues of the 1930s.

Die Stachelschweine   Since the beginning of the Cold War, the "Porcupine" has poked prickly fun at the German and American political scenes. The performance is delivered in rapid-fire German and evokes the legendary Berliner sense of satire, which can often be scathing in its humor. Although you need to understand German to really appreciate what goes on here, you'll still recognize some of the names (George W., Dick Cheney, Al Gore, and Hillary), and there's likely to be a deliberately corny selection of popular ditties ("Life is a cabaret, old chum") thrown in. Shows take place Tuesday to Friday at 8pm and Saturday at 8 and 9:30pm. The box office is open Tuesday to Friday 11am to 2pm and 3 to 7:30pm, and Saturday 10am to 2pm and 3 to 8:45pm. It's closed in July. Tauentzienstrasse and Budapesterstrasse (in the basement of Europa Center). ☏ **030/2614795.** www.stachelschweine-berlin.de. Cover 13€–28€. U-Bahn: Kurfürstendamm.

Friedrichstadt Palast   For access to talent that includes multilingual comedians and singers, jugglers, acrobats, musicians, plenty of coyly expressed sexuality, and lots of costume changes, consider an evening here. Although showtimes may vary with whatever revue is featured at the time of your visit, they tend to begin Tuesday to Saturday at 8pm, with additional performances every Saturday and Sunday at 4pm. Friedrichstrasse 107. ☏ **030/23262326.** www.friedrichstadtpalast.de. Cover 17€–100€. U-Bahn or S-Bahn: Friedrichstrasse.

Wintergarten Varieté   The largest and most nostalgic Berlin cabaret, the Wintergarten offers a variety show every night, with magicians, clowns, jugglers, acrobats, and live music. The most expensive seats are on stage level, where tiny tables are available for simple suppers costing from 13€ to 24€. Balconies have conventional theater seats, but staff members pass frequently along the aisles selling drinks. Shows usually begin Wednesday to Saturday at 8pm, Sunday at 6pm. Rarely, most often in summer, shows might also be presented on Monday and Tuesday. All times are subject to change, so call ahead. Shows last around 2¼ hours. Potsdamer Strasse 96. ☏ **030/588433.** www.winter garten-variete.de. Cover Fri–Sat 25€–55€, Sun–Thurs 15€–50€. U-Bahn: Kurfürstenstrasse.

Dance Clubs

Clärchens Ballhaus   This landmark in old East Berlin has reemerged back to its original glory during the last decade. It became a legend, opening in 1913 right before "The Great War" and miraculously surviving until the end of World War II; Nazi officers once used the top floor (with a decadent mirrored ballroom) as a private club. After the war, part of it remained closed but its downstairs great ballroom remained open throughout the Cold War. Since 2005, the mirrored ballroom was reopened for the first time since WWII, and today a hot DJ and live bands rage through the night, with occasional tango dancers and the like—even Johann Strauss music. Gypsy street musicians are a favorite. Everybody from Turks out for a night on the town to elderly East Berlin couples fill the joint. It's usually open from 7 to 11pm, but not every night, so call before heading here. Auguststrasse 24. ☏ **030/2829295.** www.ballhaus.de. S-Bahn: Oranienburger Strasse.

Club der Visionaere   Hip 20-somethings flock like birds to this Spree riverside bar in Kreuzberg. Its interior has been compared to a shipwreck. The club has become famous for its Sunday-afternoon parties that seem to last until dawn streaks the sky. House music fills the night in this very Louisiana Bayou–like atmosphere. If you're here at sunrise, take in the concrete watchtower across the street. It's one of the last surviving towers constructed by the East German police to shoot down "deserters" from the DDR. Open Monday to Friday 2pm to 4am (or beyond), Saturday and Sunday noon to 4am (or beyond). Am Flutgraben 1. ☏ **030/69518944.** www.club dervisionaere.com. Cover 1€–5€ (depending on what's happening). U-Bahn: Warschauer Strasse.

Delicious Doughnuts   This club for acid jazz and other delights still keeps its old name, though it no longer sells doughnuts. A scarlet red decor and black-leather booths have given it a more sophisticated ambience. A pocket-size dance floor is just part of the allure, along with a hot DJ. Rosenthalerstrasse 9. ☏ **030/28099274.** www.delicious-doughnuts.de. Cover Wed–Sat 8€. U-Bahn: Rosenthaler Platz.

Sage Club ★   This is one of Berlin's trendiest clubs, with a trio of dance areas and a special VIP section with a pool "reserved for the privileged," such as Mick Jagger.

This club is like a party tour for the *Sex and the City* crowd. Patrons have done everything and everybody. The music blaring away is rock, funk, "big beat," soul, indie, and house. In the rear is a much frequented wooden courtyard. It's open Thursday to Sunday 7pm to 5am. Köpenicker Strasse 76. © **030/2789830.** www.sage-club.de. Cover 6€–15€. U-Bahn: Heinrich-Heine-Strasse.

SO36 ★ 🏠 The lines begin to form here about 30 minutes before the place opens, but they move quickly as Berlin's hipsters get into the spirit of one of the city's more witty and unconventional clubs. Its name derives from the postal code for this district before World War II. Inside, you'll find two very large rooms, a stage, an ongoing rush of danceable music, and a scene that combines a senior prom in the high-school gym with some of the more bizarre aspects of Berlin nightlife. Lots of women come here, both gay and straight, and there's a higher percentage of heterosexual men than you might have expected along this strip of bars in Kreuzberg. The club is open most nights, based on an evolving schedule, 8pm to at least 4am. Oranienstrasse 190, Kreuzberg. © **030/61401306.** www.so36.de. Cover 4€–22€. U-Bahn: Görlitzer Bahnhof.

Watergate Club ★ During the Cold War, West Berliners avoided going near the Spree River, which was divided with the dreaded DDR. Today, some of the city's coolest nightlife occurs along the banks of the river. The biggest attraction is the Watergate, a beautifully designed split-level club opening onto the river with its floor-to-ceiling plate-glass windows. It is known for its LED lighting. One habitué called it "a hell of a cool locale." The dancing after-dark cognoscenti descends on this throbbing hot spot. Management draws some of the world's leading international DJs. Music is house, break-beat, and drum and bass nights. Open Wednesday, Friday, and Saturday from midnight to 4am (or beyond). Falckensteinstrasse 49. © **030/61280395.** Cover 8€–12€. U-Bahn: Schlesisches Tor.

White-Trash Don't you love that name? You can eat, party, or attend a film all under one roof. The club originated in a former Chinese restaurant where you might encounter Mick Jagger or Marilyn Manson on any given night. Much of the colorful decor, including those kitschy dragon columns, were brought along to this site. The Asian influence is complemented by Elvis memorabilia and numerous "trash" knick-knacks on the walls. The waiters look like they escaped from *A Clockwork Orange*. In the basement's Diamond Lounge, whose bar is behind bars, you might encounter totally tattooed rockers or rockabilly brides. Electroclash bands dominate the air waves. The most popular food item on the menu is a juicy burger with an X-rated name. Open Monday to Friday noon to midnight, Saturday and Sunday 6pm to midnight. Main courses cost from 4.50€ to 11€, with drink specials priced at 10€. Schönhauser Allee 6–7. © **030/50348668.** www.whitetrashfastfood.com. U-Bahn: Rosa-Luxemburg-Platz.

Live Music

A Trane This small and smoky jazz house is an excellent choice for beginning or ending an evening of barhopping in the neighborhood. It features musicians from all over the world. It's open daily at 9pm; music begins around 10pm. Closing hours vary. Pestalozzistrasse 105. © **030/3132550.** www.a-trane.de. Cover 8€–15€. S-Bahn: Savignyplatz.

Knaack-Klub This four-story club features a live-music venue, two floors of dancing, and a games floor with billiards. There are usually four live rock shows a week, with a fairly even split between German and international touring bands. Show days vary. There's dancing on Wednesday, Friday, and Saturday nights. Hours are nightly from 9pm. Greifswalderstrasse 224. © **030/4427060.** www.knaack-berlin.de. Cover 8€–17€. S-Bahn: Alexanderplatz.

Oxymoron   This is a good example of Berlin's crop of hypertrendy, high-visibility hangouts where the food is served almost as an afterthought to an exhibitionistic/voyeuristic scene that can be fun and intriguing. The setting is a high-ceilinged room with old-fashioned proportions and enough battered kitsch to remind you of a coffeehouse in Franz Josef's Vienna. Local wits refer to it as a *Gesamtkunstwerk*—a self-obsessed, self-sustaining work of art that might have been appreciated by Wagner. Most nights after around 11pm, a slightly claustrophobic, much-used annex room—all black with ghostly flares of neon—opens for business as a dance club, usually with a clientele that's about 75% hetero and 100% iconoclastic. If live bands appear at all, it will usually be on a Friday. It's open daily 11am to 2am. In the courtyard of the complex at Rosenthaler Strasse 40–41. ✆ **030/28391886.** www.oxymoron-berlin.de. Cover 8€–15€. S-Bahn: Hackescher Markt.

Quasimodo ★   This is the top Berlin jazz club. Although many styles of music are offered here, including rock and Latin, jazz is the focus. Local acts are featured on Tuesday and Wednesday, when admission is free. Summer visitors should check out the **Jazz in July** festival. Opening hours depend on the event; call for the schedule. Kantstrasse 12A. ✆ **030/3180456.** www.quasimodo.de. Cover Thurs–Sat 12€–24€. U-Bahn: Zoologischer Garten.

Wild at Heart   This club, with its kitschy knickknacks, colored lights, and wine-red walls, is dedicated to the rowdier side of rock, featuring hardcore punk, rock, and rockabilly bands from Germany and elsewhere. Live performances take place Wednesday to Saturday nights. It's open Monday to Friday 8pm to 3am, Saturday and Sunday 8pm to 10am (yes, you may miss breakfast). Wienerstrasse 20. ✆ **030/6119231.** www.wildatheartberlin.de. Cover 8€–12€ for concerts only. U-Bahn: Görlitzer Bahnhof.

THE BAR & CAFE SCENE
Beer Gardens & Wine Cellars

Historischer Weinkeller   This squat and unpretentious inn may be the site of one of your more intriguing evenings in Berlin. The setting is a highly atmospheric vaulted cellar. You can order beer or one of more than 100 German wines, as well as main courses priced at 9€ to 20€. If you plan to dine, make reservations in advance. During summer months, an outdoor rustic beer garden is open. The inn is open Tuesday to Saturday 4 to 11pm, and Sunday noon to 11pm. Alt-Pichelsdorf 32 (about 1.5km/1 mile west of the Olympiastadion). ✆ **030/36432619.** www.steile-stiege.de. U-Bahn: Olympia-Stadion.

Joe's Wirthaus zum Löwen   This cozy pub in the city center is attractively decorated with traditional Teutonic accessories. Even in winter, when you're snug and warm inside, you get the feeling you're sitting out under the chestnut trees. The kitchen offers good plain German food, including Bavarian specialties and some Italian dishes. It's open daily 11am to 1am; the best time to come here is 7pm to midnight. Hardenbergstrasse 29 (opposite the Kaiser Wilhelm Memorial Church). ✆ **030/2621020.** www.joes-berlin.de. U-Bahn: Zoologischer Garten.

Prater Garten ★   Lying in the rapidly emerging Prenzlauer Berg district, this is the city's oldest beer garden, dating from 1837. It attracts artists and families, hipsters and professional people, who occupy one of the 600 seats. A selection of local beers, including a light lager (Prater Pils) or a dark beer (Schwarzbier) are served. You can order such fare as beef goulash or *Wiener Schnitzel*, with mains costing from 9.10€ to 17€. Open April to September Monday to Saturday 6pm to midnight, Sunday noon to 10pm. Kastanienallee 7–9. ✆ **030/4485688.** www.pratergarten.de. U-Bahn: Eberswalder Strasse.

Zollpackhof   On a sunny summer day there might be no better place in Berlin for an afternoon than spending it here sitting under 130-year-old chestnut trees while enjoying a view of Berlin's Chancellery and the Spree River. Locals sip *Berliner Weisse* and watch the small boats chug along the Spree River. This beer garden is a Berlin tradition, dating from its foundation in 1685. After the wall came tumbling down and Germany's seat of government was revived, this place was restored and reopened. Main courses range from 17€ to 20€. Open Tuesday to Saturday 11am to midnight. Elizabeth-Abegg-Strasse 1. *©* **030/30099720.** www.zollpackhof.de. S-Bahn: Hauptbahnhof.

The Best Bars

Green Door   No, the name wasn't taken from one of the 20th century's most famous porno flicks, *Behind the Green Door*. There is actually a green door here at this intimate, cozy, and classic cocktail lounge. But like the famous movie itself, there is a '70s-retro feel to the place. Exotic cocktails perfectly prepared by the waitstaff are one of the best features of this place, and all of them have such names as Hot Kiss or Burning Bush. We'd rank their martinis as among the best in town. It's open Sunday to Thursday 6pm to 3am, Friday and Saturday 6pm to 4am. Winterfeldstrasse 50. *©* **030/2152515.** www.greendoor.de. U-Bahn: Nollendorfplatz.

Harry's New York Bar   Harry's is an aggressively stylized bar with minimalist decor, pop art, and photographs of all the American presidents. It's modeled after the famous watering hole Harry's New York Bar, in Paris. Its drink menu is a monument to the oral traditions of the International Bar Flies (IBF) Society and includes such favorites as Mizner's Dream (created in 1962 for the Boca Raton Hotel Club in Florida) and the 1964 classic the Petrifier (ingredients unlisted), for two. The menu lists almost 200 drinks, as well as a limited selection of food. It's open 24 hours a day, 7 days a week. In the Grand Hotel Esplanade, Lützowufer 15. *©* **030/25478821.** www.esplanade berlin.com. U-Bahn: Nollendorfplatz, Wittenbergplatz, or Kurfürstenstrasse.

Juleps New York Bar   The roaring '20s and the turbulent '30s of America are evoked at this speak-easy-type bar with bare brick walls. The only thing they don't have is Prohibition, as the liquor flows. We counted more than 120 different cocktails on the drink menu alone. On a tree-lined street in Charlottenburg, this is a warm, intimate, and welcoming place, with a long oaken bar. If you're hungry, check out those big and yummy bacon cheeseburgers, dig into pasta, or order chicken satays. The kitchen even turns out fabulous desserts such as Mississippi mud cake. The mojitos here are as good as those in Cuba. It's open Sunday to Thursday 5pm to 1am, Friday and Saturday 5pm to 2am. Giesebrechtstrasse 3. *©* **030/8818823.** www.joepenas.com. U-Bahn: Adenauerplatz.

Newton Bar   There have been more reviews about Berlin's Newton Bar than virtually any other watering hole in town. You may be rejected at the door by a bouncer who disapproves of your sense of style. Here's what you'll get if you're admitted: a high-ceilinged, well-proportioned room that evokes 1960s modernism at its best and a deeply ingrained sense of the well-heeled and socially conscious bourgeoisie looking for like-minded people. It's condemned for its sense of *chicki-micki* (self-conscious chic) by clients of counterculture bars in less expensive neighborhoods. But regardless of how you feel, you can't help but be intrigued by a huge black-and-white mural (photographed by Helmut Newton) that sweeps an entire runway of naked fashion models across your field of vision, and service rituals inspired by Old Prussia. It's open daily 10am till at least 3am, with cocktails priced at 10€. Charlottenstrasse 57. *©* **030/2029540.** www.newton-bar.de. U-Bahn: Stadtmitte.

Reingold   This bar is elegant and chic, stretching along the length of a long and narrow room. The overall effect has been called "Manet meeting Hopper." An aquarium seems de rigueur for Berlin bars, but the one here is modest. The beautiful people descend nightly to see and be seen. It's open daily from 7pm to 3am. Novalisstrasse 11. ℭ **030/28387676.** www.reingold.de. U-Bahn: Friedrichstrasse.

Times Bar   The cozy and intimate Times Bar has a quiet charm reminiscent of a wood-paneled private library in someone's home. The bar is dedicated to the *Times* (of London), whose latest edition is often displayed in the window. Guests sit in leather-upholstered chairs and read English-language newspapers. Menu items range from lobster soup to ice cream. It's open daily 11am to 2am. In the Savoy hotel, Fasanenstrasse 9–10. ℭ **030/311030.** www.hotel-savoy.com. U-Bahn: Zoologischer Garten.

Victoria Bar   One of our favorite lounge retreats is this stylishly retro bar behind blacked-out windows just a stone's throw from Potsdamer Platz in the heart of Berlin. In sophisticated surroundings, you can enjoy an excellent list of cocktails or order a sandwich if you're hungry (with choices running from barbecued beef to cucumber). The walnut tables and long bar are good points for a rendezvous with a friend. "People come here to escape the hustle and bustle," said the bartender. The tequila drinks are from Mexico, the tropical fruit punches from the Caribbean. Reduced-price drinks are served Monday to Saturday 6:30 to 9:30pm or all day Sunday. Hours are Sunday to Thursday 6:30pm to 3am, Friday and Saturday 6:30pm to 4am. Potsdamer Strasse 102. ℭ **030/25759977.** www.victoriabar.de. U-Bahn: Potsdamer Platz.

Hanging out at a *Kneipe*

A *Kneipe* is a cozy rendezvous place, a sort of lowbrow pub. Many Berliners have a favorite *Kneipe* for relaxing after work and visiting with friends, and there are hundreds in Berlin. The following is a more upscale version of a *Kneipe* known for its history and food.

Lutter und Wegner 1811 ★   This place was named after a gastronomic and social landmark, Lutter und Wegner, a hangout for actors in the 19th century. You can have a drink in the stand-up bar or make reservations in advance to dine. Try the local specialty, *Königsberger Klopse*, with potatoes and a fresh salad. The *Wiener Schnitzel* or pot roast with horseradish and *Sekt* (German sparkling wine) are also recommended. The wide selection of drinks ranges from single-malt Scotch whiskeys to Italian grappas. Main courses range from 13€ to 20€. Both the restaurant and the bar are open Tuesday to Sunday 6pm to 2am. The kitchen is open until midnight. In summer, you can sit on a terrace and observe the passing parade. Schlüterstrasse 55. ℭ **030/8813440.** www.restaurantlutterundwegner.de. S-Bahn: Savignyplatz.

Cafe Life

At its mid-19th-century zenith, Berlin was famous for its cafes. Max Krell, an editor, once wrote: "Cafes were our homeland. They were the stock exchange of ideas, site of intellectual transactions, futures' market of poetic and artistic glory and defeat." They've changed with the times, but cafes are still going strong in Berlin—particularly, these days, in what used to be East Berlin. In the heart of the old East German capital is a complex of about 100 bars, shops, and restaurants, called **Die Hackenschen Höfe** (S-Bahn: Hackescher Markt). This stylish minimall attracts hip counterculture denizens who wander between galleries, boutiques, and fashionable cafes. It has become one of the most prominent places in the city to go drinking.

Cafe Aedes   Tucked away within what were once small 19th-century factories, this is a trendy and convivial cafe with a counterculture clientele that's very, very hip to the changing face of Berlin and its cultural scene. The decor includes lots of shimmering glass and free-form concrete, and the clientele includes a mixed collection of merchants, artists, performers, writers, and businesspeople. Whiskey with soda costs 8€; platters of simple food range from 8€ to 19€. Beef consommé, salmon steaks with mango sauce, pasta with tuna and fresh tomatoes, and vegetarian salads are what it's all about—that and ongoing dialogues. Daily hours are 10am to midnight. Rosenthaler Strasse 40–41.(℃) **030/2858275.** www.cafe-aedes.de. U-Bahn: Weinmeisterstrasse.

Café Einstein ★   This legendary cafe became famous for its mellow house-roasted *Kaffee* and *Kuchen* (freshly made cakes). It became so good, in fact, that it spawned a chain of swanky coffee bars across Berlin. But we always like to go to the original, which is decorated like a gilded cafe in Vienna. It's as grand as a ballroom and is found in an old town-house mansion. We often drop in for an elaborate breakfast, which usually costs us 10€ each. You can also return later in the day for a wide range of dishes, going from prosciutto from Italy (also Italian cheeses) to such New Yorker favorites as smoked salmon, bagels, and cream cheese. Main courses cost from 14€ to 22€. We think the *Apfelstrudel* with its paper-thin pastry sheets and amber-colored fresh fruit is among the best in Berlin. Ask for it *mit Sahne* (with cream). It's open 8am to 1am daily. Kurfürstenstrasse 58.(℃) **030/2615096.** www.cafeeinstein.com. U-Bahn: Wittenbergplatz.

Cafe Wintergarten in Literaturhaus Berlin ★   Set within a Tuscan-style brick villa that was built in 1885, 1 block south of the Ku'Damm, a few steps from the Käthe-Kollwitz-Museum, this cafe is part of a private foundation that's devoted to the promotion—through lectures and research—of German literature. In addition to a prestigious and respectable bookshop that fills the building's basement, it contains lecture halls, offices that have links to Germany's academic community, and space for temporary exhibitions that cost from 5€ to 7€. The best way to unlock the secrets of this place is to head for the cafe and restaurant, with tables that fill two old-fashioned Berliner-style rooms and spill into a much-sought-after garden during clement weather. If you're hungry, the cheerful, old-Berliner-style staff will serve platters of noodles with cheese, rigatoni with beef strips, Argentine steaks with herbs and parsleyed potatoes, and cucumber-and-tuna salads. It's open daily 9:30am to 1am. Fasanenstrasse 23.(℃) **030/8825414.** U-Bahn: Kurfürstendamm.

Dachgarten   This cafe is installed in the dome of the Reichstag (p. 95). Sad to say, the food is hardly the city's finest, although we find the setting and panorama so overpowering we recommend a visit, if only for coffee and pastry. If you are a customer here, you can also avoid the long lines of people waiting to enter the dome; restaurant patrons can head for the separate entrance that opens into the Reichstag directly from the Platz der Republik. (It's technically known as the "handicapped entrance," but isn't restricted to those with disabilities.) An elevator will whisk you up to the Dachgarten restaurant. The cafe was stylishly redesigned by Sir Norman Foster, and it looks like a modern art museum. Even the Reichstag *Küchenchef* admits most diners come for the view and not the Continental menu. A waiter recently confided to us, "Come back in the morning for breakfast. We get the least complaints about the food then." Main courses cost from 25€ to 30€. The Dachgarten is open daily 9am to 4:30pm and 6:30pm to midnight. Platz der Republik, Tiergarten. (℃) **030/ 22629900.** U-Bahn: Unter den Linden.

GAY & LESBIAN BERLIN

Traditionally, lesbian and gay life centered on the **Nollendorfplatz** (U-Bahn: Nollendorfplatz), the so-called "Pink Village." There is a history of homosexuality here at the **Schwules Museum,** Mehringdamm 61 (✆ **030/69599050;** www.schwules museum.de), open Wednesday to Monday from 2 to 6pm (to 7pm Sat). Admission is 5€ adults, 3€ students. The state-supported **Spinnboden Lesbenarchiv & Bibliothek,** Anklamerstrasse 38 (✆ **030/4485848;** www.spinnboden.de), caters to all sorts of lesbian cultural events. **Mann-o-Meter,** Bülowstrasse 106 (✆ **030/2168008;** www.mann-o-meter.de), is a gay information center.

Today, Motzstrasse is the location of many gay and lesbian bars, including **Tom's** and **Prinzknecht.**

In the latter half of June, the Lesbisch-Schwules Stadtfest (Lesbian and Gay Men's Street Fair) takes place at Nollendorfplatz. This is topped in size, though not in exuberance, the last week in June by the Christopher Street Day parade, when 200,000 people congregate to have fun and drop inhibitions.

Kumpelnest 3000   Gay or straight, you're welcome here. All that's asked is that you enjoy a good time in what used to be a brothel. This crowded and chaotic place is really a bar now, but there's also dancing to disco classics. Berliners often show up here for early-morning fun after they've exhausted the action at the other hot spots. It's open daily 7pm to 5am, even later on weekends. Lützowstrasse 23. ✆ **030/2616918.** www.kumpelnest3000.com. U-Bahn: Kurfürstenstrasse.

Prinzknecht   It's large, brick lined, and mobbed with ordinary guys who just happen to be gay and who just happen to be involved in computers, media, the building trades, and show business. The combination can be unpretentious and a lot of fun, especially when frothy pink Hemingways are bought by friends for friends and the stories start getting raunchy. If you want a place that manages to be both high class and earthy, within walking distance of lots of other gay options, this might be appropriate. It's open daily 3pm to 3am. Fuggerstrasse 33. ✆ **030/23627444.** www.prinzknecht.de. U-Bahn: Viktoria-Luise-Platz.

SchwuZ   If you hadn't been warned in advance, you might not even know that this is a nightclub, hidden as it is behind the conventional-looking facade of the Café Sundström. You'll descend into a battered-looking warren of basement rooms, outfitted in a surreal combination of glossy stainless steel that alternates with structural beams and cinder block. The mostly gay, mostly male, and mostly under 35-year-old crowd comes to dance the night away, every night from 11pm to around 4am. There are two separate dance floors, one with cutting-edge music, the other with more traditional dance music. Mehringdamm 61. ✆ **030/6290880.** www.schwuz.de. Cover 5€ 0€. U-Bahn: Mehringdamm.

The Sharon Stonewall Bar   Don't you love the name? The bar honors one of Hollywood's most gay-friendly actresses as well as the Greenwich Village bar where the gay revolution was launched. The atmosphere is so congenial and laid-back that straights, in addition to gays and lesbians, frequent its easygoing loungey atmosphere in the central Mitte district. The friendly owners are from Australia, and the room is filled with comfortable, cozy couches. On some occasions, the bar sponsors theme nights honoring gay and lesbian icons, with the odd DJ. The bartender makes the best strawberry daiquiris in town, and those martinis are extra dry (stirred, not shaken). It's open Tuesday to Saturday 5pm to 2am, and Sunday 6pm to 2am. Happy hour is Tuesday to Thursday 8 to 9:30pm. Präsidentenstrasse 3. ✆ **030/24085502.** www.sharonstonewall.com. U-Bahn: Oranienburger Tor. S-Bahn: Oranienburger Strasse.

Tom's Bar   Tom's becomes crowded after 11pm with young gay men. Most of the clients show up here in rugged-looking T-shirts, flannel, jeans, and/or black leather, evocative of a Tom of Finland drawing. Upstairs, the porno action is merely on the screen; downstairs it's real. Tom's is open daily 10pm to 6am. Monday nights feature two-for-one drinks. There's a cover charge for special occasions only. Motzstrasse 19. ✆ **030/2134570.** www.tomsbar.de. U-Bahn: Nollendorfplatz.

GAMBLING THE NIGHT AWAY

Casino Berlin   This is an exclusive club on the 37th floor of the Park Inn Hotel, opening onto a panoramic view of Berlin at night. Games of chance include American roulette, blackjack, and French roulette. Nearly 100 slot machines are found on the ground floor, which is very Las Vegas. The gaming club costs 5€ to enter and is open daily from 3pm to 3am. Alexanderplatz 8.✆ **030/23894144.** www.westspiel.de. U-Bahn: Alexanderplatz.

Spielbank Berlin   It's brassy, it sparkles with lots of chrome, and the staff is about as jaded as any you'll find in a city that's legendary for its jaded citizens. The setting is a high-ceilinged, scarlet affair that might remind you of an airport. The basement is devoted to slot machines; the upper floors (Casino Royale) host a battery of more sophisticated gambling devices that include roulette and baccarat. Men must wear a necktie for access to the Casino Royale, but not to the basement-level slot machines. The cover charge of 5€ is refunded in the form of a casino chip. There are no maximum bets—the amount you lose, or can bet on any one play, depends on your credit rating with the casino. The slot machines are accessible daily 11:30am to 3am; the rest of the complex is available for bets daily 2pm to 3am. You must be 19 or over to enter and gamble, and a passport is required to enter the casino. Marlene-Dietrich-Platz 1 (Potsdamer Platz).✆ **030/255990.** www.spielbank-berlin.de. Cover 5€. U-Bahn: Potsdamer Platz.

Sports & Outdoor Pursuits

BIKING

The best place to rent bikes in Berlin is at **Fahrradstation GmbH,** Bergmannstrasse 9 (✆ **030/2151566;** U-Bahn: Platz der Luftbrücke), in Kreuzberg. Rentals cost 15€ per day or 50€ per week. Oddly enough, rentals of 3-speed, 7-speed, and 21-speed (racing) bikes all cost the same; consequently, a cyclist can rent whichever degree of high-tech savvy he or she prefers. The city maintains a labyrinth of bike paths, marked by red bricks on the walkways, through the central core of Berlin and in its parks, especially the Tiergarten. The best places for biking are the Tiergarten in central Berlin and farther afield in the Grunewald Forest (S-Bahn: Grunewald). *Note:* You can take bikes on the S- and U-Bahn, but you must board the correct carriage (look for the bike sign on the doors) and buy an extra bike ticket (1.50€ within zones AB, 2.10€ within zones ABC).

JOGGING

Head for the vast and verdant leafiness of the **Grunewald,** on the city's western edge, which is crisscrossed with pedestrian and bike paths. This area is appropriate for very long endurance tests. Closer to the center is the **Tiergarten,** which allows you to soak up a little history on your morning jog thanks to its many monuments and memorials. The grounds of **Schloss Charlottenburg** are also good for jogging.

SPECTATOR SPORTS

Among Berliners, **fussball (soccer)** is the most popular sport. For information about which teams are playing, ask your hotel receptionist or refer to a daily newspaper or the weekly magazine *Berlin Programm.*

SWIMMING

Berlin is hardly a beach resort, but each summer the banks of many of the canals are covered with sand on which rest deck chairs under rainbow-hued umbrellas, creating a series of mini-beaches. The best of these is **Bundespresse Strand,** Kapelle-Ufer 1 (✆ **030/28099119;** www.derbundespressestrand.de), across from the Reichstag in the center of Berlin. It offers two swimming pools, live music, and a glass pavilion for rainy days.

The bar here is the best-known "beach bar" in Berlin; if you're hungry, it offers, in addition to beer and cocktails, freshly made salads and grilled meats. On Thursday evenings, salsa music is a feature, and on Sunday, beginning at 3pm, a dance is staged. From May to the end of summer, volleyball is offered—free until 5pm, 15€ thereafter. The location is on the site of the old Berlin Wall in once "forbidden" territory. In summer it's open daily 10am until late at night (U-Bahn: Friedrichstrasse).

Perched on the top floor of the Europa Center's parking garage (Parkhaus Europa Center), the health and exercise club called **Thermen,** Nürnberger Strasse 7 (✆ **030/2575760;** www.thermen-berlin.de; U-Bahn: Wittenbergplatz), offers an array of heated pools, saunas, massage facilities, and solariums. You'll pay 17€ for a 3-hour use of these facilities, but most visitors find that unless they're terribly rushed and plan on just a quick dip, it's more practical to buy a full-day pass for 19€. They'll give you a key to lock up your valuables. It's a good idea to bring your own bathing suit, but if you don't have one, an attendant will drag one out of a tattered inventory in back. Know in advance that men and women share the same saunas, and in Germany, no one seems particularly adverse to sweating nude in a communal setting. Massages go for 30€ per 30-minute session and should be reserved in advance. Hours are Monday to Saturday 10am to midnight and Sunday 10am to 9pm.

For outdoor swimming during the hot months, head to one of Europe's largest lake beaches at **Wannsee.** Take the S-Bahn to Nikolaisee and follow the hordes of bathers heading toward the water's edge.

TENNIS & SQUASH

A well-respected outfit that features access to indoor tennis and squash courts is **Sport Center Buschkrug,** Buschkrugallee 84 (✆ **030/6069999;** www.sportcenter-buschkrug.de; U-Bahn: Grenzallee). Depending on the time of day you arrive, indoor tennis courts rent for between 24€ and 29€ per hour, and indoor squash courts rent for between 9€ and 18€ per hour. Know in advance that the most expensive and most sought-after playing times are between 6 and 10pm, presumably when local residents need to work off steam after a day at the office. A worthy competitor is Berlin's **Squash Tennis Nord,** Treuenbrietzenerstrasse 36 (✆ **030/4153011;** U-Bahn. Wittenau, then bus no. 124 or X-21), which charges a bit less—18€ to 24€ per hour for use of one of its half-dozen tennis courts and 10€ to 13€ per hour for use of one of its 10 squash courts, depending on when you opt to play. Advance reservations at both clubs are recommended.

WHERE TO STAY

Berlin is the scene of frequent international trade fairs, conferences, and festivals, and during these times, vacancies in the city will be hard to find. The greatest concentration of hotels, from the cheapest digs to the most expensive, lies in the center near the **Kurfürstendamm (Ku'Damm),** the main boulevard of western Berlin. Most good-value pensions and small hotels are in the western part of the city; note that many such accommodations are in older buildings where plumbing is rarely state-of-the-art.

The business convention crowd still anchors primarily in the west, as do the hordes of summer visitors on whirlwind tours of Europe. **Eastern Berlin** often attracts Germans from other parts of the country who want a glimpse of the Berlin that was shut away behind the Wall for so long. The eastern sector still doesn't have the visitor structure and facilities of the west, although several first-class and deluxe hotels have opened there, notably the Grand, Adlon, and Hilton.

Travelers can also head for hotels in **Grunewald,** close to nature in the Grunewald Forest, or **Charlottenburg,** near Olympic Park. If you like biking, jogging, and breathing fresh air and don't mind the commute into central Berlin for shopping and attractions, you'll enjoy both these areas.

Tegel Airport is only 20 minutes from Berlin by taxi, but if you have a very early departure or late arrival, and want the added security of an airport hotel, you can check into **Mercure Airport Hotel Berlin Tegel,** Kurt-Schumacher-Damm 202, 13405 Orsteil-Reinickendorf (www.mercure.com; ✆ **030/41060;** fax 030/4106700). Doubles are medium size and furnished in standard motel-chain format. The rate for a double is from 69€. There's also a restaurant on-site, plus a free shuttle service that runs back and forth between the hotel and the airport. American Express, Diners Club, MasterCard, and Visa are accepted.

On or Near the Kurfürstendamm
VERY EXPENSIVE

Brandenburger Hof ★★★　This hotel lies on a dignified street in the commercial heart of the city and dates from 1991, when it was built in the classic Bauhaus style beloved by so many Germans. As a Relais & Châteaux property, it offers better food and service than most other hotels in its price range. Rooms range from medium size to spacious and are among the most stylish in the city. The decor, with torchier lamps, black-leather upholstery, and platform beds, may appear a touch minimalist, but everybody will appreciate the original artworks that adorn the walls. Another bonus is the state-of-the-art security system and the French doors that open up onto balconies on all but the top floor.

Eislebener Strasse 14, 10789 Berlin. www.brandenburger-hof.com. ✆**030/214050.** Fax 030/21405100. 82 units. 295€–345€ double; from 425€ suite. Rates include buffet breakfast. AE, DC, MC, V. Parking 24€. U-Bahn: Kurfürstendamm or Augsburger Strasse. S-Bahn: Zoologischer Garten. **Amenities:** 2 restaurants; bar; airport transfers (65€); babysitting; concierge; access to nearby health club; room service. *In room:* TV, hair dryer, minibar, Wi-Fi (6€ per hour).

Concorde Berlin　Its 17-story limestone exterior near the Kurfürstendamm has already changed the skyline of western Berlin. The location is only 100m (300 ft.) from the landmark Kaiser Wilhelm Memorial Church. The famous Berlin architect, Jan Kleihues, went for understated elegance in the hotel design, which features minimalist interiors in warm colors and modern art on the walls. The bedrooms are the largest in Berlin. Like the public rooms, they are elegantly understated in design and most comfortable with warm colors and beautiful hardwoods. The suites, both junior and regular, are among Berlin's finest and most luxurious, each imbued with grand style.

Augsburger Strasse 41, 10789 Berlin. www.berlin.concordehotels.de. © **030/8009990.** Fax 030/80099999. 311 units. 135€–275€ double; 240€–430€ junior suite; from 550€ suite. AE, DC, MC, V. Parking 25€. U-Bahn: Zoologischer Garten or Kurfürstendamm. **Amenities:** Restaurant; bar; babysitting; concierge; exercise room; Jacuzzi; room service; sauna. *In room:* A/C, TV, hair dryer, minibar, Wi-Fi (free).

Grand Hotel Esplanade ★★★   Strikingly contemporary, this luxe hotel lies in a quiet and verdant neighborhood near several foreign embassies, some concert halls, and the massively expanding Potsdamer Platz. Thanks to river views and a swath of park, you might get the feeling that you're far from the city. It competes effectively with other Berlin hotels in its class, with a well-conceived collection of modern art. It is, in fact, the hypercontemporary alternative to the more traditional Kempinski (see below). The starkly contemporary, bright, sun-flooded, and cheerful rooms pay strict attention to sound insulation. Corner rooms are among the most spacious and have some of the best views of the surrounding area.

Lützowufer 15, 10785 Berlin. www.esplanade.de. © **866/597-8341** in the U.S., or 030/254788255. Fax 030/254788222. 392 units. 90€–166€ double; from 175€ suite. AE, DC, MC, V. Parking 20€. U-Bahn: Kurfürstenstrasse, Nollendorfplatz, or Wittenbergplatz. **Amenities:** 3 restaurants; 2 bars; babysitting; bikes; concierge; exercise room; state-of-the-art health club and spa; indoor heated pool; room service. *In room:* A/C, TV, hair dryer, minibar, Wi-Fi (7€ per hour).

Kempinski Hotel Bristol ★★★   This hotel reigns as one of Berlin's most prestigious and visible hotels, enjoying a reputation equivalent to some of the best hotels in the world. But the emergence of such luxe Berlin-Mitte properties as Adlon (p. 141) and the Regent (p. 142) has shaken the Kempinski crown. It occupies a bulky, boxy-looking building that was originally erected during the peak of the Cold War, but with an interior that has benefited from ongoing improvements and renovations. The staff is superbly trained, and the shamelessly rich-looking decor is more opulent and better designed than that of many comparably priced competitors. Rooms contain high-quality reproductions of English and Continental antiques, and enough insulation to retain an almost reverential hush.

Kurfürstendamm 27, 10719 Berlin. www.kempinski.com. © **800/426-3135** in the U.S., or 030/884340. Fax 030/8836075. 302 units. 240€–520€ double; from 500€ suite. Children 11 and under stay free in parent's room. AE, DC, MC, V. Parking 25€. U-Bahn: Kurfürstendamm. **Amenities:** 2 restaurants; 2 bars; airport transfers (90€); babysitting; concierge; exercise room; indoor heated pool; room service; sauna. *In room:* A/C, TV, hair dryer, minibar, Wi-Fi (25€ per day).

Steigenberger Berlin ★★   One of Berlin's most visible luxury hotels lies on a formal, gracefully proportioned plaza a few steps from the Kaiser Wilhelm Memorial Church. Originally built behind a nondescript facade in 1981, it caters to a demanding clientele of relatively conservative clients. This place represents western Berlin's sense of the status quo more visibly than virtually any other hotel in town. Public areas are large, well-designed, open spaces with high ceilings. Overall, expect a sense of bustling conservatism, plush and contemporary comfort, and corporate Europe at its most deeply entrenched. Rooms, for the most part, are medium in size, each maintained in good condition with tasteful modern decor and generous-size beds.

Los-Angeles-Platz 1, 10789 Berlin. www.berlin.steigenberger.com. © **800/223-5652** in the U.S. and Canada, or 030/21270. Fax 030/2127117. 397 units. 135€–345€ double; from 305€ junior suite. Children 11 and under stay free in parent's room. AE, MC, V. Parking 19€. U-Bahn: Kurfürstendamm. **Amenities:** 3 restaurants; 2 bars; babysitting; bikes; concierge; exercise room; indoor heated pool; room service; sauna. *In room:* A/C, TV, hair dryer, minibar, Wi-Fi (free).

EXPENSIVE

Bleibtreu Hotel ★   The facade of this trend-conscious hotel isn't easily recognizable from the street, as the tiny lobby is accessible via an alleyway that leads past an avant-garde garden and a big-windowed set of dining and drinking facilities. The setting is the labyrinthine premises of what was built long ago as a *Jugendstil*-era apartment house. Rooms are small, minimalist, and furnished in carefully chosen natural materials. Extras include dataports and cordless phones. Tables spill from the cafe into the tiny garden, where shrubs and flowers are surrounded with smooth-polished pieces of colored glass—a definite conversation piece.

Bleibtreustrasse 31, 10707 Berlin (1 block south of the Kurfürstendamm). www.bleibtreu.com. ✆ **030/884740.** Fax 030/88474444. 60 units. 120€–210€ double. Children 11 and under stay free in parent's room. AE, DC, MC, V. U-Bahn: Uhlandstrasse. **Amenities:** 2 restaurants; bar; babysitting; concierge; exercise room; room service; sauna. *In room:* TV, hair dryer, minibar, Wi-Fi (10€ per 24 hr.).

Savoy ★   If you don't demand the full-service facilities of the grander choices but require a bit of class, this is the hotel for you. In general, rooms are a bit small, but they are comfortable nonetheless, with such amenities as double-glazed windows and fine furnishings. Bathrooms are decent in size and maintained spotlessly. For a nightcap, try the cozy **Times Bar** (p. 129).

Fasanenstrasse 9–10, 10623 Berlin. www.hotel-savoy.com. ✆ **800/223-5652** in the U.S. and Canada, or 030/311030. Fax 030/31103333. 125 units. 148€–287€ double; 180€–320€ suite. Children 11 and under stay free in parent's room. AE, DC, MC, V. Parking 15€. U-Bahn: Kurfürstendamm. **Amenities:** Restaurant; bar; babysitting; concierge; exercise room; Internet (free; in lobby); room service; sauna. *In room:* TV, hair dryer, minibar, Wi-Fi (6.50€ per hour).

MODERATE

Art Nouveau ★ 🏨   On the fourth floor of an Art Nouveau apartment house, this little-known hotel is an atmospheric choice. Even the elevator is a historic gem of the upmarket and desirable neighborhood. Established in the late 1970s, Art Nouveau is fully renovated. The well-furnished and comfortable rooms are pleasantly decorated and high-ceilinged and are filled with excellent beds and well-kept bathrooms. Rooms in the rear are more tranquil, except when the nearby schoolyard is full of children at play. At an honor bar in the lobby, guests keep track of their own drinks. A generous breakfast is the only meal served.

Leibnizstrasse 59, 10629 Berlin. www.hotelartnouveau.de. ✆ **030/3277440.** Fax 030/32774440. 20 units. 128€–180€ double; 178€–239€ suite. Rates include continental breakfast. AE, MC, V. Parking 8€. U-Bahn: Adenauerplatz. *In room:* TV, hair dryer.

Askanischer Hof ★ 🍸   On the Ku'Damm, which was the heart of West Berlin in the Cold War era, this hotel still exudes an old-fashioned charm that is most appealing. It is not for those who get off on *Moderno*. To testify to its age, vintage photos of long-ago guests line the walls, and there is a lot of Victorian clutter. Nonetheless, it has attracted such past guests as the very hip David Bowie, so it must be doing something right.

The hotel prides itself on offering spacious, even elegant rooms, while maintaining a decor typical of Berlin, which has long ago faded at most hotels. The hotel dates from the end of the 19th century, and it miraculously survived the war. Bedrooms are most comfortable, evoking some of the charm of the 1920s. Those overlooking the Ku'Damm are double-glazed to cut down on traffic noise.

Kurfürstendamm 53, D-10707 Berlin. www.askanischer-hof.de. ✆ **030/8818033.** Fax 030/8817206. 16 units. 118€–195€ double; 200€ suite. AE, MC, V. Free parking. U-Bahn: Adenauer Platz. *In room:* TV, minibar, Wi-Fi (free).

Hollywood Media Hotel ★ 🏨 Germany has never seen a hotel quite like this before. The two replicas of the golden Oscars guarding the door set the tone for Berlin's first cinema hotel. The soundproof rooms are all dedicated to the big heroes or the beautiful divas of the screen—from Marilyn Monroe to John Wayne, from Audrey Hepburn to Humphrey Bogart. Right on the famed shopping street and the former "main street" of West Berlin, the movie-inspired hotel plays up film tie-ins, going from *High Noon* to *In the Heat of the Night*. The most spacious and the best accommodations here are apartments with a kitchenette and a balcony or terrace, each dedicated to a classic movie with a film scene painted directly on the wall. The hotel even has a 100-seat cinema. Rooms are medium to spacious in size, each comfortably and elegantly furnished with full, first-rate bathrooms. Rooms are spread across six floors.

Kurfürstendamm 202, 10719 Berlin. www.filmhotel.de. ℂ **030/889100.** Fax 030/88910280. 182 units. 117€–169€ double; 198€–480€ apt. for 2. Rates include buffet breakfast. Children 11 and under stay free in parent's room. AE, MC, V. Parking 17€. U-Bahn: Uhlandstrasse. Bus: 109, 119, or 219. **Amenities:** Restaurant; bar; airport transfers (20€–37€); babysitting; exercise room; spa. *In room:* A/C, TV, fax, hair dryer, minibar, Wi-Fi (10€ per day).

Hotel Domus 🍴 Clean, streamlined, and unpretentious, this government-rated three-star hotel dates from 1975 and lies in one of Berlin's most attractive districts in Wilmersdorf, a short walk from St. Ludwig's Church. Most of the accommodations come with a private bathroom; the occupants of two rooms share an adjoining bathroom with toilet and shower stall. It's a favorite of business travelers, who appreciate its good value and respectability. As such, it has a high proportion of single rooms. Rooms are well designed, well scrubbed, and, although not particularly large, very comfortable. There are virtually no extras on-site, except soundproof windows and a charming breakfast room.

Uhlandstrasse 49, 10719 Berlin. www.hotel-domus-berlin.de. ℂ **030/8803440.** Fax 030/88034444. 70 units. 58€–110€ double. AE, DC, MC, V. Parking 10€. U-Bahn: Hohenzollernplatz or Spichernstrasse. **Amenities:** Bar; Wi-Fi (free; in lobby). *In room:* TV, hair dryer.

Kronprinz Berlin 🏨 This hotel is located away from Berlin's center at the far western edge of the Ku'Damm. In spite of its many discreet charms and features, it remains relatively unknown. All rooms have balconies and fine appointments (often tasteful reproductions of antiques). If you want a little extra comfort, ask for one of the Bel-Etage rooms. Many guests congregate in the garden, under the chestnut trees, in summer.

Kronprinzendamm 1, 10711 Berlin. www.kronprinz-hotel.de. ℂ **030/896030.** Fax 030/8931215. 80 units. 150€–215€ double; 225€–275€ suite. Rates include buffet breakfast. AE, DC, MC, V. Parking 13€. U-Bahn: Halensee. Bus: 110, 119, 129, or 219. **Amenities:** Bar; babysitting; bikes. *In room:* TV, hair dryer, minibar, Wi-Fi (5€ per day).

Ku'Damm 101 ★ On the main drag of the former West Berlin, this boutique hotel is one of the best. Of course, you have to be pleased with its clean, almost stark lines and minimalist palette. At the western end of the Kurfürstendamm, in the district of Wilmersdorf, the hotel is both a winner and a charmer. The midsize bedrooms represent the latest in contemporary aesthetic and lifestyle, with comfortable furnishings and state-of-the-art bathrooms. You breakfast above the rooftops of Berlin, after being treated, if you wish, to everything from ear acupuncture to shiatsu body treatments the day before in the on-site spa. The interior design in both the public and private rooms is harmonious, using high-quality materials and the latest high-tech innovations.

Kurfürstendamm 101, 10711 Berlin. www.kudamm101.com. (C) **030/5200550.** Fax 030/520055555. 170 units. 119€–250€ double. Children 12 and under stay free in parent's room. AE, MC, V. Parking 14€. U-Bahn: Adenauer-Platz. **Amenities:** Bar; concierge; exercise room; room service. *In room:* A/C, TV, hair dryer, Wi-Fi (10€ per day).

INEXPENSIVE

Alexandra Hotel Pension This three-floor hotel is comfortable, centrally located, and quiet. The building dates from 1900 and was converted into a hotel in the 1920s. Certain rooms are lined with photographs of old Berlin—perfect for acquainting yourself with what to look for as you tour the streets of the city. Most rooms have modern furniture and well-kept bathrooms.

Wielandstrasse 32, 10629 Berlin. www.alexandra-berlin.de. (C) **030/8812107.** Fax 030/88577818. 13 units. 46€–120€ double. Rates include buffet breakfast. AE, MC, V. Parking nearby 6€. S-Bahn: Savigny-platz or Olivaerplatz. *In room:* TV, hair dryer, Wi-Fi (free).

Bogota Since 1964, when a quartet of separate hotels on four floors was com-bined into a cohesive whole, this hotel has been a local favorite for the frugal traveler. Typical for older Berlin apartment houses, rooms come in various shapes and sizes, but all have been recently restored. Guest rooms are well cared for and comfortable, the best opening onto an inner courtyard.

The building more or less withstood World War II bombardments. Constructed in 1911, it had been a famous address known for its frequent parties, at which a young Benny Goodman appeared on occasion. The famous entrepreneur Oskar Skaller lived here and was known for his collection of Impressionist paintings, including works by van Gogh. What is now the lounge and TV room was once the office of the infamous director, Hans Hinkel, of the Reich Chamber of Culture. Charlie Chaplin named the title character in his film *The Great Dictator* after Hinkel.

Schlüstrasse 45, 10707 Berlin. www.hotel-bogota.de. (C) **030/8815001.** Fax 030/8835887. 130 units, 60 with bathroom (12 with shower but no toilet). 75€–84€ double without bathroom; 89€–150€ double with full bathroom. Rates include continental breakfast. AE, DC, MC, V. Parking 13€. U-Bahn: Adenauerplatz or Uhlandstrasse. S-Bahn: Savignyplatz. Bus: 109. **Amenities:** Wi-Fi (free; in lobby). *In room:* TV, hair dryer.

Hotel-Pension Bregenz This dignified pension occupies the fourth and sunniest floor of a four-story, century-old apartment building, accessible by elevator. The owner, Mr. Zimmermann, works hard to maintain the cleanliness and charm of his comfortably furnished, relatively large rooms. Double doors help minimize noise from the public corridors. The staff gladly assists guests in reserving tickets for shows and tours.

Bregenzer Strasse 5, D-10707 Berlin. www.hotelbregenz-berlin.de. (C) **030/8814307.** Fax 030/8824009. 14 units, 11 with bathroom (shower only). 70€ double without bathroom; 95€ double with bathroom. Rates include continental breakfast. MC, V. Parking 10€. U-Bahn: Adenauerplatz. S-Bahn: Savignyplatz. *In room:* TV, hair dryer, minibar.

Hotel-Pension Funk ★ 🎒 Lying on a back street of the Kurfürstendamm in western Berlin, the home of actress Asta Nielsen has been restored and turned into first-rate and affordable accommodations. Nielsen, a Danish-born star (1881–1972), became one of the stellar lights of the silent era, her beauty praised by Guillaume Apollinaire. She was offered her own studio in Nazi Germany by Josef Goebbels, but turned down the offer. Many original features of her home have been preserved, including decorative ceilings and Art Nouveau windows. All the midsize bedrooms are modernized and comfortably furnished.

Fasanenstrasse 69, 10719 Berlin. www.hotel-pensionfunk.de. (C) **030/8827193.** Fax 030/883329. 14 units. 72€–114€ double. Rates include buffet breakfast. MC, V. U-Bahn: Kurfürstendamm or Uhland-strasse. *In room:* TV on request.

Pension München This pension occupies only part of the third floor of a massive four-story elevator building erected as an apartment house in 1908. It offers a simple but tasteful decor of modern furnishings accented with fresh flowers. Rooms are clean, with contemporary furniture and prints and engravings by local artists. Each comes with a compact, shower-only bathroom. Look for sculptures by the owner in some of the public areas.

Güntzelstrasse 62 (close to Bayerischer Platz), 10717 Berlin. www.hotel-pension-muenchen-in-berlin.de. ☏ **030/8579120.** Fax 030/85791222. 8 units. 78€–98€ double. AE, DC, MC, V. Parking 6€. U-Bahn: Güntzelstrasse. *In room:* TV.

Pension Nürnberger Eck 🦪 This reliable pension in Charlottenburg is refreshingly old-fashioned. It occupies the second floor of a four-story building on a relatively quiet side street near Europa Center. Rooms are large, with high ceilings, massive doors, and, in many cases, reproductions of Biedermeier-style furniture, including comfortable beds, plus small shower bathrooms. This is the kind of place where Sally Bowles from *Cabaret* might have stayed.

Nürnberger Strasse 24A (near the Europa Center), 10789 Berlin. www.nuernberger-eck.de. ☏ **030/2351780.** Fax 030/23517899. 8 units, 5 with bathroom. 70€ double without bathroom; 70€–95€ double with bathroom. Rates include continental breakfast. MC, V. Parking 6€. U-Bahn: Augsburgerstrasse. **Amenities:** Room service. *In room:* TV.

Near the Memorial Church & Zoo
VERY EXPENSIVE

Palace Berlin ★★ Although it isn't at the level of the Kempinski or the Grand Hotel Esplanade, this well-managed hotel outranks such landmarks as the Berlin Hilton and the Steigenberger Berlin. Don't be surprised by its boxy exterior (ca. 1968) that rises immediately adjacent to the Europa Center. Inside, thanks to dozens of improvements, the setting is very comfortable and, at times, even opulent. The soundproof rooms range in size from medium to spacious. All have fine beds, superb lighting, quality carpeting, and conservatively traditional styling. Known as "new deluxe rooms," the most comfortable accommodations are on the third, fourth, and fifth floors.

In the Europa Center, Budapesterstrasse 45, 10787 Berlin. www.palace.de. ☏ **800/457-4000** in the U.S., or 030/25020. Fax 030/25021161. 282 units. 145€–360€ double; 265€–415€ junior suite; from 325€ suite. AE, DC, MC, V. Parking 26€. U-Bahn: Zoologischer Garten. **Amenities:** 2 restaurants; 2 bars; airport transfers (118€–148€); babysitting; bikes; concierge; exercise room; indoor heated pool; room service; spa. *In room:* A/C, TV, hair dryer, minibar, Wi-Fi (15€ per day).

EXPENSIVE

Art'otel ★ 🏛 Chic, discreet, and avant-garde, this is unlike any other Berlin hotel. The location is ideal, in the heart of cosmopolitan Berlin, with the Ku'Damm action virtually outside the front door. The decor, strictly minimalist, includes touches from top designers. You'll find Philippe Starck bar stools, Arne Jacobsen chairs, and artwork by Berliner Wolf Vostell. Modernists will be at home here, amid chrome-legged furnishings and pedestal tables that look like cable spools. Traditionalists might not be so pleased. Rooms are all comfortable, with soundproofing, large beds, and tasteful lighting. The service here is among Berlin's finest. On weekends, a minimum stay of 2 nights is required.

Joachimstalerstrasse 29, 10719 Berlin. www.artotels.com. ☏ **030/884470.** Fax 030/88447700. 133 units. 69€–240€ double. Rates include buffet breakfast with champagne. AE, DC, MC, V. Parking 14€. U-Bahn: Kurfürstendamm. **Amenities:** Restaurant; bar; babysitting; concierge; room service. *In room:* A/C, TV, hair dryer, minibar, Wi-Fi (free).

Hecker's Hotel   For years, this establishment enjoyed a reputation as a small, private hotel, but now it's expanded. Though not in the same league as the Art'otel (see above), it's still a good choice, conveniently located near the Ku'Damm and the many bars, cafes, and restaurants around Savignyplatz. The original 42 rooms are smaller than the newer units, which are medium size. The rather severe and somewhat somber modern style may not suit everyone—certainly not those seeking romantic ambience—though the sterility is balanced by up-to-date comfort and top-notch maintenance.

Grolmanstrasse 35, 10623 Berlin. www.heckers-hotel.de. ℘ **030/88900.** Fax 030/8890260. 69 units. 110€–250€ double; 280€–500€ suite. AE, DC, MC, V. Parking 18€. U-Bahn: Uhlandstrasse. Bus: 109 from Tegel Airport to Uhlandstrasse or 119 from Tempelhof Airport. **Amenities:** Restaurant; bar; babysitting; room service. *In room:* A/C, TV, fax, hair dryer, minibar, Wi-Fi (free).

MODERATE

Ambassador Berlin ★   This hotel is an attractive choice if you'd like to lodge near the Ku'Damm. Rooms are, for the most part, spacious and comfortable for families and include traditional furnishings. Bathrooms are rather small, and only a fifth have showers; the rest have tubs. Soundproof windows are always a relief in noisy central Berlin. The hotel is sometimes overrun with large groups.

Bayreutherstrasse 42–43, 10787 Berlin. www.sorat-hotels.com. ℘ **030/219020.** Fax 030/21902380. 218 units. 129€–201€ double; 174€–226€ suite. Children 12 and under stay free in parent's room. AE, DC, MC, V. Parking 15€. U-Bahn: Wittenbergplatz. **Amenities:** Bar; babysitting; Wi-Fi (free; in lobby). *In room:* A/C, TV, hair dryer, minibar.

INEXPENSIVE

Arco Hotel   Although some of its competitors are more visible and more heavily promoted, this four-story hotel is one of the most consistently reliable and fairly priced gay-friendly hotels in Berlin. It occupies part of a 1900 Berlin apartment building. Rooms are mostly white, well scrubbed, and well organized, with tasteful, albeit simple, artwork and furnishings. A garden in back hosts breakfasts during clement weather. A polite and hardworking staff is alert to the location of emerging neighborhood bars and restaurants. Much of its business includes repeat guests.

Geisbergstrasse 30, 10777 Berlin. www.arco-hotel.de. ℘ **030/2351480.** Fax 030/21475178. 20 units. 70€–117€ double. Rates include breakfast buffet. AE, DC, MC, V. Parking 10€. U-Bahn: Wittenbergplatz, Viktoria-Luise-Platz, or Nollendorfplatz. **Amenities:** Bikes; Wi-Fi (free; in lobby). *In room:* TV, hair dryer.

In Grunewald
MODERATE

Schlosshotel im Grunewald ★★★   With only 54 gemlike rooms, this is one of the most historic and plushest hotels in Berlin. It was built in the 19th century by a friend and advisor of Kaiser Wilhelm II, who entertained him from time to time on the premises. For anyone who can afford it and prefers a stay in the city's verdant suburbs, the experience can be elegant, historic, and charming. Service is superb and invariably cheerful. Although changes have been made to the decor, its original inspiration was by German-born fashion superstar Karl Lagerfeld. The structure's monumental staircase, minstrel's gallery, and other Belle Epoque trappings remain, but Mr. Lagerfeld's contributions have added an undeniable gloss to the hotel's interior. Beds are sumptuous, with great pillows, fine linen, and elegant fabrics.

Brahmsstrasse 10, 14193 Berlin-Grunewald. www.schlosshotelberlin.com. ℘ **030/895840.** Fax 030/89584800. 54 units. 239€–279€ double; from 339€ suite. Rates include buffet breakfast. AE, DC, MC, V. Free parking. S-Bahn: Grunewald. **Amenities:** 2 restaurants; bar; airport transfers (85€–120€); babysitting; exercise room; indoor heated pool; room service; spa. *In room:* A/C, TV, hair dryer, Wi-Fi (free).

In Berlin-Mitte

VERY EXPENSIVE

Berlin Hilton ★   The Regent and Westin Grand are finer hotels, attracting some of the Hilton's former clients, but this durable landmark remains strong. Set within one of the city's most expensive and desirable neighborhoods, Gendarmenmarkt, this deluxe hotel was the first to open in what was East Berlin following the collapse of the Berlin Wall. Today, it's the third-largest hotel in the city and one of the most popular, with enough accessories and facilities within its seven floors to keep you busy for a week. Thanks to all the visual distraction in the lobby, you may even have a vague sense that you're in a resort hotel that's eager to meet the needs of both large groups and business travelers. Rooms are conservatively modern and very comfortable, with double-glazed windows, comfortable beds, and bedside controls. At least half overlook the twin churches of the dramatic Gendarmenmarkt.

Mohrenstrasse 30, 10117 Berlin. www.hilton.com. ℂ **800/445-8667** in the U.S. and Canada, or 030/20230. Fax 030/20234269. 589 units. 165€–349€ double; 365€–965€ suite. AE, DC, MC, V. Parking 20€. U-Bahn: Stadtmitte. **Amenities:** 5 restaurants; bar; babysitting; bikes; concierge; exercise room; indoor heated pool; room service; spa. *In room:* A/C, TV, hair dryer, minibar, Wi-Fi (10€ per hour).

Grand Hyatt Berlin ★★★   This is the most exciting, best-designed, and most iconoclastic hotel in Berlin, a government-rated five-star mecca. Don't expect rococo frills: Interior designer Hannes Wettstein permeated this hotel with a minimalist simplicity that may remind you of a Zen temple. Ceilings soar toward surreal-looking inverted pyramids, upstairs hallways run off into futuristic-looking infinities, and light derives from rambling expanses of glass or translucent slabs of alabaster. The large and sun-flooded rooms are among the hotel's best features. Suites are often commandeered by fashion photographers as backgrounds for cutting-edge fashion layouts.

Marlene-Dietrich-Platz 2, 10785 Berlin. www.berlin.grand.hyatt.com. ℂ **030/25531234.** Fax 030/25531235. 344 units. 205€–510€ double; from 500€ suite. AE, DC, MC, V. Parking 20€. U-Bahn: Potsdamer Platz. **Amenities:** 3 restaurants; bar; airport transfers (90€–115€); babysitting; concierge; exercise room; indoor heated pool; room service; spa. *In room:* A/C, TV, hair dryer, minibar, Wi-Fi (18€ per day).

Hotel Adlon ★★★   Berlin's most historic hotel is a phoenix, freshly risen from the ashes of 1945. No other hotel sits as close to the Brandenburg Gate, at the top of an avenue that's reasserting its claim on the city's sense of chic. Grand and historic, and permeated with the legends of the glamour and tragedies that befell it during various eras of its life, it was originally built by legendary hotelier Lorenz Adlon in 1907, and then reopened with a well-publicized flourish in 1997. Public areas, some of them illuminated with lavishly detailed stained-glass domes, contain coffered ceilings, mosaics, inlaid paneling, and lots of Carrara marble. Rooms are mostly large and have lots of state-of-the-art electronic extras. Those on the top floor offer the best views but are a bit more cramped and lack some extras.

Unter den Linden 77, 10117 Berlin. www.hotel-adlon.de. ℂ **800/426-3135** in the U.S., or 030/22610. Fax 030/22612222. 394 units. 240€–440€ double; from 700€ suite. AE, DC, MC, V. Parking 28€. S-Bahn: Unter den Linden. **Amenities:** 3 restaurants; bar; babysitting; concierge; health club and spa; indoor heated pool; room service. *In room:* A/C, TV, DVD player (in some), fax (in some), hair dryer, kitchenette (in some), minibar, Wi-Fi (12€ per hour).

Hotel de Rome ★★★ ☺   The Rocco Forte chain makes its Berlin bow in this classically designed building off Unter den Linden in the center of Berlin. The hotel is close to the Brandenburg Gate and opposite Humboldt University. This is one of the few luxury hotels in Berlin located in a prewar building (the rest were bombed).

The structure dates from 1889, when it was designed by Ludwig Helm, master builder of Berlin. The playful lobby filled with giant urns sets the tone for this exclusive hotel. A choice of bedrooms, all grand and supremely comfortable, offers classic rooms, deluxe rooms, even superior deluxe rooms, and a range of suites from junior to two historic suites. Bathrooms are among the grandest in the capital, with mosaic marble detailing. Restaurant Parioli, named for a chic district of Rome, features a terrace for alfresco dining in summer and a savory year-round Mediterranean cuisine.

Behrenstrasse 37, 10117 Berlin. www.roccofortecollection.com. © **888/667-9477** in the U.S., or 00800/76666667 in the U.K. Fax 030/460609. 146 units. 395€–495€ double; 595€ junior suite; from 700€ suite. AE, DC, MC, V. Parking 20€. U-Bahn: Französische Strasse. **Amenities:** Restaurant; bar; babysitting; children's programs; concierge; health club and spa; indoor heated pool; room service; Wi-Fi (free; in lobby). *In room:* A/C, TV, hair dryer, minibar.

The Regent ★★★ Ranking right up there with the Adlon, this is one of the most elegant and tranquil hotels in Berlin, a citadel of luxury and fine living. The location is near the Gendarmenmarkt in the heart of Berlin Mitte, near Unter den Linen and Friedrichstrasse. The spacious bedrooms, done in harmonious colors and fabrics, are oases of style, comfort, and charm, with many luxurious touches, including marble-clad bathrooms and deep soaking bathtubs and walk-in showers. Many of the rooms open onto a quiet inner courtyard. The bar is idyllic for drinks, a light meal, or after-noon tea, and the Fischers Fritz restaurant is separately recommended (p. 110).

Charlottenstrasse 49, Berlin 01017. www.theregentberlin.com. © **888/201-1806** in the U.S., or 030/20338. Fax 030/20336119. 195 units. 235€–380€ double; from 425€ suite. Rates include breakfast. AE, DC, MC, V. Parking 28€. U-Bahn: Französische Strasse. **Amenities:** Restaurant; bar; babysitting; concierge; health club and spa; room service; Wi-Fi (free; in lobby). *In room:* A/C, TV, DVD player (in some), fax (in some), hair dryer, minibar.

The Ritz-Carlton ★★★ ☺ One of Berlin's most glamorous and prestigious hotels opened at the Potsdamer Platz. The building evokes the Art Nouveau heyday of New York skyscrapers constructed in the 1920s. The club-level rooms and the suites, of course, are the most luxurious way to stay here, but even the standard guest rooms are luxuriously furnished and decorated. The hotel is full of grace notes, such as afternoon tea served in the lobby lounge by an open fireplace; live jazz or blues in the hotel bar, the Curtain Club; and an indoor pool. The dining facilities are among the finest in town, featuring a creative European cuisine, with lots of Italian influences.

Potsdamer Platz 3, 10785 Berlin. www.ritzcarlton.com. © **800/241-3333** in the U.S., or 030/337777. Fax 030/7775555. 302 units. 265€–365€ double; 355€–455€ junior suite; from 435€ suite. AE, DC, MC, V. Parking 28€. U-Bahn: Potsdamer Platz. **Amenities:** 3 restaurants; bar; babysitting; children's programs; concierge; exercise room; indoor heated pool; room service; spa. *In room:* A/C, TV, CD player, hair dryer, minibar, Wi-Fi (20€ per day).

Westin Grand Hotel ★★★ A monument to "capitalistic decadence," as they used to say during the Cold War era, amazingly, this hotel was constructed on socialist soil by the East German government. Now under management by the Westin group and devoid of its original sense of stiffness, it's one of Berlin's finest hotels. Belle Epoque features blend with contemporary styling. Guest rooms come in a wide range of styles, from beautifully appointed standard doubles all the way up to the lush-looking Schinkel Suite. Rooms contain beds with wonderfully soft linens, down pillows, and comforters, as well as terry-cloth robes, and fresh flowers.

Friedrichstrasse 158-164, 10117 Berlin. www.westin.com/berlin. © **888/625-5144** in the U.S., or 030/20270. Fax 030/20273362. 400 units. 189€–430€ double; 339€–560€ junior suite; from 489€ apt. suite. AE, DC, MC, V. Parking 26€. U-Bahn: Französische Strasse. S-Bahn: Friedrichstrasse. **Amenities:** 3

restaurants; bar; babysitting; concierge; state-of-the-art health club and spa; indoor heated pool; room service. *In room:* A/C, TV, hair dryer, minibar, Wi-Fi (18€ per day).

EXPENSIVE

Alexander Plaza ★   A short walk from both Alexanderplatz and the historic district of Hackescher Höfe, this hotel originated in 1897 as an office building. In 1997, it was converted into one of the neighborhood's most charming and best-managed hotels. A labyrinth of hallways opens into rooms with unique floor plans. Each has parquet floors, high ceilings, and neo-Biedermeier blond-wood furniture. The executive rooms are very large. Low-end rooms are smaller and less dramatic, but still very comfortable. The staff here is among the most attentive in Berlin.

Rosenstrasse 1, 10178 Berlin. www.hotel-alexander-plaza.de. *©* **800/223-5652** for reservations in the U.S. and Canada, or 030/240010. Fax 030/24001777. 92 units. 125€–235€ double; 175€–330€ suite. AE, DC, MC, V. Parking 15€. S-Bahn: Hackescher Markt. **Amenities:** Restaurant; bar; babysitting; concierge; exercise room; room service; sauna. *In room:* A/C, TV, fax, hair dryer, minibar, Wi-Fi (13€ per day).

Arcotel Velvet ★ 🛍   With its Andy Warhol–inspired decor, this hotel stands in what used to be a Cold War no man's land. Enveloped by a vibrant artist and designer scene, the hotel lies right in the midst of some of Mitte's hippest cafes, bars, and restaurants. Its glass facade conceals a comfortably modern hotel that employs minimalist design and innovative concepts in its use of modern equipment, soft furnishings, and tasteful materials. All the beautifully designed bedrooms are stylish and inviting. The on-site restaurant, Lutter & Wegner, is run by Joe Laggner, a legendary star of Austrian innkeeping, and he serves a sublime regional cuisine. That's not all: The Velvet Bar is as hip as Lady Gaga and is a Mitte hot spot, known for its to-die-for cocktails.

Oranienburger Strasse 52, 10117 Berlin. www.arcotel.at. *©* **030/2787530.** Fax 030/278753800. 85 units. 95€–230€ double. AE, DC, MC, V. Parking 18€. S-Bahn: Oranienburger Strasse. **Amenities:** Restaurant; bar; babysitting; bikes; room service. *In room:* A/C, TV/DVD, CD player, hair dryer, minibar, Wi-Fi (20€ per day).

The Mandala Hotel ★   Built in 1999, this 11-story establishment is one of the most posh and elegant hotels in the pivotal Potsdamer Platz neighborhood. The hotel's exterior is sheathed in steel and warmly textured Italian brick. Each of the units inside is configured as a suite and is upholstered in discreetly plush fabrics, decorated with top-of-the-line stone, tile, or marble, and ringed with big windows that flood the postmodern interiors with sunlight. The upper levels, including the lounge, Qiu, one floor above lobby level, are spacious and opulent, in vivid contrast to the discreet and understated scale of the reception area. One of this hotel's most charming features is its fifth-floor restaurant, **FACIL** (p. 111).

Potsdamer Strasse 3, 10785 Berlin. www.themandala.de. *©* **030/590050000.** Fax 030/590050500. 167 units. 170€–400€ standard suite; from 1,700€–3,800€ deluxe suite. AE, DC, MC, V. Parking 20€. U-Bahn: Potsdamer Platz. **Amenities:** Restaurant; bar; babysitting; bikes; concierge; exercise room; room service; spa. *In room:* A/C, TV/DVD, hair dryer, minibar, Wi-Fi (10€ per day).

Maritim ProArte ★   This is a more luxe version of Art'otel (p. 139). Set about a block from Unter den Linden, this hotel was built as an avant-garde architectural showcase in the mid-1970s by the then–East German government. Today, despite frequent renovations, it still evokes a jazzy, *Moderno,* and vaguely dated kind of architecture that features lots of chrome and stainless steel. There's a bustle here, however, thanks in part to a hardworking and polite staff, and a regular clientele of business clients and conventioneers. Avant-garde artwork is exhibited throughout, and Philippe Starck created some of the furniture. Rooms are individually designed, soothing, uncluttered, and comfortable.

Friedrichstrasse 151 (across from Friedrichstrasse station), 10117 Berlin. www.maritim.de. ☎ **030/20335.** Fax 030/20334090. 403 units. 154€–312€ double; from 254€ suite. AE, DC, MC, V. Parking 21€. S-Bahn: Friedrichstrasse. **Amenities:** 3 restaurants; bar; babysitting; bikes; concierge; exercise room; indoor heated pool; room service; sauna. *In room:* A/C, TV, hair dryer, minibar, Wi-Fi (15€ per day).

Meliá Berlin ★★   This deluxe hotel is the first Meliá hotel that the Spanish chain has opened in Berlin. It sits along the River Spree and opens onto splendid views. Since its opening, it has become a celebrity favorite. Within easy reach of all the major attractions, it is ideal for the vacationer or the business traveler. Spacious guest rooms are decorated in welcoming colors and contemporary wooden furnishings. The outward-facing rooms are soundproof. All rooms have access to the Executive Club on the seventh floor. In honor of its Spanish heritage, the hotel serves some of the best tapas in Berlin.

Friedrichstrasse 103, 10117 Berlin. www.meliaberlin.com. ☎ **030/20607900.** Fax 030/2060790444. 364 units. 177€–212€ double; 257€ junior suite; 850€ suite. Rates include buffet breakfast. AE, DC, MC, V. Parking 20€. U-Bahn: Friedrichstrasse. **Amenities:** Restaurant; bar; babysitting; concierge; exercise room; room service. *In room:* A/C, TV, hair dryer, minibar, Wi-Fi (22€ per day).

MODERATE

Arte Luise Kunsthotel ★ 🏛   This hotel boasts that it is a "home for artists." No, it's not a communal crash pad for the bohemian fringe, but a select boutique hotel where a different German artist designed and individually furnished each of the guest rooms. Under historic preservation, the hotel is in a restored 1825 city palace. Clients from the arts, media, and even the political or business world are drawn to this unusual hostelry. Each room comes as a total surprise, and, of course, you're treated to some of each artist's work, which runs the gamut from Andy Warhol–like pop to classicism. Some units evoke modern minimalism, whereas others are much more quirky.

Luisenstrasse 19, 10119 Berlin. www.luise-berlin.com. ☎ **030/284480.** Fax 030/28448448. 46 units, 29 with bathroom. 79€–110€ double without bathroom; 99€–210€ double with bathroom; 130€–240€ suite. AE, DC, MC, V. Parking 15€. U-Bahn: Friedrichstrasse. **Amenities:** Restaurant. *In room:* A/C (in some), TV, minibar (in suites), Wi-Fi (free).

Hotel Honigmond ★ 🏛   A romantic retreat today, ideal for honeymooners, this boutique hotel in a restored building from 1899 was once a retreat for East German opposition leaders. As such, it was often closed by the dreaded Stasi. The sad history of the repression of East Germany has been wiped away without a trace. Today, guests are coddled in comfort in individually furnished rooms with ornate stucco ceilings, wood floors, and even bed linen designed by Paloma Picasso. The hotel lobby is filled with oil paintings, and a half dozen caged rabbits nibble away contentedly in the inner courtyard. In the cozy restaurant, with its wooden tables and candles, you can relish old-fashioned treats that the Kaiser enjoyed, including Königsberg Klopse and Bohemian dumplings.

Tieckstrasse 12, 10115 Berlin. www.honigmond-berlin.de. ☎ **030/2844550.** 44 units. 145€–235€ double. MC, V. U-Bahn: Oranienburger Tor. **Amenities:** Restaurant; bar; room service. *In room:* A/C, TV, hair dryer, Internet (free), minibar.

Hotel Luisenhof ★   This is one of the most desirable small hotels in eastern Berlin. It lies within a severely dignified house, built in 1822. Its five floors of high-ceilinged rooms have been outfitted in a conservative and traditional style, a welcome escape from modern Berlin. The upgraded units range in size from small to spacious, but all are equipped with fine beds and individual fax machines. The neighborhood around this hotel, like many other parts of the once-dour eastern zone, is undergoing a rapid renovation.

Köpenicker Strasse 92, 10179 Berlin. ☎ **030/2462810.** Fax 030/24628160. 27 units. 120€–299€ double; 249€–399€ suite. Rates include buffet breakfast. AE, DC, MC, V. Parking 10€. U-Bahn: Märkisches

Museum. **Amenities:** Restaurant, bar; babysitting; concierge; room service. *In room:* TV, DVD (in suites), CD player, hair dryer, minibar.

Hotel MitArt ✦ This was Berlin's first organic hotel. The staff takes the eco credo seriously—100% of its raw materials are certified organic, not only in the food products—primarily local—but even in all cleaning liquids. Energy and water are used in a sustainable fashion, which is to say sparingly. Two floors of the hotel are smoke free. In addition, the designer of the hotel had a certain artistic flair. All of its bedrooms have been individually designed and present rotating exhibits of paintings and photography by international artists. Be prepared to get along without those energy-burning amenities in your room.

Linienstrasse 139–140, 10115 Berlin. www.mitart.de. ✆ **030/28390430.** 28 units. 110€–180€ double. MC, V. U-Bahn or S-Bahn: Oranienburger. **Amenities:** Cafe; Wi-Fi (free).

Lux 11 ★ ⛺ In the hip central Mitte district, among fashionable art galleries and trendy media firms, this is an oasis of charm, comfort, and style. In a chic minimalist style, its bedrooms occupy a monolithic space, with a modern, glamorous decor. The open bathrooms are furnished in honey-colored wood and concrete. Lux 11 is the latest creation from that dynamic minimalist duo Claudio Silvestrin and his wife, Giuliana Salmaso. In the basement is the Aveda Spa, and there's even a "micro" department store operated by a former buyer for Quartier 206, a posh fashion emporium in Berlin.

Rosa-Luxemburg-Strasse 9–13, 10178 Berlin. www.designhotels.com. ✆ **030/9362800.** 72 units. 149€–205€ double; 230€–295€ suite. AE, MC, V. Parking 20€. U-Bahn: Weinmeisterstrasse. **Amenities:** Restaurant; bar; babysitting; exercise room; room service; spa. *In room:* A/C, TV/DVD, fax, hair dryer, kitchenette, Wi-Fi (4€ per hour).

Mövenpick Hotel Berlin ★ ✦ East of Berlin Mitte, a 19th-century Siemen's office building that more or less survived Allied World War II bombings has been converted into a trendy, modern hotel with a starkly chic design, including Eero Saarinen-esque chairs. Opaque glass walls separate the bedroom from the spacious bathroom, which sometimes contains a quirky free-standing tub. The clientele blends German hipsters with American college kids and budget-conscious families. The onsite and space-agey Anhalter Bar at the front entrance attracts Berlin youth who live in the area. A massive breakfast buffet is served in an airy, piazza-like dining room.

Schoneberger Strasse 3, 10963 Berlin. www.moevenpick-berlin.com. ✆ **030/230060.** Fax 030/23006199. 243 units. 104€ double; 144€ junior suite; 209€ suite. AE, MC, V. S-Bahn: Anhalter Bahnhof. **Amenities:** Restaurant; bar; babysitting; exercise room; room service. *In room:* A/C, TV, hair dryer, minibar, Wi-Fi (free).

Myer's Hotel Berlin ✦ Spared from the 1945 bombings, this classical building from the 19th century has been renovated and turned into a good-value hotel that is comfortable, well maintained, and immaculate. Nostalgia and charm are combined with modern amenities. Guest rooms, midsize to spacious, come with a well-appointed bathroom with the latest fixtures, including tub and shower. The hotel offers several charming features, including a lobby bar with parquet flooring and chairs and tables that look as if they came from old Havana. Drinks are also served on the garden roof terrace.

Metzer Strasse 26, 10405 Berlin. www.myershotel.de. ✆ **030/440140.** Fax 030/44014104. 135€–189€ double; 210€–345€ suite. Rates include buffet breakfast. AE, MC, V. Free parking. U-Bahn: Senefelderplatz. Bus: 143. **Amenities:** Bar. *In room:* TV, hair dryer, minibar, Wi-Fi (15€ per day).

INEXPENSIVE

Circus Hotel ✦ This is the greenest hotel and the hippest, attracting a youth-oriented clientele intent on saving the planet. Among its many features, all papers used are recycled, some 80% of the lamps are fitted with energy-saving bulbs, and all waste is separated for recycling. There's no A/C, as the owners believe it is an unnecessary burning of resources. The well-designed bedrooms have blue, tangerine, lime, or hot-pink accents, and all have dark oak floors along with vintage flea market accessories. The staff loads iPods with the best of Berlin music, there is bike and Segway rental, and the garden courtyard is a great place to unwind. In the Fabish Restaurant, local products are featured, and you can also sip cocktails a la Sally Bowles. Across the street is a hostel of the same name, Weinbergsweg 1A (☎ **030/20003939**), offering 16 simple bedrooms, costing 19€ to 25€ if shared, 28€ in a double, and 43€ in a single. In a double with bathroom, the rate is 70€ to 85€.

Rosenthalerstrasse 1, 10119 Berlin. www.circus-berlin.de. ☎ **030/20003939**. 60 units. 80€–90€ double; 100€ junior suite; 110€ 2-room apt.; 160€ 3-room apt. MC, V. U-Bahn: Rosenthaler Platz. **Amenities:** Restaurant; bar; bike rentals. *In room:* Wi-Fi (free).

In Charlottenburg
MODERATE

Propeller Island City Lodge ★ 🏨   Associated with a record producer and songwriting studio (Propeller Island GmbH), this hotel occupies three high-ceilinged floors of an old-fashioned apartment house originally built in the 1880s. Each of the guest rooms is radically different in its decor and theme, and each may delight or appall you with its quirks. Therapie is an all-white, minimalist room whose mood changes with the color of the lighting, which you can adjust at will. Flying Bed places a mattress as an iconic temple at the top of an inclined ramp, giving your bed a cultish importance. And the room known as Galerie features a round bed, a pedal-operated mechanism that can spin the bed on a pivot, and empty picture frames wherein you can superimpose your fantasies. Weirdest of all is the Coffin Room, where those of a macabre bent can sleep in either of two (well-ventilated) closed coffins for a night of Gothic pensiveness . . . or whatever.

Note: This hotel's eccentricities (think installation art/sleeping quarters) means room types simply do not fit into traditional single, double, or suite categories; in some units, multiple guests can stay in the same rooms, or units can be connected and feature access to shared or private kitchen and bathroom facilities. Call or visit the website for details on each room's configuration and sleeping situation.

Albrecht-Achilles-Strasse 58, Charlottenburg, 10709 Berlin. www.propeller-island.de. ☎ **030/8919016** (daily 8am–noon), or 0163/2565909 (all other hours). Fax 030/8928721. 30 units, 24 with bathroom. Rooms 80€–220€ per person. Each additional person 18€ per night. DC, MC, V. U-Bahn: Adenauerplatz. *In room:* No phone.

Villa Kastania ★ 🏨   Surrounded by chestnut trees, this is a snug retreat in the Westend. A small and independently run hotel near the Berlin Exhibition, it is like staying in a villa, filled with fine fabrics, natural stone, and artworks. The spacious rooms are imbued with charm and comfort. Depending on the price you want to pay, you can book a functional yet comfortably furnished bedroom, or one of the "Comfort Rooms," with better amenities such as larger bathrooms, balconies, and more storage space. Those who want to live more luxuriously can book one of the deluxe suites, including the elegant Venetian Room. The restaurant Marron has a drinking lounge, fireplace, and romantic garden terrace; an on-site Mediterranean health spa comes with pool, Roman sauna, and sun deck.

Kastanienallee 20, 14052 Berlin. www.villakastania.com. ☎ **030/30000020**. Fax 030/30000210. 47 units. 77€–197€ double; 107€–207€ suite. AE, MC, V. U-Bahn: Theodor-Heuss-Platz. **Amenities:** Restaurant; bar; room service; sauna; spa. *In room:* A/C, TV, hair dryer, minibar, Wi-Fi (free).

In Prenzlauer

MODERATE

Ackselhaus Blue Home ★ 🦢 A majestic building from the 1800s has been restored and turned into a bastion of elegance and affordability. Although completely modernized, the hotel presents a design backdrop of the colonial era and a touch of Balinese romance. A harmonious decor prevails in the midsize to spacious bedrooms, which are bastions of comfort featuring supersize bathtubs. The stylish breakfast cafe, **Club del Mar,** opens onto a tree-lined street in the Prenzlauer Berg neighborhood.

Belforter Strasse 21, 10405 Berlin. www.ackselhaus.de. ✆ **030/44337633.** Fax 030/44312603. 35 units. 110€–170€ double; 180€–250€ studio apt. MC, V. Free parking. U-Bahn: Senefelderplatz. **Amenities:** Bar; room service. *In room:* A/C, TV, hair dryer.

A SIDE TRIP: POTSDAM & ITS PALACES ★★★

24km (15 miles) SW of Berlin, 140km (87 miles) NE of Leipzig

The best day trip from Berlin is to the baroque town of Potsdam on the Havel River. It's often been called Germany's Versailles. World attention focused on Potsdam July 17 to August 2, 1945, when the Potsdam Conference helped shape postwar Europe. The town has many historic sights and was beautifully planned, with large parks and a beautiful chain of lakes formed by the river. The palaces and gardens of **Sanssouci Park,** which lies to the west of Potsdam's historic core, are the major attractions here. A mile northeast of Sanssouci is the **Neuer Garten** on the Heiliger See, which contains the **Schloss Cecilienhof.**

Essentials

GETTING THERE   By Train   Potsdam Hauptbahnhof is on the major Deutsche Bundesbahn rail lines, with 29 daily connections to the rail stations in Berlin (23 min. to Bahnhof Zoo and 54 min. to Ostbahnhof). There are also 14 trains daily to and from Hannover (3–3½ hr.), and 15 daily trains to and from Nürnberg (6–6½ hr.). For rail information and schedules, call ✆ **01805/996633** or visit www.bahn.de.

Potsdam can also be reached by S-Bahn lines S1 and S7 from Berlin, connecting at Wannsee station with lines R1, R3, and R4. Travel time on these lines from Berlin to Potsdam is 30 minutes. For more information, call **BVG Berlin** (✆ **030/19449;** www.bvg.de).

By Bus   Verkehrsverbund Potsdam provides regional bus service with frequent connections between Berlin and Potsdam at Wannsee station (bus no. 118) in Berlin. For travel information and schedules, call **BVG Berlin** (✆ **030/19449;** www.bvg.de).

By Car Access is via the E30 Autobahn east and west or the E53 north and south. Allow about 30 minutes to drive here from Berlin.

VISITOR INFORMATION Contact **Potsdam-Information,** Brandenburger-strasse 3 (✆ **0331/275580;** www.potsdam-tourism.com), open April to October Monday to Friday 9:30am to 6pm, and Saturday and Sunday 9:30am to 4pm; from November to March, hours are Monday to Friday 10am to 6pm, Saturday and Sunday 9:30am to 2pm.

GETTING AROUND   By Public Transportation Ask at the tourist office about a **Potsdam Card.** With the card, you can ride on the city's public transportation system at a discount. The card is available for 2 days for 9.60€ or 3 days for 12€. In Potsdam, **bus no. 695,** leaving from the rail station, will deliver you to the Potsdam palaces.

By Boat   Because the area around Potsdam is surrounded by water, boat tours in fair weather are a popular diversion. For more information, call or visit the website of **Weisse Flotte Potsdam** (✆ **0331/2759210;** www.schiffahrt-in-potsdam.de).

Exploring the Parks & Palaces

A British air raid on April 14, 1945, destroyed much of the old city center, but the major attraction, Sanssouci Park and its palaces, survived.

Neuer Garten GARDEN   On Heiliger See (Holy Lake), in the northern part of Potsdam, lies the Neuer Garten. The nephew and successor to Friedrich the Great, Friedrich Wilhelm II, had these gardens laid out. Set between the park and the palace, this lovely baroque garden is well maintained, and it's a delight to take a walk into it, enjoying the flower beds, the well-trimmed hedges and arbors, and the fountains in decorated basins. The tract of land was walled in during the 18th century so that the king and his consort could walk in peace without "peeping Toms" intruding on their privacy.

On Heiliger See, about 2km (1¼ miles) northwest of Sanssouci. ✆ **0331/9694200.** Free admission. Same hours as Sanssouci (see below). Bus: 695.

Sanssouci Palace ★★★ HISTORIC BUILDING   Sanssouci Park, with its palaces and gardens, was the work of many architects and sculptors. The park covers an area of about 1.6 sq. km (⅔ sq. mile). Its premier attraction is the palace of Friedrich II ("the Great"), **Sanssouci,** meaning "free from care." Friedrich was one of the most liberal and farsighted of the Prussian monarchs. He was a great general, but he liked best to think of himself as an enlightened patron of the arts. Here he could get away from his duties, indulge his intellectual interests, and entertain his friend Voltaire. The style of the buildings he had constructed is called "Potsdam rococo" and is primarily the achievement of Georg Wenzeslaus von Knobelsdorff.

Sanssouci Palace (✆ **0331/9694200**), with its terraces and gardens, was inaugurated in 1747. The long, one-story building is crowned by a dome and flanked by two round pavilions. The elliptically shaped Marble Hall is the largest in the palace, but the music salon is the supreme example of the rococo style. A small bust of Voltaire commemorates Voltaire's sojourns here. Sanssouci Palace can be visited only with a guide. *Tip:* It is best (especially in summer) to show up before noon to buy your tickets for the palace tour. At busy times, all the slots for the rest of the day can be completely filled by noon. The palace is open April to October Tuesday to Sunday 10am to 6pm, and November to March Tuesday to Sunday 10am to 5pm. Guided tours (in English) of the palace cost 8€ to 12€ for adults, 5€ to 8€ for students and children 6 to 18, free for children 5 and under.

Bildergalerie (Picture Gallery), Östlicher Lustgarten (✆ **0331/9694181**), was built between 1755 and 1763. Its facade is similar to that of Sanssouci Palace, and the interior is one of the most flamboyant in Germany. The collection of some 125 paintings features works by Italian Renaissance and baroque artists along with Dutch and Flemish masters. Concerts of the Potsdam Park Festival take place here. The Bildergalerie is open May to October Tuesday through Sunday from 10am to 6pm. The Bildergalerie can be visited with or without a guide, and the crush of visitors here is nowhere near as intense as at Sanssouci Palace. Entrance without a guided tour costs 3€ for adults, 2.50€ for students and children 8 to 18, and free for children 7 and under. Guided tours are available only for groups and by appointment.

West of the palace is the **Orangerie** (© **0331/9694280**), built between 1851 and 1864. It was based on Italian Renaissance designs. Its purpose was to shelter southern plants during the cold months. In the central core is the Raphael Hall, which holds 47 copies of that master's paintings. In addition, you can visit five lavishly decorated salons. The Orangerie is open May 15 to October 15 Tuesday through Sunday from 10am to 5pm. The Orangerie must be visited with a guide. Though not as severe a situation of overcrowding as you'll find at Sanssouci Palace, you should still try to get your tickets before noon, especially in midsummer. Guided tours cost 4€ for adults, 3€ for students and children 8 to 18, and free for children 7 and under.

The largest building in the park is the extravagant **Neues Palais** (© **0331/ 9694361**), built between 1763 and 1769, at the end of the Seven Years' War. Crowning the center is a dome. The rococo rooms, filled with paintings and antiques, were used by the royal family. The most notable chamber is the Hall of Shells, with its fossils and semiprecious stones. At the palace theater, concerts take place every year

April to November. Neues Palais must be visited with a guide, costing 6€ for adults, 5€ for children 8 to 18, and free for children 7 and under.

Zur historischen Mühle. ℂ **0331/9694200.** www.spsg.de. Apr–Oct Tues–Sun 10am–6pm; Nov–Mar Tues–Sun 10am–5pm. Bus: 695 or X15.

Schloss Cecilienhof HISTORIC BUILDING   This palace was completed in the style of an English country house. Kaiser Wilhelm II had it built between 1913 and 1917 for Crown Prince Wilhelm. The palace was occupied as a royal residence until March 1945, when the crown prince and his family fled to the West. In addition to the regular guided tour, offered in summer, there's a tour of the private rooms of Crown Prince Wilhelm and Princess Cecilie on the upper story. The tour takes place at 11am and 2pm. Note that you can lunch and spend the night here, if you wish.

Cecilienhof was the headquarters of the 1945 Potsdam Conference, attended by the heads of the Allied powers, including Truman, Stalin, and Churchill. You can visit the studies of the various delegations and see the large round table, made in Moscow, where the actual agreement was signed. In winter you have to take a guided tour; in summer you can go with a guide or wander about on your own.

In Neuer Garten. ℂ **0331/9694244.** www.spsg.de. Admission (with tour included) 6€, 5€ students, free for children 5 and under. The palace can be visited in summer without a guide for 5€ adults, 4€ students, free for children 5 and under. Apr–Oct Tues–Sun 10am–6pm; Nov–Mar Tues–Sun 10am–5pm. Bus: 692.

Schloss Charlottenhof ★ HISTORIC BUILDING   This palace was built between 1826 and 1829 by Karl Friedrich Schinkel, Germany's greatest master of neoclassical architecture. He also designed most of the furniture inside. The nearby **Roman Baths** are on the north of the artificial lake known as Maschinenteich (Machine Pond). These baths, constructed between 1829 and 1835, were built strictly for the nostalgic love of antiquity and have no practical purpose.

South of Okonomieweg. ℂ **0331/9694228.** www.spsg.de. Admission 4€ adults, 3€ for children 17 and under. May–Oct Tues–Sun 10am–6pm. Closed Nov–Apr. Tram: 91.

Where to Eat

Friedrich-Wilhelm ★★★ GERMAN/INTERNATIONAL   The finest restaurant to open since before World War II is also romantically scenic and tranquil, in addition to serving the city's finest gourmet cuisine. In winter a fireplace blazes, with summer guests retreating to an open-air terrace to enjoy the breezes. The cuisine is market fresh, creative, and wonderfully delicate, though you pay a lot for what you get. Even though operating in an inland city, the chefs seem to obtain remarkably fresh-tasting fish such as sea bass or halibut. The menu frequently changes so we can't recommend any specialties, but the chefs seem skilled at all they turn out, especially if inspired by the Mediterranean kitchen. Perhaps you'll sample such delights as sturgeon, goose liver, breast of pigeon, or lobster.

In the Hotel Bayrisches Haus, Im Wildpark 1. ℂ **0331/55050.** Reservations required. Main courses 28€–42€; fixed-price menus 58€–85€. AE, DC, MC, V. Tues–Sat 6–10pm. Located 6km (4 miles) southwest of Potsdam.

Specker's Gaststätte zur Ratswaag ★★ CONTINENTAL   One of Potsdam's most prestigious and sought-after restaurants happens to be one of its oldest, within a thick-walled country-baroque building set midway between Potsdam's railway

Sanssouci Palace

A Friedenskirche
B Neptungrotte
C Historische Mühle
D Drachenhaus
E Belvedere
F Antikentempel
G Freundschaftstempel
H Schloss Charlottenhof
I Römische Bäder
J Chinesisches Haus

station and its historic core. The clients who file in here for the inventive cuisine of Chef Gottfried Specker tend to be deeply involved in the whirlwinds swirling around whatever political event happens to be gripping Germany at the time of your visit. Within a decor noted for thick walls, rich paneling, and mementos that evoke the glory days of Prussia, you'll dine on cuisine that changes with the seasons, the availability of local ingredients, and the inspiration of the chef. As such, it's likely to change at intervals of every 10 to 14 days. Expect a celebration of whatever's fresh (asparagus, strawberries, game, and some kinds of fish are good examples) and ongoing specialties that include, among others, a terrine of wild mushrooms and goose liver; medallions of sea wolf in a Riesling-flavored foie gras sauce; a clear oxtail soup, loaded with flavor and garnished with spinach leaves; cream of wild mushroom soup; poached crayfish on a bed of black (squid-ink-flavored) risotto; and breast of guinea fowl with a mango-flavored cream sauce.

Jägerallee 13. ✆ **0331/2804311.** www.speckers.de. Reservations recommended. Main courses 16€–35€; fixed-price menu 30€. AE, MC, V. Tues–Sat noon–2pm and 6–11pm. S-Bahn: Potsdam Hauptbahnhof.

Where to Stay

Hotel Bayrisches Haus ★★★ 🗖 The most tranquil and luxurious retreat in Potsdam today lies just a 15-minute drive from the center. In 1847, King Friedrich Wilhelm ordered the construction of this Bavarian-style chalet in a forest. Miraculously spared from the ravages of war, it has been successfully converted into an exceedingly comfortable residence of charm and grace. With its elegant atmosphere, it is the only luxury hotel in Potsdam and the only one that's rated five stars by the government. The spacious guest rooms are studies in design, comfort, and luxury. From the fireplace in winter to the panoramic terrace in summer, this is the way to live in Potsdam if you can afford it.

Im Wildpark 1, 14471 Potsdam. www.bayrisches-haus.de. ✆ **800/735-2428** in the U.S., or 0331/55050. Fax 0331/5505560. 33 units. 155€–230€ double; 230€–450€ suite. Rates include buffet breakfast. AE, DC, MC, V. Free parking. 6km (4 miles) southwest of Potsdam; take Zeppelinstrasse from the center. **Amenities:** Restaurant; bar; babysitting; concierge; exercise room; indoor heated pool; room service; spa. *In room:* TV, hair dryer, minibar, Wi-Fi (free).

NH Hotel Voltaire ★★★ This hotel is a radical renovation of the Brühlsche Palace, formerly a dour and crumbling relic built in 1732. Only the palace's baroque facade has been retained. The site belongs to the NH chain. Rooms are scattered over three floors and, in almost every case, overlook the quiet, pleasant garden in back. The rooms here are far better furnished and more elegantly appointed than those within its closest rival, Schlosshotel Cecilienhof (see below), although the latter has a richer history. The decor, in fact, is so sophisticated here that the Voltaire accurately labels itself as "a designer hotel." Some of the accommodations are large enough to be used as triples, with each guest having enough room to move about. Many families book suites here, although some of the regular rooms are large enough to accommodate extra beds. An added feature is the roof terrace, where you're treated to a panoramic view over Potsdam.

Friedrich-Ebert-Strasse 88, 14467 Potsdam. www.nh-hotels.com. ✆ **0331/23170.** Fax 0331/2317100. 143 units. 73€–143€ double; from 105€ suite. AE, DC, MC, V. Free parking. Tram: 92. **Amenities:** Restaurant; 2 bars; babysitting; bikes; concierge; exercise room; Jacuzzi; room service; sauna; Wi-Fi (free; in lobby). *In room:* TV, hair dryer, minibar.

Relexa Schlosshotel Cecilienhof ★★ 🗖 Many visitors to Potsdam don't realize that they can stay in the palace where Truman and Churchill met Stalin during the 1945 Potsdam Conference. The hotel is better located than any other in Potsdam, or Berlin for that matter, standing in the famous Neuer Garten, bordering a lake about a 15-minute stroll from Sanssouci. The German government originally converted a residential wing of this former royal residence into one of the most charming country hotels and retreats in eastern Germany. Guest rooms are midsize to spacious and are traditionally furnished and well maintained.

Neuer Garten, Potsdam 14469. www.relexa-hotels.de. ✆ **0331/37050.** Fax 0331/3705221. 41 units. 90€–201€ double; from 211€ suite. AE, DC, MC, V. Parking 8€. **Amenities:** Restaurant; bikes; room service; sauna; Wi-Fi (free; in lobby). *In room:* TV, hair dryer, minibar.

Steigenberger Maxx Hotel Sanssouci Potsdam ★ 🗖 Not your typical businessperson's chain hotel, this is more of a boutique-type establishment, with its terrace opening onto the park and palace of Sanssouci. Many guests prefer to stay in Potsdam during their Berlin visit because of the easy commute. You're given free transportation for your commute between the two cities. Like another hotel in Berlin (Hollywood Media, p. 137), the Maxx leans heavily on movie theme rooms, using stills, props, and photos from old Hollywood or else from the nearby Babelsberg studio where German films were made in the heyday of UFA, which produced them. The designers wanted to re-create a British- or American-style hotel from the 1930s and 1950s. In elegant, tasteful, and comfortable surroundings, the guest rooms are midsize to spacious and decorated in dark wood and earthy tones, with cane furniture.

Allee nach Sanssouci 1, 14471 Potsdam. www.steigenberger.de. (℃ **0331/90910.** Fax 0331/9091909. 137 units. 83€–135€ double; 150€–184€ suite. AE, MC, V. Parking 15€. Tram: 96. Bus: 606 or 631. **Amenities:** 2 restaurants; bar; babysitting; bikes; spa; Wi-Fi (free; in lobby). *In room:* TV, ceiling fan, hair dryer, minibar.

SAXONY & THURINGIA

Traveling in regions of the former East Germany is a fulfilling experience. Once difficult to visit, famous cities have been beautifully revived and are inviting and less touristy than some of the picturesque towns in southern Germany. Notable examples include Dresden, destroyed during World War II and poignantly restored, at least in part; Leipzig, where Johann Sebastian Bach spent most of his musical life as cantor (choirmaster) of St. Thomas Church; Meissen, famous for exquisite porcelain; and Weimar, glowing from its recent designation as a European City of Culture. In addition, unspoiled scenery and medieval towns such as Quedlinburg invite you to wander off the beaten track.

5

Since reunification, many visitors have come from around the world to explore the political landscape and to honor the memory of the intellectual giants who once made eastern Germany their home—Goethe, Luther, Bach, Schiller, and Brecht, among others. Hotels are being built, tourist facilities are being developed, and getting around eastern Germany is easier than ever. Some 1,600km (1,000 miles) of autobahns and about 11,000km (7,000 miles) of secondary highways cut across the region.

But travelers should be aware that the economy is weaker than in western Germany, and eastern Germany is still a region in transition. The best guess is that it will take 10 to 15 more years before eastern Germany's infrastructure is comparable to western Germany's. The upside of this is that you'll find some of Germany's most unspoiled countryside and untouched villages, where rural traditions that have disappeared from most of western Europe still linger. Outside Dresden or Leipzig, you can still see many old towns that have not succumbed to the Americanization you can find in most of western Germany. Drenched in history and medieval legend, the towns of Weimar and Wittenberg, home to Goethe and Martin Luther, give you a view of Germany that has been swept away in the more modern parts of the country. A visit can provide you with unforgettable new experiences and stories to tell your grandchildren.

WEIMAR ★★

260km (162 miles) SW of Berlin, 22km (14 miles) E of Erfurt

Weimar, a beautiful 1,000-year-old town on the edge of the Thuringian Forest, is an important destination for those interested in German history and culture. Unlike many cities in the former East Germany, Weimar

Saxony & Thuringia

GERMANY

Hamburg

Berlin ★

Frankfurt am Main

Munich

Area of detail

Hamburg

Eberswalde

POLAND

107

5

167

A11

E55

A24

102

5

273

A10

E55

BERLIN

Brandenburg

Potsdam

E51

A115

A10

E30

A10

A12

E55

189

A2

E30

2

A13

87

A2

Magdeburg

A9

102

Lübben

E51

Lübbenau

Elbe River

Wittenberg

A15

81

71

187

Dessau

Quedlinburg

6

2

87

Eisleben

Halle

101

A13

80

6

97

A4

91

A9

Leipzig

A14

Meissen

4

93

A4

Dresden

88

Dornburg

Altenburg

E40

173

E55

Buchenwald

Weimar

Chemnitz

Erfurt

A4

E40

Jena

A4

2

174

To Eisenach

Arnstadt

A9

E441

A72

Thüringer Wald

Plauen

E442

4

E49

Karlovy Vary

Hof

E49

6

Coburg

E48

CZECH

279

E51

REPUBLIC

27

A70

E48

21

E49

E50

Bayreuth

Bamberg

A9

22

A93

A73

To Nürnberg

E50

0   1 mi

0   1 km

retains much of its old flavor: Many of its important historical monuments were spared bombing in World War II. Its atmospheric, narrow, winding streets, lined with houses with high-pitched gabled roofs, seem left over from the Middle Ages. A 19th-century writer called Weimar "one of the most walkable towns of Europe," and it still fits into that category.

Weimar's history as a cultural center is centuries old. Famed Renaissance painter Lucas Cranach the Elder worked here in the 16th century. From 1708 to 1717, Bach was court organist. In 1775, the great Goethe came to reside at the court of "Dowager Duchess" Anna Amalia and her son, Karl August II, and he attracted such notables as Herder and Schiller. Later in the 19th century, Franz Liszt was musical director of the National Theater; under his auspices, Wagner's *Lohengrin* had its first performance. It was also in Weimar that the German national assembly met in February 1919, in the aftermath of World War I, to draw up the constitution for what was to be called the Weimar Republic.

Essentials

GETTING THERE

BY TRAIN   **Weimar Hauptbahnhof** is on the major Deutsche Bundesbahn rail lines, which link Erfurt and Leipzig with Dresden. There are frequent daily connections in both directions. Trains from Berlin travel via Leipzig. For rail information and schedules, call (C) **01805/996633** or visit www.bahn.de.

BY BUS   Regional buses to all parts of the city and the surrounding area are run by **Verkehrsgesellschaft Weimar** ((C) **03643/24200**).

BY CAR   Access is via the E40 Autobahn east and west.

VISITOR INFORMATION

Head for **Tourist-Information Weimar,** Am Markt 10 ((C) **03643/7450;** www.weimar.de). The office is open Monday to Friday 9:30am to 6pm, Saturday and Sunday 9:30am to 2pm.

Exploring Weimar

Weimar enjoys a scenic location on the Ilm River, set against the backdrop of the Ettersberg and Vogtland hills. The city has many popular sights, but perhaps the best thing to do here is simply wander about on foot. A walk at night through the old streets that once felt the footsteps of Goethe, Bach, Wagner, and Schiller is particularly rewarding.

The town's main square, the **Marktplatz,** or market square, retains the old flavor of the city. Instead of breakfast at your hotel, visit one of the bakeries near the square and create your own breakfast, as many locals do. The daily produce market still takes place on the Marktplatz (7am–4pm). The painter Lucas Cranach the Elder lived here during his last year, from 1552 to 1553. Today, you can view the **Lucas Cranach the Elder House** from the outside, richly decorated and bearing a coat of arms of the Cranach family. A modern gallery is inside the house but is open only Thursday and Friday from noon to 8pm, Saturday 11am to 3pm.

For a midday break from sightseeing, we suggest a visit to **Park an der Ilm** (also known as Goethe Park) flanking the river. Goethe himself landscaped this park. It sports numerous 18th-century pavilions and is the best place in Weimar for a picnic.

If you've had a little too much Schiller and Goethe, flee the inner city and escape to **Bauhaus Universität** on Marienstrasse, just across the footpath in

Weimar

ATTRACTIONS ●
Bauhaus-Museum **4**
Deutsches Nationaltheater **3**
Goethes Gartenhaus **16**
Goethe-Nationalmuseum **11**
Liszt Haus **13**
Neues Museum Weimar **1**
Schillerhaus **6**
Schloss Belvedere **15**
Schlossmuseum **9**
Wittumspalais **5**

HOTELS ■
Amalienhof Hotel **12**
Grand Hotel Russischer Hof **2**
Hotel Elephant **10**
Leonardo Hotel **14**

RESTAURANTS ◆
Hotel Elephant **10**
Ratskeller **8**
Shakespeares **7**

ⓘ Information

GERMANY
Hamburg
Berlin ★
Weimar ●
Frankfurt ●
Munich ●

front of the Bauhaus building. Here you can meet Weimar students, nearly all of whom speak English.

In the evening, head for one of the smoky beer halls near **Herderplatz,** keeping in mind that Nietzsche, who spent the last 3 years of his life here, discovered them long before you.

Bauhaus-Museum MUSEUM In 1919, Walter Gropius founded his Staatliche Bauhaus here, so it's only fitting that a museum has been established in Weimar as a testament to the elegance of modernism that was launched in the city. The Bauhaus architectural school of design was noted especially for its program that synthesized technology, craftsmanship, and design aesthetics. It was to sweep the world. From the Bauhaus school rose such towering artists as Klee, Kandinsky, and Feininger. The golden era of Bauhaus is re-created in arts and crafts, graphics, paintings, and representative works of some of the outstanding painters or teachers of the era. A school once flourished here, in the center of town, until 1925.

At Theaterplatz, across from the Deutsches Nationaltheater. ✆ **03643/545401.** www.klassik-stiftung. de. Admission 4.50€ adults, 3.50€ students, free for children 5 and under. Daily 10am–6pm. Bus: 1, 2, 3, 5, 6, or 7.

Goethe Gartenhaus ★★ HISTORIC HOUSE In a park on the Ilm River stands a plain cottage with a high-pitched roof. Goethe selected this house as his first residence when he came to Weimar. Even after he moved to other quarters, he still came here in summer to find peace and tranquillity. He described the park around him as "infinitely beautiful," and so it remains today.

Im Park an der Ilm. ✆ **03643/545375.** www.klassik-stiftung.de. Admission 4.50€ adults, 3.50€ students, free for children 5 and under. Apr–Oct daily 10am–6pm; Nov–Mar daily 10am–4pm. Bus: 1, 10, or 12.

Goethe Nationalmuseum ★★★ HISTORIC HOUSE Weimar's principal attraction is the house where Johann Wolfgang von Goethe (1749–1832) lived from 1782 to 1832. It's a typical example of a baroque German nobleman's house. There are 14 exhibition rooms, some pretty much as Goethe and his wife, Christiane Vulpius, left them. The library contains more than 5,000 volumes. The writer's mineral collection is here also, as well as much original art. Although Goethe's reputation rests today on his writing, he had wide-ranging interests, including an interest in science (he was an early advocate of the belief in the common origin of all animal life). He died in Weimar on March 22, 1832.

Am Frauenplan 1. ✆ **03643/545347.** www.klassik-stiftung.de. Admission 8.50€ adults, 7€ students, free for children 5 and under. Apr–Sept Tues–Sun 9am–6pm; Oct–Mar Tues–Sun 9am–4pm. Bus: 1, 2, 5, 6, or 8.

Kunstsammlungen zu Weimar MUSEUM This structure was begun under the guidance of Goethe in 1789 and completed in 1803. The previous castle burned down in 1774; only a tower survived. In one of the wings is a series of galleries dedicated not only to Schiller and Goethe, but also to two other famous names associated with Weimar: Johann Gottfried Herder (1744–1803), the German critic and philosopher who was a pioneer of the *Sturm und Drang* ("Storm and Stress") literary movement, and Christoph Martin Wieland (1733–1813), the poet and critic who wrote the satirical romance *The Republic of Fools.* The museum has a shop, which is open April to October Tuesday to Sunday 9am to 6pm.

The ground floor displays works by Lucas Cranach the Elder. On some of the upper floors, you can see exhibits from Walter Gropius's Bauhaus school, which started in Weimar. The primary aim of this movement was to unify arts and crafts within the context of architecture. Its appeal came from the changing sensibilities of the Industrial Age, as well as from the need for inexpensive construction techniques in an era of rising costs and exploding demand for housing. Followers around the globe may have been impressed, but not the good people of Weimar. They "tolerated" Gropius's school until 1925, and then bombarded it in the press until it finally moved to Dessau. There it stayed until the Nazis closed it in 1933, claiming it was a center of "Communist intellectualism."

Burgplatz 4. ✆ **03643/545401.** www.klassik-stiftung.de. Admission 6€ adults, 5€ students. Apr–Oct Tues–Sun 10am–6pm; Nov–Mar Tues–Sun 10am–4pm. Bus: 1.

Liszt-Haus HISTORIC HOUSE   Franz Liszt (1811–86), the Hungarian composer and pianist, spent the last period of his life here. You'll find several mementos, both personal and musical, from the composer's life, including letters exchanged between Liszt and his son-in-law, as well as the piano at which he played and taught his pupils. The house was once the home of the royal gardeners of Weimar.

Marienstrasse 17. ✆ **03643/545388.** www.klassik-stiftung.de. Admission 4€ adults, 3€ students, 1€ children 6–18, free for children 5 and under. Apr–Oct Wed–Mon 10am–6pm. Closed Nov–Mar. Bus: 1, 4, or 6.

Neues Museum Weimar MUSEUM   This is eastern Germany's first museum devoted to modern art, an artistic field frowned upon by the former Communist regime with its more traditional tastes. The exhibitions are frequently changed or alternated, so you never know what you'll be viewing at any given time. The restored building was constructed in 1869 but radically overhauled to accommodate its new role. The museum was opened to coincide with the naming of Weimar as cultural capital of Europe in 1999. Its permanent exhibition includes works of American minimal and conceptual art, as well as pieces by Italian painters and expressive works of the new "wild painters" of Germany, as they are called. In addition, such major artists as Anselm Kiefer and Keith Haring are represented extensively.

Weimarplatz 5 (directly north of center, on the square adjoining Rathenauplatz). ✆ **03643/545401.** www.klassik-stiftung.de. Admission 3.50€ adults, 2.50€ students, free for children 5 and under. Apr–Oct Tues–Sun 11am–6pm; Nov–Mar Tues–Sun 11am–4pm. From the heart of town, Goetheplatz, walk north for 10 min.

Schillerhaus ★★ HISTORIC HOUSE   After his friend Goethe, Friedrich von Schiller (1759–1805) is the greatest name in German literature. He lived here with his family from 1802 to 1805 and wrote his last works here, including *Wilhelm Tell.* The attic rooms have been furnished as they were in Schiller's day.

Schillerstrasse 9. ✆ **03643/545350.** www.klassik-stiftung.de. Admission 5€ adults, 4€ students and children 6–18, free for children 5 and under. Apr–Oct Wed–Mon 9am–6pm; Nov–Mar Wed–Mon 9am–4pm. Bus: 1, 2, 3, 5, 6, 7, or 8.

Schloss Belvedere HISTORIC BUILDING   The baroque Schloss Belvedere was a favorite retreat of Anna Amalia and the "enlightened" Weimar set. It has an orangery, along with the open-air theater and an English-style park. Inside the château are displays of dainty rococo art and a collection of historical coaches.

Belvederer Allee. ✆ **03643/545931.** www.klassik-stiftung.de. Admission 4€ adults, 3€ seniors and students, free for children 5 and under. Apr–Oct Tues–Sun 10am–6pm. Closed Nov–Mar. Bus: 12. From Weimar, follow the Belvedereschlossallee south for 3km (2 miles).

Schlossmuseum MUSEUM   This is a special art museum often overlooked by the hurried visitor but appreciated by art lovers who care to seek out its special treasures. Its collection of European art ranges from the Reformation period to the 20th

STATE-OF-THE-ART china: MEISSEN PORCELAIN

by George McDonald

In 2010, Meissen celebrated its 300th anniversary as a center for the manufacture of quality porcelain. Since 1710, the Elbe River town has been the home of Meissen porcelain, and you can visit the factory where it's produced to witness a demonstration of the traditional art of making and hand-painting so-called "Dresden" china. Meissen is just 24km (15 miles) downriver from Dresden, and the name of the larger city, which was the capital of Saxony's royal house, has attached itself indelibly to Meissen's pride and joy. The early makers of this "white gold" were virtually held prisoner here because the princes who ruled both Dresden and Meissen carefully guarded the secret to its production.

Meissen porcelain got its start when the Saxon ruler Augustus the Strong, a patron of the arts and a fanatical porcelain collector (he owned almost 15,000 pieces) commissioned the alchemist Johann Friedrich Böttger to transmute gold from base metals. That project went nowhere, naturally, but with the aid of scientist Ehrenfried Walther von Tschirnhaus, Böttger successfully produced Chinese-style porcelain instead.

That was enough to keep Augustus happy, since expensive Chinese porcelain had long bedazzled Europe, and until Böttger and von Tschirnhaus got to work, had resisted the best efforts of European craftsmen to re-create it.

The new homegrown china was made inside Meissen's medieval Albrechtsburg castle until 1865, when production shifted to the current site overlooking the town. Most of the iconic tableware patterns sold today, such as the Swan and the cobalt-enhanced Blue Onion patterns, have been in production since the 1700s at the Staatliche Porzellan-Manufaktur Meissen (Meissen State Porcelain Manufactory). Meissen porcelain is for sale in specialized stores and by mail order, but it is far more interesting to go to the workshop in the town to see how it is made. Little has changed over the centuries, and all the ornate painting, decoration, and other effects are still done by hand. This makes Meissen porcelain pricey, but each piece is a unique product, made by craftsmen. The delicacy of the brush stroke, the richness of color, or the sheen of the glazes make the items produced by the firm so highly prized.

century. The museum sprawls across three floors, with main works on the first floor, including paintings by Lucas Cranach. On the second floor is an exhibition of more German works, paintings done in the age of Goethe, and various pieces of Romantic art. There is an exceptional collection of religious icons from the 19th and 20th centuries. In the graphic collection are exhibitions of the works of the great masters such as da Vinci, Dürer, and Rembrandt.

Burgplatz 4. ✆ **03643/545960.** www.klassik-stiftung.de. Admission 6€ adults, 5€ students and seniors, free for children 5 and under. Apr-Oct Tues-Sun 10am-6pm; Nov-Mar Tues-Sun 10am-4pm. Bus: 1, 5, 6, 8, or 10. From Markt, the market square in the town center, head east along Am Markt for 5 min.

Wittumspalais HISTORIC BUILDING   If you follow Rittergasse to the end, you will come upon the 1767 Wittumspalais. This was once the residence of Dowager Duchess Anna Amalia, who presided over the German Enlightenment, which brought a stark rationalism to literature and the arts. The old ducal dower house is devoted to mementos of the movement.

Art and Technique Despite its fragile nature—which in the wrong hands can easily turn out to be tragic—Meissen porcelain is technically a "hard" or "hard-paste" porcelain, made from the feldspar (ore-free) clay kaolin, also known as china clay, that's mined at a quarry in Mehren, 5km (3 miles) west of Meissen. The ingredients are mixed in a proprietary recipe and fired in a kiln at around 1,200°C (2,192°F) to produce the famous translucent white china.

Form and Content Among the products that have emerged from the Meissen workshop are dinner services and other tableware, human and animal figurines, clocks, candlesticks, snuffboxes, and classic Chinese and Japanese scenes and motifs. Art Nouveau and Art Deco works were produced between the late 19th and early 20th centuries. Some of the most exquisite antique pieces depict classical Greek and Roman myths and legends.

Red Porcelain Production of Meissen porcelain was one of Communist East Germany's few profitable industries, so the Staatliche Porzellan-Manufaktur Meissen was of great importance to the country's economy. At that time, the factory

was owned by "the People," though few East German people outside of the Party elite could afford such a luxury. Purchasers from the capitalist West snapped up the china, causing demand to outstrip supply. Ownership of the factory reverted to the state of Saxony after Germany's reunification in 1990.

Real or Fake? To be tolerably sure that you're looking at a real piece of Meissen porcelain (though it's not an absolute guarantee), look on the bottom for the distinctive cobalt-blue crossed-swords logo, derived from Augustus the Strong's coat of arms, and an official hallmark granted in 1724.

A Porcelain Feast In addition to viewing Meissen porcelain in the workshop's own museum—and in the factory store, of course—you can take in the world's largest single collection in nearby Dresden's Zwinger Palace (p. 188). It counts 8,000 pieces. There's even a full-size glockenspiel of Meissen porcelain bells in the palace's gate tower.

Bull Market Delicate antique Meissen porcelain is considered a solid investment, a fact that gives a whole new meaning to the old saw about a bull in a china shop.

Am Palais 3. ☏ **03643/545401.** www.klassik-stiftung.de. Admission 5€ adults, 4€ students and seniors, free for children 5 and under. Apr–Oct Tues–Sun 10am–6pm; Nov–Mar Tues–Sun 10am–4pm. Bus: 1, 2, 3, 4, 5, or 6.

MORE SIGHTS

In the **cemetery** south of the town center lies the controversial **Denkmal der März Gefallenen,** a monument to the revolutionaries whose merciless and needless slaughter in 1919 (by government forces) so affected the ultraliberal Gropius and his Bauhaus followers. But most interesting today is the **Goethe-Schiller Mausoleum,** once the family vault of the Weimar dynasty, where Goethe and Schiller, friends in life, lie side by side in death. It was built in 1825 through 1826 in accordance with plans drawn up by Coudray, who consulted Goethe on the design and construction. Schiller was entombed here in 1827 and Goethe in 1832, both in oak coffins. Admission is free. Visiting hours are March to October Wednesday to Monday 9am to 1pm and 2 to 5pm, and November to February Wednesday to Monday 10am to 1pm and

2 to 4pm. A Russian-style **chapel** is on the south side of the mausoleum. It was built in 1859 for Maria Pavlovna, daughter-in-law of Duke Carl August.

BUCHENWALD CONCENTRATION CAMP & MEMORIAL SITE The Buchenwald bus (no. 6) from Weimar's Hauptbahnhof goes 6km (4 miles) northwest of Weimar to **Gedenkstätte Buchenwald** (✆ **03643/4300;** www.buchenwald.de). An estimated 250,000 Jews, Slavs, Gypsies, homosexuals, political opponents, prisoners of war, Jehovah's Witnesses, social misfits, criminals, and others were confined here from 1937 until the camp's liberation by the U.S. Army in 1945. Officially, Buchenwald was a work camp, so far fewer people were killed here than at other concentration camps.

Nonetheless, 56,000 people died here; many, many thousands of others were sent on from here to other death camps; and a quarter of a million people, from more than 30 nations, suffered unspeakable pain as prisoners here. Furthermore, atrocities practiced in Buchenwald have made its very name synonymous with human perversity. Medical experiments on prisoners were common here, and prisoners, ironically, did not get nearly the amount of care and protection that animals in the SS men's zoo received. This is also the concentration camp from which famed author and Nobel Peace Prize winner Elie Wiesel was liberated. (For more about his experiences at Buchenwald, read his best-selling book, *Night.*)

Buchenwald's sad history continued when Soviet occupation forces used the site as an internment camp from 1945 to 1950, where more than 7,000 people died and were buried in mass graves.

Today, Buchenwald is a haunting sight. Only fragments of the camp have been preserved, as much of it has vanished by deliberate destruction and through the wear and tear of many years. The clock in the gate building reflects the time of the liberation by the U.S. Army in 1945. The gate has JEDEM DAS SEINE ("To Each His Own") inscribed upon it: It is one of the only Nazi concentration camps with a gate that was not inscribed with ARBEIT MACHT FREI ("Work Will Make You Free"). All but a few buildings have been replaced with eerie black rocks filling in the foundations (which you can still see) of old barracks and more. The storehouse (as well as some other buildings) still exists in its original form, and the museum inside reflects both the Soviet and the Nazi past of the camp.

A well-planned and -executed monument/memorial lies about 1km (⅔ mile) from the remnants of the camp itself, with its own parking lot. The monument has several facets (sculpture, bell tower, and so on) built over the graves of more than 3,000 Buchenwald victims.

You can visit Buchenwald April to October Tuesday to Sunday 10am to 6pm, and November to March Tuesday to Sunday 10am to 4pm. Last admission is 30 minutes before closing. Admission is free.

Where to Eat

Hotel Elephant ★★ GERMAN/INTERNATIONAL   There are two restaurants in this hotel. The more formal, **Anna Amalia,** is modern, sky-lit, and airy, with spacious tables, a garden terrace, and good service. Its German and international dishes are the very best in the city. The chefs have unerring senses of flavor and proportion as well as fertile imaginations. They use only the best ingredients available at the local markets. Filet stroganoff, pork medallions, and *Sauerbraten* are among the menu items. Goethe, Schiller, Bach, Liszt, and Wagner all wined and dined here.

You can reach the historic **Elephantenkeller (Elephant Cellar)** by a flight of stone steps at a separate entrance. It's decorated in a rustic style, with square travertine columns. The best dishes at this informal restaurant are the traditional Thuringian platters. An autumn specialty is *Zwiebelmarkt* salads, made from onions from the famous October onion market, a tradition dating from 1653.

Am Markt 19. ⓒ **03643/8020.** Reservations recommended. Main courses 25€–33€. AE, DC, MC, V. Anna Amalia summer daily 11am–3pm, Tues–Sat 7:30–11pm; winter Sat–Sun 11am–3pm, Tues–Sat 7:30–11pm. Elephantenkeller Mon–Tues noon–3pm; daily 6pm–midnight. Closed July–Aug 25. Bus: 1 or 12.

Ratskeller THURINGIAN   A flight of stairs leads into a pair of dining rooms. The first is vaulted and white, the second more modern, paneled, and with a prominent bar. Everything is correct and proper. Some typical local specialties include neck of pork marinated in beer and served with puréed potatoes or a medallion of beef, and a pork filet with a sauce made from forest mushrooms. These dishes aren't dazzling, but they're very satisfying. The venison, when in season, is excellent, and the wild boar and duck in red-wine sauce is reason enough for a meal here.

Markt 10. ⓒ **03643/850573.** www.ratskeller-weimar.de. Reservations recommended. Main courses 9€–17€; fixed-price menus 15€–25€. AE, MC, V. Daily noon–midnight. Bus: 7 or 71.

Shakespeares INTERNATIONAL   Set in the town's center, a few steps from the Rathaus (Town Hall), this restaurant offers well-prepared food, a bar area, angular modern decor, and big windows that overlook a garden strewn with tables for warm-weather dining. Menu items are well prepared and flavorful, and include salads, soups, risottos, fresh shellfish, and several kinds of grilled fish, some of them served with a Riesling sauce. Main courses may feature savory ragouts of chicken, lamb, or veal; noodles in cream sauce studded with ham and cheese; veal cutlets; and *Wiener Schnitzel*. In addition to the street-level dining room, a small-scale auditorium (Kulturstadt Neurotika) is in the restaurant's cellar. Most of what's presented inside is scheduled for Friday and Saturday nights, with an occasional Sunday-afternoon jazz concert. Entrance to most concerts and plays costs around 15€ per person.

Windischenstrasse 4–6. ⓒ **03643/901285.** www.weimar-shakespeares.de. Reservations recommended. Main courses 6.90€–24€. No credit cards. Daily 11am–midnight.

Shopping

A visit to Weimar's antiques stores offers a chance to buy porcelain, silver, crystal, and furniture that survived the devastation of World War II. An attractive source for mostly 18th- and 19th-century German antiques, with everything from farmhouse rustic to the kind of high-style pieces you might have expected at Friedrich the Great's Sanssouci, can be found at **Thiersch Antiquitäten,** Bräuhausgasse 15 (ⓒ **03643/402540**).

Entertainment & Nightlife

A good national theater, live music venues, and dance clubs provide a variety of choices for evening entertainment. The city's bars and outdoor cafes are good places to drink and talk. Just walk down Schillerstrasse or along the Theaterplatz. All of the bars and cafes in this area carry free copies of *Schlagseite* and *Boulevard,* local entertainment papers. *Takt* is another good resource; you can save 3€ by picking it up in the tourist office (see "Visitor Information," earlier in this chapter), the only place it's free.

Weimar's main performance venue is the **Deutsches Nationaltheater,** Theaterplatz 2A (ⓒ **03643/755334;** www.nationaltheater-weimar.de), where Franz Liszt

THE THURINGIAN FOREST: GERMANY'S green HEART

"There is indeed no forest on all the earth as beautiful as the Thuringian," wrote the Danish novelist Martin Anderson Nexö. Hikers and nature lovers have long extolled the scenic beauties of this region, which has often been called "the green heart of Germany." The **Thuringer Wald ★★** was the former stamping ground of such philosophers and artists as Goethe, Schiller, Martin Luther, Ludwig Bechstein, and Bach.

The mountains within the forest, though not nearly as tall as the German Alps, are geological highlights. The highest peaks, around 985m (3,230 ft.), are composed of gneiss, porphyry, and granite; the foothills are made of softer strata of sandstone and sedimentary limestone.

The scenic, 150km (100-mile), northwest-to-southeast ramble known as the Thuringian High Road was one of the most popular destinations anywhere for East German schoolchildren and campers before reunification. You can take a lowland driving version by following Route 88 between Eisenach and Ilmenau, a city that Goethe loved.

Just as attractive as the region's scenic beauty are the dozens of unspoiled, charming medieval villages that pepper the landscape. Dornburg has a series of three palaces, perched high above the Saale River. Altenburg, directly south of Leipzig, is the home of a hilltop castle. Finally, Arnstadt, founded in 704, is the oldest town in the Thuringian Forest. It lies just beyond Erfurt. Today, the town's medieval walkways and buildings are being restored to their former glory.

and Richard Strauss once conducted. Call the box office or the tourist office for information about schedules. Tickets cost 8€ to 55€.

C-Keller Galerie, Markt 21 (✆ **03643/510521;** www.c-keller.de), combines an art gallery with a cafe that serves beer, wine, tea, and light meals. It's a popular place to unwind. The gallery has works for sale by local, national, and European artists. The cafe is open daily noon to 1:30am. The most popular and animated dance club in Weimar isn't exactly cutting edge—it's more like Hannover than Hamburg or Berlin. But if you're interested in a medley of disco favorites from the '70s and '80s, head for **Bistro Corona,** Goetheplatz 5 (✆ **03643/801756**). This is both a bar and a restaurant, open Monday to Friday 8:30am to 11pm, Saturday 10am to 2am, and Sunday 10am to 9pm. The best nights for music and dancing are Friday and Saturday when a 5€ cover is imposed.

Where to Stay

Amalienhof Hotel 🎔 Though not as roomy and comfortable as the Russicher Hof, Elephant, or Leonardo, this hotel is more affordable. Originally built in 1826 as a private villa, it was enlarged in the early 1990s, with a modern annex just across the street. Reception and breakfast facilities are in the older of the two buildings; if you're assigned a room in the annex, you'll be given a key to the annex's front door. Rooms in the annex are modern in decor and styling; rooms in the hotel's original core are Biedermeier. The hotel has a convenient location, directly south of Goethe National Museum, within an easy walk of the town's historic core and major attractions. The breakfast buffet, the only meal served here, is generous.

Amalienstrasse 2, 99423 Weimar. www.amalienhof-weimar.de. ✆ **03643/5490.** Fax 03643/549110. 32 units. 78€–105€ double; 95€–135€ suite. Rates include buffet breakfast. AE, MC, V. Free parking. Bus: 1. *In room:* A/C, TV, hair dryer.

Grand Hotel Russischer Hof ★

The Russischer Hof was built in 1805 by Russian aristocrats for their visits to the Weimar court. Such luminaries as Turgenev, Tolstoy, Schumann, and Liszt have passed through its doors. It sports a dark-green-and-white facade and opens onto an important square in the center of town. Inside, the pastel-colored public areas are elegant and intimate. The small to midsize rooms are in a somewhat lackluster modern annex behind the hotel, each with decor loosely based on 18th-century French motifs. Even if you're not a guest, consider a visit to its restaurant, Anastasia, serving an excellent Thuringian cuisine with some Austrian specialties.

Goetheplatz 2, 99423 Weimar. www.russischerhof.com. ✆ **03643/7740.** Fax 03643/774840. 126 units. 95€–302€ double; 215€–555€ suite. AE, DC, MC, V. Parking 14€. Bus: 1 or 7. **Amenities:** Restaurant; bar; babysitting; concierge; exercise room; room service; sauna. *In room:* A/C, TV/DVD, hair dryer, minibar, Wi-Fi (12€ per hour).

Hotel Elephant ★★

The Elephant is Weimar's most famous hotel, although it's actually not quite as comfortable or well accessorized as the Leonardo Hotel. Many celebrities have stayed here, including Tolstoy and Bach; the most notorious guest was Adolf Hitler. The Elephant became best known in Germany through Thomas Mann's novel *Lotte in Weimar* (published in English as *The Beloved Returns*). The elegant facade of this building (ca. 1696) is set off by a beautifully weathered terra-cotta roof, a series of elongated bay windows stretching from the second to the third floors, and, best of all, a frontage onto the old marketplace, which contains a dried-up fountain dedicated to Neptune. An Art Deco decor and bold color schemes make the rooms dramatically appealing.

Markt 19, 99423 Weimar. www.starwoodhotels.com. ✆ **03643/8020.** Fax 03643/802610. 99 units. 109€–245€ double; 211€–295€ junior suite; 235€–555€ suite. AE, DC, MC, V. Parking 13€. Bus: 5 or 7. **Amenities:** 2 restaurants; bar; babysitting; room service. *In room:* TV/DVD, CD player, hair dryer, minibar, Wi-Fi (19€ per 24 hr.).

Kay's Loungehotel Weimar 🍴

This affordable hotel in the center of town near the railway station dates from 1897 but has been completely renovated in modern style. The small rooms are clean and simply but adequately furnished, each with a compact shower-only bathroom. The focal point of the public areas is a glassed-in winter garden. The hotel is known for its *gutbürgerlich* (home-style) cookery, which one reader described as "just like my Saxon mother used to cook."

Brennerstrasse 42, 99423 Weimar. www.hotel-thueringen-weimar.de. ✆ **03643/74022.** Fax 03643/74022300. 36 units. 77€–90€ double. Rates include buffet breakfast. AE, MC, V. Parking 5€. Bus: 1 or 7. **Amenities:** Restaurant; room service. *In room:* TV, no phone.

Leonardo Hotel ★★

Ironically, credit for the excellence of this hotel's construction and the lavishness of its materials goes to the former East German government, which designed and built it shortly before reunification. The hotel stands beside Goethe Park, a swath of greenery with posh residences and embassies left over from the Weimar Republic. The lobby is dramatic, with sun-flooded skylights and glass walls. Rooms are small but comfortable. The midsize to spacious bathrooms are the best in town.

Belvederer Allee 25, 99425 Weimar. www.leonardo-hotels.com. ✆ **03643/7220.** Fax 03643/7222111. 294 units. 59€–155€ double; 245€–645€ suite. AE, DC, MC, V. Parking 12€. Bus: 1. **Amenities:** Restaurant; 3 bars; babysitting; exercise room; indoor heated pool; room service; sauna. *In room:* A/C, TV, hair dryer, minibar, Wi-Fi (15€ per day).

Side Trips from Weimar

ERFURT ★

The small city of Erfurt, on the Gera River and first mentioned in 742, is one of the most visited cities of eastern Germany because it still exudes the spirit of a medieval market town. Erfurt is filled with historic houses, bridges, winding cobblestone alleys, and church spires reaching toward the skyline, as well as decorative and colorful Renaissance and baroque facades. The city emerged from World War II relatively unscathed and remains one of the best places to see what yesterday's Germany looked like. Nearly everything of interest is concentrated in the Altstadt (Old Town) area. It's well worth your time to take 2 or 3 hours to walk around this city of "flowers and towers."

Why flowers? Erfurt is a center of the German horticultural trade. It's also Europe's largest vegetable seed producer. One of Europe's biggest horticultural shows, the **Internationale Gartenbau Ausstellung (International Horticulture Exhibition),** is held here in the Cyriaksburg Park every year from the end of March to September.

ESSENTIALS You can reach Erfurt after a 24km (15-mile) train ride from the Weimar Hauptbahnhof; there are frequent connections. For rail information and schedules, call ✆ **01805/996633** or visit www.bahn.de. Access by car is via the E40 Autobahn and State Hwy. 4. The **Erfurt Tourist-Information** center is at Bendiktsplatz 1 (✆ **0361/66400;** www.erfurt.de). From April to December, it's open Monday to Friday 10am to 7pm, Saturday 10am to 6pm, and Sunday 10am to 4pm; January to March, it's open Monday to Saturday 10am to 6pm and Sunday 10am to 4pm.

Exploring Erfurt

Well-preserved patrician mansions built in both Gothic and Renaissance styles are the town's dominant feature. Many of the narrow streets are lined with old half-timbered houses. One of Erfurt's curiosities is the **Krämerbrücke (Shopkeepers' Bridge;** www.kraemerbruecke.de), which has spanned the Gera since the 14th century. It has houses on both sides, nearly three dozen in all, and is filled with bookstalls, cafes, and antiques shops. You'll certainly want to spend some time here browsing.

The ecclesiastical center is the **Domberg,** where two Catholic churches stand side by side, their 15th-century walls almost closing in on each other. The **Dom (Cathedral;** ✆ **0361/6461265;** www.mariendom-erfurt.de), on Domplatz, was begun in the 12th century and later rebuilt in the 14th century in the Gothic style. Its stained-glass windows above the choir date from 1370 to 1420 and are unusual in Germany because they depict scenes of everyday life. The interior of the cathedral is richly baroque, but it also has some notable works from 1160: a Romanesque altar of the Virgin and the statue-candelabrum known as "the Wolfram." Note also the 13th-century tombstone of the count of Gleichen and his two wives. One local legend says that the second woman wasn't his wife at all, but a Saracen beauty from the Holy Land who, under mysterious circumstances, saved his life. The Dom is open May to October Monday to Friday 9 to 11:30am and 12:30 to 5pm, Saturday 9 to 11:30am and 12:30 to 4:30pm, and Sunday 2 to 4pm; November to April, hours are Monday to Saturday 10 to 11:30am and 12:30 to 4pm, and, in addition to Sunday Masses (usually conducted at 9 and 11am), it's open to tourists on Sunday from 2 to 4:30pm.

Its neighbor is the Gothic **Church of St. Severi** (✆ **0361/576960**), a "hall-type" church with five naves. Don't miss seeing its extraordinary font, a masterpiece of intricately carved sandstone, rising practically to the roof. You may also look for a notable sarcophagus of the saint (ca. 1365) in the southernmost aisle. St. Severi is linked to the Dom by a 70-step open staircase. It's open May to October Monday to

Friday 9am to 12:30pm and 1:30 to 5pm, and November to April Monday to Friday 10am to 12:30pm and 1:30 to 4pm. It's closed January and during most of February.

The most beautiful churches are the Romanesque **Peterskirche,** dating from the 12th and 14th centuries, and the 13th-century **Predigerkirche,** of the Order of Mendicant Friars. There are also three early medieval churches: **Agidienkirche, Michaeliskirche,** and **Allerheiligengeistkirche.** The tourist office (see above) will give you a map pinpointing all these. Most can be reached on foot.

Where to Eat

Alboth's Restaurant im Kaisersaal ★★ INTERNATIONAL   Set within part of a sprawling and stately looking building in the heart of the city, this restaurant is the most formal and most gastronomically ambitious in town. Much of its decor evokes the lavish aesthetic of the late 18th century, with plush upholsteries and tones of cream, champagne, and gold. Come here for artfully prepared dishes, each richly *neuen* (new, or nouvelle) in their presentation, each reflecting seasonal variations as interpreted by Claus Alboth, chef and namesake. Perhaps the best way to handle the gastronomy here involves ordering one of the set-price meals, one of which focuses on Thuringian regional dishes with updated, modern twists (ravioli stuffed with blood sausage and liverwurst, for example). Expect a changing array of dishes, the best examples of which include lamb stew in red wine with farmer's cheese, lobster, and champagne soup; roasted wild goat with port-wine sauce; sweetbreads in puff pastry; goose liver with asparagus-flavored cream sauce; and a chocolate charlotte with raspberries and apricots.

Futterstrasse 15–16. ☎ **0361/5688207.** www.alboths.de. Reservations recommended. Main courses 27€; fixed-price menus 30€–90€. AE, MC, V. Tues–Sat 6:30–9:30pm. Closed 3 weeks in midsummer, 3 weeks in Jan.

Where to Stay

Mercure Erfurt Altstadt   Erfurt's most up-to-date hotel, in the heart of town, is also its best. It was built as a sophisticated enlargement of a *Gasthaus* (inn) from the 1300s. The medieval part—meticulously conserved and restored—faces onto a side street, the Futterstrasse. Otherwise, the hotel is modern, restrained, and tasteful. Most rooms correspond to middle-to-upscale chain-hotel standards. An additional 13 rooms retain the wood paneling and architectural quirks of their original medieval construction.

One of the town's best restaurants, Zum Rebstock, is in the old wing of the hotel. The restaurant was part of the original structure and has since been painstakingly restored. It serves German and international dishes.

Meienbergstrasse 26–27, 99084 Erfurt. www.accorhotels.com. ☎ **0361/59490.** Fax 0361/5949100. 141 units. 76€–160€ double; 200€ suite. Rates include continental breakfast. AE, DC, MC, V. Parking 12€. **Amenities:** Restaurant; bar; babysitting; room service; sauna. *In room:* TV, hair dryer, minibar, Wi-Fi (19€ per day).

Radisson Blu Hotel   This is one of the town's better addresses. It hasn't fully escaped its East German Cold War boxy architectural quality, but the Radisson group has poured in tons of money to upgrade it and has given it a lot more than a face-lift. Its modern rooms are comfortable but a bit cramped. Bathrooms are very compact, containing tub/shower combinations and inadequate shelf space. The location is halfway between the station and the town center. The on-site restaurant serves first-rate Thuringian meals as well as some international dishes. The restaurant's lounge and bar is a popular rendezvous point.

Juri-Gagarin-Ring 127, 99084 Erfurt. www.radisson.com. ☎ **0361/55100.** Fax 0361/5510210. 284 units. 79€–159€ double; 168€–210€ suite. Rates include buffet breakfast. AE, DC, MC, V. Parking 14€. **Amenities:** Restaurant; bar; exercise room; room service; sauna. *In room:* A/C, TV, hair dryer, minibar.

EISENACH ★

This town lies on the northwestern slopes of the Thuringian Forest, at the confluence of the Nesse and Horsel rivers, 50km (30 miles) west of Erfurt. Eisenach, once a center of the East German auto industry, is not particularly charming, but it does have one of the region's finest castles and a few sights associated with Luther and Bach, who were both born here. Half-timbered houses ring its ancient market square.

ESSENTIALS   Many trains from Erfurt (see above) arrive every day. For rail information and schedules, call ℂ **01805/996633** or visit www.bahn.de. Access by car is via the A4 Autobahn east and west. For tourist information, contact **Eisenach-Information,** Markt 9 (ℂ **03691/79230**), open Monday to Friday 10am to 6pm, and Saturday 10am to 4pm. Here you can pick up a map with the locations of all the tourist sites.

Exploring Eisenach

Eisenach is best known as the site of **Schloss Wartburg ★**, Wartburg Foundation at the Wartburg (ℂ **03691/2500;** www.wartburg-eisenach.de; bus: 3, 10, or 13), reached only after a rigorous climb up a 180m (590-ft.) hill. Hitler called Wartburg Castle "the most German of German castles" and engaged in a battle with local authorities to take down its cross and replace it with a swastika. This ancient castle belonged to the landgraves of Thuringia and once hosted the medieval *Minnesinger* poets, immortalized by Wagner in *Tannhäuser*. This was also where Martin Luther hid upon his return from the Diet of Worms in 1521, so he could complete his translation of the Bible—he is said to have "fought the Devil with ink" at Wartburg. The castle has now been turned into a regional museum. Admission to the palace, the museum, and the room within the castle where Luther lived and worked is 8€ for adults and 5€ for students and children ages 6 to 18. Admission is free for children 5 and under. It's open March to October daily 8:30am to 8pm, November to February daily 9am to 5pm. The last ticket is sold 1 hour prior to closing.

Eisenach is the birthplace of Johann Sebastian Bach (1685–1750). **Bachhaus,** Am Frauenplan 21 (ℂ **03691/79340;** www.bachhaus.de; bus: 3, 7, 11, or 13), contains many mementos of the Bach family, along with a collection of musical instruments. Admission costs 6.50€ for adults, 3.50€ for students and children 6 to 18. Children 5 and under enter free. It's open daily 10am to 6pm.

If you're a die-hard Luther fan, you can also visit the **Lutherhaus,** Lutherplatz 8 (ℂ **03691/29830;** www.lutherhaus-eisenach.de; bus: 1 or 5). Martin Luther stayed here as a schoolboy; today, it contains a series of exhibitions illustrating his life. Admission is 3.50€ for adults, 3€ for seniors, and 2€ for students and children 6 to 18. Children 5 and under enter free. It's open daily 10am to 5pm.

Where to Eat & Stay

Hotel Kaiserhof ★   Much of the elegance of the late 1800s is still evoked here in the lobby and especially in the dining room. Both are stellar examples of the stately looking German Landhaus architecture. Rooms are generally spacious and tastefully renovated, each with comfortable furnishings and midsize bathroom.

Wartburgallee 2, 99817 Eisenach. www.kaiserhof-eisenach.de. ℂ **03691/88890.** Fax 03691/203653. 64 units. 112€–131€ double. Rates include buffet breakfast. AE, DC, MC, V. Free parking. Bus: 3. **Amenities:** 2 restaurants; bar; room service; sauna. *In room:* A/C, TV, hair dryer, minibar.

LEIPZIG ★

164km (102 miles) SW of Berlin, 111km (69 miles) NW of Dresden, 126km (78 miles) NE of Erfurt

If you have limited time and have to choose between Dresden and Leipzig, make it Dresden. But if you can work Leipzig into your itinerary, you'll be richly rewarded. More than any other city in former East Germany (except Berlin, of course), Leipzig brings you into the Germany of today. This once-dreary city has taken on a new life and vitality; a visit here can be absolutely invigorating. Glassy skyscrapers and glitzy nightlife add a cosmopolitan flavor you don't encounter in much of the rest of the region. The approximately 20,000 students who study in the area (as Nietzsche, Goethe, and Leibniz once did) help add a spark. One resident put it this way: "Our grunge and metal bands are just as good as those of Berlin, and our cafes just as supercool."

Leipzig is also famous for more traditional music. Johann Sebastian Bach is closely associated with Leipzig, Mozart and Mendelssohn performed here, and Wagner was born here in 1813.

Because of its strategic value as a rail center, both the RAF and the U.S. Air Force bombed the city heavily in World War II, but it's been rebuilt, more or less successfully. It still has some narrow streets and houses from the 16th and 17th centuries, as well as some *Jugendstil* (Art Nouveau) flair. And Leipzig is again a major rail terminus. From its Hauptbahnhof—the largest in Europe, with 26 platforms—lines radiate to the chief German cities and the rest of the Continent.

Essentials

GETTING THERE

BY PLANE The **Leipzig-Halle International Airport** lies 11km (7 miles) northwest of the city center. About 50 airlines link Leipzig with major German cities, such as Munich and Frankfurt, and also some continental destinations. For **airport information,** call ✆ **0341/2241155** (www.leipzig-halle-airport.de). A train called the Airport Express runs from the airport to the Hauptbahnhof every 30 minutes from 5am to midnight. The fare costs 7€ for adults and 5€ for children. Taxis are also available, meeting all arriving planes, but the 25- to 30-minute ride to the city center will cost around 30€ each way for up to four passengers.

BY TRAIN The **Leipzig Hauptbahnhof,** Willy-Brandt-Platz, lies on the major Deutsche Bundesbahn rail line, with frequent connections to German cities. Seventeen trains arrive daily from Berlin (trip time: 1 hr., 40 min., to 2 hr., 50 min.); 23 trains from Dresden (1 hr., 35 min., to 2 hr.); and 15 trains from Frankfurt (3–4 hr.). For information and schedules, call ✆ **01805/996633** or visit www.bahn.de. The **Hauptbahnhof** has recently been restored and contains many cafes, shops, and restaurants; it's one of the most happening places in Leipzig.

BY BUS Long-distance bus service to such cities as Berlin is provided by **Leipziger Verkehrsbetriebe.** Buses depart from the east side of the main rail station. For information and schedules, call ✆ **0341/19449.**

BY CAR Access is via the Halle-Dresden Autobahn east and west or the E51 Autobahn north and south.

VISITOR INFORMATION

Contact the **Tourist-Information** office at Richard Wagner Strasse 1 (© **0341/ 7104265;** www.leipzig.de), Monday to Friday 9:30am to 6pm, Saturday and Sunday 9am to 3pm. The office can supply a map pinpointing the major sights. This place becomes a beehive of activity at the time of the annual trade fairs.

SPECIAL EVENTS Upon arrival, be sure to drop in at the tourist office and see if any festivals are taking place. For a week every year, in October, for example, during the **Leipziger Jazztages,** the churches, student clubs, and opera house fill with jazz music.

GETTING AROUND

A public transit system of trams, light railways, and buses provides frequent service to all parts of the city. An S-Bahn (light railway) serves the suburbs, arriving and leaving from the Hauptbahnhof in the center of Leipzig.

Exploring Leipzig

For the latest information on what's happening in Leipzig, you can check out the website **www.rundgang-kunst.de**, which publishes a list of special exhibitions on view at the time of your visit. The magazine **Kreuzer** (www.kreuzer-leipzig.de) has detailed listings of cultural events, galleries, and restaurant data.

Goethe, who was a student in Leipzig, called the city *klein Paris* (miniature Paris). We wouldn't go quite that far, but Leipzig definitely has its charms. One of the best things to do is explore the handsomely restored Art Nouveau **Arkaden (arcades)** that thread through the historic city center core. Mädler Mall is Leipzig's finest arcade. This is the site of the famous **Auerbachs Keller** (p. 174), the setting for one of the scenes of Goethe's *Faust.* A bronze group of characters from *Faust,* sculpted in 1913, beckons you down a stone staircase into the cellar restaurant.

A gateway leads to **Nasch Markt,** which occupies the space behind the Altes Rathaus. Walk around the front of the Altes Rathaus to find yourself within Am Markt, the city's best-known square, at the edge of which stands the **Königshaus.** Originally built in the late 1700s on the site of an even older building, the Königshaus at one time functioned as the city's official guesthouse for VIPs; it housed both Napoleon and Richard Wagner during their sojourns here.

Neues Rathaus on Burgplatz was erected on the site of the old Pleissenburg, the citadel where Martin Luther held a momentous disputation in 1519. The best place in Leipzig for people-watching is on **Petersstrasse,** below Markt.

THE TOP ATTRACTIONS

Altes Rathaus ★ HISTORIC BUILDING   The 16th-century town hall stands on the 12th-century Renaissance Markt. Allied bombs rained down on the building, but it has been carefully restored. Inside, you'll find the Stadtgeschichtliches Museum (Museum of City History), chronicling the city's cultural and political history.

Markt 1. © **0341/9651320.** www.stadtgeschichtliches-museum-leipzig.de. Admission 4€ adults, 3€ students and children 6–18, free for children 5 and under. Tues–Sun 10am–6pm. Tram: 4 or 6.

Bach-Museum HISTORIC HOUSE   The reconstructed Bose House stands in the shadow of the Thomaskirche. It was once the home of the Bach family and now contains the largest Bach archives in Germany, as well as many mementos of the composer.

Thomaskirchhof 14. © **0341/9137200.** www.bach-leipzig.de. Admission 6€ adults, 4€ students, free for children 16 and under. Tues–Sun 10am–6pm. Tram: 9.

Leipzig

ATTRACTIONS ●
Altes Rathaus 23
Bach-Museum 11
Deutsche Bücherei 15
Grassimuseum 17
Königshaus 22
Museum der Bildenden Künste 7
Museum in der Runden Ecke 9
Naschmarkt 24
Neues Opernhaus 26
Neues Rathaus 13

Nikolaikirche 25
Schillerhaus 2
Thomaskirche 10
University of Leipzig 19
Zoologischer Garten
  Leipzig 1

HOTELS ■
Hotel Adagio 16
Hotel Fürstenhof 4
Markgraf 14

Seaside Park Hotel
  Leipzig 6
Victor's Residenz 5
Westin Leipzig 3

RESTAURANTS ◆
Auerbachs Keller 21
Kaiser Maximillian 20
Stadtpfeiffer 18
Thüringer Hof 12
Zill's Tunnel 8

Grassimuseum ★ MUSEUM   This museum is a three-in-one delight in an Art Deco building updated by the celebrated British architect David Chipperfield. Three distinctive museums are found under one roof.

If for no other reason, we'd go for the **Museum für Völkerkunde (Ethnological Museum)** to see its stunning exhibitions of the antique art of Southeast Asia. From Oceania to Australia, from Indonesia to Europe and the Americas, the exhibits cover all continents, along with Russian displays and artifacts from the Arctic Ocean. In the **Musikinstrumentenmuseum (Musical Instruments Museum)** you can see one of the largest collections of musical instruments in the world, including the oldest known clavichord, built in 1543 in Italy. Most of the instruments, including lutes, flutes, and spinets, date from the Renaissance era. Recorded sounds from the instruments can be heard as you look them over. Finally, the **Museum für Kunsthandwerk (Arts and Crafts Museum)** is rich in the treasures of eastern Germany, not only exquisite porcelain (among the world's finest) but tapestries, handicrafts, and even examples of the famous Bauhaus design.

Johannisplatz 5-11. ℂ **0341/21420.** www.grassimuseum.de. Museum für Völkerkunde 4€; Musikinstrumentenmuseum 4€; Museum für Kunsthandwerk 4€. Museum für Völkerkunde Tues–Fri 10am–6pm, Sat–Sun 10am–5pm; Musikinstrumentenmuseum Tues–Sun 10am–6pm; Museum für Kunsthandwerk Tues and Thurs–Sun 10am–6pm, Wed 10am–8pm.

Museum der Bildenden Künste ★★ MUSEUM   The 2,700 paintings and sculptures in this museum include works by Dürer, Rubens, Rembrandt, Rodin, and van Eyck. The museum, designed like a glass cube, is one of eastern Germany's most impressive art collections. On exhibit is art ranging from the medieval period in Germany up to contemporary art from the United States. The most important art is the work of Lucas Cranach the Elder, including 16th-century portraits. Tintoretto weighs in with his *Resurrection of Lazarus,* and there are many paintings from the German schools of the 19th and 20th centuries. The impressive pieces of sculpture are by such older masters as Rodin and Berthel Thorvaldsen, the most famous sculptor to come out of Denmark.

Katharinenstrasse 10. ℂ **0341/216990.** www.mdbk.de. Admission 5€ adults, 3.50€ students and children 4-14, free for children 3 and under. Tues and Thurs–Sun 10am–6pm; Wed noon–8pm.

Museum in der Runden Ecke MUSEUM   This museum could hardly have been imagined during the Cold War. The building was the headquarters of the dreaded Stasi, the East German Ministry for State Security. Exhibits detail how Stasi operated within East Germany through various methods, most interesting of which show the tools of espionage, such as hidden cameras and letter-opening (and resealing) machines. Other exhibits show the extent of the massive spying, with entire floors devoted to handwriting samples from Leipzig's citizens and extensive personal files on various members of the population. One exhibition, called "The Power and Banality of the East German Secret Police," documents the meticulous and paranoid methods by which the police monitored every exchange of information in the country. They constantly seized private letters and listened in on phone conversations—at times monitoring up to 2,000 calls at once. The exhibition also traces the steps local people took to throw off the Communist regime and end Stasi terror. On the nights of December 4 and December 5, 1989, local citizens seized the building. Leipzig is called *Heldenstadt,* or "city of heroes," for its role in toppling the government of East Germany.

Dittrichring 24 (north of Thomaskirche). ℂ **0341/9612443.** www.runde-ecke-leipzig.de. Free admission. Daily 10am–6pm. Tram: 1, 2, 4, 6, 15, 17, 21, or 24 to Goerderlerring or Thomaskirche.

Schillerhaus HISTORIC HOUSE   In this small farmhouse in Gohlis, a suburb about 20 minutes from the center of Leipzig, Friedrich von Schiller (1759–1805) wrote his "Ode to Joy" in 1785. Beethoven incorporated the poem into the great final movement of his Ninth Symphony.

Menckestrasse 42, Gohlis. ℗ **0341/5662170.** www.stadtgeschichtliches-museum-leipzig.de. Admission 3€ adults, 2€ students, free for children 16 and under. Apr–Oct Tues–Sun 10am–5pm; Nov–Mar Wed–Sun 10am–4pm. Tram: 4 to Menckestrasse.

Thomaskirche ★ CHURCH   Leipzig's most famous resident, Johann Sebastian Bach (1685–1750), was cantor here from 1723 until his death. He spent his most creative years as choirmaster at this church and is buried just in front of the altar. Both Mozart and Mendelssohn performed in the Thomaskirche as well, and Wagner was christened here in 1813. The church was built on the site of a 13th-century monastery and was heavily restored after World War II. Its high-pitched roof dates from 1496. When not touring, the city's *Thomanerchor* (St. Thomas Boy's Choir) presents concerts every Sunday morning and Friday evening.

Thomaskirchhof 18 (just off Marktplatz). ℗ **0341/9602855.** www.thomaskirche.org. Free admission. Daily 9am–6pm. Tram: 4, 6, 8, 10, 11, or 13.

Zoologischer Garten Leipzig ☺ ZOO   This zoo breeds animals to help conserve endangered species. It was founded in 1878, and it is internationally known for breeding carnivores. The biggest aquarium in eastern Germany outside Berlin is also here.

Pfaffendorfer-Strasse 29. ℗ **0341/5933385.** www.zoo-leipzig.de. Admission 13€ adults, 11€ students, 9€ children 4–14, 34€ family ticket, free for children 3 and under. Nov–Mar daily 9am–5pm; Apr and Oct daily 9am–6pm; May–Sept daily 9am–7pm. Tram: 12.

MORE SIGHTS & ACTIVITIES

The German Museum of Books and Scripts, the **Deutsche Bücherei,** Deutscher Platz 1 (℗ **0341/22710;** www.d-nb.de; tram: 21), is the central archive of German literature. You can visit it free from Monday to Friday 8am to 10pm, and Saturday 9am to 6pm, but only with an advance phone call. The archive was established in

SINGING THROUGH THE CENTURIES: THE ST. THOMAS boys' choir

In recent times while the Vienna Boys' Choir enjoyed worldwide fame, Leipzig's Thomanerchor (St. Thomas Choir) languished in obscurity in the eastern zone. Now all that is changing. Any musical expert can tell you that the Leipzig choir has plenty of talent, and as it tours more widely in Europe, its fame will no doubt grow.

The choir has been here since the 13th century. The boys sang on every occasion in the Middle Ages—city celebrations, the installation of bishops, and even executions. Today, the setting for this venerable musical force is Thomaskirche. Choirboys still follow an almost medieval regime within a distinctive subculture that's a world unto itself. Each newcomer is assigned a "mentor" from among the trusted older members of the choir, and all members are required to eat, sleep, study, and rehearse according to a semimonastic regimen. The most famous member was none other than Johann Sebastian Bach. He wrote his great cantatas for this choir and was cantor (choirmaster) for 27 years.

Ever since 1696, **Coffe Baum**, Kleine Fleischergasse 4 (*©* **0341/9610060; www.coffe-baum.de**), has entertained the artistic luminaries of Leipzig, including Wagner, Schumann, and Liszt. Reportedly, even the Emperor Napoleon dropped in for a "cuppa." Still going strong after all these years, the cafe dispenses its traditional *Kaffe und Kuchen* (coffee and cake). Many patrons come just for the desserts, including a buttermilk strawberry mousse on mango foam with frozen apricots in chocolate. You can also order full meals here, with main dishes costing 20€ to 23€.Typical dishes include shoulder of suckling pig with savoy cabbage and potato dumplings or braised leg of lamb in a mint and garlic sauce. Upstairs is a museum with displays of the history of Saxon coffee. Hours are daily 10am to 7pm.

1912 to showcase the fine art of German printing and bookbinding. It's said to possess every item of German literature ever published. It also has a copy of *Iskra,* the Bolshevik newspaper that Lenin came here to print secretly in 1900.

Contrary to popular belief, Thomaskirche isn't the oldest church in Leipzig. That distinction belongs to **Nikolaikirche,** on Nikolaistrasse, erected in 1165. Many works by Bach, including the *St. John Passion,* were first performed here.

If the weather is fair, head for the **Universität Leipzig Turm,** near Nikolaikirche. This metal-and-glass tower overlooks street performers who take over on summer weekends. It's the greatest free show in Leipzig. (Well, not exactly free—the performers will pass the hat at the end of their acts.) Just beware of the skateboard warriors, who make walking about a bit perilous. **Universität Leipzig,** founded in 1409, has contributed greatly to the cultural growth of the city. The East German government rechristened it Karl Marx University, but the old name was restored in 1990. **Augustusplatz** is the ideal center to rub elbows with the thousands of students who study here.

To escape the fumes and noise of the city, head for such "green lungs" as **Johannapark,** on Karl-Tauchnitz-Strasse, or one of the wildly overgrown cemeteries by the **Völkerschlachdenkmal.** On hot days, the fountains in **Sachsenplatz** are popular for splashing about.

Where to Eat
EXPENSIVE

Auerbachs Keller ★ SAXON/INTERNATIONAL   This is the famous restaurant and tavern where Goethe staged the debate between Faust and Mephistopheles in his play *Faust.* The cellar dates from 1530 and has a series of 16th-century murals representing the *Faust* legend. The chefs prepare mainly regional Saxon dishes, along with some international selections. Some of the most tempting offerings are filet of veal, beef, or saddle of lamb, prepared with special sauces and served with seasonal vegetables. The menu changes every 2 months. You can also order from a fine selection of wines and beers. Guests have a choice of the stately looking Historic Rooms (dinner only) or the sprawling, Germanic-looking Big Room, with a different menu and paneling and high ceiling to evoke an upscale beer tavern. Between 11:30am and 6pm Monday to Saturday, visitors can see the Historic Rooms for a charge of 1€.

Mädlerpassage (off the market square, close to the Altes Rathaus), Grimmaischestrasse 2-4. *©* **0341/ 216100.** www.auerbachs-keller-leipzig.de. Reservations recommended. Historic Rooms main courses

27€–31€, fixed-price menus 34€–40€; Big Room main courses 11€–23€, fixed price menu 20€–37€. AE, MC, V. Historic Rooms Mon–Sat 6pm–midnight. Big Room daily 11:30am–midnight. Tram: 4 or 6.

Stadtpfeiffer ★★★ FRENCH/CONTINENTAL   The most prestigious and best-recommended restaurant in Leipzig occupies a glass-ringed dining room that seems to pour golden light out into the angular, concrete-and-glass urban landscape it occupies. As such, it's a welcome spot of warmth and humanity in an otherwise anonymous-looking landscape. Inside, you'll find impeccably detailed service rituals and a sublime cuisine, almost a defiant contrast to a restaurant scene that until now wasn't anywhere near as sophisticated, urban, and international as what you'll find here. Depending on the day of your visit, a delightful meal here might include mussels in puff pastry; lightly smoked freshwater fish with bacon; pan-fried shrimp with fennel; various preparations of lobster; fresh fish, perhaps prepared with olives and demi-glace; and desserts that might feature a gratin of figs with almond-flavored ice cream.

In the Gewandhaus, Augustusplatz 8. ✆ **0341/2178920.** www.stadtpfeiffer.de. Reservations required. Main courses 20€–36€; fixed-price menus 88€–108€. AE, MC, V. Tues–Sat 6pm–midnight. Closed July–Aug.

MODERATE

Kaiser Maximillian ★★ MEDITERRANEAN   You may have some of your best meals in Leipzig here, especially if you like Italian and French-inspired dishes from the Mediterranean. In a sophisticated setting with modern appointments, this restaurant, with its black-leather seats and hip waitstaff, is found in the center of Leipzig in the Urban Department Store between Neumarkt Strasse and Universität Strasse.

Businesspeople in the area drop in for a quick lunch, but in the evening the ambience is more mellow and ideal for long, lingering meals over wine, especially if you order from the fixed-price gourmet menus. The candles glow as you feast on the offerings of the expert chefs who have a talent for sauces and for creating harmonious flavor combinations. Fish is a specialty, appearing as pikeperch with a calf's-head sauce or haddock with a purée of nettles. Anglerfish is a tasty treat with cheeks of beef. You may not want to dine in such an experimental fashion, settling for more familiar meat dishes such as a loin of pork with asparagus and new potatoes, or else saddle of lamb with bell peppers and a creamy polenta. The dessert chef wins our heart with his fresh rhubarb ragout with homemade vanilla ice cream.

Neumarkt 9–19. ✆ **0341/35533333.** www.kaiser-maximilian.de. Reservations required. Main courses 19€–25€. AE, DC, MC, V. Mon–Sat noon–3pm and 6pm–midnight.

INEXPENSIVE

Apels Garten GERMAN/SAXON   Its name commemorates the site of a 400-year-old garden, no longer in existence. Today, you'll find a modern mid-1980s building with a conservatively decorated street-level restaurant known for its home-style German food. Specialties include Leipzig-style onion soup or wild-duck soup with homemade noodles, roast goose with potatoes and vegetables, grilled *Wurst* with potatoes and red cabbage, and *Sauerbraten* with onions and red cabbage. The cuisine is more robust than refined; it's very filling.

Kolonnadenstrasse 2. ✆ **0341/9607777.** www.apels-garten.de. Reservations recommended. Main courses 10€–20€; set menu 16€–30€. AE, MC, V. Mon–Sat 11am–11pm; Sun 11am–3:30pm. Tram: 4, 6, 8, 10, 11, or 13.

Thüringer Hof SAXON/THURINGIAN   Martin Luther used to dine here—that's how old this mellow place is. It's been serving hearty regional fare since 1454. Goethe used to drop in, as did the composer Robert Schumann. By 1865 it became known as the Thüringer Hof and had 1,200 seats, making it one of the most famous restaurants of Germany, as fabled as the Hofbräuhaus in Munich. The restaurant had to be rebuilt after World War II, and the Luther Hall section was completely duplicated. Showing wear and tear in the 1990s, it was rebuilt once again. The tradition of good food is still maintained, with some of the recipes sounding as if they are the same that Luther himself ate. We're talking Thuringian potato soup with sausage slices or pickled beef with raisin sauce and Thuringian dumplings. Purple cabbage comes with many dishes. Among the courses we'd recommend are spicy pork goulash with cream mushrooms or rare filets of lamb in a garlic sauce with potato croquettes. Hearty eaters will go for the grill platter for two—breast of chicken, venison steak, pork medallions, and home-fried potatoes.

Burgstrasse 19. ℂ **0341/9944999.** www.thueringer-hof.de. Reservations recommended. Main courses 7.60€–17€. AE, DC, MC, V. Daily 11am–midnight.

Zill's Tunnel SAXON   This is one of the city's most atmospheric restaurants, serving tasty and reasonably priced food, including massive quantities of regionally brewed beer, to hungry diners and drinkers. The restaurant is not a real tunnel, though its barrel-ceilinged ground floor tavern suggests that. The location is at the marketplace opposite the old city hall. Today's restaurant is the end result of a once-popular eatery established here in 1841. You can also dine upstairs in the more formal wine restaurant, with its open fireplace and antiques. In addition to international vintages, there are some good-value Meissen wines. The menu is in German and very traditional, including such longtime favorites as pork *Schnitzel* with potatoes or Norwegian filet of salmon, even tender beef tournedos in a pepper sauce. Desserts are rich, wholesome, and prepared fresh daily, as are the homemade soups for appetizers.

Barfussgasschen 9. ℂ **0341/9602078.** www.zillstunnel.de. Reservations recommended upstairs. Main courses 10€–15€; fixed-price menus 14€–35€. AE, DC, MC, V. Daily 11:30am–midnight.

Shopping

Leipzig has emerged as the art-buying capital of the former East Germany. Galleries hold rich inventories of paintings and sculpture by artists whose works were once unknown to western consumers. **Galerie für Zeitgenössische Kunst,** Karl-Tauchnitz-Strasse 11 (ℂ **0341/140810;** www.gfzk-online.de), is a privately owned art gallery that displays international art, showing about 14 exhibitions a year. It charges 5€ for adults, 3€ for students and children 10 to 18 (free for those 9 and under).

If you're looking for examples of the antique furniture and art objects that many Leipzigers have dragged down from their attics since reunification, head for any of the dozen or so antiques dealers conducting business within the town's core. **Neumarkt Passage** has several antiquarian bookshops. With more than 150 outlets, including restaurants and cafes, the **Hauptbahnhof,** Willy-Brandt-Platz, is a shopper's delight, one of the best shopping experiences not just in Leipzig, but in this entire part of Germany.

Entertainment & Nightlife

Leipzig's active nightlife offers something for everyone. The area around the Markt is full of bars, cafes, and other entertainment options; it's a good place to kick off your search for a nightspot.

THE PERFORMING ARTS   The **Leipziger Oper** is one of Germany's most acclaimed opera companies. Its home is the **Neues Opernhaus** (it's sometimes referred to simply as Oper Leipzig), Augustusplatz 12 (ℂ **0341/1261275;** www.oper-unplugged.de; tram: 4, 7, 8, 10, or 11), opposite Das Gewandhaus (see below). Part of

GERMAN men of ideas: MARTIN LUTHER (1483–1546)

"I am more afraid of my own heart than of the pope and all his cardinals. I have within me the great pope, Self."

Field of Study: Priest, theologian, firebrand.

Revolutionary Insight: His *95 Theses* questioned the culture of church indulgences (donating money to guarantee salvation). It evolved into a critique of Catholic corruption and a rejection of papal infallibility, sparking the Protestant Reformation. Luther's views spread quickly, thanks to the recent invention of the printing press.

Controversy Quotient (0 to 5): (5+) Excommunicated by Pope Leo X and declared heretic/ outlaw by Holy Roman Emperor Charles V in 1521; ordained as a monk in 1507, but married in 1525; late in life spouted virulent, violent anti-Semitic views.

Little Known Fact: Met his wife, Katherina von Bora, while abetting her escape from a Cistercian convent; smuggled her (and other nuns) out in a wagon filled with herring barrels.

—Kelly Regan

its space is devoted to the **Kellertheater** (℗ **0341/1261275;** www.oper-leipzig.de), a small-scale theater that presents small-ensemble, progressive performances of all types. The box office for both the main opera house and the Kellertheater is open Monday to Friday 10am to 8pm, and Saturday 10am to 4pm. Tickets to the theater are 10€ to 32€ for adults, with students getting up to one-third off, depending on the performance. Call the box office, or ask at the tourist office, for information. Tickets to the opera cost 10€ to 60€.

The home of the famous **Gewandhaus Orchestra ★** is a modern concert hall built in 1981, **Das Gewandhaus** (℗ **0341/1270280;** www.gewandhaus.de; tram: 4, 7, or 15), which faces the Neues Opernhaus across Augustusplatz. Founded in 1781, the orchestra saw some of its greatest days under the baton of Felix Mendelssohn, who died in Leipzig in 1847. Other notable conductors have included Wilhelm Furtwängler, Bruno Walter, and Kurt Masur. Concerts, ballets, organ recitals, and other events are staged here. Tickets usually range from 5€ to 60€.

The main venue for theater in Leipzig is the **Schauspielhaus,** Bosestrasse 1 (℗ **0341/1268168;** www.schauspiel-leipzig.de; tram: 1, 2, 4, 6, 15, 17, 21, or 24), home to several arts companies that jointly stage an eclectic mix of theatrical and musical productions. Tickets cost 7€ to 27€ for adults, half-price for students. The box office is open weekdays noon to 7pm, Saturday 10am to 1pm, and 1 hour before showtime.

DANCE CLUBS Leipzigers like to dance, and the downtown area offers several animated nocturnal venues. Appealing to a youngish crowd is **Nachtcafé,** Petersstrasse 39–41 (℗ **0341/2114000;** www.nachtcafe.com). Open only on Monday and Wednesday nights from 9pm to around 3am and Saturday nights from 10pm to around 4am, it plays soul, house, funk, blues, and whatever's hip and contemporary in London and L.A., with music provided by a crew of DJs who are well known locally. Entrance is 5€, except for women under 24, who invariably talk their way in free. Attracting a young, raffish crowd is **Spizz,** Marktplatz 9 (℗ **0341/9608043;** www.spizz.info). Cramped, crowded, sweaty, hot, and usually convivial, they play jazz, reggae, pop, and disco music from the

'80s and '90s. Entrance costs 10€ per person. It's open only Friday and Saturday nights from 11pm to around 5am.

LIVE MUSIC Built against the old city wall, **Moritzbastei,** Universitätsstrasse 9 (*✆* **0341/702590;** www.moritzbastei.de; tram: 4, 6, 15, or 20), is a jaunty-looking, all-in-one entertainment complex that houses at least two stages for the presentation of concerts and cabarets, a labyrinthine pub with lots of different areas for drinking, carousing, and dancing, and a cafe. It's popular with students. Depending on the night of the week and the time you show up, you'll find either live bands or DJs playing Afropop, heavy metal, and rock mixed with contemporary dance music. Some aspect of this complex opens daily from 10am, but the nighttime energy gets wound up only Wednesday to Saturday from 8pm to 5am, when it charges a cover that ranges from 4.50€ to 21€. Sometimes, in midsummer, films (foreign and German language) are shown in an open-air terrace in a kind of "be-in" communal venue that will remind you of your college years.

For more blues, jazz, and the occasional presentation of German-language satire and cabaret, head to **Pfeffermühle,** Gottschedstrasse 1 (*✆* **0341/9603253;** tram: 4, 6, 8, 10, 11, or 13), on Monday night, when the bands start up at 10pm. Other nights, people gather to drink and talk. The courtyard here is very popular during warm weather.

GAY BARS & CLUBS The friendly, ultracool bar **RosaLinde,** Langestrasse 11 (*✆* **0341/8796982;** www.rosalinde.de), is the central focus of gay nightlife in Leipzig. It's open Sunday to Thursday as a bar from 5 to 11pm; Friday and Saturday it functions as a cafe, bar, and dance club from 5pm to 3am, with music beginning around 9pm. Come here for a drink and the chance to mingle with conventional, not particularly fetishistic gay men (and to a lesser degree, lesbians) in their 20s and 30s.

VARIETY Recommended only for visitors who really understand fluent, and highly ironic, German-language nuances, **Schaubühne Lindenfels,** Karl-Heine-Strasse 50 (*✆* **0341/484620;** www.schaubuehne.com; tram: 1, 2, 4, 6, 15, 17, 21, or 24), offers alternative theater and cinema in a laid-back cafe/bar complex and is

---

GERMAN men of ideas: GOTTFRIED LIEBNITZ (1646–1716)

"Even in the games of children there are things to interest the greatest mathematician."

Field of Study: Philosopher, lawyer, diplomat, self-taught mathematician.

Revolutionary Insight: First published theory of infinitesimal calculus in 1684; notebooks indicate his first equations employed in 1675, just 3 years after first taking up the study of math. Inspired by the classic Chinese text *I Ching,* invented the binary numerical system, now the basis of all modern computer programming.

Controversy Quotient (0to 5): (2) Dogged by (still unresolved) controversy over whether he plagiarized calculus theory after seeing Isaac Newton's unpublished writings on a 1676 visit to London.

Little Known Fact: In 1891, Hermann Bahlsen introduced a butter cookie named Liebniz-Keks, in honor of the philosopher. It remains the company's most popular product.

—Kelly Regan

open daily 10am to 2am. Admission to movies, which are shown almost nightly, costs between 5€ and 8€ per person. Admission to theater productions costs from 7.50€ to 20€ per person. Depending on the seasonal lineup, they're presented Thursday to Saturday and sometimes Sunday.

Where to Stay

EXPENSIVE

Hotel Fürstenhof ★★★ This hotel, located in the former residence of a Leipzig banker, is the best in Leipzig, a government-rated five-star hotel. Its interior has been redecorated to reflect the building's original, almost-forgotten neoclassical theme. A corps of English and Swedish designers has outfitted the rooms in a modern interpretation of neoclassical style. The rejuvenated bathrooms are the best in town. The ballroom (the Serpentinensaal) and a monumental staircase date from the 19th century.

Tröndlinring 8, 04105 Leipzig. www.starwoodhotels.com. ℂ **0341/1400.** Fax 0341/1403700. 92 units. 109€–330€ double; 240€–640€ junior suite. AE, DC, MC, V. Parking 19€. Tram: 15. **Amenities:** 2 restaurants; 2 bars; babysitting; concierge; exercise room; indoor heated pool; room service; spa. *In room:* A/C, TV, hair dryer, minibar, Wi-Fi (19€ per day).

Victor's Residenz ★ This Best Western hotel near the Hauptbahnhof is a successful reconstruction of a 19th-century building that survived World War II bombings. Today it's been completely restored and turned into an oasis of comfort in the very heart of Leipzig. The bedrooms are midsize to spacious and the latest word in modernity, and the suites in particular are among the most comfortable and best appointed in town. We have found the staff particularly helpful. The on-site restaurant is more like a brasserie in Paris, the chefs specializing in Mediterranean cuisine. When the summer sun shines, a patio opens up. The atmosphere is definitely not stuffy, the manager telling us, "We believe in our guests having a good time."

Georgiring 13, 04103 Leipzig. www.victors.de. ℂ **0341/68660.** Fax 0341/6866899. 101 units. 125€–252€ double; 195€–292€ suite. Rates include buffet breakfast. AE, DC, MC, V. Parking 13€. **Amenities:** Restaurant; bar; babysitting; concierge; room service. *In room:* A/C, TV, fridge, hair dryer, minibar, Wi-Fi (free).

Westin Leipzig ★★ Rising 27 floors, this is one of the tallest landmarks in Leipzig and one of eastern Germany's leading hotels. In this luxe category, we prefer the greater charm and comfort of the Fürstenhof (see above), although the Westin is fine in every way. Close to the railway station, it is the largest hotel in Leipzig, a businessperson's favorite, and also a popular venue for conventions. Don't expect lots of atmosphere or personal service. All the guest rooms, ranging from small to spacious, are renovated. The hotel offers more diverse dining and drinking options than its competitors, everything from a *Bierstube* with Saxon cookery to a *teppanyaki* grill with sushi and sashimi.

Gerberstrasse 15 (5 min. from Altes Rathaus), 04105 Leipzig. www.westin.com/leipzig. ℂ **800/327-0200** in the U.S. and Canada, or 0341/9880. Fax 0341/9881229. 447 units. 89€–295€ double; 269€–500€ suite. AE, DC, MC, V. Parking 19€. Tram: 4 or 6. **Amenities:** 3 restaurants; 3 bars; concierge; exercise room; indoor heated pool; room service; spa. *In room:* TV, hair dryer, minibar, Wi-Fi (20€ per day).

MODERATE

Seaside Park Hotel Leipzig Less than a kilometer (about ½ mile) from the city center, this is the latest reincarnation of a hotel that opened in 1913 near the central rail depot. Back then it was hailed as the grandest first-class hotel in the city, though today the competition is too keen for it to retain that title. Government protected as a historical monument, the hotel lies behind a facade of soundproof windows. It caters mainly to business travelers but also welcomes vacationers to its well-furnished, mid-size to spacious guest rooms, decorated in an Art Deco style with well-equipped bathrooms, mostly with tub/shower combinations. Fine dining characterizes the two restaurants here. Our favorite part of the hotel is a reconstruction of the famous Orient Express dining room.

Richard-Wagner Strasse 7, 04109 Leipzig. www.parkhotelleipzig.de.℗ **0341/98520.** Fax 0341/9852750. 288 units. 105€–155€ double; from 175€ suite. Rates include buffet breakfast. AE, DC, MC, V. Parking 13€. **Amenities:** 2 restaurants; bar; exercise room; Jacuzzi; room service; sauna. *In room:* A/C, TV, hair dryer, kitchenette (in some), minibar, Wi-Fi (20€ per hour).

INEXPENSIVE

Galerie Hotel Leipziger 🛗   Behind a baroque facade, this offbeat choice offers funky but comfortable rooms. It appeals to artists and students as well as a group of patrons who in the past would have been called "bohemians." Each small to midsize bedroom is furnished in a rather minimalist style. The saving grace is that Leipzig artists contributed paintings or sculpture to make each bedroom unique—hence, the name of the hotel. There is also an on-site art gallery.

Hedwigstrasse 1–3, 04315 Leipzig. www.leipziger-hof.de. ℗ **0341/69740.** Fax 0341/6974150. 73 units. 87€–155€ double; 165€ junior suite. AE, DC, MC, V. Parking 7€. Tram: 1, 3, or 8. **Amenities:** Spa. *In room:* TV, hair dryer, minibar, Wi-Fi (free).

Hotel Adagio ☺   This is a restored and greatly refurbished 1882 building in a tranquil location between the Neues Gewandhaus and the Grassimuseum. Each midsize guest room is individually furnished with such themes as the Roaring 1920s. The bathrooms that come with the 1920s guest rooms contain the largest tubs in the city. The hotel staff gives a special welcome to families traveling with children.

Seeburgstrasse 96, Leipzig 04103. www.hotel-adagio.de. ℗ **0341/216690.** Fax 0341/9603078. 32 units. 85€–90€ double; 140€–160€ suite. Rates include buffet breakfast. AE, DC, MC, V. Parking 8€. **Amenities:** Bar; room service. *In room:* TV, hair dryer.

Markgraf 🍴   Stay here for its affordable price—not any luxurious living. What you get are small yet comfortable rooms. Platform beds with thin mattresses prevail, and there are many blond-wood furnishings. In its modest category, this is one of the best deals in town, all modern and sleek. Maintenance and service rate high points. The hotel lies just a short walk or tram ride south of the city center.

Körnerstrasse 36, 04107 Leipzig. www.markgraf-leipzig.de. ℗ **0341/303030.** Fax 0341/3030399. 54 units. 65€–185€ double; 100€–235€ suite. AE, DC, MC, V. Parking 10€. Tram: 10 or 11 from the Hauptbahnhof. **Amenities:** Exercise room; room service; sauna. *In room:* TV, fax (in some), minibar, Wi-Fi (free).

Side Trips from Leipzig

LUTHERSTADT WITTENBERG

This is the city associated with **Martin Luther** (1483–1546), leader of the German Reformation, and it attracts pilgrims from all over the world. Wittenberg's other famous son was humanist Philipp Melanchthon (1497–1560), a Protestant reformer and scholar, and a friend of Luther's and later of Calvin's. Luther and Melanchthon are honored with statues in front of the Rathaus. Wittenberg is a handsome enough city, but a stop here isn't a must unless you're particularly interested in Luther.

ESSENTIALS   Wittenberg lies about 70km (43 miles) northeast of Leipzig and 100km (60 miles) southwest of Berlin. Access by car is via the A9 Autobahn north and south, Route 187 east, and Hwy. 2 north and south. The Wittenberg Bahnhof is on the major Deutsche Bundesbahn rail line (Halle-Berlin), with frequent connections. It's an hour by train from Leipzig. For travel information, contact **Wittenberg-Information,** Schlossplatz 2 (✆ **03491/498610;** www.wittenberg.de). November to February, it's open Monday to Friday from 10am to 4pm, Saturday from 10am to 2pm, and Sunday from 11am to 3pm. March to October, it's open Monday to Friday from 9am to 6pm, Saturday from 10am to 3pm, and Sunday from 11am to 4pm. In January and February, it's closed on weekends.

Exploring Wittenberg

Both Luther and Melanchthon are buried in the **Schlosskirche,** Friedrichstrasse 1A (✆ **03491/402585;** www.schlosskirche-wittenberg.de), which dates from the 15th century but was rebuilt in the 19th. It was on the Schlosskirche doors that Luther nailed his "Ninety-Five Theses" in 1517. The bronze doors were added in 1858 and bear the Latin text of the theses. The church is open November to April, Monday to Saturday 10am to 4pm and Sunday 11:30am to 4pm; May to October, it's open Monday to Saturday 10am to 6pm and Sunday 11:30am to 6pm. Services are held Sunday at 10am and Wednesday at noon. There's a 30-minute organ concert every Tuesday at 2:30pm. Admission to the church and to its concerts is free; a brief audio guided tour, conducted in either German or English, costs 3€. For further information contact the tourist office at ✆ **03491/498610.**

Part of an Augustinian monastery in which Luther lived has been turned into the **Lutherhalle Wittenberg,** Collegienstrasse 54 (✆ **03491/42030;** www.martin luther.de). The parish church here, where Luther preached, dates from the 14th century. An oak tree marks the spot outside the Elster gate where Luther publicly burned his papal bull (edict) of excommunication in 1520. Hours are November to March Tuesday to Sunday 10am to 5pm, April to October daily 9am to 6pm. Admission costs 5€ for adults, 3€ for students and children ages 7 to 18, free for children 6 and under.

You can also visit the **Stadtkirche,** the "Mother Church of the Reformation," Judenstrasse 35 (✆ **03491/403201**), where Luther did the majority of his preaching. Sections date from the 13th century, making it the oldest structure in Wittenberg. The altar is by Lucas Cranach the Elder, who was once *Bürgermeister* of Wittenberg and a friend to Luther. It's open November to April Monday to Saturday 10am to 4pm and Sunday 11:30am to 4pm; hours for May to October are Monday to Saturday 9am to 5pm and Sunday 11:30am to 5pm. Admission is free.

Where to Eat & Stay

Grüne Tanne ★ 🍴 In the city of Martin Luther, only a traditional, atmospheric hotel will do for some visitors. On the outskirts of town, this is a former knight's manor with a history going back 4 centuries. The estate is a warm, inviting, and cozy country manor, with a tradition of welcoming guests since 1871. The hotel maintains a shuttle between the train station and the inn. The guest rooms are midsize and comfortably and tastefully furnished, and the suites are spacious and beautifully maintained. The on-site restaurant, which serves traditional German food, is worth a visit even if you're a nonguest. In the summer, dining overflows onto the terrace, and the entire place assumes a festive atmosphere.

Am Teich 1, 06896 Wittenberg. www.gruenetanne.de. ✆ **03491/6290.** Fax 03491/629250. 40 units. 59€–79€ double; 89€–109€ suite. Rates include buffet breakfast. AE, DC, MC, V. Free parking. **Amenities:** Restaurant; children's playground. *In room:* TV, hair dryer.

QUEDLINBURG ★

In 1994, UNESCO cited Quedlinburg as "an extraordinary example of a medieval European city" and added it to its list of World Heritage Sites.

Quedlinburg, which survived World War II intact, is nestled at the foot of a rock pinnacle and crowned by a castle and an abbey church. Its origins go back to a Saxon settlement in the early 10th century. Here you'll see the church of St. Servatius, an architectural masterpiece, as well as a well-preserved castle and cobbled lanes with half-timbered houses dating from the 16th and 17th centuries. In fact, Quedlinburg has more than 1,600 half-timbered buildings, more than any other town in the country.

ESSENTIALS There are three trains a day from Leipzig (travel time: 3 hr.). Call ✆ **01805/996633** or visit www.bahn.de for information and schedules. Access by car is along B6. For tourist information, contact **Quedlinburg-Information,** Markt 2 (✆ **03946/905624;** www.quedlinburg-info.de), open April to September Monday to Friday 9am to 7pm, Saturday and Sunday 10am to 3pm; and October to March Monday to Friday 9:30am to 6pm, and Saturday 10am to 2pm.

Exploring Quedlinburg

Begin your tour in the **Altstadt (Old Town),** site of the **Markt (Marketplace).** The **Rathaus (Town Hall),** in the Renaissance style of the 1600s, was originally built in 1310. The statue (ca. 1420) on the left of the facade is of Roland, Charlemagne's knight. The buildings on the other three sides of the Markt are from the 1600s and 1700s. Branching off the square are small cobblestone lanes right out of the Middle Ages. The area around Breitstrasse has several colorful alleyways.

Take the ramp up to the castle to the broad terrace that offers a panoramic view of the medieval town. Here, on the site of the original 9th-century church, stands Quedlinburg's major attraction, the **Stiftskirche St. Servatius ★★**, Schlossberg 1 (✆ **03946/709900;** www.domschatzquedlinburg.de), an architectural masterpiece of the Romanesque era. The church was started in 1070 but wasn't consecrated until 1129. Craftsmen from northern Italy created the friezes and capitals above the central nave. Three aisles with diagonal rib vaulting divide the crypt beneath the chancel. The aisles are adorned with frescoes depicting scenes from the Bible.

The church is filled with treasures, including a *Domschatz* (treasury) with manuscripts dating from the 10th century. In 1990, a number of ecclesiastical artifacts that had disappeared after the war turned up in Texas, when the heirs of a U.S. Army officer tried to sell them. The purloined treasures have been returned and are now on permanent display. The church is open May to October Tuesday to Saturday 10am to 6pm, Sunday noon to 6pm; and November to April Tuesday to Saturday 10am to 4pm and Sunday noon to 5pm. Admission is 5€ for adults, 4€ for students and children ages 6 to 18. It's free for children 5 and under.

Burgberg Schloss, Schlossberg 1 (✆ **03946/2730**), was once part of an abbey. A Saxon stronghold in the 10th century, the castle was expanded from the late 16th to the mid–17th century. The complex includes the Schlossmuseum, with 16th- and 17th-century Italian and Flemish paintings, as well as exhibits on the town's history. You can also visit the Princes' Hall from the mid-1700s and the throne room. The castle is open April to October daily 10am to 6pm, and November to March Saturday to Thursday 10am to 4pm. Admission is 4€ for adults, 3€ for children ages 6 to 18, and free for children 5 and under.

Where to Eat

Brauhaus Lüdde GERMAN   The best place for a good regional meal and the best beer around is this restored old brewery. The Lüdde brewery was once known throughout the Harz Mountains, but shut down in 1966. After reunification, one of the Lüdde relatives took it over and converted the rotting buildings into a good hotel, brewery, and restaurant. The beer comes in four varieties, the most famous being Pubarschknall, a brown beer. In summer a beer garden flourishes between the main house and the old horse stables. Menus change seasonally but expect good, hearty cooking consisting of regional fare.

Blasiistrasse 14. ✆ **03946/705206.** Reservations not required. Main courses 8€–20€. MC, V. Mon–Sat 11am–midnight; Sun 11am–10pm.

Ratskeller GERMAN   This longtime favorite is within walking distance of the railway station. Wine buffs should order the rare Saxon wine. The food is hearty and regional. Many of the meat and game specialties are served with wine *Sauerkraut* and dumplings. In season, venison is likely to be on the menu.

Markt 1 (in the Rathaus). ✆ **03946/2768.** Reservations recommended. Main courses 10€–19€. No credit cards. Daily 11am–10pm. Closed Jan.

Where to Stay

Hotel Zum Brauhaus 🔔   This is the most atmospheric place to stay in town; it's attached to an old brewery that had been allowed to slumber for decades. In a restored half-timbered house, the hotel offers attractively furnished bedrooms, ranging in size from small to medium. Many of the wooden timbers have been exposed, giving it an old-fashioned look. In spite of its antique look, everything is modern inside.

Carl-Ritter-Strasse 1, 06484 Quedlinburg. www.hotel-brauhaus-luedde.de. ✆ **03946/901481.** Fax 03496/901483. 51 units. 80€–89€ double. Rates include continental breakfast. MC, V. Free parking. **Amenities:** Restaurant; bar. *In room:* TV.

Ringhotel Schlossmühle ★★   Set in the medieval center, this government-rated four-star hotel has emerged as the finest in Quedlinburg. It combines a historic core with a modern addition. Ancient traditions and a modern ambience are perfectly wed here, creating a special atmosphere. Guest rooms are midsize to spacious and are completely up-to-date, each one tastefully furnished and comfortably decorated, with midsize bathrooms. On-site are two restaurants, offering a variety of regional and international dishes, the best in Quedlinburg. The hotel is better accessorized than its nearest competition, Romantik Hotel am Brühl (see below).

Kaiser-Otto-Strasse 28, 06484 Quedlinburg. www.schlossmuehle.de. ✆ **03946/7870.** Fax 03946/787419. 77 units. 96€–138€ double; 138€–170€ suite. AE, DC, MC, V. Parking 10€. **Amenities:** Restaurant; bar; Jacuzzi; sauna. *In room:* TV, hair dryer, minibar, Wi-Fi (free).

Romantik Hotel am Brühl ★★   Romantic and tranquil, and set behind a richly historic brick and half-timbered facade, this hotel is run by the Schmidt family. Guest rooms come in a variety of shapes and sizes, as do the bathrooms. All rooms are well furnished with first-rate mattresses and fine linens; some open onto castle views. Virtually all major attractions are within walking distance.

Billungstrasse 11, 06484 Quedlinburg. www.hotelambruehl.de. ✆ **03946/96180.** Fax 03946/9618246. 46 units. 113€–150€ double; 155€–195€ suite. Rates include buffet breakfast. AE, DC, V. Free parking. **Amenities:** Restaurant; room service; sauna. *In room:* TV, hair dryer, minibar, Wi-Fi (free).

Zur Goldenen Sonne   This hotel, which dates from 1671, is a good traditional choice. It stands near the Mathildenbrunne, a landmark fountain. The building's timber-frame construction is typical of this part of Germany. The small rooms are cozily furnished in rustic style, and each is equipped with a small, shower-only bathroom. In summer, the garden is popular with locals and visitors.

Steinweg 11 (5-min. walk from the railway station), 06484 Quedlinburg. www.hotelzurgoldenensonne. de. ✆ **03946/96250.** Fax 03946/962530. 27 units. 69€–92€ double. Rates include buffet breakfast. AE, MC, V. Free parking. **Amenities:** Restaurant; bar. *In room:* TV, minibar.

DRESDEN ★★★

198km (123 miles) S of Berlin, 111km (69 miles) SE of Leipzig

Dresden, once known as "Florence on the Elbe," was celebrated throughout Europe for its architecture and art treasures. Then came the night of February 13, 1945, when Allied bombers rained down phosphorus and high-explosive bombs on the city. By morning, the Dresden of legend was but a memory. (When Brits heard the news that British pilots had bombed Dresden, many viewed it as Churchill's revenge for the mass aerial bombardment of the old city of Coventry earlier in the war.) No one knows for sure how many died, but the number is certainly in the tens of thousands, and perhaps more. If you're interested in the subject, you might want to read Kurt Vonnegut's novel *Slaughterhouse Five*.

Today, Dresden is undergoing a rapid and dramatic restoration, and it is once again a major sightseeing destination. Dresden boasts beautiful churches and palaces, as well as many world-class museums, among the finest in all of Germany.

In 2006, Dresden celebrated its 800th anniversary.

Essentials

GETTING THERE

BY PLANE   The **Dresden-Klotsche** airport lies 10km (6 miles) north of the city center. The airport is served by Lufthansa and most international carriers, with regularly scheduled flights from 11 German cities and other major European cities. For flight information, call ✆ **0351/8813360** or visit www.dresden-airport.de. A rail line that's linked to Dresden's S-Bahn network stretches from the airport to the city's main station, requiring 20 minutes' transit each way, and a one-way fare of 1.90€. A taxi from the airport to the center of Dresden costs about 25€.

BY TRAIN   Dresden has two main rail stations, the **Hauptbahnhof,** on Wiener Platz, and the **Dresden-Neustadt,** at Schlesischer Park. Tram no. 3 connects the two. The city is served by the Deutsche Bundesbahn rail line, with frequent connections to major and regional cities. From Berlin, 15 trains arrive daily (trip time: 2–2½ hr.); 12 trains pull in from Frankfurt (trip time: 5 hr.). For rail information and schedules, call ✆ **01805/996633** or visit www.bahn.de.

BY CAR   Access is via the E50 Autobahn from the west or the E4 Autobahn from the north (Rostock, Berlin) or south.

VISITOR INFORMATION

The **Dresden Tourist Information Office** is in the Kulturpalast on Wilsdrufferstrasse (✆ **0351/50160160;** www.dresden.de). Open April to December Monday to Friday 10am to 7pm, Saturday 10am to 6pm, and Sunday 10am to 3pm. Off-season hours are Monday to Friday 10am to 6pm, Saturday 10am to 4pm, and Sunday 10am to 2pm.

Dresden

GERMANY
Hamburg
Berlin ★
Dresden ●
Frankfurt am Main
Munich ●

0   200 yds
0   200 m

NEUSTADT

Blockhaus

Neustädter Markt

Carola-platz

Elbe

Zwingerteich

Semper-oper

Theater-platz

Schloss-platz

Brühlsche

Terrasse

Terrassenufer

Brühlscher Garten

Zwinger

Chiaveri-gasse

Residenz-schloss

Kunst-akademie

Verkehrs-museum

An der Frauenkirche

Taschen-berg

Kleine Brüdergasse

Jüdenhof

Neu-markt

Rampische Str.

Akademiestr.

Tzschirner-platz

Rathenau-platz

Post-platz

Kultur-palast

Salzgasse

Landhausstr.

ALTSTADT

Wilsdruffer Strasse

Altmarkt

Kreuz-kirche

Webergasse

Pirnaischer Platz

Grunaer Str.

Altmarkt-Galerie

Kramer-gasse

An der Mauer

Rathaus

Rathaus-platz

Pirnaische Str.

Dippoldis-walder Platz

Waisenhausstrasse

Georg-platz

Information ⓘ
Pedestrians only

Deutsches Hygiene-museum

BLÜHER-PARK

Lingner-platz

ATTRACTIONS ●
Albertinum **19**
Altmarkt **21**
Frauenkirche **17**
Gemäldegalerie
  Alte Meister **9**
Grosser Garten **23**
Katholische Hofkirche **13**
Kreuzkirche **22**
Porzellansammlung **9**
Residenzschloss **12**
Rüstkammer **9**
Semperoper **6**
Zwinger **9**

HOTELS ■
Art'otel **4**
Bülow Residenz **2**
Hilton Dresden **14**
Hotel am Terrassenufer **26**
Hotel Suitess **18**
Kempinski Hotel
  Taschenbergpalais **11**
Raskolnikoff Pension **3**
Rothenburger Hof **3**
Schlosshotel Dresden-Pillnitz **25**
Steigenberger Hotel de Saxe **20**
Westin Bellevue **1**

RESTAURANTS ◆
Alte Meister **5**
Ayers Rock **15**
Café Schinkelwache **8**
Italienisches Dörfchen **7**
Lesage **24**
Rossini **16**
Sophienkeller im
  Taschenbergpalais **10**

5

SAXONY & THURINGIA | Dresden

GETTING AROUND

By Public Transportation   If you plan to see more than the historic core of Dresden, you can use the bus and tram lines. A ride of four stops or fewer costs 1.90€, or you can purchase a 24-hour pass for 5€. Maps and tickets are sold at automated dispensers outside the main rail station. Most major lines operate every hour, though service is curtailed between midnight and 5am. Dresden's S-Bahn reaches the suburbs.

BY FUNICULAR   Dresden has two funiculars. The busier and more accessible of the two is the **Standseilbahn,** which links the suburb of Loschwitz to a hillside residential area, Weisser Hirsch. More remote, with less frequent runs, is the **Schwebebahn,** which links Loschwitz with Oberloschwitz on Saturday and Sunday only, carrying passengers to the viewing site at Loschwitzhöhe, which gives you an excellent view of the city. This funicular was the first of its kind in the world, built from 1898 to 1900. Fares on either funicular cost 3.70€ each way. For operating hours and more details, contact the transportation office at ℂ **0351/8571011.**

BY FERRY   Five ferries service Dresden, each operated by the same authorities that maintain the city's network of trams and buses. One is a vehicular ferry across the River Elbe between Dresden-Kleinschachwitz and the Pillnitz Castle. To reach its departure point, take tram no. 1 from Postplatz. For more information, call ℂ **0351/8571011.**

BUS TOURS

Responding to the flood of visitors coming to see the city's historic core, **Stadtrundfahrt Dresden,** Königsstrasse 6 (ℂ **0351/8995650;** www.stadtrundfahrt.com), has organized a flotilla of red-and-white buses that feature—via prerecorded descriptions and headsets—running commentary in eight languages. April to October daily from 9:30am to 5pm, buses depart at 30-minute intervals for circular tours of the city that incorporate overviews of all the major monuments. From November to March daily service is from 10am to 3pm. Visitors can hop on or off the bus at any of 22 points along the way, and they can even postpone some of the stops until the following day. Each tour begins at the Theaterplatz, adjacent to the Augustusbrücke. Additional stopovers include the Zwinger, the Grünes Gewölbe, the Frauenkirche, and many of the parks, gardens, and architectural highlights of the city. The price is 22€ per adult, with no discounts for students; children 13 and under are free when accompanied by an adult.

Exploring Dresden

Frauenkirche (Church of Our Lady) ★★, at Neumarkt (ℂ **0351/65606100;** www.frauenkirche-dresden.org; tram no. 4 or 8), was built between 1726 and 1743 and once was known throughout Europe for its 93m (305-ft.) dome. On the night of February 13, 1945, it was bombed by Allied planes, and during the Cold War it

---

Dresden for Less

The Dresden City-Card, which costs 21€ and is good for 48 hours, is a great deal for short-term visitors. The card gives you unlimited access to all public trams, buses, and ferries, plus free access to 12 of the city's best museums.

There are also reductions on charges for certain sightseeing tours and some cultural events. The tourist office sells the card, and it's also available at the front desks of most hotels.

---

remained the most evocative ruins in Dresden. The East German government deliberately let the blackened hulk stay as it was as a reminder of the horrors of modern warfare. Today the church has been rebuilt and was reconsecrated for the 800th anniversary of the founding of Dresden on October 30, 2005. The original pieces from the pile of rubble left over from 1945 were used, along with other materials. This is one of the most important Protestant churches in Germany, with its famous dome restored. In 2002, the duke of Kent came to Dresden to hand over a new dome cross, with a dimension of 8m (26 ft.), a symbol of reconciliation between Great Britain and Germany. The German chancellor, Gerhard Schröder, participated in the ceremony, the transfer taking place 55 years after the destruction of Dresden by Allied bombers. Admission is free, and hours are daily from 10am to noon and 1 to 6pm.

Residenzschloss, the former Dresden Royal Palace, stands at Schlossplatz (© 0351/49142000; www.skd-dresden.de; tram no. 2, 4, or 8), behind its Renaissance facade. Construction began in 1709, and Napoleon once stood here. It was destroyed by British bombers in 1945 and continues to be restored on an ongoing basis. Its Hausmannsturm (Hausmann Tower; Apr–Oct Wed–Mon 10am–6pm; 3€) can be climbed for a panoramic vista over Dresden and the Elbe, but the chief attraction here is the **Grünes Gewölbe (Green Vaults) ★★★**, a dazzling collection of 16th- to 18th-century treasures: rococo chests, ivory carvings, jewelry, intricately designed mirrors, and priceless porcelain. Many pieces were created by the craftspeople of local guilds; others were acquired from the far corners of the earth. It's open from mid-March to mid-November and accessible via timed entry (Wed–Mon 10am–6pm; 10€; buy tickets from entrance or online).

The restored **Katholische Hofkirche (Catholic Court Church) ★★**, Schlossplatz (© 0351/4844712; tram no. 4 or 8), is the largest church in Saxony. It was built by the son of August the Strong, Friedrich August II, who ruled from 1733 to 1763. The church's facade has 38 biblical and historical figures in the high baroque style. Inside, you can see the crypt with the tombs of 49 rulers of Saxony and a box allegedly containing the heart of August the Strong. On the main floor you can see a beautiful stone pulpit by the royal sculptor Balthasar Permoser (1651–1732), one of the leading sculptors of his time in Saxony. There's also an 18th-century church organ. Admission is free. This church, also known as the Cathedral of St. Trinitas, is open Monday to Friday 8:30am to 6pm, Saturday 10am to 4pm, and Sunday 1:30 to 4pm. Guided tours, conducted in German only and priced at 4€ per person, are conducted Monday to Thursday at 2pm and Saturday at 1 and 2pm.

Kreuzkirche (Church of the Cross) ★ (© 0351/4393920; tram no. 4 or 8) stands at the **Altmarkt,** or old market square. This church is the home of the *Kreuzchor,* the famous boys' choir of Dresden. Free concerts are conducted every Saturday at 5pm, unless the choir is traveling. The church's architecture is a combination of baroque and Art Nouveau. The present building is from the late 18th century, although a church stood here as early as the 13th century. You can also see the reconstructed **Rathaus (Town Hall)** and the 18th-century **Landhaus** at the Altmarkt. Very little of either is open to viewing and the Rathaus tower is also closed. However, you can appreciate their facades.

Of Dresden's many parks and gardens, the best and most popular is the **Grosser Garten,** to the southeast of the Altstadt. This park, which was mapped out in 1676, contains a zoo and a botanical garden. In the center is a minor *Lustschloss* (pleasure palace) built in 1670 that's most appealing when viewed from the outside; just don't plan a casual visit during the occasional midsummer concerts conducted there (you'll spend most of your time fighting your way through the crowd rather than admiring the palace). For more information, contact the tourist office.

THE MAJOR MUSEUMS

Albertinum ★★★ MUSEUM   This imposing imperial structure, which recently underwent extensive renovations, houses one of Germany's great galleries. It's named for the Saxon King Albert, who, between 1884 and 1887, converted this former royal arsenal into a home for a vast collection of art and precious jewelry.

On the upper two floors is the **Galerie Neue Meister ★★★**, a collection of 19th- and 20th-century art and sculpture, from Corot to Otto Dix. The desolate and haunting landscapes of Caspar David Friedrich, the German Romantic artist, are especially nice. Impressionists and post-Impressionists are well represented, including Gauguin, Degas, Manet, Monet, Corinth, Liebermann, Klimt, and van Gogh. Antifascist artists, whose works were either destroyed or banned in the Nazi era, are also on display. In the sculpture collection, the works of more than 5 millennia are presented, ranging from the ancient cultures of the Mediterranean and the Near East to virtually all epochs of European artistic developments, dating from the early Middle Ages.

Brühl Terrace. © **0351/49142000.** www.skd-dresden.de. Admission 8€ adults, free for children 15 and under. Daily 10am–6pm. Closed 2 weeks in Jan. Tram: 1, 3, 5, 7, or 8 to Rathenau Platz.

Zwinger ★★★ MUSEUM   August the Strong, elector of Saxony (also king of Poland), built this baroque masterpiece, modeled after Versailles, in 1719. Here he staged tournaments and kept dozens of concubines. His physique was called Herculean, his temperament Rabelaisian, but he also had a great love for the arts. Today, this artfully symmetrical complex of buildings holds a collection of museums. The damage caused by the British air raid in 1945 was so devastating that some locals feared the Zwinger would remain a ruin forever. However, it's been restored and it's back in business, welcoming new generations of art lovers.

M. D. Pöppelmann (1662–1736) initially conceived the Zwinger as the forecourt of the castle. In the center of the large quadrangle are formal gardens, fountains, and promenades, forming a deep curving bay enclosed by pavilions. Notable are the Wall-pavilion in the center of the semicircular arched gallery in the west end and the **Nymphenbad (Bath of Nymphs) ★★** with its graceful fountains and mythological figures by Balthasar Permoser, who helped Pöppelmann in the construction of the Zwinger. On the northeast side is a Renaissance-style building, added in 1846 by Gottfried Semper (1803–79). Semper's two-story pavilions are linked by one-story galleries. The architectural critic Sir Nikolaus Pevsner once wrote: "What exultation in these rocking curves, and yet what grace! It is joyful but never vulgar; vigorous, boisterous perhaps, but never crude."

The most important museum in the complex is the **Gemäldegalerie Alte Meister (Old Masters Picture Gallery) ★★★**, which has its entrance at Theaterplatz 1. This gallery, one of the best on the Continent, has as its showpiece Raphael's *Sistine Madonna.* You'll also find Giorgione's *Sleeping Venus,* Antonello da Messina's *The Martyrdom of St. Sebastian,* Titian's *Tribute Money,* and many famous works by Veronese, Tintoretto, Correggio, and Annibale Carracci. You'll also see Flemish, Dutch, and German paintings by Van Dyck, Vermeer, Dürer, and Rembrandt, among others. The Rubens collection includes his spectacular *Neptune,* full of rearing horses, and an exquisite *St. Jerome.* Admission is 10€ adults, free for children 15 and under.

You can take a cruise on the historic Elbe River from central moorings below the Brühl Terrace. **Sächsischer Dampfschiffahrt** (*© 0351/866090;* www. saechsische-dampfschiffahrt.de) offers a 4½-hour cruise along the Elbe from Dresden to Rathen, a German village at the border of the Czech Republic. These trips take you through some of the finest river scenery in eastern Germany, including an area known as "Swiss Saxony," one of Germany's most popular natural wonders. It's a land of table-shaped outcrops, isolated pillars, deep gorges, and sheer sandstone cliffs. The upper reaches of the Elbe flow in wide curves through these fantastically shaped rock formations. Between March and early November, boat departures occur daily, at 9am.

Because each leg of this waterborne journey requires 4½ hours, you'll have to block out an entire day for this experience if you opt for round-trip transport by boat. Alternatively, you can opt for one-way transit by boat, with a return back to Dresden from Rathen by train, a 40-minute ride. Trains depart at 30-minute intervals throughout the day between Rathen and Dresden. Boat passage, each way, costs 21€; rail transport, each way, costs 10€. While you're cruising, look for the **Blaues Wunder (Blue Wonder),** one of Dresden's most celebrated bridges, completed in 1893 and never destroyed during the wartime bombings. It is a beautiful expression of the bridge-building genius that flourished here at the turn of the 20th century.

Rüstkammer (Armory) displays a vast collection of weaponry from the 15th to the 18th century, including halberds, shields, cannons, and suits of armor for both men and horses. The **Porzellansammlung (Porcelain Collection)** displays the finery produced by the porcelain factories of Dresden during the 350 years since their founding. Admission is 6€ adults, free for children 15 and under.

Theaterplatz 1. *©* **0351/49142000.** www.skd-dresden.de. Admission 12€ for adults, 7.50€ students, free for children 16 and under. All 4 Zwinger sites: Tues–Sun 10am–6pm. Tram: 1, 2, 4, 7, 8, 11, 12, or 14. Bus: 82 or 94 to Postplatz.

Where to Eat
EXPENSIVE

Lesage ★★ GERMAN/INTERNATIONAL   One of the city's best restaurants is oddly positioned in the "Transparent Factory of Volkswagen," a stunning glass structure where you can witness new models of cars being assembled by workers in white lab jackets. The elegant restaurant itself is tucked away near the entrance. Begin with such delights as apple curry soup with baked spring chicken or lobster soup with angler fish and mango cream. You might follow with filet of pork under a tortilla crust served with paprika potatoes and guacamole. Another specialty is sautéed Barbary duckling breast with red figs and a shallot confit. If you wish, you can drive off in a new Phaeton.

Lennestrasse 1. *©* **0351/4204250.** www.lesage.de. Reservations required. Main courses 14€–26€. AE, DC, MC, V. Mon noon–2:30pm; Tues–Sat noon–3pm and 6–10pm; Sun 11am–3pm.

Rossini ★ ITALIAN   Rossini offers Italian cuisine in a stylish setting, one floor above the lobby of the Dresden Hilton. Menu items might include chicken-liver pâté in Marsala wine; a buffet of Sicilian antipasti, carpaccio of swordfish marinated in

Marsala vinaigrette, Parma ham with coarse bread, and a tapenade of olives; Sicilian-style fish soup; or grilled lamb with anchovy sauce. Dessert may be cassata made with ricotta cheese and candied fruit, or a *granita* (sorbet) of oranges and lemons floating on white wine.

In the Dresden Hilton, An der Frauenkirche 5. 📞 **0351/86420.** Reservations recommended. Main courses 18€–27€. AE, DC, MC, V. Daily 6–11pm. Tram: 4 or 8.

MODERATE

Alte Meister ★ CONTINENTAL   Established in 2001, this is the first restaurant directly within the Zwinger that anyone can remember for a very long time. Although it has its own entrance (on Theaterplatz directly opposite the entrance to the Opera House), it's close to its namesake, the Zwinger's Alte Meister collections. Within a high-ceilinged and stately room that evokes the imperial grandeur of Renaissance Saxony, you'll enjoy well-flavored and traditional food items with touches of elegance. The best examples include cream of carrot soup, studded with chunks of braised rabbit liver; soft goat cheese with toast and a ragout of tomatoes; grilled prawns served with chicory salad; and carpaccio of pressed veal with a tomato-and-mushroom salad. Main courses include filet of sea bass served with a curried version of coconut-laced vegetables; breast of free-range chicken with a sauté of Gorgonzola-flavored spinach; and a combination platter that contains, on the same plate, roasted saddle of rabbit and a braised filet of lamb.

Theaterplatz 1A–B. 📞 **0351/4810426.** www.altemeister.net. Reservations recommended. Main courses 11€–15€. AE, MC, V. Daily 10pm–1am. Bus: 91.

Brauhaus am Waldschlösschen GERMAN   This is a replica of the old-fashioned beer halls and beer gardens that played such an important role in Dresden's past. Around 250 diners and drinkers can cram into a series of dining rooms, and another 800 can be accommodated within the sprawling garden (Apr–Oct). Expect heaping platters of such favorites as marinated saddle of pork steak with roasted onions; Saxon sour beef with raisin sauce, red cabbage, and potato dumplings; sautéed fish with parsley and onions; soups; *Schnitzels, Wursts;* and roasts. Live music, usually from a jazzy pianist, is presented Monday to Saturday 8pm to midnight. Beer (Waldschlösschen) is brewed on the premises and comes in several degrees of darkness.

Am Brauhaus 8B (in the Neustadt district, 5km/3 miles northeast of the city center). 📞**0351/6523900.** www.waldschloesschen.de. Reservations required. Main courses 8€–16€. AE, DC, MC, V. Daily 11am–1am. Tram: 11. Bus: 91.

Italienisches Dörfchen ITALIAN/INTERNATIONAL   Italienisches Dörfchen is a stately looking neoclassical building that was erected in 1911 on the site of the cluster of cottages ("the Italian Village") that once housed the mostly Italian crews of laborers building the nearby monuments of the Saxon kings. Today, it contains a quartet of restaurants, each with a different theme. The best way to decide which to patronize is to wander through the formal premises of the building and inspect them. Choices include the **Biersaal,** whose painted ceiling evokes the 18th century; the neoclassical **Weinzimmer,** a formal, rather uncomfortable and fussy-looking room outfitted in red; and the **Bellotto,** an upscale Italian eatery on the top floor. There's also the **Kurfürstenzimmer,** an area that serves both Saxon and international food. Supplementing the four dining options is **Café,** a graceful-looking antique room with windows that overlook the river. Prices in all four of the restaurants are about the same, but if you're interested just in coffee, tea, a drink, and/or pastries, you'd be best advised to head directly for the cafe.

Theaterplatz 2. ℂ **0351/498160.** www.italienisches-doerfchen.de. Reservations not necessary. Main courses 10€–18€. AE, DC, MC, V. Daily 10am–midnight. Tram: 4 or 8.

INEXPENSIVE

Ayers Rock ★ 🍴AUSTRALIAN   The success of this likable restaurant is proof of the growing sophistication of Dresden. It was named and modeled after the geological oddity in central Australia that deeply impressed the owner during a holiday there. Lighthearted and breezy, the place serves almost 300 kinds of cocktails, as well as some brands of German and Aussie beer on tap. Menu items are inspired by what's cooking "down under" and include a savory version of lamb with green bean stew, grilled veal shank, fresh asparagus with strips of chicken breast, and roebuck steak with mushrooms and glass noodles. After 8:30pm, the bar area gets crowded with the young at heart and singles.

Münzgasse 8. ℂ **0351/4901188.** www.ayersrock-dresden.de. Reservations not necessary. Main courses 10€–20€. AE, DC, MC, V. Daily noon–2am. Tram: 1, 2, or 4.

Brauhaus Watzke GERMAN   One of Dresden's most famous and atmospheric beer halls lies 6.5km (4 miles) west of the city center, on a site overlooking the Elbe. Established in 1898, it confirms that while governments in Germany may rise and fall, beer halls will remain intact. If the weather is clement, you can opt for a seat within the sprawling garden, where hardworking waitresses carry impossibly heavy loads of beer mugs and heaping platters to the long tables. Inside, the venue is appropriately woodsy looking and *gemütlich* (cozy). Anything you drink here (including beers of the month) will have been brewed on the premises, with modern equipment that was installed in 1996. Regardless of which kind of beer you pick, a half-liter costs 2.70€. It's never bottled in individual containers, only in kegs, and it's almost never available anywhere except here and within a limited handful of other restaurants nearby. Menu items are appropriately hearty and include *Meltzer Schnitzel*, a filet of veal dredged in malt and fried, or *Watzke Bierfleische*, a ragout of beef stewed in dark aromatic beer. Salads, soups, and fish dishes are just as tasty.

Kötzschenbroder Strasse 1. ℂ **0351/852920.** www.watzke.de. Reservations not necessary. Main courses 8.50€–15€. AE, MC, V. Daily 11am–midnight. Tram: 4 or 13.

Café Schinkelwache CONTINENTAL   Designed like a miniature Ionic-style temple, this is one of Dresden's architectural gems. Noted architect Karl Friedrich Schinkel built this sandstone structure in 1832 to house soldiers and guards. In 1995, it was rebuilt and reconfigured into the cafe you see today. Its interior is cozier and on a smaller scale than you'd imagine from a look at its stately facade. During clement weather, tables and parasols spill onto the terrace surrounding the building. Menu selections include pastries, meal-size salads, soups, cold platters, toasts, and at least two full-fledged dishes of the day. Wine, beer, and coffee are the preferred drinks.

Theaterplatz 2. ℂ **0351/4903909.** Reservations recommended. Pastries 3€–5€; platters 11€–18€. AE, MC, V. Daily 10am–midnight. Tram: 8 or 11.

Sophienkeller im Taschenbergpalais ★ 📷GERMAN   The food here approximates the hearty medieval feasts you might have expected in the Royal Saxon Court, albeit in a more sanitary form. Your happiness in these deep but bustling cellars depends on where you happen to sit. Four distinct areas are available, but the ones that are the most authentically historic are the Grosses and Kleines Zunfi Gewölbe, where flickering candles, set beneath vaulted ceilings, provide most of the illumination. Waitresses in traditional dirndls haul steaming platters of crispy suckling pig from the spit with wine-flavored cabbage, a juicy chicken filet with fresh spinach and hearty Gorgonzola cheese, or venison goulash with dumplings. Tantalizing regional appetizers include a Saxon potato soup with fried slices of *Bockwurst* sausage or a smoky fish soup with fresh chervil and shrimp. It's a bit theme-ish, especially in its emphasis on 18th-century costumes, and at least part of its energy is devoted to the care and feeding of large tour groups, but the food is hearty and flavorful and the ambience can be very romantic.

Taschenberg 3. *C* **0351/497260.** www.sophienkeller-dresden.de. Reservations recommended. Main courses 8€–15€. AE, DC, MC, V. Daily 11am–1am. Tram: 4 or 11.

Shopping

Perhaps because of Dresden's destruction in the final days of World War II, there's an emphasis here on collecting the high-quality antiques that remain. You'll find many antiques dealers in the city. Most of the inventory has been culled from homes and estate sales in the relatively unscathed surrounding hamlets. The most interesting shops in Dresden, and many of the most glamorous ones, line either side of the **Königstrasse.** Here, look for a roster of handcrafted goods and gift items.

And don't overlook the city's role as a purveyor of modern painting and sculpture. The best of the art galleries is **Galerie am Blauen Wunder,** Pillnitzer Landstrasse 2 (*C* **0351/2684020**).

Weihnachtsland am Zwinger, Kleine Brüdergasse 5 (*C* **0351/8621230;** www. weihnachtsland-dresden.com), is the best-stocked and most interesting gift shop in Dresden, with a year-round emphasis on Christmas, New Year's, and Easter ornaments that are handmade in the nearby Erzgebirge region. Look for pieces of delicate Plauener Spitze lace that are designed to hang on hooks affixed by suction cups to the glass of your windows—it's easy to transport, and some pieces can be acquired for less than 6€. There are also elaborately detailed Easter eggs, carved wooden figurines in the shapes of either soldiers or angels, and framed still lifes and landscapes made from assemblages of dried flowers.

Other shops line **Prager Strasse** with its department stores, **Altmarkt,** and **Wilsdruffer Strasse.** Tony shops and boutiques are found along **Hauptstrasse.**

Count yourself lucky if you're in Dresden for the celebrated **Weihnachtsmarkt ★★,** the oldest Christmas market in Germany, a tradition since 1434. Handmade regional crafts, delicious homemade foods such as cakes and cookies, and dozens of other goodies are featured in the Altmarkt. The blown-glass tree decorations from Lauscha are particularly stunning and virtual heirlooms since they never go out of style.

Entertainment & Nightlife

Dresden is Saxony's cultural center. There's always a variety of options for nightlife here, whether you're looking for drama, classical concerts, punk-rock shows, dancing, or just a good place to drink.

THE PERFORMING ARTS Between the Elbe River and the Zwinger, on the western side of Theaterplatz, stands the **Semperoper (Semper Opera House) ★★★,** one of the most exquisite opera houses in the world, Theaterplatz 2 (*C* **0351/4911705;** www.semperoper.de; tram: 1, 2, 4, 7, 8, 11, 12, 14, or 17). Both Wagner and Weber conducted here. Gottfried Semper, the same architect who mapped out the famous picture gallery in the Zwinger, designed the building. Restorers have brought the Renaissance-style two-tiered facade and the interior of the building back to life. Careful attention was paid to the replacement of Semper's original paintings and decorations. More important, the fine acoustics for which the opera house was known have been reestablished. Good seats can be had for 20€ to 120€. *Note:* Seats are *extremely* difficult to get; purchase your tickets as far in advance as possible. The opera company takes a vacation mid-July to mid-August.

The **Dresden Philharmonic** appears at the **Kulturpalast,** in the Altmarkt (© **0351/4866306;** www.kulturpalast-dresden.de; tram: 3 or 5). Tickets cost 14€ to 50€. Concerts, sometimes with accompaniment by ballet recitals, are also performed during June and August in the courtyards of the Zwinger.

For musical theater, come to the **Staats Operette,** Pirnaer Landstrasse 131, about 5km (3 miles) southeast of the city center (© **0351/2079929;** www.staatsoperette-dresden.de; tram: 4), which mainly performs works from the 19th and early 20th centuries. The box office is open Sunday 1 hour before the show, Monday 11am to 4pm, Tuesday to Friday 11am to 7pm, and Saturday 4 to 7pm. Tickets cost 7€ to 25€.

The classical stage for drama in the city is **Schauspielhaus,** Postplatz (© **0351/ 4913555;** www.staatsschauspiel-dresden.de; tram: 1, 2, 4, 7, 8, 11, 12, or 14), where dramas by Goethe, Schiller, and Shakespeare (in German) are performed. Performances usually start at 7:30pm. The box office is open Monday to Friday 10am to 6:30pm, Saturday and Sunday 10am to 2pm. Tickets cost 10€ to 28€. The Schauspielhaus box office also handles tickets and inquiries for the **Residenztheater im Schloss,** Theaterplatz (© **0351/491350;** tram: 4 or 8), a small theater focusing on modern drama and small-ensemble pieces. The cost is 10€ to 72€. Both theaters are closed from July to mid-August.

For a family theater experience, check out **Theater Junge Generation,** Meissner Landstrasse 4 (© **0351/429120;** www.tjg-dresden.de; tram: 1; bus: 94), which interprets Shakespeare and fairy tales in a way that both kids and parents can enjoy. The box office is open Monday to Saturday 10am to 6pm, and 1 hour before performances. Ticket prices are 5€ to 12€. In summer, some members of the troupe bring their acts outdoors, usually to the courtyard in front of the Staffhof, an imposing building originally intended as a stable.

BARS At **Las Tapas,** Münzgasse 4 (© **0351/4960108;** www.las-tapas.de; tram: 1, 2, 4, or 14), within a stone-floored room modeled after an Iberian *tasca* (wine tavern), you'll find small tables and a stand-up bar area, where up to 40 kinds of Spanish-style marinated mushrooms, sausages, Serrano hams, salted almonds, baked artichokes, and prawns in bacon are displayed behind glass. Priced at 3€ to 8€, they go well with beer or the Spanish wines sold here. More substantial platters, priced at 12€ to 20€, include lamb tenderloins with eggplant and spits of marinated pork tenderloin served with sherry sauce. It's open daily 11am to between 1 and 2am, depending on business.

A once run-down but now gentrified nightlife destination that assembles about 20 different bars, art galleries, and restaurants into one historic site is **Kunsthof,** Alaunstrasse 70 (© **0351/8106617;** www.kunsthof-dresden.de; tram no. 6, 7, or 13), where a series of hip cafes, art galleries, and affordable restaurants line the edges of an interior courtyard. A particularly appealing bar, tapas bar, and restaurant within the complex is the Spain-inspired **El Perro** (© **0351/8036723;** www.elperro.de).

CLUBS Dance clubs that are known to virtually every 20-something resident of Dresden include **DownTown** (© **0351/8115592;** www.downtown-dresden.de)

and **Groove Station** (📞 **0351/8029594;** www.groovestation.de), set immediately adjacent to one another at Katharinenstrasse 11 and 13 (tram: 7 or 8). Clients can move freely from one to the other of this pair of cramped, sometimes convivial bars, where music rocks and rolls at high volumes and suds flow freely. Both are at their peak capacity on Friday and Saturday nights. Monday is gay and lesbian night, and on Sunday there's dinner and dancing. Both of them are open daily from 9pm "until everybody leaves." A single cover charge, ranging from 9€ to 15€, depending on the night of the week, applies to both clubs.

Projekttheater Dresden, Louisenstrasse 47 (📞 **0351/8107600;** www.projekt theater.de; tram: 7 or 8), a publicly funded organization, usually, but not always, gives live jazz performances Tuesday to Sunday at 9pm and also maintains separate areas for the presentation of avant-garde films, lectures, and art exhibitions. Don't expect a nightclub-style cabaret, as no drinks are served. Tickets, available 1 hour before showtime, cost 11€ each. Call to see if a performance is scheduled.

For an insight into Germany's newest crop of political satirists, head for the irrever-ent premises of **Herkules Keule,** Sternplatz 1 (📞 **0351/4925555;** www.herkules keule.de; tram: 1, 2, 4, 7, 8, or 11). Although it was well known during the heyday of the former GDR, its sometimes scathing pronouncements have reached their sharp-est and shrillest since reunification. Come here if your knowledge of German is extremely good and if you're prepared for caustic humor that touches on everything from politics to sex. Shows are presented Monday to Friday at 7:30pm and Saturday at 6 and 9pm. Admission is 10€ to 19€, depending on the night of the week.

Where to Stay

Since reunification and the amazing increase in tourism, Dresden's hotel prices have soared, as has the demand for rooms. Even so-called "budget" hotels can command 130€ a night for a double.

VERY EXPENSIVE

Kempinski Hotel Taschenbergpalais ★★★   Few hotels of post-reunification Germany have sparked as much pride among local citizens as this one. Its history dates from the early 18th century, when the elector of Saxony built a baroque castle for his favorite mistress, the Countess Cosel, who, for mysterious reasons, was later ban-ished from his court. For 250 years, the palace was the pride of Dresden, a site visited almost as much as the Zwinger. Only the surreal remains of a massive marble staircase survived the bombs, but now the historic Taschenberg Palace is back better than ever.

A real estate developer spent $175 million on transforming the ruin into Dresden's finest hotel, restoring the five-story baroque, sculpture-dotted facade to its original opulence. Rooms are the most luxurious in town. Those on the west and north sides overlook the Zwinger or the Opera.

Taschenberg 3, 01067 Dresden. www.kempinski-dresden.de. 📞 **0351/49120.** Fax 0351/4912812. 214 units. 219€–339€ double; from 419€ suite. AE, DC, MC, V. Parking 16€. Tram: 5 or 8. **Amenities:** 2 res-taurants; 2 bars; airport transfers (60€); babysitting; bikes; concierge; exercise room; indoor heated pool; room service; spa. *In room:* A/C, TV, hair dryer, minibar, Wi-Fi (25€ per day).

EXPENSIVE

Bülow Residenz ★★★   We prefer staying at the Bülow Residenz, a charming, gracious boutique hotel and one of the most luxurious in eastern Germany, to the Taschenbergpalais (see above). This hotel, with a restored facade from the 1700s, has been a success since its opening in the early 1990s. The formal lounge, with its plush seating, sets the tone, and the garden patio is the perfect place to be on a summer day. Individually decorated rooms are unusually spacious compared to most in Dresden. Oversize beds and contemporary redwood furnishings offer a restful ambience. The sumptuous German-style 21€ breakfast buffet is well worth it; check the Web for special rates, as many packages include breakfast and/or a pair of nearly-impossible-to-obtain Semperoper tickets (p. 192).

Rähnitzgasse 19 (near the Opera), 01097 Dresden. www.buelow-residenz.de. © **0351/80030.** Fax 0351/8003100. 30 units. 195€–250€ double; 310€–650€ suite. AE, DC, MC, V. Parking 16€. Tram: 3, 4, 8, or 11. **Amenities:** Restaurant; bar; babysitting; bikes; exercise room; spa. *In room:* A/C, TV, hair dryer, minibar.

Hilton Dresden ★ This hotel is one of the best in the region, though lacking the romance and glamour of the Taschenbergpalais or the intimacy and charm of the Bülow (see above). Its conservative mansard-roofed facade blends harmoniously with the baroque buildings on the nearby Neumarkt. A glassed-in passageway connects the hotel to a 19th-century building, the Sekundogenitur, which contains two restaurants and an array of banqueting and conference rooms. Rooms are midsize, conservatively modern, and well maintained. Double-glazed windows cut down on noise. The best rooms face the Frauenkirche.

An der Frauenkirche 5, 01067 Dresden. www.hilton.com. © **800/4458667** in the U.S. and Canada, or 0351/86420. Fax 0351/8642725. 333 units. 158€–243€ double; 248€–382€ suite. AE, DC, MC, V. Parking 20€. Tram: 3, 5, 7, 8, or 12. **Amenities:** 7 restaurants; 2 bars; babysitting; bikes; concierge; health club and spa; indoor heated pool; room service. *In room:* TV, fridge (in some), hair dryer, minibar, Wi-Fi (22€ per day).

Hotel Suitess ★★★ A member of Small Luxury Hotels of the World, this is one classy address. It was reconstructed according to a historic architectural plan behind a detailed baroque facade. The entire hotel, which is government rated as five stars, is the epitome of charm, luxury, comfort, and service, with a Biedermeier aura. The Kempinski may be grander and larger, but for grace, style, and tranquillity, Suitess is the oasis of Dresden. Each room is individually designed, with a harmonious decor and a careful attention to detail. The staff is the best trained in town. The on-site Maurice Restaurant is for serious foodies, and uses luxury ingredients.

An der Frauenkirche 13, 01067 Dresden. www.suitess-hotel.com. © **0351/417270.** Fax 0351/41727160. 21 units. 113€–280€ double; from 247€ suite. AE, DC, MC, V. **Amenities:** Restaurant; bar; airport transfers (35€); babysitting; concierge; health club and spa; room service; Wi-Fi (free; in lobby). *In room:* A/C, TV/DVD, hair dryer, minibar.

Romantik Hotel Pattis ★★★ Lying outside Dresden center in the Kemnitz section, 4km (2½ miles) to the northwest, this is one of the most romantic and atmospheric hotels in all of eastern Germany. It originated as a mill, but by 1870 it had become a popular day trip for the rich folk of Dresden, who came here to go boating on a lake and also to dance the waltz in its ballroom. The property fell into decline after World War II but was rescued by the Pattis family, which reconstructed the original house, which is surrounded by a large, landscaped park. All the spacious rooms and suites are beautifully furnished, cozy, and comfortable, with high-quality furnishings and fabrics. On-site is a gourmet restaurant. Begin the evening with a drink in the cozy bar or else in the library in front of a crackling open fire.

Merbitzerstrasse 53, 01157 Dresden-Kemnitz. www.pattis.de. © **0351/42550.** Fax 0351/4255255. 47 units. 130€–205€ double; 190€–350€ suite. AE, DC, MC, V. Parking 5€ indoors. Bus: 94. **Amenities:** 2 restaurants; bar; bikes; concierge; exercise room; Jacuzzi; room service; sauna. *In room:* TV, hair dryer, minibar, Wi-Fi (free).

Steigenberger Hotel de Saxe ★★   In the 18th century a famous hotel once stood on this spot, opening onto views of the Neumarkt. Today, this luxury hotel has risen on the spot to grace the skyline of Dresden. Directly opposite the fabled Frauenkirche, the hotel was reconstructed in the grand baroque style with rows of dormer windows. The rooms are luxuriously furnished and most comfortable—definitely a hotel of the 21st century in spite of its old-fashioned architecture. Even the simplest rooms are called "superior," although if you're willing to pay more you can get a deluxe room with even better appointments.

Neumarkt 9, 01067 Dresden. www.steigenberger.com. ✆ **0351/43860.** Fax 0351/4386888. 185 units. 145€–185€ double; 295€–395€ suite. AE, DC, MC, V. Parking 20€. **Amenities:** Restaurant; bar; exercise room; room service; spa. In room: A/C, TV, hair dryer, minibar, Wi-Fi (15€ per day).

Westin Bellevue ★   The Bellevue, which we'd rank just under the Hilton, stands by the most attractive part of the Elbe. If you look out the hotel's windows or from its terraces to the opposite riverbank, you'll know you're in the spot where Canaletto painted his magnificent scenes. The ornate walls of a pair of courtyards that survived the 1945 bombings have been integrated into the structure and are now a protected monument. Some rooms overlook the courtyards; others are in modern wings that often open onto the Elbe. Whether you stay in the old part or more modern section, you'll find well-appointed rooms.

Grosse Meissner Strasse 15, 01097 Dresden. www.westin.com/bellevue. ✆ **0351/8050.** Fax 0351/8051609. 343 units. 119€–299€ double; from 399€ suite. AE, DC, MC, V. Parking 16€. Tram: 4 or 5. **Amenities:** 2 restaurants; bar; babysitting; concierge; health club & spa; indoor heated pool; room service. In room: A/C, TV/DVD, CD player, hair dryer, minibar, Wi-Fi (18€ per day).

MODERATE

Art'otel ★ 🛍   The six floors of this dramatic postmodern hotel are the most self-consciously "arty" of any hotel in Dresden. They were designed by Denis Santachiara, whose work has been heralded in Munich, Milan, New York, and Paris. One floor is an art gallery that focuses on striking contemporary paintings and sculpture by German artists. The stylish guest rooms are well furnished and comfortable, each with a neat, efficiently organized private bathroom. The staff is very conscious of cutting-edge trends in German cities.

Ostra-Allee 33, 01067 Dresden. www.artotels.com. ✆ **0351/49220.** Fax 0351/4922777. 174 units. 129€–200€ double; from 160€ suite. Rates include buffet breakfast. AE, DC, MC, V. Parking 15€. Tram: 11. **Amenities:** Restaurant; bar; bikes; exercise room; room service; sauna. In room: A/C, TV, hair dryer, minibar, Wi-Fi (8€ per hour).

Hotel am Terrassenufer   Comfortable and reasonably priced, this hotel was built in the 1960s as a student dormitory. In the 1990s, it was renovated and enlarged into the streamlined 12-story hotel you see today. Set on the riverbank, a short walk from Dresden's historic core, it offers large, airy, big-windowed rooms with lots of sunlight and compact bathrooms.

Terrassenufer 12, 01069 Dresden. www.hotel-terrassenufer.de. ✆ **0351/4409500.** Fax 0351/4409600. 196 units. 81€–150€ double; 144€–240€ suite. AE, DC, MC, V. Parking 10€. Tram: 3, 7, or 9. **Amenities:** Restaurant; bar; room service. In room: A/C, TV, hair dryer, minibar, Wi-Fi (8€ per hour).

Rothenburger Hof ★★   Beautifully renovated, this time-honored and traditional hotel, which first opened its doors in 1685, is once again claiming its regal position as a small luxury hotel. A family run hotel, it is in Neustadt, the area rebuilt after a great fire in the late 1680s. It's within an easy walk of the historical monuments of the Old City. It's much more comfortable today than when it first opened because so many modern improvements have been made, including the addition of a swimming pool, sauna, Turkish bath, and solarium, plus a garden terrace and an elevator. The midsize rooms are traditionally furnished and comfortable, with freshly renovated, tiled bathrooms. Guest-room furnishings are tasteful reproductions of antiques.

Rothenburger Strasse 15-17, 01099 Dresden. www.rothenburger-hof.de. © **0351/81260.** Fax 0351/8126222. 39 units. 99€–160€ double; 170€–185€ suite. Rates include buffet breakfast. AE, MC, V. Parking 8€. Tram: 11. **Amenities:** Children's center; exercise room; indoor heated pool; room service; sauna. *In room:* TV, kitchen (in some), minibar, Wi-Fi (free).

Schlosshotel Dresden-Pillnitz ★★ 🎁 Set within a few steps of Schloss Pillnitz (Pillnitz Castle), about 8km (5 miles) east of downtown Dresden, this historic building functioned as a restaurant as early as 1760, often feeding the courtiers and service personnel doing business with the castle. In 1999, the Zepp family poured time and money into its restoration. Today, the upper floors are devoted to well-maintained, discreetly tasteful guest rooms, each with big windows, well-crafted furniture, and comfortable beds. The lower floors contain a cafe, a reception hall, and a high-ceilinged restaurant with excellent food.

August-Böckelstiegel-Strasse 10, 01326 Dresden-Pillnitz. www.schlosshotel-pillnitz.de. © **0351/26140.** Fax 0351/2614400. 45 units. 115€–140€ double; 200€–240€ suite. Rates include buffet breakfast. AE, MC, V. Free parking. **Amenities:** Restaurant; bikes; Wi-Fi (8€ per day; in lobby). *In room:* TV, hair dryer, minibar.

INEXPENSIVE

Raskolnikoff Pension 🔥 This is one of the better *pensiones* (boardinghouses) in town, lying across the river in Neustadt (New Town). It takes its name from a Dostoevsky character, but don't expect *Crime and Punishment* if you lodge here. Family owned and run, it is in a restored building dating from 1732 and is a rather artsy choice, with a modern gallery on-site. Special features include a courtyard garden and a cozy restaurant, serving regional specialties of Saxony. All the bedrooms have been renovated and are done in an extreme modern style, though private bathrooms have been installed in only two rooms. At these prices forget about in-room amenities.

Böhmische Strasse 34, 01099 Dresden. www.raskolnikoff.de. © **0351/8045706.** 6 units, 2 with private bathroom. 52€ double without bathroom; 55€ double with bathroom. Rates include continental breakfast. No credit cards. **Amenities:** Restaurant.

MEISSEN ★

25km (16 miles) NW of Dresden, 174km (108 miles) S of Berlin, 85km (53 miles) E of Leipzig

This "city of porcelain" is most often visited on a day trip from Dresden, although since reunification, it now has suitable accommodations for those who'd like to spend the night and get acquainted with the area.

Meissen lies on both banks of the Elbe, with the Altstadt on the left bank. It's a very old town, dating from A.D. 929. Since 1710, Meissen has been known around the world as the center for the manufacturing of Dresden china. The early makers of this so-called "white gold" were virtually held prisoner here because the princes who ruled the city wanted to keep their secrets to themselves. Today, shoppers can find the greatest selection of porcelain in all Germany. However, not wanting to undercut their distributors in such cities as Munich or Berlin, Meissen porcelain manufacturers keep their prices about the same as elsewhere.

Essentials

GETTING THERE

BY TRAIN **Meissen Bahnhof** is on the Deutsche Bundesbahn rail line, with connections departing for Dresden at 30- to 45-minute intervals throughout the day and evening. For rail information, call ✆ **01805/996633** or visit www.bahn.de.

BY BUS Regional buses connecting Dresden with Meissen are operated by **Verkehrsgesellschaft Meissen.** Consult the tourist office in Meissen for a schedule of connections or ask at the tourist office in Dresden.

BY CAR Access is via the E40 Autobahn from Dresden or the E49 from Leipzig.

BY BOAT If you're in Dresden in summer, you can go to Meissen by boat in about an hour and enjoy the scenery along the Elbe. The **Sächsischer Dampfschiffahrt,** Hertha Lindner Strasse 10 (✆ **0351/866090;** www.saechsische-dampfschiffahrt. de), leaves daily between May and late October at 9:45am from Dresden's Brühl Terrace, the fortified embankment on the other side of the Hofkirche. Boats arrive in Meissen 2 hours later. Waterborne returns to Dresden from Meissen depart at 2:45pm.

VISITOR INFORMATION

Contact **Tourist-Information Meissen,** Markt 3 (✆ **03521/41940;** www.tourist info-meissen.de), November to March Monday to Friday 10am to 5pm and Saturday 10am to 3pm (closed Sat in Jan); April to October, hours are Monday to Friday 10am to 6pm, and Saturday and Sunday 10am to 4pm.

Exploring Meissen

Towering over the town is the Gothic-style **Dom ★**, Domplatz 7 (✆ **03521/452490;** www.meiland.de), one of the smallest cathedrals in Germany, built between 1260 and 1450. Until the year 1400, the bishops of the diocese of Meissen had their seat next to the cathedral. Later, Saxon rulers were buried here, the first in 1428. Inside are works of art, including a painting by Lucas Cranach the Elder, along with rare Meissen porcelain. The cathedral has been Protestant since the 16th century. Admission costs 2.50€ per person. A 30-minute German-language guided tour, departing at virtually any time you specify, costs 5€ per person. Hours are April to October daily 9am to 6pm, and November to March daily 10am to 4pm.

Sharing the castle quarter with the cathedral is **Albrechtsburg Castle ★**, Domplatz 1 (✆ **03521/47070;** www.albrechtsburg-meissen.de), where the first Meissen porcelain was made. Construction of the castle began in 1471 and went on intermittently until 1525. From 1710 to 1864 it was the site of the Meissen Porcelain Manufactory. It is open March to October daily 10am to 6pm, November and December daily 10am to 5pm. Closed January and February. Admission is 5€ for adults, 2.50€ for children 6 to 16, and free for children 5 and under.

But the prime attraction in town is the **Porzellan-Manufaktur ★**, Talstrasse 9 (✆ **03521/4680;** www.meissen.com). At this factory, you can see how the centuries-old process of making Meissen china is still carried on, using the same traditional designs. You can rent a prerecorded audio device, priced at 9€, which will direct you (in any of several languages) on a self-guided tour lasting between 30 and 60 minutes, depending on how fast you move through the premises. You can visit the on-site **Porcelain Museum,** with 3,000 pieces, plus the workshop. Other than the cost of the guided tour, admission is free. The factory, its museum, and the audio machines are available May to October daily 9am to 6pm, and November to April daily 9am to 5pm.

Where to Eat

Romantik Restaurant Vincenz Richter ★ GERMAN/SAXON   This charming, hearty, and traditional restaurant is in a vine-sheathed 1523 building. It has a hard-working, devoted staff and a cozy setting of Germanic charm. Try the fresh chanterelles in a creamy sauce with homemade bread dumplings and a green salad, or else grilled pikeperch with sauerkraut and herb-flavored potatoes. The bar stocks an impressive inventory of local wines, and the kitchens serve ample portions of Saxon food.

An der Frauenkirche 12 (uphill from Meissen's Marktplatz). (✆ **03521/453285.** www.vincenz-richter.de. Reservations recommended. Main courses 12€–18€; fixed-price menus 31€–44€. AE, DC, MC, V. Tues-Sat noon–11pm; Sun noon–6pm.

Shopping

Porzellan-Manufaktur (see above) has recently crafted, hand-painted porcelain, which they'll ship home for you. However, don't expect prices to be much cheaper than in other German cities. The same organization also maintains a shop, with basically the same prices, in the center of Meissen at Burgstrasse 6 (✆ **03521/458015**).

Where to Stay

Welcome Park Hotel ★   This is the only first-rate hotel in town. For decades, Meissen didn't have a suitable hotel, but this Art Nouveau villa filled the void in the early 1990s. You can request a room in the original villa, although most accommodations are in the more sterile modern annexes. A suite on the top floor under the eaves is perfect for romantic couples. Most rooms open onto panoramic vistas.

Hafenstrasse 27-31 (on the Elbe, directly across the water from the castle), 01662 Meissen. www. welcome-hotel-meissen.de. (✆ **03521/72250.** Fax 03521/722904. 97 units. 78€–145€ double; 158€–210€ suite. AE, DC, MC, V. Parking 10€. **Amenities:** Restaurant; bar; exercise room; Jacuzzi; indoor heated pool; room service; sauna. *In room:* A/C, TV, hair dryer, minibar, Wi-Fi (free).

6

FRANCONIA & THE GERMAN DANUBE

The Renaissance swept across all of Germany, but it concentrated its full force on that part of northern Bavaria that had once been a Frankish kingdom. Franconia today contains many of Germany's greatest medieval and Renaissance treasures. Its hillsides are dotted with well-preserved medieval castles, monasteries, and churches. From the region's feudal cities sprang some of Germany's` most significant artists—Albrecht Dürer, Lucas Cranach the Elder, Veit Stoss, Adam Krafft. Today, Franconia draws music lovers to its annual Wagner Festival in Bayreuth (p. 201).

Franconia owes much of its beauty to the limestone range on the southern edge of the province. Between these hills and the edge of the Bavarian Forest is the upper **Danube,** which begins about 30km (20 miles) from Regensburg. The Danube gradually builds force from the smaller streams flowing out of the Alps and Swabian Jura, and by the time it reaches the Austrian border, at Passau, it's large enough to carry commercial ships and barges. Although not as important to the German economy as the Rhine, the Danube was responsible for the growth of several influential towns.

Franconia's countryside is equally compelling, especially the forest called **Frankenwald.** This scenic region stretches from the Bohemian Forest on the border of the Czech Republic in the east to the fringes of Frankfurt in the west. The most beautiful part is Frankisches Schweiz, the "Switzerland of Franconia," bounded by Bamberg on the west, Bayreuth in the east, and Kulmbach in the north.

OUTDOORS IN FRANCONIA The best **hiking** is in the northern parts of the province. Even the Germans, who rush to the Bavarian Alps, often overlook the some 25,000 hiking trails in Franconia. Local tourist officials have details of the best hikes in the area. Most trails are found in Germany's largest park, **Altmühltal Nature Park,** and in the Frankenwald.

You can also explore Franconia by **bike.** At all area train stations, you can rent a mountain bike for 10€ per day, half-price with a valid train ticket. Local tourist offices have information on the best biking routes. The **Danube Bicycle Path** cuts right through Regensburg; cyclists can ride along its 650km (400 miles) from the river's source to Passau. The Regensburg tourist office (p. 222) is the best source when you're organizing a biking trip. You can even go as far as Vienna. The **Five Rivers**

Bicycle Path is a 3- to 5-day circular route through the valleys of the Danube, Naab, and Vils. This path links Regensburg with Amberg and Nürnberg.

BAYREUTH ★

230km (143 miles) N of Munich, 64km (40 miles) E of Bamberg, 92km (57 miles) NE of Nürnberg

Bayreuth lies in a wide valley on the upper basin of the Roter Main River. In the town's early years, the counts of Andechs-Meranien gave it the protection of a fortified castle. In the Middle Ages, Bayreuth became the property of the Hohenzollerns and grew into one of the leading centers of this part of Germany. It's now the capital of the district of upper Franconia.

Bayreuth is forever associated with **Richard Wagner** (1813–83). The town is worth a visit for its baroque and rococo architectural treasures, even if you're not interested in its favorite son, but most people come here because it's the home of the annual Wagner opera festival, and the premier location for Wagnerian performance in the world.

Wagner's "endless melody" is still said to pervade Bayreuth. The composer's early success caught the eye of Ludwig II, king of Bavaria. With the king's support, Wagner opened his first **Festspielhaus** in 1876, in an old residence in Bayreuth; later he built and designed a new Festspielhaus, suited especially for his own operas. Wagner not only composed the music for his music dramas but also wrote the librettos and designed the sets. *Tristan and Isolde* remains perhaps his most daring opera; his best known is the four-opera *Ring of the Nibelungs*.

Essentials

GETTING THERE

BY TRAIN   The **Bayreuth Hauptbahnhof** is on the main Nürnberg-Pegnitz-Bayreuth and Bayreuth-Weiden rail lines, with good connections. Express trains arrive from Nürnberg every hour. For information, call ✆ **0180/5996633.**

BY BUS   Long-distance bus service to Berlin and Munich is provided by **Berlin Linien** Bus (✆ **030/8619331;** www.berlinlinienbus.de). Local and regional buses in the area are run by **OVF Omnibusverkehr Franken GmbH** in Bayreuth (✆ **0921/789730;** www.ovf.de).

BY CAR   Access by car is via the A9 Autobahn from the north and south.

VISITOR INFORMATION

Contact **Tourist-Information,** Opernstrasse 22 (✆ **0921/88588;** www.tourismus.bayreuth.de), Monday to Saturday 9am to 6pm. From May to October, it is also open Sunday 10am to 2pm.

GETTING AROUND

Many streets within the historic core of Bayreuth are exclusively reserved for pedestrians, and that, coupled with the city's small size, makes walking between points of interest both easy and efficient. Whereas the centerpiece of the old town is Marktplatz, the geographical landmark of the new town is the Hauptbahnhof. Buses no. 301 through 312 crisscross the town, and of those, about half follow a route that moves between those two points. If in doubt, ask someone at the tourist office or waiting at a bus stop. One-way bus fares for points within the town and its outskirts cost 1.60€.

Exploring Bayreuth

Altes Schloss Eremitage (Hermitage) ★ HISTORIC BUILDING In addition to the Neues Schloss (see below), the margraves of Bayreuth also had a pleasure palace outside the city, reached via a road lined with chestnut trees planted in honor of Friedrich the Great. In 1718 Georg Wilhelm built this retreat set in a park, full of formal as well as English-style gardens. In them, you can see the New Palace of the Hermitage, built around 1750. Notice the columns covered with polychrome pebbles in mosaic style, a unique structural element in German architecture. A part of the palace becomes a cafe in summer and sometimes hosts painting exhibitions.

On Rte. 22, 5km (3 miles) northeast of Bayreuth toward Weidenberg. ⓒ **0921/759690.** www. schloesser.bayern.de. Gardens free; palace 4.50€ adults, free for children 17 and under. Gardens daily 24 hr. Palace Apr–Sept daily 9am–6pm; Oct 1-15 daily 10am–4pm. Closed Oct 16–Mar. Bus: 302, 303.

Festspielhaus OPERA HOUSE The operas of Wagner are dispensed like a musical Eucharist to Wagnerian pilgrims at the Festspielhaus, at the northern edge of town. The theater, designed by the composer himself, is not a beautiful building, but it's an ideal Wagnerian facility, with a huge stage capable of swallowing up Valhalla, and excellent, beautifully balanced acoustics throughout the auditorium. Because of the design, the orchestra never overwhelms the singers. The festival was opened here in 1876 with the epic *Ring* cycle. When the composer died in Venice, his wife, Cosima, took over. In the post–World War II era, Wagner's grandsons, Wolfgang and Wieland, have produced the operas, with exciting avant-garde staging and the best musicians and singers from all over the world.

Am Festspielhügel 1-2. ⓒ **0921/78780.** www.bayreuther-festspiele.de. Guided tour 5€. Tours offered in German only; English leaflets are available. Sept–May Tues–Sun at 10 and 2pm. Tours may not be given during rehearsals or at festival time. Bus: 305.

Franz-Liszt-Museum MUSEUM Wagner's wife, Cosima, was the daughter of Franz Liszt (1811–86), the great Hungarian-born composer and piano virtuoso who revolutionized piano playing. The composer lived and died in Bayreuth, and now rests in the local cemetery. Opened on October 22 (Liszt's birthday) in 1993, this museum shows the room where the composer died, and displays memorabilia related to his life and work.

Wahnfriedstrasse 9. ⓒ **0921/5166488.** Admission 2€. Sept–June daily 10am–noon and 2-5pm; July–Aug daily 10am–5pm. Bus: 302 or 307 to Villa Wahnfried.

Markgräfliches Opernhaus (Margravial Opera House) ★ OPERA HOUSE Whereas Munich's Cuvilliés Theater is a gem of Rococo, this is the finest original baroque theater in Germany, if not Europe. Behind its weathered wooden doors is a world of gilded canopies and columns, ornate sconces, and chandeliers. The house was built under the auspices of the Margravine Wilhelmine, who was known for her taste and her cultivation of the arts; her name has been given to a special baroque style called *Wilhelmian*. Her brother, Friedrich the Great, formally opened the theater in 1748. Up until that time, operas (notably those of Telemann) had been performed in the court theater. Today, the opera house, which seats 520, is used for Bayreuth's other festival: the **Musica Bayreuth,** usually held late in May. Concerts are also given during the summer.

Opernstrasse. ⓒ **0921/7596922.** www.schloesser.bayern.de. Guided tours (in German only) 5.50€ adults, free for children 5 and under. Apr–Sept daily 9am–6pm; Oct–Mar daily 10am–4pm. Bus: 302.

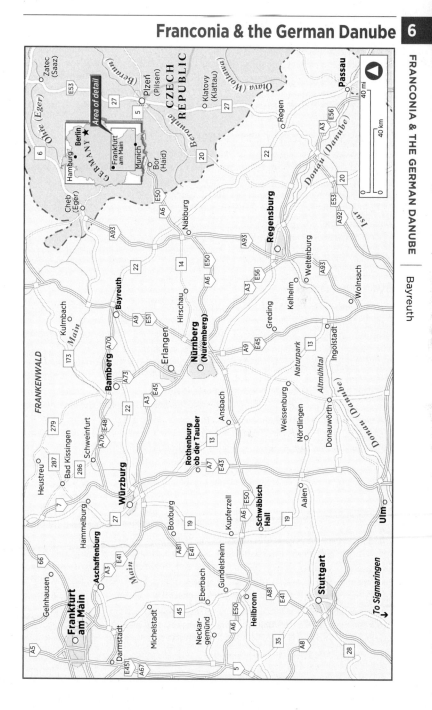

Neues Schloss (New Palace) HISTORIC BUILDING The well-preserved Neues Schloss in the center of town also shows the influence and enlightened taste of the talented and cultured Wilhelmine (1709–58). Whereas the baroque palace dates from the mid–18th century, the apartments of Wilhelmine and her husband, Margrave Friedrich, are decorated in a late-Rococo style with period furnishings.

Ludwigstrasse (1 block from the Markgräfliches Opernhaus). ✆ **0921/759690.** www.schloss.bayern.de. Guided tours (in German, with English leaflets available) 5.50€ adults, free for children 17 and under. Tours given Apr–Sept daily 9am–6pm; Oct–Mar Tues–Sun 10am–4pm. Bus: 314.

THE BAYREUTHER FESTSPIELE

The Richard Wagner opera festival takes place between mid-July and the end of August. If you arrive in Bayreuth then, you may think that the entire town has turned out to pay homage to the great composer, who built his opera house here, lived here, and was buried here following his death in Venice.

Tickets to the festival operas are almost impossible to obtain (there's an 8-year waiting list) but can sometimes be booked as part of a package tour. Tickets cost 50€ to 210€. *Warning:* During the 5 weeks of the festival, hoteliers raise their rates quite a bit. Always firmly establish the rate before booking a room and make reservations far in advance.

Where to Eat

Gendarmerie ★ FRENCH/FRANCONIAN Within the town center itself, the Bayerischer Hof (see below) contains the town's most intriguing dining choices. The hotel has a selection of restaurants offering both French and Franconian cooking. The Hans-Sachs-Stube, an air-conditioned replica of an old inn, has walls covered with pictures of famous opera singers who have performed in Bayreuth or dined here. You can also dine at the hotel's bistro, Spanische Stube. The best cuisine, however, is found at the Gendarmerie, the main a la carte restaurant. The food is superbly precise and refined here, combining inventive French dishes with the best of Franconian fare. Each dining room has a different decor, although the seasonally adjusted menu is the same in all three.

Bahnhofstrasse 14 (in front of the train station). ✆ **0921/78600.** www.gendarmerie.de. Reservations recommended. Main courses 16€–24€; fixed-price menus 28€–32€. AE, DC, MC, V. Daily 7am–11pm.

Oskar's 🏷 FRANCONIAN/INTERNATIONAL It's cozy, it's popular, and it offers some of the best value in a town that's not particularly noted for reasonable prices. Set in the heart of town, Oskar's has a large central dining room, designed like a greenhouse and flooded with sunlight, and a trio of smaller, cozier *Stuben* that have wood paneling and a sense of updated Franconian tradition. Menu items include lots of old-fashioned Franconian favorites, such as loin of beef with horseradish sauce and Bayreuther-style *Klos* (potato dumplings), roasted pork, *Schnitzels,* baked salmon, and *Sauerbraten.* There's also a short list of pastas, soups, and salads. Whenever a particular vegetable or fruit comes into season, expect lots of emphasis on it in the list of daily (or weekly) specials.

Maximilianstrasse 33. ✆ **0921/5160553.** www.oskar-bayreuth.de. Reservations not necessary. Main courses 5.50€–14€. MC, V. Mon–Sat 8am–1am; Sun 9am–1pm.

Restaurant Lohmühle FRANCONIAN Set in the Lohmühle Hotel (see below), this cozy and well-managed restaurant is partially contained in what was built in the 1600s as a mill. The rest is in a modern (but antique-looking) extension that was added in the late 1970s. Today, views from its tables encompass the Mühlbach River, and its cuisine focuses on the specialties of Franconia, particularly in the use of freshwater fish such as carp and trout. The fish are kept in large holding tanks and aquariums, and can be prepared in virtually any way you specify. Meat eaters gravitate to such dishes as calves' liver with baked apple or grilled rump steak with roasted onion rings.

In the Hotel Lohmühle, Badstrasse 37. ℰ **0921/53060.** Reservations recommended. Main courses 12€–16€. AE, DC, MC, V. June–Aug and Nov–Dec Mon–Sat noon–2pm and 6–10pm, Sun noon–2pm; Jan–May and Sept–Oct Mon–Fri 6–10pm, Sat noon–2pm and 6–10pm, Sun noon–2pm.

Where to Stay

Bayerischer Hof ★   The Bayerischer Hof remains a special favorite of Wagner fans, who find it the most convenient location for arriving by rail. The hotel is well run and offers some of the best service in town. Rooms range from midsize to spacious and are furnished in both modern and traditional pieces, usually reproductions of antiques. Some of the furnishings were shipped in from France; others are in the more functional Scandinavian modern style. The hotel dining facilities, Gendarmerie (p. 204), have even more charm and character than the hotel itself, and they're open to nonresidents, who enjoy both classical and modern dishes from an international and regional menu.

Bahnhofstrasse 14 (in front of the train station), 95444 Bayreuth. www.bayerischer-hof.de. ℰ **0921/78600.** Fax 0921/7860560. 50 units. 85€–130€ double; 121€–280€ suite. AE, DC, MC, V. Parking 11€. **Amenities:** Restaurant; bar; babysitting; indoor heated pool; room service; sauna; Wi-Fi (free; in lobby). *In room:* TV, hair dryer, minibar.

Brauerei-Gasthof Goldener Löwe ★ ♦   This unpretentious, well-managed inn serves as the town's best affordable choice. Its facade is set off by window boxes loaded with flame-red geraniums. Rooms have a Bavarian theme, with checker-patterned down comforters and light-grained pinewood trim. Guest rooms are small but comfortably furnished. The overall atmosphere is informal and homelike thanks in part to the hospitable staff.

Kulmbacher Strasse 30, 95445 Bayreuth. www.goldener-loewe-bayreuth.de. ℰ **0921/746060.** Fax 0921/47777. 13 units. 74€–119€ double; 99€–130€ suite. Rates include continental breakfast. AE, DC, MC, V. Free parking. Bus: 306. **Amenities:** Bar; room service. *In room:* TV, Wi-Fi (3€ per hour).

Goldener Anker ★★   This inn is popular locally and has a similar comfort level to the Bayerischer Hof (see above). It has hosted distinguished composers, singers, and conductors for more than 200 years. The framed photographs on the time-seasoned, oak-paneled walls are museum treasures. The guest book includes signatures of such notables as Richard Strauss, Arturo Toscanini, Fritz Kreisler, Bruno Walter, William Saroyan, Lauritz Melchior, and Patrice Chéreau. Furnishings include fine antiques and Oriental rugs. Rooms are individually designed, each with a small bathroom.

Opernstrasse 6 (next door to the Markgräfliches Opernhaus), 95444 Bayreuth. www.anker-bayreuth.de. ℰ **0921/7877740.** Fax 0921/65500. 42 units. 128€–198€ double; 450€ suite. Rates include continental breakfast. AE, DC, MC, V. Parking 10€. Bus: 306. **Amenities:** Restaurant; babysitting; room service; Wi-Fi (3€ per hour; in lobby). *In room:* TV, hair dryer.

Hotel Lohmühle ★   Located next to the Mühlbach River and a 5-minute walk from the town center, this hotel opened in 1979, when one of its oldest buildings (a 17th-c. half-timbered mill once used for tanning hides and later grinding grains into wheat) was enlarged with an architecturally compatible (new-but-old-looking) annex and radically upgraded. Today, the two separate sections of this hotel offer an appealing mix of old-fashioned Franconia that's softened with modern amenities, a polite and hardworking staff, and lots of regional charm. Guest rooms are cozy, comfortable, and rustic looking. The hotel's restaurant is recommended separately in "Where to Eat," above.

Badstrasse 37, 95444 Bayreuth. www.hotel-lohmuehle.de. © **0921/53060.** Fax 0921/5306469. 42 units. 102€–172€ double. Children 8 and under stay free in parent's room. AE, DC, MC, V. Parking 5€. Bus: 302, 307. **Amenities:** Restaurant; bar. *In room:* TV, minibar, Wi-Fi (15€ per day).

Ramada Hotel Palace ★ 🍴 One of the best deals in town is found at this government-rated four-star hotel—in some German towns, a comparable hotel would be three times the price of this one. Centrally located, the hotel is within walking distance of the major attractions. All of the spacious, comfortable, and attractively decorated bedrooms lie in the modern extension of the hotel. The older part contains a restaurant, brew house, and bar located in a restored former brewery. Modern amenities include a large conservatory and a spacious sun terrace.

Erlanger Strasse 37, 95444 Bayreuth. www.ramada.de. © **0921/75850.** Fax 0921/7585601. 104 units. 69€–104€ double. AE, DC, MC, V. Parking 7€. Bus: 301, 305, 309. **Amenities:** Restaurant; bar; exercise room; Jacuzzi; room service; sauna. *In room:* A/C, TV, hair dryer, Wi-Fi (free).

BAMBERG ★★

238km (148 miles) NW of Munich, 61km (38 miles) NW of Nürnberg, 97km (60 miles) NE of Würzburg

This little city is one of the gems of Franconia, although visitors often pass it by. Set in the rolling Franconian hills where the Regnitz River flows into the Main, this modest-sized town is loaded with attractions, including numerous architectural treasures luckily untouched by the ravages of World War II.

In the Middle Ages, Bamberg was two towns divided by the river: the powerful ecclesiastical town of the prince-bishopric, of which it was the capital for 800 years, and the secular town of the burghers. Bamberg's architecture spans more than 1,000 years, with styles ranging from Romanesque to Gothic, Renaissance to baroque, up to the eclecticism of the 19th century. There are narrow cobblestone streets, ornate mansions and palaces, and impressive churches.

Today, Bamberg and beer go together like barley and hops. The town has been called "a beer drinker's Eden" (there are more breweries here than in Munich, often at cheaper prices). The average Bamberger drinks 190 liters of beer a year, making the rest of the Germans look like teetotalers by comparison. Beer lovers come from afar for *Rauchbier,* a smoked beer first brewed in 1536.

Essentials

GETTING THERE

BY TRAIN The **Bamberg Bahnhof** is on the Stuttgart-Hof and the Berlin-Munich rail lines, with frequent connections in both directions. Most visitors arrive from Nürnberg in just 1 hour. There are direct trains running from Bayreuth to Bamberg. For information and schedules, call © **01805/996633** or visit www.bahn.de.

BY CAR Access is via the B22 from Würzburg or the A73 from Nürnberg.

VISITOR INFORMATION

Contact the **Bamberg Tourist Information Office,** Geyerswörthstrasse 5 (© **0951/2976200;** www.bamberg.info). Office hours are Monday to Friday 9:30am to 6pm, Saturday to Sunday 9:30am to 2:30pm (Jan–Mar closed Sun).

GETTING AROUND

A well-run network of buses fans out from the Zentralomnibusbahnhof on Prome-nadestrasse, next to the railway station. For more information, head to **i-Punkt** (© **0951/9685872**) in the railway station, open Monday to Thursday 7am to 7pm and Friday 7:30am to noon. Bus maps and tickets can be purchased at the station or from machines at stops along the route. A single ride for Zone 1 costs 1.50€; a single ride for Zone 1 and 2 goes for 2.10€.

Exploring Bamberg

Alte Hofhaltung, a Renaissance imperial and Episcopal palace, with a courtyard surrounded by late-Gothic framework buildings, dominates the center square. **Altes Rathaus** ★ is the strangest town hall in Germany. Determined not to play favorites between the ecclesiastical and secular sections of the city, the town authorities built this Gothic structure on its own little island in the middle of the Regnitz River, half-way between the two factions—a true middle-of-the-road (or river) political stand. From the island, you get the best view of the old fishermen's houses along the banks in the section called "Little Venice."

Alte Hofhaltung HISTORIC BUILDING   Located on the north side of Bam-berg's great cathedral, this once-glorified palace is still an impressive half-timbered pile in the Gothic style, with Renaissance styling and a spacious courtyard for peri-odic special events. Ask at the tourist office for more information. Inside, former times are reflected in the remains of the original 11th-century Diet (assembly) hall, and notable lovely rooms, such as the frescoed Kaisersaal, the main banqueting hall, or the Chinesisches Kabinet known for its walls of marquetry. Don't miss the rose garden.

The building itself is more intriguing than its on-site **Historisches Museum** (Historical Museum), filled with artifacts, documents, and maps of the history of Bamberg. To fully appreciate this museum, you must be fluent in German, be writing a book on the history of Bamberg, and/or view the city as the place of origin of your ancestors.

Domplatz 8. © **0951/5190746.** Admission 3.50€. May–Oct Tues–Sun 9am–5pm. Bus: 910.

Kaiserdom (Imperial Cathedral) ★★ CHURCH   Given its size and age, this cathedral on the hillside is stunning. Begun in 1215 in Romanesque and early-Gothic style, it has a unique double-chancel, the eastern one raised on a terrace to compen-sate for the slope. The massive towers at the four corners of the church dominate Bamberg's skyline, while the interior features some fine religious art. Best known is the 13th-century equestrian statue, the **Bamberger Reiter,** which represents the idealized Christian king of the Middle Ages. Among the many tombs is that of Emperor Heinrich II, who erected the original cathedral. Sculptor Tilman Riemen-schneider labored more than a decade over this masterpiece of a tomb, as well as the one devoted to the emperor's wife, Kunigunde (who was suspected of adultery, com-memorated in a scene on the tomb). The west chancel contains the only papal tomb north of the Alps, that of Pope Clement II, who died in 1047. The rich cathedral treasury may be seen in the adjoining **Diözesanmuseum.**

Domplatz. © **0951/502330.** Free admission. May–Oct Mon–Fri 9:30am–6pm, Sat 9:30–11:30am and 12:45–6pm, Sun 12:30–1:45pm and 2:45–6pm; Nov–Apr Mon–Sat 9:30am–5pm, Sun 12:30–1:45pm and 2:45–5pm. Diözesanmuseum 3€ adults, 2€ students and children 8–14, free for children 7 and under. Bus: 910.

Neue Residenz (New Residence) ★ ROYAL BUILDILNG   Opposite the Alte Hofhaltung is the 17th-century Neue Residenz, a much larger palace for prince-bishops, showing both Renaissance and baroque influences, and the site of one of the most famous unsolved mysteries in Germany. In 1815, a corpse found beneath the windows of the palace turned out to be the body of Marshal Berthier, Napoleon's chief of staff, who retired here after Napoleon was exiled to Elba. No one knows if Berthier was murdered or committed suicide. Upstairs are works by German masters. On the second floor are the former **Imperial Apartments,** with Gobelin tapestries, parquet floors, and baroque furnishings. The **Emperors' Hall** has portraits and frescoes.

Domplatz 8. ✆ **0951/519390.** www.schloesser.bayern.de. Admission 4€ adults, 3€ children. Apr–Sept daily 9am–6pm; Oct–Mar daily 10am–4pm. Bus: 910.

Where to Eat

Historischer Brauereiausschank Schlenkerla FRANCONIAN   Diners con-gregate here much as they did in 1405, when the place was a brewery. The long wooden tables and smallish chairs exude a genuinely rustic and *gemütlich* (cozy) atmosphere. Unpretentious and affordable Franconian fare is served, including local dishes such as *Bierbrauervesper* (Brewmaster's Break, consisting of smoked meat and sour-milk cheese) and *Rauchschinken* (smoked ham). Wash them down with the hearty malt, *Rauchbier*, which has an intense smoky aroma and flavor.

Dominikanerstrasse 6. ✆ **0951/56060.** www.schlenkerla.de. Main courses 7€–12€. No credit cards. Daily 9:30am–11:30pm. Bus: 910.

Romantik Restaurant-Weinhaus Messerschmitt ★ FRANCONIAN/INTER-NATIONAL   You'll have to look hard to find better dining or a more refined atmo-sphere in town. Following over 160 years of tradition, the cuisine's dignity shines through its simplicity. Menu items depend on available ingredients. Freshwater fish (kept in an aquarium) and game are two of the specialties. You may find some of the offerings, such as roast eel from the Main River, a bit too authentic, but the Franco-nian duck is a terrific choice.

Langestrasse 41. ✆ **0951/297800.** Main courses 14€–28€. AE, DC, MC, V. Daily 11am–11pm. Bus: 905 or 921.

Shopping

The primary shopping district in Bamberg is by the cathedral, where you will find stores of all kinds, including more than a dozen antiques shops and numerous galler-ies. An antiques store that has it all, **Sebök,** Untere Königstrasse 21 (✆ **0951/202593;** www.seboek-auktionen.de), offers paintings, books, furniture, fine jewelry, silver, glass, toys, watches, clocks, and more. Auctions are held every 2 months, with the summer auction falling in July. If you're interested in local ceramics, go to **Töpfer-laden Irene Herold,** Untere Brücke 1 (✆ **0951/56913**), where you'll find ceramic candleholders, cups, dinnerware, vases, and garden statuary.

Entertainment & Nightlife

Sinfonie an der Regnitz, Mussstrasse 1 (✆ **0951/9647200;** www.bamberger-symphoniker.de), is home to the Bamberg Symphony Orchestra from September to May. From the last week in June to mid-July, there's a summer festival with weekend symphonic concerts. Tickets are 23€ to 43€.

Hofburg Repertory Theater performs at the **E. T. A. Hoffman Theater,** E.T.A.-Hoffmann-Platz 1 (© **0951/873030;** www.theater-bamberg.de). Its season runs September through July. The productions range from 18th-, 19th-, and 20th-century classics to contemporary musicals. The box office is open daily 10am to 6pm and 1 hour before showtime. In June and July, the company moves outdoors, performing a series of German-language dramas in the courtyard of the Alte Hofhaltung (see above). Tickets for both indoor and outdoor performances are 17€ to 30€, but students with a valid ID card pay half-price. For more information about these and other cultural events in Bamberg, contact the Tourist Information Office (see "Visitor Information," above).

A young crowd gathers at **Jazzclub,** Obere Sandstrasse 18 (© **0951/55225;** www.jcbamberg.de), to listen to punk, Goth, and alternative music on Tuesday and Thursday nights from 9pm to 1am, when the cover is 5€ mid-September to April; the club opens its cellar for live jazz on Friday and Saturday 9pm to 2am, when the cover is 9€ to 17€, depending on the group. Tickets to virtually any cultural or sporting event in Bamberg are available from the city's largest ticket agency, **BVD Bamburger Ticket Agency,** Langestrasse 22 (© **0951/980820;** www.bvd-ticket.de), open Monday to Friday 9am to 6pm and Saturday 9am to 1pm.

Another option for whiling away the after-dark hours is a visit to **Haas Säle,** Obere Sandstrasse 7 (© **0951/500458** or **0951/53304;** www.haas-saele.de), where you'll find a battered-looking pub with a small stage that presents, depending on the night of the week, flamenco dancing, short plays, or political satire. Dance music follows the show. There's almost never a cover charge and everything is usually spontaneous and pulled together on short notice.

Where to Stay
EXPENSIVE

Bamberger Hof Bellevue ★ This hotel plays second fiddle to the Welcome Hotel Residenzschloss (see below), but the service and accommodations of both are roughly on par. A great old palace of stone, crowned by a tower and facing a little park, it's good for soaking up the mellow atmosphere of yesteryear. Try to book one of the large rooms with sitting areas. Each unit is well furnished and attractively maintained, most often with a generous-size bathroom.

Schönleinsplatz 4, 96047 Bamberg. www.bambergerhof.de. © **0951/98550.** Fax 0951/985562. 50 units. 165€ double; 195€–450€ suite. Rates include buffet breakfast. AE, DC, MC, V. Parking 15€. Bus: 905 or 921. **Amenities:** Restaurant; bar; room service; Wi-Fi (free; in lobby). *In room:* TV, hair dryer, minibar.

Romantik Hotel-Weinhaus Messerschmitt ★★ This hotel in the heart of the city, beloved by traditionalists, is Bamberg's most romantic choice. However, some of its antique appeal as an old German inn has been diminished by the addition of 50 new bedrooms in a modern wing. These are the most up-to-date and among the most comfortable in town. The main building of the hotel remains one of the oldest structures in the area, dating from 1422. The present exterior is 18th century, a gabled expanse of pale blue and yellow with baroque-style window frames. Inside, the mellow decor includes paneling, ceramic ovens, and antiques. Many of the beds have meticulously crafted headboards. The owner and his staff are very helpful.

Langestrasse 41, 96047 Bamberg. www.hotel-messerschmitt.de. © **0951/297800.** Fax 0951/2978029. 67 units. 135€–170€ double; 220€ junior suite. Rates include buffet breakfast. AE, DC, MC, V. Parking 8€. Bus: 905 or 921. **Amenities:** Restaurant (p. 208); Jacuzzi; sauna. *In room:* TV, minibar.

Villa Geyerswörth ★★　Four buildings in the heart of Bamberg's Old Town were connected to form this boutique hotel set close to the banks of the old Ludwig-Danube-Main Canal. The structures have been completely modernized and brought up-to-date, each with good plumbing and comfortable but traditional furnishings. Standard doubles enjoy a quiet location, opening onto views of the river. The superior doubles lie in the newer section of the hotel, with views over the garden, fountains, and a pavilion. Some 80% of the guest rooms are allergy friendly. A restaurant on-site serves a contemporary cuisine with seasonal specialties.

Geyerswörthstrasse 15, 96047 Bamberg. www.villageyerswoerth.de. ✆ **0951/91740.** Fax 0951/9174500. 40 units. 149€–169€ double; 219€ suite. AE, DC, MC, V. Parking 12€. **Amenities:** Restaurant; bar; exercise room; room service; sauna. *In room:* A/C, TV, hair dryer, minibar, Wi-Fi (8€ per hour).

Welcome Hotel Residenzschloss ★★　This elegant hotel, a blend of old and new, is the best choice in town. It lies on a bank of the Regnitz, near the Altstadt and across from the Bamberg Symphony Orchestra building. The building, with its ocher-colored baroque walls, was constructed by the local archbishop in 1787 as a hospital. Today, the original hospital chapel continues to host local weddings. A less glamorous modern annex is connected to the main building by a glass-sided breezeway. The annex contains perfectly functional rooms, but those in the main building are midsize to spacious and decorated in a classical, elegant style with supremely comfortable furnishings.

Untere Sandstrasse 32, 96049 Bamberg. www.welcome-hotels.com. ✆ **0951/60910.** Fax 0951/6091701. 184 units. 141€–204€ double; 350€ suite. Rates include buffet breakfast. AE, DC, MC, V. Parking 10€. Bus: 916. **Amenities:** 2 restaurants; bar; babysitting; exercise room; Jacuzzi; room service; sauna. *In room:* TV, hair dryer, minibar, Wi-Fi (8€ per hour).

MODERATE

Barock Hotel am Dom ★ 🍴　This hotel offers some of the same style, tradition, and romance of the pacesetters above, but at a better price. Advance reservations are recommended. The owners have retained every detail of the original ornamented facade and renovated key areas of the interior. The result is a winning combination of baroque elements in a well-lit modernized building. Guest rooms are attractively furnished, if a bit cramped, as are the shower-only bathrooms. The comfort level and maintenance are high. Rates include a nourishing breakfast served in the old cellar, with tables under the plastered stone vaulting.

Vorderer Bach 4, 96049 Bamberg. www.barockhotel.com. ✆ **0951/54031.** Fax 0951/54021. 19 units. 98€–105€ double. Rates include buffet breakfast. AE, DC, MC, V. Bus: 910, 912, or 918. *In room:* TV, hair dryer, minibar.

Hotel National　The National is still a favorite, though it no longer enjoys the renown it used to. Modernization has removed some of its quaint charm, and it lacks the style of the Romantik Hotel-Weinhaus Messerschmitt (see above), but the price is right and the rooms are first rate, each with a tidily kept bathroom. With its black mansard roof, iron balconies, baroque and classical detailing, and opulent public rooms, the hotel is attractive, if small. It has well-maintained and traditionally furnished rooms that tend to provide a comfortable stay.

Luitpoldstrasse 37, 96052 Bamberg. www.hotel-national-bamberg.de. ✆ **0951/509980.** Fax 0951/22436. 41 units. 90€–110€ double; 115€–125€ suite. Children 7 and under stay free in parent's room. Rates include buffet breakfast. AE, DC, MC, V. Parking 7€. Bus: 901, 902, 907 or 911. **Amenities:** Restaurant; bar; room service. *In room:* TV, hair dryer, minibar, Wi-Fi (free; in lobby).

INEXPENSIVE

Hotel Garni Graupner   This reasonably priced hotel has been accepting overnight guests since the 14th century. Your room may have a view over the Altstadt, but will definitely be clean and decent, although short on charm. If the main hotel is full, guests are directed to the lackluster 1960s annex, about 8 blocks away and across the canal. It offers 10 modern rooms for the same price charged in the main hotel. The same family also owns a rose-garden cafe a stone's throw from the cathedral.

Langestrasse 5, 96047 Bamberg. www.hotel-graupner.de. © **0951/980400.** Fax 0951/9804040. 30 units, 26 with bathroom. 70€ double without bathroom; 75€–90€ double with bathroom; 98€ junior suite. Rates include buffet breakfast. MC, V. Parking 6.50€. Bus: 1, 2, 4, 8, or 16. **Amenities:** Wi-Fi (free; in lobby). *In room:* TV, hair dryer.

NÜRNBERG (NUREMBERG) ★★

169km (105 miles) NW of Munich, 225km (140 miles) SE of Frankfurt, 204km (127 miles) NE of Stuttgart

When this city celebrated its 900th birthday in 1950, the scars of World War II were still fresh. Nürnberg was once a masterpiece of medieval splendor, but that legacy was lost in the ashes of war. With the exception of Dresden, no other German city suffered such devastation in a single air raid. On the night of January 2, 1945, 525 British Lancaster bombers rained fire and destruction on this city, the ideological center of the Third Reich.

Nürnberg today has regained its vitality and is now a symbol of postwar prosperity. The city swarms with people, both longtime residents and the *Gastarbeiter* (foreign workers), who have flooded the city in recent years—many from the old Soviet Bloc countries to the east. For most of the year, the city is thronged with visitors too. It's a notable industrial center, still associated with its traditional gingerbread products and handmade toys. The first pocket watches, the Nürnberg eggs, were made here in the 16th century.

Centuries of art and architecture made Nürnberg a treasure. During the 15th and 16th centuries, Nürnberg enjoyed a cultural flowering that made it the center of the **German Renaissance,** bringing together Italian Renaissance and German Gothic traditions. In the artists' workshops were found such great talents as Veit Stoss, Peter Vischer, Adam Krafft, Michael Wolgemut, and, above all, Albrecht Dürer. Koberger set up his printing press here, and Regiomontanus built an astronomical observatory. Here, too, flourished the guilds of the *Meistersingers,* composed of prosperous artisans; Wagner made their most famous member, Hans Sachs, the hero of his opera *Die Meistersinger von Nürnberg.*

Many of Nürnberg's most important buildings, including some of the finest churches in Germany, have been restored or reconstructed. The old part of the city, the **Altstadt,** lies mainly within a pedestrian zone. Today's visitors can see the ruins of the ramparts that once surrounded the city as well as more modern sites, such as the **Justice Palace,** where the War Crimes Tribunal sat in 1946.

Visitors can also see the **Zeppelinfeld arena,** the huge amphitheater where, from 1927 to 1935, Hitler staged those dramatic Nazi rallies that were immortalized by Leni Riefenstahl in *Triumph des Willens (Triumph of the Will).* Hitler's architect, Albert Speer, constructed what has been called a "concrete mecca," whose grounds today have been turned into a park with apartment blocks, a trade fair, and a concert hall. Speer's Congress Hall, larger than the Colosseum in Rome, has become a recording studio and warehouse.

Essentials

GETTING THERE

BY PLANE   **Nürnberg Flughafen** is 6km (4 miles) north of the city center. Despite its relatively small size (it's only the tenth busiest in Germany), this airport is served by 14 airlines, with flights to dozens of European destinations. These are supplemented by charter flights. For information and schedules, call © **0911/93700** or visit **www.airport-nuernberg.de**.

BY TRAIN   The **Nürnberg Hauptbahnhof** lies on several major German rail lines, with frequent connections to big cities and many smaller regional towns. Travel time to Frankfurt is 2 hours; to Berlin, 5 hours; and to Munich, 1 hour. For information and schedules, call © **01805/996633** or visit **www.bahn.de**.

BY BUS   For international destinations, check with Eurolines affiliate, **Touring** (© **069/7903501;** www.touring.de). **Berlin Linien** (© **030/8619331;** www. berlinlinienbus.de) buses provide service to Berlin, Dresden, Leipzig and other domestic points north and east. Regional service to neighboring towns within Franconia is offered by **OVF Omnibusverkehr Franken GmbH,** Nelson Mandela Platz 18 in Nürnberg (© **0911/430570;** www.ovf.de). For information on these or any other bus line coming into Nürnberg (or anywhere else in Franconia), contact one of the city's largest travel agents, **TUI Reise Center,** Lorenzerstrasse 19 (© **0911/ 2270000**).

BY CAR   From Munich, take the A9 Autobahn north; from Frankfurt, head southeast along the A3 Autobahn; from Berlin, take the A9 Autobahn south.

VISITOR INFORMATION

Contact **Tourist Information,** Hauptmarkt 18 (© **0911/23360;** tourismus. nuernberg.de), Monday to Saturday 9am to 6pm. From May to October, it is also open Sunday 10am to 4pm.

GETTING AROUND

Nürnberg has a **subway** system that consists of east-west and north-south lines that intersect at the Hauptbahnhof. One-way fares within the city cost 2.10€. A Day Ticket Solo, valid for the entire transportation network for 24 hours, costs 4.20€. The visitor-friendly **Bus no. 36** cuts through the heart of the old town and ends at the Reichsparteitagsgelände (p. 214). For more information, call © **0911/2834646** or visit **www.vag.de**.

   Walking between two points at opposite ends of the old town—the Hauptbahnhof (main railway station) and the Kaiserburg (the base of the city's medieval castle)—will take you only about 30 minutes and will lead you through the heart of the city's medieval core and past most of its historic monuments. To summon a **taxi,** call © **0911/19410**. The base fare and first kilometer cost 2.70€ each, while each additional kilometer adds on 1.35€.

Exploring Nürnberg

You can easily spend a full day here seeing the sights. Begin at the central market square, **Hauptmarkt,** the most colorful place in Nürnberg, filled with kiosks stacked tall with fresh produce brought in from the countryside. Nearly all the city's attractions lie nearby within the **medieval fortifications,** parts of which still remain. Between the main wall (which has rampart walks) and the secondary wall once ran the waters of a protective moat. At the "corners" of the Altstadt are the massive stone

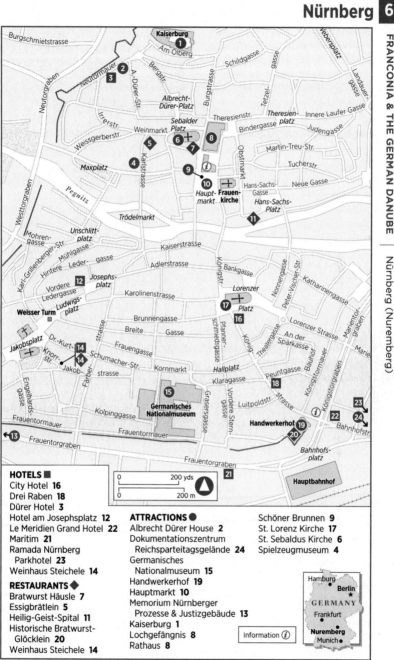

HOTELS ■
City Hotel **16**
Drei Raben **18**
Dürer Hotel **3**
Hotel am Josephsplatz **12**
Le Meridien Grand Hotel **22**
Maritim **21**
Ramada Nürnberg
 Parkhotel **23**
Weinhaus Steichele **14**

RESTAURANTS ◆
Bratwurst Häusle **7**
Essigbrätlein **5**
Heilig-Geist-Spital **11**
Historische Bratwurst-
 Glöcklein **20**
Weinhaus Steichele **14**

ATTRACTIONS ●
Albrecht Dürer House **2**
Dokumentationszentrum
 Reichsparteitagsgelände **24**
Germanisches
 Nationalmuseum **15**
Handwerkerhof **19**
Hauptmarkt **10**
Memorium Nürnberger
 Prozesse & Justizgebäude **13**
Kaiserburg **1**
Lochgefängnis **8**
Rathaus **8**

Schöner Brunnen **9**
St. Lorenz Kirche **17**
St. Sebaldus Kirche **6**
Spielzeugmuseum **4**

0   200 yds
0   200 m

Information ⓘ

213

6 | CANAL & riverboat TOURS

The Main-Danube Canal links together the Rhine, the Main, and the Danube. For information about riverboat tours on the canal and the rivers that feed it, contact **Neptun (NPS) GmbH** (✆ **0911/6002055;** www.neptun-personenschifffahrt.de). Between May and September, the company offers weekly water excursions from Nürnberg to Forchheim, which lies 4 hours away. The cost of 34€ round-trip allows several hours for strolling the streets of Forchheim before returning the same day to Nürnberg.

towers, still intact, of the city gates. The remains of dozens of other gateway towers still exist along the ramparts. Crowning the northern periphery of the Altstadt is the **Kaiserburg.**

The best example of Nürnberg's aesthetic passion is the **Schöner Brunnen (Beautiful Fountain)** on the Hauptmarkt. This stone pyramid, 18m (60 ft.) high, dates from 1396 and is adorned with 30 figures arranged in four tiers. Within it is enclosed the symbol of Nürnberg, the journeyman's ring.

At some point in your day, wander over to **Handwerkerhof,** near the main train station. In this mall, you can see artisans creating the products for which Nürnberg has been known since the Middle Ages: glassware, pewter (often in the form of beer mugs), intricate woodcarvings, and toys.

If you're interested in a famous landmark of World War II, visit the **Justizge-bäude,** Fürtherstrasse 22 (U-Bahn: Bärenschanze), where the "Judgment of Nürnberg" took place. Here, in Courtroom 600, the surviving leaders of the Third Reich stood trial in October 1946 for crimes against humanity. Afterward, 10 were hanged. The building still serves as a courthouse, and you'll have to ask the guard at the door if you can enter.

Albrecht Dürer House ★ HISTORIC HOUSE   The town's most popular shrine is the Albrecht Dürer House, just a short walk up the cobblestoned Bergstrasse from the Dürer Monument and St. Sebald Church. Typical of the half-timbered burghers' houses of the 15th century, the structure is the only completely preserved Gothic house in Nürnberg. The first floors are sandstone, surmounted by two half-timbered stories and a gabled roof with a view of the town below. Exhibits inside the house are devoted to Dürer's life and works. Many of the rooms are furnished with important historical pieces and contain original etchings and woodcuts, plus copies of Dürer's paintings.

Am Tiergartnertor, Albrecht-Dürer-Strasse 39. ✆ **0911/2312568.** www.museen.nuernberg.de. Admission 5€ adults, 3€ students and children 6–18, free for children 5 and under. Tues–Fri 10am–5pm; Thurs 10am–8pm; Sat–Sun 10am–6pm; July–Sept Mon 10am–5pm.Tram: 4. Bus: 36.

Dokumentationszentrum Reichsparteitagsgelände ★ WWII SITE   In the north wing of the unfinished Kongresshalle, the memories of the Nazi Party Congress rallies of 1934 and 1935 live on. You can visit the **Documentation Center Nazi Party Rally Grounds** to gain a greater understanding of the events in Nürnberg that shaped world history. Included are permanent and changing exhibitions, plus visits to the rally grounds. In addition, the Documentation Center considers academic and pedagogical tasks to be an integral part of its education work. One example of this is the International Study Forum, presenting film programs as well as talks and discussions with groups to assess their opinions before and after their visits to the exhibition. Political and peace education are central to the Documentation Center's vision, as is the study of human rights.

The Kongresshalle opens onto Lake Grosser Dutzendteich. Across the lake stands Zeppelinwiese, a field that's the site of the Tribüne, that mass mammoth marble platform from which Hitler ranted at more than 100,000 spectators enthralled by his violent denunciations.

Bayernstrasse 110. 🕐 **0911/2315666.** www.museen.nuernberg.de. Admission 5€ adults, 3€ students and children, 11€ family card. Mon–Fri 9am–6pm; Sat–Sun 10am–6pm. S-Bahn: 2 to Dutzendteich. Tram: 9. Bus: 36 or 55.

Germanisches Nationalmuseum (Germanic National Museum) ★★★
MUSEUM   Located just inside the south section of the medieval walls, the largest museum of German art and culture covers the entire spectrum of German craftsmanship and fine arts from their beginnings to the 20th century. The prehistoric and early historical section contains finds from the Stone Age and from the burial sites of the Merovingians. The extensive painting and sculpture sections include works by Albrecht Dürer and Veit Stoss, a sculptor and woodcarver known for his "nervous" angular forms and realism. The boundless variety and richness of German handicrafts is fully evident in this museum. (*Note:* At press time, most of the galleries have reopened following a year-long closure and renovation in 2011, though the 20th century collection is scheduled to remain closed until February 2012.)

Kartäusergasse 1 (near the Hauptbahnhof). 🕐 **0911/13310.** www.gnm.de. Admission 6€ adults, 4€ children. Tues and Thurs–Sun 10am–6pm; Wed 10am–9pm (free admission after 6pm Wed). U-Bahn: Opernhaus.

Kaiserburg ★ HISTORIC BUILDING   "The Burg" looms above the city from its hilltop at the northern edge of the Altstadt. From 1050 to 1571, it was the official residence of the German kings and emperors, including Frederick Barbarossa. The castle is divided into three complexes: the Kaiserburg (Imperial Castle), the Burgraves' Castle, and the Municipal Buildings of the Free City.

The oldest portion is the **Pentagonal Tower** (1050). It probably dates from the previous palace of the Salian kings, over which the Burgraves' Castle was constructed. Although the **Burgraves' Castle** has been in ruins since it was destroyed by fire in 1420, the remains offer visitors a look into the layout of a feudal castle. The watchmen and guards used the heavy ramparts with the parapet walks and secret passages to protect the burgraves and the emperors, who lived in the inner core of the castle complex.

Kaiserburg, grouped around the inner court within the ramparts of the Burgraves' Castle, was the residence of the kings and emperors of Germany. Most of the buildings were constructed during the 12th century and centered on the once magnificent Palas, built by Konrad III in 1138. The great Knights' Hall on the ground floor and the Imperial Hall on the floor above look much as they did when King Friedrich III rebuilt them in the 15th century, with heavy oak beams and painted ceilings. The rooms are decorated with period Gothic furnishings. Adjoining the Palas is the Imperial Chapel—actually two chapels, one above the other in cross section but united at the center by an open bay. Thus, the emperor could worship to the same liturgy with his court in the upper chapel while the lesser members of his retinue worshiped in the lower.

The third set of buildings, outside the Burgraves' Castle, was erected by the council of Nürnberg in the 14th and 15th centuries, when it took over the responsibility of protecting the emperor. This section includes the imperial stables (now a youth hostel), the massive bastions of the fortress, the Tiefer Brunnen (Deep Well), and the castle gardens. Even more impressive than the fortress is the view of the roofs and towers of Nürnberg from its terraces.

The complex also includes the new **Kaiserburg Museum** (✆ **0911/2009540**), which contains antique weaponry, armor, and paintings, and explains the history of the castle.

Burgstrasse 13. ✆ **0911/2446590.** www.schloesser.bayern.de. Admission (including all parts of the castle) 6€ adults, 4€ students, free for children 16 and under. Apr–Sept daily 9am–6pm; Oct–Mar daily 10am–4pm. Tram: 4.

Lochgefängnisse (Dungeons) HISTORIC INTEREST   This gruesome attraction under the Altes Rathaus is a medieval prison with its original cells and torture chamber. Opposite the torture chamber lie the remnants of a room that once hid the city council's treasures and important documents during wars and emergencies. An underground passage from the dungeons to the outside world existed from 1543 to 1945, when bombing rendered it impassable.

Rathausplatz. ✆ **0911/2312690.** www.museen.nuernberg.de. Admission 3.50€ adults, 1.50€ children. Tues–Sun 10am–4:30pm. Closed weekends Nov–Mar; closed Jan–Feb. Bus: 36, 46, or 47.

Memorium Nürnberg Prozesse & Justizgebäude (Memorium Nuremberg Trials & Courthouse) ★★ WWII SITE   In a recently opened wing of the Justizgebäude, this memorial sheds light on the Nürnberg Trials, the famous set of war trials that have become synonymous with the city. Beginning on November 20, 1945, 21 leading Nazi war criminals were tried in Courtroom 600 before the Allied International Military Tribunal for conspiracy and crimes against world peace, the rules of warfare, and humanity. The trials became a milestone in judicial history as a birthplace for a new law of nations: For the first time in history, sentences were pronounced according to the principle of the personal responsibility of the individual. Faced with the historical legacy of National Socialism, the trials were deliberately set in Nürnberg in order to make a statement.

Documents, photographs and artifacts such as the dock and the box for transporting evidence help reconstruct the events of the trial. Viewing the actual Courtroom 600 cannot be guaranteed, as it is still a functioning court. Contact the memorial on Fridays to find out when viewing the historic room is possible for the following week.

Bärenschanzstrasse 72. ✆ **0911/32179372.** www.memorium-nuremberg.de. Admission 5€ adults, 3€ students and children. Wed–Mon 10am–6pm. U-Bahn: Bärenschanze.

St.-Lorenz-Kirche ★ CHURCH   Across the Pegnitz River from the castle is the largest and most majestic church in Nürnberg. Although it took more than 200 years to complete, beginning in 1270, the final result is one of Gothic purity, inside and out. The twin towers (ca. 1400) flank the west portal, whose sculptures depict the theme of redemption, from Adam and Eve through the Last Judgment. Upon entering the church, turn around and note the color and detail in the stained-glass rosette above the portal. Much of the church's stained and painted glass dates from the 15th century. The interior is punctuated by pillars that soar upward and disappear in the vaulting shafts above the nave. Each pillar is adorned with sculptures carrying on the theme introduced at the entrance. The oldest of these is *Mary with Child*, chiseled around 1285. The sculptures urge you toward the single east choir, the last portion of the church to be completed (1477). *The Angelic Salutation* (1519), carved in linden wood by Veit Stoss, is suspended from the roof of the church just behind the Madonna Chandelier. To the left of the altar, the upthrusting turret of the Gothic Tabernacle, hewn from stone by Adam Kraft (1496), repeats the vertical emphasis of the church. Above the high altar is another masterpiece by Stoss, a carved crucifix.

Lorenzer Platz 10. (C) **0911/2446990.** www.lorenzkirche.de. Free admission. Mon–Sat 9am–5pm; Sun 1–4pm. U-Bahn: Lorenzkirche.

St.-Sebaldus-Kirche CHURCH   Consecrated in 1273, this church is a fine example of 13th-century transition from Romanesque to German Gothic styles. The nave and west choir are late Romanesque, with a narrow chancel containing a simple altar and an ancient bronze baptismal font. The larger east choir, consecrated in 1379, is pure Gothic and contains the church's most important treasures. Between the two east pillars is a huge 16th-century crucifixion group dominated by a life-size crucifix by Veit Stoss. Just behind the altar is the elaborate shrine of St. Sebald, whose remains are encased in a monument cast in brass by Peter Vischer in 1519. It's supported by an array of snails and dolphins and adorned with a host of statuettes. The nave of the church also holds several important **works of art ★★**, including 14th-century statues of St. Catherine and St. Sebald and the *Madonna with a Halo* (1440).

Albrecht-Dürer-Platz 1. (C) **0911/2142500.** www.sebalduskirche.de. Free admission. Jan–Mar daily 9:30am–4pm; Apr–May and Oct–Dec daily 9:30am–6pm; June–Sept daily 9:30am–8pm. Sun services 8:30 and 10am. U-Bahn: Lorenzkirche.

Spielzeugmuseum (Toy Museum) ☺ MUSEUM   Nürnberg is a major toy center and home to the International Toy Fair in February, so it's only fitting that the city devote a museum to this industry. Toys, both hand- and machine-made, fill three floors with some dating from medieval times. The collection of old dollhouses is vastly amusing, as is a mechanical Ferris wheel. You'll often see adults here (even without children).

Karlstrasse 13–15. (C) **0911/2313164.** www.museen.nuernberg.de. Admission 5€ adults, 3€ students and children, 11€ family ticket (2 parents with 1 or more children). Tues–Fri 10am–5pm; Sat–Sun 10am–6pm. Bus: 36.

Where to Eat
EXPENSIVE

Essigbrätlein ★★★ FRANCONIAN/CONTINENTAL   The oldest and best-known restaurant in Nürnberg, this 450-year-old establishment doesn't need a website. Its upscale cuisine is so inventive and refreshing, it is a good enough reason to visit the city in the first place. As the chef firmly believes in market-fresh ingredients, expect an ever-changing menu based on seasonal availability. For the traditional specialty, look no further than the name, meaning "roast loin of beef." Originally a meeting place of wine merchants, there are no doubt fine vintages here.

Weinmarkt 3. (C) **0911/225131.** Reservations required. All main courses 33€; fixed-price 4-course lunch 89€, 4- and 6-course dinner 104€. AE, DC, MC, V. Tues–Sat noon–1:30pm and 7–9:30pm. Closed Jan 1–15 and 2 weeks in Aug (dates vary). U-Bahn: Karstadt.

MODERATE

Heilig-Geist-Spital 🍴 FRANCONIAN   You can't get much more Franconian than this. Entered through an arcade above the river, Nürnberg's largest historical wine house has been in business for 650 years, serving hearty and filling Franconian fare. Carp is a specialty, as is pork knuckle—it's safe to say no one has altered this recipe since the days of Dürer himself. In season, you can order leg of venison with noodles and berries. The wine list is abundant and excellent.

Spitalgasse 16. ✆ **0911/221761.** www.heilig-geist-spital.de. Reservations recommended. Main courses 10€–18€. AE, MC, V. Daily 11am–11pm. Bus: 46 or 47.

Weinhaus Steichele ★ FRANCONIAN/BAVARIAN   Steichele's walls are covered with polished copper pots, antique display cases lit from within, and hanging chandeliers carved into double-tailed sea monsters and other mythical beasts. Try roast shoulder of pork with potato balls and *Sauerkraut*; or paprika-coated baked ham in an onion sauce, served with french fries and a salad. The wine list is superb. Surely if former patron Hermann Hesse returned today, he would notice no major alteration in the cuisine. Amid all the change in Nürnberg, this place still respects former times.

Knorrstrasse 2. ✆ **0911/202280.** www.steichele.de. Reservations recommended. Main courses 6€–20€. AE, DC, MC, V. Mon–Sat 11am–midnight; Oct–May Sun 11am–3pm. U-Bahn: Weisser Turm.

INEXPENSIVE

Bratwurst-Häusle FRANCONIAN   This is the best-known eatery serving Nürnberg's famous finger-sized sausages—stop here for lunch as you explore the historic town. Prices are kept at a 1970s level, but portions are as large as ever. In winter, you'll find an open hearth to warm you; in summer, this is a refreshingly cool retreat from the heat. Expect a cheerful, mostly non-English-speaking staff, a savory collection of soups (including potato soup and liver dumpling soup), and a strong emphasis on such garnishes as potato salad and *Sauerkraut*.

Rathausplatz 1 (opposite the Rathaus). ✆ **0911/227695.** www.die-nuernberger-bratwurst.de. Reservations recommended. Main courses 6.50€–12€. No credit cards. Mon–Sat 10am–10pm. U-Bahn: Lorenzkirche.

Historische Bratwurst-Glöcklein ★ FRANCONIAN   Nürnbergers refer to it as their *Bratwurst Lokale* (bratwurst locale), and it's the only serious rival to Bratwurst-Häusle (see above). The kitchen prepares a traditional Nürnberg-style bratwurst with *Sauerkraut* and boiled potatoes, all served on tin plates. Because beer goes perfectly with *Wurst*, you'll enjoy sampling some of the brews on tap while admiring the craftsmanship of the room, which dates from the Middle Ages. Ham hocks are an additional specialty. Be careful or you'll spend your entire afternoon on the sun terrace—it's that tempting.

Im Handwerkerhof, Königstrasse 5. ✆ **0911/227625.** www.die-nuernberger-bratwurst.de. Reservations recommended. Main courses 7€–12€. No credit cards. Mon–Sat 10:30am–10pm. U-Bahn: Hauptbahnhof.

Shopping

Located near the railway station in the center of the city, **Handwerkerhof** (U-Bahn: Hauptbahnhof) is a crafts mall in a medieval castle setting, where Franconian artisans create and sell a wide range of handicrafts. It's open March 20 to December 23, weekdays 10am to 6:30pm and Saturday 10am to 4pm. In December, it also opens Sunday 10am to 6:30pm.

At **Kistner,** Weinmarkt 6 (✆ **0911/203482;** www.kistner.de; U-Bahn: Lorenzkirche), you can step back in time. This wonderful store is full of antique books, prints, and engravings, including some by Dürer, Rembrandt, and other masters. The owner, Herr Kistner, is an expert in the field.

Villeroy & Boch, Königstrasse 13 (✆ **0911/223182;** www.villeroy-boch-nuernberg.de; U-Bahn: Lorenzkirche), sells sets of china, crystal ware, and porcelain trinkets.

The largest department store in the city, **Karstadt,** Königstrasse 14 (© **0911/2130;** U-Bahn: Lorenzkirche), carries clothing, housewares, and other home furnishings.

Adding variety to prudence, **La Condomeria,** Ludwigstrasse 57 (© **0911/232784;** www.lacondomeria.de; U-Bahn: Weisser Turm), sells condoms in various colors, textures, flavors, and scents. It also has postcards and T-shirts.

Entertainment & Nightlife

A theater complex offering quality productions of drama and opera, the **Staatstheater Nürnberg,** Richard-Wagner-Platz 2–10 (© **0180/5231600** for tickets; www. staatstheater-nuernberg.de; U-Bahn: Opernhaus), houses the Kammerspiele, Opernhaus, and Schauspielhaus. The box office is open Monday to Friday 9am to 8pm plus Saturday 9am to 6pm; tickets are 10€ to 65€. Students get 25% off, and the general public can check on discounted seats at the box office 1 hour before each performance. Tickets can also be obtained by calling the number listed above.

Touring cabaret acts play at the **Loni-Übler-Haus,** Marthastrasse 60 (© **0911/541156;** Tram: 5), on Saturday and Sunday at 8pm. The box office is open Tuesday to Friday 9am to 10pm, and tickets are 10€ to 50€. The city's premier outdoor venue, **St. Katarina,** is located in the ruins of the Katharinenkirche, Katherinenkloster 1 at Peter-Vischer-Strasse (U-Bahn: Lorenzkirche). It hosts concerts by an eclectic mix of international musical acts. The events within this evocative outdoor ruin are, by necessity, subject to sudden cancellations because of inclement weather. For events at St. Katarina Church, it is best to call the tourist office (© **0911/23360**).

An artists' hangout, **Treibhaus,** Karl-Grillenberger-Strasse 28 (© **0911/223041;** www.cafetreibhaus.de; U-Bahn: Weisser Turm), opens early for big breakfasts that run 3€ to 15€, and offers soup, salad, and sandwich specials from 5€ to 10€ throughout the day. At night, it dims the lights and keeps serving drinks. It's open Monday to Friday 8am to 1am, Saturday and Sunday 9am to 1am. Food is served until 10:30pm, and breakfast is served all day.

Another low-key arts scene, **Café Ruhestörung,** Tetzelgasse 21 (© **0911/221921;** www.ruhestoerung.org; U-Bahn: Lorenzkirche or Rathenauplatz), offers some of the best people-watching in the city. Just sit on the patio and order a drink or a sandwich and watch the world stroll by. Draft beers are 2.50€ to 4€. It's open daily 9am to 1am.

At **Mach 1,** Kaiserstrasse 1–9 (© **0911/2406602;** www.mach1-club.de; U-Bahn: Lorenzkirche), Thursday and Friday move from disco to hip-hop, warming up for Saturday's big house party. Cover is 8€ on Thursday, 9€ on Friday, and 15€ on Saturday. Hours are Thursday to Saturday 10pm to 5am.

A popular gay bistro, **Cartoon,** An der Sparkgasse 6 (© **0911/227170;** www. cartoon-nbg.de; U-Bahn: Lorenzkirche), serves beer, wine, and light meals Monday to Saturday 2pm to midnight and Sunday 2 to 11pm. For later hours, hit the dance clubs, all of which have both gay and straight clientele.

Where to Stay
EXPENSIVE

Le Méridien Grand Hotel ★★★ This old-world palace is the best place to stay in Nürnberg. The Grand is a solid six-story blockbuster built "when hotels were really hotels"—that is, before World War I. The first-rate and stylish rooms have the finest furnishings, and the roomy bathrooms are exceedingly well maintained, with deluxe toiletries. Many have a private sitting area.

Bahnhofstrasse 1–3 (across from the Hauptbahnhof), 90402 Nürnberg. www.lemeridien.com. ℂ **800/543-4300** in the U.S., or 0911/23220. Fax 0911/2322444. 192 units. 112€–330€ double; 212€–1,100€ suite. AE, DC, MC, V. Parking 17€. U-Bahn: Hauptbahnhof. **Amenities:** Restaurant; bar; concierge; exercise room; indoor heated pool; room service; sauna; Wi-Fi (21€ per day; in lobby). *In room:* A/C (in some), TV, hair dryer, minibar, MP3 docking station.

Maritim ★★   Maritim attracts those who prefer modern convenience to old-world charm. It used to be the city's most stylish hotel, until the Méridien chain upgraded the Grand. Rooms are of good size—although not as spacious as the Grand's—with large beds and many extras, such as large bathrooms with tub/shower combos. Try an upper-floor room for a panoramic view over Nürnberg's medieval fortifications and busy traffic artery.

Frauentorgraben 11, 90443 Nürnberg. www.maritim.de. ℂ **0911/23630.** Fax 0911/2363823. 316 units. 100€–310€ double; 230€–437€ suite. Rates include buffet breakfast. AE, DC, MC, V. Parking 15€. U-Bahn: Hauptbahnhof. **Amenities:** Restaurant; bar; exercise room; indoor heated pool; room service; sauna. *In room:* A/C, TV, hair dryer, minibar, Wi-Fi (8€ per hour).

Ramada Nürnberg Parkhotel ★   The Ramada is not as grand as Le Méridien Grand Hotel or even the Maritim (see above), but it's close to the top of the heap. One of the most modern in town, this hotel looks like a four-story collection of concrete cubes set up on stilts. Inside, it's flooded with natural light, with many windows offering views of the landscaped park around it. For the most part, both the guest rooms and the bathrooms are roomy; the furnishings, though not terribly stylish, are comfortable and inviting. Three rooms are specially designed for travelers with disabilities. The hotel is directly connected to the Meistersingerhalle, where concerts and conventions take place, and around the corner from the Reichsparteitagsgelände.

Münchener Strasse 25 (5-min. drive from city center), 90478 Nürnberg. www.ramada-nuernberg.de. ℂ **0911/47480.** Fax 0911/4748420. 200 units. 129€–310€ double; 240€–340€ suite. Rates include buffet breakfast. Children 11 and under stay free in parent's room. AE, DC, MC, V. Parking 10€. Tram: 9. Bus: 36. **Amenities:** Restaurant; bar; exercise room; indoor heated pool; room service; sauna. *In room:* TV, hair dryer, minibar (in some), Wi-Fi (free).

MODERATE

Drei Raben ★ ♟♙   An offbeat choice, this is the first theme hotel ever established in Nürnberg. The Three Ravens (its English name) offers individually decorated bedrooms, each chamber decorated according to a local legend. One room is devoted to Dürer, and another to a modern-day saga—Nürnberg's famous soccer team. The most unusual junior suite is called "Legend and Bathtub Enchantment," for up to three guests. Standing in the middle of the room is an enchanting bathtub. Less expensive are the standard rooms, which are equally comfortable but lacking the drama of the theme rooms. As a startling entrance, the reception area is decorated with pods to evoke the film *2001: A Space Odyssey.* The location is a 5-minute walk from the Hauptbahnhof, the main train station.

Königstrasse 63, 90402 Nürnberg. www.hotel3raben.de. ℂ **0911/274380.** Fax 0911/232611. 22 units. 120€ standard room; 150€ theme room; 185€ junior suite. AE, DC, MC, V. Parking 15€. **Amenities:** Bar; room service. *In room:* TV/DVD, CD player, Wi-Fi (free).

Dürer-Hotel ★   The Dürer has steadily grown in prestige since it opened in the late '80s beside the birthplace of its namesake, right under the castle. Following a 2009 renovation the guest rooms have modern furniture and a light, classic style with wooden furniture and carpeted floors. The bathrooms are well kept and midsize. The only meal served is breakfast, but you're only a short walk from restaurants and cafes.

Neutormauer 32, 90403 Nürnberg. www.duerer-hotel.de. ℂ **0911/2146650.** Fax 0911/214665555. 105 units. 99€–265€ double. Rates include buffet breakfast. AE, DC, MC, V. Parking 12€. Tram: 6 or 9. Bus: 36 or 46. **Amenities:** Bar; exercise room; room service; sauna. *In room:* TV, hair dryer, minibar (in some), Wi-Fi (13€ per day).

Hotel Am Josephsplatz ★★ 🏠 In the historic center of the city, this restored hotel is installed in a building dating from 1675. However, its interior has been completely modernized with all the latest gadgetry, and there are such extras as a winter garden and a rooftop sun terrace. A family-style atmosphere prevails, and the historical ambiance was preserved during wholesale renovations. Miraculously, the building survived massive damage during the heavy bombings of World War II. Bedrooms are beautifully furnished with antique styling including draped beds and swag curtains. If you prefer less traditional rooms, there are some that are decorated in a more modern style. The restaurant on-site serves a classic Franconian cuisine.

Josephsplatz 30–32, 90403 Nürnberg. www.hotel-am-josephsplatz.de. ℂ **0911/214470.** Fax 0911/21447200. 36 units. 99€–155€ double; 138€–240€ apt. Rates include buffet breakfast. AE, V. Parking 8€–15€. **Amenities:** Exercise room; sauna. *In room:* TV, minibar, Wi-Fi (free).

INEXPENSIVE

City Hotel 🌶 This serviceable, if unspectacular, hotel provides a great low-cost choice. It occupies the third, fourth, and fifth floors of an old-fashioned building on a wide pedestrian thoroughfare. Take a small elevator upstairs to the third-floor reception area, where the efficient owner will show you one of her simple, cramped, but immaculate rooms. Be sure to check out the rooftop terrace.

Königstrasse 25–27 (near St.-Lorenz-Kirche), 90402 Nürnberg. www.cityhotel-nuernberg.de. ℂ **0911/225638.** Fax 0911/203999. 20 units. 49€–80€ double. Rates include continental breakfast. AE, DC, MC, V. Parking 6€. Closed for 2 weeks after Christmas. U-Bahn: Lorenzkirche. *In room:* TV, hair dryer.

Weinhaus Steichele ★ Located on a tranquil street a few steps from the bustling Jakobsplatz, this small hotel retains its old-fashioned allure. The building is a beautifully balanced and handcrafted structure of heavy stone blocks with an elegant gambrel roof. Any overflow of guests spills into a modern annex next door that blends harmoniously with the older building. Rooms are decorated in a rustic Bavarian style, each with a small but efficiently organized bathroom.

Knorrstrasse 2–8 (near Jakobsplatz), 90402 Nürnberg. www.steichele.de. ℂ **0911/202280.** Fax 0911/221914. 49 units. 104€–180€ double. Rates include buffet breakfast. AE, DC, MC, V. Parking 10€. U-Bahn: Weisser Turm. **Amenities:** Restaurant. *In room:* TV, hair dryer.

REGENSBURG ★★

122km (76 miles) NE of Munich, 100km (62 miles) SE of Nürnberg, 114km (71 miles) NW of Passau

Regensburg is one of Germany's best-preserved cities, relatively undamaged by World War II bombings. Despite this, it remains somewhat obscure to many foreign visitors. Even if you don't have time to explore the city's museums or the interiors of its many historical monuments, try to take in the view of the Danube from one of its bridges, especially at sunset.

Regensburg started as a Celtic settlement, called Radespona, around 500 B.C. The Romans later took it over, renamed it Castra Regina, and made it their center of power on the upper Danube. From the 7th century, the town was the center from which Christianity spread over southern Germany. The architecture of Regensburg testifies to its long history and past grandeur, which reached its peak by the beginning of the Gothic era. Its buildings and towers offer an unspoiled glimpse into history, and many of its ancient structures are still in active use today. The best example is the **Stone Bridge,** built in 1146 on 16 huge arches, in continuous service for more than 800 years.

Essentials

GETTING THERE

BY TRAIN   The **Regensburg Hauptbahnhof** is on major rail lines, including Passau-Regensburg-Nürnberg and Munich-Landshut-Regensburg, with frequent connections in all directions. From Munich, more than 20 trains arrive daily (trip time: 1½ hr.), and from Frankfurt, 7 direct trains daily (trip time: 3 hr.). The trip from Nürnberg takes only 1 hour, 15 minutes; from Passau, 1¼ hours. For rail information and schedules, call ✆ **01805/996633** or visit www.bahn.de.

BY BUS   Regional buses service the nearby towns. For information about routes, scheduling, and prices of buses operating within the region, contact the **Regensburger Verkehrsverbund** (RVV; ✆ **0941/463190;** www.rvv.de) for information. For longer domestic or international stretches Munich or Nürnberg make better departure points.

BY CAR   Access by car is via the A3 Autobahn from east and west and the A93 from north and south.

VISITOR INFORMATION

Contact **Tourist-Information,** Rathausplatz 3 (✆ **0941/5074410;** www. tourismus.regensburg.de). Hours are year-round Monday to Friday 9am to 6pm, Saturday 9am to 4pm, and Sunday 9:30am to 4pm; between November and March, Sunday hours are 9:30am to 2:30pm.

GETTING AROUND

Much of the center of Regensburg and its highlights are within a short walk of each other. To get from the Hauptbahnhof to the town's medieval core (Altstadt), take any of the bright yellow Altstadt buses that line up along Maximilianstrasse, next to the station. One-way fare is 1€, but a day ticket valid for up to five people costs 2€ and must be purchased on the bus. Buses run at 6-minute intervals every Monday to Friday 8:30am to 8:30pm. There's no service on Saturday and Sunday. If you wish to go farther afield, you'll find an adequate system of bus routes fanning out from the railway station to the outer suburbs. A single ride costs 2€, and buses run 6am to midnight daily. A 24-hour ticket costs 4.20€. A list of bus routes is available at the railway station at the Presse & Buch kiosk.

Exploring Regensburg

Regensburg is a city of churches; it was once the focal point from which Christianity spread throughout Germany and even into central Europe via the Danube. The most majestic of these churches is the towering **Dom St. Peter's ★**, Domplatz (✆ **0941/5865500;** www.regensburger-dom.de; bus: 1, 6, or 11), which was begun in the 13th century on the site of an earlier Carolingian church. Because it was constructed with easily eroded limestone and green sandstone, this French Gothic edifice is constantly being restored. The massive spires of the two western towers, added in the mid–19th century, were almost completely replaced in 1955 with a more durable material. The well-preserved **stained-glass windows ★★** in the choir (14th c.) and south transept (13th c.) are impressive. Most of the pillar sculptures in the aisles of the nave were made in the cathedral workshop in the mid–14th century. The towns-folk call the two little sculptures in the niches on opposite sides of the main entrance *The Devil* and *The Devil's Grandmother*. The cathedral is home to a famous boys' choir, the **Chor Dompatzen,** which performs every Sunday morning at 10am Mass. The performance is open to all. From April to October, the cathedral is open Monday to Saturday 6:30am to 6:30pm and Sunday noon to 6pm; November to April, hours are Monday to Saturday 8am to 5pm and Sunday noon to 4pm. Admission is free.

You can also visit the cathedral treasures at the **Domschatzmuseum,** Krauterer-markt 3 (© 0941/57645; www.domschatz-regensburg.de; bus: 1, 6, or 11, or the Altstadt bus), which displays goldsmiths' work and splendid textiles from the 11th to the 20th century. Entrance is through a portal in the north aisle of the cathedral. It's open April to October Tuesday to Saturday 10am to 5pm and Sunday noon to 5pm; December to March, it's open generally only Friday and Saturday 10am to 4pm and Sunday noon to 4pm (closed in Nov). The charge is 2€ for adults and 1€ for students and children 13 and under. You can also buy a combination ticket to the Domschatz-museum and the Diözesanmuseum St. Ulrich (see below) that costs 3€ for adults and 4€ for a family ticket. (Admission to the cloister isn't included with this ticket.)

The permanent collection of the **Diözesanmuseum St. Ulrich** is on exhibit in the former Church of St. Ulrich, an early Gothic building to the side of the cathedral, Domplatz 2 (© 0941/51688; bus: 1, 2, 6, or 11). Sculptures, paintings, and gold-smiths' work form a representative selection of religious art in the diocese from the 11th to the 20th century. Of particular interest are works on loan from the monastic foundations of the diocese. The museum is open April to October Tuesday to Sunday 10am to 5pm. Admission is 2€ for adults, 1€ for children 13 and under.

Crossing the cathedral garden, you enter the **cloister** with its Romanesque Aller Heiligenkapelle (All Saints' Chapel) and Sankt Stephan Kirche (St. Stephen's Church). The ancient frescoes on the walls of the chapel depict liturgical scenes from All Saints' Day. The 11th-century church of St. Stephen contains an altar made of a hollowed limestone rock with openings connecting to early Christian tombs. You can visit the cloister and Sankt Stephan Kirche only on one of the guided tours (in Ger-man), which are given from May to October daily at 2pm with an extra 10:30am tour Monday to Friday; from November to April, contact the Tourist Information for details on the irregular tour schedule. The charge is 4€ adults, 2€ students and chil-dren, and free for children 5 and under.

Of all the remnants of Roman occupation of Regensburg, the ancient **Porta Prae-toria,** behind the cathedral, is the most impressive, with its huge stones piled in the form of an arched gateway. Through the grille beside the eastern tower you can see the original level of the Roman street, nearly 3m (10 ft.) below—which is why you often have to step down into the churches of Regensburg.

Of the four **Museen de Stadt Regensburg (City Museums of Regensburg),** the most important is the **Historisches Museum (History Museum)** ★, Dachau-platz 2–4 (© 0941/5072448; www.regensburg.de/museumsportal; bus: 1, 2, or 3), one of the most notable museums in east Bavaria. Its displays show major develop-ments in the history of the region from the earliest days up to the present. You'll see relics of the Roman period, such as a stone tablet marking the establishment of a garrison at Regensburg in the 2nd century. There's also a stone altar to the Roman god Mercury, as well as several Christian tombstones. The museum is open Tuesday, Wednesday, and Friday to Sunday 10am to 4pm, Thursday 10am to 8pm. Admission is 2.20€ for adults; 1.10€ for students, seniors, and children 8 to 18; 4.40€ for a fam-ily ticket; and free for children 7 and under.

No town hall in Germany is preserved better than Regensburg's **Altes Rathaus** ★, Rathaus Platz (© **0941/5073440;** bus: 1, 6, or 11, or the Altstadt bus). This Gothic structure, begun in the 13th century, contains a Reichssaal (Imperial Diet Hall), where the Perpetual Diet sat from 1663 to 1806. In the basement of the Rathaus are the dungeons, with the torture chamber preserved in its original setting. The Altes Rathaus is open daily, with guided tours Monday to Saturday every 30 minutes 9:30am to noon and 2 to 4pm; Sunday and holidays, every 30 minutes 10am to noon. Know in advance that all of the Rathaus tours are in rapid-fire, colloquial German. The tour in English is conducted April to October daily at 3pm; from November 1 to January 6 and March daily at 2pm. From January 7 to February 28 no tours are conducted in English. For information about tours of the Rathaus, contact either the tourist office (p. 222) or the number noted above.

Where to Eat

Gänsbauer ★ BAVARIAN/INTERNATIONAL   For elegant dining, visit Gänsbauer, one of the best restaurants in the city. The setting is mellow and old-fashioned, but the cuisine is strictly *neue Küche* (cuisine moderne) with a Continental influence. Well-known Bavarian dishes are given a lighter touch here, and only the freshest ingredients are used. The baby turbot in Pernod sauce is superb. The desserts will likely be exotic concoctions you've never seen. The restaurant occupies a 500-year-old building with an open space where you can sit in fair weather.

Keplerstrasse 10. © **0941/57858.** www.gaensbauer.de. Reservations recommended. Main courses 15€–30€; fixed-price dinners 40€. AE, DC, MC, V. Mon–Sat 6–10:30pm. Bus: Fischmarkt.

Restaurant & Bistro Rosenpalais ★★★ INTERNATIONAL   Positioned on the eastern fringe of Regensburg's historic core, this restaurant occupies a gracefully proportioned 18th-century baroque villa with an exterior painted in tones of bright pink and cream. This building has had stints as a private home as well as an upscale *Lustschloss* (wine tavern), a tradition it continues in two separate venues today. One floor above street level, you'll find the more formal venue, the restaurant, consisting of two high-ceilinged and somewhat restrained dining rooms, one of which is shaped in an octagon. Here, menu items are as posh and esoteric as you'll find anywhere in the area, with seasonal variations that might include marinated calves' livers with tomato-and-basil vinaigrette, a very generously sized crayfish salad, cream of spinach soup garnished with braised mussels, a perfectly braised filet of tuna with mango-studded couscous and bok choy, and venison cutlets with Bavarian herbs and seasonings.

Less formal and esoteric cuisine is served in the somewhat more extroverted street-level bistro, where among the salads, pastas, and old-fashioned Teutonic and Continental specialties you'll find sole meunière, *Wurst* with *Sauerkraut,* pepper steak with french fries, and French onion soup with a crusty top layer of Emmental cheese.

Minoritenweg 20. © **0941/5997579.** www.rosenpalais.de. Reservations recommended. Main courses 9€–34€; fixed-price menus 29€–85€. MC, V. Tues–Sat 11:30am–2pm and 6pm–1am.

Entertainment & Nightlife

The town's cultural center, **Alte Mälzerei,** Galgenbergstrasse 20 (© **0941/7888115;** www.alte-maelzerei.de), hosts concerts and theater productions, as well as a run-down bar and beer garden that serves cheap drinks daily 5pm to 1am. The only late-night bar in town, **Wunderbar,** Keplerstrasse 11 (© **0941/53130;** www.wunderbar. de; bus: Altstadt bus), serves drinks until 3am, 7 nights a week.

Historische Wurstküche, Thundorferstrasse 3 (© 0941/466210; www.wurst kuchl.de), celebrated its 856th birthday in 2011, making it the oldest operating fast-food joint in all of Germany. It's still the best place in town for those delicious *Regensburger* sausages, which are cooked over beechwood fires in the small kitchen. A total of six of them, served with *Sauerkraut* and fresh bread, costs 7.50€. It's located next to the Steinerne Brücke, and tables have a river view. At various times the river has risen to flood the joint. It is open April to October daily from 8am to 7pm; November to March, it is open only on Sunday 8am to 3pm.

At **Scala,** Gesandtenstrasse 6 (© 0941/52293; www.scalaclub.de; bus: Altstadt-bus), three bars hem in the dance floor and attract an under-35 crowd. It's open Wednesday to Sunday 11pm to 3am (Fri–Sat until 4am). Admission is 5€ to 10€.

Where to Stay

Bischofshof am Dom ★★ A longtime favorite, appealing to traditionalists, this hotel was constructed as an ecclesiastical academy by the bishops of Regensburg in 1810. Today it blends 19th-century monastic with modern secular. Many of the units have hosted princes, even emperors. Rooms are attractively furnished, each with a well-maintained bathroom. Part of the hotel takes in a piece of a Roman gateway. Behind the building is one of Regensburg's most popular sun terraces. Guests can also sit in the hotel's *Weinstube* (wine bar) or in one of the 350 seats in the beer garden. The beer comes from a brewery dating from 1649.

Krauterermarkt 3, 93047 Regensburg. www.hotel-bischofshof.de. © **0941/58460.** Fax 0941/5846146. 55 units. 138€–148€ double; 195€ suite. Rates include continental breakfast. AE, DC, MC, V. Parking 12€. Bus: 1. **Amenities:** Restaurant; bar; Wi-Fi (3€ per hour; in lobby). *In room:* TV, hair dryer, minibar.

Orphée Grosses Haus ★★ You get one hotel here but three different houses and three different living experiences. Our preferred choice is the splendid baroque mansion, Grand Hotel Orphée (Grosses Haus, in German), which is sumptuous with beautifully restored bedrooms at Untere Bachgasse 8, right next door to the Restaurant Orphée. You'll live in the grand style of old Germany with elaborately carved and inlaid baroque doors, period door frames with hand-wrought hinges, and ornate ceilings, along with state-of-the-art bathrooms. If you're romantic, opt for one of the rooms in the attic with baroque roof beams and panoramic views over the roofs of the town.

The Petit Hotel Orphée (Kleines Haus, in German) at Wahlenstrasse 1 is the cozi-est of the lot. It's installed in the former home of a prosperous family of merchants. Rooms here are individually furnished but with antique washstands and Turkish tiles. In some respects, this is the prettiest hotel of the lot.

A final hotel, Country Manor Orphée (also called Andreasstadel), Andreasstrasse 26, lies across an old stone bridge, north of the Danube. The hotel is installed on the second floor of a 16th-century salt warehouse, which has been turned into a cultural center with a cinema, a restaurant, and artists' studios. Ten enticing apartments are rented, six of which have a little patio overlooking the banks of the Danube. Each unit has a kitchenette and a vaguely Mediterranean look.

Grand Hotel Orphée at Untere Bachgasse 8, 93047 Regensburg; Petit Hotel Orphée at Wahlenstrasse 1, 93047 Regensburg; Country Manor Orphée at Andreasstrasse 26, 93059 Regensburg. www.hotel-orphee.de. © **0941/596020** for Grand Hotel Orphée and Petit Hotel Orphée; © **0941/59602300** for Country Manor Orphée. Fax 0941/59602199 for Grand Hotel Orphée and Petit Hotel Orphée; 0941/59602399 for Country Manor Orphée. 25 units in Grand Hotel Orphée, 15 units in Petit Hotel Orphée, 10 units in Country Manor Orphée. 125€–195€ in Grand Hotel Orphée; 75€–175€ in Petit Hotel Orphée; 135€–155€ in Country Manor Orphée. Rates include continental breakfast. AE, DC, MC, V. Park-ing 6€. **Amenities:** Restaurant; bar. *In room:* TV (in some), kitchenette (in some).

Parkhotel Maximilian ★ The next best thing to staying in one of "Mad" King Ludwig's palaces is to check into the Parkhotel Maximilian, an exquisite neorococo building. Its facade and public areas have been classified a public monument. The main salon, with a ceiling supported by columns of polished red stone, continues the theme of 18th-century opulence coupled with 21st-century convenience. Guest rooms are attractively furnished, and each comes with a roomy private bathroom.

Maximilianstrasse 28, 93047 Regensburg. www.maximilian-hotel.de. ✆ **0941/56850.** Fax 0941/52942. 52 units. 84€–175€ double. Rates include continental breakfast. AE, DC, MC, V. Parking 11€. Bus: 1, 2, 3, or 6. **Amenities:** Restaurant; room service. *In room:* TV, hair dryer, minibar, Wi-Fi (22€ per day).

Straubinger Hof ★ 🎒 This attractive, unpretentious hotel just outside the medieval Ostentor (East Gate) is little publicized, but bargain hunters should seek it out. The small rooms are simple but satisfactory, with lots of sunlight and angular, somewhat spartan furniture, plus a tiny bathroom.

Adolf-Schmetzer-Strasse 33 (15-min. walk east of the cathedral), 93055 Regensburg. www.hotel-straubinger-hof.de. ✆ **0941/60030.** Fax 0941/794826. 60 units. 65€–90€ double. Rates include buffet breakfast. AE, DC, MC, V. Free parking. Bus: 1. *In room:* TV, hair dryer, minibar.

PASSAU ★★

191km (119 miles) E of Munich, 117km (73 miles) SE of Regensburg

For years, Passau languished in a lost corner of West Germany. But since reunification, the beauty and nostalgia of this old city has been rediscovered. With its romantic river setting and stately streets, Passau is a city of great harmony. Located at the confluence of the Danube and two of its tributaries, the Ilz and Inn rivers, Passau's bustling port is worth a visit in itself.

Essentials
GETTING THERE
BY TRAIN Because Passau is a German border station, **InterCity** trains stop here, with frequent daily arrivals from such cities as Nürnberg, Munich, and Vienna. The other major rail links include Frankfurt-Nürnberg-Passau-Vienna and Nürnberg-Regensburg-Passau, with frequent connections. Trip time from Nürnberg is 2 hours; from Frankfurt, 4¼ to 6 hours; from Munich, 2¼ hours; from Regensburg, 1¼ hours; and from Vienna, 2¾ hours. For rail information and schedules, call ✆ **01805/996633** or visit www.bahn.de.

BY BUS No long-distance buses serve Passau. However, buses service the outskirts of the city. For schedules (in German), call **RBO (Regional Bus Ostbayern GmbH)** at ✆ **0851/756370** or visit www.rbo.de.

BY CAR Access is by the A3 Autobahn from the north or south.

VISITOR INFORMATION
Contact the **Tourist Information Office,** Rathausplatz 3 (✆ **0851/955980**). Hours are April to October Monday to Friday 8:30am to 6pm, Saturday and Sunday 9am to 4pm; November to March, it's open Monday to Thursday 8:30am to 5pm, Friday 8:30am to 4pm, Saturday and Sunday 10am to 5pm.

GETTING AROUND
Local inner-city buses, clearly marked CITY-BUS, run through Passau and make stops at both the Rathaus (Town Hall) and the Hauptbahnhof (railway station) every 15 minutes, charging a per-person rate of 1.50€. They connect all the attractions recommended

below. They operate Monday to Friday 8am to 6pm and Saturday 8am to 4pm. There's no service on Sunday. Call the tourist office for scheduling information.

Exploring Passau

The **Altstadt** is built on a rocky spur of land formed by the confluence of the Inn and the Danube. To best appreciate its setting, cross the Danube to the **Veste Oberhaus,** St. Georg Berg 125, a medieval Episcopal fortress towering over the town and the river. Note how arches join many of the houses, giving them a unity of appearance. As you view the town, you can sense that the architecture here is more closely allied to northern Italy and the Tyrolean Alps than to cities to the north. The fortress houses the **Oberhaus Museum** (*C* **0851/4933512;** www.oberhausmuseum.de), a museum of regional history going back to medieval times. It's open March to November Monday to Friday 9am to 5pm, and Saturday and Sunday 10am to 6pm. Admission is 5€ for adults, 4€ for children, and 10€ for a family ticket. Take the shuttle bus to the castle from Rathausplatz

Dominating the town are the twin towers of the **Dom (St. Stephen's Cathedral),** Domplatz 9 (*C* **0851/39241;** bus: City-Bus). The original Gothic plan is clear, despite its 17th-century reconstruction in grand baroque style. Its most unusual feature is the octagonal dome over the intersection of the nave and transept. The interior of the cathedral is mainly Italian baroque—almost gaudy, with its many decorations and paintings. Of particular interest is the choir, which remains from the Gothic period. A newer addition is a huge organ with 17,974 pipes, said to be the largest church organ in the world, built in 1928 and placed in an 18th-century casing. Thirty-minute concerts are given May to October Monday to Saturday at noon; there's a second performance on Thursday at 7:30pm. The noon concerts cost 4€ for adults and 2€ for students and children 13 and under. The cost of the Thursday 7:30pm concert varies based on your seat, and runs 5€ to 8€ for adults, 5€ for children. The Dom is open Monday to Saturday 8 to 11am and 12:30 to 6pm. Admission is free.

Below the cathedral, on the bank of the Danube, are the **Marktplatz** and the 13th-century **Rathaus,** with a facade decorated with painted murals depicting the history of the town. Inside, the huge knights' hall contains two large 19th-century frescoes illustrating incidents from the legend of the Nibelungen. The Town Hall has a Glockenspiel in its tower that plays at 10:30am, 2, and 7:25pm; on Saturday there's an additional performance at 3pm.

Where to Eat

Blauer Bock FRANCONIAN/GERMAN   Set in the heart of Passau, adjacent to the Danube, this nostalgia-laden building was constructed in 1374 and is one of the oldest buildings in town. Part of its allure derives from a woodsy, dark-paneled interior that reeks of 19th-century coziness. This, coupled with a riverside terrace with 250 seats, replete with views of the passing river traffic, makes it a great choice for a snack, meal, or drink. Menu items are simple, traditional, and straightforward. The best examples include *Leberknödel* (liver-dumpling) soup and pork shank, slow-cooked for hours, served with a local version of dumplings and *Sauerkraut.* A tasty and time-tested main course, prepared only for two diners at a time, is a roasted and pickled leg of pork with *Sauerkraut,* potatoes, and dumplings. At least four kinds of beer, each brewed within the city limits of Passau by any of several local brewers, are available on tap at any time. Bottled beers from the town's other local brewers are also available.

Also on the premises are four simple, conservatively decorated bedrooms, each with minibar and TV, and renting for 67€ to 90€ double, 92€ to 135€ triple. Laundry service and room service are also available.

Höllgasse 20. (© **0851/34637.** Reservations recommended. Main courses 7€–15€; fixed-price lunches 11€–17€, dinners 18€–27€. AE, DC, MC, V. Daily 7am–11pm.

Heilig-Geist-Stift-Schenke BAVARIAN/AUSTRIAN Until that great day when a first-class restaurant comes to Passau, this little gem established in 1358, remains the top choice, with hearty, stick-to-your-ribs fare. In summer, you can sit in a beautiful wine garden under chestnut trees. Indoors, the dining room has an open fireplace, decorated with old tools used to press grapes. The restaurant has its own vineyard, and you can order its wines under the label *Grüner Veltliner*. The ancient kitchen serves low-cost regional dishes, including boiled rump steak Austrian-style and roast suckling pig. *Passauer Schlosserbuam* is a dessert specialty (the waiter will explain). Bavarian, Austrian, and international dishes are featured.

Heiliggeistgasse 4. (© **0851/2607.** www.stiftskeller-passau.de. Reservations recommended. Main courses 9€–20€. AE, MC, V. Thurs–Tues 10am–1am. Closed Jan.

Peschl Terrasse 🍺 FRANCONIAN Named after the beer (Peschl) served in many variations here, this popular eatery is known for copious portions of straightforward and traditional food that tastes especially marvelous when accompanied with beer. There's a cavernous main dining room, three small areas for private parties, and a sunny Danube-fronting outdoor terrace that's invariably the most popular place on warm summer evenings. The establishment has been in the hands of the same family since 1855, and since then, lots of suds have been swilled and spilled within its folkloric-looking premises. Menu items include roasted shank of veal or pork, usually served with *Sauerkraut,* dumplings, and/or potatoes; cream of potato soup; fish goulash; heaping platters of sausages; terrine of venison; pigs' trotters *Sauerbraten;* and *Schnitzels* of pork, chicken, or veal.

Rosstränke 4. (© **0851/2489.** www.peschl-braeu.de. Reservations not necessary. Main courses 6€–13€. MC, V. Tues–Sun 10am–midnight.

Entertainment & Nightlife

Combining quality drama with a dramatic setting, the **Stadttheater Company** is housed in the **Stadttheater Passau,** Gottfried-Schäfer-Strasse (© **0851/9291913;** www.theater-passau.de), a beautiful baroque opera house built by the local prince-bishops. Call for performance schedules and ticket prices. Summertime brings drama, pantomime, opera, jazz, and classical concerts to town, scheduled as part of the **Europäische Wochen (European Weeks) Festival,** which runs June to late July. Call © **0851/4908310** for information; for schedules, tickets, or reservations, contact the **Kartenzentrale der Europäischen Wochen Passau** (© **0851/4908310;** fax 0851/49083120; www.ew-passau.de).

Home to Passau's popular cabaret company, **Theater im ScharfrichterHaus,** Milchgasse 2 (© **0851/35900;** www.scharfrichter-haus.de), has a year-round repertoire. It also hosts a series of jazz concerts throughout the year. Contact the theater for schedules, prices, and ticket availability. Tickets cost 15€ to 20€.

Café Innsteg, Innstrasse 15 (© **0851/51257;** www.innsteg.de), housed in a bungalow hanging over the Inn River, offers the town's most scenic setting in which to relax with a drink. Like every other cafe/bar in town, it's open from midmorning to 1am. **Café Kowalski,** Oberer Sandstrasse 1 (© **0851/2487;** www.kowalski.passau-live.de),

CRUISING THE danube

One reason for visiting this *Dreiflüss-estadt* (town of three rivers) on the Austrian frontier is for a boat tour along the Danube and its tributaries, the Inn and the Ilz. Trips range from a 45-minute three-river tour to a steamer cruise downriver to Vienna. The cruises depart from Fritz-Schäffer Promenade. Many passengers prefer to go by boat, and then take a train back.

You may also be tempted to board one of the passenger ferries that makes runs (Apr–Oct only) practically every day from Passau downstream to the Austrian city of Linz. The trips take 5 hours downstream and 6 hours upstream, cost 23€ per person, and depart every day except Monday from the city's riverfront piers at 9am and noon.

If you're interested in gaining even greater insights into life along the Danube, you can continue by train from Linz to Vienna, buying a ferryboat, train, and hotel package priced at a reasonable 286€ per person, which will include round-trip transit by boat and train to Vienna, via Linz, from Passau, and 1 night's stay at a four-star hotel in Vienna. For information about either the day trip to Linz or the overnight sojourn in Vienna, contact the **Donau-Schiffahrt Line** (www.donauschiffahrt.de) through its local representative, Wurm & Köck, Höllgasse 26, D-94032 Passau (*✆* **0851/929292**).

is less dramatic but also has balcony views of the river. Underground, across the river, **Joe's Garage,** Lederergasse 38 (*✆* **0851/31999**), is a friendly student dive named after a Frank Zappa album.

Where to Stay

Altstadt-Hotel ★ 🏨   The waters of the Danube, the Ilz, and the Inn converge just a few steps from this hotel. You could stay just for the view, but it's also a well-run, well-priced hotel. Guests who could afford the Holiday Inn seek out this little charmer for its ambience. Rooms are comfortably furnished in traditional style; some overlook the confluence of the rivers. All rooms come with an average-size and tidily kept bathroom. In summer, guests can enjoy meals on the terrace. The hotel has opened an annex, **Zum Laubenwirt,** lying 30m (100 ft.) from the main building. In 15 rooms that are also comfortably furnished and well equipped, it offers bathrooms with shower and such in-room amenities as Wi-Fi, dataport, minibar, and hair dryer. Doubles range from 70€ to 85€, including a buffet breakfast.

Bräugasse 23–29, 94032 Passau. www.altstadt-hotel.de. *✆* **0851/3370.** Fax 0851/337100. 36 units. 75€–135€ double; 145€–155€ suite. Rates include buffet breakfast. AE, DC, MC, V. Parking 6€ in underground garage. Bus: City-Bus. **Amenities:** Restaurant; bar. *In room:* TV, hair dryer, minibar, Wi-Fi (free).

Hotel König   Although the location isn't as scenic as that of the Altstadt-Hotel (see above), this hotel sits at the edge of a spit of land separating the Danube and Inn rivers. Behind massive stucco-covered buttresses and a salmon-colored facade, the interior is comfortably up-to-date. Each well-scrubbed room has pinewood accents. The best open onto views of the Danube or the Inn. The private bathrooms are compact, each with some shelf space.

Untere Donaulände 1, 94032 Passau. www.hotel-koenig.de. *✆* **0851/3850.** Fax 0851/385460. 40 units. 89€–140€ double. Rates include buffet breakfast. AE, DC, MC, V. Parking 10€. Bus: City-Bus. **Amenities:** Sauna; Wi-Fi (free; in lobby). *In room:* TV, hair dryer, minibar.

Passauer Wolf ★ This hotel on the Danube lies behind an elegant baroque facade. It isn't as up-to-date as the Holiday Inn but has better food and more character. Rooms are modern and comfortable and service is efficient. Bathrooms are compact, functional boxes that are well maintained.

Rindermarkt 6, 94032 Passau. www.hotel-passauer-wolf.de. ℂ **0851/931510.** Fax 0851/9315150. 40 units. 74€–159€ double; 150€–180€ suite. Rates include buffet breakfast. AE, DC, MC, V. Parking 10€. Bus: City-Bus. **Amenities:** Bar; bikes; Jacuzzi; room service; sauna; Wi-Fi (free; in lobby). *In room:* TV, hair dryer, minibar.

Schloss Ort ★ For old-fashioned charm with the comfort of today, you can seek lodging in a castle whose origin goes back to the 1200s. The bedrooms are the most spacious in town, opening onto the River Inn. Many prefer one of the bedrooms with 19th-century four-poster beds, although modern furnishings have been scattered throughout as well. Even if you don't stay here, you might want to patronize the on-site restaurant, which overflows onto a garden terrace in fair weather, with tables overlooking the Inn. The restaurant doesn't serve on Mondays and in winter.

Ort 11, 94032 Passau. www.schlosshotel-passau.de. ℂ**0851/34072.** Fax 0851/31817. 18 units. 97€–136€ double; 142€–199€ suite. DC, MC, V. Parking 4€. **Amenities:** Restaurant; bar. *In room:* TV, Wi-Fi (free; in some).

Weisser Hase ★ 🔷 This inn straddles the peninsula between the Danube and Inn rivers in the heart of Passau. Completely up-to-date, the "White Rabbit" (its English name) has been accommodating wayfarers since the 1500s. Some prefer this hotel to the more highly rated Passauer Wolf because it provides better value for your money. The guest rooms are midsize and neatly organized with functional furniture that is nonetheless comfortable; each comes with an average-size tiled bathroom. There's also a *Weinstube* with Bavarian-Austrian decor—carved wood and provincial chairs.

Heiliggeistgasse 1, 94032 Passau. www.weisser-hase.de. ℂ **0851/92110.** Fax 0851/9211100. 111 units. 89€–149€ double; 159€–175€ suite. Rates include buffet breakfast. AE, DC, MC, V. Parking 12€. Bus: City-Bus. **Amenities:** Restaurant; sauna. *In room:* TV, hair dryer (in some), Wi-Fi (free).

Wilder Mann ★ The most historic hotel in Passau has origins that may date from the 11th century. On the waterfront market square next to the ancient town hall, the hotel has hosted everybody from the Empress Elizabeth ("Sissi") of Austria to the moon-walking U.S. astronaut Neil Armstrong. The midsize to spacious rooms are furnished in a richly baroque style, each with a well-maintained private bathroom. Dining in the elaborately old-fashioned and candlelit restaurant is one of the best reasons to stay here. On-site is the small Passauer Glasmuseum, devoted to German glass.

Am Rathausplatz, 94032 Passau. www.wilder-mann.com. ℂ **0851/35071.** Fax 0851/31712. 49 units. 80€–100€ double; 200€ suite. Rates include buffet breakfast. AE, DC, MC, V. **Amenities:** Restaurant; room service; Wi-Fi (free). *In room:* A/C, TV (in some).

ULM ★★

97km (60 miles) SE of Stuttgart, 138km (86 miles) W of Munich

Visit Ulm for its architectural heritage and its history—not for great shopping, nightlife, or even an exciting local life. The city (situated at a strategic spot on the Danube) is a bit sleepy, smug, and satisfied with its monuments, especially its undeniably magnificent cathedral. Ulm's importance as a commercial river port has made it a

GERMAN men of ideas: ALBERT EINSTEIN (1879–1955)

"The release of atom power has changed everything except our way of thinking... the solution to this problem lies in the heart of mankind. If only I had known, I should have become a watchmaker."

Field of Study: Nobel Prize–winning theoretical physicist, philosopher, peace activist.

Revolutionary Insight: In his mid-20s, published papers that upended Newton's law of gravity with general & special theories of relativity. Argued that the speed of light remains constant, but space and time aren't absolute; gravity is an expression of how four-dimensional space-time curves around large masses—a seemingly simple notion that underpins modern astrophysics & the Big Bang Theory.

Controversy Quotient (0to 5): (2) Fled Nazi Germany in 1933; convinced U.S. to begin developing atomic bomb during World War II; later regretted his role in rise of nuclear technology, becoming a pacifist & fierce civil rights advocate.

Little Known Fact: In 1952, after the first president of Israel died, Einstein was offered the post. He declined, saying, "I lack both the natural aptitude and the experience to deal properly with people."

—Kelly Regan

prosperous city ever since the Middle Ages. Today, Ulm is a center of scientific and technological research, as befits the birthplace of Albert Einstein, who started life here in 1879. The old, narrow alleyways of the Altstadt lead to a modern city of riverbank promenades, beer gardens, spacious squares, and pedestrian zones.

Essentials

GETTING THERE

BY TRAIN   The **Ulm Hauptbahnhof** is on several major and regional rail lines, with frequent connections in all directions. More than 40 trains per day arrive from Munich (trip time: 1 hr., 25 min.) and some 50 or more from Stuttgart (1 hr., 10 min.). Daily trains also arrive from Cologne (3 hr., 15 min.). From Frankfurt (2 hr., 20 min.), you can take an ICE (InterCity-Express), the fastest and most comfortable way to travel by rail. For rail information and schedules, call © **01805/996633** or visit www.bahn.de.

BY BUS   There are no buses from major cities; local buses service only satellite towns—mostly bedroom communities of Ulm.

BY CAR   Access by car is via the A8 Autobahn east and west or the A7 north and south. It takes about 1½ hours to drive to Ulm from Munich and about 3 hours to drive from Frankfurt.

VISITOR INFORMATION

Tourist-Information, Marktplatz 1 (© **0731/1612830;** www.tourismus.ulm.de), is open Monday to Friday 9am to 6pm and Saturday 9am to 4pm. From April to December, it's also open Sunday 11am to 3pm.

GETTING AROUND

Ulm's only tram line runs east-west, connecting the suburban *Messe* (convention center) with the main Hauptbahnhof (railway station) and Söflingen. Ulm's historic core, Altstadt, lies within an easy walk from the Hauptbahnhof. Bus nos. 3, 7, and 8 radiate from the station to the suburbs. Buses and trams run at intervals of between 10 and 30 minutes, depending on the time of day and day of the week, and cost 1.90€ for travel within Ulm.

Exploring Ulm

If you approach the town from the Stuttgart-Munich autobahn, you'll miss the best view. So sometime during your visit, you should cross the Danube into Neu Ulm for a look at the gables and turrets of the Altstadt, which line the north bank of the river. Here is the **Fishermen's Quarter,** with its little medieval houses and tree-shaded squares. Nearby are the elaborate Renaissance patrician houses and the Gothic Renaissance **Rathaus.**

Rathaus GOVERNMENT BUILDING   The Rathaus was built in 1370 as a warehouse but has served as the town hall since 1419. It contains some ornate murals dating from the mid–16th century. On the south gable hang coats of arms of cities and countries with which Ulm is linked by commerce. On the east gable is an astronomical clock from 1520. Above the staircase is a reproduction of A. L. Berblinger's flying machine from 1811. Known as "the tailor of Ulm," he was one of the first people to make a serious attempt at flight.

Marktplatz 1. ☏ **0731/1610.** Free admission. Mon–Wed 9am–6pm; Thurs 9am–8pm; Fri 9am–6pm; Sun 11am–6pm. Closed Sat. Bus: 4, 5, 6, or 9.

Ulmer Museum ★ MUSEUM   This museum contains an important collection of arts and crafts produced in Ulm and upper Swabia from medieval times onward. There are also exhibitions of both ancient and modern art and artifacts, ranging from the region's prehistory up to the 20th century, with works by Klee, Kandinsky, and Picasso.

Marktplatz 9 (near the cathedral). ☏ **0731/1614300.** www.museum.ulm.de. Admission 3.50€ adults, 2.50€ students, free for children 14 and under, free for all Fri. Tues–Wed and Fri–Sun 11am–5pm; Thurs 11am–8pm. Bus: 2, 5, or 6.

Ulm Münster ★★★ CHURCH   Before you even get close to the city, you'll see the towering Ulm Münster on the skyline. Its 162m (531-ft.) steeple is the tallest of any cathedral in the world, and the Ulm Münster itself is second only to Cologne Cathedral in size. Without the pews, the nave of the church could hold nearly 20,000 people, more than twice the population of Ulm at the time the cathedral was begun in 1377. When Ulm joined the Protestant movement in 1531, work on the building was suspended. It was not to be continued until 1844, and wasn't completed until 1890. Miraculously, the cathedral escaped serious damage during World War II.

The exterior is almost pure German Gothic, even though bricks were often used in the walls along with the more typical stone blocks. The unusual feature of the Münster is that its architects placed as much emphasis on horizontal lines as on the vertical. Before entering, stop to admire the main porch, whose three massive arches lead to two 15th-century doors. This section dates from the 14th and 15th centuries and contains a wealth of statues and reliefs.

The five aisles of the cathedral lead directly from the hall below the tower through the nave to the east chancel. The conspicuous absence of a transept heightens the emphasis on the chancel and also increases the length of the nave. Huge pillars towering into steep arches enclose each of the five aisles. The ceiling is swept into net-vaults so high that any of Germany's church steeples could sit comfortably beneath them. The nave is so large that, even with pews, it can accommodate more than 11,000 people at one service.

The most remarkable treasure of the cathedral is the **Chorgestühl** ★★★ or choir stalls, which are some of the finest examples in Germany of woodcarving. Jorg Syrliun the Elder created these between 1469 and 1474. He depicted personages from the Bible facing those from the pagan era.

You can climb the tower as far as the third gallery (768 steps) to look out on the town and surrounding countryside over the Danube plain as far as the Alps.

Münsterplatz 1. ✆ **0731/9675023.** www.ulmer-muenster.de. Münster free; tower 4€ adults, 2.50€ children. Buy tickets an hour before the climb. Nov-Feb daily 9am-4:45pm; Mar and Oct daily 9am-5:45pm; Apr-June and Sept daily 8am-6:45pm; July-Aug daily 8am-7:45pm. Bus: 2, 7, or 9.

Where to Eat

Zunfthaus der Schiffleute BAVARIAN/SEAFOOD   Built some 6 centuries ago between the Danube and the Blau, this landmark building is the classic restaurant in the old town of Ulm. It was once the guild headquarters and pub for local fishermen, who told tall tales about how the Danube used to flood and the fish would swim right up to the kitchen door, where they were caught and put on the grill. Fresh fish is still a specialty here, but you can also order a number of well-prepared meat specialties, including delectable veal, roast beef, or entrecôte. A number of freshly made soups and hors d'oeuvres (including carpaccio) are prepared daily. Top it all off with a velvety chocolate mousse.

Fischergasse 31. ✆ **0731/64411.** www.zunfthaus-ulm.de. Reservations not needed. Main courses 9€-19€. AE, MC, V. Daily 11am-midnight.

Zur Forelle ★ SWABIAN/GERMAN   So authentically historic and so renowned as a bastion of Germanic *Gemütlichkeit* (coziness) is Zur Forelle that whenever a celebrity arrives in town, their hosts entertain them here. (Noteworthy visitors have included Albert Einstein and Herbert von Karajan.) Named after the trout that appear in succulent versions on the menu, it contains three antique, half-paneled dining rooms, an outdoor terrace with a view of the river and Ulm's historic core, masses of geraniums in its exterior window boxes, and a history of feeding hungry diners that goes back at least 375 years. Food items arrive in generous portions and reflect the best old-fashioned German cooking of the region, with special emphasis on fish. Your meal might begin with Ulm-style herb-and-salmon soup, spicy fish soup with garlic, or a platter of pickled seasonal vegetables. Main courses include beef and liver stew with roasted potatoes and green salad; filet of beef with fresh mushrooms and an herb-flavored cream sauce, served with house-made noodles and green salad; a mixed grill that offers roasted sausage, sliced pork, and hash-brown potatoes on one platter; roasted Barbary duckling in a reduction of port wine; and a wide choice of fish based on whatever is available that day from the local fish market.

Fischergasse 25. ✆ **0731/63924.** www.zurforelle.com. Reservations recommended. Main courses 10€-22€; fixed-priced menus 20€-79€. AE, MC, V. Daily 11am-3pm and 5pm-midnight.

Entertainment & Nightlife

The best beer hall in town is **Barfüsser,** Lautenberg 1 (✆ **0731/6021110;** www.barfuesser-brauhaus.de), a brewpub that also bakes its own pretzels. A beer garden overlooks the Danube. If you'd like to go on a tavern crawl, you can walk **Neue Strasse** down to the river. But if you have a beer at every place, you may not make it to the river.

Where to Stay

Hotel am Rathaus & Reblaus This is the most atmospheric place to stay in town, lying in back of the landmark Rathaus (Town Hall) in the Old Town. It consists of both the main hotel and the equally charming half-timbered annex, Reblaus. The owner of the hotel is a collector, filling the public areas with antiques, old paintings, and even 19th-century dolls. Try for a bedroom facing the front, since its windows open onto the towering spire of the famous cathedral. Bedrooms have a scattering of antiques, and all have modern appointments as well, with good lighting and crisp white sheets. Hand-painted Bavarian cupboards add more decorative touches throughout the rooms.

Kronengasse 8-10, 89073 Ulm. www.rathausulm.de. ✆ **0731/968490.** Fax 0731/9684949. 34 units. 88€–120€ double; 130€–170€ family room (maximum 5 persons). MC, V. Free parking. Closed late Dec to mid-Jan. *In room:* TV, Wi-Fi (free).

Maritim Hotel Ulm ★★★ ☺ A first-class hotel, this 16-story city-center choice is the grandest hotel in and around Ulm, which until the 1990s never had a first-rate hotel. All guest rooms are large, furnished with fine pieces and deluxe mattresses, and have roomy bathrooms. Although it claims to be a home away from home, few homes look like this palace, and even fewer have the facilities of this monument. This hotel is also the most family friendly in Ulm; it's the only one to offer rooms big enough for extra beds, babysitting services, and a pool.

Basteistrasse 40, 89073 Ulm. www.maritim.de. ✆ **0731/9230.** Fax 0731/9231000. 287 units. 117€–213€ double; from 229€ suite. AE, DC, MC, V. Parking 13€. **Amenities:** 2 restaurants; bar; babysitting; bikes; exercise room; indoor heated pool; room service; sauna. *In room:* A/C, TV, hair dryer, minibar, Wi-Fi (8€ per hour).

Neu-Ulm Mövenpick Hotel This hotel beside the Danube contains rather bland but well-maintained rooms. Fortunately, many feature views of the river. Guest rooms are in a standard chain format, but each is midsize and furnished comfortably. All units contain a compact and well-organized tiled bathroom. The English-speaking staff is helpful.

Silcherstrasse 40, 89231 Neu Ulm. www.moevenpick-hotels.com. ✆ **0731/80110.** Fax 0731/85967. 135 units. 99€–139€ double; 159€ junior suite. AE, DC, MC, V. Parking 10€. Bus: 2, 3, or 7. **Amenities:** Restaurant; bar; bikes; room service; Wi-Fi (free; in lobby). *In room:* TV, hair dryer, minibar.

THE ROMANTIC ROAD

Acollection of 28 picturesque towns, the Romantic Road (Romantische Strasse) makes for a great connection between Frankfurt and Munich, and stands as a memorable highlight of any trip through southern Germany. First drawn up in the aftermath of World War II, the 385km (239-mile) scenic route sets out in historic Würzburg, skirts the pastoral villages along the border of Bavaria and Baden-Würtemburg, and culminates in the rising foothills of Füssen and the Alps.

Although major centers such as Würzburg, Rothernburg ob der Tauber, Augsburg, and Füssen can be seen by train within a week, the entire region begs the traveler to slow down, to take a bike or hike, and to lose track of time and modernity in the well-preserved and restored communities along the way. Regardless of your means of travel, the well-connected tourist offices have detailed maps and information to get you where you need to go.

THE TOWNS OF THE ROMANTIC ROAD   Each town along the route merits a visit in its own right, but here we've included the best ones, along with a few that are not officially on the route. **Würzburg,** the bustling heart of the Franconian wine region, possesses one of Germany's finest palaces. Although often flooded with tourists, **Rotherburg ob der Tauber** offers an unparalleled medieval core that should not be missed. **Dinkelsbühl** and **Nördlingen** are less-touristy versions of Rothenburg, each with their own unique charm. **Augsburg** provides the amenities of a city, with a rich history to admire.

BUS TOURS OF THE ROMANTIC ROAD   The **Romantische Strasse Touristik Arbeitsgemeinschaft GbR,** Segringer Strasse 19, 91550 Dinkelsbühl (✆ **09851/5513487;** www.romantischestrasse.de), oversees the route and offers maps for drivers, cyclists, and walkers. The office also operates a convenient **coach** (✆ **069/719126 268,** or 0171/6532340 cellphone; www.romanticroadcoach.de) from mid-April to mid-October with daily departures from Frankfurt and Füssen at 8am. With a 6-month pass costing 104€, passengers can hop on and off anywhere along the route, usually in main squares or near partner hotels. Eurail Pass holders receive a 20% discount. In Frankfurt information is available at **Touring Tours & Travel Gmbh,** Am Römerhof 17, 60486 Frankfurt am Main (✆ **069/7903501;** www.deutsche-touring.com).

WÜRZBURG ★★

280km (174 miles) NW of Munich, 119km (74 miles) SE of Frankfurt, 109km (68 miles) NW of Nürnberg

For Germans, the south begins at Würzburg, one of the loveliest baroque cities in the country and the best place to start driving the Romantic Road. This young and lively city on the Main has a population of some 50,000 students, who give it a German version of *joie de vivre.* It's also a center of the Franconian wine region.

Würzburg remained faithful to the Roman Catholic Church throughout the Reformation. It's been called "the town of Madonnas" because of the more than 100 statues of its patron saint that adorn the house fronts. The best known of these statues is the baroque *Patrona Franconiae,* also known as the "Weeping Madonna," which stands among other Franconian saints along the buttresses of the 15th-century Alte Mainbrücke, Germany's second-oldest stone bridge.

On March 16, 1945, Würzburg was shattered by a bombing raid. Since a miraculous rebuilding program, nearly every major structure has been restored.

Essentials

GETTING THERE

By Train   The **Würzburg Hauptbahnhof** lies on several major and regional rail lines, with frequent connections to all major German cities. From Frankfurt, 30 trains arrive per day (trip time: 1 hr., 10 min.); from Munich, 20 trains (2 hr., 10 min.); from Nürnberg, 30 trains (1 hr.); and 12 trains from Stuttgart (2 hr., 15 min.). For rail information and schedules, call ✆ **01805/996633** or visit www.bahn.de.

By Bus   For bus service along the Romantic Road, see "Bus Tours of the Romantic Road," above.

By Car   Access is via the A7 Autobahn from north and south or the A3 Autobahn from east and west. The A81 Autobahn has links from the southwest.

VISITOR INFORMATION

Contact the **Tourist Information Office,** Falkenhaus am Markt (✆ **0931/372398**). It's open April to December Monday to Friday 10am to 6pm, Saturday 10am to 2pm (May–Oct also open Sun 10am–2pm); hours January to March are Monday to Friday 10am to 4pm, Saturday 10am to 1pm.

SPECIAL EVENTS   For Mozart lovers, the highlight of the cultural year is the annual **Mozart Festival,** www.mozartfest-wuerzburg.de, staged over the entire month of June. Wolfgang Amadeus fans from around the world, especially Americans and Europeans, flock to this festival. The venue for most of the Mozart concerts is the glorious baroque palace, the Residenz (see below). For information, contact the tourist office (see above). Many visitors book tours that feature the Mozart festival; the best are conducted by **Allegro Holidays** (✆ **800/838-6860;** www.allegro holidays.com).

Würzburg is also quite proud of its 4-day **Africa Festival** (www.africafestival.org), also in June, and the largest of its kind in Europe

GETTING AROUND

The quickest and most efficient means for covering the central core of Würzburg is by tram (streetcar). A single fare is 2.20€, or else you can purchase a ticket, good for 24 hours at any station, for 4.45€. The same fare applies to buses, which also serve

Würzburg

Within the map image:
- Hamburg
- Berlin ★
- GERMANY
- Frankfurt am Main
- Würzburg
- Munich
- Information ⓘ
- Veitshöchheimerstr.
- Hauptbahnhof
- Röntgenring
- Haugerring
- Friedens-brücke
- Luitpoldstr.
- Kranenkai
- Koellikerstr.
- Julius-spital
- Kaiserstr.
- Heinestr.
- Kroaten-gasse
- Berliner Platz
- Wörthstr.
- Dreikronenstr.
- Main Mainkai
- Juliuspromenade
- Schönborn str.
- Semmelstr.
- Ludwigstr.
- Kapuzinerstr.
- Rennweger Ring
- Zeller Str.
- Karmeliterstr.
- Eichhornstr.
- Theaterstr.
- ⓘ Marktplatz
- Altes Rathaus
- Dom St. Kilian
- Balth.-Neumann-Promenade
- Residenz
- Rennweg
- Alte Main-brücke
- Domstr.
- Büttnerstr.
- Augustinerstr.
- ALTSTADT
- Domerschulstr.
- HOFGARTEN
- MAINVIERTEL
- Saalgasse
- Neubaustr.
- Alte Universität
- Ottostr.
- Ebert- Ring
- Festung Marienberg
- Burkarder Tor
- Sanderstr.
- Neue Universität
- Sanderring
- Südbahnhof
- Leistenstr.
- 0 1/8 mile
- 0 125 meters
- Ludwigs-brücke
- Sanderglacisstr.
- Am Studenten-haus
- Studentenstr.
- Friedrich-
- Friedenstr.
- Kantstr.

the city. The no. 9 bus is especially convenient, linking the Marienberg Fortress and the Residenz palace. For information about routes and schedules, call ✆ **0931/361352** or visit www.vvm-info.de.

Exploring Würzburg

In spring and summer, the liveliest place in town is the **Marktplatz (central marketplace).** Here street performers entertain and vendors hawk their wares, ranging from fresh fruit to souvenir trinkets. You can also stroll down the traffic-free **Schönbornstrasse,** with its modern boutiques and cafes. The wine merchants here sell *Bocksbeutels,* the green, narrow-necked wine bottles native to the region. It's said that the shape came about because wine-drinking monks found it the easiest to hide under their robes.

Dom St. Kilian CHURCH   This cathedral, begun in 1045, is the fourth-largest Romanesque church in Germany. Its interior received a coat of high-baroque stucco after 1700. The imposing row of bishops' tombs begins with that of Gottfried von Spitzenberg (ca. 1190), who was one of the first prince-bishops to rule over the town. Look for three sandstone tombstones by Riemenschneider, constructed between

1502 and 1506. The Dom is dedicated to St. Kilian, an Irish missionary to Franconia in the 7th century.

Domstrasse (at the end of Schönbornstrasse). ✆**0931/3211830.** Free admission. Easter–Oct Mon–Sat 10am–5pm, Sun 1–6pm; Nov to the day before Easter Mon–Sat 10am–noon and 2–4:30pm, Sun 12:30–1:30pm and 2:30–6pm.

Festung Marienberg (Marienberg Fortress) ★HISTORIC BUILDING   Festung Marienberg, located across from the Altstadt, over the stone bridge, was the residence of the local prince-bishops from 1253 to 1720. The combination of age and wartime destruction has taken a serious toll on its thick walls and once-impenetrable ramparts. But what remains is worth a visit. The 8th-century **Marienkirche,** one of the oldest churches in Germany, stands within its walls.

In the former arsenal and Echter bulwark, to the right of the first courtyard, is the **Mainfränkisches Museum (Main-Franconian Museum),** housed here since 1946. Here you'll find the historical museum of the former Bishopric of Würzburg and Dukedom of Franconia, as well as the provincial museum of lower Franconia. On display is a collection of important sculptures by the great, flamboyant Gothic master Tilman Riemenschneider (1460–1531), called "the master of Würzburg." The sculptor came to live here in 1483 and was the town's mayor in 1520 and 1521. Never a totally decorative artist, Riemenschneider concentrated on the reality of people's appearances, highlighting their hands, faces, and clothing. The museum also displays paintings by Tiepolo and sandstone figures from the rococo gardens of the prince-bishops' summer palace. A tribute to one of the few industries of the city, winemaking, is paid in the press house, which contains historic casks and carved cask bases and a large collection of glasses and goblets.

Fürstenbaumuseum (✆ 0931/43838) is situated in the restored princes' wing of the fortress. Here you can glimpse the living quarters and conditions of the prince-bishops up to 1718. The urban-history section offers a stroll through 1,200 eventful years of Würzburg's history, including an exhibit relating to the discovery of X-rays by Wilhelm Conrad Röntgen in 1895. A model of the town shows its appearance in 1525, and another shows the destruction after the bombing of 1945.

Festung Marienberg. ✆ **0931/205940.** www.mainfraenkisches-museum.de. Admission to Mainfränkisches Museum 4€ adults, 2€ students, free for children 13 and under. Apr–Oct Tues–Sun 10am–5pm; Nov–Mar Tues–Sun 10am–4pm. Fürstenbaumuseum 4.50€ adults, 3.50€ students, free for children 17 and under. Apr–Oct Tues–Sun 9am–6pm. Tours of the fortress (in English and German) 3.50€ adults, 2.50€ students. Apr–Oct Tues–Sun 10am–4pm. Bus: 9.

Residenz (Schloss und Gartenverwaltung Würzburg) ★★ HISTORIC BUILDING   The Residenz of Würzburg is the last and finest of a line of baroque castles built in Bavaria in the 17th and 18th centuries. This horseshoe-shaped edifice was begun in 1720 to satisfy Prince-Bishop Johann Philipp Franz von Schönborn's passion for elegance and splendor. Its design was the joint effort of the best Viennese, French, and German architects working under the leadership of Balthasar Neumann (1687–1753). An architect and an engineer, Neumann was known for his technical virtuosity and the harmony of his compositions. This castle shows a unity of purpose and design unusual in structures of such size.

At the center of the castle is the masterful *Treppenhaus* (staircase). The high, rounded ceiling above is decorated with a huge fresco by Tiepolo. At its center, Apollo is seen ascending to the zenith of the vault. The surrounding themes represent the four corners of the world, the seasons, and signs of the zodiac. The painting appears to be overflowing onto the walls of the upper hall.

The other important attraction is the court chapel, in the southwest section. Neumann placed the window arches at oblique angles to coordinate the windows with the oval sections, thus creating a muted effect. The rectangular room is divided into five oval sections, three with domed ceilings. Colored marble columns define the sections, their gilded capitals enriching the ceiling frescoes by Johann Rudolf Byss. At the side altars, Tiepolo painted two important works: *The Fall of the Angels* on the left and *The Assumption of the Virgin* on the right. **Note:** Due to renovation, the chapel will be closed until summer 2012.

During the summer, a **Mozart festival** is held in the upper halls. For information, call © **0931/372336.**

Residenzplatz 2, Tor B. © **0931/355170.** www.residenz-wuerzburg.de. Admission 7.50€ adults; 6.50€ students, children, and seniors. Apr-Oct daily 9am-6pm; Nov-Mar daily 10am-4pm. Guided tours in English (included in admission) 11am and 3pm. Bus: 9.

Where to Eat

Try the local specialty, *Zwiebelkuchen,* which is like a quiche Lorraine, and also look for another specialty, *Meerfischle,* a well-seasoned stew made from saltwater fish. White Franconian wine goes well with the local sausage.

Backöfele FRANCONIAN/GERMAN   Because this place is a short walk from both the Residenz and the Rathaus, you'll probably eat here at least once while in Würzburg. Even the locals don't really know whether to call it a beer hall, a wine cellar, or a restaurant. Regardless, the place serves well-prepared traditional food in huge quantities. Two specialties are lamb chops with fresh potatoes and fresh vegetables, and pikeperch with noodles and a salad.

Ursulinergasse 2. © **0931/59059.** www.backoefele.de. Reservations recommended. Main courses 7€-29€. AE, MC, V. Mon-Sat noon-11pm; Sun noon-10pm. Tram: 1 or 4.

Ratskeller Würzburg 🗲 FRANCONIAN/INTERNATIONAL   This 500-year-old tavern keeps alive the tradition of a city hall cellar restaurant for its citizens, serving tasty Franconian fare at reasonable prices. Country cookery is an art here, as you'll discover if you order the boiled beef with horseradish sauce and noodles. Other specialties include marinated salmon with potato pancakes, pikeperch in a white-wine sauce, and medallions of pork gratin with cheese. Game is featured in season. Ask about local beer and Franconian white wines.

Langgasse 1 (near the Alte Mainbrücke). © **0931/13021.** www.wuerzburger-ratskeller.de. Reservations required Sat-Sun. Main courses 8€-26€. AE, DC, MC, V. Daily 11:30am-10:30pm. Tram: 1, 2, 3, or 5.

Weinhaus Zum Stachel ★ FRANCONIAN/INTERNATIONAL   No other wine house in Würzburg is as old as this one, dating from 1413. Seats and walls have been burnished by the clothing of many hundreds of drinkers and diners during the past 500 years. Some of the generous portions include the veal *cordon bleu,* tender pepper steak aromatically flavored with cognac, or more prosaic rump steak with onions. Some dishes, such as chateaubriand, are so elaborate that they're prepared only for two. Chef Richard Huth is proudest of his freshwater fish prepared according to old family recipes. In summer, you can dine in a vine-draped outdoor courtyard, and sip wines from the restaurant's own vineyards.

Gressengasse 1. © **0931/52770.** www.weinhaus-stachel.de. Reservations required. Main courses 12€-23€; 3-course meal 38€, 6-course meal 66€. MC, V. Tues-Sat 11am-midnight. Tram: 1, 3, 4, or 5.

Wein und Fischhaus Schiffbäuerin ★ 👜 SEAFOOD One of the best dining spots in the region is this combined wine house/fish restaurant, across Alte Main-brücke on the Marienberg fortress side in an old half-timbered building in a narrow street. Once the residence of shipbuilders, the house now specializes in freshwater fish such as pike, carp, char, tench, trout, wels, and eel. Most of these dishes are priced per 100 grams (3½ oz.). Soup specialties are fish, snail, and French onion.

Katzengasse 7. ☏ **0931/42487.** www.schiffbaeuerin.de. Reservations recommended. Main courses 16€–24€. No credit cards. Tues-Sat 11:30am–2:30pm and 6–11:30pm; Sun 11:30am–3pm. Closed Tues in Jun, Jul, and Aug. Tram: 2 or 4.

Entertainment & Nightlife

Much of Würzburg's nightlife takes place in its numerous *Weinstuben* (wine cellars). For music and cultural happenings, scan the flyers posted in the *Studentenhaus* (student center) on Am Exerzierplatz at Münzstrasse.

The city's oldest jazz club, **Omnibus,** Theaterstrasse 10 (☏ **0931/56121;** www.omnibus-wuerzburg.de; bus: 14 or 20), has been packing them in for live acts for over 3 decades. This cellar-level joint is also where people come to drink and play chess. It's open Monday to Thursday 8pm to 1am, and Friday and Saturday 9pm to 3am. Cover charges for performances range from 8€ to 16€. A place for a cheap meal or a drink, **Standard,** Oberthürstrasse 11a (☏ **0931/51140;** www.standard-wuerzburg. de; bus: 14 or 20), is open daily 10am to 2am. It occasionally has a live band on the weekend. **Kult Statt Kneipe,** Landwehrstrasse 10 (☏ **0931/53143;** www.kult-wuerzburg.de; tram: 1, 3, or 5), keeps the stereo cranking. It's open Monday to Friday 9am to 1am (Fri until 2am), Saturday 10am to 2am, and Sunday 10am to 1am.

The **Weinstuben Juliusspital,** Klinikstrasse 1 (☏ **0931/3931400;** www. weingut-juliusspital.de), is one of the many top addresses for wine connoisseurs, with an array of characteristic Franconian vintages. Meals are also served. It's open daily 10am to midnight.

Where to Stay
EXPENSIVE

Hotel und Weinrestaurant Schloss Steinburg ★ 👜 If you're looking for a dream castle, this pretty much fits the bill. With 13th-century roots and a 19th-century makeover, a hillside of vineyards sweeping down before it, and a breathtaking view over the Main and the steeples of Würzburg, the Steinburg provides idyllic charm within reach of the city's sights. Stay in either an exquisitely furnished Dream Castle Room, a Rural Castle Room with more country nostalgia, or a more modest but still fancy Castle Room. The location is ideal for motorists.

Auf dem Steinberg, 97080 Würzburg. www.steinburg.com. ☏ **0931/97020.** Fax 0931/97121. 46 units. 155€–245€ double. Rates include buffet breakfast. AE, DC, MC, V. Free parking. Take Rte. 27 5km (3 miles) toward Fulda. **Amenities:** Restaurant; indoor heated pool; room service; sauna. *In room:* TV, hair dryer.

Premier Hotel Rebstock ★★ This palace with a rococo facade dates from at least 1408, and is now a premier hotel run under the Best Western brand. The airy foyer with a convertible sun roof greets the guest with statues, antiques, paintings, and a Spanish sea chest. The rooms themselves are conservatively designed with less flair than you'd expect given the rococo style. A few rooms have fancy wrought-iron bed frames with drapes. Its location across the river from the Marienberg is also a plus.

Neubaustrasse 7, 97070 Wurzburg. www.rebstock.com. ℂ **800/528-1234** in the U.S., or 0931/30930. Fax 0931/3093100. 70 units. 169€–213€ double. Children 11 and under stay free in parent's room. AE, MC, V. Parking 10€. Tram: 1, 3, 4, or 5. **Amenities:** 2 restaurants; bar; babysitting; room service; Wi-Fi (free; in lobby). *In room:* TV, hair dryer, minibar.

MODERATE

Franziskaner 🍴 For homespun cleanliness, this 1909 hotel is a winner—and the price is right, too. You'll receive a hearty welcome from the staff. The lobby has attractive black panels surrounded with natural wood; the breakfast room has fine large windows looking out to the greenery beyond. All of the rooms are well furnished, each with an immaculate bathroom. The hotel serves only breakfast, but its restaurant Tamarillo offers Frankish and Mediterranean cuisine.

Franziskanerplatz 2, 97070 Würzburg. www.hotel-franziskaner.de. ℂ **0931/35630.** Fax 0931/3563333. 38 units. 106€–130€ double. Rates include buffet breakfast. AE, MC, V. Parking 10€. Tram: 1. **Amenities:** Restaurant. *In room:* TV, hair dryer, Wi-Fi (free).

Hotel Maritim ★★★ Nothing in Würzburg matches this hotel for comfort and style, not even its closest contender, Premier Hotel Rebstock (see above). The Maritim, built in 1983, has 20 rooms with views over the Main River and is linked to the city convention center. A baroque-style mansard roof tops its modern and imposing yellow facade. The comfortable rooms each contain a midsize tiled bathroom.

Pleichertorstrasse 5, 97070 Würzburg. www.maritim.de. ℂ **0931/30530.** Fax 0931/3053900. 287 units. 96€–191€ double; from 206€ suite. Rates include buffet breakfast. AE, DC, MC, V. Parking 10€. Tram: 2 or 4. **Amenities:** Restaurant; bar; babysitting; bikes; indoor heated pool; room service; sauna. *In room:* A/C, TV, hair dryer, minibar, Wi-Fi (8€ per hour).

Zur Stadt Mainz ★ 🎁 Dating from the 1400s, when it was known as the Raven, this is one of the most romantic and atmospheric of Franconian inns. Owners Margarethe and Anneliese Schwarzmann are known for their hospitality and excellent cuisine. The midsize rooms are furnished in a cozy, old-fashioned Franconian style, with comfortable beds, tasteful furnishings, and small bathrooms with shower only. The breakfast buffet is the most generous and the best in town.

Even if you're not a guest, consider visiting its restaurant, where many of the traditional dishes come from a historic cookbook. Apple strudel lures afternoon coffee drinkers.

Semmelstrasse 39, 97070 Würzburg. www.hotel-stadtmainz.de. ℂ **0931/53155.** Fax 0931/58510. 15 units. 100€ double; 130€ triple; 160€ quad. Rates include continental breakfast buffet. AE, DC, MC, V. Parking 9€. **Amenities:** Restaurant. *In room:* TV, hair dryer.

INEXPENSIVE

St. Josef ★ 🍴 St. Josef offers the best inexpensive accommodations in the Altstadt. The rooms may be small, but the Casagrande family has successfully brought them up to date. They are pleasantly furnished and well maintained, each equipped with an efficiently organized bathroom. Fresh flowers add a personalized touch to this well-run establishment.

Semmelstrasse 28-30, 97070 Würzburg. www.hotel-st-josef.de. ℂ **0931/308680.** Fax 0931/3086860. 33 units. 89€–95€ double; 124€ triple. Rates include continental breakfast. MC, V. Parking 8.50€. Tram: 1, 2, 3, or 5. **Amenities:** Restaurant. *In room:* TV, hair dryer, minibar.

Schönleber With easy access down the street to the Residenz palace, the Schönleber, meaning "one who lives beautifully," also sits in close proximity to other sites, not to mention the train station. Two boutiques occupy enormous arched windows facing the sidewalk on the ground floor, while the upper floors offer smallish but comfortably furnished rooms with modern amenities. Bathrooms are cramped but adequate. The staff is friendly and helpful.

Theaterstrasse 5, 97070 Würzburg. www.hotel-schoenleber.de. © **0931/3048900.** Fax 0931/ 30489030. 54 units, 27 with bathroom. 66€ double without bathroom; 72€–100€ double with bathroom. Rates include buffet breakfast. AE, MC, V. Parking 8€. Tram: 1, 2, 3, or 5. **Amenities:** Bikes; Wi-Fi (2€ per hour; in lobby). *In room:* TV, hair dryer.

A DETOUR TO MILTENBERG & AMORBACH

Miltenberg ★

29km (18 miles) S of Mespelbrunn, 71km (44 miles) W of Würzburg

This riverside town is located to the west of the traditional and official route of the Romantic Road, but it's very popular and well worth a visit. Miltenberg is sleepy, traditional, and full of half-timbered buildings. If you're looking for a medieval town but you want to avoid the tour-bus hordes that overrun places like Rothenburg (see "Rothenburg ob der Tauber," below), Miltenberg is for you.

The town, which is still enclosed within walls and gate towers, is attractively situated under a steep wooded hill crowned by a castle. Its municipal charter dates from 1237, but it was actually settled centuries earlier by the Romans. The best way to appreciate Miltenberg's charm is on a fast drive-through, with a pedestrian detour through its charming **Marktplatz ★**. Here, on steeply sloping terrain centered on a Renaissance-era red-sandstone fountain and a wealth of flowers, you'll find a phalanx of half-timbered houses, and one of the oldest inns in Germany, the **Haus zum Riesen.**

ESSENTIALS

GETTING THERE **By Train** There's at least one connection per hour from Würzburg, 90 minutes away, requiring a changeover in Aschaffenburg. About 25 trains per day make the 45-minute trip from this important railway junction. For railway information, call © **01805/996633** or visit www.bahn.de.

By Car From the north, take Rte. B469 into town (it's signposted). From Würzburg, take the A3 west and then minor roads.

VISITOR INFORMATION The **tourist office,** Engelplatz 69 (© **09371/ 404119;** www.miltenberg.info), offers English-language pamphlets describing brief self-guided walking tours through the town. It's open Monday to Friday 9am to 5pm. May to October, it's also open Saturday 10am to 1pm.

EXPLORING MILTENBERG

Park your car in the first convenient parking lot and walk into the center of town—don't attempt to drive. Other than the above-mentioned Marktplatz, the main attraction in town is **Schloss Miltenberg ★**. (It is sometimes identified simply as "Miltenburg."), which has recently reopened after a long-standing series of renovations. You can visit the courtyardand climb to the top of a watchtower for a sweeping view over the surrounding forest. The courtyard, the tower, and the cafe that's associated with the site are open only May to October Tuesday to Friday 2 to 5:30pm, Saturday and Sunday 1 to 5:30pm. Admission is 3€ adults and 2€ for children 11 and under.

During your exploration of Miltenberg, don't overlook the oldest and most historic bar in town, a 500-year-old hangout that locals refer to simply as **Weinhaus,** Marktplatz 185 (© **09371/5500**). Here, every evening between 5:30pm and midnight, you can order any of the local vintages, at a per-glass price of 3€ to 8€.

WHERE TO EAT

Gasthaus zum Riesen GERMAN   Although this restaurant is associated with the hotel below, it is run separately at a nearby address, lying 90m (300 ft.) away. Inside, the dining room is an antique that often features old-fashioned dishes, such as bear steak, imported from Russia. From the kitchen come such German granny favorites as either potato soup or liver dumpling soup, as well as a dish that we've seen in no other restaurant in Germany, *Ochsenfetzen* ("torn-apart ox"). This delicacy—the subject of many articles in culinary reviews and based on authentic medieval scholarship—uses brisket of beef marinated for 2 weeks in marinades that change every other day. You can also order such rib-sticking fare as loin of pork with mushrooms, or a platter piled high with pork filets, turkey filets, German sausages, *Rösti* (hash browns), and freshly made salads. Most diners order freshly made crepes or ice cream for dessert.

Hauptstrasse 99. © **09371/989948.** www.riesen-miltenberg.de. Main courses 8€–19€. AE, MC, V. Mon–Wed 11am–midnight; Thurs–Sat 11am–1am.

WHERE TO STAY

Haus zum Riesen Hotel ★   This historic hotel dates from 1190, just before it hosted Frederick Barbarossa during his expeditions in this part of Germany. During the Thirty Years' War, it housed VIPs from both sides, depending on who was in control. Today, this hotel is the most evocative in town, graced with charmingly old-fashioned rooms, usually with beamed ceilings. Bathrooms range from midsize to spacious. However, the place is more famous as a restaurant (see review above) than as a hotel. There is a major drawback here: Some members of the staff are the rudest you'll encounter along the Romantic Road.

Hauptstrasse 97, 63897 Miltenberg. www.riesen-miltenberg.de. © **09371/3644.** 15 units. 80€–105€ double; 125€ suite. Rates include continental breakfast. No credit cards. **Amenities:** Restaurant; bar; room service. *In room:* Hair dryer.

Hotel Altes Bannhaus ★   This medieval hotel on the town's main street is behind a severely dignified stone facade that's graced with an elaborate iron bracket. It treads the fine line between authentically historical and merely dowdy. Overall, its vaulted stone cellars and massive masonry are charming. Rooms are more angular and modern looking than the authentically antique public areas. Each has functional furniture, small windows, and small bathrooms.

Hauptstrasse 211, 63897 Miltenberg. www.altesbannhaus.de. © **09371/3061.** Fax 09371/68754. 10 units. 95€–100€ double. Rates include buffet breakfast. AE, DC, MC, V. **Amenities:** Restaurant; room service. *In room:* TV, hair dryer, minibar, Wi-Fi (free).

Amorbach ★

11km (7 miles) S of Miltenberg, 92km (57 miles) SW of Würzburg

This little town shouldn't take up too much of your time, but it does offer a few rewarding sights, notably the Abteikirche of St. Maria. It also has one of the finest hotels in the region. As you wander about Amorbach's center, note how local homeowners have dotted the half-timbered facades with flower boxes.

ESSENTIALS

GETTING THERE **By Train or Bus**   Sixteen trains a day make the 12-minute trip from Miltenberg to the Amorbach terminus, in addition to a handful of buses, which need 30 minutes to reach the town. From other points, passengers must arrive first in Miltenberg for a change of trains before proceeding on to Amorbach. For railway information, call *C* **01805/996633** or visit www.bahn.de.

By Car   From Miltenberg, follow Route 469 south for 11km (7 miles).

VISITOR INFORMATION   The **Stadt Verkehrsamt,** at the Rathaus, Marktplatz 1 (*C* **09373/20940;** www.amorbach.de), is open April to October Monday to Friday 9:30am to 12:30pm and 2:00 to 5:30pm, Saturday 10:30am to 2:30pm. From November to March, it is open Monday to Friday 10am to noon and 3 to 5pm.

Exploring Amorbach

Much of the fun of a visit to Amorbach lies simply in wandering through the streets of the old town, where half-timbered medieval buildings, some of them a bit artfully askew, still evoke old Germany.

The town's most important monument is the **Abteikirche St. Maria ★**, Kirchplatz (*C* **09373/971545;** www.abteikirche.de). This impressive church underwent at least a half-dozen enlargements and alterations between the 8th and the 18th centuries, but it still retains a degree of charm and cohesiveness, for example the rococo gable between Romanesque towers. The interior is a mass of ornate baroque stucco, centering on one of the most impressive baroque-era organs in Germany. Entrance is free, but a guided tour, conducted in German or English, costs 4.50€ per person. It's open Monday to Saturday 10am to noon and 1 to 2pm, and Sunday noon to 5pm.

The ruined remains of **Wildenburg Castle,** Odenwald (*C* **09373/20940**), lie 5km (3 miles) south of Amorbach. Originally built 1,000 years ago, it's now little more than a jumble of impressive medieval-looking rock piles. The restored watchtower, however, can be climbed every Sunday 11am to 5pm. Admission is free. The view over the Odenwald Forest is excellent.

Where to Eat & Stay

Der Schafhof Amorbach ★★★   The most romantic and carefully manicured hotel in the district lies within what was originally a Benedictine monastery (ca. 1450) and rebuilt in 1721 in a country-baroque style. The more historic rooms lie within the former abbey; more modern, better-equipped units are within a well-built modern annex. Our favorites lie under the eaves of the main building and are crisscrossed with a labyrinth of hand-hewn ceiling beams. Rooms are stylish and comfortably outfitted in a plush but conservative style, each with a midsize tiled bathroom.

Local gourmets fawn on the sublime cuisine served in the hotel's **Abtstube,** the finest restaurant in the district, specializing in regional and Mediterranean cuisine. Main courses range from 16€ to 26€.

Otterbachtal, 63916 Amorbach. www.schafhof.de. *C* **09373/97330.** Fax 09373/4120. 24 units. 135€–180€ double; 225€–260€ suite. Rates include continental breakfast. AE, DC, MC, V. From Amorbach, follow N47 (the Nibelungenstrasse) west for 5km (3 miles). **Amenities:** 2 restaurants; room service; sauna. *In room:* TV, hair dryer, minibar (in some).

WEIKERSHEIM

10km (6 miles) E of Bad Mergentheim, 40km (25 miles) S of Würzburg

The architecture of this riverside town is consistently 18th century; it's one of the most stylistically unified towns on the Romantic Road. Weikersheim also boasts one of the mightiest castles on the Romantic Road.

Essentials

GETTING THERE   By Train or Bus   Four direct trains pull into Weikersheim from Würzburg at intervals of 2 hours throughout the day (trip time: 90 min.). Six direct trains also make the trip from Aschaffenburg (trip time: 2 hr., 15 min.). From Stuttgart, change trains at Lauda or Crailsheim, a trip that takes over 2 hours. For information about railway schedules, call the station at 🕿 **01805/996633** or visit www.bahn.de. For bus service along the Romantic Road, see "Bus Tours of the Romantic Road," at the beginning of this chapter.

By Car   From Bad Mergentheim, take the B19 to Igersheim, then the L2251 along the Tauber.

VISITOR INFORMATION   The **Tourist Office** at Marktplatz 7 (🕿 **07934/ 10255;** www.weikersheim.de) is open May to October Monday to Friday 9am to 5:30pm, and November to April Monday to Thursday 9am to 4pm and Friday 9am to 1pm.

Exploring Weikersheim

During its formative years, the very existence of the town was dependent on its castle, **Schloss Weikersheim,** Marktplatz 11 (🕿 **07934/992950;** www.schloss-weikersheim.de). It was begun in 1586 after Count Wolfgang II reestablished Weikersheim as his family's main residence, ordering that the old moated castle be replaced with a new Renaissance palace. Work finished a century later in a severely dignified style that had nothing to do with the baroque style then popular in other parts of Germany.

You can visit the castle's interior daily April to October 9am to 6pm and November to March 10am to noon and 1 to 5pm; admission is 5.50€ adults and 2.80€ for students, seniors, and children. A family ticket is 14€. Its architectural and decorative highlight is the **Rittersaal (Knight's Hall)** ★★, which was completed in 1603 and shows the transition between the baroque and the earlier Renaissance style. This is the most sumptuous banqueting hall ever built in Germany. Note the bas-reliefs of game animals lining the walls. The entrance doorway is carved with a scene of a battle against the Turks. The castle contains one of the most remarkable collections of **antique furnishings** ★★ of any castle in Germany, a treasure-trove stretching out for 2 centuries beginning in 1550. Also, allow some time to wander through the well-preserved baroque **Schlossgarten (castle gardens).**

To one side of the castle is the **Marktplatz,** a semicircular market square that opens onto sweeping vistas. It was laid out in the early 18th century.

Where to Eat & Stay

Flair Hotel Laurentius ★   The most appealing hotel in town is an old-fashioned monument to the art of hospitality. It's an ideal stopover along the Romantic Road, for either a meal or an overnight stay. Its vaulted, street-level area is the site of a cozy restaurant and wine bar. Upstairs, a series of high-ceilinged rooms contain a pleasing, unpretentious mix of attractive reproductions and genuine antiques. Bathrooms are quirkily old-fashioned, but not without charm. Suites have whirlpool tubs and panoramic flatscreen televisions.

Marktplatz 5, 97990 Weikersheim. www.hotel-laurentius.de. © **07934/91080.** Fax 07934/910818. 13 units. 60€–125€ per person double. Rates include continental breakfast. AE, DC, MC, V. Free parking. **Amenities:** Restaurant; bar; room service; sauna. *In room:* TV/DVD, hair dryer, minibar (in some), Wi-Fi (free).

CREGLINGEN

19km (12 miles) E of Weikersheim, 40km (25 miles) S of Würzburg

With a history stretching back more than 4,000 years, Creglingen became an important Celtic stronghold north of the Limes defense border of the Roman Empire. Later on, around the year 1000, it was mentioned in written sources as a winegrowing site. In 1349, the town gained the prestigious status of a "city." Around the same time, Creglingen became an important pilgrimage site, thanks to the legend of a local farmer who claimed to have seen Jesus and a phalanx of angels. Today, Creglingen is one of the quieter hamlets along the Romantic Road, with a tiny but colorful inner core of buildings that evoke the Germany of long ago and a charming but substandard set of accommodations, usually in local farmhouses.

Essentials

GETTING THERE

By Train   Given that the nearest trains stations are at Weikersheim (see above) and the hamlet of Steinach, about 19km (12 miles) east of Creglingen, you'll need to take a local bus (see below) or taxi to reach Creglingen (the latter will run about 40€). Rail connections from Würzburg arrive in Steinach about once an hour. For railway information, call the information service for local train lines at © **01805/996633** or visit www.bahn.de.

By Bus   For convenient bus service along the Romantic Road, see "Bus Tours of the Romantic Road," at the beginning of this chapter. Otherwise, local buses operated by **Omnibusverkehr Franken** (© **0931/3528940;** www.ovf.de) also make the trip from Weikersheim via Creglingen to Rothenburg ob der Tauber. However, connections are irregular, ranging from 5 to 10 a day from either direction, and buses may be filled with school children outside high season. Inquire at local tourist offices for exact information and departure times.

By Car   From Weikersheim, either follow the L2251 for 18km (11 miles) through the scenic bend of the Tauber River valley, or cut east via the L1001 and L1003 for 12km (7½ miles)

VISITOR INFORMATION

Tourist information is at Bad Mergentheimer Strasse 14 (© **07933/631;** www.creglingen.de); it's open Monday to Friday 9am to 4:30pm.

Exploring Creglingen

Creglingen is home of one of the most quirky museums in Germany, the **Fingerhutmuseum (Thimble Museum),** Kohlesmühle 6 (© **07933/370;** www.fingerhutmuseum.de), with the largest collection of thimbles in Europe. Some of them are bone rings dating from prehistoric times; others are made of brass that was smelted in Creglingen during the Middle Ages. It's open April to October Tuesday to Sunday 10am to 12:30pm and 2 to 5pm; hours for November, December, and March are Tuesday to Sunday 1 to 4pm. Admission is 2€.

The most important local attraction is the **Herrgottskirche (Chapel of Our Lord).** Located opposite the Thimble Museum on the road to Münster, this chapel built by the counts of Hohenlohe around 1525 features an enormous altarpiece by Tilman Riemenschneider. The 10m (33-ft.) structure showing the ascension of Mary was carved in the 16th century. Figures with expressive faces are set in a filigree shrine specially constructed to catch the day's changing light effects. The chapel can be visited daily April to October 9:15am to 6pm, and November to March Tuesday to Sunday 1 to 4pm. Admission is 2€. For more information, contact the tourist office (© **07933/508**), which is set 3km (2 miles) south of Creglingen within the Herrgottstal Valley. It's clearly posted from the village center.

Where to Stay

Accommodations are not plentiful in Creglingen, since most visitors are merely passing through. You might find a small B&B operating in summer, but don't count on it. Consider Würzburg (p. 236), Weikersheim (see above), or Rothenburg ob der Tauber (see below) for food and lodgings.

ROTHENBURG OB DER TAUBER ★★★

117km (73 miles) NE of Stuttgart, 51km (32 miles) SE of Würzburg

Even those strapped for time should find the time to see Rothenburg ob der Tauber. This medieval relic has the distinction of being one of Europe's few well-preserved cities. After its heyday as an independent Free Imperial City in the Holy Roman Empire, the once important crossroads fell dormant after the Thirty Years' War (1618–48) and thus retained its character for 19th-century painters and modern-day tourists to admire. While World War II left its mark when the U.S. bombed the eastern 40% of the town (the Nazis had fled there from Nürnberg), the citizens of Rothenburg rebuilt their town with the help of financial donors, whose names adorn the stones of the ramparts.

Today, this gem on the Tauber both attracts and relies on visitors for good reason, and overcrowding is a constant concern for the city council. But to pass it off as touristy doesn't do it justice, as a hike into the Tauber valley, a walk around the ramparts, or a nighttime stroll in the off-season will reveal.

Essentials

GETTING THERE

When trying to reach this gem of a town, some travelers have suddenly discovered themselves at a Rothenburg somewhere else in Germany. To avoid the confusion, make sure to ask for a ticket to "Rothenburg ob der Tauber."

BY PLANE   The nearest regional airport is Nürnberg (see chapter 6); from there it's a 2-hour train ride to Rothenburg ob der Tauber.

BY TRAIN   Rothenburg ob der Tauber is connected with hourly trains to the junction of Steinach, which has frequent connections to Würzburg (total trip time: 1 hr.)

Connections to Munich take 3 hours, and those to Frankfurt take 2½. For information, call ☎ **01805/996633** or visit www.bahn.de.

BY BUS   For bus service along the Romantic Road, see "Bus Tours of the Romantic Road," at the beginning of this chapter. Regular long-distance buses service Rothenburg from Frankfurt, Würzburg, Augsburg, and Munich, as well as Füssen. For information and reservations, call the Frankfurt terminal number (☎ **069/7903261** in Frankfurt). Regional bus service is provided by **OVF Omnibusverkehr Franken GmbH,** Nelson-Mandela-Platz 18, D-90159 Nürnberg (☎ **0911/430570;** www.ovf.de).

BY CAR   Access by car is via the minor road south from Creglingen or by the A7 Autobahn on the Würzburg-Ulm run.

VISITOR INFORMATION

Contact **Rothenburg Tourismus Service,** Marktplatz (☎ **09861/404800;** www. rothenburg.de). November to April, it's open Monday to Friday 9am to 5pm, and Saturday 10am to 1pm; May to October, it's open Monday to Friday 9am to 6pm, Saturday and Sunday 10am to 5pm.

SPECIAL EVENTS   The cultural event of the year is the **Meistertrunk festival,** held late May to early June, celebrating the entire history of the town with more than 1,000 participants in costume. Concerts, historical exhibitions, a parade, and a play about the *Bürgermeister* Nusch's wager (see the Reichsstadtmuseum listing, below) are the festival's highlights. The play is also staged in July and October. For details, contact the visitor information office, or visit www.meistertrunk.de.

Exploring Rothenburg ob der Tauber

For an excellent view, take a walk on the **town ramparts ★**. The wall tour, from the massive 16th-century Spitaltor (at the end of the Spitalgasse) to the Klingentor, takes about a half-hour. At the **Rödertor (Röder Gate),** you can climb the tower to a small but fascinating exhibition describing the air raid of 1945, all the while enjoying the excellent **views** over the city. Entry is 1.50€ for adults, 1€ for children, but opening times vary and depend on the weather. To fortify yourself for this walk, you can stop at one of the many kiosks in town selling the local pastry called *Schneeballen* (snowballs), a round, sugarcoated pastry that's fattening but delicious.

If you want to escape the tourist hordes, you can rent a bike at **Rad und Tat,** Bensenstrasse 17 (☎ **09861/87984;** www.mietraeder.de), for about 12€ per day. Get a map from the tourist office and head out along the Tauber River with a picnic lunch.

Kriminalmuseum (Criminal Museum) MUSEUM   The only museum of its kind in Germany, the Kriminalmuseum is housed in a structure built in 1395 for the Order of the Johanniter, who cared for the sick. The building was redone in 1718 in the baroque style, making it the only example of baroque architecture in town. The museum's four floors provide a fascinating insight into the life, laws, and punishments of medieval days. You'll see chastity belts, shame masks, a shame flute for bad musicians, torture devices, and a cage for bakers who baked bread too small or too light.

Burggasse 3-5. ☎ **09861/5359.** www.kriminalmuseum.rothenburg.de. Admission 4€ adults, 2.80€ students, 2.40€ children 6-17. Jan-Feb and Nov daily 2-4pm; Mar and Dec 1-4pm; Apr daily 11am-5pm; May-Oct daily 10am-6pm.

Rothenburg ob der Tauber

THE ROMANTIC ROAD

Rathaus (Town Hall) ★ HISTORIC BUILDING   Rothenburg's town hall has an older Gothic section from 1240 and a newer Renaissance structure facing the square. From the 50m (160-ft.) tower of the Gothic hall is a great **view** ★ of the town. The tower was first used as a sentry's lookout, but after a fire destroyed the Gothic hall's twin (where the Renaissance hall now stands) in 1501, it became a lookout for fire. Guards rang the bell every quarter-hour to prove that they were awake and on the job.

The new Rathaus, built in 1572 to replace the portion destroyed in the fire, is decorated with intricate friezes, an oriel extending the building's full height, and a large stone portico opening onto the square. The octagonal tower at the center of the side facing the square contains a grand staircase leading to the upper hall. On the main floor is the large courtroom.

Marktplatz. ☎ **09861/40492.** Admission: Rathaus free; tower 1.50€ adults, 1€ children. Rathaus Mon-Fri 8am-6pm. Tower Apr-Oct daily 9:30am-12:30pm and 1-5pm; Dec daily noon-3pm; Nov and Jan-Mar Sat-Sun and holidays noon-3pm.

Reichsstadtmuseum (Imperial City Museum) MUSEUM   The historical collection of Rothenburg is housed in this 13th-century Dominican nunnery. The cloisters are well preserved, and you can visit the convent hall, kitchen, and apothecary. The museum collection includes period furniture and art from Rothenburg's more prosperous periods, including the original glazed elector's tankard, and a new section of archaeological objects from prehistoric times up to the Middle Ages. Among the artistic exhibits is the 1494 *Rothenburg Passion* series, 12 pictures by Martinus Schwartz that depict scenes from the suffering of Christ. You can also see the works of English painter Arthur Wasse (1854–1930), whose romantic pictures manage to capture the many moods of the city. Finally, there's a Jewish section, with gravestones from the Middle Ages and some religious objects.

But perhaps the most remarkable object on display is an enormous tankard that holds 3.5 liters—more than 6 pints. You'll find echoes of its story all over the city. In 1631, during the Thirty Years' War, the Protestant city of Rothenburg was captured by General Tilly, commander of the armies of the Catholic League. He promised to spare the town from destruction if one of the town burghers could drink down the huge tankard full of wine in one draft. *Bürgermeister* Nusch accepted the challenge and succeeded, thus saving Rothenburg. Look for the clock on the Marktplatz with mechanical figures representing this event.

Klosterhof 5. ☎ **09861/939043.** www.reichsstadtmuseum.rothenburg.de. Admission 4€ adults, 3€ students and children 6–18, 8€ family ticket. Apr-Oct daily 10am-5pm; Nov-Mar daily 1-4pm.

St. Jakobskirche (Church of St. James) CHURCH   This church's name and the statue on the south facade with a scallop shell remind us that Rothenburg lies on the pilgrim trail to Santiago de Compostella in Spain, site of the remains of St. James. Inside, the stained glass of the 1336 choir frames the imposing **High Altar** (1466), which merits a look for its delicate sculpture and the rear panels depicting scenes from the life of the pilgrim-attracting saint. Original statues, chancel pews, and paintings fill the rest of the interior. The main attraction is hidden from view, in the upper floor in the west gallery. The **Altar of the Holy Blood ★★**, a masterpiece by the famous Würzburg sculptor Tilman Riemenschneider (ca. 1460–1531), was executed between 1499 and 1505 to provide a worthy setting for the Reliquary of the Holy Blood. This venerated relic from the Middle Ages is contained in a rock-crystal capsule set in the reliquary cross (ca. 1270) in the center of the shrine. The central depiction of *The Last Supper* on the altar immediately makes a strong impact on the viewer. Christ is giving Judas the morsel of bread, marking him as the traitor, while the apostle John leans on Christ's bosom. The altar wings show the entry of Christ into Jerusalem (on the left) and Christ praying in the Garden of Gethsemane (on the right). Erhard Harschner, Rothenburg's master craftsman, is credited with the casing. The fine painted-glass windows in the choir date from the late-Gothic period. To the left is the tabernacle (ca. 1400), a place of sanctuary for condemned criminals.

Klostergasse 15. ☎ **09861/700620.** Admission 2€ adults, .50€ children. Apr-Oct Mon-Sat 9am-5:30pm, Sun 11am-5:30pm; Dec daily 10am-5pm; Nov and Jan-Mar daily 10am-noon and 2-4pm.

Where to Eat

Hotel Mittermeier Restaurant ★★★ FRANCONIAN/INTERNATIONAL   One of the great restaurants along the Romantic Road, this hotel is the domain of

Christian Mittermeier, whose original take on Franconian cuisine is a gastronomic beacon. He is an inventive chef who can delight you with the subtlety and flavor of his cooking, based on only the freshest of ingredients. With its garden terrace, the restaurant offers inviting service and near-faultless cuisine. Lunch menus are often ignored by chefs who concentrate on dinner. Not so here. On offer are such lunch dishes as slices of bison rib-eye on wild garlic with risotto or "on the skin" roast pike-perch with a potato and poppy seed roulade. You can finish off with a delectable cara-mel rhubarb cake. Dinner is even more elaborate, with such heavenly delights as a Ligurian fish soup with Tahiti vanilla, Norway lobster, and fresh mint. Main dishes tend to be sublime, including a roasted ridge of suckling pig on leaf spinach or else truffled filet of salmon with crayfish in puff pastry. We still remember the parfait of passion fruit with fresh raspberries and rose water sorbet.

Vorm Würzburger Tor 7-9. (℗ **09861/94540.** www.villamittermeier.de. Reservations required. Main courses 14€–32€; 4-course fixed-price menu 79€. AE, DC, MC, V. Tues–Sat noon–2pm and 7–9:30pm.

Ratsstube FRANCONIAN   This restaurant enjoys a position right on the market square, so expect a bustling center of activity throughout the day. Inside, a true tavern atmosphere prevails with hardwood chairs and tables, vaulted ceilings, and pierced copper lanterns. A recently added replica of the market square's Glockenspiel hangs in the rear, and may put on a show during your dinner. Downstairs you'll find a wine bar offering live music periodically. The a la carte menu of Franconian wines and dishes includes *Sauerbraten* and venison, both served with fresh vegetables and pota-toes. For dessert, you can order homemade Italian ice cream and espresso.

Marktplatz 6. (℗**09861/5511.** www.ratsstuberothenburg.de. Reservations recommended. Main courses 10€–15€. MC, V. Mon–Sat 9am–10pm; Sun 9am–6pm.

Shopping

Friese-Kabalo Kunstgewerbe OHG, Grüner Markt 7 (℗ **09861/7166**), special-izes in cuckoo clocks and also carries Hummel figurines, pewter beer steins, music boxes, and dolls. It's Christmas every day at Käthe Wohlfahrt's **Weihnachtswerk-statt (Christmas Workshop),** Herrngasse 1 (℗ **098614090**), which is filled with shops carrying everything from clothing and accessories to cuckoo clocks, but the real attractions are locally made toys and Christmas ornaments. If you collect teddy bears, you'll love **Teddyland,** Herrngasse 10 (℗ **09861/8904;** www.teddyland.de), which stocks more than 5,000 of them, the largest teddy bear population in Germany. Bear images are printed on everything from T-shirts to bags and watches.

Entertainment & Nightlife

The best memory some people have of Rothenburg ob der Tauber is following the cloaked **night watchman** with his lantern and halberd through the quiet cobble-stone streets of the old town, as he recounts historical episodes of hardship in the medieval days. From mid-March to December, he makes his rounds from the Mark-tplatz at 8pm in English and 9:30pm in German, with a fee of 7€ for adults and 4€ for children 17 and under.

The most idyllic place to go in the evening is **Unter den Linden,** at Kurze Steige 7B (℗ **09861/5909**), a cafe-bar on the River Tauber. You reach it by going under the arch at St. Jakobskirche and following Klingengasse through the town gate, heading down a path to Detwang. The cafe is open April to October, daily 10am to 10pm, but it shortens its hours in winter, depending on weather.

Where to Stay

EXPENSIVE

Burg Hotel ★   Tucked down the end of a lane, this old-fashioned timbered house overlooks the Tauber Valley making you understand why it's called "over the Tauber." The rooms, with spacious bathrooms, cover three floors (without an elevator). Nos. 7, 12, and 25 afford the best views. Herr Berger is proud of the newly installed basement spa with a sauna, tanning bed, whirlpool, and musical accompaniment. Parking is in the barn of a former Dominican monastery.

Klostergasse 1-3, 91541 Rothenburg ob der Tauber. www.burghotel.eu. ℂ **09861/94890.** Fax 09861/948940. 15 units. 100€–170€ double; from 170€ suite. Rates include buffet breakfast. AE, MC, V. Parking 7.50€. **Amenities:** Bikes; spa; tanning bed; Wi-Fi. *In room:* TV, hair dryer, minibar.

Eisenhut ★★★   The distinguished "Iron Helmet" is the most celebrated inn on the Romantic Road and one of the finest small hotels in Germany. Although rather expensive it's worth the money and its popularity vouches for that. The castle-like interior spreads out over four patrician houses dating from the 14th and 15th-century in the heart of the town. Each room is unique: ranging from modest to grandiose. The various luxurious touches include hand-carved and monumental pieces, a tufted satin headboard, bedside controls, spacious bathrooms, and ample closet space.

Herrengasse 3-5, 91541 Rothenburg ob der Tauber. www.eisenhut.com. ℂ **09861/7050.** Fax 09861/70545. 89 units. 90€–200€ double; 200€–300€ suite. AE, DC, MC, V. Parking 10€. **Amenities:** Restaurant; room service. *In room:* TV, hair dryer, minibar, Wi-Fi (5€ per hour).

Romantik Hotel Markusturm ★★   This is one of Rothenburg's gems, without the facilities and modern amenities of the Eisenhut, but a winner in its own right. When this hotel was constructed as a customs house in 1264, one of Rothenburg's defensive walls was incorporated into the building. Some rooms have four-poster beds, and the individual decorations range from contemporary to antique (Biedermeier or Empire, for example). Dare you ask for a room called an "Oasis of Dreams" done in Laura Ashley? Many guests request room no. 30, a cozy attic retreat. The hotel employs one of the most helpful staffs in town.

Rödergasse 1, 91541 Rothenburg ob der Tauber www.markusturm.de. ℂ **09861/94280.** Fax 09861/9428113. 25 units. 125€–190€ double. Rates include buffet breakfast. AE, DC, MC, V. Parking 12€. **Amenities:** Restaurant; room service. *In room:* TV, hair dryer, Wi-Fi (free).

MODERATE

Hotel Rappen   Located a stone's throw from the Gallows Gate, this comfortable hotel doesn't suffer from the summer crowds and parking fees of other hotels, while maintaining all the charm of old Rothenburg. The building, constructed in 1603, began as a Christian hospice and later served as the post depot. Antique furnishings like a sewing machine, crib, and spinning wheel in the halls give a nostalgic touch to the historical premises, which includes the rustic Weinstube Rappenschmiede tavern with its 200-year-old beams. The spacious rooms feature more contemporary comforts and furniture. A hit with motorists, its on-site free parking is a huge bonus in a town known for its parking woes and fees. The ground-floor restaurant dishes out delicious *Pfannkuchen*, German-style pancakes that fill the pan.

Vorm Würzburger Tor 6-10, 91541 Rothenburg ob der Tauber. www.hotel-rappen-rothenburg.de. ℂ **09861/95710.** Fax 09861/6076. 104 units. 75€–95€ double; from 125€ suite. Rates include breakfast. AE, MC, V. Free parking. **Amenities:** Restaurant, room service, Wi-Fi (free; in lobby). *In room:* TV.

Hotel Reichs-Küchenmeister ★ We are very partial to this hotel, one of the town's oldest structures. Although it sustained damage in a World War II firestorm, a massive, thoroughly sensitive restoration has rendered it both stylish and well equipped. Rooms are furnished with regional wooden furniture; some contain minibars. Bathrooms are a bit small, but maintenance is tidy. Seventeen less expensive rooms are in a less desirable annex across the street.

Kirchplatz 8 (near St. Jakobskirche), 91541 Rothenburg ob der Tauber. www.reichskuechenmeister.com. ✆ **09861/9700.** Fax 19861/970409. 45 units. 75€–120€ double; 160€–225€ suite for 2; 160€–225€ suite for 5. Rates include buffet breakfast. AE, DC, MC, V. Parking 5€ in the lot; 8€ in the garage. **Amenities:** Restaurant; bar; bikes; Jacuzzi; sauna. *In room:* TV, hair dryer, minibar (in some).

INEXPENSIVE

Bayerischer Hof This little B&B doesn't even try to compete with the grand inns of the town, offering ideal access between the train station and the medieval walled city. In spite of the sterile exterior, owners Petra and Harald Schellhaas extend a warm welcome and maintain clean, well-furnished accommodations full of cozy Bavarian touches such as traditionally painted furniture. Rooms and shower-only bathrooms are small, but the housekeeping is excellent and the staff is most hospitable.

Ansbacher Strasse 21, 91541 Rothenburg ob der Tauber. www.bayerischerhof.com. ✆ **09861/6063.** Fax 09861/86561. 9 units. 62€–105€ double. Rates include continental breakfast. MC, V. Free parking. Closed Jan. **Amenities:** Restaurant; bar. *In room:* TV.

Gasthof Goldener Greifen ★ The Klingler family proves that the essence of a stay lies in the hospitality, not just the furnishings. Originally mayor Heinrich Toppler's house, this 14th-century dwelling has been a hotel ever since, with a splendid upper floor common area that hasn't changed much over the 650 or so years. Recent renovations have resulted in larger family-friendly rooms. Have breakfast in the mayor's old office with a well-preserved oven-looking closet for his parchments. The restaurant specializes in Franconian fare with tasty dishes like marinated beef, and moist roast goose leg soaked in an unforgettable gravy, and a side of red kraut and potato dumplings. Try it with the bold Taubertäler red wine from Lauda-Königshofen.

Obere Schmiedgasse 5 (off Marktplatz), 91541 Rothenburg ob der Tauber. www.gasthof-greifen-rothenburg.de. ✆ **09861/2281.** Fax 09861/86374. 14 units. 65€–90€ double. Rates include buffet breakfast. AE, MC, V. Free parking. Closed Dec 22–Jan 3. **Amenities:** Room service. *In room:* TV (in most), no phone.

DINKELSBÜHL ★

93km (58 miles) SW of Nürnberg, 114km (71 miles) NE of Stuttgart, 105km (65 miles) SE of Würzburg

Dinkelsbühl sits like a gabled, half-timbered wonderland with pastel colors, burgundy shudders, and that typically German *Fraktur* script bedecking its facades. A complete ring of medieval fortifications surrounds the town, with 18 towers offering views of the sea of sienna tiles and storks roosting on the rooftops. The generally provincial atmosphere swells in the summertime like many towns along the Romantic Road, but offers respite from the crowds in its cellar restaurants, and outlying parks and paths.

Essentials

GETTING THERE

By Train The nearest train station is in Dombühl, a small station on the line between Crailsheim and Ansbach, which has several daily connections to Munich,

Nürnberg, and Stuttgart. From Dombühl, Dinkelsbühl can be reached by bus, taking 30 minutes. Train rides from Munich or Frankfurt take about 2½ to 3 hours, depending on the connection. For rail information, call ✆ **01805/996633** or visit www.bahn.de.

By Bus   For bus service along the Romantic Road, see "Bus Tours of the Romantic Road," at the beginning of this chapter. Buses run by **Omnibusverkehr Franken** (✆ **0931/3528940;** www.ovf.de) link Dinkelsbühl with local towns, including three to five buses a day via Dombühl to Rothenburg ob der Tauber and five to six buses a day to Nördlingen. Contact Tourist Information for exact times and points of departure.

By Car   Follow the "Romantische Strasse" signs south from Rothenburg ob der Tauber, or hop on the A-7 Autobahn south to exit 112 and head east. The B-25 connects Dinkeslbühl to Nördlingen and Donauwörth.

VISITOR INFORMATION

Contact **Touristik Service Dinkelsbühl,** Altrathaus 14 (✆ **09851/902440**), open May through October Monday to Friday 9am to 6pm, Saturday, Sunday, and holidays 10am to 5pm; November to April hours are daily 10am 5pm.

SPECIAL EVENTS   This dreamy village awakens for 10 days in July for the **Kinderzeche (Children's Festival),** which commemorates the saving of the village by its children in 1632. According to the story, the children pleaded with conquering Swedish troops to leave their town without pillaging and destroying it—and got their wish. The pageant includes concerts given by the local boys' band dressed in historic military costumes. For more information, check out **www.kinderzeche.de**.

Exploring Dinkelsbühl

Dinkelsbühl is a lively, wonderfully preserved medieval town, full of narrow, cobblestone streets. You may begin exploring at the 14th-century gateway, **Rothenburger Tor,** and then head down the wide Martin Luther Strasse to the market square. Along the way, you can take in the town's fine collection of early Renaissance burghers' houses.

Dinkelsbühl's main attraction is the late-Gothic **Münster St. Georg,** on Marktplatz, built between 1448 and 1499 around a Romanesque doorway dating from ca. 1220. Along with the 15th-century Holy Cross altar and pillar sculptures, notice the St. Sebastian Altar with St. Christopher and St. James, denoted by the scallop shell. Below lie the bejeweled remains of St. Aurelius, a Roman saint beheaded under Emperor Nero. Also worth a look is the **Haus der Geschichte Dinkelsbühl,** Altrathausplatz 14 (✆ **09851 902 440;** www.hausdergeschichte-dinkelsbühl.de), which provides an excellent overview of the pivotal periods of the town's history including the Reformation and the Thirty Years' War. Its art gallery reflects the 19th-century era when it became a painters' haunt. One of them, Joseph Kühn Jr., arrived here in 1901 and bequeathed his collection, including one of two paintings by Schmidt-Rotluff whose postexpressionist *Bäuerlinsturm* (1938) hangs on the third floor. The top floor displays a 1926 model of the city as it would have looked in medieval times.

The best evening activity here is to take a **walk** around the ramparts. Just as in medieval times, the **night watchman** makes his round from Münster St. Georg through the town daily at 9pm from May to October, and only Saturdays from November to April.

Where to Eat & Stay

Blauer Hecht ★ This inn does the best job of making you feel like you're in someone's home, from antique furnishings to the family pictures on the wall. In spite of its penchant for keeping things classical, it is the only hotel within the town walls that has a modern indoor pool and sauna. The three elegant hand-built stories of stucco, stone, and tile date from the 17th century. Rooms tend to be on the smaller side, but provide just as much comfort and quiet. The breakfast buffet is excellent and copious, but the owners don't approve of packing a sandwich for the road.

Schweinemarkt 1, 91150 Dinkelsbühl. www.blauer-hecht.de. ℂ **09851/5810.** Fax 09851/581170. 44 units. 90€–98€ double; 115€ suite. Rates include continental breakfast. AE, MC, V. Parking 8€. **Amenities:** Restaurant; bar; indoor heated pool; sauna. *In room:* TV, minibar, Wi-Fi (2€ per hour).

Deutsches Haus ★ The most central of hotels in town boasts the finest furnishings and that dignified air of tradition that you'd expect from the most central hotel in town. The facade and structure date to 1440 but the renovated interior reflects a homogenous synthesis between old and new. Ornate wood-panel doors and molded ceilings meld with modern touches like the walk-in showers on granite. Rooms either overlook the lively Weinmarkt in town or the quiet, gabled courtyard. Each room is cozy and comfortable in its own way, with a ceramic stove, or a Biedermeier desk, or a four-poster bed as a centerpiece. Even if you don't stay here, you may want to dine in the **Altdeutsches Restaurant,** one of the finest in Dinkelsbühl. It's intimate and convivial, and serves Franconian and regional specialties.

Weinmarkt 3, 91550 Dinkelsbühl www.deutsches-haus-dkb.de.. ℂ **09851/6058.** Fax 09851/7911. 18 units. 129€ double; 140€–160€ suite. Rates include continental breakfast. AE, MC, V. Parking 8€. Closed Jan 8–Feb 1. **Amenities:** Restaurant; bikes. *In room:* TV, hair dryer, minibar, Wi-Fi (free).

Eisenkrug ★★ The affable Keck family operates this hotel-cum-tavern built in a 1620 edifice overlooking the old market. Following a 2009 renovation, the rooms and bathrooms feel brand new, with a modest amount of decoration that feels authentic. Its restaurant in the vaulted Reichstadtkeller features thick pillars giving off a true medieval atmosphere. (Are those shackles on the wall?) The constantly changing menu features a variety of local dishes such as the *Schwein Rückensteak* (pork loin) with *Speckbohnen* (beans and bacon) and *Bratkartoffeln* (baked potatoes). Other tasty offerings include an onion *Rostbraten* with buttered *Spätzle,* or a *Rotbarschfilet* (red perch) with potato salad.

Dr. Martin-Luther-Strasse 1, 91550 Dinkelsbühl. www.hotel-eisenkrug.de. ℂ **09851/57700.** Fax 09851/577070. 13 units. 64€–91€ double. Rates include continental breakfast. MC, V. Free parking. **Amenities:** 2 restaurants. *In room:* TV, hair dryer, minibar, Wi-Fi (free).

NÖRDLINGEN ★

130km (81 miles) NW of Munich, 95km (59 miles) SW of Nürnberg

Along with Rothenburg ob der Tauber and Dinkelsbühl, Nördlingen still stands within its original medieval walls, in part thanks to a 1826 law by the Romantic king himself, Ludwig I, preventing the dismantling of them. Things are rather tranquil around Nördlingen today; nonetheless, the town still employs sentries to sound the reassuring message, *"So G'sell so"* ("All is well"), as they did in the Middle Ages.

The town sits in a gigantic crater called the Ries. Once thought to be the crater of an extinct volcano, it is now known that the Ries was created by a meteorite at least half a mile in diameter. It struck the ground some 15 million years ago at more than

72,500kmph (45,000 mph). Today the Ries is the best-preserved and most scientifically researched meteorite crater on earth.

Essentials

GETTING THERE

BY PLANE　The nearest major airport is in Nürnberg; from there you can make either bus or rail connections to Nördlingen.

BY TRAIN　Nördlingen lies on the main Nördlingen-Aalen-Stuttgart line, with frequent connections in all directions. Call ✆ **01805/996633** or visit www.bahn.de for schedules and more information. Nördlingen can be reached from Stuttgart in 2 hours, from Nürnberg in 2 hours, and from Augsburg in 1 hour.

BY BUS　For bus service along the Romantic Road, see "Bus Tours of the Romantic Road," at the beginning of this chapter. Local buses also make the trip from Dinkelsbühl; contact the Tourist Information for times and departure points.

BY CAR　Access by car is via the A7 Autobahn north and south and Rte. 29 from the east. From Dinkelsbühl, take Rte. 25 south.

VISITOR INFORMATION

Contact the **Verkehrsamt,** Marktplatz 2 (✆ **09081/84116;** www.noerdlingen.de), open Easter to October Monday to Thursday 9:30am to 6pm, Friday 9:30am to 4:30pm, and Saturday 10am to 2pm; November to Easter, hours are Monday to Thursday 9:30am to 5pm, and Friday 9:30am to 3:30pm; May to September, it's open Sunday 10am to 2pm.

Exploring Nördlingen

You can walk around the town on the covered parapet on top of the perfectly preserved walls. Along the way, you'll pass 11 towers and five fortified gates. At the center of the circular Altstadt, within the walls, is **Rübenmarkt.** If you stand in this square on market day, you'll be swept into a world of the past—the country people here have preserved many traditional customs and costumes, which, along with the ancient houses, evoke a living medieval city. Around the square are a number of buildings, including the Gothic **Rathaus.** An antiquities collection is displayed in the **Stadtmuseum,** Vordere Gerbergasse 1 (✆ **09081/2738230;** www.stadtmuseum-noerdlingen.de), which is open March to October Tuesday to Sunday 1:30 to 4:30pm. Admission is 4€ for adults and 3€ for children.

　St. Georgskirche ★, on the square's northern side, is one of the town's oldest buildings, and its most striking sight. This Gothic-Hall church dates from the 15th century. Plaques and epitaphs commemorating the town's more illustrious 16th- and 17th-century residents decorate the fan-vaulted interior. Although the original altarpiece by Friedrich Herlin (1462) is now in the Reichsstadtmuseum in Rothenburg, a portion of it depicting the Crucifixion, by Nikolaus Gerhart van Leydeu, remains in the church. Above the high altar stands a more elaborate baroque altarpiece. The church's most prominent feature, however, is the 90m (300-ft.) French Gothic tower, called the "Daniel." At night, the town watchman calls out from the steeple, his voice ringing through the streets. The tower is accessible daily April to October from 9am to 8pm, and admission is 2€ for adults and 1€ for students and children. It's free to visit the church, which is open Easter to October Monday to Friday 9:30am to 12:30pm and 2 to 5pm, and Saturday and Sunday 9:30am to 5pm.

Rieskrater-Museum, Eugene-Shoemaker-Platz 1 (𝒸 **09081/84710;** www.
rieskratermuseum,de), documents the impact of the meteorite that crashed into the
earth here on the Alb plateau nearly 15 million years ago. Hours are May to October
Tuesday to Sunday 10am to 4:30pm; November to April Tuesday to Sunday 10am to
noon and 1:30 to 4:30pm. Admission is 4€ for adults, 1.50€ for students and children
ages 6 through 11, and free for children 5 and under.

Where to Eat

Meyers-Keller ★ CONTINENTAL   The conservative, modern decor here seems
a suitable setting for the restrained *neue Küche* style of the talented chef and owner,
Joachim Kaiser. The cuisine changes according to the availability of ingredients and
the inspiration of the chef; typical selections are likely to include roulade of sea wolf,
salmon with baby spinach and wild rice, and John Dory with champagne-flavored
tomato sauce. There's also an impressive array of European wines, many reasonably
priced.

Marienhöhe 8. 𝒸 **09081/4493.** www.meyerskeller.de. Reservations required. Main courses 16€–24€;
fixed-price menu 75€–119€. AE, MC, V. Wed–Sun 11:30am–2pm; Tues–Sun 5:30–10pm. 2km (1¼ mile)
south of Nördlingen.

Where to Stay

Kaiser Hotel Sonne ★   The Sonne is in a bull's-eye position next to the cathedral
and the Rathaus. It has a heady atmosphere from having entertained so many illustrious personalities since it opened as an inn in 1405. Among its guests have been
emperors, kings, and princes, including Friedrich III, Maximilian I, and Karl V; the
great poet Goethe; and, in more recent times, American astronauts. Many of the
rooms contain hand-painted four-poster beds. Each is midsize to spacious, and most
are tastefully and comfortably furnished, with excellent bathrooms.

Marktplatz 3, 86720 Nördlingen. www.kaiserhof-hotel-sonne.de. 𝒸 **09081/5067.** Fax 09081/23999. 43
units, 35 with bathroom. 65€ double without bathroom; 80€ double with bathroom; 100€ suite. Rates
include continental breakfast. AE, DC, MC, V. Parking 7.80€. **Amenities:** Restaurant; bar; babysitting;
room service. *In room:* TV, hair dryer, Internet (5€ per day), minibar.

NH Klösterle Nördlingen ★★   With the NH brand of Spanish-bred luxury, you
can expect the best and most luxurious accommodations in town. This historic,
white-sided, red-roofed building was originally constructed as a monastery in the
1200s. Since then, its ziggurat-shaped gables and steep roof have been an essential
part of Nördlingen's medieval center. The hotel offers elevator access and a hardworking, polite staff. Guest rooms have dark-wood fixtures and larger-than-expected
bathrooms.

Beim Klösterle 1, 86720 Nördlingen. www.nh-hotels.de. 𝒸 **09081/87080.** Fax 09081/8708100. 98
units. 80€–145€ double. Rates include buffet breakfast. AE, DC, MC, V. Parking 10€. **Amenities:** 2 restaurants; bar; bikes; exercise room; indoor heated pool; room service; sauna. *In room:* TV, hair dryer,
minibar.

DONAUWÖRTH

40km (25 miles) N of Augsburg, 11km (7 miles) S of Harburg, 95km (59 miles) NW of Munich

Visitors come to Donauwörth for its architecture and sense of history rather than for
specific attractions. The town is located on what was the last navigable point on the
Danube, which led to its becoming a key stop on the trade route between Augsburg

and Nürnberg. Its attempted capture by the Imperial Party in 1608 led directly to the division of Germany into warring Protestant and Catholic military alliances, resulting in the Thirty Years' War.

The oldest part of town sits on an island in the middle of the stream, access to which is via the oldest surviving gate in town, the **Riederstor,** which funnels traffic along the island's most historic and evocative street, the **Reichsstrasse.** Donauwörth was badly damaged in World War II bombing raids in 1945, but it has been carefully restored. Parts of the town's fortifications have survived.

Essentials

GETTING THERE

BY TRAIN   Trains arrive from Augsburg at 30-minute intervals throughout the day (trip time: 35–45 min.). Trains also come hourly from Munich (trip time: 1 hr.). For information, call ✆ **01805/996633** or visit www.bahn.de.

BY BUS   For bus service along the Romantic Road, see "Bus Tours of the Romantic Road," at the beginning of this chapter.

BY CAR   From Augsburg, follow Rte. 2 north. From Nördlingen, take Rte. 25.

VISITOR INFORMATION

Tourist-Information is at Rathausgasse 1 (✆ **0906/789151;** www.donauwoerth. de). It's open May to September Monday through Friday 9am to noon and 1 to 6pm, Saturday and Sunday 3 to 6pm. October through April it's open Monday through Thursday 9am to noon and 1 to 5pm, Friday 9am to 1pm.

Exploring Donauwörth

The current baroque building of the dominating **Klosteranlage Heilig Kreuz,** or Monastery of the Holy Cross, dates from 1720, but its history began when Count Mangold I brought back a relic of Emperor Constantine's mother from Byzantium in 1030. It's an outstanding example of the distinctive churches built and decorated in the school of Wessobrunn, which flourished in the 17th and 18th centuries and often employed elaborate stucco decorations.

The site that draws the greatest numbers of visitors is the **Käthe-Kruse-Puppen-Museum,** Pflegstrasse 21a (✆ **0906/789170**). Inside, you'll find a small-scale collection of the dolls and dollhouses that were designed by master artisan Käthe-Kruse, whose most prolific period during the 1950s and 1960s has been called a high point in the history of doll making. April to October, it's open Tuesday to Sunday 2 to 5pm; November to March it is open Wednesday, Saturday, and Sunday 2 to 5pm. Entrance costs 2.50€ for adults, 1.50€ for children and students.

Where to Eat & Stay

Posthotel Traube ★   This hotel dates from the 1600s, with a guest list that included Goethe and Mozart. Despite a few modern conveniences, there's still the definite sense of old Europe here, thanks to a somewhat creaky staff and a no-nonsense approach to innkeeping. Rooms are nostalgically outfitted with engravings and prints of old-fashioned Germany. This is a comfortable choice with midsize to spacious bedrooms. Perhaps some of the furnishings show too much wear and tear, but tradition-minded guests like it here. Each bathroom is midsize to roomy, most often with a tub/shower combination.

On the premises is a restaurant that serves solid, reliable dishes, not inventive in any way, but hearty and filling. These Franconian recipes have been around for generations.

Kapellstrasse 14–16, 86609 Donauwörth. www.posthoteltraube.de. (C) **0906/706440.** 43 units. 85€–90€ double. Rates include continental breakfast. MC, V. **Amenities:** Restaurant; sauna. *In room:* TV, hair dryer.

AUGSBURG

68km (42 miles) NW of Munich, 80km (50 miles) E of Ulm, 160km (100 miles) SE of Stuttgart

Augsburg's 2,000 years of history have made it one of southern Germany's major sightseeing attractions. It's the Romantic Road's largest town and serves as a gateway to the Alps and the south.

Augsburg was founded under Emperor Tiberius in 15 B.C., though little remains from this period. On the other hand, the wealth of art and architecture from the Renaissance is staggering. Augsburg has hosted many distinguished visitors and boasts an array of famous native sons, including painters Hans Holbein the Elder and the Younger and playwright Bertolt Brecht. In 1518, Martin Luther was summoned to Augsburg to recant his 95 theses before a papal emissary. Today, Augsburg, with a population of about 250,000, is an important industrial center and Bavaria's third-largest city, after Munich and Nürnberg.

Essentials

GETTING THERE

BY TRAIN About 90 InterCity trains arrive here daily from all major German cities. For information, call (C) **01805/996633** or visit www.bahn.de. There are 60 trains a day from Munich (trip time: 30–50 min.) and 35 from Frankfurt (3–4½ hr.).

BY BUS For bus service along the Romantic Road, see "Bus Tours of the Romantic Road," at the beginning of this chapter.

BY CAR Access is via the A8 Autobahn east and west. From Donauwörth, take Rte. 2 south.

VISITOR INFORMATION

Contact **Tourist-Information,** Schiessgrabenstrasse 14 ((C) **0821/502070;** www. regio-augsburg.de), open Monday to Friday 9am to 6pm.

GETTING AROUND The Augsburger Verkehrs Verbund Gmbh (**0821/157000;** www.avv-augsburg.de) oversees the public transportation in Augsburg, consisting of four tram lines and 31 bus lines. They operate daily from 5am to midnight.

Exploring Augsburg

Extending southward from the Rathaus is the wide **Maximilianstrasse ★**, lined with shops and old burghers' houses and studded with fountains by the Renaissance Dutch sculptor Adrien de Vries.

Dom St. Maria CHURCH The cathedral of Augsburg has the distinction of containing the oldest stained-glass windows in the world. These Romanesque windows, dating from the 12th century, are in the south transept and depict Old Testament prophets in a severe but colorful style. They are younger than the cathedral itself, which was begun in 944 and partially Gothicized in the 14th century. The cathedral's interior, restored in 1934, contains side altars with altarpieces by Hans Holbein the Elder and Christoph Amberger. You'll find the ruins of the original basilica in the crypt beneath the west chancel.

The original 11th-century bronze doors, adorned with bas-reliefs of a mixture of biblical and mythological characters, are now located in the adjacent **Diözesanmuseum St. Afra** (𝄞 0821/3166333; www.bistum-augsburg.de), open Tuesday to Saturday 10am to 5pm and Sunday noon to 6pm. Admission is 4€ for adults, and 3€ for children and students.

Hoher Weg. 𝄞 **0821/3166353.** Free admission. Mon–Sat 7am–5pm; Sun noon–5pm. Tram: 1.

Fuggerei ★ HISTORIC INTEREST   During the 15th and 16th centuries, Augsburg became one of Europe's wealthiest communities, mainly because of its textile industry and the political and financial clout of its two banking families, the Welsers and the Fuggers. The Welsers have long since faded away. But the founders of the powerful Fugger family have established themselves permanently by an unusual legacy, the Fuggerei, set up in 1519, by Jakob Fugger the Rich, to house poorer Augsburgers. It's Europe's oldest welfare housing.

The basic features, laid down in 1521, are still in force today. The nominal rent of 1€ per annum (formerly one Rhenish guilder) has not changed in more than 450 years (the city council determines who gets the break—it's based on need). The only obligation is that tenants pray daily for the souls of their founders. The Fuggerei is a miniature, self-contained town with its own gates, which are shut from 10pm to 5am and guarded by a night watchman. Franz Mozart—great-grandfather of Wolfgang Amadeus Mozart—once lived at Mittlere Gasse 14.

A house at Mittlere Gasse 13, next to the one once occupied by Mozart's ancestor, is now the Fuggerei's **museum.** The rough 16th- and 17th-century furniture, wood-paneled ceilings and walls, and cast-iron stove, as well as other objects of everyday life, show what it was like to live here in earlier times.

At the end of Vorderer Lech. 𝄞 **0821/3198810.** www.fuggerei.de. Museum 4€ adults, 3€ students and children. Museum Apr–Sept daily 8am–8pm; Oct–Mar daily 9am–6pm. Tram: 1.

Rathaus HISTORIC BUILDING   In 1805 and 1809, Napoleon visited the Rathaus, built by Elias Holl in 1620. Regrettably, the building was also visited by an air raid in 1944, leaving it a mere shell of what had once been a palatial eight-story monument to the glory of the Renaissance. The original Goldener Saal (Golden Chamber), also laid to ruin, has been resurrected to its original form for the public to enjoy. Walking tours offer a view of the spacious chamber, celebrated for its imposing portals, gold-leaf coffered ceilings, and huge wall frescoes.

Am Rathausplatz 2. 𝄞 **0821/3242120.** Admission 2€ adults, 1€ children 7–14, free for children 6 and under. Daily 10am–6pm. Tram: 1.

St. Ulrich und St. Afra Kirche ★ CHURCH   Near the southern end of Maximilianstrasse is the Hercules Fountain, and behind it, the most attractive ecclesiastical compound in Augsburg. The churches of St. Ulrich and St. Afra were constructed between 1476 and 1500 on the site of a Roman temple. As a tribute to the 1555 Peace of Augsburg, which recognized two denominations, one Roman Catholic and the other Lutheran, these two separate churches—Catholic Basilika St. Ulrich und Afra and Protestant St.- Ulrichs-Kirche—stand next to each other. The churches are mainly 15th-century Gothic with baroque overlays. St. Afra is the most elaborate,

Augsburg

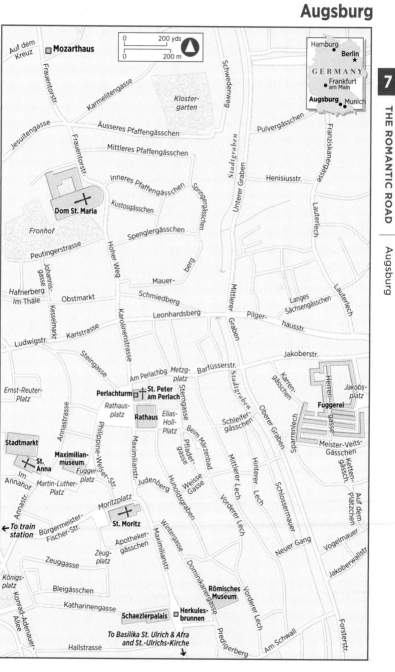

Mozarthaus

| 0 | 200 yds |
| 0 | 200 m |

Hamburg
Berlin ★
GERMANY
Frankfurt am Main
Augsburg ● ● Munich

Auf dem Kreuz
Frauentorstr.
Karmelitengasse
Klostergarten
Schwedenweg
Äusseres Pfaffengässchen
Pulvergässchen
Jesuitengasse
Mittleres Pfaffengässchen
Franziskanergasse
Frauentorstr.
Inneres Pfaffengässchen
Spenglergässchen
Henisiusstr.
Dom St. Maria
Kustosgässchen
Stadtgraben
Unterer Graben
Lauterlech
Fronhof
Spenglergässchen
Peutingerstrasse
Hoher Weg
berg
Mauer-
Langes Sächsengässchen
Lauterlech
Johannis-gasse
Hafnerberg
Im Thäle
Obstmarkt
Schmiedberg
Mittlerer
Leonhardsberg
Pilger-
hausstr.
Ludwigstr.
Karlstrasse
Karolinenstrasse
Steingasse
Graben
Jakoberstr.
Ernst-Reuter-Platz
Am Perlachbg. Metzg-platz
Barfüsserstr.
Jakobs-platz
Perlachturm
St. Peter am Perlach
Sterngasse
Karren-gässchen
Herren-gasse
Fuggerei
Annastrasse
Rathaus-platz
Rathaus
Elias-Holl-Platz
Beim Märzenbad
Schleifer-gässchen
Oberer Graben
Sparrenlech
Meister-Veits-Gässchen
Stadtmarkt
Maximilian-museum
Pfladergasse
Mittlerer Lech
Hinterer Lech
Schlossermauer
Ketten-gässchen
St. Anna
Fugger-platz
Judenberg
Weisse Gasse
Vorderer Lech
Auf dem plätzchen
Im Annahof
Martin-Luther-Platz
Philippine-Welser-Str.
Maximilianstr.
Hunoldsgraben
Moritzplatz
St. Moritz
Wintergasse
Neuer Gang
Vogelmauer
To train station
Bürgermeister-Fischer-Str.
Apotheker-gässchen
Maximilianstr.
Dominikanergasse
Jakoberwallstr.
Königs-platz
Zeug-platz
Zeuggasse
Bleigässchen
Römisches Museum
Vorderer Lech
Konrad-Adenauer-Allee
Katharinengasse
Schaezlerpalais
Herkules-brunnen
Predigerberg
Am Schwall
Forsterstr.
To Basilika St. Ulrich & Afra and St.-Ulrichs-Kirche
Hallstrasse

with a magnificent altar and finely carved baroque railings bordering the entrance. St. Ulrich is the former monastery assembly hall, taken over by the Lutherans. The shared crypt contains the tombs of the two namesake saints. The lance and saddle of St. Ulrich are displayed in the sacristy.

Ulrichplatz 15. ⓒ **0821/345560.** Free admission. Daily 9am–5pm. Tram: 1.

Schaezlerpalais MUSEUM   The Schaezlerpalais, a 60-room mansion built between 1765 and 1770, has an amazing art collection. Most of the works in the collection are by German artists of the Renaissance and baroque periods, including Hans Holbein the Elder and Hans Burgkmair. One of the most famous paintings is Albrecht Dürer's portrait of Jakob Fugger the Rich. Rubens, Veronese, Tiepolo, and others are also represented. The palace-gallery also has a rococo ballroom, with gilded and mirrored wall panels and a ceiling fresco, *The Four Continents.* On April 28, 1770, Marie Antoinette danced the night away here.

Maximilianstrasse 46 (facing the Hercules Fountain). ⓒ **0821/3244102.** Admission 7€ adults, 5.50€ for students, children 9 and under free. Tues 10am–8pm; Wed–Sun 10am–5pm. Tram: 1.

Where to Eat

August ★★ INTERNATIONAL   This is the most sophisticated restaurant in town, with a social and culinary pedigree that's nothing short of spectacular. The cuisine is the inspired and innovative work of Chef Christian Grünewald, whose light textured emphasis on seasonal vegetables has elicited praise from local and national media. The set-price menu contains no fewer than 17 courses, and can be configured either as an all-vegetarian version or as a meat, fish, and vegetable version, depending on your wishes. Specific menu items change with the availability of ingredients, but examples are likely to include cannelloni stuffed with braised black trumpet mushrooms and apples; fresh goose liver with mandarin oranges, almonds, white carrots, and celery sauce; and a manioc-based risotto flavored with chives, black truffles, and Emmental cheese. In midsummer the entire venue moves up to the rooftop garden terrace, opening onto panoramic views of the city.

Frauentorstrasse 27. ⓒ **0821/35279.** Reservations strongly recommended. Set-price menus 99€–115€. MC, V. Wed–Sat 7–10pm. Closed 2 weeks in Jan and 2 weeks in Sept–Oct. Tram: 2.

Fuggerei Stube GERMAN/SWABIAN   Connected to the historic Fuggerei, this affordable restaurant can fit 60 people at a time into its large, *gemütlich* dining room. Expect generous portions of well-prepared food such as *Sauerbraten,* pork *Schnitzel,* game, and fish dishes. The beer foaming out of the taps here is Storchenbräu; most visitors find that it goes wonderfully with the conservative German specialties that are this establishment's forte.

Jakoberstrasse 26. ⓒ **0821/30870.** www.fuggerei-stube.de. Reservations recommended. Main courses 12€–24€. AE, MC, V. Tues–Sat 11:30am–2pm and 6–11pm; Sun and public holidays 11:30am–3pm. Tram: 1.

Haupt im Prinz Karl Palais ★★ GERMAN/INTERNATIONAL   It doesn't have quite the glamour of August, but this is one of the grandest restaurants in the Augsburg area. Under vaulted ceilings, with alfresco dining in midsummer, this deceptive restaurant only seems rustic. Its market-fresh cuisine strives for perfection and is backed up by a sound technique. Each dish is a laudable effort, and the menu is seasonally adjusted. For flavor, the chefs roam the world, borrowing a teriyaki sauce from Asia, mangoes from tropical countries, or truffles from Italy. Some of their soups are laced with curry or citrus. One dish combines *Fisch und Fleisch* (fish and meat) with fresh asparagus. Some of their veal and beef dishes are worthy of a prize.

Schertlinstrasse 23. ℂ **0821/5898475.** www.restaurant-haupt.de. Reservations required. 19€–26€; fixed-price menus 48€–68€. AE, MC, V. Tues–Sat 11:30am–2:30pm and 6:30–11:30pm.

Papageno ★ BAVARIAN/INTERNATIONAL One of the leading restaurants in this historic city, Papageno is a first-class establishment known for serving a series of the finest fixed-price menus along the Romantic Road. The cooking is very good indeed, based in part on local farm products. We savor such traditional dishes as veal cutlet schnitzels sautéed to a golden brown, or even such regional fare as calf's tongue in a savory caper sauce. The chefs also carefully craft a delectable osso buco along with an array of other dishes that are creative and sometimes wonderfully delicate. Food is also presented in an on-site Wintergarten.

Theaterstrasse 8. ℂ **0821/9076464.** www.papageno-restaurant.de. Reservations required. Main courses 9.50€–27€; fixed-price menus 52€ for 3-course, 61€ for 4-course, 77€ for 5-course. AE, MC, V. Tues–Sun 11:30am–2pm and 6–11pm.

Augsburg After Dark

Kongresshalle, Güggingerstrasse 10 (ℂ **0821/3242348;** tram: 1), presents concerts by the local ballet and opera companies and the chamber and symphony orchestras. Call for schedules, prices, and reservations. It's closed in August. The internationally renowned **Mozart Festival** is held in Augsburg every September. Contact the Tourist-Information office (see above) for details. In the courtyard of the Fugger Palace, the city hosts a **musical-theater** production each June and July. Tickets run 12€ to 40€. Information and reservations are available by calling the tourist office.

Maximilianstrasse, the main shopping street with its many cafes, continues to be the focus of nightlife after the shops close. **Brauereigasthaus Drei Königinnen,** Meister-Veits-Gässchen 32 (ℂ **0821/158405;** www.augusta-brauerei.de; tram: 2 or 4), doubles as an art gallery, has a pleasant beer garden that's open 1:30 to 10pm, and has a main restaurant/bar that closes at 8pm. Another garden/bar combo that keeps the same hours is **Thorbräu,** Wertachbrucker-Tor-Strasse 9 (ℂ **0821/36561;** www. thorbraeu.de; tram: 2 or 4). **Liliom,** Unterer Graben 1 (ℂ **0821/33724;** www. liliom.de; tram: 2 or 4), is equipped with a good stereo system to go with drinks and conversation; local artwork is often available for purchase. The bar is open Monday to Saturday 5pm to 12:30am and Sunday 3pm to midnight.

Where to Stay

Dom Hotel 🏆 The Dom Hotel lacks the decorative flair of its competitors, but it is a peaceful, comfortable hotel. That, combined with the moderate rates, makes this one of the most appealing choices in town. Across the street from Augsburg's famous cathedral, it features new furnishings and spotless bathrooms in historic environs. Rooms on most floors are medium in size, although we prefer the smaller attic accommodations, where you can rest under a beamed ceiling and enjoy a panoramic sweep of the rooftops of the city. Accommodations come with neatly tiled and efficiently organized compact bathrooms. Breakfast is the only meal served; during warm weather, it can be enjoyed in a garden beside the town's medieval fortifications.

Frauentorstrasse 8, 86152 Augsburg. www.domhotel-augsburg.de. ℂ **0821/343930.** Fax 0821/34393200. 52 units. 92€–135€ double; 116€–185€ suite. Rates include buffet breakfast. AE, DC, MC, V. Free parking in lot; 6€ in garage. Tram: 2. **Amenities:** Exercise room; indoor heated pool; sauna. *In room:* TV, hair dryer, minibar, Wi-Fi (free).

Privat Hotel Riegele ✒ The Schmid family welcomes you into its little hotel opposite the Hauptbahnhof (the main rail station). They run a neat, tidy hotel with midsize to spacious bedrooms, each with comfortably modern furnishings that are renewed as needed, along with highly polished, tiled private bathrooms. On-site is the **Restaurant Bräustüble,** a tavern patronized by locals as well as visitors for its hearty regional dishes. The breakfast buffet is one of the most generous in town.

Viktoriastrasse 4, 86150 Augsburg. www.hotel-riegele.de. ✆ **0821/509000.** Fax 0821/517746. 28 units. 89€–130€ double; extra bed 25€. Rates include buffet breakfast. AE, DC, MC, V. Free parking. **Amenities:** Restaurant; bar; room service. *In room:* TV, Wi-Fi (free).

Romantik Hotel Augsburger Hof ★ Originally built in 1767, this hotel is known for its traditional, romantic atmosphere with its thick, solid walls and exposed beams and timbers. The rooms range from small to spacious, with some exuding a country-romantic air. The "Romantik Room" almost seems entirely bedecked with wood. Some bathrooms seem crowded in as an afterthought, but each is beautifully maintained. Rooms overlooking the tranquil inner courtyard are more expensive than ones facing the street.

Auf dem Kreuz 2, 86152 Augsburg. www.augsburger-hof.de. ✆ **0821/343050.** Fax 0821/3430555. 36 units. 99€–140€ double. Rates include buffet breakfast. AE, DC, MC, V. Parking 7€. Tram: 2. **Amenities:** Restaurant; bar; room service; sauna. *In room:* TV, hair dryer, minibar, Wi-Fi (free).

Steigenberger Drei Mohren ★★ The original "Three Moors," dating from 1723, was one of the most renowned hotels in Germany before its destruction in a 1944 air raid. In 1956, it was reconstructed in a modern style in four- and five-story buildings. Following a 2011 renovation, it continues to be the premier hotel in town despite competition from the Romantik Hotel Augsburger Hof (see above). The drawing room contains a slatted natural-wood ceiling and walls, along with a roomwide mural of Old Augsburg. Guest rooms are comfortable and inviting, with thick carpets and double-glazed windows. Doubles vary in size and appointments, ranging from smaller, somewhat cramped quarters to more spacious accommodations.

Maximilianstrasse 40, 86150 Augsburg. www.augsburg.steigenberger.de. ✆ **800/223-5652** in the U.S. and Canada, or 0821/50360. Fax 0821/157864. 111 units. 110€–181€ double; 235€–650€ suite. Children 11 and under stay free in parent's room. AE, MC, V. Parking 14€. Tram: 1. **Amenities:** 2 restaurants; bar; babysitting; concierge; room service. *In room:* A/C (in some), TV, hair dryer, minibar, Wi-Fi (5€ per hour).

FÜSSEN ★

92km (57 miles) S of Augsburg, 119km (74 miles) SW of Munich

Füssen marks the end of the Romantic Road, just as it touches the foothills of the Bavarian Alps. The town is mainly a base for those going on to the castles at Neuschwanstein and Hohenschwangau, but it has a number of attractive buildings, including a 15th-century castle once used by the bishops of Augsburg as a summer palace. Füssen is also ideally located for excursions into the surrounding countryside.

Essentials

GETTING THERE

BY PLANE The nearest major airport is in Munich.

BY TRAIN Trains from Munich and Augsburg arrive frequently throughout the day. For information, call ✆ **01805/996633** or visit www.bahn.de. Train time from Munich is 2 hours, or 1 hour 45 minutes from Augsburg.

BY BUS   For bus service along the Romantic Road, see "Bus Tours of the Romantic Road," at the beginning of this chapter. Regional service is provided by **Regionalverkehr Oberbyaern** (*©* **089/551640;** www.rvo-bus.de), which runs 19 buses a day to the royal castles, costing 2.10€ for the 8-minute trip.

BY CAR   Access by car is via the A7 Autobahn from the north and also the B17 from Augsburg.

VISITOR INFORMATION

Contact the **Kurverwaltung,** Kaiser-Maximilian-Platz 1 (*©* **08362/93850;** www.fuessen.de). Hours vary but are usually Monday to Friday 8:30am to 6:30pm, Saturday 9am to 2:30pm, and Sunday 10am to noon in summer; and in winter Monday to Friday 9am to 5pm and Saturday 10am to noon.

Exploring Füssen

Füssen's main attraction is the **Hohes Schloss,** Magnusplatz (*©* **08362/903164**), one of the finest late-Gothic castles in Bavaria. It was once the summer residence of the prince-bishops of Augsburg. Inside, you can visit the Rittersaal (Knight's Hall), known for its stunning coffered ceiling. There's also a collection of Swabian artwork from the 1400s to the 1700s. The castle is open April to October Tuesday to Sunday 11am to 4pm, with hours reduced November to March to 2 to 4pm. Admission is 3€ for adults, free for children 13 and under.

Immediately below the castle lies the 8th-century **St. Mangkirche** and its **abbey** (*©* **08362/6190**), which was founded by the Benedictines and grew up on the site where St. Magnus died in 750. In the 18th century it was reconstructed in the baroque style, and in 1803 it was secularized. Free tours of the abbey are given July to September on Tuesday and Thursday at 4pm and on Saturday at 10:30am; in May, June, and October the schedule is Tuesday at 4pm and Saturday at 9:30am; and from January to April tours are on Saturday at 10:30am. In November and December you might be able to arrange a tour by contacting the Kurverwaltung (see above).

Within the abbey complex, signs point the way to the **Chapel of St. Anne,** where you can view the macabre *Totentanz* or "dance of death," painted by an unknown local artist in the early 15th century. It has a certain uncanny fascination. The chapel is open April to October Tuesday to Sunday 10am to 5pm, and November to March Tuesday to Sunday 1 to 4pm. Admission is free. Nearby is the **Heimatmuseum** (*©* **08362/903146**), which displays artifacts relating to the history and culture of the region, including a collection of musical instruments. It keeps the same hours as the chapel and charges 3€ to enter.

The principal shopping spot in town is the **Reichenstrasse,** which was known in Roman times as the Via Claudia. This cobblestone street is flanked with houses from the Middle Ages, most of which have towering gables.

Where to Eat

Fischerhütte ★ SEAFOOD   This restaurant is at the edge of the lake, within sight of dramatic mountain scenery. There are four gracefully paneled, old-fashioned dining rooms, and there's a terrace in summer. As its name (Fisherman's Cottage) suggests, the establishment specializes in seafood. Menu items read like an international atlas: one-half of an entire Alaskan salmon (for two); North Atlantic lobster; a garlicky version of French bouillabaisse; fresh Alpine trout, prepared pan-fried or with aromatic herbs in the style of Provence; and grilled halibut. A limited array of meat dishes is also offered, along with a selection of succulent desserts. In summer, a beer garden serves simple Bavarian specialties.

Uferstrasse 16 (5km/3 miles northwest of Füssen), Hopfen am See. ✆ **08362/91970.** www. fischerhuette-hopfen.de. Reservations recommended. Main courses 12€–28€. AE, DC, MC, V. Daily 10am–9:30pm.

Hotel Hirsch ★ BAVARIAN   *Hirsch* in German means stag, and the hotel's trademark sets the theme for its very Bavarian, almost folkloric, decor. Even if you're not staying here, you can visit for a meal, experiencing an authentic regional cuisine either in its Bierstube section or else in its more formal dining room. The menu is seasonally adjusted, with game specialties dominating in the autumn, including wild duck with blue cabbage and dumplings. Fresh trout comes from local rivers, and fish soup is often featured, as are a number of chicken and beef dishes. Desserts and breads are luscious.

The hotel also rents comfortably appointed and traditionally furnished bedrooms—ask for the King Maximilian Room or the King Ludwig Room. Doubles rent from 96€ to 147€, with themed suites going for 138€ to 180€. Free Wi-Fi is included.

Kaiser-Maximilian-Platz 7, Füssen 87629. ✆ **08362/93980.** Fax 08632/939877. www.hotelhirsch.de. Main courses 10€–18€; fixed-price menu 20€. AE, MC, V. Daily 11:30am–2pm and 6–9:30pm.

Where to Stay

In addition to the two choices listed here, the **Hotel Hirsch** (whose Bavarian restaurants are covered in the dining section, above) is also a fine choice.

Hotel Christine   The Christine is one of the best local choices. The staff spends the long winter months refurbishing the rooms so they'll be fresh and sparkling for spring visitors. Breakfast, the only meal served, is presented on beautiful regional china as classical music plays in the background. A Bavarian charm pervades the hotel, and the small- to medium-size rooms are very cozy, though hardly fit for King Ludwig II were he to return.

Weidachstrasse 31 (5-min. ride from the train station), 87629 Füssen. www.hotel-christine-fuessen.de. ✆ **08362/7229.** Fax 08362/940554. 13 units. 95€–130€ double. Rates include continental breakfast. MC, V. Free parking. Closed Jan 15–Feb 15. *In room:* TV, hair dryer.

Steig Mühle 🍴   Owners and hosts Gunter and Hedwig Buhmann like things to be cozy—their chaletlike guesthouse is almost a cliché of Bavarian charm. Rooms open onto a view of the lake or mountains, and many have their own balconies. They're furnished in a neat, functional style and kept immaculately clean. There aren't a lot of frills, but the place offers one of the best values in the area.

Alte Steige 3, 87629 Füssen-Weissensee. www.steigmuehle.de. ✆ **08362/91760.** Fax 08362/3148. 24 units. 54€–68€ double. Rates include buffet breakfast. No credit cards. Free outside parking; 3€ in garage. From Füssen, take Rte. 310 toward Kempten, a 5-min. drive. **Amenities:** Sauna. *In room:* TV.

Beyond Füssen: a Rococo Masterpiece

From Füssen, you can take a fascinating side trip to the **Wieskirche** ★★ (✆ **08862/932930;** www.wieskirche.de), one of the most extravagant Rococo buildings in the world, a masterpiece by Dominikus Zimmermann. The Wieskirche is a noted pilgrimage church, drawing visitors from all over the globe. It's located on the slopes of the Ammergau Alps between Ammer and Lech, in an Alpine meadow just off the Romantic Road near Steingaden, where there is a **visitor information office** (✆ **08862/200**). The staff at the office can give you a map and confirm that the church is open.

With the help of his brother, Johann Baptist, Zimmermann worked on this church from 1746 to 1754. Upon entry, the interior explodes with so much decoration it almost creates a humorous effect. The great Zimmermann was so enchanted with his creation that he built a small home in the vicinity and spent the last decade of his life here. A bus heading for the church leaves Füssen Monday to Friday six times per day (once per day on the weekend). If you're driving, signs between the official Romantic Road towns of Wildsteig and Steingaden indicate the way 3km (2 miles) south to Wies. Visitors should check the timetable at the station for bus information or ask at the Füssen tourist office (see above). The trip takes 30 minutes and costs 13€ round-trip.

NEUSCHWANSTEIN ★★★ & HOHENSCHWANGAU ★

7km (4 miles) E of Füssen, 116km (72 miles) SW of Munich

Just east of Füssen are the two "Royal Castles" of Hohenschwangau and Neuschwanstein, among the finest in Germany. Hohenschwangau, the more sedate of the two, was built by Maximilian II in 1836; Neuschwanstein was the brainchild of his son, "Mad" King Ludwig II. The extravagant Ludwig was responsible for two other architectural flights of fancy besides Neuschwanstein: Linderhof, near Oberammergau, and Herrenchiemsee, on an island in Chiemsee (both are covered in chapter 9). Ludwig died under mysterious circumstances in 1886 (see "The Fairy-Tale King" box, below).

After you've fought the crowds to get into these royal castles (in summer, the lines to get in can seem endless), you can spend your remaining time hiking around the surrounding Alpine peaks and valleys for what might be some of the most memorable walks of your life. For one of the grandest panoramas in all of the Alps (in any country), hike up to the **Marienbrücke** (the trail is signposted), which spans the Pöllat Gorge behind Neuschwanstein Castle. If you're properly dressed and have stout boots, continue uphill from the gorge for another hour for the most splendid view possible of "Mad" King Ludwig's fantasy castle.

Essentials

GETTING THERE By Bus Nineteen buses a day arrive from Füssen (see above).

By Car Head east from Füssen along the B17.

VISITOR INFORMATION Information about the region and the castles is available at the **Kurverwaltung,** Kaiser-Maximilian-Platz 1, Füssen (✆ **08362/93850**). Hours vary but are usually Monday to Friday 8:30am to 6:30pm and Saturday 9am to 2:30pm in summer; in winter, hours are Monday to Friday 9am to 5pm and Saturday 10am to noon. Information is also available at the Kurverwaltung in the Rathaus, Münchenerstrasse 2, Schwangau (✆ **08362/938523**), open Monday through Friday from 9am to 5pm and Saturday from 10am to 1pm.

Visiting the Royal Castles

Be prepared for very long lines (sometimes an incredible 4- to 5-hr. wait) at the castles during summer, especially in August. On some days, 25,000 people visit. To alleviate the inconvenience of long lines and stress, RAD Data Communications has installed a network for organizing visits. Under the system, tickets displaying specific

THE fairy-tale KING

Ludwig II, often called "Mad" King Ludwig (although some Bavarians hate that label), was born in Munich in 1845, the son of Maximilian II. Only 18 years old when he was crowned king of Bavaria, handsome Ludwig initially attended to affairs of state, but he soon grew bored and turned to less subtle pursuits. A loner who never married, Ludwig gradually became more and more obsessed with acting out his extravagant fantasies.

At the baroque palace of **Nymphenburg** (p. 296), the summer residence of the Bavarian rulers, you can still see in the Marstall Royal Stables the richly decorated coaches and sleighs in which young Ludwig loved to travel, often at night, with his spectacular entourage. His crown jewels can be admired in the treasury in the Königsbau wing of the **Residenz** palace, in the heart of Munich (p. 288).

Ludwig had a long association with Richard Wagner and was a great fan and benefactor of the composer. The king had Wagner's operas performed for his own pleasure and watched them in royal and solitary splendor. At Linderhof, the first romantic palace that he built, he even reconstructed the Venus grotto from the Munich opera stage design for *Tannhäuser.*

Ludwig's architectural creations are legendary. To construct his own Versailles, he chose one of Germany's most beautiful lakes, Chiemsee. He called the palace **Herrenchiemsee,** in homage to Louis XIV, the Sun King. Today, visitors can enjoy the castle's Versailles-style Hall of Mirrors and its exquisite gardens (p. 343). **Schloss Linderhof** (p. 358), in the Graswang Valley near Oberammergau, was a smaller creation but became his favorite castle; it was the only one completed by the time of his death.

Nestled in a crag high above the little town of Hohenswangen is the most famous of the royal designer's efforts, the multiturreted Disney-like **Neuschwanstein** (see below). From a distance, the castle appears more dreamlike than real. It's the most photographed castle in Germany. The king's study, bedroom, and living room sport frescoes of scenes from Wagner's operas *Tristan and Isolde* and *Lohengrin.*

Finally, Ludwig's excesses became too much, and he was declared insane in 1886 at the age of 41. Three days later, he was found drowned in Lake Starnberg on the outskirts of Munich. He may have committed suicide, or he may have been murdered. A memorial chapel lies on the bank of the lake. Ludwig is buried along with other royals in the crypt beneath the choir of St. Michael's Church.

admission times are sold at kiosks at the base of the castle before you make your ascent. Visitors can then purchase a ticket and wait for their reserved tour instead of standing in long lines with no definite time set. Entry to the castles is controlled by a computerized turnstile that reads the tickets. Ticketing information for each castle is conveyed to the central ticket office via a microwave link, which links the two castles to an office in the valley below. **Note:** It is imperative to arrive by the time indicated on your ticket; otherwise, you will have to go back to the kiosk at the base and pick up a new ticket and start all over again.

HOHENSCHWANGAU ★

Not as glamorous or spectacular as Neuschwanstein (see below), the neo-Gothic **Hohenschwangau Castle** nevertheless has a much richer history. The original structure dates from the days of the 12th-century knights of Schwangau. When the

Third Floor

Fourth Floor

- **A** Castle entrance
- **B** Study
- **C** Throne room
- **D** King's bedroom
- **E** Sängerhalle (Singer's Hall)

knights faded away, the castle began to fade, too, helped along by the Napoleonic Wars. When Ludwig II's father, Crown Prince Maximilian (later Maximilian II), saw the castle in 1832, he purchased it and in 4 years had it completely restored. Ludwig II spent the first 17 years of his life here and later received Richard Wagner in its chambers.

The rooms of Hohenschwangau are styled and furnished in a much heavier Gothic mode than those in Neuschwanstein. Many are typical of the halls of knights' castles of the Middle Ages in both England and Germany. There's no doubt that the style greatly influenced young Ludwig and encouraged the fanciful boyhood dreams that formed his later tastes and character. Hohenschwangau, unlike Neuschwanstein, has a comfortable look about it, more like an actual home than a museum.

Among the most attractive chambers is the **Hall of the Swan Knight,** named for the wall paintings depicting the saga of Lohengrin. Note the Gothic grillwork on the ceiling with the open spaces studded with stars.

Hohenschwangau, Alpseestrasse (*C* **08362/930830**), is open April to September daily 8am to 5:30pm, and October to March daily 9am to 3:30pm. Admission is 12€ for adults and 8€ for students and children 12 to 15; children 11 and under enter free. There are several parking lots that serve both castles.

NEUSCHWANSTEIN ★★★

Neuschwanstein represents the climax of King Ludwig II's fairy-tale ambitions. Construction lasted 17 years until the king's sudden death in 1886, when all work stopped, leaving a part of the interior uncompleted. Ludwig had lived in these rooms on and off for a total of only about 6 months of his last 3 years on the throne and planet.

The doorway off to the left side of the vestibule leads to the king's apartments. The **study,** like most of the rooms, is decorated with wall paintings showing scenes from Nordic legends. The theme of the study is the Tannhäuser saga. The only fabric in the room is hand-embroidered silk, used in curtains and chair coverings, all designed with the gold-and-silver Bavarian coat of arms.

From the vestibule, you enter the **throne room** through the doorway at the opposite end. This hall, designed in Byzantine style by J. Hofmann, was never completed. The floor is a mosaic design, depicting the animals of the world. The columns in the main hall are made of deep-copper-red porphyry. The circular apse where the king's throne was to have stood is reached by a stairway of white Carrara marble. The walls and ceiling are decorated with paintings of Christ in heaven looking down on the Twelve Apostles and six canonized kings of Europe.

The **king's bedroom** is the most richly carved in the entire castle—it took 4½ years to complete this room alone. The walls are decorated with panels carved to look like Gothic windows, as well as with a mural depicting the legend of Tristan and Isolde. In the center is a large wooden pillar, completely encircled with gilded brass sconces. The ornate bed is on a raised platform with an elaborately carved canopy. Through the balcony window you can see the 50m (160-ft.) waterfall in the Pöllat Gorge, with the mountains in the distance.

The fourth floor of the castle is almost entirely given over to the **Singer's Hall,** the pride of Ludwig II and all of Bavaria. Modeled after the hall at Wartburg, the Singer's Hall is decorated with marble columns and elaborately painted designs interspersed with frescoes depicting the life of Parsifal.

The castle is open year-round. In September, visitors have the additional pleasure of hearing Wagnerian concerts along with other music in the Singer's Hall. For information and reservations, contact the tourist office, **Verkehrsamt,** at the Rathaus in Schwangau (✆ **08362/938523**). Tickets go on sale in early June and sell out rather quickly. The castle can be visited only on one of the guided tours (offered in English), which are given daily year-round, except November 1; December 24, 25, and 31; January 1; and Shrove Tuesday. April to September, tours are given 8am to 5pm, and October to March, times are 9am to 3pm. Tours leave every 45 minutes and last 35 minutes. Admission is 12€ for adults, 8€ for students and seniors over 65, and free for children 14 and under. A combination ticket for both castles is 22€ for adults and 15€ for children 14 and under. For more information, visit **www.neuschwanstein.com**.

Reaching Neuschwanstein involves a steep half-mile climb from the parking lot at Hohenschwangau Castle (see above). This can be a 30-minute walk for the athletic, an eternity for those less so (and, regrettably, there are almost no benches along the route, and they're always occupied). To cut down on the climb, you can take a bus to Marienbrücke, a bridge that crosses over the Pöllat Gorge at a height of 90m (300 ft.). From that vantage point, you, like Ludwig, can stand and meditate on the glories of the castle and its panoramic surroundings. If you want to photograph the castle, don't wait until you reach the top, where you'll be too close for a good shot. It costs

1.80€ for the bus ride up to the bridge or 1€ to return. From Marienbrücke, it's a 10-minute walk to Neuschwanstein castle. This footpath is very steep.

The traditional way to reach Neuschwanstein is by horse-drawn carriage; this costs 6€ for the ascent and 3€ for the descent. **Note:** Some readers have complained about the rides being overcrowded and not at all accessible for visitors with limited mobility. Also note there is no guarantee of arrival time. If you miss your timed entry, you're out of luck. Our recommendation is to avoid the ride unless you have plenty of time to wait in line and make the ascent before your timed entry into the castle.

Where to Eat & Stay Nearby

Hotel Lisl and Jägerhaus This graciously styled villa and its annex in a historic building across the street are among the better addresses in the area. Most rooms have a view of one or both castles, even from one of the bathroom windows. A few rooms in the main building have been decorated with exclusive wood paneling and carvings. If you're assigned to the annex, never fear, as its rooms are just as fine as—or in some cases even better than—the main building. Some of the bathrooms in the Jägerhaus are larger than some hotel rooms. For charm and price, this one is a winner.

Neuschwansteinstrasse 1–3, 87645 Hohenschwangau. www.neuschwanstein-hotels.de. © **08362/8870.** Fax 08362/81107. 47 units. 85€–170€ double; 180€–220€ suite. AE, DC, MC, V. Free parking. Closed Dec 21-26. **Amenities:** Bar; room service. *In room:* TV (in some).

Hotel Müller Hohenschwangau   This hospitable inn has an alluring location near the foundations of Neuschwanstein Castle. Each of the inviting midsize rooms possesses a bit of Bavarian charm with tasteful, comfortable furnishings, along with a small tiled bathroom. Nature lovers especially enjoy hiking the short distance to nearby Hohenschwangau Castle.

This hotel is your best bet for dining even if you're not a guest. You have a choice of savory Bavarian cuisine or superb international dishes with an emphasis on flambé. In summer, dinners are served on the Alpsee Boathouse's lakeside terrace.

Alpseestrasse 16, 87645 Hohenschwangau. www.hotel-mueller.de. © **08362/81990.** Fax 08362/819913. 41 units. 98€–200€ double; 187€–250€ suite. Rates include buffet breakfast. AE, DC, MC, V. Free parking. Closed Jan 11–Mar 26. Bus from Füssen stops here. **Amenities:** 4 restaurants; bar; outdoor pool; room service; sauna. *In room:* TV, hair dryer, minibar (in some).

MUNICH

City slickers speeding down the autobahn in top-of-the-range BMWs, endless wheat beer and oompah-pah in the Hofbräuhaus, and 20-somethings shopping for trendy Oktoberfest dirndl dresses—you'll find it all in progressive, festive, and downright traditional Munich. Some visitors come for the world-class Pinakothek galleries, some for boutique shopping on Maximilianstrasse, others for outdoor activities with views of the not-so-distant Alps. But for most Münchners, there's no place like the vast English Garden, where they can shrug off that self-consciously cool image and (quite literally) let it all hang out.

Things to Do **Marienplatz** beckons with street entertainers, pavement cafés, and the Gothic **Neues Rathaus.** Arrive at noon when the glockenspiel chimes. A short stroll away is the opulent **Residenz** palace evoking the 700-year Wittelsbach dynasty, and the twin-domed **Frauenkirche** church. Contemplate Picassos and Warhols at the **Pinakothek** galleries and motoring legends at the space-age **BMW World.** Outdoorsy Münchners enjoy the lake-dotted **English Garden,** where they cycle, row, and sunbathe in the buff during their lunch hour.

Shopping Join the morning throngs shopping for fresh produce in the **Viktualienmarkt** before quaffing *Frühschoppen* (prelunch beers) under the maypole. Designer is the word on stately **Maximilianstrasse** boulevard and the nearby **Fünf Höfe** courtyards. For more idiosyncratic tastes, dip into the galleries and boutiques in **Gärtnerplatz** and **Schwabing.** The **Bayerischer-Kunstgewerbe-Verein** showcases every form of local creativity. Oysters and champagne in Munich's centuries-old **Dallmyr** deli is very Munich, as is a tight-fitting dirndl or pair of strapping lederhosen from **Loden-Frey.**

Nightlife & Entertainment Oktoberfest's stein-swinging infuses Munich's jovial beer halls year-round. The **Hofbräuhaus** draws tourists and locals with oom-pah bands and dirndl-clad waitresses juggling liters of foaming *Weizen* (wheat beer), while the chestnut-shaded **Hirschgarten** and cavernous **Augustiner Bräu** are less crowded. Socialites hobnob over expertly mixed cocktails in **Schumann's Bar am Hofgarten** before hitting the upbeat jazz clubs in party-loving **Schwabing** or the dance floor in the ultraexclusive **P1 Club.** Book tickets to see the acclaimed Bavarian State Opera perform at the **National Theatre.**

Restaurants & Dining Münchners are never merrier than when eating and drinking. For a traditional Bavarian feel, choose a wood-paneled tavern in the **Altstadt** serving herby *Weisswurst* veal sausage (don't forget to peel it) with sweet mustard or glistening pork knuckles with sauerkraut.

Chefs get creative in minimalist-chic restaurants in **Haidhausen** and **Maxvorstadt.**
Schwabing's old artists' quarter is the place for late-night Chinese, Italian, Mexican,
and Greek food. See Munich's skyline glitter from the Olympic Tower's revolving
Restaurant 181.

ESSENTIALS

Although Germany's third largest metropolis, the heart of Munich is easily accessible
by foot and by public transportation. A few outer sites will require over 30 minutes to
reach, but you can use the great network of buses, trams, and underground rail to get
you where you need to go.

Getting There

BY PLANE   Compared to most European cities, the **Munich International Airport** (✆ **089/97500;** www.munich-airport.de) is located a bit further afield, 27km
(17 miles) northeast of central Munich. Yet, Germany's second busiest airport, inaugurated in 1992, has become one of Europe's best, with well-functioning facilities, as
well as amenities and events that may make you actually want to stick around. The
airport handles more than 400 flights a day, serving at least 65 cities worldwide with
nonstop connections to New York, Miami, Chicago, and Toronto, among other places.

    S-Bahn (✆ **01805/661010;** www.s-bahn-muenchen.de) trains connect the airport
with downtown Munich. The S1 is ideal for destinations near the Hauptbahnhof (main
railroad station), and the S8 is better for the east side of the city and the Ostbahnhof
(east railroad station.) Departures are every 10 minutes for the 45-minute trip. One-way
fare for the four-zone ticket is 10€, but you might as well get the four-zone day ticket
for 10.80€ if you plan to use public transportation again that day. A taxi into the center
costs 50€ to 60€. Airport buses, such as those operated by **Autobus Oberbayern**
(✆ **089/323040;** www.airportbus-muenchen.de), also run between the airport and
the center, costing 11€ for adults (17€ round-trip), 5.50€ for children 6 to 14.

BY TRAIN   Munich's main rail station, the **Hauptbahnhof,** west of the center
past Karlsplatz, contains a hotel, restaurants, shopping, car parking, and banking
facilities. Pretty much all of Germany is accessible from this station. Some 20 direct
high-speed trains connect Munich to Frankfurt (trip time: 3¼ hr.) and 12 to Berlin
(average trip time: 6 hr.). The **Ostbahnhof** also serves as a rail terminus for the east
side of the Isar river. For information about long-distance trains, call ✆ **01805/996633**
or visit www.bahn.de.

    Both rail stations are connected to the **S-Bahn** rapid-transit system, and the
U-Bahn (subway) system serving the Munich Innenraum (inner section). In addition, buses and trams fan out in all directions.

📷   **Prost!**

The airport may provide your first
glimpse of Munich's innovative edge, a
sight worth enjoying over a brew at the
world's first airport brewery, the Air-
bräu Restaurant & Café. From your
table in a spacious Biergarten beneath

a massive glass awning, don't be surprised to see a grandiose promotional
event occurring in between the terminals. (This writer saw the latest Audis
being driven up and down a makeshift
mountain.)

The More, the Merrier . . . and Cheaper

The **City Tour Card** offers all of the flexibility of a public transportation day pass with additional savings on many museums, tours and sights. Discounts include 1€ to 3€ off the normal price for museums like the Schloss Nymphenburg, Bier & Oktoberfestmuseum, Residenz, and BMW Museum, as well as 25% off Autobus Oberbayern day-trips.

It's worth checking it out and doing some math to see if it benefits you. A single person pass costs 9.90€ for 1 day, 20€ for a 3-day pass. Groups of up to five people save the most with a day-pass for 17€ and a 3-day pass for 30€. It's available at the Tourist Information Offices and MVV sales counters at the main U-Bahn stations.

BY BUS   Munich has long-distance bus service from many German and European cities. Depending on their point of origin, buses depart from either the section of the Hauptbahnhof called the West-Wing Starnberger Bahnhof, or from the Deutsche Touring Terminal on Arnulfstrasse 3, about a block away. For information about connections, fares, and schedules, call **Deutsche Touring GmbH** at *©* **089/88989513** (www.touring.de). Regional service to towns and villages within Bavaria can be arranged through **Oberbayern Autobus,** Heidemann-Strasse 220 (*©* **089/323040;** www.autobusoberbayern.de), or its affiliate **Greyline,** Schützenstrasse 9 (*©* **089/ 54907560;** www.greyline.com). Greyline also organizes bus tours to specific tourist destinations around Bavaria and into neighboring Austria, including the castles of King Ludwig, Innsbruck, and Salzburg.

Visitor Information

There are two tourist offices in Munich: Bahnhofplatz 2, open Monday to Saturday 9am to 8pm and Sunday 10am to 6pm; and Marienplatz in the Neues Rathaus, open Monday to Friday 10am to 8pm, Saturday 10am to 5pm, and Sunday 10am to 4pm. For information, call *©* **089/23396500** (www.muenchen.de).

City Layout

Munich's **Hauptbahnhof (rail station)** lies just west of the historic center and opens onto Bahnhofplatz. From there you can take Schützenstrasse to **Karlsplatz** (nicknamed Stachus), where the Karlstor announces entry into the medieval core that used to be surrounded by ramparts. From Karlsplatz, you can continue east along the pedestrians-only Neuhauserstrasse and Kaufingerstrasse until you reach **Marienplatz,** which is the heart of Munich's **Altstadt (Old Town).**

From Marienplatz you can head north on Dienerstrasse, which will lead you to Residenzstrasse and finally to **Max-Joseph-Platz,** a landmark square, with the Nationaltheater and the former royal palace, the Residenz. East of this square runs **Maximilianstrasse,** a fashionable shopping and dining street, while north extends the districts laid out by Ludwig I, including the Ludwigstrasse and Briennerstrasse. On the south edge of Maximilianstrasse is the **Platzl** quarter, a suitable choice for nightlife in the *Innenstadt;* here you'll find some of the finest (and also some of the worst) restaurants in Munich, along with the landmark Hofbräuhaus, the most famous beer hall in Europe.

North of the old town is **Schwabing,** a former bohemian section whose main street is Leopoldstrasse. The sprawling municipal park grounds, the **Englischer**

Munich Neighborhoods

Garten, are due east of Schwabing. To the south and west around Sendlingertor and Gärtnerplatz extend the **Glockenbachviertel,** also a popular haunt for nightlife.

FINDING AN ADDRESS/MAPS   In the Altstadt, "hidden" squares may make finding an address difficult; therefore, you may need a detailed street map, not the more general maps handed out free by the tourist office and many hotels. Kompass publishes a great map for 2.95€, which contains a detailed street index and is available at nearly all bookstores and at many newsstands.

Neighborhoods in Brief

Altstadt   This medieval core used to be surrounded by ramparts, but is bordered by the wide boulevards that connect the Sendlinger Tor (Tor means gate) and Isartor to the south, Odeonsplatz to the north, and Karlstor to the west. Marienplatz, with its Rathaus (Town Hall) and its Glockenspiel performances, serves as the hub of the district, which can be traversed in about 15 minutes.

Museum Quarter   Just north of the Altstadt lie the squares and avenues laid out by Ludwig I, an area he would be proud of given its wealth of museums containing some of Europe's most important art. The 3 **Pinakotheks,** the **Glyptothek,** and **Museum Brandhorst** are just some of the excellent offerings for art-lovers.

Schwabing   This large northern section of the city with **Leopoldstrasse** as its artery had a Bohemian heyday before World War I, and continues to be a favorite haunt of students and some artists. The Englischer Garten spreads out along its eastern border, the Studentenstadt is to its north, and Olympiapark and Josephsplatz mark its western border.

Olympiapark   Once known primarily for the Black September terrorist attack at the 1972 Olympics, in which Palestinian terrorists killed 11 Israeli athletes, the entire park is now a multipurpose complex hosting concerts, sporting events, fairs and more. At over 180m (600 ft.), the restaurant in the **Olympia Tower** provides the best Alpine view in town. For more information, see p. 296.

Nymphenburg   On warm days, you can enjoy the grounds and gardens of this summer palace just as members of the Wittelsbach dynasty did. Even in bad weather, the ornately-decorated rooms and priceless porcelain make a trip here worth the ride to the northwestern edge of town (p. 296).

Getting Around

Munich is a city for walkers, with much of the Altstadt and many of its sights free of traffic. Even those with limited mobility will find the trams, buses and U-bahn very navigable. Simply leave the car at the hotel and find a ticket that suits you best.

BY PUBLIC TRANSPORTATION

The **U-Bahn,** or underground rail, is the quickest way to get to various places in the immediate town center. It overlaps the suburban network called the **S-Bahn,** which is useful for distant destinations like the airport and Dachau. The S-Bahn lines also conveniently converge to form the main spine of transportation through the city, linking the Hauptbahnhof, Karlsplatz, Marienplatz and the Ostbahnhof, with departures in as little as a minute apart.

A ticket issued by the **MVV** transportation authority (www.mvv-muenchen.de) is valid on the U-Bahn and S-Bahn, as well as trams and buses. No transfer ticket is required. The U-Bahn is likely the most useful network, unless Dachau, the airport,

Munich U-Bahn & S-Bahn

8

MUNICH | Essentials

or the lakes to the southwest are in your plans. Some tram and bus lines are active overnight for the night owls. The Eurailpass is valid on the S-Bahn, since it's state-owned, but not the U-Bahn.

Make sure your ticket is valid for the area in which you're traveling, as a 40€ fine may be levied. Familiarize yourself with the network map, or when in doubt ask a helpful attendant before crossing the line of blue validating machines, where you'll need to stamp your ticket. A **single ticket** costs 2.50€ for the *Innenraum*, which is the innermost zone. Dachau is located in the second outer zone (5€ for a single ticket), the airport in the fourth (10€). To save money, estimate how much traveling you'll be doing and consolidate it if possible. At 5.40€ a *Tageskarte* **(day ticket)** makes sense, and is valid in the *Innenraum* until 4am the next day. For those staying several days, the 12€ *IsarCard Wochenkarte* **(week ticket)** is a good option, offering unlimited travel within two of the four rings of the *Innenraum* from Monday to the following Sunday. A week card for all four rings of the *Innenraum* costs 18€. For further details, consult maps at the stations, ask an attendant, or call ℂ **089/41424344.**

BY TAXI

The meter on cabs you hail on the street or find waiting at a taxi stand begins at 3.10€. If you phone for a taxi, 1.20€ will be added to the fare. For rides within the city of Munich, you'll be charged 1.70€ per kilometer, unless your ride is longer than 5km (6¼ miles), in which case the per-kilometer rate goes down to between 1.40€ and 1.50€, depending on the distance you travel. Drivers who wait for passengers within their cabs receive a prorated waiting fee of 24€ per hour. Each suitcase in the trunk costs an addition .60€. For more information, call ℂ **089/21610.**

BY CAR

It's usually cheaper to rent a car before leaving for Germany (see "Getting Around," in chapter 19), though you can also rent one here. Major international car-rental companies have easy-to-spot offices at the airport.

If you're already in Munich and plan on making excursions into the Bavarian countryside, it's often more convenient to rent a car in the city center than to trek out to the airport. Car-rental companies are listed under *Autovermietung* in the Yellow Pages of the Munich phone book. Contact **Sixt Autovermietung,** Grillparzerstrasse 29 (ℂ **1805/252525;** www.sixt.de), to rent a car locally.

Because of heavy traffic, don't attempt to see Munich itself by car. And beware if your hotel doesn't have parking; parking garages tend to be expensive, often 18€ to 25€ per night.

BY BICYCLE

One of the most convenient places to rent a bike is **Radius Bikes** (ℂ **089/596113;** www.radiustours.com), at the far end of the Hauptbahnhof, near lockers opposite track 32. The charge is 3€ per hour, or else 15€ to 18€ per day. Mountain bikes rent for 5€. A deposit of 50€ or a credit card number is required; students receive a 10% discount. Radius Bikes is open mid-March to October Monday to Friday 9am to 6pm, Saturday and Sunday 9am to 8pm.

[FastFACTS] MUNICH

Bookstores Most large bookshops in Munich have an English-language section, but **Word's Worth** bookshop specializes in books in English, Schellingstrasse 3 (© **089/2809141;** www.wordsworth.de).

Business Hours Most **banks** are open Monday to Friday 8:30am to 12:30pm and 1:30 to 3:30pm (many stay open to 5:30pm Thurs). Most **businesses** and **stores** are open Monday to Saturday 9am to 6pm, although some close in the early afternoon on Saturday.

Consulates See the "Embassies & Consulates" entry in chapter 19.

Currency Exchange You can get a better rate at a bank than at your hotel. On weekends or at night, you can exchange money at the Hauptbahnhof exchange, open daily 6am to 11:30pm.

Dentists & Doctors For an English-speaking dentist, go to the **Klinik und Poliklinik für Kieferchirurgie der Universität München,** Lindwurmstrasse 2A (© **089/51600;** U-Bahn: Goetheplatz), the dental clinic for the university. It deals with emergency cases and is always open. For 24-hour medical service, go to **Schwabing Hospital,** Kölner Platz 1 (© **089/ 30680;** U-Bahn: Scheidplatz).

Drugstores For an international drugstore where English is spoken, go to **Bahnhof Apotheke,** Bahnhofplatz 2 (© **089/594119;** U-Bahn/S-Bahn: Hauptbahnhof), open Monday to Friday 8am to 6:30pm and Saturday 8am to 2pm. If you need a prescription filled during off hours, call © **089/557661** for open locations. The information is recorded and in German only, so you may need to get someone from your hotel staff to assist you.

Emergencies For emergency medical aid, phone © **112.** Call the police at © **110.**

Fax Head for any of the hole-in-the-wall kiosks labeled **Deutsche Telekom.** These include locations on the Marienplatz and in the Hauptbahnhof. Deutsche Telekom phone cards are available in denominations of 6.50€ to 30€. You can use these to operate self-service fax machines.

Internet Access You can send e-mails or check your messages at the **Easy Internet Café,** Bahnhofplatz 1 (© **089/55999696;** U-Bahn: Hauptbahnhof). It's open daily from 7:30am to 11:45pm. Other Internet cafes include the **San Francisco Coffee Company,** Im Tal 15 (© **089/9952973;** U-Bahn: Isartor), near Isartor. Hours are Monday to Friday

7:30am to 9pm, Saturday 8am to 10pm, and Sunday 9am to 9pm. Most of these cafes charge 3€ per hour for the use of their services.

Laundry & Dry Cleaning A reliable dry-cleaning establishment is **SB Wasch Center,** Parkstrasse 8 (© **089/14079937**). Look in the Yellow Pages under either *Wäscherei* or *Waschsalon* for a coin-operated laundry near your hotel.

Post Office The most central post depot is the **Postbank** at Bahnhofplatz (U-Bahn/S-Bahn: Hauptbahnhof), opposite the main train station exit, and is open Monday to Friday 8am to 8pm, and Saturday 9am to 4pm. You can have your mail sent here *Poste Restante* (general delivery), but include the zip code (80335). You'll need a passport to reclaim mail, and you can't call for information, but must show up in person.

Safety Munich, like all big cities, has its share of crime, especially pickpocketing and purse and camera snatching. Most robberies occur in the much-frequented tourist areas, such as Marienplatz and the Hauptbahnhof, which is particularly dangerous at night. Many tourists also lose their valuables when they carelessly leave clothing unprotected as they join the nude sunbathers in the Englischer Garten.

Television There are two national TV channels, ARD (Channel 1) and ZDF (Channel 2). Sometimes these stations show films in the original language (most often English). The more expensive hotels often have cable TV, with such channels in English as CNN.

Toilets The center of Munich has several clean, safe, and well-kept public facilities.

Organized Tours

BY BUS

City tours encompass aspects of both modern and medieval Munich, and depart from the main railway station aboard red-sided buses. Departures, depending on the season and the tour, occur between two and eight times a day, and tours are conducted in both German and English. Most tours don't last more than 2½ hours, with the exception of a scientific odyssey that focuses on the technological triumphs of Munich as witnessed by various museums that include the Deutsches Museum. That experience usually lasts for a minimum of 4 hours, plus the time you spend wandering through museums at the end of your tour.

Depending on the tour, adults pay 11€ to 16€; children 13 and under are charged 6€ to 14€. Advance reservations for most city tours aren't required, and you can buy your ticket from the bus driver at the time you board. Tours leave from the square in front of the Hauptbahnhof.

To go farther afield and visit major attractions in the environs (such as Berchtesgaden or Ludwig II's castles), contact **Sightseeing Gray Line,** Schützenstrasse 9 (✆ **089/54907560;** www.grayline.com; U-Bahn/S-Bahn: Hauptbahnhof), open year-round Monday to Friday 9am to 6pm and Saturday 9am to 1pm. (Travel agents in Munich, as well as the concierge or reception staff at your hotel, can also book these tours.) At least a half-dozen touring options are available, ranging from a quick 1-hour overview of the city to full-day excursions to such outlying sites as Berchtesgaden, and the stunning Bavarian palaces in Oberammergau and Hohenschwangau. To participate in tours that cover attractions outside the city limits, advance reservations are required, especially if you want the bus to pick you up at any of Munich's hotels.

BY BIKE

Pedal pushers will want to try Mike Lasher's popular **Mike's Bike Tour,** Hochbrückenstrasse (✆ **089/25543988;** www.mikesbiketours.com). His bike-rental services include maps, locks, child and infant seats, and helmets at no extra charge. English and bilingual tours of central Munich run only March 1 to April 14 and September 1 to November 10 daily at 12:30pm and from April 15 to August 31 daily at 11:30am and 4pm. Customers love Mike's charm. Participants meet under the tower of the old town hall, a gray building on the east end of Marienplatz. Mike, the consummate guide, will be here—whistle in mouth—letting everyone know who he is. The tour veers from the bike paths only long enough for a lunch stop at a beer garden. Fear not, fainthearted: The bikes are new, and the rides are easy, with plenty of time for historical explanations, photo opportunities, and question-and-answer sessions. The cost for a tour, including the bike, is 24€. It is also possible to rent a bike for 12€ for same-day return.

ON FOOT

Munich Walk Tours, in English (✆ **089/24231767;** www.munichwalktours.de), is a fun way to get to know the city through various themed walks. Tours range in price from 10€ to 20€. The basic City Walk lasts just over 2 hours, and is offered daily at 10:45am and 2:45pm, except between November and April when the latter tour is offered only Friday to Sunday. An intriguing "Hitler's Munich-Third Reich Tour" leaves daily at 10:15am, and takes you to the infamous places associated with the *Führer*. Other themed tours, including the "Beer and Brewery" tour and "Haunted Munich," have irregular schedules; check the website for specifics. The main meeting point for all tours is at the main entrance of the Neues Rathaus on Marienplatz in the heart of Munich.

EXPLORING MUNICH

Although visitors can see Munich's major sights and museums within two or three days, the city's allure and history come out best while getting to know its various districts over several days. Combining the historical sights, culinary offerings, and evening activities brings out the true character of each neighborhood.

If you're pressed for time, make sure to view the sights of the Altstadt centering around **Marienplatz,** including the **Neues Rathaus, Altes Rathaus, Frauenkirche,** and **St. Peter's Church,** then stop by the **Viktualienmarkt** for a quick bite to eat. From there, be sure to visit the **Residenz** and **Schatzkammer** with a look in one of the museums in the **Kunstareal,** preferably the **Alte Pinakothek.** The **Deutsches Museum** is also a must, with **Schloss Nymphenburg** topping off your quick peek at the best of Munich.

Attractions by District

MARIENPLATZ & THE CITY CENTER

Marienplatz ★ grew from a modest medieval market square to the heart of a bustling capital as Munich and Bavaria gained importance. Having outgrown the Gothic **Altes Rathaus (Old City Hall),** the city inaugurated its proud **Neues Rathaus** in 1874, symbolizing the 'New Munich.' Crowds still gather here with cameras in hand to capture the Glockenspiel performances at 11am and noon, with an extra 5pm performance in summer. The wooden figures spin and act out the famous 1568 marriage of Wilhelm V and Renata (seated on their wooden thrones), an event that lasted some 18 days. Visitors in early 2012 will be able to see a live reenactment of the dance, called the *Schäfflertanz*, which takes place once every seven years. You may wish to climb the 55 steps to the top of the Rathaus's tower (an elevator is also available) for a view of the city center.

The Black Fisherman & Pink Triangles

In the Spring of 2012 the city of Munich will erect a new Holocaust monument at the corner of Dultstrasse and Oberanger, in memory of previously overlooked victims of Nazi persecution: homosexuals. Joining similar monuments in Berlin, Frankfurt and Cologne, the structure will stand at the site of the former gay-friendly hangout Schwarzfischer (The Black Fisherman), which stood on the corner until a Nazi raid on October 20, 1934. The Nazi regime rounded up some 50,000 homosexuals during their time in power, most of whom did not survive persecution in the concentration camps.

Central Munich Attractions

Alte Pinakothek **2**
Altes Rathaus **30**
Antikensammlungen **7**
Asamkirche **11**
Bayerisches
  Nationalmuseum **21**
Cuvilliés Theater **26**
Deutsches Museum von
  Meisterwerken der
  Naturwissenschaft und
  Technik **37**
Deutsches Theater **8**
Englischer Garten **20**
Frauenkirche **29**
Glyptothek **5**
Hofgarten **23**
Isartor **36**
Jüdisches Museum
  München **34**
Karlstor **9**
Lenbachhaus **5**
Marienplatz **31**
Matthäuskirche **12**
Michaelskirche **10**
Münchner Stadtmuseum **33**
Museum Brandhorst **3**
Nationaltheater **27**
Neue Pinakothek **1**
Neues Rathaus **28**
Peterskirche **32**
Pinakothek der Moderne **4**
Residenz **25**
Schack-Galerie **22**
Theatinerkirche **24**
University **13**
Viktualienmarkt **35**

NYMPHENBURG
Amalienburg **18**
Badenburg Pavilion **19**
Magdalenenklause **15**
Marstallmuseum **17**
Pagodenburg **14**
Schloss Nymphenburg **16**

Nymphenburg

⑭ Kleiner See
⑮
⑯
Nymphenburger Kanal

SCHLOSSPARK
NYMPHENBURG
⑱
⑰

Grosser See
⑲

Zuccalistr.
Richildenstr.

LUDWIG-MAXIMILIANS-
UNIVERSITÄT MÜNCHEN
Geschwister-
Scholl-Pl. Ⓤ
⑬ Universität

Schellingstrasse

Museum
Brandhorst ③

Pinakothek
der Moderne ④

Bayerische
Staatsbibliothek

Theresien-
strasse

Amalienstr.

Fürstenstr.

Rhein-
berger-
str.

Schönfeld-   str.

Ludwigstrasse

Von-der-Tann-(Str

ENGLISCHER
GARTEN
⑳

Ludwig-Str.

Oskar-von-Miller-Ring

Jägerstr.

Kardinal-
Döpfner-Str.

Finkenstr.

Dichtergarten
Galeriestrasse

Haus der Kunst

Prinzregentenstrasse

Lerchenfeldstrasse

Himbselstr.

Seeaustr.

Oettingenstrasse

Bayerisches
Nationalmuseum
㉑

㉒

Platz der Opfer
des National-
sozialismus

Wittelsbacher-
platz

Odeons-
platz

Hofgarten

platz

Jungfern-
turmstr.

Rochusberg

Odeonspl. Ⓤ

㉓ Hofgartenstr.

Bayerische
Staatskanzlei

Franz-Josef-Strauss-Ring

Unsöldstrasse

Alexandrastr.

Rochusstr.

㉔

Theatiner-
kirche

Christophstr.

LEHEL

Prannerstr.

Salvatorstr.

Promenade-
platz

Maffeistr.

Theatinerstrasse

Residenzstr.

㉕

Residenz ㉖

Marstallplatz

Liebig-   strasse

Bruder-

Seitz-

Karl-Scharnagl-Ring

Sankt-
Anna-
Platz

Tiftstr.

Sankt-Anna-Str.

Robert-Koch-Str.

Reitmor-

Gewürzmühlstr.

Widenmayerstr.

Löwengrube

Schäfflerstr.

Frauen-
kirche

Frauen-
platz ㉙

Kaufingerstr.

Max-
Joseph-
Platz ㉗

National-
theater

Perusa-
str.

Schramm-
str.

Hofgraben

Pfisterstr.

Maximilian-

Herzog-
Rudolf-Str.

Falcken-
bergstr.

strasse

Lehel Ⓤ

Bürkleinstr.

Sternstr.

Prater-

Maximilians-
brücke

Augustiner-

Fürstenfelder Str.

Färbergraben

㉘

Weinstr.

Dienerstr.

Marien-
hof

Alter
Hof

Platzl

Neuhauser-

Münz-
str.

Brau-
haus-

Sparkassenstr.

Maderbräustr.

Ledererstr.

Hochbrückenstr.

Hildegardstr.

Knöbel-

Thomas-Wimmer-Ring

Völkerkunde-
museum
strasse

Adelgundenstr.

PRATER-
INSEL

MAXIMILIAN-
ANLAGEN

③ ㉛

Marienpl.

㉚

㉜

Peterskirche

Rosenstr.

Rindermarkt

Tal

Hochbrückenstr.

Marienstr.

Isartor Ⓢ

Steinsdorfstrasse

㉟

Stadt-
museum ㉝

Jüdisches Zentrum
Jakobsplatz

㉞

VIKTUALIEN-
MARKT

Schrannenhalle

Prälat-Zistl-Str.

Heiliggeiststr.

Radlsteg

Westenriederstr.

Am
Einlass

Frauenstrasse

Rumford-

㊱

Isartor

Isartor-
platz

Thiersch-

Zweibrückenstr.

Liebherrstr.

strasse

Am
Gasteig

Innere Wiener Str.

Preysingstr.

Kellerstrasse

Anger-

Dultstr.

Sack-
str.

Blumenstrasse

Cornelius-
strasse

Papa-
Schmid-
Str.

Müllerstrasse

Gärtner-
platz

Klenze-

Butter-
melcherstr.

Aventinstr.

Kohl-

Baader-

Morassistr.

strasse

strasse

Ludwigs-
brücke

MUSEUMS-
INSEL

Isar

Kleine

Auer Mühlbach

Zeppelinstrasse

Lilienstrasse

Rosenheimer Str.

Gasteig

Staatstheater am
Gärtnerplatz

Jahnstr.

Frauenhoferstrasse

Klenze-

Frauenhoferstr. Ⓤ

Reichenbach-

Cornelius-

str.

Erhardt-

㊲

Deutsches
Museum

Hochstrasse

The twin domes of Munich's other landmark, the **Frauenkirche,** also keep watch over the square, while the old tower of **Peterskirche** offers excellent, if not vertigo-inducing views of the Altstadt, and perhaps the distant Alps on a clear day. The nearby food market known as **Viktualienmarkt** is the best place to catch locals at leisure, offering a variety of Bavarian and international victuals and tipples at unbeatable prices.

In addition to the sights described below, the entire Altstadt is surrounded with remnants of its former medieval ramparts, dismantled in the 19th century. To the west the **Karlstor** (aka Stachus) dates from the 1500s and makes a popular photo op. To the southwest, the **Sendlingertor** was one of the four original town gates, while the eastern **Isartor** (Isar Gate) remains Munich's best preserved. First mentioned in 1337, the Isar Gate features a 19th century fresco depicting the triumphant return of Louis the Bavarian, Holy Roman Emperor, after his defeat of the Hapsburg Frederick the Fair in 1332. It also houses a curious museum to a famous son of the city, Karl Valentin, the so-called "German Charlie Chaplin."

Frauenkirche (Cathedral of Our Lady) ★ CHURCH With her twin spires gracing the skyline and many emblematic images, Munich's largest church provides the best testament of the city's post-war perseverance. It's astonishing to consider that the massive Gothic church lay in ruins after the shelling of 1945, and even more remarkable that workers and architects rebuilt the 15th-century structure piece by piece. Simple and dignified, its interior also retains relics such as Hans Krumpper's ornate cenotaph of Ludwig the Bavarian (next to the rear entrance), for whom the church was built beginning in 1468.

Also in the rear is the "devil's footstep," created by the imp himself according to legend. From there, the visitor can appreciate the slender pillars masking the windows, a concept which made the devil laugh so hard and stamp his foot into the marble floor. Bavaria's last king, Ludwig III, lies in the royal crypt under the altar with many others from his lineage.

Since 1821 the Frauenkirche has been the seat of the archbishopric, which was held between 1977 and 1982 by Joseph Ratzinger, known these days as Pope Benedict XVI.

Frauenplatz 1. ℂ **089/2900820.** www.muenchner-dom.de. Free admission. Daily 7am–7pm (Fri until 6pm). U-Bahn or S-Bahn: Marienplatz.

Peterskirche (St. Peter's Church) CHURCH Known as Old Peter, Munich's oldest inner-city church also bore the brunt of war, leaving little more than its fragile 14th-century tower. Recent restorations have finally completed the splendid overhead fresco by Rococo master Johann Baptist Zimmermann (see Wieskirche, p. 266). Other sights include a ghastly gilded skeleton of St. Mundita in the second chapel on the left. Perhaps the best sights of the church are atop the labyrinthine staircase, 306 in total, for an all-encompassing **view** ★ 55m (184 ft.) above Munich's rooftops. On a clear day the Alps spread to the south. (A sign with a white circle at the ticket window indicates if they are visible.)

Rindermarkt 1 (near the Rathaus). ℂ **089/2604828.** Church free; tower 1.50€ adults, .50€ children. Mon–Fri 9am–5:30pm; Sat–Sun 10am–5:30pm. U-Bahn or S-Bahn: Marienplatz.

Jüdisches Museum München MUSEUM From the genesis of the idea in 1928, the creation of a Jewish museum took some 60 years to come to fruition. This building, constructed along with the adjacent synagogue and community center, opened its doors in 2007, displaying a variety of exhibits about Jewish culture. Not only is the

FROMMER'S favorite MUNICH EXPERIENCES

A Morning at the Deutsches Museum
It would take a month to see all of the largest technological museum in the world, but a morning will at least whet your appetite. Everything is here: the first automobile by Benz (1886), the original V-2 rocket (Hitler's secret weapon), the first diesel engine, and plenty of buttons to push.

An Afternoon at Nymphenburg Palace
The Wittelsbach family considered this the best place to be on a hot afternoon—and so might you. The grounds

of Germany's largest baroque palace are filled with lakes, waterfalls, and pavilions.

A Night at the Opera in the Cuvilliés Theater If you see one opera in your life, make it in the most beautiful Rococo theater in the world, an elaborately gilded tier-boxed structure from the 18th century.

A Day in the Beer Gardens Münchners gather on weekends in summer to down high tankards of beer and watch the world go by, especially at Chinesischer Turm in the Englischer Garten.

history of Munich as it concerns the Jews explored on the three floors, but also a wider background on the Diaspora and displays about traditions. Temporary and changing exhibitions help supplement the fragmented coverage offered by the few objects that have been bequeathed to the collection.

St.-Jakobs-Platz 16. © **089/23396096.** www.juedisches-museum-muenchen.de. Admission 6€ adults, 3€ students and seniors, free for children 5 and under, 9€ family ticket (2 adults and up to 4 children). Tues–Sun 10am–6pm. U-Bahn or S-Bahn: Marienplatz.

Münchner Stadtmuseum (Municipal Museum) ★ MUSEUM   For those who take the time, this museum may be the most revealing look into the history of city. Housed in a 1490s armory, the "Typically Munich!" exhibition here serves as a good introduction to Munich, and an even better wrap-up. Memorabilia including painting and models of the city offer glimpses of how the Marienplatz or Neuveste in the Residenz used to look. Notable artifacts include a 1452 bell from Marienkirche, armor, and the valuable *Moriskentanzer* (Moorish Dancers) by Erasmus Grasser, rare examples of Gothic secular art. Period furniture and decoration span the periods from the Medieval, Renaissance, Baroque and Rococo, Biedermeier, Historicism, and Jugendstil to those of the 20th century. Don't miss the separate ground-floor wing dedicated entirely to the Nazi period, complementing the displays from the main exhibit. Every Tuesday and Wednesday, and from Friday to Sunday, the film museum shows films from its extensive archives at 6:30 and 9pm. On Thursdays the showtime is at 7pm only.

St. Jacobs-Platz 1. © **089/23322370.** www.stadtmuseum-online.de. Admission 4€ adults, 2€ students, 18 and under free. Tues–Sun 10am–6pm. U-Bahn or S-Bahn: Marienplatz.

ODEONSPLATZ & LUDWIGSTRASSE

Standing at the Odeonsplatz, the visitor really gets the impression of the stately grandeur Ludwig I envisioned when the whole district was laid out in the early 19th century to reflect the status of "kingdom" bestowed upon Bavaria by Napoleon in 1806. With its trio of arches, the 1844 Feldherrnhalle forms one bookend of arches that continue down the Ludwigstrasse—via the Bavarian National Library, other municipal buildings, and the University Church—to the distant Siegestor (Victory

Gate) finished in 1852. Ludwig I himself is represented on horseback on the west side of the avenue, perhaps admiring his own creation.

On the east side of the square is the bustling Café Tambosi, where locals have been basking in the sun rays since 1775, and the entrance into the Hofgarten, laid out between 1613 and 1617, which merits a peek regardless the weather.

The Residenz complex spreads to the east along Residenzstrasse until Max-Josephs-Platz and the National Theater, which is great to check out during a performance of the Bavarian National Opera or Ballet (see "Entertainment & Nightlife," later in this chapter).

Residenz ★ HISTORIC BUILDING   Before building castles in the countryside became à la mode, the Bavarian royalty resided here. Underground portions remain from the original 1358 castle called the Neuveste, but most of what you see in this immense palace dates from at least the 16th century. The whole is a hodgepodge of styles: from the Palladian facade facing the Hofgarten, to the Renaissance sections along Residenzstrasse, to the Florentine front overlooking Max-Joseph-Platz. Its role as a royal dwelling expired with the kingdom itself in 1918, and the bombs of the subsequent World War took their toll. Yet, just like the Frauenkirche, the Münchners rebuilt the prized palace piece by piece, a fact that makes a visit here well worth it.

The complex is composed of three sites: the **Residenz Museum,** which will take over two hours to visit its 120 rooms if you let it; the engrossing **Schatzkammer,** a must-see if you are strapped for time; and the unique **Cuvilliés Theater,** which some may delight in while others shrug at.

The changing tour itineraries of the Residenz lead through countless corridors and galleries, but some are worth a longer look. When it was completed by 1571, the long **Antiquarium** ★ was the only other structure outside of the original Neuveste. Although intended to house Albrecht V's sculpture collection, the 66m-long (216-ft.) hall was converted into a banquet room. Sixteen ceiling paintings by Peter Candid portray fame and virtue, while depictions of 102 Bavarian towns by Hans Donau the Elder blanket the rest of the vaulted ceiling. Admire the marble table in front of the chimney as well as the two credenzas by Friedrich Sustris containing rare majolica porcelain.

The **Grotto Courtyard,** the royalty's secret little piece of Italy, links the Antiquarium with the **Ancestral Gallery** ★. This celebration of gilded stucco and portraits was intended to boast the Wittelbach's claim to the throne, depicted in the towering family tree midway down the gallery. The neighboring **Porcelain Cabinet** showcases fine pieces in a mirrored room with gilded stucco by Zimmermann that hints at the Rococo style.

Maximilian I's own private **Ornate Chapel** was painstakingly reconstructed to its original detailed design. In the **Imperial Hall and Staircase,** you can imagine arriving to the court as a guest. François de Cuvilliés's **Green Gallery** also arouses the imagination, given the lavish soirees that once occurred here.

The **Cuvilliés Theater** ★★ in the Brunnenhof is a highlight for fans of Rococo, for it's one of the few and best-preserved constructed in the style. The royal family sat in its box at the back of the theater rather than next to the stage. Notice the originality of and lack of repetition in the decoration: from the red draping lining the balconies, and the faux curtains lining either side of the stage, to each telemon and caryatid in between each box. Mozart's premiere of *Idomeneo* took place here, a sell-out needless to say.

The **Schatzkammer (Treasury)** ★★ rivals its counterparts in Dresden and Vienna and is one of the most important treasuries in Europe. Arranged chronologically, the first

HOFGARTENSTRASSE

State Collection of
Egyptian Art

Four-
shaft
Room

Entrance Hall

Festival Hall Building

Bavarian
Academy
of
Science

Battle
Room
Wing

Court Garden Wing

Imperial
Courtyard

Apothecary
Courtyard

Stone Room Wing

Trier Wing

Collection

Hercules Chest
Ladies' Floor

Coin

Tower Building

Cuvilliés-Theater

Foyer

Foyer
Courtyard

Chapel Courtyard

Fountain
Courtyard

Apothecaries'
Wing

Cabinet
Garden

Old Residenz
RESIDENZSTRASSE

Grotto
Courtyard

Antiquarium

Wittelsbach
Fountain

Ruins of
All Saints
Church

Vestment
Rooms

Ancestors'

Gallery

Royal Building
Courtyard

Tickets

Kitchen
Courtyard

MARSTALLPLATZ

Nibelungen Rooms

Treasury

New Residenz
Theater

Entrances to Residenzmuseum & Schatzkammer

MAX-JOSEPH-PLATZ

Ground Floor

Grotto
Courtyard

Fountain
Courtyard

Rich Rooms

Royal Building
Courtyard

Kitchen
Courtyard

Porcelain Gallery

Upper Floor *(partial)*

- **A** Treasury
- **B** Ancestors' Gallery
- **C** Antiquarium
- **D** Die Reichen Zimmer
- **E** Königsbau
- **F** Porcelain Rooms
- **G** Hofkapelle
- **H** Reliquienkammer
- **I** Altes Residenztheater

three rooms feature rare and priceless pieces, including the *Crown of an English Queen*. Cast in Paris around 1375 and bequeathed to the Wittelbachs with Blanche of England's marriage into the line, this is the oldest English crown (since 1649, when Oliver Cromwell had most the crown jewels melted down). The equally impressive 16th-century Renaissance statue of *St. George Slaying the Dragon* was likely given as a gift for Wilhelm V, whose face looked a lot like the knight's.

Numerous other priceless objects fill out the collection.

Max-Joseph-Platz 3. ☎ **089/290671.** www.residenz-muenchen.de. Combination ticket for Residenzmuseum and Schatzkammer 9€ adults, 8€ seniors, free for students and children 17 and under. Ticket for either Residenzmuseum or Schatzkammer 6€ adults, 5€ seniors, free for students and children 17 and under. Apr to mid-Oct daily 9am–6pm; mid-Oct to Mar daily 10am–5pm. U-Bahn: Odeonsplatz.

Theatinerkirche CHURCH   A few years before his death in 1768, Cuvilliés commenced work on this church's facade, which is visually arresting when viewed on a sunny day with a blue sky. Inside, the bleached interior of 17th-century Italianate baroque reminds you of an unfinished painting. Scan the interior and look at each cherub's expression; one of them is telling you to be quiet and listen. Finishing the decoration in 1675, the Italian stucco artists intentionally exaggerated the size of the heads the higher they were. Those in the interior of the cupola seem out of proportion to their own bodies. King Maximilian II rests in the third chapel on the right side with his wife Marie, who outlived her son Ludwig II by a few years.

Theatinerstrasse 22. © **089/2106960.** Free admission. Mon–Fri 10am–1pm and 1:30–4:30pm; Sat 10am–3pm. U-Bahn: Odeonsplatz.

KÖNIGSPLATZ & THE KUNSTAREAL

Reigning from 1825 to 1848, Ludwig I set out to make Munich a second Athens, best embodied in the Classical architecture of Königsplatz. On either side of the Propyläen, the Antikensammlungen and Glyptothek house the king's former collections of Greek and Roman artifacts. A nearby placard at the corner of Briennerstrasse and Arcisstrasse describes and maps out Hitler's equally ambitious plans for the square as the heart of the Nazi regime.

Two blocks to the north, the Kunstareal provides four top-notch art museums that are all worth visiting, comprising a blockbuster overview of art history from the 15th century to today. The Alte Pinakothek rivals as one of the most significant in the world, while the smaller Neue Pinakothek offers many recognizable gems from the 19th century. The Pinakothek der Moderne and Museum Brandhorst provide a one-two punch of 20th-century art for modern art fans.

To the north stretches Schwabing, Munich's former bohemian haunt that continues to provide innovative locales for creative types, students, artists, and connoisseurs of the arts.

Alte Pinakothek (Old Picture Gallery) ★★★ MUSEUM   Like the Louvre in Paris and the Uffizi in Florence, this is one of the must-see museums of Europe. You will not find a collection of Rubens like this anywhere. In fact, the building was inaugurated 1836 to house the Dutch painter's colossal *Last Judgment (Gross Jungst Gericht),* as a sort of keystone for the collection. Other recognizable masterpieces by European artists from the 14th to the 18th centuries hang from the walls among the nearly 900 on display. If pressed for time, you may want to stroll through the massive collection to see what catches your eye. Otherwise, consider getting an audio guide and canceling other plans for the day to take it all in, as the lack of descriptions leaves a lot of guessing work.

In the first room, Albrecht Altdorfer represents the Danube School with his ***Battle of Alexander at Issus*** (1529), signaling the end of Persian advance, painted the same year as the Muslims began their advance towards Vienna. Ten paintings by **Albrecht Dürer** hang nearby, including the penetrating ***Self Portrait With Fur-trimmed Robe*** ★ as a 28-year old with Christ-like details, and his last major work, ***Four Apostles*** (1526). The Italian school is well represented with **Raphael's** *The Canigiani Holy Family* (1505–06), **Leonardo da Vinci's** *Madonna with Child,* and **Botticelli's** *Mourning Christ.*

The breathtaking **Rubenssaal** ★★ displays 17 large-scale canvases by the Dutch master on a background of deep red, including the enormous 6m-high (20-ft.) ***Last Judgment (Gross Jungst Gericht)*** ★. The neighboring *Kabinette* displays more from

Alte Pinakothek

Upper Floor

I Early Netherlandish Painting

IIa

Early German Painting II

Italian Renaissance Painting IV

Venetian Painting V

17th Cent. Flemish Painting VI

D

The Rubens Room **E** VII

Flemish Painting VIII

17th Cent. Dutch Painting **F** IX

Italian Baroque Painting X

French Painting XI

XIIa

French Painting XII

IIb

14th–17th Cent. Italian Painting

17th Cent. Flemish Painting

17th Cent. Dutch Painting

XIIb

The Cologne School III

16–17th Cent. German Painting

18th Cent. French Painting

18th Cent. Italian Painting

XIII **G**

Spanish Painting

C

Ground Floor

I Exhibition Area at the Klenze-Portal Ia

BARER STRASSE

Café Klenze

Shop

XI

Tickets ←Klenze-Portal

Tickets ℹ

Early German Painting

XII **A**

IIa Exhibition Areas at the Klenze-Portal

B Flemish Painting

II

Entrance ♿

XIII

THERESIENSTRASSE

A Galleries XI–XII **C** Gallery II **E** Gallery VII **G** Gallery XIII

B Rooms 16-23 **D** Gallery IV **F** Gallery IX

the more than 50 paintings by Rubens. What is a Rembrandt, is well represented with his series of six scenes from the life of Christ, and his *Self Portrait* (1629), aged 23.

Francois Boucher's loving portrait of *Madame de Pompadour* (1756) is a highlight from the French school

Don't miss the small but excellent cabinets on the first floor located behind the gift shop, which contain among other treasures **Pieter Bruegel the Elder's** Bosch-esque *Land of Cockaigne* (1567) and *Harbor Scene with Christ Preaching* (1598).

Barer Strasse 27. ℂ **089/23805216.** www.pinakothek.de/alte-pinakothek. Admission 7€ adults, 5€ students and seniors, free for children 14 and under. Sun admission for all 1€. Tues 10am–8pm; Wed–Sun 10am–6pm. U-Bahn: Theresienstrasse. Tram: 27. Bus: 100.

Antikensammlungen (Antiquities Collections) ★ MUSEUM Ludwig I's collection of Greek vases is the centerpiece of this museum, which was celebrated by art historians as one of the greatest in the world. Meant to complement the Glyptothek, the current collection of more than 650 vases and a few other pieces of Antique art is astounding, yet leaves a lot of guessing work for those unfamiliar with German, as the lack of signage and up-to-date literature on the museum is scant, especially in English. Yet, it makes for a pleasant Sunday stroll through the world of Greek pottery the likes of which you're not likely to find anywhere else.

8

MUNICH | Exploring Munich

291

Among its prized possessions is the oldest piece, a pre-Mycenaean "goddess from Aegina" (3000 B.C.) carved out of a mussel shell. Another highlight is Exekias' finely preserved **Dionysus Cup** (540 B.C.), with a depiction of the god of wine lounging in his vessel underneath a canopy of grape leaves.

Königsplatz 1. ℭ **089/59988830.** www.antike-am-koenigsplatz.mwn.de. Admission 3.50€ adults, 2.50€ students and seniors, free for children 15 and under. Sun admission for all 1€. Tues–Sun 10am–5pm (Thurs until 8pm). U-Bahn: Königsplatz.

Glyptothek (Museum of Sculpture) ★ MUSEUM   The centerpiece of this collection is the marbles from the pediments of the temple on Aegina, an island off the coast near Athens, which ranks up there with Pergamon Altar in Berlin, the Ephesus antiquities in Vienna, and the still-disputed Acropolis marbles in the British Museum in London. No need to worry, Ludwig I got a receipt for this transaction. This is the best chance to get up close and personal with the statues that you usually have to peer up at on the real thing in Greece.

Other notable items include the "Barbarini Faun," once housed in the palace of the same name in Rome, and Roman copies of Greek statues like the "Child with a Goose." The "Drunk Old Lady with a Wine Urn" also makes for an amusing image as you leave.

Königsplatz 3. ℭ **089/286100.** www.antike-am-koenigsplatz.mwn.de. Admission 3.50€ adults, 2.50€ students and seniors, free for children 15 and under. Sun admission for all 1€. Tues–Sun 10am–5pm (Thurs until 8pm). U-Bahn: U2 to Königsplatz.

Lenbachhaus ★★ 🏛 MUSEUM   One of the most unheralded but greatest collections of art is housed in the opulent 1800s mansion of the painter Franz von Lenbach. The collection is chiefly celebrated for its works by the Blaue Reiter (Blue Rider) group, which arose in the city in the years before World War I. The group has a color theory: that blue represents the male principle, austere and spiritual; yellow the female principle, gentle, bright, and sensual; with red standing for what is brutal and heavy. The most evocative painting of that movement is the 1911 *Blue Horse* ★★, by Franz Marc. The treasure-trove of art here includes works by every artist from Wassily Kandinsky to Andy Warhol. On display is Paul Klee's 1920 *Rose Garden,* an example of what the artist called "polyphonous painting."

No portrait in the gallery is as arresting as that of the *Dancer Aleksandr Sakharov* ★★★, painted in 1909 by Alexey von Jawlensky. Sakharov hides behind kohl-rimmed eyes and a voluptuously rouged mouth while wearing a red dress. In 1926 Rudolf Schlichter depicted *Bertolt Brecht* as a common man. **Note:** Following a three-year closure, the newly renovated villa is scheduled to reopen in early 2013. Contact the museum for opening times.

Luisenstrasse 33. ℭ **089/2333200.** www.lenbachhaus.de. Admission 6€ adults, 3€ students. Tues–Sun 10am–6pm. U-Bahn: Königsplatz.

Sunday on Sale for a Euro

Many of Munich's state-owned museums celebrate lazy Sundays with an across-the-board €1 entry fee for all visitors. With treasures in the 3 Pinakotheks (Alte, Neue, der Moderne), Museum Brandhorst, Schack-Galerie, the Glyptothek, Antikensammlungen, and the Bayerisches Nationalmuseum at such a price, your Sunday may not be lazy after all.

Museum Brandhorst ★ MUSEUM   In the Museum Quarter, Udo and Anette Brandhorst have donated their collection of contemporary art, assembled over a lifetime, to this museum, which is unique in Munich. The building, using sustainable "green" features, is the most avant-garde in the city. Perfectly lit, its exhibits are arranged according to the latest in 21st-century design. Paintings and sculptures range from Andy Warhol to a dozen original editions of books illustrated by Picasso—almost the whole of his *oeuvre* in this field.

The museum owns 60 works by Cy Twombly, an American artist celebrated for his calligraphic-style graffiti paintings. Damien Hirst, the British artist famous for his series of dead animals preserved in formaldehyde, has the most gruesome works on display. Other major works are by Sigmar Polke and Gerhard Richter, the leaders of the "Capitalistic Realism" school of painting, an antistyle of art inspired by advertising. Currently, the museum owns some 700 modern works of art, although not all of them are on display at the same time.

Kunstareal, Theresienstrasse 35A. ℂ **089/238052286.** www.museum-brandhorst.de. Admission 7€ adults, 5€ children 5-16. Sun admission for all 1€. Tues–Sun 10am–6pm (Thurs until 8pm). U-Bahn: Königsplatz or Theresienstrasse. Bus: 100 or 154.

Neue Pinakothek (New Picture Gallery) ★ MUSEUM   The survey of 19th-century works in this museum has two main highlights. For one, the excellent collection surrounding Romantic works and those associated with Ludwig I provide excellent insight into the zeitgeist and zest for all things Greek. **Johann Christian Reinhart**'s quartet of *Views of Rome from the Villa Malta* plunge you into the center of Rome, where a 24-year-old Ludwig visited and drank wine with the painters and poets, as depicted in **Franz Ludwig Catel**'s *Ludwig in a Wine Tavern in Rome* (1824). **Philipp von Foltz** and **Peter von Hess** depict King Othon, the first king of the newly independent Greece—and Ludwig's son—leaving Munich, and arriving in Athens and Nafplio. Casper David Friedrich rounds out the Romantic tour with the early *Summer* (1807) and *Riesengebirge with Rising Fog* (1819), which clearly portray the development of his style.

The other main highlight is the museum's dosage of Impressionist works, starting with **Edouard Manet**'s scandalous *Luncheon in the Studio*, with three characters that have nothing to do with one another. Also, one of **Van Gogh**'s prized *Sunflowers* (1888) hangs in the next room, while Monet, Munch, Degas, Renoir, Munch, and Klimt round out the tour.

Barerstrasse 29 (across Theresienstrasse from the Alte Pinakothek). ℂ **089/23805195.** www.pinakothek. de. Admission 7€ adults, 5€ students and seniors, free for children 15 and under. Sun admission for all 1€. Thurs–Mon 10am–6pm; Wed 10am–8pm. U-Bahn: Theresienstrasse. Tram: 27. Bus: 100.

Pinakothek der Moderne ★★ MUSEUM   When this equivalent of London's Tate Gallery or Paris' Pompidou opened in 2002, it was one of world's largest museums dedicated to the visual arts of the 19th and 20th centuries. It encompasses four collections: **Staatsgalerie Moderner Kunst (State Gallery of Modern Art)** ★★★, with paintings, sculpture, photography, and video; **Die Neue Sammlung (New Collection),** which constitutes the national museum of applied art featuring design and craft work; the **Architekturmuseum der Technischen Universität (Technical University's Architectural Museum),** with architectural drawings, photographs, and models; and the **Staatliche Graphische Sammlung (State Collection of Graphics),** with its outstanding collection of prints and drawings, which can be viewed only by request.

The structure, designed by Stefan Braunfels, is a work of art itself, a veritable cathedral of light, lines and space. Your tastes may dictate which collection to see first, but the upstairs Gallery of Modern Art is not to be missed. The paintings by Matisse, Picasso, Braque, Magritte, and Dalí alone would make an amazing gallery. Yet, the museum possesses a wealth of excellent German Modern art, represented by Die Brücke artists like Kirchner and Schmidt-Rotluff, and the Blaue Reiter group with Kandinsky, Franz Marc, and Auguste Macke. Some of these turned up in a revealing collection of *Entartete Kunst*, or Degenerate Art, which the Nazis deemed as unworthy of their collections of "fine" art. Works by Warhol, Francis Bacon and Joseph Beuys wrap up the tour, leaving you with just enough energy to enjoy the rest.

Barerstrasse 40. ✆ **089/23805360.** www.pinakothek.de. Admission 10€ adults; 7€ students, seniors, and children 16 and under. Sun admission for all 1€. Wed–Sun 10am–6pm (Thurs until 8pm). U-Bahn: Odeonsplatz.

PRINZREGENTENSTRASSE & THE ENGLISCHER GARTEN

After the Ludwigstrasse, Maximilianstrasse, and Briennerstrasse, the Prinzregentenstrasse was the last monumental boulevard laid out during the short-lived Kingdom of Bavaria. It takes the name of the Prince Regent Luitpold, who stood in as ruler from 1886 to 1912 when Ludwig II's older brother Otto was deemed too insane to sit in the throne. This grand avenue slips between the Hofgarten and the Englisher Garten, passing the Nazi-built Haus der Kunst, Bavarian National Museum, and Schack Gallerie, and eventually leads over the Isar River to the Villa Stuck. At a bridge crossing a branch of the Isar as it enters the Englischer Garten, stop to have a look at courageous surfers carving waves.

Bayerisches Nationalmuseum (Bavarian National Museum) ★★ MUSEUM

In 1855, King Maximilian II inaugurated this shrine to the arts in Bavaria, with a collection that grew to be so large it moved to several other locations before settling here. The ornate building by Gabriel von Seidl, architect of the Lenbachhaus and parts of the Deutsches Museum, was finished in 1900.

The collection presents several highlights in Room I, devoted to church art from the 4th to 15th centuries. Romanesque sculptures and architectural fragments from Wessobrunn monastery are the focal point, along with a collection of absorbing ivories in haut-relief, lion-shaped silver pitchers from Nuremberg (1400), and a priceless gold-plated glass of Peter and Paul from Rome. The Bamberger Saal (Room 4) contains three large altar paintings from the early 1400s.

Room 9 presents a unique and consuming **painted wooden Amtsstube interior,** from the Zunfthaus der Weber in Augsburg. Painted at various points between 1457 and 1601, the wooden vault depicts scenes and figures from the Old Testament, as well as Jewish prophets, Greek Philosophers, and prominent politicians.

A highlight of the ground floor is the **Vaulted Gothic hall** (Room 15) with astounding altar pieces Jan Polack and Erasmus Grasser, and the 1490 Gothic Altar that used to stand in Peterskirche. Don't miss a curious 15th-century wooden Christ on a donkey with wheels, which used to be paraded through a village in the Allgäu region. The next room presents several pieces by **Tilman Riemenschneider,** including the spellbinding wood carving *St. Magdalena von Engeln erhoben* (1490–92), covered in swirling hair.

Other highlights of the museum include Bavarian beer steins (*Humpen*) and **Jakob Sandtner's models** of Bavarian cities, both in Room 22. From the Renaissance collection, Room 27 contains a unique **ceremonial hammer** used by the Pope for opening the doors of St. Peter's, given in 1550 to the Augsburg cardinal. The Baroque and Rococo collection features a fascinating **astronomical floor clock** (Room 46), with a hilarious ensemble of cherubs and animals of the zodiac. One babe is being pinched by Cancer's claw, and Scorpio is crawling up another one. Don't miss Room 52, which contains **King Othon's coronation garb** (1835), which was made for the Bavarian-born King of Greece, but never worn.

Prinzregentenstrasse 3. (ⓒ **089/2112401.** www.bayerisches-nationalmuseum.de. Admission 5€ adults, 4€ students and seniors, free for children 14 and under. Sun admission for all 1€. Tues–Wed and Fri–Sun 10am–5pm; Thurs 10am–8pm. U-Bahn: Lehel. Tram: 17. Bus: 100.

Schack-Galerie MUSEUM   To appreciate this florid and romantic overdose of sentimental German paintings of the 19th century, you've got to enjoy fauns and elves at play in picturesque, even magical, landscapes. Such art has its devotees. Obviously, if you're a Picasso cubist, you'd be better off going elsewhere. But this once-private collection adheres to the Baroque tastes of Count Adolf Friedrich von Schack of Schwerin (1815–94), who spent a rich life acquiring works by the likes of Spitzweg, Schwind, Fuerbach, and others, many others—some of whom frankly should have been assigned to the dustbin of art history. Still, in all, we find a visit here fun, at least on a rainy, gray day. It's like wandering back to a lost world.

Prinzregentenstrasse 9. (ⓒ **089/23805224.** www.pinakothek.de/schack-galerie. Admission 4€ adults, 3€ children. Wed–Sun 10am–6pm. Closed major holidays. Bus: 100.

OUTER SIGHTS

BMW Welt MUSEUM   Germany's passion for its cars almost exceeds that of its beer. BMW World is an exemplary shrine to the Bavarian brand, erected on the other side of the Autobahn from the factory itself. The Welt (World) itself is free and open to the public, showcasing several new models with a restaurant and shop. Those who wish to delve further can opt to visit the museum, or get the full experience with a tour of the plant. Plant tours (in English and German) are offered only on weekdays, last 2½ hours, and cost 8€; call in advance for schedules and information.

Lerchenauer Strasse 57. (ⓒ **0180/1118822.** www.bmw-welt.com. Museum admission 12€ adults, 6€ children 18 and under and seniors, 24€ family ticket. Daily 9am–6pm. U-Bahn: Olympiazentrum.

Deutsches Museum von Meisterwerken der Naturwissenschaft und Technik (German Museum of Masterpieces of Science and Technology) ★★★ ☺ MUSEUM   All of the displays in this Louvre of technology cannot be seen in a day, and it may be hard to drag the kids (and adults) out of here. Combined with the **Flugwerft Schleissheim** 18km (11 miles) north of town and the **Verkehrszentrum (Transportation Center)** at Theresienhöhe, this museum, Germany's largest, houses over 20,000 objects, providing a comprehensive survey of scientific and technological innovation. Highlights include the aviation hall with several suspended aircraft, including the Wright Brothers' Model A plane from 1909 (the first one they produced commercially and flew at Berlin's Tempelhof airport). The 19th century ship *Maria* sits in the same hall. Model mines, turning watermills, and musical instruments make up the over 18,000 exhibits covering topics like physics, photography, farming, and pharmacy. As if there weren't already enough levers, buttons and cranks in the museum, a special Kid's Kingdom (*Kinderreich*) provides kids aged 3 to 8 water to splash in, a large guitar to strum, and blocks for building. Upper floors provide a unique perspective of Munich's skyline.

Automobile aficionados may want to focus on just on the **Verkehrszentrum,** where vintage cars, buses, trams, trains and just about anything related to ground transport is on display. Here you'll find the Ford Model T and the first automobile (Benz, 1886). In the further-flung **Flugwerft Schliessheim,** you'll find a 1918 hangar filled with planes, helicopters, gliders and anything related to aviation.

Museumsinsel 1. ✆ **089/21791.** www.deutsches-museum.de. Admission 8.50€ adults, 7€ seniors, 3€ students, free for children 6 and under. Admission to all 3 museums 17€. Daily 9am–5pm. Closed major holidays. U-Bahn: Fraunhoferstrasse. S-Bahn: Isartor. Tram: 18. **Verkehrszentrum:** Theresienhöhe 14a. ✆ **089/500806762.** Admission 6€ adults, 4€ seniors, 3€ students, free for children 6 and under. Daily 9am–5pm. U-Bahn: Schwanthalerhöhe. **Flugwerft Schliessheim:** Effnerstrasse 18. ✆ **089/315714.** Admission and opening times same as Verkehrszentrum. S-Bahn: S1 to Oberschleissheim.

Olympia Park ★ PARK   Although the Olympic flame has long since moved on—and may soon return again—the Olympic Grounds remain a pleasant green area for picnics, walks, and sporting activities. The hall and stadium still host periodic events and concerts, and the pool is open to the public (see "Outdoor Pursuits," p. 322). Built on a pile of World War II rubble, the **Olympischer Berg (Olympic Mountain)** offers sweeping views of the city.

The vistas from the top of the **Olympiaturm (Olympia Tower;** ✆ 089/30672750) are even better, especially when combined with a night of fine dining at the **Restaurant 181** (✆ **089/350948181;** www.restaurant181.com). Head Chef Otto Koch has transformed this restaurant from an unforgettable view with nice food to unforgettable food with a nice view. Fashioned like service on an airplane, since you're so high up anyway, the First and Business meals are served at separate times with a three-course economy menu from 6 to 8pm for 36€, followed by the four-course business menu after 8:30pm 50€. The Tower Restaurant revolves around its axis in 60 minutes, giving guests who linger a changing vista of Munich. Diners Club, MasterCard, and Visa are accepted.

No one here can forget the horrific Black September attack on the Israeli team during the 1972 Olympics, in which 11 Israeli athletes, a German police officer, and five of the Palestinian terrorists perished. Just west of U-Bahn station Olympiazentrum, the building where the hostage standoff began still stands at Connolystrasse 31, with a **memorial marble** listing the names of the 11 Israelis.

Schloss Nymphenburg ★★ HISTORIC BUILDING   The birth of Maximilian II Emanuel in 1662 to Elector Ferdinand Maria and his wife, Henriette Adelaide of Savoy, was a cause for long-awaited joy, so much that the Elector called for the construction of a summer villa along with the Theatinerkirche. Once a pleasant summer retreat for the Wittelsbach royalty, the Nymphenburg Palace and Park are now a popular year-round destination for visitors and locals alike. The modest interior of the main building lacks the "room-after-room" feel of Versailles, and can be viewed in less than an hour. Be sure to devote more time to the gardens and pavilions.

Swiss architect Enrico Zuccalli completed the original core residence by 1679 consisting of the Great Hall and royal bedrooms. Under Maximilian II Emanuel the building grew to its present size, with Antonio Viscardi carrying out Zuccalli's plans for a northern and southern wing beginning in 1702. Italian baroque gave way to French styles after 1715, when architect Joseph Effner and landscape designer Dominique Girard masterminded a grand expansion resulting in the park and its decoration. In the mid-1700s Cuvilliés the Elder and stucco-master Johann Baptist Zimmermann topped it all off with the sumptuous Amalienburg, and the decoration of the **Great Hall** you see first upon entering.

Inside, Zimmermann's frescoes (1756) seem to evoke what is going on outside the park, and depict nymphs paying homage to Flora, hence the palace's name. Turning

Deutsches Museum

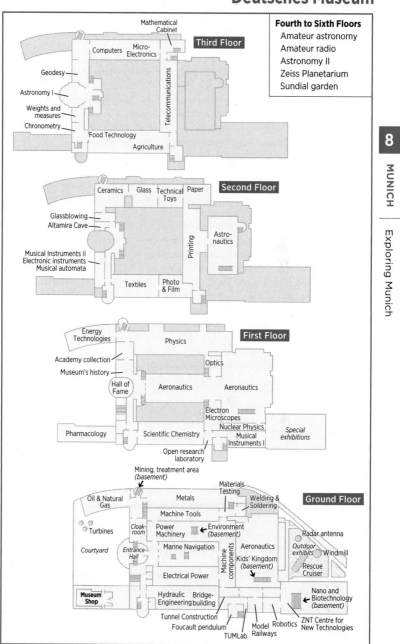

Fourth to Sixth Floors
Amateur astronomy
Amateur radio
Astronomy II
Zeiss Planetarium
Sundial garden

Third Floor

Mathematical Cabinet
Computers
Micro-Electronics
Telecommunications
Geodesy
Astronomy I
Weights and measures
Chronometry
Food Technology
Agriculture

Second Floor

Ceramics
Glass
Technical Toys
Paper
Glassblowing
Altamira Cave
Printing
Astro-nautics
Musical Instruments II
Electronic instruments
Musical automata
Textiles
Photo & Film

First Floor

Energy Technologies
Physics
Academy collection
Optics
Museum's history
Hall of Fame
Aeronautics
Aeronautics
Electron Microscopes
Pharmacology
Scientific Chemistry
Nuclear Physics
Special exhibitions
Musical Instruments I
Open research laboratory

Ground Floor

Mining, treatment area *(basement)*
Materials Testing
Oil & Natural Gas
Metals
Welding & Soldering
Turbines
Machine Tools
Cloak-room
Power Machinery
Environment *(basement)*
Radar antenna
Courtyard
Entrance Hall
Marine Navigation
Machine components
Aeronautics
Outdoor exhibits
Windmill
Kids' Kingdom *(basement)*
Rescue Cruiser
Electrical Power
Museum Shop
Hydraulic Engineering
Bridge-building
Nano and Biotechnology *(basement)*
Tunnel Construction
Foucault pendulum
TUMLab
Model Railways
Robotics
ZNT Centre for New Technologies

left from the hall, you enter the North Gallery where visitors waited for the Elector and admired the 1722 veduta paintings of other palaces in Bavaria. Nearby are Maximilian II Emanuel's Great Gallery of Beauties, five portraits of dames in Louis XIV's court, which only act as a prelude to Ludwig I's **Gallery of Beauties ★** in the South Gallery.

This splendid collection of 36 portraits painted between 1827 and 1850 by Joseph Stieler includes royal members like Ludwig II's mother Marie of Prussia, who gave birth to the "Mad King" in the nearby Queen's Bedroom. A few of the king's mistresses are portrayed as well, like the promiscuous Jane Elizabeth Digby and the scandalous Lola Montez, whose affair ended Ludwig II's reign. Don't miss Helene Sedlmayer, aka the *Schöne Münchnerin (Lovely Munich Girl)*, a humble daughter of a shoemaker whose image became emblematic of Munich's beauty.

Housed in the former stables further south, the **Marstallmuseum** displays an array of fancy state and gala coaches, ornate hunting sleighs, and even hearses. Highlights include the coronation coach of Karl Albrecht when he became Holy Roman Emperor in 1742, and a fantastic hunting sleigh from 1827 with Hercules slaying a Hydra. "Mad King" Ludwig fans can marvel at his pompous New Dress Coach (1871), and his deluxe sleigh with a moveable cabin that sits on wheels or runners. His own "Gallery of Beauties" (referring to his horses) hangs nearby.

The upstairs **Porzellansammlung (Porcelain Collection)** boasts the work of the Nymphenburg Porcelain Manufactory stretching from 1747 to 1930, with many works by Franz Anton Bustelli, active from 1754 to 1763. Individual figures like the imposing eagle (1918) designed by Theodor Kärner and Fernand Clément are impressive enough, but even more enthralling are Otto Wustlich's copies of famous Alte Pinakothek paintings that look as if they were painted yesterday.

Behind the palace, the expansive **Schlosspark Nymphenburg ★** stretches for some 200 hectares (500 acres), meaning a delightful stroll can turn into a pilgrimage if you don't watch out. Your best bet is to round clockwise through the park, beginning with the elaborately decorated **Amalienburg ★★** pavilion, which Karl Albrecht had built for his wife by 1739. Cuvilliés the Elder designed this masterpiece of Rococo, and although restrained on the exterior, the interior explodes with Zimmermann's silver stucco work. The impressive Hall of Mirrors announces the hunting theme with cherubs engaged in hunting and fishing, while Peter Jacob Horemans's canvases embedded into the wall of the Hunting Room depict the royal hunting games and festivities. The kitchen shifts themes with radiant blue tiles with biblical scenes as well as Chinese motifs. If you have time, the main canal and numerous ponds and streams in the rest of the park provide a lush playground for nature's critters and your kids alike. Joseph Effner's **Badenburg** pavilion, completed in 1721, features an interesting bath complex blending Turkish and baroque elements into an innovative ensemble that was imitated elsewhere. It offers a pleasant view of the Grosser See (Great Lake) with its circular Apollo Temple. Effner's small **Pagodenburg** on the other side of the grand canal, completed in 1719, reflects the popularity of all things Chinese at the time. If his other creation in the park, the **Magdalenclause (Hermitage)** looks run-down, that's on purpose, as it is meant to resemble a hermit's wooded retreat.

Schloss Nymphenburg 1. ℂ **089/179080.** www.schloss-nymphenburg.de. Admission to all attractions: 12€ adults, 9€ seniors, free for students and children 17 and under. Admission to Schloss Nymphenburg only: 6€ adults, 5€ seniors, free for students and children 17 and under. Admission to Marstallmuseum, Amalienburg, or Porzellansammlung only: 4.50€ adults, 3.50€ seniors, free for students and children 17 and under. Oct–Mar daily 10am–4pm; Apr–Sept daily 9am–6pm. Free parking beside the Marstallmuseum. U-Bahn: Rotkreuzplatz, then tram 12 to Romanplatz. Tram: 17.

PARKS & ZOOS

At 417ha (1,030 acres) the **Englischer Garten ★** is not only Munich's largest city park, but it's also larger than London's Hype Park or Central Park in New York. Designed in 1789, the "green lung" of the cityscape was the brainchild of the Massachusetts-born Englishman Sir Benjamin Thompson, who was employed in the Bavarian court under the assumed name "Count Rumford" after English aspirations went belly-up in the American colony. The famous **Chinesischer Turm (Chinese Tower)** went up a year later—it took quite some time before the beer garden and brass band showed up—and stands near the only bus line piercing the park. A network of some 78km (48 miles) of paths cross the lawns and woods between the eastern Isar River and western Schwabing neighborhood, offering hours of potential for walkers, joggers, and even loungers. In summer, many locals in some parts of the park seem to have forgotten to wear clothes (some claim these areas are Munich's most popular tourist attraction). One of the best sunset spots in town is the Monopteros hill just south of the Chinese Tower, from where you can watch the sun dip behind the city's steeple-studded skyline.

Hellabrunn Zoo stands in Tierpark Hellabrunn, about 6km (4 miles) south of the city center, at Tierparkstrasse 30 (✆ **089/625080;** www.zoo-munich.de; U-Bahn: Thalkirchen; bus: 52). It's one of the largest zoos in the world, with hundreds of animals roaming in a natural habitat. A walk through the attractive park is recommended even if you're not a zoo buff. There's a big children's zoo, as well as a large aviary. You can visit the zoo daily 9am to 6pm (in winter, 9am–5pm); admission is 11€ for adults, 7.50€ for students and seniors, 4.50€ for children ages 4 to 14, and free for children 3 and under.

Especially for Kids

Of all the museums in Munich, kids will most enjoy the **Deutsches Museum,** Museumsinsel 1 (✆ **089/21791;** www.deutsches-museum.de; S-Bahn: Isartor; tram: 18), which has many hands-on exhibits (p. 295).

On the third floor of the **Münchner Stadtmuseum,** St. Jakobsplatz 1 (✆ **089/23322370;** www.stadtmuseum-online.de; U-Bahn/S-Bahn: Marienplatz), is an array of marionettes and hand puppets from around the world. Another section is devoted to fairground art, including carousel animals, shooting galleries, roller coaster models, and wax and museum figures. The main exhibit has the oldest-known carousel horses, dating from 1820. For hours and admission fees, see p. 287.

The **Spielzeugmuseum,** in the Altes Rathaus, Marienplatz 15 (✆ **089/294001;** www.spielzeugmuseum-muenchen.de; U-Bahn/S-Bahn: Marienplatz), is a historical toy collection. It's open daily 10am to 5:30pm. Admission is 3.50€ for adults, 1.50€ for children, and 6€ for a family ticket.

For a truly charming experience, go to the **Münchner Marionettentheater,** Blumenstrasse 32 (✆ **089/265712;** www.muenchner-marionettentheater.de; U-Bahn: Sendlinger Tor), which was established in 1858. It stages marionette productions of operas by Mozart and other composers every Wednesday, Thursday, Saturday, and Sunday at 3pm, and every Saturday at 8pm. At matinees, adults pay 10€, children 8€. At evening shows tickets for adults cost 18€ and those for children ages 4 to 12 go for 10€; shows are not suitable for children 3 and under. Matinees tend to be more animated and crowded than evening shows and are particularly well suited for children ages 4 and up.

Bavaria Film Studio, Bavariafilmplatz 7, Geiselgasteig (© 089/64990; www. filmstadt.de; tram: 25 to Bavariafilmplatz), is Europe's largest filmmaking center—Germany's version of Hollywood. Such classics as *The Neverending Story* and *Willy Wonka and the Chocolate Factory* were filmed here. The 30-minute "Bavaria Action Show" features a stunt team demonstrating fistfights and fire stunts, tumbling down staircases, and even taking a 30m-high (100-ft.) plunge. Guided 1½-hour tours are given March to October daily 9am to 4pm, November to February daily 10am to 3pm (from April to October, tours in English are at 1pm daily). Admission is 11€ for adults, 10€ for students and seniors, 8€ for children ages 4 to 14, and free for children 3 and under.

Hellabrunn Zoo has a large children's zoo, where kids can pet the animals. For details, see p. 299.

WHERE TO EAT

Munich, one of the few European cities with more than one Michelin-rated three-star restaurant, is the place to practice *Edelfresswelle* ("high-class gluttony"). The classic local dish, traditionally consumed before noon, is *Weisswurst,* herb-flavored white-veal sausage blanched in water. Sophisticated international cuisine is popular throughout the city, too. For the location of restaurants in this section, see the "Central Munich Restaurants & Hotels" map on p. 302.

In Central Munich
VERY EXPENSIVE

Ederer ★★ MODERN INTERNATIONAL Noted as one of the poshest addresses in Munich, and the culinary domain of celebrity chef Karl Ederer, this restaurant is noted for its huge windows, several blazing fireplaces, very high ceilings, and an appealing collection of paintings. Inspiration for the menu items covers the gamut of cuisines from Bavaria, France, Italy, the New World, and the Pacific Rim. The menu changes with the seasons and the whim of the kitchen staff, but might include such starters as marinated sweet-and-sour pumpkin served with shiitake mushrooms, parsley roots, and lukewarm chunks of octopus; or terrine of duckling foie gras with a very fresh brioche and a dollop of pumpkin jelly. Representative main courses include a delectable grilled guinea fowl with shiitake mushrooms and a spicy sauce, or sautéed crispy octopus with fresh asparagus and quince.

Kardinal Faulhaber Strasse 10. © **089/24231310.** www.restaurant-ederer.de. Reservations required. Main courses 22€–33€; fixed-price 2-course lunch 25€, 4-course dinner 65€. AE, MC, V. Mon–Sat noon–3pm and 6:30–10pm. U-Bahn: Marienplatz or Odeonsplatz.

Garden-Restaurant ★ MEDITERRANEAN/INTERNATIONAL This showcase restaurant within one of Munich's showcase hotels is housed in a sleek and minimalist sunroom. Catering to a cosmopolitan crowd, the cuisine is about as cultivated and esoteric as you can find in Munich. Some of the examples include sautéed slices of calf's liver in a shallot sauce or a steak of suckling veal with truffle-laced risotto. A delectable ravioli of oxtail appears flavored with leeks, or else you can order poached catfish and a smoked salmon with a horseradish mousse. You might start with the orange and fennel soup flavored with Thai chili oil.

In the Bayerischer Hof hotel, Promenadeplatz 2–6. © **089/2120993.** Reservations recommended. Main courses 25€–43€. AE, DC, MC, V. Daily noon–3pm and 6–11:30pm. Tram: 19.

Restaurant Königshof ★★★ INTERNATIONAL/FRENCH   Overlooking the Karlstor, this remains one of Munich's grand hotel dining rooms, with its oyster-white panels of oak, polished bronze chandeliers, silver candelabras, and porcelain. The waiters are polite and skilled and the chefs highly inventive. The cuisine is simply dazzling, light, full of flavor, and prepared with only the finest of ingredients. For some of the most discerning foodies in Germany, this restaurant is a must on their gastronomic itineraries.

Among the favorite dishes here are baked turbot with mushrooms, smoked eel, and parsley oil, or smoked duck breast with chicory. Especially delectable is a saddle of bison with sautéed polenta, eggplant, and young onions. Lobster appears with a delightful vanilla butter, and loin of lamb is aromatically seasoned with fresh herbs.

In the Hotel Königshof, Karlsplatz 25 (Am Stachus). (© **089/551360.** Reservations required. Main courses 42€–49€; fixed-price menus 95€–210€. AE, DC, MC, V. Tues-Sat noon-2:30pm and 7-10pm. Closed Aug 1-Sept 5. S-Bahn: Karlsplatz. Tram: 16, 17, 18, 19, or 27.

Restaurant Vue Maximilian ★ FRENCH/INTERNATIONAL   Restaurant Vue Maximilian is in a quiet and elegant location within walking distance of the opera house. The atmosphere is dignified and refined, the service extremely competent, and the food prepared along classic French lines with imaginative variations, including Asian influences. Refreshing the menu about once a month, Chef Sven Büttner lets his culinary fancy wander at will, as exemplified by such dishes as Sautéed Dover sole with steamed spinach or a filet of turbot in a truffled potato purée. You might also try the sautéed calf's liver with glazed apple slices. Favorite starters include a tartare of Bavarian beef with caviar and crème fraîche or a boiled prime rib of beef consommé with semolina dumplings.

In the Hotel Vier Jahreszeiten Kempinski München, Maximilianstrasse 17. (© **089/21252125.** Reservations required. Main courses 26€–44€. AE, DC, MC, V. Daily noon-3:30pm and 6-11:30pm. Tram: 19.

Schuhbecks in den Südtiroler Stuben ★★★ BAVARIAN/INTERNATIONAL   This luxe restaurant is one of the very best restaurants in all of Bavaria, given serious competition only by Tantris (p. 311). Chef Alfons Schuhbeck enjoys well-deserved celebrity. East meets West in his fusion cuisine, which some critics liken to "California freestyle." At the top of his menu, the chef welcomes you with "modest greetings," but there is nothing modest about the cuisine. The menu is forever changing, based on the freshest and best ingredients in any season.

Some of our favorite starters include fish soup made with freshwater fish and crayfish, given added zest with a touch of curry; marinated tuna fish with caviar and vegetable jelly; and the truffle-infused pasta with Parmesan and summer vegetables. Main dishes have robust flavors and are most satisfying, including roast wild boar with an apple-and-pear purée, veal roulades stuffed with potatoes, and rack of lamb with curried eggplant.

Am Platzl 6-8. (© **089/2166900.** www.schuhbeck.de. Reservations required. Fixed-price menus 78€–128€. AE, DC, MC, V. Tues-Sat noon-2:30pm; Mon-Sat 6-11pm. U-Bahn or S-Bahn: Marienplatz.

EXPENSIVE

Austernkeller ★ SEAFOOD   This "oyster cellar," with the largest selection of oysters in town, from raw oysters to oysters Rockefeller, is a delight to visitors and locals. A terrific starter is the shellfish platter with fresh oysters, mussels, clams, scampi, and sea snails. Or you may begin with a richly stocked fish soup or cold hors

Central Munich Restaurants & Hotels

HOTELS ■
Anna Hotel **11**
Bayerischer Hof &
  Palais Montgelas **40**
Brack **6**
Charles Hotel **13**
Cortiina **38**
Creatif Hotel Elephant **3**
Eden-Hotel-Wolff **4**
Excelsior Hotel **10**
Gästehaus Englischer
  Garten **24**
Hotel an der Oper **34**
Hotel Exquisit **18**
Hotel Jedermann **1**
Hotel Mark **8**
Hotel Monaco **9**
Hotel München Palace **58**
Hotel Olympic **19**
Hotel Preysing **55**
Hotel Schlicker **47**
Hotel Splendid-Dollmann
  im Lehel **56**
Hotel Torbräu **50**
Hotel Uhland **5**
Hotel Vier Jahreszeiten
  Kempinski München **45**
Kriemhild **2**
Laimer Hof **2**
La Maison **22**
Mandarin Oriental **36**
Pension Westfalia **7**

RESTAURANTS ◆
Alois Dallmayr **29**
Andechser am Dom **26**
Asam Schlössl **54**
Austernkeller **46**
Bier- und Oktoberfest-
  museum **49**
Café Glockenspiel **27**
Café Ignaz **15**
Club Moritz **53**
Cohen's **21**
Der Katzlmacher **37**
Deutsche Eiche **52**
Dukatz **41**
Ederer **42**
Garden-Restaurant **40**
Hans-im-Glück
  Burgergrill **14**
Käfer-Schänke **57**
La Bouille **15**
La Galleria **32**
La Valle **31**

Lenbach **16**
Nero Pizza **51**
Nürnberger Bratwurst
  Glöckl am Dom **25**
Pfistermühle **33**
Prinz Myshkin **43**
Ratskeller München **28**
Restaurant Königshof **12**
Restaurant Mark's **36**
Restaurant Vue
  Maximilian **45**
Schelling Salon **20**
Schuhbecks in den
  Südtiroler Stuben **35**
Spatenhaus an
  der Oper **44**
Tantris **23**
Vinorant Alter Hof **30**
Weinhaus Neuner **17**
Weisses Bräuhaus **39**
Zum Alten Markt **48**

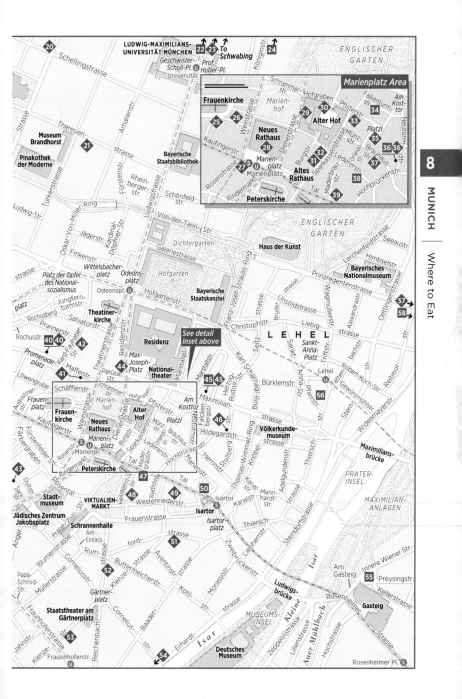

d'oeuvres. French meat specialties are also offered, but the focus is seafood—everything from lobster Thermidor to shrimp grilled in the shell. The decor is elegant and refined, and the service is attentive.

Stollbergstrasse 11. ✆ **089/298787.** www.austernkeller.de. Reservations required. Lunch main courses 13€–15€; dinner main courses 21€–24€. AE, DC, MC, V. Mon–Fri 11:30am–2pm; daily 5–11:30pm. Closed Dec 23–26. U-Bahn: Isartor.

Der Katzlmacher ★ 🏛 ITALIAN   Few Italian restaurants would have had the nerve to adopt as their name a pejorative German term referring to Italians. This one did, however, and its sense of humor has helped make it beloved by loyal local fans. The setting is a few steps from the Marienplatz and a short walk to the famous Hofbräuhaus. The modern design is bistro style, and the cooking is personalized and market fresh, focusing on dishes from the north of Italy. The chefs are imaginative, offering, for example, at least four dishes with radicchio, including a scampi tempura, risotto with red wine, sirloin strips, or lasagna. Other themes might focus seasonally on shellfish, asparagus, morels, or truffles. Year-round specialties are a mixed fish fry, a carpaccio of duck breast, or eel in a champagne sauce.

Bräuhausstrasse 6. ✆ **089/348129.** www.der-katzlmacher.de. Reservations recommended. Main courses 25€–28€; fixed-price lunches 10€–27€, dinners 41€–54€. MC, V. Mon–Sat noon–3pm and 6:30–11pm. U-Bahn: Marienplatz.

La Galleria ★ ITALIAN   This intimate and appealing Italian restaurant feels like a private art salon, but offers experimental and tasty Italian cuisine. The Italian owners provide gracious service and a carefully crafted roster of dishes that change with the availability of ingredients and the inspiration of the chefs. In addition to a range of homemade pasta dishes, you'll find grilled cuttlefish with curry sauce, tagliatelle with leeks and angler fish, or grilled tuna with candied tomatoes and eggplant.

Sparkassenstrasse 11. ✆ **089/297995.** www.ristorante-galleria.de. Reservations recommended. Main courses 15€–27€; fixed-price dinners 58€–65€. AE, DC, MC, V. Mon–Sat noon–2:30pm and 6:30–11:30pm. U-Bahn or S-Bahn: Marienplatz.

Restaurant Mark's ★★★ FRENCH/CONTINENTAL   This restaurant is appropriately elegant with an impeccably trained staff. Lunch is served in a small, cozy enclave off the lobby, Mark's Corner, and is usually limited to a fixed-price menu favored by businesspeople. Dinners are more elaborate, served one floor above street level in a formal dining room that overlooks a monumental staircase and the lobby below. On Sunday and Monday nights only, the formal dining room is closed, and dinner is served in Mark's Corner. Menus change monthly and according to the inspiration of the chef. Many dishes are somewhat experimental but still succeed beautifully, such as filet of beef with a ragout of artichokes and potatoes and deep-fried baby garlic buds; sea wolf with green lentils, bacon, and goose liver; and filet of beef with horseradish, served with dumplings and Savoy cabbage.

In the Mandarin Oriental, Neuturmstrasse 1. ✆ **089/290980.** www.mandarinoriental.com. Reservations recommended. Main courses 29€–32€; fixed-price menus 65€–169€. AE, DC, MC, V. Tues–Sun 7–11pm. U-Bahn or S-Bahn: Marienplatz.

MODERATE

Alois Dallmayr ★★ CONTINENTAL   This famous delicatessen has been serving Munich's most elegant consumers since 1700. The upstairs dining room serves a subtle German version of Continental cuisine, owing a heavy debt to France. The food array is dazzling, ranging from the excellent herring and sausages to such rare treats as vine-ripened tomatoes flown in from Morocco and papayas from Brazil. The famous French *poulet de Bresse* (this Bresse chicken is identified throughout Europe as the most flavorful and tender chicken anywhere), beloved of gourmets, is also shipped in. The smoked fish is fabulous, and the soups are superbly flavored, especially the one made with shrimp. If you're dining alone, you may prefer to sit at the counter instead of a table. Expect a busy lunch crowd.

Dienerstrasse 14-15. © **089/2135100.** www.dallmayr.de. Reservations recommended. Main courses 35€–55€; fixed-price 4-course lunch 95€, 7-course dinner 140€. AE, DC, MC, V. Tues–Sat noon–2pm and 7–11pm. U-Bahn: Marienplatz.

Café Glockenspiel ☺ PASTRIES/INTERNATIONAL

Overlooking Munich's central square, this 5th-floor perch offers the best view of the clockwork of the Neues Rathaus, not to mention pastries, tasty pies, and a few delectable dishes for dinner. You can select from the intimate Red Salon, a sunny courtyard-side veranda, or the cafe, which usually fills up around midday and 5pm for the Glockenspiel performance. The spinach and goat cheese strudel with stewed eggplants makes an excellent starter or light meal, followed by jumbo shrimp and scallops in garlic butter with asparagus, baby carrots, and saffron foam. For dessert, just join the drooling patrons eying the fruit tortes and Viennese Sacher torte in the glass counter.

Marienplatz 28. © **089/264256.** www.cafe-glockenspiel.de. Main courses 12€–24€; fixed-price menus 24€–33€. MC, V. Mon–Sat 10am–1am; Sun 10am–7pm. U-Bahn or S-Bahn: Marienplatz.

Dukatz ★ INTERNATIONAL/FRENCH

This cafe/restaurant pays tribute to the writer Oskar Maria Graf (1894–1967), and draws writers, editors, and readers from Munich's large publishing community. When called in to carry out the Graf theme, New York artist Jenny Holzer took sentences from Graf's writings and inscribed them on the cafe's leather benches and on the plates. You'll have to finish your meal to see what Graf had to say.

This is no mere coffeehouse, however. The restaurant serves full-fledged meals with some of the Bavarian countryside's finest ingredients. At lunch, try a sandwich such as the baguette with rabbit or the pastrami with *Sauerkraut.* A good dinner choice is the salmon in champagne sauce with fresh oysters. The *Blutwurst* in pastry, with diced apples, was better than the typical *boudin noir* in a French bistro. For dessert, try the pear tart with almond cream.

Maffeistrasse 3. © **089/2919600.** www.dukatz.de. Reservations not needed. Main courses 16€–28€; 4-course menus 45€–58€. No credit cards. Mon–Sat noon–2:30pm and 6:30–10:30pm. U-Bahn: Odeonsplatz.

Lenbach ★ CONTINENTAL/ASIAN

Aggressively hip and aesthetically striking, this is one of the most sought-after restaurants in Munich. It occupies a landmark building, erected in 1887, that originally functioned as the home and sales outlet for the era's most flamboyant antiques dealer, who frescoed its interior with Renaissance murals. An unusual blend of hypermodern and Renaissance motifs greets diners here, whose path to their table is along a slightly elevated catwalk that evokes a runway where supermodels might strut their stuff.

A tempting array of main dishes includes chicken stuffed with small artichokes and served with a lemony pine sauce, or curried saddle of lamb with an olive-studded polenta. A savory pasta dish is the ravioli with leek ragout and sun-dried tomatoes. The most appealing starters are a carpaccio of beef with seafood and asparagus, or a creamy soup of wild garlic with almond croutons.

Ottostrasse 6. © **089/5491300.** www.lenbach.de. Reservations recommended. Main courses lunch 9.50€–13€, dinner 15€–28€. AE, DC, MC, V. Mon–Sat 11:30am–2:30pm and 6pm–midnight. U-Bahn: Stachus.

Nürnberger Bratwurst Glöckl am Dom ★ ☺ 🍴 BAVARIAN Whether Nuremberg is on your itinerary or not, come here to sample the best finger-size white sausages made famous in the Franconian town. In this convivial tavern-style retreat, faded prints of old Bavaria bedeck the worn wooden walls, and small hand-carved chairs gather round communal tables where you're sure to rub elbows with your neighbor. The upstairs Dürerstube is equally appealing, with decorative details that make for pleasant eye-wandering.

The menu features such items as crispy roast pork with bread dumplings and cabbage salad, veal breast stuffed with a potato-and-cucumber salad, or breaded veal escalopes topped with a cream sauce. Don't be surprised when the food comes on tin plates.

Frauenplatz 9. ℂ **089/2919450.** www.bratwurst-gloeckl.de. Reservations recommended. Main courses 6€–22€. MC, V. Daily 10am–1am. U-Bahn: U2 or U3 to Marienplatz.

Pfistermühle BAVARIAN The country comes right into the heart of Munich at this authentic and old-fashioned restaurant, which is comprised of a series of charmingly decorated dining rooms in a converted old mill. A warm welcome and a refreshing cuisine await you here. Many of the dishes would be familiar to your Bavarian grandmother, and portions are generous and satisfying. Come here for some of the most perfectly prepared roasts in the city, always served with a selection of fresh vegetables. Instead of these meat courses, you can opt for a fine array of simply prepared fresh fish from the lakes and rivers of Bavaria, especially the delectable salmon trout or brown trout. Most fish dishes come with chive-flecked sour cream and a potato pancake. Finish with a pyramid of vanilla custard served with a fresh berry sauce, followed by a glass of wild-cherry schnapps.

In the Platzl Hotel, Pfisterstrasse 4. ℂ **089/23703865.** www.platzl.de. Reservations recommended. Main courses 24€–27€. AE, DC, MC, V. Mon–Sat 11:30am–11pm. U-Bahn: Marienplatz.

Ratskeller München BAVARIAN Throughout Germany, you'll find *Ratskellers,* traditional cellar restaurants in Rathaus (city hall) basements, designed to serve decent and inexpensive food and wine to all citizens. Thus, a city hall restaurant should be roomy. Whether you descend from the inner courtyard or from Marienplatz, you'll find a forest of pillars and vaults that is said to hold up to 1,100 diners. The decor, with dark wood and carved chairs, resembles a sophisticated beer cellar. The coziest tables are in the semiprivate dining nooks in the rear, under the vaulted painted ceilings. In addition to the prominent regional fare, the chefs include an array of international, vegetarian, and lighter dishes not normally found on a Ratskeller menu. Hearty-tasting regional fare includes Munich white sausages with sweet mustard, and roast Bavarian duckling with

---

☺ family-friendly RESTAURANTS

Café Glockenspiel (on the Marienplatz) Your kids can down delectable Bavarian pastries while enjoying the miniature "tournament" staged each day near the clock on the Rathaus facade (at 11am and noon, with an extra 5pm performance in summer).

Nürnberger Bratwurst Glöckl am Dom (Frauenplatz 9, facing the cathedral)

Hot dogs will never taste the same again after your child has tried one of these savory little sausages from Nürnberg.

Restaurant 181, Olympiapark (p. 296) For a panoramic view of the Alps as well as the Olympic grounds, take your kids here to dine and, later, out onto one of the observation platforms.

mustard-seed gravy. Another regional dish much in favor with diners is the roast pork shank with potato dumplings and red cabbage.

Im Rathaus, Marienplatz 8. ℂ**089/2199890.** www.ratskeller.com. Reservations required. Main courses 13€–27€. AE, MC, V. Daily 10am–midnight. U-Bahn or S-Bahn: Marienplatz.

Spatenhaus an der Oper BAVARIAN/INTERNATIONAL   The Spatenhaus, one of Munich's best-known beer restaurants, offers wide windows overlooking the opera house on Max-Joseph-Platz. You can sit in an intimate, semiprivate dining nook or at a long table. Spatenhaus has old traditions, typical Bavarian food, and generous portions at reasonable prices. If you want to know what all this fabled Bavarian gluttony is about, order the "Bavarian plate," which is loaded with various meats, including pork and sausages. (After that, you'll have to go to a spa.) Other fine choices include crispy Bavarian pork roast in a dark beer sauce or breast of veal stuffed with a bread stuffing. You can also order grilled veal liver with crispy onions. Of course, to be loyal, you should order the restaurant's own beer, Spaten-Franziskaner-Bier, with your meal. There's another dining annex on the second floor, open daily from 11:30am to 1am, specializing in an international cuisine that includes grilled filet of pikeperch in a wild garlic sauce, or filet steak of Angus beef with a red-wine sauce and a serving of potato strudel. Main courses in this restaurant annex cost 20€ to 30€.

Residenzstrasse 12. ℂ**089/2907060.** Reservations recommended. Main courses 10€–36€. AE, MC, V. Daily 9:30am–12:30am. U-Bahn: Odeonsplatz or Marienplatz. Tram: 19.

Vinorant Alter Hof ★ 🍴 FRANCONIAN   In a castle in the heart of the city (Marienplatz), this restaurant serves the best Franconian regional cuisine in Munich. In the basement is a wine bar where you can enjoy inexpensive snacks and the best of regional wines. Upstairs, a more formal cuisine is served, including an excellently prepared fixed-price menu. This old favorite is decorated in a regional style, and adjusts its menus to take advantage of the best ingredients in any season—game in autumn, fresh asparagus in the spring. Although cooking for the "masses," the chefs manage to create distinctive flavor in their dishes. Desserts are yummy and made fresh daily, great on flavor, and heavy on calories.

Alter Hof 3. ℂ **089/24243733.** www.alter-hof-muenchen.de. Reservations recommended in main restaurant. Main courses 8€–20€. DC, MC, V. Mon–Sat 11:30am–11:30pm. U-Bahn or S-Bahn: Marienplatz.

Weinhaus Neuner BAVARIAN/INTERNATIONAL   To find the *Älteste Weinhaus Münchens* (Munich's oldest wine tavern) look for the ornate gilded lion on a grapevine hanging over the door. This taste of old Munich is housed in its original 15th-century, Tyrolean vaults with black wood paneling. The delicate wood-carvings and late 19th-century oils of old Munich scenes in both the casual *Weinstube* (wine tavern) and formal Restaurant create a place that brims with warmth and charm. Once young priests were educated here, but after Napoleon brought secularization, it became a wine tavern and a rendezvous for artists, writers, and composers, including Richard Wagner. You'll relish such dishes as medallions of monkfish with a crust of chanterelles with a champagne sauce, or the roast gray partridge in a port-wine sauce, or perhaps saddle of wild pig with a juniper cream sauce. One of the most favored desserts is a white-chocolate and poppy-seed mousse with quince and a black-currant ice cream.

Herzogspitalstrasse 8. ℂ**089/2603954.** www.weinhaus-neuner.de. Reservations recommended. Main courses 19€–26€; fixed-price lunch 18€–23€, dinner 45€. AE, MC, V. Mon–Sat noon–3pm and 6pm–midnight. U-Bahn or S-Bahn: Karlsplatz/Stachus.

Zum Alten Markt ♦ BAVARIAN/INTERNATIONAL Snug and cozy, Zum Alten Markt serves beautifully presented, fresh cuisine. Located on a tiny square off Munich's large outdoor food market, the restaurant has a mellow charm and a welcoming host, Josef Lehner. The interior decor, with its intricately coffered wooden ceiling, came from a 400-year-old Tyrolean castle. In summer, tables are set up outside. Fish and fresh vegetables come from the nearby market. You may begin with a tasty homemade soup, such as cream of carrot or perhaps black-truffle tortellini in cream sauce with young onions and tomatoes. The chef makes a great *Tafelspitz* (boiled beef). You can also order classic dishes such as roast duck with applesauce or a savory roast suckling pig.

Am Viktualienmarkt, Dreifaltigkeitsplatz 3. ℂ **089/299995.** www.zumaltenmarkt.de. Reservations recommended. Main courses 15€–20€; fixed-price menu 33€–50€. No credit cards. Mon–Sat 11am–midnight. U-Bahn or S-Bahn: Marienplatz. Bus: 53.

INEXPENSIVE

Andechser am Dom GERMAN/BAVARIAN This brewery outlet manages to mix class with beer hall rowdiness, with a suave clientele that includes members of Bavarian high society. Not only is Andechs known for its beer, which is brewed near the Ammersee southwest of town, but owner Sepp Krätz also runs the Hippodrom tent at Oktoberfest, a so-called VIP tent. Although not the roomiest restaurant in town, the ground floor tavern and patio manage to pack all the guests in, while the leftovers trickle down to the cellar that has the feel of a secret chapel. The house specialty is the *Kloster Schmaus*, spicy sausages with dumplings, green beans and veggie strips served piping hot in the pan itself. The *Schweinsbraten* (pork roast) features a dark beer sauce, and Gluten-free and vegetarian offerings attest to their modern tastes in cuisine.

Weinstrasse 7A. ℂ **089/298481.** www.andechser-am-dom.de. Reservations recommended. Main courses 8.50€–18€. AE, DC, MC, V. Daily 10am–1am. U-Bahn or S-Bahn: Marienplatz.

Bier- und Oktoberfest Museum ★ 🏛 BAVARIAN This authentically Bavarian locale is part museum, part party. The Augustiner Brewery operates this unique cultural and culinary combination as a nonprofit organization in a building dating back to 1327. The multi-story museum explains the beer-making process and the history of the world-famous beer bacchanalia. The ticket includes a voucher for a glass of brew and a snack including the Bavarian cheese *Obatzda* with *Leberwurst* (liver sausage). Your doctor may not like it, but to go Bavarian all the way you can spread *Schmalz* (chicken fat) over your freshly baked rye bread.

After 6pm you can return for the regional Bavarian fare, starting perhaps with a beer-infused goulash and noodles and following with sausage salads or *Schnitzels* and the like. Naturally, everything is washed down with the Augustiner brew.

Sterneckstrasse 2. ℂ **089/24243941.** www.museumsstueberl.de. Reservations not needed. Main courses 4€–14€. No credit cards. Museum Tues–Sat 1–5pm; beer hall Tues–Sat 6pm–midnight. U-Bahn or S-Bahn: Isartor.

Club Morizz CONTINENTAL/THAI/INTERNATIONAL This is *the* hip gay restaurant of Munich. As estimated by the staff, it has a 70% gay-male clientele; lesbian women and gay-friendly straights make up the rest of the clientele. Part of the space is devoted to a sprawling, attractive bar, where red-leather chairs, mirrors, and an impeccably trained staff evoke a 1920s Paris hotel bar. You can enjoy at least 40 single-malt whiskeys, a half-dozen single-barrel bourbons, and a wide array of unusual wines. The adjacent dining room offers an appealing combination of international and

Continental food, prepared by a central European staff whose interpretation of Thai cuisine is especially enjoyable. The menu changes weekly. Try the shrimp with Thai curry or the chicken in a sweet-and-sour sauce with fresh pineapple, or perhaps sautéed filet of chicken flavored with garlic and peppers.

Klenzestrasse 43. ☎ **089/2016776.** www.club-morizz.de. Reservations recommended. Main courses 15€–23€. MC, V. Sun–Thurs 6pm–2am; Fri–Sat 6pm–3am. U-Bahn: Fraunhoferstrasse.

Cohen's JEWISH/CENTRAL EUROPEAN   This eatery tucked in a courtyard near the museum district serves the type of authentic Jewish specialties that were common before the Holocaust. In fact the family recipes stem from the 19th-century Hapsburg era of Austria and Eastern Europe. Although the office feel of the decor could use a makeover, the food doesn't disappoint. The potato salad alone is worth the trip, but you can have so much more, including gefilte fish, latkes, and wonderful goulash dishes. Roast hen appears with couscous, and a delicious green split pea soup is also served. Naturally the matzo ball–and–noodle soup is delectable. Live klezmer music accompanies your meal on Friday evenings.

Theresienstrasse 31, Maxvorstadt. ☎ **089/2809545.** www.cohens.de. Reservations recommended. Main courses 11€–17€. AE, MC, V. Mon–Sat noon–3pm and 6–10:30pm. U-Bahn: Theresienstrasse.

Deutsche Eiche GERMAN   Ever since a building was erected here in 1864, there has been a restaurant with a mostly gay, or at least arts-oriented, clientele. In the 1970s, noteworthy film director Rainer Werner Fassbinder hung out here a lot, usually dressed entirely in chains and leather. Late in the 1990s, the place was renovated into a less evocative, more streamlined-looking beer hall, still with a healthy percentage of gay clients, with direct access to a 36-room hotel and one of the busiest gay saunas in Munich. Accommodations in the hotel are relatively affordable at 139€ to 159€ for a double. Each has a TV and telephone and an all-white, efficient-looking collection of furnishings.

Most come here for the restaurant/bar, however. Simple beer hall–style food includes escalope of pork with french fries, turkey steak with mushrooms in cream and homemade noodles, and a filet of pork with roasted potatoes and fresh vegetables. For those who dare there's a "Munich breakfast" with a pair of white sausages, a pretzel, and white beer, in addition to the buffet served starting at 7pm.

Reichenbachstrasse 13. ☎ **089/2311660.** www.deutsche-eiche.com. Reservations not necessary. Main courses 10€–16€. AE, MC, V. Daily 7am–11pm. U-Bahn: Frauenhoferstrasse.

Hans-im-Glück Burgergrill ★ INTERNATIONAL   Bucking the trend of greasy-spoon burger joints, this eatery might look like a sushi bar from the outside. In fact, a German fairy tale inspired its forest decor, accented by leaf-shaped plates and sleek, black picnic tables that create a familial atmosphere. As for the burgers, the soft flour-dusted buns are baked in Belgium, and the beef hails from the nearby Allgäu region. The chefs have transformed the American staple, integrating the tastes of Teutonic and international cuisine, with such wild results as the Tyrolean burger with Alp cheese, German coleslaw, and walnuts, and an Alsatian creation with Brie and cranberries. The Shanghai with wasabi, sprouts, and chili sauce adds an international flavor. Although not central, it makes an ideal stopover on your way out to or back from Nymphenburg.

Nymphenburgerstrasse 69. ☎ **089/64299982.** www.hansimglueck-burgergrill.de. Reservations recommended. Main courses 7€–15€. AE, MC, V. Mon–Fri 11am–midnight; Sat–Sun 1pm–midnight. U-Bahn: Mailingerstrasse.

La Valle ★ ITALIAN   Given its prime location right off Munich's central square, this Italian restaurant is one of the best and most affordable in town. With dining on two floors, the classically decorated interior recalls the colors of Tuscany, while the food recalls its flavor. The friendly owners Luigi and Carlo lead the largely "south of the border" staff, and provide honest menu advice, especially about the day's fish, pasta, or meat specialties. For starters, the minestrone is about the best in Munich, as are the pastas, especially the rich spaghetti carbonara. An array of pizzas features all the necessary toppings, including a tempting one with scampi and rucola. This seafood lover raved about the pasta topped with succulent medallions of anglerfish, river crayfish, and avocado in a lobster cream sauce. There's always a grilled fish of the day, perhaps king prawns with fresh herbs, each with fresh vegetables. The best meat dish is the *piccata alla lombarda,* tender veal in a white-wine-and-lemon sauce.

Sparkassenstrasse 5. ℂ **089/29160676.** www.ristorante-lavalle.com. Reservations recommended. Small main courses and pizzas 8€–13€; main courses 9€–19€; fixed-price lunch 6.50€–9.50€. AE, MC, V. Mon–Sat 11am–11:30am. U-Bahn or S-Bahn: Marienplatz.

Nero Pizza PIZZA   Some pizza devotees claim the pies baked here, with their thin crusts, are not only the best in Munich, but are capable of competing with some of the best in Rome itself. Guests sit together at sprawling communal tables. Pies come in a wide range of flavors, at times with an astonishing array of toppings. Whole-wheat and gluten-free crust is even available. The lunch special of a pizza and a freshly made salad is a great bargain at only 7.50€. Finish off with a lush dessert such as a margherita-and-truffle cream pie.

Rumfordstrasse 34. ℂ **089/21019060.** www.nero-muenchen.de. Pizzas 7€–13€. No credit cards. Mon–Thurs noon–1am; Fri noon–2am; Sat 6pm–2am; Sun 5pm–midnight. U-Bahn: Frauenhoferstrasse.

Prinz Myshkin ★ VEGETARIAN   If you need a break from the *Lederhosen* and *Dirndls,* come here for modern, cosmopolitan cuisine that serves arguably the best vegetarian fare in Munich. The ingenuity of the chefs' creations warrants the prices and will have you ogling the dishes as they pass to neighboring tables. You can savor a stack of fried soy medallions with carrots, cauliflower, and oyster mushroom, or a truffle potato zucchini gratin and a drizzle of walnut-honey dressing. Vegan offerings include the *involtini* teriyaki containing tofu, nuts, and roasted mushroom, snug in a Swiss chard wrap. Its array of freshly made salads, Indian and Thai dishes, casseroles, soups, and zesty pizzas make this place a vegetarian's heaven.

Hackenstrasse 2. ℂ **089/265596.** www.prinzmyshkin.com. Reservations recommended. Main courses 12€–16€. AE, MC, V. Daily 11am–12:30am. U-Bahn or S-Bahn: Marienplatz.

Weisses Bräuhaus BAVARIAN/RHENISH   Weisses Bräuhaus is big, bustling, and Bavarian with a vengeance. Not for the pretentious, this informal place does what it's been doing for centuries: serving home-brewed beer. At one time, the famous salt-trade route between Salzburg and Augsburg passed by its door, and salt traders are very thirsty folk. The front room, with smoke-blackened dark-wood paneling and stained glass, is for drinking and informal eating; the back room is more formal. Sample typical Bavarian dishes such as smoked filet of trout, rich potato soup, roast pork with homemade potato dumplings and cabbage salad, or Viennese veal goulash with mushrooms and cream sauce. You have to share a table, but that's part of the fun.

Tal 7. ℂ **089/2901380.** www.weisses-brauhaus.de. Reservations recommended, especially for the back room. Main courses 8€–20€. MC, V. Daily 8am–1am. U-Bahn or S-Bahn: Marienplatz.

Near the Isar, South of Center

Asam Schlössl BAVARIAN/INTERNATIONAL   This Augustiner brewery restaurant offers a relaxed, relatively informal hideaway amid the congestion of Munich. The building was built as a private villa in 1724. Some of the original castle-like design remains, though the structure has been expanded and renovated over the years. All brews offered are products of Augustiner, including both pale and dark versions of *Weissebier*, beer fermented from wheat. Menu items include such typical Bavarian fare as *Böfflamott* (beef braised in red wine) with *Semmelknödel* (bread dumplings), and a dish beloved by Emperor Franz Josef of Austria, *gesottener Tafelspitz mit frischen Kren*, a savory form of the familiar boiled beef with horseradish.

Maria-Einsiedel-Strasse 45. (✆) **089/7236373.** www.asamschloessl.de. Main courses 9€–20€. AE, MC, V. Daily noon–1am. U-Bahn: Thalkirchen.

In Schwabing

This district, which was called "bohemian" in the 1920s, overflows with restaurants. Many of them are awful, but there are several fine choices, some of which attract a youthful clientele. The evening is the best time for a visit.

VERY EXPENSIVE

Tantris ★★★ MEDITERRANEAN/INTERNATIONAL   Tantris serves Munich's finest cuisine. Chef Hans Haas has been voted the top chef in Germany many times, and he has refined and sharpened his culinary technique since. The setting is unlikely: a drab commercial area, with bare concrete walls and a garish decor. But inside, you're transported by the fine service and excellent food that's a treat for the eye as well as for the palate. The choice of dishes is wisely limited, and the cooking is subtle and original. Feast on such savory offerings as Dover sole with roast Jerusalem artichokes or scallops with cauliflower and a curry marinade, perhaps spinach-stuffed turbot. Roast scallops come with a mango and apple marinade.

Johann-Fichte-Strasse 7, Schwabing. (✆) **089/3619590.** www.tantris.de. Reservations required. Fixed-price 4-course lunch 115€, 5-course dinner 165€. AE, DC, MC, V. Tues–Sat noon–3pm and 6:30–10:30pm. Closed public holidays, annual holidays in Jan and May. U-Bahn: Dietlindenstrasse.

MODERATE

La Bouille FRENCH/MEDITERRANEAN   The kitchen of sunny Provence is celebrated at this restaurant, which opened in 2004 and became an immediate success. In elegant surroundings, you're welcomed with a smile and invited in to peruse the menu. Friendly service, fine French wines, and, most of all, the flavor-filled cooking redolent of olive oil and the aromas of Provence prevail here. Our party recently devoured perfectly prepared dishes that included pigeon with green cabbage, rack of lamb with a fresh olive crust, and a tender and beautifully flavored breast of duck. Save room for one of the artfully crafted desserts.

Neureutherstrasse 15, at Arcisstrasse. (✆) **089/399936.** www.labouille.de. Reservations recommended. Main courses 18€–23€; fixed-price menus 48€–55€. DC, MC, V. Tues–Fri noon–2:30pm; Mon–Sat 7pm–midnight. U-Bahn: Josephsplatz or Universität.

INEXPENSIVE

Café Ignaz 🍴 VEGETARIAN   This modest and quaint vegetarian cafe-cum-restaurant serves slightly more affordable cuisine than the cross-town alternative, Prinz Myshkin (p. 310). Popular with the student crowd, it excels in its depth of

beer GARDENS, CELLARS & TAVERNS

Regardless the time of year, you will find Bavarians congregating somewhere to take part in one of their favorite pastimes: socializing over a beer. In winter, the countless *Bierkeller* (cellars) and *Bierstuben* (taverns) are packed to the brim with frothy-faced locals (and visitors, let's be honest). Once the sun peeks through in early spring, the benches and chairs of the *Biergärten* fill up on a daily basis throughout summer, culminating in the one last hurrah of Oktoberfest, when the waning sunlight of a Bavarian autumn sends everyone back into the cellars and halls. These beer joints are Munich institutions, with a tradition dating as far back as the foundation of the city. In a sense, these establishments are restaurants, bars, and sometimes nightlife wrapped in one, where Bavarians come to relax and just be themselves any time of the day or night. Check out some of the traditional garb for proof. Always be aware of table reservations for the *Stammgäste* (regulars), who will certainly show up at the time indicated on plaques or notes on the tables to down their daily rounds.

Although half-liter mugs are available, you might want to join the masses and order a *Mass,* or a liter. To order, ask for "ein Mass, bitte." You also might want to try the massive pretzels *(Breze),* and add *Obatzda,* a Bavarian cheese spread with paprika. *Radi,* white radish slices with chives on bread, are also a popular snack.

Producing what many locals call the best beer in town, the **Augustinerbräu** operates several establishments and countless affiliates, but three are worth mention. In the heart of the city, the **Augustinerbräu Stüberl/Grossgaststätten,** Neuhauserstrasse 27 (② 089/ 23183257; www.augustiner-restaurant. com; U-Bahn: Marienplatz), keeps getting bigger the farther back you explore the vaulted rooms; it feels like an indoor *Biergarten,* but remains classy enough for dining. The **Augustiner-Keller,** Arnulfstrasse 52 (② 089/594393; www. augustinerkeller.de; tram: 16 or 17), is the spacious sister-branch with the best garden, as well as medieval cellars. For the cheapest *Mass* in town (5.10€), check out the **Augustiner Bräustuben,** Landsbergerstrasse 19 (② 089/5022569; www.braeustuben.de; tram: 18 or 19), installed into the former stalls right next to the brewery itself, and a short walk from the Oktoberfest grounds.

Bamberger Haus, Brunnerstrasse 2 (② 089/3088966; www.restaurant-la-villa.de; U-Bahn: Scheidplatz), located northwest of Schwabing at the edge of Luitpold Park, is named after a city

offerings, with a variety of baked gratins, wok dishes, and risotto, couscous and gnocchi-based creations. Choose one of several Khorasan-wheat pizzas, including one topped with ginger, sea algae, and mushrooms. The *Indische Pfanne* (Indian pan) features a medley of flavors with curry, rice, dates, ginger, raisins among a mix of veggies. The adjacent cafe offers soy-based cakes and pastries using whole-wheat or white flour, great for a dessert or a take-out treat.

Georgenstrasse 67. ② **089/2716093.** www.ignaz-cafe.de. Reservations not needed. Main courses 8€–10€; lunch buffet 7€. AE, MC, V. Fri–Wed 8am–11pm. U-Bahn: Josephsplatz.

Schelling Salon GERMAN/BAVARIAN   Dating from 1872, this tavern is known for its Bavarian *Knödel* and billiards, and it's been a tradition since 1872, having survived World War II bombings. In days of yore, you could see everybody from Lenin to Hitler playing billiards here. On-site is a billiard museum, tracing the history of noted for mass consumption of beer. The street-level restaurant, **La Terrazza,** serves Bavarian and international specialties: well-seasoned soups, grilled steak, veal, pork, and sausages. If you only want to drink, you might visit the rowdier and less expensive beer hall in the cellar. Main courses in the restaurant range from 8€ to 15€.

The **Biergarten Chinesischer Turm,** Englischer Garten 3 (*☎* **089/3838730;** www.chinaturm.de; U-Bahn: Universität), may seem gaudy and touristy until you realize most of the *Mass*-raising clientele are locals. You may find an oom-pah band puffing away in the pagoda tower. The place is open every day March to November 10am to midnight, but December to February its hours depend on the weather and the number of patrons.

Hirschgarten, Hirschgartenstrasse 1, in Nymphenburg Park, near the palace (*☎* **089/17999199;** www.hirschgarten. de; S-Bahn: Laim; tram: 17 to Romanplatz), is the largest open-air restaurant in Munich, and likely in Europe for that matter, with seating for more than 8,000 beer drinkers and merrymakers. Full meals cost 7.50€ to 18€. A 1-liter stein of Augustiner beer is 6.30€. It's open daily 9am to midnight. MasterCard and Visa are accepted.

Some might claim that the world-renowned **Hofbräuhaus am Platzl ★,** Am Platzl 9 (*☎* **089/221676;** www. hofbraeuhaus.de; U-Bahn: Marienplatz), is too gaudy and touristy, but Bavarians have never shied away from kitsch. In fact, the place is so gaudy that even some locals may secretly sneak in for a *Mass* of brew and *Wurst.* Waitresses in dirndls survey the scene and others in candy cane outfits distribute pretzels bigger than your head. The brass band puffs their cheeks to the beat and everybody has a good time. Be sure to check out the lockers where denizens lock up their personal mugs for next time. Rent is only 4€ per year, but the waiting list is long—longer than it takes to grow some of the curly mustaches here.

The **Waldwirtschaft Grosshesselöhe,** George-Kalb-Strasse 3 (*☎* **089/ 74994030;** www.waldwirtschaft.de; S-Bahn: Isartal Bahnhof; tram: 7), is a popular summertime rendezvous, located above the Isar River near the zoo with seats for some 2,000 drinkers. Recorded music ranging from Dixieland to jazz to Polish polka is played throughout the week. Entrance is free, and you bring your own food. It's open daily 11am to 11pm (they have to close early because neighborhood residents complain), with live music on Friday to Sunday nights.

pool since the days of ancient Egypt. The waitstaff serves hearty fare washed down with mugs of beer. Start perhaps with the goulash soup or one of the freshly made salads, including a Russian salad. You face a selection of dishes from the cold or hot kitchen, featuring such courses as *Wiener Schnitzel* or sausage platters. A small selection of fish dishes is also offered.

Schellingstrasse 54. *☎* **089/2720788.** www.schelling-salon.de. Reservations not needed. Breakfast 3€–5€; main courses 4€–11€. AE, MC, V. Thurs-Mon 10am-1am. U-Bahn: Universität.

In Bogenhausen

Käfer-Schänke GERMAN/INTERNATIONAL   This is a great spot for casual dining with elegant style, in a setting that evokes a chalet. It's located on the second floor of a famous gourmet shop called Käfer. The cuisine roams the world for inspiration—from Lombardy to Asia. You select your hors d'oeuvres from the most dazzling display in Munich. Often Käfer-Schänke devotes a week to a particular country's cuisine. Once, the classic soup of the French Riviera (sea bass with fennel) was simply delicious. From a cold table, you can choose smoked salmon or smoked eel. Venison, quail, and guinea hen are also regularly featured.

Prinzregentenstrasse 73. © **089/4168247.** www.feinkost-kaefer.de. Reservations required. Main courses 24€–44€. AE, DC, MC, V. Mon–Sat noon–11pm. Closed holidays. U-Bahn: Prinzregentenplatz. Bus: 100. Tram: 18.

SHOPPING

The most interesting shops are concentrated on Munich's pedestrians-only streets, between Karlsplatz and Marienplatz.

Art

Bayerischer Kunstgewerbe-Verein ★★ This is one of Germany's largest, most visible, and most historic art galleries, established in the 1840s as a showcase for local artists. The complex contains an upscale art gallery and a sales outlet, the Ladengeschäft, where attractive crafts are sold at prices that begin at 25€. Works by more than 400 artists are displayed and sold here. Examples include sculpture in all kinds of mediums, crafts, textiles, and woven objects. Pacellistrasse 6–8. © **089/2901470.** www.kunsthandwerk-bkv.de. U-Bahn: Karlsplatz.

Books

Hugendubel Not only is this Munich's biggest bookstore, but it enjoys the most central location. It sells a number of English-language titles, both fiction and nonfiction, and also offers travel books and helpful maps. Marienplatz 22. © **0180/1484484.** www.hugendubel.de. U-Bahn or S-Bahn: Marienplatz.

Munich Readery This find claims it's the largest English-language secondhand bookstore in Germany, and we agree. Expect to find mint to near-mint condition books, many of which reach the shelf due to the store's trading system. Augustenstrasse 104. © **089/12192403.** U-Bahn: Theresienstrasse.platz Bus: 154

China, Silver & Glass

Kunstring Meissen ★ During the coldest days of the Cold War, this was Munich's exclusive distributor of Meissen and Dresden china, manufactured behind the iron curtain in East Germany. With reunification, Kunstring's exclusive access became a thing of the past. Despite that, the shop still contains one of Munich's largest inventories of the elegant porcelain. Briennerstrasse 4. © **089/281532.** U-Bahn: Odeonsplatz.

Crafts

Bayerischer Kunstgewerbe-Verein The Bavarian Association of Arts & Crafts is a showcase for Bavarian artisans and has excellent handicrafts: ceramics, glasses, jewelry, woodcarvings, pewter, and seasonal Christmas decorations. Pacellistrasse 6–8. © **089/2901470.** www.kunsthandwerk-bkv.de. U-Bahn: Karlsplatz.

Prinoth 👜 Most of the woodcarvings sold here are produced in small workshops in the folklore-rich Italian South Tyrol. The selection is wide-ranging, and because the shop is 6km (4 miles) west of Munich's tourist zones, prices are reasonable compared to those of shops closer to the Marienplatz. Guido Schneblestrasse 9A. © **089/560378.** www.prinoth.de. U-Bahn: Laimerplatz.

Department Stores

Kaufhof At Germany's answer to one-stop shopping, wander freely among displays that are art forms in their own right. The inventory includes virtually everything, from men's, women's, and children's clothing to housewares, and much more. Marienplatz. ©**089/231851.** www.galeria-kaufhof.de. U-Bahn or S-Bahn: Marienplatz.

Ludwig Beck am Rathauseck Most merchandise here is intended for local residents; however, visitors will also be interested in this four-floor shopping bazaar, which sells handmade crafts from all over Germany, old and new. Items include decorative pottery and dishes, etched-glass beer steins and vases, painted wall plaques, decorative flower arrangements, unusual kitchenware, fashions, textiles, and much more. Am Marienplatz 11. ©**089/236910.** www.ludwigbeck.de. U-Bahn or S-Bahn: Marienplatz.

Eyeglasses

Pupille Shelf after shelf of eyeglasses in all styles and sizes reveal why Germans are known for their optical products, which are sold around the world. Some of the most fashionable glasses in Germany are sold here, including selections from name designers such as Chanel. Theatiner Strasse 8. ©**089/24243838.** www.pupille.de. Tram: 19.

Fashion

Bogner Haus Before you head for the slopes, shop here for the latest in ski clothing and styles. Willy Bogner, the filmmaker and Olympic downhill racer, sells this flamboyant attire. The store also sells more formal clothing for men and women. Residenzstrasse 14-15. ©**089/2907040.** U-Bahn or S-Bahn: Marienplatz or Odeonsplatz.

Hirmer In the pedestrian zone, this shop has the best collection of German-made and international men's clothing in town. The staff here is especially skilled at helping people select something that looks good on them. The selection comes from such brand names as Boss, Barbour, Rene Lezard, and van Laak. Both business and leisure suits are sold at middle- to upper-bracket prices. They even cater to "big beer bellies." Kaufinger Strasse 22. ©**089/236830.** www.hirmer-muenchen.de. U-Bahn: Marienplatz.

Loden-Frey You can see the twin domes of the Frauenkirche above the soaring glass-enclosed atrium of this shop's showroom. Go here for the world's largest selection of loden clothing and traditional costumes, as well as for international fashions from top European designers such as Armani, Valentino, and Ungaro. Maffeistrasse 7. ©**089/210390.** www.loden-frey.de. U-Bahn or S-Bahn: Marienplatz.

Maendler This store is divided into a series of boutiques well known to virtually every well-dressed woman in Bavaria. You'll find the creative vision of Joop, New York New York, and Jil Sander here. Looking for that special something for your dinner with the mayor or the president of Germany? Ask to see formal evening wear by Jean-Paul Gaultier. Theatiner Strasse 7. ©**089/24228850.** www.maendler.com. U-Bahn: Marienplatz.

Wies'n Tracht & Mehr ★ 📷 The milkmaid-style dress, the dirndl, has been making a comeback. In spite of its low-cut bodice, it is considered wholesome. The best selection of dirndls in Munich is offered at this outlet, but prices are not cheap, starting at 400€. Both new and vintage dirndls are sold here. They are worn with the traditional off-the-shoulder white blouse and often an apron. Tal 19. No phone. www.wiesn-tracht-mehr.de. U-Bahn or S-Bahn: Marienplatz.

Food

Alois Dallmayr ★   What Fortnum & Mason is to London, the venerable Dallmayr is to Munich. Gastronomes as far away as Hamburg and Berlin telephone orders for exotica not readily available anywhere else. Dallmayr's list of prestigious clients reads like a who's who of German industry and letters. Wander freely among racks of food-stuffs. Some are too delicate to survive shipment abroad, but others can be shipped anywhere. Dienerstrasse 14–15.℗ **089/21350.** www.dallmayr.de. Tram: 19.

Jewelry & Watches

CADA-Schmuck ★   Herbert Kopp, a jewelry designer, is attracting lots of media attention for his stunning handmade jewelry sold here. His chic wares come in 18-carat gold or sterling silver. There is a large collection of earrings (both small and large) along with necklaces and pendants. Maffeistrasse 8.℗ **089/2554270.** www.cada-schmuck.de. Tram: 19.

Hemmerle ★★★   This is *the* place for jewelry. The original founders of this con-servative shop made their fortune designing bejeweled fantasies for the Royal Bavar-ian Court of Ludwig II. All pieces are limited editions, designed and made in-house by Bavarian craftspeople. The company also designs its own wristwatch, the Hem-merle. Maximilianstrasse 14.℗ **089/2422600.** www.hemmerle.de. U-Bahn or S-Bahn: Marienplatz.

Porcelain

Porzellan-Manufaktur-Nymphenburg ★★★   At Nymphenburg, about 8km (5 miles) northwest of the heart of Munich, is one of Germany's most famous porce-lain factories, on the grounds of Schloss Nymphenburg. You can visit its exhibition and sales rooms, Monday to Friday 10am to 5pm. Shipments can be arranged if you make purchases. A more central branch is in Munich's center at Odeonsplatz 1 (℗ **089/282428;** U-Bahn: Odeonsplatz). Nördliches Schlossrondell 8.℗ **089/1791970.** www.nymphenburg.com. Bus: 100.

Toys

Münchner Puppenstuben und Zinnfiguren Kabinette ☺   This is Germany's oldest miniature pewter foundry, dating from 1796. Many Germans visit Munich every December to purchase traditional Christmas decorations of a type once sold to Maximilian I, king of Bavaria. Managed by matriarchs of the same family, this store is one of the best sources in Germany for miniature houses, furniture, bird cages, and people, all cunningly crafted from pewter or carved wood. Some figures are made from 150-year-old molds that are collector's items in their own right. Anything here makes a great gift, not only for a child but also for an adult with a nostalgic bent. Maxburgstrasse 4.℗ **089/293797.** U-Bahn: Karlsplatz.

Obletter's ☺   Established in 1825, this is one of the largest emporiums of chil-dren's toys in Munich. The two floors of inventory contain everything from folkloric dolls to computer games. Karlsplatz 11.℗ **089/55089510.** U-Bahn: Karlsplatz.

ENTERTAINMENT & NIGHTLIFE

To find out what's happening in Munich, go to the tourist office just outside the Hauptbahnhof (℗ **89/23396500**) and ask for *Monatsprogramm* (a monthly program guide), costing 1.80€. It contains a complete cultural guide, telling you not only what's being presented—including concerts, opera, special exhibits, and museum hours—but also how to purchase tickets.

If you're looking for activity any hour of the day or night, head for **Schrannenhalle,** on the south side of the Viktualienmarkt, a former 19th-century grain depot completely restored. Today it is home to some great little shops, a bevy of bars, and every sort of restaurant, serving everything from Japanese sushi to old-fashioned Bavarian dishes. Entertainment, ranging from jazz to rock, is often provided. Locals like to drop in here before dawn to order *Weisswurst,* those Bavarian white sausages.

The Performing Arts

Nowhere else in Europe, other than London and Paris, will you find so many musical and theatrical events. The good news is that seats don't cost a fortune—so count on indulging yourself and going to several performances. You can get good tickets for anything from 10€ to 45€.

If you speak German, you'll find at least 20 theaters offering plays of every description: classic, comic, experimental, contemporary—take your pick. The best way to find out what current productions might interest you is to go to a theater-ticket agency. Head for **München Tickets** (✆ **0180/54818181**), where you can purchase tickets to cultural, entertainment, and sporting events within Bavaria, with access to each ticket provider's computer database. For some sporting events (such as soccer) and musical events (including most of the operas subsidized by the city of Munich), where season tickets and long-term subscriptions reduce availability, you'll have to go to the venue's box office, as organizers tend not to cooperate with outside ticket agencies.

Altes Residenztheater (Cuvilliés Theater) An attraction in itself (see Residenz, p. 288), this is the most beautiful theater in Germany, and it was completely restored in 2008. The **Bavarian State Opera** and the **Bayerisches Staatsschauspiel** perform smaller works here, in keeping with the tiny theater's more intimate character. Box-office hours are Monday to Saturday 10am to 7pm. Residenzstrasse 1. ✆ **089/21851940** for ticket information. www.bayerischesstaatsschauspiel.de. Building tours 5€.

Bayerischen Staatsoper The **Bavarian State Opera** is one of the world's great companies. The Bavarians give their hearts and souls to opera. Productions here are beautifully mounted and presented, and the company's roster includes some of the world's greatest singers. Hard-to-get tickets may be purchased at the box office Monday to Friday 10am to 6pm and Saturday 10am to 1pm, plus 1 hour before each performance. The Nationaltheater is also the home of the **Bavarian State Ballet.** Nationaltheater, Max-Joseph-Platz 2. © **089/21851920.** www.bayerische.staatsoper.de. Tickets 15€–264€, including standing room. U-Bahn or S-Bahn: Marienplatz.

Bayerisches Staatsschauspiel   The Bavarian State Theater is known for its performances of the classics: Goethe and Schiller, Shakespeare, and others. The box office, on Max-Joseph-Platz, is open Monday to Saturday 10am to 7pm. Max-Joseph-Platz. © **089/21851920.** www.bayerischesstaatsschauspiel.de. Tickets 15€–60€. U-Bahn or S-Bahn: Marienplatz.

Deutsches Theater   This late-19th-century venue is mainly for musicals, but operettas, ballets, and international shows are performed as well. During Carnival in January and February, the theater becomes a ballroom—the costume balls and official black-tie festivities here are famous throughout Europe. *Note:* Due to renovations expected to last until spring 2013, performances are currently held in a theater tent on the grounds of the Allianz Arena at Fröttmaning. Schwanthalerstrasse 13. © **089/55234444.** www.deutsches-theater.de. Tickets 19€–49€, higher for special events. U-Bahn: Fröttmaning.

Münchner Kammerspiele   Contemporary and classic plays are performed at the Munich Studio Theater. The season runs early October to July. You can reserve tickets by phone Monday to Friday 10am to 6pm, but you must pick them up at least 2 days before a performance. The box office is open Monday to Friday 10am to 6pm and on Saturday 10am to 1pm, plus 1 hour before performances. There's also a second, smaller theater called **Werkraum,** Hildegardstrasse 1 (same phone as below), where new works are presented. Maximilianstrasse 28. © **089/23396601.** www.muenchner-kammerspiele.de. Tickets 6€–44€. U-Bahn: Marienplatz. S-Bahn: Isartor. Tram: 19.

Münchner Philharmoniker   Although founded in 1893, the Munich Philharmonic Orchestra calls the modern Gasteig Cultural Center home, where it performs in Philharmonic Hall. The center also shelters the Richard Strauss Conservatory and the Munich Municipal Library, and has five performance halls. You can purchase tickets at the ground-level Glashalle, Monday to Friday 10am to 8pm and Saturday 10am to 4pm. The Philharmonic season runs mid-September to July. Gasteig Kulturzentrum in the Haidhausen district, Rosenheimerstrasse 5. © **089/480985500.** www.muenchnerphilharmoniker.de. Tickets 15€–64€. S-Bahn: Rosenheimerplatz. Tram: 18 to Gasteig. Bus: 51.

Live Music

Jazzclub Unterfahrt   This is Munich's leading jazz club, attracting artists from throughout Europe and North America. Reaching it requires wandering down a labyrinth of underground cement-sided corridors that might remind you of a bomb shelter during the Cold War. Inside, the space opens to reveal flickering candles, a convivial bar, high ceilings, and clusters of smallish tables facing a stage and whatever singers and musicians happen to be emoting at the time. Off to one corner is an art gallery. The bar here opens daily at 7:30pm; live music is Tuesday to Sunday 8:30pm to 1am, Friday and Saturday 7:30pm to 3am. Einsteinstrasse 42. © **089/4482794.** www.unterfahrt.de. Cover 5€–32€. U-Bahn: Max-Weber-Platz.

Mister B's   This small, dark club hosts a slightly older, mellower crowd than the rock and dance clubs. Blues, jazz, and rhythm-'n'-blues combos take the stage Thursday to Saturday, while it's open Tuesday to Sunday 8pm to 3am. Herzog-Heinrichstrasse 38. © **089/534901.** www.misterbs.de. Cover 7€–20€. U-Bahn: Goetheplatz.

Schwabinger Podium This staple of the Schwabing scene offers varying live music acts, which on some nights attracts a jazz crowd; Monday nights are reserved for a local jazz outfit. Otherwise, expect cover bands and local acts. It's open Sunday to Thursday 8pm to 1am and Friday and Saturday 8pm to 3am. Wagnerstrasse 1. ℂ **089/399482.** www.schwabinger-podium.com. Cover 7€. U-Bahn: Münchner Freiheit.

Nightclubs & Dance Halls

Bayerischer Hof Night Club Here in the extensive cellars of the Bayerischer Hof hotel (p. 323), you'll find some of Munich's most sophisticated entertainment. Within one very large room is a piano bar, where a musician plays Friday and Saturday nights 7 to 10pm. Behind a partition that disappears after 10pm is a bandstand for live orchestras, which play to a crowd of dancing patrons every night. Entrance to the piano bar is free, but there's a cover charge to the nightclub Friday to Sunday nights. Drinks begin at 9€. The club and bar are open daily until 3 or 4am, depending on business. Daily happy hour is 7 to 8:30pm, with drinks starting at 5€. In the Bayerischer Hof hotel, Promenadeplatz 2-6. ℂ **089/21200.** www.bayerischerhof.de. Cover to nightclub Fri-Sat 5€-50€. Tram: 19.

Café am Hochhaus Not for wallflowers, this entire locale is basically a dance floor with wallpaper decor that local artists design. With average-priced drinks and skilled DJs, this is as close as you get to a club without the pretense or prices. You will end up dancing before the night is over. The scene shifts around quite a bit here. One night might be soulful reggae, another night retro or disco. On Sunday there is a gay T-dance, and on Monday night management promises "anything can happen." It's open Monday to Saturday 8pm to 3am. Blumenstrasse 29. ℂ **089/89058152.** www. cafeamhochhaus.de. U-Bahn: Sendlinger Tor.

Nachtgalerie The "Night Gallery" contains two dance halls rocking to party music and hip-hop along with house, electronica, or even rhythm 'n' blues. The club attracts largely intoxicated crowds in their 20s and 30s. International student parties are often staged here. Expect various theme nights, perhaps one devoted to the sounds of a Caribbean summer. Girls dance with girls, boys with boys, and sometimes boys with girls. There is a cover, but once inside, drinks are cheap—beginning at 2€. Nachtgalerie is open Friday and Saturday 10pm to 5am. Landsbergerstrasse 185. ℂ **089/32455595.** www.nachtgalerie.de. Cover 10€. S-Bahn: Hirschgarten.

Oklahoma File under surreal. German and European bands decked out in cowboy hats and boots struggle with the nuances of an extremely foreign musical form. Even when the results are dead-on mimicry, there's something strange about watching German "cowboys" line dance or lean on the bar while guzzling Spaten. Cover is at the low end of the scale, rising when English and American acts hit the stage. Depending on your mood, this place can be a lot of fun. Pull on your jeans and come on in Tuesday to Saturday 8pm to 1am. Schäftlarnstrasse 156. ℂ **089/7234327.** www.oklahoma-saloon. com. Cover 10€-12€. U-Bahn: Thalkirchen.

The Bar & Cafe Scene

In addition to the venues listed below, see the review for Dukatz on p. 305.

Alter Simpl This classic cafe started as a literary haunt inspired by the 1890s satire publication of the same name. Its emblematic red pit bull no longer bites off the chains of censorship, but rather a champagne bottle. Frank Wedekind, who penned the play *Spring Awakening* led a circle of artists who congregated here. Nowadays, it's a spacious "beer cafe" that's still popular with students who swirl their steins into the late hours. A great selection of food will satiate late-night hunger. It's open Sunday to Thursday 11am to 3am, Friday and Saturday 11am to 4am. Türkenstrasse 57. © **089/2723083.** www.eggerlokale.de. U-Bahn: Universität.

Café Puck   A dark-paneled retreat for students, artists, and workers, this cafe plays a variety of roles for its diverse crowd. It's a bar to students; a restaurant to the locals, who like the daily menu of German, American, and Asian dishes; and a hangover cure for artists and young people who creep in after midday for a big American breakfast. There's usually plenty of conversation and someone who wants to practice English, and there are always German- and English-language newspapers. Also, most of their staff speaks fluent English. Café Puck is open daily 9am to 1am. Türkenstrasse 33. © **089/2802280.** www.cafepuck.de. U-Bahn: Universität.

Die Bank   Imagine stripping the interior of a bank, adding a stage, a bar, sofas, a foosball table, local artwork, a pizza stand, and a hair salon, and you have an idea of the vibe here. The Bank still fills with the diverse crowd that gave the Glockenbachviertel its character, proving that not all of the district has sold out. Local acts improve their gigs on Sunday nights. Müllerstrasse 42 © **089/23684171.** www.die-bank.com. U-Bahn: Sendlingertor.

Havana Club   This is not the spicy Cuban club you might expect. Employees may tell you about the bar's brush with fame, when Gloria Estefan made an appearance, but its day-to-day function is as a lively singles bar fueled by rum-based cocktails. It's open Monday to Thursday 6pm to 1am, Friday and Saturday 6pm to 3am, Sunday 7pm to 1am. Herrnstrasse 30. © **089/291884.** www.havanaclub-muenchen.de. S-Bahn: Isartor.

Killians Irish Pub/Ned Kelly's Australian Bar   This pub/bar combo offers live music, Irish and Australian drinks and food, and coverage of sporting events, especially soccer. Depending on the night, one may be rowdier than the other. On the weekend, it gets "g'zaft" Bavarian style, with wooden mallets bashing the tap into the keg. On the first Monday of the month, you may catch an evening of Irish dance with local Munichers and Irish expats pounding the floor. Both bars are open Monday to Thursday 4pm to 1am, Friday and Saturday 11am to 2 or 3am, and Sunday noon to 1am. Frauenplatz 11. © **089/24219899.** www.kiliansirishpub.com. U-Bahn or S-Bahn: Marienplatz.

Pusser's New York Bar   This is the only European franchise of a small, well-run chain of restaurant-bars based in Tortola, British Virgin Islands. Its nostalgic decor celebrates the British navy of the 18th and 19th centuries. The specialties are Caribbean-inspired dishes and rum-based drinks, such as Pusser's Painkiller (rum, coconut, fresh orange juice, pineapple, and grated nutmeg). The cellar houses a piano bar. It's open daily 5pm to 3am. Falkenturmstrasse 9. © **089/220500.** www.pussersbar.de. U-Bahn or S-Bahn: Marienplatz.

Sausalitos   For the best margaritas in town, the kind Hemingway used to slurp down in Havana, head to this welcoming Mexican cantina. If you're in your 20s, you'll fit right in. You never know what to expect: perhaps a young man walking around in a leather jockstrap or a blonde beauty showing off her latest nipple piercings. If you're ravenous, order the generous platters of main dishes ranging from 9€ to 13€, or else opt for drinks costing 6€ to 11€. During happy hour daily from 5 to 8pm, mixed drinks are half-price. It's open Monday to Thursday and Sunday 11am to 1am, Friday and Saturday 11am to 2:30am. Im Tal 16. ℂ**089/24295494.** www.sausalitos. de. U-Bahn or S-Bahn: Marienplatz.

Schumann's Bar am Hofgarten This is Munich's most legendary bar. It has an international fan club, lots of pizazz, a history that goes back forever, and new premises that have been the subject of many architectural reviews. Some of the staff members here consider the layout, the ample use of green marble, and the wooden paneling evocative of a church. All of that changes, however, when the drinks begin to flow and the crowd gets animated. This bar is a grand-slam rip-roaring affair that gets very crowded. There's a simple roster of menu items that changes with the season and the outside temperature. Schumann's is open Monday to Friday 5pm to 3am, Saturday and Sunday 6pm to 3am. Odeonsplatz 6–7, at the corner of Galerie Strasse. ℂ**089/ 229060.** www.schumanns.de. U-Bahn: Odeonsplatz.

Shamrock At this beer-lover's bar, you can compare the great brews of Germany with the best of the Irish exports. There's free entertainment every night at 9pm, when a mixed bag of Irish, rock, country, folk, funk, or blues musicians take to the stage. There are even Irish fiddlers. Should you get hungry, there's a good pizza menu to order from, costing from 6.50€, and there's a "wild" chili con carne as well. Located near the university, Shamrock gets a fair share of the student crowd. Hours are Tuesday to Thursday 6pm to 2am, Friday and Saturday 6pm to 4am. Trautenwolfstrasse 6. ℂ**089/331081.** www.shamrockmunich.com. U-Bahn: Giselastrasse.

Gay & Lesbian Nightlife

Munich's gay and lesbian scene is centered around the blocks between the Viktualienmarkt and Gärtnerplatz, particularly on Hans-Sachs-Strasse.

Bau Macho and swaggering, this gay bar encourages leather, denim, and as many uniforms as can be crammed onto the bodies that surround its street-level bar. Dimly lit and international, it's not as scary as it might look at first. Don't be surprised if you spot several New York City cop uniforms. It's open nightly 8pm to 3am. Beethovenstrasse 1. ℂ**089/269208.** www.bau-munich.de. U-Bahn: Sendlinger Tor.

Inges Karotte This is one of the major gathering places for lesbians in Munich, both foreign and domestic. One patron called the clients "a female jungle," a widely diverse group of ages, professions, and interests. Many stylish lesbians show up here escorted by their girlfriends. It's a good atmosphere for drinking and mating. Cocktails begin at 5€, and happy hour is only from 4 to 6pm. Disco music sometimes rules the night. Hours are Monday to Saturday 6pm to 1am, Sunday 4pm to 1am. Baaderstrasse 13. ℂ**089/2010669.** www.inges-karotte.de. U-Bahn: Frauenhofer Strasse.

Kr@ftakt As might be suggested by its name, this is an Internet cafe and the only gay one in Munich. Its clientele, looking for that Internet connection, is both gay and lesbian. Although we've put this listing in the nightlife section because of its late hours, it even serves a late breakfast costing from 4€—if you arrive late enough, you might even call it brunch. There's a happy hour on Wednesday from 7 to 9pm, when a beer goes for only 1€. You can also order food here throughout the day, including pasta dishes costing from 7€ to 10€. We get the impression that more gays go here to socialize in a convivial atmosphere than search the Web. It's open Sunday to Thursday 10am to 1am, Friday and Saturday 10am to 3am. Thalkircher Strasse 4. ℂ**089/21588881.** www.kraftakt.com. U-Bahn: Sendlinger Tor.

NY Club ★★   Known as New York Discotheque for nearly 2 decades, this club has reinvented itself. Attracting male fashionistas, it is now the most stylish and modern gay dance club in town. Guests enjoy two different areas, a beautifully designed lounge and a high-tech dance floor with lots of room for dancing and cruising. Both pastimes are pursued most eagerly here. Look for special events and gay parties by searching the club's website. Sonnenstrasse 25. ☎ **089/62232152.** www.nyclub.de. Cover from 5€, higher for special events. U-Bahn: Sendlinger Tor.

Teddy-Bar   Gay and neighborly, and ringed with varnished pine and a collection of teddy bears, this is a congenial bar patronized by gay men over 30. It's relatively easy to strike up a conversation, and if you're hungry, there are platters of Bavarian and German food. It's open nightly 6pm to 4am. October to April it opens for brunch at 11am on Sunday. Hans-Sachs-Strasse 1. ☎ **089/2603359.** www.teddybar.de. U-Bahn: Sendlinger Tor.

Outdoor Pursuits

BEACHES, POOLS & WATERSPORTS

On hot weekends, much of Munich heads for nearby lakes, the **Ammersee** and the **Starnbergersee,** where bathing facilities are clearly marked. You can also swim at **Maria-Einsiedel,** in the frigid, snow-fed waters of the Isar River. The city has several public swimming pools as well. The largest of these includes the giant competition-size pool in the Olympiapark, the **Olympia-Schwimmhalle** (☎ **089/23615050;** U-Bahn: Olympiazentrum). Admission is 4€ for 3 hours, or 7.20€ for a day pass. Information on both sailing and windsurfing is available from the **Bayerischer Seglerverband,** Georg-Brauchle-Ring 93 (☎ **089/15702366;** www.bayernsail.de).

JOGGING

Regardless of the season, the most lushly landscaped place in Munich is the **Englischer Garten** (U-Bahn: Universität), which has an 11km (7-mile) circumference and an array of dirt and asphalt tracks. Also appropriate are the grounds of the **Olympiapark** (U-Bahn: Olympiazentrum) or the park surrounding **Schloss Nymphenburg** (U-Bahn: Rotkreuzplatz, then tram no. 12 to Romanplatz; tram: 17). More convenient to the center of the city's commercial district is a jog along the embankments of the Isar River.

ROWING

Rowboats add to the charm of the lakes in the **Englischer Garten.** You can rent them at a kiosk at the edge of the Kleinhesseloher See starting at 6€ for 30 minutes. Rowboat rentals are also on the southern bank of the **Olympiasee,** in the Olympiapark.

SKIING

Because of the proximity of the Bavarian and Austrian Alps, many Munich residents are avid skiers. For information on resorts and snow-related activities, contact the **Bayerischer Skiverband,** Georg-Brauchle-Ring 93, 80992 München (☎ **089/15702325;** www.bsv-ski.de).

Spectator Sports

You won't leave Munich without seeing the red and white checkered emblem of Munich's most famous team **FC Bayern München** (☎ **089/699310;** www.fcbayern.de), or the sky blue and white of **1860 München** (☎ **01805/601860;** ww.tsv1860.de). Both play in the snazzy Allianz Arena, on the U6 line at Fröttmaning. **FC Bayern**

Entertainment & Nightlife

MUNICH

München's professional basketball team (☎ **089/699317877;** www.basketball.fc bayern.de) also attracts a crowd to games at the Olympia Eissportzentrum.

For something different, check out the Munich surfing scene. Opposite Prinzregentenstrasse 22 next to a bridge spanning the **Eisbach,** waves rush out in a constant (but frigid) flow for the avid (and insane) surfers in town.

WHERE TO STAY

There are many rooms available in Munich, though most are costly. Bargains are few and far between—but they do exist.

The **Munich tourist offices** (see earlier) are helpful if you arrive without a hotel reservation. Here, Bavarian personnel (most speak English), with some 35,000 listings in their files, will help you find a place to stay. Tell them what you can afford. They'll book you a room and even give you a map with instructions on how to reach it. Keep your receipt—if you don't like the room, go back to the tourist office, and they'll book you another at no extra charge. Reservations are free, but a deposit equal to 10% of the total value of your stay is collected in advance. For direct access to the hotel booking department, call ☎ **089/23396550** or fax 089/23330319.

In Central Munich

VERY EXPENSIVE

Bayerischer Hof & Palais Montgelas ★★★ Together, the Bayerischer Hof and the 17th-century Palais Montgelas make up the *crème de la crème* of Munich hotels. You can add your name to the litany of distinguished guests who have stayed here since it opened in 1841, including Ludwig I himself (due to a lack of bathtubs at the palace back then). Rooms range from medium to extremely spacious, and the decor from Bavarian rustic to R&B (red and beige tones) to Colonial African. The English designer Laura Ashley has even designed one room. Palais Montgelas has 20 of the most upscale rooms in this complex.

Promenadeplatz 2–6, 80333 München. www.bayerischerhof.de. ⓒ**089/21200.** Fax 089/2120906. 350 units. 340€–520€ double; from 1,800€ suite. AE, DC, MC, V. Parking 29€. Tram: 19. **Amenities:** 3 restaurants; 5 bars; airport transfers (120€); babysitting; concierge; exercise room; rooftop heated pool; room service; spa. *In room:* TV, hair dryer, minibar, Wi-Fi (27€ per day).

Charles Hotel ★★★ This eight-story hotel offers a sleek contemporary alternative to the more traditional hotels in town. Overlooking the old Botanical Gardens like its own front yard, this new member of the Rocco Forte group of European hotels features a relatively peaceful location in the center of Munich, with the added luxuries of five-star living. The spacious and luminous rooms don't feel stuffy, but refined with lighter shades of earthy tones like forest green and camel. Aim for the park-side rooms if you can, which offer your own quiet piece of the Munich cityscape thanks to soundproof windows and doors. The bathrooms feel brand new, with original Nymphenburger porcelain decorating those in the suites. The knowledgeable staff offer refined and friendly service without pretense.

Sophienstrasse 28, 80333 München. www.charleshotel.de. ⓒ**089/5445550.** Fax 089/5445552000. 160 units. 495€–550€ double; 790€ junior suite; from 1,500€ suite. AE, DC, MC, V. Parking 24€. U-Bahn: Karlsplatz. **Amenities:** Restaurant; bar; bikes; concierge; exercise room; indoor heated pool; room service; spa; Wi-Fi (free; in lobby). *In room:* A/C, TV, hair dryer, minibar.

Hotel München Palace ★★   It's tasteful, it's restrained, it's perfectly mannered, and it's very, very aware of how prestigious a stay here can really be. The Hotel Palace is sought out by performers at the nearby theaters and concert halls as a peaceful and nurturing address in Bogenhausen, a stylish residential neighborhood east of Munich's medieval core. Originally built in 1986 as an office building, it was later transformed into a hotel. Public areas are streamlined and contemporary, graced with elaborate hypermodern balustrades on travertine-sheathed staircases. Rooms are immaculate and upscale, and each comes with a luxurious bathroom.

Trogerstrasse 21, 81675 München. www.muenchenpalace.de. © **089/419710.** Fax 089/41971819. 74 units. 185€–400€ double; from 430€ suite. AE, DC, MC, V. U-Bahn: Prinzregentumplatz. **Amenities:** Restaurant; bar; bikes; exercise room; room service; sauna; Wi-Fi (10€ per hour; in lobby). *In room:* A/C, TV, DVD player (in some), hair dryer, minibar.

Hotel Vier Jahreszeiten Kempinski München ★★★   This grand hotel is not only the most elegant in Munich, but also Germany's most famous and distinctive, and among the finest in the world. Its tradition stretches back to 1858. Rooms and suites—which have hosted royalty, heads of state, and famed personalities from all over the world—combine the charm of days gone by with modern luxuries. The antique-style beds feature fine linen on sumptuous mattresses. The windows opening onto Maximilianstrasse are double-glazed.

Maximilianstrasse 17, 80539 München. www.kempinski-vierjahreszeiten.de. © **800/426-3135** in the U.S., or 089/21250. Fax 089/21252000. 308 units. 255€–470€ double; from 754€ suite. AE, DC, MC, V. Parking 28€. Tram: 19. **Amenities:** Restaurant; 2 bars; babysitting; concierge; exercise room; indoor heated pool; room service; sauna; Wi-Fi (12€ per hour). *In room:* A/C, TV, hair dryer, minibar.

Mandarin Oriental ★★★   Although one of Munich's smaller hotels, this is by no means a lightweight. Only the Hotel Vier Jahreszeiten Kempinski München and the Bayerischer Hof (see above) outclass this sophisticated and luxurious winner. Located within sight of the Frauenkirche, the stylish and elegant wedge-shaped 1880s building combines neo-Renaissance, neoclassical, and Biedermeier touches. A marble staircase sweeps upward to the very comfortable large rooms, each with specially crafted furniture or original antiques. Many have private terraces opening onto views of Munich.

Neuturmstrasse 1, 80331 München. www.mandarinoriental.com/munich. © **089/290980.** Fax 089/222539. 73 units. 325€–545€ double; from 585€ suite. AE, DC, MC, V. Parking 24€. U-Bahn or S-Bahn: Marienplatz. Tram: 19. **Amenities:** 2 restaurants; bar; babysitting; bikes; concierge; exercise room; rooftop heated pool; room service. *In room:* A/C, TV/DVD, CD player, hair dryer, minibar, Wi-Fi (25€ per day).

MODERATE

Anna Hotel   This building was constructed around 1900 as a four-story office block, and in 2002, when it was converted into this streamlined and stylish hotel, the developers had to evict at least one doctor's office. Today, it's a clean, charming, well-managed hotel with a minimalist and stylish decor that's loaded with wood paneling and warm tones of ocher and russet, with touches of yellow-and-black marble in all the bathrooms. A collection of postmodern sculptures in the lobby is by Stephan Ester, a locally well-known artist. Many of the clients of this hotel are business travelers, who appreciate the stylish and well-choreographed service and the comfortably secure bedrooms. Four of the suites are in a tower that affords exceptional views over the city.

Schützenstrasse 1, 80335 München. www.annahotel.de. © **089/599940.** Fax 089/59994333. 73 units. 215€–380€ double; 430€–560€ tower suite. Rates include continental breakfast and nonalcoholic minibar contents. MC, V. Parking 22€. U-Bahn: Karlsplatz or Hauptbahnhof. **Amenities:** Restaurant; bar; airport transfers (65€–130€); access to nearby health club. *In room:* A/C, TV, hair dryer, minibar, Wi-Fi (free).

Cortiina ★ 👜   Built in 2001 and run by the designing duo of Rudi Kull and Albert Weinzerl, the Cortiina exudes the fresh and trendy side of Munich that attracts the business crowd and young "elegentia." The chic receptionists straight out of a Tarantino film, and the dimmed halls for soothing bleary eyes make you forget you're in a hotel. A new annex with an additional 40 rooms features a rooftop terrace, and the latest furnishings including wooden swivel doors and marble bathrooms. The junior suites offer an added kitchenette for longer stays.

Ledererstrasse 8, 80331 München. www.cortiina.com.© **089/2422490.** Fax 089/242249100. 75 units. 195€–380€ double; 285€–500€ suite. AE, DC, MC, V. Parking 19€. U-Bahn: Marienplatz. **Amenities:** Bar; babysitting; room service. *In room:* TV/DVD, hair dryer, minibar, MP3 docking station, Wi-Fi (free).

Eden-Hotel-Wolff ★   This dignified hotel hides behind a modest facade across the street from the train station and the Airport bus terminus. If you have an early departure and still seek a touch of luxury, you'll be glad you chose this hotel. The traditional interiors vary from room to room. Some are classic with chandeliers and dark-wood paneling; others have rustic touches like antler ornaments and white clapboard walls. Hypoallergenic units are available, with special beds and a private ventilation system. Also ask about special weekend rates, which may or may not be available.

Arnulfstrasse 4-8, 80335 München. www.ehw.de.© **089/551150.** Fax 089/55115555. 210 units. 184€–325€ double; 295€–400€ suite. 1 child 6 and under stays free in parent's room. Rates include buffet breakfast. AE, DC, MC, V. Parking 17€. U-Bahn or S-Bahn: Hauptbahnhof. **Amenities:** Restaurant; bar; babysitting; concierge; exercise room; room service; spa. *In room:* TV, hair dryer, minibar, Wi-Fi (10€ per day).

Excelsior Hotel ★   This solidly comfortable hotel near the Hauptbahnhof prides itself on being one of the few hotels to survive the wartime bombings. Like the Anna Hotel (see above), it's run by the Geisel Group and stands as the first-class grandfather of the designer Anna. Its turn-of-the-20th-century design provides traditional elegance with spacious bedrooms outfitted in a tasteful and conservative style. Some seem to be a trove of antiques. Overall, this is a low-key, discreet, highly Europeanized hotel with a resolute lack of glitter.

Schützenstrasse 11, 80335 München. www.excelsior-muenchen.de.© **089/551370.** Fax 089/55137121. 114 units. 180€–310€ double; 240€–400€ suite. AE, DC, MC, V. Parking 22€. U-Bahn: Hauptbahnhof. **Amenities:** Restaurant; bar; airport transfers (65€); concierge; room service. *In room:* A/C, TV, hair dryer, minibar, Wi-Fi (free).

Hotel An der Oper   Although its name implies "at the opera," the pair of five-story buildings making up this hotel are located in a quiet street just a short walk from the Bavarian National Theater, where operas take place. Incorporating softer hues like vanilla and violet, rooms are elegantly furnished, some with chandeliers or the wider French-style beds. Somehow even the clear plastic chairs blend in to the dignified air expected of an opera hotel. And even after the fat lady sings, there's plenty going on in its neighboring streets.

Falkenturmstrasse 10, 80331 München. www.hotelanderoper.com. © **089/2900270.** Fax 089/29002729. 68 units. 195€–270€ double; 250€–390€ apt. Rates include buffet breakfast. AE, MC, V. Parking 15€. Tram: 19. *In room:* TV, hair dryer, minibar, Wi-Fi (free in lobby).

Hotel Exquisit ★ ☺   This great choice benefits from a traffic-reduced street, and is a short walk from the center, Deutsches Theater and nightlife in the Glockenbach district. The paneled lobby adjoins an inviting bar and lounge, where your night may begin. A wood-lovers dream, the interior is bedecked with bold stained mahogany wherever possible alongside salmon and hummus shades. The classically designed suites feature a separate living room, and families will enjoy the multistory maisonettes in the pitched roof. Whether your window overlooks the street or the ivy-draped courtyard, you'll sleep comfortably.

Pettenkoferstrasse 3, 80336 München. www.hotel-exquisit.com. ©**089/5519900.** Fax 089/55199499. 50 units. 185€–295€ double; 239€–355€ suite. Rates include buffet breakfast. AE, DC, MC, V. Parking 15€. U-Bahn: Sendlinger Tor. **Amenities:** Restaurant; bar; room service; sauna. *In room:* TV, hair dryer, minibar, Wi-Fi (20€ per day).

Hotel Mark 🍴   This hotel near the train station is keeping the '50s alive with in-room renovations that still echo the period wood paneling in the lobby. The trimming in the no-frills rooms matches the vintage postwar architecture that over recent years has found a place in people's hearts. Guests can use the computer in the lobby at no extra charge.

Senefelderstrasse 12, 80336 München. www.hotel-mark.de. © **089/559820.** Fax 089/55982444. 95 units. 72€–262€ double. Rates include buffet breakfast. AE, DC, MC, V. Parking 14€. U-Bahn or S-Bahn: Hauptbahnhof. **Amenities:** Room service; babysitting. *In room:* TV, hair dryer, minibar, Wi-Fi (10€ per day, in some).

Hotel Olympic ★   Built as a private villa around 1900, this hotel represents one of Munich's most appealing conversions of an antique building into a hip and attractive hotel. The lobby occupies a high-ceilinged, Victorian vestibule that retains many of the original details. Breakfast is served in a very large, graciously proportioned dining room, where memories of the grand bourgeoisie of the Industrial Revolution still seem to permeate the woodwork. Rooms are minimalist and all white, much more modern than the ground-floor reception areas, but comfortable and well engineered.

Hans Sachs Strasse 4, 80469 München www.hotel-olympic.de. ©**089/231890.** Fax 089/23189199. 38 units. 155€–200€ double; 530€–880€ apt. Rates include buffet breakfast. AE, DC, MC, V. Parking 15€. U-Bahn: Sendlinger Tor. **Amenities:** Babysitting; room service. *In room:* TV, hair dryer, minibar, Wi-Fi (free).

Hotel Splendid-Dollmann im Lehel ★ 🎁   Check in here if you want a hotel that's up-to-date yet replete with antiques, fine paintings, quality Oriental carpets, and a sense of Munich's sometimes gracious 18th- and 19th-century past. The venue is an elegant 19th-century town house, fronted with chiseled white-stone blocks, in the upscale Lehel district. Inside, an attentive staff welcomes you into a small, boutique-style hotel fitted with a library-style bar and many of the decorative accessories of an upscale private home. Bedrooms are cozy, colorful, and well maintained, each with a different theme and reproductions of antique furniture.

Thierschstrasse 49, 80538 München. ©**089/238080.** Fax 089/23808365. www.splendid-dollmann. de. 37 units. 160€–250€ double; 230€–400€ suite. AE, DC, MC, V. Parking 8.50€. U-Bahn: Lehel. **Amenities:** Bar; room service. *In room:* TV, Wi-Fi (3€ per hour).

Hotel Torbräu ★   This charmer has looked out over the Isar Gate since the 15th century, and offers an ideal spot between the German Museum and the sights around Marienplatz. All the while it offers modern amenities and furnishings with lighter wood furnishings. Given its age, the rooms may seem less spacious than others in town, but each retain a sense of old-world comfort that makes a stay here memorable.

Tal 41, 80331 München. www.torbraeu.de. ©**089/242340.** Fax 089/24234235. 90 units. 194€–282€ double; 280€–403€ suite. Rates include buffet breakfast. AE, MC, V. Parking 15€. Closed 1 week at Christmas. U-Bahn: Isartor. **Amenities:** 2 restaurants; bar; babysitting; concierge; room service. *In room:* A/C, TV, hair dryer, minibar (in some), Wi-Fi (free).

INEXPENSIVE

Brack   Located a "stein's-throw" from the Oktoberfest grounds, this hotel is usually booked long in advance of the famous festival. Yet, the rest of the year it offers easy access to the U-Bahn, and tops it off with free bike rental and a map of the cycle routes. The affordable rooms offer all the comfort and class of other Munich hotels with no-nonsense, friendly service. Soundproof windows and electrically operated windows are just some of the added modern comforts. The long breakfast hours suit both the early birds and the nighthawks.

Lindwurmstrasse 153, 80337 München. www.hotel-brack.de. © **089/747255.** Fax 089/72015015. 50 units. 99€–189€ double; 135€–220€ triple. Rates include buffet breakfast. AE, DC, MC, V. Free parking. U-Bahn: Poccistrasse. **Amenities:** Bikes. *In room:* TV, Wi-Fi (free).

Creatif Hotel Elephant ♠ This takes the cake for the most daring use of color in town, which helps offset the otherwise lackluster area around the main rail station. Its salmon-colored facade announces the brightness of the interior with simple but comfortably furnished rooms. There's nothing antique about the design, just clean, new materials and colors to brighten your stay.

Lämmerstrasse 6, Leopoldvorstadt, 80335 München. www.creatifelephanthotel.com. © **089/555785.** Fax 089/5501746. 40 units. 65€–250€ double. AE, DC, MC, V. U-Bahn or S-Bahn: Hauptbahnhof. **Amenities:** Concierge. *In room:* TV, Wi-Fi (free).

Hotel Jedermann ♠ ☺ With a name inspired from the 15th-century morality play *Everyman,* this hotel, run by the Jenke family for more than 50 years, caters to every taste. Not trying to be too exclusive or extravagant, the Jedermann provides pleasant comfort and good value in a convenient, albeit not picturesque, location. Families will appreciate the cribs, cots, and toys available.

Bayerstrasse 95, 80335 München. www.hotel-jedermann.de. © **089/543240.** Fax 089/54324111. 55 units. 75€–215€ double; 90€–219€ triple. Rates include buffet breakfast. MC, V. Parking 10€. U-Bahn or S-Bahn: Hauptbahnhof. **Amenities:** Internet (free; in lobby). *In room:* A/C (in some), TV, hair dryer (in most).

Hotel Monaco ★ The Monaco proves you shouldn't judge a hotel by its facade. This haven of comfort is located in an otherwise unremarkable area that might put many off. (The entrance is not at the adult shop below the sign, but around the corner in the Adolf-Kolping-Strasse.) Since 1998 Christine Sevdas has offered her award-winning service that receives rave reviews from repeat customers. The spacious bedrooms feature rural Bavarian touches like wood-frame beds and ornate lighting fixtures. The generous breakfast buffet is a welcome sight first thing in the morning.

Schillerstrasse 9, 80336 München. www.hotel-monaco.de. © **089/5459940.** Fax 089/5503709. 27 units. 60€–229€ double; 90€–290€ triple. Extra bed 20€–50€. AE, MC, V. Parking 15€. U-Bahn or S-Bahn: Hauptbahnhof. **Amenities:** Room service. *In room:* TV, Wi-Fi (free).

Hotel Schlicker ♠ This charming traditional hotel dates to 1544 and has been run in a friendly, inviting fashion by the Mayer family since 1897. Although sandwiched between a McDonald's and a Burger King, it's also in the heart of Munich, just steps away from the landmark Marienplatz and around the corner from one of the best food markets in Germany, Viktualienmarkt. Only the breakfast room suggests that this place was once an ancient inn—the rest of the hotel is modernized. Bedrooms are comfortable and traditional, each midsize.

Tal 8, 80331 München. www.hotel-schlicker.de. © **089/2428870.** Fax 089/296059. 69 units. 145€–185€ double; 260€ suite. Rates include continental breakfast. AE, DC, MC, V. Parking 10€. U-Bahn: Marienplatz. **Amenities:** Room service. *In room:* TV, minibar (in some), Wi-Fi (free).

Hotel Uhland Just a 10-minute walk from the Hauptbahnhof and even closer to the Oktoberfest grounds, the Uhland is a pleasant residential retreat in the city. The stately town mansion, built in Art Nouveau style, stands in its own small garden. The hotel offers friendly, personal service, and rooms are soundproof, snug, traditional, and comfortable.

Uhlandstrasse 1, 80336 München. www.hotel-uhland.de. © **089/543350.** Fax 089/54335250. 30 units. 81€–204€ double. Rates include buffet breakfast. AE, DC, MC, V. Free parking. U-Bahn or S-Bahn: Theresienwiese. Bus: 58. *In room:* TV, hair dryer, minibar, Wi-Fi (free).

Pension Westfalia ★ 🏷 Originally built in 1895, this four-story villa near Goetheplatz provides easy access to the mania on the Theresienwiese during Oktoberfest time, and overlooks the pleasant meadow and Bavaria Statue the rest of the year. Rooms are rather functional and short on extras, but they are well maintained. Parking on the street, when available, is free.

Mozartstrasse 23, 80336 München. www.pension-westfalia.de. © **089/530377.** Fax 089/5439120. 19 units, 14 with bathroom. 50€–60€ per person double without bathroom; 68€–82€ per person double with bathroom. Rates include buffet breakfast. AE, MC, V. U-Bahn: Goetheplatz. Bus: 58. *In room:* TV, Wi-Fi (free).

In Schwabing
MODERATE

Gästehaus Englischer Garten ★★ ☺ This ivy-covered retreat provides a unique experience in Munich. As one of the few hotels bordering the Englischer Garten, this villa feels more like a private home with an expansive backyard. Roselinde Zankl keeps a tidy home and does an excellent job at making you feel welcome, which may make you want to stick around longer. The genuine antiques, comfortable beds, and Oriental rugs add to the grandmotherly appeal of the interior. Although a short walk and a few U-Bahn stops from the center, the location is ideal for a bike ride or stroll through the city's largest park, or a night out in the trendy Schwabing district.

Liebergesellstrasse 8, 80802 München-Schwabing. www.hotelenglischergarten.de. © **089/3839410.** Fax 089/38394133. 31 units, 26 with bathroom. 75€–109€ double without bathroom; 129€–169€ double with bathroom; 110€–163€ apt. AE, DC, MC, V. Parking 9€. U-Bahn: Münchner Freiheit. **Amenities:** Babysitting; bikes. *In room:* TV, minibar, Wi-Fi (free).

La Maison ★ 🛍 If Goth-posh was ever possible, this hotel might embody it. Shades of black and white permeate the sleek furnishings of this oasis of class in the otherwise grungy neighborhood of Schwabing. The somber furnishings with black velvet touches seem to recall a lost era of pouting crooners in Parisian cabarets, which may make you want to leave your tuxedo on. The lounge sofas in the lobby feel like a cloud, and a recently -opened Japanese Restaurant provides refined cuisine. Whether it's your style or not, expect all the comforts and amenities of a successfully run hotel.

Occamstrasse 24, 80802 München. www.hotel-la-maison.com. © **089/33035550.** Fax 089/330355555. 31 units. 180€–220€ double. AE, MC, V. Parking 15€. U-Bahn: Münchener Freiheit. **Amenities:** Restaurant; bar; room service. *In room:* TV/DVD, CD player, hair dryer, minibar, Wi-Fi (free).

In Haidhausen
MODERATE

Hotel Preysing ★ 🛍 If you want a quiet location and don't mind a hotel a bit removed from the historic center, consider the Preysing, located across the Isar river near the Deutsches Museum. A short tram or S-Bahn ride will bring you into the center of the city. Despite the dour facade, the hotel's agreeable interior is conservatively furnished with no unnecessary extravagant decoration. Many little extras add to the overall charm: fresh flowers are everywhere, the furnishings have been carefully selected, and fresh fruit is supplied daily.

Preysingstrasse 1, 81667 München. www.hotel-preysing.de. ℂ **089/458450.** Fax 089/45845444. 76 units. 198€–280€ double; from 258€ suite. Rates include buffet breakfast. AE, DC, MC, V. Parking 12€. S-Bahn: Rosenheimer Platz. Tram: 18. **Amenities:** Babysitting; bikes; room service. *In room:* A/C, TV, hair dryer, minibar, Wi-Fi (free).

In Nymphenburg

INEXPENSIVE

Kriemhild ☺   This is one of the best choices for visitors with kids in tow, as it lies in the suburb of Nymphenburg, near the famous palace of the same name. In ten minutes, you and the children can walk over to Schloss Nymphenburg (p. 296) with its beautiful ponds and leafy parks. Even closer is the Hirschgarten, with possibly the biggest beer garden in Europe. The accommodating staff will help you get oriented and figure out the quickest connections to sights in town. Some of the rooms are spacious enough to contain a corner sofa, which can be converted for use as a three- or four-bed family room. In the morning, there's an elaborate buffet breakfast, and at night you can drink beer or wine in a cozy Bavarian-styled *Guntherstube* (beer tavern).

Guntherstrasse 16, 80639 München. www.kriemhild.de. ℂ **089/1711170.** Fax 089/17111755. 18 units. 88€–104€ double; 118€–178€ suite. Rates include continental breakfast buffet. AE, MC, V. Parking 5€. S-Bahn: Laim. Tram: 16 or 17. **Amenities:** Bar. *In room:* TV, hair dryer, minibar, Wi-Fi (free).

Laimer Hof ★ 🎒☺   This neo-Renaissance villa is in one of the most tranquil and exclusive sections of Munich. The Nymphenburg Palace and its enchanting park and ponds lies just a 5-minute walk from the hotel. The 1886 villa was turned into a hotel in 1937, but a young couple, Sebastian and Alexandra Rösch, took over and made substantial improvements and renovations, turning it into one of the most desirable private hotels of Munich. The modernized bedrooms still maintain traditional touches, like wrought-iron bed frames, that exude the aura of the era. The hotel is a hit with families, and the hotel's proximity to the park provides the opportunity to integrate jogging, biking and walking into your stay. The nearby Hirschgarten—with its massive beer garden and mini deer garden—is also alluring. The included lavish breakfast buffet will get you on your way.

Laimer Strasse 40, 80639 München. www.laimerhof.de. ℂ **089/178038.** Fax 089/1782007. 23 units. 85€–105€ double. Rates include buffet breakfast. AE, MC, V. Free parking. Tram: 12, 16, or 17. Bus: 151. **Amenities:** Bikes. *In room:* TV, minibar, Wi-Fi (free).

SIDE TRIPS FROM MUNICH

The **Bavarian Alps** are within easy reach (see chapter 9), or you can head for **Neuschwanstein** (p. 267) to see Ludwig II's fairy-tale castle.

Dachau Concentration Camp Memorial Site

In 1933, what had once been a quiet little artists' community just 15km (10 miles) from Munich became a tragic symbol of the Nazi era. Shortly after Hitler became chancellor, Himmler and the SS set up the first German concentration camp on the grounds of a former ammunition factory. The list of prisoners at the camp included enemies of the Third Reich, including everyone from communists and Social Democrats to Jews, homosexuals, Gypsies, Jehovah's Witnesses, clergymen, political opponents, some trade union members, and others.

During its notorious history, between 1933 and 1945, more than 206,000 prisoners from 30 countries were imprisoned at Dachau, perhaps a lot more. Some were forced into slave labor, manufacturing Nazi armaments for the war and helping to build roads, for example. Others fell victim to SS doctors, who conducted grotesque medical experiments on them. And still others were killed after Dachau became a center for mass murder: Starvation, illness, beatings, and torture killed thousands who were not otherwise hanged, shot by firing squads, or lethally injected. At least 30,000 people were registered as dead while in Dachau between 1933 and 1945. However, there are many other thousands who were also murdered there, even if their deaths weren't officially logged.

The SS abandoned the camp on April 28, 1945, and the liberating U.S. Army moved in to take charge the following day. In all, a total of 67,000 living prisoners—all of them on the verge of death—were discovered at Dachau and its subsidiary camps.

Upon entering the camp, **KZ-Gedenkstätte Dachau,** Alte-Römerstrasse 75 (© **08131/669970;** www.kz-gedenkstaette-dachau.de), you are faced by three memorial chapels—Catholic, Protestant, and Jewish—built in the early 1960s. Immediately behind the Catholic chapel is the Lagerstrasse, the main camp road lined with poplar trees, once flanked by 32 barracks, each housing 208 prisoners. Two barracks have been rebuilt to give visitors insight into the conditions the prisoners endured.

The museum is housed in the large building that once contained the kitchen, laundry, and bathrooms. Photographs and documents show the rise of the Nazi regime and the SS; other exhibits show the persecution of Jews and other prisoners. Every effort has been made to present the facts. The tour of Dachau is a truly moving experience.

You can get to the camp by taking the frequent S-Bahn train S2 from the Hauptbahnhof to Dachau (direction: Petershausen), then bus no. 726 to the camp. The camp is open Tuesday to Sunday 9am to 5pm; admission is free. The English version of a 22-minute documentary film, *The Dachau Concentration Camp,* is shown at 11:30am, 2pm, and 3:30pm. All documents are translated in the catalog, which is available at the museum entrance.

BEFORE HITLER, A BELOVED artists' COLONY

Unknown to many, Dachau had a glorious history long before it became infamous in the annals of human cruelty. At the end of the 19th century, it was one of the leading artists' colonies of Germany, and landscape painting was virtually developed in the Dachau moorlands. Women were not yet allowed in the Munich Art Academy, but they were educated in the town's private art schools.

If you have time to spare, you can explore Dachau's historic core, including its **Schloss Dachau,** a hilltop Renaissance castle that dominates the town at Schlossplatz (© **08131/87923**). All that's left of a much larger palace is a wing from 1715. Stand in the east terrace for a panoramic view of Munich in the distance. The highlight is the grand Renaissance hall, with its scenes of figures from ancient mythology. Chamber concerts are staged here. The on-site brewery hosts the town's beer and music festival annually during the first 2 weeks of August. Charging 2€ for admission, the castle is open April to September Tuesday to Sunday 9am to 6pm, and October to March Tuesday to Sunday 10am to 4pm.

Many paintings from the artists who settled here in the 1800s are still in town, especially the works on display in **Gemäldegalerie,** Konrad-Adenauer-Strasse 3 (© **08131/567516**), open Tuesday to Friday 11am to 5pm, Saturday and Sunday 1 to 5pm, charging an admission of 4€.

THE BAVARIAN ALPS

The huge state and former kingdom of Bavaria boasts not only the best mountainous landscape in Germany, but also one comparable to that of its Alpine neighbors further south—just don't tell that to the Austrians or the Swiss. This region along the Austrian border is a world unto itself known for the hospitality of the locals, well-preserved craft-making, and expansive vistas. Although many travelers think of the Alps as a winter vacationland, you'll find that nearly all the Bavarian resorts and villages offer unforgettable attractions throughout the year.

Munich is the major driving gateway, with autobahns leading directly to the Bavarian Alps. If you're beginning your tour in Garmisch-Partenkirchen in the west, you should fly into Munich. However, if your destination is Berchtesgaden in the eastern Alps, the nearest airport is Salzburg, Austria.

OUTDOORS IN THE BAVARIAN ALPS The Bavarian Alps are both a winter wonderland and a summer playground. The **Alpine** and **cross-country skiing** is the best in Germany, and among the best in all of Europe. A regular winter snowfall in January and February usually measures from 30 to 50 centimeters (12–20 in.), leaving about 2m (6½ ft.) of snow in areas served by ski lifts. The Zugspitze, at 2,960m (9,700 ft.) above sea level, is the tallest mountain peak in Germany. You can reach this well-known ski district in spring or autumn by a rack railway; it is inaccessible in winter. Ski slopes begin at a height of 2,650m (8,700 ft.). Call the local "Snow-Telefon" (German only) at $\textcircled{C}$ **08652/967297** for current snow conditions.

Another great ski district in the Alps is **Berchtesgadener Land,** with Alpine skiing around Jenner, Rossfeld, Götschen, and Hochschwarzeck. Snow conditions are consistently good until March. You'll find a cross-country skiing center, many kilometers of tracks in first-class condition, natural toboggan runs, an artificial ice run for toboggan and skibob (or snow-bike) runs, and artificial ice-skating and curling rinks.

There's also skating between October and February at the world-class ice-skating rink in Berchtesgaden. Less reliable, but more picturesque, is skating on the surface of the Hintersee, once it's sufficiently frozen.

Alpine hiking is the major attraction in summer, when many visitors come just to hike through **Berchtesgaden National Park,** bordering the Austrian province of Salzburg. The 2,470m (8,100-ft.) Watzmann Mountain, the Königssee (Germany's cleanest, clearest lake), and parts of the Jenner—the pride of Berchtesgaden's four ski areas—are within the park, which has well-mapped trails through protected areas, leading the hiker through spectacular natural beauty. For more on hiking in the park, contact **Nation-alparkhaus,** Franziskanerplatz 7, 83471 Berchtesgaden (℡ **08652/64343;** www.nationalpark-berchtesgaden.bayern.de), open daily 9am to 5pm. ***Note:*** In 2012 the park's glistening new **Haus der Berge** will replace the Nationalparkhaus, at the site of the former Berchtesgadener Hof at Hanielstrasse 7.

Back to the southwest of Munich, one of the best areas in summer is the 1,240m (4,070-ft.) **Eckbauer,** lying on the southern fringe of Partenkirchen (the local tourist office will supply maps and details). From Garmisch-Partenkirchen, serious hikers can embark on full-day or overnight Alpine treks, following clearly marked footpaths and staying in isolated mountain huts. Some huts are staffed and serve meals. For truly remote unsupervised huts, you'll be provided with information on how to gain access. For information, ask at the local tourist office or write to the government-subsidized **German Alpine Association,** Am Franziskanerplatz 7, 83471 Berchtes-gaden (℡ **08652/64343;** www.alpenverein.de), which will also direct you to a privately owned tour operator, the **Summit Club** (www.summitclub.de), an outfit devoted to the organization of high-altitude expeditions throughout the world.

You can use the somewhat touristy facilities of Garmisch-Partenkirchen as a base for explorations of the rugged Zugspitze and Eckbauer areas. Stay at one of the inns in Mittenwald or Oberammergau and take advantage of a wide roster of outdoor diversions there. Any outfitter will provide directions and linkups with their sports programs from wherever you stay.

Berchtesgaden also makes a great base for its stunning backyard. Street maps of the town and its environs are usually available free from the **Berchtesgaden-König-see Tourist Office,** Königsseer Strasse 2, Berchtesgaden (℡ **08652/9670;** www.berchtesgadener-land.info); intricately detailed maps of the surrounding Alpine topography are available for a fee.

Weather permitting, another summer activity is **ballooning,** which can be arranged through **Outdoor Club Berchtesgaden,** Metzgerstrasse 7 (℡ **08652/97760;** www.outdoor-club.de).

Anglers will find plenty of **fishing** opportunities (especially salmon, pikeperch, and trout) at Hintersee and the rivers Ramsauer Ache and Königsseer Ache. To acquire a fishing permit, contact the **Berchtesgaden-Königsee Tourist Office** (see above) at Berchtesgaden, which will direct you to any of four different authori-ties, based on where you want to fish. For fishing specifically within the Hintersee, contact tourist officials at the **Kurverwaltung,** ImTal 2 (℡ **08657/988920**), at Ramsau, 12km (7½ miles) from Berchtesgaden.

Despite the obvious dangers, **hang gliding** or **paragliding** from the vertiginous slopes of Mount Jenner can be thrilling. To arrange it, contact **Summit Club** (see above).

Practice your **kayaking** or **white-water rafting** techniques on one of the area's many mountain rivers (called Ache in German), such as the Ramsauer, Königsseer, Bischofswiesener, and Berchtesgadener Aches. For information and options, contact the above-mentioned **Outdoor Club Berchtesgaden.**

If you would like to go **swimming** in an Alpine lake—not to everyone's taste, due to frigid temperatures—there are many tarns found in the Bavarian Forest.

Exploring the Region by Car

Acclaimed as one of the most scenic drives in all of Europe, the **Deutsche Alpen-strasse (German Alpine Road)** ★ stretches for some 480km (300 miles) between Berchtesgaden in the east and Lindau on Lake Constance in the west (see chapter 10). The road goes through or past mountains, lakes, forests, and "castles in the sky." The best times to drive are in early spring or early autumn. In winter, mountain passes are often shut down, and even those highways that remain open can be dangerous.

IF YOU HAVE 1 DAY   After your stopover in Munich (see chapter 8), head south along Autobahn A8 (drive in the right lane if you want to avoid the speeders on the left). Turn south on Rte. B20 for **Berchtesgaden,** 158km (98 miles) southeast of Munich. After settling in and having lunch, take an afternoon excursion to **Obersalzberg** and **Kehlstein** (you can go by bus).

IF YOU HAVE 2 DAYS   While still based in Berchtesgaden, explore the **Königssee,** to the south (about 2 hr. by boat). This long, narrow lake, famed for its steep banks and dark waters, is one of Europe's most dramatic and romantic sights. In the afternoon, drive west along the Alpine road and then north on Rte. B20 some 20km (12 miles) to **Bad Reichenhall,** one of Germany's most famous spas. Return to Berchtesgaden for the night.

IF YOU HAVE 3 DAYS   Get back on Autobahn A8 toward Munich but turn off at **Prien am Chiemsee,** 85km (53 miles) southeast of Munich. The premier attraction here is the Neues Schloss, a fantastic castle begun by Ludwig II in 1878 on the island of Herrenchiemsee. You can find food and lodging at Prien.

IF YOU HAVE 4 DAYS   Get back on the autobahn to Munich, but take a cross-country route (472) toward Bad Tölz, which is one of Bavaria's leading spas, although it lacks any major attractions. Continue west from Bad Tölz along Rte. 472 to the town of Bichl, at which point you head south along Rte. 11 until you reach Benediktbeuern, a distance of 14km (9 miles) from Bad Tölz. Here you'll find **Benediktbeuern,** the most ancient Benedictine monastery in upper Bavaria. Records trace it back to the year 739. After a look, continue 6km (4 miles) south along Rte. 11 to **Kochel am See,** with its Alpine vistas. Follow Rte. 11 south to the express highway, Rte. 2, which you then follow about 30km (20 miles) to **Mittenwald** on the Austrian border. Plan an overnight stay.

IF YOU HAVE 5 DAYS   You'll want to spend as much time as possible in **Mittenwald.** Goethe called it a "living picture book"—you may think it looks like part of *The Sound of Music* film set. It's also a major center for violin making. Give it at least a morning before driving northwest for 20km (12 miles) on Rte. 2 to **Garmisch-Partenkirchen.** After checking in, head for the major attraction, the **Zugspitze,** the highest peak in German territory. Wear warm clothing. This could be the highlight of your trip to Bavaria.

IF YOU HAVE 6 DAYS   Leaving Garmisch-Partenkirchen, head north on Rte. 2 for 20km (12 miles) toward **Oberammergau.** Along the way, you'll pass **Kloster Ettal,** founded in 1330. Its original 10-sided church is a stunning example of the Bavarian rococo style. Some 10km (6 miles) to the west is **Schloss Linderhof,** one of "Mad" King Ludwig's royal residences, built between 1874 and 1878 on the grounds of his hunting lodge. These two attractions will take up most of your day, but you'll still arrive in the little old woodcarver's village of Oberammergau, 11km (7 miles) northeast of Linderhof, in time to wander about. Later, enjoy a hearty Bavarian dinner before turning in to your Alpine bed.

BERCHTESGADEN ★★

158km (98 miles) SE of Munich, 18km (11 miles) SE of Bad Reichenhall, 23km (14 miles) S of Salzburg

Ever since Ludwig I of Bavaria chose this resort as a favorite hideaway, the tourist business in Berchtesgaden has been booming. The village is situated below the many summits of Watzmann Mountain—2,713m (8,900 ft.) at its highest point. According to legend, the mountain peaks were once a royal family who were so evil that God punished them by turning them into rocks.

Berchtesgaden is a quiet old Alpine village with ancient winding streets and a medieval marketplace and castle square. Its name is often linked with Hitler and the Nazi hierarchy, but this impression is erroneous. Hitler's playground was actually at Obersalzberg, on a wooded plateau up the mountain.

Essentials

GETTING THERE

BY AIR The nearest airport is **Salzburg Airport** (© 0662/85800; www.salzburg-airport.com). It has regularly scheduled air service to Frankfurt, Berlin, Düsseldorf, Hamburg, London, and Zürich. Major airlines serving the Salzburg airport are **Air Berlin** (© 0820/737800; www.airberlin.com), **Austrian Airlines** (© 0517/661000; www.aua.com), **British Airways** (© 0179/567567; www.ba.com), and **Lufthansa** (© 0180/5838426; www.lufthansa.com). From Salzburg you can take a 1-hour train ride to Berchtesgaden, changing trains at Freilassing.

BY TRAIN The **Berchtesgaden Bahnhof** lies on the Munich-Freilassing line. Fourteen trains a day arrive from Munich with a connection in Freilassing (trip time: 1½ hr.). For information, call © **01805/996633** (www.bahn.de). Berchtesgaden has three mountain rail lines—Obersalzbergbahn, Jennerbahn, and Hirscheckbahn—going to mountain plateaus around the resorts. For information, contact **Berchtesgadener Bergbahn AG** (© **08652/95810**; www.jennerbahn.de) and **Obersalzbergbahn AG** (© **08652/2561**; www.obersalzbergbahn.de).

BY BUS Regional bus service to Alpine villages and towns around Berchtesgaden is offered by **RVO Regionalverkehr Oberbayern** at Berchtesgaden (© **08652/94480**; www.rvo-bus.de).

BY CAR Access by car is via the A8 Autobahn from Munich in the north or Rte. 20 from the south. The drive from Munich takes about 2 hours.

VISITOR INFORMATION

Contact the **Kurdirektion,** Königsseerstrasse 2 (© **08652/9670**; www.berchtes gadener-land.info). It's open mid-June to mid-October Monday through Friday 8:30am to 6pm, Saturday 9am to 5pm, and Sunday 9am to 3pm; mid-October to mid-June Monday through Friday 8:30am to 5pm, and Saturday 9am to noon.

Exploring Berchtesgaden

The **Stiftskirche (Abbey Church),** dating from 1122, is adjacent to the Königliches Schloss Berchtesgaden. The church is mainly Romanesque, with Gothic additions. One of its ancient twin steeples was destroyed by lightning and rebuilt in 1866. The interior contains many fine works of art; the high altar has a painting by Zott dating from 1669. In the vestry is a small silver altar donated by Empress Maria Theresa of Austria.

Schlossplatz ★, partially enclosed by the castle and Stiftskirche, is the most attractive plaza in town. On the opposite side of the square from the church is a 16th-century arcade that leads to **Marktplatz,** with typical Alpine houses and a wooden fountain from 1677 (restored by Ludwig I in 1860). Some of Berchtesgaden's oldest inns and houses border this square. Extending from Marktplatz is the **Nonntal,** lined with more old houses, some built into Lockstein Mountain, which towers above the town.

Heimatmuseum, Schloss Aldelsheim, Schroffenberg-Allee 6 (© **08652/4410**; www.heimatmuseum-berchtesgaden.de), is a minor but charming museum devoted

to Alpine woodcarving. The craft here predates the more fabled woodcarving at Oberammergau. Some of the best examples in Germany are on display. The museum is open Tuesday to Sunday 10am to 5pm. Admission is 2.50€ for adults and free for children 18 and under. It's closed in November.

Königliches Schloss Berchtesgaden MUSEUM   In the Middle Ages, Berchtesgaden grew up around a powerful Augustinian monastery. Its monks introduced the art of woodcarving, for which the town is still noted. When the town became part of Bavaria in 1809, the abbey was secularized and eventually converted to a palace for the royal Wittelsbach family. Now it is a museum, mostly devoted to the royal collection of sacred art, including wood sculptures by the famed artists Veit Stoss and Tilman Riemenschneider. There's also a gallery of 19th-century art, a collection of Italian furniture from the 16th century, and a display of 17th- and 18th-century firearms. Visitors are ushered through about 30 of the castle's showcase rooms as part of tours that depart at 20-minute intervals throughout the day. Tours last an hour each, and are conducted mostly in German, with a smattering of English. (English-language written texts and descriptions of the castle are passed out in advance.) Note that the castle is closed for the last half of August every year, during which time HRH Franz, the duke of Bavaria, heir to the throne of Bavaria and owner of the castle, comes for his summer vacation.

Schlossplatz 2. ✆ **08652/947980.** www.haus-bayern.com. Admission 7€ adults, 3.50€ students and seniors, 3€ children 6–17, free for children 5 and under. Mid-May to mid-Oct Sun–Fri 10am–noon and 2–4pm; mid-Oct to mid-May Mon–Fri 11am–2pm. Closed last half of Aug.

Salzbergwerk Berchtesgaden ☺ NATURAL ATTRACTION   These salt mines at the eastern edge of town were once owned by the Augustinian monastery. Operations began here in 1517. The deposits are more than 300m (1,000 ft.) thick and are still processed from four galleries or "hills." Visitors are given protective miner's clothing. Older children will enjoy the guided tours that begin with a ride into the mine on a small wagonlike train. After a nearly 1km (½-mile) journey, visitors leave the train and explore the rest of the mine, sliding down a miner's slide and riding on the underground salt lake in a ferry. The highlight of the tour is the "chapel," a grotto containing unusually shaped salt formations illuminated for an eerie effect. The 1½-hour tour can be taken any time of the year, in any weather.

Bergwerkstrasse 83. ✆ **08652/60020.** www.salzzeitreise.de. Admission 15€ adults, 9.50€ students and children 4–16, 41€ Family Card. Children 3 and under not admitted. May–Oct daily 9am–5pm; Nov–Apr daily 11am–3pm. Bus: 840.

Where to Eat

Hubertusstube INTERNATIONAL   You'll get an undeniable sense of Bavarian *Gemütlichkeit* in this richly paneled restaurant, where a trio of old-fashioned dining rooms, each with a century-old history of hospitality, offers well-prepared food and a view of the Alps. Specialties include roast salmon with herb butter and creamy mushroom-laced noodles, or catfish in a white wine and cream sauce with baby shrimp. More standard dishes feature a breaded veal steak stuffed with ham and cheese or a small sirloin steak flavored with mustard. Service is traditional and very polite.

In the Hotel Vier Jahreszeiten, Maximilianstrasse 20. ✆ **08652/9520.** Reservations recommended. Main courses 9€–25€. AE, DC, MC, V. Daily 11:30am–2pm and 6–11pm.

Where to Stay

Alpenhotel Denninglehen ★ 🏨   Set in a high Alpine meadow 6km (4 miles) east of Berchtesgaden, at an altitude of 900m (3,000 ft.) above sea level (Berchtesgaden is

500m/1,600 ft. above sea level), this solid, traditional-looking mountain chalet was built in 1980. Ringed with snow in winter and grassy meadows and flower beds in summer, and within a short schuss from the ski slopes, it's a refreshingly rustic (albeit manicured) getaway for urbanites, with comfortable lodgings, clean air, and views that stretch for miles. Bedrooms are outfitted in either rustic, wood-sheathed contemporary style or more folkloric Bavarian and old-fashioned decor. Although efficient and modernized, they are rather small.

Am Priesterstein 7, 83471 Berchtesgaden/Oberau. www.denninglehen.de. ℂ **08652/97890.** Fax 08652/64710. 25 units. 35€–79€ per person. Rates include buffet breakfast. MC, V. Free parking. Closed last week of Dec and Jan 15–29. From Berchtesgaden, drive along Rte. 305, following signs to Unteran; take Rte. 319, following the signs to Oberau. **Amenities:** Restaurant; bar; exercise room; indoor heated pool; sauna; Wi-Fi (free; in lobby). *In room:* TV.

Hotel Krone 🍴 One of the most appealing bargains in Berchtesgaden is this well-built chalet-inspired hotel. Operated by live-in managers, the Grafe family, and permeated with a sense of Alpine thrift and good cheer, it offers cozy rooms sheathed with varnished pine. Each has a balcony or terrace and a compact bathroom.

Am Rad 5, 83471 Berchtesgaden. www.hotel-krone-berchtesgaden.de. ℂ **08652/94600.** Fax 08652/946010. 21 units. 35€–53€ per person. Rates include buffet breakfast. MC, V. Closed Nov–Dec 28. **Amenities:** Restaurant; Jacuzzi; sauna; Wi-Fi (free; in lobby). *In room:* TV, hair dryer.

Hotel Wittelsbach Quiet, serene, and sedate, with a loyal clientele that tends to include many elderly guests who return year after year, this is a well-maintained hotel with century-old, four-story premises. It resembles a private *Jugendstil* (Art Nouveau) chalet with pink exterior walls, lavish balustrades (most rooms have a private balcony), and a location within a small but verdant garden on one of the major thoroughfares of the town center. Bedrooms are comfortable, quiet, high ceilinged, and generously sized. The only meal offered is breakfast, served within a rustic, charming, *gemütlich* (cozy) room loaded with local artifacts and a sense of Teutonic charm.

Maximilianstrasse 16, 83471 Berchtesgaden. www.hotel-wittelsbach.com. ℂ **08652/96380.** Fax 08652/66304. 29 units. 88€–98€ double; 130€ suite. Rates include breakfast buffet. AE, DC, MC, V. Parking 5€. **Amenities:** Room service. *In room:* TV, minibar.

Vier Jahreszeiten ★ This old inn with modern extensions in the heart of the village has been remodeled and improved over the years, and is quite comfortable now. Some of the newer units, with tiny sitting rooms and balconies, resemble suites. There's a terrace for your summer viewing pleasure.

Maximilianstrasse 20, 83471 Berchtesgaden. www.hotel-vierjahreszeiten-berchtesgaden.de. ℂ **08652/9520.** Fax 08652/5029. 59 units. 86€–104€ double; 110€–144€ junior suite. Rates include buffet breakfast. AE, DC, MC, V. Free outdoor parking; 8€ in garage. **Amenities:** Restaurant; bar; indoor heated pool; sauna. *In room:* TV, hair dryer, minibar, Wi-Fi (free).

Side Trips to Königssee & Obersalzberg

KÖNIGSSEE ★★

This is the "jewel in the necklace" of Berchtesgaden. The waters of this scenic lake appear to be dark green because of the steep mountains that jut upward from its shores. Low-lying land on the lake's northern edge contains a parking lot and a few charming inns and bathing facilities, but mountains enclose the rest of the lake, making it impossible to walk along the shoreline. The only way to explore the water, unless you're like one of the mountain goats you may see above, is by boat. Electric motorboats—no noisy gas-powered launches allowed—carry passengers on tours around the lake throughout the summer and occasionally even in winter.

The most popular spot on Königssee is the tiny, flat peninsula on the western bank, the site of a basilica as early as the 12th century. Today the Catholic **Kirche Sankt Bartholomä (Chapel of St. Bartholomew)** is still used for services (except in winter). The clergy must arrive by boat because there's no other way to approach the peninsula.

The adjacent buildings include a fisher's house and a restaurant, which was once a favorite hunting lodge of the Bavarian kings. Here you can sample trout and salmon caught in the crisp, clean waters. At the southern end of the lake you come to the Salet-Alm, where the tour boats make a short stop near a thundering waterfall. If you follow the footpath up the hillside, you'll reach the summer pastures used by the cattle of Berchtesgaden. Just over the hill is **Lake Obersee,** part of Königssee until an avalanche separated them 8 centuries ago. If you prefer a shorter trip, you can take the boat to St. Bartholomew and back.

To reach Königssee from Berchtesgaden by car, follow the signs south from the town 5km (3 miles). It's also a pleasant hour's walk or a short ride by electric train or bus from the center of town.

For information about boat excursions, call **Schiffahrt Königssee** at ✆ **08652/ 96360** or visit www.seenschiffahrt.de. An entire tour of Königssee requires about 2 hours. There are boats in summer every 30 minutes, so getting off one boat and climbing aboard another is easy if you want to break up the tour. During the summer, the first boat departs every morning at 8am and the last boat leaves at 5:15pm. In winter, boats leave about every 45 minutes beginning at 9:30am. The important stops are at St. Bartholomä and Salet Obersee, the latter off limits in winter A round-trip fare for a lake tour is 16€ for adults, 8€ for children 6 to 17.

OBERSALZBERG ★★

The drive from Berchtesgaden to Obersalzberg at about 1,000m (3,300 ft.) is one of Bavaria's most scenic routes. Obersalzberg was where Hitler settled down in a rented cottage after his prison term while he completed *Mein Kampf*. After he came to power in 1933, he bought Haus Wachenfeld and had it remodeled into his residence, the Berghof. Obersalzberg became the center for holiday living for Nazis such as Martin Bormann and Hermann Göring.

Today, you can walk around the **ruins of Hitler's Berghof.** This was where the famous 1938 meeting took place between Hitler and British Prime Minister Neville Chamberlain. The result was the Munich Agreement, which Chamberlain so mistakenly declared would bring "peace in our time." The Berghof was destroyed in 1945 by Bavarian government authorities at the request of the U.S. Army—the Americans did not want a monument to Hitler.

An eerily fascinating point of interest is the **Kehlstein (Eagle's Nest) ★★,** which was erected on a high-altitude site by Bormann, who intended it as a 50th-birthday gift for Hitler. Built on a rocky plateau and never intended as a military installation, its access was made possible by the construction of a 7km (4½-mile) road that was blasted out of solid rock beginning in 1937—an outstanding act of engineering. Ironically, Hitler visited the site very rarely, perhaps three times in all. Unlike Hitler's larger lodgings at Obersalzberg, which were demolished by the Allies at the end of World War II, the original granite-built teahouse on the mountain summit at Kehlstein is still standing. Today it's the site of a restaurant, the **Kehlsteinhaus.** In winter, the site is completely closed because of snow blockages on its access road.

Between May and October, if you want to reach Kehlstein, you can either sign up for an organized tour with Eagle's Nest Tours (see below), or set out by yourself from the railway station at Berchtesgaden. Modern buses operated by the **RVO Regional-verkehr Oberbayern** (for information, call the Berchtesgaden Tourist Office at ☏ **08652/9670**) charge 7€ per person for round-trip transit from the Berchtesgaden railway station up to the Alpine hamlet of **Berchtesgaden-Hintereck.** Here you'll find some souvenir shops, a documentation center, and a small museum showcasing the region's role as a place of rest and relaxation for Hitler. Also at Hintereck, you'll have the option of visiting a bunker and a grim series of rooms used as a military prison by the Nazi regime. Access to the museum, the documentation center, the bunker, and the prison cells at Hintereck costs 8€ for adults. Access is free for students, children 15 and under, and military personnel. From May to October, they're open daily from 9am to 5pm; from November to March, they're open Tuesday to Sunday 10am to 3pm (closed Jan 1, Nov 1, Apr, and Dec 24–25 and 31).

To continue uphill from Hintereck to Kehlstein, you'll have to transfer to the **Kehlstein Bus** that hauls passengers uphill, past sweeping panoramas, along a tight and winding Alpine road, to the base of an elevator shaft that will carry you the remaining way to the Kehlstein. Total transit time from Berchtesgaden to Kehlstein, without stops, is about 50 minutes each way. The Kehlstein bus line operates at roughly 25-minute intervals daily from 9am to 5pm from mid-May to mid-October. Round-trip passage, including the fee for the elevator, costs 16€ per person (free for children 4 and under). If you're hardy, you can skip the elevator and take a 30-minute uphill climb along a well-marked hiking trail instead. The **restaurant** at the summit, within the Kehlsteinhaus, is open during hours that correspond to the bus access described above.

The Kehlstein road is closed to private traffic. The only option for drivers of private cars involves parking in the lot at Hintereck and then riding the Kehlstein bus to the base of the elevator described above.

If you prefer to visit Kehlstein by guided tour, you'll find English-language options at the American-run **Eagle's Nest Tours,** Königsseer Strasse 2 (☏ **08652/64971;** www.eagles-nest-tours.com). Tours, including Obersalzberg, Eagle's Nest, and the bunker system as an afternoon history package, are conducted daily mid-May to mid-October starting at 1:15pm, departing from the Berchtesgaden Visitor Center. A 4-hour tour costs 50€ for adults, and 35€ for children 6 to 12. Children 5 and under are not permitted on the tour. In addition, Eagle's Nest Tours also offers a popular "Sound of Music" tour to nearby Salzburg, which costs 35€ for adults, 25€ for children 6 to 12, and is free for children 5 and under.

Where to Stay

Hotel zum Türken The Hotel zum Türken, located in Obersalzberg, is legendary. It's designed in the Alpine style and has terraces with views. On its facade is a large painted sign of "the Turk"—legend has it that the first owner was a veteran of the Turkish war. In the 1930s, anti-Nazi remarks led to trouble for the proprietor, Herr Schuster, who was arrested. Afterward Bormann used the building as a Gestapo headquarters; it then fell victim to air raids and looting in April 1945. Herr Schuster's daughter, Therese Partner, was able to buy the ruin from the German government in 1949. There is an old air-raid shelter directly under the hotel that can be visited every day from 9am to 3pm. The small- to medium-size rooms are well maintained, with neatly kept bathrooms. Most rooms have balconies with views of the valley.

83471 Berchtesgaden-Obersalzberg. www.hotel-zum-tuerken.com. ☏ **08652/2428.** Fax 08652/4710. 15 units, 12 with shower or tub. 102€–105€ double without bathroom; 112€–158€ double with bathroom. Rates include continental breakfast. AE, DC, MC, V. Free parking. Obersalzberg bus from Berchtesgaden. **Amenities:** Bar. *In room:* Hair dryer, no phone.

InterContinental Resort Berchtesgaden ★★★ Set against snowcapped mountains, Herman Göring's former rural retreat has been turned into one of the best hotels in the Bavarian Alps. It is just over a rise from the Berghof, the house where Hitler plotted his infamous deeds. You can ski here in the winter or golf and hike, certainly swim, and also go rafting in the summer. The opening of this luxurious spa and retreat on land formerly inhabited by Nazis plotting mass murder has generated unfavorable press comment worldwide. But until the Nazis made it their private preserve, the Obersalzberg area was a vacation retreat in the 19th century. So, in a sense, the resort is returning to its origins with the opening of this hotel. The spacious bedrooms are furnished with deluxe styling, comfort, charm, and grace.

Hintereck 1, 83471 Berchtesgaden. www.ichotelsgroup.com. ℰ **08652/97550.** Fax 08652/97559999. 138 units. 204€–285€ double; from 414€ suite. AE, DC, MC, V. Parking 15€. **Amenities:** 3 restaurants; bar; babysitting; concierge; exercise room; 2 heated pools (1 indoor, 1 outdoor); room service; sauna; indoor tennis court (lit). *In room:* A/C, TV, fax, hair dryer, minibar, Wi-Fi (15€ per day).

BAD REICHENHALL ★

135km (84 miles) SE of Munich, 20km (12 miles) SE of Salzburg

The best German spas can call themselves *Staatsbad* (where the standards of maintenance and cleanliness, quality of the waters, and breadth of facilities are high enough for the government to recognize them as among the top-rated spas in the country), and Bad Reichenhall bears that title with pride. This town is the most important curative spa in the Bavarian Alps. Its brine springs, with a salt content as high as 24%, are the most powerful saline springs in Europe, and the town has been a source of salt for more than 2,400 years. The combination of the waters and the pure air has made Bad Reichenhall a recognized spa for centuries.

In 1848, King Maximilian of Bavaria stayed here, popularizing Bad Reichenhall as a fashionable resort. Today, visitors come from all over the world to take the waters, which supposedly treat asthma and other respiratory ailments. Treatment sessions take place almost exclusively in the morning at seven resort institutes, the therapy ranging from simply drinking the water to pneumatotherapy—even electronic lungs for the most serious cases.

Essentials

GETTING THERE

BY AIR   The nearest airport is Salzburg (see "Berchtesgaden," earlier in this chapter). From Salzburg, it's a 20-minute train ride into Bad Reichenhall, with trains leaving every hour throughout the day, with a change in Freilassing. There are also frequent bus and rail connections to and from Berchtesgaden, either trip taking about 45 minutes. Buses or trains leave every hour from Berchtesgaden heading for Bad Reichenhall.

BY TRAIN   Bad Reichenhall is connected to the airport at Munich (see chapter 8) by frequent train service through Rosenheim. The trip takes about 2½ hours. For information and schedules, call ℰ **01805/996633** or check out www.bahn.de.

BY BUS   Regional bus service to and from Bad Reichenhall is provided by **RVO Regionalverkehr Oberbayern** (ℰ 08821/948274; www.rvo-bus.de). From the spa, you can take a bus to various stops in the Bavarian Alps, including Berchtesgaden.

BY CAR   Access is by the A8 Autobahn, from Munich in the north and Salzburg in the south. Exit on Federal Hwy. 21 into Bad Reichenhall.

VISITOR INFORMATION

For tourist information, go to the **Kur- und Verkehrsverein im Kurgastzentrum,** Wittelsbacherstrasse 15 (© 08651/6060; www.bad-reichenhall.com). It's open Monday to Friday 8:30am to 5pm and Saturday 9am to noon.

Exploring Bad Reichenhall

The climate permits a complete spectrum of outdoor events, from excursions into the mountains for skiing or hiking to tennis tournaments. Gardeners and botanists will enjoy the spa gardens; the sheltered location of the town amid the lofty Alps permits the growth of several varieties of tropical plants, giving the gardens a lush, exotic appearance. There's also a wide choice of indoor activities, from symphony concerts to folklore presentations to gambling.

The great fire of 1834 destroyed much of the town, but many impressive churches survived. An outstanding example is **St. Zeno,** a 12th-century Gothic church with a later baroque influence. Its most remarkable feature is its painted interior, centering on the carved altarpiece of the *Coronation of the Virgin.*

Bad Reichenhaller Saltmuseum, Alte Saline Reichenhall (© 08651/7002146; www.alte-saline-bad-reichenhall.de), a short walk from the Kurgarten, is home of the industry responsible for Bad Reichenhall's growth and prosperity from Celtic times to today. Parts of the old plant still stand, but most of it was reconstructed in the mid–19th century by Ludwig I of Bavaria. The large pumps and huge marble caverns are impressive. Tours run May to October daily 10 to 11:30am and 2 to 4pm, and November to April Tuesday and Friday 2 to 4pm. Admission is 6.90€ for adults and 4.60€ for children.

Where to Eat

Restaurant die Holzstube GERMAN/ITALIAN/INTERNATIONAL   The old-fashioned tradition and service here attract many regular patrons. In a garden setting, you can watch flowers bloom and enjoy a wide selection of cuisine (with many diet-conscious selections). You may try one of the kitchen's own original recipes—for example, marinated and roasted medallions of venison *Königin Luise,* served with bacon, chanterelles, and whortleberries. A more modern dish is roasted saltwater shrimp with a lemon purée and pesto sauce. One of the most requested dishes is beef stroganoff with a bacon roulade.

In the Parkhotel Luisenbad, Ludwigstrasse 33. © **08651/6040.** Reservations recommended. Main courses 15€–25€. DC, MC, V. Daily noon–2pm and 6–9pm.

Shopping

Shops are predictably upscale, rather limited in scope, and conservative. Since 1856, **Josef Mack Co.,** Ludwigstrasse 36 (© 08651/78280), has been the region's best place for medicinal herbs, many grown in the Bavarian Alps.

Entertainment & Nightlife

Most guests looking for a night out head for the **Bayerische Spielbank Casino,** Wittelsbacherstrasse 17 (© 08651/95800; www.spielbanken-in-bayern.de), which offers roulette, American roulette, blackjack, and 50 types of slot machines. You must show your passport if you plan to do any gaming. It's open daily 3pm to 2am; admission is 2.50€. Men must wear jackets and ties. The **theater,** also located here at the Kurgastzentrum, site of the casino, is a setting for operas, operettas, plays, ballets, musicals, symphonies, folkloric evenings, and chamber-music recitals. The tourism office (see "Visitor Information," above) keeps a complete list of events and ticket prices. When weather permits, performances are staged in an open-air pavilion. Tickets are 15€ to 40€.

Where to Stay

Parkhotel Luisenbad ★★   A world unto itself, Parkhotel Luisenbad is an 1860s hotel with a new wing in a garden setting. Rooms range from medium to spacious. The more modern ones are handsome, with bold colors and tasteful furnishings, but many guests prefer the older, more traditional rooms. Bathrooms are well maintained, with deluxe toiletries.

Ludwigstrasse 33, 83435 Bad Reichenhall. www.parkhotel.de. ✆ **08651/6040.** Fax 08651/62928. 83 units. 118€–218€ double. Rates include continental breakfast. DC, MC, V. Parking 5€. **Amenities:** 3 restaurants; bar; bikes; indoor heated pool; room service; spa. *In room:* TV, hair dryer, minibar, Wi-Fi (free).

Salzburger Hof 🏆   This three-story hotel is one of the best deals in town. Its public areas are filled with old Bavarian charm. Best of all are the compact rooms, most of which contain streamlined sofas, beds with built-in headboards, and armchairs around a breakfast table; all open onto tiny balconies. Price depends on the view.

Mozartstrasse 7, 83435 Bad Reichenhall. www.salzburgerhof.de. ✆ **08651/97690.** Fax 08651/976999. 24 units. 76€–86€ double. Rates include buffet breakfast. No credit cards. Free parking. **Amenities:** Restaurant. *In room:* TV.

Villa Erika ★ 🧳   Charming, intimate, and personalized, this Italianate hotel was built in a grandiose Renaissance style in 1898 by an architect who based his inspiration on a small palace he had admired near Venice. Today, with an interior that has been much modernized by its hardworking owner, Anton Oberarzbacher, it welcomes overnight guests into a verdant garden in a location in the heart of Bad Reichenhall. Bedrooms are outfitted in a combination of contemporary and vaguely *Jugendstil* design, in monochromatic color schemes of red, blue, yellow, or green, with lots of exposed wood. Virtually everyone who stays here opts for the half-board plan. The dining room is open only to residents of the hotel.

Adolf-Schmid-Strasse 3, 83435 Bad Reichenhall. www.hotel-pension-erika.de. ✆ **08651/95360.** Fax 08651/9536200. 33 units. 60€–96€ double; 92€–120€ suite. Rates include buffet breakfast. AE, MC, V. Free parking. Closed Nov–Feb; in-house restaurant closed Sun year-round. **Amenities:** Restaurant. *In room:* TV.

CHIEMSEE ★

85km (53 miles) SE of Munich, 22km (14 miles) E of Rosenheim, 64km (40 miles) W of Salzburg

Chiemsee, known as the "Bavarian Sea," is one of the most beautiful lakes in the Bavarian Alps. Surrounded by a serene wooded landscape, the lake greets a silhouette of mountains to the south. Resorts line the shores and sailboats swarm the seas in summer, but the main attractions are its two islands, **Frauenchiemsee** and **Herrenchiemsee,** where Ludwig II built his palace, Neues Schloss.

Essentials

GETTING THERE

BY TRAIN   The station at Prien Bahnhof is on the major Munich-Rosenheim-Freilassing-Salzburg rail line, with frequent connections in all directions. Ten trains arrive daily from Munich (trip time: 1 hr.). For information, call ✆ **01805/996633** or visit www.bahn.de.

BY BUS   Regional bus service is offered by **RVO Regionalverkehr Oberbayern** (☎ **08821/948274;** www.rvo-bus.de).

BY CAR   Access by car is via the A8 Autobahn from Munich.

VISITOR INFORMATION

Contact the **Kur- und Verkehrsamt,** Alte Rathaus-Strasse 11, in Prien am Chiemsee (☎ **08051/69050**). It's open Monday to Friday 8:30am to 6pm. From May to September it is also open on Saturday during the same hours.

GETTING AROUND

BY STEAMER   From the liveliest resort, Prien, on the lake's west shore, you can reach either Frauenchiemsee or Herrenchiemsee via lake steamers. The round-trip fare to Herrenchiemsee is 6.90€, and the round-trip fare to Fraueninchiemsee is 8€. Children 13 and under travel free. The steamers, operated by **Chiemsee-Schiffahrt Ludwig Fessler** (☎ **08051/6090;** www.chiemsee-schifffahrt.de), make trips year-round covering the entire lake.

As an added treat especially for kids, the same company operates the vintage **Chiemsee Bahn** that connects Prien harbor with the train station, but only on Saturday and Sunday in May and daily during the summer season. Unfortunately, the 7 minute-ride may be over before you know it. A combination train and boat ticket to Herrenchiemsee costs 9€ and Frauenchiemsee 10€. Connections can also be made from Gstadt, Seebruck, Chieming, Übersee/Feldwies, and Bernau/Felden. Large boats leave Prien/Stock for Herrenchiemsee May to September daily, about every 20 minutes from 9am to 5pm. The last return is at 6:50pm.

BY BUS   Bus service is from the harbor to the DB station in Prien (Chiemsee-Schiffahrt) and around the lake by RVO.

Exploring the Islands

FRAUENCHIEMSEE

Frauenchiemsee (or Fraueninsel) is the smaller of the lake's two major islands. On its sandy shore is a fishing village that holds an elaborate festival at Corpus Christi (usually late May). Fishing boats are covered with flowers and streamers, fishers are outfitted in Bavarian garb, and young women of the village dress as brides. As the boats circle the island, they stop at each corner for the singing of the Gospels. The island is also the home of a Benedictine convent, Frauenchiemsee Abbey, founded in 782, which makes it the oldest in Germany. The convent is known for a liqueur called Kloster Likör—it's supposed to be an "agreeable stomach elixir."

You can walk around the island in about 30 minutes, enjoying panoramic views of the lake. **Torhalle** (☎ **08054/7256**), a summer-only art gallery, is in the ancient hall that used to be the gatehouse of the Frauenwörth convent. Admission is 2.50€ for adults, 1.50€ for students, and free for children 11 and under. The hall is open only May to October daily 11am to 6pm.

HERRENCHIEMSEE ★★

Herrenchiemsee (or Herreninsel) is home to the fantastic **Neues Schloss** (also known as Königschloss), Herrenchiemsee 3 (☎ **08051/68870;** www.herren-chiemsee.de), begun by Ludwig II in 1878 (see "The Fairy-Tale King," in chapter 7). Never completed, the castle was to have been a replica of Versailles, which Ludwig admired. When work stopped with Ludwig's death in 1886, only the center of the palace had been completed.

Nonetheless, the palace and its formal gardens, surrounded by woodlands of beech and fir, remain one of the grandest and most fascinating of Ludwig's constructions.

The palace **entrance** is lit by a huge skylight over the sumptuously decorated staircase. Frescoes depicting the four states of existence alternate with Greek and Roman statues in niches on the staircase and in the gallery above. The vestibule is adorned with a pair of enameled peacocks, Louis XIV's favorite bird.

The **Great Hall of Mirrors ★★** is unquestionably the most splendid room, and the most authentic replica of Versailles. The 17 door panels contain enormous mirrors reflecting 33 crystal chandeliers and 44 gilded candelabras. The vaulted ceiling is covered with 25 paintings depicting the life of Louis XIV.

Practically every inch of the **state bedroom ★** has been gilded. On the dais, instead of a throne, is a richly decorated bed, its purple-velvet draperies weighing more than 135 kilograms (300 lb.). Separating the dais from the rest of the room is a carved wooden balustrade covered with gold leaf. On the ceiling, a huge fresco depicts the descent of Apollo, surrounded by the other gods of Olympus. The sun god's features bear a strong resemblance to those of Louis XIV.

The **dining room** is a popular attraction for visitors because of the so-called "little table that sets itself." A mechanism in the floor permitted the table to go down to the room below to be cleared and relaid between courses. Over the table hangs an exquisite chandelier of Meissen porcelain, the largest in the world and the single-most-valuable item in the palace.

You can visit Herrenchiemsee year-round. From April to September, tours run daily 9am to 6pm. Off season, they run daily 9:40am to 4pm. Admission (in addition to the round-trip boat fare) is 8€ for adults, 7€ for students, and free for children 17 and under.

Where to Eat

Restaurant Mühlberger ★★★ CONTINENTAL   A 2-minute drive (or 5-min. walk) from the center of Prien, this is a relatively modern building whose exposed pine and coziness make it look older. The hospitable staff present menu items that reflect the diversity of local culinary traditions, and although lots of imagination is shown in the kitchens, some of the recipes evoke strong memories of childhood in many patrons. Examples including *Saibling* (a local freshwater whitefish) served in herb sauce with new potatoes, filet of veal with exotic wild mushrooms and a sauce made from a local white wine, and such saltwater fish dishes as tuna steak with a curried tomato sauce or turbot with béarnaise sauce. You may begin a meal here with a terrine of guinea fowl with pearl onions and end it with a house-made strudel that's layered with wild cherries, vanilla ice cream, and chocolate sauce.

Bernauerstrasse 40. ℭ **08051/966888.** www.muehlberger-restaurant.de. Reservations recommended. Main courses 28€–53€; fixed-price lunch 35€, dinner 89€. MC, V. Thurs–Mon 11:30am–2pm and 6–10pm. Closed 3 weeks in June.

Where to Stay

Bayerischer Hof   Rustic decor such as the painted ceiling in the dining room creates the illusion that this relatively severe, modern hotel is older than it is. The rest of the hotel is more streamlined—modern, efficient, and appealing—though the Yachthotel (below) has more style and flair. Nonetheless, rooms are comfortable and bathrooms well equipped.

Bernauerstrasse 3, 83209 Prien am Chiemsee. www.bayerischerhof-prien.de. ℭ **08051/6030.** Fax 08051/62917. 46 units. 80€–120€ double. Rates include buffet breakfast. AE, MC, V. Parking 7€. Restaurant closed

Nov; restaurant and hotel closed last 2 weeks of Jan. **Amenities:** Restaurant; bar; babysitting; bikes. *In room:* TV, minibar, Wi-Fi (free).

Inselhotel zur Linde 🏄 Set on the highest hillock on the Fraueninsel, this is a solid, richly textured, and historic inn with a tradition of welcoming overnight guests that dates from 1396. Its premises are scattered among a pair of steep-roofed, old-fashioned Teutonic-looking buildings surrounded with a lush flowering garden and flanked by the island's largest beer garden. Bedrooms feature high ceilings and are old-fashioned and conservatively outfitted with lace curtains, various tones of beige and champagne, and traditional, Mittel-European style. Don't expect much in the way of amenities here. You'll be comfortable, but other than a telephone, it's fairly gadgetless.

Haus 1, 83256 Fraueninsel im Chiemsee. www.inselhotel-zurlinde.de. ℂ**08054/90366.** Fax 08054/7299. 14 units. 117€–126€ double. Rates include continental breakfast. MC, V. Closed mid-Jan to mid-Mar. **Amenities:** Restaurant.

Yachthotel Chiemsee ★ With docks of sailboats at its shore, you can expect the boating crowd flocks to this hotel. Its attractively furnished rooms all feature balconies or terraces, some opening onto the water. Lakeside rooms are equipped with two double beds and a pullout sofa for groups of four or more. Most rooms are fairly spacious and all of them are well furnished.

Harrasser Strasse 49, 83209 Prien am Chiemsee. www.yachthotel.de. ℂ**08051/6960.** Fax 08051/5171. 97 units. 150€–190€ double; 190€–280€ suite. Rates include buffet breakfast. AE, DC, MC, V. Free parking. **Amenities:** Restaurant; bar; bikes; children's center; exercise room; Jacuzzi; indoor heated pool; room service; sauna. *In room:* TV, hair dryer, Wi-Fi (free).

MITTENWALD ★

106km (66 miles) S of Munich, 18km (11 miles) SE of Garmisch-Partenkirchen, 37km (23 miles) NW of Innsbruck

The idyllic mountain resort of Mittenwald is wedged in a pass of the Karwendel Range just before the Austrian border. The Alpine architecture is in effect here, from frescoed facades to wooden balconies and overhanging eaves. On the square stands a monument to Matthias Klotz, who introduced violin making to Mittenwald in 1684, and sparked the industry of this highly specialized craft that continues today.

Essentials
GETTING THERE
BY TRAIN Hourly train service runs on the express rail line between Munich and Innsbruck, Austria. From Munich, trip time is 1½ hours. Call ℂ **01805/996633** or visit www.bahn.de for information.

BY BUS Regional bus service from Garmisch-Partenkirchen and nearby towns is frequently provided by **RVO Regionalverkehr Oberbayern** at Garmisch (ℂ **08821/948274** for schedules and information).

BY CAR Access by car is via the A95 Autobahn from Munich.

VISITOR INFORMATION
Contact the **Tourist-Information Mittenwald,** Dammkarstrasse 3 (ℂ **08823/33981;** www.mittenwald.de). It's open Monday to Friday 8:30am to noon and 1 to 5pm, and Saturday 9am to noon.

Exploring Mittenwald

Mittenwald's chief attraction is the town itself, its most notable feature being the **painted houses ★★** that line the main street. The village can be explored in about an hour and a half. In winter it's a picture postcard of snow-laden charm, and in summer a mass of flowering facades with pots of geraniums, clinging to houses with their richly decorated gables.

The town's museum, which contains a workshop, has exhibits that trace the history of violins and other stringed instruments from their invention through various stages of their evolution. The **Geigenbau- und Heimatmuseum,** Ballenhausgasse 3 (✆ **08823/2511;** www.geigenbaumuseum-mittenwald.de), is open Tuesday to Sunday 10am to 5pm in the high season, and 11am to 4pm in the low season. Admission is 4.50€ for adults, 3.50€ students, and 2€ for children. The museum is closed November 5 to December 10.

In the surrounding countryside, the scenery of the Wetterstein and Karwendel ranges constantly changes. Some 130km (80 miles) of hiking paths wind up and down the mountains around the village. You can hike through the hills on your own, take part in mountain-climbing expeditions, or take horse-and-carriage trips and motorcoach tours to nearby villages. The **Karwendelbahn Mittenwald** (✆ 08823/8480;** www.karwendelbahn.de) is a cable car operating in winter and summer, costing 22€ round-trip and running daily 9am to 4:30pm, and until 7:30pm in summer. It climbs to a height of 2,244m (7,360 ft.), where numerous ski trails become hiking trails in summer. In winter, the 7km-long (4-mile) Dammkar downhill slope offers some of the best skiing and snowboarding around.

In the evening, various inns offer typical Bavarian entertainment, such as folk dancing and singing, zither playing, and yodeling. Concerts during the summer are held in the music pavilion.

Where to Eat

Restaurant Arnspitze ★ BAVARIAN   This traditionally decorated restaurant, in a modern chalet hotel on the outskirts of town, is the best in Mittenwald. The cuisine is solid, satisfying, and wholesome. Try sole with homemade noodles or veal steak in creamy smooth sauce. Two other specialties are a delicate sautéed veal liver or lamb baked under on olive crust with fresh vegetables. You can finish off with one of the freshly made desserts.

Innsbrucker Strasse 68. ✆ **08823/2425.** www.arnspitze-mittenwald.de. Main courses 16€–23€. MC, V. Thurs–Mon noon–2:30pm and 6–9pm. Closed 2 weeks in Apr and Nov–Dec 15.

Shopping

Professional musicians have sought out the classical stringed instruments crafted here for centuries. Prices may be steep, but a visit to **Geigenbau Leonhardt,** Mühlenweg 53A (✆ **08823/8010;** www.violin-leonhardt.de), is educational—even if you're just browsing the array of instruments.

Where to Stay

Die Alpenrose ★ 🎺   This particularly inviting hotel in the heart of the village features an ornately decorated facade with bursting window boxes. Its original 14th-century structure was once part of a monastery, which has been supplemented with its annex, the Bichlerhof. Try to stay in the main older building, where rooms have a great deal of charm, with finely woven fabrics, old-fashioned farmhouse cupboards, and dark-wood paneling. Bathrooms in both buildings are a bit cramped. The tavern room overlooking the street has many fine features, including handmade chairs, flagstone floors, and a square-tile stove in the center.

Obermarkt 1, 82481 Mittenwald. www.hotel-alpenrose-mittenwald.de. ✆**08823/92700.** Fax 08823/ 3720. 19 units. 35€–44€ per person double. Rates include buffet breakfast. AE, DC, MC, V. Free parking. **Amenities:** Restaurant; bar; room service; Wi-Fi (free; in lobby). *In room:* TV, hair dryer, minibar.

Gästehaus Sonnenbichl 🍴
This modest chalet on the edge of the village offers good value and comfort in a green setting. Built in 1977, it resembles a private country home with a view of the village set against a backdrop of the Alps. The small but exceedingly well-kept rooms are freshly decorated in vivid natural colors, and all contain neatly kept bathrooms. Reserve well in advance.

Klausnerweg 32, 82481 Mittenwald. www.sonnenbichl-tourismus.de. ✆**08823/92230.** Fax 08823/5814. 18 units. 32€–49€ per person double; 37€–51€ per person apt. Rates include buffet breakfast. MC, V. **Amenities:** Bikes; room service; sauna. *In room:* TV, hair dryer, minibar, Wi-Fi (free).

Hotel Post ★★
Mittenwald's finest lodging, the Post is the most seasoned and established chalet hotel in the village, dating from 1632, when stagecoaches carrying mail and passengers across the Bavarian Alps stopped here to refuel. A delightful lunch and dinner are served on the sun terrace, with a view of the Alps. Beds are among the most comfortable in town, with duvets and beautiful linen. All the midsize bathrooms are efficiently organized.

Obermarkt 9, 82481 Mittenwald. www.posthotel-mittenwald.de. ✆ **08823/9382333.** Fax 08823/ 9382999. 73 units. 50€–70€ per person double; 70€–95€ per person suite. Rates include buffet breakfast. MC, V. Parking 6€. **Amenities:** Restaurant; bar; indoor heated pool; room service; sauna. *In room:* TV, hair dryer, minibar, Wi-Fi (free).

GARMISCH-PARTENKIRCHEN ★★★

97km (60 miles) SW of Munich, 117km (73 miles) SE of Augsburg, 60km (37 miles) NW of Innsbruck

The villages of Garmisch and Partenkirchen make up Germany's top Alpine resort. In spite of their urban flair, the towns maintain the charm of an ancient village, especially Partenkirchen. Even today, you occasionally see country folk in traditional dress, and you may be held up in traffic while the cattle are led from their mountain-grazing grounds down through the streets of town.

Essentials

GETTING THERE

BY TRAIN The **Garmisch-Partenkirchen Bahnhof** lies on the major Munich-Weilheim-Garmisch-Mittenwald-Innsbruck rail line, with frequent connections in all directions. Twenty trains per day arrive from Munich (trip time: 1 hr., 25 min.). For information and schedules, call ✆ **01805/996633** or visit www.bahn.de. Mountain rail service to several plateaus and the Zugspitze is offered by the **Bayerische Zugspitzbahn** at Garmisch (✆ **08821/7970;** www.zugspitze.de).

BY BUS Both long-distance and regional buses through the Bavarian Alps are provided by **RVO Regionalverkehr Oberbayern,** Finkenstrasse 3, in Garmisch-Partenkirchen (✆ **08821/948274;** www.rvo-bus.de).

hiking IN THE BAVARIAN ALPS

Hiking is Bavaria's favorite pastime. Locals believe firmly in the emotional and spiritual benefits of walking and hill climbing and tend to hit the trails the moment the snows melt.

The tourist office in Garmisch-Partenkirchen will point you to hiking trails of varying degrees of difficulty, all clearly marked with signs. The office also offers a brochure outlining the half-dozen best trails. You don't have to be an Olympic athlete to enjoy them. Most hikes will take an energetic person 4 to 5 hours, but some of them are shorter and easy enough for children.

An easily accessible destination is the 1,240m (4,070-ft.) **Eckbauer** peak, which lies on the southern fringe of Partenkirchen. The easy trails on its lower slopes are recommended for first-time Alpine hikers. You can even take a chairlift to the top, where, in real Bavarian style, the *Berggasthof* (a guesthouse or cafe, usually in a high-altitude rural location) will serve you a glass of buttermilk. In less than an hour, you can

descend on relatively easy trails through a forest. The cable car stretching from Garmisch to the top of the Eckbauer departs year-round from the Eckbauer-bahn (℡ **08821/3469;** www.eckbauer bahn.de), adjacent to the ski stadium in Garmisch. A round-trip fare costs 12€ for adults, 7€ for children ages 6 to 16, and free for children 5 and under.

More demanding are the slopes of the rugged **Alpspitz** ★ region, which begins about 1.6km (1 mile) southwest of Garmisch. The area is interlaced with wildflowers, unusual geology, meadows, and a network of cable cars and hiking trails spread over a terrain ranging in altitude between 1,200m (4,000 ft.) and 1,800m (6,000 ft.). The highest trails are around the summit of the Alpspitz at 2,600m (8,500 ft.).

One of the most appealing ways to gain a high-altitude panorama over this region is to take a trip up the Alpspitz. Begin your journey at the Kreuzeckbahn/Alpspitzbahn cable car terminus, a mile south of Garmisch. The cable car will carry you uphill

BY CAR   Access is via the A95 Autobahn from Munich; exit at Eschenlohe.

VISITOR INFORMATION

Contact the **Verkehrsamt,** Richard-Strauss-Platz 2 (℡ **08821/180700;** www.garmisch-partenkirchen.de). It's open Monday to Saturday 8am to 6pm, and Sunday and holidays 10am to noon. The tourist office arranges free bookings in local guest houses.

GETTING AROUND

An unnumbered municipal bus services the town, depositing passengers at Marien-platz or the Bahnhof, from which you can walk to all centrally located hotels. This free bus runs daily every 15 minutes from 6am to 8pm.

Exploring the Area

Garmisch-Partenkirchen is a center for winter sports, summer hiking, and mountain climbing. The symbol of the city's growth and modernity is the **Olympic Ice Stadium,** built for the 1936 Winter Olympics and capable of holding nearly 12,000 people. On the slopes at the edge of town is the **Ski Stadium,** with two ski jumps and a slalom course. In 1936, more than 100,000 people watched the events in this stadium. Today it's still an integral part of winter life in Garmisch—the World Cup Ski Jump is held here every New Year's Day.

along the Kreuzeckbahn for a 4-minute ride across a jagged landscape to the lowest station of the Hochalm cable car. Here the Hochalmbahn will carry you uphill for another 4 minutes to the top of the Osterfelderkopf, 1,950m (6,400 ft.) above sea level. Cable cars for both stages of this trip depart at 30-minute intervals daily 8:15am to 5:15pm. After your visit to the Osterfelderkopf summit, you can return to Garmisch via a different route, a direct downhill descent via the Alpspitzbahn, a 10-minute ride above jagged gorges, soaring cliffs, and grassy meadows.

Round-trip passage along this three-tiered Alpine itinerary costs 24€ for adults and 18€ for children. These fares and times of departure can fluctuate. For the latest details, either call the information service for the above-mentioned cable cars (© **08821/7970**) or check with the Garmisch **Verkehrsamt (tourist office)** on Richard-Strauss-Platz 2 (© **08821/180700**).

From Garmisch-Partenkirchen, many other peaks of the Wetterstein range are accessible as well, via the 10 funiculars ascending from the borders of the town. From the top of the 1,780m (5,840-ft.) **Wank** to the east, you get the best view of the plateau on which the villages of Garmisch and Partenkirchen sit. This summit is also a favorite with the patrons of Garmisch's spa facilities because the plentiful sunshine makes it ideal for the *Liegekur* (deck-chair cure).

Another hearty hike is through the **Partnachklamm ★★**, a gorge with a roaring stream at the bottom and sheer cliff walls rising on either side of the hiking trail. Take the Graseck Seilbahn from its departure point at the bottom of the gorge, less than 1km (½ mile) south of Garmisch's ski stadium, and get off at the first station, which is adjacent to a cozy hotel, the **Forsthaus Graseck** (© **08821/ 943240;** www.forsthaus-graseck.de). The 3-minute cable car ride costs 6€ per person each way (free for hotel guests) and operates from 7am to 10pm, midnight on weekends. You may want to get a meal or drink at the hotel first.

The town and its environs offer some of the most panoramic views and colorful buildings in Bavaria. The pilgrimage **Chapel of St. Anton,** on a pinewood path at the edge of Partenkirchen, is all pink and silver, inside and out. Its graceful lines are characteristic of the 18th century, when it was built. In the park surrounding the chapel, the **Philosopher's Walk ★** is a delightful spot to wander, just to enjoy the views of the mountains around the low-lying town.

This area has always attracted German romantics, including "Mad" King Ludwig (see the box "The Fairy-Tale King," on p. 268). Perhaps with Wagner's music ringing in his ears, the king ordered the construction of a hunting lodge here in the style of a Swiss chalet but commanded that the interior look like something out of *The Arabian Nights*. The lodge, **Jagdschloss Schachen,** is still here. It can be reached only after an arduous climb. The tourist office will supply details. Mid-June to mid-September, tours to the lodge usually leave from the Olympic Ski Stadium at 11am and 2pm, but check before you go.

TO THE TOP OF THE ZUGSPITZE ★★★

From Garmisch-Partenkirchen, you can see the tallest mountain in Germany, the **Zugspitze,** 2,960m (9,700 ft.) above sea level. Ski slopes begin at a height of 2,650m (8,700 ft.). For a panoramic view of both the Bavarian and the Tyrolean (Austrian)

Alps, go all the way to the summit. There are two ways to reach the Zugspitze from the center of Garmisch. The first begins with a trip on the cog railway, the Zugspitz-bahn, which departs from the back of Garmisch's main railway station daily every hour from 8:15am to 2:15pm. The train travels uphill, past lichen-covered boulders and coursing streams, to a high-altitude plateau, the Zugspitzplatt, where views sweep out over all Bavaria. At the Zugspitzplatt, you'll transfer onto a cable car, the Gletscher Seilbahn, for a 4-minute ride uphill to the top of the Zugspitze. There, far-reaching panoramas, a cafe and restaurant, a gift shop, and many Alpine trails await. Total travel time for this itinerary is about 55 minutes, but you may want to linger at the first stop, the Zugspitzplatt, before continuing up.

The other way to get to the summit is to take the Zugspitzbahn for a briefer trip, disembarking 14km (9 miles) southwest of Garmisch at the lower station of the Eib-see Seilbahn (Eibsee Cable Car), next to a clear Alpine lake. The cable car will carry you from there directly to the summit of the Zugspitze, for a total transit time of about 40 minutes. The Eibsee Seilbahn makes its run at least every half-hour 8:30am to 4:30pm (July–Aug to 5:30pm).

Round-trip tickets allow you to ascend one way and descend the other, in order to enjoy the widest range of spectacular views. May to October, round-trip fares are 47€ for adults, 33€ for ages 16 to 18, and 26€ for children 6 to 15. November to April, round-trip fares are reduced to 37€ for adults, 27€ for ages 16 to 18, and 21€ for ages 6 to 15. For more information, contact the **Bayerische Zugspitzbahn,** Olympias-trasse 27, Garmisch-Partenkirchen (✆ **08821/7970;** www.zugspitze.de).

Where to Eat

MODERATE

Alpenhof ★ 🍴 INTERNATIONAL   Alpenhof is widely regarded as one of the finest restaurants in Garmisch, as are the hotel dining rooms at the Posthotel Parten-kirchen and Reindl's Partenkirchner Hof. The cuisine here is grounded in tradition. Robert Leipold offers a variety of Bavarian specialties, as well as trout meunière or pikeperch with a savory peppercorn sauce. Locals love the roast duck with red cab-bage and potato dumplings. For dessert, try a soufflé with exotic fruits. In summer, the outside tables are lovely, and in winter you can retreat to the cozy interior, which is flooded with sunlight from a greenhouse.

Am Kurpark 10. ✆ **08821/59055.** www.alpenhof-garmisch.de. Reservations recommended. Main courses 15€–24€. MC, V. Daily 11am–2pm and 6–10pm.

Husar ★ BAVARIAN   Behind a historical facade, this elegant restaurant serves one of the finest cuisines in the area. The welcome is warm; the service is efficient; and the ingredients, when possible, are market fresh. If you wish, a suitable wine will be sug-gested for you to sip while you peruse the menu. Specialties are carefully crafted, includ-ing a tenderloin of beef flavored with cognac and served with a tangy pepper sauce along with potatoes gratin and a freshly made salad. One of the more desirable dishes is a platter containing a variety of fish, many from Bavarian rivers and lakes. This dish is bound together with a Riesling sauce and served with a medley of different vegetables.

Fürstenstrasse 25. ✆ **08821/9677922.** www.restauranthusar.de. Reservations required. Main courses 20€–50€. MC, V. Tues–Sun 6–10:30pm; Sun only noon–2pm.

Joseph-Naus-Stub'n ★ GERMAN/CONTINENTAL   One of the most charm-ing dining spots in town lies on the lobby level of a prominent and very visible hotel, the Zugspitze, which, with its traditional Alpine design, evokes a very large mountain chalet on steroids. Within a country-baroque decor that manages to be elegant and woodsy, but with a definite sense of almost ladylike grace, you can enjoy some of the most upscale and sophisticated cuisine in town. Menus change with the season, but the best examples include selections from an oft-changing array of oysters, crabs, North Sea sole and flounder, trout, and zander, each prepared in a different way every night or according to your specifications. During the autumn and winter, the focus is on game dishes, including filet of venison.

In the Hotel Zugspitze, Klammstrasse 19. © **08821/9010.** Reservations recommended Fri–Sat nights. Main courses 12€–24€. AE, DC, MC, V. Daily 5:30–10pm; Sun noon–2pm.

Reindl's Restaurant ★★ INTERCONTINENTAL   One of the best places to eat in Partenkirchen is Reindl's, a first-class restaurant in every sense of the word. The seasonal menu offers modern cuisine as well as regional Bavarian dishes. Two notable appetizers are the scampi salad *Walterspiel* with fresh peaches, lemon, and tarragon, and the homemade goose-liver pâté with Riesling jelly. For a main dish, rack of lamb flavored with fresh herbs; crispy suckling pig with potato dumplings, or poultry breast in curry sauce. For dessert, try either the Grand Marnier sabayon with strawberry and vanilla ice cream or something more spectacular: a *Salzburger Nockerl* (a dessert soufflé made with egg white, sugar, butter, and flour) for two.

In the Partenkirchner Hof, Bahnhofstrasse 15. © **08821/943870.** Reservations required. Main courses 12€–22€. DC, MC, V. Daily noon–2:30pm and 6:30–11pm. Closed Nov 10–Dec 15.

INEXPENSIVE

Café Riessersee BAVARIAN/INTERNATIONAL   This cafe/restaurant on the shores of a small emerald-green lake is the ideal place to stop after you explore the Zugspitze. It's a great place for a leisurely lunch or afternoon coffee with cakes, ice cream, and chocolates, but it's worth visiting for the Bavarian dinner dishes as well. Dinner main courses center on fresh fish served from a big aquarium-style holding tank. Seasonal dishes are based on, for example, wild game, fresh fruits and wild berries, and forest mushrooms. During *Spargel* (asparagus) season from early April to June 24th, there is a menu devoted entirely to asparagus. The priciest main course (50€) features the most elaborate mixed grill in the region—succulent cuts of beef, pork, veal, and chicken (don't worry, this price is not indicative of the rest of the menu!).

Riess 6 (3km/2 miles from the center of town). © **08821/95440.** www.riessersee.de. Main courses 9€–21€. AE, MC, V. Daily 11:30am–9pm.

Shopping

Your best bets are in the traffic-reduced Ludwigstrasse in Partenkirchen and in the almost traffic-free zone from Richard-Strauss-Platz to Marienplatz in Garmisch. A vast array of stores sells boots, boutique items, clothing, jewelry, art, antiques, and more. If you like traditional Bavarian dress but don't want to spend a lot of money, head for **Loisachtaler,** Burgstrasse 20 (© **08821/52390**). Here, Petra Ostler has assembled the area's finest collection of secondhand clothing. Take your pick: a Jägermeister loden coat, an Alpine hat with pheasant feathers, or a castoff dirndl. They all look like new.

Entertainment & Nightlife

You can test your luck at the town's casino, **Spielbank Garmisch-Partenkirchen,** Am Kurpark 10 (© **08821/95990;** www.spielbanken-in-bayern.de). Admission costs 2.50€ per person, and you must be 18 or over (you must present a passport).

The casino is open daily 3pm to 2am. Beginning at 8pm, blackjack tables are open. Friday and Saturday, games of seven-card stud poker are arranged (book in advance). Men must wear a jacket and tie.

If you'd like to meet locals at night, head for one of the taverns. All major hotels have bars, but for a change of pace, go to the **Irish Pub,** Rathausplatz 8 (© **08821/ 3938;** www.theirishpub.de), and order a Guinness. This pub, in the center of town, attracts one of the most convivial crowds in the area.

Many hotels have dance floors that keep the music pumping into the wee hours, but for dancing of a different sort, check out the summer program of **Bavarian folk music and dancing,** held every Saturday night mid-May to September in the Bayernhalle, Brauhausstrasse 19. During the same season Saturday to Thursday, **classical concerts** are held at the Garmisch park bandstand. On Friday, these live shows move to the Partenkirchen bandstand. Check with the local tourist office (see "Visitor Information," earlier in this section) for details about these programs as well as a 5-day **Richard Strauss Festival** held in June.

Where to Stay

To make extra money in a bad economy, more than 40 *Gästehäuser* (guesthouses) have opened, offering a room with breakfast for 30€ to 50€per person, although the price could go much higher, depending on the comfort of the establishment. The tourist office will help you arrange accommodations in these private rooms.

EXPENSIVE

Grand Hotel Sonnenbichl ★★   The most upscale hotel in the area is on the hillside overlooking Garmisch-Partenkirchen, 1.5km (1 mile) from the city center and 3km (2 miles) from the Bahnhof. It has excellent views of the Wetterstein mountain range and the Zugspitze (from front rooms only; rear rooms open onto a forested hillside). Bedrooms are well kept and range from midsize to spacious. The decor is generally Art Nouveau.

Burgstrasse 97, 82467 Garmisch-Partenkirchen. www.sonnenbichl.de. © **08821/7020.** Fax 08821/702131. 93 units. 178€–198€ double; 300€–470€ suite. Rates include buffet breakfast. AE, DC, MC, V. Free parking. Take Rte. 23 toward Oberammergau. **Amenities:** 2 restaurants; bar; bikes; exercise room; Jacuzzi; indoor heated pool; room service; sauna; Wi-Fi (15€ per day; in lobby). *In room:* TV, hair dryer.

Staudacherhof ★★   The Staudacher family runs one of the most tranquil hotels at the resort, offering old-fashioned Bavarian hospitality at its best. In winter you may look out your window to see a horse-drawn sleigh arriving with fur-clad passengers. The bedrooms are among the coziest at Garmisch, each beautifully maintained and attractively and comfortably furnished. You'll feel at home when you see an armchair waiting, along with a footstool, bedroom slippers, and a pot of tea resting beside a reading lamp.

Höllentalstrasse 48, 82467 Garmisch-Partenkirchen. www.staudacherhof.de. © **08821/9290.** Fax 08821/929333. 39 units. 180€–210€ double; 280€ junior suite; 310€ suite. Rates are on full-pension basis. MC, V. Parking 9€. **Amenities:** Restaurant; bar; children's center; health club and spa; 2 pools (1 indoor); room service; Wi-Fi (free; in lobby). *In room:* TV, hair dryer.

MODERATE

Atlas Grand Hotel ★   The Atlas Grand Hotel, which was founded in 1492, is one of the town's most prestigious hotels. Now bearing a four-star rating, the Grand features old-world living in stylish, U-shaped rooms containing Bavarian baroque carved furnishings and antiques. The sunny balconies overlook a garden and offer a view of the Alps. Rooms are generally medium size, though some are quite spacious, and each comes with a midsize bathroom.

Ludwigstrasse 49, 82467 Garmisch-Partenkirchen. www.atlas-grandhotel.com. © **08821/93630.** Fax 08821/93632222. 59 units. 120€–160€ double; 300€–420€ suite. Rates include buffet breakfast. MC, V. Free parking. **Amenities:** Restaurant; bar; room service; Wi-Fi (free; in lobby). *In room:* TV, hair dryer, minibar.

Atlas Posthotel ★   The history and identity of Garmisch are bound up in events that took place at this hotel in the heart of town. What started out as a tavern in 1512 turned into a shelter for refugees from besieged Munich during the Thirty Years' War. In 1891, it was bought by the Berlin beer baron who invented *Berliner Weisse,* which quickly became one of the most popular brands in Garmisch. Rooms range from spacious to rather small and cozy, successfully mingling Bavarian antique charm with modern comforts. Bathrooms are beautifully kept, containing tub/shower combos.

Marienplatz 12, 82467 Garmisch-Partenkirchen. www.atlas-posthotel.com. ©**08821/7090.** Fax 08821/ 709205. 44 units. 90€–130€ double. Rates include buffet breakfast. AE, MC, V. Parking 10€. **Amenities:** 2 restaurants; bar; room service; sauna. *In room:* TV, hair dryer, minibar, Wi-Fi (free).

Waxenstein ★ 🛏   One of the most delightful places to recharge your batteries is not in Garmisch itself, but in Grainau, lying in a sunny spot, 2km (1¼ miles) from the center. The spacious and elegantly furnished bedrooms and suites open onto panoramic vistas of the Zugspitze. Even if you're not an overnight guest, but touring the area, consider a visit to their Toedt's Restaurant, which serves market-fresh ingredients with excellent regional cooking.

Höhenrainweg 3, 82491 Grainau. www.waxenstein.de. © **08821/9840.** Fax 08821/8401. 41 units. 140€–165€ double; 205€ suite. Rates include continental breakfast. AE, DC, MC, V. Free parking. **Amenities:** Restaurant; bar; bikes; exercise room; indoor heated pool; room service; sauna. *In room:* TV, hair dryer, minibar, Wi-Fi (free).

INEXPENSIVE

Gasthof Fraundorfer 🛏   The family owned Gasthof Fraundorfer lies just a 5-minute walk from the old church on Partenkirchen's main street near shops and restaurants. One of the original unchanged buildings in town, you can't miss the hotel's fancy facade of lively murals depicting a family feast. The traditional Alpine manner prevails in the interior rooms. Two of them have four-poster beds, but all of them have firm mattresses. Some larger units are virtual apartments, suitable for up to five guests. The rear Gästehaus Barbara offers 20 additional beds, including a *Himmelbett* (heaven bed) loaded with soft, feather-stuffed pillows and comforters.

Ludwigstrasse 24, 82467 Garmisch-Partenkirchen. www.gasthof-fraundorfer.de. ©**08821/9270.** Fax 08821/92799. 31 units. 86€–98€ double; 115€–192€ family room for 2–5 people. Rates include buffet breakfast. MC, V. Free parking. **Amenities:** Restaurant; room service; sauna. *In room:* TV, hair dryer, kitchenette (in some), Wi-Fi (free; in some).

Haus Lilly   Many visitors appreciate this small, spotlessly clean guesthouse. It wins points for its large breakfasts and the personality of its smiling owner, Maria Lechner, whose English is limited but whose hospitality transcends language. Each small room comes with a comfortable bed and free access to a kitchen.

Zugspitzstrasse 20–22, 82467 Garmisch-Partenkirchen. www.fewo-lilly.de. ©**08821/52600.** 8 units. 55€–70€ double, triple, or quad. Rates include buffet breakfast. No credit cards. Free parking. 15-min. walk from the Bahnhof. *In room:* TV, hair dryer.

Hotel Hilleprandt 🏂   This cozy, tranquil chalet is a great budget choice, lying 450m (1,500 ft.) from the train station. Its wooden balconies, attractive garden, and backdrop of forest-covered mountains give the impression of an old-time Alpine building. However, a complete renovation has brought streamlined modern comfort. Rooms are small but comfortable, each with a private balcony.

Riffelstrasse 17, 82467 Garmisch-Partenkirchen. www.hotel-hilleprandt.de. ☏ **08821/943040.** Fax 08821/74548. 13 units. 36€–64€ per person double; from 54€ per person suite. Rates include buffet breakfast. MC, V. Free parking. Near Zugspitze Bahnhof and Olympic Ice Stadium. **Amenities:** Restaurant; exercise room; Jacuzzi; room service; sauna; Wi-Fi (free; in lobby). *In room:* TV, hair dryer.

Reindl's Partenkirchner Hof ★   Reindl's opened in 1911 and has continuously attracted a devoted following. Owners Bruni and Karl Reindl maintain a high level of luxury and hospitality in this Bavarian retreat. The annexes, the Wetterstein and the House Alpspitz, have balconies, and the main four-story building has wraparound verandas, giving each room an unobstructed view of the mountains and town. All the rooms are among the most attractive in town, but the best are suites with panoramic views of mountains or the garden. Fine carpeting and rustic pine furniture add to the allure.

Bahnhofstrasse 15, 82467 Garmisch-Partenkirchen. www.reindls.de. ☏ **08821/943870.** Fax 08821/94387250. 63 units. 115€–204€ per person double; from 230€ suite. Rates include continental breakfast. DC, MC, V. Parking 10€. Closed Nov 10–Dec 15. **Amenities:** 2 restaurants; bar; exercise room; indoor heated pool; room service; sauna. *In room:* TV, CD player (in some), hair dryer, minibar, Wi-Fi (free).

9 OBERAMMERGAU ★

95km (59 miles) SW of Munich, 20km (12 miles) N of Garmisch-Partenkirchen

Oberammergau is best known for its famous Passion Play, which is staged only every 10 years; the next one will take place in 2020. Surely the world's longest-running show, it began in 1634 when the town's citizens took a vow to give dramatic thanks after they were spared from the devastating plague of 1633.

However, a visit to Oberammergau is ideal at any time, even without the performance. The town is in a wide valley surrounded by forests, green meadows, and mountains. It offers first-class hotels and cozy inns, and has long been known for the skill of its woodcarvers. Numerous hiking trails lead through the nearby mountains to hikers' inns. You can also simply go up to the mountaintops on the Laber cable railway or the Kolben chairlift.

Oberammergau is often used as a base for visiting Schloss Linderhof, the Benedictine monastery at Ettal, or the fairy-tale Neuschwanstein and Hohenschwangau castles (see chapter 7).

Essentials

GETTING THERE

BY TRAIN   The **Oberammergau Bahnhof** is on the Murnau-Bad Kohlgrum-Oberammergau rail line, with frequent connections in all directions. Through Murnau, all major German cities can be reached. Daily trains arrive from Munich in 2 hours and from Frankfurt in 5½ hours. For rail information and schedules, call ☏ **01805/996633** or visit www.bahn.de.

BY BUS   Regional bus service to nearby towns is offered by **RVO Regionalverkehr Oberbayern** in Garmisch-Partenkirchen (☏ **08821/948274;** www.rvo-bus.de). An unnumbered bus goes back and forth between Oberammergau and Garmisch-Partenkirchen.

BY CAR   Many visitors drive here; the trip takes 1½ hours from Munich and 5½ hours from Frankfurt. Take the A95 Munich-Garmisch-Partenkirchen Autobahn and exit at Eschenlohe.

VISITOR INFORMATION

Contact the **Oberammergau Tourist Information Office,** Eugen-Papst-Strasse 9A (*© **08822/922740;** www.oberammergau.de). It's open Monday to Friday 8:30am to 6pm, and Saturday 9am to noon and 1 to 5pm.

Exploring Oberammergau

Oberammergau has much to offer. Consider taking an excursion to either the **Berg Laber,** the mountain that rises to the east of the town, or **Berg Kolben,** to the west. Berg Laber, slightly more dramatic, is accessible via an enclosed cable-gondola (*© **08822/4770;** www.laber-bergbahn.de) that offers a sweeping Alpine view. The 10-minute ascent costs 14€ per person. The top of Berg Kolben is accessible via a two-passenger open-sided chairlift (*© **08822/4760;** www.kolbensesselbahn.de), with exposure to high winds that is a lot more primal. The cost is 7.50€ round-trip. Both are open mid-July to mid-October and mid-December to March daily 9am to noon and 1 to 4:30pm.

Aside from the actors in the Passion Play, Oberammergau's most respected citizens are **woodcarvers,** many of whom have been trained in the village woodcarver's school. In the **Pilatushaus,** Ludwig-Thoma-Strasse 10 (*© **08822/949511**), you can watch local carvers, as well as painters, sculptors, and potters, as they work. June to October, their hours are Tuesday to Sunday 3 to 5pm. Many examples of their art can be found throughout the town, on painted cottages and inns, and in the churchyard.

Heimatmuseum, Dorfstrasse 8 (*© **08822/94136;** www.oberammergaumuseum. de), has a notable collection of 18th-, 19th-, and 20th-century Christmas crèches, all hand carved and painted. It's open mid-May to mid-October Tuesday to Sunday 10am

---

SHOPPING FOR woodcarvings

Oberammergau's woodcarvings are among the most sought after in the Germanic world, and many an example has graced the mantelpieces and shelves of homes around the globe. Most subjects are religious, deriving directly from 14th-century originals; however, to cater to the demands of modern visitors, there's been an increased emphasis lately on secular subjects, such as drinking or hunting scenes. Competition is fierce for these woodcarvings, many of which are made in hamlets and farmhouses throughout the region. Know before you buy that even some of the most expensive "handmade" pieces might have been roughed in by machine before being finished off by hand.

The **Schnitzschule** (**Woodcarving School;** *© **08822/3542**) has conditions of study that may remind you of the severity of the medieval guilds. Students who labor over a particular sculpture are required to turn it in to the school, where it's either placed on permanent exhibition or sold during the school's once-a-year sell-off, usually over a 2-day period in July.

Baur Anton, Dorfstrasse 27 (*© **08822/ 821;** www.holzschnitzerei-tonibaur.de), has the most sophisticated inventory of woodcarvings. The shop employs a small cadre of carvers who create works inspired by medieval originals. The outgoing and personable sales staff is quick to admit that the forms of many of the pieces are roughed in by machine, but most of the intricate work is completed by hand. Pieces are crafted from maple, pine, or linden (basswood). Prices start at 9€. Carvings are in their natural grain, stained, or polychromed (some of the most charming), and in some instances, are partially gilded.

to 1pm and 2 to 6pm; in the off season (Jan–Mar and the last 2 weeks of Nov), visits are Saturday only by guided tour at 2pm. Admission is 6€ for adults, 5€ for students, and 2€ children ages 6 to 16, and free for children 5 and under.

When strolling through the village, note the **frescoed houses** named after fairy-tale characters, such as the "Hansel and Gretel House" and "Little Red Riding Hood House." The citizens of Oberammergau have a long tradition of painting frescoes on their houses, most often based on scenes from fairy tales. The most famous frescoed house is **Pilatushaus** on Ludwig-Thoma-Strasse (see above), which today is a home to artisans. The frescoes here are the most beautiful in town, the creation of Franz Seraph Zwinck, who was the greatest of the town's fresco artists. They were known as *Lüftmalerei* painters. Zwinck based his fresco not on a fairy tale, but on a depiction of Jesus Christ coming before Pilate—hence the name of the house, Pilatushaus.

Where to Eat & Stay

The cost of accommodations in Oberammergau includes a universally imposed *Kur-taxe* (special tax) of 1.30€. This entitles visitors to a card providing small discounts at local attractions.

Alte Post   First mentioned in 1612 this provincial, chalet-style inn is thought to be the oldest in the village. It has a wide overhanging roof, green-shuttered windows painted with decorative trim, a large crucifix on the facade, and tables set on a side-walk under a long awning. Also the village's social hub, its interior exudes storybook charm, with a ceiling-high green ceramic stove, Alpine chairs, and shelves of pewter plates. The rustic rooms range in size from cozy to spacious and have wood-beamed ceilings and wide beds with giant posts; most have views.

Dorfstrasse 19, 82487 Oberammergau. www.ogau.de. ✆ **08822/9100.** Fax 08822/910100. 32 units. 75€–113€ double. Rates include buffet breakfast. AE, DC, MC, V. Free parking. **Amenities:** Restaurant; Internet (free; in lobby). *In room:* TV.

Hotel Café-Restaurant Friedenshöhe ✍   This bargain villa enjoys a beautiful location on a quiet street near the river, which Thomas Mann experienced for 2 months in the summer of 1906 while working on *Royal Highness*. Rooms range from rather small singles to spacious doubles. They're furnished in tasteful modern style and are well maintained, each with a compact, tiled bathroom. Opt for one of the corner rooms if possible (they're bigger). Bathrooms tend to be too small but do con-tain showers. There's an indoor terrace with a panoramic view.

König-Ludwig-Strasse 31, 82487 Oberammergau. ✆ **08822/94484.** Fax 08822/4345. www.friedenshoehe. com. 14 units. 45€–65€ double. Rates include buffet breakfast. AE, DC, MC, V. Free parking. Closed Nov–Dec 14. **Amenities:** Restaurant; bar; bikes. *In room:* TV (on request).

Hotel Der Schilcherhof ✍   This hotel is divided among three old-fashioned and charming structures, each built between 1861 and 1938. This is old, and rather courtly, *Deutschland*. With its surrounding gardens, the Schilcherhof offers good-value rooms, all of which are midsize. In summer, the terrace overflows with festive, beer-drinking patrons. Nearby is the Ammer River, which flows through the village. Although the house is built in the old style, the wooden front balconies and tiers of flower boxes add a fresh look.

Bahnhofstrasse 17, 82487 Oberammergau. www.hotel-schilcherhof.de. ✆ **08822/4740.** Fax 08822/ 3793. 26 units. 35€–43€ per person double. Rates include full breakfast. AE, MC, V. Parking 5€. Closed Nov 15–Christmas. **Amenities:** Bar; room service. *In room:* TV, hair dryer, no phone, Wi-Fi (free).

Hotel Restaurant Böld ★   This well-designed chalet hotel steadily improves in quality and now is among the town's premier choices, in a neck-to-neck race with Parkhotel Sonnenhof (see below). Shortly after receiving the Nobel Prize in 1929, Thomas Mann opted to stay here. Rooms are well furnished and most have balconies. All of the accommodations are equipped with a midsize bathroom.

König-Ludwig-Strasse 10, 82487 Oberammergau www.hotel-boeld.de.. © **08822/9120.** Fax 08822/ 7102. 57 units. 87€–127€ double; from 147€ suite. Rates include buffet breakfast. AE, MC, V. Free outdoor parking; 10€ in garage. **Amenities:** Restaurant; bar; bikes; Jacuzzi; room service; sauna; Wi-Fi (free; in lobby). *In room:* TV, hair dryer, minibar.

Hotel Wolf 🐾   The fact that this overgrown Bavarian chalet is decidedly dog-friendly may have something to do with its name. Like others in the village, its facade has an encircling balcony, heavy timbering, and window boxes spilling cascades of geraniums. Inside, it retains some local flavor, although concessions to modernity have been made, such as an elevator. Don't be deterred by room names like Quicky, Jacky, and Assi; they're German dogs' names.

Dorfstrasse 1, 82487 Oberammergau. www.hotel-wolf.de. © **08822/92330.** Fax 08822/923333. 32 units. 120€–145€ double. Rates include buffet breakfast. DC, MC, V. Free parking. **Amenities:** Restaurant; bar; outdoor heated pool; room service; sauna; Wi-Fi (free; in lobby). *In room:* TV, hair dryer.

Parkhotel Sonnenhof ★ ☺   Although short on charm and Alpine rusticity, this modern hotel is far enough from the summer crowds to offer guests peace and tranquillity, while within walking distance of the center. The hotel overlooks the Ammer River and a beautiful *Pfarrkirche* (parish church). Rooms are well maintained, filled with first-class comforts, and have balconies with an Alpine vista, often of Oberammergau's mountain, the Kobel. All rooms are nonsmoking.

König-Ludwig-Strasse 12, 82487 Oberammergau. www.parkhotellerie-sonnenhof.de. © **08822/9130.** Fax 08822/3047. 61 units. 120€–155€ double; 135€–170€ suite. AE, DC, MC, V. Free parking. **Amenities:** 3 restaurants; bar; children's center; exercise room; indoor heated pool; sauna; Wi-Fi (free; in lobby). *In room:* TV, hair dryer, minibar (in some).

Schlosshotel Linderhof 🍴   This is about as close as you can get to spending the night in King Ludwig's Linderhof palace (see "Side Trips from Oberammergau," below). Rebuilt in 1876 about 350m (1,150 ft.) away from its original location now occupied by the palace, this farmhouse hotel has gables, shutters, and half-timbering in the style of a Bavarian chalet. Rooms are dignified and high ceilinged, with tasteful hints of 19th-century gentility but with modern conveniences, such as in the bathrooms.

Linderhof 14 (near the palace), 82488 Ettal. www.schlosshotel-linderhof.com. © **08822/790.** Fax 08822/4347. 29 units. 94€–130€ double. Rates include buffet breakfast. AE, DC, MC, V. Free parking. **Amenities:** Restaurant; bar. *In room:* TV, fridge, hair dryer.

Turmwirt ★ 🍴   This cozy Bavarian-style 18th-century inn offers small, snug rooms, many with private balconies opening onto mountain views. Each comes with a small, well-maintained private bathroom. The present building was constructed in 1889 and has since been altered and renovated many times, most recently to incorporate a fitness room and sauna. The owners consist of four generations of the Glas family, which often presents Bavarian folk evenings.

Ettalerstrasse 2 (5 min. from the town center), 82487 Oberammergau. www.turmwirt.de. © **08822/ 92600.** Fax 08822/1437. 22 units. 99€–140€ double. Rates include buffet breakfast. AE, DC, MC, V. Free parking. **Amenities:** Restaurant; bikes; fitness room; room service; sauna. *In room:* TV, hair dryer, minibar.

9

THE BAVARIAN ALPS

Oberammergau

Side Trips from Oberammergau

SCHLOSS LINDERHOF ★★

Until the late 19th century, a modest hunting lodge, owned by the Bavarian royal family, stood on a large piece of land 13km (8 miles) west of the village. But in 1869, "Mad" King Ludwig II struck again, this time creating a French rococo palace in the Ammergau Mountains. This is his most successful creation. Unlike his palace at Chiemsee (p. 342), Schloss Linderhof was not meant to copy any other structure. And unlike the Neuschwanstein palace (p. 267), its concentration of fanciful projects and designs was not limited to the palace interior. In fact, the gardens and smaller buildings at Linderhof are, if anything, more elaborate than the two-story main structure.

Our favorite rooms are on the second floor, where ceilings are much higher because of the unusual roof plan. Ascending the winged staircase of Carrara marble, you'll find yourself at the **West Gobelin Room** (also called the Music Room), with carved and gilded paneling and richly colored tapestries. This room leads directly into the **Hall of Mirrors,** where the mirrors are set in white-and-gold panels, decorated with gilded woodcarvings. The hall's ceiling is festooned with frescoes depicting mythological scenes.

In the popular style of the previous century, Ludwig laid out the **gardens ★★** in formal parterres with geometrical shapes, baroque sculptures, and elegant fountains. The front of the palace opens onto a large pool where, from a gilded statue in its center, a jet of water sprays 30m (100 ft.) into the air.

The park also contains several other small but exotic buildings, including a **Moorish Kiosk** where Ludwig could indulge his wildest Arabian Nights fantasies. He would retreat here by himself for hours, smoking a *chibouk* (a Turkish tobacco pipe) and dreaming of himself as an Asian prince. The pavilion is a mammoth artificial grotto that is amazingly realistic, created out of artificial rock that looks real, complete with stalagmites and stalactites and three separate chambers.

Schloss Linderhof, Linderhof 12, 82488 Ettal (**℃ 08822/92030;** www.linderhof. de), is open to the public throughout the year and makes an ideal day trip from Munich, as well as from Oberammergau. It's open April to October 15 daily 9am to 6pm. From October 16 to March, the grotto and Moorish Kiosk are closed, but the castle is open daily 10am to 4pm. Admission in the summer is 8.50€ for adults, 7.50€ for students, and free for children 14 and under. In winter, admission is 7.50€ for adults, 6.50€ for students, and free for children 14 and under.

Bus line 9622 runs between Oberammergau (from the railway station) and Schloss Linderhof six times per day, beginning at 10:25am; the last bus leaves Linderhof at 6:56pm. Round-trip fare is 13€. For bus information, call **RVO Bus Company** (**℃ 08821/948274;** www.rvo-bus.de) at their regional office in Garmisch-Partenkirchen. Motorists from Oberammergau should follow the signs to Ettal, about 5km (3 miles) away, and then go another 5km (3 miles) to Draswang; from there follow the signs to Schloss Linderhof.

KLOSTER ETTAL ★

Kloster Ettal, on Kaiser-Ludwig-Platz at Ettal (**℃ 08822/740;** www.kloster-ettal. de), lies in a lovely valley sheltered by the steep hills of the Ammergau. Duke Ludwig the Bavarian founded this abbey in 1330. Its statue of the Virgin is attributed to Giovanni Pisano. In the 18th century, the golden age of the abbey, there were about 70,000 pilgrims here every year.

The **Church of Our Lady,** within the abbey, is one of the finest examples of Bavarian rococo architecture in existence. The impressive baroque facade was built from a plan based on the designs of Enrico Zuccali. Around the polygonal core of the church is a two-story gallery. Visitors stand under a vast dome and admire the **fresco,** painted by John Jacob Zeiller in the summers of 1751 and 1752.

The abbey stands 3km (2 miles) south of Oberammergau, along the road to Garmisch-Partenkirchen. Admission is free, and it's open daily 8am to 7pm year-round. Buses from Oberammergau leave from the Rathaus and the Bahnhof once per hour during the day, with round-trip fare 12€. Call the **RVO Bus Company** in Garmisch-Partenkirchen (© **08821/948274;** www.rvo-bus.de) for information.

LAKE CONSTANCE (BODENSEE)

A mild climate and plentiful sunshine make Lake Constance (Bodensee in German) a top vacation spot for lovers of sun and sand, as well as for sightseers and spagoers. The hillsides that slope to the water's edge are covered with vineyards and orchards and are dotted with colorful hamlets and busy tourist centers. Cruise ships and ferries link every major center around the lake. Although the lake's 260km (160-mile) shoreline is shared by three nations—Austria, Germany, and Switzerland—the area around the lake is united in a common cultural and historical heritage.

Lake Constance is actually divided into three lakes, although the name is frequently applied only to the largest of these, the Obersee. The western end of the Obersee separates into two distinct branches: the Überlingersee is a long fiord, while the Untersee is more irregular, jutting in and out of marshland and low-lying woodland. The two branches are connected by a narrow channel—which is actually the upper Rhine.

The lake offers a wealth of **activities,** including swimming, sailing, windsurfing, diving, and rowing. You can swim either in the cold waters of the lake itself, or in one of the heated lakeside pools. The Eichwald Lido at Lindau boasts a 1km-long (½-mile) "beach," with plenty of lawns for sunbathing German-style. The other popular place for lakeside swimming at a heated pool is the Jakob Lido at Constance. One of the best ways to see the lake is to cycle around it. You can rent **bicycles** at or near all the major train stations.

Sailing on Lake Constance is a major attraction. Some boatyards and sailing schools rent boats; you'll be asked to show some proof of proficiency (a certification from a sailing school, for example). Or you can rent rowboats and motorboats at all major hotels along the lake.

From Munich, motorists should take the A96, via Landsberg and Kempten, to reach the lake. Drivers from Frankfurt head south along the A7 Autobahn to Memmingen, transferring to A96. The nearest international airport to Lake Constance is at Zürich, 79km (49 miles) southwest of the town of Konstanz. The Munich airport is about 225km (140 miles) north of the lake.

LINDAU ★★

179km (111 miles) SW of Munich, 32km (20 miles) S of Ravensburg

Crossing the causeway to an island city symbolized by lions may give the brief impression that you're in Italy. Yet Lindau doesn't need comparisons to Venice to impress the visitor. From its origins in the 9th century, and throughout the Middle Ages as a free imperial town of the Holy Roman Empire, Lindau became the center of trade between Bavaria and Switzerland. In 1804 it joined Bavaria and welcomed the lion that keeps watch at the harbor entry. Today you can wander at will through the charming maze of winding narrow streets lined with houses that have stood the test of time. At the harbor stand two **lighthouses:** One, Mangturm, was built in the 1200s, the other in 1856. Each tower is some 37m (120 ft.) tall and can be climbed by the athletic via narrow spiral staircases. The reward is a panoramic vista of the Alps, both Swiss and Austrian.

Essentials

GETTING THERE

Lindau is connected to the mainland by a road bridge and a causeway for walkers and trains. It's a transportation link between the western part of Lake Constance and the towns of Austria and Switzerland, which lie directly across the water. Regional flights come in to the Friedrichshafen airport (see "Essentials" under "Friedrichshafen, below). The nearest major airport is Zürich.

BY TRAIN   The Lindau Bahnhof is on the major Basel-Singen-Radolfzell-Lindau and Lindau-Kissleg-Memmingen-Buchloe rail lines, with frequent connections in all directions. Direct trains from both Munich and Stuttgart leave every 2 hours and take 2¾ hours. Call ℭ **01805/996633,** or visit www.bahn.de for information.

BY BUS   Regional bus service along Lake Constance is offered by **RAB Regionalverkehr Alb-Bodensee GmbH** (ℭ **0751/2766;** www.zugbus-rab.de).

BY FERRY   Three to five ferries per day (depending on the season) link Lindau with Konstanz and Bregenz in Austria. Boats from Konstanz stop at Mainau, Meersburg, and Friedrichshafen before Lindau and Bregenz; the entire trip takes no less than 3 hours. Call **BSB** (ℭ **08382/275840;** www.bsb-online.com), or the tourist office for information and schedules.

BY CAR   Access by car from Munich is via the north-south A96 and the B31, skirting the northern shore of the lake.

VISITOR INFORMATION

Tourist-Information is at Alfred-Nobel-Platz 1 (ℭ **08382/260031;** www.lindau. de). The office is open April to September Monday to Friday 9am to 1pm and 2 to 6pm, Saturday 10am to 1pm and 3 to 6pm, and Sunday 10am to 1pm; from October to March, it is open Monday to Friday 9am to noon and 2 to 5pm.

Exploring Lindau

A tour of this *Ferieninsel* (holiday island) begins with the **old harbor,** seen from the lakeside promenade. The **Mangturm,** the old lighthouse, stands on the promenade as a reminder of the heavy fortifications that once surrounded the city. It also marks where Lindau was once divided into two islands. The harbor entrance is marked by the 33m (108-ft.) **New Lighthouse** and the **Bavarian Lion,** standing guard as yachts and commercial ships pass by below.

Hauptstrasse, in the center of the town, is the main street of the Altstadt. The most easily recognizable building is the **Altes Rathaus,** erected in 1422. The stepped gables are typical of the period, but the building's facade also combines many later styles of architecture. The interior, once used as a council hall, is the town library. Frescoes represent scenes from a session of the 1496 Imperial Diet.

Just north of Hauptstrasse is the town's most familiar landmark, the round **Diebsturm (Thieves' Tower),** with its turreted roof. Next to it is the oldest building in Lindau, the 11th-century **St. Peter's Church,** which houses a war memorial chapel. In the church is a group of frescoes by Hans Holbein the Elder.

Returning to Hauptstrasse, which cuts through the exact center of the island, follow the street eastward to the **Haus zum Cavazzen,** Am Marktplatz 6 (© **08382/ 944073**), the handsomest patrician house on Lake Constance. It holds the municipal art collection. Included are exhibits of sculpture and painting from the Gothic, Renaissance, and baroque periods. Some of the rooms are furnished with period pieces showing how wealthy citizens lived in the 18th and 19th centuries. Among the rarities is a collection of mechanical musical instruments. This attraction is open April to October Tuesday to Friday and Sunday 11am to 5pm, plus Saturday 2 to 5pm. Admission is 3€ adults, 1.50€ students and children 6 to 15; for a guided tour there is an extra charge of 3€ per person.

Passing across Am Marktplatz and by the Collegiate Church and St. Stephen's Church, both baroque, you come to the strange pile of rocks known as **Heathen's Wall,** dating from Roman times. Beyond this is the **Stadtgarten (Town Garden),** which, although peaceful during the day, livens up at night when the wheels of the town's casino begin to spin.

Where to Eat

Hotel Villino ★★ 🏨 ITALIAN/ASIAN   In the suburb of Hoyren, this hotel is better known for its excellent Italian restaurant than for its bedrooms. Only dinner is served, in a comfortable room decorated in high-tech Milanese style. The elegant menu includes pesto-laced spaghetti, Sicilian-style fish soup, a heaping platter of scampi served with stuffed squid and fresh tomatoes, anglerfish and lobster fried with cardamom, and a particularly succulent version of leg of lamb with garlic sauce. A fine Asian menu features sushi, Thai soup, and such dishes as filet of veal or pikeperch with Asian spicing.

The establishment maintains 16 rooms, priced at 190€ to 260€ each, plus five suites at 410€. Each unit has a private balcony, minibar, TV, and telephone. Rates include continental breakfast, and parking is free.

Hoyren, Hoyerberg 34. © **08382/93450.** Fax 08382/934512. www.villino.de. Reservations recommended. Main courses 32€–48€; fixed-price 5-course menu 98€. MC, V. Tues–Sun 6pm–midnight. 1km (½ mile) north of Lindau's center. Bus: 2.

Hoyerberg Schlössle ★★★ FRENCH   This fine restaurant, in a former private residence from 1864, lies about a 15-minute drive from the Altstadt (Old Town). The inner dining room is beautifully decorated, with a view of the mountains and lake. You can also dine on the two terraces overlooking the town and lake. Continental delicacies include cream of scampi soup, Bodensee pikeperch stuffed with champagne-flavored

herbs, and Allgäuer saddle of venison with small flour dumplings and French beans. Meals here are memorable; the chef has great flair and doesn't oversauce the food. In the afternoon the restaurant serves as a cafe, offering light snacks and drinks.

Hoyerbergstrasse 64, at Lindau-Aeschach. © **08382/25295.** www.hoyerbergschloessle.de. Reservations required for dinner. Main courses 24€–32€; fixed-price menus 62€–89€. AE, DC, MC, V. Restaurant Wed–Sun noon–2pm; Tues–Sun 6–10pm. Cafe Tues–Sun 2–4:30pm. Closed Feb. Bus: 2.

Zum Sünfzen GERMAN/BAVARIAN   This 14th-century, all-wood restaurant at the end of Maximilianstrasse serves good, reasonably priced food. Dishes range from roast pork with vegetables to filet of venison. Fresh fish from Lake Constance is a specialty. The food is the type you might be served in a middle-class private home along the lake.

Maximilianstrasse 1. © **08382/5865.** www.suenfzen.de. Reservations recommended. Main dishes 9€–20€. AE, DC, MC, V. Daily 11am–10:30pm.

Shopping

Michael Zeller is known throughout Bavaria for a twice-yearly **Internationale-Bodensee-Kunstauktion (art auction)** held in the spring and fall (dates vary) and a much smaller auction in December. His year-round store, **Michael Zeller,** Bindergasse 7 (© **08382/93020;** www.zeller.de), has Lindau's best selection of watercolors, engravings, and prints, along with jewelry, porcelain, and furniture.

Entertainment & Nightlife

NIGHTLIFE

Lindau's **Spielbank Casino,** Chelles-Alle 1 (© **08382/27740;** www.spielbanken-in-bayern.de), offers slot machines from noon to 2am and blackjack and roulette from 3pm to 2am (until 3am Fri–Sat). The bet ceiling is 12,000€ for roulette. Admission is free, and a passport is required as proof of age. Men should wear a jacket and tie.

OUTDOOR PURSUITS

For decades it was possible to rent bikes at the train station, but no more. Today, rentals are available at **Unger's Fahrradverleih,** Inselgraben 14 (© **08382/943688;** www.fahrrad-unger.de), close to the train station. The price ranges from 6€ to 15€ per day. The outfitter is open Monday to Friday 9am to 1pm and 3 to 6pm, Saturday and Sunday 9am to 1pm. Lindenhofpark is the most scenic area (it's also ideal for a picnic).

The town has three lakeside **beaches,** all open in summer Monday to Friday 10:30am to 7:30pm and Saturday and Sunday 10am to 8pm. The biggest beach is **Eichwald,** about a half-hour walk away along Uferweg (to the right if you're facing the harbor); or take bus no. 1 or 2 to Anheggerstrasse, then bus no. 3 to Karmelbuckel. Admission is 3€ for adults, 2€ for children. To reach **Lindenhofbad** (© **08382/6637;** www.seebad-lindenhof.de), take bus no. 1 or 2 to Anheggerstrasse, then bus no. 4 to Alwind. Admission is 3€ for adults and 2€ for children. If you're driving, follow the signs to B31; stay on B31 until you see the exit marked Schachen.

You can rent **windsurfers** at **Kreitmeir,** In der Grub 17 (© **08382/23330;** www.hermanno.de), for 15€ per hour. At the little dock next to Lindau's rail bridge, you can rent a **paddleboat** for 10€, a motorboat for 25€, or an electric boat for 23€ from **Bootsvermietung Hodrius** (© **08382/297771;** www.bootsverleih-lindau.de).

Where to Stay

Hotel Bayerischer Hof ★★★   This harbor-front hotel guards the promenade like the nearby stone lion surveying the lake scene. Looking as if it had been plucked from a Mediterranean resort, the atmosphere and service here are first rate. Its large rooms are Lindau's finest, each well furnished with traditional styling. Most have good views, although the less desirable units overlook a narrow thoroughfare.

Seepromenade, 88131 Lindau. www.bayerischerhof-lindau.de. © **800/223-5652** in the U.S. and Canada, or 08382/9150. Fax 08382/915591. 97 units. 185€–335€ double; 310€ junior suite; 475€–495€ suite. Children 9 and under stay free in parent's room. Rates include buffet breakfast. AE, DC, MC, V. Parking 12€. **Amenities:** 2 restaurants; bar; exercise room; outdoor heated pool; room service; spa. *In room:* TV, hair dryer, minibar, Wi-Fi (10€ per day).

Hotel-Garni Brugger ⚓ This modest, charming little hotel is the best affordable choice on the island. It possesses pleasant proportions, with a gabled attic and French doors that open onto the balconies in the back. The small rooms are up-to-date, furnished in a functional modern style, with lots of light; each comes with a small, tiled bathroom. The location is an easy walk from the lake and casino, and ideal for those with a car.

Bei der Heidenmauer 11, 88131 Lindau. www.hotel-garni-brugger.de. © **08382/93410.** Fax 08382/4133. 23 units. 92€–106€ double. Additional bed 26€. Rates include buffet breakfast. AE, DC, MC, V. Parking 8€. **Amenities:** Spa. *In room:* TV, hair dryer, minibar, Wi-Fi (2€ per day).

Hotel Reutemann und Seegarten ★★ Located on the harbor front next to its parent, the superior Bayerischer Hof, this hotel has two villas. The Reutemann has large rooms and bathrooms with showers and huge tubs. The Seegarten, with little flower-filled balconies and trailing vines, has spacious and handsome rooms, especially those with lake views (which cost more, naturally). Both villas have their own waterfront gardens with furniture for sunbathing.

Seepromenade, 88131 Lindau. www.bayerischerhof-lindau.de. © **08382/9150.** Fax 08382/915591. 64 units. 135€–245€ double. Children 9 and under stay free in parent's room. AE, DC, MC, V. Parking 12€. **Amenities:** Restaurant; babysitting; bikes; exercise room; outdoor heated pool; room service; sauna. *In room:* TV, hair dryer, minibar, Wi-Fi (free).

FRIEDRICHSHAFEN

22km (14 miles) W of Lindau, 20km (12 miles) S of Ravensburg

Friedrichshafen is at the northeastern corner of the Bodensee, near the lake's widest point. This mostly modern city was almost completely rebuilt after World War II. It has one of the longest waterfront exposures of any town along the lake. Besides that, the town's highlights are two interesting museums and the dome-capped **Schlosskirche,** the premier reminder of Friedrichshafen's baroque past.

Essentials
GETTING THERE
BY AIR The **Friedrichshafen** airport (© **07541/28401;** www.fly-away.de) lies 5km (3 miles) north of town. Flights to Friedrichshafen come in from Frankfurt, Vienna, Cologne, and Berlin. For access to flights deriving from cities not mentioned above, consider flying into Zürich's airport, which lies about 100km (60 miles) away.

BY TRAIN Friedrichshafen is the largest railway junction along the northern edge of the Bodensee and is a major transfer point for rail passengers going on to other cities and resorts along the lake. The town has two railway stations, the **Stadtbahnhof** (© 07541/31390), in the center, and the **Hafenbahnhof** (© 07541/372717), along the Seestrasse, about 1km (½ mile) away. Both of these stations are interconnected by bus nos. 1, 2, 3, 5, 6, and 7. Trains arrive from Ulm and Stuttgart at intervals of 1 hour or less throughout the day. For information and schedules, call **✆ 01805/996633.**

BY BUS Bus service along the lake is provided by **RAB Regionalverkehr Alb-Bodensee GmbH** (✆ 075/2766; www.stadtverkehr-fn.de).

BY CAR Friedrichshafen is easily reached from Stuttgart and Munich. From Stuttgart, follow Autobahn 8 east to the city of Ulm, then turn south onto Route 30 into Friedrichshafen. From Munich follow Autobahn 96 west/southwest to Lindau, then head west on Rte. 31 along Lake Constance to Friedrichshafen.

BY BOAT April to October, about eight lake steamers ply the waters from Friedrichshafen to Lindau, Bregenz (Austria), and Konstanz. For departure times and details, call **BSB** at ✆ 07541/92380 or visit www.bsb-online.com. A ferry runs year-round between Friedrichshafen and Romanshorn, Switzerland (trip time: 40 min.), and costs 8€ (4.50€ for children ages 6–15).

VISITOR INFORMATION

The city's **Tourist Information Office** is at Bahnhofplatz 2 (✆ 07541/30010; www.friedrichshafen.info). It's open July to August Monday to Friday 9am to 6pm, and Saturday 9am to 1pm; May, June and November Monday to Friday 9am to noon and 1 to 6pm, and Saturday 9am to 1pm; April and October Monday to Thursday 9am to noon and 2 to 5pm, and Friday 9am to noon; and November to March Monday to Thursday 9am to noon and 2 to 4pm, and Friday 9am to noon.

Exploring Friedrichshafen

The best thing to do in town is to stroll the lake-fronting **Seepromenade,** with its sweeping view that extends on clear days all the way to the Swiss Alps. Cycling along the broad Seestrasse is also a delight. A kiosk within the Stadtbahnhof rents bikes for 8€ to 10€ a day.

The town's architectural highlight is the 17th-century **Schlosskirche,** Schlossstrasse 33 (✆ 07541/21308). The palatial ecclesiastical buildings that were once part of the church's monastery were converted in the 1800s into a palace for the kings of Württemberg. Today, they're privately owned. The church is well worth a visit, but it's open only Easter to October daily 9am to 6pm.

The **Zeppelin-Museum** (✆ 07541/38010; www.zeppelin-museum.de), in the Hafenbahnhof, Seestrasse 22, is a tribute to Count Ferdinand von Zeppelin. Around 1900, this native of Konstanz invented and tested the aircraft that bore his name. The museum has a re-creation of the giant and historic zeppelin *Hindenburg*, including a full-scale replica of its passenger cabins. The famous blimp exploded in a catastrophic fire in New Jersey in 1937, possibly because of sabotage. The museum also has memorabilia associated with zeppelins and their inventor. May to October, it's open daily 9am to 5pm; November to April, hours are Tuesday to Sunday 10am to 5pm. Admission is 7.50€ for adults and 3.50€ for children 16 and under.

Of interest to students of educational techniques is Friedrichshafen's **Schulmuseum,** Friedrichstrasse 14 (✆ 07541/32622; www.friedrichshafen.de), which traces the development of education between 1850 (when classes were taught by monks and nuns) and 1930 (when education was the responsibility of the German state). The museum is near the Schlosskirche in the historic heart of town. Look for reconstructions of schoolrooms from periods in the 19th and 20th centuries. April to October, it's open daily 10am to 5pm; November to March, hours are Tuesday to Sunday 2 to 5pm. Admission is 3.50€ for adults and 1.50€ for children.

REBIRTH OF THE zeppelin

The zeppelin fell out of favor in 1937 when the *Hindenburg* blew up in New Jersey, but its postmillennium sibling glides peacefully over Lake Constance. (Don't worry. The new zeppelin is much smaller and rises with inert helium gas, not the explosive hydrogen used by the *Hindenburg*.) The airship, named *Bodensee*, can climb to about 2,300m (7,500 ft.). The newer vessel carries 12 passengers and a crew of two, as opposed to the *Hindenburg*, which carried 100 aboard. Cruising at approximately 54kmph (33 mph) over the scenic lake, it takes passengers on hour-long flights scheduled daily, costing 395€ per person Monday to Friday, or 200€ for a half-hour. For more information and takeoff points along the lake, visit **www.zeppelinflug.de**.

Where to Eat

Hotel-Restaurant Maier ★ 👜 INTERNATIONAL/GERMAN   In the center of the hamlet of Fischbach, at the edge of the lake, this hotel is best known for its restaurant. Local diners appreciate the generous, well-prepared dishes, the attentive service, and the sweeping views over the lake. One dining room is contemporary and modern, the other a re-creation of a traditional *Stube* in the mountains. Some of the best items on the menu include chicken breast in lemon sauce, pork filet with herbs and a sweet-pepper sauce, or else pork filet with fresh mushrooms and roasted onions.

The hotel contains 50 rooms, each with TV, minibar, and telephone. Doubles cost 90€ to 139€ and include breakfast and free parking. Most rooms are air-conditioned.

Poststrasse 1-3, Fischbach. ✆ **07541/4040.** www.hotel-maier.de. Reservations recommended. Main courses 10€–23€. AE, DC, MC, V. Sat-Thurs 11:30am-2pm; daily 5:30-10pm. 6km (4 miles) west of Friedrichshafen.

Restaurant Kurgarten INTERNATIONAL   Depending on the time of day, this place might look like a cafe, a bar, or a restaurant. It has a beautiful view over its own garden and the lake, and there's a wide range of tasty menu items. Vegetarian choices include mushrooms stuffed with spinach and zucchini stuffed with ratatouille. Other good options include an Argentine beefsteak with herb butter and grilled scampi on noodles with slices of local vegetables and salad.

Olgastrasse 20. ✆ **07541/32033.** Reservations not necessary. Main courses 13€–22€; fixed-price menus 30€–38€. MC, V. Daily 11:30am-11pm.

Where to Stay

Buchhorner Hof ★   This charming lakeside hotel, the best in town, provides a compromise between the luxurious, modern comfort of larger hotels and the traditional hospitality of smaller inns. It's housed in Friedrichshafen's oldest building. Rooms are well furnished, and each comes with a midsize modern bathroom. The restaurant serves adequate fare at lunch and dinner, and the bar is a cozy retreat.

Friedrichstrasse 33, 88045 Friedrichshafen. www.buchhornerhof.de. ✆ **07541/2050.** Fax 07541/32663. 98 units. 100€–260€ double; 255€ suite. Rates include buffet breakfast. AE, DC, MC, V. Parking 10€. **Amenities:** Restaurant; bar; bikes; exercise room; Jacuzzi; room service; spa. *In room:* TV, hair dryer, minibar, Wi-Fi (12€ per day).

Hotel Goldenes-Rad   Located in the pedestrian center in the middle of town, this traditional hotel is a short walk from Lake Constance, the ferry, and the

10

LAKE CONSTANCE (BODENSEE)

Friedrichshafen

Zeppelin-Museum. Rooms are comfortable and modern, as befitting the Best Western brand. Although the location is not very car-friendly, there is a parking lot nearby, and the English-speaking staff is courteous and helpful.

Karlstrasse 43, 88045 Friedrichshafen. www.goldenes-rad.de. © **800/528-1234** or 07541/2850. Fax 07541/285285. 70 units. 119€–129€ double; 129€–189€ suite. Rates include buffet breakfast. AE, DC, MC, V. Parking 6€. **Amenities:** Restaurant; bikes; exercise room; room service; sauna. *In room:* TV, hair dryer, minibar, Wi-Fi (free).

Seehotel ★ 📷 This is one of the most appealing hotels in town, almost in the same league as the Buchhorner Hof. Right between the railway station and Seepromenade, its small rooms are decorated sensibly, even stylishly. Some have air-conditioning; most have views of the water. All the bedrooms have midsize bathrooms. The staff is sensitive and well trained.

Bahnhofplatz 2, 88045 Friedrichshafen. www.seehotelfn.de. © **07541/3030.** Fax 07541/303100. 132 units. 109€–185€ double; 176€–272€ suite. AE, DC, MC, V. Free outside parking; 11€ inside. **Amenities:** Restaurant; bar; room service; spa. *In room:* A/C (in some), TV, fax, hair dryer, minibar, Wi-Fi (free).

MEERSBURG ★

190km (118 miles) S of Stuttgart, 143km (89 miles) SE of Freiburg

Like the towns of Italy's Lake District, this village on the northern shore of Lake Constance cascades in terraces down the hillside to the water. The heart of Meersburg is a pedestrian area. You can drive into town as far as the Stefan-Lochner-Strasse garage, where you must leave your car and continue on foot. In the center, the streets become narrow promenades and steps wander up and down the hillside. From the dock, large and small boats set out for trips on the water. Many watersports are available. One charming feature of Meersburg is the town watchman who still makes nightly rounds, keeping alive an ancient tradition.

Essentials

GETTING THERE

BY PLANE Regional flights come into the Friedrichshafen airport, 20km (12 miles) from Meersburg. The nearest international airport is at Zürich, 80km (50 miles) away.

BY TRAIN The nearest rail station is in **Uhldingen-Mühlhofen,** 5km (3 miles) away, on the Basel-Singen-Radolfzell-Lindau rail line, with frequent connections in all directions. Call © **01805/996633** for more information. From Uhldingen-Mühlhofen station, buses depart for Meersburg at 30-minute intervals every day from 6am to 10pm, charging 1.90€ each way. Buses are marked either MEERSBURG or FRIEDRICHSHAFEN but always bear no. 7395 on the front.

BY BUS Buses arrive about every 30 minutes throughout the day from Friedrichshafen. Regional bus service along Lake Constance is provided by **RAB Regionalverkehr Alb-Bodensee GmbH** in Friedrichshafen (© **07541/30130;** www.zugbus-rab.de).

BY FERRY Between April and October regular ferries make the 30-minute trip to Konstanz. Depending on the season, anywhere from 6 to 12 boats leave between 8:30am and 6pm, with just as many making the return trip.

BY CAR Access by car is via the A7 and A96 autobahns from the north or Hwy. B31. You can drive from Munich in about 3 hours, from Frankfurt in about 4½ hours, and from Stuttgart in about 2 hours.

VISITOR INFORMATION

For tourist information, contact the **Meersburg Tourismus,** Kirchstrasse 4 (© **07532/440400;** www.meersburg.de). May to September, it's open Monday to Friday 9am to 12:30pm and 2 to 6pm; and Monday to Friday 9am to noon and 2 to 4pm in the off-season.

SPECIAL EVENTS The surrounding vineyards produce excellent wine, and on the second weekend in September, winemakers around the lake come to Meersburg for the **Bodensee Weinfest** (Lake Constance Wine Festival).

Exploring Meersburg

After you enter the town through the ancient **Obertor (Upper Gate),** you'll be on Marktplatz. Here stands the 16th-century **Rathaus,** which contains a typical German *Ratskeller.* Leading off from this is **Steigstrasse,** the most interesting artery, passing between rows of half-timbered houses whose arcades serve as covered walkways above the street.

Nearby, at Schlossplatz, the **Altes Schloss ★** (© **07532/80000;** www.meersburg. com) dates from 628 and is the oldest intact German castle. All the relics of a warring age are here—clubs, flails, armor, helmets, and axes—along with 30 fully furnished rooms, decorated with pieces from various epochs. The bishops of Konstanz lived in this castle until the 18th century, when they moved to the Neues Schloss (see below). The baron of Lassberg, an admirer of medieval romance, then took over and invited Annette von Droste-Hülshoff (1797–1848), his sister-in-law and Germany's leading female poet, to come as well. She had the castle turned into a setting for artists and writers. You can visit her luxuriously furnished chambers, as well as the murky dungeons and the castle museum with its medieval jousting equipment. The castle is open March to October daily 9am to 6:30pm, and November to February daily 10am to 6pm. Admission is 8.50€ for adults, 6.50€ students, 4.50€ for children 6 to 13, and free for children 5 and under. Next to the castle is **Castle Mill** (1620), with a 9m (30-ft.) wooden water wheel, the oldest of its kind in Germany.

You go from the medieval to the baroque when you enter the **Neues Schloss,** Schlossplatz (© **07532/4404900**). The leading architect of the 18th century, Balthasar Neumann, was responsible for some of the castle's design, while ceiling paintings and frescoes were done by other prominent artists and craftsmen. Elegant stucco moldings grace the ceilings and walls. The Spiegelsaal, or Hall of Mirrors, is the setting for an international music festival in summer. Admission is 4.50€ for adults and 1.50€ for children 12 and under. It's open April to October daily 10am to 1pm and 2 to 6pm.

A Taste of Honey

Just 10km (6 miles) from Meersburg is the famous **Wallfahrtskirche at Birnau** (© 07556/92030; www.birnau.de), 5km (3 miles) southeast of Überlingen. This pilgrimage basilica, which dates from the mid-18th century, was built in rococo style, with rose, blue, and beige marble predominating. A celebrated statuette— the *Honigschlecker* (honey taster)— shows a baby sucking a finger as he's yanked out of a nest of bees. It's to the right of the St. Bernard altarpiece. The church is open daily 7:30am to 7pm, and until 5:30 pm in winter. Admission is free.

On the promenade below stands the **Gred House,** which dates from 1505. It now holds ticket offices for the railway and steamer lines on Lake Constance. Regular ferry service to Konstanz leaves from the dock on the outskirts of town.

Where to Eat

Winzerstube zum Becher ★ REGIONAL/GERMAN   Year after year this little independently run restaurant manages to serve better food than any hotel in town. If you've come to Germany with images of a handcrafted *Weinstube* that radiates warmth, then you should dine here. A pea-green tile oven tucked away in a corner provides heat in winter. The chairs are not that comfortable, but the rest of the flow-ered, paneled, and happily cluttered room provides a cozy atmosphere. The specialty of the chef is onion-flavored Swabian *Zwiebelrostbraten* with *Spätzle,* along with a host of other specialties, including fresh fish from Lake Constance. A superb fixed-price dinner cuts down on the cost. The restaurant also offers drinks (mostly wine from its own winery) and snacks.

Höllgasse 4, near the Altes Schloss. ✆ **07532/9009.** www.winzerstube-zum-becher.de. Reservations required. Main courses 10€–22€; fixed-price lunches 24€–32€, dinners 36€–52€. AE, DC, MC, V. Tues-Sun 10am–2pm and 5pm–midnight. Closed 3 weeks in Jan.

Entertainment & Nightlife

NIGHTLIFE

The **Spiegelsaal (Hall of Mirrors),** in the Neues Schloss at Schlossplatz, is the splendid backdrop for an annual international chamber-music festival. It takes place from the end of April to May. You may hear, for example, baroque ensembles, a string quartet, or a pianist playing the works of Schumann. Tickets start at 16€. Call ✆ **07541/2033300** for information.

The **Stadttheater Konstanz,** the oldest theater in Germany, dating from 1609, moves to its summer theater in Meersburg during July and August. For more details about the Meersburg program offerings, call ✆ **07531/900150.**

Other than the cultural offerings mentioned above, after dark in Meersburg means taking a romantic stroll along the Uferpromenade bordering the lake and visiting one of the bars or *Bierhalles.* The most charming and traditional place for a drink is at the **Winzerstube zum Becher,** which also is our preferred choice for dining (see above), although you can visit just for drinks. On the Market Square, another fun place to go in the evening is the **Weinstube Löwen** (see below), a delightful, cen-turies-old inn covered in vines. If you like to enjoy a lake view with your drinks, head for the **Seehotel Off,** Uferpromenade (✆ **07532/44740;** www.hotel.off.mbo.de), fronting the Bodensee. It's especially romantic around here at night.

OUTDOOR PURSUITS

Rock-strewn beaches lie west of the town center; here you can go swimming or just soak up the sun for free. But the amenities are better at the **Beheiztes Freibad,** Uferpromenade 9–11 (✆ **07532/4402850;** www.meersburg-therme. de), a 5-minute walk east of the harbor. Here you can lie on the grass on a strip of sand adjacent to the lake, or immerse yourself in any of three outdoor swimming pools. A sauna is also on-site, plus refreshment stands and a small restaurant. Mondays are women-only. A day pass to the compound costs 19€ for an adult. Three hours cost 9€ for adults and 6.50€ for children. It's free for children 3 and under. Hours are daily 9am to 10pm.

Where to Stay

Gasthof zum Bären ★ 🗡 This picture-book hotel in the heart of town offers the best value in Meersburg. There's an ornately decorated corner tower, purple wisteria covers most of the facade, and window boxes overflow with red geraniums. The hotel was built in 1605 on the foundations of a building from 1250 (the cellar of the original Bären is still here). Its small rooms are attractive, snug, and cozily furnished.

Marktplatz 11, 88709 Meersburg. www.baeren-meersburg.de. ℂ **07532/43220.** Fax 07532/432244. 20 units. 82€–108€ double. Rates include buffet breakfast. No credit cards. Parking 6€. Closed mid-Nov to mid-Mar. **Amenities:** Restaurant. *In room:* TV.

Hotel Garni Eden Built in 1971, this modern and contemporary-looking, white-walled chalet is a 5-minute uphill walk from the lake's edge. Most visitors come for rest, relaxation, and calm, spending quiet time reading in their rooms or on their private terrace or balcony, strolling around the lake, or exploring Meersburg—its flower-filled center (and its restaurants) lies about 450m (1,500 ft.) away. Bedrooms have simple, angular furniture and a well-scrubbed sense of tidiness. Other than breakfast, no meals are served, but in light of the many restaurants within a very short walk, no one seems to care.

Menizhoferweg 4, 88709 Meersburg. www.hotel-meersburg.de. ℂ**07532/43050.** Fax 07532/430533. 19 units. 98€–139€ double. Rates include continental breakfast. AE, MC, V. Free parking. *In room:* TV, hair dryer, minibar, Wi-Fi (free).

Romantik Hotel Residenz am See ★★★ In an idyllic waterfront setting, this hotel is not only the town's best, with the best cuisine, but it's enveloped by vineyards, and its rooms open onto panoramic vistas of the Bodensee. Most of the Romantik hotels in the chain are traditional German, but this one is contemporary in styling, with tasteful, elegantly furnished rooms, both public and private. Rooms, ranging from mid-size to spacious, are individually furnished, each most comfortable with a first-rate bathroom. Even if you're not a guest, consider dining here, though you should call first for a reservation. As befits its lakeside setting, fish is the chef's specialty, especially pikeperch. It's a choice little gem, so reserve early in the peak of the summer.

Uferpromenade 11, 88709 Meersburg. www.hotel-residenz-meersburg.com. ℂ**07532/80040.** Fax 07532/800470. 24 units. 135€–250€ double; 270€–380€ suite. Rates include continental breakfast. AE, MC, V. Parking 4.50€. **Amenities:** Restaurant; bar; room service. *In room:* TV, hair dryer, minibar, Wi-Fi (free).

Seehotel Off ★ 🛎 Unique on the lake, this little charmer lies on the waterfront near vineyards. Its lake terrace and winter garden are just some of the special features of the domain of Elisabeth Off and her husband, Michael Off, a master chef. Most of the attractively furnished, midsize bedrooms have a view of the lake, often from a private balcony. This is a very ecosensitive hotel—for example, all units can be insulated from electricity so as to avoid any "electrosmog." Throughout the hotel its furnishings are modern, harmonious, and well balanced, and about a dozen rooms are designed according to feng shui principles. An on-site health center features everything from aromatherapy to Reiki.

Uferpromenade 51, 88709 Meersburg. www.seehotel-off.de. ℂ **07532/44740.** Fax 07532/447444. 19 units. 47€–76€ per person double; 99€ per person suite. Rates include half board. DC, MC, V. Parking 8€. **Amenities:** Restaurant; outdoor pool; spa. *In room:* TV, Wi-Fi (free).

Seehotel zur Münz If you want to save some money, and don't need glamour or a romantic atmosphere, consider checking in here. This is the simplest of our recommendations, but it's well maintained, decent, and comfortable in every way. Only a pedestrian walkway and an iron railing separate this hotel from the tree-lined lakefront. The ambience within lets you forget urban bustle. The rooms are neatly kept, all with well-maintained bathrooms.

Seestrasse 7, 88709 Meersburg. www.seehotel-zur-muenz.de. ℭ **07532/43590.** Fax 07532/7785. 11 units. 90€–130€ double. Rates include buffet breakfast. MC, V. Parking 3€ uncovered; 5€ covered; 8€ in garage. *In room:* TV.

Weinstube Löwen ★   Weinstube Löwen is a centuries-old, charming inn on the market square. Its facade has green shutters on a red background, geranium-filled window boxes, and vines reaching the upper windows under the steep mansard roof. The Fischer family has updated its interior while keeping a homelike ambience. All but a few rooms have been modernized in a streamlined functional style. They are a bit cramped, however.

Marktplatz 2, 88709 Meersburg. www.hotel-loewen-meersburg.de. ℭ **07532/43040.** Fax 07532/430410. 20 units. 90€–120€ double. Rates include buffet breakfast. AE, MC, V. Parking 4.50€. **Amenities:** Restaurant; room service. *In room:* TV.

KONSTANZ (CONSTANCE) ★

179km (111 miles) S of Stuttgart, 76km (47 miles) NE of Zürich

Crowded against the shores of Lake Constance by the borders of Switzerland, the medieval town of Konstanz had nowhere to grow but northward across the river. Today this resort city lies on both banks of the Rhine, as the river begins its long journey to the North Sea. Its strategic position made Konstanz the most important city on the lake. Nowadays tourists come to enjoy the shops, the largest beach in the area, and the magical beauty of nearby **Mainau Island.**

Essentials
GETTING THERE
BY TRAIN   Konstanz is on the main Konstanz-Singen-Villingen-Offenburg rail line, the Schwarzwaldbahn, with frequent connections to the major cities of Germany, as well as Switzerland. For information, call ℭ **01805/996633.**

BY BUS   Regional bus service around Konstanz is provided by **SBG Südbaden Bus GmbH** at Radolfzell (ℭ **07732/994724;** www.suedbadenbus.de).

BY BOAT   Ferry service and lake cruises operate between Konstanz, Mainau Island, Meersburg, Lindau, and Bregenz. The operator is **Bodensee-Schiffsbetriebe,** Hafenstrasse 6 (ℭ **07531/3640389;** www.bsb-online.com).

BY CAR   Access by car is via the B33.

VISITOR INFORMATION
Contact **Tourist-Information,** Bahnhofplatz 43 (ℭ **07531/133030;** www.konstanz-tourismus.de). April to October, the office is open Monday to Friday 9am to 6:30pm, Saturday 9am to 4pm, and Sunday 10am to 1pm; November to March, hours are Monday to Friday 9:30am to 6pm.

Exploring Konstanz
The best way to see Konstanz is from the water. The **shoreline ★** is fascinating, with little inlets that weave in and out around ancient buildings and city gardens. Several

pleasure ships offer tours along the city shoreline and across the lake to Meersburg and several other destinations. Contact **Bodensee-Schiffsbetriebe,** Hafenstrasse 6 (© **07531/3640389;** www.bsb-online.com). The timetable for ferries changes every month, so check locally. The cost is 8€ to 17€ with a car, 5€ without a car. For information, contact **Stadtwerke Konstanz** (© **07531/8030;** www.sw.konstanz.de).

During the summer, outdoor concerts are presented in the **city gardens.** Below the gardens is the **Konzilgebäude (Council Building),** where the Council of Constance met. The building was originally constructed as a storehouse in 1388 but came to be used for meetings. The hall was restored in 1911 and decorated with murals depicting the history of the town. On the harbor in front is an **obelisk** erected in memory of Count Ferdinand von Zeppelin, the citizen of Konstanz who invented the dirigible in the late 19th century.

The towers of the Romanesque **basilica** rise behind the city garden. Begun in 1052, this church took centuries to complete. The neo-Gothic spire was added only in 1856. During the Council of Constance, the members of the synod met here. From the top tower, a view opens onto the lake and the city.

MAINAU ISLAND ★★   The unusual, almost tropical island of Mainau lies 6km (4 miles) north of Konstanz, in the arm of the Bodensee known as the Überlingersee. Here, palms and orange trees grow and fragrant flowers bloom year-round, practically in the shadow of the snow-covered Alps. The Baden princes discovered long ago that the island, protected from harsh winter winds, enjoys a freak microclimate where vegetation can grow year-round; the most delicate of tropical plants are given greenhouse protection, however. The late Swedish Count Lennart Bernadotte is credited with this botanical oasis, and his daughter Countess Bettina Bernadotte resides in the ancient castle, once a residence of the Knights of the Teutonic Order. Only the island's gardens and parks can be visited by the public. They're open daily March to October 7am to 8pm; in winter, hours are shortened to 9am to 6pm.

There are four restaurants on the island but no overnight accommodations. You can reach Mainau either by tour boat from Konstanz or by walking across the small footbridge connecting the island to the mainland, north of the city. Admission is 16€ for adults, 8.50€ for students and children, 32€ for families, free for children 12 and under. For more information, call © **07531/3030** or visit www.mainau.de.

Where to Eat

O'lac ★ INTERNATIONAL   If you happen to lose at roulette during one of your outings in Konstanz, you can revive your spirits (and drink a few, too) on the lakeside terrace of this casino restaurant. The view is lovely and the food first rate. The restaurant offers a good choice of dishes; try the fresh fish or saddle of lamb. Light and delectable fare includes a soup of coconut and lemon grass, followed by sautéed perch in a white-wine sauce served with green asparagus. The food is complemented by a good wine cellar.

Seestrasse 21. © **07531/815765.** www.o-lac-de. Reservations required. Jacket required for men in the casino. Main courses 19€–25€; fixed-price menus 28€–46€. AE, DC, MC, V. Sun–Thurs 6pm–1am; Fri–Sat 6pm–3am.

NEARBY DINING

Schwedenschenke 🍽 GERMAN/SWEDISH   Visitors sometimes make a pilgrimage to Mainau Island in Lake Constance for a meal in this old-fashioned restaurant. The chef's specialty is assorted lake fish, including perch, pikeperch, and trout. You can also try Hungarian goulash, Swedish meatballs in cream sauce, and *Tafelspitz* (boiled beef with horseradish sauce).

Insel Mainau. ✆ **07531/303156.** Reservations recommended. Main courses lunch 13€–23€, fixed-price menus 41€–56€. AE, DC, MC, V. Daily 11am–11pm. Bus: 4 from the center of Konstanz.

Shopping

The main commercial artery, **Hussenstrasse,** has the best shopping options in this cosmopolitan town. **Jacqueline,** Hussenstrasse 29 (✆ **07531/22990**), has stylish garments for women who seek a more mature look. Men can find tuned-in fashion, both formal and sporty, at **Pierre,** Hussenstrasse 3 (✆ **07531/22150**), and **Holzherr,** Rossgartenstrasse 32 (✆ **07531/128730**).

Entertainment & Nightlife

NIGHTLIFE

Classical music offerings throughout the year are numerous. The concert season of the **Südwestdeutsche Philharmonie Konstanz** (✆ **07531/900810;** www.philharmonie-konstanz.de) runs September to April, and a **summer music festival** is held mid-June to mid-July. There's also an **outdoor music festival** on the island of Mainau for 3 days in July. Contact the visitor information office (see above) for tickets, schedules, and venues. From mid-May to mid-June, the **Bodensee Festival** (✆ **07541/2033300;** www.bodenseefestival.de) offers a mix of classical concerts and theatrical productions, presented at various locations around the shores of the lake. Tickets are 15€ to 40€.

Plays have been staged at the **Stadttheater Konstanz,** Konzilstrasse 11 (✆ **07531/900150;** www.theaterkonstanz.de), Germany's oldest active theater, since 1609. It has its own repertory company. In July and August, the company moves to its summer theater in Meersburg (see "Meersburg," earlier in this chapter). Ticket prices depend on the production.

In the main room of the **Konstanz Casino,** Seestrasse 21 (✆ **07531/81570;** www.casino-konstanz.de), try your luck at blackjack, seven-card stud poker, or roulette. Slot machines are in a side room. Entry requires a passport as proof of age, and there's a cover of 3€. Men are required to wear jackets and ties. The casino is open daily 2pm to 3am and until 4am Friday and Saturday. There's a restaurant on the premises (see "Where to Dine," above), open from 6pm to 1am (until 3am Fri–Sat)

On weekends, the **Theatercafé,** Konzilstrasse 3 (✆ **07531/9785456;** www.theatercafe-kn.de), plays a mix of hip-hop and house late into the night. Good Dixieland jazz and country are found at **Hafenhalle,** Hafenstrasse 10 (✆ **07531/21126;** www.hafenhalle.com), every Sunday. Call for details.

Two **music festivals** featuring contemporary rock, jazz, and cabaret music are held during the summer. For **Sommernächte** (www.sommernaechte.com) an international menagerie of bands descends on the town in late June and early July for a series of concerts held in huge tents. Ticket prices are 8€ to 18€, and 20€ for a 3-day pass, with a few free shows, too. Throngs of revelers flood the town at the end of August for the annual **Rock Am See Festival** (✆ **07531/908844;** www.rock-am-see.de), where a 58€ ticket buys you admission to an all-day event that draws international stars.

OUTDOOR PURSUITS

If you'd like to go biking along the lake, visit **Velotours,** Bücklestrasse 13 (✆ **07531/98280;** www.velotours.de), where rentals cost from 13€ per day. Bike tours are available. The shop is open April to October daily 8am to 5pm.

Where to Stay

Barbarossa ★ ☺   The Wiedemann family welcomes you to this time-tested favorite, which has both modern and traditional architectural elements. Rooms come in a wide array of options, from a small, simple single to a large double. All the accommodations have been modernized and are comfortably furnished. Rooms are individually decorated and many have their own themes, such as Romeo and Juliet for romantic stopovers or Barbarossa for more "warlike" guests. A number of family rooms are also rented, suitable for three to four guests.

Obermarkt 8-12, 78462 Konstanz. www.hotelbarbarossa.de. ⓒ **07531/128990.** Fax 07531/12899700. 55 units. 95€-130€ double; 155€ family unit. AE, DC, MC, V. Parking 7€. **Amenities:** Restaurant; bar; room service. *In room:* TV.

Buchner Hof   Though located in Petershausen, this hotel is just a short walk from most points of interest. The pleasantly furnished rooms range from small to medium. Some bathrooms have showers only, others tub/shower combos. The hotel is named after composer Hans Buchner, who became organist at the town cathedral in 1510 and was one of the first musicians to arrange and catalog the wealth of Gregorian chants found in the region.

Buchnerstrasse 6, 78464 Konstanz. www.buchner-hof.de. ⓒ **07531/81020.** Fax 07531/810240. 13 units. 110€-140€ double. Rates include buffet breakfast. AE, DC, MC, V. Free outdoor parking; 10€ in garage. In Petershausen, across the Rhine from Konstanz. **Amenities:** Bikes; spa. *In room:* TV, hair dryer, minibar.

Steigenberger Inselhotel ★★★   The Insel started life as a Dominican monastery in the 13th century; now it's the single finest place to stay along the German side of the lake. It has a prime location on an island, with its own lakeside gardens and dock. The white step-gabled building holds an inner Romanesque cloister. Most of the spacious doubles have a living-room look, with sofas, armchairs, and tidy bathrooms with tub/shower combos.

Auf der Insel 1, 78462 Konstanz. www.konstanz.steigenberger.com. ⓒ **800/223-5652** in the U.S. and Canada, or 07531/1250. Fax 07531/125250. 102 units. 237€-282€ double; 320€-440€ suite. Rates include buffet breakfast. AE, DC, MC, V. Parking 12€. **Amenities:** 2 restaurants; bar; babysitting; bikes; exercise room; room service; sauna. *In room:* TV, hair dryer, minibar, Wi-Fi (5€ per hour).

REICHENAU ★

10km (6¼ miles) NW of Konstanz

In the more southerly of the two arms that stretch westward from the Bodensee, Reichenau is a small historic island that was only recently connected to the mainland by a causeway. By the end of the 800s, it was the site of three separate monasteries, the oldest of which had been established in 724. Later, Reichenau became a political force within the Holy Roman Empire. Today, much of the island is devoted to cultivating vegetables and salad greens, and consequently has a sedate aura, much prized by escapists looking for a quiet getaway.

Essentials

GETTING THERE

BY TRAIN   Reichenau's railway station lies midway between the larger railway junctions of Radolfzell (to the west) and Konstanz (to the east). Trains from throughout Germany and Switzerland make frequent stops at both those cities, from which passengers heading to Reichenau can transfer onto a small railway line that makes runs at hourly intervals on to Bahnhof Reichenau. Buses from Bahnhof Reichenau to Insel Reichenau (the city's historic core) take 10 minutes each way. For information, call ℂ **01805/996633.**

BY BUS Bus service to Reichenau is limited and inconvenient. For information, call **SBG GmbH** (ℂ **07732/99470;** www.suedbadenbus.de).

BY CAR From Konstanz, take Rte. 33 east to Reichenau.

BY BOAT For information about the ferryboats that ply the waters between Reichenau and the German lakeside hamlet of Allensbach, running April to October only, call ℂ **07533/98848** or visit www.schifffahrtbaumann.de.

VISITOR INFORMATION

The tourist office is the **Verkehrsbüro,** Pirminstrasse 145 (ℂ **07534/92070;** www. reichenau.de). April to October, it's open Monday to Friday 9am to 12:30pm and 1:30 to 5pm; November to March, hours are Monday to Friday 9am to 12:30pm and 1:30 to 4pm.

Exploring Reichenau

The island is divided into three separate villages (Oberzell, Mittelzell, and Niederzell), each of which is centered on the remains of a medieval monastery. The most impressive of these is the **Münster St. Maria und Markus,** Burgstrasse (ℂ **07534/249**), in Mittelzell. Originally founded in 725, it became one of the most important centers of learning in the Carolingian era. It reached its peak around 1000, when it was the home of about 700 monks. The structure is beautiful in its simplicity. Its treasury displays several reliquaries, including the original St. Mark reliquary, as well as a rare 9th-centruy Evangeliary containing the four gospels. Entrance is free, but a visit to the treasury costs 2€ for adults, 1€ for students, and free for children 14 and under. The church is open daily year-round 9am to 6pm; its treasury is open only May to October Monday to Saturday 11am to noon and 3 to 4pm. While you're in the vicinity, notice the **Kräutergarten (Herb Garden),** in the shadow of the cathedral on the Hermann Contractus Strasse. It emulates the herb and vegetable gardens maintained by monks in the Middle Ages.

The hamlet of Niederzell is home to **Stiftskirche St. Peter and St. Paul,** Egino-Strasse (no phone). If it's not open when you arrive, the tourist office will call someone to unlock the gates for you. In 1990, during restorations of the church's apse, a series of Romanesque frescoes were uncovered and are now on view.

The nearby hamlet of Oberzell houses **Stiftskirche St. George,** Seestrasse (no phone). Rising abruptly from a cabbage field, it has a severely dignified, very simple facade and a series of charmingly naive medieval frescoes inside. It's open daily 9am to 6pm. Admission is free.

A final site in Mittelzell worth a stop is the **Heimatmuseum,** Ergat 1 (ℂ **07534/999321;** www.museumreichenau.de). This is a showcase for the handicrafts and folklore that developed on Reichenau and the surrounding region. It's open April to October Tuesday to Sunday 10:30am to 4:30pm, plus November to March only Saturday and Sunday 2 to 5pm. Entrance costs 3€ adults, 1.50€ children. For further information, contact the local tourist office (see above).

Where to Eat

Restaurant Strandhotel Löchnerhaus GERMAN/INTERNATIONAL This restaurant, with its hardworking, kindly staff, is the traditional favorite of many locals. The modern-style dining room has lake views. Menu items include sea bass cooked either in Riesling sauce or in a potato crust, whitefish from the Bodensee, rack of lamb with horseradish and mint, grilled meats such as steak, and a savory version of goulash.

Schiffslände 12. (✆) **07534/8030.** Reservations recommended. Main courses 15€–28€. AE, DC, MC, V. Daily noon–2pm and 6–9pm. Closed Nov–Feb.

Shopping

For a sampling of the many wines produced within the Bodensee region, head for **Winzer Vereins,** Münsterplatz ((✆) **07534/293;** www.winzerverein-reichenau.de), where you'll be able to see rack upon rack of local vintages. You can even try a single glass to decide if you want to buy a bottle.

Entertainment & Nightlife

Those seeking a night on the town often drive over to nearby Konstanz. Life is considerably quieter in the more demure Reichenau after dark. Most visitors who come in summer prefer to sit out on one of the *Terrassen am See* (lakeside terraces), enjoying the beer, the company, and mostly the romantic views of the town at night. The best of these are at the two hotels recommended below, **Seehotel Seeschau** and **Strandhotel Löchnerhaus.** When the weather is foul, the best place for a drink is the **Kaminstube,** also at the Seehotel Seeschau.

Where to Stay

Seehotel Seeschau ★ This comfortable, well-maintained hotel is set directly beside the lake. It features good-size rooms with upscale reproductions of antique furniture and, in many cases, views over the lake. This hotel is especially appealing in the midsummer, when the flowers around its windows burst into bloom.

An der Schiffslände 8, 78479 Reichenau. www.seeschau.mdo.de. (✆) **07534/257.** Fax 07534/7264. 23 units. 128€–180€ double; from 240€ suite. Rates include continental breakfast. AE, DC, MC, V. Free parking. **Amenities:** 2 restaurants; bar; babysitting; room service. *In room:* TV, hair dryer, minibar, Wi-Fi (free).

Strandhotel Löchnerhaus ★ This is a good, well-managed hotel, close to the lakefront and its own boat pier. It's set within a pleasant garden and offers well-maintained rooms, many of which have private verandas or terraces and lake views.

An der Schiffslände 12, 78478 Reichenau. www.strandhotel-reichenau.de. (✆) **07534/8030.** Fax 07534/582. 42 units. 75€–125€ per person double. Rates include buffet breakfast. AE, DC, MC, V. Parking 12€. Closed Nov–Feb. **Amenities:** Restaurant. *In room:* TV, hair dryer, minibar.

ÜBERLINGEN ★

40km (25 miles) N of Konstanz, 46km (29 miles) E of Ravensburg, 24km (15 miles) W of Friedrichshafen

Locals call the town of Überlingen, founded in the 1200s, a German version of Nice because of its sunny weather and lakeside location. It's also one of the best-preserved medieval sites along the Bodensee.

Essentials

GETTING THERE

BY TRAIN Rail passengers are funneled through nearby Friedrichshafen, from where a smaller rail line goes through Überlingen to Radolfzell. Trains run in either direction along that line at hourly intervals throughout the day. Überlingen's railway station lies on the extreme western edge of town. For rail information, call ✆ **01805/996633.**

BY BUS   Regional bus service along Lake Constance is provided by **RAB Regionalverkehr Alb-Bodensee GmbH** in nearby Weingarten (✆ **0751/509220;** www.zugbus-rab.de).

BY CAR   Überlingen is off Rte. 31, just north of Konstanz. From Stuttgart via Ulm, take Rte. 30 south, then Rte. 31 west at Friedrichshafen. From Munich, follow Autobahn 96 west/southwest to Lindau, then Rte. 31 west to Friedrichshafen and Überlingen.

BY BOAT   April to October, 8 to 10 ferryboats a day carry passengers to Überlingen from Konstanz (trip time: up to 2 hr.) for 9.50€ each way. For information, call the **Weiss Flote,** an armada of lake steamers maintained by the BSB Bodensee Schiffs-betriebe GmbH (✆ **07531/3640389;** www.bsb-online.com). No cars are carried on any of these ferries.

VISITOR INFORMATION

Tourist information is available at Landungsplatz 5 (✆ **07551/991122;** www.ueber lingen.de), May to September Monday to Friday 9am to 6pm, Saturday 10am to 3pm, and Sunday 10am to 1pm; November to March Monday to Wednesday and Friday 9am to noon and 1 to 4pm, Thursday 9am to noon and 1 to 6pm; and April and October Monday to Friday 9am to noon and 1 to 5pm, and Saturday 10am to 1pm.

Exploring Überlingen

The most important of the city monuments is the **Münster St. Nikolaus** ★, a surprisingly large medieval structure that required 200 years to build. The larger of its two towers functioned during wars as a military watchtower and was later capped with an eight-sided Renaissance lantern. The severely dignified exterior is offset by an elaborate and intricate Gothic interior. Take special notice of the main altarpiece, carved in the early 1600s by Jorg Zürn. It is open daily 8am to 6pm. Entrance is free.

On the opposite side of the square is Überlingen's **Rathaus** ★, built in the late 1400s. Most of its interior is devoted to municipal offices, except for the Ratsaal, whose vaulted ceiling and lavishly paneled walls make it the most beautiful public room in town. Notice the coats of arms representing various factions of the Holy Roman Empire. Hours are Monday to Friday 9am to noon and 2:30 to 5pm; in summer, it is also open Saturday 9am to noon. Entrance is free.

The city maintains a **Heimatmuseum (Museum of Folklore)** within one of its most prized buildings, the Reichlin-von-Meldegg Haus, Krummeberggasse 30 (✆ **07551/991079;** www.museum-ueberlingen.de). This building artfully emulates the style of the Florentine Renaissance. Inside, you can also visit both a chapel and a lavishly ornate rococo ballroom. The museum is open only April to October Tuesday to Thursday and Saturday 9am to 12:30pm and 2 to 5pm, and Friday and Sunday 10am to 3pm. Admission is 5€ adults, 1€ children, and free for children 5 and under.

Also look for the **Franziskanerkirche,** Spitalgasse. Especially striking is the contrast between this church's severely dignified exterior and its lavishly baroque interior. It is open daily 8am to noon and 2 to 5pm.

The townspeople of Überlingen took great care to ornament the medieval fortifications that protected them from outside invaders. The best preserved of these walls is the **Stadtmauer,** which in recent times was landscaped into a graceful ramble lined with trees and shrubbery. It's part of the encircling walls that flank the north and east sides of town.

The pleasant Seepromenade (lake promenade) offers a panoramic view of the faraway Swiss Alps. Nearby stands the **Greth,** one of the largest old buildings in town and originally a market and storage vault for corn.

Where to Eat & Stay

Landgasthöf zum Adler   In the confines of a bucolic hamlet (Lippertsreute), this hotel/restaurant occupies two antique buildings, the older of which was built 300 years ago. Rooms are cozy, unpretentious, and appealingly (and artfully) rustic. All rooms contain neat, modern bathrooms.

The restaurant serves heaping, well-prepared portions of German/Swabian dishes such as *Spanferkel* (roast suckling pig), *Zwiebelrostbraten* (onion-flavored roast beef), and Bodensee whitefish prepared with white-wine sauce. Main courses cost 10€ to 22€. It's open Friday to Wednesday from 11:45am to 2pm and Friday to Tuesday from 5 to 9pm.

Hauptstrasse 44, Lippertsreute, 88662 Überlingen. www.adler-lippertsreute.de. ✆ **07553/82550.** Fax 07553/825570. 16 units. 72€–102€ double. Rates include continental breakfast. MC, V. Parking 5€. Closed Nov. 10km (6¼ miles) north of the center. **Amenities:** Restaurant; room service; Wi-Fi (free; in lobby). *In room:* TV, hair dryer.

Parkhotel St. Leonhard ★★   Set on a hilltop, this hotel allows urban visitors to rest and recharge. The woodsy-looking chalet is flanked by more angular, modern annexes. Rooms are of good size, modern, conservative, comfortable, and well designed. The kitchen succeeds admirably in serving both regional and international cuisine in three unpretentious restaurants. The food is consistently good and is prepared with market-fresh ingredients. Main courses cost 9.50€ to 24€.

Obere St. Leonhard-Strasse 71, 88662 Überlingen. www.parkhotel-st-leonhard.de. ✆ **07551/808100.** Fax 07551/808531. 170 units. 145€–205€ double; 350€–640€ suite. Rates include buffet breakfast. AE, MC, V. Free parking. 1.5km (1 mile) north of the center. **Amenities:** 3 restaurants; bar; babysitting; exercise room; indoor heated pool; spa; 3 lit tennis courts (1 indoor). *In room:* TV, hair dryer, minibar, Wi-Fi (free).

Schäpfle ★ 👶   With bedrooms opening onto balconies, most of which are decorated in a romantic style with eiderdowns and draped fabrics, this hotel has a lot of character. In the heart of the resort, the hotel might as well be in the country, with its rustic design touches and a slightly old-fashioned aura in spite of the up-to-date furnishings. Bedrooms are spread across two buildings, one opening right on the lake. Guests and locals gather in the on-site tavern, serving specialties of southern Germany.

Jakob-Kessenringstrasse 14, 88662 Überlingen. www.schaepfle.de. ✆ **07551/63494.** Fax 07551/67695. 32 units. 89€–102€ double. No credit cards. **Amenities:** Restaurant; bar; room service. *In room:* TV.

RAVENSBURG

20km (12 miles) N of Friedrichshafen, 32km (20 miles) N of Lindau

Ravensburg isn't on Lake Constance, but it's nearby and makes a good side trip. The town boasts one of the most impeccably preserved medieval cores in the region. During the 1400s, the linen trade made Ravensburg into one of the richest towns in Germany, but economic stagnation set in during the 1600s as a result of the Thirty Years' War. Today, this quiet town is a tourist's delight.

Essentials

GETTING THERE

BY TRAIN   Most passengers change trains in nearby Ulm. From Ulm, trains depart at hourly intervals for Friedrichshafen, stopping en route in Ravensburg (trip time: 1 hr.). For information call ℂ **01805/996633.**

BY BUS   Most bus routes into Ravensburg start at nearby villages and hamlets. For information, call ℂ **0751/2766.**

BY CAR   From Stuttgart, follow Autobahn 8 east to the city of Ulm, then turn south onto Rte. 30 directly into Ravensburg. From along Lake Constance, you can take routes B33, B30, or 467 north to Ravensburg.

VISITOR INFORMATION

Head to the **Stadtverkehrsamt,** Kirchstrasse 16 (ℂ **0751/82800;** www.ravensburg. de). It's open Monday to Friday 9am to 5:30pm and Saturday 10am to 1pm.

Exploring Ravensburg

You'll appreciate that cars are banned from the narrow labyrinth of alleyways within Ravensburg's historic core. Two of the most evocative streets are **Untere Breite Strasse** and **Charlottenstrasse,** both of which lie near the town's central square. Lining the Marienplatz are the late-Gothic **Rathaus;** the 14th-century **Kornhaus,** once one of the largest corn exchanges in the region and now the town's library; and the **Waaghaus,** originally built in the 1400s as a warehouse for municipal supplies and now a bank. Look also for the old city **watchtower** and the Renaissance-era **Lederhaus,** the town's post office.

Also on the Marienplatz is the **Karmelitenklosterkirche.** Originally a monastery in the 14th century, it later housed a mercantile association devoted to the promotion of the linen trade. The complex's church can be visited every day from 8am to 6pm. Nearby, at the corner of Kirchstrasse and the Herrenstrasse, is the **Liebfrauenkirche,** the parish church of Ravensburg. Deceptively simple on the outside, the 14th-century structure has been radically but authentically reconstructed on the inside. Look for remnants of original stained glass and a heavy somberness reminiscent of the Middle Ages.

Ravensburg's only noteworthy museum is its **Heimatmuseum,** devoted to local folklore and handicrafts. It lies within the Volkhaus, Torplatz 7 (for information contact the tourist office), and is open Tuesday to Friday 2 to 8pm, Saturday and Sunday 2 to 3pm. Admission is free.

📷 Scaling the Ramparts

Part of Ravensburg's allure is its well-preserved network of medieval fortifications, studded with defensive towers. The most visible is the 52m (170-ft.) **Mehlsack Tower,** adopted as the municipal symbol of Ravensburg itself. You can climb to its heights by means of 240 heavily worn, circular steps, but only on Saturday and Sunday from April to October, 10am to 3pm. The central, 51m (167-ft.) **Blaserturm** at Marienplatz is open Monday to Friday 2 to 5pm, and Saturday 10am to 3pm. Entrance to either tower is 1.50€ for adults, 1 € for children 12 to 18, and free for children 11 and under.

Where to Eat

Romantik Hotel Waldhorn Restaurant ★★★ MODERN INTERNATIONAL
This sophisticated restaurant is run by celebrity chef Albert Bouley. The stylish, gracefully antique dining room has massive ceiling beams. The Asian-influenced cuisine is among the most subtle, celebrated, and exotic in Germany. Menu items combine Eastern and Western culinary traditions with verve and zest, and change according to the seasons and the inspiration of the much-praised chef. You can order such delectable dishes as tender, well-flavored medallions of lamb with miso, lemon zest, and a mint tempura. Grilled sole is a wake-up to the palate with its exotic flavorings of chili and tamarind. If you want to become both a gourmet and a gourmand, opt for the fixed-price menu. Although it changes nightly, it usually features such inspired dishes as salad of breast of duck in lemon oil with a ragout of shrimp, lobster, and mussels seasoned with fresh herbs; sole with goose liver and fresh asparagus; and filet of stag with goat cheese. Desserts are spectacular.

Marienplatz 15. (*C*) **0751/36120.** Reservations recommended. Main courses 20€–32€. AE, DC, MC, V. Wed–Sat 11:30am–2pm; Tues–Sat 6–10:30pm.

Where to Stay

Hotel-Gasthof Obertor *⬧* This is the town's best choice for frugal travelers. This hotel was built in the 12th century as a farmhouse and is almost as old as the town. It has a lovely garden terrace in front and a park in the back. Rooms vary greatly in size and personality, so you may want to take a peek at a couple before deciding which to take. Turn-of-the-20th-century antiques abound, mostly made of cherrywood—typical of the Bodensee area.

Marktstrasse 67, 88212 Ravensburg. www.hotelobertor.de. (*C*) **0751/36670.** Fax 0751/3667200. 31 units. 110€–125€ double; from 160€ suite. Rates include continental breakfast. AE, DC, MC, V. Free outdoor parking; 7€ in the garage. **Amenities:** Restaurant; babysitting; Jacuzzi; room service; sauna. *In room:* TV, hair dryer, Wi-Fi (12€ per day).

Romantik Hotel Waldhorn ★★ The most appealing hotel in Ravensburg occupies a late-18th-century building and a more modern annex. Because both buildings lie within the town's all-pedestrian zone, it's easy to get a sense of the relaxed local lifestyle. Rooms are comfortable and cozy, and the staff is very charming. All rooms have a midsize to large bathroom. Das Rebleutehaus, one of the hotel's restaurants, serves Swabian specialties such as *Spätzle* and large ravioli stuffed with meat and spinach.

Marienplatz 15, 88212 Ravensburg. www.waldhorn.de. (*C*) **0751/36120.** Fax 07151/3612100. 42 units. 135€–150€ double; 190€ suite. Rates include buffet breakfast. AE, MC, V. Parking 8€. **Amenities:** 2 restaurants; babysitting; room service. *In room:* TV, hair dryer, minibar (in some), Wi-Fi (15€ per day).

A Side Trip to Weingarten

A major archaeological excavation is located within the agrarian hamlet of Weingarten, a sleepy village 5km (3 miles) north of Ravensburg. To reach the village, take bus no. 1, 2, or 5 from Marienplatz. In the 1950s, teams of archaeologists discovered one of the richest troves of German graves in the country. Artifacts from the dig lie in the **Alamannen Museum,** located in Kornhaus, Karlstrasse 28 ((*C*) **0751/405125**). It's open Tuesday to Sunday 2 to 5pm (Thurs until 6pm). Admission is 3.50€.

Weingarten is also home to the largest baroque church in Germany, the **Weingarten Basilica** ((*C*) **0751/561270**), which rises to about 60m (200 ft.). It was established in 1056 by the wife of a prominent official in the Guelph dynasty. Inside is one of the holiest relics in Germany, a mystical vial, which, according to legend, contains several drops of Christ's blood. The relic was entrusted to the convent by the sister-in-law of William the Conqueror, the Guelph Queen Juditha. Another highlight of the church is the organ with 6666 pipes, one of the largest in the country. Its installation required 13 years, beginning in 1737. Also noteworthy are the ceiling frescoes by Cosmas Damian Asam, one of the leaders of the Baroque School. The church is open daily 8am to 6pm.

Finally, if you can manage to schedule your visit for the day after Ascension (the Thurs 40 days after Easter), you can witness the *Blutritt*, a massive **procession** of pilgrims, at the head of which are more than 3,000 horsemen. The breeding of horses for this procession is a matter of quiet pride among local farmers. For information, visit www.blutfreitag.de.

For information on Weingarten, call the **tourist office** at Münsterplatz (© **0751/405232;** www.weingarten-online.de).

10

Ravensburg

LAKE CONSTANCE (BODENSEE)

THE BLACK FOREST (SCHWARZWALD)

Although called "black," this very green region in southwest Germany, roughly 145km (90 miles) long and 40km (25 miles) wide, possesses some of the country's purest nature, as well as its most fervent aficionados of everything green. Known as Silva Nigra to the Romans, this once dark and uncharted forest has long since been cultivated and inhabited, but still retains plenty of sky-bound pine and birch trees blanketing the mountainsides. The streams and lakes provide relaxing fishing and swimming opportunities, while the countless trails entice the wandering spirit. In the valleys village artisans preserve local crafts like clock-making, while drivers enjoy the serpentine routes strewn across the landscape (to the possible dismay of any nausea-prone passengers).

GETTING TO THE BLACK FOREST   International airports serve the area from Stuttgart (see chapter 12) and the Swiss city of Basel, which is 70km (43 miles) from Freiburg im Breisgau, the "capital" of the Black Forest. Trains run north and south through the Rhine Valley, with fast, frequent service to such Black Forest towns as Freiburg and Baden-Baden. Motorists should take the A5 Autobahn, which runs the length of the Schwarzwald. From Lake Constance (see chapter 10), continue along the B31 for 65km (40 miles) until you reach the Black Forest.

EXPLORING THE REGION BY CAR   Roads through the forest are excellent, especially the **Schwarzwaldhochstrasse** (Black Forest High Rd. or Ridgeway, Rte. B500), which runs through the northern part the region, from Baden-Baden to Freudenstadt. Another unforgettable route, the **Schwarzwald Panoramastrasse** (Black Forest Panorama Rd.), winds through the southern half of the region from Waldkirch near Freiburg to Hinterzarten just west of Titisee. On either road you'll have many opportunities to park your car and explore the countryside or to turn off on one of the side roads leading to hospitable villages, ancient castles, and rolling farmlands. Other themed routes include the Uhrenstrasse (Clock Road), not to be confused with the hiking paths used by clock makers, and the Deutsche Fachwerkstrasse (German Half-timber Rd.). For information, visit www.schwarzwaldhochstrasse.de, www.deutsche-uhrenstrasse.de, and www.deutsche-fachwerkstrasse.de.

FREIBURG IM BREISGAU ★★

208km (129 miles) SW of Stuttgart, 70km (44 miles) N of Basel (Switzerland), 280km (174 miles) S of Frankfurt

Because of its climate—the city is in the path of warm air currents that come up from the Mediterranean—Freiburg is a year-round attraction and sports center. In early spring, the town usually bursts into bloom while the surrounding mountain peaks remain covered with snow. In the fall, the smell of new wine fills the narrow streets even as snow falls on nearby peaks.

Essentials

GETTING THERE **By Train** Frequent trains connect Freiburg to major airports in Basel (Switzerland) and Stuttgart. Daily trains arrive from Frankfurt (trip time: 2 hr.) and Hamburg (trip time: 6 hr.), as well as from Berlin and Zürich (Switzerland). For information, call ✆ 01805/996633 or visit www.bahn.de.

By Bus Long-distance bus service is provided by **Südbaden Bus GmbH,** Central Bus Station, Freiburg (✆ 0761/3680388; www.suedbadenbus.de), with service from Freiburg to EuroAirport Basel-Mulhouse; and by **EuroRegioBus** (✆ 0761/3680388), which has a bus between Freiburg and the French cities of Mulhouse and Colmar.

By Car Access by car is via the A5 Autobahn north and south.

VISITOR INFORMATION For tourist information, contact **Freiburg Tourist Board,** Rathausplatz 2–4 (✆ 0761/3881880; www.freiburg.de). The office is open June to September Monday to Friday 8am to 8pm, Saturday 9:30am to 5pm, and Sunday 10am to noon (Oct–May Mon–Fri 8am–6pm, Sat 9:30am–2:30pm, and Sun 10am–noon).

GETTING AROUND Freiburg is well served by buses and trams, the latter running in the inner city. A one-way fare costs 2.10€; a 24-hour day pass is 5.30€. For schedules and information, or to buy passes, go to VAG Plus-Punkt, Salzstrasse 3 (✆ 0761/4511500; www.vag-freiburg.de), in the Altstadt. Hours are Monday to Friday 8am to 7pm and Saturday 8:30am to 4pm. Most of the city's public transportation network shuts down from 12:30 to 5:30am.

Exploring Freiburg

Augustiner Museum ★ MUSEUM Housed in the former church and monastery of the Order of St. Augustine, this museum contains the town's finest collection of art, including religious art spanning more than 1,000 years. Among the treasures are some of the cathedral's original stained-glass windows, as well as the most important of its medieval gold and silver treasures, brought here for safekeeping. Among the best works in the collection are *The Snow Miracle* by Matthias Grünewald and works by Hans Baldung Grien, who was a pupil of Albrecht Dürer. There's also a rich collection of fine late-Gothic wooden sculpture, as well as Art Nouveau glass objects.

Augustinerplatz. ✆ 0761/2012531. www.augustinermuseum.de. Admission 6€ adults, free for children 17 and under. Tues–Sun 10am–5pm. Tram: 1.

Freiburg Cathedral ★★ CHURCH This cathedral is one of the great masterpieces of Gothic art in Germany. Its unique spire is of filigree stonework; the steeple sits on an octagonal belfry, which holds a historic 4,500-kilogram (5-ton) bell dating

0   10 mi

0   10 km

Canal de la Marne au Rhin

Willgottheim

Haguenau

Moder

Rhine

Kuppenheim

Gaggenau

Brumath

Rheinau

Baden-Baden

To Calw →

Weyersheim

36

A5

500

462

294

Marlenheim

Bühl

Raumündzach

Strasbourg

Achern

Schwarzwaldhochstrasse

Molsheim

28

3

Oberkirch

A35

Offenburg

28

500

Barr

Neuried

28

Freudenstadt

F R A N C E

Gengenbach

83

36

Rhine

500

462

Lahr/Schwarzwald

Alpirsbach

Selestat

3

Zell am Harmersbach

Waldmössingen

Rhein

468

Ettenheim

Wolfach

Herbolzheim

294

Hornberg

462

Dunningen

Elsenheim

Kenzingen

33

Zimmern

Muntzenheim

Waldkirch

Triberg

A5

Schwarzwald Panoramastrasse

Triberger Wasserfälle

A81

Kandel

Furtwangen

Freiburg im Breisgau

St. Peter

Schwenningen

St. Märgen

500

A864

Hirtzfelden

Bad Krozingen

Schauinsland

31

Donaueschingen

Hüfingen

Hinterzarten

Titisee

Staufen

Titisee

Löffingen

Belchen

Feldberg

Lenzkirch

Blumberg

Badenweiler

Schluchsee

Todtnau

Bernau

Bonndorf

3

317

500

Häusern

314

Kandern

Zell im Wiesental

Schopfheim

Waldshut-Tiengen

A5

Wehr

A35

Lörrach

GERMANY

A98

Hamburg

• Berlin ★

Frankfurt am Main •

Area of detail

Basel

Rhein (Rhine)

• Munich

Prätteln

Döttingen

SWITZERLAND

from 1258. Although begun in 1200 in the Romanesque style, by the time it was completed in 1620, the builders had incorporated various Gothic styles.

Upon entering by the south door, you'll be in the transept facing an early-16th-century sculpture of the adoration of the Christ Child by the Magi. If you turn left into the nave, you'll see at the far end of the aisle, by the entrance to the tower, a fine 13th-century statue of the Virgin flanked by two adoring angels. The high altar has an altarpiece built between 1512 and 1516 by Hans Baldung Grien. Resting against one of the Renaissance pillars along the aisle is a carved 16th-century pulpit, with stairs winding around the curve of the column. The figures below the stairs are likenesses of the townspeople, including the sculptor.

In the aisles are 14th-century stained-glass windows. The oldest stained glass, dating from the 13th century, is in the small round windows of the south transept. Some pieces, however, have been removed to the Augustiner Museum and replaced by more recent panels.

Münsterplatz. ✆ **0761/202790.** www.freiburgermuenster.info. Admission: Cathedral free; tower 2€ adults, 1€ students, free for children 14 and under. Cathedral year-round Mon–Sat 10am–5pm; Sun 1–7:30pm. Tower May–Oct Mon–Sat 9:30am–5pm, Sun 1–5pm; Nov–Apr Wed–Sat 9:30am–5pm. Tram: 1, 2, 3, or 5.

Museum für Neue Kunst MUSEUM   This modern art collection was formerly housed in the Augustiner Museum. Painting and sculpture, beginning with examples of German expressionism, *Neue Sachlichkeit,* and other classic modern works, especially by artists of southwest Germany, are displayed here.

Marienstrasse 10A. ✆ **0761/2012581.** www.museen.freiburg.de. Admission 3€ adults, 2€ students, free for children 6 and under. Tues–Sun 10am–5pm. Tram: 1, 2, 3, or 5.

MORE SIGHTS IN THE ALTSTADT

In Münsterplatz, across from the cathedral, is the **Kaufhaus (Customs House),** the most colorful building in Freiburg. This Gothic structure, with oriel windows at each end, was originally an ancient emporium, to which a balcony was added in 1550. Above the massive supporting arches, the facade is decorated with the statues of four emperors of the Habsburg dynasty, of whom all but one visited Freiburg during his reign. Unfortunately, the inside cannot be visited.

Where to Eat

Even if you're not staying at the **Kühler Krug,** recommended below, consider it for lunch or dinner.

Eichhalde ★★ FRENCH/GERMAN   This notable French bistro lies in the Herden district, a 20-minute walk from the center. It gets a lot of neighborhood patronage. Fixed-price lunches and dinners are available. The chef has steadily built up a local reputation, and the cuisine is based on the clever handling of first-rate, often luxurious ingredients. The appetizers are tantalizing, including the likes of grilled marinated salmon with a papaya sauce, or a salad of fresh artichokes seasoned with chili pepper and served with sautéed octopus.

Stadtstrasse 91. ✆ **0761/54817.** www.eichhalde.online.de. Reservations required. Main courses 21€–29€; fixed-price menus 26€–46€. MC, V. Wed–Sun noon–3pm and 6–10pm. Closed 2 weeks in mid-Apr. Bus: 27.

Markgräfler Hof GERMAN   This restaurant and *Weinstube* serves a savory cuisine with market-fresh ingredients. The former 1741 mansion of the von Kagenneck family, this neoclassical villa has been restored and is today an elegant setting for dining, with a decor that features both antiques and modern art. Fresh, local products

AN EXCURSION TO THE upper BLACK FOREST

From Freiburg, you can make a 145km (90-mile) 1-day circuit through one of the most scenic parts of the Black Forest, returning in time for dinner. Along the way, you'll pass a trio of the highest summits in the Black Forest and two of the region's most beautiful lakes.

Head immediately south to **Schauinsland** along Rte. 317, a narrow twisting road. At the car park, you can climb some 100 steps to the belvedere tower for a panoramic view of the area.

Continuing south, you reach **Belchen Mountain,** which rises to a height of 1,414m (4,640 ft.). From where the road ends, it is an easy 20-minute hike to the summit. On a clear day, you can look out from the observation platform here and take in a panoramic sweep of the Rhine plain, plus a view of the Alps from Säntis to Mont Blanc.

Continue east to the hamlet of Todtnau, where visitors can walk up a footpath to the **Falls of Todtnau,** about 1.6km (1 mile) away. Back at Todtnau, continue east along Rte. 317 to Feldberg, at 1,493m (4,898 ft.) the highest peak in the region. Here a chairlift takes visitors to the 1,425m (4,675-ft.) **Seebuck** peak, which is crowned by the Bismarck monument and offers another sweeping panoramic view of the Black Forest.

On the road again, follow Rte. 317 east until it becomes Rte. 500 heading south to **Schluchsee,** one of the loveliest lakes of the area and the most important body of water in the Black Forest.

After a visit here, head north along Rte. 500 to the hamlet of **Lenzkirch,** from which you'll have a view of Lake Titisee. The road then continues to the resort of **Titisee** itself (see below). After a visit, you can return to Freiburg by heading west along Rte. 31.

---

are used whenever available. The wine list is limited but choice. Dishes range from asparagus-stuffed ravioli to sautéed butterfish laced with ginger. For dessert, try the elderberry ice cream if featured.

Gerberau 22. ⓒ **0761/32540.** www.markgraeflerhof.de. Reservations recommended. Main courses 17€–26€. AE, DC, MC, V. Tues-Sun noon–2pm and 6–10pm.

Oberkirch's Weinstube 🔥 GERMAN The innkeeper provides excellent regional cooking and comfortable rooms in this traditional establishment. The setting, on a colorful square, is pure picture postcard. The main *Weinstube* is old, with a monumental ceiling-high ceramic stove made with ornate decorative tiles. You get good old-fashioned food here—tasty soups, meat dishes, and poultry—and large helpings. Some of the best-tasting dishes include venison medallions in a cognac-and-pepper sauce; turkey breast medallions in an orange-pepper sauce, or braised veal tongue in a tarragon sauce. In season, you might want to try young pheasant. In the rear is a modern complex fronting an open patio with a fishpond.

The *Weinstube* also has 26 excellent rooms, all with private bathrooms or showers. Doubles cost 146€ to 169€, with continental breakfast included.

Münsterplatz 22. ⓒ **0761/2026868.** Fax 0761/2026869. www.hotel-oberkirch.de. Reservations recommended. Main courses 13€–25€. AE, MC, V. Mon-Sat noon–2pm and 6:30–9:30pm. Closed for 2 weeks in Jan. Tram: 1, 2, 3, or 5.

Zirbelstube ★★ REGIONAL/FRENCH This is one of the most acclaimed restaurants in the area, with a sumptuous setting and gracious and skillful service. Choice ingredients, masterful preparation, and creative presentation delight both the eye and the palate. The menu changes frequently but might include sautéed calf's liver in a Cassis-laced mustard sauce, served with black salsify and potato "cookies," breast of guinea fowl with goose liver and dried fruits on a truffle-laced polenta, or tournedos filet of veal under a caper crust with lime-flavored risotto.

In the Colombi Hotel, Rotteckring 16. ℂ **0761/21060.** www.colombi.de. Reservations required. Main courses 28€–39€. AE, DC, MC, V. Daily noon–3pm and 7–11pm. Tram: 1, 3, or 5.

Entertainment & Nightlife

An impressive entertainment complex, the **Konzerthaus,** hosts a variety of events, ranging from classical music to theater to pop concerts. In June and July, huge tents are raised to house the annual **Zeltmusik festival,** which emphasizes jazz but includes other musical styles as well. Visit www.zmf.de for details. Summer also brings a series of **chamber-music concerts** to the Kaufhaus, in Münsterplatz, and a program of **organ recitals** to the Freiburg Cathedral. Information about all venues and events listed above, including program schedules and ticket sales, is available from **Freiburg Tourist Board** (see above).

The city also has a thriving bar and club scene that goes on into the wee hours. **Jazzhaus,** Schnewlinstrasse 1 (ℂ **0761/2923446;** www.jazzhaus.de; tram: 1, 3, or 5), hosts pop, folk, blues, and jazz shows by international, regional, and local bands. The club is open Wednesday to Sunday 7pm until 1am, with a cover of 10€ to 29€. Until 8pm, the **Café Atlantik,** Schwabentorring 7 (ℂ **0761/33033;** www.cafe-atlantik.de; tram: 1), serves spaghetti platters for 3.50€ to 5€, but later on it's mainly a bar, occasionally with a band. It's open Saturday to Thursday 11am to 2am, Friday 11am till 3am.

Hausbräuerei Feierling, Gerberau 46 (ℂ **0761/243480;** www.feierling.de; tram: 1), is a brewpub, with a beer garden across the street. It's open daily 11am to midnight. Those who want a dark, smoky bar should head to the local Irish pub, the **Isle of Innisfree,** Augustinerplatz 2 (ℂ **0761/22984;** www.isleofinnisfree.de; tram: 1, 2, 3, or 5), which sometimes has live music. **Cafe Brasil,** Wannerstrasse 21 (ℂ **0761/289888;** www.brasil-freiburg.de; tram: 1, 3, or 5), has a tropical feel. It's open daily 10am to 1am.

Where to Stay

In addition to the establishments listed in this section, Oberkirch's Weinstube offers rooms for rent (see "Where to Eat," above).

Best Western Premier Hotel Victoria This is a bastion of Black Forest hospitality, and the location is among the best in town. Founded in 1875, it lies 200m (650 ft.) from the main rail station near the cathedral. Although a historical hotel, it is thoroughly modernized and "green," using many energy-saving devices such as toilet tissue from recycled paper and solar panels to provide much of its heat. The bedrooms are beautifully designed and furnished, with every gadget from electronic key card locks to in-room movies.

Eisenbahnstrasse 54, 79098 Freiburg www.victoria.bestwestern.de.. ℂ **0761/207340.** Fax 0761/20734444. 66 units. 120€–145€ double. AE, DC, MC, V. Parking 10€. **Amenities:** Bar; airport transfers 100€; children's programs; concierge; room service. *In room:* TV, CD player (in some), hair dryer, Wi-Fi (free).

Colombi-Hotel ★★★   The Colombi is the most luxurious hotel in town, and its white walls and angular lines make it easy to spot. Despite its downtown location, the hotel is quiet and peaceful. Many business conferences take place here, but the Colombi caters to independent travelers as well. Rooms are well furnished and appointed, and the suites are especially luxurious.

Rotteckring 16, 79098 Freiburg. www.colombi.de. © **0761/21060.** Fax 0761/31410. 114 units. 250€–275€ double; 298€–320€ junior suite; 550€–850€ suite; 360€ apt. AE, DC, MC, V. Parking 14€. Tram: 1, 3, or 5. **Amenities:** 3 restaurants; bar; babysitting; exercise room; indoor heated pool; room service; spa. *In room:* A/C, TV, hair dryer, minibar, Wi-Fi (free).

Kühler Krug   This cozy inn is better known for its dining than for its rooms, although it makes a good choice if you prefer a familyrun hotel; it lies only 2km (1¼ miles) from the center of town (in the suburb of Günterstal). Fixed-price menus range from 20€ to 45€. A classic regional cuisine with a modern twist is served, with the chefs specializing in fish, which is not just thrown on the grill, but often served with creative sauces such as fresh salmon in a saffron foam. In autumn, many game dishes are offered, including wild rabbit in a hazelnut sauce. The bedrooms upstairs are small to medium in size, comfortably furnished, and well maintained. Walkers and hikers in the Black Forest sing the praise of this old-fashioned inn.

Torplatz 1, 79100 Freiburg-Günterstal. www.kuehlerkrug.de. © **0761/29103.** Fax 0761/29782. 85€–95 double. Rates include buffet breakfast. MC, V. Free parking. Tram: 2. **Amenities:** Restaurant; bar; room service; Wi-Fi (free; in lobby). *In room:* TV.

Park Hotel Post ★   This baroque hotel, with an elaborate zinc cap on its octagonal turret, is within walking distance of Freiburg's major attractions and the rail station. This has been one of the top hotels in town for a long time, although its services and style aren't as good as the Colombi's. The attractively furnished rooms come in a variety of shapes and sizes and are among the most comfortable in town. Breakfast is the only meal served.

Eisenbahnstrasse 37, 79098 Freiburg. www.park-hotel-post.de. © **0761/385480.** Fax 0761/31680. 44 units. 129€–189€ double; 199€–319€ apt. Rates include buffet breakfast. AE, MC, V. Parking 8€. Tram: 1, 3, or 5. **Amenities:** Room service. *In room:* TV, hair dryer, minibar, Wi-Fi (free).

Rappen 👔   This charming inn in the pedestrians-only Altstadt has a lot more cozy Black Forest ambience than its nearby competitors. It's marked with a wrought-iron hanging sign, little dormer windows in its steep roof, window boxes, and shutters. Rooms are small and simply but comfortably furnished; the most desirable have views of the cathedral.

Münsterplatz 13, 79098 Freiburg. www.hotelrappen.de. © **0761/31353.** Fax 0761/382252. 18 units, 13 with bathroom. 124€–150€ double. Rates include buffet breakfast. AE, MC, V. Parking 9€. All trams stop 20m (70 ft.) behind the hotel. Tram: 1, 2, 3, or 5. **Amenities:** Restaurant; room service. *In room:* TV, Wi-Fi (free).

Zum Roten Bären ★   With parts dating from 1120, this is one of the oldest buildings in Freiburg and can claim to be the oldest inn in Germany. Yet, modernity has blended in pleasantly with a recently built wing. The interior is delightfully decorated, emphasizing original construction elements along with scattered pieces of antique furniture. Rooms are well styled and furnished. Try for a unit in the older section, which has more tradition and atmosphere.

Oberlinden 12, 79098 Freiburg. www.roter-baeren.de. © **0761/387870.** Fax 0761/3878717. 25 units. 152€–172€ double; 193€ suite. Rates include buffet breakfast. AE, DC, MC, V. Parking 9€. Tram: 1. **Amenities:** Restaurant; room service; sauna; Wi-Fi (8€ per hour; in lobby). *In room:* TV, hair dryer (in some), minibar (in some).

TITISEE ★

53km (33 miles) E of Freiburg, 160km (99 miles) W of Stuttgart

Titisee is the quintessential German retreat, favored by thousands for its ability to soothe, relax, and refresh the spirit and body. This small lakeside resort, which can be traversed on foot within about 12 minutes, offers access to all the natural bounty of the Schwarzwald. Well-marked hiking trails lead up the hillsides. Motorized vehicles are forbidden on the lake, for the sake of swimmers and general tranquillity. Nearby rises the Feldberg, at 1,500m (5,000 ft.) the highest point in the Black Forest.

Titisee has a year-round population of 2,000, although on busy summer days when visitors come in from nearby cities such as Freiburg, the population can easily swell to three times that amount. More facilities are available at the more workaday community of Neustadt, about 6km (4 miles) away.

Essentials

GETTING THERE   By Train   From Freiburg, trains arrive at intervals of every 30 minutes (trip time: 40 min.). The Titisee rail station is on Parkstrasse. For information call ✆ **01805/996633** or visit www.bahn.de.

By Bus   Bus connections into Titisee are mostly limited to rural hamlets within the surrounding Schwarzwald. For information, call the local bus company at their office in Neustadt, **Südbaden Bus GmbH,** at ✆ **07651/9365880** (www.suedbadenbus.de).

By Car   Titisee is set near the junction of highways B31 and B317, clearly marked from the larger towns that surround it. Driving time from Freiburg is 45 to 60 minutes, depending on traffic; from Stuttgart the trip takes 90 minutes.

VISITOR INFORMATION   Contact the tourist office at Strandbadstrasse 4 (✆ **07651/98040;** www.titisee.de). May to October, it's open Monday to Friday 9am to 6pm, and Saturday and Sunday 10am to 1pm; November to April, it's open Monday to Friday 9am to noon and 1:30 to 5pm.

Exploring the Area

You won't find museums or monuments at this outdoorsy resort, but the cold, clear waters of Lake Titisee are among the most sought-after in the region. The premier bathing spot is **Schwimmbad Titisee,** Strandbadstrasse (✆ **07651/8272**), which combines the chlorinated waters of the town's largest swimming pool with access to a sandy beach adjacent to the lake, complete with cabanas, showers, and refreshment stands. Entrance to the complex costs 3.50€ for adults, 1.90€ for students and children. It's open from mid-May to September daily 9am to 7pm (closed Oct to mid-May).

Except for a handful of medium-size steamers that slowly circumnavigate the lake (see below), local ordinances allow only rowboats, foot-operated paddle boats, and electric (not gas-operated) motorboats on the water's surface, a rule that keeps noise, pollution, and rowdiness to a minimum. You can rent rowboats and paddle boats for 6€ to 9€ per half-hour. About a half-dozen purveyors of these rental craft line the edges of the Seestrasse, the town's main lakefront promenade; the two best are **Drubba** (✆ **07651/981200;** www.drubba.com) and **Schweizer-Winterhalder** (✆ 07651/8214; www.bootsbetrieb-schweizer-titisee.de).

Schweizer-Winterhalder also operates **lake steamers,** which provide a more comfortable excursion. June to September, they depart during the day at hourly intervals from the company's pier. Trips last about 25 minutes and are priced at 4.50€ per person.

Spa clients within Titisee head for the facilities within the **Hotel Brugger,** am See, Strandbadstrasse 14 (**☎ 07651/8010;** www.hotel-brugger.de), which are open to residents of other hotels. In nearby Neustadt, the **Kneipp-Kur** (**☎ 07651/1270;** www.kneipp-kurmittelhaus.de), in the Kurpark, offers an equivalent spa facility, with treatments for cardiac and vascular disorders, rheumatism, and intestinal diseases.

Shoppers and boaters head to the stores that line the lakefront **Seestrasse.** In the early evening, a Bavarian-style marching band promenades along the lakefront, its members stopping at various hotels en route.

Where to Eat

Trescher's Schwarzwaldhotel am See ★ INTERNATIONAL/BLACK FOREST
The formal dining room in this hotel (recommended below), with picture windows opening onto the lake, is the best choice for dining in Titisee. Many of the chef's specialties are regional. Recommended appetizers include sautéed king prawns with a Béarnaise sauce, followed by carefully crafted mains such as slices of duck breasts in a peppery orange sauce or grilled lamb with gratin potatoes. You might also sample the Scottish wild salmon with grilled scampi, bound together with a lobster sauce, or pikeperch filet with truffles and a white port sauce. For dessert, try the Black Forest Cherry Bomb.

Seestrasse 10. **☎ 07651/8050.** Reservations required. Main courses 17€–35€. AE, DC, MC, V. Daily 11:30am–2pm and 6:30-10:30pm.

Where to Stay

Hotel Brugger am See ☛ One of the most affordable lakefront options, this spa hotel offers alluring relaxation and beauty treatments. The building is a modified chalet, with balconies and an all-window dining room for enjoying the view. Rooms are contemporary and mostly a good size, with exceedingly comfortable furnishings and bathrooms.

Strandbadstrasse 14, 79822 Titisee. www.hotel-brugger.de. **☎ 07651/8010.** Fax 07651/8238. 65 units. 130€–158€ double. Rates include buffet breakfast. Half board 28€ per person. AE, MC, V. Free parking. **Amenities:** Restaurant; bar; indoor heated pool; room service; spa; outdoor tennis court (lit). *In room:* TV, hair dryer, Wi-Fi (free).

Parkhotel Waldeck ★ ☛ This hotel is extremely popular, and for good reason— it offers tremendous value and numerous luxuries. A richly decorated interior with Oriental rugs, hexagonal floor tiles, and a beamed and paneled wooden ceiling is very welcoming, as are the helpful staff. The exterior is sheltered against a pine-covered hillock. The small rooms are colorful and comfortable.

Parkstrasse 6, 78922 Titisee. www.parkhotelwaldeck.de. **☎ 07651/8090.** Fax 07651/80999. 66 units. 64€–80€ per person double; 82€–99€ per person suite. Rates include buffet breakfast. AE, DC, MC, V. Parking in garage 7€. **Amenities:** Restaurant; bar; exercise room; indoor heated pool; room service; spa. *In room:* TV, hair dryer, minibar, Wi-Fi (22€ per day).

Trescher's Schwarzwaldhotel am See ★★ This sprawling hotel in the center of the resort is the most comprehensive in Titisee, with three massive annexes, each bordering a flower-filled courtyard constructed on a platform built directly into the waters of the lake. The spacious rooms are graceful and conservatively decorated, all with spick-and-span bathrooms.

Seestrasse 10, 79822 Titisee-Neustadt. www.schwarzwaldhotel-trescher.de. **☎ 07651/8050.** Fax 07651/8116. 84 units. 85€–125€ per person double; 130€–180€ per person suite. Rates include buffet breakfast. AE, DC, MC, V. Parking 14€. **Amenities:** Restaurant; bar; babysitting; bikes; exercise room; indoor heated pool; room service; sauna. *In room:* TV, hair dryer, minibar, Wi-Fi (free).

Where to Eat & Stay Nearby

Just 5km (3 miles) west of Titisee, or 30km (19 miles) east of Freiburg, lies **Hinterzarten,** one of the major pockets of posh within the Black Forest. You may want to retreat here instead of Titisee, as Hinterzarten is more tranquil and luxurious. In the town stands **St. Oswald's,** a church constructed in 1146.

Hotel Reppert ★   Although not rated as highly as the Park Hotel Adler (below), this is a good second choice, a luxurious and traditional hotel in a sunny and central location in a church meadow fronting the village pond. Its many rooms open onto balconies, each shaded by an umbrella. A rich, warm ambience inhabits the comfortable, well-furnished rooms. The lobby is filled with antiques.

The regional/international food served here is exceedingly good and the salad buffet is the best and freshest in the area.

Adlerweg 21–23, 79856 Hinterzarten. www.reppert.de. ⓒ **07652/12080.** Fax 07652/120811. 43 units. 113€–158€ per person double; 150€–156€ per person suite. Rates include half board. AE, DC, MC, V. Free parking. **Amenities:** Restaurant; babysitting; bikes; concierge; exercise room; 3 heated pools (outdoor, indoor, and indoor seawater); room service; spa. *In room:* TV/DVD, CD player, hair dryer, minibar, Wi-Fi (free).

Park Hotel Adler ★★★   This is one of the Black Forest's great inns. Chic and country estate–like with a wealth of leisure facilities, the inn suggests luxury at every turn. Not only is it in the middle of a lovely 4-hectare (10-acre) park, the rooms are sumptuously appointed and beautifully maintained, and many are quite spacious. Beds are so comfortable you won't want to get out of them, and the beautiful bathrooms are well equipped.

The **Wirtshus** attracts serious foodies with finely honed cuisine that ranges from Black Forest specialties such as calves' heads, to international favorites such as filet of sole with scallops in a mushroom cream sauce. For dessert, try the strawberry mousse.

Adlerplatz 3, D-79856 Hinterzarten. www.parkhoteladler.de. ⓒ **07652/1270.** Fax 07652/127717. 146 units. 198€–298€ double; 298€–428€ junior suite; 398€–638€ per person suite. Rates include buffet breakfast. AE, DC, MC, V. Parking 12€. **Amenities:** 2 restaurants; bar; babysitting; exercise room; indoor heated pool; room service; spa. *In room:* TV, hair dryer, minibar, MP3 docking station, Wi-Fi (free).

TRIBERG ★

138km (86 miles) SW of Stuttgart, 48km (30 miles) NE of Freiburg

Triberg, deep in the heart of the Black Forest, is home to the highest waterfall in the country. It also claims to be the birthplace of the cuckoo clock, so if you're in the market for a traditional timepiece, this is the place to find it. You'll also find many little shops selling woodcarvings, music boxes, and other local crafts. *Warning:* Triberg is virtually overrun with tour buses in summer, and the traffic tie-ups on the road to Triberg can be horrendous.

Essentials

GETTING THERE   By Plane   The nearest major airport is at Stuttgart, 2½ hours away by train (see chapter 12).

By Train   Trains arrive daily from Munich (trip time: 4½ hr.) and from Frankfurt (trip time: 3 hr.). The **Triberg Bahnhof** is on the picturesque Schwarzwaldbahn rail line connecting Konstanz, Singen, Villingen, and Offenburg, with frequent connections in all directions. There are also hourly direct trains from Karlsruhe between 6am and 8pm. Call ⓒ **01805/996633** or visit www.bahn.de for schedules and information.

wunderhiking IN THE BLACK FOREST

You can see the loveliest parts of the Black Forest by hiking the ancient trail of the cuckoo clock traders. Really. The trail follows the route of the traders who, centuries ago, carried the famous Black Forest clocks across Europe. On the village-to-village journey, you pass through deep, fragrant pinewoods and sunny pastures where farmhouses are set scenically on hillsides.

The circle trail starts at Triberg, with its waterfalls. An arrangement with a series of hotels along the trail, beginning with the **Parkhotel Wehrle** (see below), allows you to hike with only a small rucksack; vans haul your luggage on to the next hotel. You can hike from 1 to 10 days and more if you have the time (but most hikers have their fill long before this). Distances for a day's hike between hotels range from 20 to 27km (12–17 miles).

Clearly marked signs guide you across this easy trail, and the Parkhotel Wehrle provides a road map and detailed road descriptions (in English) to set you on your way. Restaurants and farmhouses offering food and refreshment are not far apart, and the area is quite safe, even for a woman walking alone.

By Bus Regional bus service in the Black Forest area is provided by **SBG Süd-baden Bus GmbH,** located in the nearby town of Furtwangen (✆ **07723/19449;** www.suedbadenbus.de).

By Car Access is via the A5 Autobahn north and south; exit at Offenburg and then follow the signs along Rte. 33 south.

VISITOR INFORMATION Contact the tourist office, Wallfahrtstrasse 4 (✆ **07722/ 866490;** www.triberg.de), open year-round daily 10am to 5pm (summer to 6pm).

Exploring the Area

Triberg is the home of the highest waterfall in Germany, **Wasserfälle Gutach (Gutach Falls)** ★, which drops some 160m (525 ft.), spilling downhill in seven misty and poetically evocative stages. They're accessible only on foot. To get here you park your car in a designated area in the town center, near the Gutach Bridge, and then walk along a clearly signposted trail. Signs point to DEUTSCHLAND'S HOCHSTE WASSERFÄLLE (Germany's Highest Waterfalls), which requires, round-trip, about an hour of moderately difficult hill climbing. Seeing the falls is possible only between April and late October. (The rest of the year, snow makes trails dangerously slippery, and access to the falls is closed.) At the bottom of the falls are some souvenir shops; a cafe and restaurant that serves bracing, rib-sticking German food and portions of Black Forest cake; and a kiosk that collects an entrance charge of 3.50€ for adults and 2€ for students and children ages 8 to 17.

Schwarzwald-Museum Triberg, Wallfahrtstrasse 4 (✆ **07722/4434;** www. schwarzwaldmuseum.com), brings the olden days of the Black Forest vividly to life, with displays of dresses, handicrafts, furnishings, bird music boxes, and, of course, clocks and clock making. You can also see a working model of the famed Schwarz-waldbahn railway; opened in 1873, it led to the development of Triberg as an international winter sports and health resort. There is also a mineral exhibit of the area, and Europe's largest barrel organ collection. The museum is open daily May to September 10am to 6pm, and October to April 10am to 5pm. Admission is 5€ adults and 3€ students and children ages 5 to 17. Children 4 and under enter free.

⛧ Stop for Clocks

You may want to make a stop along the B33 between Triberg and Hornberg at the **Haus der 1000 Uhren (House of 1,000 Clocks),** Am Bach 17, 78098 Triberg-Gremmelsbach (② 07722/963030; www.hausder1000uhren.de). You'll recognize the shop immediately by the giant cuckoo clock and water wheel in front. A painter of clock faces, Josef Weisser, launched the business in 1824; today his great-great-grandson owns the place. The shop is open Easter to October Monday to Saturday 9am to 5pm and Sunday 10am to 4pm. It ships to the United States and Canada and takes all major credit cards. There's another branch in the center of Triberg, near the entrance to the waterfall.

One of the most beautiful churches in the Black Forest, the **Wallfahrtskirche Maria in der Tanne (Church of Our Lady in the Fir Tree),** Clemens-Maria-Hofbauer Strasse (② 07722/4566), lies on the western edge of town, an 8-minute walk from the center. Built during the 18th century, it has superb baroque finishings, including a remarkable ornate pulpit. It's open year-round, daily from 8am to 7pm. Entrance is free.

After a visit to the church, consider driving to the **Schwarzwälder Freilichtmuseum** in the village of Gutach (② 07831/93560; www.vogtsbauernhof.org), which lies 17km (11 miles) north of Triberg. Here, you'll find a collection of looms and paraphernalia related to the weaving industry that in some cases are as much as 4 centuries old. In summer, guides demonstrate weaving techniques on some of the looms. The museum is open April to October daily from 9am to 6pm. Admission costs 7€ for adults, 6€ for students, and 4€ for children ages 5 to 18. A family ticket is 16€. From the A5, turn off at the Offenburg exit and follow B33 toward Gengenbach, Hausach, and Triberg. At Hausach, turn right toward Gutach.

A 15km (10-mile) drive south of Triberg is the **Deutsches Uhrenmuseum (German Clock Museum),** Gerwigstrasse 11, in the village of Furtwangen (② 07723/920800; www.deutsches-uhrenmuseum.de). To get here, drive for 20 minutes west along the B500, following the signs to Furtwangen.

It's open daily November to March 10am to 5pm and April to October 9am to 6pm. Admission is 4€ for adults and 3€ for children. This museum presents a history of timepieces, including displays of a wide variety of Black Forest clocks, some from the early 18th century. Many are elaborate and complicated. Look for the mechanical music automata and the cuckoo clocks.

Where to Eat

Parkhotel Wehrle ★ CONTINENTAL   People come from great distances to eat at this famous restaurant, where the cuisine is intelligent and imaginative, with a focus on natural flavors. Even simple dishes have flair. Try the filet of tilapia baked in a pastry shell and served with white wine, figs, and lentils, or the soufflé of pumpkin and chutney, lamb lettuce, and roasted quail breast. A traditional dessert is apples baked with pine honey and flambéed with *Kirschwasser,* a black-cherry brandy. Some of the game specialties are prepared for two.

Gartenstrasse 24. ② **07722/86020.** Reservations required. Main courses 18€–25€; fixed-price 4-course menu 55€. AE, DC, MC, V. Daily noon–2pm and 7–10pm.

Where to Stay

Romantik Parkhotel Wehrle ★★ You can't find a finer and more traditional inn in this area. Built in the early 1600s, Parkhotel Wehrle was acquired around 1730 by the family that has owned it ever since. Its lemon yellow walls and gabled mansard roof occupy one of the most prominent street corners in town. The main house offers an old-world atmosphere, but forest-loving vacationers often request accommodations near the woods in a separate chalet, where a pool and breeze-filled balconies create a modern sylvan retreat. The good-size rooms are beautifully furnished and individually decorated, sometimes with antiques.

Gartenstrasse 24, 78098 Triberg. www.parkhotel-wehrle.de. ✆ **07722/86020.** Fax 07722/860290. 50 units. 149€–210€ double; from 265€ suite. Rates include buffet breakfast. AE, DC, MC, V. Free parking outdoors; 6€ in garage. 1.5km (1 mile) from the train station. **Amenities:** 3 restaurants; bar; exercise room; 2 heated indoor pools; room service; spa. *In room:* TV, hair dryer, Wi-Fi (free).

Römischer Kaiser 🍴 You get old-style charm here, and old-style prices too. This comfortable, charmingly preserved hotel has been owned by several generations of the same family since 1840. The exterior has lots of exposed wood. Rooms come in a wide range of shapes and sizes, but all are pleasant and well maintained.

Sommerauerstrasse 35, 78098 Triberg-Nussbach. www.roemischer-kaiser.com. ✆ **07722/96940.** Fax 07722/969429. 27 units. 36€–44€ per person double. Rates include buffet breakfast. AE, DC, MC, V. Free parking. 1.5km (1 mile) outside Triberg. **Amenities:** Restaurant; bar; children's center. *In room:* TV, hair dryer, Wi-Fi (free).

FREUDENSTADT

92km (57 miles) N of Freiburg

One of the most important transportation hubs in the northern tier of the Black Forest is Freudenstadt, a riverside town known for clear air, streaming sunshine, and a sense of cleanliness and conservatism. Originally founded in 1599 by Duke Friedrich I of Württemberg, Freudenstadt provided a home at the time for Protestants fleeing religious persecution within Carinthia, in southern Austria. French troops set most of the town ablaze in the closing days of World War II, but it was completely rebuilt, close to the original plans, by 1950.

Essentials

GETTING THERE By Train Trains arrive hourly throughout the day from Frankfurt (trip time: 3 hr.) and from Munich (trip time: 4 hr.). Freudenstadt has two railway stations, the **Stadtbahnhof,** an older and smaller station in the center of town, and the **Hauptbahnhof,** about .5km (⅓ mile) south of the center. Most trains stop at both. For information on trains throughout Germany and Europe, call ✆ **01805/996633** or visit www.bahn.de.

By Bus Bus travel tends to be convenient only for those coming from surrounding hamlets. Buses stop at both the Bahnhofplatz and the Marktplatz. For information, call ✆ **07441/860130.**

By Car Driving from Stuttgart, following the B28, takes about 15 minutes; from Karlsruhe via the B462, about 30 minutes.

VISITOR INFORMATION The **Tourist Information Office** is at Marktplatz 64 (✆ **07441/8640;** www.freudenstadt.de). It's open May to September Monday to

Friday 10am to 6pm, Saturday and Sunday 10am to 2pm. From October to April, hours are Monday to Friday 10am to 5pm, and Saturday and Sunday 11am to 1pm.

Exploring Freudenstadt

Freudenstadt's appeal is its location in the midst of the best hiking, skiing, and camping country in the Black Forest. It's one of the best centers for exploring the fabled **Schwarzwald Hochstrasse** ★★. This highway stretches for 80km (50 miles) from Baden-Baden to Freudenstadt and can be traveled in 1½ hours (although most tourists prefer to take much longer due to the many charming shops and cafes along the way). Many points along the route approach a height of 1,000m (3,300 ft.) and you'll find a number of belvederes and car parks where you can take in the view. Along the route are dozens of winter ski slopes.

In summer, visitors hike in the country's largest nature preserve, the **Parkwald** ★★ abutting Freudenstadt. The park is riddled with miles of walking trails. You can pick up excellent trail maps at the Freudenstadt tourist office (see above) before setting out, in either winter or summer.

Unlike many German towns, Freudenstadt has no castle overshadowing it, but it certainly does have an enormous castle square. This plot of land, the largest **Marktplatz** ★ in Germany, was laid out in the 16th century for a castle that was never built. History's loss is today's gain. The market square that greets the visitor to Freudenstadt is a maze of lawns and concrete, broken by patches of flowers and kiosks. The buildings surrounding the square are mainly postwar because the air raids and fires of World War II almost completely destroyed the city. A few of the old Renaissance structures on the square have been reconstructed, up to their neat little archways and gabled roofs.

The town takes pride in its **Stadtkirche,** Marktplatz (✆ **07441/6554**), dating from the 17th century. The unique and odd L-shaped architecture of the church brings the two main aisles together at right angles. Over the entrance stand identical towers, topped with rounded domes and narrow spires. The church's most important treasure is the 12th-century reading desk, supported by carved and painted likenesses of the Evangelists. It's open daily 10am to 5pm. Entrance is free.

Freudenstadt's only other attraction worth mentioning is a small regional folk and crafts museum, the **Museum im Stadthaus,** in the Stadthaus as the name implies, Marktplatz (✆ **07441/6177**), open Monday and Friday 3 to 5pm, every other day of the week 10am to 5pm. From April to October, opening hours are extended until 6pm. Entrance is free.

Where to Eat

Jägerstüble SWABIAN/GERMAN   Like most of the buildings around it, this is an excellent re-creation of a medieval house that was severely damaged during World War II. Inside, foaming mugs of beer and hardworking waitresses in folkloric costumes contribute to an unpretentious re-creation of the Germany of another era. The hearty and savory dishes include *Eisbein* (veal shank) with *Sauerkraut,* farmers' omelets, venison steak prepared with garlic and red wine, and goulash of venison.

Marktplatz 12. ✆ **07441/2387.** www.jaegerstueble-fds.de. Reservations recommended. Main courses 10€–22€. MC, V. Tues–Sat 8am–11pm; Sun 8am–6pm.

Warteck ★ SWABIAN/GERMAN   One of the most durable restaurants in Freudenstadt opened in 1951 in a location that's a 3-minute walk from the town's Marktplatz. A pair of charming dining rooms are lined with flowers and outfitted in tones of ocher and turquoise. You'll enjoy savory, relatively formal cuisine that includes braised oxtail with herbs and vegetables, roasted pigeon, and a preparation of sweetbreads for which the chef is especially well known. Fish crops up often on the menu, often simply braised and served in an herb-enriched butter sauce. Everything here is in good taste, with lots of elegant, low-key charm. The restaurant lies within a cozy, government-rated three-star hotel with 13 well-furnished doubles, costing from 88€ to 95€, including breakfast.

Stuttgarter Strasse 14. ℭ **07441/91920.** Fax 07441/919293. www.warteck-freudenstadt.de. Reservations recommended. Main courses 18€–35€. AE, DC, MC, V. Wed–Mon noon–2pm and 6–10pm. Closed 2 weeks during Jan and Nov.

Where to Stay

Hotel Bären   This establishment's cozy interior may remind you of the inside of a prosperous local farmhouse. Rooms are snug, traditionally decorated, and well maintained. The Montigel family and its staff are charming and polite, conveying a nostalgic sense of traditional Germany.

The hotel is perhaps best known for its restaurant, which serves well-prepared Swabian food under the direction of chef Louis Montigel, with main courses costing 11€ to 25€.

Langestrasse 33, 72250 Freudenstadt. www.hotel-baeren-freudenstadt.de. ℭ **07441/2729.** Fax 07441/2887. 36 units. 95€–160€ double. MC, V. Free parking. Near the Marktplatz. **Amenities:** Restaurant; room service. *In room:* TV, hair dryer.

Hotel Hohenried im Rosengarten ★   This three-story hotel is designed to look like a modern version of an Alpine chalet, with a splendid garden that contains more than 2,000 rosebushes. The comfortable and contemporary-looking rooms overlook a golf course and billowing trees. In summertime, the balconies are adorned with geranium-filled flower boxes. All the accommodations come with neatly tiled bathrooms with shower units. The staff is polite and speaks English.

Zeppelinstrasse 5–7, 72250 Freudenstadt. www.hotelhohenried.de. ℭ **07441/2414.** Fax 07441/2559. 25 units. 86€–118€ double. AE, MC, V. Bus: 14. 1.5km (1 mile) south of Freudenstadt's center. **Amenities:** Restaurant; bar; exercise room; indoor heated pool; room service; sauna. *In room:* TV, hair dryer, Wi-Fi (in some rooms; free).

Where to Eat & Stay Nearby

If you want to experience the Schwarzwald at its most isolated and remote, consider a stay at either of the following two hotels, which are positioned south and north of the hamlet of Baiersbronn, respectively. Baiersbronn lies 6km (4 miles) northwest of Freudenstadt. Trains arrive in Baiersbronn about once an hour from Stuttgart and Karlsruhe, stopping in Baiersbronn before continuing south for another 6km (4 miles) to Freudenstadt. Local buses (marked BAIERSBRONN) depart from the Marktplatz in Freudenstadt for Baiersbronn, but there are only about four per day, and they won't take you anywhere near either of the two hotels. For the short distance involved, it's a lot more convenient to take any of the taxis lined up in Freudenstadt's Marktplatz.

Hotel Bareiss ★★ ☺   This deluxe resort hotel is equivalent in most ways to the Hotel Traube Tonbach (see below), but a bit less formal and a lot less stiff. It provides a soothing, carefully orchestrated, well-manicured environment, where peace, quiet, and access to the surrounding forest are fiercely guarded. You'll find lots of urban refugees on-site, recuperating from stressful careers. Rooms are spacious, carefully maintained, conservatively modern, and very comfortable. All have views over the forest.

Gärtenbühlweg 14, 072270 Baiersbronn/Mitteltal. www.bareiss.com. ℗ **07442/470.** Fax 07442/47320. 127 units. 183€–224€ double; 299€–391€ suite; 215€–286€ apt. All rates are per person. Rates include buffet breakfast. AE, DC, MC, V. Parking 9.50€. From the center of Baiersbronn, head south following signs pointing to Hotel Bareiss for 10km (6 miles). **Amenities:** 3 restaurants; bar; babysitting; bikes; children's programs; exercise room; 4 heated pools (2 indoor); room service; spa; outdoor tennis court (lit). *In room:* A/C (in some), TV, hair dryer, minibar, Wi-Fi (free).

Hotel Traube Tonbach ★★★   This is the grande dame of Black Forest resorts. In 1957, it was massively enlarged into the stately, multibalcony resort you see today and immediately attracted one of the grandest resort clienteles in Germany. Set closer to Baiersbronn (only about 1.6km/1 mile north of town) than its competitor, the Bareiss (see above), the Traube Tonbach prides itself on its conservatism, its strictly enforced sense of peace and quiet, and the glamour of its very upscale clientele. Rooms are good size, solid, well built, quiet, and very, very comfortable. Ask the staff for advice on nearby hiking trails. Be sure to dine at the Schwarzwaldstube, home to renowned chef Harald Wohlfahrt for over 30 years.

Ortsteil Tonbach, Tonbachstrasse 237, 72270 Baiersbronn. www.traubetonbach.de. ℗ **07442/4920.** Fax 07442/492692. 170 units. 143€–182€ double; 227€–314€ suite. Rates include buffet breakfast. Half board 19€ per person. AE, DC, MC, V. Parking 5€–8.50€. **Amenities:** 4 restaurants; bar; babysitting; bikes; children's center; health club and spa; 3 heated pools (2 indoor); room service. *In room:* A/C (suites only), TV, hair dryer, minibar, Wi-Fi (free).

Entertainment & Nightlife

In lieu of any real nightlife, locals head for a local *Stube,* or beer hall, for a night out. Most of these drinking places are within hotels. Two of the best are at the previously recommended Hotel Bären and the Jägerstüble (see above), the latter serving the largest mugs of beer in town.

CALW

20km (12 miles) S of Pforzheim, 66km (41 miles) N of Freudenstadt

Many residents of other parts of Germany call Calw (the *w* is silent) the most appealingly folkloric town in the Black Forest. Hermann Hesse, who was born here in 1877, described Calw as "the most beautiful place I know."

Essentials

GETTING THERE By Train   Trains arrive at Calw's Bahnhof at hourly intervals from both Stuttgart and Karlsruhe. Both cities are about an hour away. For railway information, call ℗ **01805/996633** or visit www.bahn.de.

By Bus   Buses that travel between Horb am Neckar, Nagold, and Pforzheim make stops at Calw's Bahnhofplatz. For information, call ℗ **07051/96890.**

By Car   Calw lies midway between Pforzheim and Nagold, along Hwy. B463. From the A8 Autobahn, exit at the signs indicating CALW.

VISITOR INFORMATION   The **Tourist Information office** in Calw is at Sparkassenplatz 2 (℗ **07051/167399;** www.calw.de). It's open October to April Monday to Friday 9:30am to 1pm and 2 to 4:30pm, and also May to September Monday to Friday 9:30am to 4:30pm and Saturday 9:30am to 12:30pm.

The environs of Calw also merit some attention if you have the time. Of exceptional interest is the hamlet of **Zavelstein,** which is signposted in Calw. Follow the road south for 5km (3 miles). A drive to this little hamlet is especially spectacular in late March and April, when the meadows blossom with edelweiss and crocuses. You may want to continue south in the direction of Talmühle-Seitzental, where you'll see a sign pointing along a twisting road leading to **Neubulach** (ⓒ **07053/969510**). Until it closed in the mid-1920s, this was one of the most active silver mines in the Black Forest. Long after it was abandoned, the medical profession learned that its dust-free interior was beneficial in the treatment of asthma. A therapy center is now located inside. The mine's ancient shafts can be visited on guided tours given April to November daily from 10am to 4pm, costing 5€ for adults and 3€ for children. Call ⓒ **07053/ 7346** or visit www.bergwerk-neubulach. de for details.

Exploring Calw

Calw's allure derives from its impressive and meticulously maintained roster of late-17th- and early-18th-century houses, whose half-timbered facades add an undeniable charm to such sites as the Marktplatz. The town's most prominent bridge, the 14th-century **Nikolausbrücke,** in the center, merits a stroll in admiration of its carefully chiseled masonry.

The birthplace of Herman Hesse, the **Hesse Haus,** Marktplatz 30 (ⓒ **07051/ 7522;** www.hermann-hesse.com), is a literary shrine for scholars and fans. Entrance is 5€ adults, 3€ students and children. The only other formal attraction in town is a small-scale folklore museum called **Palais Vischer,** Bischofstrasse 48 (ⓒ **07051/ 167260**). It's open April to October Tuesday to Sunday 11am to 5pm, and November to March Tuesday to Sunday 2 to 5pm. Admission is 1.50€ adults, free for children 11 and under.

Where to Eat

Ratsstube 🍴 SWABIAN/INTERNATIONAL   This is the most popular and reliable restaurant in town, not to be confused with the more down-market and sudsier Ratskeller, whose entrance lies a few feet away. The Ratsstube, built in the early 1800s, has two separate dining rooms, each evocative of a bygone Germany. It's very rustic and ethnic German; very little English is spoken by the staff. The interior is a labyrinth of masonry-sided rooms. The well-prepared but not particularly innovative dishes include *Zwiebelrostbraten* (roast beef with onions), filet of sole in wine sauce, stingray in black-butter sauce, trout with almonds or meunière style, and an array of sausages served with cabbage and roasted potatoes. Service is competent.

Marktplatz 12. ⓒ **07051/92050.** www.hotel-ratsstube-calw.de. Reservations recommended. Main courses 12€–18€. MC, V. Daily 11:30am–9pm (last order).

Restaurant Klosterschanke SWABIAN/INTERNATIONAL   Located in the above-mentioned Kloster Hirsau, this historically authentic restaurant occupies a trio of dining rooms with beamed and/or vaulted ceilings, which, in some cases, are hundreds of years old. Menu items include fresh house-marinated sardines, rack of lamb with white beans, *Zwiebelrostbraten,* monkfish braised in olive oil with herbs, and several kinds of *Schnitzel*. Although the food never reaches the sublime, it's always fresh and competently prepared.

Wildbader Strasse 2. (?) **07051/96740.** Reservations recommended. Main courses 15€–22€; fixed-price menu 15€–30€. MC, V. Daily lunch noon–2pm; *Kaffe mit Kuchen* (coffee and cakes) 2–6pm; dinner 6–10pm.

Where to Stay

Hotel Kloster Hirsau   The best place for overnighting lies right outside of town 2km (1¼ miles) to the north in the direction of Hirsau. Parts of the foundation of this historic hotel date from 1092, when the site functioned as a monastery that was noted for housing overnight visitors. Today, the establishment retains its medieval touches and antique charm. The good-size rooms have lots of Schwarzwald-inspired features, including pinewood trim and reproductions of traditional furniture. The oldest, most atmospheric, and charming bedrooms are nos. 114 to 235.

Ortsteil Hirsau, Wildbader Strasse 2, 75365 Calw. www.hotel-kloster-hirsau.de. (?) **07051/96740.** Fax 07051/967469. 40 units. 117€–129€ double. Half board 18€ per person. AE, MC, V. Free street parking; parking in garage 8€. **Amenities:** Restaurant; exercise room; indoor heated pool; sauna; 2 indoor tennis courts (lit); Wi-Fi (free; in lobby). *In room:* TV, hair dryer (in some), minibar.

PFORZHEIM

35km (22 miles) S of Karlsruhe, 53km (33 miles) SW of Stuttgart

Set at the northern edge of the Black Forest, at the junction of three rivers (the Würm, the Enz, and the Nagold), Pforzheim is one of the Schwarzwald's largest settlements. It was founded by the Romans as a fortified camp and developed into an important mercantile center during the Middle Ages. Key industries have traditionally included the crafting of jewelry and clock making. Although it was severely damaged by bombs during World War II, Pforzheim is a worthwhile site for an overnight stay between forays into the Black Forest.

Essentials

GETTING THERE   By Train   Trains pull into Pforzheim at least once an hour from Munich (trip time: 3 hr.), Frankfurt (trip time: 2 hr.), and Stuttgart (trip time: 1½ hr.). The railway station lies within an 8-minute walk of the center. For information, call (?) **01805/996633** or visit www.bahn.de.

By Bus   Bus travel to Pforzheim is a lot less practical than rail travel. The main bus stop is at Leopoldplatz, in the town center.

By Car   Pforzheim lies beside the rapid A-8 Autobahn that stretches between Munich and Karlsruhe. Transit from Stuttgart takes between 45 and 90 minutes; from Munich, around 2½ hours; and from Frankfurt, around 2 hours.

VISITOR INFORMATION   Head to **Tourist Information** in the Neues Rathaus at Marktplatz 1 ((?) **07231/393700;** www.pforzheim.de), open Monday to Friday 10am to 6pm, and Saturday 10am to 1pm.

Exploring Pforzheim

Allied bombs demolished much of Pforzheim in World War II. Of the limited number of buildings that have been restored to their former grandeur, **Schloss- un Stiftskirche**

(**Castle and Monastery Church**), Schlossberg 10 (☎ **07231/102484**), is the most dramatic. It was built in stages between the 1200s and 1400s and combines aspects of both Romanesque and Gothic architecture. It's open daily 8:30am to 6pm. A fine example of a more modern church is the **Stadtkirche,** on Melanchthonstrasse (no phone), in the town center across from the Parkhotel. Rebuilt from the town's rubble during the 1960s, this is a symbol of Pforzheim's rebirth from the devastation of World War II.

For insights into the role that clock making has traditionally played in Pforzheim, head for the city's **Technisches Museum,** Bleichstrasse 81 (☎ **07231/392869;** www.technisches-museum.de), where souvenirs and mementos of the clock-making trade commemorate humankind's painstaking efforts to organize time. On the premises is a reconstruction of a clock-making studio from the early 1800s. The museum is open every Wednesday 9am to noon and 3 to 6pm, and every second and fourth Sunday 10am to 5pm. Admission is free, although donations are appreciated.

The equally nostalgic **Schmuckmuseum,** Jahnstrasse 42 (☎ **07231/392126;** www.schmuckmuseum.de), is devoted to Pforzheim's jewelry-making trade. Its collection includes ornaments from the 3rd century B.C. to modern times. The museum is open Tuesday to Sunday 10am to 5pm. Admission is 3€, free for children under 14.

Where to Eat

Parkrestaurant GERMAN   This well-managed restaurant offers solid home-style cuisine, a view over the Stadt Theater and the banks of the Enz River, and a polite, well-trained staff. This is a preferable alternative to the Galarestaurant, its more upscale sibling within the same hotel. Menu items include *Schnitzel,* stews, roulades and grills, soups, salads, and hearty, regional desserts layered with chocolate and whipped cream.

In the Parkhotel, Deimlingstrasse 36. ☎ **07231/16101.** Reservations not necessary. Main courses 12€– 25€. AE, DC, MC, V. Daily noon–2pm and 6–11:30pm.

Where to Stay

Parkhotel ★   Set in the center of town, the four-story, contemporary Parkhotel is the meeting place for most of the civic and charitable organizations in Pforzheim.

medieval EXCURSION FROM PFORZHEIM

One of the Schwarzwald's most evocative sights lies 18km (11 miles) to the northeast of Pforzheim, within the agrarian hamlet of Maulbronn. **Kloster Maulbronn** (☎ **07043/926610;** www.kloster-maulbronn.de) has been called the best-preserved medieval monastery north of the Alps. Most of its more than 30 stone-sided buildings were constructed between 1150 and 1390, within an encircling wall that protected the monks and their allies from outside attackers. The most visible of the buildings is the compound's **church,** which combines aspects of Romanesque and Gothic architecture, and which influenced the design of later structures throughout central and northern Europe. Most visitors arrive by car or taxi from the center of Pforzheim, although there's also a bus that departs for Maulbronn from Pforzheim's Leopoldplatz at 50-minute intervals throughout the day. The monastery is open March to October daily 9am to 5:30pm, and November to February Tuesday to Sunday 9:30am to 5pm. Admission is 6€ adults, 3€ students and children. Anticipate potential closings throughout 2012 due to renovation.

Inside, you'll find a streamlined, tasteful decor with lots of exposed wood and stone. Rooms are good-size, airy, and comfortable.

Deimlingstrasse 36, 75175 Pforzheim. www.parkhotel-pforzheim.de. (✆ **07231/1610.** Fax 07231/161690. 208 units. 118€–170€ double; from 190€ suite. Rates include buffet breakfast. AE, DC, MC, V. Parking 8.50€. **Amenities:** 2 restaurants; bar; babysitting; exercise room; Jacuzzi; room service; sauna. *In room:* A/C, TV, hair dryer, minibar, Wi-Fi (free).

Royal Hotel   Equivalent in most ways to the Parkhotel (see above), the Royal's only drawback is its location on the outskirts of town. It was built in 1995 in a two-story, modern format. Rooms are small to medium size, contemporary, sunny, comfortable, clean, and utterly without pretension. The staff is polite and well trained.

Wilhelm-Becker-Strasse 3A, 75179 Pforzheim. www.hotel-royal-pforzheim.de. (✆ **07231/14250.** Fax 07231/142599. 43 units. 115€–117€ per person double. Rates include buffet breakfast. AE, DC, V. Free parking. Bus: 6. 1.5km (1 mile) west of the center. **Amenities:** Restaurant; bar; access to nearby exercise room and sauna; Internet (free; in lobby); room service. *In room:* TV, hair dryer, minibar.

BADEN-BADEN ★★

111km (69 miles) W of Stuttgart, 111km (69 miles) NE of Freiburg, 174km (108 miles) S of Frankfurt

In the 19th century, European nobility rediscovered Baden-Baden, where the bath-conscious Roman emperor Caracalla once came to ease his arthritic aches. Swanky clients such as Queen Victoria, Kaiser Wilhelm I, Napoleon III, Berlioz, Brahms, and Dostoevsky helped make Baden-Baden the most elegant and sophisticated playground in Germany. Tolstoy set a scene in *Anna Karenina* here, though he gave the town a different name. Today, the clientele may have changed, but Baden-Baden still evokes an aura of privilege, combined with the most up-to-date facilities.

Baden-Baden is the ideal choice for sports and outdoor enthusiasts. Golf, tennis, and horseback riding are all popular. Lovers of horse racing will enjoy the international racing season each August at Iffezheim Track. The surrounding countryside is filled with hiking and mountain-climbing options. During the winter, Baden-Baden is a convenient center for skiing: After a day on the slopes, you can return to a soothing swim in a thermal pool and a night out at the casino.

Essentials

GETTING THERE By Train   Baden-Baden is on major rail lines connecting Frankfurt and Basel, and Stuttgart and Munich. There are 20 trains daily from Stuttgart (trip time: 1¼ hr.); 25 from Munich (trip time: 4 hr., 10 min.), and 45 from Frankfurt (trip time: 3 hr.). For information, call (✆ **01805/996633** or visit www.bahn.de. The railway station is at Baden-Oos, northwest of town; regrettably, it's an expensive 20-minute taxi ride from the town center.

By Car   Access to Baden-Baden is via the A5 Autobahn north and south or the A8 Autobahn east and west. The drive south from Frankfurt takes 2 hours; from Munich, it's about 4 hours.

VISITOR INFORMATION   For information, contact **Tourist-Information,** Schwarzwaldstrasse 52 (✆ **07221/275200;** www.baden-baden.com), Monday to Saturday 9am to 6pm and Sunday 9am to 1pm. After the morning shift on Sunday in the tourist office, information can be obtained in the Trinkhalle from 2 to 5pm (see below).

GETTING AROUND   Baden-Baden is serviced by a network of buses whose routes coincide at the Leopoldsplatz, in the center. Bus no. 201, which runs at

10-minute intervals, interconnects most of the important sites with the railway station, about 5km (3 miles) from the center. One-way fare is 2.20€, and a day pass, good for 24 hours of unlimited public transport for up to five people, is 7.70€. Visit www.stadtwerke-baden-baden.de for details.

Discovering Baden-Baden: From Art to Spas

Caracalla-Therme BATHS   These baths have been made more pleasing visually by the addition of a round colonnaded extension with splashing and cascading pools. You can decide on your own bath temperature here. Medicinal treatment includes mud baths, massages, and whirlpools. The slightly radioactive water, rich in sodium chloride, comes from artesian wells 1,800m (6,000 ft.) under the Florentiner Mountain. Its temperature is around 160°F (71°C). Bathers usually begin in cooler pools, working up to the warm water. The baths also have a sauna area, with foot baths and sun baths; sauna temperatures go from 185° to 200°F (85°–93°C). You must wear bathing suits in the pools, but everyone goes nude in the saunas.

Römerplatz 1. ✆ **07221/275940.** www.carasana.de. Admission 14€ for 2 hr., 17€ for 3 hr., 20€ for 4 hr. Daily 8am–10pm. Bus: 201.

Friedrichsbad BATHS   Friedrichsbad, also known as the Old Baths, was built from 1869 to 1877 at the behest of Grand Duke Friedrich von Baden. Following the Roman-Irish method, it takes about 2 hours to have the complete program, which involves a shower, two saunas 130° to 160°F (54°–71°C), a brush massage soaping, thermal steam baths, and three freshwater baths ranging from warm to 60°F (16°C). After a 30-minute period of rest and relaxation, you're supposed to feel rejuvenated. Other types of therapy, including massage, electrotherapy, and hydrotherapy, are also offered. Massages are 10€ for cream massage, 24€ for a 30-minute neck and back massage, and 48€ for a 1-hour full-body massage.

Römerplatz 1. ✆ **07221/275920.** www.carasana.de. Admission 21€ without soap-brush massage, 31€ with soap-brush massage. Daily 9am–10pm.

Sammlung Frieder Burda ★★★ MUSEUM   One of Germany's most extensive collections of modern art has opened in an airy Richard Meier–designed building standing at the edge of a park. Its primary focus is on the works of postwar German expressionists. The scion of a famous publishing family, Frieder Burda spent nearly 4 decades amassing this amazing collection of some 580 works of contemporary art ranging from George Baselitz to Sigmar Polke, from Max Beckmann to Gerhard Richter. Our favorite is anything by Ernst Ludwig Kirchner. Not all the works are German—note the late *oeuvre* by Picasso or the examples of American abstract expressionism, works by Willem de Kooning, Mark Rothko, and Jackson Pollock.

Lichtentaler Allee 8B. ✆ **07221/398980.** www.museum-frieder-burda.de. Admission 9€ adults; 7€ students, children, and seniors. Tues–Sun 10am–6pm.

Trinkhalle (Pump Room) BATHS   The spa gardens contain the Pump Room, where visitors can sip the water that has been bubbling for over 17,000 years. The loggia of the hall is decorated with frescoes depicting Black Forest legends. The springs of Baden-Baden have been recognized for more than 2,000 years, and their composition is almost the same today as when the Romans built their baths here in the 3rd century.

Kaiserallee 3. No phone. Free admission. Apr–Oct daily 10am–6:30pm. Bus: 201.

The center of Baden-Baden activity is **Lichtentaler Allee ★★**, the park promenade along the bank of the Oosbach River (affectionately called the Oos—pronounced *Ohs*), which runs through the center of town. As you stroll along this walk, you'll be amazed at the variety not only of exotic shrubs and trees but also of the rhododendrons, azaleas, and roses. At the north end of the park, on the banks of the stream, are the buildings of the **Kurgarten**, including the classical Kurhaus, used as an entertainment complex.

Where to Eat

Le Jardin de France ★★★ MODERN/FRENCH   The most highly recommended and most elegant restaurant in Baden-Baden lies in a baronial-looking building in the center of town. Defining itself as a "small corner of France set within Germany," it's enhanced by the creative cuisine and service of Alsatian-born Stephan and Sophie Bernhard. During clement weather, an outdoor terrace provides alternative seating. You might begin with freshwater whiting in puff pastry with a horseradish-flavored cream sauce and winter vegetables, or fried scallops of foie gras with pineapple, fava beans, and essence of balsamic vinegar. Main courses include a turbot with olives, artichokes, and a bay leaf sauce, or Alsatian pigeon with morels and fresh asparagus. Plan on spending an evening tableside.

Lichtentalerstrasse 13. 🕻 **07221/3007860.** www.lejardindefrance.de. Reservations required. Main courses 24€–42€; set lunch 29€; set dinners 49€–95€. AE, DC, MC, V. Tues–Sat noon–2pm and 7–9:30pm. Closed for 10 days in mid-July.

Löwenbräu GERMAN/BAVARIAN   Though Baden-Baden has many fine restaurants dispensing haute cuisine, this isn't one of them—the food here is simple and affordable. The terrace is beneath a copse of clipped and pruned linden trees, and the indoor dining room, with its curved glass walls, is up a flight of stone steps at the rear. Many kinds of German sausage are offered, along with Bavarian specialties such as roast pork in a beer sauce. Regional devotees order pork knuckles fresh from the "pork-knuckle grill." Regulars often ask for the "Löwenbräu platter of bites," which is a hearty plate with everything from black pudding to sliced pork. For dessert, the apple fritters won't disappoint. The restaurant also has a popular beer garden.

Gernsbacher Strasse 9 (in the Altstadt). 🕻 **07221/22311.** www.loewenbraeu-baden-baden.de. Main courses 11€–27€. AE, DC, MC, V. Daily 10am–11pm. Bus: 201.

Park-Restaurant ★★ FRENCH/ALSATIAN   Park-Restaurant serves some of the best food in the center of Baden-Baden, although its cuisine is not quite as refined as that of Zum Alde Gott (see below) on the outskirts. This is one of the renowned spa dining rooms of Europe, and the cuisine and service are definitely worth the high price. The emphasis is on French (Alsatian) dishes. Based on market-fresh produce, some of the more alluring specialties are saddle of venison with cranberries, or the roasted monkfish with a tomato confit. A spectacular dessert is the warm chocolate cake with a liquid core.

In Brenner's Park Hotel, Schillerstrasse 6 (at the corner of Lichtentaler Allee). 🕻 **07221/9000.** www.brenners.com. Reservations required. Main courses 39€–60€. AE, DC, MC, V. Daily 7–11pm. Bus: 201.

Stahlbad ★ CONTINENTAL   Stahlbad is a luxury restaurant with an elegant decor. Although its food may not be as good as Park-Restaurant's (see above), it's the most tranquil and charming choice in the center of town, mainly because of its garden terrace. The owner, Ursula Mönch, welcomes you in the dining room. The decor and atmosphere evoke a tavern, with prints, copper vessels, antique pewter plates, mugs, and engravings. Some of the best specialties are sliced goose liver with apples and Calvados sauce; sautéed monkfish with tagliatelle; venison medallions with chanterelles, chestnuts, and cranberries; and breast of quail with broiled gooseliver.

Augustaplatz 2. ℂ **07221/24569.** www.stahlbad.com. Reservations required. Main courses 15€–30€. AE, DC, MC, V. Tues–Sun noon–2pm and 6–10pm. Bus: 201.

DINING AT NEUWEIER
Many of Baden-Baden's visitors dine at the satellite resort of Neuweier, 10km (6 miles) southwest via Fremersbergstrasse.

Zum Alde Gott ★★ BADISCHER   This is where true gourmets come to dine. In an attractive and very old wine cellar, Wilfried Serr, the most distinguished chef in the Baden-Baden area, mixes his palette of flavors with astounding skill and imagination. Wild game in season is a fine art here. Try also the Black Forest trout or the sea bass. There are only 12 tables, and the ambience is bright and cheerful. An added bonus is an open-air terrace.

Weinstrasse 10. ℂ **07223/5513.** www.zum-alde-gott.de. Reservations required. Main courses 24€–36€. DC, MC, V. Fri–Wed noon–3pm and 6:30–11pm. Bus: 216.

Shopping

A flower-flanked pedestrian zone includes **Sophienstrasse** and **Gernsbacher Strasse,** streets lined with upscale boutiques, among the most expensive in Germany. Women's clothing by one of Germany's most emulated designers is available at **Escada Boutique,** Sophienstrasse 18 (ℂ **07221/390448**). Another shop, **Münchner Moden,** Lichtentalerstrasse 13 (ℂ **07221/31090**), carries women's designs in loden-colored wool during autumn and winter and offers Austrian and Bavarian silks, linens, and cottons during warmer months.

Entertainment & Nightlife

Baden-Baden has a busy annual schedule of concert, dance, and dramatic performances. The centerpiece for most of the resort's cultural activities is the oft-photographed **Kurhaus,** Kaiserallee 1 (ℂ **07221/9070;** www.kurhaus-baden-baden.de). Originally built in the 1870s as the focal point of the resort, the Kurhaus does not contain spa facilities, as its name implies, but is rather a catchall entertainment complex. In the same building is Baden-Baden's casino, the **Spielbank** (see "The Casino," below).

   Theater am Goetheplatz, Goetheplatz (ℂ **07221/932700;** www.theater. baden-baden.de), is a well-maintained and beautiful baroque-style theater that presents opera, ballet, and drama productions. It opened auspiciously with the world première of the Berlioz opera *Beatrice et Benedict* in 1862. Every summer, the verdant core of Baden-Baden is home to several outdoor concerts, many of which focus on jazz or classical music, often informal late-afternoon or early-evening affairs organized on short notice by the tourist office. More elaborate concerts, many of them performed by the town's resident orchestra, the **Philharmonie Baden-Baden (Philharmonic Orchestra of Baden-Baden),** are part of the resort's **Musikalischer Sommer Festival,** usually conducted during an 8-day period in mid-July. Although the orchestra is likely to perform mostly within the echoing interior of one of the largest concert halls in Germany, the **Festspielhaus,** in the Alter Bahnhof (see below for ticket information), smaller events are likely to crop up within venues scattered throughout the town. For tickets to any cultural or musical event within Baden-Baden, contact either the tourist office (✆ **07221/275200**), which sells tickets on its premises, or the **Ticket Service Trinkhalle,** in the Trinkhalle on Kaiserallee (✆ **07221/932700**).

After a long slumber, Germany's most famous spa is percolating once again. Attracting visiting celebrities, the bar at **Medici,** Augustaplatz 8 (✆ **07221/2006;** www.medici.de), has become the most fashionable in town.

Bars in the resort hotels often have low-key entertainment. Try the **Jockey Bar,** in the lobby of the Radisson Blu Badischer Hof (✆ **07221/9340**), or the **Oleander Bar** in Brenner's Park Hotel, Schillerstrasse 4–6 (✆ **07221/9000**).

THE CASINO

Spielbank   Open year-round, this is the oldest casino in Germany, popular for more than 200 years. Dostoevsky is said to have written *The Gambler* after he lost his shirt, and almost his mind, at the tables here. The casino rooms were designed in the style of an elegant French château. Jackets and ties for men are mandatory, as is evening wear for women. To enter during gambling hours, you must possess a valid passport or identification card and be at least 21 years old.

The historic gaming rooms may be viewed daily 9:30am to noon on a tour costing 5€ for adults, 3€ for children 15 and under. For those who want to gamble later, a full day's ticket is available for 3€. The minimum stake is 5€, but visitors are not obligated to play. Hours are daily noon to 2am (Fri–Sat until 3am).

Kaiserallee 1. ✆ **07221/30240.** www.casino-baden-baden.de. Bus: 1.

SPORTS & OUTDOOR PURSUITS

For an entirely new perspective on the area, go hot-air ballooning. **Ballooning 2000** offers rides between the Black Forest and the Vosges. Contact pilot Rainer Keitel (✆ **07223/60002;** www.ballooning2000.de) for details. A 2-hour champagne breakfast trip over the Rhine Valley goes for 253€ per person.

For a more up-close-and-personal experience, **rock climbing** at all levels and altitudes can be enjoyed on the Battert rocks directly over the city. For a climber's guide, contact the **German Alpine Club,** Rathausplatz 7 (✆ **07221/17200;** www.alpenverein.de). You can also walk the 8km (5-mile) nature trail from the Strouzda chapel via Friesenberg to Fremersberg.

Horse races and horseback riding provide additional entertainment in Baden-Baden. Most races take place at the racetrack at Iffezheim, 30km (19 miles) from Baden-Baden, but for tickets and information about the races, contact their organizers, the **Internationaler Club,** Lichtentaler Allee 8 (✆ **07229/187332;** www.baden-galopp.com). Highlights of Baden-Baden's racing season, of which the Internationaler Club is the primary architect, occur during Spring Meeting (a week in late May and early June) and Grand Week (the last 8 days of Aug) with races on Tuesday, Thursday, Saturday, and Sunday.

Many other outdoor sports are offered as well. The local 18-hole course in Fremersberg is one of the most scenic in Europe; contact the **Baden-Baden Golf Club** at ✆ **07221/23579;** www.golf-club-baden-baden.de. Monday to Friday greens fees are 50€, Saturday and Sunday 65€.

For tennis, contact **Tennis Club Rot Weiss,** at Lichtentaler Allee 5 (*℃* **07221/ 24141;** www.tc-rw-baden-baden.de), which offers only outdoor tennis courts. At this complex, outdoor courts are available daily late April to October (weather permitting) from 8am to an hour before sundown for around 6€ per hour.

Swimmers can exercise and splash around at the **Bertholdbad,** on the Ludwig-Wilhelm-Strasse 24 (*℃* **07221/277581**). The complex contains a *Hallenbad* (indoor heated pool) that's open to the general public Tuesday to Friday 7:30 to 9:15am and 1 to 8pm (Wed until 9pm), Saturday 7:30am to 3pm, and Sunday 7:30am to 1pm; and a *Freibad* (outdoor swimming pool) that's open mid-May to mid-September daily from 9am to 7pm. Daily entrance to the compound costs 3.50€ for adults and 2.50€ for students and children 8 to 16.

Where to Stay
VERY EXPENSIVE
Brenner's Park-Hotel & Spa ★★★   This sumptuously furnished hotel is one of the finest in the world, far outdistancing the Steigenberger (see below). It lies in a large private park facing the River Oos and Lichtentaler Allee. The spa facilities here, Baden-Baden's best, are a major draw. Some of its international habitués wouldn't dare let a year go by without an appearance at this glamorous place. Rooms and suites are the last word in luxurious appointments. Beds are sumptuous, and bathrooms are state of the art.

Schillerstrasse 4–6, 76530 Baden-Baden. www.brenners.com. *℃* **07221/9000.** Fax 07221/38772. 100 units. 350€–575€ double; 650€–1,500€ suite. AE, DC, MC, V. Parking 22€. Bus: 201. **Amenities:** 2 restaurants; bar; babysitting; exercise room; indoor heated pool; room service; spa. *In room:* A/C (in some), TV, hair dryer, minibar, Wi-Fi (27€ per day).

EXPENSIVE
Der Kleine Prinz ★ 🛏 ☺   This small hotel in a century-old building exudes the world of Saint-Exupéry's *The Little Prince*, which your kids should read before staying here. Norbert Rademacher, who owns the themed hotel with his wife, has had 25 years' experience in the United States as director at the Waldorf-Astoria and the New York Hilton. Lying in the central pedestrian zone, the two elegant city mansions were combined to form the most personalized, cozy, and intimate nest at the spa. Each of the good-size rooms has its own special feature: an open fireplace, a tower, a balcony, or a whirlpool bathtub. Personalized service adds to the attractiveness of this intimate, immaculate hotel.

Lichtentalerstrasse 36, 76530 Baden-Baden. www.derkleineprinz.de. *℃* **07221/346600.** Fax 07221/38264. 40 units. 199€–299€ double; 335€–850€ suite. Rates include buffet breakfast. AE, MC, V. Parking 16€. **Amenities:** Restaurant; bar; babysitting; room service; Wi-Fi (free; in lobby). *In room:* A/C, TV, hair dryer, minibar.

Hotel Belle Epoque ★★   This is one of the most charming hotels in Baden-Baden, and it's operated by the same people who run the romantic Der Kleine Prinz (see above). Constructed as a private home in 1870, this gem lives up to its namesake. Each room is different, medium in size, and luxuriously furnished with swag draperies, lace curtains, and either antiques or reproductions. The owners will, if possible, give you the style of furnishings you request—Empire, Louis XV, Louis XVI, Biedermeier, Victorian, or Louis Philippe.

Maria-Viktoria-Strasse 2C, 76530 Baden-Baden. www.hotelbelleepoque.de. *℃* **07221/300660.** Fax 07221/300666. 20 units. 199€–299€ double; 325€–750€ suite. Rates include buffet breakfast. AE, DC,

MC, V. Parking 16€. Bus: 201, 207, or 216. **Amenities:** Room service; Wi-Fi (free). *In room:* A/C, TV, CD player, fax, hair dryer, minibar.

Privathotel Quisisana ★★ Although Brenner's Park-Hotel and even the Steigenberger properties are far superior (see above and below), this runner-up is more tranquil. It's set in a spacious park, 8 minutes away from the town center on foot. Some of the most up-to-date health facilities in the Black Forest are here. You can spend an early morning in group calisthenics, for example, followed by treatments with any of a dozen skin- and muscle-toning techniques. One of the more unusual facilities is the *Tepidarium,* where a room is warmed to body temperature as you sit and listen to meditation music. All rooms are suites and well kept, spacious, and well appointed, furnished with both traditional and modern styling.

Bismarckstrasse 21, 76530 Baden-Baden. www.privathotel-quisisana.de. (?) **07221/3690.** Fax 07221/369269. 45 units. 230€–430€ double. Rates include buffet breakfast. AE, MC, V. Parking 10€. Bus: 216. **Amenities:** Restaurant; bar; babysitting; health club and spa; indoor heated pool; room service. *In room:* TV, hair dryer, Wi-Fi (free).

Radisson Blu Badischer Hof ★★ A Baden-Baden landmark, this famed traditional hotel isn't quite as highly rated as Brenner's (see above), but it's neck and neck with its sibling, the Europäischer Hof (see below). Blu Badischer Hof is on a busy street in the center of town, but in the back you'll find an elegant garden with a wide balustraded terrace, flower beds, and a lawn around a stone fountain. The hotel began its career in 1809 as a social center for famous personalities, who came here for "the season." The well-furnished rooms are priced according to size and view. Many have private balconies. Each is elegantly appointed with tasteful fabrics and comfortable beds. Those in the monastery have thermal water piped into the bathrooms.

Lange Strasse 47, 76530 Baden-Baden. www.radissonblu.com/hotel-badenbaden. (?) **800/223-5652** in the U.S. and Canada, or 07221/9340. Fax 07221/934470. 139 units. 129€–270€ double; 276€–326€ suite. Rates include buffet breakfast. AE, MC, V. Parking 13€. Bus: 201. **Amenities:** Restaurant; bar; babysitting; bikes; concierge; exercise room; Jacuzzi; 3 heated pools (1 outdoor and 2 indoor); room service; spa. *In room:* A/C (suites only), TV, hair dryer (in some), minibar, Wi-Fi (free).

Steigenberger Europäischer Hof ★★ This is the liveliest and most social of the centrally located hotels, with a far more bustling atmosphere than Brenner's. The elegant Europäischer Hof is adjacent to the Oos River, which runs at the edge of the Kurpark. The hotel has a pair of joined structures that were built back when spacious living facilities were more affordable. Its colonnaded central hallway is stunning, and many suites and rooms open onto balconies. The staff is a bit too formal for some, but highly efficient.

Kaiserallee 2, 76530 Baden-Baden www.steigenberger.com/Baden_Baden.. (?) **800/223-5652** in the U.S. and Canada, or 07221/9330. Fax 07221/28831. 125 units. 195€–278€ double; 778€–978€ suite. AE, MC, V. Parking 18€. Bus: 201. Opposite the Kurgarten and the casino. **Amenities:** Restaurant; bar; babysitting; bikes; concierge; exercise room; room service; spa. *In room:* A/C (in some), TV, hair dryer, minibar, Wi-Fi (10€ per hour).

MODERATE

Haus Reichert The five-floor 19th-century Haus Reichert is an inviting place in a central location, not far from the casino. Rooms are of good size, high ceilinged, and comfortable, though little of the original furniture or detailing has survived the many renovations. Most are priced at the lower end of the scale given below.

Sophienstrasse 4, 76530 Baden-Baden. www.hausreichert.de. ℰ **07221/9080.** Fax 07221/29534. 23 units. 95€–125€ double. Rates include continental breakfast. AE, DC, MC, V. Parking 11€. Bus: 201. **Amenities:** Indoor heated pool; room service; sauna; Wi-Fi (free; in lobby). *In room:* TV, hair dryer, minibar.

INEXPENSIVE

Hotel am Markt ✦ On the old marketplace, this hotel is far removed from the grander social life of Baden-Baden and its deluxe palace hotels. Though it may be at the bottom of the pecking order, it's number one in town for economy. The location is first rate, with the quiet interrupted only by chimes from the church across the square. A tiny terrace cafe in front has petunia-filled window boxes. The hotel offers small, simply furnished, comfortable rooms.

Marktplatz 18, 76530 Baden-Baden. www.hotel-am-markt-baden.de. ℰ **07221/27040.** Fax 07221/ 270444. 27 units, 12 with bathroom or shower. 65€–68€ double without bathroom or shower; 82€–88€ double with bathroom or shower. Rates include buffet breakfast. MC, V. Parking 4€. Bus: 201. *In room:* TV, Wi-Fi (free).

HEIDELBERG, STUTTGART & THE NECKAR VALLEY

Ancient castle ruins in the midst of thick woodlands, quiet university towns, busy manufacturing centers—you'll find all these in the countryside of southwestern Germany. This seldom-visited area extends along the Neckar River from Heidelberg past medieval towns and modern cities as far as Tübingen. Although the river is open to commercial shipping vessels as far as Stuttgart, much of the valley has remained unspoiled. The castles that rise around every bend in the river were once home to the German royal families of Hohenstaufen and Hohenzollern. Today, castles and country palaces sometimes offer bed and board to travelers.

HEIDELBERG ★★★

120km (75 miles) NW of Stuttgart, 20km (12 miles) SE of Mannheim, 89km (55 miles) S of Frankfurt

Heidelberg, located about 89km (55 miles) south of Frankfurt, was fortunate to escape destruction by air raids in World War II. Consequently, original buildings from the later Middle Ages and early Renaissance are still standing. Historically, though, Heidelberg is a young person's place; the oldest university in Germany is based here, dating to 1386. The student population and university life impart a palpable energy, felt especially in the narrow lanes and lively inns of the Altstadt. It's no surprise Mark Twain cavorted in its lively streets in *A Tramp Abroad.*

Things to Do   Looming over the town among terraced gardens, the **Heidelberg Castle** beckons you to climb up the Gothic-Renaissance beauty; its cellar houses the **Heidelberg Tun,** the world's largest wine cask. The Bergbahn (mountain train) whisks you up from the **Kornmarkt** in the center in a flash. In the **Altstadt** (old town), cross over the **Alte Brücke** (Old Bridge) and visit the **Heidelberg monkey** bronze statue—touch his mirror to get rich, touch the paw to ensure a return to Heidelberg.

Shopping   Take a wander down boutique-lined **Hauptstrasse,** one of Europe's longest pedestrian zones and home to a third of all the city's stores. Poke your head into the shops selling handicrafts, ceramics and

glass and be sure to step into **Leder Meid,** purveyors of exceptional leather accessories. Heidelberg's known for its bustling **markets,** held on Tuesday and Friday mornings at Friedrich-Ebert-Platz and Saturday mornings at Marktplatz.

Nightlife & Entertainment   Typical of any university town, Heidelberg is full of lively, youthful bars and pubs; the majority cluster around **Hauptstrasse** and **Markplatz,** both in the **Altstadt.** Don't miss **Zum Sepp'l,** a well-known student pub in town. Here you can examine the names of previous patrons carved into the ancient tables while you sip a beer in the 17th-century structure. For a more subdued evening, head to **Max Bar,** a French-style cafe and beer bar overlooking the **Marktplatz** action.

Restaurants & Dining   Heidelberg's best dining is peppered in and around the **Altstadt.** For hearty German cuisine the **Kulturbrauerei,** a cavernous beer hall with a tranquil garden, is perfect for summer meals with a mug of frothy beer. Or head to **Zur Herrenmühle,** a family owned stalwart in a 17th-century structure with wooden beams. Regional German cuisine dominates in the cozy, antique-filled space, like *rindsrouladen* (rolled strips of beef) with red cabbage and spaetzle.

Essentials
GETTING THERE
BY PLANE   The nearest major airport is Frankfurt (see chapter 13), with a direct bus link to Heidelberg. The shuttle bus between Frankfurt and Heidelberg costs 20€ per person. Call ℰ **0621/651620** or visit www.ics-logistik.de for shuttle information.

BY TRAIN   **Heidelberg's Hauptbahnhof** is a major railroad station, lying on the Mannheim line, with frequent service to both regional towns and major cities. From Frankfurt, 26 direct trains arrive per day (trip time: 1 hr.); from Stuttgart, 25 direct trains (trip time: 45 min.). Travel time to and from Munich is about 3½ hours. For information, call ℰ **01805/996633** or visit www.bahn.de.

BY BUS   Regional bus service is provided by **BRN Busverkehr Rhein-Neckar** at Heidelberg (ℰ **06221/60620;** www.brn.de).

BY CAR   Motorists should take the A5 Autobahn from the north or south.

VISITOR INFORMATION
Contact the **Heidelberg Tourist Bureau,** Willy-Brandt-Platz 1 (ℰ **06221/19433;** www.heidelberg-marketing.de). It's open April to October Monday to Saturday 9am to 7pm, and Sunday 10am to 6pm; and November to March Monday to Saturday 9am to 6pm. Here, visitors can purchase a **Heidelberg Card,** which provides discounts on attractions and free use of public transportation. Cards valid for any consecutive 2-day

---

Exploring on Two Wheels

Unique in Germany, the **Neckar Valley Cycle Path** ★ allows you to ride all the way from the source of the Neckar, in Villingen-Schwenningen, 375km (233 miles) to the confluence of the Rhine at Mannheim. The path is marked with a signpost showing a green bicycle and a red wheel mark. The route follows the river the whole way, though many cyclists go only as far as Heidelberg. Along the way, you'll pass castles, manor houses, vineyards, country inns, and such old towns as Rottweil and Esslingen. Most cyclists average about 50km (30 miles) per day on the trail.

Heidelberg

ATTRACTIONS ●

Heidelberg Castle **20**
Heiligeistkirche **16**
Kornmarkt **19**
Kurpfälzisches Museum **11**
Marktplatz **17**
Ruprecht-Karl University **13**
Rathaus **18**
Studentenkarzer **14**

HOTELS ■

Arthotel **10**
Der Europäische Hof-Hotel Europa **8**
Heidelberg Marriott Hotel **7**
Heidelberg Suites **1**
Hip Hotel **12**
Hotel Anlage **9**
Hotel Hirschgasse **2**
Hotel Vier Jahreszeiten **4**
NH Heidelberg **8**
Parkhotel Atlantic Schlosshotel **21**
Romantik-Hotel Zum Ritter St. Georg **15**
Schnookeloch **5**
Villa Marstall **6**
Zur Alten Brücke **3**

period cost 13€ per person; cards valid for any consecutive 4-day period go for 16€ per person. A family card is available as well. Valid for two adults and two children 15 and under for any consecutive 2-day period, it sells for 28€ and carries the same provisions.

GETTING AROUND

Heidelberg is crisscrossed with a network of trams and buses, many of which intersect at the Bismarckplatz in the town center. Bus nos. 31 and 32 travel frequently between the railway station and the Universitätsplatz. The Altstadt stretches on either side of the Hauptstrasse between the Bismarckplatz and the Universitätsplatz. Bus or tram fares cost 2.20€ for a single ride.

Exploring Heidelberg

Summertime in Heidelberg, according to the song from *The Student Prince,* is a time for music and romance. Today, it's also a time when droves of visitors invade this beautiful city. Heidelberg was not leveled by air raids in World War II and therefore still has original buildings from the later Middle Ages and early Renaissance. Modern Heidelberg centers on Bismarckplatz at the foot of the Theodore-Heuss-Brücke; in this part of the city, you'll find many of the best hotels and restaurants, and the tall buildings and shopping plazas contrast with the Altstadt nearby. Across the Neckar are sports grounds, a zoo, and a large botanical garden.

Heidelberg is, above all, a university town and has been since 1386. Students make up much of the population. The colorful atmosphere that university life imparts to the town is felt especially in the old student quarter, with its narrow streets and lively inns. This oldest university in Germany is officially named **Ruprecht-Karl-University** (unofficially called Heidelberg University), honoring both its founder, Elector Ruprecht I of the Palatinate, and the man who, in 1803, made it the leading university in the state of Baden, Margrave Karl Friedrich. The school was founded after the Great Schism of 1378, when conflicting claims to the papacy created unrest and German teachers and students fled the Sorbonne in Paris.

TOURING HEIDELBERG CASTLE ★★★   You can reach the huge red-sandstone Heidelberg Castle (✆ **06221/538421**), set amid woodlands and terraced gardens, by several routes. A paved road winds up the Neue Schlossstrasse past the old houses perched on the hillside. Yet, walking is the most rewarding approach because of the constantly changing scenic view of the town and surrounding countryside. You can take the more gradual slope from the Klingentor, or make the shorter walk up the steep Burgweg from Kornmarkt. The easier walk from Klingentor takes about 20 minutes, while the steep Burgweg walk from Kornmarkt can last 30 or 40 minutes, depending on your stamina.

The castle is a dignified ruin, but even in its deteriorated state, it's one of the finest Gothic-Renaissance castles in Germany. Entering at the main gate, the huge **Gun Park** is to your left, from which you can gaze down upon Heidelberg and the Neckar Valley. Straight ahead is the **Thick Tower,** or what remains of it after its 8m (26-ft.) walls were blown up by the French in the late 17th century. Leaving Gun Park via Elizabeth's Gate (erected by Friedrich V in 1615 for his Scottish wife, the daughter of James I), you come to the Bridge House and the bridge crossing the site of the former moat.

Along the north side of the courtyard stretches the stern **palace of Friedrich IV ★★**, erected 1601 to 1607. The palace is less damaged than other parts of the castle, and its rooms are almost completely restored, including the gallery of princes and kings of the German empire from the time of Charlemagne. The ancient bell tower, at the northeast end of the Altan, dates from the early 1500s.

Boating in the Neckar

Heidelberg is an ideal point from which to explore the romantic Neckar Valley. From mid-April to early October, you can take a boat tour along the river as far as Neckarsteinach. There are usually four or five round-trips daily, and you need not return on the same boat. Boats are operated by the **Rhein-Neckar-Fahrgastschiffahrt GmbH,** Stadthalle, Heidelberg (© 06221/ 20181; www.rnf-schifffahrt.de). Trips between Heidelberg and Neckarsteinach cost 13€ round-trip, and those between Heidelberg and Hirschhorn (which operate mid-June to early Sept) cost 20€ round-trip. The same families have been working the Neckar since the early 1600s.

At the west end of the terrace, in the cellars of the castle, is the **Wine Vat Building ★**, built in the late 16th century and worth a visit for a look at the Great Cask, symbol of the abundant and exuberant life of the Rhineland-Palatinate. This huge barrel-like monstrosity, built in 1751, is capable of holding more than 208,000 liters (55,000 gal.) of wine.

To the east, connecting the palace of Friedrich IV to the **Ottheinrich Building,** itself an outstanding example of German Renaissance architecture, is the **Hall of Mirrors Building,** constructed in 1549—a Renaissance masterpiece. Only the shell of the original building remains, enough to give you an idea of its former glory, with arcades and steep gables decorated with cherubs and sirens.

Next to Ottheinrich's palace is the Chemist's Tower, housing the **Pharmaceutical Museum ★** (© 06221/25880), with utensils and laboratory equipment from the 18th and 19th centuries. Entrance is free to those who paid admission already to enter the castle precincts.

A 1-hour guided tour of the castle costs 5€ for adults and 3€ for children. Tours are frequent, especially in summer, and some are conducted in English. The castle is open April to October daily 10am to 6pm, November to March daily 10am to 5:30pm.

EXPLORING THE ALTSTADT   All the important sights of Heidelberg lie on or near the south bank of the Neckar. However, you should cross to the north side of the river (via the 18th-c. Karl Theodore Bridge) for the best overall view. **Philosophenweg (Philosopher's Way),** halfway up the hill on the north bank, offers an especially fine vista.

In the town itself, a tour of the main attractions begins with **Marktplatz** in front of the **Rathaus.** On market days, the square is filled with stalls of fresh flowers, fish, and vegetables. At the opposite end of the square is the late-Gothic **Heiliggeistkirche,** built around 1400, the largest Gothic church in the Palatinate. For nearly 300 years, the church was the burial place of the electors, but most of the graves were destroyed in the French invasion late in the 17th century. Around the corner is the famous old mansion **Romantik Hotel Zum Ritter St. Georg** (p. 417).

Kurpfälzisches Museum (Museum of the Palatinate) ★   MUSEUM   The baroque Palais Morass houses a large collection of painting and sculpture spanning 6 centuries. The most notable piece is the Riemenschneider Altar from Windsheim (1509), showing Christ and the Twelve Apostles. There's also an archaeological collection with a cast of the jawbone of the 500,000-year-old Heidelberg Man and a section on the history of the Palatinate. The restaurant makes a great lunch stop (see below).

Hauptstrasse 97. ✆ **06221/5834020.** www.museum-heidelberg.de. Admission 3€ adults, 1.80€ students and children 17 and under. Tues–Sun 10am–6pm. Bus: 31, 32, or 35.

Studentenkarzer (Student Jail) HISTORIC BUILDING   Unruly and drunken students were incarcerated here anywhere from 3 days to 4 weeks. (Any longer and they would not have done their studying.) Prisoners bedecked the walls and even the ceilings with graffiti and drawings, including portraits and silhouettes, until the last ones left in 1914. Ring the caretaker's bell for admission.

Augustinergasse 2. ✆ **06221/543593.** Admission 3€ adults, 2.50€ students and children 14 and under. Ticket includes entry for the University Museum and Alte Aula. Apr–Sept Tues–Sun 10am–6pm; Oct Tues–Sun 10am–4pm; Nov–Mar Tues–Sat 10am–4pm. Bus: 31, 32, or 35.

Where to Eat

VERY EXPENSIVE

Kurfürstenstube ★★ FRENCH   A fine hotel should offer fine food, and Der Europäische Hof-Hotel doesn't disappoint. Located in the ground-floor wing, the wood-paneled grill room is attractively decorated with provincial furnishings—real Old Heidelberg with coffered ceilings, and lots of nostalgic kitsch. The menu is in English, but the cuisine is mainly French, with both fixed-price and a la carte meals. Only the highest-quality seasonal ingredients are used. Dishes are creative, refined, and balanced, as evoked by such main courses as roast filet of codfish in a purple mustard sauce with green asparagus and truffled risotto, or steamed filet of local beef with two types of beetroot and a foam of horseradish. The wine list is the most impressive in town.

In Der Europäische Hof-Hotel Europa, Friedrich-Ebert-Anlage 1. ✆ **06221/5150.** Reservations required. Main courses 29€–33€; fixed-price menu 92€. AE, DC, MC, V. Daily noon–2:30pm and 6:30–10:30pm. Tram: Bismarckplatz.

Schwarz Das Restaurant ★★★ GERMAN/MEDITERRANEAN   Almost from the moment it opened, this beautifully designed restaurant on the 12th floor of the Print Media Academy was hailed by the press as serving the best cuisine in the city. Given the Schwarz's lofty perch overlooking the city, this is more than a "mushroom with a view." The darling of critics, Manfred Schwarz earned his reputation by cooking for numerous state guests to Germany. His gourmet fixed-price menus, ranging from three to seven courses, change every month. Who knows what will grace your plate when you visit? Let's just say he's big on truffles and caviar, along with luxe products. You might try scallops in a black sesame crust with sautéed radicchio, or roast beef tournedos with asparagus, or even a smoked salmon roll filled with Canadian lobster and served with a cucumber and wasabi salad. The restaurant also features the town's most elegant aperitif bar, and even a smoker's lounge.

Kurfürsten-Anlage 60. ✆ **06221/757030.** www.schwarzdasrestaurant.com. Reservations required. Main courses 23€–39€; fixed-price menus 89€–105€. AE, DC, MC, V. Tues–Sat 11:30am–2pm and 6–10pm. Closed a week in Jan and 3 weeks in Aug. Bus: 32, 33, 34, and 35.

EXPENSIVE

Simplicissimus ★★ FRENCH   This elegant spot is ideal for a gourmet rendezvous, and in summer it features an outdoor courtyard for dining. Johann Lummer, one of the finest chefs in Heidelberg, prepares a cuisine moderne with consummate skill. *Gourmet* magazine said that Herr Lummer "paints with food," and you'll agree. Not only are his dishes delectable, but their presentation is equally pleasing. The menu varies but is likely to include braised pork cheeks from Spain with bread dumplings, or filet of sole in lobster sauce with a risotto.

Ingrimstrasse 16. ℂ **06221/183336.** www.restaurant-simplicissimus.de. Reservations required. Main courses 20€–29€; fixed-price menus 30€–65€. MC, V. Tues-Sat 6pm–midnight. Closed 1 week in late Aug, 1 week in Sept, and 2 weeks in Jan. Bus: 31, 32, or 35.

MODERATE

Kurpfälzisches Museum Restaurant GERMAN   This quiet culinary oasis at the museum makes a good stopover for lunch. The setting is baroque and very grand, with one enormous dining hall and two satellite dining rooms. You can order such dishes as slices of veal liver in port-wine sauce or duck breast sautéed in honey and pepper, while you enjoy the view of the little garden and splashing fountain. The food is satisfying, though hardly gourmet.

Hauptstrasse 97. ℂ **06221/24050.** www.restaurantkurpfaelzischesmuseumheidelberg.com. Reservations required. Main courses 16€–19€, fixed-price menus 23€–39€. AE, DC, MC, V. June–Sept Sun-Thurs 11am–11pm, Fri-Sat 11am–midnight; off season Sun-Thurs 11am–3pm and 5:30–10pm, Fri-Sat 11am–11pm. Bus: 31 or 32.

Romantik Hotel Zum Ritter St. Georg ★ GERMAN/INTERNATIONAL   This restaurant (in one of Heidelberg's most famous Renaissance buildings) is popular with students and professors, who know that they can get great German cooking here. You dine either in the first-class Rittersaal (Great Hall) or in the smaller Councillors' Chamber. Aim for the elegant larger room, with its sepia ceilings, wainscoting, and Oriental rugs. Locals flock here when the house specialty is offered: a saddle of Odenwald venison for two (in season). Start with the St. Hubertus game soup with brandy foam, and end with the crêpes suzette. In between those courses you can order spit roasted jumbo shrimp and salmon with a garlic-laced chili mousse or fried filet of pikeperch with a Martini lime sauce.

Hauptstrasse 178. ℂ **06221/1350.** www.ritter-heidelberg.de. Reservations recommended. Main courses 10€–23€. AE, DC, MC, V. Daily noon–2pm and 6–10pm. Bus: 31, 32, or 35.

Schlossweinstube★ GERMAN   On the grounds of Heidelberg Castle, this is one of the most dramatic places to dine in the city, with Heidelberg laid out down below. On a summer night, a table on its panoramic terrace is the most desired in town. A selection of soups or appetizers, ranging from a mango and endive salad to a fish terrine, gets you started. Every night a carefully crafted array of main dishes features the freshest of fish, meats, and poultry, along with vegetarian options. Seasonal specialties may include Swabian saddle of pork with lintels and apple-potato cakes in a dark beer and cumin sauce.

Adjoining is the less expensive Bistro Backhaus, serving regional fare in a rustic setting with the largest *Backkamin* (baking oven) in Heidelberg. You can even stop in here for coffee and cake.

Schlosshof, on the grounds of Heidelberg Castle. ℂ **06221/97970.** Reservations required. Main courses 13€–28€; 3-course menu 49€; 4-course menu 62€. AE, DC, MC, V. Wed-Sat 5:30pm–midnight; Sun 11am–3pm.

Zur Herrenmühle ★ GERMAN/INTERNATIONAL   The service at this family-owned restaurant, located in a 17th-century house with thick walls and antique paneling, is equaled only at the Kurfürstenstube (see above), and the sophisticated maitre d' adds both glamour and an appropriate theatricality. Its cuisine is classic, based on the freshest ingredients. Try the rack of lamb with herbs and homemade green noodles, or the roast roebuck with a vinegar-and-honey sauce. The desserts, such as the sorbet flavored with blood oranges served with a parfait of mandarin oranges, make better use of fresh fruit than any other place in town.

Hauptstrasse 237. (©) **06221/602909.** www.herrenmuehle-heidelberg.de. Reservations recommended. Main courses 16€–26€; fixed-price menu 29€. AE, DC, MC, V. Mon–Sat 6–11pm. Closed last 2 weeks of Mar. Bus: 33.

INEXPENSIVE

Dorfschänke ★ 🍴 GERMAN Hidden down a back street in the Neuenheim section, this is one of the simplest restaurants in Heidelberg, and its affordable prices make it popular with students. Okay, so it doesn't have tablecloths—just plain wooden tables—but it's been packed since 1908. The cooks must be doing something right. Their specialty is *Flammkuchen,* a regional dish from Alsace resembling a square pizza with onions and cheese but no tomato sauce. It's a real tasty treat, as are the garlic-studded lamb and the steak served with bubbling mozzarella cheese, spinach, and fried potatoes. Tables spill outside in summer.

Lutherstrasse 14. (©) **06221/419041.** www.dorfschaenke-hd.com. Reservations recommended Fri–Sat for dinner. Main courses 8€–18€. No credit cards. Daily 5pm–midnight. Tram: 5 or 23. Bus: 31.

Shopping

The main shopping street is the traffic-free **Hauptstrasse,** which is filled with stores selling glass, crystal, handicrafts, and other items. Heidelberg is also known for its markets, including the one held on Wednesday and Saturday mornings at Marktplatz and another held Tuesday and Friday mornings at Friedrich-Ebert-Platz. One Saturday a month, based on a flexible schedule that corresponds to the events being presented in the city's convention center, a giant *Flohmarkt* (flea market) sprawls along the Kirchheimer Weg, on the city's southwestern edge, beginning at the Messeplatz. Come here for a streetside collection of junk, knickknacks, and castaways from another era.

Spiess & Walther, Friedrich-Ebert-Anlage 23a (© **06221/22233;** www.spiess undwalther.de; bus: 30, 31, 32, or 35), features exclusive designs in contemporary furniture, antiques, and textiles. For all items in leather, stop by **Leder-Meid,** Hauptstrasse 88 (© **06221/22570;** bus: 31, 32, or 35), which sells the crafts of German and other manufacturers. Some of the best women's clothing in Heidelberg is inventoried at **Caroline,** just around the corner from the entrance to the Hotel Europäischer Hof, at Friedrich-Ebert-Anlage 1 (© **06221/602963**). Come here for casual but elegant sportswear, and also for upscale formalwear.

If you want more variety under one roof, go to either branch of Heidelberg's best department store, **Kaufhof,** Hauptstrasse 30 (© **06221/5040;** www.galeria-kaufhof. de; tram: 5, 21, 22, 23, 24, or 26), or Bergheimerstrasse 1 (© **06221/9160;** tram: 5, 21, 22, 23, 24, or 26).

Entertainment & Nightlife

Nights here are alive with the youthful enthusiasm of Heidelberg's students. Early evenings often start in the bars along Hauptstrasse; then late nights get rolling in the clubs around Marktplatz.

THE PERFORMING ARTS The main performance stage is **Theater der Stadt,** Theaterstrasse 4 (© **06221/5820000;** www.theaterheidelberg.de; bus: 31 or 32), where nightly entertainment includes plays, opera, and dance productions. From mid-June to mid-August, the **Schlossfest-Spiele** festival brings opera, classical music, jazz, and theater to venues around the area, including Heidelberg Castle. Contact **Heidelberg Ticket Service,** Theaterstrasse 4 (✆ **06221/5820000**), for tickets.

HISTORIC STUDENT DRINKING CLUBS Heidelberg's most famous and revered student tavern, **Zum Roten Ochsen (Red Ox Inn)** ★, Hauptstrasse 217 (✆ **06221/20977;** www.roterochsen.de; bus: 33), opened in 1703. For six generations, it has been in the Spengel family; they have welcomed everybody from Bismarck to Mark Twain. It seems that every student who has attended the university has left his or her mark (or initials) on the walls. The series of rooms, where revelers sit at long oak tables under smoke-blackened ceilings, is arranged in horseshoe fashion; the U part has a pianist who sets the musical pace. As the evening progresses, the songs become louder and louder. A mug of beer costs 3€ and up, and wine is 4€ per glass. Meals go from 9€ to 17€. The tavern is open from April to October Monday to Saturday 11:30am to 2pm and 5pm to midnight, November to March Monday to Saturday 5pm to midnight.

Next door is **Zum Sepp'l,** Hauptstrasse 213 (✆ **06221/23085;** www.zum-seppl. de; bus: 11 or 33), open since 1634, the second most famous drinking club in Heidelberg. It's also filled with photographs and carved initials of former students, along with memorabilia that ranges from old Berlin street signs to Alabama license plates. Meals cost 8€ to 18€. A mug of beer goes for 3€. There's live piano music Monday, Tuesday, Friday, and Saturday from 7pm to midnight. When the university is closed, the activity dies down considerably. It's open Monday to Friday noon to 11pm, and Saturday and Sunday 11:30am to 3:30pm and 5pm to midnight.

BARS & CAFES When you tire of beer and want a more spirited drink, wander over to **Sonderbar,** Unterestrasse 13 (✆ **06221/25200;** bus: 31 or 32), which stocks more than 150 brands of whiskey, 10 kinds of vodka, and sundry other potions, besides its 11 types of beer. It's open daily 2pm to 2am (Fri–Sat until 3am).

Catch up on the latest news and trends at **Café Journal,** Hauptstrasse 162 (✆ **06221/161712;** bus: 31 or 32), where drinkers linger over beer while scanning newspapers and magazines from all over Europe and the United States. The cafe is open daily 8am to midnight. **Hard Rock Cafe,** Hauptstrasse 142 (✆ **06221/22819;** www.hard-rockcafe.de; bus: 31 or 32), has a branch here, open 10am to 1am.

LIVE MUSIC & CLUBS Once-sleepy Heidelberg now has a thriving music scene. A welcome addition on the scene for salsa lovers is **Havana Cocktailbar-Restaurant,** Neckarstaden 24 (✆ **06221/3894330;** www.havana-heidelberg.de), adding some Latino zest to this university town. Tapas and mojitos, along with some 100 cocktails, brighten the evening, as does the live piano music. The trendy **Print Media Lounge,** Kurfürstenanlage 60 (✆ **06221/653949;** www.printmedialounge. de), has opened across from the rail station. Serving full meals, it's mainly known for its music and exotic cocktails. There's soul, funk, and jazz on Sundays; DJs play on Friday and Saturday nights.

Where to Stay

If you want to stick with the familiar, you can stay at the **Crowne Plaza Heidelberg,** Kurfürstenanlage 1 (www.crowneplaza-heidelberg.de; ✆ **06221/9170**), in the center of town, offering all the comforts of a top-tier hotel but lacking any Heidelberg atmosphere. Doubles cost 135€ to 310€.

VERY EXPENSIVE

Der Europäische Hof-Hotel Europa ★★★ This glamorous hotel is by far Heidelberg's best. It fronts the city park in the heart of town, within walking distance of the castle and the university. Its interior is like that of a gracious home, with antiques, crystal chandeliers, and Oriental rugs. Some rooms and several suites face a quiet inside garden; front rooms in the oldest section tend to be noisy (from traffic). Nineteen have whirlpool tubs. The most dramatic recent improvement has been the addition of the Panorama Spa Club and the latest fitness equipment.

Friedrich-Ebert-Anlage 1, 69117 Heidelberg. © **06221/5150.** Fax 06221/515506. www.europaeischerhof. com. 118 units. 148€–384€ double; 338€–440€ junior suite; 420€–620€ 2-room apt. AE, DC, MC, V. Parking 19€. Tram: Bismarckplatz. **Amenities:** 2 restaurants; bar; babysitting; concierge; health club & spa; indoor heated pool; room service. *In room:* A/C, TV, fax, hair dryer, minibar, Wi-Fi (27€ per day).

EXPENSIVE

Arthotel ★★ 🎁 This is a carefully restored and very hip designer hotel lying in the Altstadt just below the famous castle. It attracts a trendy crowd, often young, and is imbued with sophistication and taste. Special features include a big roof terrace with panoramic views and an inner courtyard for open-air drinking and dining. A pedestrian area is found on the street in front, ideal for shopping and sightseeing. Bedrooms and suites are as modern as tomorrow, with simple yet elegant furnishings, including soothing pastels and oak parquet floors.

Grabengasse 7, 69117 Heidelberg. www.arthotel.de. © **06221/650060.** Fax 06221/65006100. 24 units. 125€–198€ double; 258€–390€ suite. AE, MC, V. Parking 12€. **Amenities:** Restaurant; bar; concierge; room service. *In room:* A/C, TV/DVD, CD player, hair dryer, Wi-Fi (10€ per day).

Heidelberg Marriott Hotel This hotel sits on the banks of the Neckar, just a few minutes from the Altstadt and the main train station. Although it doesn't have the flair and traditional style of Der Europäische Hof (above), it's far superior to its nearest rival, Holiday Inn Crowne Plaza. The exit from the autobahn is only minutes away, making it convenient for motorists. Rooms are comfortably furnished, many with views over the river or the hills beyond. As an added perk, the hotel operates a shuttle service to and from Frankfurt International Airport.

Vangerowstrasse 16, 69115 Heidelberg. www.marriott.com. © **06221/9080.** Fax 06221/908660. 248 units. 98€–246€ double; 225€–698€ suite. AE, DC, MC, V. Parking 18€. Tram: 2. **Amenities:** 2 restaurants; bar; babysitting; concierge; exercise room; indoor heated pool; room service; spa. *In room:* A/C, TV, fax, hair dryer, minibar, Wi-Fi (13€ per 24 hr.).

Heidelberg Suites Across from the Karl Theodor Bridge, this boutique hotel is a charmer. Designed by accomplished Italian architect Michele Bönan, these rooms possess a traditional character with etched mirrors, heroic busts, and deer antlers. The furniture was designed exclusively for the hotel, and there's a good chance you can buy a piece you fancy. Each spacious unit comes with two rooms and a fully equipped kitchen, and could be ideal for a family. Most of the bedrooms offer a view of Heidelberg Castle. The hotel is also equipped with special features, such as a fireplace in the lounge, a wonderful garden, and a panoramic rooftop terrace.

Neuenheimer Landstrasse 12, 69120 Heidelberg. www.heidelbergsuites.com. © **06221/655650.** Fax 06221/6556513. 25 units. 285€ double; 355€ junior suite; 435€–585€ suite. AE, MC, V. Parking 15€. **Amenities:** Bar; free bikes; exercise room; room service. *In room:* A/C, TV, hair dryer, kitchen, MP3 docking station, Wi-Fi (free).

Hip Hotel ★★ 🎁 This boutique hotel is the only designer inn in town to surpass Arthotel in modern flair. Both attract a similar clientele of fashionistas to their elegant, sophisticated precincts. The little hotel is part of the historic inn, Zum Güldenen Schaf, which for decades has been operated by the welcoming Kischka family, which is known for its historical menus and theme evenings. Although the hotel is more than 250 years old, don't expect antique, creaky rooms.

Hip, incidentally, means "Hyper Individual Place" in this context. Everything is fresh and contemporary—Claudia and Karim Kischka traveled the world picking up furnishings and accessories for the bedrooms. Each room is also individually designed and named for some of the most famous cities in the world, including New York, Tokyo, Marrakesh, and Amsterdam.

Hauptstrasse 115, 69117 Heidelberg. www.hip-hotel.de. ✆ **06221/20879.** Fax 06221/160409. 15 units. 150€–210€ double; 190€–240€ triple. AE, DC, MC, V. Parking 12€. **Amenities:** Restaurant; bar; room service. *In room:* A/C, TV, minibar, Wi-Fi (free).

Hotel Hirschgasse ★★ This country-home-style hotel, nestled on the hillside of a historic lane adjoining Philosopher's Way, is tops in Heidelberg for its tranquil and romantic setting. It dates from 1472 and has lodged Otto von Bismarck, and hosted Mark Twain as he attended a student duel. Rooms are all suites decorated in Laura Ashley designs, and all come equipped with modern bathrooms.

Hirschgasse 3, 69120 Heidelberg. ✆ **06221/4540.** Fax 06221/454111. www.hirschgasse.de. 20 units. 150€–195€ junior suite; 195€–245€ deluxe suite; 245€–340€ salon suite. AE, DC, MC, V. Free parking. Bus: 34. **Amenities:** 2 restaurants; babysitting; room service. *In room:* TV, hair dryer, minibar, Wi-Fi (10€ per hour).

Romantik Hotel Zum Ritter St. Georg ★ A glorious old inn right out of the German Renaissance, the Zum Ritter is a well-preserved rarity, although it's inferior to the Hirschgasse (above) in comfort and antique charm. Built in 1592 by Frenchman Charles Bèlier, it's now listed among the major sightseeing attractions of this university town. There are no public lounges. Many rooms are somewhat cramped, but beds are comfortable and the bathrooms have been renewed. See the review of one of its restaurants above.

Hauptstrasse 178, 69117 Heidelberg. www.ritter-heidelberg.de. ✆ **06221/1350.** Fax 06221/135230. 37 units. 118€–176€ double; 206€–246€ suite. AE, DC, MC, V. Bus: 31, 32, or 35. **Amenities:** 3 restaurants; room service. *In room:* TV, hair dryer, minibar.

MODERATE

Parkhotel Atlantic Schlosshotel ★ Removed from the bustle of Heidelberg, this grand hotel lies a 20-minute walk from the center on the wooded outskirts behind the castle. Its setting makes it the best in its price range; hotels in the city center, unless soundproof, get a lot of traffic noise. Guests are assured calm, modern comfort in annexes built around the core of an older villa. Although the decor is lackluster, the rooms are comfortable enough after a walk through town or on one of the many woodland trails extending through the Neckar Valley.

Schloss-Wolfsbrunnen-Weg 23, 69118 Heidelberg. www.parkhotel-atlantic.de. ✆ **06221/60420.** Fax 06221/604260. 24 units. 79€–100€ double; 105€–145€ suite. Rates include buffet breakfast. AE, DC, MC, V. Free parking. Head east from the Hauptbahnhof, along Kurfürstenanlage, go through the tunnel, and take the 2nd right, bringing you to Heidelberg Castle; continue straight beyond the castle to the hotel. **Amenities:** Room service. *In room:* TV, minibar, Wi-Fi (free).

Villa Marstall★★ This riverfront hotel not only offers panoramic views of the Old Town, but also lies just a short walk from the Hauptstrasse, the bustling main shopping drag of Heidelberg. It possesses the personalized service, comfort, style, and sense of romance that you'd expect from a boutique hotel. The bright and airy bedrooms, often with a four-poster, are fitted with floors of Brazilian cherrywood and contain exclusively designed classic wooden furniture. It's the thoughtful extras that count here, including such items as hypoallergenic blankets and pillows. To top it off, the candlelit breakfast buffet is the best of any hotel in the city.

Lauerstrasse 1 Heidelberg. www.villamarstall.com. ℂ **06221/655570.** Fax 06221/6555779. 18 units. 115€–185€ double. AE, DC, MC, V. Parking 8€. Bus: 31, 32, or 35. **Amenities:** Room service. *In room:* A/C, TV, hair dryer, minibar, Wi-Fi (free).

Zur Alten Brücke ★ ⚑   Next to the Restaurant Wirtshaus zum Nepomuk, this discovery is in an early-18th-century town house that has been restored and much improved over the years. The hotel borrows its name from the nearby famous bridge spanning the Neckar. Even though the building is a golden oldie, the small hotel boasts bright and fresh bedrooms furnished comfortably and tastefully in a modern style. Each has a different floor plan, but all have a panoramic view—some overlook the river, others Heidelberg Castle. The suites here are some of the most romantic in town, especially the roomy penthouse ones. Each comes with a bamboo floor, designer beds, a large bathroom, and a great view.

Obere Neckarstrasse 2, 69117 Heidelberg. www.hotel-zur-alten-bruecke.de. ℂ **06221/739130.** Fax 06221/ 7391320. 16 units. 139€–159€ double; from 199€ suite. Rates include buffet breakfast. No credit cards. Parking 12€. **Amenities:** Restaurant; bar; Wi-Fi (free; in lobby). *In room:* TV.

INEXPENSIVE

Hotel Anlage ⚑   Housed in a lavishly built, late-19th-century palace, this hotel remains one of Heidelberg's more affordable. It features an ideal location, wedged between the base of the castle hill and the heart of the city. Rooms are comfortably furnished with no unnecessary eccentricities, and have tidy bathrooms.

Friedrich-Ebert-Anlage 32, 69117 Heidelberg. www.hotel-anlage.de. ℂ **06221/5850960.** Fax 06221/ 585096130. 19 units. 79€–104€ double. Rates include continental breakfast. AE, MC, V. Parking 7€. Bus: 30, 31, 32, or 33. **Amenities:** Room service. *In room:* TV, Wi-Fi (free).

Hotel Vier Jahreszeiten   Named the Four Seasons, this hotel is a worthy choice any time of the year. With an unbeatable location, its location makes a great starting point for many interesting walks. Several famous student inns (drinking taverns patronized mainly by students of the university at Heidelberg, although open to all) and the castle are also nearby, not to mention the shopping of the Hauptstrasse and the Alte Brücke. The hotel has been improved over the years, and the rooms are comfortable.

Haspelgasse 2, 69117 Heidelberg. www.4-jahreszeiten.de. ℂ **06221/24164.** Fax 06221/163110. 22 units. 105€–150€ double. Rates include continental breakfast. AE, DC, MC, V. Parking 9€. Bus: 35. Near the Alte Brücke. *In room:* TV, Wi-Fi (free).

NH Heidelberg ★   In a brilliant example of recycling, a classic old brewery was successfully converted into this affordable hotel, now lying conveniently between the Old Town and train station. The former courtyard once filled to the brim with kegs of beer awaiting shipment has made way for a huge, glass-covered entrance hall. The owners have turned the upstairs rooms into a series of comfortable, well-furnished bedrooms. Locals visit the hotel for its collection of restaurants, three in all, including the Bräustüberl, a typically German restaurant with many Bavarian specialties. From spring to autumn an adjoining beer garden hosts special barbecues. You may also stumble upon various live music events and fondue evenings.

Bergheimer Strasse 91, 69115 Heidelberg. www.nh-hotels.com. ℂ **06221/13270.** Fax 06221/1327100. 174 units. 82€–225€ double; from 235€ suite. AE, MC, V. Parking 15€. Tram: 22. Bus: 35. **Amenities:** 3

restaurants; bar; bikes; health club and spa; room service. *In room:* A/C, TV, hair dryer, minibar, Wi-Fi (11€ per day).

Schnookeloch 🔔 This is one of the most historic old taverns of Heidelberg, dating from 1703—back when the winner of the latest student duel would retire here with his friends to celebrate with lots and lots of beer. Things might get a little raucous here on weekends, and if you're bothered with noise, you might want to seek lodgings elsewhere. Otherwise, you'll find small- to medium-size bedrooms upstairs that are beautifully maintained, modernized, and most comfortable. Even if you're not a guest, consider stopping in for a beer or a full meal. Regional specialties such as sausages and *Schnitzels* dominate the menu, with an occasional fish dish thrown in.

Haspelgasse 8, 69117 Heidelberg. www.schnookeloch.de. ✆ **06221/138080.** Fax 06221/1380813. 11 units. 88€–110€ double; 140€ triple. AE, MC, V. Parking 8€. **Amenities:** Restaurant; bar; room service. *In room:* TV, Wi-Fi (free).

HIRSCHHORN, EBERBACH & HEILBRONN

From April to early October, you can take a boat tour in the Neckar Valley as far as Neckarsteinach and back (see "Boating in the Neckar," p. 415). You can also see the many attractions along the banks of the Neckar by car, driving eastward along the right bank of the river.

Hirschhorn ★

This medieval town, 26km (16 miles) east of Heidelberg, is known as the gem of the Neckar Valley.

ESSENTIALS

GETTING THERE Access by car is via Rte. 37 east from Heidelberg. Hirschhorn lies on the Neckarelz-Heidelberg rail line with frequent local service between the two towns with the S-1 and S-2. For information, call ✆ **01805/996633** or visit www.bahn.de.

VISITOR INFORMATION Hirschhorn's Tourist Information (**06272/1742**), Untere Gasse 1, is open May to September Tuesday to Friday 8am to noon and 2 to 5pm, Saturday 9am to 1pm; October to April Monday to Friday 8am to noon and 2 to 5pm.

EXPLORING HIRSCHHORN

Overlooking the town and the river from a fortified promontory is the 18th-century **Hirschhorn Castle.** The castle defenses are from the 14th century, and wall paintings from that period can be seen in the chapel. The castle is now a hotel and restaurant (below). For a view of the sharp bend of the Neckar below the town, climb to the top of the tower.

WHERE TO EAT & STAY

Schloss-Hotel ★ This hotel, in a hilltop castle looming over the center of town, offers rooms with river views and collections of antiques. Some are in a guesthouse annex, but those in the castle have more space, style, and tradition. Central heating and an elevator have been installed. The restaurant, which serves traditional dishes, is open to nonresidents as long as they phone in advance. Specialties include roast pork loin with fresh asparagus or rump steak with hollandaise sauce.

Auf Burg Hirschhorn (on Rte. B37), 69434 Hirschhorn www.schlosshotel-hirschhorn.de.. (℃ **06272/92090.** Fax 06272/3267. 25 units. 110€–138€ double; 148€ suite. Rates include buffet breakfast. AE, MC, V. Free parking. Closed mid-Dec to Jan. **Amenities:** Restaurant; room service. *In room:* TV, fridge.

Eberbach

The imperial city of Eberbach, established in 1227, is 11km (7 miles) farther along the Neckar, at a point where the river twists to make a wide bend to the south. Its castle, which dates all the way from 1190, was mostly destroyed in the 15th century, but its ivy-covered ruins attract many visitors today. The old Pfarrhof, the medieval center of the town, is within the city walls.

Eberbach was once heavily fortified, but only the ruins of a trio of castles remain. Today you can walk along its ancient streets and take in views of the facades of its historic houses.

ESSENTIALS

GETTING THERE Rtes. 37 and 45 connect to the A5 Autobahn heading north and south or the A6 going east and west. From Heidelberg, head east along Rte. 37. Eberbach lies on the Neckarelz-Heidelberg rail line, with frequent service. Call ℃ **01805/996633** or visit www.bahn.de for information.

VISITOR INFORMATION Contact the **Tourist Office** at Leopoldplatz 1 (℃ **06271/87242;** www.eberbach.de), open May to October Monday to Friday 8am to 5pm, and Saturday 10am to noon; November to April, the office is open Monday to Thursday 8am to 5pm, and Friday 8am to noon. On Wednesday throughout the year, the office is open until 6pm.

EXPLORING EBERBACH

Begin your tour at the **Alter Markt,** or old market square. The most colorful facade here is the frescoed **Hotel Karpfen,** Alter Market 1. Many visitors can be seen photographing what the Germans called its *sgraffito* (frescoed) facade.

You can visit the tourist office in the historic **Haus Thalheim,** Kellereistrasse 36 (℃ **06271/4899**). This is the house, or so it is believed, where Great Britain's future Queen Victoria was conceived. Victoria's parents were on an extended holiday, living in Haus Thalheim, 9 months prior to her birth. In a controversial claim, some local historians assert that Victoria was actually born aboard the family's yacht moored in the Neckar. The same historians also claim, for reasons having to do with public relations and anti-German sentiment among the British at the time, that soon thereafter, the family took their newborn daughter to England and announced that Victoria had actually been born on British soil. The debate continues, quietly, in Eberbach.

Upstairs, above the tourist office, is the headquarters of the **Naturpark Informationszentrum,** the organization that dispenses maps and advice about hiking or walking through the enveloping Odenwald forest. They'll tell you about overnight shelters, give you a list of guesthouses, and outline the carefully marked footpaths leading through the forest. Be sure to ask about the nearby 60m (197-ft.) Douglas fir, purportedly the tallest tree in Germany. These offices are open May to October Monday to Friday 8:30am to noon and 2 to 5pm, Saturday 10am to noon; from November to April, they're open Monday to Thursday 8:30am to noon and 2 to 5:30pm, Friday 8:30am to noon.

Tours of Eberbach's old town are given each Saturday from May to October in English and German. The 1-hour guided walk kicks off from the tourist office at 10:30am and costs 2€.

Burg Eberbach (Eberbach Castle) lies about 1km (⅔ mile) from the town center; it's a steep uphill climb. It is only a ruin, a jumble of once-fortified walls and arches that visitors can wander through without charge, at any hour of the day or night. Views from the base of the ruin are panoramic.

From Burg Eberbach, signs point to a forest path that leads, after a relatively flat 90-minute walk, to Katzenbuckl. Here, you'll see the Turm Katzenbuckl, a tower built during the Victorian age of the "Grand Tour" that marks the highest point in the Odenwald Forest at 626m (2,053 ft.). The stone-sided tower (a 19th-c. mock-medieval folly) is open without charge day and night. Views are also panoramic. From Eberbach to Katzenbuckl requires a total walk of 2 hours, a distance of about 6km (4 miles).

WHERE TO EAT & STAY

Hotel zum Karpfen ★   This is the best and most colorful hotel in town. On its facade are authentic *Sgraffiti* (scratched-on paintings) that depict the story of Eberbach. The building is more than 2 centuries old. Each room contains a well-maintained bathroom. The old-world restaurant serves well-prepared meals.

Am Alten Markt 1, 69412 Eberbach. www.hotel-karpfen.com. © **06271/71015.** Fax 06271/71010. 50 units. 79€–107€ double; 120€ suite. Rates include buffet breakfast. AE, MC, V. Free parking. **Amenities:** Restaurant (closed Tues); room service. *In room:* TV, hair dryer.

Heilbronn

The bustling commercial and cultural center of Heilbronn started out in A.D. 741 as Villa Heilbrunna, near a holy spring.

ESSENTIALS

GETTING THERE   Access by car is via the A6 Autobahn east and west and the A81 north and south. From Heidelberg, drive south along Rte. 45, and then take A6 east. Heilbronn lies on the major Stuttgart-Würzburg rail line with frequent service. Call © **01805/996633** or visit www.bahn.de for information. Bus service to Stuttgart is provided by **Regional Bus Stuttgart GmbH** at Heilbronn (© **07131/78560;** www.rbs-bus.de). For local transport information, call Heilbronner Verkehrsverbund at © **07131/888860** (www.heilbronner-verkehrsverbund.de).

TOURIST INFORMATION   Contact the **Stadtisches Verkehrsamt,** Kaiserstrasse 17 (© **07131/562270;** www.heilbronn-tourist.de), Monday to Friday 10am to 6pm, and Saturday 10am to 4pm.

EXPLORING HEILBRONN

After Emperor Karl IV bestowed the status of imperial city upon it in 1371, Heilbronn flourished and eventually saw one of the Germany's earliest constructions of Renaissance architecture, the 64m (210-ft.) tower of **St. Killian's Church**. The old city was largely destroyed in World War II, but the church has been rebuilt in its original Gothic and High Renaissance style. Excellent original woodcarvings preserved during the war now adorn the elaborate choir and altar. The holy spring bubbles beneath the high altar.

Opposite the church is the reconstructed **Rathaus,** a combination of Gothic and Renaissance architecture. On its balcony is an astronomical clock dating to 1580. It was designed by the best-known horologist of the time, Isaak Habrecht, who created the famous clock inside the cathedral at Strasbourg, France.

Some 4,000 hectares (9,900 acres) of wooded parkland surround the city, accessible by footpaths and nature trails.

WHERE TO EAT

Ratskeller GERMAN/SWABIAN   This is your best bet for dining in Heilbronn. It's an authentic *Ratskeller*, unlike so many others, but it's been given the modern treatment, with upholstered banquettes and wrought-iron grillwork. The rib-sticking fare here is solid and reliable. Main dishes include goulash, pepper steak with french fries and salad, and grilled sole. Fish specialties and vegetarian meals are also featured. There's an impressive wine list, although many diners consider the "wine of the cellar" (house wine) perfectly adequate.

Im Rathaus, Marktplatz 7. © **07131/84628.** www.ratskeller-heilbronn.eu. Reservations recommended. Main courses 8€–24€; fixed price menus 20€–42€. MC, V. Mon–Sat 11am–11pm. Closed 10 days in Sept.

WHERE TO STAY

Insel-Hotel ★   The leading first-class choice in town and the finest hotel in the area, Insel is on an island (*Insel* in German) in the river, right in the heart of Heilbronn. Its midsize to spacious rooms are well furnished, each with a good-size tiled bathroom. Many of the rooms have private balconies opening to a view of the weeping willows in the hotel's private park. The hotel's recreational facilities include an indoor heated pool.

The front terrace of the hotel is the virtual nerve center of town, with locals stopping in to order a beer and catch up on all the gossip. The in-house restaurant is also an excellent choice, even if you're a nonguest. The chefs specialize in Swabian dishes that include onion-flavored roast beef and homemade *Spätzle*.

Friedrich-Ebert-Brücke, 74072 Heilbronn. www.insel-hotel.de. © **07131/6300.** Fax 07131/626060. 125 units. 178€–198€ double; 280€–380€ suite. AE, DC, MC, V. Free parking. **Amenities:** Restaurant; bar; babysitting; exercise room; indoor heated pool; room service; sauna. *In room:* TV, hair dryer, Wi-Fi (free).

STUTTGART ★

203km (126 miles) SE of Frankfurt, 222km (138 miles) NW of Munich, 126km (78 miles) SE of Heidelberg

Stuttgart manages to master the blend of technological innovation and green initiatives protecting and enhancing the environment. After all, two-thirds of the land inside the city limits is devoted to parks, gardens, and woodland. Yet Stuttgart maintains its manufacturing, with the logos of Mercedes, Porsche, and Zeiss optical equipment adorning their respective headquarters. Throughout the year, the fairgrounds swell with international trade fairs and congresses.

As a cultural center, this city of 600,000 inhabitants is without peer in southwestern Germany. The Stuttgart Ballet is known throughout the world, and its State Opera and Philharmonic Orchestra are also highly regarded. In addition, Stuttgart boasts an abundance of theater groups, cultural festivals, and museums, and is also the largest winegrowing city in Germany.

The name "Stuttgart" comes from a stud farm owned by one Luidolf, Duke of Swabia, and son of Emperor Otto the Great. By 1427, Stuttgart had become the capital and residence of the counts of Württemberg. The city expanded under the reign of Kaiser Wilhelm I (1816–64). At the turn of the 20th century, it had a population of 175,000 that expanded to the Neckar River by the outbreak of World War I.

During World War II, bombing attacks leveled 60% of Stuttgart's buildings, sparing not a single landmark or historic structure. After the war, Stuttgart became the capital of the newly formed state of Baden-Württemberg (many still call it by its former name, Swabia).

Stuttgart

**Map labels:**

Kriegsbergstrasse · Schellingstrasse · Hubelstr · Friedrichstrasse · Lautenschlagerstr. · Thouretstr. · Stephan-str. · Kronenstr. · Königstrasse · Marstall-str. · Arnulf-Klett-Platz · Hauptbahnhof · Schillerstrasse · Mittlerer Schlossgarten · Willy-Brandt-Str.

Börsen-platz · Börsenstr. · G.-Heinemann-Platz · Fürstenstr. · Bolzstrasse · Stauffenbergstr. · Oberer Schloss-garten · Gebhard-Müller-Platz · Urbanstrasse

Königsbau · Königstr. · Kunst-gebäude · Theater-see · Staatstheater Stuttgart · Alte Staats-galerie · Neue Staats-galerie · Moserstrasse · Eugenstr.

Kleiner Schloss-platz · Kunstmuseum Stuttgart · Schloss-platz · Neues Schloss · Haus des Landtags · Konrad-Adenauer-Strasse · Ulrichstrasse

Calwer Strasse · Kienestr. · Schiller-platz · Altes Schloss · Stauffen-berg-platz · Karls-platz · Akademie-garten · Urban- · Archivstr.

Kronprinzstr. · Königstrasse · Stiftskirche · Stiftstr. · Dorotheenstr. · Geßlerstr. · Charlotten-platz · Uhland- · Olgastr.

Johannes-Brenz-Platz · Schulstr. · Markthalle · Spörerstr. · Münzstr. · Lederstr. · Karlstr. · Charlottenstrasse · Galsburgstr. · str.

Turmstr. · Neue Str. · Neue Brücke · Markt-platz · Karls-passage · Marktstr. · Holzstr. · Esslinger Str. · Rosen-str. · strasse

Schmale Str. · Hirschstr. · Nadlerstr. · Rathaus · Brennerstr. · Weberstr. · Alexander-str. · Steinstr. · Geiss-str. · Eberhard- · Hauptstätter Strasse · Leonhards-platz · Wagnerstr. · Olgastr. · Blumen- · Hohenheimer Strasse

Eberhard-str. · Leonhards-kirche · Pfarrstr. · Katharinen-platz

ATTRACTIONS ●

Altes Schloss and Württembergisches Landesmuseum **9**
Fernsehturm **16**
Liederhalle **8**
Mercedes-Benz Museum **14**
Neues Schloss **10**
Rathaus **11**
Staatsgalerie **6**
Staatstheater **7**

HOTELS ■

Alter Fritz **1**
Am Schlossgarten **5**
City Hotel **13**
Der Zauberlehrling **12**
Hotels Mack & Pflieger **2**
Hotel Stuttgart 21 **3**
Hotel Wörtz– Zur Weinsteige **15**
Steigenberger Hotel Graf Zeppelin **4**

Inset map: Hamburg · Berlin ★ · GERMANY · Frankfurt am Main · Stuttgart · Munich

0 — 200 yds
0 — 200 m

Essentials

GETTING THERE

BY PLANE The **Stuttgart Echterdingen Airport** (© **0711/9480;** www. flughafen-stuttgart.de) is 14km (9 miles) south of the city near Echterdingen. The airport has connections with most major German and European cities with Frankfurt 50 minutes away, and flights to Hamburg or Berlin lasting 1¼ hours. The commuter S-Bahn to Stuttgart leaves from below the arrivals level of Terminal 1. Trains depart every 20 minutes, taking 27 minutes. A one-way fare valid in 3 zones is 3.40€. A taxi to the city center costs from 30€.

BY TRAIN Stuttgart has rail links to all major German cities, with frequent connections. The train station is directly north of the historic area. Twenty-seven daily trains run from Munich (trip time: 2½ hr.), and 19 trains run from Frankfurt (trip time: 1½ hr.). For information, call © **01805/996633** or visit www.bahn.de.

BY BUS Long-distance bus service into Stuttgart from cities outside Germany, including London, Paris, Vienna, and Amsterdam, is maintained by **Deutsche Touring GmbH** (© **0711/2730962;** www.touring.de). Passengers coming into Stuttgart from other cities within Germany almost always opt to take the train.

BY CAR Access by car is via the A8 Autobahn east and west, or the A81 north and south.

VISITOR INFORMATION

Information about transportation, sightseeing, and hotels is available at the **i-Punkt,** Königstrasse 1A (© **0711/22280;** www.stuttgart-tourist.de), which is open year-round Monday to Friday 9am to 8pm and Saturday 9am to 6pm; Sunday hours are 11am to 6pm the whole year.

GETTING AROUND

A single ride between points that fall within Stuttgart's historic core on the city's bus or subway system costs 2€. Rides to the outer suburbs, depending on where you travel, range from 2.50€ to 6.75€. Often, the most economical way of handling multiple rides on the system involves buying a *Tageskarte* (day ticket), which costs 6.10€; it's valid for a day of unlimited transport within the city core and also within zones 1 (central Stuttgart) and 2 (immediate suburbs). A 1-day pass that's valid for transport within the entire network (in other words, the city center and zones 1–5) sells for 14€. For more information about the city's transport system, its routes, and its prices, call © **0711/19449** or visit www.vvs.de.

Exploring Stuttgart

Many of the most remarkable structures in today's Stuttgart are progressive designs created by such architects as Ludwig Mies van der Rohe, Walter Gropius, Hans Scharoun, and Le Corbusier. The **Liederhalle,** Schloss-Strasse, constructed in 1956 of concrete, glass, and glazed brick, contains three auditoriums and is fascinating inside and out.

The town's older section is clustered around **Schillerplatz** and the statue of the great German poet and dramatist, Schiller. Visible only by group tour, the **Neues Schloss,** on Schlossplatz, was originally constructed between 1746 and 1807 and rebuilt beginning in 1958. Today, it houses state government rooms. The modern **Rathaus** faces the old Marktplatz, where vendors in open stalls sell flowers, fruit, and vegetables.

For the best view of Stuttgart, climb to the top of the 510m (1,670-ft.) **Birken-kopf,** west of the city, on a hill created from the debris of Stuttgart dumped here after World War II. After the 20-minute walk to the top, you'll be rewarded by a view of the city and the surrounding Swabian Hills, covered with vineyards and woods.

Between April and October, every day at 11am, the local tourist office organizes an English-language guided tour through the city's historic core. Beginning on the side-walk in front of the tourist office (Königstrasse 1A; ℂ 0711/22280) and lasting for 90 minutes, it costs 8€. There's no discount for students or most age groups, but children 4 and under can tag along for free.

Altes Schloss and Württembergisches Landesmuseum (Old Castle and Württemberg Regional Museum) ★ MUSEUM One of Stuttgart's oldest standing structures, this huge ducal palace was originally a moated castle built in the 13th century and was redone in the 16th century in Renaissance style. Now it houses the Württembergisches Landesmuseum, which traces the art and culture of Swabia from the Stone Age to the present. The most valuable items include a survey of Euro-pean glass through the ages, the ducal art chamber, and the crown jewels. The museum also houses a large collection of Swabian sculptures; an exhibition of clocks, coins, and musical instruments; the famous treasures of the tomb of the Celtic prince of Hochdorf (ca. A.D. 530); and a collection from the Merovingian period in the early Middle Ages.

Schillerplatz 6. ℂ **0711/2793498.** www.landesmuseum-stuttgart.de. Admission 4.50€ adults, 3€ stu-dents, free for children 13 and under. Tues–Sun 10am–5pm. U-Bahn: Schlossplatz.

Fernsehturm (Television Tower) ARCHITECTURE This 217m (712-ft.) tower, capped with a red-and-white transmitter, soars above a forested hillock south of Stuttgart. It was designed and built in 1956 using radically innovative applications of aluminum and prestressed reinforced concrete, and served as a prototype for larger towers in Toronto and Moscow. Acrophobes can dine in the restaurant at the tower's base, while height seekers will find a cafe, bar, restaurant, observation platform, and information about the tower's construction at the top of a 150m (490-ft.) elevator. Food is served daily 10am to 8pm. Look outside for the mobile platforms used by window washers.

Jahnstrasse 120, Stuttgart-Degerloch. ℂ **0711/232597.** www.fernsehturm-stuttgart.com. Admission 5€ adults, 3€ children. Daily 9am–10:30pm. Tram: 15. South of the city, just off B3.

Gottlieb Daimler Memorial HISTORIC INTEREST The life and the work of inventor Gottlieb Daimler is revealed here, along with the first models of the Daimler ever made. On this spot the first internal-combustion engine turned in 1883. Car buffs enjoy looking at some of the tools mechanics used to perfect the cars that led to the creation of the chic Mercedes line of vehicles. In the re-created workshop you can see blueprints and models of Daimler and Wilhelm Maybach's first horseless carriage and the groundbreaking "grandfather clock" engine.

Taubenheimstrasse 13, Bad Cannstatt-Stuttgart. ℂ **0711/569399.** Free admission. Tues–Sun 10am–4pm. U-Bahn: Kursaal.

Mercedes-Benz Museum ★ MUSEUM This museum honors the oldest auto-mobile factory in the world and the invention of the motorcar by Carl Benz and Got-tlieb Daimler. Nearly 75 historical vehicles are on display, including a Daimler Reitwagen from 1885, the first motor-bicycle. Other vintage items include Daimler's first Mercedes of 1902, Race cars from 1899 like the Blitzen-Benz, the Silver Arrow,

GERMAN men of ideas: JOHANNES KEPLER (1571–1630

"Truth is the daughter of time, and I have no shame in being her midwife."

Field of Study: Astronomer, mathematician, astrologer.

Revolutionary Insight: Kepler's laws of planetary motion posited, for the first time, that planets make elliptical orbits around the sun, sweeping out equal areas in equal times. His discoveries were essential to the development of Newton's laws of universal gravitation.

Controversy Quotient (Oto 5): (1) The Catholic Church opposed heliocentrism, but Kepler, a Protestant, avoided the scrutiny that caused his contemporary, Galileo, to be tried for heresy.

Little Known Fact: His posthumously published novel, *Somnium,* describes a man's voyage to the moon. Displays an uncanny, prescient understanding of the challenges of space travel.

—Kelly Regan

the Sauber Mercedes, the Indy car, and some vehicles built especially to achieve speed records.

Mercedesstrasse 100, Stuttgart-Bad Cannstatt. ✆ **0711/1730000.** www.museum-mercedes-benz.com. Admission 8€, free for children 14 and under. Tues–Sun 9am–6pm. S-Bahn: 1 to Gottlieb-Daimler-Stadion; then walk to the entrance of the plant, where you'll be taken on a special bus to the museum.

Porsche Museum ★ MUSEUM   The much-expanded Porsche Museum lets you see around 80 of these legendary cars that trace the history of this highly prized automobile. Ferdinand Porsche set up his own business on Porsche Square in Zuffenhausen in 1931, launching a business that would become world famous for its sporty serial autos and racing cars. Surprisingly, the Volkswagen was also launched here in 1936 and called the "Beetle" or "Rounded Porsche."

On exhibit are such prizes as the first Porsche-branded car (a Boxster precursor from 1948), as well as the Formula 1 champions of the mid-1980s and the 911 GTI that won the Le Mans competition in 1998. Two great specimens from 1964 include the legendary Porsch 911 and the Porsche 904 Carrera GTS, the first car with a plastic body. Tours of the factory show how an entire sports car comes together, with gigantic robotic claws lowering finished bodies onto drivetrains and chassis. You'll also see how fenders, engines, and dashboards come together to make the 911s or Boxsters.

Porscheplatz 1. ✆ **0711/91125685.** www.porsche.com. Admission 8€. Factory tours in English Mon–Fri 10am. Museum Tues–Sun 9am–5pm. S-Bahn: Neuwirtshaus/Porscheplatz.

Staatsgalerie (State Gallery of Stuttgart) ★ MUSEUM   The city's finest art museum exhibits various works spanning some 550 years. However, the best collection is from the 19th and 20th centuries, especially the works of the German expressionists—Kirchner, Barlach, and Beckmann—as well as representatives of the Bauhaus school and Blue Rider group, such as Klee and Feininger. There are also examples of French art of the 19th and 20th centuries and of the European and American postwar avant-garde.

Konrad-Adenauer-Strasse 30–32. ✆ **0711/470400.** www.staatsgalerie.de. Admission 5.50€ adults, 4€ students, free for children 13 and under. Wed and Fri–Sun 10am–6pm; Tues and Thurs 10am–8pm. U-Bahn: Staatsgalerie.

Where to Eat

Wielandshöhe ★★★ INTERNATIONAL   Vincent Klink, one of the most celebrated chefs in Germany, runs the greenest restaurant in Stuttgart. He focuses on food raised without pesticides or chemical additives. Every month, he changes the menu, posting the new carte like a work of art. Klink is an inventive chef, and he has an almost sensual approach to food, giving his cuisine a seductive charm that can wake up a terminally jaded palate. You're likely to be captivated by such dishes as braised rye bread with fresh oysters or baked venison with herbs, and especially the rack of veal with sweetbreads and fresh morels. The thornback ray filet with capers and Amalfi lemons might well be the best version of this dish you ever order. If it's featured, start with his minestrone with olives and basil; it should win an award.

Alte Weinsteige 71. ✆ **0711/6408848.** www.wielandshoehe.de. Reservations required. 4-course menu 78€; 6-course menu 110€. AE, DC, MC, V. Tues–Sat noon–2pm and 6–9pm. Tram: U-1 or U-14, then the Zahnradbahn, no. 10.

Zeppelin-Stüble SWABIAN   Although many restaurants in Stuttgart have abandoned true Swabian cuisine for more international fare, the chefs here still turn out the old-fashioned specialties preferred by locals. In this elegantly appointed restaurant furnished with Swabian antiques, each dish uses fresh, seasonal ingredients. Such Swabian specialties as *Rostbraten* (roast beef) and *Maultaschen* (a type of ravioli made with a variety of fillings) are offered. The kitchen does an excellent *Schwäbischer Sauerbraten* (a Swabian version of marinated beef) with *Spätzle* and salad. Other specialties include arctic char with leafy spinach, homemade Swabian ravioli, and pork medallions with pan-fried wood mushrooms.

In the Steigenberger Hotel Graf Zeppelin, Arnulf-Klett-Platz 7. ✆ **0711/2048184.** Reservations recommended. Main courses 11€–21€. AE, DC, MC, V. Mon–Sat 11:30am–2:30pm and 6–10:30pm. U-Bahn: Hauptbahnhof.

Zur Weinsteige ★ INTERNATIONAL   The interior of this restaurant celebrates German handicrafts that look handmade, from the handblown leaded glass in the small-paned windows to the carved columns and tables and chairs. The chef offers international cuisine, with a number of Swabian specialties. In summer, you can sit among the grapevines stretching over the sun terrace. Also worth seeing is the wine cellar, well stocked with the best regional wines and a wide selection of German and international wines. Next to the cellar, you can taste and buy wine directly from the hotel's vineyards.

In the Hotel Wörtz, Hohenheimerstrasse 30. ✆ **0711/2367000.** Fax 0711/2367007. Reservations recommended. Main courses 19€–35€; 3-course menu 35€; 6-course menu 85€. AE, DC, MC, V. Tues–Sat noon–2pm and 6–10pm. Closed holidays, 3 weeks in Jan, and 2 weeks in Aug. S-Bahn: Dobelstrasse.

Shopping

Home to clothing designers Hugo Boss and Ulli Knecht, Stuttgart has its fair share of boutiques that range from interesting to elegant. **Klett Passage,** across from the train station, is an underground mall full of upscale shops. If you follow the Königstrasse from the station for about 1km (½ mile), you'll likely find anything you want in one of the retail stores that line the street. There are somewhat more expensive boutiques along the Calwer Strasse, especially in the gleaming chrome-and-glass arcade, **Calwer Passage.** Bargains galore can be found at the Saturday morning **flea market** on the Karlsplatz between the old castle and the new palace, where clothes, books, furniture, household items, art, and just about anything else are likely to turn up.

In business since 1723, **Tritschler,** Am Marktplatz 7 (✆ **0711/1204574;** www.tritschler.com; U-Bahn: Charlottenplatz), stocks glass, porcelain, and fine china, as well as cutlery and decorative housewares. **Pavillon,** Eberhardstrasse 31–33 (✆ **0711/243134;** www.antiquitaeten-pavillon.de; U-Bahn: Rathaus), specializes in silver from the 19th and 20th centuries, and also sells glass, crystal, Meissen porcelain, and a few paintings.

The city's largest bookstore, **Wittwer,** Königstrasse 30 (✆ **0711/25070;** www.wittwer.de; S-Bahn: Hauptbahnhof), carries many books in English and has tables placed throughout the store so that you can comfortably scan potential purchases. For a bit of everything, head to the city's largest department store, **Breuninger,** Marktstrasse 1–3 (✆ **0711/2110;** www.breuninger.de; U-Bahn: Charlottenplatz), where glass elevators whisk you through several floors of housewares, furnishings, and fashion.

Entertainment & Nightlife

Listings of the various cultural events, as well as tickets, are available from the tourist office (see "Visitor Information," above). The magazine *Lift,* available at newsstands, lists all the happenings around Stuttgart.

THE PERFORMING ARTS **Staatstheater,** Oberer Schlossgarten (✆ **0711/202090;** www.staatstheater.stuttgart.de; S-Bahn: Hauptbahnhof), is the leading cultural venue in Stuttgart. The theater consists of the Grosses Haus for opera and ballet, the Kleines Haus for theater, and the Kammer-Theater, which puts on experimental works. This is home to the world-class **Stuttgart Ballet,** established by the American choreographer John Cranko in the 1960s and now led by Reid Anderson. It also houses the respected **Staatsoper (State Opera).** Tickets are 8€ to 126€ and can be purchased at the Staatstheater box office (closed Aug).

Classical and other concerts may be heard in the three halls of the **Liederhalle,** Berliner Platz 1–3 (✆ **0711/2027710;** www.liederhalle-stuttgart.de; U-Bahn: Liederhalle/Berlinerplatz), which is home to the **Stuttgarter Philharmoniker,** under the baton of Gabriel Feltz, and the **Radio-Sinfonieorchester Stuttgart.** Tickets for all concerts are on sale at **SKS Russ,** Charlottenplatz 17 (✆ **0711/1635321;** www.sks-russ.de; U-Bahn: Charlottenplatz). Prices are 8€ to 40€.

THE BAR, CAFE & CLUB SCENE Start your evening with a drink at **Amadeus,** Charlottenplatz 17 (✆ **0711/292678;** www.amadeus-stuttgart.de; U-Bahn: Charlottenplatz), where students and locals gather. It's open Monday to Saturday at 9am for breakfast and on Sunday at 10am for brunch, and all week until 2am.

For a trendier locale, and one where you're likely to meet counterculture Stuttgart (complete with purple hair and piercings in unpredictable places), head to **Palast der Republik,** Friedrichstrasse 27 (✆ **0711/2264887;** U-Bahn: Keplerstrasse), a century-old bar that has tended to draw an arts-conscious crowd throughout its long history. DJs play funk and soul. It's open Monday to Wednesday 11am to 2am, Thursday to Saturday 11am to 3am, and Sunday 3pm to 1am. **Café Stella,** Hauptstätter Strasse 57 (✆ **0711/6402583;** www.cafe-stella.de; U-Bahn: Österreichischerplatz), is a see-and-be-seen kind of place that serves drinks and food; it hosts local jazz bands, on a varying schedule, several times a month. Sunday brunch is a particularly stylish venue for the hip and hipster wannabes.

Where to Stay

No matter when you come to Stuttgart, you'll probably find an international trade fair in progress, from the January glass-and-ceramics exposition to the December book exhibition. (Stuttgart is also southern Germany's most important publishing center.) Good accommodations may be difficult to find at almost any time, so you should always reserve in advance, or contact the i-Punkt for assistance.

EXPENSIVE

Am Schlossgarten ★★★　The Steigenberger Hotel Graf Zeppelin (see below) is the market leader in Stuttgart, attracting the Porsche crowd, but this government-rated five-star hotel wins the race for charm and tranquility. Both the landscaped Oberschlossgarten park and the Königstrasse shopping zone sit a stone's throw away, and it's even only a few minutes on foot from the central train station. Listed as one of the "Leading Hotels of the World," this epitome of luxury living in Stuttgart boasts the town's most enjoyable hotel dining and drinking facilities.

Bedrooms and suites are elegant, with individual character, comfortable furnishings, and deluxe bathrooms with tub and shower. The on-site **Zirbelstube** offers a grand cuisine under the direction of Bernhard Diers and his team of talented chefs. Innovation and craftsmanship mark the cuisine. In summer the outdoor tables of the **Restaurant am Schlossgarten** provide one of the most romantic settings for dining in Stuttgart. The wine bar serves an innovative Mediterranean cuisine, with perhaps the finest wine carte in Stuttgart.

Schillerstrasse 23, 70173 Stuttgart. www.hotelschlossgarten.com. ✆ **0711/20260.** Fax 0711/2026888. 116 units. 205€–311€ double; from 223€ junior suite; from 426€ suite. AE, DC, MC, V. Parking 18€. **Amenities:** 3 restaurants; bar; airport transfers (55€); bikes. In room: A/C, TV, fax, hair dryer, minibar, Wi-Fi (27€ per day).

Hilton Garden Inn Stuttgart Neckar Park ★★ ☺　At long last Stuttgart has a Hilton, although it lies east of the center in the leafy suburb of Bad Cannstatt next to the Mercedes Museum. As German Hiltons go, this is one of the more modest choices, but it's first class in all respects, ranging from the comfort of its bedrooms to the quality of its food and service. It is especially popular with commercial travelers in Stuttgart on automobile business.

All the bedrooms are built to the highest modern standards with all the latest gadgets. Furnishings are tasteful with modern sophistication, and the sleek bathrooms come with tub/shower combos. The Palm Beach restaurant on the ground floor is particularly delightful with its cocktails, light Mediterranean food, and typical American dishes. A special feature is the 24-hour Pavilion Pantry stocked with snacks, drinks, and "everything you forgot."

Mercedesstrasse 75, 70372 Stuttgart-Bad Cannstatt. www.hilton.com. ✆ **0711/900550.** Fax 0711/90055100. 150 units. 220€–305€ double. AE, DC, MC, V. **Amenities:** Restaurant; children's programs; concierge; exercise room; room service. In room: A/C, TV, hair dryer, minibar, Wi-Fi (free).

Steigenberger Hotel Graf Zeppelin ★★　This is the best hotel for those who come to wheel and deal with Stuttgart businesspeople. Although situated at the train station, it's not only attractive but dignified and stylish, once you get past its plain postwar exterior. The spacious, soundproof rooms are colorfully decorated, all with tidily kept bathrooms.

Arnulf-Klett-Platz 7, 70173 Stuttgart. www.stuttgart.steigenberger.com. ✆ **800/223-5652** in the U.S. and Canada, or 0711/20480. Fax 0711/2048542. 155 units. 135€–255€ double; 305€–355€ suite. AE, DC, MC, V. Parking 20€. U-Bahn: Hauptbahnhof. **Amenities:** 3 restaurants; bar; babysitting; bikes; exercise room; indoor heated pool; room service; spa. In room: A/C, TV, fax (in some), hair dryer, minibar (in some), Wi-Fi (free).

MODERATE

Alter Fritz Pleasant, conservative, quiet, and isolated in a verdant location about a mile north of the center of Stuttgart, this imposing stone-sided building dates from 1903, when it was constructed at the edge of a wooded stretch of land known as Killesberg Park. Many visitors opt for at least some exposure to the great outdoors, often with morning jogs or brisk walks through the footpaths in the park. The building's interior was radically modernized in the mid-1980s, leaving a clean, efficient, and blandly modern collection of public areas flooded with sunlight and, in many cases, views of the park.

The cuisine has French and international overtones. Residents of the hotel dine in a room devoted exclusively to them; nonresidents eat in a cozy dining room known as **Der Kleine Fritz.**

Feuerbacher Weg 101, Killesberg 70192. www.alter-fritz-am-killesberg.de. ✆ **0711/135650.** Fax 0711/ 1356565. 10 units. 88€–110€ double. Rates include continental breakfast. No credit cards. Free parking. Bus: 43. **Amenities:** Restaurant. *In room:* TV, minibar.

Der Zauberlehrling ★ 📷 This offbeat choice has a lot of bohemian charm. Each of its individually designed bedrooms conjures up a theme, ranging from 1,001 Nights to Seventh Heaven. Likewise, the decor in minimalist settings roams the world—perhaps the Hermitage, a country estate in some far and distant land with ruby-red brocades and sultry salons. As you enter Paddington, you're brought back to antiques from Queen Victoria's times, with Miss Marple looking down from above. The most modern of all is the Media Suite, with its high-tech efficiency where communication is everything. If you want to perform dirty deeds in private while in Stuttgart, behind carefully concealed doors, you won't be exposed if you check into the Black Box.

Rosenstrasse 38, 70182 Stuttgart. www.zauberlehrling.de. ✆ **0711/2377770.** Fax 0711/237775. 9 units. 150€–280€ double; from 320€ suite. AE, MC, V. Parking 15€. U-Bahn: Charlottenplatz. **Amenities:** Restaurant; bar; room service. *In room:* A/C, TV, CD player, minibar, Wi-Fi (free).

Hotel Wörtz-Zur Weinsteige 🍷 The amber lights of a *Weinstube* (wine bar) welcome visitors to this local favorite in Stuttgart, which has the best rooms and the best food of all local hotels in this price range. The small soundproof rooms are paneled and sometimes have massive hand-carved armoires. For royal treatment, check out the Louis XVI Suite with rococo furnishings and marble columns surrounding a whirlpool. The *Weinstube* evokes the feeling of a remote corner of Swabia—it's perfect for relaxing after a long trip, especially on its garden terrace.

Hohenheimerstrasse 28–30, 70184 Stuttgart. www.hotel-woertz.de. ✆ **0711/2367000.** Fax 0711/ 2367007. 32 units. 130€–150€ double. Rates include buffet breakfast. AE, DC, MC, V. Parking 8€. U-Bahn: Dobelstrasse. **Amenities:** Restaurant; room service. *In room:* TV, hair dryer, Wi-Fi (free).

INEXPENSIVE

City Hotel The City is a bed-and-breakfast-type hotel, within walking distance of the sights in the city center. It offers pleasantly furnished but hardly spectacular rooms equipped with private showers (no tubs) and direct-dial telephones. The generous breakfast buffet, the only meal served, is offered in a sunny winter garden.

Uhlandstrasse 18, 70182 Stuttgart. www.cityhotel-stuttgart.de. ✆ **0711/210810.** Fax 0711/2369772. 31 units. 99€–115€ double. Rates include buffet breakfast. AE, DC, MC, V. Free parking. U-Bahn: Olgaeck. Directly east of Charlottenplatz. *In room:* TV, minibar, Wi-Fi (free).

Hotels Mack & Pflieger These two hotels share the same management and basically the same design. Set within a few steps of one another just a short walk from the railway station, they were built in stages between around 1960 and 1980. Each rises between three and four stories and has roughly the same decor and architectural style. All the rooms are small and somewhat basic, but are nonetheless completely adequate and comfortable.

Kriegerstrasse 7 (Hotel Mack) and Kriegerstrasse 11 (Hotel Pflieger), 70191 Stuttgart. Mack: www.hotel-mack-stuttgart.de; ✆ **0711/292942;** fax 0711/2536919. Pflieger: www.hotel-pflieger.de; ✆**0711/221878;** fax 0711/293489. 54 units. 50€–130€ double. Rates include buffet breakfast. AE, DC, MC, V. Free parking. U-Bahn: Hauptbahnhof. **Amenities:** Bar. *In room:* TV.

Hotel Stuttgart 21 ★ 🍴 This hotel, though not as centrally located as the City Hotel, offers more style and better rooms. Other benefits are a nicely tiled indoor pool with a sauna and a manicured garden where a waiter will take your drink order. Rooms are well maintained and inviting. Most are medium in size, although some are quite small.

Friedhofstrasse 21, 70191 Stuttgart. stuttgart21.bestwestern.com. ✆**0711/25870.** Fax 0711/2587404. 90 units. 98€–130€ double; 120€–300€ suite. Rates include buffet breakfast. AE, DC, MC, V. Parking 10€. U-Bahn: Turlenstrasse/Burgerhospital. **Amenities:** Restaurant; babysitting; concierge; indoor heated pool; room service; sauna. *In room:* TV, hair dryer, minibar, Wi-Fi (free).

TÜBINGEN ★★

47km (29 miles) S of Stuttgart, 153km (95 miles) NE of Freiburg

Though it's often compared to Heidelberg, this quiet old university town on the upper Neckar has a look and personality all its own. Gabled medieval houses crowd against the ancient town wall at the bank of the river, and students pole gondola-like boats up and down the Neckar in summer. This far upstream, the Neckar is too shallow for commercial vessels, so Tübingen has been spared the industrial look of a trading community.

Progress has not passed the city by, however. In spite of its medieval aspect, it has a new residential and science suburb in the shadow of the Schönbuch Forest north of the city, with medical facilities, research institutes, and lecture halls affiliated with the university. The buildings of the old university, founded in 1477, are north of the botanical gardens. The humanist Melanchthon taught here in the 16th century, and later on Schiller, Hegel, and Hölderlin were students.

Essentials
GETTING THERE
BY AIR The nearest major airport, at Stuttgart, has good connections to Tübingen, including a direct bus link.

BY TRAIN The Stuttgart-Tübingen rail line offers frequent service. Tübingen also has good rail ties to other major cities in Germany, including Frankfurt (trip time: 2½ hr.), Berlin (trip time: 6½ hr.), and Hamburg (trip time: 8½ hr.). For information, call ✆ **01805/996633** or visit www.bahn.de.

BY BUS Because of Tübingen's position astride some of the major rail lines of central Europe, most visitors get here from other parts of Germany by train. But if you're committed to the idea of bus transport in and out of town, contact **Deutsche Touring GmbH** in Frankfurt (✆ **069/7903501;** www.touring.de) for information about the buses that service Tübingen and its surrounding region.

BY CAR Access is via Rte. 27 south from the A8 Autobahn running east and west, or via Rte. 28 east from the A81 Autobahn running north and south.

VISITOR INFORMATION

Contact the **Verkehrsverein,** An der Neckarbrücke 1 (© **07071/91360;** www. tuebingen-info.de), open Monday to Friday 9am to 7pm and Saturday 10am to 4pm. From May to September, the office is also open on Sunday from 11am to 4pm.

Exploring Tübingen

Standing on the Eberhardsbrücke over the Neckar River running through town, you'll see a long and narrow island in the river's center created with landfill. Nearby, locals enjoy the tree-shaded promenade **Platanenallee ★★**, which fills with strollers in warm weather. From there, you get a panoramic view of the town, with its willows and houses reflected in the river. Towering above the other buildings is the Renaissance **Schloss Hohentübingen (High-Tübingen Castle)** now used by the university. It's worth climbing up to the castle for the dramatic view from the terraces.

The narrow streets of the Altstadt wind up and down the hillside, but they all seem to lead to **Marktplatz ★**, where festive markets are held on Monday, Wednesday, and Friday. You'll feel as if you're stepping into the past when you come upon country people selling fruit and vegetables in the open square. Facing the square is the **Rathaus ★**, which dates from 1435 but also has more recent additions, including the 19th-century painted designs on the facade.

On a hillside above Marktplatz is **Stiftskirche,** Holzmarkt, the former church of the Augustinians. The monastery became a Protestant seminary in 1548, and its church became the Collegiate Church. Inside, the tombs of the dukes of Württemberg in the chancel and the 15th-century French Gothic pulpit and rood screen are all noteworthy. The **tower** (enter on the left of the chancel) provides a panoramic view of the town. The church is open daily 9am to 5pm, whereas the chancel and tower are open Tuesday to Friday 10:30am to 5pm, and Saturday and Sunday 2 to 5pm. Admission to the tower is 2.50€ for adults and 2€ for children.

Hölderlinturm, Bursagasse 6 (© **07071/22040**), lies at the end of a walk by the Neckar River. This was the home of the lyric poet Friedrich Hölderlin, who resided here with the Zimmer family from the onset of his mental illness at age 36 until his death in 1843, at age 73. Although Hölderlin is not well known outside Germany, try reading a few of his poems in translation before coming. Most tours of the museum are in German, but you can request one in English. The house is open Tuesday to Friday 10am to noon and 3 to 5pm, Saturday and Sunday 2 to 5pm. Admission is 2.50€ adults, 1.50€ students and children.

Where to Eat

Restaurant Museum ★ 🍴 INTERNATIONAL/SWABIAN This is one of Tübingen's foremost restaurants. It's a pleasant place to dine on international specialties such as Marseille snail soup, or regional dishes such as Swabian medallions of veal. The lunches here are considered by many locals (including students) to be not only the best in town but also the best value.

Wilhelmstrasse 3. © **07071/22828.** www.restaurant-museum.de. Reservations recommended. Main courses 11€–25€; fixed-price menu 30€. AE, MC, V. Daily 11:45am–3pm and Tues–Sat 6pm–midnight.

Restaurant Rosenau ★★ GERMAN/SWABIAN This restaurant, near the botanical gardens, offers the finest food in the town center. The owner serves modern cuisine along with superb Swabian specialties, listed under the *gutbürgerlich* selections. Try the tasty and filling Swabian hot pot with *Spätzle* (egg noodles) and fresh mushrooms or the delectable veal steak with morels. Desserts are often elaborate. In fair weather, guests can order drinks out in the sun.

Beim Neuen Botanischen Garten. ✆ **07071/68866.** www.restaurant-rosenau.de. Reservations recommended. Main courses 18€–25€; fixed-price 3-course lunch 19€. AE, DC, MC, V. Tues–Sun 10am–midnight. Bus: 5, 13, 17.

NEARBY DINING

Gasthof Waldhorn ★★★ GERMAN/FRENCH   The finest restaurant in the area is not in Tübingen but on its outskirts, at Tübingen-Bebenhausen. Many locals make the trip to this elegant manor house, where Herr and Frau Schulz offer a light German and French cuisine based on regional ingredients, backed up by an impressive wine list (with many half bottles). With a chef who combines inventiveness and solid technique, this is one restaurant that truly deserves its stars. The menu changes daily but may include trout terrine and wild venison with forest mushrooms, along with the in-season vegetable. The dessert specialty is a soft cream concoction flavored with rose hips. Behind the house, the garden has five tables for summer dining.

Schönbuchstrasse 49. ✆ **07071/61270.** www.waldhorn-bebenhausen.de. Reservations required. Main courses 12€–34€; fixed-price menus 69€–92€. No credit cards. Wed–Sun noon–2pm and 6:30–9pm. Closed 2 weeks in Aug. 6km (4 miles) from the town center. Bus: 754, 826, 828.

Entertainment & Nightlife

Student-inspired nightlife makes this old town very young at heart. Just head into the Marktplatz at night and follow the sound of partying. You can order a beer and read the comics hanging on the walls of **Marktschenke,** Am Markt 11 (✆ **07071/22035**), then join the students spilling outside into the square. Daily hours are 9am to 1am; Friday and Saturday it closes at 2am. Or start your evening in the ancient **Boulanger,** Collegiumsgasse 2 (✆ **07071/23345**), where you could offer to pick up Hegel's bar tab, which has gone unpaid for more than 200 years. **Ammerschlag,** Ammergasse 13 (✆ **07071/51591;** www.ammerschlag.de), is a cramped and smoky hole-in-the-wall dive that has live music one Sunday a month, ranging from blues to rap. Hours are daily 3pm until 1am.

Better suited for drinks and gossip than dancing is the cramped, but fun, hole-in-the-wall **Blauer Turm Lounge,** Friedrichstrasse 21 (✆ **07071/360390;** www. blauer-turm-tuebingen.de), which is open Wednesday and Thursday from 8pm to 3am, Friday and Saturday from 9pm to 5am. Wednesday nights feature swing bands, and there are live DJs every Friday and Saturday night. Entrance is free.

Where to Stay

Hotel am Bad 🍃   This hotel, located in the center of one of Tübingen's well-maintained public parks, offers woodland calm not far from the city center. Its rambling rose-colored exterior complements the masses of red flowers on the sun terrace. Rooms are modest and a bit small but still comfortable, all containing neatly kept bathrooms.

Europastrasse Freibad 2, 72072 Tübingen. www.hotel-am-bad.de. ✆ **07071/79740.** Fax 07071/75336. 35 units. 97€–115€ double. Rates include buffet breakfast. AE, MC, V. Free outdoor parking; 6.50€ in garage. Closed 3 weeks over Christmas and New Year's. **Amenities:** Bar; bikes; room service. *In room:* TV, hair dryer, minibar, Wi-Fi (free).

Hotel am Schloss ★ 🎁   One of the most atmospheric hotels in town is a group of steep-gabled antique buildings in the town's historic core; each is accented in summer with window boxes loaded with flowers, and the oldest dates to 1491. You'll register in the main building and be assigned a room, and if it's within either of the two very old, and very historic, outbuildings, you'll get a key for access to their respective entrances. None of the three buildings have an elevator, but each has thick walls, and each has benefited from a renovation that retains the old-fashioned charm while adding modern conveniences and a scattering of traditional furnishings.

The main building contains at least half of the hotel's accommodations, as well as its restaurant, where Swabian food is served daily at both lunch and dinner (closed Tues Oct–Apr). Main courses range from 10€ to 20€.

Burgsteige 18, 72070 Tübingen. www.hotelamschloss.de. ✆ **07071/92940.** Fax 07071/929410. 35 units. 108€–135€ double. Rates include buffet breakfast. AE, DC, MC, V. Parking 7€. **Amenities:** Restaurant; bar; Wi-Fi (2.50€ per hour). *In room:* TV, hair dryer (in some), minibar (in some).

Krone Hotel ★   The town's most prestigious and central hotel is located right off the river. Traditional and conservative, its homey decor includes a generous use of antiques or fine reproductions. Many of the personalized rooms have decorative tiling, and all contain bathrooms with tub/shower combos.

Among hotel dining rooms, the Uhlandstube Restaurant serves some of the most sophisticated fare in town. Both international dishes and regional specialties are available; main courses range from 19€ to 25€.

Uhlandstrasse 1, 72078 Tübingen. www.krone-tuebingen.de. ✆ **07071/13310.** Fax 07071/133132. 47 units. 139€–159€ double; 169€–199€ suite. Rates include buffet breakfast. AE, DC, MC, V. Free parking. Closed Dec 23–31. **Amenities:** Restaurant; room service. *In room:* TV, hair dryer (in some).

SCHWÄBISCH HALL ★★

97km (60 miles) NE of Stuttgart, 138km (86 miles) W of Nürnberg

Technically, this medieval town is not in the Neckar Valley; however, if you skip it in your travels through this region, you'll have missed one of southwestern Germany's treasures. Schwäbisch Hall is located in the heart of the forests of the Schwäbische Alb, where it clings to the steep banks of the Kocher River, a tributary of the Neckar. From the opposite bank, the houses of the Altstadt set on terraces built into the hillside appear to be arranged in steps, overlooking the old wooden river bridges.

Essentials
GETTING THERE
BY TRAIN   Trains run daily from Stuttgart and Nürnberg into the Bahnhof Schwäbisch Hall. For information, call ✆ **01805/996633** or visit www.bahn.de.

BY BUS   Regional bus service in the area is offered by **Stuttgart GmbH.** Call ✆ **0791/930090** for schedules and information.

BY CAR   Access is via the A6 Autobahn running east and west, or Rte. 14 from the east and Rte. 19 from the north.

VISITOR INFORMATION
The **Verkehrsverein,** Am Markt 9 (✆ **0791/751384;** www.schwaebischhall.de), is open October to April Monday to Friday 9am to 5pm; from May to September, hours are Monday to Friday 9am to 6pm, and Saturday and Sunday 10am to 3pm.

Exploring Schwäbisch Hall

Ths **Marktplatz ★★** may win the prize for the most attractive in Germany. Fine half-timbered patrician houses flank the sloping square to the baroque Rathaus at the lower end. A 16th-century Gothic fountain adorned with statues of St. Michael with St. George and Samson stands in the center. The Marktplatz is the scene of festive occasions, such as the annual Kuchenfest, celebrating the ancient salt industry that grew around the salt springs in Schwäbisch Hall.

At the upper side of the Marktplatz, 54 imposing but delicately curved stone steps rise to the **Michaelskirche.** This 15th-century Gothic church cathedral retains a 12th-century tower. Many pews date from the 15th century, as does St. Michael's altarpiece in the side chapel. The church is open March to November 14, Monday noon to 5pm, Tuesday to Friday 10am to 5pm, and Sunday 11am to 5pm; November 15 to February, hours are Monday noon to 2pm, and Tuesday to Sunday 11am to 3pm. It costs 1.50€ to visit the church tower.

Where to Eat & Stay

Der Adelshof ★   In an attractive stone building dating from 1400, the Adelshof boasts a prime location right in the center of town. Rooms are clean and comfortable, if a bit small. An octet of themed rooms provides a range of ambiences, from the wine-swilling *chambre rouge* to the baby-blue Wedgewood room. The refurbished, 500-year-old Kellerbar has become one of the town's most popular bars.

Am Markt 12 (on Marktplatz), 74523 Schwäbisch Hall. www.hotel-adelshof.de. (C) **0791/75890.** Fax 0791/6036. 46 units. 110€–145€ double; 150€ suite. Rates include buffet breakfast. AE, DC, MC, V. Parking 5€. **Amenities:** Restaurant; bar; spa. *In room:* TV, hair dryer, Wi-Fi (free).

Hotel Hohenlohe ★★   The Hohenlohe is on the left bank of the Kocher River, in the historic Freie Reichsstadt district opposite the town center. Rooms are pleasant and compact, with bright color accents. Most of the accommodations open onto scenic views, best enjoyed over breakfast on the open-view roof deck. The restaurant offers regional meals; a cafeteria and a bar are also on the premises.

Am Weilertor 14, 74523 Schwäbisch Hall. www.hotel-hohenlohe.de. (C) **0791/75870.** Fax 0791/758784. 114 units. 67€–100€ per person double; 149€–180€ per person suite. Rates include buffet breakfast. AE, DC, MC, V. Parking 7€ inside; free outside. **Amenities:** 2 restaurants; bar; babysitting; concierge; exercise room; 3 heated pools (1 outdoor, 2 indoor); room service; spa. *In room:* TV, DVD (in some), CD player (in some), hair dryer, minibar, Wi-Fi (10€ per day).

FRANKFURT

Cosmopolitan and bustling, Goethe's hometown flanking the River Main is the undisputed financial powerhouse of Germany. It rightly earns it its nickname "Mainhattan," but it's a fun-loving city at heart. Frankfurt's also known for luring 1.5 million visitors annually to its international trade fairs. The best known is the International Book Fair, when some 5,500 publishers from nearly 100 countries converge, lending the city a distinctly intellectual reputation. Overall, Frankfurt is surprisingly contradictory—soaring skyscrapers sit next to half-timbered houses and frenetic shopping streets hide cozy apple-wine taverns.

Things to Do   Start at the **Altstadt** (old town) in the city center and admire the **Römerberg's** (square) 14th and 15th-century half-timbered houses. Nearby is the **Goethe-Haus,** the writer's birth abode showcasing his original desk and library. Gaze down at the Altstadt from inside the elegant, Gothic tower of **Dom St. Bartholomäus,** then meander south over the pretty **Eiserner Steg** foot bridge to the museum-lined **Museumsufer** embankment. Don't miss **Städel Museum,** full of works by Renoir and Monet, and 14th- to 16th-century masterpieces.

Nightlife & Entertainment   Nightlife centers around **Sachsenhausen,** south of the **River Main.** This entire area feels like one big open-air bar on the weekend—stroll along Schweizer Strasse or Textorstrasse for the widest selection of drinking spots, from cocktail bars to wine taverns. Try Frankfurt's famously tart **Ebbelwei** (apple wine) when you stopy by Adolf Wagner for a convivial evening Frankfurt-style.

Restaurants & Dining   Small bites like sausages with rolls fill the food-minded **Fressgasse** (literally "Munch Alley") northwest of the **Altstadt**— it's lined with snack stalls and small restaurants. Or choose from Asian menus on banker-populated Schillerstrasse. Sample regional Hessian cuisine like *Tafelspitz* (boiled beef) or pork schnitzel; try either with green sauce (a mix of seven herbs including parsley and chives). Don't miss the **Kleinmarkthalle** market with regional specialties, fresh produce and several sausage stands, often with long lines. Both are available south of the **Altstadt** at **Historix,** a historic wine cellar with modern, vast glass windows.

Relaxation   Stroll through the park and botanic garden **Palmengarten** in the **Westend,** especially its Tropicarium, a brilliant explosion of tropical vegetation. In summer, take your towel to Frankfurt's **Main River** lidos; the shady **Freibad Brentano** is a favorite. Or lounge on the open deck aboard the **Primus Line,** while it takes you down the river through the city. For a leisurely tour, passengers on the **Apple Wine Express** lumber through town on a tram and sip local apple wine.

ESSENTIALS
Getting There

BY PLANE   **Flughafen** (✆ 180/53724636; www.airportcity-frankfurt.de) lies 11km (7 miles) from the city center at the Frankfurter Kreuz, the intersection of two major expressways, A3 and A5. This airport, continental Europe's busiest, serves more than 290 destinations in about 110 countries worldwide. Not only is it the country's primary international gateway, all major airports can be reached via Frankfurt. Flying time from Frankfurt to Berlin or Hamburg is 70 minutes; to Munich, 60 minutes. For the status of flights coming in and out of the Frankfurt airport, call ✆ **180/53724636.**

At the **Airport Train Station** beneath Terminal 1, you can connect to German InterCity trains and S-Bahn commuter trains to Frankfurt and nearby cities. Terminal 2 is linked to Terminal 1 by a people-mover system, Sky Line, which provides quick transfers.

For information about S-Bahn trains and regional trains departing from the Frankfurt airport to other points in and near Frankfurt, or for information about trains headed from the Frankfurt airport to more distant destinations, call ✆ **01805/996633** or visit www.bahn.de. S-Bahn lines S-8 and S-9 between the airport and Frankfurt center runs every 10 minutes and deposit passengers at the main rail station in 11 to 15 minutes. A one-way ticket costs 3.90€. Purchase tickets before boarding.

BY TRAIN   Frankfurt's main rail station, the **Hauptbahnhof,** the busiest in Europe, is the arrival point for some 1,700 trains per day carrying about 350,000 passengers. Trains arrive from most major cities in Germany every hour until 8pm. Many other European cities also have direct rail links with Frankfurt. For travel information, ticket reservations, and seat information, call **Deutsche Bahn** (✆ **01805/996633**) or visit www.bahn.de.

BY BUS   Frankfurt has long-distance bus service to about 700 German and European cities. Buses depart from the south side of the Hauptbahnhof. For information, contact **Deutsche Touring GmbH,** Am Römerhof 17 (✆ **069/7903501;** www.touring.de).

BY CAR   The A3 and A5 autobahns intersect at Frankfurt. The A3 comes in from the Netherlands, Cologne, and Bonn, and continues east and south to Würzburg, Nürnberg, and Munich. The A5 comes from the northeast (Hannover and Bad Hersfeld) and continues south to Heidelberg, Mannheim, and Basel (Switzerland). From the west, the A60 connects with the A66, which leads to Frankfurt and the inner city, hooking up with the A3. Road signs and directions are frequently posted.

Visitor Information

The **tourist office** is in two locations: at the Hauptbahnhof, opposite the main entrance (✆ **069/21238800;** www.frankfurt-tourismus.de), open Monday to Friday 8am to 9pm, and Saturday and Sunday 9am to 6pm; and in Römerberg 27 (✆ **069/21238800**), open Monday to Friday 9:30am to 5:30pm, and Saturday and Sunday 10am to 4pm.

City Layout

Most of Frankfurt's sights, nightlife, restaurants, and hotels lie in the **Stadtmitte (town center).** However, chances are you'll cross the Main River to visit the museums or *Apfelwein* (apple-wine) taverns in the **Sachsenhausen** area as well. It is also

Frankfurt

ATTRACTIONS ●
Alte Oper **14**
Deutsches Filmmuseum **31**
Goethe-Haus **21**
Historisches Museum
  (Historical Museum) **46**
Kaiserdom St.
  Bartholomäus **44**
Liebieghaus **33**
Museum für Angewandte
  Kunst **30**
Museum für Moderne
  Kunst **42**
Palmengarten **2**
Römerberg **45**
Städel Museum **32**

HOTELS ■
Admiral **39**
Am Berg **49**
An Der Messe **10**
Art Hotel Robert Mayer **9**
Continental **26**
Fleming's Deluxe Hotel **12**
Fleming's Hotel Messe **23**
Gerbermühle **41**
Goldman 25hours
  Frankfurt **40**
Hotel Amadeus **40**
Hotel Hessischer Hof **18**
Hotel Liebig **5**
Hotel Neue Kräme **43**
Hotel Palmenhof **7**
Hotelschiff Peter Schlott **25**
Le Méridien Parkhotel **27**
Maritim Hotel Frankfurt **19**
The Pure **24**
Steigenberger
  Frankfurter Hof **20**
25hours by Levi's **22**
Villa Diana **11**
Villa Kennedy **34**
Villa Orange **35**

RESTAURANTS ◆
Adolf Wagner **48**
Bull + Bear **16**
Café Laumer **8**
Chicago Meatpackers **29**
Gargantua **4**
Im Herzen Afrikas **28**
Kameha Suite **15**
Maingau Stuben **47**
Main Tower Restaurant
  & Bar **17**
Pacific Colors **13**
Restaurant Français **20**
San San Restaurant **36**
Silk **6**
Solberfäss'je **37**
Surf 'n Turf **3**
Tiger Palast Restaurant/
  Palastbar & Tigerbistro **38**
Villa Merton **1**

13

FRANKFURT | Essentials

443

possible that you'll seek out both restaurants and hotels in the increasingly fashionable **Westend.** Most of the other areas of Frankfurt probably will not concern you, unless you're hunting for intriguing restaurants in the **Nordend (North End)** or even nightlife in the **Ostend (East End).**

Most of the heart of Frankfurt can be covered on foot. Nearly all the main sights lie within the boundaries of the old town walls, which today form a 5km-long (3-mile) stretch of narrow parkland, almost a perfect half-moon around the **Altstadt (Old City).** Once one of the great old towns of Europe, around 85% of the Altstadt was blasted to rubble in two horrendous air raids in 1944. Some of its buildings have been sympathetically reconstructed in the old style.

The Römerberg, in the historic heart of the city, is an ideal place to begin your exploration of Frankfurt. Once the site of Charlemagne's fort, it grew into a prominent marketplace in the Middle Ages. Now, its reconstructed half-timbered houses look out over the animated square. Just east of the Römerberg, the red-sandstone **Kaiserdom** rises over the foundations of buildings dating back to the Roman times. Although called a "Dom," it isn't technically a cathedral, though it did host the coronation of ten Holy Roman emperors between 1562 and 1792.

The **Zeil** runs to the north of the Dom/Römerberg area between the twin transportation hubs of Konstablerwache and Hauptwache. Frankfurt's prime shopping district lies in this area, with the MyZeil mall and all the international brands in a pleasant pedestrian zone. The **Hauptwache** itself, an 18th-centruy baroque guardhouse, stands just a stone's throw from the **Börse** (stock exchange). The **Goethe Haus** and **Goethe Museum** lie a few minutes away by foot to the west of the Dom/Römerberg area. Continuing further west, the skyscrapers of the **financial district,** jokingly called "Main-hatten," rise out of where the western ramparts stood until the 19th century. The **Main Tower** with its candy-cane antenna is the only one accessible to the public.

Even further west, and past an admittedly unappealing district that often tarnishes visitor's impressions and should be avoided if possible, stands the **Hauptbahnhof.** If you're arriving by train, walk down the safer Kaiserstrasse straight in front of the station to get to the financial district and Stadtmitte, or take the U-Bahn two stops to Dom/Römer.

The **Main River** is south of the Dom/Römerberg area, flowing from east to west. At some point during your stay, you'll want to cross it on one of the pedestrian bridges or the Alte Brücke, which offers a nice view of the entire downtown. A row of no less than eight **museums** line the south bank between Friedensbrücke and the Eiserner Steg. In the evening, this often overlooked area also draws locals and visitors alike to the **Alt-Sachsenhausen** district with its congenial apple-wine taverns. Other attractions, like the Frankfurt Zoo and the Palmengarten, lie further afield, but are only a short ride away via the handy U-Bahn.

STREET MAPS Arm yourself with a detailed street map, not the general overview handed out by the tourist office. Maps are sold at most bookstores and news kiosks. See "Bookstores" in "Fast Facts: Frankfurt," below.

Getting Around
BY PUBLIC TRANSPORTATION
The **RMV (Rhein-Main Verkehrsverbund),** Mannheimer Strasse 15 (© **01805/7684636;** www.rmv.de) administers the network of metro lines (U-Bahn), trams (Strassenbahn), and buses. Additional express lines (S-Bahn) thread

below the city with trains nearly every 1 to 3 minutes during the day. Any of these forms of transportation can be used within their fare zone, including transfers between them. Purchase tickets at coin-operated machines marked "Fahrscheine." Although they accept all denominations, it's a good idea to have small bills and coins ready, as change is given in coins. Zone charts and additional information in six languages are displayed on all the automatic machines. Except for bus travel (where you have the option of paying the driver directly for your passage), be sure to buy your ticket before you board any of the public transport conveyances of Frankfurt. If you're caught traveling without the proper ticket, you may be fined 40€.

If you want to simplify the ticket-buying process—for both public transport and museum admissions within Frankfurt—consider the purchase of a **Frankfurter Tageskarte (Frankfurt Card)** from either of the city's tourist offices. These cards allow unlimited travel anywhere within the greater Frankfurt area, transport on the shuttle bus going to and from the airport, and half-price admission to any of the city's museums. The cost is 9€ for a 1-day card and 13€ for a 2-day card. Children age 14 and under go free when traveling with an adult. *Warning:* The card expires on midnight of the day of purchase (or midnight the following day, for the 2-day card). Use after that can subject you to a fine. For more information, contact the tourist office.

For more information about Frankfurt's public transportation system, call **RMV,** the city transport office, at ☎ **01805/7684636,** or visit www.rmv.de and look for the information listed in English.

BY TAXI

There's no surcharge for calling for a taxi; dial ☎ **069/792020,** 230033, or 250001. Otherwise, you can get a cab either by standing at any of the city's hundreds of clearly designated taxi stands or by hailing one that has an illuminated dome light. Taxis charge by the trip and by the carload, without surcharge for pieces of luggage. Some are suitable for carrying up to six passengers, others for a maximum of only four. Regardless of their size, the initial fee you'll pay for a Frankfurt taxi is 2.75€ plus 1.65€ per kilometer for rides between 6am and 10pm; from 10pm to 6am, the basic rate is 3.25€ plus 1.75€ per extra kilometer.

BY RENTAL CAR

The big rental companies each maintain offices at the airport and at central locations throughout Frankfurt. The most reliable are **Avis,** whose downtown branch is inside the Hauptbahnhof (☎ **069/27997010;** www.avis.com), and **Hertz,** whose offices are in the Hauptbahnhof (☎ **069/230484;** www.hertz.com) and at the airport (☎ **069/69593244**). Also recommended is **Europcar,** which maintains offices at the Hauptbahnhof (☎ **069/2429810;** www.europcar.com) and at the airport (☎ **069/697970**).

[FastFACTS] FRANKFURT

Bookstores The best English-language bookstore is **British Bookshop,** Börsenstrasse 17 (☎ **069/ 280492;** U-Bahn/S-Bahn: Hauptwache). It's open Monday to Friday 9:30am to 7pm and Saturday 9:30am to 6pm.

Currency Exchange There are multiple facilities for the exchange of international currencies at the Frankfurt airport.

Dentists & Doctors For an English-speaking dentist or doctor, call ☎ **069/19292** to arrange an appointment.

Drugstores For information about pharmacies

open near you, call ⓒ **069/19292.** Otherwise, you can go to Kissel-Apotheke, Mörfelder Landstrasse 235 (ⓒ **069/68974730**).

Emergencies Dial ⓒ **110** for the police; ⓒ **112** for a fire, first aid, and ambulance; and ⓒ **069/6607271** for emergency dental service.

Internet Access Head for **CyberRyder,** Tongegasse 31 (ⓒ **069/91396754;** www.cyberyder.de), open Monday to Friday 9:30am to 10pm, Saturday 10am to 10pm, and Sunday noon to 10pm. Internet connections cost 1.60€ for 15 minutes. There are several other Internet cafes in Frankfurt as well; the best place to search for Internet cafes is along Elisabethenstrasse, not far from the Hauptbahnhof in central Frankfurt. Those looking for a Wi-Fi connection will find that many cafes and bars offer free access, most notably Cafe Moloko+ (p. 462) and any Burger King.

Luggage Storage & Lockers Lockers can be rented and luggage stored at the Hauptbahnhof.

Post Office There's a post office at the Hauptbahnhof (ⓒ **069/97511004**), open Monday to Friday 6:30am to 9pm, Saturday 8am to 6pm, and Sunday and holidays 11am to 6pm.

Safety Frankfurt is a relatively safe city, but you should still stay alert at all times. Stay out of the area around the Hauptbahnhof at night, as muggings are frequent. Also be aware of bogus police officers in civilian clothes asking to check your cash. Real officers show a green ID, and never ask about money.

Toilets There are many decent public facilities in central Frankfurt, especially in the Altstadt.

EXPLORING FRANKFURT

When bombs rained down on Frankfurt in 1944, nearly all the old half-timbered buildings were leveled. In what seemed like record time, residents of Frankfurt rebuilt their city into a fine mélange of modern and traditional architecture and faithfully restored some of their most prized old buildings as well.

Although Frankfurt doesn't have the monuments or museums to equal Munich or Berlin, its museums and exhibition halls still lure some two million visitors annually. As the cultural director of the city of Frankfurt, Dr. Hans Bernhard Nordhoff, said, "We offer you everything from Goethe to Andy Warhol, from *Tyrannosaurus Rex* to the female ideal of Botticelli."

Many of the grandest museums lie along the Main on the south bank—often called "Museum Embankment," in itself a dazzling array of contemporary architecture even before you go inside to look at the exhibits.

The easiest way to sightsee in Frankfurt is to take a cruise on the Main River aboard one of the vessels operated by **Primus-Linie,** Mainkai 36 (ⓒ **069/1338370;** www.primus-linie.de). From March to October, boats leave from the North Bank of the Main at Mainkai during the day, offering a 50-minute excursion for 9€ or a 100-minute excursion for 11€. The trip gives you a preview of the skyline of Frankfurt.

See the map on p. 442 for the location of Frankfurt's major attractions.

The Top Attractions

ALTSTADT ★★

You can take in the sights of the old town in about a half a day, beginning at the historic core of the **Römerberg.** This pleasant and often lively square is bordered on one side by a trio of medieval patricians' houses known as the **Römer,** home to the city hall since 1405. Opposite stands a row of half-timbered houses reconstructed in 1986 to original plans. They recall they way the historic and cramped inner city looked before the fire bombs of World War II reduced it to dust.

Among the more intriguing sights is the **Kaiserdom** (detailed below), which was consecrated in 1239 and hosted ten imperial coronations between 1562 and 1792. The **Archeological Gardens** in the square to the west of the Kaiserdom presents scant foundations of the Roman military outpost and Carolingian royal palace.

The nearby **Paulskirche** has historical significance as site of the first German National Assembly in 1848. A short walk west you'll find the **Goethe Haus,** birthplace of Germany's greatest writer in 1749.

Nearing the northern edge of the old town, the squat **Hauptwache** greets you. This old guardhouse from 1730 used to mark the exact center of town, until it was moved 6m (18ft.) during post-war rebuilding. A short stroll down Eschenheimerstrasse brings you to the only remaining gate of the former ramparts, the **Eschenheimer Tor,** dating from around 1400.

Although not technically in the Altstadt, the row of museums on the opposite bank of the Main are another main attraction, including the not-to-be-missed **Städel** and **Liebieghaus.**

Goethe Haus ★ HISTORIC HOUSE Not much of Frankfurt, the great Goethe's house included, survived the ravages of World War II. Yet, careful (and costly) reconstruction of the German literary figurehead's birthplace, with the installation of preserved furnishings, has recreated the 18th century splendor of an aristocratic life. The young writer entered the world at this location in 1749 and spent his formative years here until the age of 26, when he heeded a call to Weimar. With the useful hand-held placards in English, you can roam as you please through the four floors of antique rooms, giving you the true feeling of family life in old Frankfurt.

Once you pass through a Rococo garden hall bearing busts of his parents, note the massive water pump in the kitchen on the ground floor, a true luxury at the time. His parents' initials (JCG and CEG) have been wrought into the iron banister leading to the second floor. There, the music room presents a touching portrait of the Goethe children, including the others who didn't live long. A unique astronomical clock from 1746 stands on the next floor. On the top floor, you'll find the poet's puppet theater, as well as his private room, an inspiring place to work on the first version of *Faust.* The complementary **Frankfurter-Goethe Museum** on the ground floor features a collection of portraits of the writer at various ages, as well as period works like Caspar David Friedrich's *The Evening Star.*

Grosser Hirschgraben 23-25. (✆ **069/138800.** www.goethehaus-frankfurt.de. Admission 5€ adults, 2.50€ students, 1.50€ children 7-18, free for children 6 and under. Mon–Sat 10am–6pm; Sun and holidays 10am–5:30pm. U-Bahn or S-Bahn: Hauptwache.

Liebieghaus ★★★ MUSEUM The absorbing collection of sculpture on display in this museum is not its only draw, but also wandering through the creaking halls of this 1896 villa as if it's yours, and stumbling upon ancient statues of virgins in the niches of the round tower, or antique cabinets with miniature sculpture spanning from the Egyptian to Baroque. Larger rooms in an adjacent building display impressive pieces like a Roman copy of the Myron's *Athena,* Naukydes' *Discus Thrower,* and a striking Syrian Room with a beautiful and well-preserved *Mummy Portrait of a Girl* from the 2nd century. The medieval collection features Riemenschneider's *Virgin Mary,* as well as the earliest example of a *Virgin Enthroned* from the Middle Rhine.

Schaumainkai 71. (✆ **069/6500490.** www.liebieghaus.de. Admission 9€ adults, 7€ seniors and students, free for children 11 and under. Tues and Fri–Sun 10am–6pm; Wed–Thurs 10am–9pm. Tram: 15 or 16 to Otto-Hahn-Platz.

13

FRANKFURT | Exploring Frankfurt

frankfurt's TOWERS

Many visitors to Frankfurt miss out on one of the city's great points of interest, never having taken the time to look up. You'll find several interesting skyscrapers lying along the Neue Mainzerstrasse, known jokingly as "Bankenklamm" (bank gorge), or "Little Wall St." Except for the Europaturm, you'll find the others in the grid stretching to the train station district and fairgrounds.

Europaturm At 337.5m (1107 ft.), a tad taller than the Eiffel Tower, this needle-shaped structure north of the city center has been Frankfurt's highest structure since its construction in 1979. Used today as a communications tower, it is not open to the public.

Commerzbank Tower The tallest office building in the European Union rises to a height of 258.7m (848.5 ft.), just shy of San Francisco's Transamerica Pyramid. Famed British architect Norman Foster, creator of London's bullet-shaped 30 St. Mary Axe known as "The Gherkin," designed the tower, erected by 1997, with a distinct triangular floor plan

and 19th-floor park, which is unfortunately not open to the public.

Messeturm (Trade Fair Tower) Some say this 256.5m (841.3-ft.) tower finished in 1991 is the displaced twin of the Bank of America Plaza in Atlanta. Its designer, German-American Helmut Jahn, is also known for Berlin's futuristic Sony Center at Potsdamer Platz.

Kronenhochhaus Also known as the Westend Tower, this distinctive 208m (682.2-ft.) tower gets its name from its bill-shaped crown. It also features a giant sculpture at its entry called "Inverted Collar and Tie," by Claes Oldenburg and Coosje van Bruggen, which reminds us bankers can also have a sense of humor.

Main Tower If your neck aches from looking up all the time, let the elevator here whisk you imperceptibly to the 54th floor. At a height of 200m (656 ft.) the splendid views extend across the city and its skyscrapers to the distant Feldberg (826m, 2709 ft.) mountain visible to the northwest.

Städel Museum ★★★ MUSEUM Frankfurt's premier art gallery houses a prominent collection of European art, from 15th-century Dutch, German and Italian masterpieces to works by contemporary German and international artists. The museum is proud of its new expansion under the courtyard garden with round, ground-level openings that create a bright space for displaying artwork. Botticelli's exquisite *Idealized Portrait of a Lady* and Lucas Cranach the Elder's impish *Venus* hang among other works by Albrecht Dürer, his pupil Hans Baldung Grien, and Hieronymus Bosch. Jan van Eyck's intimate *Madonna* (1433) also draws the viewer nearer. Don't miss Rembrandt's gory *The Blinding of Samson,* or Tischbein's portrait of a reclining Goethe. Alongside a few Impressionists the Städel also boasts notable works from modernists like Kirchner, Schmidt-Rotluff, Picasso and Yves Klein.

Schaumainkai 63 (on the south bank of the Main). (C) **069/6050980.** www.staedelmuseum.de. Admission 12€ adults, 10€ children 12–16, 20€ family ticket, free for children 11 and under. English audio guide 4€. Tues, Fri, and Sun 10am–6pm; Wed–Thurs 10am–9pm. U-Bahn: Schweizer Platz.

RÖMERBERG ★

The Altstadt (U-Bahn: Dom/Römer) centers on three Gothic buildings with stepped gables, known collectively as the **Römer,** Römerberg (C) **069/21234814**). These

Trianon Like the Commerzbank Tower, this 186m (610.1 ft.) tower features a triangular floor plan in addition to a glass facade that makes it look like a prism on end.

Silver Tower At 166.7m (546.8 ft.), the seat of Dresdner Bank is notable for its aluminum exterior, giving it a silver sheen, and the only rounded corners on a Frankfurt skyscraper.

Deutsche Bank Towers These twin towers have taken on the nickname "Soll & Haben," meaning Debits and Credits, which apparently sounds funny to Frankfurt's bankers. Although built between 1979 and 1984, these 158m (518 ft.) towers were rebuilt from within as "Green Towers," which now use half the electricity.

Skyper Based on the common, though unofficial, convention of defining a skyscraper as a building 150m (492 ft.) tall or more, this 154m (505.1-ft.) favorite of many is Frankfurt's shortest skyscraper. Its quarter-circle floor plan blends in with the neighboring Silver Tower. A great selection of shops and restaurants fills the ground floor.

Gallileo The name of this 136.8m (448.7-ft) building had little to do with the Italian astronomer Galileo, but rather with its proximity to the former Gallus Gate (hence the extra 'l'). Built between 1999 and 2003, its 4,000 windows provide natural heating, not to mention a transparent view of what's going down inside. Its original plans called for it to be taller, but were reduced to these 37 stories after September 11, 2001.

Kastor und Pollox These Gemini twins may look more like an odd couple, but the squatter Castor, 91.4m (299.8 ft.), and taller Pollox 126.9m (416.2 ft.) with the Messeturm form the portrait of the fairgrounds.

Japan Center Although far from the tallest, you may find this unsung hero of the bunch is the most charming, if a skyscraper can be such. Completed in 1996 and rising to 115m (377.2 ft.), the humble Japan Center features a hanging roof and a red granite, square-paneled facade, of which the measurements are based on a Japanese tatami mat measuring roughly 180cm by 90cm.

houses were originally built between 1288 and 1305 and bought by the city a century later for use as the Rathaus. The second floor of the center house is the **Kaisersaal (Imperial Hall),** lined with the romanticized 19th-century portraits of 52 emperors; 13 of them celebrated their coronation banquets here. You can visit this hall daily 10am to 1pm and 2 to 5pm. An hourly tour costing 2€ is obligatory. Tours are conducted in English and German and tickets can be purchased at the entrance to the Römer.

The elaborate facade of the Römer, with its ornate balcony and statues of four emperors, overlooks **Römerplatz (Römerberg Square).** On festive occasions in days gone by, the square was the scene of oxen roasts that featured flowing wine. Today, unfortunately, the Fountain of Justitia pours forth only water, but oxen are still roasted on special occasions.

KAISERDOM ★

The dominant feature of the Altstadt is the 15th-century, red-sandstone tower of the **Kaiserdom St. Bartholomäus,** in whose chapels the emperors of the Holy Roman Empire were elected and crowned for nearly 300 years. The church was constructed between the 13th and 15th centuries on the site of a Carolingian building. It is most

GERMAN men of ideas: JOHANN WOLFGANG VON GOETHE (1749–1832)

"That is the true season of love; when we believe that we alone can love, that no one could ever have loved as much before, and that no one will ever love in the same way again."

Field of Study: Romanticist, poet, playwright, philosopher, scientist.

Revolutionary Insight: The towering figure in German literature, his book *The Sorrows of Young Werther* was a seminal inspiration for the Romantic movement. His epic *Faust* inspired such artists as Mozart, Liszt, Beethoven, and Mahler. Nonfiction writing heavily influenced

Hegel, Nietzsche, Jung, Darwin, and others.

Controversy Quotient (0to 5): (3) Favored a highly sexualized writing style at a time of repressive social mores; some of his poems were suppressed from publication in his lifetime. *Werther,* one of his first works, was criticized as glorifying suicide.

Little Known Fact: His poem *Der Zauberlehrling* was adapted for "The Sorcerer's Apprentice" segment in the 1940 animated Disney film *Fantasia*.

—Kelly Regan

noted for its west tower or **Westturm ★★**, which is greatly ornamented and crowned by a polygonal gable. It's topped by both a lantern and a dome. Surprisingly, the cathedral was not completed until 1877, but it was based on plans created by the Dom's original architect, Madern Gerthener. Destroyed by Allied bombs in 1944, it was rebuilt in 1953. One of its chief treasures is its **choir stalls ★**, which represent brilliant Upper Rhine craftsmanship, dating from around the mid–14th century. In the north chancel, look for **Maria Schlafaltar (Altar of Mary Sleeping),** dating from 1434. It is the only altar remaining from the church's original interior. The Dom is open daily, at no charge, from 9am to noon and 2 to 6pm.

In the cloister is the **Dom Museum** (⌀ **069/13376186;** www.dommuseum-frankfurt.de) which, among other things, exhibits robes of the imperial electors. Dating back as far as the 1400s, these robes, which are still quite sumptuous, were worn at coronation ceremonies. Walk west of the cathedral to an "archaeological garden" called **Archäologischer Garten,** with ruins of both Roman and Carolingian fortifications. The site is open and free to the public at all times.

Other Top Museums

Deutsches Filmmuseum (German Film Museum) ★ MUSEUM   You don't have to be a cinephile to enjoy one of the best film museums in Germany. A newly renovated series of three floors walk you through the history of cinema, beginning with tools and items from the 19th century and techniques that create illusion. Exhibits include Emile Reynaud's 1882 Praxinoscope, Edison's Kinetoscope from 1889, and a copy of the Lumière brothers' Cinematograph from 1895. There are also models illustrating how special effects are shot, including those in the original *King Kong*. In addition to changing special exhibitions, the museum also screens films from its vast collection of classics.

Schaumainkai 41, at the corner of Schweizerstrasse. ⌀ **069/21238830.** www.deutschesfilmmuseum. de. Admission 3.50€ adults, 1.50€ students and children; film screenings 8€ adults, 5.50€ students, 4€ children. Tues, Thurs–Fri, and Sun 10am–5pm; Wed 10am–8pm; Sat 2–8pm. U-Bahn: Schweizer Platz.

Historisches Museum (Historical Museum) ★ MUSEUM Since this dignified museum was established in a stately looking building near Town Hall in 1878, its curators have systematically added exhibits that showcase the history and culture of Frankfurt. After undergoing a complete renovation in 2011, its exhibitions help recapture the history of Frankfurt that may not be so apparent in the modern metropolis. Items include examples of gold and silver plate ware and jewelry; pottery and porcelain; and paintings, lithographs, and photographs. Most absorbing are the scaled-down models of the Altstadt at various periods of its development.

Saalgasse 19. *☏* **069/21235599.** www.historisches-museum.frankfurt.de. Admission 4€ adults, 2€ children 6–18, free for children 5 and under. Tues and Thurs–Sun 10am–6pm; Wed 10am–9pm. U-Bahn: Römer.

Museum für Angewandte Kunst (Museum of Applied Arts) ★ MUSEUM Contained in the 1877 in a 19th-century Villa Metzler and a 1985 structure designed by New York–architect Richard Meier, this museum explores the interior worlds of design through the more than 30,000 objects from across Europe and Asia. With a collection begun in 1877 the first floor covers nearly 800 years of European history through statues, tapestries, and everyday objects like tables and chairs. Fascinating pieces such as massive beer mugs are highlights of the glassware collection, and some stem from 15th-century Venice. Persian carpets bedeck the second floor, along with rich faience from the 9th century and a porcelain collection.

Schaumainkai 17. *☏* **069/21234037.** www.angewandtekunst-frankfurt.de. Admission 8€ adults, 4€ students and children 7–18, free for children 6 and under. Tues and Thurs–Sun 10am–5pm; Wed 10am–9pm. U-Bahn: Schweizer Platz.

Museum für Moderne Kunst (Museum of Modern Art) MUSEUM This museum opened in 1991 in a building created by Hans Hollein, the Viennese architect. The structure is designed like a boat, but in spite of its somewhat bizarre shape, the gallery has a bright, spacious air. (Some critics claim the dazzling architecture is more interesting than the exhibits.) Major artists since the 1950s are displayed here, including Roy Liechtenstein (see his *Brush-stroke*), Andy Warhol, and George Segal, with his *Jazz Combo.*

Domstrasse 10 (in the center of the Altstadt, near Römerberg). *☏* **069/21230447.** www.mmk-frankfurt.de. Admission 8€ adults, 4€ students, free for children 5 and under, free for all last Sat of each month. Tues and Thurs–Sun 10am–6pm; Wed 10am–8pm. U-Bahn: Dom/Römer. Tram: 11 or 12.

Parks

Given such a soaring skyline, Frankfurt is remarkably green. The entire ring where the ramparts once ran is now a veritable shady oasis popular with joggers. **Bethmann Park,** with its Chinese gardens and rose garden, lies along this route, reachable by bus no. 30 or tram no. 12. Both banks of the Main provide a riverside retreat for lunch breaks, and are often the venues for summertime festivals.

Farther north, the city's two major parks can be found next to one another. Once the grounds of the Rothschild family's former castle, the **Grüneburg Park** is the city's largest, and a popular sunbathing haunt in summer. The neighboring **Palmengarten** ★, Siesmayerstrasse 61 (*☏* **069/21233939;** www.palmengarten.frankfurt. de; U-Bahn: Westend; bus: 32), is a park and a botanical garden. Renewals and reconstructions have enhanced the gardens in recent years, and they're now home to a perennial garden, an expanded rock garden, and a beautiful rose garden. A huge gallery that serves as an exhibition hall for flower shows and other botanical exhibitions surrounds the 1869 palm house. Don't miss the Tropicarium and its tropical vegetation, the Entrance Conservatory and its insectivorous plants and bromeliads, and the Sub-Antarctic House with plants from southern Chile, Argentina, and New Zealand. Collections of orchids, palms, succulents, waterlilies, and many others are also on display.

Admission to the botanical garden is 5€ for adults and 2€ for children, or 9.50€ for a family ticket. It's open daily March to October 9am to 6pm, and November to January 9am to 4pm. In the park area, there's a small lake where people can row boats. In summer, concerts are given in the band shell; evening events include open-air dancing, jazz, and fountain illumination. There are some facilities for food. For guided tours in English call ℂ **069/21233391.**

WHERE TO EAT

Almost overnight, without much of the world being aware, the city of Frankfurt has become one of Europe's great dining capitals. Though it's still fighting to overcome a terrible culinary reputation, Frankfurt now ranks with Berlin and Munich as a dining mecca. Everybody knows it for its banking and business, but serious gourmets now also descend on the city, which offers one of Europe's most varied cuisines. It still doesn't have as eclectic a mixture of cuisine as New York (which has virtually every cuisine served on earth), but Frankfurt is getting there.

For years, visitors to the famous book fair always came home to tell visitors, "You can't get a decent meal in Frankfurt." That wasn't even true way back then, and it's gross libel today.

See the map on p. 442 for restaurant locations.

In the Center
VERY EXPENSIVE

Restaurant Français ★★★ FRENCH   This restaurant is very stylish, and very conscious of maintaining the top-notch standards usually associated with upscale hotel restaurants in Paris. It occupies a duet of stately rooms, outfitted in tones of imperial blue and gold, on the lobby level of Frankfurt's most prestigious hotel. Don't think you can go slumming if you drop in for a bite here: jackets and ties are recommended for men. Menu items are cultivated, posh, and beautifully prepared and presented—the descriptions alone will make you drool. Look for brilliant combinations, such as Alsatian goose liver with smoked eel and apple sorbet, or else caviar with an iced cucumber gratiné. You can also sample such dishes as Atlantic sole with potato purée and morels, or lamb from Roussillon with eggplant and garlic chips.

In the Steigenberger Frankfurter Hof, Am Kaiserplatz. ℂ **069/21502.** www.steigenberger.com. Reservations required. Main courses 30€–38€; fixed-price 8-course menu 129€. AE, DC, MC, V. Mon–Fri noon–2:30pm and 6:30–10:30pm. U-Bahn: Willy-Brandt-Platz.

Tiger Restaurant/Palastbar & Tigerbistrot ★★★ INTERNATIONAL   No one expected a restaurant associated with a cabaret (Tigerpalast, p. 460) to be this exceptional, but when Michelin first granted it a star in 2000, the city took notice. In the basement below the theater you're greeted with whimsical murals that could have been painted by a latter-day Jean Cocteau. Menu items are impeccably presented. Try the sea bass with a mild pepper crust with chanterelles, risotto, and baked calves'-head ravioli, or the sole rolls with Périgord truffle with fried artichokes and potato foam.

Meals in the Palastbar & Tigerbistrot are less elaborate and cheaper, served under the vaulted brick ceiling of what was built as a warehouse about a century ago.

Examples include vegetarian paella in saffron sauce or breast of chicken stuffed with tomato, sage, and Parma ham, served with an eggplant mousse and potato gnocchi. One of the best dishes is a glazed filet of turbot with a truffle mousse.

Heiligkreuzgasse 16–20. ✆ **069/9200220.** www.tigerpalast.com. Reservations required. Restaurant main courses 49€–64€. Palastbar & Tigerbistrot main courses 23€–38€. AE, DC, MC, V. Restaurant Tues–Sat 7pm–midnight. Palastbar & Tigerbistrot Tues–Sun 5pm–1am. U-Bahn: Konstablerwache.

EXPENSIVE

Pacific Colors ★ CALIFORNIAN   This intensely dramatic lobby-level restaurant in Frankfurt's most avant-garde hotel boasts a New Age design in (what else?) Pacific tones of sea green and blue, with big-windowed views over the trees and walkways of the Friedberger Anlage Park. The food is what keeps gastronomes coming back—particularly those with a fondness for a Mediterranean-inspired cuisine that manages to be both airy and earthy. As conceived by culinary artist Manfred Breuer, the exact composition of the menu changes about every 3 months, but the best examples include a seafood medley—a trio of red snapper, whitefish, and prawns served with spicy chili-laced noodles and a coriander syrup. The steak, a filet mignon with an olive-and-potato tapenade, is also sumptuous.

In the lobby of the Hilton Hotel, Hochstrasse 4. ✆ **069/133802450.** www.hilton.com. Reservations recommended. Main courses 24€–39€. AE, DC, MC, V. Daily 6:30–11pm. U-Bahn: Eschenheimer Tor.

San San Restaurant ★★ CHINESE   Aficionados of Chinese food flock to this hotel restaurant, which arguably hires the finest chefs from the Far East in all of Frankfurt. These artists in the kitchen concoct a modern interpretation of Chinese culinary delights from carefully chosen products. You can select a seat in the modern Bamboo Lounge, in the authentically decorated Shanghai Suite, or even the Separee bathed in natural light. Savor such specialties as spicy chicken served in a sizzling pot or else wok-stir-fried prawns, squid, and scallops. A chicken is served stuffed with bell peppers and prawns and accompanied by fine Chinese noodles in a black-bean sauce.

In the Westin Grand Frankfurt, Konrad-Adenauer-Strasse 7. ✆ **069/29810.** Reservations required. Main courses 16€–26€. AE, DC, MC, V. Mon–Sat noon–2:30pm and 5–11:30pm. U-Bahn: Konstablerwache.

MODERATE

Kameha Suite ★★ INTERNATIONAL   Frankfurt fashionistas converge on this sophisticated enclave in a wonderfully preserved neoclassical villa with a sweeping marble staircase. "We're whatever you want us to be," the manager told us. Perhaps he was referring to the multipurpose role of his establishment—chic lounge, bar, cafe, restaurant, and, yes, even a nightclub. In a historic building across from the opera house, the dining room is on the second floor.

Exceptional products are featured with a finely honored technique. The cooking has flair and imagination, including such dishes as roast lamb with Périgord truffles. A lot of grill specialties are featured, and the pastas are homemade, including ravioli of wild garlic filled with sautéed mushrooms.

Taunusanlage 20. ✆ **069/4800370.** www.kamehasuite.de. Reservations required for dining. Main courses 18€–35€. AE, DC, MC, V. Mon–Fri 11:30am–3pm and 6–11pm; Sat 6–11pm; Sun 10am–3pm. S-Bahn: Tanusanlage.

Main Tower Restaurant & Bar ★ EUROPEAN   For the highest fine dining experience in town, let the Main Tower elevator whisk you up to the 53rd floor for unbeatable fare and an unforgettable view. The long line of diners who ascend every day for lunch, dinner, and after-work cocktails makes up one of the most diverse clientele in town, including grandmothers showing the view to their offspring, media hipsters affiliated with the building's TV stations, and newcomers trying to figure out the geography of Frankfurt.

The chefs don't try to get by on the view alone, but instead boast a solid and reliable cuisine prepared with fresh ingredients. Appetizers range from a smoked salmon with a pesto sauce to goose liver with black currants, followed by such main courses as a succulent rib of beef with anchovy jus or eggplant lasagna flavored with young leeks.

Neue Mainzer Strasse 52-58. (✆ **069/36504777.** www.maintower-restaurant.de. Reservations required. Main courses 18€–30€; fixed-price menus 59€–99€. AE, MC, V. Tues–Fri noon–3pm and 6pm–1am; Sat–Sun 1–5pm and 6pm–1am. U-Bahn: Willy-Brandt-Platz.

INEXPENSIVE

Bull + Bear INTERNATIONAL/MEDITERRANEAN   Its name, referring to the types of financial markets, may seem like a nerdy stock broker creation, but this hip bistro next to the stock exchange is far from it. The decor here may remind you of a glass-sided cube, thanks to soaring ceilings and a glittery, metallic look that evokes the waiting room of an international airport. Well-prepared menu items include pork filet with an asparagus ragout, tortellini stuffed with ricotta and spinach, saddle of lamb with Provençal vegetables, and a wide selection of grilled Angus steaks.

Bull + Bear also serves as a singles bar and a late-night dance spot. In the basement Börsenkeller, there's a dance floor that's usually mobbed, especially on Friday and Saturday, with a young, hip, after-work crowd. A live DJ plays house, techno, and trance music; the cover charge is 10€. Drinks start at 5€ each during happy hour, which is every day from 4 to 7pm.

Börsenplatz/Schillerstrasse 11. (✆ **069/13388733.** www.bullandbear.de. Reservations recommended for parties of 6 or more. Main courses 7€–22€; lunch salads, sandwiches, and platters 7€–16€. AE, DC, MC, V. Mon–Thurs 8am–1am; Fri–Sun 8am–3am. U-Bahn or S-Bahn: Hauptwache.

Chicago Meatpackers ☺ AMERICAN   For a piece of Americana not involving meal deals and triple soy lattes, your best bet is this eatery seemingly plucked from a 1940s Chicago stockyard. Its ornate 19th-century facade overlooking the backside of the Neues Opernhaus (New Opera House) shields the wood-planked interior with pizzeria tablecloths and tons of good-ol' American clutter, including a model train suspended on its track in the air. Despite the emphasis on Chicago and its meatpacking expertise, most of the beef served here is Argentinean. The steaks are tender, the ribs are zesty, the fried chicken is juicy, and everything is dished up in generous portions. Kids will love the burgers, which are the juiciest in town. Cocktails include such fanciful names as the "Beverly Hills."

Untermainanlage 8. (✆ **069/231659.** www.chicago-meatpackers.de. Main courses 10€–30€. AE, DC, MC, V. Mon–Thurs and Sun 11:30am–midnight; Fri–Sat 11:30am–1 or 2am. U-Bahn: Willy-Brandt-Platz.

Im Herzen Afrikas ☺ ERITREAN   A local favorite, this African oasis in the cityscape will make you forget you're in Frankfurt. Relax on low seats and at straw tables in the sand, or slide in at a candlelit table with patrons you'll know by the end of the night. You won't find silverware here, but instead a bread wrap called injera. Some of the Eritrean specialties include Tzhada kulwa (lamb meat with bell peppers) accompanied by spinach, lentils and potatoes, and Dorho (spicy chicken in a tomato sauce.) Vegetarian concoctions with spinach, potatoes, carrots, onions, and chick peas are also available.

Gutleutstrasse 13. (✆ **069/24246080.** www.im-herzen-afrikas.de. Main courses 4€–10€. No credit cards. Daily 6pm–1am. U-Bahn: Willy-Brandt-Platz.

Solberfäss'je ★ 🍴 HESSIAN   Cramped, old-fashioned, and gregarious, this restaurant is firmly committed to maintaining its role as the kind of beer bar and working-class restaurant that thrived in this neighborhood a century ago, when its clientele included mostly the horse-cart drivers delivering supplies to homes and stores along the nearby Zeil. Food items focus on *Schnitzel, Sauerbraten, Rouladens* of beef, and the kinds of roasted knuckles and joints that dyed-in-the-wool beer lovers savor, and which have been associated with *Bierkellers* since anyone can remember. These include roasted shanks of lamb, veal, pork, beef, and turkey, each of which emerges savory and crackling from the ovens. There are also three versions of *Eisbein* (pork knuckle), roasted, smoked, or steamed. Regulars rave about the *Strudel*. The hardworking and English-proficient Sänger family keeps the 112-year-old tradition alive. Its name, in Hessian dialect, refers to a medieval technique of preserving meat in barrels filled with salt.

Grosse Friedberger Strasse 8. ✆ **069/296767.** www.solberfaessje.com. Reservations recommended. Main courses 10€–18€. AE, DC, MC, V. Mon–Sat 10am–midnight. U-Bahn: Konstabler Hauptwache.

In Westend
VERY EXPENSIVE

Gargantua ★★★ CONTINENTAL   One of Westend's genuinely stylish restaurants, Gargantua evokes an upscale and somewhat snobbish 1920s-era bistro in Paris. With a new location behind the Alte Oper, its decor of olive hues whets the palate before you feast your eyes on the menu. The guiding force behind the cuisine is local food writer and columnist Klaus Trebes who, with his wife, Monika, usually directs the restaurant in a discreet, well-versed way that includes a sophisticated knowledge of German, Italian, and Austrian wines. Patrons expect—and receive—a near-perfect dining experience. Flavors, textures, and colors combine to delight in such dishes as a creamy soup with black sausage and Périgord truffles, or a zesty risotto with radicchio, squid, and spicy chorizo sausage. The chef is at his best when he prepares guinea fowl braised with cinnamon or rack of veal with a morel cream sauce. Rib-eye steak comes with a vegetable flan and rosemary potatoes, or else you can sample filet of sea bass with Amalfi lemons.

An der Welle 3. ✆ **069/720718.** www.gargantua.de. Reservations required. Main courses 19€–28€; fixed-price dinners 44€–68€. AE, DC, MC, V. Mon–Fri noon–2:30pm and 6pm–1am. U-Bahn: Alte Oper.

EXPENSIVE

Surf 'n Turf Steakhouse ★ AMERICAN/SEAFOOD   Although the name conjures up a West Coast sports bar, this fine restaurant is actually a shrine to steak. The dark hues of the wooden interior set the tone for the meat delicacies to come. Expect the usual suspects like steak tartare, Porterhouse, and rib-eye, from cattle fed exclusively corn and grain. The beef is fantastic, especially the "Butter Knife," a triple-star filet mignon, hailed as the best filet in the world. If you don't want steak, the double-cut lamb chops or the rack of lamb with rosemary and sage is delectable. For fishlovers, there's a catch of the day.

Grüneburgweg 95 (near the Palmengarten). ✆ **069/722122.** www.the-steakhouse.de. Reservations required. Main courses 19€–50€. MC, V. Mon–Fri noon–3pm; Mon–Sat 6pm–midnight. Closed for July. U-Bahn: Grüneburgweg.

Villa Merton ★★★ CONTINENTAL/INTERNATIONAL   This 1925 neoclassical villa located in the leafy diplomat's district feels more like the private home of a dignitary than a restaurant. Its demure dining rooms overlook an inviting terrace that seems to be an extension of the nearby park. Chef de cuisine Matthias Schmidt concocts imaginative creations that make the Merton one of the most exquisite dining experiences in town. A typical meal might start out with trout stained in its own caviar with asparagus and cress. Main courses include locally raised Angus loin cooked sous-vide and bathed in walnut gravy. In autumn gourmets flock here for venison ragout with fresh chanterelles.

At the Union International Club, Am Leonhardsbrunn 12. *℘* **069/703033.** www.koflerkompanie.com. Main courses 21€–39€. AE, DC, MC, V. Mon–Fri noon–2pm and 6–10pm. U-Bahn: Leipziger Strasse or Bockenheimer Warte.

INEXPENSIVE

Café Laumer ★ ⭐ GERMAN/AUSTRIAN   There are many cafes scattered throughout Frankfurt, but this one is proud of literary antecedents that are a bit deeper, broader, and more authentic than those that are cited by some of its competitors. No one will mind if you adopt this place as a cafe, but if you want full-fledged meals, be aware that they are available only until 6pm. Menu items include crisp *Schnitzel,* freshly made salads, grilled steaks with peppercorn sauce, roulades of beef or pork stuffed with herbs and bread crumbs, and, when it's available, fresh game and fish dishes. Framed honorariums on the walls of this place refer to its most historically famous client, musicologist and philosopher Theodor Adorno (1903–69), who used to come here every day in the 1930s for coffee and conversation before moving on to professorships at Oxford and Princeton.

Bockenheimer Landstrasse 67. *℘* **069/727912.** www.cafe-laumer.de. Reservations recommended for meals. Main courses 7.50€–12€. MC, V. Mon–Fri 8am–7pm; Sat 8:30am–7pm; Sun 9:30am–7pm. U-Bahn: Westend.

Across the Main

MODERATE

Maingau Stuben ★ HESSIAN/GERMAN   One of the best loved of the Sachsenhausen restaurants, this South Bank eatery does a thriving business, although food critics sometimes complain of a variance in the quality of the cuisine. The menu isn't as old-fashioned as you might think by the traditional setting of subdued lighting and linen tablecloths. The chef does duck extremely well, and is also noted for his rack of venison served in a walnut crust. He also on occasion prepares a saddle of rabbit wrapped around fresh asparagus.

Schifferstrasse 38–40. *℘* **069/610752.** www.maingau.de. Main courses 18€–28€. AE, DC, MC, V. Tues–Sun noon–3pm; Tues–Sat 6–10pm. U-Bahn: Schweizer Platz.

INEXPENSIVE

Adolf Wagner ☺ HESSIAN   This familial and sometimes rowdy Apfelwein tavern may not be ideal for an intimate dinner for two, but it provides an authentic, entertaining experience found only in Frankfurt. Local specialties fill the menu, like pork knuckle with home fried potatoes, grilled pork belly with fried onions, the ubiquitous Grüne Sosse (green sauce) with at least seven herbs, and schnitzels galore. The vegetable Rösti with herb sour cream acts as a token meal in what is really a shrine for meat lovers. A ribbed glass of refreshing apple wine adds just the right accent to the lively dining experience.

Schweizer Strasse 71. *℘* **069/612565.** www.apfelwein-wagner.com. Main courses 7€–15€. AE, DC, MC, V. Daily 11am–midnight. U-Bahn: Schweizer Platz.

In the East End
VERY EXPENSIVE

Silk ★★ 🎁 FUSION/AUSTRO-GERMAN   This "bed restaurant" embodies chic decadence. Patrons, mostly in their 20s and 30s, lounge barefooted on white leather beds savoring some of the best food in Frankfurt. All guests dine at the same time, with the reception beginning at 7:30pm and dinner service following at 8pm and lasting for most of the evening. With free entry into the adjoining exclusive Cocoon Club, your night might as well end there.

Critically acclaimed chef Mario Lohninger dishes out the 11-course menu to a backdrop of ambient and innovative music. Mediterranean diversity meets Asian minimalism, as you sample such delights as a succulent lobster spiked with mango, Serrano ham, and lemon grass. Perhaps you'll have a rack of lamb with a *Sauerkraut* risotto, or else corn ravioli with pumpkinseed oil, or smoked salmon with marinated fresh fennel. The Micro Restaurant on the premises serves comparable fare a la carte, with main courses ranging from 18€ to 39€.

Carl-Benz-Strasse 21. ✆ **069/900200.** www.hoeren-sehen-schmecken.net. Reservations required. 11-course fixed-price menu 119€. AE, MC, V. Tues–Sat 7:30pm–2am. Tram: 11 or 12.

SHOPPING

When it comes to shopping, Frankfurt has everything that you'd expect from an international financial center, with international brands and specialty shops that have convenient opening hours. Most stores are open Monday to Saturday 9 or 10am to 6 or 6:30pm.

In Frankfurt, the shopping scene is divided into different regions. On "the Golden Mile," the **Zeil,** a pedestrian zone between the Hauptwache and Konstablerwache, you'll find department stores, clothing shops, shoe stores, and furniture outlets. Once a 14th-century cattle market, it is now home to the **MyZeil** mall, which from an architectural standpoint is more than just a mall. Designed by Italian architect Massimiliano Fuksas and opened in 2009, its spider-web glass facade caves inward, creating an inner funnel of glass and metal that creates a sense of movement within the space. Ride the six-story escalator, the longest shopping mall escalator in Europe, to the top to appreciate the impressive work of modern architecture.

Nearby is the **Kleinmarkthalle,** a pleasant and often-missed covered market with international and regional grocery products. It's open Monday to Friday 8am to 6pm, and Saturday 10am to 4pm.

The **Hauptwache,** in the center of Frankfurt, has two shopping areas, one above and one below ground. Groceries, book dealers, flowers, clothing, tobacco, photo supplies, recordings, and sporting equipment abound. In the Hauptwache-Passage are restaurants, travel agencies, and banks.

Schillerstrasse, another pedestrian zone, lies between Hauptwache and Eschenheimer Turm, near the stock exchange. Walking from Schillerstrasse northeast toward Eschenheimer Tor, you'll pass many elegant boutiques and specialty shops. West of the Hauptwache is the Alte Oper. You can reach it by taking either the **Goethestrasse,** with exclusive stores evocative of Paris or Milan, or the parallel **Grosse Bockenheimerstrasse,** traditionally nicknamed Fressgasse or "Pig-Out Alley." Most wine dealers, delis, and butcher shops here look back on a long and venerable past. **Opernplatz** has a variety of restaurants and cafes.

West of the Hauptwache is Rossmarkt, leading to **Kaiserstrasse.** It passes the **BFG skyscraper,** which has three floors of exclusive retail stores, boutiques, and restaurants, and directly connects the downtown area to the Hauptbahnhof. Kaiserstrasse is also known for its large selection of stores selling clothing, audio and photography equipment, and stainless-steel ware. The heart of the fur trade in Frankfurt is **Düsseldorfer Strasse,** opposite the Hauptbahnhof. Most book dealers are located around the Hauptwache and **Goetheplatz.** Antiques, old books, etchings, and paintings on **Braubachstrasse** can be found near the Römer, at the Dom, and on Fahrgasse.

Art and antiques are the domain of **Alt-Sachsenhausen,** an appealing and original neighborhood. The **Frankfurt Flea Market** takes place here every Saturday 8am to 2pm along the Main River on the Sachsenhausen side. To get here, walk from the Römer toward the river and cross the Eisener Steg bridge.

Art Galleries

Galerie Adler   This is the most avant-garde gallery in Frankfurt, presenting all media from paintings to photographs and video to plastic. It features a talented array of fresh faces, both young Frankfurters and international artists. Various exhibitions are staged throughout the year. Hanauer Landstrasse 134. ✆ **069/43053962.** www.galerieadler. com. U-Bahn: Zoo.

Department Stores

Karstadt   A Frankfurt shopping tradition along the Golden Mile, this vast store offers clothes and shoes for every mood, while catering to a wide range of budgets. Families with small children may want to check out the selection of toys, and foodies will delight in the food hall in the basement, with tidbits from all over the globe. On the ground floor is a selection of jewelry and cosmetics, among other items. Zeil 90. ✆ **069/929050.** www.karstadt.de. U-Bahn: Konstablerwache.

Kaufhof   This department store accurately touts its one-stop shopping. On its seven floors it's got just about everything—porcelain, accessories, clothes, jewelry, glassware, and a food hall. Tired of shopping? Retreat to the top-floor restaurant, which has one of Frankfurt's most panoramic views. Zeil 116–126. ✆ **069/21910.** www. kaufhof.de. U-Bahn: Hauptwache.

Fashion

For basics, check out the vast array of clothing at the previously recommended department stores.

Kleidoskop   Even though this shop specializes in secondhand clothing, much of it appears to be new. For those who like designer labels, there is an array of Gucci, Armani, Prada, and other big names—all up for grabs at cut-rate prices. Oeder Weg 56. ✆ **069/550837.** www.kleidoskop.de. U-Bahn: Eschenheimer Tor.

Peek & Cloppenburg   In business since 1900, this large emporium, a branch of the well-known German name, attracts the frugal shopper but also sells designer labels. Its clothing for both women and men ranges far and wide, ideal for sports, office wear, or nightclubbing. Zeil 71–75. ✆ **069/298950.** www.peek-cloppenburg.de. U-Bahn or S-Bahn: Konstablerwache.

Jewelry

House of Silver   This little shop set in the midst of the apple-wine taverns of Sachsenhausen is a discovery. Savvy Frankfurter collectors go here to indulge their taste in silver jewelry. The store is small, but the range is wide, going from classic motifs to more modern lines. Schweizer Strasse 73. (C) **069/627681.** www.house-of-silver.com. U-Bahn: Schweizer Platz.

Porcelain

Höchster Porzellan Manufacture GmbH ★★   This gilt and blue-painted showroom contains one of Germany's largest inventories of what's been created by Höchst Porcelain for more than 150 years. The quality of the "white gold" is almost flawless, and the prestige level of virtually anything associated with this outfit is about as good as it gets in Frankfurt today. (Even Goethe's mother collected the stuff, praising its virtues to her impressionable and articulate young son.) If the object of your desire lies on the sale table, there may be a markdown to 60% off retail prices. You can request particular color schemes for whatever object you select, as long as it's within the historical/aesthetic framework of the era when the original item was produced. Look in particular for illustrated platters inspired by the Struwwelpeter legends, beloved by children in Mittel Europa for generations. Palleskestrasse 32. (C) **069/3009020.** www.hoechster-porzellan.de. S-Bahn: Höchst.

ENTERTAINMENT & NIGHTLIFE

Nightlife

For details of what's happening in Frankfurt, you can pick up copies of *Journal Frankfurt* at newsstands throughout the city. Also listing events are *Frizz* and *Strandgut,* both free and available at the tourist office.

To purchase tickets for many major cultural events, go to the tourist office at the Hauptbahnhof. Or you can head for a bona fide ticket agent, one of the biggest in Frankfurt, for tickets to concerts, plays, and sporting events throughout town. **Best Tickets** lies in the ZeilGalerie (Shop no. 47), Zeil 112–114 ((C) **069/91397621**).

Of course, one of the greatest ways to spend an evening in Frankfurt is at one of the *Apfelwein* (apple-wine) taverns across the south bank of the Main in the district of Sachsenhausen.

THE PERFORMING ARTS

Theater der Stadt Frankfurt, Untermainanlage 11 ((C) **069/1340400;** U-Bahn: Willy-Brandt-Platz), has three stages. One belongs to the **Frankfurt Municipal Opera,** whose productions have received worldwide recognition in recent years. Two stages are devoted to drama. If your German is adequate, you may want to see a performance of **Städtische Bühnen/Schauspiel** ((C) **069/21249494;** www.schauspielfrankfurt.de), a forum for classic German plays as well as modern drama. A variety theater, **Kunstlerhaus Mouson Turm,** Waldschmidtstrasse 4 ((C) **069/40589520;** www.mousonturm.de; U-Bahn/S-Bahn: Merianplatz), hosts plays, classical music concerts, and dance programs almost every night of the week. Tickets run 12€ to 22€.

Count yourself lucky if you're in Frankfurt when the **Forsythe Company** presents its classical ballets. Many of these are held at the Bockenheimer Depot, and ballet programs can be searched at **www.theforsythecompany.com**. The company is a smaller version of the now-defunct Frankfurt Ballet, with fewer than 20 dancers. When not at its home base, the troupe tours Europe and the United States.

Alte Oper Although not a stage for opera per se, the old opera house is still the pride of Frankfurt. Reopened in 1981 after wartime destruction, the current hall recalls the original, which was opened in 1880 under Kaiser Wilhelm I and hailed as one of the most beautiful theaters in Europe. Today the Alte Oper is the site of frequent symphonic and choral concerts, and worth the ticket price. The box office is open Monday to Friday 10am to 6:30pm, and Saturday 10am to 2pm. Opernplatz. (☏) **069/13400.** www.alteoper.de. Tickets 21€–80€. U-Bahn: Alte Oper.

English Theatre The spirit of the English-language theater founded by the actress Judith Rosenbauer has been kept alive at the base of the Gallileo Tower. It began in a Sachsenhausen backyard and became the largest English-language production company on the European continent. Its program features musicals, comedies, dramas, and thrillers. During the season (Sept–July), performances are Tuesday to Saturday at 7:30pm and Sunday at 6pm. The box office is open Monday from noon to 6pm, Tuesday to Friday from 11am to 6:30pm, Saturday from 3 to 6:30pm, and Sunday from 3 to 5pm. Gallusanlage 7. (☏) **069/24231620.** www.english-theatre.org. Plays 22€–34€; musicals 29€–47€. S-Bahn: Willy-Brandt-Platz.

Oper Frankfurt This is Frankfurt's premier showcase for world-class opera and ballet. Acclaimed for its dramatic artistry, the **Frankfurt Opera** is currently under the direction of conductor Sebastian Weigle. The box office is open Monday to Friday 10am to 6pm, and Saturday 10am to 2pm. Willy-Brandt-Platz (btw. the Hauptbahnhof and the Innenstadt). (☏) **069/1340400.** www.oper-frankfurt.de. Opera and ballet 9€–130€. U-Bahn: Willy-Brandt-Platz.

THE CLUB & MUSIC SCENE
Cabaret

Tigerpalast The most famous and sought-after cabaret in Frankfurt, this was named after cofounder Johnny Klinke's Chinese zodiac birth year (the Tiger). Klinke founded the club with Margarita Dillinger in the late 1980s. Shows are presented in a not very large blue-and-black theater, where guests sit at tiny tables to see about eight different artists per show. The acts include a variety of international acrobats, puppeteers, jugglers and crooners. A tiger, a panther, and a sea lion all make carefully choreographed appearances as well, each presented with an emphasis on razzmatazz, nostalgia, and schmaltz. Each show lasts 2 hours with breaks for drinks and snacks, and each is presented as child-approved, family style entertainment without nudity. Two restaurants are associated with this cabaret (p. 452). Shows are Tuesday through Thursday 7 and 10pm, Friday to Saturday 7:30 and 10:30pm, and Sunday 4:30 and 8pm. Heiligkreuzgasse 16–20. (☏) **069/9200220.** www.tigerpalast.de. Tickets 53€–60€; half-price for children 11 and under. Drinks from 10€. U-Bahn: Konstabler Wache.

Dance Clubs

In a 16-square-block area in front of the Hauptbahnhof, you'll find a rowdy kind of entertainment, what the Germans call *erotische Spiele*. Doormen will practically pull you inside to view porno movies, sex shows, sex shops, and dance clubs teeming with prostitutes. ***Warning:*** This area can be dangerous—don't come here alone. For less lurid activities in a safer environment, head to the live-music clubs, dance clubs, bars, and cafes across the Main River in the **Sachsenhausen** district. Most gay bars and clubs are located in a small area between Bleichstrasse and Zeil.

Cocoon Club   Thanks to the worldwide success of DJ Sven Väth, this has become the premier nightspot in Frankfurt, attracting visitors from all over Europe to experience a night when he spins here. Considered among some to be the best in Germany, if not Europe, the techno club complex also features the top-notch restaurant Silk (p. 457). Open Fridays and Saturdays 10pm to 7am. Carl-Benz-Strasse 21. ✆ **069/900200.** www.cocoonclub.net. Tram: 11 or 12.

King Kamehameha Club   The launch of this club on a street once filled with abandoned warehouses helped make the industrial East End of Frankfurt a chic after-dark address. Called "King Ka" by its loyal devotees, the club remains the hottest weekend address in this part of Frankfurt. On Thursday nights a live band is usually presented, with DJs taking over on Friday and Saturday nights. The club is open only from Thursday to Saturday 10pm to 4am. (See p. 453 for a review of **Kameha Suite.**) Hanauer Landstrasse 192. ✆ **069/48009610.** www.king-kamehameha.de. Tram: 11.

Living XXL   On Friday and Saturday night it seems that half of Frankfurt—both gay and straight—is here dancing the night away. The club is one of the largest bars and restaurants in Germany, with a widely mixed clientele. The most action and dancing are on Friday and Saturday nights. The location is in the Eurotower, the headquarters of the European Central Bank, and the terraced interior is architecturally dramatic. The compound opens Monday to Friday at 11:30am, but closing times can vary from 11pm to 4am. On Saturday it is open 7pm to 5am. Kaiserstrasse 29. ✆ **069/2429370.** www.livingxxl.de. U-Bahn: Seckbacher Landstrasse.

The Odeon Club ★   To find this club, look for the pulsating white villa on a hill, which by day is the 1808 Bethmann Pavilion. This popular club doesn't sell out or try to be exclusive, attracting a varied crowd depending on the night of the week. On Thursdays students dance off the free buffet and reduced-price drinks, while a 30s-to-40s crowd comes on Friday. The younger crowd tends to return on Saturday for the R&B music as well as hip-hop and soul. The ground floor offers two bars and a spacious dance floor, with more tranquil seating in the winter garden. For those who want to sit, talk, and cuddle, there is the upper-floor bar with its many cushions. The Odeon is open only on Monday 5pm to 4am, Thursday 9pm to 4am, and Friday and Saturday 10pm until dawn. Seilerstrasse 34. ✆ **069/285055.** www.theodeon.de. Cover 5€–8€. U-Bahn: Konstablerwache.

Live Music

Der Jazzkeller   This basement club, established in 1952, is one of the most famous and atmospheric jazz clubs in Germany. Its reputation is as solid as the 200-year-old red-brick walls that surround it. The place has played host to such jazz luminaries as Louis Armstrong, Dizzy Gillespie, and Gerry Mulligan. Thursday and Saturday, live music usually begins at 10pm. On nights when there is no live music, the club becomes a late-night pub. It's open Wednesday to Sunday 9:30pm to 3am. Kleine Bockenheimerstrasse 18A (near Goethestrasse). ✆ **069/288537.** www.jazzkeller.com. Concerts 5€–20€. U-Bahn or S-Bahn: Alte Oper.

Sinkkasten   This live-music institution began 40 years ago hosting varied names like Charles Mingus, Canned Heat, and Peter Green. Nowadays an array of styles including jazz may be heard here, except on Thursday, Saturday, and late Friday, when the club turns disco. Come early to beat the crowd, or risk being turned away. It's open Sunday to Thursday 9pm to 2am, Friday and Saturday 9pm to 3am. Brönnerstrasse 5-9. ✆ **069/280385.** www.sinkkasten-frankfurt.de. Dance club 5€–8€; concerts 6€–27€. U-Bahn or S-Bahn: Konstablerwache.

BARS & CAFES

Balalaika For one of the most charming evenings Frankfurt can offer, head to Sachsenhausen—not for an *Apfelwein* tavern, but to visit this shoebox-size club. It is the domain of Anita Honis, an American from Harlem, who imbues the club with her personal charm and her music. Several times a night she'll bring out her guitar and entertain guests while perched on a wooden bar stool. Balalaika is open Sunday to Thursday 8pm to 2:30 or 3am, and Friday and Saturday 8pm to 4am. Schifferstrasse 3. © **069/612226.** www.balalaika-frankfurt.de. Bus: 30 or 36.

Cafe Moloko+ This airy cafe has a great location near the river with an inviting terrace that fills up on sunny days. The interior is equally comfortable with leather bucket seats and original furnishings that look like chic leftovers from an attic sale. Its relaxed denizens sell the place best, radiating a friendly vibe that provides a personal touch to the otherwise rushed Frankfurt cityscape. Open daily 10am to 1am, Friday and Saturday until 2am. Kurt-Schumacher-Strasse 1 © **069/13886932.** www.moloko-am-meer.de. Bus: 36.

Irish Pub Bornheim Given the villagelike atmosphere of the laid-back Bornheim district, you may think you're in Ireland when you see this pub near a few half-timbered houses. Not far from the happening nightlife in Berger Strasse, it's worth popping in here to meet the locals—or the expats who have become so. It's a modest-size pub that lacks the chain-feel at the other Irish pubs in town, with a predictable selection of pints, and even apple wine. Berger Strasse 255. © **069/800603.** www.irishpub bornheim.de. U-Bahn: Bornheim Mitte.

Jimmy's Bar To impress that really big client, take him or her to Frankfurt's most elegant bar in its most elegant hotel, Hessischer Hof (p. 465). Against a backdrop of gentle piano music, you can drink your Tom Collins in style with the city's smoothest service. The bartenders seem able to fill all requests, no matter how unusual. Jimmy's is open daily 8pm to 4am. Hessischer Hof, Friedrich-Ebert-Anlage 40. © **069/75400.** www. hessischer-hof.de. S-Bahn: Platz der Republik. Bus: 32 or 33.

Luna This hip bar is always packed with Frankfurt's young professionals drinking cocktails and listening to the cool jazz playing in the background. The bartenders perform gymnastics (reminiscent of the Tom Cruise film *Cocktail*) in making such drinks as grasshoppers, juleps, champagne fizzes, and tropical coladas. Drink prices start at 6€. The place is packed on weekends. Hours are Monday to Thursday 7pm to 2am, Friday and Saturday 7pm to 3am. Stiftstrasse 6. © **069/294774.** www.luna-bar.de. U-Bahn: Hauptwache.

GAY & LESBIAN FRANKFURT

Harvey's This gay and lesbian restaurant and bar, which also attracts a lot of liberal-minded straight couples, is named for the gay city supervisor, Harvey Milk, of San Francisco. He was gunned down, as depicted in the Sean Penn film *Milk*. In spite of the grim namesake, the atmosphere is fun loving, in a pre–World War II setting (it escaped the bombing raids). In summer, tables overflow into an outdoor garden filled with revelers and beer drinkers. Main courses cost 9€ to 19€. It's open Monday to Friday 10am to 1am, Saturday 10am to 2am, and Sunday 10am to midnight. Bornheimer Landstrasse 64, Nordend. © **069/48004878.** www.harveys-ffm.de. Tram: 12.

Lucky's Manhattan Best described as a gay cafe and bar wrapped into one, Lucky's also has aspects of a conservative tearoom. Most folks come here to drink beer or apple wine, or perhaps to nibble on the limited array of toasts and crepes. It's a worthwhile place to begin an evening on the town. Lucky's operates Sunday through Thursday 3pm to 1am, and Friday and Saturday 3pm to 2am. Schäfergasse 27. ℂ **069/ 284919.** www.luckys-manhattan.com. U-Bahn or S-Bahn: Konstablerwache.

Pulse   This is a cafe with an active bar trade; a clientele that's mostly fashionable, male, and gay; and a throbbing Valentine-hued decor of red, black, and gray. Come here for breakfasts after a late night out, salads, sandwiches, and late-night platters that include miniquiches. Menu items cost from 4€ to 18€; mixed drinks are from 8€ to 11€, unless they're alcohol free (such as the Safe Sex on the Beach), when they go for 8€. Some nights, house and garage music begins after 10pm, transforming the place into something that you may define as a dance club with food service. Pulse is open Monday to Saturday 11am to 1am (Sat till 3 or 4am), and Sunday 10am to 1am. Bleichstrasse 38A. ℂ **069/13886802.** www.pulse-frankfurt.de. U-Bahn: Konstablerwache.

Sports & Outdoor Pursuits
JOGGING
A pretty jogging route is along the quays of the River Main, using both sides of the river and the bridges to create a loop. Another choice is the above-mentioned Grüneburg Park, with walkways that are suitable for jogging.

TENNIS
Few of the tennis courts in Frankfurt allow nonmembers to play. A noteworthy exception is the **Tennisplatz Eissporthalle,** Am Bornheimer hang, 60486 Frankfurt (ℂ **069/21239308** or 069/21230810; www.eissporthalle-ffm.de; U-Bahn/S-Bahn: Eissporthalle), which has a half-dozen courts. They're open May to October daily 8am to sundown. The cost is 10€ per hour.

WHERE TO STAY

Finding a room, not to mention one at an affordable price, depends largely on the busy trade fair schedule. On average, there is one a month; the tourist office maintains a schedule online at www.frankfurt-tourismus.de. It's best to reserve well in advance, but if you need to make a last-minute booking, contact the friendly staff at the tourist office.

Most of Frankfurt's accommodations lie around the fairgrounds and the train station (the latter is designed for convenient arrival and a quick escape). The station can be considered central, although it may require a walk through the less-than-picturesque Bahnhofviertel in front of the main station, and bordered by Mainzer Landstrasse, Taunusanlage, Gallusanlage, and Münchnerstrasse. Unfortunately, this is the only side of Frankfurt that many see, leaving them with a dim view of the city. Alternatively, consider hotels in Westend, Ostend, or across the Main to get a perspective of the city that many casual visitors miss.

In the Old Town (Altstadt)
VERY EXPENSIVE
Steigenberger Frankfurter Hof ★★★   This is the most famous, most prestigious, and most legendary hotel in Frankfurt, with both service and a historic location that are unmatched anywhere else in town. The only hotel in Frankfurt that really measures up is a personal favorite, the Hessischer Hof (see below), but the restaurant (Restaurant Français, p. 452) is better here. The highly visible five-story flagship of one of Germany's most elegant hotel chains, it was established in 1872 behind a

landmark stone facade that's very central, very prominent, and very grand. Its rooms are in high demand by visiting dignitaries, especially during the book fair, when guests as prominent as the former king of Greece have been denied a room. Public areas are discreet and plush; bedrooms are high ceilinged, sun flooded, and gracefully furnished. Some of the more traditional rooms have valuable antiques, but those in the Bethmann Wing have been newly renovated with sleek and modern touches.

Am Kaiserplatz, 60311 Frankfurt. www.frankfurter-hof.steigenberger.de. *(C)* **800/223-5652** in the U.S. and Canada, or 069/21502. Fax 069/215900. 321 units. 199€–479€ double; 590€–1,670€ suite. AE, DC, MC, V. Parking 20€. U-Bahn: Willy-Brandt-Platz. **Amenities:** 4 restaurants; bar; babysitting; concierge; room service; spa. *In room:* A/C, TV, fax, hair dryer, minibar, Wi-Fi (12€ per hour).

EXPENSIVE

Fleming's Deluxe Hotel ★★★   Next to Frankfurt's only remaining tower gate from the 15th century, this classy hotel peers out over the rooftops of Frankfurt to the Taunus Hills in the distance. Its postwar exterior may look bleak at first, but then you realize it looks like a treasure chest being opened. Indeed, the interior provides a trove of amenities and appointments using top-quality materials. It's worth every one of its five stars, and the warm earth tones like amber and bordeaux red soften the metallic fixtures of the interiors. A sophisticated sense of modern design is evident throughout, especially in the glamorous rooms and suites—don't be surprised to find the glass shower near your bed. The health club is one of the best in Frankfurt.

Eschenheimer Tor 2, 60313 Frankfurt. www.flemings-hotel.com. *(C)* **069/4272320.** Fax 069/42723999. 113 units. 208€–380€ double; from 419€ suite. Rates include buffet breakfast. AE, DC, MC, V. Parking 19€. U-Bahn: Eschenheimer Tor. **Amenities:** Restaurant; bar; concierge; state-of-the-art health club; room service. *In room:* A/C, TV, hair dryer, minibar, MP3 docking station (in some), Wi-Fi (free).

Villa Orange ★★ 🎁   This hotel resulted from the radical renovation of a century-old building with lots of architectural character. A team of architects and decorators with taste and talent created a conservative and elegant interior that combines lots of natural hardwoods into radiant hues of orange. Although technically in the Northend, it provides easy access to the leafy park surrounding the center and the Altstadt. Overall, the hotel is comfortable, intimate, tasteful, and well mannered—a fine alternative to one of the megahotels.

Hebelstrasse 1, 60318 Frankfurt. www.villa-orange.de. *(C)* **069/405840.** Fax 069/40584100. 38 units. 90€–255€ double. AE, DC, MC, V. Free parking. U-Bahn: Musterschule or Merienplatz. **Amenities:** Bar; babysitting. *In room:* A/C, TV, hair dryer, Wi-Fi (free).

MODERATE

Hotel Neue Kräme   There aren't many quaint, family run hotels in the heart of Frankfurt, but this one located in a pedestrian street fits the bill. Outside you're within view of the Römerberg to the south and the Liebfrauenkirche to the north, and many of the city's sites lie within a 10-minute walk. Behind the unassuming facade, the bright blue and soft yellow tones of the interior invite the daylight in. Your host Frau Wenzl makes you feel at home in basic but lovingly maintained rooms with spotless bathrooms.

Neue Kräme 23, 60311 Frankfurt. www.hotel-neuekraeme.de. *(C)* **069/284046.** Fax 069/296288. 21 units. 79€–130€ double. Rates include buffet breakfast. AE, DC, MC, V. Parking 10€. U-Bahn: Dom/Römer. **Amenities:** *In room:* TV; hair dryer; Wi-Fi (free).

INEXPENSIVE

Admiral ☺   This modern hotel on the eastern edge of the old town provides basic comfort and easy access to the zoo—a huge plus for families. The location is also on a side of Frankfurt not many see, within walking distance to the nightlife along Berg-erstrasse in Bornheim. Rooms have classic Scandinavian furnishings with wood touches on bold swaths of color. Bathrooms are tight, but pristine. A copious buffet breakfast will energize you before tackling the wildlife in the zoo.

Hölderlinstrasse 25, 60136 Frankfurt. www.hoteladmiral.de. ✆ **069/448021.** Fax 069/439402. 47 units. 65€–82€ double. Rates include buffet breakfast. AE, DC, MC, V. Parking 10€. U-Bahn: Zoologischer Garten (Zoo). **Amenities:** Bar. *In room:* TV, minibar, Wi-Fi (free).

Around the Fairgrounds (Messe) & Main Station
VERY EXPENSIVE

Hotel Hessischer Hof ★★★   Frankfurt hotels don't get much better than this. If it wasn't for the Steigenberger Frankfurter Hof (see above), it would be the top-ranking hotel in the city. A private and traditional place opposite the trade-fair build-ing, this boxy, nine-story hotel may have a relatively modest postwar exterior, but shines with an interior that radiates luxury. Many of the bedrooms are furnished with antiques, and those in the older building in front feature added touches like chande-liers strung from high ceilings and 19th-century lithographs. Rooms here are not quite as elegant as those at the Frankfurter Hof and Meridien. But in the newer wing, the *Nordflügel*, the bedrooms outrank even the stiffest Frankfurt competitors. In the evening, enjoy its great jazz bar, Jimmy's.

Friedrich-Ebert-Anlage 40, 60325 Frankfurt. www.hessischer-hof.de. ✆ **069/75400.** Fax 069/ 75402924. 117 units. 291€–600€ double; from 300€ and way up suite. Children 12 and under stay free in parent's room. AE, DC, MC, V. Parking 24€. U-Bahn: Festhalle/Messe. **Amenities:** Restaurant; bar; airport transfers (110€); babysitting; bikes; concierge; exercise room; room service. *In room:* A/C, TV, fax, hair dryer, minibar, Wi-Fi (free).

Le Méridien Parkhotel ★★   Le Méridien Parkhotel provides warmth and per-sonal attention to its guests (mainly from the world of commerce), who can walk over to the fairgrounds in mere minutes. It opens onto its own verdant, park-like square. The hotel has been built in two sections—an ornately decorated 1905 palace and a sleek but duller 1970s boxy wing. Go for the older, more traditional rooms in the *palais*, which have a luxurious atmosphere and are individually designed. As you can imagine, they are more expensive than those in the annex, where units are albeit larger with high ceilings and built-in furnishings.

Wiesenhüttenplatz 28–38, 60329 Frankfurt. www.lemeridien-frankfurt.com. ✆ **866/500-8320** in the U.S. and Canada, or 069/26970. Fax 069/2697884. 300 units. 211€–520€ double; 329€–679€ suite. AE, DC, MC, V. Parking 27€. U-Bahn: 8. Near the Hauptbahnhof. **Amenities:** Restaurant; bar; babysitting; concierge; room service; spa. *In room:* A/C, TV, hair dryer, minibar, Wi-Fi (21€ per day).

EXPENSIVE

An Der Messe ★   This quiet charmer is the choice of seasoned and discriminating visitors to Frankfurt. Its location opposite the university offers ideal access to the fairgrounds and train station, but a few stops on the U-Bahn away from the sights and center. The staff is friendly enough and the rooms are stylishly furnished, especially the superior class units with Asian, African, or Thai motifs.

Westendstrasse 104, 60325. www.hotel-an-der-messe.de. ✆ **069/747979.** Fax 069/748349. 45 units. 100€–395€ double. Rates include buffet breakfast. AE, DC, MC, V. Underground garage parking 15€. Tram: 16 or 17. **Amenities:** Babysitting; concierge; room service. *In room:* TV, hair dryer, minibar, Wi-Fi (free).

Maritim Hotel Frankfurt ★★   This behemoth of a hotel feels like a city within a city. With more than 500 rooms, this may be the best choice for those interested in visiting a trade fair, especially given the direct covered walkway leading to the fairgrounds (be sure to book early though). The hotel also provides decent access to the rest of the city, if you don't mind a longer walk or a short ride on the U-Bahn. The anonymous service and neutral decor are what you would expect from a place that caters to so many, but the friendly staff and comforts like reclined armchairs are still appealing. Bedrooms may be neutral, but they're very comfortable. The long writing desks make excellent workspaces.

Theodor-Heuss-Allee 3, 60486 Frankfurt. www.maritim-hotels.de. ℂ **069/75780.** Fax 069/75781000. 543 units. 145€–585€ double; 315€–795€ suite. AE, DC, MC, V. Parking 27€. U-Bahn: Festhalle/Messe. **Amenities:** 2 restaurants; 2 bars; bikes; concierge; exercise room; Jacuzzi; indoor heated pool; room service; sauna. *In room:* A/C, TV, hair dryer, minibar, Wi-Fi (18€ per day).

The Pure ★★ ■ The Pure is like no other hotel in all of Frankfurt. A new concept in hotel design, it carries modernism, not to mention all things white, to its extremes. Walking a few minutes from the train station, you come to a nondescript facade with a barely visible sign, and enter a bleached lobby straight out of a Kubrick film, if not a *Star Wars* spacecraft. It seems like the only colors allowed line the liquor shelf behind the bar. The sleek rooms make way for a few more tones from the color spectrum, with hints of darker shades and wood paneling accentuating the bleached linens and leather headboard of the bed.

Niddastrasse 86, 60329 Frankfurt. www.the-pure.de. ℂ **069/7104570.** Fax 069/710457177. 50 units. 120€–450€ double. AE, DC, MC, V. Parking 15€. **Amenities:** Bar; exercise room; room service; sauna. *In room:* A/C, TV, hair dryer, minibar, Wi-Fi (free).

25hours Hotel by Levi's ★★ ■ This clever boutique hotel is an attraction itself. The name Levi's should give you a hint about its decoration of choice: denim. From the upholstery of the chairs in the lobby and rooms to the head boards, the blue jeans fabric sets the tone for an ambience that reflects more than just the material. The entire Levi's lifestyle is reflected in such unique additions as Wurlitzer jukeboxes in some rooms and a music practice space with Gibson instruments for jams. The weft and warp of the jeans fabric form the pattern of the wallpaper, and chrome fixtures revive that fifties feel in the lobby.

Niddastrasse 58, 60329 Frankfurt. www.25hours-hotels.com. ℂ **069/2566770.** Fax 069/256677288. 76 units. 75€–110€ double. AE, DC, MC, V. Parking 15€. U-Bahn: Hauptbahnhof. **Amenities:** Restaurant; bar; room service. *In room:* A/C, TV, hair dryer, minibar; MP3 docking station, Wi-Fi (free).

MODERATE

Fleming's Hotel Messe ★ The flagship hotel of the Fleming's brand has entered its seventh year of providing sleek design at an affordable rate. Less expensive than the previously mentioned sibling, this hotel boasts a convenient location near the fairgrounds, train station, and financial district. Making good use of wood and elegant fabrics, the bedrooms have a sleek contemporary look and are quite comfortable. Some of the superior rooms have a large desk. Especially appealing is the on-site French brasserie and deli. The dining section sells succulent grill and seafood specialties, and the deli has some top-quality treats, including freshly filled baguettes and a selection of cheese or antipasti to go.

Mainzer Landstrasse 87, 60329 Frankfurt. www.flemings-hotels.com. ℂ **069/8080800.** Fax 069/808080499. 96 units. 135€–355€ double. AE, DC, MC, V. Parking 15€. U-Bahn or S-Bahn: Hauptbahnhof. **Amenities:** Restaurant, bar; babysitting; concierge; room service. *In room:* A/C, TV, hair dryer, minibar, Wi-Fi (free).

INEXPENSIVE

Continental   Located in the area around the Hauptbahnhof, this relic of the Belle Epoque era provides a hint of nostalgia behind an unassuming facade for a decent price. Often the choice of business travelers, its decor varies from subdued tones of black, white, and tan, to a circus of color. You can't get any closer to the station, and street noise from the nearby bars is not an issue here.

Baselerstrasse 56, 60329 Frankfurt www.hotelcontifrankfurt.de.. (℃ **069/42729990.** Fax 069/232914. 88 units. 57€–262€ double. AE, DC, MC, V. Parking 20€. U-Bahn or S-Bahn: Hauptbahnhof. **Amenities:** Restaurant. *In room:* TV, hair dryer.

In Westend

EXPENSIVE

Hotel Palmenhof ★   A short walk from the botanical gardens, this five-story Art Nouveau building retains some of its original architectural features. Behind its grand facade of 1890 reddish sandstone, the interior has such architectural features as skylights beaming light down onto a Belle Epoque set of furniture. Rooms have somewhat fussy furnishings but are well kept and often contain high ceilings. Not only is it near the Palmengarten, it stands across from the Cafe im Literaturhaus, a wining-and-dining spot that seduces authors away from book fairs.

Bockenheimer Landstrasse 89–91, 60325 Frankfurt. www.palmenhof.com. (℃ **069/7530060.** Fax 069/75300666. 45 units. Mon–Thurs 162€–182€ double, 235€ suite; Fri–Sun 85€–100€ double, 165€ suite. AE, DC, MC, V. Parking 15€. U-Bahn: Westend. **Amenities:** Room service. *In room:* TV, hair dryer, minibar, Wi-Fi (free).

MODERATE

Art Hotel Robert Mayer ★ 🎁   The manager of this villa found a creative solution when it came time to renovate the rooms back in 1994: commission local visual artists. Each of the twelve interiors in the century-old villa features a personal vision associated with a designer from Frankfurt. You may find a thought-provoking jumble of furniture inspired by Frank Lloyd Wright or an anonymous Milanese postmodernist piece set adjacent to pop art. No matter the design, the creature comforts provide a good night's rest.

Robert-Mayer-Strasse 44, 60486 Frankfurt am Main. www.arthotel-frankfurt.de. (℃ **069/9709100.** Fax 069/97091010. 12 units. 85€–275€ double. Rates include continental breakfast. AE, DC, MC, V. Nearby parking 7€. U-Bahn: Bockenheimer Warte. *In room:* TV, Wi-Fi (free).

Hotel Liebig ★ 🎁   The aura within this upscale B&B is small-scale, intimate, and luxurious, with an intensely "decorated" look that could have been lifted directly from the pages of a Laura Ashley (or Versace) catalog. As such, it presents a welcome change for business travelers looking for something more personalized and less anonymous than what's available within one of the blockbuster hotels closer to the fairgrounds. The town house that contains it was built in 1905 and still retains its ornate maroon sandstone facade, its curving interior staircase, and proportions that hint at its origins as an upscale private home.

Liebigstrasse 45, 60323 Frankfurt am Main. www.hotelliebig.de. (℃ **069/24182990.** Fax 069/24182991. 20 units. 118€–215€ double; 195€–290€ suite. AE, MC, V. Free parking. U-Bahn: Westend. *In room:* A/C, TV, minibar, Wi-Fi (free).

Villa Diana 🗡   A self-proclaimed needle in a haystack, this spotless and homey abode provides villa elegance at a reasonable price. Its location in the relaxed Westend district in a pleasant residential street is ideal for strolls in the Palmengarten, or a night at the opera. An inviting drawing room and an intimate breakfast salon make up the common areas. The small bedrooms are lackluster but comfortable and well maintained, each with a neat little bathroom with a shower stall.

Westendstrasse 83, 60325 Frankfurt. www.villadianafrankfurt.de. ✆ **069/9074420.** Fax 069/90744277. 26 units. 135€–265€ double; 165€–295€ junior suite or triple. Rates include continental breakfast. AE, DC, MC, V. Parking 15€. U-Bahn: Westend or Festhalle/Messe. **Amenities:** Breakfast room. *In room:* TV, hair dryer, minibar, Wi-Fi (free).

Across the Main
VERY EXPENSIVE

Villa Kennedy ★★★   On the south bank of the Main River, this luxurious five-star hotel occupies a trio of recently constructed buildings and the 1904 Villa Speyer. It lies close to the center of Frankfurt's Left Bank nightlife district, Sachsenhausen, with its vibrant bars and restaurants. Along with the Pure, Villa Kennedy is the epitome of Teutonic cool. "We are more than a crash pad," the manager claims. "We are a way of life."

The hotel respects the past but is as modern as the 21st century. Surprisingly for a city hotel, the villa is set in landscaped gardens. The bedrooms are spacious and among the swankiest in town, with beautiful furnishings, subtle lighting, wooden floors, and full-length-mirrored walls; the suites are the pride of Frankfurt, fit for a visiting president. Off the central courtyard and garden is the colonnaded Gusto, a first-class restaurant serving both German and international cuisine. Guests and nonresidents alike meet in JFK's Bar & Lounge.

Kennedyallee 70, 60596 Frankfurt am Main. www.villakennedy.com. ✆ **069/717120.** Fax 069/717122430. 163 units. 550€–590€ double; from 685€ suite. AE, DC, MC, V. Parking 27€. U-Bahn: Schweizer Platz. **Amenities:** Restaurant; bar; concierge; health club and spa; indoor heated pool; room service. *In room:* A/C, TV, minibar, Wi-Fi (free).

MODERATE

Am Berg ★ 🏨   Deep down in Sachsenhausen, this is a great location for those seeking offbeat accommodations in a romantic old villa with towers and turrets. It's a glimpse of how life used to be before the bombs of World War II rained down on Frankfurt. Only a 5-minute ride from the city center, it stands in a leafy residential section near the Südbahnhof (the south train station). Each of the midsize to spacious bedrooms has an individual decor, but all are well maintained, inviting, and comfortable. The hotel itself dates from 1900, and many of the rooms rest under high ceilings. The smallest rooms are on the second and third floors.

Grethenweg 23, Sachsenhausen, 60598 Frankfurt. www.hotelamberg.com. ✆ **069/612021.** Fax 069/615109. 21 units. 68€–252€. AE, MC, V. Free parking. U-Bahn or S-Bahn: Südbahnhof. **Amenities:** Wi-Fi (free; in lobby). *In room:* TV, hair dryer, minibar.

Gerbermühle ★★ 🏨   When Goethe was a young man and this building was a romantic villa, he met his first love here. After years of being dilapidated, this building, which originally was a 16th-century flour mill, has emerged as a favorite address for the *Schickimicki* (fashionistas). Guest rooms are imbued with a sense of the romantic, with beautiful furnishings including French beds and bathrooms in Belgian marble. Each individually decorated bedroom is in a country-house style. All signs of Goethe's day are now gone except for the first-rate *Biergarten* overlooking the Main River. To honor the writer, the chefs still serve his favorite dish, veal *Tafelspitz* with a green sauce made with nine fresh herbs.

Deutschherrnufer 105, 60594 Frankfurt am Main. www.gerbermuehle.de. ✆ **069/9652290.** Fax 069/689777966. 20 units. 180€ double; from 400€ suite. AE, MC, V. Bus: 46. **Amenities:** Restaurant; room service. *In room:* A/C, TV, minibar, Wi-Fi (free).

In the East End
MODERATE
Goldman 25hours Frankfurt ★ 🎁   Artists and media types tend to favor this hotel with its often mischievous design, including lamps that are penguin replicas wearing shades on their heads. After work, its bar scene becomes boisterous and is the place to be seen. The designers loved color and saturated the hotel with it—and they're not afraid to use purple. A *Schickimicki* (fashionista) admitted, "I always stay here because it's cool and sexy." Think of it as an urban retreat for night owls, with individually decorated bedrooms that are stylishly comfortable, and very avant-garde.

Hanauer Landstrasse 127, 60314 Frankfurt am Main. www.25hours-hotels.com. ✆ **069/40586890.** Fax 069/4058689890. 49 units. 75€–125€ double. AE, DC, MC, V. Free parking nearby. U-Bahn: Zoo. **Amenities:** Restaurant; bar; room service. *In room:* A/C, TV, hair dryer, minibar, Wi-Fi (free).

On the Outskirts
EXPENSIVE
Hotel Amadeus ★ 🎁   Set within the leafy residential suburb of Bergen-Enkheim, an easy 15-minute tram ride east from central Frankfurt, this is a warm and friendly hotel with well-designed rooms. It's also one of the leading architectural highlights of its neighborhood, featuring a soaring, atrium-style lobby fronted with glass, marble floors, and three wings that join in a design that emulates an airplane propeller. The staff here is especially charming, and on-site is a cozy bar that stays open late, a restaurant that attracts residents of the surrounding community, and a concierge who knows how to get things done.

Röntgenstrasse 5, 60338 Frankfurt am Main. www.hotel-amadeus-frankfurt.de. ✆ **06109/3700.** Fax 06109/370720. 160 units. Mon–Fri 109€–188€ double; Sat–Sun 68€–98€ double. AE, MC, V. Free parking. U-Bahn: Hessen Center. **Amenities:** Restaurant; bar; babysitting; concierge; access to nearby health club. *In room:* A/C, TV, hair dryer, kitchenette (in some), minibar, Wi-Fi (free).

INEXPENSIVE
Hotelschiff Peter Schlott 🎁   For something completely different, experience the Main river by sleeping on it in this 1950s riverboat. Its only drawback is its location in the western suburb of Höchst, a 10-minute ride on the S-Bahn—the experience of feeling like you're at sea makes the trip worth it, though. As expected, the cabins are snug and the mattresses thin, but the gently lapping waters beneath you will lull you into slumber. Night owls and those with lots of luggage might want to find another hotel.

Mainberg, 65929 Frankfurt. www.hotel-schiff-schlott.de. ✆ **069/30067680.** Fax 069/307671. 19 units, all with wash basins, 10 with shower, none with toilet. 65€ double without shower; 100€ double with shower. Rates include continental breakfast. AE, DC, MC, V. S-Bahn: Höchst. **Amenities:** Restaurant. *In room:* No phone.

SIDE TRIPS FROM FRANKFURT
Picturesque Aschaffenburg and some of the leading spas of Germany lie on Frankfurt's doorstep. Another memorable side trip is to Mainz (p. 489).

Aschaffenburg

40km (25 miles) SE of Frankfurt, 77km (48 miles) NW of Würzburg

Aschaffenburg was originally a Roman settlement on the right bank of the Main River and later became an important town in the Middle Ages. In recent years, it's grown industrially, but even with 250 garment manufacturers, the town has remained peaceful and provincial. Tucked in the northwestern corner of Bavaria, its many parks and shady lanes make it a fitting gateway to the streams and woodlands of the Spessart Hills. Weekly fairs are held on the square, where fishers along the banks of the Main sell seafood straight from their buckets. Many traditional shops are in a pedestrian zone, with lamps, fountains, and flowers.

ESSENTIALS

GETTING THERE By Train The **Aschaffenburg Bahnhof** is on the major Nürnberg-Würzburg-Frankfurt line and on the regional Maintal Aschaffenburg-Mittenburg-Wertheim line, with frequent connections in all directions. From Frankfurt, 36 trains arrive daily (trip time: 30 min.–1 hr.). For information, call ☏ **01805/996633** or visit www.bahn.de.

By Bus There is no direct bus service between Frankfurt and Aschaffenburg.

By Car Access by car is via the A3 Autobahn east and west.

VISITOR INFORMATION Contact **Tourist-Information,** Schlossplatz 1 (☏ **06021/395800;** www.info-aschaffenburg.de). It's open April to September Monday to Friday 9am to 6pm and Saturday 9am to 1pm, October to March Monday to Friday 9am to 5pm and Saturday 10am to 1pm.

GETTING AROUND Aschaffenburg and the immediate region around it are served by a network of green-painted buses whose junction is the Hauptbahnhof, the city's main railway station. Because many of the streets within the city's historic core are reserved for pedestrians, many sightseers take bus no. 1, 4, 5, or 8 between the Hauptbahnhof and the Stadthalle (town hall), immediately adjacent to the Altstadt. Buses run daily 5:30am to 9pm. Rides within the central zone cost 1.50€ per person each way. An all-day ticket goes for 2.80€. For information, call the city tourist office (☏ **06021/395800**).

EXPLORING ASCHAFFENBURG

The best park in Aschaffenburg is **Schönbusch Park,** Kleine Schönbuschallee 1 (☏ **06021/625478;** bus: 4), located 3km (2 miles) across the Main southwest of the center. It's a marvel of planning, using the natural surroundings as a setting for formal 18th-century gardens, shady lanes, temples, and gazebos. At the edge of the mirror-smooth lake is a small neoclassical castle, really a country house, once used by the electors of Mainz. The house is open April to September Tuesday to Sunday 9am to 6pm. Admission is free. In summer, it's possible to rent a small boat to go on the lake. There's also a cafe/restaurant open daily 8am to 8pm.

The most impressive sight in Aschaffenburg is the huge Renaissance **Schloss Johannisburg ★**, Schlossplatz 4 (☏ **06021/386570;** bus: 1, 4, or 8), reflected in the waters of the Main. Erected from 1605 to 1614, it became the residence of the rulers of the town, the prince-electors of Mainz. The red-sandstone castle is almost perfectly symmetrical, with four massive lantern towers surrounding an inner courtyard. April to September, the castle is open daily 9am to 6pm; October to March, hours are daily 10am to 4pm. Admission is 5.50€ for adults and 4.50€ for children 14 and under. While here you can visit the Schlossweinstuben (see below). From the castle gardens you can reach the **Pompeiianum,** built by Bavaria's King Ludwig I as a replica of the Castor and Pollux palace discovered among the ruins of Pompeii. The Pompeiianum is open April to mid-October Tuesday to Sunday 9am to 6pm. Admission is 5.50€ for adults, 4.50€ for students, and free for children 14 and under. The **combination ticket** for Schloss Johannisburg and the Pompeiianum is 9€ for adults, 7€ for children 14 and under.

Stiftskirche St. Peter and St. Alexander, Stiftsgasse 5 (✆ **06021/22420;** www.stiftsbasilika.de; bus: 1, 4, or 10), has overlooked the town for 1,000 years and its varied architecture reflects the periods of remodeling and reconstruction, culminating as a combination of Romanesque, Gothic, and baroque. Its most precious treasure is the painted retable *The Lamentation of Christ,* by Mathias Grünewald. The interior is decorated with several paintings of the school of Lucas Cranach, as well as a marble-alabaster pulpit by Hans Juncker. One of the oldest pieces is a Roman-style crucifix from A.D. 980. Adjacent to the north side of the church is a Romanesque cloister from the 13th century. The church is open Wednesday to Monday 11am to 5pm. Admission is free, but a tour costs 3€ adults, 2€ students and children, and 6€ for a family ticket.

WHERE TO DINE

Meals are also offered at the two hotels listed below.

Schlossweinstuben FRANCONIAN/BAVARIAN One of the most alluring corners of this historic castle is its popular wine cellar, where you'll find a wide variety of German wines to complement the conservative but well-prepared menu items. A meal may begin with liver-dumpling soup, and then follow with a game specialty (depending on the season). The selection of very fresh fish is likely to include trout and pike. There is no pretension to this cuisine—it's just hearty, rib-sticking fare.

Schloss Johannisburg. ✆ **06021/12440.** Reservations recommended. Main courses 8.50€–18€. No credit cards. Apr–Oct daily 11am–midnight; Nov–Mar Tues–Sun 11am–midnight. Bus: 1, 3, or 4.

WHERE TO STAY

Hotel Dalberg Built in 1994, this hotel occupies a prominent site that's within a 5-minute walk from Aschaffenburg's historic core and its pedestrian zone. Rising behind an all-white, four-story facade, it offers cozy, well-designed rooms, each with a tiled shower. On the premises you'll find a rustic-looking *Weinstube* (wine bar) serving regional cuisine and drinks from a bar.

Pfaffengasse 12-14, 63739 Aschaffenburg. www.hotel-dalberg.de. ✆ **06021/3560.** Fax 06021/219894. 26 units. 95€–220€ double. Rates include continental breakfast. AE, MC, V. Parking 11€. Bus: 1 or 4. **Amenities:** Restaurant; bar; airport transfers 46€. *In room:* TV, minibar, Wi-Fi (free).

Hotel Post This is the town's premier hotel, offering greater comfort than its rivals. Close to the heart of town and built in 1919, rooms are well maintained and decorated in traditional style. Some units come with a tub and shower, others only a shower. The dining room is a stylized version of an old posting inn; it includes an original mail coach, timbered walls and ceiling, and lead-glass windows. Reasonably priced Franconian meals are served here.

Goldbacherstrasse 19-21, 63739 Aschaffenburg. www.post-ab.de. ✆ **06021/3340.** Fax 06021/334144. 69 units. 103€–126€ double; 125€–149€ junior suite. AE, DC, MC, V. Parking 4€. Bus: 1, 3, 4, 6, or 10. **Amenities:** Restaurant; babysitting; indoor heated pool; room service; sauna. *In room:* A/C, TV, hair dryer, minibar, Wi-Fi (free).

Wiesbaden ★

40km (25 miles) W of Frankfurt, 151km (94 miles) SE of Bonn

This sheltered valley, between the Rhine and the Taunus mountains, has held a spa since Roman times. Today, Wiesbaden competes with Baden-Baden for the title of Germany's most fashionable resort. Its success is based partly on its 26 hot springs, with temperatures of 117° to 150°F (47°–66°C), and partly on its proximity to Frankfurt's transportation centers, which gives the spa a distinctly international flavor.

Wiesbaden also boasts its cultural side. Every spring it plays host to the International May Festival of music, dance, and drama. The major concert halls are in the **Kurhaus,** a lively, multiroomed structure centered on a cupola-crowned hall. In addition to concerts, the complex hosts plays and ballets, plus a variety of social gatherings, such as international conferences, congresses, exhibitions, and trade fairs. It also holds a casino, a lively restaurant, and an outdoor cafe.

For more active visitors, Wiesbaden offers horseback riding, a golf course, swimming, tennis, and hiking. The streets of the city are nice to stroll, as is the **Kurpark,** which has a lake surrounded by old shade trees. It's especially beautiful at night, when the water reflects the lights of the spa and the huge fountains are lit. The park stretches for about a kilometer (½ mile) northward along the Kuranlagen, ending in a fancy residential quarter, the Sonnenberg.

ESSENTIALS

GETTING THERE   By Train   Trains run between Frankfurt airport and Wiesbaden about every hour, leaving from the airport's lower level (trip time: 30 min.). Tickets can be purchased at machines in the station area or at the airport's railway ticket counter. There's also frequent service from the center of Frankfurt on S-Bahn S-1 and S-9 (trip time: 30–40 min.). For information, call ✆ **01805/996633** or visit www.bahn.de.

By Car   Wiesbaden lies at a major crossroads, with access via the A3 Autobahn from the north and south, connecting with the A66 Autobahn from the west and east. Travel time by car from Frankfurt is about 20 to 30 minutes, depending on traffic. From the Frankfurt airport to Wiesbaden by car is about 20 minutes.

VISITOR INFORMATION   The **Verkehrsbüro,** Marktplatz 1 (✆ **0611/ 1729930;** www.wiesbaden.de), is open October to March Monday to Friday 10am to 6pm, and Saturday 9:45am to 3pm; April to September Monday to Friday 10am to 6pm, Saturday 9:45am to 3pm, and Sunday 11am to 3pm.

GETTING AROUND   The Hauptbahnhof is the junction point for most of the city's bus lines. Buses are blue-sided, and charge, depending on the distance within the city limits you travel, 2.40€ to 5.80€ per ride. City buses operate Monday to Friday between 5am and midnight, at intervals of between 10 and 15 minutes, with less frequent service on Saturday and Sunday. Kirchgasse and Langgasse are two of the most prominent streets in the pedestrian zone, but the closest point to catch a bus to either of them is in front of the Staatstheater.

THERMAL BATHS   The big, modern, and well-maintained Kaiser Friedrich Therme, Langgasse 38–40 (✆ **0611/1729660;** www.wiesbaden.de), are famous within Germany for their ability to soothe the aches and pains of arthritis, gout, indigestion, and other ailments induced by age and everyday stress. The saunas and thermally heated swimming pools are open daily from 10am to 10pm (Fri and Sat until midnight). Admission costs 3.50€ per hour from May to August, going up to 5€

per hour from September to April. Remember that the venue here involves both men and women who mingle freely within the facilities. Tuesday, however, is reserved for women. Also pleasant is the surrounding park whose landscaping includes hundreds of seasonal flowers.

WHERE TO DINE

Ente Restaurant ★★★ CONTINENTAL/MEDITERRANEAN   This restaurant serves the best food in town, and the innovative chef makes sure that meals are as pleasing to the eye as they are to the palate. The light, modern cuisine features weekly changing specialties; typical offerings include ravioli of Canadian lobster with a crustacean foam or breast of pigeon with roast black pudding and a mace foam. Other good dishes include milk-fed suckling pig cutlet and U.S. roast beef glazed with honey. Desserts, especially the lemon soufflé with strawberries and the mountain-honey ice cream, are reason enough to visit. Ente also has one of the best wine lists in Europe, including many moderately priced bottles. A boutique, delicatessen, wine cellar, and bistro are attached.

In the Hotel Nassauer Hof, Kaiser-Friedrich-Platz 3–4. 🕿 **0611/133666.** www.nassauer-hof.de. Reservations required. Main courses 28€–42€. AE, DC, MC, V. Tues–Fri 6–11pm; Sat noon–3pm and 6–11pm. Bus: 1, 2, 8, or 16.

Käfer's INTERNATIONAL   Käfer's directs two restaurants within one at the stately and prestigious Kurhaus. The more appealing of the two is Käfer's Bistro, a replica of the kind of bustling, upscale, well-run bistro you may find in Lyon or Paris. In an adjoining room is the airier, quieter, and more self-consciously formal Casino Restaurant. The menu and prices are the same as in the bistro, but the atmosphere is calmer and, frankly, a bit more stuffy. Men are required to wear a jacket and tie. Menu items change every 4 weeks. Examples may include smoked salmon served with a *Rösti* pancake, crème fraîche, and chives; Canadian lobster with yogurt-flavored cocktail sauce and lemon; penne pasta with pesto sauce and grilled giant prawns; vegetarian dishes; and, in springtime, asparagus with filet mignon, bacon, or salmon steak. Dessert may be a mousse, flavored with three kinds of chocolate.

In the Kurhaus, Kurhausplatz 1. 🕿 **0611/536200.** www.kurhaus-gastronomie.de. Reservations recommended. Main courses 18€–32€. AE, MC, V. Daily 11:30am–1am. Bus: 1, 2, or 8.

Restaurant M AUSTRIAN/INTERNATIONAL   Set on the street level of the Hotel de France, a stately looking structure built in 1880, this is an upscale brasserie that attracts actors, politicians, and in-the-know yuppies who appreciate good food and conversation. Surrounded by decor that includes memorabilia from upscale cigar companies, movie stills from the '30s and '40s, and African hunting trophies, you can enjoy mostly Austrian food with international touches, all of it prepared by Markus Seegert. Some of the most appealing menu items include wild garlic risotto with grilled prawns in a white-wine sauce, and a classic *Wiener Schnitzel* with pan-fried potatoes and cranberries. The hotel that contains this restaurant is a four-star place with 37 rooms and doubles priced from 132€ to 192€. Each room has a TV, telephone, minibar, safe, and contemporary decor.

In the Hotel de France, Taunusstrasse 49. 🕿 **0611/2048765.** www.mrestaurant.de. Reservations recommended. Main courses 19€–30€. AE, DC, MC, V. Mon–Sat 5–10:30pm. Bus: 1.

WIESBADEN AFTER DARK

"Rien ne va plus" is the call when the ball starts to roll on the gaming tables at the historic **Spielbank Wiesbaden,** Im Kurhaus, Kurhausplatz 1 (🕿 **0611/536100;**

www.spielbank-wiesbaden.de; bus: 1, 8, or 16). Opened in 1771, this is where Fyodor Dostoyevsky blew his credit in 1865 and dictated *The Gambler* in record time to compensate. You'll find roulette, blackjack, and poker. To enter, you must present a passport or an identification card. You must be 18 to enter and gamble, and men must wear jackets and ties. The casino is open daily 3pm to 3am and admission is 2.50€.

Music and **theater** flourish in Wiesbaden throughout the year. For information on performances during your visit, check the Wiesbaden tourist office (see "Visitor Information," above). For information about any of the conference and cultural facilities in the **Kurhaus** compound, including the casino and theater, call ✆ **0611/17290.**

Hessisches Staatstheater, Christian-Zais-Strasse 3 (✆ **0611/1321;** www.staats theater-wiesbaden.de; bus: 1), built in 1894 by Emperor Wilhelm II, is one of the most beautiful theaters in Germany. From September to June it presents a program of operettas, musicals, ballets, and plays. Tickets are 8€ to 50€.The important **International May Festival** features concerts, classical in-house drama productions, and a wide selection of guest performances by internationally renowned theater companies. For information and tickets, call ✆ **0611/1321,** or visit www.maifestspiele.de.

The sprawling and gentrified **Park Café,** Wilhelmstrasse 36 (✆ **0611/3413246;** www.park-cafe-wiesbaden.de; bus: 1), incorporates a cafe, brasserie, and a nightclub. The cover ranges from 8€ to 12€, and it's open daily 9pm to 4am.

WHERE TO STAY

Admiral Hotel 🏅   The centrally located Admiral is a favorite of traditionalists and one of Wiesbaden's best values. Readers consistently praise the owners (a retired U.S. Army officer and his German-born wife) for their hospitality. Rooms are furnished in a charmingly old-fashioned way, often with brass beds. Bathrooms are small yet well maintained. The hotel offers a healthy, hearty breakfast to start your day.

Geisbergstrasse 8, 65193 Wiesbaden. www.admiral-hotel.de. ✆ **0611/58660.** Fax 0611/521053. 23 units. 79€–139€ double; 98€–149€ triple. Rates include buffet breakfast. AE, DC, MC, V. Parking 14€. Bus: 1 or 8. A 5-min. walk from the Kurhaus. *In room:* TV, hair dryer, Wi-Fi (free).

Hotel am Landeshaus   This central hotel is one of the spa's best reasonably priced hotels. It balances fresh modernity with warmth and comfort. Rooms are well kept, with small but immaculate bathrooms. Guests can enjoy drinks in a rustic ale tavern on-site.

Moritzstrasse 51, 65185 Wiesbaden. www.hotel-am-landeshaus.de. ✆ **0611/996660.** Fax 0611/996666. 15 units. 69€–135€ double. Rates include buffet breakfast. MC, V. Free parking. Bus: 3, 6, 16, 22, 28, or 33. Within walking distance of the railroad station. *In room:* TV, Wi-Fi (free).

Hotel Klee am Park ★★ 🏅   This hotel is highly recommend for those who find the older, more luxurious Nassauer Hof a bit too monumental. Klee am Park is a modern hotel in a tranquil setting, surrounded by its own informal gardens. The theater, casino, and shopping area are nearby. Rooms have French doors opening onto balconies; some have sitting areas large enough for entertaining.

Parkstrasse 4, 65189 Wiesbaden. www.klee-am-park.de. ✆ **0611/90010.** Fax 0611/9001310. 60 units. 148€–188€ double. AE, DC, MC, V. Free parking. Bus: 8. **Amenities:** Restaurant; bar; room service. *In room:* TV, hair dryer, minibar, Wi-Fi (12€ per hour).

Hotel Klemm ★ 🏅   This little hotel occupies a late-19th-century *Jugendstil* villa with solid stone walls, attracting many repeat visitors who are drawn to its charm and its good value. The midsize bedrooms are attractively decorated, often with small sitting areas. The staff is one of the most gracious and helpful in town, and the break-fast buffet is generous.

Kapellenstrasse 9, 65193 Wiesbaden. www.hotel-klemm.de. ℘ **0611/5820.** Fax 0611/582222. 60 units. 100€–180€ double. AE, DC, MC, V. Bus: 1, or 8. Near the Kurhaus. *In room:* TV, hair dryer, minibar, Wi-Fi (free).

Hotel Nassauer Hof ★★★   The superluxurious Nassauer Hof is among the most appealing hotels in town. Often referred to as the grande dame of Wiesbaden, its spacious rooms have up-to-date conveniences like soundproof windows, elegant furnishings, and comfortable appointments. Bathrooms contain tub/showers, deluxe beauty products, and robes. The hotel stands in the city center, within walking distance of the Kurhaus, Spielbank, theaters, and a shopping area.

Kaiser-Friedrich-Platz 3-4, 65183 Wiesbaden. www.nassauer-hof.de. ℘ **800/2236800** in the U.S., or 0611/1330. Fax 0611/133632. 159 units. 328€–358€ double; from 460€ suite. AE, DC, MC, V. Parking 20€. Bus: 1, 2, 8 or 16. **Amenities:** 2 restaurants; bar; babysitting; concierge; exercise room; indoor heated pool; room service; spa. *In room:* A/C, TV, hair dryer, minibar, Wi-Fi (free).

pentahotel Wiesbaden ★   Lots of businesspeople stay here instead of staying in Frankfurt, as it's only 20 minutes from the Frankfurt airport. Because of its location outside of the center, the hotel is more suited for motorists who don't want to face the traffic of Wiesbaden. Think of it as a good roadside motel, one that is almost equally convenient for visiting Wiesbaden or Frankfurt. Rooms are modern and comfortably furnished. If you want the old spa ambience of Wiesbaden, opt for Klee am Park or Hotel Nassauer Hof.

Abraham-Lincoln-Strasse 17, 65189 Wiesbaden. www.pentahotels.com. ℘ **0611/7970.** Fax 0611/797731. 209 units. 75€–180€ double; from 239€ suite. AE, DC, MC, V. Parking 15€. Bus: 5 or 28. **Amenities:** Restaurant; bar; babysitting; room service. *In room:* A/C, TV, hair dryer, minibar, Wi-Fi (5.50€ per day).

Bad Homburg ★

16km (10 miles) N of Frankfurt, 45km (28 miles) NE of Wiesbaden

Bad Homburg is one of Germany's most attractive spas, still basking in the grandeur left over from turn-of-the-20th-century Europe. The spa's saline springs are known to treat various disorders, especially heart and circulatory diseases. This popular watering spot has attracted commoners and royalty from all over the world since Roman times. King Chulalongkorn of Siam (Thailand) was so impressed that he built a Buddhist temple in the Kurpark. Czar Nicholas I erected an onion-domed Russian chapel nearby. The name of the town was popularized by England's Edward VII when, as Prince of Wales, he visited the spa and introduced a new hat style, which he called the "homburg." The town became the gaming capital of Europe when the Blanc brothers opened the casino in 1841.

The **Spa Park ★** is a verdant, carefully landscaped oasis in the middle of an otherwise rather commercial-looking town. The actual spa facilities are in the **Kaiser Wilhelms Bad im Kurpark** (℘ **06172/178178;** www.kur-royal.de). They're open daily 10am to 10pm. Entrance to the facilities is 40€ per person for 4 hours, 60€ for a full-day admission. Patrons have access to a wide range of facilities, including thermally heated pools, saunas, steam baths, and herb-enriched hot-water baths. Massage facilities and special mud baths require additional fees. The immaculately tended gardens in the surrounding Kurpark are filled with brooks, ponds, arbors, and seasonal flowers. The town center has a sprawling pedestrian-only district with many shops, restaurants, and cafes.

ESSENTIALS

GETTING THERE   **By Train**   Visitors from Frankfurt usually opt to take the S-5 train, which runs from Frankfurt's main railway station to Bad Homburg for a cost of 3.90€ each way. The trip takes about 20 minutes. Call ℭ **01805/996633** or visit www.rmv.de for information.

By Car   Access by car from the north or south is via the A5 Autobahn, exiting at Bad Homburg.

VISITOR INFORMATION   For information, go to the **Verkehrsamt im Kurhaus,** Louisenstrasse 58 (ℭ **06172/1783710;** www.bad-homburg.de). It's open Monday to Friday 8:30am to 6:30pm and Saturday 10am to 2pm.

GETTING AROUND   Public transport in Bad Homburg is provided by a network of green-and-white buses, with main junction points at the Hauptbahnhof, a 10-minute walk southwest of the city center, and in front of the Kurhaus, in the city center. Buses, which run daily 4:30am to midnight, charge 2.40€ per ride.

EXPLORING BAD HOMBURG

Schloss Homburg HISTORIC BUILDING   This palace was the residence of the landgraves of Hesse-Homburg from its construction in 1680 until the mid–19th century. Its builder, Prince Friedrich II von Homburg, preserved the White Tower from the medieval castle that stood on the site. In the late 19th century, the palace became a summer residence for Prussian kings and, later, German emperors. The interior contains 18th-century furniture and paintings, including a bust of Prince Friedrich II by Andreas Schlüter, Germany's greatest baroque sculptor. The former "telephone room of the empress" features *Cleopatra* by Pellegrini.

Schloss. ℭ **06172/9262148.** www.schloesser-hessen.de. Admission 4€ adults, 2.50€ children. Tues–Fri 10am–4pm; Sat–Sun 11am–5pm. Bus: 1, 4, or 11. A few blocks from the spa gardens.

Taunus Therme BATHS   A large recreation area, Taunus Therme boasts several pools, a sauna, a solarium, and a health center, plus TVs, cinemas, and two restaurants.

Seedammweg. ℭ **06172/40640.** www.taunus-therme.de. Admission Mon–Fri 13€ for 2 hr., 17€ for 4 hr., 24€ all day; Sat–Sun and holidays 15€ for 2 hr., 26€ for all day; free for children 3 and under. Sun–Tues 9am–11pm; Wed–Sat 9am–midnight. Bus: 6.

WHERE TO DINE

Casino-Restaurant ★ FRENCH/GERMAN   Until a few years ago, this was the only restaurant in Germany that directly adjoined the gaming tables of a casino. And while not in the same class as Sängers, it's also one of the finest restaurants in town. The dining room is decorated in a formal, vaguely English style. It offers attentive service and a winning combination of light French and German cuisine. Head chef Udo Finkenwirth begins each workday searching for fresh, seasonal ingredients at the local markets. Lobster is a popular choice. Although the main kitchen service stops at 10:30pm, there's a reduced menu until 12:30am.

Im Kurpark. ℭ **06172/170170.** Reservations required. Jacket and tie required for men. Main courses 15€–25€; fixed-price menu 34€. AE, DC, V. Daily 6pm-12:30am. Tram: 5.

Sängers Restaurant ★★★ FRENCH   Local food lovers and spa devotees crowd this restaurant to enjoy the highly personal and inventive cuisine, the best in town. The two elegant dining rooms are outfitted in the style of 18th-century England. Menu items may include carpaccio of turbot with Iranian caviar, goose-liver terrine served with brioche and gelatin of wild berries, a foam-capped celery soup with quail eggs, roast breast of duck on a bed of rhubarb, and a succulent array of desserts.

Kaiser-Friedrich-Promenade 85. ℰ **06172/928839.** www.saengers-restaurant.de. Reservations required. Main courses 26€–35€; 5-course set menu 59€; 7-course set menu 99€. AE, MC, V. Mon–Sat noon–2pm and 7–11pm. Closed 2 weeks in July. Bus: 1, 4, 11, or 12. Near the Steigenberger Bad Homburg.

WHERE TO STAY

Das Hardtwald Hotel ★   This hotel, resembling a chalet set in a forest, is an ideal retreat near the spa gardens. In spring, flowers overflow from its window boxes. The comfortably furnished rooms overlook the forest and come with a compact tiled bathroom. The chef in the excellent, flower-filled dining room uses only the freshest ingredients to prepare his well-known international and German dishes. In summer, tables are set on the large patio. As an added treat, you can rent horses at a stable next to the hotel

Philosophenweg 31, 61350 Bad Homburg. www.hardtwald-hotel.de. ℰ **06172/9880.** Fax 06172/82512. 39 units. 105€–220€ double. Rates include buffet breakfast. AE, DC, MC, V. Bus: 3. A 20-min. walk from the center of town. **Amenities:** 2 restaurants; bar; room service. *In room:* TV, hair dryer, minibar.

Haus Daheim 🐾   This light-blue corner building is one of the finest small hotels in town, with a loyal following of repeat business. The comfortable, soundproof rooms have firm beds, plus tiled bathrooms. Admittedly a modest choice compared to the hotels reviewed above, but for value, it's hard to beat.

Elisabethenstrasse 42, 61348 Bad Homburg. www.hotel-haus-daheim.com. ℰ **06172/677350.** Fax 06172/67735500. 19 units. 89€–149€ double. Rates include buffet breakfast. AE, DC, MC, V. Parking 12€. Tram: 5. A short walk from the Kurhaus. **Amenities:** Wi-Fi (free; in lobby). *In room:* TV, hair dryer, minibar.

Maritim Kurhaus-Hotel ★   As sleek and up-to-date as this hotel near the spa facilities is, the Steigenberger Bad Homburg far outclasses it. Double rooms feature king-size beds and singles have queen-size beds, but all rooms are plush. Some rooms have balconies or terraces, permitting wide-angle views over the greenery of the surrounding park; many have tall bay windows.

Kurpark, Ludwigstrasse 3, 61348 Bad Homburg. www.maritim.de. ℰ **06172/6600.** Fax 06172/660100. 148 units. 84€–245€ double; 155€–265€ suite. AE, DC, MC, V. Parking 13€. Bus: 1, 2, 3, 4, 11, or 12. **Amenities:** Restaurant; bar; babysitting; indoor heated pool; room service; sauna. *In room:* TV, hair dryer, minibar, Wi-Fi (15€ per day).

Parkhotel Bad Homburg 🐾   This is your best bet for a moderately priced spa vacation. This hotel has an enviable location in the middle of the Kurpark's well-maintained gardens, near the thermal springs. Although its design is modern and angular, its edges are softened with window boxes. Rooms are conservatively furnished. On the premises are a bar and a sunroom. One of the hotel's restaurants serves a savory Italian cuisine; the other offers excellent Asian fare.

Kaiser-Friedrich-Promenade 53–55, Am Kurpark, 61348 Bad Homburg. www.parkhotel-bad-homburg.de. ℰ **06172/8010.** Fax 06172/801400. 124 units. 106€–222€ double; 148€–228€ suite. Rates include buffet breakfast. AE, DC, MC, V. Parking 12€. Tram: 5. **Amenities:** 2 restaurants; bar; babysitting; bikes; exercise room; Jacuzzi; room service; sauna. *In room:* TV, kitchenette (in some), minibar, Wi-Fi (15€ per day).

Steigenberger Bad Homburg ★★★   This is the resort's best and most prestigious hotel. Europe's high society used to stroll here in days of yore, and an ambience of luxury still prevails. Rooms are beautifully furnished, each with individually adjustable air-conditioning and extra-long beds. The spacious, soundproof bathrooms contain deluxe luxury items and sumptuous robes.

Kaiser-Friedrich-Promenade 69–75, 61348 Bad Homburg. www.bad-homburg.steigenberger.com.
© **800/2235652** in the U.S. and Canada, or 06172/1810. Fax 06172/181630. 169 units. 99€–260€ double; from 199€ suite. AE, DC, MC, V. Parking 20€. Bus: 1, 2, 3, 4, 11, or 12. Opposite the spa gardens and casino. **Amenities:** Restaurant; bar; babysitting; exercise room; room service; sauna. *In room:* A/C, TV, fax, hair dryer, minibar, Wi-Fi (5€ per hour).

ENTERTAINMENT & NIGHTLIFE

Spielbank im Kurpark (© **06172/17010;** www.casino-bad-homburg.de; tram: 5), called the "Mother of Monte Carlo," is the spa's major attraction. This casino opened way back in 1841 and helped make Bad Homburg famous. Roulette, blackjack, and baccarat are the games here. Passports are required for entrance (you must be 18 to enter and gamble), and men must wear jackets and ties. Admission is 2.50€; hours are daily 2:30pm to 3am.

The town's favorite beer hall and *Weinstube* is **Zum Wasserweibchen,** Am Mühlberg 57 (© **06172/29878;** www.wasserweibchen.de; bus: 1, 4, or 11). About 1.5km (1 mile) east of the town center in Ober-Erlenbach, you'll find another folkloric place, **Gasthaus Rupp,** Homburgerstrasse 6 (© **06172/42484;** bus: 2 or 12), whose home-style cuisine is enhanced by the establishment's homemade apple wine. The **Kurhaus** also contains a handful of bars, cafes, and shops that usually stay open late.

THE RHINELAND

F ew rivers can claim such an important role in the growth of a nation as the Rhine. The Rhine rises in Switzerland and ultimately flows through the Netherlands in its progress to the sea, but most of its 1,370km (850 miles) snake through the mountains and plains of Germany. For more than 2,000 years, it has been a chief trade route, its deep waters enabling modern seagoing vessels to travel downstream from the North Sea as far as Cologne.

From its earliest times, the Rhine has also been a main road for religious, intellectual, and artistic ideas. It has been called a "triumphal avenue of the muses," and a trip along its banks today reveals endless treasures.

From Mainz north to Koblenz, the winding river cuts through steep vine-covered hillsides dotted with towns whose names are synonymous with fine German wine. Here you'll find the dramatic Lorelei, the legendary rock from which a siren lured men to their doom. The saga of *The Nibelungenlied,* the best known of the Rhine legends, is associated with the topography from the Siebengebirge (the Seven Mountains) near Bonn, where Siegfried slew the dragon, to the city of Worms, where Brunhild plotted against the dragon slayer.

The Rhine is also the home of many of Germany's largest and most modern cities. **Cologne (Köln)** and **Düsseldorf** vie for trade and tourism. Cologne is also a common starting point for boat tours of the river.

Roadways along the Rhine tend to be heavily trafficked, so allow adequate time if you're driving. Main roads hug both the left and the right banks of the river, and at many points you'll come across car ferries that can take you across. The most scenic stretch for driving is the mid-Rhine, between Koblenz and Mainz. EuroCity and InterCity trains connect all the major cities, including Cologne, Düsseldorf, Bonn, and Mainz. Rail service also extends as far north as Hamburg and as far south as Munich.

SPEYER ★

93km (58 miles) S of Mainz, 21km (13 miles) SW of Heidelberg

One of the oldest Rhine cities, Speyer celebrated its 2,000th jubilee in 1990. It became a significant religious center early on when the Diet of Speyer, in 1529, united the followers of Luther in a protest against the Church of Rome.

WATCH ON THE rhine

The Rhine carries more freight than any other river in Europe, and its once famous salmon were caught at the rate of 250,000 annually. But by the 1950s the river had simply become too poisonous for the fish to survive. By the 1970s and 1980s, the fabled Rhine was called "the sewer of Europe." That has now changed and the salmon are back. Billions of euros spent on water-treatment plants led to a cleaner river. However, the salmon you see today heroically leaping about aren't the same salmon of yore. The new salmon were brought in from Ireland, France, Scotland, and Scandinavia. Therefore, we must rely on old cookbooks to tell us of the glorious taste of the salmon Rhinelanders once enjoyed. One species of small crab is not as welcome. This alien amphipod that came from the Danube is now spreading to all the major rivers of Germany, including the Rhine, devouring native species at a rapid rate, and reducing biodiversity.

Essentials

GETTING THERE

By Train   Trains reach Speyer only by connections at Mannheim. The trip from Frankfurt takes 1 to 1½ hours; from Munich, 3½ to 4 hours. Call 𝄢 **01805/996633** for schedules (www.bahn.de).

By Bus   About one bus per hour arrives from Heidelberg. Regional service is provided by **BRN Busverkehr Rhein-Neckar GmbH** at Ludwigshafen (𝄢 **0621/12003;** www.brn.de).

By Car   You can drive from Frankfurt in about an hour, from Munich in about 4 hours. Access is by the A61 Autobahn east and west connecting with Route 9 south.

VISITOR INFORMATION

For information, go to the **Verkehrsamt,** Maximilianstrasse 13 (𝄢 **06232/142392;** www.speyer.de). It's open November to March Monday to Friday 9am to 5pm, and Saturday 10am to noon; and April to October Monday to Friday 9am to 5pm, Saturday 10am to 3pm, and Sunday 10am to 2pm.

GETTING AROUND

Walking city tours in English and other languages are available from April 1 to November 30, regularly on Saturday and Sunday. The walking tour costs 3.60€ per person. The tour leaves at 11am at the tourist information office (see above).

Exploring Speyer

Nothing brings back the medieval German empire as much as the **Kaiserdom (Imperial Cathedral)** ★★ in Speyer (𝄢 **06232/1020**), the greatest building of its time. This cathedral, consecrated in the early 11th century, is the largest Romanesque edifice in Germany. Having weathered damage by fires, wars, and restorations, the cathedral was finally brought back to its original shape during a restoration that ran from 1957 to 1961. When you enter the church through the single west door set in a stepped arch, you're at once caught up in the vastness of its proportions; the whole length of the nave and east chancel opens up, lit by the muted daylight from above. The church contains the royal tombs of four emperors, three empresses, and four German kings, as well as a row of bishops' tombs. It is open April to October Monday to Friday 9am to 7pm, Saturday 9am to 6pm, and Sunday 1:30 to 6pm; off-season hours are daily from 9am to 5pm.

Other attractions include the **Historisches Museum der Pfalz (Palatinate Historical Museum;** ✆ **06232/13250;** www.museum.speyer.de), whose main attraction is the Domschatz, or cathedral treasury. Inaugurated in 1910, this museum is housed in a castle with four wings and lies next to the cathedral. In all, there are 300,000 artifacts here related to the history of the Palatinate and the city of Speyer. Relics date from prehistoric times, with a strong emphasis on the Roman and medieval eras.

Increasing numbers of travelers are opting for views of some of the most legendary panoramas in Germany directly from the deck chairs of yachts and cruise ships. We highly recommend one in particular.

Viking River Cruises, 5700 Canoga Ave., Woodland Hills, CA 91367 (© **800/304-9616;** www.vikingrivers. com), is the world's largest river cruise line. It maintains a total of 14 river cruisers, each designed for between 100 and 230 passengers. Efficient and, in some cases, infused with touches of luxury, the cruises traverse the muddy waters of the Rhine between Amsterdam and Basel (Switzerland), traveling for between 8 and 15 nights. For views of Germany's eastern regions, cruises along the Elbe usually begin in Magdeburg and end in Decin, on the border of the Czech Republic, and focus heavily on day trips through the majestic core of such revered cities as Dresden.

The per-person rate, depending on the onboard accommodations and the season, ranges from $184 to $457 per day double occupancy. Onboard attendants deliver commentaries in several languages (including English) of the sights and monuments en route. Food is served at tables for between four and eight diners, cruise-ship-style. All meals, onboard lodgings, and shore excursions are included in the price.

On-site is the **Wein Museum (Wine Museum),** with exhibits showing how the Romans produced their *vino.* The world's oldest bottle of wine (ca. A.D. 300) is also exhibited. Objects found in tombs of former emperors under the Dom are exhibited in the treasury. The most celebrated exhibit is the Bronze Age *Golden Hat of Schifferstadt.* This is a golden, cone-shaped object used in religious celebrations in ancient times. The entrance to the Historisches Museum is on Domplatz. Hours are Tuesday to Sunday 10am to 6pm. Entrance is 4€ adults, 3€ children 16 and under.

The **Technik-Museum (Museum of Technology),** Geibstrasse 2 (© **06232/ 67080;** www.technik-museum.de), is housed in a former 1913 aircraft hanger. Here you can view a vast array of airplanes, locomotives, vintage automobiles, fire engines, and even automatic musical instruments. For many, the biggest thrill is going inside a 20-ton U-boat once used to terrorize Allied shipping in the Atlantic.

Annexed to the museum is the **Marine Museum,** displaying a rich collection of historical model ships. Part of the attraction is a monumental 3-D IMAX cinema. Entrance to the two museums costs 15€ for adults, 11€ for children 15 and under. It's open daily 9am to 6pm.

Dreifaltigkeitskirke (Trinity Church), on Grosse Himmelsgasse, dates from 1701 to 1717, when it was constructed in an elaborate baroque style. It's one of the most richly adorned and decorated churches along the Rhine, and the only elaborate, baroque-style church that still exists in the Rhine-Main-Neckar region; the interior contains a two-story gallery with a splendid balustrade of wooden-capped vaulting painted by artisans. Johann Peter Grabner, architect to the court of Palatinate, designed the church. Check with the Speyer tourist office to see if the church is open on the day of your visit.

Speyer was one of the most important centers of Jewish culture along the Rhine, although precious little of that settlement remains today. However, some ruins from the old **Jüdisches Viertel (Jewish quarter)** can still be seen behind the Palatinate Historical Museum. Enter the ruins from Judengasse and pay the entry fee at the gatehouse (© **06232/291971**). The east wall of the ancient synagogue is the *Judenbad* (called *Mikwe* in Hebrew), a 12th-century ritual bathhouse for women. The masons who constructed the Dom also built this bathhouse, the oldest and best-preserved relic of its kind in the country and a poignant, nostalgic reminder of a vanished culture. The site is open from April to October daily 10am to 6pm, costing 2€ admission.

Where to Eat

Backmulde ★ 🛄 FRENCH/SEAFOOD   This restaurant, a staple in town since the 1970s, occupies a 400-year-old house. The decor is nostalgic with lots of wood paneling. Gunter Schmidt, the owner, serves not only fresh fish and Continental specialties but a few modern Rhineland-Palatinate recipes. You can order such dishes as braised scallops with olive oil and balsamic vinegar, a salad of wild greens and prawns, or roasted lamb baked under a salt crust.

Karmeliterstrasse 11-13. © **06232/71577.** www.backmulde.de. Reservations required. Main courses 18€-30€; fixed-price menus 35€-68€. AE, DC, MC, V. Tues-Sat 11:30am-2:30pm and 7-11:30pm. Closed 3 weeks late Aug to mid-Sept.

Kutscherhaus ★ GERMAN/RHINELANDER   You're transported back to old Germany at this beer garden, once a depot for *Kutschen* (stagecoaches) in the 1890s. Its gabled, half-timbered architecture is an inviting oasis, with climbing vines and plenty of summer flowers. The food is regional, hearty, and filling, and served in generous portions. Begin with appetizers such as a smoked salmon or cream soup with garden vegetables. Main courses feature fresh ingredients and are well prepared, including *loup de mer* (sea bass) or filet of halibut, perfectly grilled rump steak, or a delicious plate of herring with a creamy sauce.

The inn has three attractive, modern bedrooms, costing 78€ to 120€ for a double. Each room comes with private bathroom, TV, and minibar, and rates include buffet breakfast.

Am Fischmarkt 5A. © **06232/70592.** www.kutscherhaus-speyer.de. Main courses 18€-24€; fixed-price menus 19€-40€. AE, DC, MC, V. Fri-Tues 11:30am-2pm and 6-11pm.

Zum Alten Engel ★ 🍷 RHINELANDER   Zum Alten Engel, one of the finest restaurants in Speyer, is animated, loud, convivial, and extremely popular. To reach it, you'll descend a flight of antique masonry steps to a century-old brick-vaulted cellar, flickering with candles and awash with German antiques. Set in Speyer's historic core, and much in demand among locals, it specializes in hearty regional cuisine accompanied by the perfect glass of wine—more than 180 kinds of wine from around Germany and the world are available. Menu items usually include hearty *gutbürgerlich* fare of the kind many locals remember from their childhoods. The best examples of this old-fashioned "home and hearth" cookery include fried sausages, liver dumplings, a Rhenish version of *Sauerbraten*, pepper steak, veal cutlets, and at least two different preparations of lamb.

Mühlturmstrasse 7. © **06232/70914.** www.zumaltenengel.de. Reservations required. Main courses 10€-20€. MC, V. Mon-Sat 11:30am-2:30pm and 6-11pm; Sun 5-11pm. Closed 2 weeks in Aug.

Where to Stay

Goldener Engel This centrally located inn lies near the Gothic town gate at Maximilianstrasse, adjoining one of Speyer's finest restaurants, Zum Alten Engel (see above), and is the most atmospheric choice in town. Imbued with lots of character in the spirit of old Rhinelander hotels, the Goldener Engel comes complete with many traditional touches and antiques such as baroque free-standing clothes closets. In contrast, the midsize bedrooms are completely modern and up-to-date, with well-maintained private bathrooms.

Mühlturmstrasse 5–7, 67346 Speyer. www.goldener-engel-speyer.de. © **06232/13260.** Fax 06232/132695. 46 units. 92€–110€ double. Rates include buffet breakfast. AE, DC, MC, V. **Amenities:** Bikes. *In room:* A/C, TV.

Rhein-Hotel Luxhof This hotel is imbued with an unusual character. It's modern in style, but somehow retains the spirit of a rambling country inn. The blandly decorated rooms are well designed and compact, often featuring small sitting areas that open onto tiny balconies. All come equipped with well-maintained bathrooms.

An der Speyerer Rheinbrücke, 68766 Hockenheim. www.luxhof.de. © **06205/3030.** Fax 06205/30325. 45 units. 99€–118€ double. Rates include buffet breakfast. AE, DC, MC, V. Free parking. At the Rhine Bridge, just outside the town. **Amenities:** Restaurant; bikes; exercise room; sauna; outdoor tennis court (lit). *In room:* TV, minibar (in some), Wi-Fi (free).

WORMS ★

45km (28 miles) S of Mainz, 43km (27 miles) SW of Darmstadt

Before the Romans came, Germanic peoples had made Worms their capital. Here, Siegfried began his legendary adventures, recorded in *The Nibelungenlied*. Later on, Martin Luther arrived under less than desirable circumstances. He was "invited" to appear before the Imperial Diet at Worms, and after he refused to retract his grievances against the Church of Rome, Holy Roman Emperor Karl V declared him an outlaw. A huge monument to Luther and other giants of the Reformation has been erected.

Worms also makes an excellent base for a tour of the **Deutsche Weinstrasse,** an 80km (50-mile) route through local wine towns (see "A Driving Tour of the German Wine Road," below).

Essentials
GETTING THERE

By Plane The nearest airport is at Frankfurt (see chapter 13), 69km (43 miles) away. From Frankfurt, you can drive to Worms in a rented car. Take A5 south to A3 west to A65 south.

By Train Worms enjoys good rail connections to major German cities. It lies on the main Mainz-Mannheim line. At Mannheim, one train per hour runs south in to Speyer (trip time: 30 min.). For rail information and schedules, call © **01805/996633** (www.bahn.de).

By Bus Regional bus service for the area is provided by **BRN Busverkehr Rhein-Neckar GmbH** (© **06241/207312;** www.brn.de) in Worms.

By Car From Mainz, continue south along Route 9.

VISITOR INFORMATION

For tourist information, go to the **Verkehrsverein,** Neumarkt 14 (© **06241/25045;** www.worms.de). It's open year-round Monday to Friday 9am to 6pm; from April to October, it's also open Saturday 9:30am to 1:30pm.

GETTING AROUND

A network of cream-colored buses traverses most neighborhoods of the town and its suburbs. The city's main junction point is the Hauptbahnhof. Buses run 6am to midnight and charge 2.50€ and 4€ depending on how far you go, paid directly to the driver.

Exploring Worms

Towering physically and historically above all the other ancient buildings of the city is the majestic **Dom St. Peter ★★,** Lutherring 9 (© **06241/6151;** bus: 2). This basilica is a fine example of High Romanesque style. The east choir, with a flat facade and semicircular interior, is the oldest section, dating from 1132. It was designed as the sanctuary, where the clergy performed the rites of divine service. The chancel glows with the gold and marble of the pillared enclosure of the **baroque high altar** by the famous 18th-century architect Balthasar Neumann. This opulent work was so large that there was no place for a proper transept. In Gothic times the choir stalls stood in the apse, but later they were built into the transept. The interior has a quiet elegance, with little decoration other than the rosette window and several memorial slabs and monuments. Well worth seeing is the highly decorated 14th-century **side chapel of St. Nicholas,** with its Gothic baptismal font and new stained-glass windows. This was the setting of history's famous Diet of Worms, an assembly of august figures of the Catholic hierarchy, an imperial court that banished Martin Luther into exile when he refused to renounce his so-called "heretical doctrine." (Luther adamantly maintained that religious truth exists in Scripture, not in papal power or edicts.) The cathedral is open for visitors April to October daily 9am to 6pm, and November to March daily 9am to 5pm.

North of the Altstadt is the restored **Jüdisches Viertel** (**Jewish Quarter;** bus: 2). Before World War II, Worms had one of the oldest Jewish communities in Germany. The still-functioning **synagogue,** Hintere Judengasse 6 (© **06241/8534700**), which dated from the 11th century, was destroyed in 1938 and has since been rebuilt. The synagogue is open November to March daily 10am to noon and 2 to 4pm, and April to October 10am to 12:30pm and 1:30 to 5pm. Inside, you'll find the **Raschi-Haus Museum** (same phone; www.worms.de), containing memorabilia from the original synagogue and references to the Holocaust. The museum is open November to March Tuesday to Sunday 10am to 12:30pm and 1:30 to 4:30pm, and April to October Tuesday to Sunday 10am to 12:30pm and 1:30 to 5pm. Admission is 1.50€ adults, .80€ children 13 and under. A staff member inside will point you in the direction of the **Judenfriedhof** (**Jewish cemetery**) ★, off the Lutherring, one of the oldest and largest in Europe, with hundreds of tombstones, some more than 900 years old.

Where to Eat

Rôtisserie Dubs ★ CONTINENTAL   The prices are a bit steep for the area, but you're paying for imaginative cookery and quality ingredients. Despite rustic ceiling beams and the massive stonework of the fireplace, Rôtisserie Dubs has a feeling of elegant airiness. The light Continental cuisine adds to that impression. Owner Wolfgang Dubs features such French-inspired dishes as salmon in champagne marinade and delicately seasoned pike-and-cabbage soup. His steak in snail sauce is worth the trip outside of town (it may not sound appealing but it's quite sublime).

Kirchstrasse 6. ℂ **06242/2023.** www.dubs.de. Reservations required. Fixed-price menus 34€–84€. MC, V. Wed–Mon noon–2:30pm and 6pm–midnight. At Rheindurkheim, take Rte. 9 north for 8km (5 miles).

Entertainment & Nightlife

The city's most important showcase for music, classical drama (in German only), and opera is the **Städtisches Spiel und Festhaus,** Rathenaustrasse 11 (ℂ **06241/ 22525;** bus: 2).

Don't expect raucous nightlife in Worms. The best advice, if you want a drink in the town center, is to head for the **Judengasse** (bus: 2), a street with a denser collection of nightlife options than any other in town. One of the most appealing is the **Affenhaus,** Judengasse 17 (ℂ **06241/22216**), which opens for business every day at 10am, carrying on into the wee hours.

Where to Stay

Central Hotel Worms 🗡 One of the best small hotels in the city, this is a modest and unassuming choice. Innkeeper Alexandra Hill rents comfortably furnished but rather small rooms. All contain bathrooms with tub/shower combos. The reception staff speaks English, and the hotel has an ideal central location, within walking distance of all major historic monuments.

Kämmererstrasse 5, 67547 Worms. www.centralhotel-worms.de. ℂ **06241/64570.** Fax 06241/27439. 19 units. 80€–90€ double. Rates include buffet breakfast. AE, DC, MC, V. Parking 5€. Closed late Dec to late Jan. Bus: 2, 4, or 5. *In room:* TV.

Dom-Hotel This is an ideal choice for the in-and-out traveler. The all-purpose hotel is a postwar structure built in a complex of shops and boutiques. Rooms are a little boxy and functionally furnished, but all are well maintained and contain spick-and-span bathrooms.

Am Obermarkt 10, 67547 Worms. www.dom-hotel.de. ℂ **06241/9070.** Fax 06241/23515. 60 units. 105€–125€ double; 140€ apt. Rates include buffet breakfast. AE, DC, MC, V. Free parking. Bus: 2. About a block from the cathedral. **Amenities:** Restaurant. *In room:* TV, hair dryer, minibar, Wi-Fi (free).

Parkhotel Prinz Carl ★★ At long last Worms has a hotel that befits its status as such an important and historic German city. Architecturally distinguished in the old Rhinelander style with step gables, it is completely modernized inside, decorated in a warm, elegant style. There are five room categories ranging from standard to deluxe, but all of the accommodations are furnished comfortably and tastefully, with sleek bathrooms. In the morning, guests enjoy the most generous breakfast buffet in town. The formal restaurant features first-class and international specialties backed up with an impressive wine list from the Rhineland itself.

Prinz-carl-Anlage 10, 67547 Worms. www.parkhotel-prinzcarl.de. ℂ **06241/3080.** Fax 06241/308309. 90 units. 95€–125€ double; 115€–145€ junior suite; 125€–155€ deluxe studio. AE, DC, MC, V. Free parking. **Amenities:** Restaurant; bar; babysitting; bikes; room service. *In room:* A/C, TV, hair dryer, minibar, Wi-Fi (free).

A Driving Tour of the German Wine Road ★★

Germany's oldest designated tourist route, the **Deutsche Weinstrasse,** runs south for 80km (50 miles) from Bockenheim, a small town 14km (8½ miles) west of Worms, to Schweigen-Rechtenbach on the frontier with France. This is a land of old castles (most in ruins) and venerable vineyards. Most of the wines produced here are whites, with special emphasis on clear, aromatic Rieslings and *Weissburgunders.* The area also abounds in old Rhineland-Palatinate inns and wine taverns, serving hearty local specialties such as *Sauerbraten* (beef marinated in wine vinegar).

Armed with a map (available at the Worms tourist office), you can set out to explore the area beginning in the north at **Bockenheim.** From Bockenheim, follow Rte. 271 directly south to Grünstadt, where signs point the way to the village of **Neuleiningen,** 10km (6 miles) away. The locals here are known rather unflatteringly as *Geesbocke* or "billy goats," a reference to their longtime poverty—goats (supposedly) were the only livestock they could afford. Today they bear the label with a certain pride. While here, sample the local fare at **Alte Pfarrey,** Untergasse 40, Neuleiningen (✆ **06359/86066;** www.altepfarrey.de), where fixed-price menus cost 70€ to 90€. It is open Thursday to Monday noon to 1:30pm and 6:30 to 9:30pm.

From here, Hwy. 271 leads south to Kallstadt, a distance of 10km (6 miles), where the next stopover at **Bad Dürkheim** is signposted. Here you can view the remains of the **Monastery of Limburg,** once one of the most significant Romanesque structures in the country. The best restaurant is **Weinrefugium,** Schlachthausstrasse 1A (✆ **06322/8910980;** www.weinrefugium-bad-duerkheim.de), which charges 29€ to 35€ for fixed-price menus of regional food. It is open Wednesday to Sunday 1 to 2:30pm and 6 to 9:30pm.

Route A65 and B9 en route to Kaiserslautern, west of Bad Dürkheim, leads to **Frankenstein Schloss,** a castle from the Middle Ages (now in ruins). Local legend claims it was this *Schloss* that inspired Mary Shelley's classic monster.

A journey 8km (5 miles) south along 271 leads to the **Deidesheim,** the medieval seat of the bishops of Speyer. The grounds that surround their former *Schloss,* now a picturesque ruin, have been turned into a lovely park. Some of the wine road's most charming half-timbered buildings are found on the main square, Marktplatz. Deidesheim is your best bet for wine tastings in this area. Our favorite place is the **Basserman-Jordan Wine Estate,** Kirchgasse 10 (✆ **06326/6006**), dating from 1775. On-site is a **Museum of Historical Wines,** a collection containing wines from every year up until 1880. Admission is free and you can visit the estate Monday to Friday from 8am to 6pm and Saturday from 10am to 3pm.

The most elegant hotel in the neighborhood is the very stylish **Deidesheimer Hof,** Am Marktplatz 1 (✆ **06326/96870;** www.deidesheimerhof.de), where doubles cost 125€ to 290€. Inside are two restaurants, the **Schwarzer Hahn,** where fixed-price menus go from 90€ to 180€, and the more artfully rustic **St.-Urban,** which charges 50€ for fixed-price menus.

From Deidesheim, continue along Rte. 271 for another 15 minutes, following the signs to **Neustadt-an-der-Weinstrasse,** the largest town on the Weinstrasse, lying at the foot of the Haardt hills. Pass quickly through its ugly suburbs to reach the heart of the old town, with its narrow, often-crooked streets. There are some 2,000 hectares (5,000 acres) of vineyards within the town limits, and the main streets are lined with taverns and wine shops. For wine tastings, visit **Weingut Probsthof,** Probstgasse 7 (✆ **06321/6315;** www.weingut-probsthof.de). Open Monday to Saturday from 8am to 6pm, this estate offers tastings for 10€. If you prefer *Sekt* (sparkling wine), the cost rises to 12€.

From Neustadt, you can drive 5km (3 miles) south to historic **Schloss Hambach** (**©** 06321/30881; www.hambacher-schloss.de), 1km (½ mile) outside the village of Hambach. The castle is open November to March daily 11am to 5pm, April to October daily 10am to 6pm. Admission is 5€.

An 8km (5-mile) drive south takes you into the sleepy hamlet of **St. Martin,** which for our money is the loveliest village along the wine road, filled with antique houses draped with flowering vines. A castle here, whose nostalgic ruins still tower over St. Martin, happens to have the best food and lodging along the wine road. Its name is **St. Martiner Castell ★★**, Maikammer Strasse 2 (**©** 06323/9510; www. hotelcastell.de), and each of its 26 rooms rents for around 100€ double occupancy, with breakfast included. In its restaurant, main courses are 10€ to 25€ and fixed-price menus are 33€ to 67€.

Yet another 5km (3 miles) south (the road is signposted) takes you to **Gleisweiler,** a wine-producing hamlet known as the warmest village in Germany. Fig trees flourish in its rich soil and almost subtropical climate.

From Gleisweiler, it's 13km (8 miles) south along Rte. B38 to **Annweiler,** site of **Burg Trifels ★★** (**©** 06346/8470), the Rhineland's most fabled castle, set imperiously on a jagged crag. In 1193, Richard the Lionhearted was captured and imprisoned here until he was bailed out with a huge ransom. From the panoramic peak, you can also view the ruins of Scharfenberg Castle and Anebos Castle to the south. Burg Trifels is open January to March and October to November daily 9am to 5pm, April to September daily 9am to 6pm. The last ticket (5€) is sold 30 minutes before closing.

The most idyllic place for food and lodging in the area is **Landhaus Herrenberg,** Lindenbergstrasse 72, 76829 Landau-Nussdorf (www.landhaus-herrenberg.de; **©** 06341/60205), 3km (2 miles) north of Landau in der Pfalz, a 15-minute drive east of Annweiler. This is a movie cliché of a charming country inn along the wine road, although its nine rooms are contemporary and well appointed, costing 95€ a night. The owners, the Lergenmüller family, have won awards for their red wines. Naturally, their bottles are the wines of choice in the excellent on-site regional restaurant, which offers three- or four-course menus for lunch Friday to Wednesday; meals cost from 35€. The inn is closed 3 weeks in January. American Express, MasterCard, and Visa are accepted.

The B38 leads next to **Klingenmünster,** a journey of only 8km (5 miles) south. From here, a sign points the way to the ruins of **Burg Landeck,** reached after a 30- to 40-minute stroll through a chestnut-tree forest. At the end, the castle ruins stand at one of the most scenic spots along the wine road, with views extending as far as the Black Forest.

From here, B38 goes yet another 8km (5 miles) to reach **Bad Bergzabern,** an old spa, without equal for its old half-timbered houses.

From Bad Bergzabern, a 10km (6-mile) drive along Highway B38 (the final lap of your journey) will deliver you to **Schweigen-Rechtenbach,** a village at the French frontier. In the summer of 1935, local vintners constructed a gargantuan stone arch, the **Deutsches Weintor (German Wine Gate),** marking the southern end of this oft-traveled tourist route. From a gallery atop the gate, you can view miles of vineyards and even see a panorama of the Vosges in France. Visitors can cross the border, about 250m (800 ft.) from the arch, to sample the vintages on the French side as well, as there are no border formalities here. You can follow a trail known as the Weinlehrpfad (wine inspection path), going on for 1.5km (1 mile) until you reach the vineyards at the hamlet of Sonnenberg. This is one of the most rewarding walks along the wine route.

In Schweigen-Rechtenbach, one of the best values for lodging is found in the town center at **Am Deutschen Weintor,** Bacchusstrasse 1 (www.hotelgarni-amdeutschen weintor.de; ℂ **06342/7335**), which charges 52€ to 75€ for a double room, breakfast included. We suggest getting a meal at the **Hotel Schweigener Hof,** Hauptstrasse 2 (ℂ **06342/9250**; www.schweigener-hof.com), open daily 11:30am to 3pm and 5 to 9pm. A fixed-price lunch or dinner is 16€ to 24€; wine is extra.

MAINZ ★

13km (8 miles) S of Wiesbaden, 82km (51 miles) NW of Mannheim, 40km (25 miles) SW of Frankfurt

Mainz is located on the left bank of the Rhine, across from the Rhine's intersection with the Main River. It is thought that there may have been wine-producing vines in the area even before the coming of the Romans in 38 B.C., although it was from that time that the regions of the Rheingau and Rheinhessen became widely known for fine viticulture.

At the beginning of the Christian era, a bridge connected the settlement on the Rhine's left bank and the Roman fortifications opposite. In the 8th century, the town became a primary archbishopric. Over the centuries, church politics and a series of wars shuffled control of the city back and forth between the French (who called it "Mayence") and various German factions. Today Mainz is a bustling city, with a prosperous trade in wine and other businesses.

Most visitors will be interested in the relatively compact **Altstadt,** which has been restored tastefully and carefully.

Essentials

GETTING THERE

By Plane   The nearest airport is at Frankfurt (see chapter 13). There is direct rail service from the airport (S-14 train) via Wiesbaden to Mainz. For information, call the Mainz Railway Station at ℂ **06131/151055.**

By Train   From Frankfurt, an express train takes 30 minutes to reach Mainz, while the S-Bahn arrives in 40 minutes. There are also trains leaving Mainz for Heidelberg and Koblenz (trip time: 1 hr.) or Cologne (trip time: 2 hr.). Daily trains to and from Munich take about 4½ hours. For more rail information, call ℂ **01805/996633** (www.bahn.de).

By Bus   Regional bus service is provided by **ORN Omnibusverkehr Rhein-Nahe GmbH,** at Mainz (ℂ **06131/5767470**; www.orn-online.de).

By Car   Access by car to Mainz is via the A60 east and west, and the A63 south and A643 north.

VISITOR INFORMATION

Go to **Touristik Centrale,** Brückenturm am Rathaus (ℂ **06131/286210;** www. info-mainz.de). It's open Monday to Friday 9am to 6pm, Saturday 10am to 4pm, and Sunday 11am to 3pm.

SPECIAL EVENTS   The most celebrated merrymaking in festive Mainz is the All Fools capers at **Carnival** each spring, on the Monday and Tuesday before Ash

Wednesday, where merrymakers act like fools, jesters, and clowns. This festival is broadcast throughout Germany the way the Macy's parade is throughout the U.S. There's also an annual **Wine Fair** the first week in August and the first week in September. For information, contact the tourist office at $℮$ **06131/286210.**

GETTING AROUND
Trams and buses fan out across the city from the Hauptbahnhof from 5am until around midnight. Fares start at 2.50€ and vary depending on how far you go.

Exploring Mainz

Dom und Diözesan Museum (Cathedral and Diocesan Museum) ★
CHURCH   Above the roofs of the half-timbered houses in the Altstadt rise the six towers of St. Martin's Cathedral, the most important Catholic cathedral in the country after Cologne's. It dates from A.D. 975 but was continually rebuilt and restored, reaching its present form mainly in the 13th and 14th centuries. Below the largest dome, a combination of Romanesque and baroque styles, is the transept, separating the west chancel from the nave and smaller east chancel. Many of the supporting pillars along the aisles of the nave are decorated with carved and painted statues of French and German saints.

The cathedral's Diocesan Museum houses a collection of religious art. In it are exhibitions of reliquaries and medieval sculpture, including works by the Master of Naumburg. In the 1,000-year-old cathedral crypt is a contemporary gold reliquary of the saints of Mainz. Among the most impressive furnishings in the sanctuary are rococo choir stalls and an early-14th-century pewter baptismal font.

Domstrasse 3. $℮$ **06131/253344.** www.dommuseum-mainz.de. Cathedral free; Diocesan Museum 3.50€ adults, 2€ students and children 15 and under. Cathedral Apr–Sept Mon–Fri 9am–6:30pm, Sat 9am–4pm, Sun 2–5pm; Oct–Mar Mon–Fri 9am–5pm, Sat 10am–3:30pm, Sun 1–3pm. Museum Tues–Sat 9am–5pm. Bus: 1, 7, 13, 17, or 23.

Gutenberg Museum ★★ MUSEUM   This museum is a unique memorial to the city's most famous son. In the rebuilt Gutenberg workshop, visitors can trace the history of printing, beginning with Johannes Gutenberg's hand press, on which he printed his 42-line-per-page Bible from 1452 to 1455. The collections cover the entire spectrum of the graphic arts in all countries, past and present, as well as printing, illustration, and binding. Two Gutenberg Bibles are the most popular exhibits.

Liebfrauenplatz 5. $℮$ **06131/122640.** www.gutenberg-museum.de. Admission 5€ adults, 2€ children 8–18, free for children 7 and under. Tues–Sat 9am–5pm; Sun 11am–1pm. Closed Jan. Bus: 54, 57, 60, or 71. Opposite the east towers of the cathedral.

Landesmuseum Mainz (Provincial Museum of the Central Rhineland)
MUSEUM   It's worth a visit here to get a pictorial history of Mainz and the middle Rhineland ranging from prehistoric times to the present. The Lapidarium shows one of the most important collections of Roman monuments in Europe. The most impressive exhibits are the Roman tombstones of soldiers and civilians of the 1st century A.D. and the towering Column of Jupiter, erected in Mainz at the time of Nero, around A.D. 65 to 68. There's a true-to-life replica of the column in front of the Parliament building.

Grosse Bleiche 49–51. $℮$ **06131/23295557.** www.landesmuseum-mainz.de. Admission 5€ adults, free for children 5 and under; free for all Sat. Tues 10am–8pm; Wed–Sun 10am–5pm. Bus: 6, 15, or 23.

Where to Eat

Palatinate, the regional cuisine of the area in which Mainz is located, is basic German fare with regional subtleties based on the availability of local ingredients.

Geberts Weinstuben ★ 🎒 PALATINATE   This traditional *Weinstube* is housed in one of the oldest buildings in Mainz, built in 1879, with a decor that's almost spartan. But people flock here for the food, not the ambience. Once seated, you're treated to a traditional meal of game, fish, or regional specialties such as goose *à l'orange*. The cuisine includes other hearty regional fare such as roast pork with *Sauerkraut*.

Frauenlobstrasse 94. ✆ **06131/611619.** www.geberts-weinstuben.de. Reservations required. Main courses 18€–28€; fixed-price menu 31€. AE, MC, V. Sun and Tues–Fri 11:30am–2pm; Tues–Sat 6–10pm. Closed mid-July to mid-Aug. Bus: 21 or 70.

Haus des Deutschen Weines GERMAN   Set in Mainz's historic core, immediately adjacent to the Stadttheater, this modern, contemporary-looking restaurant focuses on a savory combination of German food and mostly German wines. Said wines run the gamut of virtually every vintage produced within Germany, and the staff is well versed in their compatibility with menu items that include fresh or marinated salmon, all kinds of venison (available year-round), a savory version of rump steak, and perfectly grilled fish. Expect lots of emphasis on whatever vegetable is in season at the moment of your arrival. In spring, for example, asparagus is celebrated with at least a dozen variations served either as starters or as main courses. No one will object if you order just wine and a small platter of food; examples include *Spundekäse,* an age-old recipe that mingles local cheese whipped with onions and cream into a soft paste. It's best served with rough-textured bread.

Gutenbergplatz 3. ✆ **06131/221300.** www.hdw-gaststaetten.de. Reservations recommended. Main courses 10€–18€. AE, MC, V. Daily 11:30am–midnight.

L'Angolo ITALIAN   This informal Italian-inspired trattoria is known for its congenial staff and its excellent pizza and pasta. You can also order freshly made salads, with shrimp or prosciutto, and meat dishes with escalopes of either pork or veal. Reasonable prices and a full bar generally keep this place packed.

Augustinerstrasse 8. ✆ **06131/231737.** www.l-angolo.de. Pizzas and pastas 8€–12€; meat platters 10€–20€. No credit cards. Daily 11am–midnight. Bus: 6, 15, or 23.

Weinstube Lösch 🍴 RHINELANDER   This old-fashioned *Weinstube* in the heart of the Altstadt has been popular for generations and is rich in tradition. The menu offers regional hot and cold dishes and light salads, plus lots of Rhine wine. The pork *Schnitzel* with mushrooms is particularly savory. Two regional dishes include *Jägerschnitzel* with mushrooms and *Zigeunerschnitel* with paprika, both served with boiled potatoes and a green salad. Tender rump steak is also a huge specialty here. The 12 tables seat 85 guests. Six additional tables are placed out front in summer on the pedestrian mall.

Jakobsbergstrasse 9. ✆ **06131/220383.** Reservations recommended. Main courses 12€–20€; daily specials 5€–11€. No credit cards. Tues–Sat 3:30–10:30pm. Bus: 6 or 23.

Shopping

The city's most active shopping area is **Am Brand,** a short boulevard near the cathedral that's lined with shops on either side (bus: 1 or 54). One of the town's best clothing emporiums is **Peek & Cloppenburg,** Am Brand 38 (✆ **06131/669200;** www.peek-cloppenburg.de), which sells clothing for men, women, and children, in styles ranging from very formal to chic and casual. For German designer fashions, head to **Sinn,** Markt 19 (© **06131/971560;** www.sinnleffers.de), which carries men's and women's clothing.

Whatever you can't find along the Am Brand will almost certainly be available among the vast inventories of Mainz's most visible department store, **Kaufhof,** Schusterstrasse 41 (© **06131/2540;** www.galeria-kaufhof.de; bus: 54). For a treasure-trove of secondhand goods, shop the **Krempelmarkt;** this flea market is held along the banks of the Rhine on the first Saturday of each month, February to October (bus: 54).

Mainz After Dark

The cultural center of the city is **Frankfurter Hof,** Augustinerstrasse 55 (© **06131/220438;** www.frankfurter-hof-mainz.de; bus: 54), which stages concerts of classical music, jazz, folk, and pop. The center also hosts an annual tent festival featuring an eclectic mix of international performers. Tickets to all events cost 10€ to 75€. Call for scheduled shows, festival dates and performers, and ticket information.

Although you can buy tickets at the offices of any of the theaters and entertainment venues in Mainz, a more convenient way is to contact the **Ticket Service,** which is a division of the town's tourist office at Brückenturm am Rathaus, 55116 Mainz (© **06131/286210;** bus: 54).

In terms of its nightlife, Mainz is sleepy enough to compel many residents to head to Cologne or Düsseldorf after dark. But if you don't want to get out of town too quickly, consider dancing the night away at the **Disco Kuz,** Dagobertstrasse 20 (© **06131/286860;** www.kuz.de; bus: 60 or 61), where you'll find attractive people drinking, dancing, and talking. It's open Wednesday, Friday, and Saturday 10pm until at least 4am, charges a 6€ to 10€ cover, and attracts ages 20 to around 35. The hottest address is **Red Cat,** Emmerich-Josef-Strasse 13 (© **06131/225656;** www. redcat-club.de), in the heart of town, right off the landmark Schillerplatz. The club is tiny, as is its dance floor, but hip young Mainzers pack the joint anyway. **Chapeau Claque,** Kleine Landgasse 4 (© **06131/223111;** www.chapeau-mainz.de; bus: 9), is a gay bar that's open nightly 6pm to 4am.

Where to Stay

Favorite Parkhotel ★ Set in isolated privacy within a park on a hillside above the Rhine and the old city of Mainz, which lies within a 12-minute downhill walk, this three-story hotel was established in the early 1960s, and enlarged in 2005 with a five-story modern wing. It's a respectable, conservative, family-managed hotel. Accommodations in the old wing are actually preferred for their solid sense of comfort, pastel colors, and conservative sense of modernity. Rooms within the newer wing are trendier, more artfully contemporary, and more minimalist and monochromic, but still very comfortable. The morning breakfast buffet is very complete, a reflection of the good service and food in the gourmet-conscious **Stadtpark Restaurant,** and its *Bierkeller*-style cohort, the **Bierkutscher.** Then, of course, there is an outdoor beer garden (open May to late Sept daily noon–10pm).

Karl Weiser Strasse 1, 55131 Mainz. www.favorite-mainz.de. © **06131/80150.** Fax 06131/8015420. 121 units. 133€–245€ double; 239€–285€ suite. Rates include buffet breakfast. AE, DC, MC, V. Parking 15€. Bus: 60 or 61. **Amenities:** 2 restaurants; babysitting; bikes; concierge; exercise room; Jacuzzi; indoor heated pool; room service; sauna. *In room:* TV, CD player, hair dryer, minibar, Wi-Fi (free).

Hilton Mainz City ★★ Occupying two desirable plots of land near the center of town, the Hilton is one of the most imaginatively designed and strikingly modern hotels along the Rhine Valley. Its twin sections are sheathed in reflective mirrors and soaring spans of steel, and are connected by a glass-sided, covered walkway above the traffic below. The labyrinthine interior has sun-flooded atriums with live plants and acres of marble flooring. The spacious rooms are the most artfully decorated in the region.

Rheinstrasse 68, 55116 Mainz. www.hilton.com. *C* **800/445-8667** in the U.S. and Canada, or 06131/2450. Fax 06131/245589. 437 units. 195€–320€ double; from 304€ suite. AE, DC, MC, V. Parking 20€. Bus: 7, 13, 17, 34, or 37. A 5-min. walk from the cathedral. **Amenities:** 3 restaurants; bar; babysitting; concierge; exercise room; room service; sauna. *In room:* A/C, TV, hair dryer, minibar, Wi-Fi (22€ per day).

Hotel Ibis This chain hotel is modern and functional, its two chief attractions being its convenient location at the edge of the Old Town and its affordable prices. Bedrooms are small to midsize and are suitably comfortable in a chain-format sort of way. Rooms are climate controlled.

Holzhofstrasse 2, 55116 Mainz. www.ibishotel.com. *C* **016131/2470.** Fax 016131/234126. 144 units. 79€–99€ double. AE, DC, MC, V. Free parking. **Amenities:** Bar; Wi-Fi (free; in lobby). *In room:* A/C, TV, no phone.

Hotel Mainzer Hof ★ Mainzer Hof is six floors of modernity directly on the Rhine, almost at the point where some of the boats dock. This hotel is a clean-cut, convenient stopover. The medium-size rooms are well furnished and maintained.

Kaiserstrasse 98, 55116 Mainz. www.hotel-mainzerhof.de. *C* **06131/288990.** Fax 06131/228255. 80 units. 75€–165€ double. Rates include buffet breakfast. AE, DC, MC, V. Parking 8€. Bus: 9. A 10-min. walk from the Hauptbahnhof. **Amenities:** Restaurant; bar; exercise room; room service; sauna. *In room:* TV, hair dryer, minibar, Wi-Fi (free).

Hyatt Regency Mainz ★★★ Opening onto the Rhine, this deluxe palace has eclipsed the two Hiltons and now reigns supreme. It is the best hotel south of Cologne, done in a strikingly modern architectural style. A glittering 21st-century aura prevails in the public rooms, restaurants, and guest accommodations. The room furnishings are tasteful and sleekly sophisticated, with modern art decorating the walls. The more desirable units open onto the Rhine, and these have even larger bathrooms. The public facilities are among the best in this part of Germany, with a wine bar and the **Römische Weinstube** restaurant, featuring a grand terrace along the Rhine. In summer a beer garden goes full blast.

Malakoff-Terrasse 1, 55116 Mainz. www.mainz.regency.hyatt.com. *C* **06131/731234.** Fax 06131/731235. 268 units. 130€–255€ double; from 368€ junior suite. AE, DC, MC, V. Parking 20€. **Amenities:** 2 restaurants; bar; babysitting; concierge; exercise room; indoor heated pool; room service; spa. *In room:* A/C, TV, hair dryer, Wi-Fi (21€ per day).

Mainz City Hilton ★★ In the historic zone of Mainz, about a 3-block walk from the rail terminus, this Hilton is particularly lively. Although the rooms are about the same in both Hiltons, we prefer the relatively subdued atmosphere here and the more personal staff. We also like the architectural touches, including an ancient wall discovered during reconstruction. The wall was preserved and now frames the courtyard terrace. Rooms are a bit cookie-cutter, but tasteful and spacious, each with a deluxe bathroom. They're priced according to view and location; those on the top cost the most money because of their panoramic views and balconies. The least desirable are on the lower floors, facing a park.

Munsterstrasse 11, 55116 Mainz. www.hilton.com. *C* **06131/2780.** Fax 06131/2782099. 128 units. 145€–290€ double; 200€–360€ suite. Rates include buffet breakfast. AE, DC, MC, V. Parking 20€. **Amenities:** Restaurant; 2 bars; babysitting; concierge; exercise room; room service. *In room:* A/C, TV, hair dryer, minibar, Wi-Fi (22€ per day).

THE RHEINGAU ★★★

Legend says that when God was looking for a place to set up Paradise, the sunny slopes between the Taunus Mountains and the Rhine nearly won the prize. Today the Rheingau is the kingdom of another god: Bacchus. Nearly every town and village from Wiesbaden to Assmannshausen is a major wine producer. The names suddenly seem familiar—Bingen, Johannesburg, Rüdesheim, Oestrich—because they're featured on the labels of many wines.

The Rheingau is also rich in old churches and castles, as well as landmarks. The **Niederwald Monument,** on a hill halfway between Rüdesheim and Assmannshausen—it can be reached by cable car from either town—is a huge statue of Germania, erected by Bismarck in 1883 to commemorate the unification of Germany. Below it, on a small island at the bend of the Rhine, is the **Mäuseturm (Mouse Tower),** where, according to legend, the greedy archbishop of Mainz was devoured by a swarm of hungry mice. But the real attraction of the Rheingau is the cheerful character of the wine villages and their people. Rüdesheim and Assmannshausen are the most visited towns.

Essentials

GETTING THERE

By Plane The nearest airport is at Frankfurt (see chapter 13), 50km (30 miles) away.

From the airport, you can rent a car. Otherwise, take the train or bus from Wiesbaden (see the "By Train" or "By Bus" section, below). There are bus links from the Frankfurt airport to Wiesbaden's bus and train transport hubs.

By Train The main rail station at Rüdesheim is on the Wiesbaden-Koblenz line, with frequent service to regional towns and connections to all major cities. For rail information and schedules, call ℂ **01805/996633** (www.bahn.de). Train service from Frankfurt is via Wiesbaden and takes 1 hour.

By Bus Bus service for the region is provided by **ORN Omnibusverkehr Rhein-Nahe GmbH,** in Wiesbaden (ℂ **0611/977580;** www.orn-online.de).

By Car Access by car is via the A61 Autobahn from the north and Hwy. 42 connecting with the A671 from the west. From Frankfurt, motorists can take the A66 until they reach the junction with Rte. B42, which is signposted and leads right to Rüdesheim. Motorists heading from Koblenz on the west bank of the Rhine can use the A61 to Bingen, and then follow the signs for the ferryboats that cross the river to Rüdesheim. For information on the ferry service, call ℂ **06722/2972.** From Koblenz, you can also take B42 along the east bank of the river, which will lead directly into Rüdesheim. Rte. B42 links Rüdesheim with Assmannshausen.

VISITOR INFORMATION

For information about Rüdesheim and Assmannshausen (see below), go to the **Stadt Verkehrsamt,** Geissenheimer 22 in Rüdesheim (ℂ **06722/906150;** www. ruedesheim.de). It's open January to mid-April and November to December Monday to Friday 11am to 5pm, and mid-April to October Monday to Friday 9am to 6:30pm, Saturday and Sunday 11am to 5pm; Christmas market (the weeks before Christmas) they are also open Saturday and Sunday 11am to 5pm.

Rüdesheim ★

With its old courtyards and winding alleyways lined with half-timbered houses, Rüdesheim is the epitome of a Rhine wine town. The vineyards around the village date back to the Roman emperor Probus. The full-bodied Riesling is produced here, as well as brandy and *Sekt* (sparkling wine). Rüdesheim is also the scene of the annual August wine festival, when the old taverns on the narrow and very touristy **Drosselgasse (Thrush Lane)** are crowded with visitors from all over the world. Drosselgasse has been called "the smallest but the happiest street in the world." From April to November, you can listen to music and dance in these taverns daily noon to 1am.

To prove how seriously Rüdesheimers take their wine, they have opened a wine museum in Bromserburg Castle. The **Rheingau- und Weinmuseum,** Rheinstrasse 2 (☎ **06722/2348;** www.rheingauer-weinmuseum.de), charges 5€ for adults, and 3€ for children 11 and under; it's open mid-March to October daily 10am to 6pm (last admission 5:15pm). It traces the history of the grape and has an exhibition of wine presses, glasses, goblets, and drinking utensils from Roman times to the present. Wine tastings are 7.50€ to 16€ extra, depending on how many samples you drink.

WHERE TO EAT & STAY

Breuer's Rüdesheimer Schloss ★★   This hotel is the first choice for staying and dining in town. The Breuer family is noted for its wine cellars and plentiful food and drink. The wine cellar dates from 1729. The mostly medium-size rooms are immaculately kept, and a few are even quite spacious. The hotel staff will help you prepare a tailor-made package of excursions or perhaps a "gastronomic feast" and a musical evening on their premises. German and Rhineland specialties are served here. The chef prides himself on his *Zehnthofplatte,* consisting of regional sausages, smoked pork, grilled knuckle of pork, and *Sauerkraut.*

Steingasse 10, 65385 Rüdesheim. www.ruedesheimer-schloss.de. ☎ **06722/90500.** Fax 06722/905050. 26 units. 125€–155€ double; 155€–175€ suite. Children 12 and under stay free in parent's room. Rates include buffet breakfast. AE, DC, MC, V. Free parking. **Amenities:** Restaurant; bikes. *In room:* TV, hair dryer, minibar, Wi-Fi (free).

Gasthof Krancher ★ 👔   This is a home-and-hearth choice. Gasthof Krancher has been in the Krancher family for four generations and it's located next to the inn's own vineyards. Naturally, the Kranchers make their own wines, and they'll gladly show you the cellar where they store bottles that have won gold and silver medals. Everything is decorated in a regional motif. Rooms are a bit cramped but are reasonably comfortable. From your window you can look out on the vineyards. Local German food, mostly Rhinelander specialties, is served here; a simple three-course meal costs around 20€.

Eibinger-Oberstrasse 4, 65385 Rüdesheim. www.gasthof-krancher.de. ☎ **06722/2762.** Fax 06722/47870. 62 units. 28€–38€ per person double. Rates include buffet breakfast. MC, V. Free parking. 10-min. hike uphill from the town center. **Amenities:** Restaurant. *In room:* TV.

Hotel und Weinhaus Felsenkeller   The beautifully carved timbers on the facade of this 1613 building suggest the traditional aura you'll find inside. A sampling of Rhine wine can be enjoyed in a room with vaulted ceilings and murals with vine leaves and pithy pieces of folk wisdom. In fair weather, guests can eat on the terrace. The hotel serves regional Rhineland cuisine and complete meals, which are huge and cost from 18€ to 43€. The small, attractively modern, and freshly painted rooms open onto views of the vineyards surrounding the house.

Oberstrasse 39–41, 65385 Rüdesheim. www.ruedesheim-rhein.com. © **06722/94250.** Fax 06722/47202. 60 units. 85€–125€ double; 116€–145€ triple. Rates include buffet breakfast. AE, MC, V. Free parking. Closed Nov–Easter. In the center of the old town. **Amenities:** Restaurant. In room: TV, hair dryer, Wi-Fi (free).

Rüdesheimer Hof 🍴 This village inn, set back from the Rhine, boasts a side garden and terrace where wine tasters gather at rustic tables. Most of the units are roomy and comfortably furnished. The atmosphere is informal. If you stay here, you can sample the lifestyle of a Rhine village by mingling with the townspeople, eating the regional food, and drinking the Rheingau wines. Guests dine at cafe tables placed under a willow tree. Food is served daily 11:30am to 9:30pm and meals cost 15€ to 22€.

Geisenheimerstrasse 1, 65385 Rüdesheim. www.ruedesheimer-hof.de. © **06722/91190.** Fax 06722/48194. 38 units. 92€–119€ double. Rates include buffet breakfast. AE, DC, MC, V. Free parking. Closed Dec to mid-Feb. 10-min. walk from the Bahnhof. **Amenities:** Restaurant. In room: A/C, TV.

Assmannshausen

This old village at the northern edge of the Rheingau is built on the slopes of the east bank of the Rhine. Its half-timbered houses and vineyards seem precariously perched on the steep hillsides, and the view of the Rhine Valley from here is awe-inspiring. Assmannshausen is known for its fine burgundy-style wine. It lies 5km (3 miles) northwest of Rüdesheim and 60km (37 miles) west of Frankfurt.

WHERE TO EAT & STAY

Alte Bauernschanke-Nassauer Hof ★ The winegrower owners have turned two of the oldest mansions in town into a hotel and restaurant. The interior decor is luxurious, the comfort fine, and the welcome hearty. Rooms are beautifully furnished in traditional style. The restaurant has live folk music every night. Try goulash soup, pepper steak with fresh green beans and french fries, and a bottle of the growers' red wine. Meals cost 22€ to 30€.

Niederwaldstrasse 23, 65385 Rüdesheim-Assmannshausen. www.altebauernschaenke.de. © **06722/49990.** Fax 06722/47912. 53 units. 85€–115€ double; 115€–145€ suite. Rates include buffet breakfast. AE, MC, V. Closed Dec 16–Mar 8. Near the church, about .5km/¼ mile from the Rhine. **Amenities:** Restaurant; bar; room service. In room: TV, hair dryer, Wi-Fi (free).

Krone Assmannshausen ★★★ This distinguished hotel offers the most luxurious accommodations in the entire Rüdesheim am Rhein district. It's on the banks of the Rhine, surrounded by lawns, gardens, and a pool. Its origins can be traced back 400 years. The inn is a great big gingerbread fantasy with fairy-tale turrets and wooden balconies evocative of the Romantic architecture of the 16th century. A small second-floor lounge is virtually a museum, with framed letters and manuscripts of some of the famous people who have stayed here—Goethe, for one, and also Kaiser Wilhelm II. There's a stack of about 40 autograph books dating from 1893 signed by writers, painters, diplomats, and composers. You may stay in a medieval, Renaissance, or postwar building. The spacious rooms have an old-inn character, with traditional furnishings.

Rheinuferstrasse 10, 65385 Rüdesheim-Assmannshausen. www.hotel-krone.com. © **06722/4030.** Fax 06722/3049. 65 units. 195€–245€ double; 325€ junior suite; 375€–705€ suite. AE, DC, MC, V. Parking 10€. **Amenities:** Restaurant; babysitting; outdoor pool; room service. In room: TV, hair dryer, minibar, Wi-Fi (free).

KOBLENZ ★

88km (55 miles) SE of Cologne, 63km (39 miles) SE of Bonn, 100km (62 miles) NW of Frankfurt

Koblenz has stood at the confluence of the Rhine and the Mosel for more than 2,000 years. Its strategic location in the mid-Rhine region has made the city a vital link in the international river-trade routes of Europe. The city is surrounded by vine-covered hills dotted with castles and fortresses. Koblenz is also the place where many cruises through the Rhine begin or end.

Essentials

GETTING THERE

By Plane   The nearest airports are Frankfurt (see chapter 13) and Cologne (later in this chapter). From there, you can rent a car or go by train. See below for train information.

By Train   The **Koblenz Hauptbahnhof** lies on a major rail line, with frequent connections to important German cities. For train information, prices, and schedules, call ✆ **01805/996633** or visit www.bahn.de. Thirty trains per day arrive from Frankfurt (trip time: 2 hr.) and 16 from Berlin (trip time: 8½ hr.). Trains also arrive every 30 minutes from Cologne (trip time: 45 min.–1 hr.).

By Bus   Rail is by far the best way to get to Koblenz, but information on bus service is available at ✆ **0261/3038823.**

By Car   Access by car to Koblenz is via the A48 Autobahn east and west, connecting with the A3 north to south.

VISITOR INFORMATION

For information about tours, boat trips on the Rhine, and bus and train connections, contact the **Koblenz Tourist Office,** Bahnhofplatz 17 (✆ **0261/31304;** www.koblenz.de). It's open Monday to Saturday 9am to 6pm, and Sunday 10am to 6pm.

GETTING AROUND

The city is served by 10 main bus lines. Fare is 1.70€ to 2.45€ depending on how far you go, paid on the bus (the bus driver will help you get the proper ticket, though most tourists will stay in the central zone and pay the cheaper fare).

Exploring Koblenz

Koblenz was heavily bombed during World War II, but many of its historic buildings have been restored. The focal point of the Altstadt is the **Liebfrauenkirche (Church of Our Lady),** a 13th-century Gothic basilica built on a Romanesque foundation, with twin towers topped by onion-shaped spires. The early-18th-century **Rathaus** was formerly a Jesuit college. In the courtyard behind the hall is a fountain dedicated to the youth of Koblenz called *Das Schängelchen (The Spitting Boy),* and that's just what he does. At the edge of the old town, near the Deutsches Eck, is Koblenz's oldest, biggest, and most attractive church, **St. Castor's,** originally built in 836, though in its present form it dates mostly from the 12th century.

   Festung Ehrenbreitstein (✆ **0261/9742441;** www.festungehrenbreitstein.de), across the Rhine from Koblenz, can be reached by chairlift between May and September. You can also drive there via the Pfaffendorfer Bridge just south of the Altstadt or take bus no. 8, 9, or 10 from the rail station. The fortress was constructed on a rock and towers 120m (400 ft.) above the Rhine. The present walls were built in the

For the most panoramic view of Koblenz, go to the point where the two rivers meet. It is called Deutsches Eck, or the "corner of Germany." From the top of the base where a huge statue of Wilhelm I once stood, you can see the Altstadt and across the Rhine to the Festung Ehrenbreitstein.

19th century. From the stone terrace is one of the best views along the Rhine; the panoramic vista includes not only Koblenz but also several castles on the river and many terraced vineyards. To reach the fortress, make the 3.50€ one-way passage across the river from the main Rhine dock. Ferries operate mid-March to late November daily 9am to 5:15pm. The chairlift operates April to October daily 9:30am to 4:30pm. Round-trip tickets cost 8€ for adults, 5€ for children 13 and under.

Where to Eat

Café-Restaurant Palais INTERNATIONAL This old building, a former furniture store, has been converted into a cafe set against a backdrop of Art Nouveau styling. The exterior is a 19th-century Victorian facade, and the interior is filled with fine antiques and original paintings. The chefs roam the world borrowing recipes to create a finely tuned modern cuisine enhanced by attentive service. Try the platter-wide Wiener Schnitzel filet steak, or a succulent chicken breast with curry sauce, diced pineapples, and pears. The pastas are succulent, especially the penne with a Gorgonzola sauce, served with an herby garlic bread.

Firmungstrasse 2. ☏ 0261/1005833. www.palais-koblenz.de. Reservations recommended. Main courses 10€–19€. MC, V. Mon-Thurs 8am–1am; Fri-Sat 8am–3am; Sun 10am–midnight.

Da Vinci ★★ MEDITERRANEAN One of the most appealing restaurants in Koblenz, Da Vinci is plush and richly accessorized, with backlit bars lighting up like displays in an art museum, plus plenty of polished copper, wood paneling, and leather. And in honor of the restaurant's namesake, it contains replicas—either framed or painted like murals directly onto the walls—of da Vinci's most famous art. Conveniently central, with a location near Centralplatz, the venue focuses on Mediterranean cuisine, but with presentations that are a lot more sophisticated than anything *mamma mia* ever made. The best examples include carpaccio of beef with fresh Parmesan and arugula; grilled quail with forest mushrooms and paprika sauce; and a "strudel" stuffed with Italian cured ham, grilled vegetables, olive paste, and mushrooms. Dessert? How about sweet ravioli stuffed with lemon grass ice cream and drizzled with caramel sauce.

Firmungstrasse 32B. ☏ 0261/9215444. www.davinci-koblenz.de. Reservations recommended. Main courses 14€–28€. AE, DC, MC, V. Daily 11am–11pm. Bus: 8.

Weinhaus Hubertus GERMAN Weinhaus Hubertus looks like a half-timbered country inn. It's the oldest wine tavern in town, dating from 1696. The place offers German wines accompanied by a choice of homemade dishes—soups, sandwiches, and light platters, all designed to go well with the wines offered. The furnishings and decor are family style, providing a homelike atmosphere. There's a choice here of 100 wines from all over Germany, 30 of these by the glass. In summer, you can enjoy the view of the Altstadt from the terrace.

Florinsmarkt 6. ✆ **0261/31177.** www.weinhaus-hubertus.de. Reservations recommended. Main courses 15€–24€. MC, V. Wed–Mon 4–10pm. Bus: 1. Across from the Old Rathaus.

Entertainment & Nightlife

THE PERFORMING ARTS   The **Rheinische Philharmonie Orchestra** performs in the **Rhein-Mosel-Halle,** Schlossstrasse 35 (✆ **0261/300160;** www.rheinische-philharmonie.de; bus: 9 or 10), which also hosts other performances. Tickets cost 15€ to 60€. Call for listings, dates, and prices of other performances. The **Stadttheater (City Theater),** housed in the **Grossehaus,** Dinehartplatz (✆ **0261/1292804;** www.theater-koblenz.de; bus: 9 or 10), stages dramas, comedies, and musicals (in German) September to June. The box office is open daily 9am to noon. Tickets are 20€ to 55€, but can be higher depending on the event.

BARS   A pub-oriented crowd, mostly under 40, hangs out late at night at the previously recommended **Palais,** Firmungstrasse 2, Am Görresplaz (✆ **0261/1005833;** www.palais-koblenz.de), before heading for one of the many pubs on Florinsmarkt for a nightcap. **Club Abaco** (same phone), in the basement of this building, attracts a mostly 20-ish crowd to dance to the music provided by a live DJ. The club is open Thursday to Saturday from 9pm to 4am, charging a cover that ranges from 5€ to 15€.

At **Irish Pub Koblenz,** Burgstrasse 7 (✆ **0261/9737797;** www.irishpub koblenz.de; bus: 1), copious amounts of Guinness, Kilkenny, hard cider, and German beers are served as accompaniment to everything from traditional Gaelic songs to progressive rock 'n' roll. Hours are Monday to Thursday 4pm to 1am, Friday 4pm to 2am, Saturday 1pm to 2am, and Sunday 1pm to 1am.

Where to Stay

Hotel Brenner ★   This hotel is your best bet if you're seeking a moderately priced choice. The small- to medium-size rooms are spotlessly maintained. Each bathroom is immaculately kept. The garden retreat is a pleasant spot for getting back to nature.

Rizzastrasse 20–22, 56068 Koblenz. www.hotel-brenner.de. ✆ **0261/915780.** Fax 0261/36278. 24 units. 87€ double. Rates include buffet breakfast. AE, DC, MC, V. Parking 6€. Bus: 1 or 5 to Christuskirche. Near the Kurfürstl Schloss. *In room:* TV, hair dryer, minibar.

Hotel Scholz   Scholz is a personally run, well-maintained family hotel offering sparsely furnished units that make for a reasonably priced overnight stopover. Rooms are small, but the beds are comfortable and the bathrooms beautifully maintained.

Moselweisserstrasse 121, 56073 Koblenz. www.hotelscholz.de. ✆ **0261/94260.** Fax 0261/942626. 67 units. 78€ double. Rates include buffet breakfast. AE, DC, MC, V. Free parking. Bus: 6 or 16. A 5-min. bus ride from the town center. **Amenities:** Restaurant. *In room:* TV, Wi-Fi (5€ per hour).

Kleiner Riesen   This is one of the few hotels in central Koblenz that sits directly on the banks of the Rhine. Its rooms are close enough to view the boats as they go by. Within the city proper, only the Mercure is better. The Kleiner Riesen is a large, informal chalet, with several lounges and comfortable rooms. It's away from town traffic, so it has a peaceful small-town quiet.

Kaiserin-Augusta-Anlagen 18, 56068 Koblenz. www.hotel-kleinerriesen.de. ✆ **0261/303460.** Fax 0261/160725. 28 units. 88€ double. Rates include buffet breakfast. AE, DC, MC, V. Parking 8€. *In room:* TV, Wi-Fi (free).

Mercure ★★   Glittering and stylish, the Mercure is easily the best hotel in town. It's perched on a hillock at the edge of the Rhine. Its streamlined architecture contrasts with the century-old trees and ancient stones of the surrounding medieval town. Rooms are well insulated against sound, and each has a neatly kept bathroom. One of the city's loveliest riverside promenades is just a short walk away.

Julius-Wegeler-Strasse 6, 56068 Koblenz. www.mercure.de. © **0261/1360.** Fax 0261/1361199. 168 units. 117€–168€ double; 260€ suite. 2 children stay free in parent's room. AE, DC, MC, V. Parking 12€. Bus: 9 or 10. Pets accepted. **Amenities:** 2 restaurants; babysitting; bikes; exercise room; Jacuzzi; room service; sauna. *In room:* A/C, TV, hair dryer, minibar, Wi-Fi (in some; free).

BONN ★

72km (45 miles) S of Düsseldorf, 27km (17 miles) S of Cologne, 174km (108 miles) NW of Frankfurt

Until 1949, Bonn was a sleepy little university town, basking in its 2,000 years of history. Then suddenly it was shaken out of this quiet life and made capital of the Federal Republic of Germany. But in 1991, after the reunification of Germany, Berlin again became the official capital.

From the 13th century to the 18th century, Bonn was the capital of the prince-electors of Cologne, who had the right to participate in the election of the emperor of the Holy Roman Empire. The city is also proud of its intellectual and musical history—Beethoven was born here; composer Robert Schumann and his wife, pianist Clara Schumann, lived here; and Karl Marx and Heinrich Heine studied in Bonn's university.

Bonn is also within sight of the **Siebenbirge (Seven Mountains),** a volcanic mountain range rising up on the eastern bank of the Rhine. The local wine produced on these slopes is known as *Drachenblut* (Dragon's Blood) and is better than most German reds.

Essentials

GETTING THERE

By Plane   The nearest airport is **Flughafen Köln/Bonn** (see "Cologne [Köln]," later in this chapter). Buses from the airport to Bonn's main rail station run every 30 minutes daily 5:40am to 10:30pm.

By Train   The **Bonn Hauptbahnhof** is on a major rail line, with connections to most German cities. There are 12 trains daily to Berlin (trip time: 5 hr.), more than 30 trains to Frankfurt (trip time: 2 hr.), and service to Cologne every 15 minutes (trip time: 20 min.). For information, call © **01805/996633** (www.bahn.de).

By Bus   Long-distance bus service connects with such cities as Munich, Stuttgart, Aachen, Brussels, and London. For information, call **Deutsches Touring GmbH** in Frankfurt (© **069/7903501;** www.touring.de). Regional bus service from Bad Godesberg and nearby towns is provided by **Regionalverkehr Köln GmbH at Meckenheim** (© **0228/7111;** www.rvk.de).

By Car   Access is by the A565 Autobahn connecting with the A3 Autobahn from the north or south.

VISITOR INFORMATION

Go to the **Bonn Tourist Office,** Windeckstrasse 1 (© **0228/775000;** www.bonn. de), open Monday to Friday 9am to 6:30pm, Saturday 9am to 4pm, and Sunday 10am to 2pm.

GETTING AROUND

If you visit the Reisenzentrum under the Bonn railway station, you can pick up a free map outlining the city's transportation network. The office is open Monday to

Saturday 5.30am to 10pm and Sunday 6:30am to 10pm. Bus or S-Bahn/U-Bahn tickets cost 1.60€ to 9.80€. You can also purchase a day ticket costing 5.60€ to 21€.

TOURS

The best way to get acquainted with Bonn is to take a **walking tour,** the meeting point of which is the Bonn Tourist Office (see above). Call ✆ **0228/775000** for reservations. Tours lasting 2½ hours cost 15€ for adults or 8€ for children 6 to 14, free for children 5 and under, with a family ticket (two adults and two kids) going for 30€. Tours depart January to April 4 and November 2 to December 15 only on Saturday at 2pm. The "Big City Tour" is conducted on a bus with commentary in English and German, taking in all the scenic highlights and going by the major monuments. The last part of the tour involves a walk through the historic core.

Exploring Bonn

The **government quarter,** along the west bank of the Rhine, is a complex of modern, rather nondescript white buildings. The two most impressive, both along Koblenzerstrasse, are the former residences of the president and chancellor. These empire-style villas are reminiscent of the older Bonn, before it became an international center of diplomatic activity. They are not open to the public. Running north along the Rhine from the government buildings is a tree- and flower-lined promenade, which ends at the **Alter Zoll.** This ruined ancient fortress makes a fantastic viewing point from which visitors can see across the Rhine to the Siebengebirge and the old village of Beuel. These grounds, in essence, have become a city park.

Beethoven Haus ★ HISTORIC HOUSE   Beethoven House is Bonn's pride and joy. Beethoven was born in 1770 in the small house in back, which opens onto a little garden. On its second floor is the room where he was born, decorated only with a simple marble bust of the composer. Many of Beethoven's personal possessions are in the house, including manuscripts and musical instruments. In the Vienna Room, in the front of the house overlooking the street, is Beethoven's last piano (it was custom made, with a special sounding board to amplify sound for the hearing-impaired composer).

Bonngasse 20. ✆ **0228/981750.** www.beethoven-haus-bonn.de. Admission 5€ adults, 4€ students and children, 10€ family ticket. Apr–Oct Mon–Sat 10am–6pm, Sun 11am–6pm; Nov–Mar Mon–Sat 10am–5pm, Sun 11am–5pm. Tram: 62 or 66. In the old section of town, just north of the marketplace.

Haus der Geschichte der Bundesrepublik Deutschland (House of History of the German Republic) MUSEUM   All the sweep and drama of Germany's modern history is brought to life in this museum, in artifacts, photographs, and other displays. Exhibits trace the history of Germany after 1945, up to the breakdown of law and order in the eastern sector that led to reunification. The museum made headlines in 2001 when Emilie Schindler, the 93-year-old widow of Oskar Schindler, donated some of her famous husband's documents to the museum. Oskar Schindler was the subject of Steven Spielberg's film *Schindler's List,* one of the best-known movies ever made of the Holocaust. The bequest includes excerpts from the diary of one of hundreds of Jews who Schindler, a German industrialist, saved from the Nazi death camps. The donation also includes a photo album of the making of the Spielberg movie and a congratulatory letter from then American president Bill Clinton.

Willy-Brandt-Allee 14. ✆ **0228/91650.** www.hdg.de. Free admission. Tues–Sun 9am–7pm. U-Bahn: Heussallee/Museumsmeile.

Kunstmuseum Bonn MUSEUM This triangular structure, flooded with light, contains one of the most important art collections along the Rhine. The highlight is 20th-century art, including works by Rhenish expressionists, most notably August Macke. There are also works by Kirchner, Schmidt-Rottluff, Campen-Donk, Ernst, Seehaus, and Thuar.

Friedrich-Ebert-Allee 2. ℂ **0228/776260.** http://kunstmuseum.bonn.de. Admission 7€ adults, 3.50€ children, 14€ family ticket. Tues–Sun 10am–6pm (Wed until 9pm). U-Bahn: Heussallee.

Where to Eat

Em Höttche 🦪 GERMAN Em Höttche enjoys a long and colorful history, going all the way back to 1389. It's fed thousands over the centuries with its rib-sticking fare—perhaps changing the recipes every 100 years or so. The interior has been restored, with carved-wood paneling, natural brick, old beamed ceilings, decoratively painted plaster, and curlicue chandeliers. Favorite dining spots are tables set inside the walk-in fireplace. On the a la carte list, you'll find specialties for two, including entrecôte. Fresh salmon is often available. Complement your meal with a carafe of local wine—the best buy in the house. However, the drink of choice for most visitors is *Kölsch,* a famous Rhineland beer for which the establishment is well known.

Markt 4. ℂ **0228/690009.** www.em-hoettche.de. Reservations not accepted. Main courses 12€–24€. No credit cards. Daily 11am–1am. Tram: 47. Bus: 618. Next to the Rathaus.

Ristorante Grand'Italia ★ ITALIAN/INTERNATIONAL This is one of the most appealing Italian restaurants along the Rhine. Main courses might include a *filletto della casa* (filet of beef prepared in a "special sauce," the composition of which the chefs won't discuss), *tagliorini* with white truffles, and an autumnal version of roast pheasant. Also look for Roman-style *osso buco* (veal shank layered with prosciutto), a succulent risotto Milanese, and such desserts as a velvety version of zabaglione.

Bischofsplatz 1. ℂ **0228/638333.** Reservations recommended. Main courses 17€–28€. AE, DC, MC, V. Daily noon–3pm and 6pm–midnight. Tram: 62 or 66. Adjacent to the old market square.

Zur Lese GERMAN This restaurant's polite service and outdoor terrace with a sweeping view over the Rhine attract many local residents, especially in the afternoon, when visitors drop in for coffee, cakes, and glasses of wine after strolling in the nearby Hofgarten. Elegant, well-prepared lunches are also offered. Dinner is served in the cafe. A menu of German specialties (with English translations) includes pork with curry sauce and the chef's superb *Gulasch Lese* (goulash). You can also choose rainbow trout or lobster from the terrace aquarium. The food is home-style and hearty, with no pretense.

Adenauerallee 37. ℂ **0228/223322.** www.zurlese.de. Reservations recommended. Main courses 12€–23€; fixed-price menu 39€. AE, DC, MC, V. Restaurant Tues–Sun noon–midnight. Cafe Tues–Sun noon–2pm and 6–10pm.

Shopping

Not surprisingly, you'll find lots of shops in town specializing in garments suitable for diplomacy and business. Most of the best are on the **Sternstrasse** (S-Bahn: Hauptbahnhof), partly a pedestrian-only street at certain times of day.

Eighteenth-century German and French furniture as well as Biedermeier is found at **Paul Schweitzer,** Loebestrasse 1 (ℂ **0228/362659;** S-Bahn: Godesberger Bahnhof), which also handles Oriental carpets, silver, French glass, and estate jewelry. A

GERMAN men of ideas: FRIEDRICH NIETZSCHE (1844-1900)

"Man is something that shall be overcome.... You have made your way from worm to man, and much in you is still worm... Man is a rope, tied between beast and overman—a rope over an abyss... What is great in man is that he is a bridge and not an end."

Field of Study: Philosopher, philologist, ethicist.

Revolutionary Insight: Believed Christianity promoted a "slave morality" in which meekness, submission, and piety are valued. The "death of God" meant it was impossible to know objective, divine truth; against this backdrop of relativism the solitary, exceptional *übermensch* (overman) creates his own inner, superior morality.

Controversy Quotient (Oto 5): (4) Intellectual combativeness alienated contemporaries, including Richard Wagner. In life, Nietzsche despised nationalism and anti-Semitism; posthumous reputation suffered when Hitler corrupted the *übermensch* into a Nazi eugenic ideal.

Little Known Fact: Some historians now believe the sickly Nietzsche went insane not from late-stage syphilis, but from a vascular disease that manifested in migraines, stroke, and dementia.

—Kelly Regan

market called the **Flohmarkt,** at Rheinaue, Ludwig-Erhard-Strasse (tram: 66), is where you'll find all manner of secondhand goods and collectibles. It's held the third Saturday of each month April to October. A weekly market, **Wochenmarkt,** on the square of the same name, is held Monday to Saturday. You can enjoy a good lunch here, buying cooked food as you walk along inspecting the produce and various flea market items.

Entertainment & Nightlife

Once a dismal place to go out on the town, Bonn now has a thriving fine-arts community and a brisk nightlife. If you're in the area around the first Saturday in May, don't miss the Rhine in Flames event which features a spectacular annual fireworks display, visible for a distance of about 25km (15 miles) south of the city.

THE PERFORMING ARTS   Bonn has always struggled with the perception that it can't compete with the larger arts communities in Hamburg and Berlin, and consequently it compensates (or overcompensates) with an impressive roster of cultural events. One of the most visible is "La Scala of the Rhineland," the **Oper der Stadt Bonn,** Am Boeselagerhof (© **0228/778008;** www.theater-bonn.de; S-Bahn: Hauptbahnhof), where ballet and opera are performed at regular intervals mid-August to June. Box office hours are Monday to Friday 10am to 3:30pm, Saturday 9:30am to noon, and Sunday 10am to 2pm. Tickets are 9€ to 115€ each, depending on the event.

The **Klassische Philharmonie Bonn (Bonn Symphony Orchestra)** performs in Beethovenhalle, Wachsbleiche 16 (© **0228/654965;** www.klassische-philharmonie-bonn.de; S-Bahn: Hauptbahnhof), September to June, with occasional free concerts given on Sunday mornings. Otherwise, tickets cost 15€ to 62€. On a more intimate scale, chamber music is sometimes presented within a small but charming concert hall within the **Beethoven Haus** (see above for contact information).

During the Bonner Summer Festival, mid-May to August, an international selection of dance and music groups performs, mostly for free, in open-air locations around the city. Contact ☏ **0228/201030** or 2010345 for details. In addition, the **BeethovenFest Bonn,** a rekindling of both the nostalgia and the music associated with Bonn's greatest musical genius, takes place in late August and September. Visit **www.beethovenfestbonn.de** for information.

Bonn's **Theater-Kasse,** Windeckstrasse 1 (☏ **0228/775000;** www.theater.bonn. de; S-Bahn: Hauptbahnhof), is a well-known and highly resourceful ticket agency associated with the city's tourist office. It has access to tickets for virtually every sporting, entertainment, and cultural venue in Bonn. Also call for information on performers, schedules, and prices.

LIVE MUSIC & CABARET   The **Pantheon Theater,** Bundeskanzlerplatz (☏ **0228/212521;** www.pantheon.de; bus: 610), stages jazz and pop concerts, comedy shows, and political cabaret. Nearly every weekday there is a performance of some sort. Friday and Saturday, the facility becomes a dance club. The box office is open Monday, Wednesday, Thursday, and Friday noon to 6pm.

GAY BARS   The most crowded gay bar is **Boba's Bar,** Josefstrasse 17 (☏ **0228/650685;** www.bobasinn.de; S-Bahn: Hauptbahnhof), near the railway station, adjacent to the Rhine. It welcomes a drinking (but not dancing) crowd in their 20s and 30s. It's open Tuesday to Sunday 8pm to 3am and Friday and Saturday 8pm to 5am. There's also **Le Copain,** Berliner Platz 5 (☏ **0228/639935;** S-Bahn: Berliner-von-Suttner-Platz), which attracts a somewhat older clientele and is open 4pm to 1 or 2am.

Where to Stay

Dorint Sofitel Venusberg ★★★   This elegant and intimate hotel, built in a style evocative of a French country home, is surrounded by the beauty of the Venusberg nature reserve, part of the larger Kottenforst. It is the grandest choice for Bonn. About half the units offer private balconies overlooking the hills. Bathrooms are well accessorized.

An der Casselsruhe 1, 53127 Bonn. www.dorint.de. ☏ **0228/2880.** Fax 0228/288288. 85 units. 119€–280€ double; 365€–409€ junior suite; 425€–569€ suite. AE, DC, MC, V. Parking 11€. 2.5km (1½ miles) southwest of Bonn, via Trierer Strasse. **Amenities:** 2 restaurants; babysitting; concierge; access to nearby health club; Jacuzzi; room service; sauna. *In room:* A/C, TV, hair dryer, minibar, Wi-Fi (5€ per hour).

Günnewig Bristol Hotel ★★   This somewhat sterile, Cold War–era concrete-and-glass tower is still a suitable address. The good-size rooms are the best in Bonn, featuring double-glazing on the windows, along with fashionable and well-equipped bathrooms. The staff is also excellent.

Prinz-Albert-Strasse 2, 53113 Bonn. www.guennewig.de. ☏ **0228/26980.** Fax 0228/2698222. 116 units. 119€–217€ double; 230€–390€ suite. Children 12 and under stay free in parent's room. Rates include American breakfast. AE, DC, MC, V. Parking 15€. Tram: 61 or 62. Near Poppelsdorf Castle. **Amenities:** 3 restaurants; bar; babysitting; indoor heated pool; room service; sauna. *In room:* A/C, TV, hair dryer, minibar, Wi-Fi (in some; 8€ per hour).

Hotel Domicil ★★   This modern and convenient hotel, like the Kaiser Karl (see below), is an oasis of charm and grace in Bonn's rather sterile environment. It's like an exclusive London town house and provides a viable alternative to the Günnewig Bristol (see above). In the front, a glass-and-steel portico stretches over the sidewalk.

The interior is one of the most elegant in the capital. The handsomely designed and spacious rooms range from Belle Epoque to Italian modern.

Thomas-Mann-Strasse 24–26, 53111 Bonn. www.bestwestern.de. © **800/780-7234** in the U.S., or 0228/729090. Fax 0228/691207. 44 units. 108€–222€ double; 250€ suite. Rates include buffet breakfast. AE, DC, MC, V. Parking 25€. U-Bahn: Hauptbahnhof. 4 blocks north of the cathedral, near the Hauptbahnhof. **Amenities:** Restaurant; bar; babysitting; Jacuzzi; room service; sauna. *In room:* TV, hair dryer, minibar, Wi-Fi (free).

Kaiser Karl ★★ 🎁 Kaiser Karl is one of Bonn's gems. Like the Domicil (see above), it has more style and atmosphere than other luxury leaders. Constructed in 1905 as a private town house, it was converted in 1983 into a stylish four-story hotel. The attractive decor includes lacquered Japanese screens, English antiques, Oriental carpets, Venetian mirrors, and Edwardian potted palms. Each beautifully furnished room has a sleek bathroom.

Vorgebirgstrasse 56, 53119 Bonn. www.kaiser-karl-hotel-bonn.de. © **0228/985570.** Fax 0228/9855777. 42 units. 89€–420€ double; from 250€ suite. Children 6 and under stay free in parent's room. AE, DC, MC, V. Parking 12€. Bus: 645 or 607. Pets allowed. **Amenities:** Restaurant; babysitting; bikes; room service. *In room:* TV, hair dryer, minibar, Wi-Fi (free).

Sternhotel This is one of the best of Bonn's moderately priced hotels. It offers an informal, cozy atmosphere. Rooms are homey, all with comfortable furnishings and bathrooms are well equipped.

Markt 8, 53111 Bonn. www.sternhotel-bonn.de. © **0228/72670.** Fax 0228/7267125. 80 units. 115€–185€ double; 145€–230€ suite. Rates include buffet breakfast. DC, MC, V. U-Bahn: Uni-Markt. Bus: 624, 625, or 626. Next to the Rathaus. **Amenities:** Exercise room; sauna. *In room:* TV, minibar.

BAD GODESBERG

6km (4 miles) S of central Bonn

Part of greater Bonn, Bad Godesberg is one of the Rhine's oldest spa towns. It's located just opposite the legendary Siebengebirge (Seven Mountains), with a view of Drachenfels (Dragon's Rock), where, according to legend, Siegfried slew the dragon. You can still see some ancient castle ruins on the hills, such as **Godesberg Castle,** built in the 13th century by the electors of Cologne (its ruins have been incorporated into the Ringhotel Rheinhotel Dreesen; see below). From the promenade along the Rhine, you can watch a flow of boats and barges wending their way up and down the river.

Most of the spa's activities center on the small but elegant 18th-century **Redoute Palace.** Theaters, concerts, and social functions offer a constant whirl of events. Since these events are not permanent, check with the **Bonn tourist office** (p. 500), which publishes a weekly list of current events happening at the time of your visit and can provide additional information about the town.

GETTING THERE You can reach Bad Godesberg from Bonn by taking tram no. 16 or 63 from Bonn's central rail station (trip time: 20 min.). If you're driving from the center of Bonn, take the B9 (driving time: 20 min.).

Where to Eat

Halbedel's Gasthaus ★★ CONTINENTAL Here, amid many nostalgic souvenirs and antique tables and chairs, the courtly owners will welcome you to their turn-of-the-20th-century villa. The kitchen prides itself on using mostly German-grown produce. The chefs are true artists, using ingredients of superlative quality to create harmonious flavors and textures. Some of the dishes will be familiar; others are imaginative inventions. Perhaps the most experimental dish on the menu is pigeon with a dark chocolate and chili sauce. In spite of the sound of it, it is a great flavor to many gourmets. Also reaching heights of culinary bliss is the goose liver with a brioche that's accompanied by apples and a passion fruit sauce. Lobster tartare appears delectably with avocados and mangoes. We are also impressed with the turbot with fresh artichokes and morels.

Rheinallee 47. ⓒ **0228/354253.** www.halbedels-gasthaus.de. Reservations recommended. Main courses 35€–42€; fixed-price menu 85€–105€. AE, MC, V. Tues–Sun 6–10:30pm. Closed 3 weeks July–Aug. Tram: 16. Bus: 610.

Where to Stay

Ringhotel Rheinhotel Dreesen ★ Directly beside the river, a 10-minute ride from the center of Bonn, this noble structure offers rooms opening onto the banks of the river. Across the river, guests can see the national park areas of Siebengebirge and Petersberg. Bedrooms are elegant and comfortable, each tastefully furnished and ranging from midsize to spacious, with first-class bathrooms. Bikes are available for cycling tours along the banks of the Rhine or else in the park. Freshly prepared meals with quality ingredients are served in the on-site bistro and restaurant.

Rheinstrasse 45, 53179 Bad Godesberg. www.rheinhoteldreesen.de. ⓒ **0228/82020.** Fax 0228/8202153. 72 units. 120€–185€ double; 200€–250€ suite. Rates include buffet breakfast. AE, DC, MC, V. Parking 10€. Tram: 16. **Amenities:** Restaurant; bar; room service. *In room:* A/C, TV, minibar, Wi-Fi (16€ per day).

AACHEN (AIX-LA-CHAPELLE) ★

64km (40 miles) W of Cologne, 80km (50 miles) SW of Düsseldorf

The ancient Imperial City of Aachen (Aix-la-Chapelle), at the frontier where Germany, Belgium, and the Netherlands meet, is inseparably connected with Charlemagne. He selected this spot as the center of his vast Frankish empire. History is important here, but today there's also a youthful *joie de vivre* that attracts young people from all over the world. Visitors also come for the sulfurous hot springs and the magnificent cathedral.

Aachen has an even longer history as a spa than as an imperial city. Roman legionnaires established a military bath here in the 1st century A.D. By the end of the 17th century, Aachen was known as the "Spa of Kings" because royalty from all over Europe came here to take the cure. Its springs are among the hottest in Europe. The treatment includes baths and the *Trinkkur* (drinking the water). The spa gardens are the center of resort activity, with attractive ponds, fountains, and shade trees.

Essentials

GETTING THERE **By Train** The Hauptbahnhof at Aachen receives some 200 trains a day from all parts of Germany and from Paris, with easy connections from most major cities as well as nearby Cologne (trip time: 45 min.). Frankfurt is 2 hours and 45 minutes away, and Munich, 5 hours and 40 minutes. For information, call ⓒ **01805/996633** (www.bahn.de).

By Car Access is by the A4 Autobahn east and west or the A44 north or south. Driving time from Cologne is 50 to 60 minutes, depending on traffic. Frankfurt is 3½ hours away by car; Munich, 6½ hours.

VISITOR INFORMATION You'll find the **Tourist Office Aachen** on Friedrich-Wilhelm-Platz (© 0241/1802960; www.aachen.de). Office hours are Monday to Friday 9am to 6pm, Saturday 9am to 2pm. From April to December the tourist office is also open on Sunday 10am to 2pm.

GETTING AROUND Buses pull into the main railway station in the center of town at Peterskirchhof and Peterstrasse. Tickets are 1.55€ to 7.30€. A 24-hour pass, available at the bus station, offers unlimited travel within Aachen for 6.45€.

Exploring Aachen

Aachen's Altstadt is small enough to be covered on foot. Marktplatz, in the heart of town, is overshadowed by the Gothic **Rathaus,** which contains the city archives. From here, you can head down one of the most popular and busiest pedestrian precincts in the city, Krämerstrasse, which will lead to **Münsterplatz (Cathedral Square)** and the famous cathedral (see below), one of the masterpieces of architecture in the Western world. Past the cathedral you reach the Elisengarten, bordered on the south by the symbol of Bad Aachen, the **Elisenbrunnen,** a rotunda with a thermal drinking fountain. From Münsterplatz you can go through the great iron gate to the **Fischmarkt,** with old merchants' houses and the Fischpuddelchen fountain with spouting fish.

Wingerstberg **Kurgarten** and the **Stadtgarten,** with its thermal bath and casino, lie to the northeast of town, and the **Hauptbahnhof** is on the southern ring, opening onto Römerstrasse.

Couven Museum ★ MUSEUM This gracefully designed villa gives you an insight into the decorative traditions of the late 18th and 19th centuries. It has one of the best collections of antique furnishings of any museum in the region. On the ground floor is a reproduction of a small-scale chocolate factory. You'll find treasures, some of them low key and discreet, virtually everywhere you look.

Huhnermarkt 17. © **0241/4324421.** www.couven-museum.de. Admission 5€ adults, 2.50€ students and children. Tues–Sun 10am–5pm; 1st Sun of every month 1–5pm. Bus: 4.

Dom (Cathedral) ★★ CHURCH About A.D. 800, Emperor Charlemagne built the "octagon," the core of the Imperial Cathedral. Within stands the marble *Königsstuhl,* Charlemagne's throne, one of the most venerable monuments in Germany. (Visitors to the cathedral can view the throne only with a guide; request one at the treasury or call ahead.) The Holy Roman emperors were crowned here from 936 to 1531, when Frankfurt became the coronation city.

The cathedral is an unusual mixture of Carolingian (the well-preserved dome), Gothic (the choir, completed in 1414), and baroque (the Hungarian chapel), all united into a magnificent upward sweep of architecture. The **treasury ★★★**, in the adjoining house (entry: Klostergasse), is the most valuable and celebrated ecclesiastical treasure-trove north of the Alps. But the cathedral itself holds its own share of wealth. The elaborate gold shrine (1215) in the chancel contains the **relics of Charlemagne ★★★**. The **pulpit ★★★** of Henry II (ca. 1002) is copper studded with precious gems.

Klosterplatz 2. © **0241/47709127.** www.aachendom.de. Cathedral free; treasury 4€ adults, 3€ students and children. Cathedral daily 7am–7pm. Treasury Mon 10am–1pm; Tues–Wed and Fri–Sun 10am–6pm; Thurs 10am–9pm. Bus: 1, 11, or 21.

Rathaus HISTORIC BUILDING The 14th-century Rathaus was built on the original site of Charlemagne's palace. Part of the ancient palace structure can still be seen in the so-called Granus Tower at the east side of the hall. The richly decorated facade, facing the marketplace, is adorned with the statues of 50 German rulers, 31 of them crowned in Aachen. In the center, standing in relief, are the "Majestas Domini," the two most important men of their time in the Holy Roman Empire, Charlemagne and Pope Leo III.

On the second floor of the Rathaus is the double-naved and cross-beamed Imperial Hall, where coronation banquets took place from 1349 to 1531. Built as the successor to the Carolingian Royal Hall, today it contains exact replicas of the imperial crown jewels, true in size and material to the originals, presently in the Vienna Secular Treasury. On the walls are the Charlemagne frescoes, painted in the 19th century by Alfred Rethel, illustrating the victory of the Christian Franks over the Germanic heathens.

Am Markt. ✆ **0241/4327310.** Admission 5€ adults, 2.50€ students and children. Daily 10am–6pm. Closed sometimes for official events. Bus: 4 or 11.

Suermondt Ludwig Museum ★ MUSEUM   The impressive collection of medieval German sculpture, one of the finest in the land, includes a *Madonna in Robes* (1420) from the Swabian school and a *Virgin and Child* from the 14th-century Tournai school. The second landing has a good collection of primitive Flemish and German works, along with 17th-century Dutch and Flemish paintings. Look for works by Van Dyck and Jordaens. The museum also has modern works, especially from the 1920s and 1930s.

Wilhelmstrasse 18. ✆ **0241/479800.** www.suermondt-ludwig-museum.de. Admission 5€ adults, 3€ children. Tues–Sun noon–6pm (Wed until 8pm). Bus: 3, 4, or 13.

Where to Eat

Magellan TURKISH/INTERNATIONAL   Set within a 5-minute walk from Aachen's Rathaus (Town Hall), with a sprawling outdoor terrace that overlooks trees and flowers, this restaurant encompasses cuisine from terrain that its namesake, the famed explorer Magellan, might have visited. The venue is rustic, with thick wooden tables, durable chairs, and a magisterial chandelier that somehow evokes something akin to a Greek Orthodox church. The menu includes choices from Turkey (*mezes*, the succulent and savory dishes like mashed eggplant, olives, and hummus), Italy (pizzas and pastas), and Germany (*Schnitzel* and sausages), as well as a wide choice of grilled lamb and beefsteaks.

Pontstrasse 78. ✆ **0241/4016440.** www.magellan-ac.de. Reservations not necessary. Main courses 12€–16€. MC, V. Daily 10am–midnight; last order for hot food at 11pm. Bus: 3 or 13.

Ratskeller CONTINENTAL/GERMAN   This old-fashioned restaurant is a long-established favorite among locals. A rather formal dining area is in the cellar of the Rathaus, and meals from a mainly Continental menu are served here. In addition to various specialties, solid German food is also offered, including potato soup, grilled steaks, and *Sauerkraut* with *Wurst,* followed by fresh berries and pastries for dessert. The **Postwagen,** a pub dating back to 1901, serves heaping portions of good home cooking.

Markt 40, Am Markt (in the Rathaus). ✆ **0241/35001.** www.ratskeller-aachen.de. Reservations needed in restaurant. Ratskeller main courses 20€–36€; 4-course set menu 40€, 6-course 60€. Postwagen main courses 14€–25€. AE, MC, V. Ratskeller daily 11am–3pm and 6–10pm. Postwagen daily noon–9:30pm (drinks till 11pm). Bus: 2, 11, or 25.

Entertainment & Nightlife

For information about what's happening in Aachen, pick up a copy of the booklet *Tourist-Information*, published and given away free by the tourist information office. You can also download a copy at www.aachen.de. Alternatively, you can buy a copy of the monthly glossy, *Klenkes*, a magazine available in news kiosks around the city for 2€.

THE PERFORMING ARTS   Classical concerts are presented in the town's convention center, **Kongresszentrum Eurogress,** Mondheimsallee 48 (☎ **0241/91310;** www.eurogress-aachen.de; bus: 57), by the local symphony orchestra and by visiting chamber orchestras. The **Theater Aachen** (formerly the Stadttheater), Theaterplatz (☎ **0241/47841;** www.theater-aachen.de; bus: 33, 34, or 57), hosts opera, theater, and dance recitals. Ticket prices in both places are 14€ to 100€. If you understand German and want to see experimental theater and plays by Bertolt Brecht and the like, head for the small and rather cramped **Theater 99 Akut,** Gasborn 9–11 (☎ **0241/27458;** www.akut-theater99.de; bus: 166). Tickets are 19€ to 56€.

BARS & CAFES   There are at least a half-dozen bars in or around Aachen's Marktplatz. One of the most appealing is **Café Kittel,** Pontstrasse 39 (☎ **0241/36560;** www.cafekittel.de; bus: 13), which somewhat resembles a greenhouse; its menu concentrates on beer, wine, sandwiches, and quiche. It's open Monday to Thursday 10am to 2am, Friday and Saturday 10:30am to 2am, and Sunday 10am to 1am.

LIVE MUSIC   A final nightlife venue is the **Domkeller,** Hof 1 (☎ **0241/34265;** www.domkeller.de; bus: 1, 11, or 21), which offers live blues or jazz on some nights and lots of hubbub every night. It is open Sunday to Thursday 10am to 2am and to 3 or 4am Friday and Saturday.

Where to Stay

Am Marschiertor ★ 🛍   This charming hotel stands in the center of Aachen, not far from the Hauptbahnhof and next to the medieval town gate for which it's named. The hotel is quiet, with a courtyard and a view over the Altstadt and cathedral. The lobby and connecting hall are attractive, with antique furniture. The recently refurbished rooms have a cozy atmosphere, and each—generally medium in size—is well appointed and well maintained.

Wallstrasse 1–7, 52064 Aachen. www.hotel-marschiertor-aachen.de. ☎ **0241/31941.** Fax 0241/31944. 50 units. 88€–140€ double. AE, DC, MC, V. Parking 10€. Bus: 1, 11, or 21. Pets accepted. **Amenities:** Room service; babysitting. *In room:* TV, hair dryer, Wi-Fi (free).

Aquis Grana City Hotel ★   Aquis Grana City Hotel is your best bet in the town center. The comfortable rooms offer all the modern extras and range from spacious to medium. The staff is very alert to all your needs. Housekeeping rates an A-plus.

Büchel 32, 52016 Aachen. www.hotel-aquisgrana.de. ☎ **0241/4430.** Fax 0241/443137. 97 units. 88€–230€ double; 270€–420€ suite. Children 10 and under stay free in parent's room. AE, DC, MC, V. Parking 10€. Bus: 1, 11, or 21. **Amenities:** Restaurant; room service; Wi-Fi (free; in lobby). *In room:* TV, hair dryer, minibar.

Hotel Benelux 🥄   The warm and inviting Benelux is within walking distance of many major attractions. It's a small family run hotel, tastefully decorated and personalized. Americans from the Southwest will feel at home in the lobby/reception area—it has probably the only cactus collection in Aachen. Rooms range from small to medium.

Franzstrasse 21–23, 52064 Aachen. www.hotel-benelux.de. ℂ **0241/400030.** Fax 0241/40003500. 33 units. 120€–154€ double. Rates include continental breakfast. AE, DC, MC, V. Parking 8€. Bus: 5, 25, or 35. A 5-min. walk from the Hauptbahnhof. **Amenities:** Restaurant; exercise room; room service; Wi-Fi (free; in lobby). *In room:* A/C, TV, hair dryer, minibar.

Hotel Pullman Aachen Quellenhof ★★★ Once a country home for the kaiser during World War I, this has been turned into a charming, welcoming hotel that appeals to traditionalists. Operated by the Accor chain, the hotel and its spa are reason enough to go to Aachen. Both the public and the private rooms are spacious and beautifully decorated, resting under tall ceilings. An antique and conservatively modern decor is successfully blended. Rooms are furnished comfortably and attractively. Many guests use the hotel as a spa, and it has the Royal Spa with a pool, Turkish bath, Finnish sauna, bio-sauna, ice grotto, and solarium, along with beauty-treatment rooms. The drinking and dining facilities are first-class.

Monheimsallee 52, 52062 Aachen. www.accorhotels.com. ℂ **0241/91320.** Fax 0241/9132100. 185 units. 170€–365€ double; 220€–530€ suite. 1 child stays free in parent's room. AE, DC, MC, V. Parking 16€. Pets allowed. **Amenities:** Restaurant; 2 bars; babysitting; exercise room; indoor heated pool; room service; spa. *In room:* A/C, TV, hair dryer, Wi-Fi (in some; free).

COLOGNE (KÖLN) ★★★

27km (17 miles) N of Bonn, 40km (25 miles) S of Düsseldorf, 188km (117 miles) NW of Frankfurt

Cologne (Köln), the largest city in the Rhineland, is so rich in antiquity that every time a new foundation is dug, the excavators come up with archaeological finds. Today there is much to see from every period of the city's 2,000-year history. However, Cologne is also a vibrant, modern city and is fast becoming the fine art capital of Germany, with museums dedicated to postmodern art, old masters like Rembrandt and a hopping gallery scene.

Things to Do Cologne's centerpiece is the French Gothic **Dom** (Cathedral) with its towering twin spires. Inside, admire its crowning jewel, **The Shrine of the Three Magi**—the gilded sarcophagus of The Three Kings. Next door, stop by for a dose of Roman History at the **Römisch-Germanisches Museum** (Roman-Germanic Museum) or explore American Pop art at the **Museum Ludwig.** After, hit the **Chocolate Museum,** south of the center, where you'll learn about its origins as you enjoy fabulous samples.

Shopping Cologne has become home to a thriving community of emerging, avant-garde artists. Gallery hop along **St. Apernstrasse,** east of the center near the **Neumarkt** (a square), and pop into **Galerie der Spiegel,** one of the first to hit the scene in the 1950s and still the most prominent. If you're in town in December, explore the stalls selling handcrafts and gingerbread at **Christkindlmarkt,** Europe's most famous Christmas Market. It wraps around the **Dom,** which at night sparkles in holiday splendor.

Nightlife & Entertainment **Kölsch** beer is the drink of choice in Cologne, a light and slightly bitter concoction available at more than a dozen local breweries. Sip it at the lofty **Früh am Dom,** a rustic beer hall next to the cathedral, or head to the loveliest quarter in town, the **Zülpicher Viertel,** which buzzes with even more pubs and bars. Alternatively, relax with classical music at the **Kölner Philharmonie** (Cologne Philharmonic), a round, elegant concert venue in the city center.

Cologne (Köln)

14

THE RHINELAND | Cologne (Köln)

HOTELS ■
Antik-Hotel Bristol **7**
Barceló Cologne City Center **34**
Brandenburger Hof **5**
Chelsea **32**
Coellner Hof **1**
Dom Hotel **17**
Excelsior Hotel Ernst **10**
Hopper Hotel et cetera **33**
Hopper Hotel St. Antonius **4**
Hotel im Wasserturm **31**
Hyatt Regency **15**
Santo **2**

ATTRACTIONS ●
Gross St. Martin Church **20**
Käthe Kollwitz Museum Köln **23**
Kölner Dom **11**
Kölner Philharmonie **13**
Museum für Angewandte
  Kunst **18**
Museum Ludwig **14**
Museum Schnütgen **25**
Oper der Stadt Köln **16**
Römisch-Germanisches
  Museum **12**
St. Andreas Church **9**
St. Aposteln Church **22**

St. Cecilia's Church
  (Cäcilienkirche) **24**
St. Georg Church **28**
St. Gereon Church **8**
St. Kunibert Church **3**
St. Maria im Kapitol
  Church **26**
St. Maria Lyskirchen **27**
St. Panteleon Church **30**
St. Severin Church **29**
St. Ursula Church **6**
Schauspielhaus **21**
Wallraf-Richartz Museum/
  Fondation Corboud **19**

Restaurants & Dining   Head to the Old Town, just south of the Dom and spend an evening at the antique-filled **Das Kleine Stapelhäuschen,** a convivial wine tavern that faces the old fish market. This tavern is the place to feast on the region's signature dish, *sauerbraten* (braised beef marinated with vinegar) with potato dumplings. Or splurge on top-shelf international fare such as Angus steak with asparagus and truffle jus, at the wood-paneled **Hanse Stube** in the city center.

Essentials

GETTING THERE

By Plane   Cologne and Bonn are served by the same airport, **Flughafen Köln/ Bonn Konrad Adenauer** (℗ **02203/404001;** www.airport-cgn.de), 14km (9 miles) southeast of Cologne. Flights come from most major European cities. Bus no. 670 from the airport to the center of Cologne operates every 12 minutes, from 5am to 7pm. Travel takes 20 minutes, and the fare is 13€ per person. A taxi, suitable for up to four passengers, costs from 25€.

By Train   The **Cologne Hauptbahnhof** is in the heart of the city, next to the cathedral. For schedules, call ℗ **01805/996633** (www.bahn.de). This depot has frequent rail connections to all major German cities and many continental destinations. There are 18 trains per day from Berlin (trip time: 4 hr., 20 min.), 30 from Frankfurt (trip time: 1 hr., 22 min.), and 25 from Hamburg (trip time: 4½ hr.).

By Bus   Cologne is linked to several major cities, including Frankfurt, by bus. For complete information and schedules, call **Deutsche Touring GmbH** (℗ **0221/7598660;** www.touring.de). Regional bus service to nearby cities such as Trier (see chapter 15) is provided by **Regionalverkehr Köln GmbH** (℗ **0221/ 16370;** www.rvk.de).

By Car   Cologne is easily reached from major German cities. It's connected north and south by the A3 Autobahn and east and west by the A4 Autobahn.

VISITOR INFORMATION

For tourist information, go to the **Köln Tourismus Office,** Kardinal-Höffner-Platz 1 (℗ **0221/22130400;** www.cologne-tourism.com), a few steps from the cathedral. October to June, it's open Monday to Saturday 9am to 9pm and Sunday 10am to 6pm; July to September, hours are Monday to Saturday 9am to 10pm and Sunday 10am to 6pm.

GETTING AROUND

For 1.60€ to 9.80€, depending on where you're going, you can purchase a ticket allowing you to travel on Cologne's excellent **bus, tram, U-Bahn,** and **S-Bahn** connections. A day ticket, the **Kölner Tageskarte,** which costs 5.60€, allows you to travel throughout the city's transportation network from 9am to 3am. For more information, call ℗ **0221/5470** or go to **www.kvb-koeln.de.**

For a taxi, call ℗ **0221/19410** for a recorded message and then press 1 in reply. Meters start at 3€ and rise 1.55€ per kilometer for rides between 6am and 10pm, and 1.70€ per kilometer for rides between 10pm and 6am.

Exploring Cologne

One of the best panoramas over the ancient city of Cologne is from within one of the cars of the Rhein-Seilbahn, the first and only cable car in Europe that was designed to span a major river. The Rhein-Seilbahn stretches between a point near the zoo, in the district of Cologne-Riehl, to the Rheinpark in Cologne-Deutz, a total of about 900m (3,000 ft.). From the air, you'll get a good view of the busy river traffic along the Rhine. The cable car operates April 1 to November 2 daily 10am to 6pm. A one-way ticket costs 4€ for adults, 2.40€ for children; a round-trip ticket costs 6€ for adults, 3.50€ for children. For more information, call ℂ **0221/5474184** or visit www.koelner-seilbahn.de.

THE TOP ATTRACTIONS

Käthe Kollwitz Museum Köln MUSEUM   This is the second museum in Germany devoted to the works of this major German figure (1867–1945), the country's most celebrated female artist of the 20th century. This museum has more of her works than its sibling museum in Berlin. Capturing human emotions, both tender and arresting, the Berlin-born artist focuses on such subjects as death, hunger, war, love, grief, and even happiness. In addition to the works of Kollwitz, presented in drawings, sketches, and sculpture, the museum has special exhibitions, such as those devoted to Picasso, William Hogarth, or even contemporary artists.

Neu-Markt 18-24. ℂ **0221/2272363.** www.kollwitz.de. Admission 3€. Tues–Fri 10am–6pm; Sat-Sun 11am–6pm. In Neu-Markt Galerie, Innenstadt.

Kölner Dom (Cologne Cathedral) ★★★ CHURCH   This majestic structure is one of the world's great cathedrals—the spiritual and geographical heart of the city. It's the largest Gothic cathedral in Germany. From the top of the south tower, you get panoramic views of the city and surrounding area.

Construction began in 1248, in order to house the relics of the three Magi brought to Cologne in 1164 by Archbishop Reinald von Dassel, chancellor to Frederick Barbarossa. After the completion of the chancel, south tower, and north-side aisles (around 1500), work was halted and not resumed until 1823. In 1880, the great enterprise was completed, and unlike many time-consuming constructions that change styles in midstream, the final result was in the Gothic style, true to the original plans.

At the end of the war in 1945, this great cathedral appeared relatively unscathed, even though the entire district around it was leveled. According to legend, Allied bombers used the Dom as a landmark to guide their flights to more strategic military targets and could not bring themselves to destroy such an architectural triumph.

For the best overall view of the cathedral, stand back from the south transept, where you can get an idea of its actual size and splendor. Note that there are no important horizontal lines—everything is vertical. The west side (front) is dominated by two towering spires, perfectly proportioned and joined by the narrow facade of the nave. The first two stories of the towers are square, gradually merging into the octagonal form of the top three stories and tapering off at the top with huge finials. There is no great rose window, so characteristic of Gothic architecture, between these spires—nothing detracts from the lofty vertical lines.

Entering through the west doors (main entrance), you are immediately caught up in the cathedral's grandeur. Although this portion of the church is somewhat bare, the clerestory and vaulting give a feeling of the size of the edifice. The towering windows on the south aisles include the Bavarian windows, donated by King Ludwig I of Bavaria in 1848. Like most windows in the nave, they are colored with pigments that have been burned on rather than stained. In the north aisles are the stained-glass Renaissance windows (1507–09).

In the center of the transept is an elegant bronze-and-marble altar that can be seen from all parts of the cathedral. Behind the high altar, in the chancel, is *The Shrine of the Three Magi* ★★★, the most important and valuable object in the cathedral. It's designed in gold and silver in the form of a triple-naved basilica and decorated with relief figures depicting the life of Christ, the Apostles, and various Old Testament prophets. Across the front of the chancel are two rows of **choir stalls** ★ divided into richly carved partitions. The oak choir dates from 1310 and is the largest extant in Germany.

Surrounding the chancel are nine chapels, each containing important works of religious art. The Chapel of the Cross, beneath the organ loft, shelters the oldest full-size cross in the Occident, the painted, carved oak cross of Archbishop Gero (900–976). Directly across the chancel, behind the altar in Our Lady's Chapel, is the famous *Altar of the City Patrons* ★★★ painted by Stephan Lochner (1400–51). When closed, this triptych masterpiece shows the *Annunciation,* and when opened, it reveals the *Adoration of the Magi* in the center, flanked by St. Ursula, the patron saint of Cologne, and St. Gereon.

English-language tours are given Monday to Saturday at 10:30am and 2:30pm, and Sunday at 2:30pm. German-language tours are conducted Monday to Saturday at 11am, 12:30, 2, and 3:30pm, and every Sunday at 2 and 3:30pm. Tours last an hour and cost 7€ for adults and 5€ for students and children.

Domkloster. ℂ **0221/92584731.** www.koelner-dom.de. Cathedral free. Cathedral tower 2.50€; treasury 4€; combination ticket to treasury and tower 5€. Cathedral daily 6am–7:30pm, except during religious services; cathedral tower and treasury daily 10am–6pm. U-Bahn: Dom/Hauptbahnhof.

Museum für Angewandte Kunst (Museum of Applied Art) ★ MUSEUM
This is a showcase for the arts and crafts of Germany dating from the Middle Ages, with the 20th century prominently featured. This museum is one of the best of its kind in Germany.

An der Rechtsschule. ℂ **0221/22126735.** www.museenkoeln.de. Admission 4.20€ adults, 2.60€ children 6–12, free for children 5 and under. Tues–Sun 11am–5pm. U-Bahn: Hauptbahnhof.

Museum Ludwig ★★★ MUSEUM
This stunningly upgraded museum is the home of one of the world's largest collections of the works of Pablo Picasso, bested only by the Picassos in Paris and Barcelona. Irene Ludwig, widow of the late German art patron Peter Ludwig, for whom the museum is named, donated numerous Picassos to the museum, including 49 paintings, 29 ceramics, 37 works on paper, 15 relief plates, and 681 graphic prints, which previously had been on loan to the museum.

In 1976, Ludwig first gave more than 300 works of art to Cologne to form the basis of this museum. Some of these paintings are the most celebrated and reproduced Picassos in the world, including *Harlequin with Folded Hands* from 1923 and the disturbingly forceful *Woman with Artichoke* from 1941.

The museum is also home to a great collection of modern art from Dalí to Warhol. The American pop art collection, which also includes Roy Lichtenstein, Rauschenberg, and Jasper Johns, rivals the Guggenheim in New York. Our two favorites are Dalí's *Railway Station at Perpignan* and Ed Kienholz's *Portable War Memorial.*

Museum Ludwig is also the home of **Agfa-Historama,** which chronicles the art of photography for the past century and a half, with works by all the greats. This collection of historic photographs and cameras is the largest in the world.

Bischofsgartenstrasse 1. ℂ **0221/22126165.** www.museenkoeln.de. Admission 9€ adults, 6€ students and children. Tues–Sun 10am–6pm; 1st Fri of each month 10am–10pm. U-Bahn: Dom/Hauptbahnhof.

Museum Schnütgen ★★ MUSEUM   This is Cologne's best collection of religious art and sculpture. It's all displayed in an original setting, Cäcilienkirche (St. Cecilia's Church), which is a fine example of Rhenish-Romanic architecture. The works displayed include several medieval ivories, woodwork, and tapestries, including one showing rosy-cheeked Magi bringing gifts to the Christ Child (1470). There are also many Madonnas, of all sizes and descriptions, carved in stone, wood, and metal. Cäcilienstrasse 29. (C) **0221/22122310.** www.museenkoeln.de. Free admission. Tues–Fri 10am–5pm; Sat–Sun 11am–5pm. U-Bahn: Neumarkt.

Römisch-Germanisches   Museum   (Roman-Germanic   Museum) MUSEUM   The most compelling treasure in this museum is the Dionysos-Mosaik, from the 3rd century A.D., discovered in 1941, when workers were digging an air-raid shelter. This elaborately decorated and colored mosaic was once the floor of an *oecus* (main room) of a large Roman villa. It depicts Dionysus, the Greek god of wine. On the second floor of the museum is an unusual collection of Roman antiquities found in the Rhine Valley, including Roman glass from the 1st to the 4th century, as well as pottery, marble busts, and jewelry. Roncalliplatz 4. (C) **0221/22124438.** www.museenkoeln.de. Admission 8€ adults, 5€ children, free for children 5 and under. Tues–Sun 10am–5pm. U-Bahn: Hauptbahnhof.

Wallraf-Richartz Museum/Foundation Corboud ★★★ MUSEUM   This is Cologne's oldest museum, begun in the 19th century with a collection of Gothic works by local artists, still one of the main attractions. The Wallraf-Richartz shows art from 1300 to 1900. Several well-known works from churches are exhibited as well, including the triptych of the *Madonna with the Vetch Flower* (1410). The painting collection represents nearly every period and school, from the Dutch and Flemish masters to the French Impressionists. Stephan Lochner's *Madonna in the Rose Garden* (1450) is a fine example of the German Gothic style, as are his frightening *Last Judgment* and Dürer's *Drummer and Piper*. The museum also houses Germany's largest collection of works by Wilhelm Leibl, as well as paintings by Max Ernst, Paul Klee, and Ernst Ludwig Kirchner. Obenmarspforten. (C) **0221/22121119.** www.museenkoeln.de. Admission 9.50€ adults, 7.50€ students and children 5–16, free for children 4 and under. Tues–Fri 10am–6pm; Thurs 10am–10pm; Sat–Sun 11am–6pm. U-Bahn: Hauptbahnhof.

CHURCHES

Cologne has 12 important Romanesque churches, all within the medieval city wall. Devastated during World War II, they have been almost completely restored and again recapture Cologne's rich early medieval heritage. **St. Panteleon,** Am Pantaleonsberg 2 (U-Bahn: Poststrasse), built in 980, has the oldest cloister arcades remaining in Germany. **St. Gereon,** Gereonsdriesch 2–4 (U-Bahn: Christophstrasse), is elliptically shaped, with a decagon between its two towers. It contains the tomb of St. Gereon and other martyrs, and its crypt still has mosaics from the 11th century. **St. Severin,** Severinstrasse 1 (U-Bahn: Severinstrasse), originated as a 4th-century memorial chapel; the present church dates from the 13th to the 15th century.

The church of **St. Ursula** (1135), Ursulaplatz (U-Bahn: Hauptbahnhof), is on the site of a Roman graveyard. Legend has it that St. Ursula, patron saint of Cologne, was martyred in the city with her 11,000 virgin companions in about 451. **St. Maria im Kapitol,** Kasinostrasse 6 (U-Bahn: Heumarkt), is on the site where Plectrudis, wife of Pippin (dim figures of the Dark Ages, significant because Plectrudis is one of the few women who had political power in the area, as she was the daughter of an important landowner), built a church in the early 8th century. The cloverleaf choir of the present structure was modeled on that of the Church of the Nativity in Bethlehem. **St. Aposteln,** Neumarkt 30 (U-Bahn: Neumarkt), and **Gross St. Martin,** on the Rhine in the Altstadt (U-Bahn: Heumarkt), also have the cloverleaf choir design.

St. Georg, Am Waidmarkt (U-Bahn: Poststrasse), the only remaining Romanesque pillared basilica in the Rhineland, contains an impressive forked crucifix from the early 14th century. **Cäcilienkirche (St. Cecilia's Church),** Cäcilienstrasse 29 (U-Bahn: Neumarkt), is the site of the Museum Schnütgen for sacred art (see above). **St. Andreas,** near the cathedral (U-Bahn: Hauptbahnhof), contains a wealth of late Romanesque architectural sculpture. The remaining two Romanesque churches are on the Rhine: **St. Kunibert,** Kunibertskloster 2 (U-Bahn: Hauptbahnhof), and **St. Maria Lyskirchen,** Am Lyskirchen 12 (U-Bahn: Heumarkt), both of 13th-century origin.

Where to Eat
VERY EXPENSIVE
Hanse Stube ★★ FRENCH   One of Cologne's best restaurants, Hanse Stube offers top-drawer service and food better than that served in the dining room of the Dom Hotel. Prodigious talent and imagination go into shaping the cuisine. Unusual and tasty main courses include breast of guinea fowl stuffed with herbs or medallions of venison with savoy cabbage and a sweet-corn potato *Rösti*. Also delectable are a galantine of quail with pigeon breast served with pistachios in aspic, or else a filet of lamb with spinach and a tomato ragout.

On the ground floor of the Excelsior Hotel Ernst, Domplatz. (©) **0221/2701.** Reservations recommended. Main courses 27€–38€; fixed-price lunches 19€–39€. AE, DC, MC, V. Daily noon–3pm and 6pm–midnight. U-Bahn: Hauptbahnhof.

EXPENSIVE
Le Moissonnier ★★ FRENCH   This charming brasserie is steeped in the aesthetic and culinary traditions of the early 20th century, with mirrors, cove moldings, dark paneling against ocher-colored walls, bentwood chairs, and tiled floors. Here you'll enjoy the carefully crafted cuisine of chef Eric Menchon. Menu items change with the season and the inspiration of the chef, but are likely to include risotto with almonds and truffle oil; crayfish sautéed in vanilla oil; carpaccio of turbot; and a house specialty that combines braised filet of goose breast with tarragon and strips of goose liver, and is served with prosciutto-studded mashed potatoes. Salads and fresh fish are all delicious, as are the *Sauerkraut* and a Toulouse-inspired version of cassoulet loaded with pork, small sausages, and white beans.

Krefelder Strasse 25. (©) **0221/729479.** www.lemoissonnier.de. Reservations recommended. Main courses 34€–49€; 4-course lunch menu 65€; 6-course dinner 103€ on Fri–Sat. V. Tues–Sat noon–3pm and 6:30–9:30pm. U-Bahn: Hansaring.

MODERATE
Brauhaus im Walfisch GERMAN/FRENCH   Brauhaus im Walfisch isn't easy to find, but it's a good choice for atmospheric dining. This step-gabled inn with a black-and-white timbered facade dates from 1626. More important, it serves excellent food. There are many German specialties, often influenced by French cuisine. You might try the sole meunière or venison for two. You'll find the restaurant on a narrow street set back from the Rhine, near Heumarkt.

Salzgasse 13. (©) **0221/2577879.** www.walfisch.net. Reservations required. Main courses 12€–22€. No credit cards. Mon–Thurs 5pm–midnight; Fri 3pm–midnight; Sat–Sun 11am–midnight. U-Bahn: Heumarkt.

Das Kleine Stapelhäuschen ★ GERMAN This is one of the most popular wine taverns in Cologne. It's housed in an office building and opens onto the old fish-market square and the Rhine. The two-story dining room and service bar are antique in style. Provincial cabinets hold a varied wine collection. A wide cantilevered wooden staircase leads to mezzanine tables. Though the wine is the main reason for coming here (it's that special), the cuisine is also excellent. A specialty is *Rheinischer Sauerbraten* with almonds, raisins, and potato dumplings. You can also order marinated roast beef in a dark-brown vinegar sauce with raisins, or else escalope of veal with roast potatoes and a mixed salad.

Fischmarkt 1–3 (Am Rheinufer). ✆ **0221/2727777.** Reservations recommended. Main courses 18€–28€. AE, MC, V. Daily 11:30am–11pm. Closed late Dec to early Jan. U-Bahn: Heumarkt. A few minutes from the cathedral.

Fischer's ★ 🎁 INTERNATIONAL Part of Fischer's appeal is the fact that it's owned and directed by one of Germany's best-known women sommeliers, Christina Fischer. Don't expect to see her hawking wines on the floor, however. These days she's more of an *éminence grise,* leaving the day-to-day wine pouring to a staff of underlings. A 10-minute walk from the cathedral, Fischer's has a large, modern dining room that's lined with wine racks and paintings celebrating grape harvesting, the production of wine, and its uncorking rituals. The chefs are proud of the restaurant's policy of combining culinary tenets from both Europe and Asia, often on the same platter. The finest examples include *Tafelspitz* (boiled beef) served with potato/arugula salad; sashimi of tuna with bean sprout salad and lemon sauce; and fried sea bream with strips of foie gras. There are at least 40 kinds of wine available by the glass and more than 700 vintages from around the world available in bottles.

Hohenstaufenring 53, Ringe. ✆ **0221/3108470.** www.fischers-wein.com. Reservations required. Main courses 20€–37€; 3-course menu 79€; 4-course menu 89€. DC, MC, V. Tues–Fri noon–2pm; Fri–Sat 6:30–11pm. Tram: 12, 16, or 18.

INEXPENSIVE

Früh am Dom GERMAN Within the cathedral precincts, this former brewery is known for its economy and hearty portions of old-fashioned German cooking, like your German grandmother made. Früh-Kolsch beer, a very special brew, is the right liquid to wash it down. It's a top-fermented brew with a dry, inimitable taste and a tradition stretching back 1,000 years. Well-cooked meals are served on scrubbed wooden tables, with different specialties every day. A favorite dish for any day is the Cologne specialty of cured smoked knuckle of pork served with *Sauerkraut* and potato purée. The beer garden is a summer delight.

Am Hof 12–18, Altstadt. ✆ **0221/26130.** www.frueh.de. Reservations not needed. Main courses 9€–20€. MC, V. Daily 11am–midnight. U-Bahn: Hauptbahnhof.

Heising & Adelmann ★ RHINELANDER/FRENCH "We come here to eat, drink, and be merry," a local patron told us. "And no German does that better than a Rhinelander." Although that assertion may be arguable, he more or less stated why young residents of Cologne flock to this place with its good German beer, its French and German specialties, and its lively atmosphere. Start with such delights as a lobster cream soup with fresh mussels and follow with any number of good-tasting dishes such as pan-fried filets of sole with braised mussels and white asparagus or penne with fresh tuna. One imaginative dish is a carpaccio of goose with a chicory strudel.

Friensenstrasse 58–60, Neustadt-Nord. ✆ **0221/1309424.** www.heising-und-adelmann.de. Main courses 19€–23€. AE, MC, V. Tues–Sat 6–10:30pm. U-Bahn: Friesenplatz.

beer TAVERNS

Some of the best inexpensive places to eat (and drink) in Cologne are beer taverns. Come to **Bräuhaus Sion,** Unter Taschenmacher 5–7 (© 0221/2578540; www.brauhaus-sion.de; U-Bahn: Heumarkt; tram: 5 or 7), if you want a traditional local tavern where the beer is good, the wood paneling is smoky with time and frequent polishing, and the food portions are generous. The main courses are traditional and filling Westphalian fare, and the best dish is *Kölsch Kaviar* (blood sausage with onion rings). On tap is the famed local beer, *Kölsch,* a light brew with an alcohol content of about 3%. It's served in *Stangen* (rods) about 18 centimeters (7 in.) tall. Main courses are 16€ to 26€. No credit cards are accepted. It's open daily 10am to midnight, but closed Christmas Eve.

Haus Töller, Weyerstrasse 96 (© 0221/2589316; www.haus-toeller.de; U-Bahn: Barbarossaplatz), a 15-minute walk south of the cathedral, has thrived as a brew house since 1876 by selling copious portions of two-fisted Teutonic food and foaming mugs of a local brew, Sion. The menu includes a local specialty, *Schinkenhempsel* (roast leg of pork), served with *Sauerkraut* and roast potatoes. Main courses are 12€ to 20€; a mug of Sion will set you back 1€. No credit cards are accepted. It's open daily 5pm to midnight.

Shopping

Shopping is not taken quite as seriously here as in Düsseldorf—with one exception. Increasingly, Cologne is emerging as the capital of contemporary art in Germany, and lately the city seems to be brimming with galleries.

ART GALLERIES We'll recommend the major ones to get you started, but there are many more than we can list here. You might want to walk along **St. Apernstrasse** (U-Bahn: Neumarkt), where many leading art galleries are located. The gallery that launched Cologne as a European art mecca is **Galerie der Spiegel,** Richartstrasse 10 (© 0221/255552; U-Bahn: Hauptbahnhof). Established amid the ruins of the wartime bombings in 1945, it was a focal point for the contemporary art that evolved from the shattered dreams of the postwar years. Since then, it has managed to hold its own against rising competition. **Galerie Greve,** Drususgasse 1–5 (© 0221/2571012; www.galerie-karsten-greve.com; U-Bahn: Dom Hauptbahnhof), changes its exhibits every season, specializing in international postwar avant-garde painting. Another excellent gallery for both modern and experimental art is **Galerie Michael Werner,** Gertrudenstrasse 24 (© 0221/9254620; www.michaelwerner.com; U-Bahn: Neumarkt), which sells contemporary European, particularly German, painters.

CLOTHING Looking almost like a modern cathedral, the home of one of Germany's leading retailers of clothing, **Peek & Cloppenburg,** Schildergasse 65 (© 0221/453900; www.peek-cloppenburg.de), lies under a translucent nave that evokes a large crystal egg, using 6,800 handmade panels of glass held together by strips of metal and wooden beams. Renzo Piano designed the store in what he termed a "rather classical cubic form." Shoppers behind the diaphanous walls browse through one of Germany's most elegant, but often affordable, selections of clothing. The company has been selling clothing to well-dressed Germans for more than a century.

Long surpassed by Düsseldorf for fashion, Cologne's pedestrian-friendly layout is blossoming with some of the chicest stores along the Rhine. Fashionistas are flocking to **Apropos Coeln,** Mittelstrasse 12 (© **0221/2725190;** www.apropos-coeln.de), for the latest from Prada or Jil Sander. Storefronts continue to open in the Friesen district, including the Lebanese-born **Perla Zayek's** namesake boutique at Richmondstrasse 7 (© **0221/256022;** www.perlazayek.de), or **Atelier Ludvik,** Palmstrasse 43 (© **0221/2774568;** www.ludvik-cologne.de), where you'll find funky, feminine clothing by designer Fenja Ludwig.

OUTDOOR MARKETS   If you're interested in the kitschy artifacts that pour out of estate sales, be alert to the flea markets in Cologne's inner city. The most appealing are held within the **Alter Markt** (U-Bahn: Hauptbahnhof), at irregular intervals throughout the year, usually at least once a month (ask at the tourist office). More regular are the outdoor food and vegetable markets, the largest of which is held on the **Wilhelmsplatz,** in the Nippes district (U-Bahn: Florastrasse), Saturdays 8am to at least 2pm.

Entertainment & Nightlife

As one of Germany's major cultural centers, Cologne has a variety of fine arts and nightlife options. Many clubs stay open into the early-morning hours. You can pick up a copy of *Stadt Revue* or *Kölner* for 3€ each to find out what's happening in the city. If you're interested in attending a sporting, entertainment, or cultural event within Cologne, you can always head to the box office for tickets. More convenient, however, is the well-orchestrated service of **Köln-Ticket,** Grosse Neugasse 2 (© **0221/2801;** www.koelnticket.de; U-Bahn: Hauptbahnhof), which has many different event tickets for sale. Depending on the ticket, the service charge is around 5€.

THE PERFORMING ARTS

The most impressive grouping of theaters in Cologne is within the **Schauspielhaus,** Offenbachplatz (© **0221/22128256;** www.schauspielkoeln.de; U-Bahn: Neumarkt), the site of three theaters, each with its own agenda and schedule. Performances range from the avant-garde to the classic. **Der Keller,** Kleingedankstrasse 6 (© **0221/318059;** www.theater-der-keller.de; U-Bahn: Ulrepsorte), hosts contemporary plays, usually in German, and dance performances. Tickets are 14€ to 34€ each; call either the number listed above or **Köln-Ticket** (© **0221/2801;** www.koelnticket.de) for schedules and showtimes.

Kölner Philharmonie   This architectural showcase was completed during the late 1980s. The concert hall features a soaring roof, enviable acoustics, and some of the

---

Cologne Water

The word *cologne* has been a part of the common language since the introduction many years ago of the scented water called *Kölnisch Wasser* (eau de cologne). **Eau de Cologne,** Glockengasse 4711 (© **0221/57289250;** U-Bahn: Neumarkt), sells the scented water first developed at this address by Italian chemist Giovanni Maria Farina in 1709. Originally employed to hide the stench of aristocrats who rarely bathed, cologne is now simply a sweet-smelling tradition and a cheap way to take home a little piece of Cologne. The smallest 25-milliliter flacon costs a mere 5€.

finest classical music along the country's western tier. The building is the home of two separate orchestras, the **Gürzenich Kölner Philharmoniker** and the **Westdeutscher Rundfunk Orchestra.** Pop and jazz programs are also presented. Performances are given almost every night at 8pm, except Monday. Bischofsgartenstrasse 1. ✆ **0221/204080.** www.koelner-philharmonie.de. Tickets 17€–140€. U-Bahn: Hauptbahnhof.

Oper der Stadt Köln This is the leading opera house of the Rhineland, known for its exciting productions and innovative repertory of classical and contemporary works. Performances take place almost every evening except Tuesday, usually at 7:30pm. Dance programs are also presented. The box office is open Monday to Friday 9am to 6pm and Saturday 9am to 2pm. Offenbachplatz. ✆ **0221/22128400.** www.buehnen koeln.de. Tickets 10€–77€. U-Bahn or S-Bahn: Neumarkt.

THE CLUB & MUSIC SCENE

DANCE CLUBS One of the city's most dramatic and surreal nightlife options is **E-Werk,** Schanzenstrasse 28 (✆ **0221/9627910;** www.e-werk-cologne.com; U-Bahn: Keupstrasse), a combination of a dance club and a large concert hall. It's housed within what used to be an electrical power plant. Recorded music alternates with live acts. It's open every Friday and Saturday night at 10pm until about 3am most nights. Cover is 5€. Concert prices are 19€ to 49€.

JAZZ CLUBS **Klimperkasten** (also known as **Papa Joe's Biersalon**), Alter Markt 50–52 (✆ **0221/2582132;** www.papajoes.de; U-Bahn: Hauptbahnhof), is an intimate jazz and piano bar open from 11am to 3am, with live music every night beginning around 8pm. The jazz is also hot at **Papa Joe's Jazzlokal,** Buttermarkt 37 (✆ **0221/2577931;** U-Bahn: Heumarkt). Sunday, when the music begins at 4pm and lasts until 1am, is the best day to come. The club is also open for live jazz Monday to Saturday 8pm to 3am. Surprisingly, there's never a cover.

LIVE MUSIC CLUBS Some of the best music in Cologne is played at the aptly named **Loft,** Wissmannstrasse 30 (✆ **0221/952155;** www.loft-koeln.de). The club was established in 1989 when Hans-Martin Müller, a jazz flutist, converted his apartment into a place to listen to great music. Along with what is perhaps the finest acoustics of any club in the city, the **Loft** has a large Steinway grand piano as its centerpiece. Some of the best jazz pianists visiting Germany show up here. Call to find out what's happening and when to show up.

Prime Club (formerly known as Luxor), Luxemburgstrasse 40 (✆ **0221/2714180;** www.prime-entertainment.de; U-Bahn: Barbarossaplatz), offers some kind of live music most nights of the week except Monday. You'll never know what to expect. The management books unknown, inexperienced bands, some of which show great promise. Hours vary, but usually music starts around 9pm. Cover ranges from 10€ to 20€.

BARS

A 110-year-old bar, **Päffgen Bräuhaus,** Friesenstrasse 64–66 (✆ **0221/135461;** www.paeffgen-koelsch.de; U-Bahn: Friesenplatz), serves its *Kölsch* brand of beer, along with regional cuisine. Seating is available indoors and out. It's open Sunday to Thursday 10am to midnight, Friday and Saturday 10am to 12:30am. **Altstadt Päffgen,** Heumarkt 62 (✆ **0221/2577765;** www.max-paeffgen.de; U-Bahn: Heumarkt), also serves the local brew and German dishes, and is open Tuesday to Sunday noon to midnight.

At **Hotelux,** Von Sandt Platz 10 (✆ **0221/241136;** www.hotelux.de), both its food and its scarlet decor are self-consciously Soviet. You can eat platters of Russian food, drink Russian beer or more than two dozen brands of Russian vodka, and sit in a garden with greenery that is thankfully apolitical. It's open Sunday to Thursday 6pm to 1am, Friday and Saturday 6pm to 3am. The major gay and lesbian scene is **Gloria,** Apostelnstrasse 11 (© **0221/660630;** www.gloria-theater.com; U-Bahn: Neumarkt), a sophisticated rendezvous which also welcomes hip straights This was once a movie house showing feature films, but today it's a bustling cafe and club known for its occasional themed parties. If there's music playing, there's a cover of 5€ to 22€. The club is open Monday to Thursday 9am to 1am, Friday and Saturday 9am to 3am, and Sunday 11am to 1am.

GAY NIGHTLIFE

Cologne offers more diversions and distractions for gay men and women than any other city in the Rhineland.

Schampanja, Mauritiuswall 43 (© **0221/2409544;** www.schampanja-koeln.de; U-Bahn: Neumarkt), is a small pub that sometimes books live bands (often punk).

Another easygoing pub is **Zum Pitter,** Alter Markt 58–60 (© **0221/2583122;** www.zum-pitter-cologne.de), which is open daily noon to 1am, attracting a young crowd, particularly on a summer night when its courtyard opens to beer drinkers.

The major gay and lesbian scene takes place at **Gloria** (see above). It also presents theatrical performances with tickets costing 8€ to 30€. It's open Monday to Thursday 9am to 1am, Friday and Saturday 9am to 3am, and Sunday 11am to 1am.

For more information on Cologne's LGBT scene, pay a visit to **Checkpoint,** Pipinstrasse 7 (© **0221/92576868;** www.checkpoint-cologne.de; U-Bahn: Zurticherplatz), a privately owned dispenser of nightlife information that performs some of its functions in cooperation with the city's official tourism authorities. It's open Wednesday and Thursday 5 to 9pm, Friday and Saturday 2 to 7pm, and Sunday 2 to 6pm.

The first weekend in July is devoted to the city's **Gay Pride Parade,** when as many as 500,000 spectators line the parade route for a glimpse of the floats and marchers. For specifics on the parade, contact Checkpoint (see above) or go to **www. colognepride.de**.

Where to Stay

VERY EXPENSIVE

Excelsior Hotel Ernst ★★★   In spite of increased competition, notably from the Hyatt Regency, Cologne's longtime prestige hotel continues to hold its own as the premier address in Cologne. Founded in 1863, the hotel is known for its Empire-style lobby. The public areas contain old-master paintings, including an original work by Van Dyck. The breakfast room has a Gobelin tapestry. Rooms are spacious and up-to-date.

Trankgasse 1–5, Domplatz, 50667 Köln. www.excelsiorhotelernst.de. © **0221/2701.** Fax 0221/2703333. 152 units. 265€–440€ double; from 360€ suite. Rates include continental breakfast. AE, DC, MC, V. Parking 25€. U-Bahn: Hauptbahnhof. **Amenities:** 2 restaurants; babysitting; concierge; exercise room; room service; sauna. *In room:* A/C, TV, hair dryer, minibar, Wi-Fi (22€ per day).

Grandhotel Schloss Bensberg ★★★   The most romantic place to stay in the area is this restored baroque castle constructed 300 years ago by Prince Jan Wellem. Crowning a hill 14km (9 miles) from Cologne, it offers panoramic views of the city.

After lavish renovations, it has been successfully transformed and elegantly furnished with all the modern amenities. Rooms vary in size, but all of them are handsomely equipped with such extras as three phones. Our favorite is no. 307, with its panorama of Cologne and its black-marble bathroom with Jacuzzi. The atmosphere is more intimate and friendly than some drafty castle might suggest. It features special grace notes such as a collection of 10,000 wines in the cellar, a state-of-the-art spa, and 66,000 lights around the pool imitating a night sky.

Kadettenstrasse, 51429 Bergisch Gladbach. www.schlossbensberg.com. ✆ **02204/420.** Fax 02204/42888. 120 units. 265€–370€ double; from 540€ suite. AE, DC, MC, V. Parking 22€. **Amenities:** 3 restaurants; bar; airport transfers (75€); babysitting; concierge; exercise room; indoor heated pool; room service; spa. *In room:* A/C, TV, hair dryer, minibar, Wi-Fi (18€ per day).

Hotel im Wasserturm ★★★

When the tallest water tower in Europe was converted into an 11-story deluxe hotel-in-the-round, at a cost of $75 million, one of the most avant-garde and daring reincarnations of an existing structure in all of Germany was born. Even if living in a water tower is not your idea of a good time, check out the hotel anyway. It's southwest of the city center, just a mile from the cathedral. The design and decor are ingenious, from the Warhol paintings to the tiled lobby with stunning dark woodwork. The structure is 19th century, but everything else is contemporary. Rooms come in unusual configurations, but each is cleverly designed for comfort, flair, and convenience. Original art and exquisite carpeting fill the spacious rooms, and the bathrooms are deluxe, tiled in mosaics and containing such extras as triptych mirrors, robes, and power showers.

Kaygasse 2, 50676 Köln. www.hotel-im-wasserturm.de. ✆ **0221/20080.** Fax 0221/2008888. 88 units. 175€–385€ double; from 274€ suite. AE, DC, MC, V. Parking 25€. **Amenities:** Restaurant; bar; babysitting; concierge; room service; sauna. *In room:* A/C, TV, hair dryer, minibar, Wi-Fi (13€ per day).

Hyatt Regency ★★

This is the most spectacular and up-to-date hotel in Cologne. It's an architectural triumph: a mixture of reddish granite, huge expanses of glass, and a facade that combines Art Deco and neo-Aztec styles. The lobby is dramatic, with a 4m (13-ft.) waterfall. Rooms are stylishly furnished and come with walk-in closets. Many have views of the Rhine and the cathedral on the other side. Bathrooms have private phones, deep tubs with showers, robes, and deluxe toiletries. To get to the Altstadt from here, you can take the Hohenzollernbrücke, a bridge across the Rhine.

Kennedy-Ufer 2A, 50679 Cologne-Deutz. www.hyatt.com. ✆ **888/591-1234** in the U.S., or 0221/8281234. Fax 0221/8281370. 306 units. 160€–265€ double; from 338€ junior suite. AE, DC, MC, V. Parking 21€. Tram: 1 or 9. Across the Rhine from the Altstadt, a short walk from the train station. **Amenities:** 2 restaurants; bar; babysitting; concierge; exercise room; indoor heated pool; room service; spa. *In room:* A/C, TV, hair dryer, minibar, Wi-Fi (18€ per day).

EXPENSIVE

Dom Hotel ★★

Few hotels in Germany have been so consistently awarded the official government five stars or maintained such a standard of excellence as this old-world hotel right across from the cathedral. We prefer the Excelsior Hotel Ernst (see above), but there are many clients who will stay nowhere else but the Dom. The hotel's location, in the shadow of the cathedral, assures it a steady clientele. In summer, the side portico overlooking the square is filled with cafe tables. Rooms have all modern conveniences and a wide collection of period furniture. Try for one of the corner units, which are the most spacious and have the best views. To reach the hotel by car, drive into the square to the side of the Dom's flying buttresses.

Domkloster 2A, 50667 Köln. www.cologne.lemeridien.com. ✆ **800/543-4300** in the U.S., or 0221/20240. Fax 0221/2024444. 124 units. 215€–390€ double; from 340€ suite. AE, DC, MC, V. Parking 20€. U-Bahn: Hauptbahnhof. **Amenities:** Restaurant; bar; babysitting; bikes; concierge; room service. *In room:* A/C, TV, hair dryer, minibar, Wi-Fi (24€ per day).

MODERATE

Antik-Hotel Bristol ★★   The Bristol is exceptional in that each of its rooms is furnished with genuine antiques, either regal or rustic. There's a different type of antique bed in almost every room, ranging from French baroque and rococo to something reminiscent of High Rhenish ecclesiastical art; the oldest four-poster dates from 1742. The Bristol stands in a little park, with lots of greenery, flowers, and fountains. It's near a U-Bahn stop and within walking distance of the cathedral.

Kaiser-Wilhelm-Ring 48, 50672 Köln. www.antik-hotel-bristol.de. ✆ **0221/120195.** Fax 0221/131495. 44 units. 118€ double; from 136€ suite. Rates include buffet breakfast. AE, DC, MC, V. Parking 12€. U-Bahn: Christophstrasse. **Amenities:** Bar; babysitting; concierge; room service. *In room:* TV, hair dryer, minibar, Wi-Fi (free).

Barceló Cologne City Center ★   Opening directly onto the Rudolfplatz, one of Cologne's most famous squares, this is a modern first-class hotel with a lot of special features, such as a heated indoor pool. Rooms come in a wide range, beginning with standard accommodations and going up to superior rooms with views of the cathedral. Special features include double-glazed windows and sleek, contemporary decor with first-rate amenities. Rooms often come with three phones. Both regional and French cuisine are served, attracting an international crowd that feels at home in this cosmopolitan neighborhood.

Habsburgerring 9–11, 50674 Köln. www.barcelocolognecitycenter.com. ✆ **0211/2280.** 301 units. 89€–129€ double; from 189€ junior suite. AE, MC, V. Parking 16€. U-Bahn: Neumarkt. **Amenities:** Restaurant; bar; babysitting; concierge; exercise room; indoor heated pool, room service. *In room:* A/C, TV, hair dryer, minibar, Wi-Fi (free).

Chelsea ★ 👔   This is one of Cologne's most chic designer boutique hotels, a favorite of painters, art-gallery owners, and other artists. The artfully designed and glamorously contemporary bedrooms have huge, beautifully maintained bathrooms. Original pieces of art fill this well-designed hotel. If you'd like more space and don't mind spending extra euros, you can opt for one of the junior suites or apartments. The on-site restaurant and cafe is a sophisticated rendezvous point and features a finely honed blend of art and food. It takes about 20 minutes to walk to the center of town.

Jülicherstrasse 1, Belgisches Viertel, 50674 Köln. www.hotel-chelsea.de. ✆ **0221/207150.** Fax 0221/239137. 35 units. 92€–149€ double; 120€–235€ junior suite or apt. AE, DC, MC, V. Parking 8€. U-Bahn: Rudolfplatz. **Amenities:** Restaurant; bar. *In room:* TV, hair dryer, minibar, Wi-Fi (free).

Hopper Hotel et cetera ★ 👔   The unusual name of this hotel provides no clue as to its former role as one of the monasteries of Cologne. Only the statue of a bishop in the lobby evokes any former ecclesiastical role. The interior, which received a radically contemporary overhaul, contrasts dramatically with the older landmark-status exterior. Some of Cologne's finer artists have their works on display in the bedrooms, which are elegantly but a bit sparsely furnished. The parquet floors are made of eucalyptus, and the units are fitted with handsomely designed cherrywood furnishings. Try to avoid the small so-called "cloister cells," rooms better suited for the monks of old. Two of the double rooms have connecting doors, making them suitable for families. We'd opt for one of the junior suites if available, as they come with such extra amenities as a kitchenette. The top-floor room boasts a roof terrace and deck chair. The hotel lies in the fashionable district of Cologne known as Belgisches Viertel.

Brüsselerstrasse 26, 50674 Köln. www.hopper.de. ✆/fax **0221/924400.** 49 units. 120€–140€ double; 150€–170€ suite. Rates include continental breakfast. AE, DC, MC, V. Parking 13€. U-Bahn: Molttestrasse. **Amenities:** Restaurant; exercise room; sauna. *In room:* TV, hair dryer, minibar, Wi-Fi (free).

Hopper Hotel St. Antonius Named after a statue of St. Antonius that stands in the garden (the owners bought it during a holiday in Portugal), this hotel rises five very modern floors from a location in the heart of Cologne's historic core. You'll register in a lobby sheathed with slabs of gray stone and floored with stone mosaics. The same colors are repeated within the very contemporary-looking bedrooms, with wooden floors, marble-sheathed bathrooms, and teak-wood furniture. This is a well-selected and popular choice with lots of comfort and style and an articulate staff.

Dagobertstrasse 32, 50668 Köln. www.hopper.de. ℰ **0221/16600.** Fax 0221/1660166. 54 units. 145€–180€ double; 170€–220€ suite. AE, DC, MC, V. Parking 13€. U-Bahn: Ebertplatz or Dom/Hauptbahnhof. **Amenities:** Restaurant; bar; room service. *In room:* TV, fax, kitchenette (in some), minibar, Wi-Fi (free).

Santo ★ 🛏 This hotel comes as a surprise in Cologne because it's so different from its competitors—an oasis of feng shui with an array of orchids and open spaces, plus a beautiful teak bar in the front. Light is the focal point of the architects' philosophy, and the staff is trained in offering individualized hospitality. The hotel is a unique blend of materials, some of it old, such as fine oak wood. But it's also as modern as tomorrow with its Kreon lamps creating shifting patterns of light. The bathrooms are laid out in a sleek, contemporary fashion, and the minimalist bedrooms are comfortable with an elegant design that relies on simplicity more than clutter. Only breakfast is provided, but there are many good restaurants nearby.

Dagoberstrasse 22, 50668 Köln. www.hotelsanto.de. ℰ **0221/9139770.** Fax 0221/913977777. 69 units. 119€–160€ double. Rates include buffet breakfast. AE, DC, MC, V. Parking 15€. U-Bahn: Ebertplatz. **Amenities:** Bar; room service. *In room:* A/C, TV, hair dryer.

INEXPENSIVE

Brandenburger Hof In this family style hotel, all rooms are small and pleasantly decorated, and many come with a private bathroom. For those that don't, corridor bathrooms are adequate, with a couple on each floor. A full breakfast, including orange juice and eggs, is served in a cozy room or, in summer, in the garden. The hotel is about 3 blocks from the river and within walking distance of the cathedral.

Brandenburgerstrasse 2–4, 50668 Köln. www.brandenburgerhof.de. ℰ **0221/122889.** Fax 0221/135304. 45 units, 28 with bathroom. 50€–95€ double without bathroom; 70€–155€ double with bathroom; 75€–120€ triple without bathroom; 85€–195€ triple with bathroom; 85€–130€ quad without bathroom. Rates include continental breakfast. No credit cards. Free parking. U-Bahn: Hauptbahnhof. **Amenities:** Wi-Fi (free; in lobby). *In room:* No phone.

Coellner Hof 🍴 Set within a 10-minute walk north of the cathedral, this six-story, turn-of-the-20th-century building houses a well-maintained, comfortable hotel that has received well-deserved praise from several readers. Public areas are distinguished looking, and some, including the dining room, are richly paneled. Each room is decorated in a conservative, solid style that evokes a baronial German home. The newer bedrooms have been updated in a crisp, comfortable, and clean modern international style that's soothing in its use of neutral, monochromatic colors and dark hardwoods. Bedrooms are larger than the norm in government-rated three-star hotels.

Hansaring 100, 50670 Köln. www.coellnerhof.de. ℰ **0221/16660.** Fax 0221/1666166. 78 units. 80€–195€ double. Rates include continental breakfast. AE, DC, MC, V. Parking 8€. U-Bahn: Ebertplatz. **Amenities:** Bar; restaurant; sauna. *In room:* TV, hair dryer, Wi-Fi (free).

DÜSSELDORF ★

40km (25 miles) N of Cologne (Köln), 230km (143 miles) NW of Frankfurt

Wealthy Düsseldorf, the richest city in Germany, is situated in the western North Rhine-Westphalia region. It's large, full of banks, offices and skyscrapers, but it's also refreshingly clean. Düsseldorf began as a settlement on the right bank of the Rhine, but today it's spread out on both sides—the older part on the right, and the avant-garde, commercial, and industrial part on the left. Parks and esplanades line the riverbanks and today it's the most elegant metropolis in the Rhine Valley.

Things to Do   Wander through the **Altstadt** (Old Town), a thick ribbon of cobbled lanes in the center of town and admire its 1573 Gothic **Rathaus** (City Hall). North of the **Rathaus** you'll spy the 13th-century **St-Lambertus Basilika** (St. Lambertis Church)—it stands out like a brilliant giant with its splendid, twisted spire. After, head east to the **Kunstsammlung Nordrhein-Westfalen: K20,** a contemporary black glass museum. Its post-WWII art includes more than 100 Paul Klee paintings.

Shopping   The Rhine Valley's most famous shopping street, **Königsallee,** resides in the center of town. Lined with high-end designer shops like Gucci and Chanel to make your credit card ache, it's fun to window-shop. On a slow stroll, ponder the elaborate displays of haute couture and take in the elegant, swanky feel. Don't be surprised if you pass ladies in fur coats boutique-hopping—Düsseldorf is a magnet for fashionistas.

Nightlife & Entertainment   Nightlife centers around the **Altstadt,** which brims with inviting bars and historic beer taverns. The area feels like one big bar on weekends and it can get rather boisterous, but it's all in good, friendly fun. Many venues here serve Düsseldorf's signature **Altbier,** a dark, semisweet brew. Drop by **Bräuerei Schumacher,** a well-loved stalwart with exposed timber overhead and tile-decorated walls. This brewpub only serves its own beers, including Schumacher Alt, its version of the city's popular Altbier, of course.

Restaurants & Dining   Düsseldorf's most historic restaurant (notables from Napoleon to Arthur Miller allegedly once ate here) is **Zum Schiffchen.** Settle into the atmospheric, rustic space for belly-filling *Wursts* and *Schnitzels*, plus lighter seasonal specialties like white asparagus in May. A 180-degree turn literally awaits you at **Rheinturm Top 180 Restaurant,** where you can sample international fare, like rack of lamb with rosemary potatoes and salmon with lime crust, while slowly spinning atop the otherworldly **Rheinturm,** a silvery communication tower and Düsseldorf's tallest building.

Essentials
GETTING THERE

By Plane   Düsseldorf International Airport, 6km (4 miles) north of the city, has regularly scheduled connections to 14 German, 47 European, and 132 international airports. You can fly from Frankfurt to Düsseldorf in just 45 minutes or from Munich or Berlin in an hour. For flight information, call ℂ **0211/4210** or visit www.duesseldorf-international.de.

The airport is linked to the **GermanRail** network. Transfer to the Düsseldorf main rail station is via S-Bahn 11, offering service daily 4:03am to 12:30am, with trains every 20 minutes (trip time: 12 min.). One-way fare is 3€. For information, call ℂ **01805/996633** (www.bahn.de). Regular airport buses also connect the airport with Bonn and Cologne. A taxi ride to central Düsseldorf takes about 20 to 30 minutes and costs from 25€, depending on traffic.

By Train   The main train station, the **Düsseldorf Hauptbahnhof,** on Konrad-Adenauer-Platz in the southeastern sector, offers frequent connections to all major cities. The trip time to Frankfurt is about 2½ hours; to Munich, about 7 hours. For information, call © **01805/996633** (www.bahn.de). Düsseldorf also has extensive regional rail links; for information on regional trains or trams, call © **0211/58228.** Luggage-storage facilities are available at the Hauptbahnhof.

By Bus   Access to Düsseldorf is a lot easier by rail than by bus. The region's largest carrier is **Adorf GmbH** (© **0211/418970;** www.adorf.de), most of whose buses service small towns within the Rhineland that don't necessarily have railway stations of their own. Buses usually pull into Düsseldorf at the northern edge of the Bahnhofplatz.

By Car   Access to Düsseldorf is by the A3 Autobahn north and south or the A46 east and west.

VISITOR INFORMATION

For information, go to the **Tourist Office,** Immermannstrasse 65B (© **0211/ 17202844;** www.duesseldorf-tourismus.de), opposite the railway station. It's open Monday to Saturday 9:30am to 7pm. The office also has a hotel reservations service, which charges a one-time booking fee of 5€, along with a deposit that equals the price of the first night's accommodations. For the tourist office's room reservation services, call © **0211/1720224** Monday to Saturday 9:30am to 6:30pm.

GETTING AROUND

Düsseldorf is a big, sprawling city, so you'll probably want to rely on public transportation. The city and environs are served by a network of **S-Bahn railways** that fan out to the suburbs, along with **buses, Strassenbahn (trams),** and a **U-Bahn** system. Ask at the tourist office (© **0211/17202844**) about purchasing a **Düsseldorf WelcomeCard,** offering free use of public transportation as well as free entrance to city museums, and reductions on city tours, boat rides, and opera and ballet tickets. Valid for 24 hours, the welcome card costs 9€ for an adult or 18€ for a group/family card (two adults plus two children 14 and under, or three adults). A welcome card valid for 48 hours goes for 14€ for an adult or 28€ for a group/family card. A 72-hour card is available for 19€ for individuals and 38€ for groups/families.

Taxi meters begin at 5.50€ for the first 2km, after which you'll be billed 1.70€ per kilometer. To call for a taxi in Düsseldorf, dial © **0211/33333.**

Exploring Düsseldorf

As in most German cities, there's an **Altstadt (Old Town),** with a **Marktplatz (Marketplace),** a Gothic **Rathaus (Town Hall),** and a few old buildings and churches. Near the Rathaus on Burgplatz are two of the city's most famous landmarks, the twisted spire of **St-Lambertus Basilika (St. Lambertus Church)** and the **Schlossturm (Castle Tower),** both of 13th-century origin. A short walk to the east takes you to **St-Andreas Basilika (St. Andreas Church).**

The Altstadt has been called "the longest bar in the world" because of the 200-plus bars and restaurants found here. The favorite drink is a top-fermented Altbier (old beer); it's a dark, mellow brew that must be consumed soon after it's made.

A walk up **Königsallee,** called the "Kö" by Düsseldorfers, will give visitors a quick overview of the city and its residents. This street flanks an ornamental canal, shaded

Düsseldorf

ATTRACTIONS ●

Deutsche Oper am Rhein **13**
Goethe-Museum Düsseldorf **9**
Heinrich-Heine-Institut **18**
Hofgarten **7**
Königsallee **11**
Kunsthalle Düsseldorf **5**
Kunstsammlung
  Nordrhein-Westfalen:
  K20 Kunstsammlung
  am Grabbeplatz **4**

Kunstsammlung
  Nordrhein-Westfalen:
  K21 Kunstsammlung
  im Ständehaus **20**
Museum Kunst Palast **2**
Rathaus **17**
St. Andreas Basilika **14**
St. Lambertus Basilika **15**
St. Rochus Basilika **8**
Schauspielhaus **10**
Schlossturm **16**

Thyssen-Haus **6**
Tonhalle (Düsseldorf
  Symphony Orchestra) **3**

HOTELS ■

Ashley's Garden **1**
Fürstenhof **21**
Radisson SAS Media Harbour
  Hotel **19**
Steigenberger Park-Hotel **12**
Wurms Hotel **22**

by trees and crossed by bridges. One bank is lined with office buildings, the other with elegant shops, cafes, and restaurants. Here you'll see women dressed in the very latest styles. Düsseldorf is the fashion center of Germany. It's known for its Fashion Weeks, which attract designers and buyers from all over Europe.

If you walk up the Kö toward the Trident Fountain at the northern end of the canal, you'll reach the **Hofgarten,** a huge, rambling park. Here you can wander along paths or sit and relax amid shade trees, gardens, fountains, and statues, almost forgetting you're in the very center of the city. Among the monuments is one to the poet Heinrich Heine. The Hofgarten is a good central point for seeing the city's major attractions—nearly all museums and cultural attractions are on its perimeter. Towering over the Hofgarten is Düsseldorf's most impressive skyscraper, the **Thyssen-Haus.** Residents call it the Dreischeibenhaus ("three-slice house"), because it actually looks like three huge monoliths sandwiched together. Northeast of the Hofgarten is **Basilika St. Rochus,** one of the city's finest modern churches.

Düsseldorf continues its bold march into the 21st century, especially in its once dilapidated but now trendy **MedienHafen** district. Originally this was a flourishing warehouse sector in the 19th century. Today it is often a showcase for modern architecture, especially in the office buildings and other works of Frank O. Gehry, winner of the Pritzker prize, the Nobel Prize of architecture. Of course, Gehry's far better known work is his celebrated titanium masterpiece, the Guggenheim Museum in Bilbao, Spain.

Düsseldorf's most striking example of his work is the ensemble of "organic-looking" high-rises at Neuer Zollhof. This trio of buildings with their wavy lines can easily be spotted along the waterfront. Yachts and luxury cruisers stud the harbor at the foot of the Rhine Tower of MedienHafen. For the best view of these avant-garde buildings, including Gehry's controversial architecture, walk down the water-bordering promenade, Am Handelshafen, beginning at the **Rheim Turm (Rhine Tower),** heading toward Franziusstrasse.

Goethe-Museum Düsseldorf MUSEUM   The Anton and Katharina Kippenberg Foundation sponsors this literary museum dedicated to Goethe's life and work. It emerged from the Kippenbergs' private collection of some 35,000 items, including autographs, books, busts, paintings, coins, medals, plaques, and china. About 1,000 pieces are shown in the permanent exhibition, including first drafts of well-known poems. The displays present a chronology of Goethe's life and work. There are also exhibits on various topics of the Goethe era.

Schloss-Jägerhof, Jacobistrasse 2. *©* **0211/8996262.** www.goethe-museum.com. Admission 3€ adults, 1.50€ children. Tues–Fri and Sun 11am–5pm; Sat 1–5pm. Tram: 704 or 707. Bus: 722 or 800.

Heinrich-Heine-Institut MUSEUM   Heinrich Heine (1797–1856) was Germany's greatest lyric poet. More than 10,000 volumes, as well as the manuscript bequest of this Düsseldorf-born poet, are found here. Born into a Jewish family, Heine nominally converted to Christianity so that he could attend law school. He was the author of the famous *Die Lorelei,* and his poems were set to music by Schubert, Schumann, and Hugo Wolf. His work was prohibited during the Nazi era, during which *Die Lorelei* was officially attributed to an unknown author. In the Altstadt, you visit the house where Heine was born. It's at Bolkerstrasse 53 and is marked by a plaque.

Bilkerstrasse 12–14. *©* **0211/8895574.** Admission 3€ adults, free for children 17 and under. Tues–Fri and Sun 11am–5pm; Sat 1–5pm. Tram: 704 or 707.

Kunsthalle Düsseldorf MUSEUM   The Kunsthalle Düsseldorf is devoted to contemporary art from the Rhineland and throughout Europe. No other museum in the city keeps up with changing trends in art as well as this one. Visiting exhibits of every shape and size, often bizarre, are displayed here. If time remains, visit the museum's latest attraction, KIT (Kunst im Tunnel). This is an "art tunnel" literally under the museum. Here up-and-coming artists display their work, and exhibitions are frequently changed.

Grabbeplatz 4. ⓒ **0211/8996243.** www.kunsthalle-duesseldorf.de. Admission 5.50€ adults, 3.50€ students and children 10–15, free for children 9 and under. Tues–Sun 11am–6pm. U-Bahn: Heinrich-Heine-Allee. Across from the Kunstsammlung Nordrhein-Westfalen, west of the Hofgarten.

Kunstsammlung Nordrhein-Westfalen: K2O Kunstsammlung am Grabbeplatz ★ MUSEUM   This museum is divided into two museums, but the K20 Grabbeplatz location is the older and superior art center (see next review below for the second location). The black-glass edifice here is one of the most stunning modern buildings in the city. The most important exhibit is a collection of nearly 100 paintings by Paul Klee, the famous Swiss painter who once taught at Düsseldorf's National Academy of Art. The museum also displays an outstanding exhibition of surrealist art, including Salvador Dalí. Some of the major modern 20th-century artists are on display, including works by everybody from Picasso to Matisse, along with Bonnard, Léger, Johns, and Pollock. You'll also see a series of American masterpieces dating from 1946, as well as some of the lesser known but very celebrated painters of the 20th century, including art by Markus Lüpertz, Per Kirkeby, and Gerhard Richter. Six major temporary exhibits of art land here annually.

Grabbeplatz 5 (opposite the Kunsthalle). ⓒ **0211/8381130.** www.kunstsammlung.de. Admission 6.50€ adults, 4.50€ students and children. Tues–Fri 10am–6pm (until 10pm 1st Wed of every month); Sat–Sun 11am–6pm. U-Bahn: Heinrich-Heine-Allee.

Kunstsammlung Nordrhein-Westfalen: K21 Kunstsammlung im Ständehaus MUSEUM   This is the second division of the more famous K20 Kunstsammlung (see above). On display at K21 is international art that dates from 1980 and extends into the postmillennium period. It defines itself—and certainly its future—as a museum for the art of the 21st century. This is a museum in the making, and it is expected that its fledgling collection will be beefed up every year as bequests come in. The present collection is augmented by contributing museums that agree to lend great art for a limited period. K21 also displays works from some of the great collections in private hands in Germany. Don't expect all future art to be paintings. As a showplace of the 21st century, photography is embraced, as are moving images on film and video. If you have limited time, head for K20. But if you want to take "potluck," see what's being displayed at K21. It will certainly be worth your while.

Ständehausstrasse 1. ⓒ **0211/8381600.** www.kunstsammlung.de. Admission 6.50€ adults, 4.50€ students and children. Tues–Fri 10am–6pm (until 10pm 1st Wed of every month); Sat–Sun 11am–6pm. Tram: 703, 706, 712, 713, or 715 to Graf-Adolf-Platz.

Museum Kunst Palast ★ MUSEUM   This is one of the largest and most comprehensive museums in the Rhineland. The painting collection includes works by Rubens, Caspar David Friedrich, and the Die Brücke and Der Blaue Reiter schools. The sculpture collection ranges from the late Middle Ages to the 20th century. There are also some 80,000 prints and drawings, as well as early Persian bronzes and ceramics, a glass collection, textiles from late antiquity to the present, and a design collection.

Ehrenhof 5. ⓒ **0211/8990200.** www.museum-kunst-palast.de. Admission 11€ adults, 9€ students and children. Tues–Sun 11am–6pm, until 9pm Thurs. Tram: 701, 706, 711, or 715.

Where to Eat

VERY EXPENSIVE

Im Schiffchen ★★★ FRENCH/SEAFOOD   The chefs at Im Schiffchen deliver a refined, brilliantly realized repertoire of the finest cuisine you'll find in any city along the Rhine. The ingredients that go into the meals are unimpeachably authentic— every tomato, every onion, every fish or piece of meat seems to have been thoroughly evaluated for quality before purchasing. The menu is ever-changing, based on seasonal variations, but you might find homemade goose-liver pâté with green peppercorns, Brittany lobster in chamomile petals, a delectable Norwegian salmon in Vouvray sauce, or lobster cooked in chamomile tea. We could return again and again for the pikeperch cooked aromatically in puff pastry. The desserts are luscious; try the granulated fruit mélange with almond cream.

Kaiserswerther Markt 9. ✆ **0211/401050.** www.im-schiffchen.com. Reservations required. Main courses 32€–56€. AE, DC, MC, V. Tues–Sat 7–10:30pm. Tram: 79 to Klemensplatz. On the outskirts of the city, at Kaiserswerth.

Victorian Restaurant ★★★ CONTINENTAL/INTERNATIONAL   This is the finest restaurant in the city center. The decor features sparkling crystal, black-leather banquettes, and masses of flowers. The food represents the best of both traditional and modern schools. The best examples include heavenly deep-fried zucchini flowers stuffed with lobster mousse and flavored with a sauce of champagne vinegar and coriander, apple salad with slices of goose liver, and three-vegetable purée. The delectable desserts change with the inspiration of the pastry chef but might include terrine of oranges served with raspberry liqueur and fresh mint.

Nearby is the **Bistro im Victorian,** with a minimalist interior design. The kitchen area is wide open, so you can watch as the fresh ingredients are whipped into meals. Main courses in the Bistro cost from 18€ to 26€.

Königstrasse 3A. ✆ **0211/865500.** www.restaurant-victorian.de. Reservations required for the restaurant, recommended for the bistro. Main courses 24€–68€; fixed-price menus lunch 34€–48€, dinner 78€–118€. AE, DC, MC, V. Mon–Sat noon–3pm and 7–11pm. Tram: 77 or 79.

EXPENSIVE

Rheinturm Top 180 Restaurant ★ GERMAN/INTERNATIONAL   This futuristic restaurant is set atop the spool-shaped summit of the city's tallest tower (172m/564 ft.) and revolves slowly, affording a 360-degree panorama of Düsseldorf's buildings and parks. Most people come here for the view, but the food is competently prepared and includes grills, game dishes, fish, and soups. Try the slices of smoked duck breast with creamy savoy cabbage, or rolls of salmon stuffed with turbot filling and served in Riesling-and-saffron sauce. Vegetarian courses are also featured. Menu items focus on fresh seasonal ingredients, and the menu sometimes celebrates the arrival of fresh asparagus in springtime, as well as fresh fish and fresh game whenever it's in season. A trip to the tower's observation deck costs 3.60€ for adults, 2.90€ for children 13 to 17, and 2€ for children 6 to 12; kids 5 and under go free. The tower is open daily 10am to 11:30pm.

Stromstrasse 20. ✆ **0211/8632000.** www.guennewig.de. Reservations recommended. Main courses 23€–31€. AE, DC, MC, V. Daily noon–2:30pm and 6:30–11:30pm. Tram: 704, 709, or 719. Bus: 725.

MODERATE

Zum Schiffchen ★ RHINELANDER   Come here if you're looking for Düsseldorf's most traditional and atmospheric restaurant. Zum Schiffchen, in the heart of the Altstadt, is the city's oldest restaurant. A golden model ship on top of the step-gabled building (which dates from 1628) reminds you of its location, near the river. The interior follows the tavern tradition of scrubbed wooden tables and rustic artifacts. Good, hefty portions of regional cuisine are the rule here. Menu items include such two-fisted German specialties as *Wursts, Sauerbraten, Schnitzels,* knuckle of pork with roast potatoes, and great emphasis on seasonal specialties like asparagus. The menu is large, and the service by the blue-aproned waiters (called *Köbesse*) is rather hectic. Zum Schiffchen is the perfect place to sample Frankenheim, Düsseldorf's local beer. Over the years, the restaurant has attracted a host of famous diners, ranging from Napoleon and Heinrich Heine to Arthur Miller.

Hafenstrasse 5. ⓒ **0211/132421.** www.brauerei-zum-schiffchen.de. Reservations required. Main courses 10€–29€. AE, DC, MC, V. Mon–Sat 11am–10:45pm. U-Bahn: Heinrich-Heine-Allee. A block from the Rhine.

INEXPENSIVE

Im Alten Bierhause RHINELANDER   Lying 1.5km (1 mile) from the center, this place is actually more of a wine tavern than a restaurant. The building dates from 1641. Style connoisseurs will recognize it as typical of the Rhine's left bank (as opposed to the right, the left bank has more of a bohemian aura). Traditional German specialties are served here. The house specialty is *Speck-Pfannenkuchen,* a bacon pancake; a similar version is made with marmalade. On Sunday the beer drinkers pile in at 11am. The specialty of the house is that dark and foamy local brew, Altbier.

Alt-Niederkassel 75. ⓒ **0211/551272.** www.meuser1853.de. Reservations required. Main courses 10€–25€. No credit cards. Tues–Sat 3–11:30pm; Sun 11am–11pm. Closed 3 weeks in July–Aug (dates vary). Bus: 834. On the outskirts.

Zum Schlüssel GERMAN   As Germanic as the Rhine and set within the pedestrian zone in the heart of town, Zum Schlüssel thrived as a brewery under the name Alt Gatzweiler during the early 20th century, then folded, and was reborn as a smaller-scale brewery. Today, its fermentation vats and elaborate pipes are visible from the wood-sheathed dining room. The beer that arrives in frothy mugs is the Alt Schlüssel brand, available in various degrees of darkness, depending on the season. Menu items are Germanic dishes that complement the beer, and include *Sauerbraten, Schnitzel, Eisbein* (pork knuckles), homemade soups, freshly made salads, and succulent steaks.

Zum Schlüssel Bolkerstrasse 43–47. ⓒ **0211/8289550.** www.zumschluessel.de. Reservations recommended. Main courses 8€–16€; fixed-price menus 21€–27€. AE, DC, MC, V. Daily 10am–midnight (Fri–Sat until 1am). U-Bahn: Heinrich-Heine-Allee.

Shopping

Düsseldorf is a city of high fashion and high prices. Many chic Europeans visit the city just to shop for what's new and hot. The best and trendiest fashions are sold on the opulent east side of the Königsallee. The two largest concentrations of designer shops are found at the **Kö Galerie,** Königsallee 60, and the **Kö Center,** Königsallee 30. Each gallery has some 100 shops. Those not interested in dishing out lots of euros for designer duds should head for the more recently opened **Schadow Arcade,** off Schadowplatz, at the end of the Kö. Fashion here isn't so haute, but neither are the prices. Shoppers spend some 500 million euros in the shops on Schadowstrasse annually—more than is spent on any other street in the country.

ANTIQUES   Düsseldorf's historic core contains a fine selection of antiques stores. **Lothar Heubel,** Bastionstrasse 27 (© 0211/134103; U-Bahn: Heinrich-Heine-Allee), specializes in Asian and African antiques, including jewelry, ceramics, and Chinese items from the Han, Ming, and Tang dynasties, mixed in with a handful of antiques from Provence and the south of France.

DEPARTMENT STORES   **Carsch Haus,** Heinrich-Heine-Platz (© 0211/83970; www.galeria-kaufhof.de; U-Bahn: Heinrich-Heine-Allee), carries a good selection of fashions, as well as quality home furnishings, jewelry, and other items.

DESIGNER CLOTHING & ACCESSORIES   **Bogner Haus,** Königsallee 6–8 (© 0211/134222), carries functional sportswear that's meant for action on the golf course, tennis court, and ski slopes. The designers have their workshop on the second floor.

Chanel, Kö Center (© 0211/325935; www.chanel.com), offers the company's complete line of products, from clothing to cosmetics and fragrances.

Shoes and more shoes fill the racks at **Walter Steiger Schuhe,** Grunstrasse 4 (© 0211/134104), the German designer of high-quality, high-fashion footwear. In the boutique of **Louis Vuitton,** Kö Center (© 0211/323230; www.louisvuitton. com), leather accessories, luggage, and handbags are sold.

JEWELRY & WATCHES   Located in the heart of the designer shopping district, **Wempe Juwelier,** Königsallee 14 (© 0211/324077; www.wempe.de), is one of a chain of 23 shops scattered throughout Düsseldorf that carries Swiss watches and jewelry designs in gold, silver, and precious stones.

Entertainment & Nightlife

The place to go for nightlife in Düsseldorf is the **Altstadt.** This .8 sq. km (⅓ sq. mile) of narrow streets and alleyways, between Königsallee and the Rhine River, is jam-packed with restaurants, dance clubs, art galleries, boutiques, nightclubs, and some 200 song-filled beer taverns. Düsseldorfers refer to a night cruising the Altstadt as an *Altstadtbummel.*

THE PERFORMING ARTS   Classical music has long had an illustrious association with this city, once home to Brahms, Mendelssohn, and Schumann (though there are no specific tourist sites relating to them in Düsseldorf). Therefore, it's not surprising that both the **Düsseldorfer Symphoniker** and its home, **Tonhalle,** Ehrenhof 1 (© 0211/8996123 box office; www.tonhalle-duesseldorf.de; U-Bahn: Tonhalle), are world famous. The Tonhalle is perhaps Germany's most successful modern concert hall after Berlin's Philharmonie. The highly regarded orchestra gives about a dozen concerts a year, with tickets running 25€ to 89€. **Deutsche Oper am Rhein,** Heinrich-Heine-Allee 16A (© 0211/8908211; www.rheinoper.de; U-Bahn: Heinrich-Heine-Allee), is one of the city's renowned opera and ballet companies. Tickets are 11€ to 120€.

Schauspielhaus, Gustav-Gründgens-Platz 1 (© 0211/85230; www.duesseldorfer-schauspielhaus.de; U-Bahn: Heinrich-Heine-Allee), is known all over Germany for its outstanding productions and acting. Performances (in German) take place September to June, and tickets cost 14€ to 44€.

BARS & BEER HALLS   The oldest brewery-bar in the city is **Bräuerei Schumacher,** Oststrasse 123 (© 0211/8289020; www.schumacher-alt.de; U-Bahn: Oststrasse), a popular establishment that serves only beer brewed by its parent company. It's open daily 10am to midnight. Two other breweries, each serving beer brewed on the premises, are **Brauerei im Füchschen,** Ratingerstrasse 28 (© **0211/137470;** www.fuechschen.de; U-Bahn: Heinrich-Heine-Allee), and **Bräuerei zum Schlüssel,** Bolkerstrasse 43 (© **0211/828955;** www.hausbrauerei-zum-schluessel.de; U-Bahn: Heinrich-Heine-Allee), both of which also offer platters of German food.

DANCE CLUBS A hot dance spot, **Stahwerk,** Ronsdorferstrasse 134 (© **0211/730350;** www.stahlwerk.de; U-Bahn: Langenbergerstrasse), intersperses recorded dance music with live acts from throughout Europe. The club draws a mixed, fashion-conscious crowd. Charging a cover of 6€ to 18€, it is open Friday and Saturday 10pm to about 6am.

LIVE MUSIC CLUBS A popular piano bar, **Bei Tino,** Königsallee 21 (© **0211/326463;** www.beitino.com; U-Bahn: Königsallee), has music noon to 3am nightly; guests are often allowed to play the piano. **McLaughlin's Irish Pub,** Kurzestrasse 11 (© **0211/324611;** www.mclaughlins.de; U-Bahn: Heinrich-Heine-Allee), serves Guinness and Murphy's as well as traditional Irish food, and presents touring Irish bands on the weekend. It's open Sunday to Thursday 5pm to 1am and Friday and Saturday 11am to 3am.

GAY CLUBS You'll find Düsseldorf's gay nightlife integrated into straight clubs (a trend happening all over western Europe these days).

Where to Stay
VERY EXPENSIVE
Steigenberger Park-Hotel ★★ This traditional deluxe German hotel has been completely modernized and reequipped to meet modern demands. Its central location, overlooking the Hofgarten Park, is virtually unbeatable, which may explain why it attracts so many conventions and groups. The Steigenberger maintains a high level of service in the old-world style. All rooms, refitted to the latest standards, are cozy and comfortable. Bathrooms have makeup mirrors, robes, and the latest plumbing.

Königsallee 1a, 40212 Düsseldorf 1. www.steigenberger.de. © **800/223-5652** in the U.S. and Canada, or 0211/13810. Fax 0211/1381592. 134 units. 240€–265€ double; from 700€ suite. Rates include buffet breakfast. AE, DC, MC, V. Free parking. Tram: 78 or 79. Bus: 778. **Amenities:** Restaurant; 2 bars; babysitting; concierge; exercise room; room service; spa. *In room:* A/C (in some), TV, hair dryer, minibar, Wi-Fi (18€ per day).

EXPENSIVE
Ashley's Garden ★★ Posh, upscale, distinguished, and very quiet, this hotel occupies what was built in 1938 as a stately looking villa in the wealthy residential suburb of Golzheim, 5km (3 miles) north of the city center. Set within a 5-minute walk of both the Rhine and the Düsseldorf *Messe* (fairgrounds), it's completely outfitted, in both the bedrooms and the public areas, with English antiques and yard upon yard of Laura Ashley fabrics. The overall feel is that of an English country house. Terraces overlook a pleasant garden. Bedrooms are exceedingly comfortable, beautifully furnished, and spacious for the most part.

Karl-Kleppe-Strasse 20, 40474 Düsseldorf Ortsteil Golzheim. www.ashleysgarden.de. © **0211/5161710.** Fax 0211/453299. 42 units. 150€–365€ double. Rates include continental breakfast. AE, DC, MC, V. Free parking. U-Bahn: Reeserplatz. **Amenities:** Restaurant; bar; bikes; outdoor pool. *In room:* TV, Wi-Fi (free).

Radisson Blu Media Harbour Hotel ★ The architect of this hotel was inspired by the harbor, creating a stunning V-shaped facade of Brazilian slate with panoramic windows. The outer walls not only look transparent, but also slant. In the center of MedienHafen, an emerging district south of the center, the hotel offers luxurious and stylish bedrooms, furnished in a dramatically modern style. Its lounge with a fireplace is a cozy retreat, and the Italian food at **Amano** is among the best in the city. Both the vacationer and the business traveler will find comfort here.

Hammer Strasse 23, 40219 Düsseldorf. www.mediaharbour.duesseldorf.radissonsas.com. © **800/333-3332** or 0211/311190. Fax 0211/3119110. 135 units. 146€–370€ double; from 488€ suite. AE, DC, MC, V. **Amenities:** Restaurant; bar; concierge; exercise room; room service; sauna. *In room:* A/C, TV, hair dryer, minibar, Wi-Fi (free).

MODERATE

Maritim Hotel Düsseldorf ★ This is the largest hotel in the region, a magnet for conventions from many of the major corporations within the surrounding North Rhine and Westphalia region. Conveniently positioned near the airport, it is also suitable for both vacationers and business travelers. It boasts one of the best, most modern, and sophisticated decors of any hotel in Düsseldorf. The higher up you go, the better your room and facilities. Most accommodations are spacious and beautifully furnished. There are all sorts of special rooms here, even for those with vision or hearing impairments, and units for those with allergies.

Maritim Platz 1, 40474 Düsseldorf. www.maritim.de. © **0211/52090.** Fax 0211/52091000. 533 units. 135€–255€ double; 229€–605€ suite. AE, DC, MC, V. Parking 21€. **Amenities:** 3 restaurants; 2 bars; babysitting; concierge; exercise room; room service. *In room:* A/C, TV, hair dryer, minibar, Wi-Fi (19€ per day).

INEXPENSIVE

Fürstenhof This hotel is a good choice in the center of town. It's modern but not glaringly so and opens onto a tree-filled square. Rooms are handsomely furnished, each ranging in size from medium to spacious. Most of the guest rooms are at the lower end of the price scale. Half the breakfast room is reserved for nonsmoking guests.

Fürstenplatz 3, 40215 Düsseldorf 1. www.fuerstenhof-duesseldorf.de. © **0211/386460.** Fax 0211/379062. 43 units. 75€–245€ double. Rates include buffet breakfast. AE, DC, MC, V. Parking 7€. Closed Dec 24–Jan 2. Tram: 701, 707, or 708. Bus: 725. Pets allowed. **Amenities:** Babysitting; children's center; exercise room; room service; sauna. *In room:* A/C, TV, hair dryer, minibar, Wi-Fi (free).

Wurms Hotel 🔱 The Wurms Hotel, set in a five-story stucco building, is a good budget choice, even though it has an expensive room or two. The small rooms are done in dark wood offset by bright bedspreads and curtains. The buffet breakfast is the only meal served. The hotel is a short walk from the central landmark square, Graf-Adolf-Platz.

Scheurenstrasse 23, 40215 Düsseldorf. www.hotel-wurms.de. © **0211/375001.** Fax 0211/375003. 27 units. 85€–395€ double. Rates include buffet breakfast. MC, V. Parking 8€–15€. Tram: 734, 741, or 752. Bus: 835. Near Graf-Adolf-Strasse, about 4 blocks from the Hauptbahnhof. **Amenities:** Room service. *In room:* TV, Wi-Fi (10€ per day).

THE MOSEL VALLEY

I f ever you were searching for a river that was "off the beaten path," the Mosel would make a great candidate. More meandering and pastoral than the world-renowned Rhine into which it flows, the Mosel valley's verdant vineyards and lush forests blanket the hillsides, topped with castles both ruined and restored. Every village here tells a story, one that recalls the region's prominent status in Roman times, and its precarious proximity to France. If the scenery is not enough of a reason to visit, the region's excellent wines provide an added treat.

The Mosel (*Moselle* in French) springs out of the Vosges hills of France, and is at its most scenic in the 193 serpentine kilometers (120 miles) between Trier and Koblenz. Traveling downstream from Trier offers the chance to use the museums of the former Roman city as an introduction to the region. Also, one-way boat trips are slightly shorter, but who's in a rush? Trier caps off nicely a trip upstream from Koblenz, and is an ideal destination for visitors coming from the Rhine Valley, or the international airports at Frankfurt and Düsseldorf.

15

COCHEM ★

92km (57 miles) NE of Trier, 51km (32 miles) SW of Koblenz

A memorable highlight of your valley trip may be rounding a bend in the river and seeing this medieval town for the first time. At the base of a vineyard-covered hill topped with a castle, Cochem features three medieval gates (the Endertor, Martinstor, and Balduinstor), several half-timbered houses, and a large selection of inns. Its rail and road connections also make it a great overnight stopover between Koblenz and Trier.

Essentials

GETTING THERE

BY TRAIN   The architecturally striking **Cochem Bahnhof** is on the Trier-Koblenz rail line, with frequent service between these connecting cities. For information, call ℂ **01805/996633** (www.bahn.de).

BY BUS   Regional bus service along the Mosel is provided by **RMV Rhein Mosel Verkehrsgesellschaft** (ℂ **01805/7684636;** www.bahn. de) and by **Moselbahn, GmbH** (ℂ **06531/96800;** www.moselbahn.de).

BY CAR   Access is via the A48 Autobahn on the Koblenz-Trier express highway; exit either at Ulmen or at Kaisersesch.

BY BOAT   Boat rides on the Mosel River operate between Trier and Cochem. Contact **Gebrüder Kolb,** Briedern/Mosel (✆ **02673/1515;** www.moselfahrplan.de).

VISITOR INFORMATION
For tourist information, contact the **Verkehrsamt,** Endertplatz 1 (✆ **02671/60040;** www.cochem.de), open Monday to Friday 9am to 1pm and 2 to 5pm, in June also Saturday 9am to 3pm; from July to October, it is also open Saturday 9am to 5pm and Sunday 11am to 4pm.

SPECIAL EVENTS   Wine festivals celebrating the region's wines with tasting booths fill the small streets in the summer months, beginning with the **Mosel-Wein-Woche** in the last week in May or the first week of June. The **Cochemer Weinlagenfest** follows suit in late June and early July; a similar **Weinfest** wraps up the festivities in the last weekend of August. For information on either of these events, contact the tourist office (see above). They'll provide details on dates, activities, and accommodations.

Exploring Cochem

The town is a typical wine village, with tastings and festivals. But the biggest attraction is **Reichsburg Cochem ★** (✆ **02671/255;** www.burg-cochem.de). Like many castles in the valley, the original 1027 castle was laid to ruin by Louis XIV's army in 1689. Rebuilt in 1868 in the neo-Gothic style, its medieval ramparts and turrets create a dramatic backdrop for the town. To reach the castle, follow the steep footpath from the center of town; the 15-minute walk is well worth it for the rewarding views of the town and the Mosel below. Although you can visit the grounds anytime, the interior of the castle is open daily mid-March to mid-November 9am to 5pm. Guided tours (in English) are conducted at regular intervals. Admission is 5€ for adults, 4€ for students, 3€ for children 6 to 17 years old, and 15€ for a family ticket.

Where to Eat

L'Auberge du Vin ★ RHINELANDER   Within the town of Cochem itself, the best food, a traditional cuisine, is served by the Beth family. Their aim is to offer you the finest of their market-fresh shopping every day. Connoisseurs flock here to enjoy soup made with some of the fattest and most delectable snails in Germany. Fresh fish and game dishes, such as venison in autumn, round out the menu. Among the fish courses, you might enjoy the filet of pikeperch with fresh asparagus, or the scallops with tomato and noodles in a lobster sauce. Other praiseworthy dishes include breast of pigeon with "smashed" celery in a red-wine sauce, or saddle of lamb with ratatouille.

In the Lohspeicher, Obergasse 1. ✆ **02671/3976.** Reservations recommended. Main courses 25€–30€. MC, V. Thurs–Tues noon–2pm and 6–10pm. Closed Feb.

💬 **In Vino Veritas . . . with a Little Less Alcohol**

Due to the cold winter months Mosel wines have the lowest alcohol content (about 9%) of any white wine in the world. According to the German Wine Institute in Mainz, white wines make up 90% of the region's production, the highest output of any region in Germany. Sixty-five percent of the overall grapes are crisp Rieslings, with Müller-Thurgau coming in a distant second at 15%. Be sure to enjoy them young.

Weissmühle im Enderttal GERMAN   Set within the nearby shady and secluded valley of Enderttal, this restaurant's fine cuisine is popular with locals. You can dine within either the Müllerstube—a woodsy, antique-looking room that might remind you of an inn high in the Swiss Alps—or the brighter, sunnier, and larger Sommer-restaurant. A trademark dish is fresh trout from the small nearby lake, stuffed with herbs, baked, and kept warm at your table with a hot stone. The inn also rents 36 well-furnished bedrooms, each individually furnished in a rustic country style. The price per person for bed-and-breakfast ranges from 48€ to 58€.

Endertstrasse 1. © **02671/8955.** Fax 02671/8207. www.weissmuehle.de. Reservations recommended. Main courses 18€–28€. MC, V. Daily noon–2pm and 6–9pm. From Cochem's center, drive toward the A48, following the signs for Koblenz/Trier; the inn is on the left of the road, 1.5km (1 mile) northwest of Cochem.

Where to Stay

Alte Thorschenke ★   Both a hotel and a wine restaurant, the centrally located Alte Thorschenke is one of the oldest and best-known establishments along either side of the Mosel. The romantically conceived building, with its timbers and towers, was originally built in 1332. It became a hotel in 1960, when a modern wing was

Guests of the Alte Thorschenke can visit the 500-year-old **Schloss Landesberg,** Ediger-Eller (www.mosel-weinproben.de), about 7km (4½ miles) from Cochem. Here in the old cellars, you can taste some of the best wines produced along the banks of the Mosel. To arrange a visit if you're not staying at the hotel, call ✆ **02675/277.**

added. Most rooms are reached via a cantilevered wooden staircase that has creaked for centuries (there's also an elevator in the rear). Six rooms have four-poster beds; all units contain tub/shower combinations. There's also a romantic Napoleon suite.

Brückenstrasse 3, 56812 Cochem. www.castle-thorschenke.com. ✆ **02671/7059.** Fax 02671/4202. 35 units. 89€–130€ double; from 125€ suite. Rates include buffet breakfast. AE, DC, MC, V. Parking 6€ in garage. **Amenities:** Restaurant; room service. *In room:* TV, hair dryer, minibar.

Lohspeicher   This inn is good for an overnight stopover, although it's better known for its restaurant L'Auberge du Vin (see above) than for its rooms. This generously proportioned 1832 building with hand-hewn beams was once a warehouse. Rooms, though generally a bit small, are comfortably furnished, and have modern bathrooms. The team of Ingo, Birgit, and Laura Beth are the warmest hosts in the area.

Obergasse 1, 56812 Cochem. www.lohspeicher.de. ✆ **02671/3976.** Fax 02671/1772. 9 units. 45€–60€ per person double. Rates include buffet breakfast. MC, V. Parking 8€. Closed Feb. **Amenities:** Restaurant. *In room:* TV, hair dryer.

A Side Trip to Burg Eltz

Burg Eltz ★★ (✆ **02672/950500;** www.burg-eltz.de), a stately castle tucked up the Elzbach valley north of the river, is nearest to Moselkern and makes for a nice stopover between Cochem and Koblenz. It lies 20km (12 miles) northeast of Cochem and 29km (18 miles) southwest of Koblenz with access via the A48 and A61 autobahns and Route 416 on the left bank. A parking lot, Antoniuskapelle, less than 800m (½ mile) from the castle, can be reached via Münstermaifeld. A bus runs to the castle every 5 minutes and costs 1.50€. Outdoor enthusiasts can take a 35-minute hike on a marked path through the valley from Moselkern.

Burg Eltz can stake the claim to be the most beautiful authentic castle in Germany, surpassing any 19th century mimics like Neuschwanstein in Bavaria. The original structure, built from the 12th century to the 17th century, has been preserved in all its glory thanks in part to one family member who served in the French army to keep the "Sun King" Louis XIV from laying it to ruin. The castle houses different families in four separate residences, with original medieval furnishings that include some fine old paintings and tapestries. A treasury contains works by goldsmiths and silversmiths, armor, weapons, and other objects acquired by the family over the centuries. The castle is open daily April to November 1 9:30am to 5:30pm. Admission is 8€ for adults, 5.50€ for children, and 24€ for a family ticket. There are two small self-service restaurants in the castle.

BEILSTEIN

11km (7 miles) E of Cochem, 111km (69 miles) W of Mainz

This unspoiled medieval wine town on the east bank of the Mosel has a memorable marketplace dwarfed by the adjacent hillside. Above the town stand the former cloister church with a 13th century **Black Madonna** of Spanish origin, and the ruins of the 12th-century **Metternich Castle,** also destroyed by Louis XIV's army.

Essentials

GETTING THERE
BY TRAIN   The nearest rail station is at Cochem (see above).

BY BUS   Service from Cochem and other points along the Mosel is available from **RMV Rhein Mosel Verkehrsgesellschaft** (✆ **01805/7684636;** www.rmv.de) and from **Moselbahn GmbH** (✆ **06531/96800;** www.moselbahn.de).

BY CAR   Access by car is via the A48 Autobahn on the Koblenz-Trier run; exit at Kaisersesch.

VISITOR INFORMATION
The nearest information office is at Cochem (see above).

Where to Eat & Stay

Haus Burgfrieden   This hotel's simple but comfortable rooms are outfitted in an uncluttered modern style. They aren't very spacious, but the maintenance is good. All units contain neatly kept bathrooms. On the premises is a dining room featuring international cuisine. Main courses cost 9.50€ to 23€.

Im Muhlental 17, 56814 Beilstein. www.hotel-burgfrieden.de. ✆ **02673/93639.** Fax 02673/936388. 39 units. 78€–88€ double. Rates include buffet breakfast. No credit cards. Free parking. Closed Nov–Mar. 5-min. walk west of the town center. **Amenities:** Restaurant. *In room:* TV.

Hotel Haus Lipmann ★ 🛏   You can sample the wines that made Beilstein famous at this oft-photographed inn in the town center. The six guest rooms are located in the main half-timbered house dating from 1714. They're all small, cozy, and very inviting, with tiny bathrooms.

For six generations, the same family has tended the vast riverside vineyards that have won them acclaim. Try their Ellenzer Goldbäumchen or their Beilsteiner Schlossberg. In summer, the most popular place at the inn for drinking and dining is the vine-covered terrace with a statue of Bacchus, overlooking the Mosel. You can also try the antiques-filled tavern or the wood-paneled Rittersaal, with its collection of old firearms and pewter. In the cooler months, fires burn in the tall walk-in fireplace and the tiny open hearth. German food is served.

Marktplatz 3, 56814 Beilstein. www.hotel-haus-lipmann.com. ✆ **02673/1573.** Fax 02673/1521. 5 units. 100€–120€ double. Rates include buffet breakfast. No credit cards. Free parking. Closed Nov–Mar. **Amenities:** Restaurant; bar; room service. *In room:* TV.

ZELL AN DER MOSEL

69km (43 miles) NE of Trier, 105km (65 miles) W of Mainz, 35km (22 miles) S of Cochem

This old town, along the east bank of the Mosel, is best known for its excellent wine, Schwarze Katze ("Black Cat"). The grape is king here, as you'll quickly realize if you visit during the annual autumn wine festival. Nearby, on the left bank of the Mosel, 8km (5 miles) from Zell, stands the little wine village of **Alf.** The surroundings are idyllic, especially if you climb up to the Marienburg, which has a fine view over the Mosel and the vineyards of Zell.

Essentials

GETTING THERE

BY TRAIN   The nearest rail station is at Bullay, some 5km (3 miles) away. For information, call ℂ **01805/996633** (www.bahn.de).

BY BUS   Regional bus service is provided by **RMV Rhein Mosel Verkehrsgesellschaft GmbH** (ℂ **01805/7684636;** www.rmv.de) and **Moselbahn GmbH** (ℂ **06531/96800;** www.moselbahn.de).

BY CAR   Access by car is via the A1 Autobahn north and south, and Rte. 49 from the west.

VISITOR INFORMATION

Go to **Tourist-Information,** in the Rathaus, Marktstrasse 2 (ℂ **06542/96220**), Monday to Friday 9am to 5pm and Saturday 10am to 1pm.

Where to Eat & Stay

Haus Notenau   Solid, comfortable, and well maintained, this three-story building was erected in 1960 on the forested outskirts of town, one mile south along the river. Your hosts, members of the Saxler family, will offer you a cheerful, no-nonsense stay in rooms that are outfitted with contemporary-looking furniture and pale pastel-color schemes, each quiet, calm, and uncontroversial. Come here for rest, relaxation, and contemplation. If Haus Notenau is full, additional accommodations are available at its comparably priced sibling, **Haus Brandenburg,** Brandenburger Strasse 1 (ℂ **06542/5010**). The Notenau does not have its own restaurant, but the staff will direct you to eateries nearby.

Notenau 7–8, 56856 Zell an der Mosel. www.haus-notenau.de. ✆ **06542/5010.** Fax 06542/5280. 20 units. 65€ double. Rates include buffet breakfast. AE, MC, V. Free parking. Bus: From Zell's center, take bus 333, direction Bernkastel. *In room:* No phone.

Zur Post   This hotel sits directly on the river. Its small rooms are carpeted, with French doors opening onto balconies. The owner takes pride in looking after her guests and ensuring their comfort. The restaurant is open for lunch and dinner Tuesday to Sunday, serving German cuisine and an extensive selection of Mosel wines. Enjoy a glass in the warmly decorated *Weinstube* or on the inviting sun terrace as you watch the river traffic go by.

Schlossstrasse 19–25, 56856 Zell an der Mosel. ✆ **06542/4217.** Fax 06542/41693. www.hotel-zur-post-zell.de. 14 units. 71€–75€ double. Rates include buffet breakfast. AE, DC, MC, V. Free parking. Closed Feb to mid-Mar. **Amenities:** Restaurant. *In room:* TV, no phone.

TRABEN-TRARBACH

60km (37 miles) NE of Trier, 103km (64 miles) W of Mainz, 18km (11 miles) SW of Zell

Thanks to their central location on the Mosel, halfway between Koblenz and Trier, the twin towns of Traben and Trarbach have become the wine capitals of the Mosel Valley. Their gardenlike promenades offer splendid views of the surroundings and occasional speedboat and water-skiing competitions. The **July wine festival** attracts visitors from all over Europe to the old wine cellars and taverns of the towns.

Essentials

GETTING THERE
BY TRAIN   Rail passengers for Traben-Trarbach can arrive either at Trier or Bullay, then go the rest of the way by bus. Call ✆ **01805/996633** (www.bahn.de) for schedules and times.

BY BUS   Regional bus service among the Mosel River towns is provided by **RMV Rhein Mosel Verkehrsgesellschaft** (✆ **01805/7684636;** www.rmv.de) and by **Moselbahn GmbH** (✆ **06531/96800;** www.moselbahn.de).

BY CAR   Access is via the A48 Autobahn (Trier-Koblenz); exit at Wittlich.

VISITOR INFORMATION
For tourist information, contact the **Kurverwaltung und Verkehrsamt,** Bahnhof 5, Traben (✆ **06541/83980;** www.traben-trarbach.de), open Monday to Friday 10am to 4pm; from May to October, additional hours are Saturday 11am to 3pm.

Exploring Traben-Trarbach

Above Trarbach, on the east bank of the river, are the now-diminished remains of the 14th-century **Grevenburg Castle,** the scene of hard-fought battles to gain control of its strategic position. On the opposite bank, above Traben, are the ruins of **Mont Royal,** a 1687 fortress built by the invading Louis XIV, and destroyed by him 11 years later. You can wander about these testimonials to faded grandeur at any time, without charge. The towns also possess excellent examples of **Jugendstil architecture,** the German version of Art Nouveau, stemming from the time when architect Bruno Möhring resided here. The fancy bridge gate in Trarbach and Hotel Bellevue are just a few of his works.

A quick look at the map will show that an ideal way of traveling between Traben-Trarbach and its sister Bernkastel-Kues just may be by your own two feet. The two towns lie within a 2- to 3-hour walk over the hill along a marked path that offers fine views of the area. A glass of Riesling in either town at the end of your hike makes for a great reward.

Where to Eat & Stay

Hotel Moseltor ★ 🛍️ You'll find this gay-friendly hotel on the outskirts of town at Im Otsteil Trarbach. Inside this masterpiece of 19th-century fieldstone masonry, a charming combination of new construction and antique elements creates a warm mixture of comfort and convenience. The inviting rooms have neatly kept bathrooms.

Chef George Bauer's reputation for light cuisine has spread so widely that German urbanites come here for gastronomic weekends (meals cost 25€–38€). The hotel is open year-round, but the restaurant is closed in February and on Monday and Tuesday year-round.

Moselstrasse 1, 56841 Traben-Trarbach. www.moseltor.de. © **06541/6551.** Fax 06541/4922. 11 units. 100€–140€ double. Rates include continental breakfast. AE, DC, MC, V. Parking 10€ in garage. **Amenities:** Restaurant; room service. *In room:* TV, hair dryer, Wi-Fi (free).

Romantik Art Nouveau Hotel Bellevue ★★ This Art Nouveau residence on the riverbank is one of the finest hotels along the Mosel. It was designed in 1903 by the noted architect Bruno Möhring and features elaborate timberwork, a domed tower, a high-pitched roof, gables, and dormers. Many of the cozy rooms are furnished with antiques. Forty-two rooms make up the hotel itself, while 26 more offer a fine view from a building along the riverfront promenade The Clauss-Feist Restaurant is a romantic spot for both breakfast and dinner, with stained-glass windows and an old-German ambiance. There's a cozy fireplace as well as an ivy-covered terrace for dining outside.

An der Mosel 11, 56841 Traben-Trarbach. www.bellevue-hotel.de. © **06541/7030.** Fax 06541/703400. 70 units. 135€–190€ double; 160€–380€ suite. Rates include buffet breakfast. AE, DC, MC, V. Free outdoor parking; 10€ in garage. **Amenities:** Restaurant; bar; bikes; exercise room; indoor heated pool; room service; spa. *In room:* TV, hair dryer, minibar, Wi-Fi (free).

BERNKASTEL-KUES ★

48km (30 miles) NE of Trier, 113km (70 miles) W of Mainz

In a valley full of wine towns, the right-bank Bernkastel stands out as the most colorful.

Essentials

GETTING THERE

BY TRAIN The nearest rail station is the Wittlich Hauptbahnhof, 20km (12 miles) west, with a bus or taxi connection to Bernkastel-Kues. For information, call © **01805/996633** (www.bahn.de).

BY BUS Regional bus service along the Mosel River is provided by **RMV Rhein Mosel Verkehrsgesellschaft** (✆ 01805/7684636; www.rmv.de) and **Moselbahn GmbH** (✆ 06531/96800; www.moselbahn.de).

BY CAR Access by car is via the A48 Autobahn on the Koblenz-Trier run; exit at Wittlich.

VISITOR INFORMATION

Contact **Tourist-Information,** Gestade 6, in Bernkastel (✆ 06531/4023), open May to October Monday to Friday 8:30am to 12:30pm and 1:30 to 5pm, Saturday 10am to 5pm, and Sunday 10am to 1pm; from November to April, hours are Monday to Thursday 8:30am to 12:30pm and 1 to 5pm, and Friday 8:30am to 3:30pm.

Exploring Bernkastel-Kues

Half-timbered buildings dating from as early as 1608 surround the handsome **Marktplatz** and the **St. Michael's Fountain,** which flows with wine during the annual September wine festival. Its conjoined town across the river, Kues, features the late-Gothic **Cusanusstift,** resting place of 15th-century cardinal and influential scholar Nicolas of Cusa.

Where to Eat

Waldhotel Sonnora ★★★ CONTINENTAL One of the most spectacular restaurants in Germany is 18km (11 miles) west of Bernkastel-Kues. With only 12 tables, it often books 3 months in advance on weekends and 2 weeks in advance on weeknights. *Hint:* Consider lunch instead of dinner, when demand for tables is less intense. If you're lucky enough to snare a reservation for dinner, you may prefer to overnight in one of the hotel's 20 bedrooms. Doubles cost from 115€ to 280€, including breakfast.

Menu items are concocted from hyper-upscale ingredients under the supervision of master chef Helmut Thieltges. Main courses, depending on the season, might feature turbot strips of sole with grilled lobster with chicory in a lemon-butter sauce or filet of Bresse pigeon with a carrot tart. In late autumn and winter, the venison and other game dishes are delightful. The restaurant has one of the most comprehensive wine lists in the area.

Auf dem Eichelfeld. ✆ **06578/406.** www.hotel-sonnora.de. Reservations essential. Main courses 45€–52€; fixed-price menus 128€–158€. AE, MC, V. Wed–Sun noon–2pm and 7–9pm. Closed late Dec to late Jan and July 15–29.

📷 For a Grand Panorama

On a rocky promontory, 3km (2 miles) to the southeast of the town, stands **Burg Landshut.** Once the domain of the archbishops of Trier, the property dates from the 11th century but fell into ruins at the hands of Louis XIV. You don't come here for these ruins but for one of the grandest **panoramas** ★★ in the entire Rhineland and Mosel areas. Even the steepest slopes on the way to this belvedere are covered with vines.

THE TASTE OF THE grape & AN OVERNIGHT TOO

Since 1156, the Prüm family has operated a winery at this spot. Today **S. A. Prüm Winery,** Uferallee 25–26, 54470 Bernkastel-Wehlen (✆ **06531/3110;** fax 06531/8555; www.sapruem.com), allows visitors onto the estate for a wine tasting, costing from 14€. Reservations are advised. For centuries, the winery has been known for its Rieslings but now offers *Weissburgunder*/Pinot Blanc, which is a delight. Visits are possible Monday to Friday 10am to noon and 2 to 4pm, and Saturday 10am to 4pm.

There is a beautifully decorated guesthouse of eight spacious bedrooms, furnished in part with antique pieces. A patio garden opens onto the Mosel. Doubles rent for 69€ to 89€ a night and are equipped with neatly tiled bathrooms with showers. Each unit comes with a TV and Internet, and rates include buffet breakfast. The winery and guesthouse are closed December to mid-February. American Express, MasterCard, and Visa are accepted.

Where to Stay

Doctor Weinstuben   This intricately half-timbered building in the town center dates from the late 17th century. Today it's the most visually arresting hotel in Bernkastel. Transformed into a tavern in 1830, it still has many of its original woodcarvings. Its public areas are traditional, and the cozy (but often too-small) rooms are furnished in a simple, modern style. Look for the 150-year-old plant called *Blau Regen* (Blue Rain) in the garden.

Hebegasse 5, 54470 Bernkastel-Kues. www.doctor-weinstuben.de. ✆ **06531/96650.** Fax 06531/6296. 29 units. 80€–120€ double; 100€–139€ suite. Rates include buffet breakfast. AE, DC, MC, V. Parking 10€. **Amenities:** Restaurant; bar; bikes; Wi-Fi (free). *In room:* TV, hair dryer, minibar.

Hotel Moselpark ★★   This government-rated four-star hotel is the best in the area and also one of the largest—many of its rivals are mere inns with only a few bedrooms. This three-story hotel also boasts the widest range of leisure facilities and activities in the area, including a fitness studio, dance bar, and large swimming pool. Bedrooms are midsize to spacious and are exceedingly comfortable and well maintained. You could spend a week here, treating the place like a resort. Many distractions are right on the grounds, everything from a *Bierstube* to a massage parlor.

Im Kurpark, 54470 Bernkastel-Kues. www.moselpark.de. ✆ **06531/5080.** Fax 06531/508612. 143 units. 135€–252€ double. Rates include buffet breakfast. AE, DC, MC, V. Free parking. **Amenities:** 2 restaurants; babysitting; bikes; exercise room; indoor heated pool; room service; sauna; 4 indoor and 2 outdoor tennis courts (lit). *In room:* TV, hair dryer, minibar, Wi-Fi (in some; free).

Zur Post ★   Even though relatively modest, this is the winegrowing town's finest inn. This centrally located hotel was once a stopover for horseback riders on the local postal routes. The well-maintained but small rooms have both traditional and modern furnishings. Public areas include an elegantly crafted stairwell flanked by half-timbered walls and a paneled, beamed dining room that feels like the interior of a ship. Hearty dishes include a selection of grilled cuts of Angus steak with potatoes as you like them, and pork medallions with creamed mushrooms and *Spätzle*. Meals cost 13€ to 28€.

Gestade 17, 54470 Bernkastel-Kues. www.hotel-zur-post-bernkastel.de. ✆ **06531/96700.** Fax 06531/967050. 42 units. 90€–110€ double; 150€ junior suite. Rates include buffet breakfast. DC, MC, V. Free parking. Closed Jan. **Amenities:** Restaurant; sauna. *In room:* TV, minibar.

TRIER ★★

124km (77 miles) SW of Koblenz, 143km (89 miles) SW of Bonn, 193km (120 miles) SW of Frankfurt

The city known to the Romans as Augusta Treverorum possesses some of the best-preserved remnants from the era north of the Alps. Founded under Augustus in 16 B.C., its former grandeur earned it the title Roma Secunda—the second Rome. For nearly five centuries, well into the Christian era, Trier remained one of Europe's power centers.

But this city, Germany's oldest, actually dates back much farther. In 2000 B.C., according to legend, the Assyrians established a colony here, and archaeological findings indicate a pre-Roman Celtic civilization. The buildings and monuments still standing today, however, date from Roman and later periods.

Trier lies only 10km (6 miles) from Luxembourg on the western frontier of Germany, where the Ruwer and Saar rivers meet the Mosel. The city is rich not only in art and tradition but also in wine—it's one of Germany's largest exporters.

Essentials

GETTING THERE

BY TRAIN **Trier Hauptbahnhof** is on the Wasserbillig-Trier-Koblenz "Moselbahn" line and also the Trier-Saarbrücken line. Trier has frequent regional connections. There are hourly express trains each day to Koblenz (trip time: 1 hr., 25 min.), 17 direct trains to Cologne (trip time: 2 hr., 30 min.), and over 30 trains to Saarbrücken (trip time: 1 hr., 20 min.). For information, call ☎ **01805/996633** (www.bahn.de).

BY BUS Buses between Trier and Bullay run along the Mosel River, leaving from the main station in Trier at Bussteig 3. Service is provided by **RMV Rhein Mosel Verkehrsgesellschaft** (☎ **01805/7684636;** www.rmv.de) and **Moselbahn GmbH** (☎ **06531/96800;** www.moselbahn.de).

BY BOAT Boat rides on the Mosel River operate between Trier and Cochem (see "Cochem," earlier in this chapter). Contact **Mosel Personen Schiffahrt Gebrüder Kolb,** Briedern/Mosel (☎ **02673/1515;** www.mosel-personenschifffahrt.de).

BY CAR Access by car to Trier is via the A1 Autobahn north and south, the A48 east, and Rte. 51 from the north.

VISITOR INFORMATION

Contact **Tourist-Information,** An der Porta Nigra (☎ **0651/978080;** fax 0651/9780876; www.trier.de), open daily; hours vary greatly by season, so call ahead or visit the website for exact hours (closed Dec 25–26 and Jan 1).

GETTING AROUND

Most of Trier's attractions are within walking distance of each other, and few visitors need to take the bus. Tickets (purchased on the bus) cost 1.85€ within zone 1 (the city). Outside normal operating times (Mon–Fri 6:30am–6:45pm), bus numbers 81 through 87 run special routes until 2am, as well as on Saturday and Sunday. For information, call ☎ **1805/131619,** or visit www.vrt-info.de.

BOAT TOURS

Trier owes much of its majesty to the river that nurtured its medieval commerce. You can take a day cruise for a waterside view of its historic banks. Easter to October, boats depart Tuesday to Sunday at 9am from the Zurlauben (city docks) for a 4-hour trip along the river to **Bernkastel** (see "Bernkastel-Kues," earlier in this chapter), passing vineyards, wine hamlets, historic churches, and semi-ruined fortresses. Participants spend 2 hours exploring Bernkastel before returning on the same boat to Trier, arriving back at 7:30pm. The cost is 26€ per person.

If you don't want to spend so much time on the river, you can take a shorter, hour-long excursion to the nearby historic hamlet of **Pfalzel.** Boats depart from Trier's docks Easter to October daily at 10 and 11:15am, 12:30, 1:45, 3, and 4:15pm. Round-trip is 8€. You can prolong your excursion with a walk along the riverbanks in Pfalzel or return on the next boat almost immediately after your arrival.

For information on either of these excursions, contact the tourist office (see "Visitor Information," above) or the boat operator **Gebrüder Kolb** (© **0651/26666;** www.kolb-mosel.de).

Exploring Trier

Every day April to October, the tourist office (see above) conducts a 2-hour **walking tour** of the town in German, starting at 10:30am and 2:30pm. Tours in English are conducted only on Saturday at 1:30pm from May to October. The cost is 7.50€ per adult, 5€ for children 6 to 14.

VISITING THE ROMAN RUINS

When the last Roman prefect departed from Trier in about A.D. 400, he left behind a vast collection of monuments from centuries of Roman domination. Built around A.D. 180, **Porta Nigra (Black Gate)** ★★ (© **0651/75424**) is the best-preserved Roman structure in Germany, the only survivor of the great wall that once surrounded Trier. The huge sandstone blocks, assembled without mortar, were held together with iron clamps—the marks can still be seen. From outside the gate, the structure appeared to be simply two arched entrances between rounded towers leading directly into the town, but intruders soon discovered that the arches opened into an inner courtyard where they were at the mercy of the town's defenders. During the Middle Ages, the Greek hermit Simeon, later canonized, chose the east tower as his retreat. After his death, the archbishop turned the gate into a huge double church, contributing to its preservation. When Napoleon came this way, however, he ordered all the architectural changes to be removed and the original Roman core restored. Porta Nigra is open daily April to September 9am to 6pm, October and March 9am to 5pm, and November to February 9am to 4pm. Admission is 3€ for adults and 1.50€ for children. A family pass is 6€.

The Imperial Palace district, stretching along the site of the former medieval wall of the city, begins with the Roman building known today as the **Basilica,** Basilikaplatz (© **0651/72468**). Although much of the structure has been demolished, the huge hall that remains—believed to be the throne room—gives some idea of the grandeur of the original palace. The two tiers of windows are arranged within high-rising arches in which fragments of the original wall paintings can be seen. Five large heating chambers outside the walls sent warm air through the hollow floor, in the unique method of Roman central heating. Today the Basilica serves as the main Protestant church in the city. It's open April to October Monday to Saturday 10am to 6pm and Sunday noon to 6pm; November to March hours are Tuesday to Saturday 11am to noon and 3 to 4pm, and Sunday noon to 1pm. Admission is free.

Next to the Basilica stands the 17th-century **Kurfürstliches Palais (Electoral Palace;** © **0651/9494202**), begun in the German Renaissance style as a residence

Trailing Bacchus into the Underground

Since medieval times, Trier has served as a warehouse and distribution center for thousands of liters of wine fermented in its underground cellars. At least 40 of these cellars lie beneath the streets of the city and surrounding suburbs and hamlets. The oldest and most venerable of these is owned by **Vereinigte Hospitien,** Krahnen Ufer Strasse 19 (✆ **0651/9451210;** www.vereinigte hospitien.de), an organization that's

also involved in running a network of local hospitals and hospices. Tours include tastes of some of the vintages and cost 11€ per person. Be warned that if it's inconvenient for the staff to receive you, they'll be quick to tell you. The local tourist office will usually help you arrange a tour of either of these cellars or of others belonging to local competitors.

for the archbishop-electors, the town's governors. Johannes Seiz completed its fancy rococo facade and interior, which cannot be visited due to its use as city offices. The adjoining **Palastgarten (Palace Gardens)** ★, full of ponds, flowers, and rococo statues, are always open and free.

The **Imperial Baths (Kaiserthermen)** ★★ (✆ **0651/44262**), at the south end of Palastgarten, were erected in the early 4th century by Constantine I. Of the huge complex, only the ruins of the hot baths remain. These were among the largest in the Roman Empire, and although never completed, they were used in connection with the Imperial Palace. They're open daily April to September 9am to 6pm, October and March 9am to 5pm, and November to February 9am to 4pm. Admission is 3€ for adults and 1.50€ for children.

The **Amphitheater,** Amphitheaterplatz (✆ **0651/73010**), is the oldest Roman construction in Trier, dating from A.D. 100. The stone seats, arranged in three circles separated by broad promenades, held at least 20,000 people. The ruins are open daily April to September 9am to 6pm, October and March 9am to 5pm, and November to February 9am to 4pm. Admission is 3€ adults, 1.50€ children. A family pass is 6€.

A **collective ticket,** which grants admission to the amphitheater, the two sets of Roman baths, and the Porta Nigra, costs 8€ for adults and 5.60€ for students and 4€ ages 17 and under. It is available from the tourist office.

Der Trierer Dom (Trier Cathedral) ★ CHURCH   From the outside, this cathedral, with its rough-hewn stonework, looks more like a fortress than a church. It's the third church to stand on the site of the former 4th-century palace of the Empress Helena, mother of Constantine. It was begun in 1035 in Romanesque style, but later Gothic and baroque additions have only helped give the ecclesiastical architecture a timeless unity. The interior combines baroque decoration with Gothic vaulting and archways. On the south aisle is a magnificent tympanum depicting Christ between the Virgin and St. Peter. **Die Schatzkammer (Treasury Museum)** contains many important works of art, including the 10th-century St. Andrew's Altar, an unusual portable altar made of wood and covered with gold and ivory.

Domfreihof (north of the Palace Gardens and Basilica). ✆ **0651/9790790.** Cathedral free; treasury 1.50€ adults, .50€ children 15 and under. Cathedral Apr–Oct daily 6:30am–6pm; Nov–Mar daily 6:30am–5:30pm. Treasury Apr–Oct Mon–Sat 10am–5pm, Sun 12:30–5pm; Nov–Mar Tues–Sat 11am–4pm, Sun–Mon 12:30–4pm.

15

THE MOSEL VALLEY | Trier

547

Karl-Marx-Haus HISTORIC HOUSE   This old burgher's house is where Karl Marx (1818–83) was born and where he lived until 1835, when he left to attend university. The museum has exhibits on Marx's personal history, volumes of poetry, original letters, and photographs with personal dedications. There's also a collection of rare first editions and international editions of his works, as well as exhibits on the development of socialism in the 19th century. In the vicinity of the museum is a study center, **Studienzentrum Karl-Marx-Haus,** Johannestrasse 28 (same phone), for research on Marx and Engels.

Brückenstrasse 10. (𝄐 **0651/970680.** www.fes.de. Admission 3€ adults, 2€ children. Apr–Oct daily 10am–6pm; Nov–Mar Mon 2–5pm, Tues–Sun 11am–5pm. Bus: 1, 2, 3, or 4.

Liebfrauenkirche ★ CHURCH   This parish church, separated from the cathedral by a narrow passageway, is more pleasing aesthetically than its older neighbor. Begun in 1235, it was among the first German examples of Gothic architecture. The ground plan is in the shape of a Greek cross, creating a circular effect with all points equidistant from the central high altar. The structure is supported by 12 circular columns, rather than the typical open buttresses. The interior is bathed in sunlight, which streams through the high transoms. Although its restoration after the war changed some of the effect of the central construction, it's still unique among German churches.

Some of the church's more important works of art are now in the **Bischöfliches Museum,** Windstrasse 8 (𝄐 **0651/7105255;** www.bistum-trier.de). The sepulcher of Bishop Karl von Metternich, who represented the archbishopric during the Thirty Years' War, is among the most interesting items. Admission is 3.50€ for adults and 2€ for children.

Liebfrauenstrasse 2. (𝄐 **0651/9790790.** Free admission. Apr–Oct daily 7:30am–6pm; Nov–Mar daily 7:30am–5:30pm. Bischöfliches Museum: Apr–Oct Mon–Sat 9am–5pm, Sun 1–5pm; Nov–Mar Tues–Sat 9am–5pm, Sun 1–5pm.

Rheinisches Landesmuseum ★★ MUSEUM   This is one of the outstanding museums of Roman antiquities north of the Alps. Numerous reliefs from funerary monuments show daily life in Roman times. The museum's most popular exhibit is the *Mosel Ship,* a sculpture of a wine-bearing vessel crowning a big burial monument of the 3rd century A.D. Also on display are many mosaics and frescoes, ceramics, glassware, a 2,700-year-old Egyptian casket complete with mummy, an outstanding numismatic collection, and prehistoric and medieval art and sculpture.

Weimarer Allee 1 (btw. the Imperial Baths and the Basilica, at the edge of the Palace Gardens). (𝄐 **0651/97740.** www.landesmuseum-trier.de. Admission 6€ adults, 3€ children. Tues–Sun 10am–5pm. Bus: 2, 6, 16, 26, or 30.

Where to Eat

Pfeffermühle ★★ FRENCH   This is clearly the best dining in Trier. The restaurant occupies two pale-pink-and-white dining rooms, elegant and restrained, of a historic 18th-century house whose windows overlook the Mosel. While Angelika Walde maintains a bright, well-decorated dining room her husband Siegberg does his magic in the kitchen using the freshest ingredients possible. From a freshly made goose-liver terrine appetizer to the petits fours for dessert, the nouvelle French cuisine here is terrific. Try the assorted fresh fish with homemade noodles as your main course. Another specialty is breast of guinea fowl in a tarragon sauce with homemade pasta. The list of Mosel wines is extensive. In summer, guests can enjoy their meals on a terrace.

Zurlaubener Ufer 76, Zurlauben. (𝄐 **0651/26133.** www.pfeffermuehle-trier.de. Reservations required. Main courses 22€–31€. MC, V. Tues–Sat noon–2pm; Mon–Sat 6:30–9:30pm. Bus: 5.

Schlemmereule ★ GERMAN/CONTINENTAL At a location opposite the Dom, culinary whiz Peter Schmalen has brought some excitement to bored taste buds in the city. First, the setting is romantic—in the Palais Walderdorff complex that dates from the 1800s. In summer, try for a table in the courtyard. One specialty is plain old spaghetti, given a sublime twist with fresh truffles. A delectable pikeperch steams under a golden-brown potato crust. Finish off with the town's best crème brûlée. Schmalen proudly boasts one of the town's finest wine lists, with some marvelous Mosel vintages.

Palais Walderdorff, Domfreihof 1B. ✆ **0651/73616.** www.schlemmereule.de. Reservations required. Main courses 20€–28€. AE, DC, MC, V. Mon–Sat noon–2:30pm and 6–11pm. Closed 1 week in Feb.

Weinstube Kesselstatt ★ GERMAN This *Weinstube* lies in the baroque landmark, Palais Kesselstatt, which was the residence of the counts of Kesselstatt. Its wine cellar prides itself on stocking only Rieslings produced in nearby vineyards—an excellent selection. Anyone interested in sampling the region's legendary wines should head down to the cellar here. You get not only wine but platters of traditional German food. In summer the shady terrace fills up quickly. Inside you dine at old wooden tables resting under exposed beams. Menu items are made with fresh ingredients and change with the seasons. Try such dishes as slices of duck breast in an herb vinaigrette or else filet of turbot with vegetables, even pork medallions in a pepper sauce.

Liebfrauenstrasse 10. ✆ **0651/41178.** www.weinstube-kesselstatt.de. Reservations recommended. Main courses 12€–18€. MC, V. Daily 10am–midnight. Bus: 1.

Zum Domstein ★ 🏛 RHINELAND Charming Zum Domstein overlooks the flower stands and the fountain in Trier's central plaza. Try one of the wine tastings starting at 9€, which will get you three glasses of wine from the Mosel, the Ruwer, or the Saar. Otherwise, taste one of a dozen local and international wines by the glass, or select one of the hundreds of bottles stored in the cellars.

The food here is as tempting as the wine; a typically savory offering is a platter of filet of trout in a Riesling sauce or knuckle of lamb with vegetables. All the dishes are redolent of old-fashioned flavors; it is said that some were even served by the Romans, who preferred them with rich sauces. In winter, you'll want to find a spot near the huge tiled stove.

This restaurant is constructed above one of the oldest cellars in town, the **Römischer Weinkeller (Roman wine cellar),** originally built around A.D. 326. Original Roman artifacts, many connected with food and cooking, decorate the room. Dishes here are prepared according to recipes attributed to Marcus Gavius Apicius, said to have been the foremost chef at the court of Emperor Tiberius.

Hauptmarkt 5. ✆ **0651/74490.** www.domstein.de. Reservations recommended. Main courses lunch 8€–15€, dinner 13€–20€; fixed-price menus in the Roman wine cellar 16€–40€. MC, V. Daily 8:30am–10pm. Bus: 1, 2, or 12.

Entertainment & Nightlife

The cathedral hosts a series of free **organ recitals** in May, June, August, and September. Contact the tourist office (see "Visitor Information," earlier in this section) for schedules.

TUFA (✆ 0651/7182412; www.tufa-trier.de) presents theater, established touring bands, and the occasional dance party. Across from the cathedral stands **Walderdorffs,** Domfreihof (✆ 0651/9944412; www.walderdorffs.de), a cafe by day, but an action-packed bar and dance club at night. The club runs late (10pm–4am) and only on Thursday to Saturday, with the dancing not launched until 12:30am. The cafe and bar are open Sunday to Thursday from 9:30am to 1am, Friday and Saturday until 2am. A cover is sometimes imposed at the dance club, but the actual fee varies depending on the evening. Sometimes live bands are brought in. A club with a beer garden, **Exhaus,** Zurmaiener Strasse 114 (② **0651/25191;** www.exhaus.de), has both dancing and bands, usually Wednesday to Saturday. Days vary, but the hours are 8pm to 2am. Call to see what's scheduled. Cover is 8€ to 15€.

The aptly named **Irish Pub,** Jakobstrasse 10 (② **0651/49539;** www.irishpub-trier.de), serves toasted sandwiches, along with Guinness and Harp. Many evenings you'll find an Irish, English, or German band entertaining a rowdy drinking crowd.

The area's nightlife hot spot is **Riverside,** a complex of bars and restaurants, about 1.5km (1 mile) north of the town center.

Where to Stay

EXPENSIVE

Mercure Porta Nigra ★   The six-story Mercure Porta Nigra combines style, comfort, and location, making it one of the best choices in Trier. Most rooms have sitting areas and ornately tiled bathrooms. The hotel doesn't escape its chain format, but nonetheless is exceedingly comfortable.

Porta-Nigra-Platz 1, 54292 Trier. www.accorhotels.com. ② **0651/27010.** Fax 0651/2701170. 106 units. 105€–170€ double; 246€ suite. AE, DC, MC, V. Parking 12€. Bus: 2, 3, 12, 13, 14. Across from the Roman ruins. **Amenities:** 2 restaurants; bar; babysitting; room service; sauna. *In room:* A/C, TV, hair dryer, minibar, Wi-Fi (20€ per 24 hr.).

Park Plaza ★★   Although the Villa Hügel has a more traditional and tranquil location, the Park Plaza has shot to the top of the line as the finest hotel at which to stay in Trier, based on its amenities and modern comforts. Lying just a 3-minute walk from the Dom, it is stylish, tastefully furnished, and supremely comfortable. Extras include everything from the city's best health club (styled in the Roman tradition) to a winter garden lounge. Bedrooms are superior in styling and design, and there are hypoallergenic accommodations as well as family rooms with connecting doors. Maids even place a bathrobe and slippers in the state-of-the-art bathrooms. Caesar's Restaurant specializes in both regional and international cuisine.

Nikolaus-Koch-Platz 1, 54290 Trier. www.parkplaza-trier.de. ② **0651/99930.** Fax 0651/9993555. 150 units. 112€–162€ double; 192€–332€ junior suite. AE, DC, MC, V. Parking 12€. **Amenities:** Restaurant; bar; health club and spa; room service. *In room:* A/C, TV, hair dryer, minibar, Wi-Fi (free).

pentahotel Trier ★   This hotel is located in the heart of the sightseeing zone, near the old Roman monuments. It may be too sleek and impersonal for some, but it's serviceable in every way. Rooms are spacious, with streamlined modern furnishings and bathrooms.

Kaiserstrasse 29, 54290 Trier. www.pentahotels.com. ② **0651/94950.** Fax 0651/9495666. 127 units. 68€–132€ double; 118€–230€ suite. AE, DC, MC, V. Parking 6€ outdoors; 8.50€ in garage. Bus: 1, 3, 5, 6, 7, 8, 16, or 40. **Amenities:** Restaurant; bar; babysitting; room service. *In room:* A/C (in some), TV, hair dryer, minibar, Wi-Fi (5.50€ per day).

Villa Hügel ★★ ☺   This lovely Art Nouveau villa, built in 1914, offers more style and ambience than some of the other hotels, such as the pentahotel Trier. The windows overlook either a private garden with old trees or the city. Rooms are spacious and high ceilinged, and all contain modern bathrooms. Four double rooms are so large that they're almost suites, making them favorites with families.

Bernhardstrasse 14, 54295 Trier. www.hotel-villa-huegel.de. ☎ **0651/937100.** Fax 0651/37958. 36 units. 128€–188€ double. Rates include buffet breakfast. AE, DC, MC, V. Free outdoor parking; 10€ in garage. Bus: 2 or 82. **Amenities:** Restaurant; bar; Jacuzzi; indoor heated pool; room service; sauna; Wi-Fi (free; in lobby). *In room:* TV, hair dryer, minibar.

MODERATE

Hotel Kessler 🗡   The sunny Kessler is managed by the English-proficient Jörg Müller, who does everything he can to make your stay pleasant. Rooms are small but attractively maintained and furnished in a clean, modern style, all with neatly kept bathrooms. The generous breakfast will get you on your way.

Brückenstrasse 23, 54290 Trier. www.hotel-kessler-trier.de. ☎ **0651/978170.** Fax 0651/9781797. 18 units. 72€–135€ double. Rates include buffet breakfast. No credit cards. Parking 5€ outside; 9€ in garage. Bus: 1, 3, 5, 6, 7, 8, 16, or 40. Next to the Karl-Marx-Haus. *In room:* TV, hair dryer, minibar, Wi-Fi (free).

Hotel Petrisberg   Petrisberg boasts a pleasant location where a forest, a vineyard, and a private park meet. The Roman amphitheater is also just a short walk down the road. All units contain neat furnishings and well-maintained bathrooms, and offer a view of the lush greenery outside, or the city. The ground-floor *Weinstube* is the gathering place for many locals, particularly on weekends.

Sickingenstrasse 11-13, 54296 Trier. www.hotel-petrisberg.de. ☎ **0651/4640.** Fax 0651/46450. 35 units. 97€–105€ double; 150€–185€ suite. Rates include buffet breakfast. MC, V. Free outdoor parking; 5€ in garage. Bus: 6, 7, or 16. A 10-min. walk from the Altstadt. *In room:* TV, Wi-Fi (free).

Römischer Kaiser ★   In a landmark building that has been beautifully restored, this hotel is a style setter in town. Modern technology and comfort blend in well with the 19th-century beauty of this hotel right at the Porta Nigra. Bedrooms are well designed and exceedingly comfortable, with a certain minimalism. The substantial breakfast buffet is one of the finest in the city. You may also want to dine in, at least for 1 night of your stay. The chefs are noted for their use of first-class ingredients deftly handled in both German and international dishes.

Porta Nigra Platz, 54292 Trier. www.friedrich-hotels.de. ☎ **0651/9770100.** Fax 0651/97701999. 43 units. 95€–115€ double. AE, DC, MC, V. Free parking. *In room:* A/C, TV, hair dryer, minibar, Wi-Fi (free).

INEXPENSIVE

Becker's Hotel ★   For Mosel wine lovers, this estate in the suburb of Olewig is the place for both food and lodgings. In summer head here for an alfresco meal on the terrace. On-site are a trio of dining choices, including an expensive gourmet restaurant specializing in an international cuisine, an informal wine cellar, and another restaurant featuring a regional cuisine. Management arranges guided tours, wine tastings, and cellar visits to its own estate offerings.

You can also lodge here in beautifully kept and individually decorated bedrooms, most with light-wood furnishings. Several rooms open onto private balconies overlooking the vineyards.

Olewiger Strasse 206, 54295 Trier-Olewig. www.weinhaus-becker.de. ☎ **0651/938080.** Fax 0651/9380888. 30 units. 70€–85€ double; 105€–110€ junior suite; 120€ suite. Rates include buffet breakfast. AE, MC, V. Bus: 6 or 16. **Amenities:** 3 restaurants; bar; room service; Wi-Fi (free; in lobby). *In room:* TV.

THE FAIRY-TALE ROAD

The area between Frankfurt and Hamburg is Germany's most neglected tourist destination, yet it holds many discoveries. Some of Germany's best-preserved medieval towns, as well as some major spas, lie in the flatlands and rolling hills of Lower Saxony and North Hesse. The character of the area ranges widely, from the bustle of the port of Bremen to the isolation of the Lüneburg Heath.

You'll also find the beautiful Harz Mountains, perhaps the country's last stronghold of paganism, still a land of legends and fanciful names. It is said that the last bear was killed in the Harz in 1705, the last lynx in 1817, but wildcats, badgers, deer, and foxes remain, as well as many limestone caves. The beech trees that grow in the Harz range have unusual size and great beauty, and walnut trees abound.

The highlight of this area is a drive along the **Fairy-Tale Road ★★★**, stretching for 595km (370 miles) from the town of Hanau in the south to Bremen in the north. For an abbreviated form of this relatively long tour, see "The Fairy-Tale Road" in chapter 3.

As you travel this winding route, your childhood memories will live again, as you encounter such characters as Sleeping Beauty, Rumpelstiltskin, and the Pied Piper. The dark forests and countryside inspired the Brothers Grimm and their fairy tales, which are read to children all over the world today.

Train service is available to the larger cities and towns, but it's best to rent a car and explore the region at random, scurrying down some country road when you spot Little Red Riding Hood along some mysterious lane.

Although the Fairy-Tale Road tour ends in Bremen, some of the most fascinating cities of Lower Saxony and the Harz Mountains are yet to be explored if you have the time. These include the ancient cities of Lüneburg, Celle, Goslar, and Göttingen.

HANAU

20km (12 miles) E of Frankfurt, 89km (55 miles) SW of Fulda

The Fairy-Tale Road begins in the gateway town of Hanau, where the Brothers Grimm were born. Now virtually a far eastern suburb of Frankfurt, it is not a pretty town but its association with the Brothers Grimm leads to a never-ending stream of visitors.

Essentials

GETTING THERE **By Train and Bus** From the main rail station at Frankfurt, take the S8 or S9 train to the Hanau Hauptbahnhof. The trip takes only 30 minutes, and a one-way ticket costs 6€. The fare includes a bus ride from the train station to the Marktplatz.

By Car Motorists from Frankfurt can head east along Autoroute 66 into Hanau.

VISITOR INFORMATION The **Tourist Information Center** sits behind the Rathaus (Town Hall) at Am Markt 14 (✆ **06181/295950;** www.hanau.de), open Monday to Thursday 9:30am to 6pm, Friday 8:30am to 1pm, and Saturday 9am to 1pm.

Exploring Hanau

At the Marktplatz (the central square) you encounter **Nationaldenkmal Brüder Grimm,** a memorial erected in 1898 to the famous brothers. More Grimm memorabilia is found at **Schloss Philippsruhe & Schlosspark** at Philippsruher Allee 45 (✆ **06181/20209;** www.museen-hanau.de), open Tuesday to Sunday 10am to 4pm, charging 2.50€ for adults and 1.50€ for children. A short ride on bus no. 10 delivers you to the castle. The baroque castle, with its extensive park and orangery, was built on the banks of the Main River at the beginning of the 18th century. Today it houses the Hanau Historical Museum with splendid rooms, including some devoted to relics of the Brothers Grimm. The attraction's **Papiertheatermuseum** is a delight for children, presenting paper toy shows for them.

Also opening onto Marktplatz at no. 14 is the **Rathaus,** dating from the 1700s. Every day at 10am, noon, 4, and 6pm, it honors another celebrated native son, composer Paul Hindemith (1895–1963), by presenting a concert of one of his canons.

The **Altes Rathaus (Old Town Hall)** stands at Alstädter Markt 6 (✆ **06181/256556;** www.museen-hanau.de), open Tuesday to Sunday 10am to noon and 2 to 5pm, charging an admission of 2.50€ for adults or 1.50€ for children. It was the town hall from 1537 to 1900, but today is home to the Deutsches Goldschmiedehaus (German Goldsmiths' House). This museum celebrates Hanau's history beginning in the latter 18th century when it became one of the German centers for goldsmiths. The museum has a permanent collection of silver and gold artifacts and also hosts changing exhibitions.

Where to Eat & Stay

Best Western Premier Hotel Villa Stokkum ★ The premier place for food and lodging lies 4km (2½ miles) southwest of the center. Overlooking the River Main Valley, this is a Mediterranean-style hotel, rated four stars by the government. Rooms are furnished comfortably, but not lavishly, with modern pieces, soundproof windows, and marble bathrooms. Each unit comes with a bedside table and desk. The on-site restaurant, **Atrium,** serves a savory regional cuisine, with meals costing 25€ to 35€.

Steinheimer Vorstadt 70, 63456 Hanau-Steinheim. www.villastokkum.bestwestern.de. ✆ **06181/6640.** Fax 06181/661580. 135 units. 128€–185€ double. AE, MC, V. Parking 10€. **Amenities:** Restaurant; bar; room service; Wi-Fi (free; in lobby). *In room:* TV, CD player, hair dryer, minibar.

GELNHAUSEN

35km (22 miles) NE of Frankfurt, 20km (12 miles) NE of Hanau

More attractive than Hanau, Gelnhausen makes a better choice for an overnight stop along the Fairy-Tale Road. Lying in the Kinzig Valley in eastern Hesse, it is situated about midway between Frankfurt and Fulda.

Gelnhausen once stood on the old trading route, the Via Regia, between Frankfurt and Leipzig. For that reason, in 1170 the Emperor Friedrich I (Barbarossa) combined three older villages to create this town. The town thrived until the Thirty Years' War (1618–48), which ruined it. In the latter 19th century, it came back. Germans claim that one of Gelnhausen's native sons, Philipp Reis (1834–74), was the "co-inventor" of the telephone.

Essentials

GETTING THERE **By Train** Trains leave Frankfurt's Hauptbahnhof for Gelnhausen every 30 minutes during the day. Most of these trains are direct, but some require a transfer at Hanau.

By Car From Hanau (see above), follow the autobahn (A66) into Gelnhausen.

VISITOR INFORMATION The local **Tourist Office,** at Obermarkt 24 (© **06051/830300**; www.gelnhausen.de), is usually open Monday to Friday 8am to noon and 2 to 4:30pm. From May to October the office is also open Saturday and Sunday 2 to 4:30pm.

Exploring Gelnhausen

You might begin your tour at the **Untermarkt (lower market square).** Even though it's called that, it is the highest point in town and is dominated by the towers of **Marienkirche (St. Mary's Church).** You can enter through the south door (usually) daily from 9am to 5pm. Built in the Rhineland Romanesque style, it is known for its *Chorraum* ★★ or chancel, one of the masterpieces of 13th-century decorative architecture. The church was built between 1170 and 1250. In its present form, it was finally completed in 1467. Other attractions include the following:

Barbarossaburg (Imperial Palace) RUINS Now in ruins, the castle was built by "Red Beard" Barbarossa at the end of the 12th century, and the German Imperial Diet met here in 1180. Although with only a fraction of its original grandeur, it is the best-preserved imperial palace remaining from the Hohenstaufen period in Germany. The living quarters of the emperor, a fine example of Romanesque architecture, can still be seen. The castle lies on an island in the Kinzig River, and you can walk beneath the ruined ramparts along the water.

Burgstrasse 14. © **06051/3805.** Admission 3.50€. Mar–Oct Tues–Sun 10am–5pm; Nov–Dec Tues–Sun 10am–4pm.

Hexenturm Tower HISTORIC BUILDING Built around 1420, this is one of the guard towers remaining from the city's once-fortified walls. Crowned by a pointed spire, it was named "witches' tower" because women suspected of witchcraft were locked up here before facing burning at the stake or drowning (their hands and feet were bound, and they were thrown into the river). A collection of instruments of torture from the Middle Ages can be viewed inside. *Note:* The tower is accessible only via the weekly tour.

Am Fretzenstein. © **06051/830300.** Tour 5€. Tours May–Oct Sun 2:30pm.

Where to Eat & Stay

Romantisches Hotel Burg Mühle ★ The best place for food and lodgings in town takes its name, *Mühle,* meaning mill, from its former role as both the mill and the sawmill for Red Beard's castle nearby. Bedrooms show a little wear and tear but they are otherwise well maintained and comfortable, as well as affordable. Most rooms are quite spacious, and some of them open onto private balconies. The hotel is primarily known for its restaurant, where full meals cost from 25€ to 40€. In the restaurant, the old water wheel of the former mill still turns, as diners enjoy well-prepared regional cuisine, along with a wide variety of German beers including the original Budweiser.

Burgstrasse 2, 63571 Gelnhausen. www.burgmuehle.de. *©* **06051/82050.** Fax 06051/820554. 40 units. 105€–125€ double. Rates include buffet breakfast. DC, MC, V. **Amenities:** Restaurant; bar; room service; spa; Wi-Fi (free; in lobby). *In room:* TV, minibar.

STEINAU AN DER STRASSE

30km (19 miles) NE of Gelnhausen, 65km (40 miles) NE of Frankfurt

A major stop along the Fairy-Tale Road, this little town was the childhood home of the Brothers Grimm, sons of a local magistrate. The town grew up in the 1200s, and many of its antique half-timbered houses, which open onto cobblestone streets, are here to greet you today.

A former mayor once informed us—after a few beers—that if we went walking in the surrounding forests, we were sure to come upon not only Little Red Hiding Hood and Snow White, but also Hansel and Gretel. Steinau still follows its medieval layout with its castle dominating the town and its surrounding walls.

Essentials

GETTING THERE By Train From Frankfurt's Hauptbahnhof, trains arrive in Steinau at the rate of every 75 to 90 minutes during the day after stopping at such small towns as Hanau and Gelnhausen. From Steinau, the same train continues to our next destinations—Fulda and Kassel.

By Car From our last stopover at Gelnhausen, continue northeast along the A66 into Steinau.

VISITOR INFORMATION The **Tourist Information Office** is at Brüder-Grimm-Strasse 70 (*©* **06663/96310;** www.steinau.de), open Monday to Friday 8am to 4:30pm and Saturday 9am to 4:30pm.

Exploring Steinau

Brüder Grimm Haus & Museum Steinau HISTORIC HOUSE The Brothers Grimm lived in this house from 1791 to 1796. Today, the half-timbered house, along with its adjoining courtyard, has been attractively restored and is filled with memorabilia of the brothers, including picture books. Many old household objects and examples of agricultural equipment are also displayed.

Adjacent to the house, a museum displays memorabilia of Steinau—it's like an "attic" of the town, with old inn signs, an antique coach, and other artifacts.

Brüder-Grimm-Strasse 80. *©* **06663/7605.** www.museum-steinau.de. Admission 3€ for either the house or the museum, 2€ for children; combination ticket to both 4€ adults, 3€ children. Daily noon–5pm. Closed Dec 24–Jan 1.

Schloss Steinau ★ HISTORIC BUILDING   Towering over the town, the castle, with its towers and turrets, does indeed look like something out of a fairy tale by the Brothers Grimm. The original castle was constructed in the Middle Ages, but the present building is Renaissance (1528–55), and was the country residence of the counts of Hanau. The complex is shaped like an irregular pentagon, with four wings, four pavilions, and two gatehouses. The foundation walls can still be seen today, and it's surrounded by a deep moat.

On-site is the **Grimm Museum,** with mementos of the Grimm family, including the family Bible and spoons with which they ate their porridge. There's also an exhibition of marionettes from the Steinauer Marionettentheater installed in the former stables. Performances are held here most weekends at 3pm, tickets costing 6.50€. For more information call ✆ **06663/245** or visit www.die-holzkoeppe.de.

The castle doesn't have an official address but you don't need it. It's clearly evident.

✆ **06663/6843.** www.schloesser-hessen.de. Admission 4€ adults, 3.50€ children. Mar–Oct Tues–Thurs and Sat–Sun 10am–5pm; Nov–Dec 12 Tues–Thurs and Sat–Sun 10am–4pm.

Where to Eat & Stay

Brathähnchen Farm ★ 🎁🛏   Your best bet lies outside of the center and is reached by climbing up a steep hill. You're greeted by a friendly staff that welcomes you into the well-maintained and comfortably furnished bedrooms. The rooms may be a little on the small side, but they are nicely equipped and open onto views of the neighboring mountains.

Most guests show up to sample the restaurant's cuisine, which features specialties that are thrown on the grill and cooked to perfection. The name of the hotel/restaurant, Brathähnchen Farm, means "roast chicken farm," and that just happens to be the specialty of the chef. Diners come from miles around to feast on it. Of course, you can order many other mains, ranging from spareribs on the grill to pork knuckle. We like to finish off with the baked apple flambé. The restaurant doesn't serve on Mondays.

Im Ohl 1, 36396 Steinau an der Strasse. www.brathaehnchenfarm.de. ✆ **06663/228.** Fax 06663/1579. 14 units. 65€ double. Rates include buffet breakfast. AE, MC, V (hotel only). Closed mid-Dec to mid-Feb. **Amenities:** Restaurant; bar; room service. *In room:* TV.

FULDA ★

100km (62 miles) NE of Frankfurt, 32km (20 miles) NE of Steinau an der Strasse

The economic center of East Hesse, the Episcopal city of Fulda dates from 744. Today it's chiefly visited because of its baroque core, with a cathedral and a palace.

In the Christian world, it is forever linked to St. Boniface, the "Apostle of Germany." This English missionary was sent here by Pope Gregory II in the 700s to preach the gospel to the pagan Germans. He was murdered in 754 and his body brought back to Fulda, where a cult formed around his tomb (see Dom, below).

Much of the extensive building activity that began in Fulda in the early 18th century remains to delight visitors today. With some justification, Fulda is called the "City of Baroque."

Essentials

GETTING THERE   By Train   Trains from Frankfurt's Hauptbahnhof arrive daily every 75 to 90 minutes. Trip time is about 1 hour and 15 minutes.

By Car   From Steinau an der Strasse, our last stopover, continue northeast along A66 into Fulda.

VISITOR INFORMATION   The **Fulda Tourist Information Office** is at Bonifatiusplatz 1, Palais Buttlar (📞 **0661/0021814;** www.tourismus-fulda.de), open Monday to Friday 8:30am to 6pm, Saturday and Sunday 9:30am to 4pm.

Exploring Fulda

Dom (Cathedral) ★ CHURCH   The object of a pilgrimage from the devout who flock here to see the tomb of St. Boniface, the cathedral was built in the Italian baroque style by Johann Dientzenhofer between 1704 and 1712. It is the best-known baroque building in Fulda, with the tomb of the saint lying in the Bonifatiusgruft, a crypt beneath the high altar. A funerary monument in an alabaster bas-relief from the 1700s represents the saint.

The Dom's tall twin spires dominate the Altstadt. On-site is the **Dommuseum** containing liturgical robes, sacred vessels, and a collection of reliquaries from Boniface. You can even see such relics as the sword and the book with which he tried to hold off his murderers. Organ matinees are held in the cathedral every Saturday in May, June, September, and October.

Eduard Schick Platz 1-3. 📞 **0661/87207.** Admission to cathedral free, museum 2.50€. Cathedral Apr–Oct daily 6am–6pm; Nov–Mar daily 6am–5pm. Museum Apr–Oct Tues–Sat 10am–5:30pm, Sun 12:30–5:30pm; Nov–Dec and mid-Feb to Mar Tues–Sat 10am–12:30pm and 1:30–4pm, Sun 12:30–4pm.

Stadtschloss (City Palace) HISTORIC BUILDING   This is the most spectacular baroque building in Fulda, the former resident of the prince-bishops. You can visit the large Banqueting Hall and the famous **Hall of Mirrors** ★★, even the restored 18th-century princely apartments, as well as several classically designed exhibition rooms from the 19th century. A stunning collection of Fulda and Thuringian porcelain is also on display.

Schlossstrasse 1. 📞 **0661/1021813.** Admission 3€. Jan–Nov Sat–Thurs 10am–6pm, Fri 2–6pm; Dec daily 10am–2pm. Closed Dec 24-31.

Vonderau Museum MUSEUM   Housed in a former Jesuit seminary, the town's major museum offers a trio of permanent exhibitions, including a history of Fulda from prehistoric times until the present. You'll see everything from ancient burial sites to the famous Fulda Mobil, a small car built in Fulda and prized by collectors. Paintings and sculptures are exhibited in one gallery, and there is also a natural history department with life-size dioramas depicting local flora and fauna. The **planetarium** seats only 35 visitors, so reservations are needed for performances Thursday at 7pm, Friday at 5 and 8pm, Saturday at 3 and 8pm, and Sunday at 10:30am and 3pm.

Jesuitenplatz 2. 📞 **0661/928350.** www.museum-fulda.de. Admission 3.50€ to museum, 4€ to planetarium. Tues–Sun 10am–5pm.

Where to Eat & Stay

Maritim Hotel am Schloss Garten ★   This is one of the most luxurious stopovers along the Fairy-Tale Road, one of the nuggets of the Maritim chain of first-class hotels. Its rooms overlook Fulda Palace Park, where visitors can take a leisurely stroll. The midsize guest rooms, completely modernized and filled with comfortable, tasteful furnishings, are in a contemporary wing opening into a central atrium. Part of the hotel, including a spacious breakfast room, is in a beautiful Orangery dating from the

1700s and completely restored. In the cellar you can enjoy good regional cooking under medieval vaulted arches in the Dianakeller Restaurant, where complete meals range in price from 26€ to 40€.

Pauluspromenade 2, 36037 Fulda. www.maritim.de. ✆ **0661/2820.** Fax 0661/282499. 112 units. 121€–210€ double; 395€ suite. AE, DC, MC, V. Parking 12€. **Amenities:** Restaurant; bar; indoor heated pool; room service; sauna; Wi-Fi (free; in lobby). *In room:* TV, hair dryer, minibar, Wi-Fi (free).

Romantik Hotel Goldener Karpfen ★★ For the lover of the baroque who wants a more romantic hotel than the Maritim, this centuries-old inn is a viable option. It's much smaller than the Maritim, with fewer facilities, but it is more glamorous for those who love antiques. Its baroque facade is from the mid–18th century but was vastly altered at the beginning of the 20th century, though many architectural adornments remain. The bedrooms are modernized, exceedingly comfortable, beautifully furnished, and inviting. This hotel is another good choice for dining. In fact, we prefer the cuisine at its first-class restaurant—with its Persian rugs and elegant furnishings and meals ranging in price from 28€ to 50€—to the other hotel restaurants in the area.

Simpliziusbrunnen 1, 36037 Fulda. www.hotel-goldener-karpfen.de. ✆ **0661/868800.** Fax 0661/0100. 50 units. 130€–270€ double; 280€–480€ suite. AE, DC, MC, V. **Amenities:** Restaurant; bar; room service. *In room:* TV, hair dryer, minibar, Wi-Fi (free).

MARBURG ★★

60km (37 miles) NW of Fulda, 93km (58 miles) SW of Kassel

From Fulda you can head directly north into the little city of Kassel, or else you can detour west slightly to one of the most rewarding towns along the Fairy-Tale Road.

Once a great pilgrimage center, Marburg forms the heart of a triangle of Cologne, Frankfurt, and Kassel. Pilgrims came to venerate the relics of St. Elisabeth (1207–31) of Hungary. Known during her short life for her generous deeds to others, Elisabeth was canonized in 1235, and the site of her tomb in the Gothic church built for her made Marburg a major center of pilgrimage for Christians.

Today, the town, lying on a rocky outcrop, consists of half-timbered houses rising along the hill upward from the Lahn River and crowned by a castle.

A free elevator on Pilgrimstein (site of the tourist office) will deliver you from the bottom of town at the river to the peak of the Old Town to avoid a steep climb.

Essentials

GETTING THERE By Train Trains from Frankfurt's Hauptbahnhof depart at hourly intervals throughout the day, and then travel directly, with stops but without transfers, to Marburg, a trip that takes about an hour. There are also direct trains, several per day, from Kassel to Marburg, a trip that takes about an hour with no transfers needed.

By Car From Fulda (our last stopover) follow the B254 northwest to the village of Alsfeld, 34km (21 miles), where you might want to stop for a bite to eat and a tour of its narrow streets and half-timbered houses. You can follow Rte. B62 west into Marburg.

VISITOR INFORMATION The **Marburg Tourist Office** is at Pilgrimstein 26 (✆ **06421/99120;** www.marburg.de), open Monday to Friday 9am to 6pm, Saturday 10am to 2pm.

Exploring Marburg

The most beautiful illustrations in the Grimm fairy tales were done in Marburg—the Brothers Grimm studied here at the university from 1802 to 1805, and Jacob once remarked of the town, "I think there are more steps in the streets than in the houses." Today there are more than **100 pubs,** many quaint and rustic, catering to the student population.

Most of the restaurants, bars, and student cafes center around the **Marktplatz** or Obermarkt, with some of the best-preserved houses, especially no. 14 and no. 21, dating from the mid–16th century. The oldest preserved house, which is still inhabited, dates from 1323 and stands at no. 18 on the square.

> ### Stack 'Em Up
>
> **As amazing as it sounds, some of Marburg's houses can be reached only through a skylight, as some of them are stacked one on top of another. That means that in some cases a house will have a back door five floors above the front door.**

Phillips University of Marburg is not exactly a tourist attraction, although its life dominates the town today. From St. Elisabeth's church follow Steinweg, Neustadt, Wettergasse, and Reitgasse to reach the university.

The main part of the university was founded in 1527 by Landgrave Philipp of Hesse, becoming the first German Protestant university. Except for a church from the 14th century, most of its buildings are from the latter 19th century, including the largest university library in western Germany. A professor here from 1892 to 1917, Emil von Behring, won the Nobel Prize in 1901 for discovering a vaccine for diphtheria.

On Pilgrimstein you can take an elevator from below to the highest peak in Marburg, where the **Marburg Schloss** stands in Schlosspark, with panoramic views in all directions. Luther and Zwingli debated in this castle in 1429, and today it is part of the university buildings.

Students gather to catch up on the latest gossip around a fountain dedicated to St. Georg. Also opening onto the Marktplatz is the 16th-century Gothic **Rathaus,** known for its mechanical cock crowing the hours from its gable. Allow at least 2 hours for a walking tour of the Old Town.

Elisabethkirche ★★ CHURCH   Constructed from 1235 to 1283, this remarkable church is the first truly Gothic church to be built in Germany. The landmark structure is graced with two 80m (260-ft.) towers housing 700-year-old bells. The town's most beloved daughter, St. Elisabeth, is entombed here. A Hungarian princess, she was betrothed at age 4 to marry (at 12) Ludwig IV of Thuringia. He lost his life in the Crusades, and she gave up all her wealth to share with the poor, dying of exhaustion at the age of 24.

In the sacristy is the 13th-century reliquary containing the saint's bones and other artifacts. Her shrine is a masterpiece in gold completed by craftsmen from the Rhineland in 1250. Religious art, statues, and frescoes fill the cathedral, making it a virtual ecclesiastical museum.

Elisabethstrasse 3. ✆ **06421/65497.** www.elisabethkirche.de. Admission 2€ for St. Elisabeth's Shrine. Apr–Sept daily 9am–6pm; Oct daily 9am–5pm; Nov–Mar daily 10am–4pm.

Where to Eat & Stay

At some point during your day, stop in for drinks at the **Café Vetter,** Reitgasse 4 (✆ **06421/25888;** www.cafe-vetter-marburg.de), which has the most panoramic vistas of Old Marburg from its outdoor terrace. For four generations, members of the same family have been welcoming the world to their famous old cafe, which now features Internet access. On weekends, piano music fills the air.

Vila Vita Hotel Rosenpark ★★ Such an elegant luxury hotel in such a small town comes as a delightful surprise. Close to the center, the hotel stands in the meadows of the Lahn River, with one of the best spas along the Fairy-Tale Road. Its dramatic pavilion, with its glass dome, shelters the finest restaurants and bars in the city. Bedrooms are good size, each beautifully furnished and comfortably appointed, so much so you'll think you're at a resort hotel. The creative cuisine served in a trio of restaurants is the finest in the area, especially at the gourmet restaurant, **Bel Etage.** More affordable food is served at the **Rosenkavalier,** with traditional regional recipes a feature in the most rustic **Zirbelstube.**

Rosenstrasse 18, 35037 Marburg. www.vilavitahotels.com. ✆ **06421/60050.** Fax 06421/6006100. 233€–313€ double; 420€–690€ suite. AE, DC, MC, V. Parking 15€. **Amenities:** 3 restaurants; 3 bars; bikes; room service; indoor heated pool; spa. *In room:* A/C, TV, hair dryer, minibar, Wi-Fi (free).

Welcome Hotel Marburg ★ This longtime favorite stands near the river where the elevator rises to the Old Town. Its developers weren't afraid to use color, employing fire-engine red, Halloween orange, sunflower yellow, and a fruity apricot. Bedrooms are midsize and attractively and comfortably furnished. In the Tartaruga Restaurant, with its open-air terrace and beer cellar, regional meals range in price from 16€ to 19€. Am Schlossberg serves the best breakfast buffet in town.

Pilgrimstein 29, 35037 Marburg www.schlossberg-marburg.de.. ✆ **06421/9180.** Fax 06421/918444. 146 units. 102€ double; 142€–160€ suite. AE, DC, MC, V. Parking 10€. **Amenities:** Restaurant; bar; bikes; exercise room; room service. *In room:* TV, fridge, hair dryer, Wi-Fi (free).

KASSEL

100km (62 miles) NE of Marburg

The city of Kassel is the capital of the Fairy-Tale Road, and the Brothers Grimm lived here as teenagers from 1805 to 1830 (it was the hometown of their mother). They worked as librarians at the court of Napoleon's youngest brother, Jerome Bonaparte, who was the King of Westphalia. The brothers were greatly inspired by the storyteller Dorothea Viehmann (see Autobahnrastätte Knallhütte, below).

Much of Kassel's 1,000-year-old history went down in ruins in World War II, and rebuilding was haphazard, with little regard for its rich architectural past. But from the rubble rose a city of both cultural and industrial significance, its grace note being its series of parks and gardens that take the curse off many modern buildings. Kassel was designed with many traffic-free promenades and pedestrian tunnels. Some two-thirds of Kassel consists of "green lungs" in the form of parks, tree-lined streets, and woodlands.

The town was first mentioned in A.D. 913 as Chassala or Chassela. In medieval times it was spelled "Castle" and was for a time a stronghold of the Franconian kings.

This former seat of the Landgraves is known for its grottoes, Wilhelmshöhe Park, its waterfalls, and Schloss (Castle), all of which are documented below.

Kassel sits on the banks of the Fulda River in a heavily wooded part of Germany between the Meissner-Kaufungen and the Habischswald natural parks on government-protected land.

Essentials
GETTING THERE

BY TRAIN   Trains arrive from Frankfurt's Hauptbahnhof every 75 to 90 minutes during the day (trip time: 1½ hr.). Trains stop at such places as Steinau and Fulda. Once at Kassel, train routes become fragmented, fanning out in many directions across Lower Saxony.

BY CAR   From Marburg (our last stopover), follow Rte. A49 northeast into Kassel. The A44 (to Dortmund) and the A7 (Fulda to Hannover) autobahns cross in Kassel.

VISITOR INFORMATION

For information, **Kassel Tourist Office GmbH** is at Obere Königstrasse 15 (© **0561/7077707;** www.kassel-tourist.de), open Monday to Friday 9am to 6pm, Saturday 9am to 2pm. Here you can purchase the **Kassel Card,** sold only to pairs of travelers (not to individuals) and costing 13€ for 24 hours or 16€ for a 72-hour period. The card grants free transport on the city's trams and buses, discounted admission to its museums and attractions, and even discounts at some shops. It also grants free participation in tourist office walking tours and discounts on bus tours, which normally cost 15€ but are only 7€ with the card.

SPECIAL EVENTS   Documenta ★★★ is a famous art fair that has taken place every 5 years in Kassel since 1955, with musical and dramatic presentations at the Freericianum at Friedrichsplatz 18, 34117 Kassel (© **0561/707270;** www.documenta.de). The festival has been hailed in the press as an erudite heavyweight of global art exhibitions. Originally its goal was to show the world that Nazi-era nationalism was passé in Germany. Art lovers, some 650,000 of them, pour into the city for the festival, with celebrity attendees ranging from David Bowie to Queen Beatrix of the Netherlands.

Exploring Kassel

Brüder Grimm Museum MUSEUM   The surrounding Waldeck region and Reinhards Forest, as well as Kassel itself, were responsible for the birth of many legends about witches, sleeping princesses, strange beasts, and magic spells. These tall tales had a profound influence on the Brothers Grimm as teenagers. Their lives and creative output are documented in this museum of their memorabilia, containing letters, portraits, and mementos of the famous brothers, including a collection of their fairy tales from the first copy printed up until today. You'll also see art, including drawings, by the third brother, Ludwig Emil Grimm. The exhibition rooms are located in the baroque-style Palais Bellevue, which was originally designed as an observatory for Hesse's Landgrave Karl in 1714.

Brüder Grimm Platz 4A. © **0561/103235.** www.grimms.de. Admission 2€. Thurs–Tues 10am–5pm; Wed 10am–8pm.

Wilhelmshöhe Park ★★ PARK   This is the chief attraction of Kassel, and you will want to spend a minimum of 3 hours taking in all its attractions. (Sometimes visitors, mainly German, spend all day exploring the park.) Europe's largest hill park, Wilhelmshöhe sprawls across 350 hectares (865 acres) at the western edge of the city, a magnificent garden with 800 species of trees dating from 1701 when it was laid out in the baroque style.

   The crowning achievement is the **Statue of Hercules** at the highest point of the park. This giant is a copy of a statue originally created in 1717, and it's mounted atop the castle-like octagonal base. You can climb the stairs of the base for one of the **greatest panoramas ★★★** in the area. Try to time your visit for a Wednesday or Sunday afternoon at 2:30pm from mid-May to September, when water gushes down a series of cascades from a fountain below the statue. The total height of the monument is 72m (236 ft.).

Also in the park stands **Löwenburg (Lion Fortress),** a faux castle from 1800, which was constructed at the height of the sentimental Romantic period. The castle contains a collection of medieval armor and weapons along with tapestries and antique furniture.

The **Schloss** itself, completed in 1803, is in the neoclassical style. Built on a wooded slope where a monastery once stood, it was the summer residence of the landgraves and the electors of Hessen-Kassel. For 7 years, it was the residence of Napoleon's brother, Jerome, during the Napoleonic era, and it also became the summer palace of Kaiser Wilhelm II. Napoleon III was imprisoned here from 1870 to 1871.

The state apartments are lavishly furnished with antiques, including the *Kassel Apollo,* a statue from the 2nd century A.D.

The main reason to visit is to see the **Old Masters Gallery ★★★**, a treasure-trove of art collected by the landgraves. The collection features 11 Rembrandts, including a trio of self-portraits of the artist. Other highlights include Dürer's *Portrait of Elizabeth Tucher* and landscapes by Jan Bruegel. The Italian School is represented by works by Titian and Tintoretto, with the Spanish School featuring paintings by Murillo and Ribera. There are also eight paintings by Rubens and seven by Frans Hals.

The city arranges summer concerts in the park.

Schlosspark 3. ⓒ **0561/312456.** www.wilhelmshoehe.de. Admission 6€. Mar–Oct Tues–Sun 10am–5pm; Nov–Feb Tues–Sun 10am–3pm.

Where to Eat

Autobahnrastätte Knallhütte GERMAN   Dating from 1752, this brewery-cum-tavern was the home of Dorothea Viehmann, the famous storyteller and the main source of many of the fairy tales later published by the Brothers Grimm, including "Hansel and Gretel," "Little Red Riding Hood," and "Rumpelstiltskin." Today the old road that runs by the inn is now Autobahn A49 between the Baunatal Mitte and Baunatal Nord exits. The local brew is still served here, alongside regional specialties including *Biersuppe.* Expect old-fashioned German dishes such as tender veal and roast pork with dumplings and cabbage. *Schnitzels* fill the platters and herring is always a feature, as is rump steak with fried potatoes.

Knallhütterstrasse 1, Baunatal-Rengershausen. ⓒ **0561/492076.** www.knallhuette.de. Reservations not needed. Main courses 12€–18€. MC, V. Daily 11am–midnight.

Shopping

The main street for shopping is the traffic-free **Königstrasse,** in the center of the city. It's lined with many specialty shops and department stores, along with cafes with outdoor terraces in summer. Check out the **Königsgalerie** at Obere Königstrasse 39, a glass-roof atrium filled with boutiques, taverns, cafes, and restaurants.

Entertainment & Nightlife

Friedrich-Ebert-Strasse is the center of dance clubs and bars, but more sophisticated nightlife centers around the **Kassel Casino,** Maurerstrasse 11 (ⓒ **0561/930850;** www.spielbank-kassel.de), costing 2.50€ to enter. It is entered

GERMAN legends & THE BROTHERS GRIMM

by George McDonald

The brothers Jacob (1785-1863) and Wilhelm (1786-1859) Grimm traveled around Germany in the early 19th century to gather local folklore tales. They published these in their compendium, *Kinder-und Hausmärchen,* the famous *Grimm's Fairy Tales.* Although not purely morality tales, the stories were instructive and had strict rules of reward and punishment. Their enduring appeal lies in their giving a voice to childhood anxieties while affording children a safe vantage point from which to observe and explore the adult world.

From Hanau, on the Main River just east of Frankfurt, where the Brothers Grimm were born, the Fairy-Tale Road (Märchenstrasse) stretches northward along the Weser River for 595km (369 miles), past gnarled forests, and timber-frame cottages, cobblestone streets, medieval villages, and castles, to end in Bremen. Your ideal reading companion for the trip is a copy of *Grimm's Fairy Tales.* Little Red Riding Hood, the Big Bad Wolf, the Pied Piper of Hamelin, Hansel and Gretel, Rumpelstiltskin, the Pied Piper, Cinderella, fairies, wizards, dwarfs, goblins, and wicked witches are all associated with the Fairy-Tale Road. Some stops along the way include:

○ **Hameln (Hamelin)** The Weser River town is the setting for the famous tale of the Pied Piper, recalled in a weekly open-air theater performance in summer.

○ **Höxter** Noted for its timber-frame buildings and a crooked old tower, this Weser River town lays claim to having inspired *Hansel and Gretel,* and presents the drama on the first Saturday of each month from May to September.

○ **Kassel** The Waldeck region and the Reinhardswald forest around Kassel were the birthplace of many legends about witches, sleeping princesses, strange beasts, and magic spells. These tales had a profound influence on the Grimm brothers, who lived in Kassel from 1798 to 1830.

○ **Neustadt** A circular tower here is said to be the one from which Rapunzel let down her golden tresses.

○ **Sababurg** The Dornröschenschloss, a castle near Hann. Münden, is a persuasive setting for the Sleeping Beauty (Dornröschen) legend. Briar roses bloom in the courtyard.

○ **Schwalm River** Germans have dubbed the route along this river *Rotkäppchenland,* or Little Red Riding Hood country.

---

through the Kurfürsten Galerie, and it features roulette and card games, plus the latest slot machines. The casino is open Monday to Saturday 9am to 3am, Sunday noon to 3am.

Where to Stay

Ramada Hotel Kassel City Centre ★ This leading hotel in the town center rises 14 floors, and while it's not an architectural masterpiece, it offers the most comfortable and best-furnished rooms. It also has the most amenities of all its competitors. Bedrooms are midsize to spacious, and the hotel is geared to both the business traveler and the visitor intent on discovering Kassel. Its recreation area on the top floor is the best in Kassel, with a fitness center, solarium, and steam bath. Its drinking and dining facilities are also first-class, with a market-fresh cuisine.

Baumbachstrasse 2, 34119 Kassel. www.ramada.com. (℃) **0561/78100.** Fax 0561/7810100. 169 units. 120€–140€ double; from 169€ suite. AE, DC, MC, V. Parking 7€. **Amenities:** Restaurant; bar; exercise room; Jacuzzi; sauna. *In room:* A/C, TV, fridge (in some rooms), hair dryer, minibar, Wi-Fi (20€ per day).

Residenz Domus   This longtime favorite near the Hauptbahnhof (train station) was erected in 1905 as the first reinforced concrete building in Kassel and was once the headquarters of a local trading house. Its red clinker facade was strong enough to withstand the bombs of World War II. Over the years the four-story hotel has been much altered and improved to stay abreast of the changing times. Today it has a light, airy decor and modern furnishings and amenities. Many rooms and bathrooms are extremely spacious.

Erzbergerstrasse 1–5, 34117 Kassel. (℃) **0561/703330.** Fax 0561/70333498. 55 units. 99€–130€ double. Rates include buffet breakfast. AE, DC, MC, V. Parking 6€. **Amenities:** Room service. *In room:* TV, hair dryer, minibar.

Schlosshotel Bad Wilhelmshöhe ★★   This hotel is misnamed. It's not an old castle at all, but a completely modern building constructed directly across the street from the palace. As early as 1767, an inn here was receiving guests, and German troops were once billeted here after World War I. However, Allied bombings leveled the hotel in World War II, and it was rebuilt in 1955. Today, it has large, individually furnished bedrooms, some with balconies overlooking the sprawling castle park and its buildings. Quality materials such as hardwood floors in the bedrooms and green marble in the bathrooms add a touch of elegance.

Schloss 8, 34131 Kassel. www.schlosshotel-kassel.de. (℃) **0561/38880.** Fax 0561/3088428. 101 units. 94€–139€ double; 159€–179€ junior suite. AE, DC, MC, V. Free parking. **Amenities:** Restaurant; bar; room service; Wi-Fi (free; in lobby). *In room:* TV, hair dryer.

HANN. MÜNDEN ★

150km (93 miles) S of Hannover, 24km (15 miles) NE of Kassel

This little gem of a town with the odd name (once known as Hannoversch Münden) is filled with some 700 half-timbered houses. Parts of it look like a movie set. It lies at the confluence of the Werra and Fulda rivers, which join to form the Wester River.

Many of its houses are 6 centuries old. The poet Alexander von Humboldt claimed that the town is one of the seven most beautifully situated in the world.

The little city's fortified towers and remains of its old wall speak of its importance in the Middle Ages.

Essentials

GETTING THERE

BY TRAIN   Trains arrive from Kassel throughout the day, taking 16 minutes, and from Göttingen, taking 36 minutes. There are also major rail links with Hannover (trip time: 1½ hr.) and Frankfurt (trip time: 2¼ hr.).

BY CAR   From Kassel (see earlier in this chapter) follow Autobahn E45 northeast until you see the turnoff to Hann. Münden.

VISITOR INFORMATION

The **Tourist Information Office** is at the Rathaus on Lotzestrasse ((℃) **05541/75313;** www.hann.muenden-tourismus.de), open May to October Monday to Friday 8am to

5:30pm, Saturday 10am to 3pm, and Sunday 11am to 3pm; and November to April Monday to Thursday 9am to 4pm and Friday 9am to 1pm.

SPECIAL EVENTS   In summer the town celebrates its connection with the notorious quack Dr. Johann Andreas Eisenbart (1663–1727). The Doctor Eisenbart Theatre Company, founded in 1957, stages a play about the man who "could make the blind walk and the lame see."

On one Sunday in May and June and every Sunday in July and August at 11:15am, plays are staged in front of the historic Rathaus, with tickets costing 5€ for adults or 1.50€ for children ages 4 to 12. For information on these plays, contact the tourist office above.

The doctor became the subject of a ribald drinking song that immortalized him. In the song he performs such feats as shooting out an aching tooth with a gun. There's a statue of Eisenbart in front of his former home at Langestrasse 79.

Exploring Hann. Münden

Allow at least 1½ to 2 hours to walk around the central core of the old town, taking in (or photographing) all those half-timbered buildings.

St. Blaise's Church CHURCH   This is the one church of general interest to visitors, as it dates from the end of the 13th century. The chancel, the southern lateral apse, and the eastern bay were constructed at this time. The rest of the church was finished at various times, including the vaulting of the tower chamber in 1519 and the landmark tower itself in 1584. That tower is adorned with a lantern cupola. In the nave is the tomb of William of Brunswick, who died in 1503.

Kirchplatz. ☎ **05541/75313** (tourist office). Free admission. Summer only, daily 11am–4pm.

Where to Eat

Ratsbrauhaus GERMAN   The Rathaus of Münden, dating from 1605, is a fine example of the Weser Renaissance style with its gabled peaks. Its cellar is no less an architectural curiosity, with much of its original decor intact. You get good hearty fare here, including such dishes as venison pâté as an appetizer, followed by veal chops with a mustard sauce and, on occasion, breast of goose with red cranberries or a tender rack of lamb. Seafood such as oysters and lobsters is also featured.

Marktplatz 3. ☎ **05541/957107.** www.ratsbrauhaus.de. Reservations not needed. Main courses 10€–20€. MC, V. Tues–Sat 6–10:30pm; Sat–Sun 11am–2pm.

Where to Stay

Alte Rathausschanke   In the historic town center, this is the most atmospheric place to stay. It often hosts cyclists following the routes through the Weser Valley. Its bedrooms are just above the hostel level but are comfortable and individually furnished. Since many young people on a budget patronize the hotel, the staff provides a washing machine and dryer for them. A generous breakfast buffet is included every morning.

Ziegelstrasse 12, 34346 Hann. Münden. www.ratsbrauhaus.de. ☎ **05541/75313.** Fax 05541/75404. 10 units. 65€ double. No credit cards. *In room:* TV, Wi-Fi (free).

An Excursion to Sababurg

For your next stopover, head north from Hann. Münden on B80. At the village of Veckerhagen follow the signposts left into Sababurg, which lies about 100km (60 miles) south of Hannover, 60km (37 miles) west of Göttingen, and 38km (24 miles) north of Kassel. After driving through the luxuriant Forest of Reinhard, one of the largest in Germany, you come up to **Sababurg Castle,** a distance of 24km (15 miles) from Hann. Münden. The castle has been turned into a hotel (see below).

This castle is where Sleeping Beauty, in the fairy tale by the Brothers Grimm, slept for a century. The castle has had a long and turbulent history since it was built in 1334 by the archbishop of Mainz. It eventually fell into ruins, but in 1490 Count Wilhelm I constructed a hunting lodge on the site. Troops plundered the castle during the Thirty Years' War, and Friedrich II turned the castle back into a hunting lodge in 1765, but that, too, was allowed to deteriorate until its present restoration. In the castle courtyard, where briar roses bloom, you can almost expect to see the handsome prince preparing to awaken Sleeping Beauty with a kiss.

Surrounding the castle is **Tierpark Sababurg** ★, Sababurgstrasse (© **05671/ 80012251;** www.tierpark-sababurg.de), one of the oldest wildlife refuges in Europe, home to such animals as the bison and reindeer as well as a vast array of waterfowl. The surrounding acres of ancient oaks and beech trees added to the fairy-tale atmosphere of the area. Charging 5€ admission, the park is open daily as follows: April to September 8am to 7pm, October 9am to 6pm, November to February 10am to 4pm, and March 9am to 5pm.

WHERE TO STAY

Dornröschenschloss Sababurg ★ In a section of Sleeping Beauty's castle, a luxury hotel and restaurant has been constructed. Bedrooms are furnished in a period style, and, in spite of the medieval atmosphere, modern amenities have been installed. Rooms are beautifully furnished in modern or traditional style and carry various themes, including a dedication to a unicorn. For the most panoramic units, ask for one of the tower rooms. Some of the bedrooms are found in a wing dating from 1572. Afternoon tea is served on the courtyard terrace, overlooking ancient trees. A formal restaurant serving an international cuisine opens onto views of the park.

Im Reinshardswald, 34369 Hofgeismar. www.sababurg.de. © **05671/8080.** Fax 05671/808200. 17 units. 155€–195€ double; 220€ tower room. AE, DC, MC, V. **Amenities:** Restaurant; bar; babysitting; room service. *In room:* TV, hair dryer.

HÖXTER

66km (41 miles) N of Hann. Münden, 70km (43 miles) S of Hannover

On the left bank of the Weser River, the walled town of Höxter merits at least an hour of your time as you explore its historic core.

Essentials

GETTING THERE   By Train   There are no direct trains from Hann. Münden; rail passengers approach Höxter via Hannover, which is a complicated and time-consuming affair (routing from Hannover to Gottingen to Ottbergen to Höxter). If taking a train is your only option, allow plenty of time, and note that there are only 3 to 4 trips daily.

By Car   From Hann. Muenden, follow B80 northwest to the junction with B83, which will take you north to B64 which continues north into Höxter.

VISITOR INFORMATION   The **Touristik- und Kulturinformation** is in the Historisches Rathaus, Weserstrasse 11 (© **05271/19433;** www.hoexter.de), open Monday to Friday 9am to 6pm, Saturday 10am to 4pm.

Exploring Höxter

The **Dechanei (Deanery)** standing in the Markt (the market square) in the center of town dates from 1561, and the **Rathaus,** also on the square, from 1613. This municipal building is a classic example of the Weser Renaissance style, a trio of half-timbered structures with a crooked old tower that looks like something from a Brothers Grimm fairy tale.

Höxter, among other towns, lays claim for the inspiration of the tale of "Hansel and Gretel." On the first Saturday of each month from May to September the town presents the drama. Ask at the tourist office (see above) for more details.

After visiting the market square, you can walk down **Westerbachstrasse** to discover many more half-timbered houses dating from the Middle Ages. Another church to visit is **St. Kilian's** at An der Kiliankirche, dating from the 11th century. Its treasures include a 15th-century aisle and an early-16th-century Crucifixion group of sculpture. Its pulpit was built in 1597 and is an outstanding piece of Renaissance craftsmanship, decorated with motifs in alabaster.

From the center of town, take Corveyer Allée for 3km (2 miles) to **Reichsabtei Corvey (Imperial Abbey of Corvey)** in the village of Corvey (✆ **05271/694010;** www.schloss-corvey.de). Schloss Corvey (its other name) stands on a hillside overlooking the Weser River and was one of the oldest Benedictine abbeys in Germany. It was planned by Charlemagne himself but constructed by his son, Ludwig the Pious, in 822. In the 9th and 10th centuries, the abbey was one of the major cultural centers of north Germany.

During the Thirty Years' War, most of Corvey Abbey was destroyed, the only section remaining being the west facade of the church with its two spires. The abbey was rebuilt around 1730 in its present form, together with the church, monastery, and farm buildings. Guided tours take you through the library and imperial halls, and on the second floor is an exhibition of folkloric objects and prehistoric relics. In May and June a music festival is held in the great hall, the Kaisersaal. Admission to the castle is 5€, or 1€ to the abbey church. It's open April to October daily 9am to 6pm.

You can have lunch at the on-site **Schlossrestaurant** (✆ **05271/83230**) under centuries-old linden trees, enjoying regional specialties.

Where to Eat & Stay

Ringhotel Niedersachsen ★　One of the better members of the Ring chain, this venerated hotel is the best place to stay in the area. It's known for its thermal baths and for its spacious garden. The bedrooms are the finest in the area, 15 of them containing a balcony opening onto views. Rooms are equipped with up-to-date amenities and even suggest a touch of luxury. This antique Höxter building has kept abreast of the times. The restaurant, popular with locals and visitors alike, has a garden terrace. The chefs specialize in fresh river fish and other regional dishes, with main courses costing 17€ to 23€.

Grubestrasse 3–7, 37671 Höxter. www.hotelniedersachsen.de. ✆ **05271/688444.** 80 units. 110€–170€ double; 180€–200€ junior suite. AE, DC, MC, V. Parking 6.50€. **Amenities:** 2 restaurants; bar; bikes; indoor heated pool; room service; spa; Wi-Fi (free; in lobby). *In room:* TV, minibar.

BODENWERDER

25km (16 miles) S of Hameln, 34km (21 miles) N of Höxter, 70km (43 miles) S of Hannover

This is the hometown of Lügenbaron (the lying baron) von Münchhausen (1720–97). This spinner of tall tales was the biggest liar in the history of Germany—unless you want to get political and include Hitler in that competition.

The Münchhausen name has gone down in literary history. His narrative about his travels and campaigns in Russia increased his renown and was translated into many languages. The actual author was Rudolph Erich Raspe, who became acquainted with Von Münchhausen upon his retirement in 1760 from Russian service against the Turks. The baron was widely known for his exploits, including a claim that he rode a cannonball toward the enemy stronghold. Reconsidering as he neared his target, he jumped onto a cannonball shot by the enemy and rode it safely back to his troops.

From May to October during the first Sunday of every month, the **Münchhausenplay** is performed in front of the Rathaus. Locals reenact scenes from Münchhausen's colorful, if distorted, life.

Essentials

GETTING THERE **By Train** From Hannover's Hauptbahnhof, trains depart every hour for Hameln, a travel distance of 1 hour and 5 minutes. At Hameln, in front of its railway station, bus no. 520 continues on, at hourly intervals, to Bodenwerder, a travel time of 50 minutes.

By Car From Höxter, continue north along B83 into Bodenwerder.

VISITOR INFORMATION The **Tourist Information office** is at Münchhausenplatz 3 (✆ **05533/40541;** www.muenchhausenland.de), open Monday to Friday 9am to noon and 2 to 5pm, and Saturday 10am to 12:30pm.

Exploring Bodenwerder

Münchhausen-Erinnerungszimmer HISTORIC HOUSE This memorial room devoted to the great liar was the family home of the Von Münchhausen family. Today it is the Rathaus, and it's filled with mementos of this storyteller, including that cannonball he allegedly rode. You can trace some of his "adventures" in the museum—but don't believe a word of it. The fountain in front evokes a tale he told about his horse. He became suspicious when he noticed that the horse had an insatiable thirst; then he discovered that the horse had been cut in two parts. No sooner did it drink water than the liquid ran out the rear of the half horse into the fountain.

Münchhausenplatz 1. ✆ **05533/409147.** Admission 3€. Apr–Oct daily 10am–noon and 2–5pm.

Where to Eat & Stay

Goldener Anker This half-timbered old favorite, under the direction of the Schoppe family, dates from 1837 but has been modernized. The Weser River, where boats tie up, virtually runs by its front door. In summer the action overflows onto a *Biergarten* fronting the river. Most people come here for food and drink in the tavern, and it attracts both visitors and locals. The menu features an array of regional specialties, including the best steaks in town. Meals begin at 20€ per person. Bedrooms listed as standard are cozy and comfortably furnished; those rated deluxe are roomier with better plumbing fixtures.

Brückenstrasse 5, 37619 Bodenwerder. www.bodenwerder-hotel.de. ✆ **05533/400730.** Fax 05533/400733. 16 units. 50€ double. MC, V. **Amenities:** Restaurant; bar; bikes; room service. *In room:* TV, Wi-Fi (free).

Parkhotel Deutsches Haus ★   Next door to the former home of Baron von Münchhausen (now the city hall) stands this half-timbered hotel that is the most inviting and comfortable in town. A country aura is evoked by its oak paneling and old wooden beams. The bedrooms have been modernized and are attractively furnished. The hotel stands on its own landscaped grounds, which appear even larger since they lie next to the city park. Meals cost 28€ and in summer are served on a terrace near the Weser River. In honor of the baron, the house dish is named *Kugeln* or "cannonballs" (turkey, pork, and fresh vegetables).

Münchhausenplatz 4, 37619 Bodenwerder. www.hotel-deutsches-haus-bodenwerder.de. ✆ **05533/400780.** Fax 05533/4113. 42 units. 87€–105€ double. AE, MC, V. **Amenities:** 2 restaurants; bar; room service. *In room:* TV, hair dryer, minibar, Wi-Fi (free).

HAMELN ★

45km (28 miles) SW of Hannover, 48km (30 miles) W of Hildesheim

Hameln has many interesting buildings and a history dating from the 11th century, but its main claim to fame is the Pied Piper folk tale, immortalized by the Brothers Grimm, Goethe, and Robert Browning, among others. According to legend, in 1284 the town was infested by rats. Soon after, a piper appeared and offered, for a fee, to lure the vermin into the Weser River. The rat catcher successfully performed the service, but the stingy denizens of Hameln refused to pay, claiming that he was a sorcerer. So the piper reappeared the next Sunday and played a tune that lured the town's children, except one lame boy, into a mysterious door in a hill. The children and the Pied Piper were never heard from again.

There is some historical basis for the story. It appears that, several centuries ago, for some unknown reason, the children of Hameln did indeed leave the town. The story of the Pied Piper is retold every summer Sunday at noon in a special performance at the **Hochzeitshaus (Wedding House)** on Osterstrasse. In the town shops, you can buy rat figures made of almost every conceivable material, including candy.

Essentials
GETTING THERE
BY PLANE   The nearest major airport is Hannover-Langenhagen, 55km (34 miles) away.

BY TRAIN   The **Hameln Bahnhof** lies on the Hannover-Hameln-Altenbeken line, with frequent connections. Depending on the train, trip time from Hannover ranges from 45 to 55 minutes. For information, call ✆ **01805/996633** (www.bahn.de).

BY BUS   Local and regional bus service to nearby towns and Hannover is available from Grossraum-Verkehr Hannover (✆ **01803/19449;** www.gvh.de). Buses stop in front of the Hauptbahnhof.

BY CAR   It takes 3 hours to reach Hameln from Frankfurt and 6 to 7 hours from Munich. From Frankfurt, head northeast along the A5 Autobahn, then north on the

A7, and finally west on A27. From Munich, take the A9 Autobahn north to Nürnberg, the A3 west to Würzburg, then the A7 north toward Hannover, and finally take the A27 west to Hameln.

VISITOR INFORMATION

Contact the **Hamelin Marketing und Tourismus GmbH,** Deisterallee 1 (✆ **05151/957823;** www.hameln.de), open May to September Monday to Friday 9am to 6:30pm, Saturday 9:30am to 4pm, and Sunday 9:30am to 1pm; October to March Monday to Friday 9am to 6pm and Saturday 9:30am to 1pm; and April Monday to Friday 9am to 6:30pm and Saturday 9:30am to 4pm.

Exploring Hameln

Hameln's most historic building is the Gothic **Münsterkirch,** at the end of Bäcker-strasse, overlooking the Weser River. Other attractions include the **Rattenfänger-haus** (see below), with frescoes illustrating the Pied Piper legend, and the **Hochzeitshaus (Wedding House)** on Osterstrasse, with its three attractive gables. The finest houses in the town are built in what is known as Weser-Renaissance style. You can admire these nicely sculpted late-16th-century houses as you stroll along the pedestrians-only streets. One of the best examples of the Weser-Renaissance style, which can be enjoyed by looking at its facade, is **Dempterscheshaus,** built in 1607. This house, at Pferdemarkt, standing in the middle of town, has protruding bay windows. This patrician building is also characterized by fine chiseled stones and decorations of ornaments and coats of arms.

Where to Eat

Rattenfängerhaus GERMAN The "Rat-Catcher's House" dates from 1603. A meal here is practically like eating in a museum. The place is a little too touristy and crowded for some tastes, but it's an enduring favorite nonetheless. You can order traditional German dishes, including various kinds of *Schnitzels,* roasted goose, or filets of salmon with hollandaise sauce.

Osterstrasse 28. ✆ **05151/3888.** www.rattenfaengerhaus.de. Reservations recommended. Main courses 8€–22€. AE, DC, MC, V. Daily 11am–3pm and 6–11pm. Bus: 1 or 2.

Shopping

There are lots of opportunities to buy folkloric art objects here. One of the best bets for souvenir and gift hunting, **Renner,** Am Markt 6 (✆ **05151/94420**), has some genuinely charming objects. You might also want to go window-shopping along the town's best shopping streets, the **Osterstrasse** and the **Bäckerstrasse.**

Entertainment & Nightlife

The town's **Weserbergland Festhalle,** Rathausplatz (✆ **05151/916220;** www. theater.hameln.de), hosts an array of concerts, opera and ballet performances, and theatrical productions. Call the theater or the visitor information office (see above) for upcoming events and ticket information. Tickets are 10€ to 26€.

Where to Stay

Hotel zur Börse This balconied hotel within the walls of the Altstadt can be identified by the four peaks of its modern roofline. The interior is refreshingly uncluttered. Rooms are spacious and well maintained with sleek bathrooms.

Osterstrasse 41A, 31785 Hameln. www.hotel-zur-boerse.de. ✆ **05151/7080.** Fax 05151/25485. 31 units. 93€ double. Rates include buffet breakfast. AE, DC, MC, V. Parking 7€. Bus: 1 or 2. **Amenities:** Restaurant; bar; bikes; room service. *In room:* TV, fax, hair dryer, minibar, Wi-Fi (9.50€ per day).

Komfort-Hotel Garni Christinenhof   The gabled windows of this half-timbered, 300-year-old building overlook a cobblestone street in the middle of the Altstadt. Despite the antique facade, much of the hotel's interior is streamlined and modern, with many conveniences. All units contain neatly kept bathrooms and are small yet well furnished.

Alte Markstrasse 18, 31785 Hameln. www.christinenhof-hameln.de. ✆ **05151/95080.** Fax 05151/43611. 30 units. 100€–120€ double. Rates include buffet breakfast. MC, V. Free parking. Closed Dec 20–Jan 6. **Amenities:** Indoor heated pool; sauna. *In room:* TV, hair dryer, minibar, Wi-Fi (free).

Mercure Hotel Hameln   This hotel stands in a park with lots of trees but is within walking distance of the heart of the Altstadt, at the northern edge of the Burgergarten. It rises like a modern collection of building blocks, with oversize glass walls. Rooms are standard and functional, and all contain up-to-date bathrooms.

164er Ring 3, 31785 Hameln. www.mercure.com. ✆ **05151/7920.** Fax 05151/792191. 105 units. 95€–270€ double. AE, DC, MC, V. Parking 10€. Bus: 1 or 2. **Amenities:** Restaurant; bar; babysitting; exercise room; indoor heated pool; room service; sauna. *In room:* TV, hair dryer, minibar, Wi-Fi (18€ per day).

HANNOVER

122km (76 miles) SE of Bremen, 151km (94 miles) S of Hamburg, 288km (179 miles) W of Berlin

This modest little city south of Hamburg still basks in the glow of Expo 2000, when more foreigners visited than ever before. It remains one of Germany's hubs of industry, transportation, and commerce, and its annual industrial trade fair is still the largest such fair in the world, attracting producers and buyers from around the globe.

Even with a big-money investment in its inner city, Hannover is hardly a city of grace and beauty. Although it has certain idyllic sections, including one of the finest baroque gardens in the world; a 2.5km (1½-mile) man-made lake, the Maschsee; and the encircling Eilenriede Forest, Hannover is a mere shadow of its former self. The royal court checked out in the early 19th century, heading for greener fields and greater power in London.

Essentials

GETTING THERE

BY PLANE   Hannover is served by **Hannover-Langenhagen International Airport,** 10km (6 miles) north of the city center. Many international airlines fly here. Flying time between Hannover and Munich is 1 hour, 10 minutes; between Frankfurt and Hannover, 50 minutes. For flight information, call ✆ **0511/9770** or visit www. hannover-airport.de. Catch the S-Bahn to the Hauptbahnhof. The cost is 3€ each way. Service is 5am to midnight, every 30 minutes.

BY TRAIN   Hannover lies at the junction of an important network of rail lines linking Scandinavia to Italy and Paris to Moscow. Some 500 trains per day pass through, with frequent connections to major German and European cities. Nineteen trains arrive daily from Berlin (trip time: 1 hr., 35 min.), 40 trains from Frankfurt (trip time: 2 hr., 21 min., or 3 hr., depending on the train), and 40 trains from Hamburg (trip time: 1 hr., 11 min. to 1½ hr.). For information call ✆ **01805/996633** (www. bahn.de).

BY BUS Long-distance bus service to and from major German cities is offered by **Deutsche Touring** GmbH, Hamburger Allee 19, opposite the Hauptbahnhof (☏ 0511/329419; www.touring.de).

BY CAR Access is via the A1 Autobahn north or south and from the A2 east and west.

VISITOR INFORMATION

Contact **Hannover Tourist Information,** located at Ernst-August-Platz 2 (☏ 0511/12345111; www.hannover.de). Here you can reserve hotel rooms (ask about special weekend packages), book sightseeing tours, obtain general information about the city, and purchase tickets for local events as well as for trains, trams, and buses. The office is open Monday to Friday 9am to 6pm and Saturday 9am to 2pm.

GETTING AROUND

The local public-transport system includes commuter trains, an extensive underground network, trams, and buses operated by several companies. Service is frequent and extensive. For information and schedules, contact **Grossraum-Verkehr Hannover** (☏ 0511/16683000; www.gvh.de).

Exploring Hannover

Marktkirche (Market Church), the Gothic brick basilica on Marktplatz, is one of Hannover's oldest structures, built in the mid–14th century. **Altes Rathaus (Old Town Hall),** facing the square, dates from 1425. It was badly damaged in the war but has been restored and now houses the civic archives.

Herrenhäuser Garten (Royal Gardens of Herrenhäusen) ★★ GARDEN No matter where you go in Hannover, you won't be far from a park or garden. But make sure you don't miss this one, the only surviving example of Dutch/Low German early baroque-style gardening. Designers from France, the Netherlands, England, and Italy, as well as Germany, worked together to create this masterpiece of living art. **Grosse Garten,** from 1666, is the largest garden, consisting of a rectangle surrounded by a moat. Within the maze of walks and trees are examples of French baroque, rococo, and Low German rose and flower gardens. The Grosse Garten also contains one of the highest fountains in Europe, shooting jets of water 72m (236 ft.) into the air, and the world's only existing baroque hedge-theater (1692), where plays by Shakespeare, Molière, and Brecht are still performed, along with ballets and jazz concerts. The smaller 17th-century **Berggarten,** across Herrenhäuser Strasse from the Grosse Garten, is a botanical garden with houses containing rare orchids and other tropical flowers.

Herrenhäuser Strasse 4. ☏ **0511/16844543.** Admission 4€ adults, free for children 13 and under. Daily 9am–8pm. Waterworks display May–Sept Mon–Fri 11am–noon and 3–5pm, Sat–Sun and holidays 11am–noon and 2–5pm. U-Bahn: Herrenhäuser Gärten.

Niedersächsisches Landesmuseum Hannover (Lower Saxony State Museum) ★ ☺ MUSEUM The Landesmuseum is one of the most important regional museums in Germany. There are exhibits on northern European biology and geology, ethnomedicine and ethnobotany, and the history of Lower Saxony from the Paleolithic Age up to the Middle Ages. The aquarium shows a world of exotic fish, amphibians, and reptiles. In the **Kindermuseum,** children can learn about prehistoric times with activities such as grinding corn or working with stone tools.

A Twist in the Tale

by George McDonald

You might not recognize some plot elements of early versions of these famous fairy tales.

- **Cinderella (Aschenputtel)** In the Grimm version, there is no fairy godmother. It is the beautiful tree she planted on her mother's grave that comes to her aid in attending the ball. Cinderella is a passive heroine, rescued from a life of drudgery by the handsome prince.

- **Hansel and Gretel (Hänsel und Gretel)** Early versions of the story were sanitized to make it more child-friendly, with the evil mother being changed to a stepmother, thus creating the evil-stepmother trope.

- **Little Red Riding Hood (Rotkäppchen)** In the French oral version, the hunter doesn't save Little Red Riding Hood from the Big Bad Wolf—she distracts the predatory beast herself by performing a striptease, and then escapes. The Grimms sanitized the tale into a warning to children not to stray from the approved path.

- **Rapunzel** In early versions of this tale, Rapunzel asks why her dress is getting so tight, thus naively revealing to her wicked stepmother that she is pregnant following a dalliance with the prince.

The museum's art gallery contains treasures spanning 7 centuries. A highlight is Meister Bertram von Minden's *Passion Altar* (1390–1400). You'll also see paintings by Rembrandt, Van Dyck, and Rubens (his *Madonna*), as well as the *Four Times of Day* series by Caspar David Friedrich.

Willy-Brandt-Allee. ✆ **0511/9807686.** www.nlmh.de. Admission 4€ adults, 3€ students and children. Tues-Wed and Fri-Sun 10am-5pm; Thurs 10am-7pm. Tram: 1, 2, 4, 5, 6, 8, 11, 16, or 18. Bus: 131, 132, or 267. Near the Maschpark.

Rathaus GOVERNMENT BUILDING The "new" Rathaus is a large structure, built between 1901 and 1913. An inclined elevator—the only one in Europe other than the elevator at the Eiffel Tower—takes visitors up to the 10m (33-ft.) dome. The building is attractive because of its location in the Maschpark, by a small lake. It's just a short distance from the extensive artificial Maschsee, frequented by Hannoverians for its beach, boats, and restaurants.

Trammplatz 2. ✆ **0511/1680.** Elevator ride to dome 3€ adults, 2€ students and children. Apr-Oct Mon-Fri 9:30am-6:30pm; Sat-Sun 10am-6:30pm. U-Bahn: Markthalle. Tram: 3, 7, or 9. Bus: 120.

Sprengel Museum ★★ MUSEUM Although this museum of modern art, one of the best in Germany, has been around since 1979, it is gaining increasing renown for its two dozen annual exhibitions, now among the most cutting edge in Europe. These temporary shows stand side by side with the museum's permanent collection, which includes some of the greatest names in modern art—Picasso, of course, but also Paul Klee, Max Ernst, Max Beckman, and the like. The museum is named for Dr. Bernhard Sprengel, who started the original collection with its array of French modern and expressionism.

Over the years the museum has expanded to include some of the most significant artists of the 20th century, and it also created one of the best departments of photography in Germany. In 1993, it acquired the Kurt Schwitters archives. He was a native son of Hannover and one of the leading Dadaists; in fact, the square on which the museum sits was named after him.

Kurt-Schwitters-Platz 2. ℂ **0511/16843875.** www.sprengel-museum.de. Admission 7€ adults, 4€ students, free for children 11 and under. Tues 10am–8pm; Wed–Sun 10am–6pm.

Where to Eat

EXPENSIVE

Basil ★★ INTERNATIONAL   The hippest restaurant in Hannover draws a chic clientele to a dining room known for its modern cuisine, fresh ingredients, and alert waitstaff. The setting is a riding hall built in 1867 for the Royal Prussian military. Guests dine in an antique atmosphere under a vaulted ceiling. We prefer a table in the delightful garden where we've spotted Hannover's most famous son, former Chancellor Gerhard Schröder, dining. Like Clichy (see below), where the food is only slightly better, Basil changes each menu at least every 3 weeks, and it's always based on what's fresh and flavorful at the market. Recipes range from the coasts of the Mediterranean to Asia. We recently arrived in spring to enjoy a *Spargel* (asparagus menu). Had it been autumn, game dishes would have been featured. The accent of the menu is always on fish, as exemplified by the likes of sea bream in a zesty lime sauce with spring onions, or perhaps moist and tender trout stuffed with fresh spinach.

Dragonerstrasse 30A. ℂ **0511/622636.** www.basil.de. Reservations required. Main courses 18€–25€. AE, MC, V. Mon–Sat 6:30pm–2am. U-Bahn: U1 or U2 to Dragonerstrasse.

Clichy Restaurant ★★ CONTINENTAL/MEDITERRANEAN   This haven of refined cuisine is the most consistently reliable dining choice in the city. For more than 2 decades, its guiding light, Ekkehard Reimann, has coddled his guests with fine cuisine backed up by a well-stocked cellar. A Hannover food critic recently wrote, "For the inexperienced gourmet, a visit here is unforgettable." We'd include experienced gourmets in that appraisal as well. Specials rely on the day's shopping, as Chef Reimann believes in using the best seasonal ingredients available. Year after year, his cooking lives up to a superb standard, and his dishes are marked by intense flavors and precise techniques.

Weissekreuzstrasse 31. ℂ **0511/312447.** www.clichy.de. Reservations required. Main courses 24€–30€; fixed-price menus 54€–66€. AE, MC. Mon–Fri noon–2:30pm; daily 6–11pm. Tram: 3 or 7.

Wichmann ★ GERMAN/FRENCH   This family owned, white-walled, shuttered inn, with its slate walks and carefully tended flower beds, is worth the trip. The garden serves as a pleasant setting for dining in the summer months. The place is an oasis of comfort. Cooking is German *gutbürgerlich*—wholesome and hearty. Try specialties such as fish terrine, rack of lamb, homemade noodles, and wine and cheese from all over Germany. The place lies 4km (2½ miles) south of central Hannover in the satellite town of Hannover-Döhren.

Hildesheimer Strasse 230, Hannover-Döhren. ℂ **0511/831671.** www.gastwirtschaft-wichmann.de. Reservations required. Main courses 22€–35€. AE, MC, V. Daily noon–3pm and 6–11pm. Tram: 1 or 8.

MODERATE

Altdeutsche Bierstube GERMAN   With a decor that has changed little since its original construction around 1860, this old-fashioned *Bierstube* remains stable and solid, despite the monumental changes that have transformed the society around it. The unpretentious food is hearty, wholesome, and filling, with the regular fare augmented by seasonal specialties. Favorites include medallions of beef in a peppercorn sauce; and marinated pork cutlets with roasted onions, served with buttered beans and fried potatoes. Most dishes are priced at the lower end of the scale.

Köbelingerstrasse 1. ⓒ **0511/344921.** www.altdeutsche-bierstube.net. Reservations required. Main courses 8€–34€. AE, DC, MC, V. Mon–Fri 11:30am–3pm; Mon–Sat 6pm–1am. Closed holidays. U-Bahn: Lister Platz.

Steuerndieb ★ 🏠 INTERNATIONAL   In 1329, a stone-sided tower was erected about 1.5km (1 mile) east of central Hannover to guard the lumber produced in Eilenriede Forest. The tower's name, Steuerndieb, translates from the archaic German as "Stop, thieves!" Around 1850 a rustic restaurant was built on the site, and it has been known ever since for hearty and flavorful food. Many of the specialties are cooked over an open fire, and the restaurant offers a locally inspired menu that, unlike those of many other restaurants, features game year-round. Two popular dishes are venison with red cabbage, dumplings, and black-cherry sauce; and rabbit with black-pepper sauce and red cabbage.

The establishment also has a modern wing containing seven simple, white-walled rooms, each with a private bathroom, TV, telephone, and view overlooking the forest. Doubles cost 80€, including a buffet breakfast.

Steuerndieb 1. ⓒ **0511/909960.** www.steuerndieb.de. Reservations not required. Main courses 16€–24€. AE, DC, MC, V. Mon–Sat 11am–3pm and 6–11pm; Sun 11am–3pm. Tram: 3 or 7.

INEXPENSIVE

Brauhaus Ernst August HANNOVERIAN   This is a beer-lover's Valhalla, established both as a brewery and a restaurant 2 decades ago. It specializes in only one kind of brew, a *Pils,* with no preservatives added, priced at 3.20€ for a half-liter. At the on-site gift shop you can buy all sorts of items related to beer, including mugs and the evocative beer bottles with porcelain stoppers, which invading GIs in 1945 named "snap daddies." Old-fashioned Hannoverian specialties are featured, and everything is tasty and filling, including a goulash that's a meal in itself and a rich cream-of-potato soup. *Wursts* are the most popular items, although steaks, *Schnitzels,* spareribs, and chicken cutlets are also available. In spring, asparagus dishes dominate the menu. It's customary to precede your beer drinking or eating with a bolting shot of *Brauerschluck* (Brewer's Gulp), a lethal schnapps brewed on-site.

Schmiedstrasse 13. ⓒ **0511/365950.** www.brauhaus.net. Reservations not required. Main courses 10€–20€. V. Beer Sun–Thurs 8am–3am, Fri–Sat 8am–5am; warm food daily 11:30am–11pm.

Shopping

The oldest and largest flea market in Germany, the **Flohmarkt,** sprawls across Am Hohen Ufer (U-Bahn: Markthalle) every Saturday from 7am to 4pm. Stalls are set up along the banks of the Leine River. The city is hardly confined to flea markets, however. Hannover is one of the most fashion-conscious cities of the country, sometimes called "the Milan of Germany." It is the home of stylish clothing, and Hannoverians are among the most fashionably dressed Germans.

Your first destination may be the glassed-over **Galerie Luise,** a multilevel shopping mall at the corner of Luisenstrasse and Rathenaustrasse (bus: 120), with upscale shops for clothing and home furnishings. **Terner,** Luisenstrasse 9 (ⓒ **0511/363931;** tram: 5), has designer-inspired clothing for men, women, and children.

Entertainment & Nightlife

Hannover Vorschau, a monthly newspaper devoted exclusively to the city's nightlife and cultural venues, is available at news kiosks and in the city's hotels.

THE PERFORMING ARTS The **Nieder Sächsische Stadttheater Hannover GmbH,** Opernplatz 1 (✆ **0511/99991111;** www.staatstheater-hannover.de; U-Bahn: Kröpcke), built between 1845 and 1852, is the region's leading venue for ballet, concerts, and opera. Depending on the performance, tickets cost from 15€ to 65€ each. Less formal, with popular as well as classical offerings, is the **N. D. R. Symphoniker,** Rudolf Benigsen Ufer 22 (✆ **0511/9880;** bus: 2 or 6), an ugly postwar building whose charm derives from what goes on inside. You can hear poetry readings, jazz and rock-'n'-roll concerts, and chamber orchestras. Tickets cost 15€ to 35€.

BARS Many of Hannover's most appealing bars are Irish pubs. The biggest and best of the lot is **MacGowan's Irish Pub,** Bruderstrasse 4 (✆ **0511/14589;** www. irishpub-hannover.de; U-Bahn: Steintor or Hauptbahnhof). It's open daily 5pm to 2am, and serves Guinness and Murphy's on tap, along with sandwiches, fish and chips, and Irish stew. When Irish music bands are booked, a cover ranging from 8€ to 10€ is imposed.

DANCE CLUBS The best place for mainstream dance is **Osho Disco,** Raschplatz 7L (✆ **0511/6422785;** www.osho-disco.de; U-Bahn: Hauptbahnhof), a longtime survivor of the club scene. It plays funk, house, and other dance music. It's open Wednesday to Sunday 10pm to "whenever." Cover is 4€ to 10€. One of its leading competitors is **Palo Palo,** Raschplatz 8A (✆ **0511/331073;** www.palopalo-club. com; U-Bahn: Hauptbahnhof), where house, funk, blues, reggae, and Motown play every night 9:30pm until dawn, for a cover of 5€ to 8€.

LIVE MUSIC An alternative venue, **Café Glocksee,** Glockseestrasse 35 (✆ **0511/1614712;** www.cafe-glocksee.de; tram: 10), stages hard-core, punk, and techno shows. Thursday concerts start at 9pm. On Friday and Saturday, it's disco mania 11pm to 7am and again on Wednesday 6pm to 2am. The cover charge ranges from 3€ to 15€.

GAY CLUBS **Schwul Sau,** Schaufeldstrasse 30A (✆ **0511/7000525;** www. schwulesauhannover.de; tram: 6), hosts dance parties, theater performances, and private parties, attended by a crowd of gay and straight arts-conscious patrons. It's open Tuesday, Wednesday, and Friday 8pm to 3am; Saturday 9pm to at least 7am; and Sunday 3pm to 2am. Cover is 8€ to 15€ for parties or theater events, and 5€ for dancing. There's no cover Tuesday, Wednesday, or Sunday.

A CASINO The **Spielbank,** Osterstrasse 40 (✆ **0511/980660;** www.spielbankenniedersachsen.de; U-Bahn: Kröpcke), has an impressive roster of blackjack, roulette, and slot machines. It's set within a modern building, with none of the Belle Epoque trappings or decorations you might have hoped for, and contains both a bar and a restaurant. Men are required to wear jackets and ties, and women are requested to dress appropriately. The casino is open daily 3pm to 3am. Admission costs 2.50€, and you must show your passport to enter (you must be 18 or older to enter and gamble).

Where to Stay

Crowne Plaza ★ This is one of the most imaginatively designed hotels in Hannover, with a lot more charm and atmosphere than other leading contenders. It sits on a quiet street in the central business district. Inside you'll find illuminated Plexiglas columns and sweeping expanses of russet-colored marble. The hotel serves an affluent clientele, often including visiting celebrities. Rooms are spacious and elegantly furnished, all with immaculately kept bathrooms.

Hinuberstrasse 6, 30175 Hannover. www.ichotelsgroup.com. ✆ **0511/34950.** Fax 0511/3495123. 201 units. 118€–201€ double; from 250€ suite. Rates include buffet breakfast. AE, DC, MC, V. Parking 19€. Tram: 16. **Amenities:** 2 restaurants; bar; babysitting; bikes; concierge; exercise room; room service; spa. *In room:* A/C, TV, hair dryer, minibar, Wi-Fi (22€ per day).

Hotel Königshof am Funkturm ★   Both the skylights and the modernized crenellations on this hotel's mansard roof make it look like an updated feudal fortress. The hotel was built in 1984 above a glass-and-steel shopping arcade in the town center. Each plushly carpeted room has a couch that converts to a bed. Only breakfast is served at the hotel, but there's an Italian restaurant across the street.

Friesenstrasse 65, 30161 Hannover. www.koenigshof-hannover.de. ✆ **0511/33980.** Fax 0511/3398111. 91 units. 79€–281€ double; 102€–338€ suite. AE, DC, MC, V. Parking 7.50€. Bus: 20 or 39. **Amenities:** Restaurant; bar. *In room:* TV, minibar, Wi-Fi (9€ per day).

Kastens Hotel Luisenhof ★★   This is the leading hotel in town. Its stately glass-and-stone facade is just minutes from the Hauptbahnhof in the city center. A series of modernizations have enhanced comfort while maintaining conservative good taste. Rooms are spacious, stylishly furnished, and impeccably kept, all with neat bathrooms.

Luisenstrasse 1–3, 30159 Hannover. www.kastens-luisenhof.de. ✆ **0511/30440.** Fax 0511/3044807. 145 units. 177€–427€ double; 590€–990€ suite. Children 11 and under stay free in parent's room. Rates include buffet breakfast. AE, DC, MC, V. Parking 12€. Tram: 16. Near the Hauptbahnhof. **Amenities:** Restaurant; bar; bikes; exercise room; Internet (free; in lobby); room service; sauna. *In room:* A/C (in some), TV, DVD (in suites), CD player (in some), hair dryer, minibar, Wi-Fi (free).

Loccumer Hof 🗲   Situated near the train station, this is one of Hannover's best deals, a good, clean, and decent choice. The utilitarian rooms and bathrooms are small, with tub/shower combinations. Service and frills are minimal, but the beds are comfortable and the hotel is well maintained. There are six deluxe doubles and two suites dating from 2004 that are more spacious and better equipped than the standard doubles.

Kurt-Schumacher-Strasse 14–16, 30159 Hannover. www.loccumerhof.com. ✆ **0511/12640.** Fax 0511/131192. 95 units. 139€–520€ double; 159€–590€ deluxe double; 169€–640€ suite. Higher rates during trade fairs. Rates include buffet breakfast. AE, DC, MC, V. Parking 7.50€. Tram: 16. Near the Hauptbahnhof. **Amenities:** Restaurant; bar. *In room:* TV, hair dryer, minibar, Wi-Fi (free).

BREMEN ★★

119km (74 miles) SW of Hamburg, 122km (76 miles) NW of Hannover

Bremen, Germany's oldest coastal city, is second only to Hamburg among German ports. As soon as you arrive at "this ancient town by the gray river," you see how closely Bremen is tied to the sea. The sights and smells of coffee, cacao, tropical fruit, lumber, and tobacco give the city an international flavor.

Bremen grew from a little fishing settlement on a sandy slope of a river. It was already a significant port when it was made an Episcopal see in 787. In the 11th century, under the progressive influence of Archbishop Adalbert, Bremen became known as the "Rome of the North." During the Middle Ages, it was one of the strongest members of the Hanseatic League, and in 1646 it became a free imperial city. It remains one of Europe's most important ports.

Böttcherstrasse **3**
Dom Museum **5**
Dom St. Petri **5**
Focke-Museum **8**
Kunsthalle **9**
Kunstsammlungen
  Böttcherstrasse **2**
Marktplatz **4**
Rathaus **6**
Schnoor **1**
Wallanlagen **7**

Essentials
GETTING THERE
BY PLANE The **Bremen Flughafen** (② 0421/55950; www.airport-bremen.de) lies only 3km (2 miles) southeast of the city center (take S-Bahn 5). It is used mainly as a commuter airport for flights within Germany.

BY TRAIN Bremen has excellent rail connections with leading German cities. Its **Hauptbahnhof** lies on major rail lines, including Hamburg-Bremen-Osnabrück-Münster and Hannover-Bremen-Bremerhaven. Thirty trains arrive daily from Hamburg (trip time: 1 hr.), 35 trains from Hannover (trip time: 1 hr.), 13 trains from

Berlin (trip time: 5 hr.), and 50 trains from Frankfurt (trip time: 4 hr., 15 min.). For information call ℂ **01805/996633** (www.bahn.de).

BY BUS   Rail travel to Bremen is far more efficient, but the city does have some bus links to other towns. Call ℂ **0421/5596333** for information. The bus station is in front of the railway station.

BY CAR   Access by car is via the A7 Autobahn east and west and the A27 north and south.

VISITOR INFORMATION

Contact the **Bremer Touristik Zentrale GmbH,** Findorffstrasse 105 (ℂ **0421/ 3080010;** www.bremen-tourism.de). Hours are Monday to Friday 8:30am to 6pm and Saturday 9:30am to 1pm. There's also a second branch at **Liebfrauenkircher Hof,** near Marktplatz, open Monday to Friday 10am to 6:30pm, Saturday and Sunday 10am to 4pm. There is yet another branch at the **Main Railway Station,** open Monday to Friday 9am to 7pm and Saturday and Sunday 9:30am to 6pm.

GETTING AROUND

For information about public transportation within Bremen, call ℂ **01805/826826.** The cost is .10€ per minute. A single ticket, good for one trip on the city's network of buses and trams, costs 2.30€ to most destinations. For 7.60€, two adults and up to five children may ride all day on the network. The meter on local taxis begins at 2.50€.

ORGANIZED TOURS

Bremen has both bus and walking tours of its historic sites. **Bus tours,** conducted in both German and English, depart from the Hauptbahnhof Tuesday to Sunday at 10:30am. They cost 18€ for adults and 12€ for children 11 and under. **Walking tours** depart every day at 2pm, last 2 hours, and cost 6.50€ or free for ages 11 and under. From April 14 to October 6, there is an additional walking tour conducted on Saturday at 11am. The combination of a morning bus tour with an afternoon walking tour offers a broadly comprehensive overview of Bremen. Tickets should be reserved in advance, then picked up at the tourist office (see "Visitor Information," above).

The city also sponsors **boat trips** around the harbor. They depart from the jetty in front of the Martinikirche every day March to October. Tours depart at 11:45am, 1:30, and 3:15pm. From May to September there's an additional tour at 10:30am. You can reach the jetty from Marktplatz by walking southwest along Böttcherstrasse for about 3 minutes. The cost is 14€ for adults and 9€ for children 13 and under. For more information, call the tourist office (see above) or **Hal Över** (ℂ **0421/338989;** www.hal-oever.de).

Exploring Bremen
THE TOP ATTRACTIONS

The main sights center on **Marktplatz ★★**, the "parlor" of Bremen life for more than 1,000 years. The 9m (30-ft.) statue (ca. 1404) of the city's protector, Roland, bears the "sword of justice" and a shield decorated with an imperial eagle. Local legend has it that as long as the statue stands in Marktplatz, Bremen will survive as a free city. During World War II, when this area was hard hit by Allied bombs, extensive measures were taken to protect the statue.

Across the square from the Rathaus stands an example of a happy merger of Gothic and Renaissance architecture, the **Schötting,** a 16th-century guildhall used by the chamber of commerce. Somewhat in contrast to these ancient masterpieces is the **Haus der Bürgerschaft,** home of Bremen's Parliament. The 1966 structure was scaled down to fit in with its surroundings. Even though it's a maze of glass, concrete, and steel, it doesn't look entirely out of place.

Dom St. Petri (St. Peter's Cathedral) ★★ CHURCH St. Peter's, set back from the square, towers majestically over all other buildings in the Altstadt. Originally designed in 1043 as the archbishop's church, it was rebuilt in the 13th, 16th, and 19th centuries. There's a 12th-century bronze baptismal font in one of the Romanesque crypts. In the Bleikeller (Lead Cellar), there's a bizarre collection of mummified corpses of workers who fell from the roof during the construction, along with several others who met with violent ends.

You can also visit the **Dom Museum** (✆ **0421/3650475**), which displays artifacts found during the large-scale restoration of the Dom, including medieval tombs and 15th-century wall paintings. Other exhibits include the remains of an early Romanesque building and a collection of historic altar implements.

Sandstrasse 10-12. ✆ **0421/365040.** www.stpetridom.de. Cathedral free; museum and tower 3€ adults, 1.70€ students, seniors, and children; lead cellar 1.40€ adults, 1€ children. Cathedral year-round Mon-Fri 10am-5pm; Sat 10am-2pm; Sun 2-5pm. Museum May-Oct Mon-Fri 10am-5pm, Sat 10am-1:30pm, Sun 2-5pm; Nov-Apr Mon-Fri 11am-4pm, Sat 10am-noon, Sun 2-5pm. Lead cellar and tower May-Oct Mon-Fri 10am-5pm; Sat 10am-noon (cellar also Sun 10am-noon). Museum, cellar, and tower closed May 1, Oct 3, Dec 24-25 and 31, and Good Friday. Bus: 24, 25, N3, or 56. Tram: 2, 3, 4, 5, 68, or N1.

Focke-Museum ★ MUSEUM This is one of the best regional museums in this area of Germany, and we particularly applaud the user-friendly way in which the various exhibitions are displayed. The glory days of Bremen as a maritime power in the Middle Ages and through the Renaissance era are evoked in the main gallery. For safekeeping, and because they were deteriorating in the weather, the original statues carved for the facade of the Rathaus are on display here, along with ecclesiastical art, secular art, and various objets d'art, much of it retrieved from town houses of the long-departed Bremen aristocracy. Lots of portraits of fat merchants also attest to the former prosperity of Bremen. In addition, you can wander back into history to the days of the conquering Romans. Although the Roman collection is the richest, there are artifacts from prehistoric times along with Saxon antiquities. Americans may be particularly interested in documents showing the massive transport of German emigrants to the U.S. on the steamers operated by the Norddeutscher Lloyd Shipline. In the park on the museum grounds is a typical thatched farmhouse once common to Lower Saxony.

Schwachhauser Heerstrasse 240. ✆ **0421/6996000.** www.focke-museum.de. Admission 8€ adults, 6€ children 6-18, free for children 5 and under. Tues 10am-9pm; Wed-Sun 10am-5pm. S-Bahn: Focke Museum. Tram: 4 or 5.

Rathaus ★ GOVERNMENT BUILDING The 560-year-old Rathaus has seen several periods of transformation. Outside, at the west end, is one of the more recent additions: a sculpture of Bremen's visitors from the land of Grimm—the Bremen town musicians. The donkey, dog, cat, and cock are stacked, pyramid style, in a constant pose for ever-present cameras. The original Gothic foundations of the Rathaus remain basically unchanged, but the upper section reflects the 17th-century Weser-Renaissance style in the facade; the tall windows alternate with relief statues of Charlemagne and the electors of the Holy Roman Empire. The upper hall, part of the original structure, contains a beautifully carved early-17th-century oak staircase. A

This walk, which the Germans call **Wallanlagen** ★ (tram: 4, 5, or 6), is a peaceful green park where the ramparts protecting this Hanseatic city used to stand. Its gardens divide the Altstadt from the newer extensions of the city. The park is just a few short blocks from Marktplatz, along the canal (once Bremen's crown-shaped moat). Its major attraction is a still-functioning ancient windmill.

mural of *The Judgment of Solomon* (1537) reminds us that the hall was originally a council chamber and courtroom. Below the lower hall lies the historic Ratskeller (see below).

Marktplatz. 📞 **0421/3610.** www.rathaus-bremen.de. Admission 5€ adults, free for children 11 and under. For tours, inquire at the tourist office (see "Visitor Information," earlier in this section). Tours generally begin Mon–Sat at 11am, noon, 3, and 4pm, and Sun 11am and noon. Tram: 1, 2, 3, or 5. Bus: 30, 31, or 34.

MORE SIGHTS

One of Bremen's biggest attractions, **Böttcherstrasse** ★ (📞 0421/338820; www.boettcherstrasse.de; tram: 4), running from Marktplatz to the Weser River, is a brick-paved reproduction of a medieval alley, complete with shops, restaurants, a museum, and galleries. The street was designed to present a picture of Bremen life, past and present. It was the brainchild of a wealthy Bremen merchant, Ludwig Roselius, and was dedicated in 1926 and rebuilt after World War II. Try to visit around noon, 3, or 6pm, when the Meissen bells strung between two gables set up a chorus of chimes for a full 15 minutes. Besides fine handicraft and pottery shops, the street also contains buildings of historical significance.

Kunstsammlungen Böttcherstrasse ★, Böttcherstrasse 6–10 (📞 0421/3365077; tram: 4), consists of two adjoining buildings. The **Roselius Haus** is a 16th-century merchant's home with a collection of medieval objets d'art and furniture. Next door, the **Paula-Becker-Modersohn Haus** (📞 0421/3365066; www.pmbm.de) is dedicated to Bremen's outstanding painter (1876–1907) and contains many of her best works, including paintings, drawings, and prints. The two upper floors house works of the sculptor, painter, and architect Bernhard Hoetger (1874–1949). The museum is open Tuesday to Sunday 11am to 6pm. Admission is 5€ for adults and 3€ for children ages 7 to 16.

Schnoor (tram: 4, 5, or 6), the old quarter of Bremen, has undergone restoration. The cottages of this east-end district, once homes of simple fishermen, have been rented to artists and artisans in an effort to revive many old arts and crafts. Sightseers visit not only for the atmosphere but also for the unusual restaurants, shops, and art galleries.

Where to Eat

As a seaport, Bremen has developed its own style of cooking, concentrating much of its effort, naturally, on seafood from Scandinavia and the North Sea.

VERY EXPENSIVE

L'Orchidée im Bremer Ratskeller ★★★ FRENCH/MODERN GERMAN
Year after year, this restaurant continues its run as Bremen's best and most lauded.

It's operated by Hotel zur Post (see below), but enjoys a location at a different address in the old Bremer Rathaus. Veteran chefs watch over a well-trained kitchen crew, and the service is sophisticated and skillful. The dishes are simply delicious. Try the terrine of smoked eel and shrimp followed either by filet of turbot with lobster or breast of pigeon in a red-wine sauce. The desserts are made fresh daily, and the wine list is extensive.

Am Markt. © **0421/3347927.** www.lorchidee.de. Reservations required. Main courses 34€–38€. AE, MC, V. Tues–Sat 6:30–10pm. Closed 2 weeks at Easter, closed July–Aug. Tram: 1, 5, 6, or 10.

EXPENSIVE

Grashoff's Bistro ★★ 🏛 INTERNATIONAL   This restaurant is well managed, charming, and concerned with quality and ambience. Its only real flaw is that the bistro caters to mobs of office workers and shoppers at lunchtime. Dinner is a quieter affair. You'll get a distinct sense of the arts here and a few memories of Paris, thanks to dozens of framed pictures hung edge to edge across the cream-colored, bistro-inspired walls. Menu items include a succulent version of spaghetti with lobster; flank steak in a pepper sauce; an oft-changing roster of fresh fish; and desserts such as crème brûlée, fresh pastries, and tarts.

Contrescarpe 80. © **0421/14749.** www.grashoff.de. Reservations recommended. Main courses 22€–32€. AE, DC, MC, V. Mon–Fri noon–7:30pm; Sat noon–4pm. Tram: 4, 6, or 8.

Meierei im Burgerpark ★ CONTINENTAL   This lovely restaurant, in the center of a city park, is managed by the Park Hotel (see below). Locals often combine a meal here with a promenade in the park. The restaurant occupies what was originally a local aristocrat's summerhouse, sheathed in lacy gingerbread and ringed with ornate verandas. It contains an assortment of dining rooms furnished in Hanseatic style. Typical, and very good, dishes include fresh fish, consommé with scallops and saffron, fried breast of duck filled with herbs, sautéed squab with forest mushroom risotto, and medallions of monkfish with orange butter-and-basil sauce.

Im Burgerpark. © **0421/3408619.** www.meierei-bremen.de. Reservations required. Main courses 17€–23€. AE, DC, MC, V. Tues–Sun noon–2:30pm and 6:30–10pm. Tram: 8.

MODERATE

Ratskeller ★ GERMAN/INTERNATIONAL   This Ratskeller is one of Germany's most celebrated—and certainly one of the best. It's traditional for friends to gather in the evening over a good bottle of Mosel or Rhine wine (no beer is served). Appetizers include an assortment of smoked fish as well as creamy fish soup flavored with saffron; main courses often include fried pikeperch in a basil sauce and chicken ragout Bremen style (in a crayfish sauce with calves' sweetbreads and tongues, mushrooms, sausages, and a vegetable risotto). The outstanding wine list is one of the longest lists of German vintages in the world. Some of the decorative kegs have contained wine for nearly 200 years. There's also a less formal bistro, with a limited list of less expensive traditional dishes that include corned-beef hash and simple platters of fresh fish.

Am Markt. © **0421/321676.** www.ratskeller-bremen.de. Reservations recommended. Restaurant main courses 14€–30€; bistro main courses 12€–20€. AE, DC, MC, V. Restaurant daily noon–2:30pm and 7–10:30pm; bistro daily 11am–midnight. Tram: 1, 3, 5, 24, or 25. In the Rathaus.

INEXPENSIVE

Alte Gilde GERMAN   Alte Gilde is located in one of the most ornately decorated houses in Bremen. In spite of the new building surrounding it, the 17th-century structure, with its gilt gargoyles and sea serpents, clings tenaciously to the past. The restaurant is in the vaulted cellar. The chef prepares many fresh fish dishes, along with such specialties as braised calves' livers, breast of chicken with a curry-flavored cream sauce, and pan-fried filet of pork with mushrooms. An especially good dish is rump steak Provençale with paprika, onions, tomatoes, and fresh mushrooms.

Ansgaritorstrasse 24. © **0421/171712.** Reservations recommended. Main courses 12€–23€. AE, DC, MC, V. Mon–Sat 11:30am–11pm. Tram: 2 or 3. Bus: 25, 26, or 27. Entrance on Obernstrasse.

Shopping

Bremen has thrived on business and commerce since it was founded. Today, you'll find lots of shopping options along two streets, **Obernstrasse** and **Sögestrasse,** as well as dozens of boutique-inspired gift shops in the **Schnoor.** The city's cutest stuffed teddy bears, available in all sizes and degrees of fuzziness, are sold at **Bären-haus,** Stavendamm 9 (© **0421/3378419;** tram: 4, 5, or 6), for prices that begin at 14€ for your garden-variety bear and can go much, much higher.

The best shop for women's fashions is **Roland Kleidung,** Sögestrasse 18–20 (© **0421/4788570;** tram: 4, 5, or 6), although the town's largest department store, **Karstadt,** Obernstrasse 1 (© **0421/30710;** www.karstadt.de; tram: 4, 5, or 6), also stocks an impressive selection of less expensive garments. Antiques, including some brass fixtures salvaged from old ships, are sold at **Antikitäten B&M,** Fedelhörn 19 (© **0421/328282;** tram: 10).

Leder-Koopman, Postbrookstrasse 58 (© **0471/302829;** tram: 4, 5, or 6), has been making quality wallets, belts, bags, and other leather products for 100 years. Visit their shop to admire a level of craftsmanship that has become a rare commodity, and chances are you won't leave empty-handed. Bargain hunters swarm over the city's riverfront **flea markets.** The Weserflohmarkt is held at the Schlactel and Weser promenade every Saturday 10am to 4pm.

Entertainment & Nightlife

Bremen nightlife offers a full range of activities. Many pubs and clubs, including those geared toward the gay community, are located in the **Ostertorsteinweg** district (tram: 10).

THE PERFORMING ARTS Classical concerts, opera, and dance performances by visiting companies are held in the **Theater am Goetheplatz** complex, Am Goetheplatz 1–3 (© **0421/36530;** www.theater-bremen.de; tram: 2 or 3). Call for a list of scheduled performers, ticket prices, and available seating. One of its stages, Schauspielhaus (© **0421/36530**), houses a theatrical company that occasionally performs in English. Tickets are 15€ to 30€ during the September-to-June season. Opera and other musical performances are scheduled in the **Musiktheater,** Am Goetheplatz (© **0421/36530;** tram: 2 or 3), where tickets are 12€ to 35€. Experimental theater and modern dance can be found in the **Concordia,** Schwachhauser Heerstrasse 3 (© **0421/9868966;** www.concordia-bremen.de; tram: 1 or 4; bus: 25), where a seat costs 14€ to 25€. To attend productions of the Bremen Shakespeare Company, head for the **Theater am Leibnitzplatz,** Friedrich-Ebert-Strasse at Leibnitzplatz (© **0421/500333;** www.shakespeare-company.com; tram: 6), where tickets are 11€ to 20€.

BARS An early evening bar, **Achim's Beck Haus,** Carl-Ronning-Strasse 1 (© **0421/15555;** www.beckshaus.de; tram: 4, 5, or 6), is a gathering place for drinks and simple pub fare. It's open Monday to Thursday 10am to 11pm, Friday and Saturday 10am to 12:30am.

CASINO Bremen's centrally located casino, **Casino Bremen,** Boettcher Strasse 3 (☏ **0421/329000;** www.westspiel.de; tram: 4, 6, or 8), contains roulette and blackjack tables. Admission is 2.50€, and a passport is required (you must be 18 years old to enter and gamble), as are jackets and ties for men. The casino is open daily 3pm to 3am.

DANCE CLUBS One of Bremen's clubs-of-the-minute is **Stubu Club,** Rembertiring 21 (☏ **0421/326398;** www.stubu.de). Open only Thursday to Saturday from 9:30pm to 3am, it offers high-energy dance music on its street level and a somewhat calmer, more contemplative ambience upstairs. Expect doses of house, punk rock, and garage music, and clients ranging in age from 23 to 50. The cover charge runs from 5€ to 10€. In winter, **Modernes,** Neustadtswall 28 (☏ **0421/505553;** www. modernes.de; tram: 1, 4, 5, 6, or 8), is a movie house during the week, with dancing and live music on the weekend. The rest of the year, bands usually play from 7 to 11pm; afterward, it's a dance club. The cover charge is 10€ when there's just dancing; when there's live music, it's 15€ to 26€. Twice monthly, there's a free show.

GAY CLUBS Much of the gay nightlife in and around Bremen is diverted into the clubs of nearby Hamburg, but there are still a few good spots. A gay and lesbian bar of note (though it mostly caters to men) is **Rat und Tat,** Theodor-Körner-Strasse 1 (☏ **0421/700007;** www.ratundtat-bremen.de; tram: 10).

LIVE MUSIC For music in a bar setting, check out the band lineup at **Aladdin's,** Hannoverschestrasse 11 (☏ **0421/435150;** www.aladin-bremen.de; bus: 40), which also houses a two-room dance club and a bar with rock-'n'-roll memorabilia. It's open Wednesday to Saturday 10pm to 7am; cover is 9€ to 15€. **Moments,** Vordem Stein Tor 64 (☏ **0421/7926633;** www.club-moments.de; tram: 2, 3, or 10), hosts live rhythm and blues as well as jazz for a crowd of loyal regulars. Cover is 5€ to 8.50€. The place functions as a dance club on some nights; cover is then 7.50€. Moments is open Tuesday to Sunday from 8pm until dawn.

VARIETY Popular with children and adults, the ambitious puppet theater **Theatrium,** Wüste Stätte 11 (☏ **0421/326813;** www.theatrium-puppentheater.de; tram: 2 or 3), produces entertaining interpretations of books, plays, and movies, ranging from classical works to Woody Allen. Tickets cost 7.50€ for adults, 5€ for children. In the same building, **Theater im Schnoor** (☏ **0421/326054;** www.packhaus theater.de) presents cabaret and underground theater productions. Tickets are 16€ to 22€.

Where to Stay
VERY EXPENSIVE

Park Hotel Bremen ★★★ This hotel is the most outstanding and charming in Bremen. It occupies an enviable site, in a park whose meandering lakes, exotic trees, and zoo are the pride of the city. It's also just a short ride from the center of town. The hotel's terra-cotta dome and evenly proportioned side wings were rebuilt in 1955 to emulate a turn-of-the-20th-century pleasure pavilion. Rooms are generally spacious and well appointed, with large windows overlooking the park.

Im Burgerpark, 28209 Bremen. www.park-hotel-bremen.de. ☏ **0421/34080.** Fax 0421/3408602. 177 units. 195€–340€ double; from 345€ junior suite; from 585€ suite. AE, DC, MC, V. Free parking in front of the hotel; 20€ in the garage. Tram: 5 or 6. Bus: 26. **Amenities:** 2 restaurants; bar; babysitting; bikes; concierge; exercise room; outdoor heated pool; room service; spa. *In room:* A/C (in some), TV, hair dryer, minibar, Wi-Fi (22€ per day).

EXPENSIVE

Hilton Bremen ★★   At long last the city of Bremen has a Hilton. Even so, it's not as glamorous or as luxurious as the Park Hotel (see above), but the local Hilton is a modernized, tasteful bastion of comfort, ideal for both the commercial traveler and the vacationer. The Hilton stands on the historic Böttcherstrasse, near the Weser River, a block from the shopping district and within an easy walk of many of the major sights.

Bedrooms are spacious and decorated in cool, soothing pastels. Furnishings are in a stylish modern setting with tiled bathrooms, and accommodations range from standard to deluxe, with the junior suites being among the best units in town, complete with a separate working and seating area.

Böttcherstrasse 2, 28195 Bremen. www.hilton.com. ✆ **0421/36960.** Fax 0421/3696960. 235 units. 145€–191€ double; 215€–270€ junior suite. AE, DC, MC, V. Parking 20€. Tram: 1, 2, or 3. **Amenities:** 2 restaurants; bar; babysitting; bikes; concierge; exercise room; indoor heated pool; room service; sauna. *In room:* A/C, TV, hair dryer, minibar, Wi-Fi (22€ per day).

Star Inn Columbus   This hotel offers attractive and tasteful rooms, all with private, well-maintained bathrooms. An elegant recent renovation has set a higher standard for this hotel, putting it on the same footing as Munte am Stadtwald or Hotel zur Post (see both below).

Bahnhofsplatz 5–7, 28195 Bremen. www.starinnhotels.com/de/bremen-columbus. ✆ **0421/30120.** Fax 0421/3012123. 148 units. 79€ double; from 109€ suite. Rates include buffet breakfast. AE, DC, MC, V. Parking 11€. Tram: 1, 5, 6, or 10. **Amenities:** Restaurant; bar; babysitting; exercise room; room service; sauna. *In room:* TV, hair dryer, minibar, Wi-Fi (22€ per day).

MODERATE

Best Western Wellness Hotel zur Post ★   Hotel zur Post offers top-notch facilities and comfort, as well as Bremen's leading restaurant. Rooms are first-rate and slightly larger than average. All units contain tidily kept bathrooms with tub/shower combinations. Its proximity to the Hauptbahnhof makes it an ideal choice for train passengers.

Bahnhofsplatz 11, 28195 Bremen. www.bestwestern.com. ✆ **800/780-7234** in the U.S. and Canada, or 0421/30590. Fax 0421/3059591. 177 units. 148€–178€ double; from 245€ suite. AE, DC, MC, V. Parking 12€. Tram: 1, 5, 6, or 10. **Amenities:** 3 restaurants; 2 bars; babysitting; exercise room; indoor heated pool; room service; spa. *In room:* TV, hair dryer, minibar, Wi-Fi (free).

Hotel Munte am Stadtwald ★ 🔥   You'll think you're in the country at this brick hotel because it fronts directly on one of Bremen's biggest parks. The handsome rooms range from medium to spacious; all contain neatly kept bathrooms. The public rooms are inviting and comfortable, often filled with greenery to make them more homelike. The hotel is bright and friendly, with a helpful staff. For such a reasonably priced hotel, the swimming pool, sauna, steam bath, and solarium come as added luxuries.

Parkallee 299, 28213 Bremen. www.hotel-munte.de. ✆ **0421/22020.** Fax 0421/2202609. 134 units. 127€–170€ double; 181€–246€ suite. Rates include buffet breakfast. AE, DC, MC, V. Free outdoor parking; 8€ in garage. Bus: 22 or 23. In the Burgerpark, about 2.5km (1½ miles) from the center. **Amenities:** 2 restaurants; bar; bikes; indoor heated pool; room service; sauna. *In room:* TV, hair dryer, minibar, Wi-Fi (5€ per hour).

Residence   Residence advertises itself as an Art Deco hotel. The elegant public areas have high ceilings with polished crisscrossed timbers and chandeliers. Rooms

In 2005, the first emigration museum opened in Europe, appropriately sited at Bremerhaven, where seven million people departed to the New World between 1830 and 1974. These various periods of mass exodus were not just to the United States but to Canada as well as South America and Australia. The **Deutsches Auswandererhaus (German Emigration Center)** lies at Columbusstrasse 65 (✆ **0471/902200**; www.dah-bremerhaven.de). Since its opening, many emigrants, or their descendants, have visited the research facility in search of their roots. One of the most moving exhibits is of mannequins depicting emigrants as they gathered to board the ship that will carry them into "the unknown." Motives for emigration included poverty, adventure, ambition, family quarrels, and, later, escape from the Nazis. Old photos reveal how the people lived in a self-contained village awaiting passage across the seas. Perhaps the most evocative of the exhibits are the old and battered suitcases in which the emigrants stuffed the few items they were taking from the old world to the new. Admission is 13€ for adults, 8.50€ for children 4 to 14. Bremerhaven is a 50-minute drive north of Bremen. Hours are March to October daily 10am to 6pm, November to February daily 10am to 5pm.

are comfortably furnished but small, all equipped with bathrooms containing tub/shower combinations.

Hohenlohestrasse 42, 28209 Bremen. www.hotelresidence.de. ✆ **0421/348710.** Fax 0421/342322. 37 units. 94€–145€ double. Rates include buffet breakfast. AE, DC, MC, V. Free outdoor parking; 9€ in garage. Tram: 4, 5, 6, or 10. **Amenities:** Bar; room service; sauna. *In room:* TV, hair dryer, minibar, Wi-Fi (4€ per hour).

INEXPENSIVE

Best Western Hotel Schaper-Siedenburg   Near the train station, this hotel is short on style but big on comfort and maintenance—all at an affordable price. It's in a commercial section of town with a lot of noise and traffic, but rooms on the inner side of the atrium are fairly peaceful. Rooms are in a minimalist style with modern furniture and small tiled bathrooms with showers or tubs. The marketplace and the historic sections of the Altstadt (Old Town) are an easy walk away.

Bahnhofstrasse 8, 28195 Bremen. www.schaper-siedenburg.de. ✆ **800/780-7234** in the U.S. and Canada, or 0421/30870. Fax 0421/308788. 88 units. 106€–120€ double; 120€–158€ apt. Rates include buffet breakfast. AE, DC, MC, V. Parking 10€. **Amenities:** Restaurant; bikes; room service. *In room:* TV, hair dryer, minibar, Wi-Fi (free).

Hotel Buthman 🛏   This is an old but restored *Bürger* house on a tranquil side street within an easy walk of both the rail station and the Altstadt. For nearly half a century, the helpful Buthman family has operated this inn. Many frugally minded locals from the countryside, in Bremen on business or vacation, guard this as a cherished address kind to their pocketbooks. The rooms are cozy and midsize, each with traditional furnishings and a small bathroom with shower. We prefer no. 5 on the upper floor, with its high ceiling and its snugness away from the bustle of the city.

Löningstrasse 29, 28195 Bremen. www.hotel-buthmann.de. ✆ **0421/326397.** Fax 0421/3398816. 10 units. 75€–100€ double. MC, V. Parking 6€. Bus: Any to Town Center. *In room:* TV, Wi-Fi (free).

LÜNEBURG ★★

124km (77 miles) NE of Hannover, 132km (82 miles) E of Bremen, 55km (34 miles) SE of Hamburg

Motorists driving south from Scandinavia through the Baltic port of Lübeck often find themselves on the Old Salt Road leading to the Hanseatic city of Lüneburg. This was the route over which the "white gold" of Lüneburg's salt mines was transported to the Scandinavian countries during the Middle Ages. Because of its heavy salt deposits, Lüneburg became a spa, which it still is today. In the **Kurpark** is a bathing house where visitors can take brine mud baths. In the **spa gardens,** there are indoor swimming pools, sauna baths, and tennis courts.

Lüneburg is also the ideal starting point for excursions into the **Lüneburg Heath,** especially beautiful in late summer when the heather is in bloom.

Essentials

GETTING THERE

BY TRAIN　The **Lüneburg Bahnhof** (✆ **01805/996633;** www.bahn.de) lies on two major rail lines, the Hamburg-Hannover line and the Lüneburg-Lübeck-Kiel-Flensburg line, with frequent connections.

BY BUS　Long-distance bus service into Lüneburg is provided by **KVG GmbH** (✆ **04131/405303;** www.kvg-reisen.com). The bus station is in front of the railway station.

BY CAR　Access is via B4 from Hamburg.

VISITOR INFORMATION

Lüneburg Tourist Information is in the Rathaus, Am Markt 1 (✆ **04131/2076620;** www.lueneburg.de). It's open Monday to Friday 9am to 6pm, Saturday and Sunday 9am to 4pm (closed Sat–Sun Dec–Feb).

Exploring Lüneburg

Although the buildings in this 1,000-year-old city are largely from its most prosperous period, the 15th and 16th centuries, a total of 7 centuries of architecture are represented. The **Rathaus ★★**, Am Markt 1, reached along Auf der Meere, is a perfect example of several trends in architecture and design. You enter through a Gothic doorway into a Renaissance hall. The Great Council Room is the building's most outstanding feature, with sculptures and bas-reliefs by Albert von Soest (1566–84). Daily guided tours are conducted all year at 10 and 11:30am, and 1, 2:30, and 3:30pm. The cost is 5€ for adults and 4€ for students and children. For information, call ✆ **04131/309230.**

To understand Lüneburg's role as "the Salt City," visit the **Deutsches Salzmuseum,** Sülfmeisterstrasse 1 (✆ **04131/45065;** www.salzmuseum.de). Inside, a series of exhibits explore life in the Middle Ages and the role of salt in the region's economy and culture. Admission is 6€ for adults, 5€ for students and children, and 19€ for a family ticket. The museum is open May to September Monday to Friday 9am to 5pm, Saturday and Sunday 10am to 5pm; daily hours off season are 10am to 5pm. Tours are Monday to Friday at 11am, 12:30, and 3pm, and Saturday and Sunday 11:30am and 3pm.

Where to Eat

Ratskeller　GERMAN/CONTINENTAL　The Ratskeller serves satisfying but unspectacular meals in a town not known for its restaurants. The varied menu

THE LÜNEBURG heath ★

The Lüneburger Heide (Lüneburg Heath) is one of the major attractions of northern Germany. The heath covers nearly 775 sq. km (300 sq. miles) and includes many beautiful spots. The sandy soil is mainly covered with brush and heather, although there are a few oak and beech forests in the northern valleys. Toward late summer, the flowering heath turns from green to purple; August and September are the most beautiful months. The best way to approach the heath is via the old town of Lüneburg, the area's transportation hub.

You'll find dramatic, wind-swept, and bleakly evocative scenery in the **Naturschützpark Lüneburger Heide ★★**, a 260-sq.-km (100-sq.-mile) sanctuary for plants and wildlife. Its highest point is the Wilsederberg, a low-lying peak only 168m (550 ft.) above sea level, accessible via a network of footpaths from the hamlet of Wilsede. This reserve, in the center of the heath, is a peaceful, pastoral scene of shepherds, sheep, and undulating hills. Strict laws enforce the maintenance of the thatch-roofed

houses and rural atmosphere. One of the park's most charming hamlets is Undeloh, which has a good hotel, the Heiderose, Gästehaus Heideschmiede, Wilseder Strasse 29 (www.hotel-heiderose.de; ✆ 04189/311), renting doubles for 94€ to 100€, including breakfast. Also, a number of villages—listed on only the most detailed of maps—post ZIMMER FREI (ROOM FOR RENT) signs. These accommodations may be on a heath farm or even a horse farm.

For information, contact Fremdenverkehrsverbund Lüneburger Heide e.V., Barkhausenstrasse 35, Lüneburg (✆ 04131/73730), the park's administrative headquarters, which can furnish maps and information on horseback riding and cycling; it's open Monday to Friday 8am to 6pm. To reach the park from Lüneburg, drive 35km (22 miles) west, following the signs to Salzhausen. After you cross the bridge over the A7 Autobahn, follow the brown-and-white signs to the park. The tourist office (see above) compiles a list every summer of places where you can rent a bike.

includes game and regional specialties, according to the season. You can always count on good home-style cooking in a pleasant setting, backed up by a fine wine list. Parts of the decor date from 1328.

Am Markt 1. ✆ **04131/31757.** www.zum-ratskeller.de. Reservations recommended. Main courses 12€–24€. AE, MC, V. Thurs–Tues 11am–10pm. Closed Jan 6–20. Bus: 3. On the Market Sq.

Zum Heidkrug ★★★ CONTINENTAL   Set within a stone-sided antique building (ca. 1470) in Lüneburg's historic core, this is the best-recommended and most sought-after dining option in town. Within a contemporary dining room with vaguely medieval touches, you'll order from the most creative menu in town. Items are sumptuous and change frequently, according to the inspiration of Chef/owner Michael Röhm. Expect dishes that include, for example, a medley of cheeses from small farms along the north coast of Germany; strips of roasted suckling pig with wild mushrooms; grilled monkfish with tahini and grilled zucchini with curried soup; or roasted saddle of lamb with tomatoes, white garlic crust, onion jam, and gnocchi. The restaurant maintains seven comfortably appointed bedrooms upstairs, each priced at 88€ to 110€ for two occupants, with breakfast included.

Am Berge 5. ✆ **04131/24160.** www.zumheidkrug.de. Reservations required. Main courses 26€–28€. AE, MC, V. Wed–Sat noon–2pm and 6–9:30pm.

Shopping

The heath area is known for its craftspeople. Some of the best local arts and crafts are on sale at the tourist office (see above). The town's largest department store is **Karstadt,** Grosse Bäckerstrasse 31 (*C* **04131/3040;** www.karstadt.de). The main shopping streets are **Bäckerstrasse** and **Grapengiesserstrasse,** both lying in pedestrian zones.

Entertainment & Nightlife

Students make this a rowdier place with a later nightlife than most other small towns. Bars are located along the river on **Am Stintmarkt.** The most popular place for drinking and dancing is **Garage,** Auf der Hude 72 (*C* **04131/35879;** www.disco thek-garage.de). DJs play varied styles of popular music on Friday and Saturday from 10pm to around 4am. It has a cover charge ranging from 6€ to 10€.

Another important nightlife area is the **Schroederstrasse,** which is lined chocka-block with bars and *Nacht-cafés* (night cafes), some of which provide live music. Locals like to duck in and out of as many bars as possible along this street during the course of an evening.

Where to Stay

Bremer Hof   The logo of this hotel is an illustration of the animal musicians of Bremen, who, with their noise, frightened away robbers. The facade looks like something out of the 16th century. Rooms are modern and sunny, but a bit small. A 400-year-old wine cellar is open on weekends.

Lünestrasse 12–13, 21335 Lüneburg. www.bremer-hof.de. *C* **04131/2240.** Fax 04131/224224. 53 units. 93€–135€ double. Rates include buffet breakfast. AE, DC, MC, V. Parking 5€. Bus: 3. A 2-min. walk from Marktplatz. **Amenities:** Restaurant; room service. *In room:* TV, hair dryer, Wi-Fi (free).

Hotel Bargenturm   This three-story hotel at the edge of Lüneburg's historic center is one of the most modern in town. Its concrete walls and large expanses of glass make no concessions to the antique architecture of other parts of the city. Rooms are decorated with a no-nonsense, comfortable modernity. The staff is multilingual and efficient.

St. Lambertiplatz, 21335 Lüneburg. www.hotel-bargenturm.de. *C* **04131/7290.** Fax 04131/729499. 40 units. 119€–129€ double; 149€–159€ junior suite. DC, MC, V. Parking 7.50€. **Amenities:** Restaurant; bar; room service; sauna. *In room:* TV, hair dryer, minibar, Wi-Fi (free).

Hotel Berggström ★★★   One of the best hotels in northern Germany, this charming pocket of posh lies on the river. Instead of checking in, you may want to move in. Our favorite spot here is the terrace opening onto a view of the Märchentürm (fairy-tale tower), enjoying light Mediterranean dishes from the on-site **Marina Café.** Later you can retreat to the Piano Bar for entertainment and drinks. The hotel is convenient to all the attractions of town and lies only a 5-minute walk from the rail station.

Each of the spacious and well-furnished bedrooms comes with a state-of-the-art bathroom. Furnishings are in a tasteful modern style with a range of antique reproductions.

Bei der lüner Mühle, 21335 Lüneburg. www.bergstroem.de. *C* **04131/3080.** Fax 04131/308499. 125 units. 144€–186€ double; 213€ junior suite; 243€ suite. Children 15 and under stay free in parent's room. AE, V. Parking 9€. **Amenities:** Restaurant; 2 bars; babysitting; exercise room; indoor heated pool; room service; sauna. *In room:* A/C, TV, minibar, Wi-Fi (in some; free).

CELLE ★★

45km (28 miles) NE of Hannover, 111km (69 miles) SE of Bremen, 117km (73 miles) S of Hamburg

The well-preserved town of Celle stands at the edge of a silent expanse of moorland, looking like something out of a picture book. Its ancient half-timbered houses were untouched by the war. Look for the wooden beams on the facades of the houses, which are often engraved with biblical quotations. Most of the houses date from the 16th and 17th centuries—the oldest was built in 1526—but they're in such good condition that they could have been constructed in the 1900s.

Essentials

GETTING THERE   By Train   Celle Hauptbahnhof is on the Hamburg-Hannover rail line, with frequent connections to major German cities. Forty trains arrive daily from Hannover (trip time: 20–30 min.), and the same number pull in from Hamburg (trip time: 1 hr., 10 min. to 1½ hr.). For information call ✆ **01805/996633** (www.bahn.de).

By Car   Access by car is via the A7 Autobahn north and south, or Rte. 214.

VISITOR INFORMATION   Contact the **Verkehrsverein,** Markt 14–16 (✆ **05141/1212;** www.region-celle.de), open October to April Monday to Friday 9am to 5pm, Saturday 10am to 1pm; May to September hours are Monday to Friday 9am to 6pm, Saturday 10am to 4pm, and Sunday 11am to 2pm.

Exploring Celle

Bomann Museum MUSEUM   For a picture of 16th- to 20th-century everyday life in Celle and the surrounding countryside, visit this fine regional museum. Included is a complete 16th-century farmhouse, as well as rooms from old cottages, period costumes, and Hannoverian uniforms from 1803 to 1866. In the portrait gallery of the Brunswick-Lüneburg dukes, you can see pictures of the electors, later kings of England and Hannover.

Schlossplatz 7. ✆ **05141/12372.** www.bomann-museum.de. Admission 5€ adults, 3€ children, 8€ family ticket. Tues–Sun 10am–5pm. Bus: 2, 3, or 4.

Herzogschloss HISTORIC BUILDING   One of the landmarks of the town, the Herzogschloss is a square Renaissance castle, with a tower at each corner, surrounded by a moat. It once was the palace of the dukes of Brunswick and Lüneburg. The palace's bizarre 16th-century chapel was designed by Martin de Vos, with galleries and elaborate ornamentation. The pride of the castle, and of the town, is its baroque theater, the oldest still in regular use today—it dates from 1674. Call the tourist office (see "Visitor Information," above) to arrange for a tour given by an English-speaking guide.

West of the Altstadt. ✆ **05141/12373.** www.schloss-celle.de. Admission 5€ adults, 3€ children. Tours Apr–Oct Tues–Sun on the hour noon–4pm; Nov–Mar Tues–Sun 11am and 3pm. Bus: 2, 3, or 4.

Where to Eat

Historischer Ratskeller ★ GERMAN   Historischer Ratskeller is plusher than the typical beer hall and has better food. It occupies a historic site within the 14th-century walls of the town hall. Attentive waiters are constantly passing by, carrying silver platters heaped with spicy, flavorful German dishes, such as a carpaccio of salmon and sole flavored with fresh lemon and black pepper, or an especially good filet of pork tenderloin with fresh asparagus and other vegetables. Another specialty is a tender Argentine roast beef with fresh mushrooms and grilled tomatoes.

Markt 14. ☎ **05141/29099.** www.ratskeller-celle.de. Reservations recommended. Main courses 14€–24€. AE, MC, V. Mon–Sat 11:30am–2:30pm and 5:30pm–midnight; Sun 11:30am–2:30pm. Bus: 3, 5, or 10.

Restaurant Endtenfang ★★★ FRENCH/GERMAN   Celle's most prestigious and stylish restaurant occupies an appealingly old-fashioned dining room on the street level of the Fürstenhof Celle (see below). Service is efficient, helpful, and friendly. The menu focuses on game dishes, including two succulent versions of duck. (The word *Endtenfang*, from an old regional dialect, means "the hunting reserve for duck shooting.") Traditional accompaniments include a pepper-cream sauce, cabbage roulade, a potato-and-pear gratin, and fresh mushrooms, along with slices of red apples. Main dishes are quite creative, including saddle of lamb from the Pyrenees in a lemon crust flavored with anise licorice jus, or else sea bass seasoned with Amalfi lemons and capers. Atlantic cod appears with a basil and olive oil emulsion served with an onion ravioli.

In the Fürstenhof Celle, Hannoverschestrasse 55. ☎ **05141/2010.** Reservations recommended. Main courses 29€–44€; fixed-price menus 4-course 75€, 5-course 89€, 7-course 105€. AE, DC, MC, V. Tues–Sat noon–2pm and 6:30–10pm.

Ringhotel Celler Tor GERMAN/INTERNATIONAL   The Celler Tor is a cliché of German charm, with its gabled red-tile roof and banks of geraniums. When local residents want to celebrate a special occasion, they head here, knowing they can get a great selection of *gutbürgerlich* fare—that is, food fondly remembered from childhood. In season, that means wild game, such as ragout of stag with mushrooms. But the chefs also excel in preparing more modern dishes, including medallions of anglerfish in an herby crust with a paprika mousse and wild rice. Another tasty dish is the filet of roast salmon with an orange-butter sauce.

The Celler Tor also rents 73 good rooms. A double costs 125€ to 245€, including buffet breakfast; eight suites are also available, at 170€ to 265€ each. Facilities include two indoor heated pools, a workout room, a sauna, a solarium, and massage facilities.

Scheuener Strasse 2. ☎ **05141/5900.** Fax 05141/590490. www.celler-tor.de. Reservations recommended. Main courses 17€–25€. AE, DC, MC, V. Daily noon–3pm and 6–10pm. Bus: 8. About 3km (2 miles) outside town.

Where to Stay

Fürstenhof Celle ★★   This hotel, quite sophisticated for such a provincial town, is by far the best in Celle. It's a small-scale 17th-century manor house flanked by timbered wings. A towering chestnut tree shades the brick courtyard in front of the salmon-colored mansion. We prefer the comfort and style of the older rooms in the main house to the more modern rooms in an annex beyond the rear courtyard. Rooms range from medium to spacious, and all have bathrooms.

Hannoverschestrasse 55, 29221 Celle. www.fuerstenhof.de. ☎ **05141/2010.** Fax 05141/201120. 73 units. 185€–255€ double; 250€–340€ suite. AE, DC, MC, V. Parking 14€. Bus: 3, 5, or 10. At the edge of town. **Amenities:** 3 restaurants; bar; babysitting; bikes; exercise room; indoor heated pool; room service; sauna. *In room:* TV, CD player (in some), hair dryer, minibar, Wi-Fi (in some; free).

Hotel Celler Hof ★ 🍴   Celler Hof stands on the street where jousting tournaments were once held. The old-world 1890 architecture of the hotel and its neighboring half-timbered houses renders the interior furnishings incongruously modern, though they are quite pleasing. Rooms, ranging from medium to spacious, have neatly kept bathrooms. Many have a view of the castle. No dinner is served.

Stechbahn 11, 29221 Celle. www.cellerhof.de. ✆ **05141/911960.** Fax 05141/9119644. 47 units. 103€ double. Rates include buffet breakfast. AE, DC, MC, V. Parking 13€. Bus: 3, 5, or 10. **Amenities:** Breakfast room; bar; babysitting; exercise room; sauna. *In room:* TV, hair dryer, minibar, Wi-Fi (free).

Hotel Schifferkrug   This is an old-time favorite. The brick-and-timber walls of this comfortable hotel have witnessed more than 3 centuries of innkeeping. The small- to medium-size rooms have lace curtains and eiderdowns. All units have neatly kept bathrooms.

Speicherstrasse 9, 29221 Celle. www.schifferkrug-celle.de. ✆ **05141/374776.** Fax 05141/3747788. 12 units. 110€ double. Rates include buffet breakfast. AE, MC, V. Free parking. Bus: 3, 5, or 10. **Amenities:** Restaurant; bar. *In room:* TV, Wi-Fi (in some; free).

GOSLAR ★★

90km (56 miles) SE of Hannover, 43km (27 miles) S of Braunschweig, 60km (37 miles) SE of Hildesheim

In spite of Goslar's growth, the old portion of the town looks just as it did hundreds of years ago. This ancient Hanseatic and imperial town at the foot of the Harz Mountains owed its early prosperity to the Harz silver mines, which were worked as early as 968. The 600-year-old streets are still in use today, as are the carved, half-timbered houses.

For hikers and other outdoor enthusiasts, Goslar is a good starting point for day trips and excursions into the **Harz Mountains ★★**, where some of the area's best ski resorts and several spas are found. Bus tours into the Harz Mountains can be booked at the tourist office (see below).

The legends and folklore associated with the Harz Mountains are perhaps more intriguing than the mountains themselves. Walpurgis Eve (the famous Witches' Sabbath) is still celebrated each year on the night of April 30. The mountain on which the witches supposedly danced in olden times was the **Brocken,** whose granite top has been flattened by erosion. The area around the Brocken is now a national park.

Essentials

GETTING THERE

BY PLANE   The nearest major airport is in Hannover.

BY TRAIN   The **Goslar Bahnhof** is on the Hannover-Hildesheim-Goslar-Bad Harzburg rail line, with frequent connections. It takes about 1½ hours to get to Goslar from Hannover. For information, call ✆ **01805/996633** (www.bahn.de).

BY BUS   Long-distance bus service to Goslar is available through **Reisebüro Bokelmann,** Marktkirchhof 1 (✆ **05321/381990**). Regional bus service to all parts of the city and nearby towns is offered by **Regionalbus Braunschweig GmbH,** Hildesheimer Strasse 53 (✆ **05321/34310;** www.rbb-bus.de).

BY CAR   Access is via the A7 Autobahn north and south; exit at either Seesen or Rüden.

VISITOR INFORMATION

Contact the **Kur- und Fremdenverkehrs-Gesellschaft,** Markt 7 (✆ **05321/78060;** www.goslar.de), open November to April Monday to Friday 9:15am to 5pm and Saturday 9:30am to 2pm; and May to October Monday to Friday 9:15am to 6pm, Saturday 9:30am to 4pm, and Sunday 9:30am to 2pm.

Exploring Goslar

To explore this 1,000-year-old town, park your car, put on a pair of comfortable shoes, and set out on foot through the **Altstadt ★★★**, which has more than 1,000 half-timbered buildings from the 15th to the 18th century. The impressive **Rathaus ★** was built in 1450. The portico, with Gothic cross-vaulting, opening on to the Marktplatz, was used by merchants for centuries. Above this is the citizens' meeting hall and the councilmen's meeting chamber, lavishly decorated in the early 1300s with a cycle of 55 paintings depicting biblical and heathen iconography and believed to incorporate the zinc miners returning home from the Rammelsberg mines.

Marktplatz ★, in front of the Rathaus, was for a long time the town's hub of activity. In the center of the large square is a 13th-century fountain with two bronze basins and the German imperial eagle at the top. Many visitors think seeing the **Glockenspiel** perform is the highlight of their visit. Every day at noon, 3, and 6pm (there's a smaller version of the spectacle at 9am), a procession of mechanized miners, representing the silver trade of long ago, traipses out of the innards of the clock tower.

The churches of Goslar provide a look into the architectural history of the area. Many of the oldest—five had already been built by 1200—have been expanded and altered from their original Romanesque style to their current Gothic appearance. The Romanesque **Marktkirche,** just behind the Rathaus, has 700-year-old stained-glass windows and a 16th-century bronze baptismal font. From Marktplatz, take Rosentorstrasse north to reach the 11th-century **Jakobikirche,** later transformed into a Gothic masterpiece, complete with baroque altars. The church contains a *Pietà* by Hans Witten (1520). Farther down the street, the **Neuwerkkirche,** in a garden, has retained its purely Romanesque basilica, and its well-preserved sanctuary contains a richly decorated choir and stucco reliefs. It was originally constructed as a Cistercian convent in the late 1100s.

The 12th-century **Frankenberg Kirche,** on Bergstrasse, was completely remodeled in the 1700s. Over the elaborate baroque pulpit and altars hangs the intricately carved Nun's Choir Gallery, bedecked with gilded saints and symbols.

One of the reminders that Goslar was once a free imperial and Hanseatic city is the **Breites Tor (Broad Gate),** a three-towered town gate with walls up to 4m (13 ft.) thick. From here, you can follow the old town fortifications to the **Kaiserpfalz,** Kaiserbleek 6 (*✆* **05321/3119693**), a Romanesque palace that was the ruling seat of the emperors in the 11th and 12th centuries. You can view the 19th-century murals that cover its walls and visit the Ulrichskapelle, where the heart of Heinrich III was placed inside a large sarcophagus. The site is open April to October daily 10am to 5pm, and November to March daily 10am to 4pm. Admission is 4.50€ for adults and 2.50€ for children.

For a quick overview of Goslar's history, visit the **Goslarer Museum,** at the corner of Abzuchstrasse and Königstrasse 1 (*✆* **05321/43394**), which has displays of the architecture of the early town and several relics of the past. The museum also contains a large geological collection from the Harz Mountains. It's open April to October Tuesday to Sunday 10am to 5pm, and November to March Tuesday to Sunday 10am to 4pm. Admission is 4€ for adults and 2€ for children.

Where to Eat

Die Worth ★ NORTH GERMAN   This is the most rustic and most attractive dining room in Goslar. The restaurant is in a Gothic stone crypt with vaulted ceiling and arches, stained-glass windows, wrought-iron lanterns, and trestle tables. The

Just outside Goslar, about 1.5km (1 mile) south of the town center (follow the signs), you can explore an ancient mine. As early as the 3rd century A.D., lead, zinc, copper, silver, tin, and a little gold were being mined here. The **Welt-kulturerbe Rammelsberg**, Bergtal 19 (✆ 05321/7500; www.rammelsberg. de), conducts guided tours at hourly intervals, on foot or on a small underground train. The museum is open daily 9am to 6pm (closed Dec 24 and 31). Walking tours cost 12€ for adults and 7€ for children. Prices include a ride on the underground train. For more information, call either the museum or the tourist office in Goslar (✆ 05321/78060).

food is good and the portions are hearty, although all the recipes are very familiar. In season, roast game is featured with wild mushrooms, mashed apples, and berries. Rump steak is always an excellent choice, as is the more unusual *Harzer Blaubeer Schmandschnitzel*, a local recipe that combines pork *Schnitzel* with blueberry-flavored cream sauce.

In the Kaiserworth, Markt 3. ✆ **05321/7090.** www.kaiserworth.de. Main courses 11€–32€. AE, DC, MC, V. Daily breakfast 6–11am, lunch 11:30am–2pm, coffee and cake 2:30–5pm, dinner 5:30–11pm. Bus: A or B.

Where to Stay

Goldene Krone 🔥 This 300-year-old village inn has enjoyed a long history of providing a good and decent shelter for some of the most illustrious visitors to Goslar. If you enjoy local color, this is a real find. Rooms are small and simple but homelike and clean, with bathrooms containing tub/shower combos; they're a great value for the price.

Breitestrasse 46, 38640 Goslar. www.goldene-krone-goslar.de. ✆ **05321/34490.** Fax 05321/344950. 17 units. 85€–120€ double. Rates include buffet breakfast. AE, DC, MC, V. Free parking. Bus: A or B. Near the Breites Tor. **Amenities:** Bar. *In room:* TV, hair dryer.

Hotel Der Achtermann ★ This hotel is a bustling but somewhat dowdy government-rated three-star hotel whose extras rival those of four-star hotels nearby. Just after World War II, one of the round-sided 500-year-old watchtowers in the city's wraparound fortifications was enlarged with a white-sided extension, thereby creating an intriguing but rather cumbersome-looking amalgam of old and new architecture. Rooms are well furnished and comfortable, except for a few that are a bit too small (most, however, are spacious).

Rosentorstrasse 20, 38640 Goslar. www.der-achtermann.de. ✆ **05321/70000.** Fax 05321/7000999. 152 units. 104€–154€ double; 200€–280€ suite. Rates include buffet breakfast. AE, DC, MC, V. Parking 9€. **Amenities:** Restaurant; bar; bikes; exercise room; indoor heated pool; room service; spa. *In room:* TV, DVD (in some), hair dryer, minibar, Wi-Fi (8€ per hour).

Kaiserworth ★★ The Kaiserworth is a big, old-fashioned hotel, right in the heart of town. The building dates from 1494 and is itself a sightseeing attraction. The exterior is Gothic, with an arched arcade across the front, topped by a turreted oriel window facing Marktplatz. The large rooms are designed for comfort; the corner rooms are big enough to be suites. All rooms contain tub/shower combos. Room nos. 102, 106, 110, 202, and 206 have the best views of the nearby Glockenspiel.

Markt 3, 38640 Goslar. www.kaiserworth.de. © **05321/7090.** Fax 05321/709345. 66 units. 122€–185€ double; 210€ suite. Rates include buffet breakfast. AE, DC, MC, V. Parking 8€. Bus: A or B. **Amenities:** Restaurant; bar; room service. *In room:* TV, hair dryer, Wi-Fi (free).

GÖTTINGEN

132km (82 miles) S of Hannover, 47km (29 miles) NE of Kassel, 109km (68 miles) SW of Braunschweig

Heinrich Heine described the Gothic town of Göttingen as "famed for its sausages and university." The latter is one of the oldest and most respected in Germany and, in time, Göttingen became the most popular university town in Europe. The university was established in 1737 by George II, king of England and elector of Hannover.

Medieval romanticism and lively student life make Göttingen worth a day's visit. By making a slight detour, you can explore the town before dipping into the fairy-tale country of the upper Weser Valley. Göttingen is halfway between Bonn and Berlin.

Essentials

GETTING THERE

BY TRAIN Göttingen has frequent daily rail connections from Munich (trip time: 6 hr.), Frankfurt (2½ hr.), and Hannover (1 hr.). It lies on the major Kassel-Bebra-Göttingen-Hannover line, with frequent connections in all directions. For information, call © **01805/996633** (www.bahn.de).

BY BUS Regional bus service with other parts of Lower Saxony is offered by **Regionalbus Braunschweig GmbH** (© **0551/19449;** www.rbb-bus.de).

BY CAR Access is via the A7 Autobahn, which runs north to Hannover and Hamburg.

VISITOR INFORMATION

Contact **Tourist-Information,** Altes Rathaus, Markt 9 (© **0551/499800;** www.goettingen-tourismus.de), open Monday to Friday 9:30am to 6pm, Saturday 10am to 6pm (Apr–Oct also open Sun 10am–4pm).

GETTING AROUND

A network of buses runs throughout the city daily from 6am to around 10:30pm. Their main junction point is at the corner of the Judenstrasse and Friedrichstrasse, at the edge of the Altstadt. Fare is 1.90€, with a four-ticket package priced at 6.20€. The tourist office (see above) sells a **Go Card** allowing free transfer on all municipal buses and reduced admission to a few tourist sites, costing 5€ for 1 day or 12€ for 3 days.

Exploring Göttingen

In the center of Göttingen, you can wander down narrow streets, looking at wide-eaved, half-timbered houses. Many of the facades are carved and painted, and some bear marble plaques noting the famous people who lived inside, such as the more than 40 Nobel Prize winners who temporarily made their home here.

Altes Rathaus (bus: 4, 8, 10, 11, or 14) was originally built for trade purposes around 1270, but it wasn't completed until 1443. Its highlights are the open arcade, the Gothic heating system, and the Great Hall, in which the people of Göttingen once received princes and dignitaries, held courts of law, and gave feasts. **Marktplatz,** in front of the Town Hall, is the most interesting section of Göttingen. Here, since 1910, stands the "most-kissed girl in the world," the smiling statue of the

Ganseliesel on the market fountain. By tradition, every student who attains a degree must plant a kiss on the lips of the little goose-girl.

The **Stadtisches Museum,** Ritterplan 7–8 (© **0551/4002845;** bus: 3, 8, or 9), chronicles the history and culture of southern Lower Saxony. The most intriguing exhibits are in the Göttingen history wing on the second floor. Surprisingly, the museum takes an uncompromising look at the town's Nazi past—most German towns tend to downplay it. Everything is here, from *Hitlerjugend* memorabilia to pages ripped from the local Nazi-run newspaper. The museum is open Tuesday to Friday 10am to 5pm and Saturday and Sunday 11am to 5pm. Admission is 2€ for adults and 1€ for children.

Where to Dine

Ratskeller ★ NORTH GERMAN   This 600-year-old restaurant lies in the historic cellar of the Altes Rathaus. This is the best place to eat in town (faint praise, as Göttingen is not known for its restaurants) and the menu is varied and extensive. The chef is known for his *Tafelspitz* (boiled beef). Other specialties include *Alte Platte des Deutsch Landwirt* (Old German Farmer's Plate, consisting of chicken breast and pork steak with fried potatoes and roast onions) or fresh trout *au bleu* with parsley potatoes.

Markt 9. © **0551/56433.** www.rathskeller-goettingen.de. Reservations recommended. Main courses 14€–22€. AE, DC, MC, V. Daily 11:30am–midnight. Closed Christmas Eve. Bus: 4, 8, 10, 11, or 14.

Zum Schwarzen Bären NORTH GERMAN   This fine restaurant is housed in a black-and-white half-timbered building (ca. 1500) that still has the original stained-glass leaded windows. Inside, the ambience is tavern style, with a ceramic stove in the corner and dining rooms with intimate booths. The innkeeper recommends (and we agree) the brook trout from the Harz Mountains or *Bärenpfanne* (various filets with *Spätzle*).

Kurzestrasse 12. © **0551/58284.** Reservations required. Main courses 15€–28€; set lunches 12€–15€, dinners 15€–25€. AE, MC, V. Tues–Sun noon–2pm; daily 6–10pm. Bus: 4, 8, 10, 11, or 14.

Shopping

The commercial heart of town is **Wenderstrasse** and **Grönestrasse,** both of which are pedestrian malls during most of the shopping day. Here, you'll find an appealing roster of cafes and delicatessens selling sausages and cakes, as well as purveyors of the German-style good life. If you want souvenirs, the local tourist office (see above) sells T-shirts, cigarette lighters, beer mugs, and posters. Antiques are found at **Bohm,** Barfusserstrasse 12 (© **0551/4886988;** www.sbohm.de). For the works of local and international painters and sculptors, try **Galerie Apex,** Burgstrasse 46 (© **0551/46886;** www.apex-goe.de).

Entertainment & Nightlife

THE PERFORMING ARTS   The local symphony orchestra and boys choir are very active, and an annual Handel music festival is held in late May or early June. You can get information on schedules, venues, and tickets by calling © **0551/56700** or by contacting the tourist office (above). Tickets are 12€ to 133€.

For 100 years, the **Deutsches Theater,** Theaterplatz 11 (© **0551/49690;** www.dt-goettingen.de), has been staging classical and contemporary drama. Its counterpart, the **Junges Theater,** Hospitalstrasse 6 (© **0551/495015;** www.junges-theater.de), has produced experimental works for 40 years. Performances of both are

held Tuesday to Sunday, with tickets costing 10€ to 15€ for adults and 7.50€ to 11€ for students. The box office is open Monday to Saturday 11am to 1pm and 6 to 8:30pm.

BARS **Ratskeller** (see above) has already been recommended as the place to dine in this university center. Its beer cellar is also the most evocative spot to have a beer, or many beers if you like to drink as the locals do in this 600-year-old establishment. More half-liters are consumed here than at any other place in town. As you lift a mug, imagine that you're standing in the footsteps of previous patrons such as Otto von Bismarck, the Brothers Grimm (they were former faculty members at the university), or, more ominously, Werner Heisenberg, head of the German A-bomb project. One of the more offbeat social centers is **KAZ (Kommunikations Aktions-Zentrum),** Hospitalstrasse 6 (© 0551/53062; www.kaz-goettingen.de), where everyone from seniors to anarchists meet for drinks in one of the two on-premises pubs. One also serves traditional German cuisine; the other offers sandwiches. Within the complex, political forums, local discussion groups, and cultural associations meet regularly. Opening hours change with the seasons and the scheduling of volunteers and group discussion leaders, but in most cases, the center is open Monday to Thursday noon to 2am, Friday noon to 4am, and Saturday 11am to 1am.

LIVE MUSIC Live jazz is featured 1 night a week (exact night varies—call for details) at the excellent **Blue Note,** Wilhelmsplatz 3 (© **0551/46907);** on other nights, musicians explore blues, salsa, African, reggae, and other Caribbean styles. It's open Sunday to Thursday 10pm to 2am, Friday and Saturday to 3am. Cover for most bands is 10€ to 18€; cover when there is no live music is usually 5€. Popular with locals and students, **Irish Pub,** Mühlenstrasse 4 (© **0551/45664),** hosts live music every night of the week, from local rockers to visiting Irish folk bands. The pub serves Guinness, Kilkenny, and hard cider. There's never a cover, and it's open nightly 5pm to 2am.

STUDENT TAVERNS A visit to Göttingen is traditionally capped by a trip to one of the student taverns, such as the cramped but convivial **ADe,** Prinzenstrasse 16 (© **0551/56545),** open daily 6pm to 1am, or **Irish Pub** (see above).

Where to Stay

Central Hotel ★ 🎁 Although this quiet hotel on a pedestrian walkway is centrally located, its best feature is the imaginative care the designers have used to decorate the rooms. For example, one is flamboyantly wallpapered and curtained in vivid yellow-and-white tones, and another appears to be covered in pink silk. Each unit comes with a small, tiled bathroom with shower.

Judenstrasse 12, 37073 Göttingen. www.hotel-central.com. © **0551/57157.** Fax 0551/57105. 32 units. 80€–150€ double; from 150€ suite. Rates include buffet breakfast. AE, DC, MC, V. Parking 8€. Bus: 4, 8, 10, 11, or 14. Near the university. **Amenities:** Jacuzzi; indoor heated pool. *In room:* TV (in some rooms).

Eden-Hotel ★ The centrally located Eden-Hotel is the best choice in town after Gebhards (see below). The comfortable rooms have more amenities than most in this price range. Both business travelers and vacationers appreciate the health club and the pool. Even if you're not a guest, you may want to check out the on-site Italian restaurant **La Locanda,** with main courses costing 8€ to 25€. In addition, top-rate German and international dishes are served at **Pampel-Muse,** where main courses range from 10€ to 25€.

Relnhäuser Landstrasse 22A, 37083 Göttingen. www.eden-hotel.de. ✆ **0551/507200.** Fax 0551/5072111. 100 units. 94€–228€ double; 107€–268€ triple. Rates include buffet breakfast. AE, DC, MC, V. Free parking. Bus: 4, 8, or 10. Near the new Rathaus. **Amenities:** 2 restaurants; babysitting; bikes; exercise room; indoor heated pool; room service; sauna. *In room:* TV, hair dryer, minibar, Wi-Fi (3.50€ per hour).

Romantik Hotel Gebhards ★★   Gebhards is the best hotel in town. It's housed in a grand building that evokes a Tuscan villa, with a modern balconied annex built onto the back. The interior offers high-ceilinged public areas and a pleasant bar. Rooms are well designed and furnished. The cheapest double has a toilet and shower; the most expensive is an apartment with a complete private bathroom.

Goethe-Allee 22–23, 37073 Göttingen. www.gebhardshotel.de. ✆ **0551/49680.** Fax 0551/4968110. 61 units. 145€–200€ double; 220€–260€ suite. Rates include buffet breakfast. AE, DC, MC, V. Free parking. Bus: 4, 8, 10, 11, or 14. In front of the Bahnhof. **Amenities:** Restaurant; bar; Jacuzzi; room service; sauna. *In room:* TV, hair dryer, minibar.

HAMBURG

Hamburg has many dynamic faces. A walk down the neon-lit Reeperbahn at night will revive old memories of "Sin City Europe." A ride around Alster Lake in the city center will reveal the elegance of its finest parks and buildings. And a stroll along one of Hamburg's many canals explains why this city has been called the "Venice of the North." Contrasts are evident wherever you look in Hamburg. Amid the steel-and-glass structures of the modern city is the old baroque Hauptkirche St. Michaelis. A Sunday-morning visit to the Altona fish market will give you a good look at early shoppers mingling with late-night partiers.

Hamburg has had to be flexible to recover from the many disasters of its 1,200-year history. This North Sea port was almost totally destroyed during World War II. But out of the rubble of the old, the industrious Hamburgers rebuilt a larger and more beautiful city, with huge parks, impressive buildings, and important cultural institutions. Today, Hamburg is the greenest city in Europe, with nearly 50% of its surface area marked with water, woodlands, farmland, and some 1,400 parks and gardens. Green is, in fact, the city's official color.

Hamburg, Germany's second-most populated city (after Berlin), lies on the Elbe River, 109km (68 miles) from the North Sea, 285km (177 miles) northwest of Berlin, 119km (74 miles) northeast of Bremen, and 150km (93 miles) north of Hannover.

ESSENTIALS

Getting There

BY PLANE The **Airport Hamburg-Fuhlsbüttel** is 8km (5 miles) north of the city center. It's served by many scheduled airlines and charter companies, with regular flights to major German airports and many European and intercontinental destinations. **Lufthansa** (✆ **01803/805805;** www.lufthansa.com) offers flights to Hamburg from most major German cities, and many national carriers fly into Hamburg, including Air France from Paris and British Airways from London. United Airlines, Delta, and Lufthansa offer direct flights from the United States. For flight information in Hamburg, call ✆ **040/50750** or visit www.ham.airport.de.

An ultramodern terminal and passenger pier at the airport has a roof shaped like an enormous aircraft wing. This terminal contains an array of shops and boutiques—even a branch of Harrods of London—as well as restaurants and other establishments.

During the day the S-Bahn (suburban rail network) line S1 operates every 10 minutes between Hamburg airport and the central railway station, Hauptbahnhof (trip time to the center: 25 min.). The Hamburg Airport (Flughafen) S-Bahn station is directly in front of the air terminals and is reached by elevator, escalator, or stairs. The one-way fare to the center is 3€, or 1.50€ for ages 11 and under.

BY TRAIN   There are two major rail stations, the centrally located **Hamburg Hauptbahnhof,** Hachmannplatz 10 (© **040/39183046;** www.bahn.de), and **Hamburg-Altona** (© **040/39182387;** www.bahn.de), in the western part of the city. Most trains arrive at the Hauptbahnhof, although trains from the north of Germany, including Westerland and Schleswig, pull into Altona. The two stations are connected by train and S-Bahn. Hamburg has frequent train connections with all major German cities, as well as frequent continental connections. From Berlin, 15 trains arrive daily (trip time: 2½ hr.), 37 from Bremen (trip time: 54 min. to 1 hr., 16 min.), and 33 from Hannover (trip time: 1½ hr.). For information, call © **01805/ 996633** (www.bahn.de).

BY BUS   Because of Hamburg's location astride most of the rail lines of north Germany, the majority of passengers arrive by train. But if the bus appeals to you, call **Central Omnibus** (© **040/247576;** www.zob-hamburg.de). From their headquarters across from the railway station, they'll supply information on fares and schedules for the buses that funnel passengers in from other cities. Information about short-haul buses from surrounding towns and villages is available from **Hamburger Verkehrsverbund** (© **040/19449;** www.hvv.de).

BY CAR   The A1 Autobahn reaches Hamburg from the south and west, the A7 from the north and south, the A23 from the northwest, and the A24 from the east. Road signs and directions to Hamburg are frequently posted.

Visitor Information

For visitors to Hamburg, information is offered at several centers. **Tourist-Information,** Hauptbahnhof, Kirchenallee exit (© **040/30051300**), is open Monday to Saturday 8am to 9pm, Sunday 10am to 6pm (phone inquiries are accepted Mon–Sat 9am–7pm). **Port Information,** St. Pauli Landungsbrücken (© **040/30051300**), is open April to October daily 8am to 6pm, and November to March daily 10am to 6pm. There is another tourist office at the airport, at terminals 1 and 2 (arrivals area), open daily 6am to 11pm. For tourist information in Hamburg contact the visitor information hot line at © **040/30051300** or see www.hamburg-tourism.de.

City Layout

Hamburg is a showplace of modern architecture; historic structures stand side by side with towering steel-and-glass buildings. The 12 sq. km (4½ sq. miles) of parks and gardens are a vital part of the city, as are the 57 sq. km (22 sq. miles) of rivers and lakes. The city is not compact and can't be easily covered on foot. Many sections of interest are far apart; you'll have to depend on public transportation or taxis.

   The **Alster** is the perfect starting point for a pleasurable exploration of Hamburg. This lake, rimmed by the city's most significant buildings, sparkles with the white sails of small boats and ripples with the movement of motor launches. The lake is divided by the Lombard and John F. Kennedy bridges into the **Binnenalster (Inner Alster)** and the larger **Aussenalster (Outer Alster).** The Binnenalster is flanked on the south and the west by the **Jungfernstieg,** one of Europe's best-known streets and Hamburg's most vital artery and shopping district. For landlubbers, the best view of the Alster is from this "maiden's path."

From the Hauptbahnhof, on the eastern fringe of the heart of town in the vicinity of the Binnenalster, two major shopping streets fan out in a southwesterly direction, toward St. Petri Church and the Rathaus. They are **Spitalerstrasse** (reserved for pedestrians) and **Mönckebergstrasse,** paralleling it to the south. These streets contain some of the city's finest stores. Stay on Mönckebergstrasse to reach **Rathausmarkt,** which is dominated by the Rathaus, a Renaissance-style city hall palace.

The center of Hamburg offers fine opportunities for walking; for example, the eastern shoreline of the Binnenalster opens onto **Ballindamm,** which contains many elegant stores. At the foot of this lake is the Jungfernstieg, already mentioned, and along its western shoreline is yet another main artery, the Neuer Jungfernstieg. At the intersection of the Jungfernstieg and Neuer Jungfernstieg is one of the more fascinating streets in Hamburg, the **Colonnaden,** a colonnade of shops and cafes. In this neighborhood stands the **Hamburgische Staatsoper,** the famous modern opera house.

A "city within a city" is growing up in the former docklands that extend 3km (2 miles) along the Elbe River. Known as **HafenCity,** this emerging borough is expected to double the population of central Hamburg with a concert hall, bars, slick office buildings, and hundreds of waterfront apartments. The Hafen City tour leaves only on Saturday at 3pm, and from May to September also on Thursday at 6:30pm. Tours leave from Am Sandtorkai 30 (✆ **040/36901799**).

Neighborhoods in Brief

Central Hamburg This is Hamburg's commercial and shopping district, seat of many of its finest hotels and restaurants. The district centers on Binnenalster and the Rathaus (City Hall). Boat rides on the Alster lakes are a major attraction. Many historic buildings that withstood World War II are here, including St. Petri, the oldest surviving structure.

The Harbor The Port of Hamburg is the world's fifth-largest harbor, stretching for nearly 40km (25 miles) along the Elbe River. More than 1,500 ships from all over the world call each month. Since 1189, this has been one of the busiest centers for trade on the Continent, making Hamburg one of Germany's wealthiest cities.

St. Pauli This is Hamburg's nightlife center, with lots of erotica. The district is split by its famous street, the Reeperbahn, neon-lit and dazzling, offering all sorts of nighttime pleasures—cafes, sex shows, bars, dance clubs, and music halls.

Altona Formerly a city in its own right, this western district is now integrated into greater Hamburg. It was once populated mainly by Jews and Portuguese. Today it's the scene of Hamburg's famous Fischmarkt, which takes place at dawn every Sunday.

Pöseldorf Northwest of Aussenalster, this is a tree-filled residential district, with many villas dating from the 1800s. A large number of exemplary *Jugendstil* buildings can still be seen here. The district is mostly occupied by upwardly mobile professionals, including a lot of media stars.

HafenCity Locals are calling this maritime and media center a "city within a city," and it's being created in former docklands that extend 3km (2 miles) from the Elbe River. It is Europe's largest inner-city urban development project. The location is between the flood-protection line of the city center and the north arm of the Elbe River. The emerging borough is expected to double the population of central Hamburg with hundreds of waterfront apartments, and includes a concert hall, bars, and slick office buildings. A free guided tour takes place every Saturday at 3pm, and advance notice is not required. Show up at the **HafenCity InfoCenter,** Kesselhaus, Am Sandtorkai 30 (✆ **040/36901799**). U-Bahn stops include the Messberg Station and the Baumwall Station.

The Hamburg Card offers unlimited travel on all public transport in Hamburg, as well as 50% discounts to several museums and a 20% discount on city tours. A 1-day card goes for 8.50€ for individuals (for one adult and up to three children 14 years old and under) or 14€ for families. A 3-day card costs 20€ for individuals and 32€ for families. You can get these cards at some hotels, major U-Bahn stations, and the tourist office, or call ✆ **040/30051300.**

Getting Around

A word to the wise: Park your car and use public transportation in this busy city. Practically all public transportation services in the Hamburg area—the **U-Bahn** (subway), **S-Bahn** (city rail), **A-Bahn** (commuter rail), **buses,** and **harbor ferries**—are run by **Hamburger Verkehrsverbund (HVV),** Steinstrasse 12. For information, call ✆ **040/19449** (www.hvv.de). Tickets are sold at Automats and railroad ticket counters.

BY PUBLIC TRANSPORTATION Hamburg's **U-Bahn,** one of the best in Germany, serves the entire central area and connects with the **S-Bahn** surface trains in the suburbs. This network is the fastest means of getting around, but buses provide a good alternative. The advantage of surface travel, of course, is that you get to see more of the city. For information, call ✆ **040/19449.**

Fares for both U-Bahn and the bus are as follows: Most single tickets will cost 2.40€, although a very short trip will go for 1.20€. Otherwise you will be able to purchase a 1-day pass for the city center for 5.20€, or 7€ for a more extended area, or even 10€ for the entire MVV network.

BY TAXI Taxis are available at all hours; call ✆ **040/211211;** www.taxi211211. de. Taxi meters begin at 2.70€ and charge 1.70€ per kilometer after that.

[FastFACTS] HAMBURG

Business Hours Most **banks** are open Monday to Friday 8:30am to 12:30pm and 1:30 to 3:30pm (many until 5:30pm Thurs). Most **businesses** and **stores** are open Monday to Friday 9am to 6pm and Saturday 9am to 2pm (to 4 or 6pm on the first Sat of the month).

Car Rentals We don't recommend that you rent a car for touring Hamburg, but an automobile is ideal for the environs. Rentals are available at **Avis,** Gleis 12 in the Hauptbahnhof (✆ **040/32873800;** www. avis.com; U-Bahn: Hauptbahnhof), or at **Hertz,** Kirchenallee 34–36 (✆ **040/2801201;** www. hertz.com; U-Bahn: Hauptbahnhof).

Consulates Consulate General of the U.S., Alsterufer 27–28 (✆ **040/ 41171100**); British Consulate-General, Harvestehuder Weg 8A (✆ **040/4480320**).

Currency Exchange The most convenient place for recent arrivals to exchange currency is the **ReiseBank** at the Hauptbahnhof (✆ **040/323483**), which is open daily 7:30am to 10pm. The same bank maintains a branch at the Altona Station (✆ **040/ 3903770**), open Monday to Friday 7:30am to 8pm, and Saturday 9am to 2pm and 2:45 to 5pm. There's also a branch in Terminal 2 of Hamburg's airport (✆ **040/ 50753374**), open daily 8am to 9pm.

Doctors & Dentists Ask at the British or American

consulates, or go to **Allge-meines Krankenhaus Sankt Georg,** Lohmühlenstrasse 5, 20099 Hamburg (✆ **040/1818850;** U-Bahn: Lohmühlenstrasse), where you'll find an English-speaking staff.

Drugstores Pharmacies that stock foreign drugs include **Roth's Alte Eng-lische Apotheke,** Jungfern-stieg 48 (✆ **040/343906;** U-Bahn: Jungfernstieg), open Monday to Friday 8:30am to 8pm and Satur-day 9am to 6pm.

Emergencies Dial ✆ **110** for the police; for an ambu-lance, an emergency doctor or dentist, or the fire bri-gade, dial ✆ **112;** and dial ✆ **01805/101112** for the

German Automobile Asso-ciation (ADAC).

Post Office The post office at the Hauptbahnhof, Hachmannplatz 13, is cen-trally located. You can make long-distance calls here far more cheaply than at your hotel. Telegrams, telexes, and faxes can also be sent. It's open Monday to Friday 8am to 8pm, Saturday 8am to 6pm, and Sunday 10am to 4pm. A branch office located at the airport is open Monday to Friday 6:30am to 9pm, Saturday 8am to 6pm, and Sunday 10am to 6pm. For informa-tion on either post office, call ✆ **01802/3333.**

Safety Hamburg, like all big cities of the world, has

its share of crime. The major crimes that tourists encounter are pickpocket-ing and purse/camera snatching. Most robberies occur in the big tourist areas, such as the Reeper-bahn and the area around the Hauptbahnhof, which can be dangerous at night, but much less so than in Frankfurt or Munich.

Toilets There are several decent public facilities in the center of Hamburg. See chapter 19 for additional information.

Transit Information For U-Bahn and S-Bahn rail information, call the Haupt-bahnhof, Hachmannplatz 10 (✆ **01805/996633;** www. bahn.de).

Boat Tours

You can tour Hamburg by water, on both the Inner and the Outer Alster, experiencing all the charm of the Alsterpark, the villas, and the sailing boats set against the pan-orama of towers and church spires. **ATG-Alster-Touristik,** Am Anleger Jungfern-stieg (✆ **040/3574240;** www.alstertouristik.de), has daily departures about every 30 minutes from 10am to 6pm, with trips lasting 50 minutes. November to March, tours depart daily at 10:30am, noon, 1:30, and 3pm. The ships leave from the Jungfernstieg quayside (U-Bahn: Jungfernstieg). Audio devices with a description of the tour in English and a brochure in four languages (including English) are available from the captain. Trips cost 11€ for adults and 5.50€ for children 15 and under.

HADAG Seetouristik und Fährdienst AG, Bei den St. Pauli, Fischmarkt 28 (✆ **040/3117070;** www.hadag.de), also conducts tours through the watery channels of Hamburg, in a comfortable heated pleasure boat. Tours are conducted in both German and English. They depart at hourly intervals every day April to September 10:30am to 4:30pm, and from October to March 11am to 3:30pm. Boats leave from the Landungsbrücken, Pier 3. The fare is 11€ for adults, 5.50€ for children 13 and under, and 20€ for a family ticket.

EXPLORING HAMBURG

Before you tour the city, you can get a sweeping view of Hamburg from the tower of the finest baroque church in northern Germany, **Hauptkirche St. Michaelis ★,** Michaeliskirchplatz, Krayenkamp 4C (✆ **040/376780;** www.st-michaelis.de; U-Bahn: Rödingsmarkt or St. Pauli). Take the elevator or climb the 449 steps to enjoy the sweeping view from the top of the hammered-copper tower. The crypt is one of the largest in Europe and contains the tombs of such famous citizens as composer

What to See & Do in the Altstadt

1/5 mi

0.2 km

HAFENCITY

Pedestrians only

ST. GEORG

Museum für
Kunst und
Gewerbe

Steintor-
platz

Kirchenallee

Deichtor-
hallen

Haus der
Photografie

Hachmann-
platz

Haupt-
bahnhof

Steintor-
platz

Steintorwall

Altmann-
brücke

Klosterwall

Kloster-
wall

Johanniswall

Deichtor-
platz

Deichtor-
str.

Oberhafen

Holzdamm

Hamburger
Kunsthalle 7

An der Kunsthalle

Glockengiesserwall

Ernst-Merck-Str.

Georgs-
platz

Lange Mühren

Kurze
Mühren

Lilienstr.

Rosenstr.

Steinstrasse

Bugenhagenstr.

St.-Jacobi-
Kirche 9

Burchard-
platz

Alster-
tor

Feldbrunnenstr.

Brandsende

Raboisen

Ferdinandstr.

Thalia
Theater 6

Gerhart-
Hauptmann-
Pl.

Mönckebergstr.

Spitalerstr.

St.-Petri-
Kirche 5

Bergstr.

Alstertor

Alter
Fisch-
markt

Brandstwiete

Dovenfleet

Zollkanal

Bei St.
Annen

Zippel-
haus

Aussenalster

Kennedybrücke

Lombardsbrücke

Binnenalster

Rathaus-
markt

Börse 4

St.-Nikolai-
Kirche (ruin)

Domstrasse

ALTSTADT

Willy-Brandt-Str.

Katharinenstr.

Matten-
twiete

Nikolai-
fleet

Bei den Mühren

Zoll-

Esplanade

Colon-
naden

Neuer Jungfernstieg

Jungfernstieg

Kleine
Alster

Grosse
Alster

Alster
fleet

Alter Wall

Neuer Wall

Mönkedamm

Grosser Burstah

Hopfen-
markt

Rödingsmarkt

Deichstr.

Binnen-
hafen

Stephans-
platz

Gr. Theaterstr.

naden

Gänse-
markt

Poststr.

Hohe Bleichen

Grosse Bleichen

Herrlichkeit

Neuer Wall

Stadthausbrücke

Admiralität-
str.

Alsterfleet

Herrengraben
Herrengrabenfleet

Kajen

Katharinenstr.

Baumwall

Binnenhafen

Dammtorstr. 3

Drehbahn

kamp

ABC

Fuhlentwiete

Dustern-
str.

Axel-
Springer-
Platz

Westri-

Alter
Steinweg

Ludwig-Erhard-Str.

Schaar-
markt

Martin-Luther-Str.

Stubbenhuk

NEUSTADT

Caffamacherreihe

Valentins

Kaiser-Wilhelm-Str.

Laeiszhalle 2

Johannes-
Brahms-
Platz

Poolstr.

Kohlhöfen

Thiel-
beck

Gross-
neumarkt

Neander-

Encke-
platz

Hütten-

Holstenwall

Peterstr.

Neuer Steinweg

Pilatuspool

Sieveking-
platz

Gorch-Fock-Wall

Kleine
Wallanlagen

Hauptkirche
St. Michaelis 1

Böhmkenstr.

Rothe-
soodstr.

Kray-
enkamp

Schaar-
steinweg

Venusberg

Neustädter
Neuer Weg

Grosse
Wallanlagen

Museum für
Hamburgische
Geschichte

Millerntor-
damm

Zeughaus-
markt

Alter
Elbpark

Seewartenstr.

Stint-
fang

Ellpark

Ditmar-Koel-Str.

Johannis-
bollwerk

Vorsetzen

Deutsches
Schauspielhaus 8

Hamburgische
Staatsoper 3

Hauptkirche
St. Michaelis 1

Kunsthalle 7

Laeiszhalle 2

Rathaus 4

St.-Jacobi-Kirche 9

St.-Petri-Kirche 5

Thalia Theater 6

Carl Philipp Emanuel Bach and the church's builder, Ernst Georg Sonnin. Hours are daily May to October 9am to 7:30pm, and November to April 10am to 5:30pm. Entrance to the church is free, but to use the stairs or elevator costs 3.50€ for adults, 2.50€ for children. A combination ticket for the tower and crypt costs 5€ for adults, 3€ for children.

The **Altstadt** actually has little old architecture left, but there are a few sights among the canals that run through this section from the Alster to the Elbe. The largest of the old buildings is the **Rathaus,** Rathausplatz (✆ **040/428310;** U-Bahn: Rathausmarkt), which is modern in comparison to many of Germany's town halls. This Renaissance-style structure was built in the late 19th century on a foundation of 3,780 pinewood piles. It has a sumptuous 647-room interior and can be visited on guided tours costing 2€. Tours in English are given hourly Monday to Friday 10am to 3pm, and Saturday and Sunday 10am to 1pm (there are no tours during official functions). The Rathaus's 49m (161-ft.) clock tower overlooks Rathausmarkt and the **Alster Fleet,** the city's largest canal.

A few blocks away is the 12th-century **St. Petri Kirche,** Speersort 10 (✆ **040/ 3257400;** www.sankt-petri.de; U-Bahn: Rathausmarkt). The lion-head knocker on the main door is the oldest piece of art in Hamburg, dating from 1342. The church is open Monday to Friday 10am to 6pm, Saturday 10am to 5pm, and Sunday 9am to 9pm.

The nearby 14th-century Gothic **St. Jacobi Kirche,** Jakobikirchhof 22, with an entrance on Steinstrasse (✆ **040/3037370;** www.jacobus.de; U-Bahn: Mönckebergstrasse), was damaged in World War II but has been restored. It contains several medieval altars, pictures, and sculptures, as well as one of the largest baroque organs in the world (Arp-Schnitger, ca. 1693). The church is open Monday to Saturday 10am to 5pm. Guided tours in English can be arranged.

The Top Attractions

Carl Hagenbeck's Tierpark ★★ ☺ ZOO   Hamburg's zoo, one of Europe's best, was founded in 1848 and today is home to about 2,500 animals belonging to 360 species. The unfenced paddocks and beautifully landscaped park are world famous. There are sea lion shows, rides on elephants and camels, a train ride through "fairyland," and a spacious children's playground. In 2007 a tropical aquarium opened, which makes Hagenbeck competitive with the more famous aquarium in Berlin. A restaurant serves well-prepared fixed-price menus at 15€ to 28€, 11:30am to closing time.

Hagenbeckallee at Steilingen. ✆ **040/5300330.** www.hagenbeck.de. Admission 16€ adults, 11€ children 4–16, free for children 3 and under, 49€ family ticket. Parking 2.50€. Mar–Oct daily 9am–5pm (closes later in nice weather); Nov–Feb daily 9am–4:30pm. U-Bahn: Hagenbeck's Tierpark. In the northwest suburbs.

Kunsthalle ★★ MUSEUM   This is northern Germany's leading art museum, which reopened in the spring of 2006 after extensive renovations and much improved lighting. Be sure to see the outstanding **altarpiece** painted for the St. Petri Church in 1379 by Master Bertram, Hamburg's first painter known by name and a leading 14th-century German master. The 24 scenes on the wing panels depict the biblical story of humankind from creation to the flight into Egypt. Note the panel showing the creation of the animals, in which a primitive Christlike figure is surrounded by animals. As a sardonic note, one little fox is chewing the neck of the lamb next to it.

The museum also contains works by Master Francke, a Dominican monk. The altar of St. Thomas à Becket (ca. 1424) is the first known work to depict Becket's murder in Canterbury cathedral.

The collection also includes the distinctive visions of Philipp Otto Runge and Carl David Friedrich; German Impressionists Max Liebermann and Lovis Corinth; and 20th-century artists Munch, Warhol, Beuys, Picasso, Kirchner, Dix, Beckmann, Kandinsky, and Klee. In addition, the museum has an entire wing devoted to contemporary art.

Glockengiesser Wall. ✆ **040/428131200.** www.hamburger-kunsthalle.de. Admission 10€ adults, 5€ children 4–12, free for children 3 and under, 14€ family ticket. Tues–Sun 10am–6pm (Thurs until 9pm). U-Bahn: Hauptbahnhof.

Nearby Attractions

Every ship that passes the landscaped peninsula at **Willkomm-Höft (Welcome Point)** is welcomed in its own language, as well as in German, from sunrise to sunset (8am–8pm in summer). The ships' national anthems are played as a salute. The station was founded in the late spring of 1952, at the point where a sailor first catches sight of the soaring cranes and slipways of the Port of Hamburg. As a vessel comes in, you'll see the Hamburg flag on a 40m (131-ft.) mast lowered in salute. The ship replies by dipping its flag. More than 50 arriving ships, and as many departing ones, pass Willkomm-Höft each day.

The point can be reached by car from Hamburg via the Elbchaussee or Ostdorfer Landstrasse to Wedel in half an hour. You can also go to Wedel by S-Bahn; a bus will take you from the station to the point, or you can enjoy the 15-minute walk. In the summer, you can take a HADAG riverboat, leaving from St. Pauli Landungsbrücken, an hour's ferry ride.

In Wedel, you can have lunch at **Schulauer Fährhaus,** Parnastrasse 29 (✆ **04103/92000;** www.schulauer-faehrhaus.de; S-Bahn: Wedel), attractively situated on the wide lower Elbe. The sons of Otto Friedrich Behnke, who founded Willkomm-Höft, run the restaurant. It has large enclosed and open verandas, as well as a spacious tea garden. Guests are welcomed for breakfast, lunch, tea, or dinner. Fish dishes are a specialty, and the restaurant's bakery turns out a tempting array of goodies. Children, especially, will delight in watching the ships go by as they eat. Main courses run 10€ to 17€. It's open daily 9:30am to 10pm. No credit cards are accepted.

In the cellars of the Schulauer Fährhaus is the **Buddelschiff-Museum** (✆ **04103/920016;** www.buddel.de), where more than 200 little vessels are carefully preserved in bottles. The museum is open March to October, daily 10am to 6pm; November to February, hours are Saturday and Sunday only 10am to 6pm. Admission is 3€ for adults and free for children.

Gardens & Parks

Alsterpark lies on the northwest banks of Alster Lake, spread across 72 well-manicured hectares (178 acres). Beautiful shade trees and cultivated gardens greet you at every turn. From many places, you'll also have a panoramic view of the Hamburg skyline. Enter on Harvestehuderweg.

The **Hirschpark** (S-Bahn: Blankensee) is Hamburg's deer park. Its main entrance is at Mühlenberg. The park is landscaped and has a game enclosure. You can visit the Hirschparkhaus for an old-fashioned tea with pastries.

Although Hamburg is known for its X-rated entertainment, the city is actually ideal for a family vacation. **Carl Hagenbeck's Tierpark** (✆ **040/ 5300330;** www.hagenbeck.de) is one of Europe's great zoos (see above), and many other parks in Hamburg have amusements for children—for example, the **Wallringpark** has a roller-skating rink. Boat tours of the Alster and more lengthy tours of the Port of

Hamburg will also delight kids. **Willkomm-Höft** and the **Buddelschiff-Museum** (see above for details) are also fun for children.

Language is often not a problem for children, so they may enjoy the children's theater, **Theater für Kinder,** Max-Brauer-Allee 76 (✆ **040/382538;** www. theater-fuer-kinder.de; U-Bahn: Altona). All tickets cost 11€ to 20€; call for showtimes.

Stadtpark (U-Bahn: Borgweg, in Winterhude), spread across 182 hectares (450 acres) north of the center, has some 30km (19 miles) of footpaths and numerous recreational facilities. These include a planetarium, sunbathing areas (Hamburgers often prefer their sun sans attire), and open-air pools. Music concerts are often staged here during summer. For your safety, avoid this place after dark.

Finally, **Wallringpark** (U-Bahn: Stephansplatz) is a quartet of beautifully maintained parks and gardens, including the flower garden Planten und Blomen, the Alter Botanischer Garten (Old Botanical Garden), and the Grosse and Kleine (Big and Little) Wallanlagen parks, with many recreational facilities. A miniature railway connects all four. The entire complex is a popular leisure park, with a roller-skating rink, playgrounds, greenhouses filled with tropical plants, restaurants, and an ice-skating rink in winter. A particular highlight is the illuminated-fountain concert, with classical or pop music, at the onset of darkness—June to August 10pm, earlier as the summer wanes. The largest Japanese garden in Europe is in **Planten und Blomen.** Here, rock gardens, flowering plants, miniature trees, and winding pathways attract garden enthusiasts.

WHERE TO EAT

Hamburg life is married to the sea, and that includes the cuisine: lobster from Helgoland; shrimp from Büsum; turbot, plaice, and sole from the North Sea; and huge quantities of fresh oysters. Of course, there's also the traditional meat dish, *Stubenküchen* (hamburger steak), and the favorite sailor's dish, *Labskaus,* made with beer, onions, cured meat, potatoes, herring, and pickles. *Aalsuppe* (eel soup) is the best known of all Hamburg's typical dishes. To locate the restaurants in this section, see the "Where to Stay & Dine in Hamburg" map on p. 622.

Near the Hauptbahnhof
MODERATE
Fillet of Soul ★ INTERNATIONAL   This cozy, postmodern dining room is positioned on the ground floor of the wing of the Deichtorhallen that's devoted to the photography exhibits. Within a minimalist setting you'll find a restaurant favored by local residents who seek it out as an entity unto itself, with little or no intention of ever actually visiting the museum that contains it. The place does a somewhat

languid business as a morning and midafternoon cafe, but its real heart and soul is devoted to its role as a restaurant. The kitchen changes its menu according to the seasons and the availability of fresh ingredients, but regular menu items are likely to include pink-roasted breast of goose with saffron-flavored rice and Thai basil; pan-fried zanderfish with bacon-studded *Sauerkraut* and parsley sauce; and, for lighter appetites, spinach salads accented with grilled strips of salmon. Raspberry-flavored tiramisu makes for a tempting dessert.

In the Deichtorhallen Museum, Deichtorstrasse 2. © **040/70705800.** www.fillet-of-soul.de. Reservations recommended. Main courses lunch 8.50€–12€, dinner 14€–28€. No credit cards. Cafe and bar Tues–Sun 11am–midnight. Restaurant Tues–Sun noon–3pm and 6–10pm. U-Bahn: Steinstrasse.

In Binnenalster & Neustadt

MODERATE

Fischküche ★ SEAFOOD   Breezy and unpretentious, this restaurant prides itself on specializing exclusively in fish. It's in a modern building, with a dining room brightly outfitted in bold colors and extravagant chandeliers. Menu items include a changing array of reasonably priced seafood brought in fresh daily. Choices vary with the day's catch but might include several different preparations of clear or creamy lobster soup, marinated crabmeat salad, flounder with spaghetti and *tandoori* sauce, codfish with potatoes and mustard sauce, and filet of monkfish with king prawns, vegetables, and balsamic rice. It's hardly haute cuisine, but locals flock here for the robust specialties and no-nonsense service.

Kajen 12. © **040/365631.** www.die-fischkueche.de. Reservations recommended. Main courses 15€–40€. AE, DC, MC, V. Mon–Fri noon–midnight; Sat 4pm–midnight. U-Bahn: Rödingsmarkt. A 1-min. walk from the Elbe.

Tarantella ★ GERMAN/INTERNATIONAL   Fashionistas, models, the media elite, and soccer stars flock to this restaurant in the Casino Esplanade. The open-to-view kitchen hides no secrets as the chefs concoct such sublime plates as Canadian lobsters plucked from a tank or such grandmotherly dishes as crispy suckling pig with creamy *Sauerkraut*. Begin with such imaginative appetizers as octopus carpaccio with arugula pesto and a sorbet, or sautéed foie gras with kumquats. Among the more delightful main courses are a braised saddle of venison on lentils or a saddle of veal with fried asparagus. Monkfish comes with fried baby calamari and a wild garlic risotto studded with almonds.

Stephansplatz 10. © **040/65067790.** www.tarantella.cc. Reservations required. 15€–35€. AE, MC, V. Sun–Wed 11:30am–midnight; Thurs–Sat 11:30am–1am. U-Bahn: Stephansplatz.

In Altona

EXPENSIVE

Fischereihafen Restaurant ★★ SEAFOOD   Fischereihafen, established some 4 decades ago, is the best seafood restaurant in town if you prefer true local fare to the internationally oriented cuisine of other restaurants. Every day, the staff buys only the freshest fish and shellfish at the Hamburg auction hall. The menu changes daily, depending on what seafood is available. The second floor is said to be full of "fish and VIPs." Other specialties include filet of salmon with potato salad and a rémoulade sauce, Arctic trout with wild garlic, and rare tuna steak with peppercorns and honey-laced soy sauce. Appetizers include filet of sole and lobster or a plate of fresh oysters; the house special is turbot with salmon mousse dotted with truffles. A favorite local main course is a plate of giant shrimp with exotic fruits in a curry-cream sauce. Picture windows open onto a view of the Elbe.

Grosse Elbstrasse 143. ☏ **040/381816.** www.fischereihafenrestaurant.de. Reservations required. Main courses 18€–46€; fixed-price menu 60€. AE, DC, MC, V. Sun–Thurs 11:30am–10pm; Fri–Sat 11:30am–10:30pm. S-Bahn: Königstrasse. A 10-min. taxi ride from the wharf area of Landungsbrücken.

Landhaus Scherrer ★★★ NORTHERN GERMAN/CONTINENTAL   Once a brewery, the Landhaus is now a citadel of gastronomy on the Elbe at Altona. It has gained a reputation for impeccable service and imaginatively prepared cuisine. The chef's inventive cookery combines northern German and international flavors with stunning results. A special dish for two is crispy whole north German duck with seasoned vegetables and au gratin potatoes. An unusual variation might be roast goose with rhubarb in cassis sauce. Other specialties include roasted slices of calf's liver with a cherry balsamic jus or ribs of lamb with ratatouille and a rosemary jus. Yet another tasty dish is turbot flavored with horseradish and wasabi.

Elbchaussee 130. ☏ **040/8801325.** www.landhausscherrer.de. Reservations required. Main courses 28€–39€; fixed-price menu 111€. AE, DC, MC, V. Mon–Sat noon–3pm and 6:30–10:30pm. Bus: 135.

MODERATE

Eisenstein INTERNATIONAL/PIZZA   The food here is representative of the wide range of cultures that Hamburgers have been exposed to, thanks to the city's role as a great port. The menu lists specialties from Thailand, Japan (including sushi and sashimi), southern France, and Italy, as well as traditional and very fresh versions of the North German cuisine that Hamburg excels in—particularly fresh Atlantic fish prepared virtually any way you want. The chefs are known for turning out some of the most savory pizzas in town, emerging piping hot from the oven nightly until midnight. Many patrons drop in for a beer and pizza in the late evening. The setting is a solid-looking, much-restored factory and former warehouse with soaring, russet-colored brick walls that envelop diners in a cozy womb against the sometimes gray weather outside. The clientele is artsy, hip, and stylish; the staff is cooperative; and the food is surprisingly flavorful, considering its diversity.

Friedensallee 9. ☏ **040/3904606.** www.restaurant-eisenstein.de. Reservations recommended. Main courses 18€–25€; fixed-price dinners 33€–37€; pizzas 8€–14€. No credit cards. Daily 11am–11pm. U-Bahn: Altona Bahnhof.

Landhaus Dill ★★ CONTINENTAL   This restaurant is imbued with a country charm, its windows opening onto views of the River Elbe. Although it's close to the street, the terrace is an ideal place to enjoy a warm Hamburg night. The young chefs are completely at ease with their recipes, which, for diversity, cross borders from Germany to Austria, with significant inspiration from western France. Nothing beats the green asparagus soup with a truffle dumpling. After that, you can order such mains as saddle of lamb with an herb crust, or roast cod filet in a thyme sauce, perhaps sautéed slices of beef filet in a peppercorn-laced butter sauce.

Elbchaussee 94. ☏ **040/3905077.** www.landhausdill.com. Reservations required. Main courses 15€–22€; set-price menus 25€–50€. AE, DC, MC, V. Tues–Sun noon–3pm and 5:30–10:30pm. S-Bahn: Altona Bahnhof.

Rive ★ 🍴 SEAFOOD   This riverside restaurant near the ferry terminal on the Elbe River specializes in some of the best and freshest fish dishes in the city. You get not only a panoramic view of the water, with container ships going by, but delectable seafood such as lobster and clams. Its harborside oyster bar is reason enough to make the journey. Other than shellfish, specialties include herring with a choice of three sauces and pan-fried fish with mustard sauce. Outdoor tables are placed on a waterfront terrace that's heated in spring and fall.

Van-der-Smissen-Strasse 1, Altona. © **040/3805919.** www.rive.de. Reservations recommended. Main courses 18€–38€. MC, V. Daily noon–midnight. U-Bahn: Königstrasse.

In St. Pauli
EXPENSIVE

Old Commercial Room ★ 🎁 NORTHERN GERMAN This restaurant, founded in 1643, is so tied into Hamburg maritime life that many residents consider it the premier sailors' stopover. It's the best place in town for *Labskaus* (sailor's hash); if you order it, you're given a numbered certificate proclaiming you a genuine *Labskaus* eater. You can also order many other traditional north German dishes. Very well prepared are such dishes as stuffed pork filet medallions with sheep's cheese in a Calvados sauce; or Scottish wild salmon filet—fried or poached—with truffled lead spinach and a creamy pepper sauce. The restaurant's name, along with that of the street, speaks of the historic mercantile links between Hamburg and England.

Englische Planke 10. © **040/366319.** www.oldcommercialroom.de. Reservations required. Main courses 18€–42€. AE, DC, MC, V. Daily noon–midnight. Closed Dec 24. U-Bahn: St. Pauli. At the foot of St. Michaelis.

MODERATE

Restaurant Nil INTERNATIONAL Even though the name of this restaurant refers to Egypt's River Nile, don't imagine a decor influenced by either the desert or the Arab world. What you get is upscale French bistro, replete with mirrors, oiled mahogany, and polished brass. The name refers to the bounty provided by the Nile, as interpreted by north German tastes, and the cooking is superb. Clients tend to be in publishing and the arts; many are cultural movers and shakers who have adopted this place as a favorite hangout. Dishes include a carpaccio of beef with a black-olive marinade and shiitake mushrooms; saltimbocca of ham and calves' livers prepared with artichoke hearts; braised leg of turkey stuffed with sautéed leeks and served with noodles in an orange-flavored whiskey sauce; and beef bourguignon with braised shallots, mushrooms, and mashed potatoes.

Neuer Pferdemarkt 5. © **040/4397823.** www.restaurant-nil.de. Reservations recommended. Main courses 18€–22€; fixed-price menu 41€. No credit cards. Wed–Mon 6pm–midnight. U-Bahn: Feldstrasse.

In Bahrenfeld
VERY EXPENSIVE

Tafelhaus ★★ MEDITERRANEAN A favorite of visiting celebrities, Tafelhaus lies in one of the less attractive industrial neighborhoods. But once you get inside, you're treated to a fresh and varied medley of Mediterranean dishes, some with a hint of Asia as well. The Saarbrücken-born chef, Christian Rach, is a whiz in the kitchen, concocting such delights as curried-apple soup or an herby risotto with tiger shrimp. One of the most imaginative dishes we've sampled here is veal shank with a bed of avocado mousse and mango salsa. For dessert, a real change-of-pace flavor is provided by the curd-cheese torte with a fresh rhubarb sauce. The decor is modern, a single artfully designed room outfitted in tones of soft red and ocher. The restaurant overlooks a garden, where in summer tables are set out.

Neumühlen 17. © **040/892760.** www.tafelhaus-hamburg.de. Reservations required. Main courses 36€–46€. AE, DC, MC, V. Tues–Fri noon–3pm and 7–9:30pm; Sat 7–9:30pm. Closed 2 weeks in Jan, 3 weeks in July. U-Bahn: Bahrenfeld.

In Overlgönne

VERY EXPENSIVE

Das Weisse Haus ★ 🍴 GERMAN/SEAFOOD   This is an offbeat dining choice worth seeking out. It lies in a converted old fisherman's cottage. Even fishermen patronize the place along with Hamburg yachties. Forget about a menu, as there is none. You tell the waiter how hungry you are, and you might mention your food likes and dislikes, or any allergies you have. The chef takes care of your menu, which often begins with that Hamburg classic, *aalsuppe* (eel soup). You might also start with a honey almond salad with watermelon, a refreshing change of pace. Not all the menu is devoted to seafood; you can, for example, order a tender rack of lamb with a tarragon-laced hollandaise on the side.

Neumühlen 50, Overlgönne. ✆ **04/309016.** www.das-weisse-haus.de. Reservations required. 2-course menu 28€; 3-course menu 34€; 4-course menu 42€. AE, MC, V. Mon–Sat noon–3pm and–6–9pm. U-Bahn: Altona.

SHOPPING

Hamburg is a city of merchants. In general, stores are open Monday to Friday 9am to 6 or 6:30pm (some Thurs until 8pm) and on Saturday 9am to 2pm (until 4 or 6pm on *langer Samstag,* the first Sat of the month). Unfortunately, the best shops are not concentrated in one location. Two of the oldest and most prestigious shopping streets, **Grosse Bleichen** and **Neuer Wall,** run parallel to the canals, connected transversely by Jungfernstieg and Ufer Strasse on the Binnenalster. Less expensive shopping streets are Spitalstrasse and Mönckebergstrasse.

Hamburg has nine major shopping malls. The glass-roofed **Hanse Viertel Galerie Passage** is some 200m (660 ft.) long. There's a scattering of upscale cafes here and even a stand-up seafood bar where glasses of beer or *Sekt* (sparkling wine) are served at tiny tables.

Mönckebergstrasse (U-Bahn: Hauptbahnhof), a street connecting the main station with the Rathaus, is the city's traditional shopping district. Here you'll find big department stores such as **Karstadt,** Mönckebergstrasse 16 (✆ 040/30940; www. karstadt.de), part of a chain that carries many of the same brands and items as the other leading department stores, all competitively priced. The store is open Monday to Friday 9am to 8pm and Saturday 9am to 4pm. A thrifty alternative, **Kaufhof,** Mönckebergstrasse 3 (✆ 040/333070; www.galeria-kaufhof.de), carries less expensive items than the surrounding department stores and also offers better deals on merchandise markdowns. Bargain hunters combing the store are apt to be successful. Hours are Monday to Saturday 9:30am to 8pm. More fashionable and upscale than any of the three mentioned above is **Alsterhaus,** Jungfernstieg 16–20 (✆ 040/ 359010; www.alsterhaus.de), which some New Yorkers have compared favorably to Bloomingdale's (same hours as Karstadt).

If you walk down Bergstrasse to the second part of the city center, you pass along **Jungfernstieg,** with tourist boats of the Alster Fleet on the right and a teeming shopping street on the other side. About a block farther along, you come to the **Hamburger Hof,** the elegant entrance to one of the most attractive chains of shopping galleries in Europe. At the end of Jungfernstieg, you can cross Gänsemarkt to **Gänsemarkt Passage,** another shopping gallery, with stores on three levels.

An upmarket and youthfully fashionable shopping area is in **Eppendorf** (U-Bahn: Eppendorfer Baum), Hamburg's oldest village, first mentioned in written history in 1140. Many prosperous and avant-garde Hamburgers live in the stately area's 19th-century homes and apartments. The shopping district, from Klosterstern to Eppendorfer Markt, has exclusive boutiques selling fashions from Paris, Milan, and New York; colorful shops with odds and ends for your home; antiques shops; and places where you can not only make purchases but also watch goldsmiths, hat makers, potters, and weavers at work.

The Hamburg **Fischmarkt (fish market),** between Hexenberg and Grosse Elbstrasse (U-Bahn: Landungsbrücken), is held every Sunday from 5am in summer or 7am otherwise. Flowers, fruit, vegetables, plants, and pets are also for sale at this traditional market, in existence since 1703. It sometimes seems that the fish are just an afterthought nowadays. The nearby taverns are open to serve Fischmarkt visitors and vendors.

Jil Sander, Neuer Wall 43 (✆ **040/37518704;** www.jilsander.com; S-Bahn: Dammtor), is the best place to go for chic women's styling. Jil Sander burst upon Europe's fashion scene from her native city of Hamburg and has taken special efforts to make this three-floor store the flagship of her increasingly successful operation. Part of the success of her designs derives from their wearability—they are appropriate for the office, the boardroom, or cocktail hour. Another popular choice for women's fashions is **Escada Boutique,** Neuer Wall 32 (✆ **040/363296;** www.escada.com; U-Bahn: Hauptbahnhof), owned by the German design company of the same name. This store carries the firm's complete collection of women's sports-, evening, business, and knitwear, plus accessories that include hats, bags, gloves, and shoes. A less expensive division of Escada, **Laurel Boutique,** Neuer Wall 41 (✆ **040/3743270;** U-Bahn: Hauptbahnhof), appeals to an active, younger clientele with alternative takes on casual day and elegant evening wear.

For high-fashion men's clothing, go to **Thomas-i-Punkt,** Gänsemarkt 24 (✆ **040/342009;** U-Bahn: Hauptbahnhof), where you'll find suits, jackets, shirts, shoes, and belts carrying the exclusive Omen label. Ties, handkerchiefs, and other accessories are also available. Shoes, well made and fashionably styled, are sold to both men and women at **Schuhhaus Prange,** Jungfernstieg 38 (✆ **040/343151;** www.schuhhaus-prange.de; U-Bahn: Jungfernstieg).

One of the city's leading hairdressers, for both men and women, is **Marlies Müller,** Königsbergerstrasse 6 (✆ **040/6403829;** S-Bahn: Dammtor). Besides hair styling and beauty treatments, a large perfume and cosmetic selection is also offered here.

Brahmfeld & Gutruf, Jungfernstieg 12 (✆ **040/346103;** www.brahmfeldgutruf.de; U-Bahn: Jungfernstieg), is one of Germany's oldest jewelers, founded in 1743.

A store with a nautical nature, **Binikowski,** Lokstedter Weg 68 (✆ **040/462852;** U-Bahn: Eppendorfer Baum), established in 1955, is the place to find a *Buddelschiff* (ship in a bottle), as well as ship models and clocks. **Captain's Cabin,** Bei Dim St. Pauli Landungsbrücken 3 (✆ **040/316373;** S-Bahn: Landungsbrücken), stocks ship models, telescopes, barometers, figureheads, lamps, nautical clothing for the whole family, prints, posters, and more.

ENTERTAINMENT & NIGHTLIFE
Nightlife
THE PERFORMING ARTS

Hamburgische Staatsoper (Hamburg State Opera) ★★★ This modern opera house was built after the bombings of World War II. Its acoustics and technical facilities are among the most advanced in the world. The venue is the home of the **Hamburg State Opera** and the **Hamburg Ballet,** the latter directed by Californian John Neumeier. Grosstheaterstrasse 25. ✆ **040/356868.** www.hamburgische-staatsoper.de. Tickets 10€–146€. U-Bahn: Stephansplatz. S-Bahn: Dammtor.

Musikhalle ★★ This survivor of Germany's romantic age lies about 1km (½ mile) from the Staatsoper, with which it shares some facilities and staff members. The building was painstakingly restored after World War II. It hosts concerts by the **Hamburg Symphony,** the **Hamburg Philharmonic,** the **NDR Symphony,** and the renowned **Monteverdi-Chor,** known for its interpretations of baroque and Renaissance music. Touring orchestras also perform here. For tickets, call either the number listed below or the number listed for the Staatsoper (see above). Johannes-Brahms-Platz 1. ✆ **040/357666.** www.laeiszhalle.de. Tickets up to 45€. U-Bahn: Stephansplatz. S-Bahn: Dammtor.

THEATER Hamburg is blessed with more than 40 theaters, but for most of these, a good knowledge of German is necessary. An exception, the **English Theatre of Hamburg,** Lerchenfeld 14 (✆ **040/2277089;** www.englishtheatre.de; U-Bahn: Mundsburg), is the only English-speaking theater in the northern part of Germany. Tickets are 13€ to 32€. Performances are Tuesday to Saturday at 7:30pm; a matinee is presented on Tuesday and Friday at 11am.

If you understand German, try the **Deutsches Schauspielhaus** ★, Kirchenallee 39 (✆ **040/248713;** www.schauspielhaus.de; U-Bahn: Hauptbahnhof). It's one of the outstanding theaters in the German-speaking world, performing both classics and modern plays.

Other theaters are the cutting-edge **Thaliatheater,** Alstertor (✆ **040/328140;** www.thalia-theater.de; U-Bahn: Jungfernstieg), and the **Kammerspiele,** Hartungstrasse 9–11 (✆ **040/44123660;** www.hamburger-kammerspiele.de; U-Bahn: Hallerstrasse). Both stage a wide range of plays as well as musical shows. A new production usually opens every month. Tickets at these theaters range from 10€ to 45€. Small ensemble performances such as *Evening with Marlene Dietrich* are the specialty of the **Schmidt Theater,** Spielbudenplatz 24 (✆ **040/3177880;** www.tivoli.de; S-Bahn: Reeperbahn). Its companion, **Schmidts Tivoli,** Spielbudenplatz 27–28 (same phone), hosts musicals and other popular performances. Tickets are 9€ to 55€. All of these are closed on Monday.

⌕ Ticket-Buying Tips

Tickets to sporting events, including soccer matches, are best acquired through the **Hamburger Sportbund (Hamburg Sports Association),** Schäferkampsallee 1, 20357 Hamburg (✆ **040/419080;** www.hamburger-sportbund.de). Another option, for cultural (not necessarily sporting) events, is to contact Hamburg's **Tourismus Centrale (Tourist Information Office),** in the "Wandelhalle" of the city's main railway station (✆ **040/30051300).**

Two of Hamburg's busiest theaters are the **Neue Flora Theater,** Stresemannstrasse 159A (© **01805/4444;** U-Bahn: Altona), and the **Operettenhaus,** Spielbudenplatz 1 (same phone; S-Bahn: Reeperbahn), which have enjoyed an unprecedented success with German-language versions of U.S. and British musicals. The cost of seeing shows is 32€ to 126€, depending on your seat and the night you attend.

THE BAR SCENE

Bar Hamburg ★   This is one of the chicest bars in north Germany, attracting the likes of Mick Jagger and Bryan Adams when they're in town, plus Hamburg's most beautiful models (of either sex), artists, media types, and interior designers. It lies between the elegant Kempinski Hotel Atlantic and the red-light district near the train station. From 7pm nightly to "indecently late," patrons sip drinks and dig into tasty snacks. Some of the best DJs in Hamburg keep you entertained with jazz, house, and lounge music. Rautenbergstrasse 6-8. © **040/28054880.** www.barhamburg.com. U-Bahn: Hauptbahnhof.

Neo   This bustling bar attracts a roiling mass of single—or at least permissively semiattached—people, many of them rather good-looking, who congregate within a venue that combines aspects of a cafe with a cocktail bar and restaurant. The decor is minimalist and modern, centered on a very large rectangular bar area in its center. Large windows flood the place with light during the day, and furniture is painted in neon tones of pink, green, and blue. The specialty here, other than mating games, is cocktails, prepared by a staff of mixologists, at least one of whom always seems to be shaking up a container of martinis. Other choices include *caipirinhas;* a Prince of Wales (made with *Sekt,* Cointreau, and fresh oranges); and a Swimming Pool (with vodka, Blue Curaçao, and several kinds of rum). If you get hungry, know in advance that the menu consists mostly of small dishes that are meant to be combined with other small dishes into something resembling a two-fisted meal. Perfect for the mannequins and photo models who favor this place might be a diet-conscious California Body Shaper, made with turkey breast, pineapple slices, and cheese. It's open Monday to Thursday 9am to 1am, Friday and Saturday 9am to 2am, and Sunday 9am to midnight. Martinistrasse 11, in Eppendorf. © **040/46779936.** www.neogastro.de. Small platters 6.90€-14€; cocktails 7€-9€. S-Bahn: Kellinghusenstrasse.

Shamrock   The oldest Irish pub in Hamburg, the Shamrock has been in business for nearly 2 decades. It's a popular hangout for students and a transient English-speaking crowd that comes to soak up the Guinness, Kilkenny, Harp, and hard cider on tap. Every Tuesday night, the pub hosts quiz night. It's open Sunday to Thursday 1pm to 2am and Friday and Saturday 5pm to 4am. Feldstrasse 40. © **040/43277275.** www. shamrockirishbar.com. U-Bahn: Altona.

THE CLUB & MUSIC SCENE

Jazz

Cotton Club ★★   The legendary Cotton Club is the oldest (some 36 years) and best established of the Hamburg jazz clubs. Jazz and Dixieland bands come here from throughout Europe and the United States. Hours are Monday to Saturday 8pm to 1am. Alter Steinweg 10. © **040/343878.** www.cotton-club.de. Cover 6.50€-15€. S-Bahn: Stadthausbrücke.

Rock

Club Grosse Freiheit 36 ★★   This club, now world famous, is where the Beatles performed in their earliest days. Today, it's a free-for-all venue whose acts change

THE reeperbahn: A WALK ON THE WILD SIDE

Commercialized sex flourishes in many towns, but hardworking, entrepreneurial Hamburg has succeeded better than almost anywhere else at transforming it into a tourist attraction. The place where it all hangs out is the **St. Pauli district** (U-Bahn: St. Pauli; S-Bahn: Reeperbahn), just east of the center. St. Pauli's mid-section—the "genital zone," as it's sometimes called—is the **Reeperbahn,** a 1km (½-mile) thoroughfare whose name literally translates as "rope street," referring to the massive amounts of hempen rope produced here during the 18th and 19th centuries for ships in Germany's biggest harbor.

In the 19th century, most forms of entertainment, including theaters, were banned from the city's more respectable medieval core. As one resident of the district remarked, "Bourgeois Protestants don't know how to have fun." Consequently, this neighborhood near the great port developed entertainment options of its own, and sailors from around the world were safely channeled into a neighborhood where their recreational activities were out of sight (and out of mind) of the city's sober business establishment. Hamburg's first theater opened on the Reeperbahn in 1842. By the 1860s, the question, "Whatcha

doing, sailor?" became the unofficial motto of an army of prostitutes who set up shop (with the legal sanction of municipal authorities) in the district.

The city's official line is that the Reeperbahn is Hamburg's second-greatest attraction and asset (the first is the port itself). The authorities see their policies as a rare instance of civic and moral enlightenment unparalleled in any other city, except for Amsterdam's more sanitized sex scene. They make frequent references to their requirement that every officially sanctioned working girl submit to a medical examination every 2 weeks—and pay income tax on her profits. Hamburg's most-talked-about police station, **Davidwache,** at the corner of the Davidstrasse and the Reeperbahn, provides highly visible and omnipresent police protection.

What are the rules of the game, and what should you do to survive such an "in-your-face" neighborhood? Throw your sense of scheduling to the wind and take a nap on the day of your visit. Mornings in St. Pauli are burned-out, unenthusiastic times, when virtually everyone is recovering from the bacchanals of the night before. Midafternoons perk up a bit. But regardless of the fogs that roll in from the Baltic and the damp chill that's an inseparable part of the

almost nightly and whose guests in the recent past have included Prince and Willie Nelson. Even the civic and municipal authorities of Hamburg view it as one of their preeminent cultural treasures. For recorded information about upcoming acts, call ✆ **040/31777811.** Grosse Freiheit 36. ✆ **040/3177780.** www.grossefreiheit36.de. Cover 4€–20€. S-Bahn: Reeperbahn.

Fabrik   This cultural center is similar in style to the Markthalle (see below). Originally it was an old ammunition depot (ca. 1830), until it burned down; later, it was reconstructed in the same style. Open 8pm to midnight (later Sat–Sun), Fabrik is a nightclub beloved by those who survived the 1970s more or less intact. It offers a mixed program likely to feature African bands, jazz, and blues. Barnerstrasse 36 (5 min. from Bahnhof Altona). ✆ **040/391070.** www.fabrik.de. Cover 10€–35€. U-Bahn: Altona.

Hamburg experience, by 8pm the district's bars and theaters (legitimate and otherwise) are roaring away. Between midnight and 5am, you'll find thousands of women and men in drag, strutting their stuff along the turf. German enterprise has honored these women (and their reputation for a good time) by naming one of Hamburg's native beers in their honor—the famous "St. Pauli Girl."

There's a distinct pecking order among the working girls, based on the neighborhood, or street, where they're headquartered. The most exclusive and expensive area is **Herbertstrasse,** where plate-glass windows allow the women to display their charms to window-shoppers. By city ordinance, this street is open only to men 19 and over (women are officially banned, but this does not seem to be enforced). Less expensive rents can be found on the streets near Herbertstrasse: Gunterstrasse, Erichstrasse, Friedrichstrasse, Davidstrasse, and Gerhardstrasse. Lots of the women here are from the Eastern Bloc, and lately there's been a distressing trend for runaway teenagers to join their ranks. Cross-dressing and transgender workers ply their trade here, too.

If it's erotic theater you're looking for, you'll have to move a few blocks away to **Grosse Freiheit,** a street whose name appropriately translates as "Great Freedom." Any act of sexual expression, with every conceivable permutation, except those that involve animals (bestiality is one of the few things expressly forbidden), is shown in these theaters. Be it joyful, be it disgusting, it's all here, often performed by artists whose barely concealed boredom sometimes permeates the setting in a way that elsewhere would be embarrassing, but here seems merely surreal.

You aren't likely to be solicited at a performance—municipal regulations forbid prostitution, or overt solicitation, inside erotic theaters. But there's nothing to prevent a member of the audience from suddenly deciding to be a performer—it's been known to happen, if rarely. And there's nothing that prevents performers from setting up an off-premises rendezvous. In any event, caveat emptor.

Off-the-record theaters include **Safari,** Grosse Freiheit 24 (✆ **040/313233;** www.safari-hamburg. de; S-Bahn: Reeperbahn), where you're likely to find the press agent for the city of Hamburg entertaining foreign travel writers. Expect to pay a fixed price of around 25€ for one beer.

Logo   Because of its position near Hamburg's university, this club attracts lots of college students, although many *Big Chill* survivors in their 40s and 50s gravitate toward this spot as well. It's a small, informal place that often features rock bands. Sometimes well-known singers appear in concert. It's open daily 8pm (live music begins at 9pm) to 2 or 3am. Audiences often sit on the floor. Grindelallee 5. ✆ **040/ 362622.** www.logohamburg.de. Cover 3€–20€. S-Bahn: Dammtor.

Markthalle ★   This is one of the most visible live-music venues in Hamburg, with a special emphasis on up-and-coming British groups and sometimes heavy metal and high-volume electronics. The building functioned early in the 20th century as a covered marketplace. Inside is an amphitheater with a stage and a large area for standing or sitting on notoriously uncomfortable benches. Performances usually begin at 9pm, with the ticket office opening about an hour before. Klosterwall 11. ✆ **040/339491.** www. markthalle-hamburg.de. Cover 11€–28€. S-Bahn: Hauptbahnhof; U-Bahn: Steinstrasse.

John Lennon once said, "I was born in Liverpool, but I grew up in Hamburg." As all Beatles fans know, the group really got its start in Hamburg in the early 1960s. Radio Station Ondie 95 has dedicated a monument to the Beatles, which stands at the corner of the St. Pauli district in the Reeperbahn where the Beatles sang "Love Me Do" in 1962. In the middle of what is now known as "Beatles Square" on the Reeperbahn, the monument consists of a black circle, symbolizing a record, and life-size statues of the Beatles in glass. The radio station raised $625,000 among Beatles fans to pay for the monument.

Drag Shows

Pulverfass The best-known drag show in town, Pulverfass is usually featured on the "Hamburg by Night" tours, which are escorted bus tours that take travelers to a few nightclubs. This place is not for the timid. Female impersonators from all over Europe appear, and you might find the shows downright vulgar, especially if you know German. There are shows nightly (for which you need reservations) at 8:30 and 11:30pm, and also at 2:30am Friday and Saturday. Within the same building, with a view of the stage, there's a restaurant, **Teatro-Café,** which is open daily 5pm to 3am and serves French- and German-inspired fixed-price menus for 39€ to 59€ each. Reeperbahn 147. ✆ **040/249791.** www.pulverfasscabaret.de. Cover 15€–24€. U-Bahn: Steindamm.

Dance Clubs

Golden Cut ★ Set at the junction of three historic neighborhoods (St. Georg, the Innenstadt, and the Altstadt), this is a well-known and likable restaurant that expands after 10:30pm on weekends into a high-powered dance club. The restaurant and its club are separated by what management calls "a chill-out lounge." After you've chilled out for a while, you might want to move deeper into an environment of black-lacquered tables, wood paneling, cream-colored walls, a ceiling that's swathed in fabric as a means of keeping the noise from reverberating, and a color scheme of pale green and copper. Menu items in the restaurant are international and well prepared, deriving from Japan (sushi and Kobe beef), Thailand (curries and dishes laced with lemon grass), and continental Europe (filet steak layered Rossini-style, with foie gras; medallions of monkfish in butter-flavored parsley sauce). Main courses in the restaurant cost from 18€ to 28€. The club is open Friday to Sunday, plus the first Thursday of every month from 10pm to 5am; the restaurant is open Tuesday to Saturday noon to 5pm and 6pm to 1am. Ages for clients of the club average around 23 to 25 for women and around 32 to 35 for men. Holzdamm 61. ✆ **040/85103532.** www.goldencut.org. U-Bahn: Hauptbahnhof.

Molotow This is the place to dance to funk—George Clinton and Bootsy Collins have been elevated to god status here. Say you've seen Parliament-Funkadelic, and you may make lifelong friends. Opening hours may vary, but usually it opens Wednesday and Sunday at 8pm, Thursday to Saturday at 11pm; closing time depends on the energy of the dancers. Spielbudenplatz 5. ✆ **040/310845.** www.molotowclub.com. Cover 5€–16€. S-Bahn: Reeperbahn.

Gay Clubs

Hamburg, like Berlin, is one of the major gay havens of Europe, with a particularly dense concentration of gay boutiques and cafes along the Lange Reihe in St. Pauli. A little journal, *Dorn Rosa,* distributed at most gay and lesbian bars, lists (in German) the clubs, restaurants, bars, and events that cater to a gay, lesbian, and bisexual clientele.

Café Gnosa   More than any other eatery in Hamburg, this comes the closest to fulfilling the need for an official "gay restaurant." Set near the railway station, it's open daily 10am to 1am. Platters of food range from 6€ to 25€ and feature all-day breakfasts, steaks, fish, salads, and all kinds of coffee and drinks. Café Gnosa's bar is one of the most frequented gay bars in the area of the Hauptbahnhof and is quite cruisy. Lange Reihe 93. © **040/243034.** www.gnosa.de. U-Bahn: Hauptbahnhof.

Tom's Saloon & Tom's Dancehall   This is the best-established and most popular gay men's bar in Hamburg, known to virtually every gay male in town. Begin your night in the street-level dance club, work your way up to a watering hole one floor above, and end your evening in the cellar, where leather is optional but encouraged. Women, if they come here at all (which is rare), usually remain in the street-level club. At least one part of this place is open every night 10pm until dawn; every Wednesday to Sunday, additional sections open for greater space. The cover is 5€. Pulverteich 17. © **040/25328943.** www.toms-hamburg.de. U-Bahn: Hauptbahnhof.

A CASINO

Spielbank Hamburg   This casino offers roulette, blackjack, and poker, played according to international rules. You can also enjoy a drink at the bar, taking in the panoramic view over the roofs and lakes of Hamburg. The minimum stake for roulette is 2€, for blackjack 5€. Men should wear jackets and ties. Everyone needs a passport to get in (you must be 18 or over to enter and gamble). The casino is open daily 3pm to 3am. Stephansplatz 10. © **040/4501760.** www.spielbank-hamburg.de. U-Bahn: Stephansplatz.

Sports & Outdoor Pursuits

BOATING

A paddle on the Aussenalster (Outer Alster Lake) can be one of the most relaxing and charming warm-weather activities in Hamburg. **H. Pieper** (© **040/247578;** www. segelschule-pieper.de) rents rowboats, paddle boats, and one-occupant sailing dinghies; prices begin at 15€ to 22€ per hour. This outfitter is open only April to late September, daily 10am to 8pm.

GOLF

Hamburg has many golf clubs, including **Hamburger Golf-Club Falkenstein,** In de Bargen 59 (© **040/812177;** www.hamburgergolf-club.de). Greens fees range from 45€ to 75€ for 18 holes.

JOGGING & WALKING

Our favorite route, for either long walks or jogging, is the pedestrian walkway that circumnavigates the Alster lakes. The total perimeter of the larger of the two lakes measures about 6km (4 miles); that of the more congested Binnenalster is about 1.5km (1 mile). The public parks flanking the northwestern edge of the inner city are also suitable.

SPECTATOR SPORTS

For information about soccer matches and other spectator events, contact the **Hamburger Sportbund (Hamburg Sports Association),** Schäferkampsallee 1, 20357 Hamburg (© **040/419080;** www.hamburger-sportbund.de).

SWIMMING

The rivers and lakes in Hamburg are being cleaned up and are quite pretty but still rather cold for dipping into—luckily there are many swimming pools. Two of the most popular are the **Alster-Schwimmhalle,** Ifflandstrasse 21 (✆ **040/223012;** www. baederland.de; U-Bahn: Lohmühlenstrasse), and the **Holthusenbad,** Goernestrasse 21 (✆ **040/474754;** www.baederland.de; U-Bahn: Eppendorfer Baum). The latter has the advantage of artificial waves, thermal baths, and steam baths. Both pools charge 9.50€ per day.

TENNIS

Not surprisingly, the country that gave the world Steffi Graf and Boris Becker has no lack of tennis facilities. For names and addresses of tennis facilities, as well as information about upcoming tournaments, contact the **Deutscher Tennis Bund,** Hallerstrasse 89 (✆ **040/411780;** www.dtb-tennis.de).

Hamburg is also the home of the **Hamburg Tennis Masters Series,** one of the nine Masters Series events that rank just below the Grand Slams. Previously known as the German Open, it is also a major warm-up for the famous French Open, the only Grand Slam event to be played on clay. The Hamburg tournament is also played on clay, usually in May.

WHERE TO STAY

Hamburg is an expensive city with an abundance of first-class hotels but a limited number of budget accommodations, especially in the center of the city. During a busy convention period, you may have trouble finding a room. A department within **Hamburg's Tourismus Centrale (Tourist Information Office),** in the Hauptbahnhof, at Kirchenallee in the Wandelhalle (✆ **040/30051300;** www.hamburg-tourism.de), can book accommodations. Rooms from more than 200 hotels in all price categories are available. There's a fee of 5€ per reservation. You can use this agency on a last-minute basis, but no more than 7 days in advance of the time you'll need the room. Hotel-booking desks can also be found at the airport in Arrival Hall A.

Near the Hauptbahnhof

VERY EXPENSIVE

Kempinski Hotel Atlantic ★★★ This sumptuous hotel, the Kempinski chain's flagship, is one of the two great hotels of the north. It's in a central location filled with trees and imposing villas and was one of the few buildings in the neighborhood to escape the bombs of World War II. Prince, Madonna, and the late Michael Jackson cast their votes for this hotel, but we still think Fairmont Hotel Vier Jahreszeiten (see below) is number one. Many of the high-ceilinged, spacious bedrooms open onto lakeside views. All have lots of extras, including windows that open (as opposed to being permanently sealed), deluxe toilet articles, bathroom scales, and maid and butler service round-the-clock.

An der Alster 72–79, 20099 Hamburg. www.kempinski.atlantic.de. ✆ **800/426-3135** in the U.S., or 040/28880. Fax 040/247129. 252 units. 179€–400€ double; from 423€ suite. AE, DC, MC, V. Parking 32€. U-Bahn: Hauptbahnhof. Near the Aussenalster. **Amenities:** 2 restaurants; bar; babysitting; bikes; concierge; exercise room; indoor heated pool; room service; spa. *In room:* TV, hair dryer, minibar, Wi-Fi (12€ per hr.).

Le Royal Méridien Hamburg ★★★   Opening in the heart of Hamburg on Lake Aussenalster, the city's latest government-rated five-star hotel features what it calls "Art + Tech" bedrooms spread over nine floors. These rooms, designed by London-based Yvonne Golds, feature such attractions as the signature Le Méridien giant bed, 42-inch flatscreen plasma TVs, high-speed Internet access, and separate power showers with assorted massage nozzles, among other endearments such as hand-crafted etched-glass headboards. Using a neutral backdrop, color is used dramatically in either painted wall panels or soft furnishings. Furniture is designed using a mini-mal palette of materials such as pale maple or stained steel and glass (clear, frosted, or etched). The majority of the bedrooms and six two-story suites offer sweeping views of the lake, and the top-floor restaurant and bar enjoys one of Hamburg's best panoramic views from a hotel. At all times, 600 original pieces of art, the work of 50 Hamburg artists, are on exhibit.

An der Alster 52–56, 20099 Hamburg www.starwoodhotels.com.. ✆ **040/21000.** Fax 040/21001111. 284 units. 179€–299€ double; from 339€ suite. AE, DC, MC, V. Parking 26€. S-Bahn or U-Bahn: Haupt-bahnhof. **Amenities:** Restaurant; 2 bars; airport transfers (135€); bikes; concierge; exercise room; indoor heated pool; room service; spa. *In room:* A/C, TV, CD player, hair dryer, minibar, Wi-Fi (20€ per day).

Park Hyatt Hamburg ★★ ☺   Hyatt took the Levantehaus, a traditional 1912 warehouse, and transformed it into one of Hamburg's best government-rated five-star hotels. In the heart of Hamburg, close to the rail station, the Hyatt occupies the top seven floors of the building, which means rooms with views. Rooms are somewhat minimalist but nonetheless tastefully and comfortably appointed. Even the standard units are large, each with a contemporary bathroom with lots of gadgets. The suites at the Hyatt feature such additional facilities as whirlpools and saunas. A special feature is Club Olympus with its mammoth pool, gym and aerobic studio, and mas-sages and beauty treatments.

At **Apples Restaurant,** Mediterranean dishes are creatively prepared in an open kitchen in front of guests.

Bugenhagenstrasse 8–10, Neustadt 20095 Hamburg. www.hamburg.park.hyatt.com. ✆ **040/33321234.** Fax 040/33321235. 252 units. 225€–410€ double; from 410€ suite. Children 11 and under stay free in parent's room. AE, DC, MC, V. Parking 28€. U-Bahn: Hauptbahnhof. **Amenities:** 2 restaurants; bar; air-port transfers (25€); babysitting; children's programs; concierge; health club and spa; indoor heated pool; room service. *In room:* A/C, TV/DVD, hair dryer, minibar, Wi-Fi (18€ per 12 hr.).

EXPENSIVE

Aussen Alster ★   Small and exclusive, and on a quiet residential street, Aussen Alster attracts actors, advertising directors, executives, writers, and artists. Its stylish, ultramodern interior was designed by one of Germany's most famous interior design-ers, Burkardt Stoelck, who along with his partner, Hamburg film producer Klaus Feddermann, manages the place with panache. Rooms are small to medium size, white walled, angular, and consciously simple. Everything is designed for style and comfort, from the luxurious beds to the immaculate bathrooms.

Schmilinskystrasse 11, 20099 Hamburg. www.aussen-alster.de. ✆ **040/241557.** Fax 040/2803231. 27 units. 130€–175€ double. Rates include buffet breakfast. AE, DC, MC, V. Parking 14€. Closed Dec 22–29. U-Bahn: Hauptbahnhof. A 5-min. walk from the rail station and a 3-min. walk from the Alster. **Ameni-ties:** Restaurant; bar; bikes; concierge; room service; sauna. *In room:* TV, hair dryer, Wi-Fi (free).

Maritim Hotel Reichshof ★   When this long-venerated hotel was built in 1910, it was the largest hotel in Europe. In World War II, it lost most of its upper floors, but the landmark Art Nouveau lobby remained intact. The Reichshof is a favorite with

Where to Stay & Eat in Hamburg

HOTELS ■

Aussen Alster **29**
East **4**
Fairmont Hotel
  Vier Jahreszeiten **19**
Fritzhotel **1**
Garden Hotels Hamburg **18**
Gastwerk Hotel Hamburg **2**
The George **30**
Hafen Hamburg **8**
Hamburg Marriott Hotel **14**

Hamburg Renaissance
  Hotel **13**
Hotel Abtei **17**
Hotel Garni Mittelweg **17**
Hotel Miramar **32**
Hotel SIDE **15**
Hotel Village **23**
Kempinski Hotel
  Atlantic **26**
Le Royal Méridien
  Hamburg **27**

Lindner Hotel Am Michel **10**
Louis C. Jacob **7**
Maritim Hotel Reichshof **24**
Nippon Hotel **31**
Park Hyatt Hamburg **20**
Sofitel Hamburg
  Alter Wall **12**
Steens Hotel **25**
Superbude **22**
25Hotel **2**
Wedina **28**

RESTAURANTS ◆
Eisenstein **5**
Fillet of Soul **21**
Fischereihafen
 Restaurant **6**
Fischküche **11**
Landhaus Dill **6**
Landhaus Scherrer **6**
Old Commercial
 Room **9**
Restaurant Nil **3**
Rive **6**
Tafelhaus **6**
Tarantella **16**

0 — 1/5 mi
0 — 0.2 km

Pedestrians only

business travelers, so more than half its rooms are classified as singles. The comfortable rooms are medium to spacious and have double-glazing; those on the top floor feature views of the city. Bathrooms are small but have up-to-date plumbing.

Kirchenallee 34-36, 20099 Hamburg. www.maritim.de. © **040/248330.** Fax 040/24833888. 305 units. 100€–196€ double; 210€–310€ suite. AE, DC, MC, V. Parking 17€. U-Bahn: Hauptbahnhof. Across from the Hauptbahnhof. **Amenities:** 2 restaurants; bar; babysitting; indoor heated pool; room service; sauna. *In room:* TV, hair dryer, minibar, Wi-Fi (15€ per day).

Sofitel Hamburg Alter Wall ★★ Between the harbor and the Hamburg city hall, this deluxe hotel opens onto the Alster Canal, with views from its front windows. For both the business traveler and the vacationer, it is a good choice for supreme comfort, with such features as king-size beds and large marble bathrooms, along with plush luxuries such as bathrobes. The Mediterranean cuisine in its Ticino restaurant lures hundreds of nonguests. Rooms come in various configurations depending on your needs and your purse. In the 19th century, Postsparkassenamt, the Hamburg mail service customer's bank, opened in this building behind a stunning Hanseatic-styled facade, which is still preserved today.

Alter Wall 40, Alstadt, 20457 Hamburg. www.sofitel.com. © **040/369500.** Fax 040/36950100. 257 units. 155€–313€ double; from 264€ suite. AE, DC, MC, V. Parking 24€. U-Bahn: Rödingsmarkt. **Amenities:** Restaurant; bar; exercise room; indoor heated pool; room service; spa. *In room:* A/C, TV, hair dryer, minibar, Wi-Fi (15€ per day).

MODERATE

Steens Hotel 🪶 Despite its classy location, a short walk from the much more expensive Atlantic Hotel, this century-old house charges reasonable rates. Rooms are carefully maintained but short on style. Each has a private shower; all but two have a private toilet. Breakfast is the only meal served. This simple but clean and safe hotel is a great option for families on a budget.

Holzdamm 43, 20099 Hamburg. www.steens-hotel.com. © **040/244642.** Fax 040/2803593. 11 units, 2 without bathroom. 85€ double without bathroom; 190€ double with bathroom. Rates include continental breakfast. AE, MC, V. Parking 10€. U-Bahn: Hauptbahnhof. Near the Alster. **Amenities:** Bikes; exercise room; Internet (free, in lobby); sauna. *In room:* TV, hair dryer, minibar, Wi-Fi (free).

Wedina This converted 18th-century town house is a quiet retreat. Most rooms open onto a small, informal Tuscan-style garden. All are tastefully styled and range from small to medium, each with a firm bed and a tidy bathroom. The hotel is owned and run by an English-speaking family. *Note:* This hotel has no elevator. If you lodge on the third floor, be prepared to carry luggage up 55 steps.

Gurlittstrasse 23, 20099 Hamburg. www.wedina.de. © **040/2808900.** Fax 040/2803894. 59 units. 118€–170€ double. Rates include buffet breakfast. AE, DC, MC, V. Bus: 6. Near the lake, a 5-min. walk from the Hauptbahnhof. **Amenities:** Bar. *In room:* TV, hair dryer.

INEXPENSIVE

Hotel Village Originally built a century ago, this hotel was a brothel for many years. Rising five turquoise-colored stories above a busy neighborhood near the central railway station, the hotel retains some of its now artfully seamy overtones, including public areas outfitted with touches of toreador scarlet and black, an elegantly paneled breakfast room, and a number of bedrooms with naughty-looking ceiling mirrors and/or racy baldachins. Each room has a different color scheme: for example, gold-toned brocade wallpaper or bright magenta.

Steindamm 4, Altstadt 20099 Hamburg. www.hotel-village.de. © **040/806490.** Fax 040/48064949. 20 units, 16 with bathroom and 4 with shared bathroom. 65€ double without bathroom; 85€–100€

double with bathroom. Rates include continental breakfast. AE, MC, V. Parking nearby 10€. U-Bahn: Hauptbahnhof. *In room:* TV.

In St. Pauli
MODERATE

Lindner Hotel Am Michel ★★ Built in a typical Hanseatic style, with a redbrick facade, this government-rated four-star hotel is centrally located, offering elegantly furnished rooms and suites. Equipped with state-of-the-art technology, the stream-lined, midsize bedrooms are soundproof with lots of little extras, including multimedia entertainment. Guests receive a free pass to the health club on the seventh floor.

Neanderstrasse 20, 20459 Hamburg. www.lindner.de. ☏ **040/403070670.** Fax 040/40307067777. 259 units. 149€–169€ double; from 199€ suite. AE, DC, MC, V. Parking 20€. U-Bahn: St. Pauli. **Amenities:** 2 restaurants; bar; exercise room; room service. *In room:* A/C, TV, hair dryer, minibar, Wi-Fi (free).

INEXPENSIVE

Fritzhotel ★ 🛍 Close to the nightlife center of Hamburg, this small hotel is part of an old apartment block. Rather minimalist in decor, it is a house of personality, taste, and comfort. The better rooms open onto private balconies, and each is individually decorated in a modern style, containing a tiled bathroom with shower kept sparkling clean. Those seeking more tranquillity should ask for one of the rooms overlooking the tree-studded courtyard. The district in which the hotel lies has been gentrified and contains the studios of many artists who live and work nearby. The little hotel does not serve breakfast, but there are many cafes in the neighborhood.

Schanzenstrasse 101–103, 20357 Hamburg. www.fritzhotel.com. ☏ **040/82222830.** Fax 040 /822228322. 17 units. 90€ double; from 125€ suite. AE, MC, V. Free parking. U-Bahn: Sternschanze. *In room:* TV, minibar, Wi-Fi (free).

In St. Georg
MODERATE

The George ★ As the name suggests, this sleek modern hotel pays homage to British style within its elegant precincts, including an English garden and a library evoking a gentleman's club in Mayfair. The good-size bedrooms are luxuriously furnished, and the suites and penthouses are worthy of visiting royalty or presidents of nations. Views of the Alster can be seen from all seven floors, and the expansive glass front opens onto a panorama of the St. Georg district. The restaurant and bar (both named **Da Caio**) are desirable places for great cocktails or savory Mediterranean cuisine. The hotel's special feature is its rooftop, which offers one of the most dramatic views over Hamburg's cityscape.

Barcastrasse 3, 22087 Hamburg. www.thegeorge-hotel.de. ☏ **040/2800300.** Fax 040/28003030. 125 units. 155€–216€ double; 205€–256€ junior suite; 316€–376€ suite. Rates include continental breakfast. AE, DC, MC, V. Parking 16€. U-Bahn: Uhlandstrasse. **Amenities:** Restaurant; bar; bikes; concierge; health club and spa; room service. *In room:* A/C, TV, hair dryer, minibar.

Superbude 🚣 Visitors looking for the budget deal of Hamburg can book into this small hotel and hostel, lying in the St. Georg district, not far from the Alster River and the city center. Simplicity itself prevails at this government-rated two-star hotel, but so do cleanliness and comfort. The living is basic, and so is the price. The two- or four-bed units are set up with individual color schemes. With four people sharing a four-bed room, the cost is only 16€ per person, a remarkable bargain for Hamburg.

Spaldingstrasse 152, 20097 Hamburg. www.superbude.de. ☏ **040/3808780.** Fax 040/380878100. 64 units. 59€–133€ double. AE, MC, V. Parking 5€. U-Bahn: Berliner Tor. **Amenities:** Bikes. *In room:* No phone, Wi-Fi (free).

In Binnenalster & Neustadt

VERY EXPENSIVE

Fairmont Hotel Vier Jahreszeiten ★★★   This warm, mellow hotel is the finest in Germany and one of the best in the world. It was founded in 1897 by Friedrich Haerlin, but today it's run by a Japanese company. Its position is ideal, right on the Binnenalster. Built in the baronial style, it evokes the grand Edwardian hotels. Antiques are used profusely throughout. Despite the large size, personal service is a hallmark. Although no two rooms are alike, they are all beautiful, with period furnishings, Oriental rugs, and all the modern luxuries, including bedside controls, double-glazing on the windows, and luxurious bathrooms. This is a hotel for connoisseurs.

Neuer Jungfernstieg 9-14, 20354 Hamburg. www.fairmont.com/hamburg. ⓒ **888/425-8227** in the U.S. and Canada, or 040/34940. Fax 040/34942600. 157 units. 300€–385€ double; from 385€ junior suite; from 580€ suite. AE, DC, MC, V. Parking 25€. U-Bahn: Hauptbahnhof. On the Binnenalster. **Amenities:** 3 restaurants; 2 bars; babysitting; concierge; health club and spa; room service. *In room:* TV/DVD, hair dryer, minibar, MP3 docking station, Wi-Fi (free).

EXPENSIVE

Hamburg Marriott Hotel ★   This traditionally styled hotel is one of the finest in Hamburg. It was built on the site of the old Gänsemarkt, where geese were sold in the Middle Ages. The hotel is also near the Hanse Viertel shopping complex. The fashionable surrounding area is filled with boutiques, wine bars, shops, and restaurants. Rooms range from small to large. The lower price listed in the range below is for standard rooms, the higher for studios. Lavish suites are also available.

ABC Strasse 52, 20354 Hamburg. www.marriott-hotels.com. ⓒ **800/228-9290** in the U.S., or 040/35050. Fax 040/35051777. 277 units. 149€–319€ double; from 319€ suite. AE, DC, MC, V. Parking 26€. U-Bahn: Gänsemarkt. **Amenities:** Restaurant; bar; babysitting; concierge; exercise room; indoor heated pool; room service; spa; Wi-Fi (free, in lobby). *In room:* A/C, TV, hair dryer, minibar.

Hamburg Renaissance Hotel ★★   Occupying a 19th-century building, this nine-story hotel offers 20th-century comforts. From the sunken, antiques-furnished lobby to the carpeted bar area, you'll be welcomed by the staff and serenaded by a resident pianist. Rooms range from well-appointed doubles to sumptuously upholstered suites. Most are quite spacious, with paired queen-size, king-size, or twin beds, plus large bathrooms with robes, makeup mirrors, and phones. The hotel was constructed behind the facade of a historic building, and the entire complex was designed with connections to the Hanse Viertel Galerie Passage, Europe's longest shopping arcade.

Grosse Bleichen, Hanse-Viertel, 20354 Hamburg. www.renaissancehotels.com. ⓒ **800/228-9290** in the U.S. and Canada, or 040/349180. Fax 040/34918969. 205 units. 149€–279€ double; from 259€ suite. AE, DC, MC, V. Parking 25€. U-Bahn: Jungfernstieg. **Amenities:** Restaurant; bar; babysitting; concierge; exercise room; indoor heated pool; room service; sauna. *In room:* A/C, TV, hair dryer, minibar, Wi-Fi (13€ per day).

Hotel SIDE ★★   Angular, offbeat, and postmodern, this hotel, which opened in 2001, is a favorite destination of journalists and fashionistas. It rises 11 stone- and glass-sheathed floors above the street, with an additional four stories underground. Rooms are built around a central atrium, in a dramatic cream, white, and brown color scheme that was created by Matteo Thun, the well-known Milan designer. (He even designed the hotel ashtrays.) The top two stories are reserved for suites, all encased in an architectural "box" that seems to float over the structure below. On the eighth floor guests can enjoy a terrace that opens onto panoramic views of Hamburg. Bedrooms are efficiently organized with secret closets and storage space, and each contains deep upholsteries of a tasteful modern design, along with luxurious bathrooms. Each suite has a kitchenette and two washbasins.

Drehbahn 49, 20354 Hamburg. www.side-hamburg.de. ℗ **040/309990.** Fax 040/30999399. 178 units. 150€–300€ double; 325€–680€ suite. AE, DC, MC, V. Parking 20€. U-Bahn: Gänsemarkt or Stephansplatz. **Amenities:** Restaurant; bar; babysitting; bikes; concierge; exercise room; indoor heated pool; room service; spa. *In room:* A/C, TV, fax, hair dryer, minibar, Wi-Fi (21€ per day).

MODERATE

Hafen Hamburg ★ This Hamburg landmark, constructed in the Wilhelmin style, offers panoramic views of the river and the harbor traffic. It attracts the commercial traveler who's not on an expense account. The functionally furnished rooms are unusually spacious. If they're within your budget, book the more expensive harbor-view rooms. Each comes with a well-equipped private bathroom.

Seewartenstrasse 9, 20459 Hamburg. www.hotel-hafen-hamburg.de. ℗ **040/311130.** Fax 040/ 3111370601. 355 units. 100€–200€ double. AE, DC, MC, V. Parking 14€. U-Bahn: Landungsbrücken. **Amenities:** Restaurant; 3 bars; sauna; Wi-Fi (free, in lobby). *In room:* TV, hair dryer, minibar.

In the Reeperbahn
VERY EXPENSIVE

East ★★ 🛍 This sophisticated hotel originated in the early 20th century as a brick-fronted, industrial-looking iron foundry. A team of designers transformed it, achieving a radical, postmodern feel with a high-tech design motif. Whiffs of the Industrial Age are artfully celebrated. The tasteful bedrooms fall into five categories, ranging from "Small" to "XX-Large." In all, this is the first swanky retreat ever to open in the funky red-light district.

Everything is minimalist, with "rainfall" shower heads, luxe toiletries, stained-glass windows, and undulating columns. In summer, local guests recline on the rattan chaise longues in the open-air courtyard or take to the rooftop terrace.

Simon-von-Utrecht Strasse 31, 20359 Hamburg. www.east-hotel.de. ℗ **040/309930.** Fax 040/303200. 78 units. 155€–290€ double; 380€–850€ suite. AE, DC, MC, V. Parking 14€. U-Bahn: St. Pauli. **Amenities:** Restaurant; bar; babysitting; concierge; exercise room; room service; spa. *In room:* A/C, TV, hair dryer, minibar, Wi-Fi (in most; free).

In Harvestehude
EXPENSIVE

Garden Hotels Hamburg ★ ☺ 🛍 This hotel dates from 1791, and over the years it has entertained many luminaries, including King Christian VIII of Denmark in 1824. The location, however, isn't for everyone. It stands in the Hamburg-Harvestehude district on the western sector of the Outer Alster Lake, about a mile from the historic heart of town and some 10km (6 miles) from the airport. This feature makes it attractive to families with kids, since boating on the lake is available. Families also appreciate the helpfulness of the friendly staff and the hotel pool. Modern art and well-chosen antiques add to the sophisticated comfort of the rooms. Most are generously sized, and bathrooms are luxurious.

Magdalenenstrasse 60, 20148 Hamburg. www.garden-hotels.de. ℗ **040/414040.** Fax 040/4140420. 60 units. 125€–195€ double; 230€–280€ suite. AE, MC, V. Parking 15€. U-Bahn: Hallerstrasse. 1.5km (1 mile) from the center. **Amenities:** Bar; babysitting; room service. *In room:* TV, CD player, hair dryer, kitchenette (in some), minibar, Wi-Fi (in some; free).

Hotel Abtei ★★ 🛍 This discovery is 2km (1¼ miles) north of the center of Harvestehude, a highly desirable if somewhat out-of-the-way address for a little hotel.

Small-scale and charming, this bijou-style hotel was a posh private home in the 1890s and then fell into disrepair in the early 1970s, when it became a shelter for the indigent. Today, it's a plush, smart hotel with decor and ambience that recall an English country house. Rooms are cushy, conservative, and rich looking, in tones of green, red, and yellow. Antiques, including pieces of mahogany and cherrywood, are scattered about, and a trio of suites have their own private conservatories.

Abteistrasse 14, Harvestehude, 20149 Hamburg. www.abtei-hotel.de. *✆* **040/442905.** Fax 040/449820. 11 units. 170€–250€ double; 250€–300€ suite. AE, MC, V. U-Bahn: Klosterstern. **Amenities:** Babysitting; room service; Wi-Fi (free, in lobby). *In room:* TV, minibar.

MODERATE

Hotel Garni Mittelweg ★ 🎁   A real discovery, this stylishly decorated family hotel lies in the upscale Pöseldorf, within an easy stroll of the Aussenalster. The place is imbued with a country charm. Once the town house of a wealthy merchant and his family in the 19th century, the hotel has now been tastefully converted to receive guests, with modern amenities added. Bedrooms are attractively furnished and comfortable.

Mittelweg 59, Hamburg 20149. www.hotel-mittelweg.de. *✆* **040/4141010.** Fax 040/41410120. 39 units. 125€–168€ double. Rates include buffet breakfast. AE, MC, V. Parking 10€. S-Bahn: Dammtor. **Amenities:** Room service. *In room:* TV, hair dryer, minibar, Wi-Fi (6.50€ per hr.).

In Nienstedten

VERY EXPENSIVE

Louis C. Jacob ★★★   Lying outside the city center along the Elbe, this tranquil deluxe hotel compares to the Vier Jahreszeiten and Kempinski Hotel Atlantic (see above). In summer, you can sit out under linden trees 2 centuries old and enjoy views of the river traffic. Built in 1791 as a guesthouse, it has been brought up to modernity after a major overhaul. The owners believe in spectacular luxury and coddling their guests. The hotel owns one of the biggest private art collections in the north of Germany. The medium-size to spacious rooms are elegantly appointed and decorated, with walk-in closets and state-of-the-art bathrooms, each with deluxe toiletries.

Elbchaussee 401, 22609 Hamburg. www.hotel-jacob.de. *✆* **040/82255405.** Fax 040/82255444. 85 units. 210€–435€ double; from 345€ suite. AE, DC, MC, V. Parking 20€. 13km (8 miles) west via Elbchaussee. **Amenities:** 2 restaurants; bar; babysitting; room service. *In room:* A/C, TV, hair dryer, minibar, Wi-Fi (free).

In Uhlenhorst

MODERATE

Hotel Miramar ★ 🎁   One of the most hospitable couples in Hamburg welcomes visitors to their hotel outside the central area (but still convenient to public transportation). The establishment is a bit modest, but most comfortable and well maintained—plus infinitely affordable. The hotel lies in a safe neighborhood only a block from the nearest subway station. Across the street is one of Hamburg's colorful canals. The hotel is in a restored *Jugendstil* house constructed in 1904. Most of the well-furnished bedrooms are on the ground floor, and those in the rear open onto a forested area. The breakfast buffet is one of the most elaborate we've encountered in Hamburg.

Armgartstrasse 20, 22087 Hamburg-Uhlenhorst. www.hotelmiramar.de. *✆* **040/2209395.** Fax 040/2273418. 12 units. 105€–130€ double. Rates include buffet breakfast. AE, DC, MC, V. Free parking on street. U-Bahn: Uhlandstrasse. **Amenities:** Babysitting. *In room:* TV, no phone (in some).

Nippon Hotel ★★   You'll have to take off your shoes before going into your room at this remarkable modern hotel where you cross Tatami floor mats to sleep on a futon mattress. If you're used to Western-style luxury, the minimalist decor might be a bit disconcerting at first. But one guest found the ambience "relaxing for both body and soul." The style is defined by a series of straight lines and clear forms, along with light-wood furnishings and traditional rice-paper *shoji* partitions. Naturally, there's an on-site Japanese restaurant and sushi bar.

Hofweg 75, Uhlenhorst, 22085 Hamburg. www.nippon-hotel-hh.de. ℂ **040/22711490.** 42 units. 122€–158€ double; 191€ junior suite. AE, DC, MC, V. Parking 10€. U-Bahn: Mundsburg. **Amenities:** Restaurant; bar; babysitting; bikes; concierge; room service. *In room:* A/C, TV, hair dryer, minibar, Wi-Fi (8€–12€ per hr.).

In Bahrenfeld
EXPENSIVE

Gastwerk Hotel Hamburg ★★ ▮▮   In one of the most stunning rescues of a decaying industrial building in Hamburg, an old public gasworks has been recycled and given new life as a modern boutique hotel. Developers preserved as much of the industrial structure—they call it "culture"—as was possible when they converted it into a comfortable hotel with a mixture of contemporary and traditional design and all the amenities you'd expect from a high-end hotel. Bedrooms range from luxurious suites to classic loft spaces with exposed brick walls and mahogany furnishings. All the rooms, both public and private, are imbued with a light, intimate feeling. Bedrooms, midsize to spacious, are inviting and beautifully maintained, and each has a balcony.

Forum Altes Gastwerk, Daimlerstrasse 67, 22761 Hamburg. www.gastwerk-hotel.de. ℂ **040/890620.** Fax 040/8906220. 141 units. 136€–182€ double; 192€–373€ suite. AE, DC, MC, V. Free parking. U-Bahn: Bahrenfeld. **Amenities:** Restaurant; bar; babysitting; bikes; exercise room; spa. *In room:* A/C, TV, hair dryer, minibar, Wi-Fi (free).

25Hotel ★ ▮▮   In the western business district, this designer hotel lies 1km (½ mile) from the Altona Station and the River Elbe. Young designers individually created the bedrooms, which come in three sizes: small, medium, and large. There is a certain chic charm here if you like minimalism. The manager claims that the hotel was created to "meet the demands of creative metropolitan nomads." The lobby and restaurant, the latter serving excellent food, flow into each other.

Paul-Dessau-Strasse 2, 22761 Hamburg. www.25hours-hotel.com. ℂ **040/855070.** Fax 040/8555507. 89 units. 125€–155€ double. AE, DC, V. Free parking. S-Bahn: Bahrenfeld. **Amenities:** Restaurant; 2 bars; babysitting; bikes. *In room:* A/C, TV, hair dryer.

SCHLESWIG-HOLSTEIN

18

In this region, you can walk along the dunes and hear the roaring sea break fiercely on the rocks, or you can lie on a tranquil beach while tiny waves lap at your feet. Sound inconsistent? Not in Schleswig-Holstein, Germany's northernmost province, which borders both the turbulent, chilly North Sea and the smooth, gentle Baltic. Between these two bodies of water are rolling groves and meadows, lakes and ponds, and little fishing villages with thatched cottages. Fashionable seaside resorts dot both shorelines and nearby islands. Even in the coldest weather you can swim in heated seawater at the resorts of Westerland and Helgoland. In Kiel, you can wander around the harbor or explore Schleswig with its Viking memories.

Hamburg is the ideal gateway to the region, and it is easily traversed without a car. Where the trains end, local buses take you the rest of the way, linking small towns and villages. Should you decide to rent a car, bear in mind that roads are overcrowded in July and August, when many Germans head to the unspoiled beaches.

LÜBECK ★★★

92km (57 miles) SE of Kiel, 66km (41 miles) NE of Hamburg

Lübeck is a city of high-gabled houses, massive gates, strong towers, and towering steeples. It was made a free imperial city in 1226, and was the capital of the Hanseatic League, which controlled trade along the Baltic as far as Russia.

The Hanseatic merchants decorated their churches with art treasures and gilded their spires to show off their wealth. Many of these survivors of history stand side by side with postwar housing developments, and the neon lights of the business district shine on the streets and narrow passageways of bygone days.

Lübeck has had several famous sons. As a young man, Willy Brandt, who later became West German chancellor and won the Nobel Peace Prize, opposed the Nazis so vehemently that he had to flee on a boat to Norway. Thomas Mann's 1902 novel *Buddenbrooks,* set here, catapulted the 27-year-old author to international fame. In 1929, he won the Nobel Prize in Literature.

Essentials
GETTING THERE
BY TRAIN   The **Lübeck Hauptbahnhof** lies on major rail lines linking Denmark and Hamburg, and on the Hamburg-Lüneburg-Lübeck-Kiel-Flensburg and Lübeck-Rostock-Stralsund lines, with frequent connections. From Hamburg, 32 trains arrive daily (trip time: 48 min.), 23 from Berlin (trip time: 3–4 hr.). For information, call ✆ **01805/996633** (www.bahn.de).

BY BUS   Long-distance bus service to and from such cities as Berlin and Kiel is provided by **Autokraft GmbH** (✆ **0431/6660;** www.autokraft.de).

BY FERRY   Ferryboat service from the region around Lübeck to Denmark lies astride the main railway lines between Hamburg and Copenhagen, and is therefore among the busiest in Europe. Service is offered by **ScandLines** (✆ **0381/5435850;** www.scandlines.de), with boats arriving every 30 minutes, 24 hours a day, every day of the year. The port on the German side is in Puttgarden; the one on the Danish side is in Rødby, a 2-hour train ride from Copenhagen. The trip takes about 45 minutes. Railway cars, trucks, and conventional automobiles are all taken onboard. Round-trip transport for a car with up to four passengers averages 120€, with slight variations depending on the season.

TT Line operates between the German port of Travemünde and the Swedish port of Trelleborg. Call ✆ **04502/80181** for bookings and departure times (www.ttline.com).

BY CAR   Access to Lübeck is via the A1 Autobahn north and south.

GETTING AROUND

The Altstadt and the attractions outlined below can be reached by taking bus no. 1, 5, 11, or 21. Fare is 2.20€.

VISITOR INFORMATION

For tourist information, contact the **Lübeck-Informations-Zentrum,** Holstentor-platz 1–5 (✆ **0451/8899700;** www.luebeck-tourismus.de), January to May and October to December Monday to Friday 9:30am to 6pm and Saturday 10am to 3pm; June to September Monday to Friday 9:30am to 7pm, Saturday 10am to 3pm, and Sunday 10am to 2pm.

SPECIAL EVENTS   Lübeck is the center of the **Schleswig-Holstein Music Festival** (✆ 0451/389570; www.shmf.de), with performances during July and August every year. At the **Christmas market,** vendors from northwestern Germany sell their wares—many of them handmade items from toys to pottery—during the 3 weeks before Christmas on the Rathausplatz.

Exploring Lübeck

Lübeck's **Altstadt ★★★** is surrounded by the Trave River and connecting canals, giving it an island-like appearance. It suffered heavily during World War II, when about one-fifth of the city was leveled. Damaged buildings have been restored or reconstructed, and Lübeck still offers a wealth of historic attractions.

Just across the west bridge from the Altstadt, the **Holstentor (Holsten Gate) ★★** is the first monument to greet visitors emerging from the train station. Once the main town entrance, it was built in the 15th century as much to awe visitors with the power and prestige of Lübeck as to defend it against intruders. To the outside world, the towers look simple and defiant, rather like part of a great palace. But on the city side, they contain a wealth of decoration, with windows, arcades, and rich terra-cotta friezes. Within the gate is the **Museum Holstentor** (✆ **0451/1224129;** www.die-luebecker-museen.de), housing a model of Lübeck as it appeared in the mid–15th century. Hours are Tuesday to Friday 10am to 4pm, Saturday and Sunday 11am to 5pm. Admission is 5€ for adults and 2€ for children 17 and under.

Der Salzspeicher (Salt Lofts), viewed from the riverside, near the Holstentor, are among Lübeck's most attractive sights. In the 16th century, these buildings stored the salt from Lüneburg before it was shipped to Scandinavia. Each of the six buildings is different, reflecting trends in Renaissance gabled architecture.

The **Rathaus ★**, Rathausplatz (✆ **0451/1221005**), traces its origins from 1230. It has been rebuilt several times, but remains of the original structure are in the vaulting and Romanesque pillars in the cellar and the Gothic south wall. The towering walls have been made with open-air medallions to relieve the pressure on the Gothic-arcaded ground floor and foundations. Tours in English and other languages are Monday to Friday at 11am, noon, and 3pm, costing 3€ for adults and 1.50€ for children.

Marienkirche (**St. Mary's Church;** no phone), across Marktplatz from the Rathaus, is the most exceptional church in Lübeck, possibly in northern Germany. Built on the highest point in the Altstadt, it has flying buttresses and towering windows that leave the rest of the city's rooftops at its feet. Some of its greatest art treasures were bombed and destroyed in 1942, but after the fire was put out, earlier painted decorations on the walls and clerestory were discovered. The bells fell in a World War II air raid and became embedded in the floor of the church, where they remain to this day. Organ concerts take place during the summer months, carrying on the tradition established by St. Mary's best-known organist and composer, Dietrich Buxtehude (1668–1707).

Buddenbrookhaus, Mengstrasse 4 (✆ **0451/1224192;** www.buddenbrookhaus. de), near Marienkirche, is the house where author Thomas Mann's grandparents lived. It's a big, solid stone structure with a gabled roof and a recessed doorway. Above a leaded-glass fan over the heavy double doors is the date 1758. This is the house Mann (1875–1955) described as the home of the family in *Buddenbrooks*. The museum also highlights Thomas's brother, Heinrich Mann (1871–1950), author of *Professor Unrat,* the inspiration for the movie *The Blue Angel.* The house is open daily 10am to 5pm; admission is 5€ for adults, 2.60€ for students, free for children 13 and under, and 9€ for a family ticket.

In addition to Thomas Mann, Lübeck was the home of Germany's most prominent living writer, Günter Grass (born in 1927). He is still known all over the world for his most famous novel, *The Tin Drum,* published in 1959. Grass won the Nobel Prize in Literature in 1999. The museum at the **Günter Grass-Haus,** Glockengiesserstrasse 21 (✆ **0451/1224190;** www.buddenbrookhaus.de), explores the author's "double gifts" in literature, sculpture, graphics, and music—or, in the words of the curator, "we are a crossroads forum where literature and the visual arts meet." Exhibits include manuscripts of Grass—with bold corrections—and even the machines on which he wrote, going from an old-fashioned Olivetti typewriter to computer. In the courtyard garden, you'll get a rare look at some of his sculptures. Admission is 5€. It is open April to December daily 10am to 6pm, January to March daily 11am to 5pm.

It's said that within an area of 5 sq. km (2 sq. miles) around the Marktplatz stand 1,000 medieval houses. Nearby is **Petersgrube,** the finest street in Lübeck, lined with restored houses. A walk through the old streets of Lübeck reveals a continuing use of brick (the city insisted on this after fires in the 13th c.). The effect is one of unity among all the houses, churches, shops, and guildhalls.

Haus der Schiffergesellschaft (Seamen's Guild House) ★, on Breitestrasse, is one of the last of the elaborate guild houses of Hanseatic Lübeck, built in 1535 in Renaissance style, with stepped gables and high-Gothic blind windows. It's worth seeing just for the medieval furnishings and the beamed ceilings in the main hall, now a restaurant (p. 634).

Museen Behnhaus/Drägerhaus, Königstrasse 9–11, north of Glockengiesser Strasse (✆ **0451/1224148;** www.die-luebecker-museen.de), was formed from two patrician houses. Like many such houses in the town, they are tall and narrow, constructed that way to avoid heavy taxes based on frontage. The museum displays mostly German Impressionists and paintings from around 1900. There is an outstanding collection of German Romantic and "Nazarene" paintings and drawings, especially by Johann Friedrich Overbeck and his school. The Behnhaus has a permanent exhibition of contemporary paintings, including Schumacher, Schultze, Rainer, Antes, and Kirkeby, along with such 20th-century artists as Kirchner, Beckmann,

Lehmbruck, and Barlach. Both houses are open April to September Tuesday to Sunday 10am to 5pm; October to March hours are Tuesday to Friday 10am to 4pm, and Saturday and Sunday 11am to 5pm. Admission is 5€ for adults, 2€ for students and children 6 to 18, and free for children 5 and under.

You can take an excursion boat around **Lübeck Harbor,** departing from Trave Landing, right in front of the Jensen hotel. Boat tours of the harbor are available March to October daily every half-hour, 10am to 6pm.

Where to Eat

Haus der Schiffergesellschaft ★ NORTHERN GERMAN/INTERNATIONAL

Entering this restaurant, with ship models and other nautical memorabilia, is like going inside a museum of Hanseatic architecture. The restaurant was once patronized exclusively by sailors. Today, good food (and lots of it) is served on scrubbed-oak plank tables with high-backed wooden booths carved with the coats of arms of Baltic merchants. Often, you must share a table. One of the most expensive items is an elaborate sole meunière with salad. Many regional dishes are featured, such as baked black pudding with slices of apple and lamb's lettuce. Try the roast rack of lamb with rosemary sauce, green beans, and homemade noodles. You may want to have a drink in the cocktail bar of the historic **Gotteskeller.**

Breitestrasse 2. ℗ **0451/76776.** www.schiffergesellschaft.com. Reservations required. Main courses 12€–20€. MC, V. Daily 10am–midnight. Bar Tues–Sat 5pm–4am. Bus: 1 or 2.

Historischer Weinkeller ★★ INTERNATIONAL

This first-class restaurant and 12th-century wine cellar, in the basement of Holy Ghost Hospital, is the third-best dining spot in town, topped only by the Wullenwever, which has better (and more expensive) food, and Das Schabbelhaus, which has a more refined atmosphere (see both below). You may begin with North Sea shrimp served with a quail egg and caviar or assorted fish in aspic. For a main dish, try venison cutlet in garlic butter with fried potatoes, Atlantic sole with buttery potatoes, or Barbary duck with a sauce flavored with cranberries and balsamic vinegar. A few meat dishes are also featured.

Heiligen-Geist-Hospital, Koberg 8. ℗ **0451/76234.** www.historischer-weinkeller-hl.de. Reservations recommended. Main courses 10€–20€. AE, MC, V. Daily 11:30am–midnight. Bus: 1 or 3.

Roberto Rossi in Das Schabbelhaus ★★ MEDITERRANEAN

A classic example of Hanseatic architecture on a medieval street, the Schabbelhaus is encased in two patrician buildings from the 16th and 17th centuries. In the restaurant, ceiling-high studio windows overlook the small gardens. The more tradition-minded were shocked when one of the most historically evocative German restaurants was transformed into an upscale venue for artfully prepared Italian food. Today you can sample such delights as spinach salad with strips of goose meat and a sweet-and-sour walnut sauce, followed by veal steak under an apple and celery crust. Another delectable dish is the asparagus salad with Parma ham with a tartare of red beets. You might also sample such dishes as roast turbot with herbs and fresh vegetables or grilled shrimp with garlic and spicy peppers.

Mengstrasse 48–52. ℗ **0451/72011.** www.schabbelhaus.de. Reservations recommended. Main courses 18€–35€. AE, MC, V. Mon–Sat noon–2:30pm and 6–11pm. Bus: 5, 7, 11, 12, 14, or 16.

Wullenwever ★★★ FRENCH/CONTINENTAL

Roy Petermann, in his elegant 16th-century house, has established himself as one of the finest chefs in northern Germany. Scion of a distinguished culinary family, he has brought a refined and imaginative cuisine to Lübeck. Chandeliers and oil paintings enhance the ambience and, in summer, tables overflow onto a flower-filled courtyard. Using only the best and freshest produce, his dishes have subtle depths of flavor and texture. Game is featured in the autumn, and seafood is always available. Specialties include sautéed sole with capers and lemon butter, or grilled swordfish with eggplant and sweet peppers.

Beckergrube 71. ©**0451/704333.** www.wullenwever.de. Reservations required, as far in advance as possible. Main courses 26€–38€; fixed-price menus 55€–130€. AE, MC, V. Tues–Sat 7–11pm. Closed 2 weeks in Mar and Oct. Bus: 12.

Zimmermann's Lübecker Hanse ★ FRENCH/REGIONAL   This is one of Lübeck's most praised restaurants. It has an authentically weathered exterior and dark paneling inside. French food, regional meals, and lots of seafood are offered. You may want to try the *plats du jour;* they are invariably fresh and well prepared. Fresh fish from the Baltic is another good choice. In season, wild game is featured.

Kolk 3–7. ©**0451/78054.** www.luebecker-hanse.de. Reservations recommended. Main courses 14€–19€. AE, DC, MC, V. Tues–Sat noon–3pm and 6pm–midnight. Closed Jan 1–14. Bus: 1, 3, or 11.

Shopping

Lübeck is a center for antiques stores. One of the best is **Antiquitäten Bannow Günther,** Fleischhauerstrasse 87 (© 0451/77338), carrying antique silver, crystal, porcelain, books, pewter, and English, Danish, and German furniture; any article can be shipped to your home. And if you're looking for souvenirs that celebrate Lübeck's rich maritime traditions, head for the town's best handicrafts shop, **Kunsthaus Lübeck,** Königstrasse 20 (© 0451/75700; www.kunsthaus-luebeck.de), where tin, pewter, glass sculpting, pottery, and antique books will help you remember your visit. **Breitestrasse,** a pedestrian walkway throughout most of the day, is the main shopping street in town. Much of Lübeck's Altstadt is banned to cars, which makes for a pleasant afternoon of wandering.

J. G. Niederegger, Breitestrasse 89 (© 0451/53010; www.niederegger.de), sells that "sweetest of all sweetmeats," famous Lübeck marzipan. It's been across from the main entrance to the Rathaus since 1806. On the ground floor, you can buy treats to take away, or you can go upstairs to a pleasant cafe, where you can order dessert and the best brewed coffee in Lübeck. Ask for their pastry specialty, a nut torte resting under a huge slab of fresh marzipan. You'll pay around 30€ per kilo (about 15€ per pound) for marzipan. The shop is open 9am to 6pm daily. Master-Card and Visa are accepted.

Entertainment & Nightlife

A newsletter, *Piste,* free at most hotels, offers news of local happenings.

Lübeck is known for its organ concerts; about two a week are presented in various churches during summer. The tourist office (see "Visitor Information," above) has complete details, or check with **Musik und Kongresshallen Lübeck,** Willy-Brandt-Allee 10 (© 0451/79040; www.muk.de), about the many concert and theater opportunities in town. The most important theater venue is **Theater Combinale,** Huxstrasse 115 (© 0451/78817; www.combinale.de; bus: 11). Its plays range from experimental to classic. Most performances are on Friday and Saturday from August to June. Tickets are 10€ to 21€ for adults and 7.50€ to 15€ for students and children 16 and under.

Finnegan, Mengstrasse 42 (© 0451/71110; bus: 12), won an award in 1996 and 1999 from Guinness as the best Irish pub in northern Germany. Naturally, Guinness is on tap, as well as Kilkenny, and five or six whiskeys. On Wednesday, Thursday, and Saturday, bands play rock and Irish music from 8pm to midnight. The pub is open Tuesday to Saturday 7pm to 4am.

Where to Stay

Hotel Excelsior This is a good, functional hotel and not a lot more. It's in a symmetrical baroque building with splendid proportions and a modernized interior. It's especially convenient if you're traveling to Lübeck by rail. Rooms are small to medium and are well furnished.

Hansestrasse 3, 23558 Lübeck. www.hotel-excelsior-luebeck.de.© **0451/88090.** Fax 0451/880999. 61 units. 85€–130€ double; 130€–210€ suite. Rates include buffet breakfast. AE, DC, MC, V. Free outdoor parking; 6€ underground. Bus: 11 or 12. Near Lindenplatz, opposite the central bus station and next to the train station. *In room:* TV, hair dryer, minibar (in most).

Kaiserhof ★ 🍴 The Kaiserhof, frankly, could probably demand a higher price for its rooms, as it ranks up near the top with the Radisson (see below). Built as it is from two former patrician town houses outside the city center on a tree-lined boulevard, this hotel has a fashionable yet homelike environment. Rooms come in various shapes and sizes and are individually furnished. Some overflow guests stay in a more sterile but still quite comfortable annex.

Kronsforder Allee 11–13, 23560 Lübeck. www.kaiserhof-luebeck.de.© **0451/703301.** Fax 0451/795083. 60 units. 135€ double; 215€ suite. Rates include buffet breakfast. AE, DC, MC, V. Free outdoor parking. Bus: 2, 7, 10, 16, or 32. **Amenities:** Restaurant; bar; indoor heated pool; room service; sauna; Wi-Fi (free, in lobby). *In room:* TV, hair dryer, minibar.

Radisson Blu Senator Hotel Lübeck ★★ 😊 This well-designed and -run hotel is the best in town. Although the bulk of its clients are businesspeople, it has equal appeal to other visitors. The soundproof and medium-size rooms are well kept and attractively furnished. The sleekly maintained bathrooms come with a basket of toiletries.

Willy-Brandt-Allee 6, 23554 Lübeck. www.lubeck.radissonsas.com. © **800/333-3333** in the U.S., or 0451/1420. Fax 0451/1422222. 224 units. 125€–200€ double; from 400€ suite. AE, DC, MC, V. Parking 13€. Bus: 12. On the banks of the river, connected to the Altstadt by pedestrian bridge. **Amenities:** 2 restaurants; 2 bars; babysitting; children's center; concierge; indoor heated pool; room service; sauna. *In room:* A/C, TV, DVD player, hair dryer, minibar, Wi-Fi (in some; free).

Ringhotel Jensen 🍴 The Jensen is one of Lübeck's best moderately priced hotels, a good value if your expectations aren't too high. The small to medium rooms are modestly furnished in traditional German style. Some have fine views of the Hanseatic architecture across the canal. The buffet breakfast is served in a delightful room with picture windows overlooking the canal.

An der Obertrave 4–5, 23552 Lübeck. www.ringhotel-jensen.de.© **0451/702490.** Fax 0451/73386. 42 units. 98€–115€ double; 179€ suite. Children 9 and under stay free in parent's room. Rates include buffet breakfast. AE, DC, MC, V. Parking 7€ nearby. Bus: 1, 3, or 11. Near the Holstentor. **Amenities:** Restaurant; room service. *In room:* TV, hair dryer, minibar, Wi-Fi (15€ per day).

Scandic Hotel ★ 😊 This first-class hotel is close to the ferry docks and as a result attracts many Scandinavians as well as businesspeople. The medium-size rooms are well maintained. Half are nonsmoking, and some accommodate people with allergies. All units have neatly kept bathrooms.

Travemünder Allee 3, 23568 Lübeck. www.scandic-hotels.com. © **0451/37060.** Fax 0451/3706666. 158 units. 138€–193€ double; 244€–350€ suite. AE, DC, MC, V. Free outdoor parking; 12€ in garage. Bus: 12. Near the Burgtor entrance of the Altstadt. **Amenities:** Restaurant; bar; babysitting; bikes; children's center; exercise room; indoor heated pool; room service; sauna. *In room:* A/C, TV, hair dryer, minibar (in some), Wi-Fi (free).

Zur alten Stadtmauer ★ 🍴   In the heart of Old Town, this historic hotel is a safe, snug, and inexpensive nest for the night. Its front rooms open onto a view of St. Marien Kirche. Personalized service and a homelike atmosphere make this an intriguing choice. Rooms are spread across two floors, each modestly but nicely decorated, and all but a few singles come with private bathrooms. The large buffet breakfast will fortify you for the day.

An der Mauer 57, 23552 Lübeck. www.hotelstadtmauer.de. 🕾 **0451/73702.** Fax 0451/73239. 24 units. 55€–100€ double. Rates include buffet breakfast. AE, DC, MC, V. Parking 5€. **Amenities:** Babysitting. *In room:* TV, Wi-Fi (free).

KIEL ★

88km (55 miles) SE of the Danish border at Flensburg, 97km (60 miles) N of Hamburg, 92km (57 miles) NW of Lübeck

A natural harbor at the end of a 15km (10-mile) extension of the Baltic Sea made Kiel a center for commerce with northern European countries. The opening of the Kiel Canal in 1895 connected the Baltic with the North Sea and western trade.

It celebrated its 750th anniversary in 1992, but streets and buildings do little to suggest that Kiel was ever anything other than a modern city. Almost all its buildings were destroyed during World War II, and the town was rebuilt with broad streets, spacious squares, and green parks. Nearby resorts make this a vacation spot as well.

Essentials
GETTING THERE
BY TRAIN   The **Kiel Hauptbahnhof** is on two major rail lines, the Neumünster-Hamburg and the Flensburg-Kiel-Lübeck-Lüneburg lines, with frequent connections. From Hamburg, there are 40 trains daily (trip time: 1 hr., 10 min.). For information, call 🕾 **01805/996633** (www.bahn.de).

BY BUS   Long-distance bus service to and from Berlin and Flensburg, as well as local and regional service, is provided by **Autokraft GmbH,** in Kiel (🕾 **0431/6660;** www.autokraft.de). Buses pull into the Bahnhofplatz. The tourist office (see below) will provide you with schedules.

BY FERRY   Service between Kiel and Oslo, Norway, is provided by **Color Line GmbH,** in Kiel (🕾 **0431/73000;** www.colorline.com). **Stena Line,** in Kiel (🕾 **0431/9090;** www.stenaline.de), offers service between Kiel and Gothenburg (Göteborg), Sweden.

BY CAR   To reach Kiel from Hamburg, head north along the A7 Autobahn; from Lübeck, take Rte. 76 west.

GETTING AROUND
Most attractions in Kiel center around the harbor, reached by bus no. 41 or 42. Fare is 2.20€.

VISITOR INFORMATION
Contact **Tourist Information Kiel,** Andreas-Gayk-Strasse 31 (🕾 **0180/5656700;** www.kiel-tourist.de). It's open year-round Monday to Friday 9am to 6pm, and from May to September, also Saturday 10am to 2pm.

SPECIAL EVENTS   **Kieler Woche (Kiel Week),** held each June, celebrates the port's close ties to the sea. This week of special events, held for more than 100 years, includes a spectacular regatta in which more than 1,500 yachts race on the water of the Kieler Förde. In 1936 and 1972, the Olympic yacht races were held on the waters at Schilksee. For information, call the **Kieler Wochenbüro** at ✆ **0431/901905,** or check out www.kieler-woche.de.

Exploring the Harbor & Beyond

For the best overall look at the city and harbor, go to the Rathaus's 107m (350-ft.), **century-old tower,** much of which was restored after the devastating bombs of World War II. May to September, guided tours (in English and German) are offered Wednesday at 2pm for 9€ per person. For a closer view over the harbor, take a stroll along the **Hindenburgufer (Hindenburg Embankment)** ★, which stretches for 3km (2 miles) along the west side of the fiord, opposite the shipyards. Perches along this embankment are especially favored by spectators during regattas. Call Tourist Information Kiel (above) for additional details.

If you'd like to go to the beach, take a short steamer trip to one of the nearby Baltic towns, such as Laboe, about 15km (10 miles) to the north. Besides the beach, the town's main attraction is the restored World War II submarine **U-Boot 995,** Strandstrasse 92, Kiel-Laboe (✆ **04343/42700;** www.deutscher-marinebund.de; bus: 100 from the Kiel Hauptbahnhof). April to October, you can tour it every day 9:30am to 7pm (Nov–Mar to 5pm). Admission is 3.50€ adults, 2.30€ students and children ages 6 to 17.

The open-air **Schleswig-Holsteinisches Freilichtmuseum** ★★, Alte Hamburger Landstrasse (✆ **0431/659660;** www.freilichtmuseum-sh.de; bus: 501 or 502), is in Molfsee, 6km (4 miles) south of Kiel. Farms and rustic country homes, dating from the 16th to the 19th century, have been assembled here. Craftspeople operate shops while working animals perform their tasks. A half-timbered inn serves tasty lunches. The site is open April to October daily 9am to 5pm, November to March Sundays and holidays 11am to 4pm. Admission is 7€ for adults, 5€ students and children, free for children 5 and under, and 14€ for a family ticket.

Where to Eat

Kieler Yacht Club CONTINENTAL   The food here is solid and reliable, though not dazzling. The main attraction, naturally, is seafood. Try the filet of haddock with mustard sauce and potatoes. Other chef's specialties are saddle of venison with savoy cabbage, roasted lamb in wine sauce with herbs, and an assortment of meal-size salads. The bar, a local hangout, attracts the yachting set.

Hindenburgufer 70. ✆ **0431/8813442.** Reservations recommended. Main courses 13€–32€. AE, DC, MC, V. Daily 5:30–10:30pm. Bus: 41 or 51.

Quam ★ 🍴 INTERNATIONAL   Charming and cosmopolitan, with an eclectic cuisine that draws on the culinary traditions of Europe and Asia, this restaurant fills three rooms of a stone-fronted building in the historic core of Kiel, a few steps from the waterfront. You'll pass through a pleasant, flower-studded garden to reach the interior, where a maximum of only 65 diners at a time dine within a warm and cozy ocher- and russet-colored decor. Menu items are flavorful and imaginative—a world's tour of flavor. The best examples include carpaccio of rump steak with pesto-flavored beans; sashimi of salmon with soy-flavored dressing; marinated and grilled young hen with seasonal vegetables; duckling with braised shallots and wine sauce; oven-baked dorado studded with herbs, served with mushroom-flavored butter sauce; and a pungent version of slow-cooked *tandoori* chicken.

Düppelstrasse 60. ✆ **0431/85195.** Reservations recommended. Main courses 18€–25€. AE, MC, V. Mon–Sat 6–11pm. Bus: 62.

Restaurant im Schloss ★ CONTINENTAL   The most elegant formal restaurant in Kiel offers superb cuisine, service, and wine. The Schloss, a stone building (ca. 1965) overlooking the harbor, looks like a museum set in a park. If you reserve, you can get a window table that opens onto the water. The cuisine has a creative and lighthearted style, using the freshest of produce and exquisite versions of lamb. Many fish dishes are from the north German seas. Temptations include salmon fritters stuffed with spinach and served with a saffron sauce, or sautéed shrimps in a mango sauce served with wild rice.

Wall 74. ✆ **0431/91155.** www.restaurant-im-schloss.de. Reservations required. Main courses 18€–28€. AE, DC, MC, V. Tues–Fri 11am–3pm; Tues–Sun 6–9:30pm. Bus: 1.

Restaurant Jakob ★ CONTINENTAL   Set in the lobby of one of Kiel's most comfortable hotels, this restaurant boasts a plush, modern decor and views over the harbor. The chef's menu specialties are quite seductive and imbued with subtle flavors. Try such temptations as filet of beef flavored with fresh rosemary, sherry, and shallots and thyme potatoes, or else medallions of pork in a cognac sauce. Other good-tasting dishes include a seafood medley of pikeperch, "seadevil," salmon, and king prawns. A carpaccio of beef is offered in a balsamic vinaigrette with fresh parmesan cheese.

In the Steigenberger Conti-Hansa, Schlossgarten 7. ✆ **0431/5115407.** Reservations recommended. Main courses 18€–29€. AE, DC, MC, V. Mon–Sat 11:30am–2:30pm and 6–10:30pm. Bus: 1 or 12.

Entertainment & Nightlife

Take a stroll after dark through the salt air and fog of this seafaring city, admiring the Hanseatic architecture and the ever-present sense of gloomy nostalgia. Along the way, you can stop at any of the small bars of the Altstadt. One of the most visible old-fashioned nightlife options in Kiel is **Kieler Bräuerei,** Alter Markt 9 (✆ **0431/906290;** www.kieler-brauerei.de), which brews and serves, on-site, a medium-dark beer that locals compare to the better-known Düsseldorfer. Most clients come just for the beer, which starts at about 4€ for approximately a pint, but if you're hungry, head for the self-service cafeteria, also on-site, for heaping platters of *Sauerkraut,* sausage, salads, and prepared meats (try the pig on a spit, rotating behind glass for your viewing pleasure), sold by the kilo. Expect to pay around 5€ to 15€ for a platter.

Hemingway, Alter Markt 19 (✆ **0431/96812**), named in honor of Papa, is the hippest bar in town, drawing a chic young crowd nightly.

Where to Stay

Hotel Kieler Yacht Club ★ 👔   This yacht club offers unusually fine guest facilities. It's in an old classical building, standing back from the harbor, with an adjoining contemporary motel annex. Rooms are comfortable but unexciting. For style, we prefer those in the main building. All units have neatly arranged bathrooms.

Hindenburgufer 70, 24105 Kiel. www.hotel-kyc.de. ✆ **0431/88130.** Fax 0431/8813444. 57 units. 165€–300€ double; 195€–330€ suite. Rates include buffet breakfast. AE, DC, MC, V. Free outdoor parking; 10€ in garage. Bus: 41. **Amenities:** Restaurant; bar; room service. *In room:* TV, hair dryer, minibar, Wi-Fi (free).

Hotel Wiking   The Wiking, in the center of town, has well-furnished rooms for reasonable prices. The dark facade is ornamented with balconies painted a vividly contrasting white. Rooms are a bit small but are well maintained, each equipped with a comfortable bed plus a compact bathroom.

Schützenwall 1–3, 24114 Kiel. **www.hotel-wiking.com.** © **0431/661090.** Fax 0431/6610966. 42 units. 89€–95€ double. Rates include continental breakfast. AE, DC, MC, V. Parking 8€. Bus: 51 or 91. **Amenities:** Bar; sauna. *In room:* TV, hair dryer, Wi-Fi (free).

Steigenberger Conti-Hansa ★★ Conti-Hansa, located between the edge of the harbor and a well-groomed city park, is Kiel's premier hotel. It's well maintained, modern, and solidly comfortable. The medium-size rooms are outfitted in streamlined contemporary furniture; most look out over the harbor or the park.

Schlossgarten 7, 24103 Kiel. www.kiel.steigenberger.de. © **800/223-5652** in the U.S. and Canada, or 0431/51150. Fax 0431/5115444. 165 units. 95€–179€ double; 189€–403€ suite. AE, DC, MC, V. Parking 18€. Bus: 22, 32, 33, or 62. **Amenities:** 2 restaurants; bar; exercise room; room service; sauna. *In room:* TV, hair dryer, minibar, Wi-Fi (15€ per day).

SCHLESWIG ★

48km (30 miles) NW of Kiel, 34km (21 miles) S of Flensburg

This one-time Viking stronghold on the Schlei (an arm of the Baltic) is Schleswig-Holstein's oldest town, with 1,200 years of history. Everything is steeped in legend, even the sea gulls. According to tradition, the birds nesting on Seagull Island in the middle of the Schlei are fellow conspirators of Duke Abel, who in 1250 murdered his brother, King Eric. The crime was discovered when the king's body washed ashore. The duke went mad, eventually died, and was impaled and buried in the Tiergarten. His followers became sea gulls, doomed to nest forever on Seagull Island.

Essentials

GETTING THERE

BY TRAIN The **Schleswig Bahnhof** is on the Flensburg-Neumünster-Hamburg and Westerland-Hamburg rail lines, with frequent connections. Trains from Hamburg arrive daily (trip time: 2 hr., 20 min.). For information, call © **01805/996633** (www.bahn.de).

BY BUS Long-distance bus service to and from Hamburg, Flensburg, and Kiel is provided by **Autokraft GmbH** in Kiel (© **0431/6660;** www.autokraft.de).

BY CAR Access by car is via the A7 Autobahn north or south.

GETTING AROUND

Buses fan out from Königstrasse and Plessenstrasse, in the town center. Fare is 2.20€. Buses operate every day 6am to 9pm.

VISITOR INFORMATION

For information, contact **Tourist-Information,** Plessenstrasse 7 (© **04621/850056;** www.schleswig.de). Hours are May to September Monday to Friday 9:30am to 5:30pm, and Saturday 9:30am to 12:30pm; October to April, hours are Monday to Thursday 10am to 4pm, and Friday 10am to 1pm.

Exploring Schleswig

Dom St. Petri (St. Peter's Cathedral) ★ CHURCH The jewel of Schleswig is St. Peter's Cathedral, a brick Romanesque-Gothic Hallenkirche (hall church) begun in the 12th century. Its towering spire makes the rest of the Altstadt seem like so many dollhouses by comparison. Inside is the outstanding 16th-century *Bordesholm Altarpiece,* a powerful work carved in oak by Hans Bruggeman for the convent at Bordesholm. Its elaborately carved Gothic panels contain nearly 400 figures. The cathedral and cloisters also possess art treasures, including the *Blue Madonna* by J. Ovens and 13th-century frescoes.

Süderdomstrasse 1. © **04621/963054.** www.schleswiger-dom.de. Free admission. May–Sept Mon–Sat 9am–5pm, Sun 1:30–5pm; Oct–Apr Mon–Sat 10am–4pm, Sun 1:30–4pm. Bus: 1, 2, 3, 4, or 5.

Schloss Gottorf MUSEUM   A dam and a bridge connect this castle, located on a small island, with the town. As you walk around the harbor, the panorama of the Altstadt and the widening bay opens up behind you. The castle is the largest in Schleswig-Holstein. The foundations date from the original 13th-century ducal palace; the present structure was built mainly in the 16th and 17th centuries and has been reconditioned since 1948 to house two museums.

The **Archäologisches Landesmuseum (Provincial Museum of Archaeology)** ★ (© 04621/8130) has a most remarkable exhibit (in a separate building): the **Nydam Boat** ★★★, a 4th-century ship found in the Nydam marshes in 1863. In the same room are artifacts and weapons discovered with the ship and Viking corpses preserved in the moor, all adding up to one of the major archaeological finds in northern Germany.

The **Schleswig-Holstein Staatsmuseum (Schleswig-Holstein State Museum)** ★ (© 04621/8130), also housed in the castle, contains an exceptional collection of fine and applied art from medieval times to the 20th century, including painting, sculpture, furniture, textiles, and weapons. Outstanding are the late-Gothic King's Hall, the 17th-century ducal living rooms with rich stucco ceilings, and the Renaissance chapel with a private pew for the ducal family, decorated with intricate and elaborate carvings and inlays. Two buildings east of the castle house collections of contemporary art, including outstanding works of German expressionism and modern sculpture, plus the ethnological collection of implements and tools used by farmers, artisans, and fishermen.

On a small island in the Burgsee, a bay at the west end of the Schlei. © **04621/8130.** www.schloss-gottorf.de. Admission (including both museums) 8€ adults, 5€ children, free for children 5 and under, 17€ family ticket. Apr–Oct daily 10am–6pm; Nov–Mar Tues–Fri 10am–4pm, Sat–Sun 10am–5pm. Bus: 1, 2, 3, or 4.

Wikinger Museum Haithabu MUSEUM   Haithabu was one of the most prominent settlements of northern Europe during the Viking era. This Viking museum, opened in 1985, contains the finds of archaeological excavations of the Viking-age town of Haithabu. Exhibits cover all aspects of daily life. There's even a Viking long ship. In summer, you can reach this site via a scenic 20-minute boat ride. Departures are from Stadthafen, the town quay in Schleswig, south of the cathedral. After you dock, it's a 10-minute walk to the museum. In winter, you'll have to walk 3km (2 miles) from the rail station.

Durchwahl, 2.5km (1½ miles) from Schleswig. © **04621/8130.** www.schloss-gottorf.de. Admission 6€ adults, 3.50€ children, free for children 5 and under, 13€ family ticket. Mar 10–Oct daily 10am–6pm; Nov–Mar 9 Tues–Sun 10am–5pm.

Where to Eat

Stadt Flensburg GERMAN   Set in an architecturally distinguished town house dating from the late 17th century, this is a small-scale and cozy restaurant that's a short walk from the Schloss Gottorf. Designed with a simple decor that seats only 60 diners at a time, it's outfitted in tones of brown and beige, with wood paneling, a sense of sudsy beeriness, and an aura of old-fashioned protocol. Menu items include lots of fresh fish, including a well-flavored version of zander (pikeperch) with herbs, butter sauce, salad, and roasted potatoes; a succulent version of roasted lamb; steaks; and roast duck and, when it's available, goose, served with red cabbage and potatoes in a style that many locals remember from their childhoods. It's the kind of cuisine that's marvelously accompanied by beer, available on tap in both light and dark versions.

Lollfuss 102. ℂ **04621/23984.** Reservations recommended. Main courses 15€–22€. AE, DC, MC, V. Thurs–Tues noon–3pm and 6–11pm. Bus: 1 or 2.

Entertainment & Nightlife

If you're looking for action, head for **Lollfuss,** running parallel to the Schlei between Schloss Gottorf and a north-side residential area. Many places here are cafes during the day and bars at night. The best and most popular pub of the lot is **Patio,** Lollfuss 3 (ℂ **04621/29999;** www.patio-online.de; bus: 1 or 2), an intimate two-story structure that usually stays open until midnight or 1am (considered very late in this small town). It also has Schleswig's most popular outdoor terrace. If you get hungry, you'll find pastas, salads, pizzas, and steaks for 4.50€ to 16€.

Where to Stay

Hotel Waldschlösschen ★   This elegant country hotel, finer than any of the in-town properties, is equipped with every convenience to make your stay comfortable. Rooms range from small to medium, each with a compact bathroom. Outside, there's a rock garden, a gabled house, an elongated annex, and lots of trees.

Kolonnenweg 152, 24837 Schleswig-Pulverholz. www.hotel-schleswig.com. ℂ **04621/3830.** Fax 04621/383105. 115 units. 129€–149€ double; 228€ suite. Rates include buffet breakfast. AE, DC, MC, V. Free parking. Bus: 1, 2, 3, or 4. 1.5km (1 mile) southwest of town. **Amenities:** Restaurant; bar; babysitting; Jacuzzi; indoor heated pool; room service; sauna. *In room:* TV, hair dryer, minibar, Wi-Fi (free).

Ringhotel Strandhalle Schleswig 🏄   Established a century ago, with frequent renovations, the Strandhalle may not be as good as the Waldschlösschen, but it has many winning features, especially for those who'd like to stay within Schleswig and absorb the atmosphere of this ancient town. Actually, this hotel is more of a holiday resort—right on the water, with its own rowboats available. The owners maintain an informal atmosphere. Rooms are small but neatly kept, each with a somewhat cramped bathroom. Nonetheless, the hotel is good value for the area. Ask for a room opening on the water, with a view of the yacht harbor.

Strandweg 2, 24837 Schleswig. www.hotel-strandhalle.de. ℂ **04621/9090.** Fax 04621/909100. 25 units. 110€–145€ double. Rates include buffet breakfast. AE, DC, MC, V. Parking 9€. Bus: 1, 2, 3, 4, or 5. **Amenities:** Restaurant; bikes; indoor heated pool. *In room:* TV, hair dryer, minibar, Wi-Fi (10€ per day).

THE ISLAND OF SYLT ★★

20km (12 miles) W of the Danish border, 193km (120 miles) NW of Hamburg

The long, narrow island of Sylt (pronounced *Zoolt*) and its capital, Westerland, form the northernmost point of Germany. Sylt lies in the North Sea off the coasts of Denmark and Schleswig-Holstein, the largest island of the Frisian archipelago, which stretches from Denmark to the Netherlands. The "Watt" is the name given to the coast facing the mainland.

People come to breathe the iodine-rich air and enjoy the rain-soaked North Sea climate that Germans call *Reizklima*. Sylt is the most exclusive resort in Germany, and its hotel prices reflect that status. Sylt also has a sizable gay and lesbian population and is often called "The Fire Island of Europe." In the 1960s, Sylt became famous for "the rich and the naked," when the entire island was reportedly an ongoing bacchanalian frenzy. It's quieted down since then. Temperatures in midsummer are usually in the low 70s (low to mid-20s Celsius), but rain can come at any minute, and winds on the beach are a constant, giving rise to the Sylt "mink," or yellow oilskin, which chic visitors wear to protect themselves from the elements.

The spa here has facilities for the treatment of everything from heart disease to skin irritations. The basic therapy is sunshine, pure air, and seawater, but in recent years, mud baths have also become a method of treatment. Some of the more remote sections of the dunes have been turned into nudist beaches for purists in the art of sunshine therapy. In addition to bathing, there are facilities in and around Westerland for horseback riding, surfing, golf, and tennis, as well as theater and concerts.

Essentials
GETTING THERE
BY PLANE   The nearest international airport is at Hamburg (see chapter 17). From there you can fly to the regional **Sylt Airport** (© **04651/920612;** www. flughafen-sylt.de). There's also regularly scheduled air service from Berlin and Düsseldorf.

BY TRAIN   The only link between the mainland and the island of Sylt is the railroad causeway running from the mainland town of Niebüll. If you wish to bring your car to the island, you'll have to load it on the train at Niebüll for the slow ride (see "By Car," below). No advance booking is necessary—you just arrive and take your chances. Passengers are carried free.

Westerland Bahnhof lies on the Westerland-Hamburg and the Westerland-Lübeck lines, with frequent connections. Seventeen trains arrive from Hamburg daily (trip time: 2 hr., 40 min. to 3 hr., 20 min., depending on the train). For information, call © **01805/996633** (www.bahn.de).

BY CAR-FERRY   An alternative way of reaching Sylt is to take a car-ferry between the Danish port of Havneby, on the island of Rømo (easily accessible via highway from Germany), and the German port of List, at the northern tip of Sylt. There are at least a dozen daily crossings between those points in summer, with a much-reduced schedule in winter. Reservations for your car are possible. Round-trip passage for a car with a driver and up to three passengers costs 85€. For information, call the **Rømo-Sylt Line** (© **0180/3103030;** www.syltfaehre.de).

BY BUS   The few buses that pull into Sylt are forced to ride the flatcars on the rail line across the Hindenburg Causeway for the final stretch of their journey. Many passengers prefer to get off in Niebüll and transfer onto one of the passenger trains that make the frequent crossings to Westerland from other parts of Germany and Europe. Rail fare between Niebüll and Westerland costs 28€ per person, round-trip. The ride takes between 30 and 45 minutes each way.

BY CAR   Construction of a conventional bridge from Schleswig-Holstein to Sylt has never really been feasible. Therefore, cars headed to Sylt are loaded onto flatcars at the mainland railway junction of Niebüll and hauled out across the Hindenburg Damm (Hindenburg Causeway) to the railway station of Westerland. Drivers must stay in their cars, with the doors closed, eventually arriving at Westerland 30 to 40 minutes later. For information on these and all other (conventional) trains between the German mainland and Sylt, call the **Deutsche Bahn** information service in Westerland at © **01805/996633** (www.bahn.de). Trains depart at 30-minute intervals daily

5am to midnight. No reservations are accepted for hauling your car across. Round-trip transport for most cars costs 85€. Access to Niebüll is possible via the A7 Auto-bahn north or south.

VISITOR INFORMATION

For information, contact the **Sylt Tourismus Zentrale,** Keitumer Landstrasse 10B (© **04651/6026;** www.sylt-tourismus.de). It's open May to October daily 9am to 5pm, and November to April Monday to Saturday 9am to 4pm.

Where to Eat

Alte Friesenstube ★ 🏠 NORTHERN GERMAN/FRISIAN   This restaurant is refreshingly down to earth amid the pretentiousness of Sylt. Its thatched building was constructed in 1648. The menus are written on the wall in a German dialect, but someone will assist you in deciphering the offerings, which include regional pork, fish, and beef dishes. Carefully crafted dishes include grilled tuna steak with capers and lemon butter, or else baked lamb flavored with rosemary jus. Especially popular is duck with orange sauce and *Panfische* (a local saltwater fish) with roasted potatoes and mustard sauce. No one puts on airs, and the kitchen sticks to the robust fare the islanders have been eating for decades.

Gaadt 4, Westerland.© **04651/1228.** www.altefriesenstube.de. Reservations required. Main courses 18€–29€. No credit cards. Tues–Sun 6–10:30pm. Closed Jan.

Hardy auf Sylt ALSATIAN/GERMAN   This round, thatched restaurant offers a nostalgic interior featuring furniture dating from about 1890. Finely worked columns, old oil portraits, beautiful glass lamps, and skillfully wrought candlesticks combine to create a relaxed, intimate feeling. The menu is adjusted seasonally. Perhaps at the time of your visit you'll be tempted by the grilled salmon filet with Béarnaise sauce or the roast duck breast in a shallot sauce. There's a fine selection of French and German wines.

Norderstrasse 65, Westerland.© **04651/22775.** www.hardyaufsylt.de. Reservations required. Main courses 16€–24€. No credit cards. Tues–Sun 6–11:30pm. Closed Jan 10–Feb 15 and Nov 8–Dec 20.

Jörg Müller ★★★ CONTINENTAL/FRENCH   This is Sylt's most elegant res-taurant. Its brick building is almost a landmark in itself, thanks to its thatched roof, steep gables, and Frisian architecture. Menu items change with the seasons and feature a blend of contemporary Continental cuisine with imaginative variations of French recipes, which may include lobster salad with herb-flavored vinaigrette sauce, sliced and braised goose liver with segments of glazed apples, or roast salt-marsh lamb flavored with herbs and served with ratatouille-flavored cream sauce. You can also enjoy local oysters with compote of red shallots and champagne sauce or halibut baked in fennel.

Süderstrasse 8, Westerland.© **04651/27789.** Reservations required. Main courses 32€–56€; fixed-price menus 96€–128€. AE, DC, MC, V. Tues–Sun 6–10pm. Closed Nov 25–Dec 18. A 5-min. walk from the center of Westerland.

Restaurant Stadt Hamburg ★★   GERMAN/INTERNATIONAL   Top-rate cuisine is offered here in an attractive, luxurious setting of dark colors and hardwood paneling. The menu is so wide ranging it may be hard to make up your mind. A great way to begin is with the smooth cream-of-lobster soup. Many seafood specialties are featured, such as pan-fried fresh North Sea sole and turbot medallions in saffron sauce with zucchini. Another good dish is the rack of lamb (raised on the salty

A disappearing PLAYGROUND

Scientists warn that the western coast of Sylt is one of the most fragile ecosystems in Germany and may one day be reclaimed by the sea. The entire island is little more than a strip, only 550m (1,800 ft.) wide at its narrowest point, that's composed mostly of sand and very little rock. As such, it presents little resistance to the onslaught of erosion and deterioration. The sand dunes, warmed by the Gulf Stream, are forever shifting, and the winds sweeping in from the North Sea can move them by as much as 3.5m (11 ft.) in only a year. Although the winter months in general, and storms at any time of the year, are highly destructive, it's during strong south winds that most erosion takes place, and on some mornings after violent storms, huge amounts of sand migrate from the beachfront out into the North Sea.

In the 1970s, a series of *Tetrapoden* (four-legged concrete structures that look like giant jacks) were built on the sands of Westerland and Hornum beaches, in an unsuccessful attempt to hold back erosion. (They were later judged useless, and their construction was discontinued.)

Today, everyone's favorite solution is one of the simplest: Whenever funds are allocated by the municipal budget, you'll see one or more barges moored offshore, pumping sand from deepwater sites back onto beaches of Sylt. Severe penalties exist for anyone removing salt grasses and scrub from the beachfronts, as do strict regulations against building new houses on fragile land.

If there is an air of desperation about the Germans who love and frolic in this North Sea playground, it is because they know it won't be here forever.

grasslands of the island). For dessert, try homemade *rote Grütze*—berries and cherries topped with vanilla ice cream.

Strandstrasse 2, Westerland. (✆) **04651/8580.** Reservations recommended. Main courses 19€–32€. AE, MC, V. Daily 6–10pm. Bus: Centrale Omnibus Bahnhof.

Web Christel 🔱 NORTHERN GERMAN   Favored by local residents for its reasonable prices and cozy ambience, this restaurant occupies a century-old Frisian house in the center of Westerland, opposite its more glamorous (and more expensive) rival, Jörg Müller (see above). Menu items include a wide selection of fish, such as classic versions of turbot in an herb-butter-mustard sauce, and sole prepared in the meunière style or grilled and served with hollandaise sauce. Roast duck with two different sauces is also available. A signature dish is fettuccini with lobster and fresh vegetables. The staff is warm and polite.

Süderstrasse 11, Westerland. (✆) **04651/22900.** www.webchristel.de. Reservations recommended. Main courses 18€–34€; fixed-price menus 29€–41€. No credit cards. Thurs–Tues 5–11pm.

Shopping

Few other vacation destinations in Germany are as frenetic about clothing as Sylt. Garments are removed and put on again with abandon on this island with fickle weather and an extremely clothes-conscious population. You'll find impressive inventories of expensively casual clothing on Sylt—items that are artfully simple, easy to don, easy to doff, and easy to look at. The island's best shopping streets are the

Friedrichstrasse, in Westerland, and the **Strönwai,** in Kampen, both lined with boutiques associated with the great names of European fashion.

Entertainment & Nightlife

Disco Pony, Strönwai, in Kampen (© **04651/42182;** www.pony-kampen.com), where both indoor and outdoor bar areas encompass views of the sea and the scrub-covered coastline that flanks it, mostly attracts a clientele under 40. There's no cover charge.

Also in Kampen is Disco Pony's major competitor, **Club Rotes Kliff,** Alte Dorfstrasse (© **04651/43400;** www.club-rotes-kliff.de), distinguished by its hip but not necessarily young crowd. There's no cover charge.

Where to Stay

Hotel Clausen   This four-story building has long been a local favorite. Today, its congenial English-speaking owners occupy the upper (fourth) floor. On the building's lower stories is a series of small but tidily maintained rooms, each fitted with a quality mattress on a good bed. Breakfast is the only meal served, but many restaurants are nearby.

Friedrichstrasse 20, 25980 Westerland/Sylt. www.hotel-clausen-sylt.de. © **04651/92290.** Fax 04651/28007. 20 units. 95€–150€ double; 130€–165€ suite. Rates include buffet breakfast. MC, V. Parking 6€. In Westerland's pedestrian zone, a 3-min. walk from the beach. **Amenities:** Room service; Wi-Fi (free, in lobby). *In room:* TV, hair dryer.

Hotel Miramar ★   This hotel, on a bluff above the beach, has the second-best accommodations in Westerland, just below Stadt Hamburg (see below). Surrounded by an arched veranda, its public areas are graced with large arched windows with views of the sea. An octagonal light, left over from the building's 1903 construction, illuminates the salon from above. The high-ceilinged rooms are quite comfortable and each comes with a luxurious bed and bathroom.

Friedrichstrasse 43, 25980 Westerland/Sylt. www.hotel-miramar.de. © **04651/8550.** Fax 04651/855222. 67 units. 190€–395€ double; 280€–780€ suite. Rates include buffet breakfast. AE, DC, MC, V. Parking 12€. **Amenities:** Restaurant; bar; babysitting; exercise room; indoor heated pool; room service; sauna; outdoor tennis court (lit). *In room:* TV, hair dryer, minibar, Wi-Fi (free).

Hotel Wünschmann   This hotel is in the heart of the tourist belt of Westerland, yet only minutes from the sand dunes. Rooms are in a complex of modern buildings (with more than two dozen boutiques), but the hotel's interior exudes old-world tranquillity. The midsize bedrooms are individually decorated so you won't feel you're staying in a peas-in-a-pod motel. Each is cheerful and inviting, with comfortable furnishings and medium-size bathrooms.

Andreas-Dirks-Strasse 4, 25980 Westerland/Sylt. www.hotel-wuenschmann.de. © **04651/5025.** Fax 04651/5028. 35 units. 116€–286€ double; 242€–321€ suite. Rates include continental breakfast. AE, V. Parking 12€. Closed mid-Nov to mid-Dec. **Amenities:** Bikes; room service; sauna; Wi-Fi (free, in lobby). *In room:* TV, hair dryer.

Stadt Hamburg ★★★   This is the best hotel on the island, though it looks more like a well-appointed country home than a hotel. Built in the 1880s as a grand Belle Epoque summer hotel, it was enlarged in 1991 with the construction of an elegant annex, in which the hotel's suites and its more expensive rooms are housed today. Less expensive rooms, and the restaurant, still lie within the hotel's original core. The gleaming white entrance is reached through a white picket fence, and its rear windows overlook a well-kept lawn. Each spacious room is individually furnished, with homey touches. Mattresses and linens are the island's finest, and the bathrooms are state-of-the-art.

Strandstrasse 2, 25980 Westerland/Sylt. www.hotelstadthamburg.com. *(C)* **04651/8580.** Fax 04651/858220. 72 units. 220€–340€ double; 340€–585€ suite. AE, MC, V. Parking 13€. Next to the casino. **Amenities:** 2 restaurants; babysitting; exercise room; indoor heated pool; room service; spa. *In room:* TV, fax, hair dryer, Wi-Fi (free).

PLANNING YOUR TRIP TO GERMANY

GETTING THERE

By Plane

Lufthansa (☎ **800/645-3880** in the U.S., 800/563-5954 in Canada, or 01805/805805 in Germany; www.lufthansa.com) operates the most frequent service and flies to the greatest number of Germany's airports. From North America, Lufthansa serves 23 gateway cities. In any season, there are more than 100 weekly flights from these cities to Germany. The largest of the gateways is the New York City area, where flights depart from both JFK and Newark airports. Lufthansa has an alliance with **United Airlines** and **Air Canada** to provide seamless air service to Germany and other parts of the globe from North America. Dubbed "Star Alliance," the union allows cross-airline benefits, including travel on one or all of these airlines on one ticket and frequent-flier credit to the participating airline of your choice.

American Airlines (☎ **800/443-7300**; www.aa.com) flies nonstop from Chicago and Dallas to Frankfurt daily, and American's flights connect easily with ongoing flights to many other German cities on Lufthansa or British Airways. **Continental Airlines** (☎ **800/525-0280**; www.continental.com) offers daily nonstop service from Newark to Frankfurt. **Delta Airlines** (☎ **800/241-4141**; www.delta.com) offers daily connecting service to Hamburg (via Paris) and nonstop to Frankfurt from Atlanta, Cincinnati, and New York's JFK; nonstop to Munich from Atlanta; and nonstop to Berlin from JFK. **United Airlines** (☎ **800/538-2929**; www.united.com) offers daily nonstops from Los Angeles, New York, and Chicago to Frankfurt and Munich, and because of the Star Alliance, discussed above, all German flights by Lufthansa or Air Canada will also be honored as a part of a United ticket. **US Airways** (☎ **800/428-4322**; www.usairways.com) also flies to Frankfurt and Munich daily (with nonstops from Charlotte and Philadelphia).

From London, **British Airways** (☎ **0870/8509850**; www.britishairways.com) and **Lufthansa** (☎ **01805/805805**; www.lufthansa.com) are the most convenient carriers to the major German cities, including Düsseldorf, Cologne, Frankfurt, Munich, and Berlin. **British Midland** (☎ **0870/6070555**; www.flybmi.com) has daily flights to Cologne, Düsseldorf, Frankfurt, Hamburg, and Munich.

FLYING FOR LESS: TIPS FOR GETTING THE BEST AIRFARE

o Passengers who can book their ticket either **long in advance** or **at the last minute,** or who **fly midweek** or **at less trafficked hours,** may pay a fraction of the full fare. If your schedule is flexible, say so, and ask if you can secure a cheaper fare by changing your flight plans.

o Search **the Internet** for cheap fares. The most popular online travel agencies are **Travelocity** (www.travelocity.com), **Expedia** (www.expedia.com), and **Orbitz** (www.orbitz.com). In the U.K., go to **Travelsupermarket** (✆ 0845/345-5708; www.travelsupermarket.com), a flight search engine that offers flight comparisons for the budget airlines whose seats often end up in bucket shop sales. Other websites for booking airline tickets online include **Cheapflights.com, Smarter-Travel.com, Priceline** (www.priceline.com), and **Opodo** (www.opodo.com). Meta-search sites (which find and then direct you to airline and hotel websites for booking) include **Sidestep.com** and **Kayak.com**—the latter includes fares for budget carriers such as JetBlue and Spirit as well as the major airlines. **Lastminute. com** is a great source for last-minute flights and getaways. In addition, most **airlines** offer online-only fares that even their phone agents know nothing about.

o Keep an eye on local newspapers for **promotional specials** or **fare wars,** when airlines lower prices on their most popular routes.

o **Consolidators,** also known as bucket shops, are wholesale brokers in the airline-ticket game. Consolidators buy deeply discounted tickets ("distressed" inventories of unsold seats) from airlines and sell them to online ticket agencies, travel agents, tour operators, corporations, and, to a lesser degree, the general public. Consolidators advertise in Sunday newspaper travel sections (often in small ads with tiny type), in both the U.S. and the U.K. They can be great sources for cheap international tickets. On the downside, bucket shop tickets are often rigged with restrictions, such as stiff cancellation penalties (as high as 50%–75% of the ticket price). And keep in mind that most of what you see advertised is of limited availability. Several reliable consolidators are worldwide and available online. **STA Travel** (www.statravel.com) has been the world's leading consolidator for students since purchasing Council Travel, but their fares are competitive for travelers of all ages. **Flights.com** (✆ 201/541-3826) has excellent fares worldwide, particularly to Europe. They also have "local" websites in 12 countries. **FlyCheap** (✆ 800/359-2432; www.flycheap.com) has especially good fares to sunny destinations. **AirTicketsDirect** (✆ 888/858-8884; www.airticketsdirect.com), based in Montreal, is another good source.

o Join **frequent-flier clubs.** Frequent-flier membership doesn't cost a cent, but it does entitle you to free tickets or upgrades when you amass the airline's required number of frequent-flier points. You don't even have to fly to earn points; **frequent-flier credit cards** can earn you thousands of miles for doing your everyday shopping. But keep in mind that award seats are limited, seats on popular routes are hard to snag, and more and more major airlines are cutting their expiration periods for mileage points—so check your airline's frequent-flier program so you don't lose your miles before you use them. *Inside tip:* Award seats are offered almost a year in advance, but seats also open up at the last minute, so if your travel plans are flexible, you may strike gold. To play the frequent-flier game to your best advantage, consult the community bulletin boards on **FlyerTalk** (www.flyertalk.com) or go to Randy Petersen's **Inside Flyer** (www.insideflyer.com). Petersen and friends review all the programs in detail and post regular updates on changes in policies and trends.

GETTING THROUGH THE airport

- Arrive at the airport at least 2 hours before an international flight to Germany. You can check the average wait times at your airport by going to the TSA **Security Checkpoint Wait Times** site (http://waittime.tsa.dhs.gov).

- Know what you can carry on and what you can't. For the latest updates on items you are prohibited to bring in carry-on luggage, go to **www.tsa.gov/travelers/airtravel**.

- Beat the ticket-counter lines by using the self-service electronic ticket kiosks at the airport or even printing out your boarding pass at home from the airline website. Using curbside check-in is also a smart way to avoid lines.

- Help speed up security before you're screened. Remove jackets, shoes, belt buckles, heavy jewelry, and watches and place them either in your carry-on luggage or the security bins provided. Place keys, coins, cellphones, and pagers in a security bin. If you have metallic body parts, carry a note from your doctor. When possible, keep liquids in checked baggage.

- Use a TSA-approved lock for your checked luggage. Look for Travel Sentry certified locks at luggage or travel shops and Brookstone stores (or online at www.brookstone.com).

By Train

Many passengers, especially holders of the **Eurailpass,** travel to Germany by train from other European cities. (See "Getting Around," below, for information on purchasing rail passes.)

British Rail runs four trains a day to Germany from Victoria Station in **London,** going by way of the Ramsgate-Ostend ferry or jetfoil. Two trains depart from London's Liverpool Street Station, via Harwich-Hook of Holland. Most trains change at Cologne for destinations elsewhere in Germany. You can purchase tickets through British Rail travel centers in London (© **866/274-8724** in the U.S. and Canada; www.britrail.com). See "Via the Chunnel," below, for information about the Eurostar service running between London and Brussels via the Channel Tunnel.

Unless you pay a premium for rail travel on the Eurostar, which connects London's St. Pancras station via the Chunnel (see below) with either Paris or Brussels, train travel from the U.K. to points within Germany can be lengthy and tedious, with multiple transfers en route and with long, bouncing segments aboard either hovercrafts or conventional ferryboats between the English port of Ramsgate and the Belgian port of Oostende. If you opt to save money and embark upon one of these non-Chunnel methods of transport, expect transit times between London and Cologne of up to 12 hours, and from London to either Berlin or Munich of between 18 and 22 hours, depending on the train and the ferryboat or hovercraft crossing.

Frankly, it's far better to pay the extra premium aboard Eurostar, the name given to each of the trains running under the English Channel, between London and Brussels, and from there, taking a high-speed train onward to your destination within Germany. Even so, transit time from London to Cologne, requiring a change in Brussels, would take 4 hours and 45 minutes; from London to Berlin, requiring a single change in Brussels and Cologne, would take 9 hours; and from London to Munich, requiring a single change in Brussels, would require between 9 and 10 hours, depending on the day of the week.

By Car & Ferry

To bring a car over from England, you face a choice of ports from which you'll continue driving to Germany. **P & O Ferries** (© 08716/645645 in the U.K.; www. poferries.com) has 30 to 35 ferryboat crossings a day, depending on the season, between Dover and Calais. The crossing can take as little as 1 hour and 15 minutes. Once you're in Calais, the drive to Cologne takes about 3 hours. Other options involve passage from Harwich to the Hook of Holland, a sea crossing of about 8 hours. You can also take your car via the Chunnel (see below).

Via the Channel Tunnel

The $15-billion **Channel Tunnel,** one of the greatest engineering feats of all time, is the first link between Britain and the Continent since the Ice Age. The tunnel was built beneath the seabed through a layer of impermeable chalk marl and sealed with a reinforced concrete lining. The 50km (30-mile) journey between Britain and France takes 35 minutes, although actual time in the Chunnel is only 19 minutes. Once on the Continent, you can connect to Germany fairly easily.

Rail Europe (www.raileurope.com) sells tickets on the **Eurostar** direct train service between London and Paris or Brussels (© 800/622-8600 in the U.S., or 800/361-7245 in Canada; www.eurostar.com). In the U.K., make reservations for Eurostar at © 0870/5186186. The train operates 24 hours a day, 365 days a year, running every 15 minutes during peak travel times and at least once an hour at night.

The tunnel also accommodates passenger cars, charter buses, taxis, and motorcycles from Folkestone to Calais. Tickets may be purchased at the tollbooth.

GETTING AROUND

By Plane

From Frankfurt, most **Lufthansa** (© 800/645-3880 in the U.S., or 800/563-5954 in Canada; www.lufthansa.com) destinations in Germany can be reached in an average of 50 minutes, with at least four flights daily.

All German cities with commercial airports have an airport shuttle service, offering reduced fares and fast connections between the city center and the airport. Departure points are usually the airlines' town offices and the city's main rail terminal. Luggage can be checked at the DB (Deutsche Bahn/German Rail) baggage counter at the airport for delivery to the railroad station at your ultimate destination.

By Train

Whether you travel first- or second-class, you'll find that the trains of **German Rail** (**DB Rail;** © 0800/1507090; www.bahn.de) deserve their good reputation for comfort, cleanliness, and punctuality. All are modern and fast, and all cars are nonsmoking. A snack bar or a dining car, serving German and international cuisine as well as good wine and beer, can usually be found on all trains except locals.

For city sightseeing, you can leave your baggage in a locker or check it at the station's baggage counter. In many cities, German Rail provides door-to-door baggage service, allowing passengers to have luggage picked up at or delivered to their hotels. Accompanying baggage can be checked for a nominal fee. Suitcases, baby carriages, skis, bicycles, and steamer trunks are permitted as baggage. Insurance policies of various kinds, including a travel medical plan, are also available.

About 20,000 **InterCity** (**IC;** www.bahn.de) passenger trains offer express service every hour between most large and medium-size German cities. IC trains have adjustable cushioned seats and individual reading lights, and often offer telephone and secretarial services. Bars, lounges, and dining rooms are available, too. A network of **EuroCity** (**EC**) trains connecting Germany with 13 other countries offers the same high standards of service as those of IC.

> ## Don't Stow It—Ship It
>
> Though pricey, it's sometimes worthwhile to travel luggage-free, particularly if you're toting sports equipment, meetings materials, or baby equipment. Specialists in door-to-door luggage delivery include **Skycap International** and **Sports Express**. Both services use the same website (www.sportsexpress.com).

Germany's high-speed rail network, known as **InterCity Express (ICE),** is among the fastest in Europe—their trains reach speeds of 280kmph (174 mph). One of these trains runs from Hamburg, via Würzburg and Nürnberg, to Munich; another from Frankfurt, via Stuttgart, to Munich; and yet another from Berlin, via Frankfurt, to Munich. Each train makes stops along the way. ICE significantly reduces travel time, making transits north to south across the country easily possible in the course of a single day. Some 200 east-west connections have been added to the German Rail timetable to link the Deutsche Bundesbahn (west) and the Deutsche Reichsbahn (east). Additional connections make Leipzig and Dresden more accessible.

InterCity Night (ICN)—one of the most comfortable night trains in Europe—operates between Berlin and Bonn, and Berlin and Munich. Even though the train doesn't depart until 10 or 11pm, you may board as early as 8 or 8:30pm. Arrival the next morning is between 6:55 and 7:55am, and you have the option of remaining aboard until 9 or 9:30am.

The ICN offers first and tourist class. Sleeping accommodations in first class include single or double compartments with shower and toilet, and they are equipped with key cards, phones for wake-up service, luggage storage, and other amenities. Tourist class offers open seating with sleeperettes (reclining seats). The ICN is equipped with a restaurant and bistro car, and a breakfast buffet is included in the first-class fare. For an extra cost, a limited menu for dinner is offered. Advance reservations are mandatory for all sleeping accommodations.

German Rail issues tickets for the ICN and also makes reservations. Eurail and German Rail pass holders are accepted on this train but have to pay for the seat or sleeper reservation and also for meals. Youth-pass holders are accepted only in tourist class. Children 3 and under travel free, provided they do not require a separate seat; those between 4 and 12 are charged half fare.

Before leaving for Germany, you can get complete details about **German Rail** and the many plans it offers, as well as information about Eurailpasses, at Rail Europe (© **877/272-7245;** www.raileurope.com).

GERMAN RAIL TOURIST PASSES The **German Rail Passes** offer several options beginning with 3 days and going up to 10 days in 1 month. For example 3 days of travel in 1 month costs 230€ first class or 175€ second class.

If you're age 12 to 25, ask about a **Youth Pass,** or inquire about a **Twin Pass,** which is shared by two adults traveling together at all times.

The passes also entitle the bearer to additional benefits, such as free or discounted travel on selected bus routes operated by **Deutsche Touring/Europabus,** including destinations not serviced by trains, or excursions along particularly scenic highways such as the Romantic Road and the Castle Road. The pass also includes free travel on **KD German Line steamers** (day trips only) along the Rhine, Main, and Mosel rivers.

These passes are available from www.bahn.com or buy them from travel agent **Rail Europe** (℘ 877/272-7245). Rail Europe can also arrange cost-effective "Rail and Drive" packages that combine a certain number of days on the train with a certain number of days in a rental car. Here's an example of how it might work: Ride the train from Frankfurt to Munich, spend 3 days exploring the city, and then rent a car for a 2-day excursion to Berchtesgaden and the Bavarian Alps. The German Rail Flexipass is also sold by **Premier Gateway** (℘ 800/777-8369 in the U.S. and Canada; www. premiergateway.com).

WHERE TO BUY RAIL PASSES　Travel agents in all towns and railway agents in major North American cities sell all these tickets, but the biggest supplier is **Rail Europe** (℘ 877/272-7245; www.raileurope.com), which can also give you informational brochures.

Many different rail passes are available in the U.K. for travel in Britain and continental Europe. Stop in at the **International Rail Centre,** Victoria Station, London SW1V 1JY (℘ 0870/5848848 in the U.K.). Some of the most popular passes, including Inter-Rail and Euro Youth, are offered only to travelers 25 years of age or under; these allow unlimited second-class travel through most European countries.

By Car

British travelers who want to bring their own cars over should see "By Car & Ferry" under "Getting There," earlier in this chapter.

Competition in the European car-rental industry is fierce, so make sure you comparison shop. You can make reservations by calling these toll-free numbers: **Avis** (℘ 800/331-1212; www.avis.com), **Budget** (℘ 800/472-3325; www.budget. com), **Hertz** (℘ 800/654-3001; www.hertz.com), **Kemwel Drive Group** (℘ 877/820-0668; www.kemwel.com), and **Auto Europe** (℘ 800/223-5555; www.autoeurope.com). You can often rent a car in one German city and return it to another for no additional charge.

There are some advantages to **prepaying rentals** in your native currency before leaving home. You get an easy-to-understand net price, the rental process is more streamlined, and you can avoid unpleasant surprises caused by sudden unfavorable changes in currency exchange rates. Remember, however, that if you opt to prepay and your plans change, you'll have to go through some rather complicated paperwork for changing or canceling a prepaid contract.

DRIVING RULES　In Germany, you drive on the right side of the road. Both front- and back-seat passengers must wear safety belts. Children 5 and younger cannot ride in the front seat.

Easy-to-understand international road signs are posted, but U.S. travelers should remember that road signs are in kilometers, not miles. In congested areas, the speed limit is about 50kmph (about 30 mph). On all other roads except the autobahns, the speed limit is 100kmph (about 60 mph).

In theory, there is no speed limit on the autobahns (in the left, fast lane), but many drivers going too fast report that they have been stopped by the police and fined, and the government recommends a speed limit of 130kmph (81 mph). Reasonable caution is recommended, for safety if nothing else. A German driver on the autobahn can be a ferocious creature, and you may prefer the slow lane.

Note: Drinking while driving is a very serious offense in Germany. Be sure to keep any alcoholic beverages in the trunk or other storage area.

BREAKDOWNS/ASSISTANCE The major automobile club in Germany is **Automobilclub von Deutschland (AvD),** Lyoner Strasse 16, 60528 Frankfurt (© 069/660600; www.avd.de). If you have a breakdown on the autobahn, you can call from one of many emergency phones, spaced about a mile apart. On secondary roads, go to the nearest phone. If you don't belong to an auto club, call © 01802/222222. In English, ask for "road service assistance." Emergency assistance is free, but you pay for parts and materials.

DRIVER'S LICENSES American drivers, and those from E.U. countries, need only a domestic license to drive. However, in Germany and throughout the rest of Europe, you must also have an international insurance certificate, known as a *carte verte* (green card). Any car-rental agency will automatically provide one of these as a standard part of the rental contract, but it's a good idea to double-check all documents at the time of rental, just to be sure that you can identify the card if asked by border patrol or the police.

By Bus

An excellent, efficient bus network services Germany. Many buses are operated by **Bahnbus,** which is owned by the railway. These are integrated to complement the rail service. Bus service in Germany is particularly convenient during slow periods of rail service, normally around midday and on Saturday and Sunday. German post offices often operate local bus services (contact local post offices for schedules and prices).

The most popular bus ride is along the Romantic Road (see chapter 7), where special green-and-white buses carry tourists regularly from town to town. For more information, ask a travel agent or call **Deutsche Touring GmbH,** Am Römerhof 17, Frankfurt (© 069/7903501; www.touring.de).

By Boat

Perhaps Germany's most beautiful features are its lakes and rivers. The mighty Rhine is the country's most traveled waterway. German cruise ships also run on the Main River between Mainz and Frankfurt; on the Danube from Nürnberg to Linz (Austria), going on to Vienna and Budapest; and on the Mosel between Cochem and Trier.

To cruise the mythically rich rivers of Germany, especially the legendary Rhine, you can book cruises on the principal carrier, **Viking River Cruises** (© 800/304-9616 in the U.S., or 0800/319-6660 in the UK; www.vikingrivers.com).

TIPS ON ACCOMMODATIONS

In general, Germany has one of the highest standards of innkeeping in the world. Hotels range from five-star palaces of luxury and comfort to plain country inns and simple *Gasthäuser* (guesthouses), with a huge variation in rates. The cheapest accommodations are in *Fremdenheime* (pensions) or rooms in private homes (look for a sign

Tips on Accommodations

PLANNING YOUR TRIP TO GERMANY

saying ZIMMER FREI, meaning there are rooms for rent). Hotels listed as *garni* provide no meals other than breakfast.

Also, tourist offices will often book you into a room for a small charge. Obviously, the earlier you arrive in these offices, the more likely you are to get a good room at the price you want.

Surfing for Hotels

In addition to the online travel booking sites **Travelocity, Expedia, Orbitz, Priceline,** and **Hotwire,** you can book hotels through **Hotels.com, Quikbook** (www.quikbook.com), and **Travelaxe** (www.travelaxe.com).

HotelChatter.com is a daily webzine offering smart coverage and critiques of hotels worldwide. Go to **TripAdvisor.com** or **HotelShark.com** for helpful independent consumer reviews of hotels and resort properties.

It's a good idea to **get a confirmation number** and **make a printout** of any online booking transaction.

Throughout Germany, as in many tourist centers worldwide, hotels routinely overbook, so booking by credit card doesn't automatically hold your room if you arrive later than expected or after 6pm. The hotel clerk always asks when you expect to arrive, and the hotel usually holds the room until that time. Always pad your expected arrival by a few hours to be safe. However, all bets are off after 7pm, and the hotel is likely to give your room away unless you call and specifically ask them to hold it. If you've made a reservation very far in advance, confirm within 24 hours of your expected arrival. If you're experiencing a major delay, alert the hotel as soon as you can.

Beware of billing. Readers report that sometimes in Germany they booked a room online (say, $100 a night) but were charged $125 when they checked out. Keep your online confirmation in case of a dispute.

Saving on Your Hotel Room

The **rack rate** is the maximum rate that a hotel charges for a room. Hardly anybody pays this price, however, except in high season or on holidays. To lower the cost of your room:

○ **Ask about special rates or other discounts.** You may qualify for corporate, student, military, senior, frequent-flier, trade union, or other discounts.

○ **Dial direct.** When booking a room in a chain hotel, you'll often get a better deal by calling the individual hotel's reservation desk rather than the chain's main number.

○ **Book online.** Many hotels offer Internet-only discounts, or supply rooms to Priceline, Hotwire, or Expedia at rates much lower than the ones you can get through the hotel itself.

○ **Remember the law of supply and demand.** You can save big on hotel rooms by traveling in a destination's off season or shoulder seasons, when rates typically drop, even at luxury properties.

○ **Look into group or long-stay discounts.** If you come as part of a large group, you should be able to negotiate a bargain rate. Likewise, if you're planning a long stay (at least 5 days), you might qualify for a discount. As a general rule, expect 1 night free after a 7-night stay.

○ **Sidestep excess surcharges and hidden costs.** Many hotels have adopted the unpleasant practice of nickel-and-diming their guests with opaque surcharges. When you book a room, ask what is included in the room rate, and what is extra. Avoid dialing direct from hotel phones, which can have exorbitant rates. And don't be tempted by the room's minibar offerings: Most hotels charge through the nose for water, soda, and snacks. Finally, ask about local taxes and service charges, which can increase the cost of a room by 15% or more.

○ Carefully consider your hotel's meal plan. If you enjoy eating out and sampling the local cuisine, it makes sense to choose a **Continental Plan (CP),** which includes breakfast only, or a **European Plan (EP),** which doesn't include any meals and allows you maximum flexibility. If you're more interested in saving money, opt for a **Modified American Plan (MAP),** which includes breakfast and one meal, or the **American Plan (AP),** which includes three meals. If you must choose a MAP, see if you can get a free lunch at your hotel if you decide to do dinner out.

○ **Book an efficiency.** A room with a kitchenette allows you to shop for groceries and cook your own meals. This is a big money saver, especially for families on long stays.

○ **Consider enrolling in hotel chains' "frequent-stay" programs,** which are upping the ante lately to win the loyalty of repeat customers. Frequent guests can now accumulate points or credits to earn free hotel nights, airline miles, in-room amenities, merchandise, tickets to concerts and events, discounts on sporting facilities—and even credit toward stock in the participating hotel, in the case of the Jameson Inn hotel group. Perks are awarded not only by many chain hotels and motels (Hilton HHonors, Marriott Rewards, and Wyndham ByRequest, to name a few), but by individual inns and B&Bs. Many chain hotels partner with other hotel chains, car-rental firms, airlines, and credit card companies to give consumers additional incentive to do repeat business.

For more tips on surfing for hotel deals online, visit Frommers.com.

Landing the Best Room

Somebody has to get the best room in the house. It might as well be you. You can start by joining the hotel's frequent-guest program, which may make you eligible for upgrades. A hotel-branded credit card usually gives its owner "silver" or "gold" status in frequent-guest programs for free. Always ask about a corner room. They're often larger and quieter, with more windows and light, and they often cost the same as standard rooms. When you make your reservation, ask if the hotel is renovating; if it is, request a room away from the construction. Ask about nonsmoking rooms and rooms with views. Be sure to request your choice of twin, queen-, or king-size beds. If you're a light sleeper, ask for a quiet room away from vending or ice machines, elevators, restaurants, bars, and dance clubs. Ask for a room that has been recently renovated or refurbished.

If you aren't happy with your room when you arrive, ask for another one. Most lodgings will be willing to accommodate you.

In resort areas, ask the following questions before you book a room:

○ What's the view like? Cost-conscious travelers may be willing to pay less for a back room facing the parking lot, especially if they don't plan to spend much time in their room.

○ Does the room have air-conditioning or ceiling fans? Do the windows open? If they do, and the nighttime entertainment takes place alfresco, you may want to find out when showtime is over.

○ What's included in the price? Your room may be moderately priced, but if you're charged for beach chairs, towels, sports equipment, and other amenities, you could end up spending more than you bargained for.

B&B Stays

Many travelers prefer to go the B&B route when touring Germany. This can be an inexpensive alternative to all those pricey hotels. However, some B&Bs, just as in America, are more luxurious than even a first-class hotel. Naturally, these come with a higher price tag. Breakfast, as promised in the name, is served, and often the staff at a B&B will pack you a picnic lunch if you're staying over in the area and want to go hiking. In some cases, and only if arranged in advance, a home-cooked German dinner might be served.

For reservations, contact **Bed & Breakfast Inns Online** (© **800/215-7365** or 310/280-4363; www.bbonline.com) or **BnB Finder.com** (© **888/547-8226** or 212/432-7693; www.bnbfinder.com).

Bungalow, Villa & Apartment Rentals

Dozens of agencies handle such rentals, the best of which include **At Home Abroad, Inc.** (© **212/421-9165;** www.athomeabroadinc.com). **Drawbridge to Europe** (© **888/268-1148;** www.drawbridgetoeurope.com) offers vacation rentals in Mittel Europa, including not only Germany but also Switzerland and Austria. The staff will even rent you a private castle. **Interhome** (© **800/882-6864** or 954/791-8282; www.interhomeusa.com) offers properties in 21 countries, including Germany.

Castle Hotels

There are more *Schlosshotels* (castle hotels) in Germany than anywhere else in Europe. After unification, many castles in the old East Germany were restored and opened to the public. Some are rather basic, having more character than comfort, but others are luxurious, with antiques such as four-poster beds and a baronial atmosphere, often harking back 3 centuries or more. Most of them have installed modern plumbing. Some visitors with a sense of the romantic book castle hotel packages throughout Germany. The best source for such vacations is **Euro-Connections** (© **800/645-3876** in the U.S.; www.traveldata.cc).

Farm Vacations

Growing in its appeal to tourists, a vacation down on the farm—*Urlaub auf dem Bauernhof* in German—cuts costs and is an adventure as well. Nearly every local tourist office has a list of farmhouses in its area that take in paying guests. Sometimes only bed-and-breakfast is offered; at other places a farm-style home-cooked dinner can be included if you wish. For more information, you can contact **DLG** (German Agricultural Association) at © **069/247880** (www.landtourismus.de).

House Swapping

House swapping is becoming a more popular and viable means of travel; you stay in their place, they stay in yours, and you both get a more authentic and personal view of a destination, the opposite of the escapist retreat many hotels offer. Try **Home-Link International** (www.homelink.org), the largest and oldest home-swapping organization, founded in 1952, with more than 11,000 listings worldwide ($115 yearly membership). **HomeExchange.com** ($9.95 a month for 6,000 listings) and **InterVac.com** ($100 for more than 10,000 listings) are also reliable.

Romantik Hotels

Throughout Germany you'll encounter hotels with a "Romantik" in their names. This is not a chain, but a voluntary association of small inns and guesthouses that have only one theme in common: They are usually old and charming, and romantic in architecture. If you like a traditional ambience as opposed to bandbox modern, then a Romantik hotel might be for you. The requirement is that the hotel be in a historic building (or at least one of vintage date) and personally managed by the owner. Usually you get a regional cuisine and good, personal service, along with an old-fashioned setting and cozy charm. Sometimes the plumbing could be better, and standards of comfort vary widely, but all of them have been inspected.

For more information, contact **Romantik Hotels and Restaurants (© 800/650-8018** in the U.S., or 069/6612340 in Germany; www.romantikhotels.com).

Spa Hotels

More than any other country in Europe, Germany has developed the spa process to a high art. The heyday of German spa construction coincided with the rise of the bourgeoisie in the 19th century, when a lavish series of resorts was built around the dozens of mineral springs bubbling from the soil. Many of these springs had been known since the Middle Ages, or even Roman times, and to each was attributed specific cures for arthritis, gout, infertility, hypertension, and gynecological problems. (The German word *Kur—Kurort* means "spa"—is derived from the Latin *cura*, meaning "care.") Going to a spa became an intensely ritualized social experience.

Regardless of the various medical claims made at the spas of Germany, the real reason to go to any spa, in our view, is to momentarily escape the stress of everyday life.

For more information, contact **Deutschen Heilbaderverbandes,** Reinhardtstrasse 46, 10117 Berlin (© **030/2463629-0;** www.deutscher-heilbaederverband.de).

Youth Hostels

Germany has some of the best and most modern youth hostels (*Jugendherbergen*) in the world—some 550 of them are scattered throughout the country. Reservations are imperative in all cases, but especially in July and August. Venues range from rather bleak modern buildings to old castles in bucolic settings.

For more information and requirements, contact **DJH Service GmbH,** Bismarckstrasse 8, 32756 Detmold (© **05231/74010;** www.jugendherberge.de). Most hostels in Germany are affiliated with **Hostelling International USA (© 301/495-1240;** www.hiusa.org).

[FastFACTS] GERMANY

Business Hours Most **banks** are open Monday to Friday 8:30am to 1pm and 2:30 to 4pm (Thurs to 5:30pm). Money exchanges at airports and border-crossing points are generally open daily from 6am to 10pm. Exchanges at border railroad stations are kept open for arrivals of all international trains. Most **businesses** are open Monday to Friday from 9am to 5pm and on Saturday from 9am to 1pm. Store hours can vary from town to town, but **shops** are generally open Monday to Friday 9 or 10am to 6 or 6:30pm (Thurs to 8:30pm). Saturday hours are generally from 9am to 1 or 2pm, except on the first Saturday of the month, when stores may remain open until 4pm.

Car Rental See "By Car" under "Getting Around," earlier in this chapter.

Cellphones See "Mobile Phones," later.

Crime See "Safety," later.

Customs You can take into Germany most personal effects and the following items duty-free: one video camera or two still cameras with 10 rolls of film each; a portable radio, a tape recorder, and a laptop PC, provided they show signs of use; 400 cigarettes, 50 cigars, or 250 grams of tobacco; 2 liters of wine or 1 liter of liquor per person 18 and over; fishing gear; one bicycle; skis; tennis or squash racquets; and golf clubs.

Returning **U.S. citizens** who have been away for at least 48 hours can bring back, once every 30 days, US$800 worth of merchandise duty-free. You'll be charged a flat rate of 4% duty on the next US$1,000 worth of purchases. Be sure to have your receipts handy. On mailed gifts, the duty-free limit is US$200. With some exceptions, you cannot bring fresh fruits and vegetables into the United States. For specifics on what you can bring back, download the invaluable free pamphlet *Know Before You Go* online at **www.cbp. gov**. Or contact the **U.S. Customs & Border Protection (CBP),** 1300 Pennsylvania Ave. NW, Washington, DC 20229 (✆ **877/287-8667**), and request the pamphlet.

For a clear summary of **Canadian rules,** you can download the booklet *I Declare* at www.cbsa-asfc.gc.ca/publications. It is issued by Canada Border Services Agency (✆ **800/461-9999** in Canada, or 204/983-3500; www.cbsa-asfc.gc.ca). Canada allows a C$750 exemption, which can be used only once a year and only after an absence of 7 days. You're allowed to bring back duty-free one carton of cigarettes, one can of tobacco, 40 imperial ounces of liquor, and 50 cigars. In addition, you're allowed to mail gifts to Canada valued at less than C$60 a day, provided they're unsolicited and don't contain alcohol or tobacco (write on the package "Unsolicited gift, under C$60 value"). You should declare all valuables on the Y-38 form before departing Canada, including serial numbers of valuables you already own, such as expensive foreign cameras.

Citizens of the U.K. who are **returning from an E.U. country** will go through a separate Customs exit (called the "Blue Exit"). In essence, there is no limit on what you can bring back from an E.U. country, as long as the items are for personal use (including gifts) and you have already paid the necessary duty and tax. However, Customs law sets out guidance levels. If you bring in more than these levels, you may be asked to prove that the goods are for your use. Guidance levels on goods bought in the E.U. for your own use are 3,200 cigarettes, 200 cigars, 400 cigarillos, 3 kilograms of smoking tobacco, 10 liters of spirits, 90 liters of wine, 20 liters of fortified wine (such as port or sherry), and 110 liters of beer. For information, contact **HM Revenue Customs** at ✆ **0845/0109000** (✆ 02920/501261 from outside the U.K.), or consult their website at **www.hmrc.gov.uk**.

The duty-free allowance in **Australia** is A$900 or, for those 17 and under, A$450. Citizens can bring in 250 cigarettes or 250 grams of loose tobacco, and 2.25 liters of alcohol. If you're returning with valuables you already own, such as foreign-made cameras, you should file form B263. A helpful brochure available from Australian consulates or Customs offices is *Know Before You Go.* For more information, call the **Australian Customs Service** at ✆ **1300/363263,** or log on to www.customs.gov.au.

The duty-free allowance for **New Zealand** is NZ$700. Citizens 18 and over can bring in 200 cigarettes, 50 cigars, or 250 grams of tobacco (or a mixture of all three if their combined weight doesn't exceed 250g); plus 4.5 liters of wine and beer, or 1.125 milliliters of liquor. New Zealand currency does not carry import or export restrictions. Fill out a certificate of export, listing the valuables you are taking out of the country, so you can bring them back without paying duty. Most questions are answered in a free pamphlet available at New Zealand consulates and Customs offices: *New Zealand Customs Guide for Travellers, Notice no. 4.* For more information, contact **New Zealand Customs Service,** The Customhouse, 17–21 Whitmore St., Box 2218, Wellington (✆ **0800/428786** or 04/4736099 in New Zealand, or 04/4736099; www.customs.govt.nz).

Disabled Travelers   Germany is one of the better countries for travelers with disabilities. All the large cities have excellent facilities. The local tourist offices can issue permits for drivers to allow them access to parking areas for people with disabilities. Newer hotels are more sensitive to the needs of those with disabilities, and the more expensive restaurants, in general, are wheelchair accessible.

Older, smaller towns may pose more of a problem, however, especially where the streets are cobblestone. Also, because of Germany's many hills and endless flights of stairs, visitors with disabilities may have difficulty getting around outside of major cities, but conditions are slowly improving. If the areas you wish to visit seem inaccessible or you are not certain, you may want to consider taking an organized tour specifically designed to accommodate travelers with disabilities.

Organizations that offer assistance to travelers with disabilities include **MossRehab** (*C* **800/225-5667;** www.mossresourcenet.org), which provides a library of accessible-travel resources online; **Society for Accessible Travel & Hospitality (SATH;** *C* **212/447-7284;** www.sath.org), which offers a wealth of travel resources for all types of disabilities and informed recommendations on destinations, access guides, travel agents, tour operators, vehicle rentals, and companion services; and the **American Foundation for the Blind (AFB;** *C* **800/232-5463** or 212/502-7600; www.afb.org), a referral resource for those who are blind or visually impaired that provides information on traveling with Seeing Eye dogs.

Air Ambulance Card (*C* **877/4247633;** www.airambulancecard.com) is now partnered with SATH and allows you to preselect top-notch hospitals in case of an emergency.

Access-Able Travel Source (*C* **303/232-2979;** www.access-able.com) offers a comprehensive database on travel agents from around the world with experience in accessible travel; destination-specific access information; and links to such resources as service animals, equipment rentals, and access guides.

Many travel agencies offer customized tours and itineraries for travelers with disabilities. Among them are **Flying Wheels Travel** (*C* **507/451-5005;** www.flyingwheelstravel.com) and **Accessible Journeys** (*C* **800/846-4537** or 610/521-0339; www.disabilitytravel.com).

Flying with Disability (www.flying-with-disability.org) is a comprehensive information source on airplane travel.

Also check out the quarterly magazine ***Emerging Horizons*** (www.emerginghorizons.com), available by subscription ($17 per year in the U.S.; $22 outside the U.S.).

The "Accessible Travel" link at **Mobility-Advisor.com** (www.mobility-advisor.com) offers a variety of travel resources to persons with disabilities.

British travelers should contact **Holiday Care** (*C* **0845/124-9971** in the U.K. only; www.holidaycare.org.uk) to access a wide range of travel information and resources for seniors and people with disabilities.

For more on organizations that offer resources to travelers with disabilities, go to Frommers.com.

Doctors   Contact the **International Association for Medical Assistance to Travelers (IAMAT;** *C* **716/754-4883** or 416/652-0137; www.iamat.org) for tips on travel and health concerns in Germany and lists of local, English-speaking doctors. You can find listings of reliable medical clinics in Germany at the **International Society of Travel Medicine** (www.istm.org).

Drinking Laws   As in many European countries, drinking laws are flexible, enforced only if a problem develops. Officially, you must be 18 to consume any kind of alcoholic beverage. Bars and cafes rarely request proof of age. Drinking while driving, however, is treated as a very serious offense.

Driving Rules   See "Getting Around," earlier in this chapter.

Electricity   In most places, the electricity is 220 volts AC (50 cycles). You will need a transformer and a plug that fits the German socket for your U.S. appliances. Many leading hotels will supply these

Embassies & Consulates   The following embassies and consulates are in Berlin. The embassy of the **United States** is at Pariser Platz 2 (© **030/83050;** http://germany.us embassy.gov; U-Bahn: Brandenburger Tor), open Monday to Friday 8:30am to 3pm. The **U.K. Embassy** is at Wilhelmstrasse 70 (© **030/204570;** http://ukingermany.fco.gov.uk/ de; U-Bahn: Anhalter Bahnhof), open Monday to Friday 8am to 4:30pm. The **Australian Embassy** is at Wallstrasse 76–79 (© **030/8800880;** www.germany.embassy.gov.au/beln/ home.html; U-Bahn: Spittel-markt), open Monday to Thursday 8:30am to 5pm and Friday 8:30am to 4:15pm. The **Canadian Embassy** is at Leipziger Platz 17 (© **030/203120;** www. canadainternational.gc.ca; U-Bahn: Potsdamer Platz), open Monday to Friday 9am to noon. The **Irish Embassy** is at Friedrichstrasse 200 (© **030/220720;** www.embassyof ireland.de; U-Bahn: Uhlandstrasse), open Monday to Friday 9:30am to noon and 2:30 to 3:45pm. The **New Zealand Embassy** is at Friedrichstrasse 60 (© **030/206210;** www. nzembassy.com; U-Bahn: Friedrichstrasse), open Monday to Friday 9am to 1pm and 2 to 5:30pm.

Emergencies   Throughout Germany the emergency number for **police** is © **110;** for fire or to call an ambulance, dial © **112.**

Family Travel   To locate accommodations, restaurants, and attractions that are particularly kid-friendly, look for the "Kids" icon throughout this guide.

Health   Germany should not pose any major health hazards. The heavy cuisine may give some travelers mild diarrhea, so take along some antidiarrhea medicine and moderate your eating habits. The water is safe to drink throughout Germany; however, don't drink from mountain streams, no matter how clear and pure the water looks.

German medical facilities are among the best in the world. If a medical emergency arises, your hotel staff can usually put you in touch with a reliable doctor. If not, contact the American embassy or a consulate; each one maintains a list of English-speaking doctors. Medical and hospital services aren't free, so be sure that you have appropriate insurance coverage before you travel.

If you suffer from a chronic illness, consult your doctor before your departure. Pack **prescription medications** in your carry-on luggage and carry them in their original containers, with pharmacy labels—otherwise they won't make it through airport security. Carry the generic name of prescription medicines, in case a local pharmacist is unfamiliar with the brand name.

For conditions such as epilepsy, diabetes, or heart problems, wear a **MedicAlert Identification Tag** (© **888/633-4298;** www.medicalert.org), which will immediately alert doctors to your condition and give them access to your records through MedicAlert's 24-hour hot line.

Insurance   For travel overseas, most U.S. health plans (including Medicare and Medicaid) do not provide coverage, and the ones that do often require you to pay for services upfront and reimburse you only after you return home.

As a safety net, you may want to buy travel medical insurance. If you require additional medical insurance, try **MEDEX Assistance** (© **800/732-5309** or 410/453-6300; www.medexassist.com) or **Travel Assistance International** (© **800/821-2828;** www. travelassistance.com; for general information on services, call **Worldwide Assistance Services, Inc.** at © **800/777-8710;** www.worldwideassistance.com).

Canadians should check with their provincial health-plan offices or call **Health Canada** (© **866/225-0709;** www.hc-sc.gc.ca) to find out the extent of their coverage and what documentation and receipts they must take home if they are treated overseas.

Travelers from the U.K. should carry their European Health Insurance Card (EHIC), which replaced the E111 form as proof of entitlement to free/reduced-cost medical treatment abroad (℃ **0845/605-0707;** www.ehic.org.uk). Note, however, that the EHIC covers only "necessary medical treatment"; for repatriation costs, lost money, baggage, or cancellation, travel insurance from a reputable company should always be sought. Call ℃ **0870/033-9985** or visit **www.travelinsuranceweb.com** for quotes from several companies.

Travel Insurance The cost of travel insurance varies widely, depending on the destination, the cost and length of your trip, your age and health, and the type of trip you're taking, but expect to pay between 5% and 8% of the vacation itself. You can get estimates from various providers through **InsureMyTrip.com** (℃ **800/487-4722**). Enter your trip cost and dates, your age, and other information, for prices from more than a dozen companies.

U.K. citizens and their families who make more than one trip abroad per year may find that an annual travel insurance policy works out cheaper. Check **www.moneysupermarket.com** (℃ **0845/345-5708**), which compares prices across a wide range of providers for single- and multitrip policies.

Most big travel agents offer their own insurance and will probably try to sell you their package when you book a holiday. Think before you sign. **Britain's Consumers' Association** recommends that you insist on seeing the policy and reading the fine print before buying travel insurance. The **Association of British Insurers** (℃ **020/7600-3333;** www. abi.org.uk) gives advice by phone and publishes "Holiday Insurance," a free guide to policy provisions and prices. You might also shop around for better deals: Try **Columbus Direct** (℃ **0870/033-9988;** www.columbusdirect.net).

Trip-Cancellation Insurance Trip-cancellation insurance will help retrieve your money if you have to back out of a trip or depart early, or if your travel supplier goes bankrupt. Trip cancellation traditionally covers such events as sickness, natural disasters, and State Department advisories. The latest news in trip-cancellation insurance is the availability of **expanded hurricane coverage** and the **"any-reason"** cancellation coverage—which costs more but covers cancellations made for any reason. You won't get back 100% of your prepaid trip cost, but you'll be refunded a substantial portion. **TravelSafe** (℃ **888/885-7233;** www.travelsafe.com) offers both types of coverage. Expedia also offers any-reason cancellation coverage for its air-hotel packages. For details, contact one of the following recommended insurers: **Access America** (℃ 800/284-8300; www.accessamerica.com), **Travel Guard International** (℃ 800/826-4919; www.travelguard.com), **Travel Insured International** (℃ 800/243-3174; www.travelinsured.com), and **Travelex Insurance Services** (℃ 800/228-9792; www.travelex-insurance.com)..

Internet & Wi-Fi Many hotels, cafes, and retailers are signing on as Wi-Fi "hot spots." **Boingo** (www.boingo.com) and **Wayport** (wayport.com) have set up networks in airports and high-class hotel lobbies. IPass providers (see below) also give you access to a few hundred wireless hotel lobby setups. To locate other hot spots that provide **free wireless networks** in cities in Germany, go to **www.jiwire.com**.

A few thousand hotels in Germany now offer free high-speed Internet access. In addition, major Internet service providers (ISPs) have **local access numbers** around the world, allowing you to go online by placing a local call. The **iPass** network also has dial-up numbers around the world. You'll have to sign up with an iPass provider, who will then tell you how to set up your computer for your destination(s). For a list of iPass providers, go to www3.ipass.com and click on "Individuals Buy Now." One solid provider is **i2roam** (℃ **866/811-6209** or 920/233-5863; www.i2roam.com).

To find cybercafes, check **www.cybercaptive.com** and **www.cybercafe.com**. Cybercafes can be found on almost every business street in large cities.

Aside from formal cybercafes, most **youth hostels** and **public libraries** have Internet access.

Language German, of course, is the official language, but English is widely understood. Germans start learning English in grade school.

LGBT Travelers Although Germany is one of the "gayest" countries of Europe, there is also prejudice and hostility here. Violence against gays and foreigners (especially nonwhite) is not unknown. On the other hand, homosexuality is widely accepted by a vast number of the country's millions, especially young people. All major cities have a wide and varied gay and lesbian nightlife. Keep in mind that western Germany is far more gay-friendly than the more isolated outposts of the former East Germany. The legal minimum age for consensual homosexual sex is 18.

The **International Gay and Lesbian Travel Association** (IGLTA; ✆ 954/630-1637; www.iglta.org) is the trade association for the gay and lesbian travel industry and offers an online directory of gay- and lesbian-friendly travel businesses; go to its website and click on "Members."

Many agencies offer tours and travel itineraries designed specifically for gay and lesbian travelers. **Now, Voyager** (✆ 800/255-6951; www.nowvoyager.com) is a well-known San Francisco–based gay-owned and -operated travel service. **Olivia Cruises & Resorts** (✆ 800/631-6277; www.olivia.com) charters entire resorts and ships for exclusive lesbian vacations and offers smaller group experiences for both gay and lesbian travelers. **Gay. com** (✆ 415/834-6500; http://daily.gay.com/travel) provides regularly updated information about gay-owned, gay-oriented, and gay-friendly lodging, dining, sightseeing, nightlife, and shopping establishments in every important destination worldwide.

The Canadian website **GayTraveler** (www.gaytraveler.ca) offers ideas and advice for gay travel all over the world.

The following travel guides are available at many bookstores, or you can order them from any online bookseller: *Spartacus International Gay Guide,* 38th edition (Bruno Gmünder Verlag; www.spartacusworld.com/gayguide); and the *Damron* guides (www.damron.com), with separate annual books for gay men and lesbians.

For more gay and lesbian travel resources, visit Frommers.com.

Mail Street mailboxes are painted yellow. It costs 1.70€ for the first 5 grams (about ⅕ oz.) to send an airmail letter to the United States or Canada, and 1€ for postcards. All letters to the U.K. cost .70€.

Medical Requirements Unless you're arriving from an area known to be suffering from an epidemic (particularly cholera or yellow fever), inoculations or vaccinations are not required for entry into Germany.

Mobile Phones The three letters that define much of the world's wireless capabilities are GSM, which stands for Global System for Mobiles, a big, seamless network that makes for easy cross-border cellphone use. In general, reception is good. But you'll need a Subscriber Identity Module (SIM) card. This is a small chip that gives you a local phone number and plugs you into a regional network. In the U.S., T-Mobile and AT&T Wireless use this quasi-universal system; in Canada, Microcell and some Rogers customers are GSM, and all Europeans and most Australians use GSM. Unfortunately, per-minute charges can be high.

For many, **renting** a phone is a good idea. While you can rent a phone from any number of overseas sites, including kiosks at airports and at car-rental agencies, we suggest renting the phone before you leave home. North Americans can rent one before leaving home from **InTouch USA** (✆ 800/872-7626 or 703/222-7161; www.intouchglobal.com) or **RoadPost** (✆ 888/290-1616 or 905/272-5665; www.roadpost.com). InTouch will also, for free, advise you on whether your existing phone will work overseas.

Buying a phone can be economically attractive, as many nations have cheap prepaid phone systems. Once you arrive at your destination, stop by a local cellphone shop and get the cheapest package; you'll probably pay less than $100 for a phone and a starter calling card. Local calls may be as low as 10¢ per minute, and in Germany incoming calls are free.

Money & Costs The **euro** (€) is the single European currency of Germany and other participating countries. Exchange rates of participating countries are locked into a common currency fluctuating against the dollar.

The major cities of Germany are some of the world's most expensive. So, if you want to see the country without breaking the bank, you may want to cut short your time in Frankfurt, Munich, or Berlin and concentrate on regional capitals such as Freiburg in the Black Forest, where you can cut your travel cost by anywhere from 20% to 40%. You may also want to consider a rail pass.

Although prices in Germany are high, you generally get good value for your money. The inflation rate has remained low. Hotels are usually clean and comfortable, and restaurants generally offer good cuisine and ample portions made with quality ingredients. Trains are fast and on time, and most service personnel treat you with respect.

Many people come to Germany just for winter sports. The most expensive resorts are places like Garmisch-Partenkirchen. However, if you avoid the chic places, you can enjoy winter fun at a moderate cost. Some of the winter spots in the Bavarian Alps that haven't been overrun by the beautiful people give you great value for your money. And prices in a village next to a resort are often 30% lower than at the resort itself.

In Germany, many prices for children (generally defined as ages 6–17) are considerably lower than for adults. And fees for children 5 and younger are often waived entirely.

THE VALUE OF THE EURO VS. OTHER POPULAR CURRENCIES

Euro (€)	Aus$	Can$	NZ$	UK£	US$
€1	A$1.33	C$1.37	NZ$1.79	£0.87	$1.41

Frommer's lists exact prices in the local currency. The currency conversions quoted above were correct at press time. However, rates fluctuate, so before departing consult a currency exchange website such as **www.oanda.com/currency/converter** to check up-to-the-minute rates.

ATMs The easiest way to get cash away from home is from an ATM (automated teller machine), sometimes referred to as a *Geldautomat*. **Note:** Remember that many banks impose a fee every time you use a card at another bank's ATM, and that fee can be higher for international transactions. In addition, the bank from which you withdraw cash may charge its own fee. For international withdrawal fees, ask your bank.

Note: Banks that are members of the **Global ATM Alliance** charge no transaction fees for cash withdrawals at other Alliance member ATMs; these include Bank of America, Scotiabank (Canada, Caribbean, and Mexico), Barclays (U.K. and parts of Africa), Deutsche Bank (Germany, Poland, Spain, and Italy), and BNP Paribas (France).

Credit Cards Credit cards are another safe way to carry money. They also provide a convenient record of all your expenses, and they generally offer relatively good exchange rates. You can withdraw cash advances from your credit cards at banks or ATMs, but high fees make credit card cash advances a pricey way to get cash. Remember that you'll pay interest from the moment of your withdrawal, even if you pay your monthly bills on time. Also, note that many banks now assess a 1% to 3% "transaction fee" on *all* charges you incur abroad (whether you're using the local currency or your native currency).

WHAT THINGS COST IN BERLIN	EUROS
Taxi from Tegel airport to Europa-Center	25.00
Average ride on the Underground (U-Bahn)	2.10
Double room at the Brandenburger Hof (very expensive)	295.00
Double room at the Savoy (expensive)	146.00
Double room at Askanischer Hof (moderate)	118.00
Double room at Alexandra Hotel Pension (inexpensive)	45.00
Lunch for one at Arlecchino (moderate)	24.00
Lunch for one at Lubitsch (inexpensive)	16.00
Dinner for one, without wine, at Alt-Luxemburg (very expensive)	48.00
Dinner for one, without wine, at Funkturm Restaurant (moderate)	30.00
Dinner for one, without wine, at StäV (inexpensive)	16.00
Half a liter of beer	3.50
Coca-Cola in a restaurant	2.20
Cup of coffee	2.00–2.50
Glass of wine	3.00–3.50
Admission to Alte Nationalgalerie	8.00
Movie ticket	8.00–20.00
Ticket to Berlin Philharmonic Orchestra	20.00–85.00

In Germany, American Express, Diners Club, MasterCard, and Visa are commonly accepted, with the latter two cards predominating.

Beware of hidden credit-card fees while traveling. Check with your credit or debit card issuer to see what fees, if any, will be charged for overseas transactions. Recent reform legislation in the U.S., for example, has curbed some exploitative lending practices. But many banks have responded by increasing fees in other areas, including fees for customers who use credit and debit cards while out of the country—even if those charges were made in U.S. dollars. Fees can amount to 3% or more of the purchase price. Check with your bank before departing to avoid any surprise charges on your statement.

For help with currency conversions, tip calculations, and more, download Frommer's convenient Travel Tools app for your mobile device. Go to www.frommers.com/go/mobile and click on the "Travel Tools" icon.

Passports Visas are not needed by citizens of the U.S., Canada, Ireland, Australia, New Zealand, or the U.K. for visits of less than 3 months. You do need a valid passport, unless you're a citizen of the E.U., EEA or Switzerland (in which case you need only an identity card, though we recommend you always carry a passport anyway).

Passport Offices

Australia   Australian Passport Information Service (☎ 131-232, or visit www.passports. gov.au).

Canada   Passport Office, Department of Foreign Affairs and International Trade, Ottawa, ON K1A 0G3 (☎ 800/567-6868; www.ppt.gc.ca).

Ireland   Passport Office, Setanta Centre, Molesworth Street, Dublin 2 (📞 01/671-1633; www.foreignaffairs.gov.ie).

New Zealand   Passports Office, Department of Internal Affairs, 47 Boulcott Street, Wellington, 6011 (📞 0800/225-050 in New Zealand or 04/474-8100; www.passports. govt.nz).

United Kingdom   Visit your nearest passport office, major post office, or travel agency or contact the Identity and Passport Service (IPS), 89 Eccleston Square, London, SW1V 1PN (📞 0300/222-0000; www.ips.gov.uk).

United States   To find your regional passport office, check the U.S. State Department website (travel.state.gov/passport) or call the National Passport Information Center (📞 877/487-2778) for automated information.

Police   Throughout the country, dial 📞 **110** for emergencies.

Safety   Overall, the security risk to travelers in Germany is low. However, Germany experiences a number of demonstrations every year on a variety of political and economic themes. These demonstrations have a tendency to spread and turn violent, and anyone in the general area can become the victim of a random attack. Prior police approval is required for public demonstrations in Germany, and police oversight is routinely provided to ensure adequate security for participants and passersby. Nonetheless, situations may develop that could pose a threat to public safety. All foreign visitors are cautioned to avoid the area around protests and demonstrations and to check local media for updates on the situation.

In addition, hooligans, most often young and intoxicated "skinheads," have been known to harass or even attack people whom they believe to be foreigners or members of rival youth groups. While U.S. citizens have not been specific targets, several Americans have reported that they were assaulted for racial reasons or because they appeared "foreign."

Violent crime is rare in Germany, but it can occur, especially in larger cities or high-risk areas such as train stations. Most incidents of street crime consist of theft of unattended items and pickpocketing. You should take the same precautions against becoming a crime victim as you would in any city.

Report the loss or theft abroad of your passport immediately to the local police and the nearest embassy or consulate. If you are the victim of a crime while in Germany, in addition to reporting to local police, contact the nearest embassy or consulate for assistance. The embassy/consulate staff, for example, can assist you in finding appropriate medical care, contacting family members or friends, and explaining how funds could be transferred. Although the investigation and prosecution of the crime is solely the responsibility of local authorities, consular officers can help you understand the local criminal-justice process and find an attorney if needed

Senior Travel   Mention that you're a senior when you make your travel reservations. Although all major U.S. airlines have canceled their senior-discount and coupon-book programs, many hotels still offer discounts for seniors. In most cities, people 60 and over qualify for reduced admission to theaters, museums, and other attractions, as well as discounted fares on public transportation.

Members of **AARP,** 601 E St. NW, Washington, DC 20049 (📞 **888/687-2277;** www. aarp.org), get discounts on hotels, airfares, and car rentals. AARP offers members a wide range of benefits, including *AARP The Magazine* and a monthly newsletter. Anyone 50 and over can join.

Many reliable agencies and organizations target the 50-plus market. **Exploritas**'s (📞 **800/454-5768;** www.exploritas.org) programs include a wide spectrum in Germany. The most popular is a 10-night program in both Berlin and Munich, where participants join local experts to learn about the history and culture of Germany. For the more athletic, there is a 13-night program spent biking along the Danube. Those interested in opera and classical music can join a 12-night cultural and fine arts program that takes place in the vibrant cultural cities of Berlin, Dresden, and Leipzig.

Recommended publications offering travel resources and discounts for seniors include the quarterly magazine *Travel 50 & Beyond* (www.travel50andbeyond.com) and the best-selling paperback *Unbelievably Good Deals and Great Adventures That You Absolutely Can't Get Unless You're Over 50* (McGraw-Hill), by Joann Rattner Heilman.

Frommers.com offers more information and resources on travel for seniors

Smoking   Check before lighting up. In general, you cannot smoke in most restaurants and many bars in Germany, but it is in a continuous state of flux and rules vary by federal state—in some cases smoking is banned by law and enforced. In other cases the official law is not enforced in bars of a certain size, or after the kitchen closes at restaurants that are open late and morph into a barlike setting as the night goes on. Throughout the country, smoking is banned in all public buildings and transport.

Taxes   As a member of the European Union, Germany imposes a tax on most goods and services known as a **value-added tax (VAT)** or, in German, *Mehrwertsteuer.* Nearly everything is taxed at 16%, including vital necessities such as gas and luxury items such as jewelry. Food and books are taxed at 7%. VAT is included in the prices of restaurants and hotels. Goods for sale, such as cameras, also have the 16% tax already factored into the price. Stores that display a tax-free sticker will issue you a **Tax-Free Shopping Check** at the time of purchase. When leaving the country, have your check stamped by the German Customs Service as your proof of legal export. You can then get a cash refund at one of the Tax-Free Shopping Service offices in the major airports and many train stations, even at some of the bigger ferry terminals. Otherwise, you must send the checks to Tax-Free Shopping Service, Mengstrasse 19, 23552 Lübeck, Germany. If you want the payment to be credited to your bank card or your bank account, mention this. There is no airport departure tax.

Telephones   The country code for Germany is 49. To call Germany from the United States, dial the international access code 011, then 49, then the city code, then the regular phone number. *Note:* The phone numbers listed in this book are to be used within Germany; when calling from abroad, omit the initial 0 in the city code.

For directory assistance: Dial ℂ **11837** if you're looking for a number inside Germany, and dial ℂ **11834** for numbers to all other countries.

For operator assistance: If you need operator assistance in making a call, dial ℂ **0180/200-1033.**

Local and long-distance calls may be placed from all post offices and from most public telephone booths, about half of which operate with phone cards, the others with coins. Phone cards are sold at post offices and newsstands in denominations of 6€ to 25€. Rates are measured in units rather than minutes. The farther the distance, the more units are consumed. Telephone calls made through hotel switchboards can double, triple, or even quadruple the base charges at the post office, so be alert to this before you dial. In some instances, post offices can send faxes for you, and many hotels offer Internet access—for free or for a small charge—to their guests.

German phone numbers are not standard. In some places, numbers have as few as three digits. In cities, one number may have five digits, whereas the phone next door might have nine. Germans also often hyphenate their numbers differently. But since all the area codes are the same, these various configurations should have little effect on your phone usage once you get used to the fact that numbers vary from place to place.

Be careful dialing **toll-free numbers.** Many companies maintain a service line beginning with 0180. However, these lines might appear to be toll-free but really aren't, costing .12€ per minute. Other numbers that begin with 0190 carry a surcharge of 1.85€ per minute—or even more. Don't be misled by calling a 1-800 number in the United States from Germany. This is not a toll-free call but costs about the same as an overseas call.

To call the U.S. or Canada from Germany, dial 01, followed by the country code (1), then the area code, and then the number. Alternatively, you can dial the various telecommunication companies in the States for cheaper rates. From Germany, the access number for **AT&T** is ✆ **0800/8880010,** and for **MCI,** ✆ **0800/8888000. USA Direct** can be used with all telephone cards and for collect calls. The number from Germany is ✆ **013/00010. Canada Direct** can be used with Bell Telephone Cards and for collect calls. This number from Germany is ✆ **013/00014.**

If you're calling from a public pay phone in Germany, you must deposit the basic local rate.

Tipping   If a restaurant bill says *Bedienung,* that means a service charge has already been added, so just round up to the nearest euro. If not, add 10% to 15%. Bellhops get 1€ per bag, as does the doorperson at your hotel, restaurant, or nightclub. Room-cleaning staffs get small tips in Germany, as do concierges who perform some special favors.

Toilets   Use the word *Toilette* (pronounced twah-*leh*-tah). Women's toilets are usually marked with an F for *Frauen,* and men's toilets with an H for *Herren.* Germany, frankly, doesn't have enough public toilets, except in transportation centers. The locals have to rely on bars, cafes, or restaurants—and using them isn't always appreciated if you're not a paying customer

VAT   See "Taxes," above.

Visas   See "Passports," above.

Visitor Information   All cities and nearly all larger towns in Germany have tourist offices. The **German National Tourist Board** headquarters is at Beethovenstrasse 69, 60325 Frankfurt am Main (✆ **069/751903;** www.germany-tourism.de or www.cometo germany.com).

In the U.S., they can be reached at 122 E. 42nd St., Ste. 2000, New York, NY 10017 (✆ **212/661-7200**).

In **Canada,** tourist offices are at 480 University Ave., Ste. 1500, Toronto, ON M5G 1V2 (✆ **877/315-6237** or 416/968-1685). In the **U.K.,** you can write P.O. Box 2695, London W1A ETN (✆ **020/7317-0808**).

Water   See "Health," earlier.

Wi-Fi   See "Internet & Wi-Fi," earlier.

USEFUL TERMS & PHRASES

GETTING THERE & GETTING AROUND

I am looking for...	Ich suche…
…a porter.	…einen Träger für mein Gepäck.
…the check-in counter.	…den Abfertigungsschalter.
…the ticket counter.	…den Kartenschalter.
…arrivals.	…den Ankunftsbereich.
…departures.	…den Abreisebereich.
…the waiting area.	…den Wartebereich.
…the men's restroom.	…die Herrentoilette.
…the women's restroom.	…die Damentoilette.
…the police station.	…die Polizeidienststelle.
…a security guard.	…einen Sicherheitsbeamten.
…the smoking area.	…den Raucherbereich.
…the information booth.	…den Informationsstand.
…a public telephone.	…ein öffentliches Telefon.
…an ATM.	…einen Geldautomaten.
…baggage claim.	…die Gepäckausgabe.
…a luggage cart.	…einen Gepäckwagen.
…a currency exchange.	…eine Geldwechselstube.
…a café.	…ein Café.
…a restaurant.	…ein Restaurant.
…a bar.	…eine Bar.
…a bookstore or newsstand.	…eine Buchhandlung oder einen Zeitungsstand.
…a duty-free shop.	…einen Duty-Free-Shop.

Is there Internet access here? Gibt es hier einen Internetzugang?
I'd like to page someone. Ich möchte jemanden ausrufen lassen.
Do you accept credit cards? Akzeptieren Sie Kreditkarten?

Common Airport Signs

Ankunft	Arrivals	**Ziehen**	Pull
Abreise	Departures	**Rauchen verboten**	No Smoking
Terminal	Terminal	**Eingang**	Entrance
Gate	Gate	**Ausgang**	Exit
Tickets	Ticketing	**Herren**	Men's
Zoll	Customs	**Damen**	Women's
Gepäckausgabe	Baggage Claim	**Pendelbusse**	Shuttle Buses
Drücken	Push	**Taxis**	Taxis

Security Lingo

Bitte ziehen Sie Ihre Schuhe aus.   Please remove your shoes.
Ziehen Sie Ihre Jacke aus.   Remove your jacket / sweater.
Legen Sie Ihren Schmuck ab.   Remove your jewelry.
Legen Sie Ihre Taschen auf das Band.   Place your bags on the conveyor belt.
Treten Sie zur Seite.   Step to the side.
Wir müssen Sie abtasten.   We have to do a hand search.

Road Signs

Geschwindigkeitsbegrenzung   Speed Limit
Stopp   Stop
Vorfahrt gewähren   Yield
Gefahr   Danger
Sackgasse   No Exit
Einbahnstrasse   One Way
Einfahrt verboten   Do Not Enter
Strasse gesperrt   Road Closed
Maut   Toll
Nur Bargeld   Cash Only
Parken verboten   No Parking
Parkgebühr   Parking Fee
Parkhaus   Parking Garage

GENERAL TERMS

Basic Greetings & Expressions

Hello.   Hallo.
How are you?   Wie geht es Ihnen?
I'm fine, thanks.   Mir geht es gut, danke.
And you?   Und Ihnen?
My name is ____.   Ich heiße ____.
And yours?   Wie heißen Sie?
It's a pleasure to meet you.   Freut mich, Sie kennen zu lernen.
Please.   Bitte.
Thank you.   Danke.
Yes.   Ja.
No.   Nein.
Okay.   OK.
No problem.   Kein Problem.
I'm sorry, I don't understand.   Entschuldigung, ich verstehe Sie nicht.
Would you speak slower please?   Könnten Sie bitte etwas langsamer sprechen?
Would you speak louder please?   Könnten Sie bitte etwas lauter sprechen?
Do you speak English?   Sprechen Sie Englisch?
Do you speak any other languages?   Sprechen Sie irgendeine andere Sprache?
I speak ____ better than German.   Ich spreche besser ____ als Deutsch.
Would you spell that?   Könnten Sie das bitte buchstabieren?
Would you please repeat that?   Könnten Sie das bitte wiederholen?
Would you point that out in this dictionary?   Könnten Sie mir das bitte in diesem Wörterbuch zeigen?

Common Words

Allee Avenue

Altes Rathaus Old town hall (a historical monument; no longer used as the headquarters of the city's officials)

Altstadt Old part of a city or town

Anlage Park area

Apotheke Pharmacy

Auf Wiedersehen Goodbye

Ausgang Exit

Bad Spa (also bath)

Bahn Railroad, train, course

Bahnhof Railroad station

Berg Mountain

Bitte Please

Brücke Bridge

Burg Fortified castle

Danke Thank you

Dom Cathedral

Domplatz Cathedral square

Drogerie Shop selling cosmetics, sundries

Eingang/Einfahrt Entrance

Eintritt Admission

Fahrrad Bicycle

Flughafen Airport

Gasse Lane

Gasthaus Inn, tavern, restaurant

Gasthof Inn

Gutbürgerliche Küche German home cooking

Hallo Hello

Hauptbahnhof Main railroad station

Hotelgarni Hotel that serves no meals or serves breakfast only

Insel Island

Kammer Room (in public building)

Kapelle Chapel

Kaufhaus Department store

Kino Cinema

Kirche Church

Kloster Monastery

Kneipe Bar for drinking; may serve snacks

Konditorei Cafe for coffee and pastries

Kunst Art

Land State

Marktplatz Market square

Neue Küche Cuisine moderne

Neues Rathaus New town hall (the seat of current city business)

Neustadt New part of city or town

Palatinate A region of Germany bordering France

Platz Square

Polizei Police

Postamt Post office

Rathaus Town or city hall

Ratskeller Restaurant in a Rathaus cellar serving traditional German food

Reisebüro Travel agency

Residenz Palace

Schauspielhaus Theater for plays

See Lake (*der See*) or sea (*die See*)

Seilbahn Cable car

Speisekarte Menu

Spielbank Casino

Stadt Town, city

Stadtbahn (S-Bahn) Commuter railroad

Steg Footbridge

Strasse Street

Strassenbahn Streetcar, tram

Tagesmenu Menu of the day

Tankstelle Filling station

Teller Platter

Tor Gateway

Turm Tower

Ufer Shore, riverbank

Untergrundbahn (U-Bahn) Subway, underground transportation system

Verkehrsamt Tourist office

Weg Road

Weinstube Wine bar or tavern serving meals

Zimmer Room

MENU TERMS

Meats & Poultry (Wurst, Fleisch & Geflügel)

Aufschnitt Cold cuts
Beefsteak Hamburger steak
Brathuhn Roasted chicken
Bratwurst Grilled sausage
Eisbein Pigs' knuckles
Ente Duck
Frankfurter Hot dog
Gans Goose
Hammel Mutton
Kalb Veal
Kassler Rippchen Pork chops
Lamm Lamb
Leber Liver

Ragout Stew
Rinderbraten Roast beef
Rindfleisch Beef
Sauerbraten Marinated beef
Schinken Ham
Schnitzel Cutlet
Schweinebraten Roast pork
Tafelspitz Boiled beef usually served with applesauce and horseradish—a famous staple of Austria
Truthahn Turkey
Wiener schnitzel Breaded veal cutlet
Wurst Sausage

Fish (Fisch)

Aal Eel
Forelle Trout
Hecht Pike
Karpfen Carp
Lachs Salmon

Makrele Mackerel
Muschel Mussel
Rheinsalm Rhine salmon
Schellfisch Haddock
Seezunge Sole

Eggs (Eier)

Eier in der Schale Boiled eggs
Mit Speck With bacon
Rühreier Scrambled eggs

Spiegeleier Fried eggs
Verlorene Eier Poached eggs

Vegetables (Gemüse)

Artischocken Artichokes
Blumenkohl Cauliflower
Bohnen Beans
Bratkartoffeln Fried potatoes
Champignon Mushroom
Erbsen Peas
Grüne Bohnen Green or string beans
Gurken Cucumbers
Karotten Carrots
Kartoffel Potato
Kartoffelbrei Mashed potatoes
Kartoffelsalat Potato salad
Knödel Dumplings

Kohl Cabbage
Reis Rice
Rettich Radish
Rote Rüben Beets
Rotkraut Red cabbage
Salat Lettuce
Salzkartoffeln Boiled potatoes
Sellerie Celery
Spargel Asparagus
Spinat Spinach
Steinpilze Boletus mushrooms
Tomaten Tomatoes
Weisse Rüben Turnips

Desserts (Nachtisch)

Auflauf Soufflé
Bienenstich Honey almond cake
Blatterteiggebäck Puff pastry

Bratapfel Baked apple
Dolce di Castagne Chestnut roll
Eis Ice cream

Kaffeecreme   Coffee mousse
Käse   Cheese
Kirschtorte   Black Forest cake
Kompott   Stewed fruit
Obstkuchen   Fruit tart
Obstsalat   Fruit salad
Pfannkuchen   Sugared pancakes
Pflaumenkompott   Stewed plums

Schlagsahne   Whipped cream
Schokolademus   Chocolate mousse
Tarte Tatin   A tart filled with, most often, apples
Topfenpalatschinken   Cottage cheese pancakes
Zwetschkenknodel   Plum dumplings

Fruits (Obst)

Ananas   Pineapple
Apfel   Apple
Apfelsine   Orange
Banane   Banana
Birne   Pear
Erdbeeren   Strawberries

Himberren   Raspberries
Kirschen   Cherries
Pfirsich   Peach
Weintrauben   Grapes
Zitrone   Lemon

Beverages (Getränke)

Bier   Beer
Ein dunkles   A dark beer
Ein helles   A light beer
Eine Tasse Kaffee   A cup of coffee
Eine Tasse Tee   A cup of tea
Eistee   Ice tea
Geist   Brandy
Hiesse Schokolade   Hot chocolate
Kaffee   Coffee
Kaffee mit Rahm/Milch/Zucker   Coffee with cream/milk/sugar
Kaffee mit Suss-stoff   Coffee with artificial sweetener
Kaffee Schwarz   Black coffee
Koffeinfrei   Decaffeinated coffee
Kräutertee   Herb tea
Leicht   Light (wine)
Likör   Liqueur
Limonade   Lemonade
Milch   Milk

Mineralwasser   Mineral water
Mit Eis   With ice
Mit Wasser   With water
Ohne Eis   Without ice
Ohne Wasser   Without water
Pur   Straight
Rotwein   Red wine
Saft   Juice
Schaumwein   Sparkling wine
Schnaps   Schnapps
Schokolade   Chocolate
Soda   Club soda
Soda mit gas   Soda with gas (to make sure your club soda is carbonated)
Süss   Sweet (wine)
Tee mit Milch   Tea with cream
Tee mit Zitrone   Tea with lemon
Trocken   Dry (wine)
Wasser   Water
Weisswein   White wine

Condiments & Table Items (Würze & Tafelgeschirr)

Brot   Bread
Brötchen   Rolls
Butter   Butter
Eis   Ice
Essig   Vinegar
Flasche   Bottle
Gabel   Fork

Glas   Glass
Kalte pikante sosse   Ketchup
Löffel   Spoon
Messer   Knife
Öl   Oil
Pfeffer   Pepper
Platte   Plate

Sahne Cream
Salat Zubereitung Salad dressing
Salz Salt
Senf Mustard

Tasse Cup
Teller Platter
Tischzeug Napkin
Zucker Sugar

Cooking Terms

Gebacken Baked
Gebraten Fried
Gedämpft Steamed
Gefüllt Stuffed
Gekocht Boiled
Geröstet Roasted
Gut durchgebraten Well done

Heiss Hot
Kaltes Cold
Mittep Medium
Nicht durchgebraten Rare
Paniert Breaded
Pochiert Poached

Index

A

Aachen (Aix-la-Chapelle), 506–510
Abercrombie & Kent, 46
Abteikirche St. Maria (Amorbach), 244
Accommodations, 655–658
  best, 9–10
Achim's Beck Haus (Bremen), 584
ADe (Göttingen), 598
Affenhaus (Worms), 486
Africa Festival (Würzburg), 236
Agfa-Historama (Cologne), 514
Air travel, 648–651
Aladdin's (Bremen), 585
Alamannen Museum (Weingarten), 381
Albertinum (Dresden), 188
Albrecht Dürer House (Nürnberg), 214
Albrechtsburg Castle (Meissen), 198
Alexanderplatz (Berlin), 72
Alois Dallmayr (Munich), 316
Alpine hiking, 46, 331–332
Alpspitz region, 348
Alsterhaus (Hamburg), 612
Alsterpark (Hamburg), 607
Altar of Mary Sleeping (Frankfurt), 450
Alte Hofhaltung (Bamberg), 207
Alte Mälzerei (Regensburg), 224
Alte Nationalgalerie (Berlin), 95–96
Alte Oper (Frankfurt), 460
Alte Pinakothek (Old Picture Gallery; Munich), 290–291
Alter Markt
  Cologne, 519
  Eberbach, 424
Alter Simpl (Munich), 319–320
Alter Zoll (Bonn), 501
Altes Museum (Berlin), 96–97
Altes Rathaus (Old Town Hall)
  Bamberg, 207
  Göttingen, 596
  Hanau, 554
  Hannover, 573
  Leipzig, 170
  Lindau, 362
  Regensburg, 224
Altes Schloss (Meersburg), 369
Altes Schloss and Württembergisches Landesmuseum (Stuttgart), 429
Altes Schloss Eremitage (Bayreuth), 202
Altmühltal Nature Park, 200
Altstadt
  Düsseldorf, 532
  Frankfurt, 446–448
  Goslar, 594
  Hamburg, 606
  Lübeck, 632
  Mainz, 489
  Nürnberg, 211
  Passau, 227
Altstadt Päffgen (Cologne), 520
Amadeus (Stuttgart), 432
Amalienburg (Munich), 298
Ambiente (Frankfurt), 42
Ammerschlag (Tübingen), 437
Ammersee (Munich), 322
Amorbach, 243–244
Amphitheater (Trier), 547
Annweiler, 488
Antikensammlung (Museum of Antiquities; Berlin), 96–97
Antikensammlungen (Antiquities Collections; Munich), 291–292
Antikitäten B&M (Bremen), 584
Antiquarium (Munich), 288
Antiquitäten Bannow Günther (Lübeck), 635
Apartment rentals, 657
Apropos Coeln (Cologne), 519
AquaDom (Berlin), 103
Archäologischer Garten (Frankfurt), 450
Archäologisches Landesmuseum (Schleswig), 641
Architecture, 26–29
Architekturmuseum der Technischen Universität (Munich), 293
Arndt & Partner Berlin (Berlin), 117
Art, 23–26
Arts and Crafts Museum (Leipzig), 172
Aschaffenburg, 470–471
Assmannshausen, 494, 496
Atelier Ludvik (Cologne), 519
ATMs (automated-teller machines), 664
A Trane (Berlin), 126
Augsburg, 259–264
Augustinerbräu (Munich), 312
Augustiner Museum (Freiburg), 384

B

Bach, Johann Sebastian, 32, 34, 174
  Bachhaus (Eisenach), 168
Bachhaus (Eisenach), 168
Bach-Museum (Leipzig), 170
Bad Bergzabern, 488
Bad Dürkheim, 487
Baden-Baden, 402–409
Baden-Baden Golf Club, 406
Badenburg (Munich), 298
Bad Godesberg, 505–506
Bad Homburg, 475–478
Bad Reichenhall, 340–342
Bad Reichenhaller Saltmuseum, 341
Balalaika (Frankfurt), 462
Ballooning, 332
Ballooning 2000 (Baden-Baden), 406
Bamberg, 206–211
Barbarossaburg (Imperial Palace; Gelnhausen), 555
Bärenhaus (Bremen), 584
Barfüsser (Ulm), 233
Bar Hamburg, 615
Basilica (Trier), 546
Basilika St. Rochus (Düsseldorf), 528
Basserman-Jordan Wine Estate (Deidesheim), 487
Bau (Munich), 321
Bauer & Hieber (Berlin), 122
Bauhaus Archive (Berlin), 120
Bauhaus-Archiv Museum für Gestaltung (Bauhaus Design Museum; Berlin), 83
Bauhaus-Museum (Weimar), 158
Bauhaus Universität (Weimar), 156, 158
Baur Anton (Oberammergau), 355
Bavaria, suggested itinerary, 56–58
Bavaria Film Studio (Munich), 300
Bavarian Alps, 49, 331–359
  exploring by car, 332
  outdoor activities, 331–332
Bavarian Lion (Lindau), 362
Bavarian State Ballet (Munich), 318
Bavarian State Opera (Munich), 317–318
Bayerischer Hof Night Club (Munich), 319
Bayerischer Kunstgewerbe-Verein (Munich), 314
Bayerischer Skiverband, 322
Bayerisches Nationalmuseum (Bavarian National Museum; Munich), 294–295
Bayerische Spielbank Casino (Bad Reichenhall), 341
Bayerisches Staatsschauspiel (Munich), 317, 318
Bayreuth, 201–206
Bayreuther Festspiele, 204
Beaches
  Lindau, 364
  Meersburg, 370
  Munich, 322
The Beatles, 618
Bebelplatz (Berlin), 90
Bed & breakfasts (B&Bs), 657
Beer, 39
Beer halls and taverns, best, 11
Beethoven, Ludwig van, 32–34
BeethovenFest Bonn, 504
Beethoven Haus (Bonn), 501
Beheiztes Freibad (Meersburg), 370
Beilstein, 539
Bei Tino (Düsseldorf), 533
Belchen Mountain, 387
Belvedere (Berlin), 82
Berchtesgaden, 333–340
Berchtesgadener Land, 331

Berchtesgaden-Hintereck, 339
Berchtesgaden National Park, 46, 331–332
Berggarten (Hannover), 573
The Berggruen Collection: Picasso and His Era (Berlin), 80
Berghof (Obersalzberg), 338
Berg Kolben, 355
Berg Laber, 355
Berlin, 47, 65–153. *See also* specific neighborhoods
  accommodations, 133–147
  average daytime temperature and rainfall, 41
  business hours, 76
  dentists and doctors, 76
  drugstores, 76
  emergencies, 76
  entertainment and nightlife, 123–132
  exploring, 78–103
    sightseeing suggestions, 78
  finding addresses in, 68
  Frommer's favorite experiences, 88
  gay and lesbian nightlife, 131–132
  getting around, 73–74
  getting there, 66–67
  hospitals, 76
  hot lines, 76–77
  Internet access, 77
  laundry and dry cleaning, 77
  layout of, 68
  lost property, 77
  maps, 69
  neighborhoods in brief, 69–73
  organized tours, 74–76
  post office, 77
  restaurants, 103–116
  safety, 77
  shopping, 116–123
  side trip to Potsdam, 147–153
  sports and outdoor pursuits, 132–133
  toilets, 77
  visitor information, 67–68
  water, 77
Berlin Brandenburg International Airport, 66
Berliner Dom (Berlin), 89
Berliner Ensemble (Berlin), 124
Berliner Philharmonisches Orchester (Berlin Philharmonic Orchestra), 123
Berliner Trödelmarkt (Berlin), 121–122
Berliner Zinnfiguren (Berlin), 122
Berlinische Galerie (Berlin), 89
Berlin-Mitte, 72
  accommodations, 141–146
  exploring, 88–94
  restaurants, 110–115
Berlin Wall, 20–22, 96
Berlin Wall Memorial (Berliner Mauer Dokumentationszentrum), 96

Berlin Zoo-Aquarium (Zoologischer Garten Berlin), 102, 103
Bernkastel-Kues, 542–544
Bertholdbad (Baden-Baden), 407
Bertolt Brecht (Munich), 292
Bethmann Park (Frankfurt), 451–452
Biking
  Berlin, 74, 132
  best, 8
  Franconia, 200–201
  Konstanz, 374
  Lindau, 364
  Munich, 280, 282
  Neckar Valley, 412
  Rothenburg, 248
  tours, 45
Bildergalerie (Picture Gallery; Potsdam), 148–149
Binikowski (Hamburg), 613
Biosphefere Expedition, 44
Birkenkopf (Stuttgart), 429
Bischöfliches Museum (Trier), 548
Bismarck, Otto von, 17
Bistro Corona (Weimar), 164
The Black Forest (Schwarzwald), 49, 383–409
  exploring by car, 383
  traveling to, 383
Black Madonna (Beilstein), 539
Blaserturm (Ravensburg), 380
Blauer Turm Lounge (Tübingen), 437
Blaues Wunder (Dresden), 189
Bleibgrün (Berlin), 120–121
Blue Note (Göttingen), 598
BMW Welt (Munich), 295
Boating (boat rentals)
  Hamburg, 619
  Lindau, 364
  Titisee, 390
Boat tours and cruises, 45, 482, 654–655
  Berlin, 75–76
  Bremen, 580
  the Danube (from Passau), 229
  Hamburg, 604
  Königssee, 338
  Main-Danube Canal, 214
  Neckar Valley, 415
  Titisee, 390
  Trier, 545–546
Boba's Bar (Bonn), 504
Bockenheim, 487
Bode-Museum (Berlin), 97
Bodensee (Lake Constance), 49, 360–382
Bodensee Festival (Konstanz), 374
Bodenwerder, 569–570
Bogner Haus
  Düsseldorf, 532
  Munich, 315

Bomann Museum (Celle), 591
Bonn, 500–505
Bonn Symphony Orchestra, 503
Books, recommended, 30–34
Boros, Christian, 92
Botanischer Garten (Botanical Garden), Berlin, 102
Böttcherstrasse (Bremen), 582
Boulanger (Tübingen), 437
Brachiosaurus Brancai (Berlin), 93
Brahmfeld & Gutruf (Hamburg), 613
Brahms, Johannes, 33
Brandenburger Tor (Brandenburg Gate; Berlin), 89–90
Brauereigasthaus Drei Königinnen (Augsburg), 263
Brauerei im Füchschen (Düsseldorf), 533
Bräuerei Schumacher (Düsseldorf), 532–533
Bräuerei zum Schlüssel (Düsseldorf), 533
Breites Tor (Goslar), 594
Breitestrasse (Lübeck), 635
Bremen, 578–587
Brendan Vacations, 45
Breuninger (Stuttgart), 432
British Bookshop (Frankfurt), 445
Brocken, 593
Bröhan Museum (Berlin), 78
Brothers Grimm, 31, 32
  Brüder Grimm Museum (Kassel), 562
  Grimm Museum (Steinau an der Strasse), 557
  Kinder-und Hausmärchen (Grimm's Fairy Tales), 564
  Nationaldenkmal Brüder Grimm (Hanau), 554
  Schloss Philippsruhe & Schlosspark (Hanau), 554
Brücke Museum, 98–99
Brüder Grimm Haus (Steinau an der Strasse), 556
Brüder Grimm Museum (Kassel), 562
Buchenwald Concentration Camp & Memorial Site, 162
Buddelschiff-Museum (Hamburg), 607
Buddenbrookhaus (Lübeck), 633
Bundespresse Strand (Berlin), 133
Burgberg Schloss (Quedlinburg), 182
Burg Eberbach, 425
Burg Eltz, 538
Burg Landeck, 488
Burg Landshut, 543
Burgraves' Castle (Nürnberg), 215
Burg Trifels (Annweiler), 488
Burial Cult Room (Berlin), 98
Bus travel, 654

C

Cabaret, 18–19
Cäcilienkirche (St. Cecilia's Church; Cologne), 516
CADA-Schmuck (Munich), 316
Cafe Aedes (Berlin), 130
Café am Hochhaus (Munich), 319
Café Atlantik (Freiburg), 388
Cafe Brasil (Freiburg), 388
Café Einstein (Berlin), 130
Café Glocksee (Hannover), 577
Café Gnosa (Hamburg), 619
Café Innsteg (Passau), 228
Café Journal (Heidelberg), 419
Café Kittel (Aachen), 509
Café Kowalski (Passau), 228–229
Cafe Moloko+ (Frankfurt), 462
Café Puck (Munich), 320
Café Ruhestörung (Nürnberg), 219
Café Stella (Stuttgart), 432
Cafe Wintergarten in Literaturhaus Berlin, 130
Calendar of events, 41–43
Calw, 398–400
Calwer Passage (Stuttgart), 431
Canal barge cruises, 45
Captain's Cabin (Hamburg), 613
Caracalla-Therme (Baden-Baden), 403
Carl Hagenbeck's Tierpark (Hamburg), 606
Carnival, Mainz, 489–490
Caroline (Heidelberg), 418
Carsch Haus (Düsseldorf), 532
Cartoon (Nürnberg), 219
Car travel, 651, 653–654
Castle hotels, 657
Castle Mill (Meersburg), 369
Castles and palaces, best, 4–5
Cathedrals. See also Dom
    best, 5–6
Catholic Court Church (Dresden), 187
Celle, 591–593
Cellphones, 663–664
Ceramics Studio (Berlin), 121
Chanel (Düsseldorf), 532
Channel Tunnel, 651
Chapeau Claque (Mainz), 492
Chapel of Reconciliation (Kapelle der Versöhnung; Berlin), 96
Chapel of St. Anne (Füssen), 265
Chapel of St. Anton (Partenkirchen), 349
Chapel of St. Bartholomew (Königssee), 338
Charlottenburg (Berlin), 69
    accommodations, 146
    restaurants, 109–110
    sights and attractions, 78–82
Checkpoint (Cologne), 521
Chiemsee, 342–345
Children's Festival (Kinderzeche; Dinkelsbühl), 254
Chinesischer Turm (Chinese Tower; Munich), 299

Chor Dompatzen (Regensburg), 223
Chorgestühl (Ulm), 233
Christmas Fair (Mainz), 43
Christmas market (Lübeck), 632
Church of Our Lady (Kloster Ettal), 359
Church of Our Lady in the Fir Tree (Triberg), 394
Church of St. Severi (Erfurt), 166–167
Church of the Cross (Dresden), 187
CityTourCard (Berlin), 80
City Tour Card (Munich), 275
C-Keller Galerie (Weimar), 164
Clärchens Ballhaus (Berlin), 125
Climate, 41
Club Abaco (Koblenz), 499
Club der Visionaere (Berlin), 125
Club Grosse Freiheit 36 (Hamburg), 615–616
Club Rotes Kliff (Sylt), 646
Cochem, 535–538
Cochemer Weinlagenfest (Cochem), 536
Cocoon Club (Frankfurt), 461
Coffe Baum (Leipzig), 174
Collette Vacations, 45–46
Cologne (Köln), 510–524
    accommodations, 521–524
    beer taverns, 518
    exploring, 512–516
    getting around, 512
    getting there, 512
    nightlife and entertainment, 519–521
    restaurants, 516–518
    shopping, 518–519
    visitor information, 512
Commerzbank Tower (Frankfurt), 448
Concordia (Bremen), 584
Constance (Konstanz), 372–375
Consulates, 661
Corner Berlin, 120
Cotton Club (Hamburg), 615
Couven Museum (Aachen), 507
Cranach, Lucas, the Elder, House (Weimar), 156
Credit cards, 664–665
Creglingen, 246–247
Criminal Museum (Kriminalmuseum; Rothenburg), 248
Cross-country skiing, Bavarian Alps, 331
Cruises and boat tours, 45, 482, 654–655
    Berlin, 75–76
    Bremen, 580
    the Danube (from Passau), 229
    Hamburg, 604
    Königssee, 338
    Main-Danube Canal, 214
    Neckar Valley, 415
    Titisee, 390
    Trier, 545–546

Cusanusstift (Bernkastel-Kues), 543
Customs regulations, 659
Cuvilliés Theater (Altes Residenztheater; Munich), 288, 317

D

Dachau Concentration Camp Memorial Site, 329–330
Dachgarten (Berlin), 130
Dalí Museum (Berlin), 90
The Danube, 48
Danube Bicycle Path, 200
Danube River, 200
Das Gewandhaus (Leipzig), 177
Davidwache (Hamburg), 616
DDR Museum (Berlin), 90
The Dechanei (Deanery; Höxter), 568
Deidesheim, 487
Delicious Doughnuts (Berlin), 125
Dempterscheshaus (Hameln), 571
Denkmal der März Gefallenen (Weimar), 161
Departmentstore Quartier 206 (Berlin), 120
Der Jazzkeller (Frankfurt), 461
Der Keller (Cologne), 519
Der Salzspeicher (Lübeck), 632
Deutsche Bank Towers (Frankfurt), 449
Deutsche Bücherei (Leipzig), 173–174
Deutsche Guggenheim Berlin, 90–91
Deutsche Oper am Rhein (Düsseldorf), 532
Deutsche Oper Berlin, 123
Deutsches Auswandererhaus (Bremerhaven), 587
Deutsches Filmmuseum (Frankfurt), 450
Deutsches Historisches Museum (Berlin), 91
Deutsches Museum (Munich), 299
Deutsches Museum von Meisterwerken der Naturwissenschaft und Technik (Munich), 295
Deutsches Nationaltheater (Weimar), 163–164
Deutsches Salzmuseum (Lüneburg), 588
Deutsches Schauspielhaus (Hamburg), 614
Deutsches Theater
    Göttingen, 597
    Munich, 318
Deutsches Uhrenmuseum (Triberg), 394
Deutsches Weintor (German Wine Gate; Schweigen-Rechtenbach), 488–489
Deutsche Weinstrasse (German Wine Road), 487–489

Die Bank (Munich), 320
Diebsturm (Lindau), 362
Die Hackenschen Höfe (Berlin), 129
Die Neue Sammlung (Munich), 293
Die Sammlung Berggruen: Picasso und Seine Zeit (Berlin), 80
Die Schatzkammer (Treasury Museum; Trier), 547
Die Stachelschweine (Berlin), 124-125
Dinkelsbühl, 253-255
Diözesan Museum (Mainz), 490
Diözesanmuseum St. Afra (Augsburg), 260
Diözesanmuseum St. Ulrich (Regensburg), 223
Disabled travelers, 660
Disco Kuz (Mainz), 492
Disco Pony (Sylt), 646
Doctors, 660
Documenta (Kassel), 562
Documentation Center Nazi Party Rally Grounds, 214-215
Dokumentationszentrum Reichsparteitagsgelände (Nürnberg), 214-215
Dom (Cathedral)
    Aachen, 507
    Augsburg (Dom St. Maria), 259-260
    Bremen (Dom St. Petri), 581
    Cologne (Kölner Dom), 513-514
    Dinkelsbühl (Münster St. Georg), 254
    Erfurt, 166
    Frankfurt (Kaiserdom St. Bartholomäus), 449-450
    Freiburg, 384, 386
    Fulda, 558
    Mainz (St. Martin's Cathedral), 490
    Meissen, 198
    Munich, Frauenkirche (Cathedral of Our Lady), 286
    Passau (St. Stephen's), 227
    Regensburg (St. Peter's), 222-223
    Schleswig (Dom St. Petri), 640-641
    Trier (Der Trierer Dom), 547
    Ulm Münster, 232-233
    Worms (St. Peter), 485
    Würzburg (St. Kilian), 237-238
Domberg (Erfurt), 166
Dome Gallery (Berlin), 89
Domkeller (Aachen), 509
Dom Museum
    Bremen, 581
    Frankfurt, 450
Dommuseum (Fulda), 558

Domschatzmuseum (Regensburg), 223
Donauwörth, 257-259
DownTown (Dresden), 193-194
Dreifaltigkeitskirke (Speyer), 482
Dresden, 48, 184-197
    accommodations, 194-197
    bus tours, 186
    exploring, 186-189
    getting around, 186
    getting there, 184
    nightlife and entertainment, 192-194
    restaurants, 189-192
    shopping, 192
    visitor information, 184
Dresden Philharmonic, 193
Drinking laws, 660
Driving tours, best, 7
Drosselgasse (Rüdesheim), 495
Düsseldorf, 525-534
Düsseldorfer Symphoniker, 532

E

Eagle's Nest (Kehlstein; Obersalzberg), 338, 339
Earthwatch, 44
East Side Gallery (Berlin), 96
Eating and drinking, 37-41
Eau de Cologne, 519
Eberbach, 424-425
Eberbach Castle, 425
Eckbauer, 332, 348
Egyptian Museum (Berlin), 97
Eichwald, 364
1860 München (Munich), 322
Einstein, Albert, 231
Eisenach, 168
Elbe River, cruises, 189
Electricity, 661
Elisabethkirche (Marburg), 560
Elisenbrunnen (Aachen), 507
Embassies and consulates, 661
Emergencies, 661
Englischer Garten (Munich), 294, 299, 322
English Theatre (Frankfurt), 460
English Theatre of Hamburg, 614
Eppendorf (Hamburg), 613
Erfurt, 166-167
Erotik-Museum (Berlin), 83-84
Escada Boutique
    Baden-Baden, 405
    Hamburg, 613
E. T. A. Hoffman Theater (Bamberg), 209
Ethnological Museum (Leipzig), 172
Ethnologisches Museum (Berlin), 100
Europa Center (Berlin), 99, 117
Europäische Wochen (European Weeks) Festival, 228
Europaturm (Frankfurt), 448
European Barging, 45
E-Werk (Cologne), 520
Exhaus (Trier), 550

F

Fabrik (Hamburg), 616
The Fairy-Tale Road, 51, 552-599
    suggested itinerary, 61-64
Fairy tales, 574. See also Grimm, Jakob and Wilhelm
Falls of Todtnau, 387
Families with children, 661
    Berlin attractions, 102
    Hamburg activities, 608
    Munich
        attractions, 299-300
        restaurants, 306
    suggested itinerary, 58-61
Farm vacations, 657
Fasching (Carnival), 42
FC Bayern München (Munich), 322-323
Fernsehturm (Television Tower)
    Berlin, 88
    Stuttgart, 429
Festspielhaus
    Baden-Baden, 406
    Bayreuth, 201, 202
Festung Ehrenbreitstein (Koblenz), 497-498
Festung Marienberg (Marienberg Fortress; Würzburg), 238
Filmmuseum Berlin (Berlin), 84
Films, 36-37
Fingerhutmuseum (Thimble Museum; Creglingen), 246-247
Finnegan (Lübeck), 635
Fischmarkt (Aachen), 507
Fischmarkt (fish market; Hamburg), 613
Fishermen's Quarter (Ulm), 232
Fishing, 332
Five Rivers Bicycle Path, 200-201
Flohmarkt (flea market)
    Bonn, 503
    Bremen, 584
    Frankfurt, 458
    Hannover, 576
    Heidelberg, 418
    Stuttgart, 431
Flugwerft Schleissheim (near Munich), 295
Flugwerft Schliessheim (Munich), 296
Focke-Museum (Bremen), 581
Forsythe Company (Frankfurt), 459-460
Franconia, 48, 200-201
Frankenberg Kirche (Goslar), 594
Frankenstein Schloss, 487
Frankenwald, 200
Frankfurt, 50, 440-478
    accommodations, 463-469
    average daytime temperature and rainfall, 41
    doctors and dentists, 445
    drugstores, 445-446
    emergencies, 446

entertainment and nightlife, 459–463
exploring, 446–452
getting around, 444–445
Internet access, 446
layout of, 441, 444
post office, 446
restaurants, 452–457
safety, 446
shopping, 457–459
side trips from, 469–478
street maps, 444
towers of, 448–449
traveling to, 441
visitor information, 441
Frankfurt Book Fair, 43
Frankfurter-Goethe Museum (Frankfurt), 447
Frankfurter Hof (Mainz), 492
Frankfurter Tageskarte (Frankfurt Card), 445
Frankfurt Municipal Opera, 459
Frankfurt Opera, 460
Franziskanerkirche (Überlingen), 378
Franz-Liszt-Museum (Bayreuth), 202
Frauenchiemsee (Fraueninsel), 342, 343
Frauenkirche (Cathedral of Our Lady; Munich), 286
Frauenkirche (Church of Our Lady; Dresden), 186–187
Freiburg Cathedral, 384, 386
Freiburg im Breisgau, 384–389
Freiburg Wine Tasting, 42
Freudenstadt, 395–398
Friedrich IV, palace of (Heidelberg), 414
Friedrichsbad (Baden-Baden), 403
Friedrichshafen, 365–368
Friedrichstadt Palast (Berlin), 125
Friedrichswerdersche Kirche-Schinkelmuseum (Berlin), 91
Friese-Kabalo Kunstgewerbe OHG (Rothenburg), 251
Fuggerei (Augsburg), 260
Fulda, 557–559
Fürstenbaumuseum (Würzburg), 238
Füssen, 264–267

G

Galerie Adler (Frankfurt), 458
Galerie am Blauen Wunder (Dresden), 192
Galerie Brusberg (Berlin), 118
Galerie der Spiegel (Cologne), 518
Galerie für Zeitgenössische Kunst (Leipzig), 176
Galerie Greve (Cologne), 518
Galerie Luise (Hannover), 576
Galerie Michael Werner (Cologne), 518
Galerie Neue Meister (Dresden), 188

Galerie Pels-Leusden (Berlin), 118
Galeries Lafayette (Berlin), 120
Galerie Thomas Schulte (Berlin), 118
Galerie Wohnmaschine (Berlin), 118
Gallery of Beauties (Munich), 298
Gallileo (Frankfurt), 449
Ganseliesel (Göttingen), 597
Garage (Lüneburg), 590
Garmisch-Partenkirchen, 347–354
Gasthaus Rupp (Bad Homburg), 478
Gay Pride Parade (Cologne), 521
Gays and lesbians, 663
   Berlin, 131–132
   Bonn, 504
   Bremen, 585
   Cologne, 521
   Düsseldorf, 533
   Frankfurt, 462–463
   Hamburg, 618–619
   Hannover, 577
   Leipzig, 178
   Munich, 283, 321
Gedenkstätte Buchenwald, 162
Geigenbau Leonhardt (Mittenwald), 346
Geigenbau- und Heimatmuseum (Mittenwald), 346
Gelnhausen, 555–556
Gemäldegalerie (Portrait Gallery)
   Berlin, 84
   Dachau, 330
Gemäldegalerie Alte Meister (Dresden), 188
German Clock Museum (Triberg), 394
German Emigration Center (Bremerhaven), 587
German Film Museum (Frankfurt), 450
Germanisches Nationalmuseum (Nürnberg), 215
Gewandhaus Orchestra (Leipzig), 177
Gipsformerei der Staatlichen Museen Preussischer Kulturbesitz (Berlin), 122
Gleisweiler, 488
Globus & Cosmos Tours, 46
Glockenspiel (Goslar), 594
Gloria (Cologne), 521
Glyptothek (Museum of Sculpture; Munich), 292
Godesberg Castle, 505
Goethe, Johann Wolfgang von, 30–31, 450
   Gartenhaus (Weimar), 158
   Goethe-Museum Düsseldorf, 528
   Goethe-Schiller Mausoleum (Weimar), 161–162
   Nationalmuseum (Weimar), 158
Goethe Haus (Frankfurt), 447

Goethestrasse (Frankfurt), 457
Golden Cut (Hamburg), 618
Golf, 46
   Baden-Baden, 406
   Hamburg, 619
Goslar, 593–596
Goslarer Museum (Goslar), 594
Göttingen, 596–599
Gottlieb Daimler Memorial (Stuttgart), 429
Grassimuseum (Leipzig), 172
Great Hall of Mirrors (Herrenchiemsee), 344
Gred House (Meersburg), 370
Green Door (Berlin), 128
Green Vaults (Dresden), 187
Greth (Überlingen), 379
Grevenburg Castle (Traben-Trarbach), 541
Grimm, Jakob and Wilhelm (Brothers Grimm), 31, 32
   Brüder Grimm Museum (Kassel), 562
   Grimm Museum (Steinau an der Strasse), 557
   Kinder-und Hausmärchen (Grimm's Fairy Tales), 564
   Nationaldenkmal Brüder Grimm (Hanau), 554
   Schloss Philippsruhe & Schlosspark (Hanau), 554
Grips-Theater (Berlin), 102
Groove Station (Dresden), 194
Grosse Bockenheimerstrasse (Frankfurt), 457
Grosse Freiheit (Hamburg), 617
Grosse Garten (Hannover), 573
Grossehaus (Koblenz), 499
Grosser Garten (Dresden), 187–188
Gross St. Martin (Cologne), 516
Grotto Courtyard (Munich), 288
Grüneburg Park (Frankfurt), 451–452
Grünes Gewölbe (Dresden), 187
Grunewald (Berlin), 69, 132
   accommodations, 140
Gun Park (Heidelberg), 414
Günter Grass-Haus (Lübeck), 633
Gutach Falls (Triberg), 393
Gutenberg Museum (Mainz), 490

H

Haas Säle (Bamberg), 209
Hackesche Höfe (Berlin), 89
Hafenhalle (Konstanz), 374
Hall of Mirrors (Fulda), 558
Hall of Mirrors Building (Heidelberg), 415
Hall of the Swan Knight (Hohenschwangau), 269
Hamburg, 51, 600–629
   accommodations, 620–629
   business hours, 603
   consulates, 603
   currency exchange, 603
   drugstores, 604
   emergencies, 604

Hamburg (cont.)
  entertainment and nightlife, 614–619
  exploring, 604–608
  getting around, 603
  getting there, 600–601
  layout of, 601–602
  neighborhoods in brief, 602
  post office, 604
  restaurants, 608–612
  safety, 604
  shopping, 612–613
  spectator sports, 619, 620
  sports and outdoor pursuits, 619
  toilets, 604
  transit information, 604
  visitor information, 601
Hamburg Ballet, 614
Hamburg Card, 603
Hamburger Sportbund, 614
Hamburgische Staatsoper (Hamburg State Opera), 614
Hamburg Summer, 42
Hameln, 570–572
Hameln (Hamelin), 564
Hanau, 552–554
Handel, George Frideric, 34
Handwerkerhof (Nürnberg), 214, 218
Hang gliding, 332
Hann. Münden, 565–566
Hannover, 572–578
Hansaviertel (Hansa Quarter; Berlin), 99
Hanse Viertel Galerie Passage (Hamburg), 612
Hard Rock Cafe (Heidelberg), 419
Harmel's (Berlin), 117
Harry Lehmann (Berlin), 122
Harry's New York Bar (Berlin), 128
Harvey's (Frankfurt), 462
Harz Mountains, 593
Hauptbahnhof (Leipzig), 176
Hauptkirche St. Michaelis (Hamburg), 604, 606
Hauptmarkt (Nürnberg), 212
Hauptstrasse (Heidelberg), 418
Hauptwache (Frankfurt), 447, 457
Hausbräuerei Feierling (Freiburg), 388
Haus der Bürgerschaft (Bremen), 581
Haus der Geschichte der Bundesrepublik Deutschland (Bonn), 501
Haus der Geschichte Dinkelsbühl, 254
Haus der Schiffergesellschaft (Lübeck), 633
Haus der 1000 Uhren (Triberg), 394
Haus der Wannsee-Konferenz (Berlin), 100
Haus Thalheim (Eberbach), 424

Haus zum Cavazzen (Lindau), 362
Havana Club (Munich), 320
Havana Cocktailbar-Restaurant (Heidelberg), 419
Haydn, Franz Joseph, 34
Health concerns, 661
Heathen's Wall (Lindau), 362
Heidelberg, 49, 410–423
  accommodations, 419–423
  exploring, 414–416
  floodlighting of the Castle, 42, 43
  getting around, 414
  nightlife and entertainment, 418–419
  restaurants, 416–418
  shopping, 418
  traveling to, 412
  visitor information, 412, 414
Heidelberg Castle, 414–415
Heilbronn, 425–426
Heiliggeistkirche (Heidelberg), 415
Heimatmuseum
  Berchtesgaden, 334, 336
  Oberammergau, 355–356
  Ravensburg, 380
  Reichenau, 376
  Überlingen, 378
Heinrich-Heine-Institut (Düsseldorf), 528
Hellabrunn Zoo (Munich), 299
Hemingway (Kiel), 639
Hemmerle (Munich), 316
Herbertstrasse (Hamburg), 617
Hercules, Statue of (Kassel), 562–563
Herderplatz (Weimar), 158
Herkules Keule (Dresden), 194
Hermitage
  Bayreuth, 202
  Munich (Magdalenclause), 298
Herrenchiemsee (Herreninsel), 268, 342–344
Herrenhäuser Garten (Hannover), 573
Herrgottskirche (Chapel of Our Lord; Creglingen), 247
Herzogschloss (Celle), 591
Hesse Haus (Calw), 399
Hessisches Staatstheater (Wiesbaden), 474
Hexenturm Tower (Gelnhausen), 555
Hiking, 46
  Bavarian Alps, 348–349
  best walks, 7–8
  the Black Forest, 393
  Franconia, 200
Hindenburgufer (Kiel), 638
Hindenburg zeppelin, 367
Hinterzarten, 392
Hirmer (Munich), 315
Hirschhorn, 423–424
Hirschhorn Castle, 423
Hirschpark (Hamburg), 607

Historischer Weinkeller (Berlin), 127
Historisches Museum (History Museum)
  Bamberg, 207
  Frankfurt, 451
  Regensburg, 223
Historisches Museum der Pfalz (Speyer), 481
Historische Wurstküche (Regensburg), 225
History of Germany, 13–23
Hitler, Adolf, 18–20
  Führer Bunker (Berlin), 94
  Nürnberg, 211
  Obersalzberg, 338
Höchster Porzellan Manufacture GmbH (Frankfurt), 459
Hochzeitshaus (Wedding House; Hameln), 570, 571
Hofburg Repertory Theater (Bamberg), 209
Hofgarten (Düsseldorf), 528
Hohenschwangau, 267–269
Hohes Schloss (Füssen), 265
Hölderlinturm (Tübingen), 436
Holidays, 41
Holocaust Memorial, 83
Holstentor (Lübeck), 632
Holy Roman Empire, 16
Holzherr (Konstanz), 374
Horseback riding, Baden-Baden, 406
Horse racing, Baden-Baden, 406
Hotel Brugger (Titisee), 391
Hotel Karpfen (Eberbach), 424
Hotels, 655–658
  best, 9–10
Hotelux (Cologne), 520–521
House of 1,000 Clocks (Triberg), 394
House of Silver (Frankfurt), 459
House swapping, 657
Höxter, 564, 567–568
Hugendubel (Munich), 314

I

Imperial Baths (Kaiserthermen; Trier), 547
Inges Karotte (Munich), 321
Insurance, 661–662
Internationale-Bodensee-Kunstauktion (Lindau), 364
Internationale Gartenbau Ausstellung (International Horticulture Exhibition; Erfurt), 166
International Film Festival (Berlin), 42
International May Festival (Wiesbaden), 474
Internet and Wi-Fi, 662–663
Irish Pub
  Garmisch-Partenkirchen, 352
  Göttingen, 598
  Koblenz, 499
  Trier, 550

Irish Pub Bornheim (Frankfurt), 462
Ishtar Gate (Berlin), 98
Isle of Innisfree (Freiburg), 388
Itineraries, suggested, 51–64

J

Jacqueline (Konstanz), 374
Jagdschloss Schachen (Garmisch-Partenkirchen), 349
Jakobikirche (Goslar), 594
Japan Center (Frankfurt), 449
Jazzclub (Bamberg), 209
Jazzclub Unterfahrt (Munich), 318
Jazz-Fest Berlin, 43
Jazzhaus (Freiburg), 388
Jewish Museum Berlin (Jüdisches Museum Berlin), 91–92
Jewish War Memorial (Berlin), 98
J. G. Niederegger (Lübeck), 635
Jil Sander (Hamburg), 613
Jimmy's Bar (Frankfurt), 462
Jockey Bar (Baden-Baden), 406
Jody Lexow Yacht Charters, 45
Joe's Garage (Passau), 229
Joe's Wirthaus zum Löwen (Berlin), 127
Johanna Petzoldt (Berlin), 118
Josef Mack Co. (Bad Reichenhall), 341
Judenfriedhof (Jewish cemetery), Worms, 485
Judengasse (Worms), 486
Jüdischer Friedhof (Jewish Cemetery; Berlin), 100
Jüdisches Museum Berlin (Jewish Museum Berlin), 91–92
Jüdisches Museum München (Munich), 286–287
Jüdisches Viertel (Jewish Quarter), Worms, 485
Jüdisches Viertel (Jewish quarter), Speyer, 483
Jugendstil architecture, 29, 169, 541, 602, 628
Juleps New York Bar (Berlin), 128
Junges Theater (Göttingen), 597–598
Justizgebäude (Nürnberg), 214

K

Kaiserburg (Nürnberg), 215
Kaiserburg Museum (Nürnberg), 216
Kaiserdom (Imperial Cathedral)
  Bamberg, 207
  Frankfurt (St. Bartholomäus), 449–450
  Speyer, 480–481
Kaiser Friedrich Therme (Wiesbaden), 472–473
Kaiserpfalz (Goslar), 594

Kaisersaal (Imperial Hall; Frankfurt), 449
Kaiser-Wilhelm Gedächtniskirche (Kaiser Wilhelm Memorial Church; Berlin), 84, 86
  accommodations near, 139–140
  restaurant, 109
Kaiser Wilhelms Bad im Kurpark (Bad Homburg), 475
Kammerspiele (Hamburg), 614
Kapelle der Versöhnung (Berlin), 96
Karl-Marx-Haus (Trier), 548
Karmelitenklosterkirche (Ravensburg), 380
Karstadt
  Bremen, 584
  Frankfurt, 458
  Hamburg, 612
  Lüneburg, 590
  Nürnberg, 219
Karwendelbahn Mittenwald, 346
Kassel, 561–565
Kassel Casino, 563–564
Kastor und Pollox (Frankfurt), 449
Käthe-Kollwitz-Museum (Berlin), 86
Käthe Kollwitz Museum Köln, 513
Käthe-Kruse-Puppen-Museum (Donauwörth), 258
Katholische Hofkirche (Dresden), 187
Katzenbuckl, 425
Kaufhaus (Customs House; Freiburg), 386
Kaufhaus des Westens (KaDeWe; Berlin), 120
Kaufhaus Schrill (Berlin), 122
Kaufhof
  Frankfurt, 458
  Hamburg, 612
  Heidelberg, 418
  Mainz, 492
  Munich, 315
Kayaking, 332
KAZ (Kommunikations Aktions-Zentrum; Göttingen), 598
Kehlstein (Eagle's Nest; Obersalzberg), 338, 339
Kellertheater (Leipzig), 177
Kempinski Plaza (Berlin), 117
Kennedy Museum (Berlin), 92–93
Kepler, Johannes, 430
Kiel, 637–640
Kieler Bräuerei (Kiel), 639
Killians Irish Pub/Ned Kelly's Australian Bar (Munich), 320
Kindermuseum (Hannover), 573–574
Kinderzeche (Children's Festival; Dinkelsbühl), 254
King Kamehameha Club (Frankfurt), 461
Kirche Sankt Bartholomä (Königssee), 338
Kistner (Nürnberg), 218

Klassische Philharmonie Bonn, 503
Kleidoskop (Frankfurt), 458
Kleinmarkthalle (Frankfurt), 457
Klett Passage (Stuttgart), 431
Klimperkasten (Cologne), 520
Klingenmünster, 488
Klosteranlage Heilig Kreuz (Donauwörth), 258
Kloster Ettal, 358
Kloster Maulbronn, 401
Knaack-Klub (Berlin), 126
Kneipp-Kur (Titisee), 391
Koblenz, 497–500
Kölner Philharmonie (Cologne), 519–520
Komische Oper Berlin, 123–124
Kongresshalle (Augsburg), 263
Kongresshalle (Congress Hall; Berlin), 99
Kongresszentrum Eurogress (Aachen), 509
Königliche Porzellan-Manufaktur (KPM; Berlin), 119
Königliches Schloss Berchtesgaden, 336
Königsallee (Düsseldorf), 526, 528
Königsgalerie (Kassel), 563
Königshaus (Leipzig), 170
Königsplatz (Munich), 290–294
Königssee, 337–338
Konstanz (Constance), 372–375
Konstanz Casino, 374
Konzerthaus (Freiburg), 388
Konzerthaus Berlin, 124
Konzilgebäude (Council Building; Konstanz), 373
KPM (Berlin), 119
Kr@ftakt (Munich), 321
Krämerbrücke (Erfurt), 166
Kräutergarten (Herb Garden; Reichenau), 376
Krempelmarkt (Mainz), 492
Kreuzberg (Berlin), 69, 72
Kreuzkirche (Dresden), 187
Kriminalmuseum (Criminal Museum; Rothenburg), 248
Kronenhochhaus (Frankfurt), 448
Kult Statt Kneipe (Würzburg), 240
Kulturpalast (Dresden), 193
Kumpelnest 3000 (Berlin), 131
Kunstareal (Munich), 290–294
Kunstgewerbemuseum (Museum of Applied Arts; Berlin), 86
Kunsthalle (Hamburg), 606–607
Kunsthalle Düsseldorf, 529
Kunsthaus Lübeck, 635
Kunsthof (Dresden), 193
Kunstlerhaus Mouson Turm (Frankfurt), 459
Kunstmuseum Bonn, 502
Kunstring Meissen (Munich), 314
Kunstsammlungen Böttcherstrasse (Bremen), 582
Kunstsammlungen zu Weimar, 158–159

Kunstsammlung Nordrhein-Westfalen: K2O
Kunstsammlung am Grabbeplatz (Düsseldorf), 529
Kunstsammlung Nordrhein-Westfalen: K21
Kunstsammlung im Ständehaus (Düsseldorf), 529
Kurfürstendamm (Ku'damm; Berlin), 67, 69
  accommodations, 134–139
  restaurants, 104–109
  shopping, 116
Kurfürstliches Palais (Trier), 546–547
Kurgarten (Baden-Baden), 404
Kurhaus
  Baden-Baden, 405
  Bad Homburg, 478
  Wiesbaden, 472, 474
Kurpark (Wiesbaden), 472
Kurpfälzisches Museum (Heidelberg), 415–416
KW Institute for Contemporary Art (Berlin), 118–119
KZ-Gedenkstätte Dachau, 330

L

La Condomeria (Nürnberg), 219
Lake Constance (Bodensee), 49, 360–382
Lake Obersee, 338
Landesmuseum Mainz, 490
Landhaus Herrenberg, 488
L. & M. Lee (Berlin), 117
Language, 663
Las Tapas (Dresden), 193
Laurel Boutique (Hamburg), 613
Le Copain (Bonn), 504
Leder-Koopman (Bremen), 584
Leder-Meid (Heidelberg), 418
Leipzig, 48, 169–184
  accommodations, 179–180
  exploring, 170–174
  getting around, 170
  getting there, 169
  nightlife and entertainment, 176–179
  restaurants, 174–176
  shopping, 176
  side trips from, 180–184
  visitor information, 170
Leipziger Jazztages, 170
Leipziger Oper, 176
Lenbachhaus (Munich), 292
Lenzkirch, 387
LGBT travelers, 663
  Berlin, 131–132
  Bonn, 504
  Bremen, 585
  Cologne, 521
  Düsseldorf, 533
  Frankfurt, 462–463
  Hamburg, 618–619
  Hannover, 577
  Leipzig, 178
  Munich, 283, 321

Lichtentaler Allee (Baden-Baden), 404
Liebfrauenkirche (Church of Our Lady)
  Koblenz, 497
  Ravensburg, 380
  Trier, 548
Liebieghaus (Frankfurt), 447
Liebnitz, Gottfried, 178
Liederhalle (Stuttgart), 428, 432
Liliom (Augsburg), 263
Lindau, 361–365
Lindenhofbad, 364
Linderhof, 358
Liszt, Franz, Franz-Liszt-Museum (Bayreuth), 202
Liszt-Haus (Weimar), 159
Literature, 30–31
Literaturhaus Berlin (Berlin), 119
Living xxl (Frankfurt), 461
Lochgefängnisse (Dungeons; Nürnberg), 216
Loden-Frey (Munich), 315
Loft (Cologne), 520
Logo (Hamburg), 617
Loni-Übler-Haus (Nürnberg), 219
Lothar Heubel (Düsseldorf), 532
Louis Vuitton (Düsseldorf), 532
Löwenburg (Lion Fortress; Kassel), 563
Lower Saxony, 51
Lübeck, 630–637
Lübeck Harbor, 634
Lucas Cranach the Elder House (Weimar), 156
Lucky's Manhattan (Frankfurt), 462–463
Ludwig Beck am Rathauseck (Munich), 315
Ludwig II, "Mad" King
  Neuschwanstein, 267, 268, 270
  Schloss Linderhof, 358
Ludwigstrasse (Munich), 287–288
Luna (Frankfurt), 462
Lüneburg, 588–590
Lüneburger Heide (Lüneburg Heath), 589
Luther, Martin, 30, 177
  Lutherhaus (Eisenach), 168
  Lutherstadt Wittenberg, 180–181
Lutherhalle Wittenberg, 181
Lutherhaus (Eisenach), 168
Lutherstadt Wittenberg, 180–181
Lutter und Wegner 1811 (Berlin), 129

M

MacGowan's Irish Pub (Hannover), 577
Mach 1 (Nürnberg), 219
McLaughlin's Irish Pub (Düsseldorf), 533
Madame Tussauds Berlin, 93
Maendler (Munich), 315

Magdalenclause (Hermitage; Munich), 298
Mail, 663
Mainau Island, 372, 373
Main-Danube Canal, 214
Mainfränkisches Museum (Main-Franconian Museum; Würzburg), 238
Main Tower (Frankfurt), 448
Mainz, 489–493
Mangturm (Lindau), 361–362
Marburg, 559–561
Marburg Schloss, 560
Maria-Einsiedel (Munich), 322
Maria Schlafaltar (Frankfurt), 450
Marienbrücke, 267
Marienkirche (St. Mary's Church)
  Berlin, 88–89
  Gelnhausen, 555
  Lübeck, 633
  Würzburg, 238
Marine Museum (Speyer), 482
Marionettentheater, Münchner (Munich), 299
Market Gate of Miletus (Berlin), 98
Markgräfliches Opernhaus (Margravial Opera House; Bayreuth), 202
Märkisches Museum (Berlin), 93
Markthalle (Hamburg), 617
Marktkirche (Market Church)
  Goslar, 594
  Hannover, 573
Marktplatz
  Berchtesgaden, 334
  Bernkastel-Kues, 543
  Bremen, 580
  Goslar, 594
  Göttingen, 596–597
  Heidelberg, 415
  Marburg, 560
  Miltenberg, 242
  Schwäbisch Hall, 438–439
  Triberg, 396
  Tübingen, 436
  Weimar, 156
  Würzburg, 237
Marktschenke (Tübingen), 437
Marlies Müller (Hamburg), 613
Marstallmuseum (Munich), 298
Martin-Gropius-Bau (Berlin), 93
Marx, Karl, 540
  Karl-Marx-Haus (Trier), 548
Maupintour, 46
Mäuseturm (Mouse Tower; between Rüdesheim and Assmannshausen), 494
Mausoleum (Berlin), 82
May Theatre Festival (Wiesbaden), 42
Medical requirements for entry, 663
Medici (Baden-Baden), 406
MedienHafen district (Düsseldorf), 528
Meersburg, 368–372

Mehlsack Tower (Ravensburg), 380

Meissen, 160–161, 197–199

Meissen porcelain, 160–161

Munich, 314

Meistertrunk festival (Rothenburg), 248

Memorial to the Murdered Jews of Europe (Stiftung Denkmal für die ermordeten Juden Europas; Berlin), 83

Memorium Nürnberg Prozesse & Justizgebäude (Memorium Nuremberg Trials & Courthouse), 216

Mercedes-Benz Museum (Stuttgart), 429–430

Merkel, Angela, 23

Messeturm (Frankfurt), 448

Metternich Castle (Beilstein), 539

Michaelskirche (Schwäbisch Hall), 439

Michael Zeller (Lindau), 364

Mike's Bike Tour (Munich), 282

Miltenberg, 242–243

Mister B's (Munich), 318

Mittelzell, 376

Mittenwald, 345–347

Mobile phones, 663–664

Modernes (Bremen), 585

Molotow (Hamburg), 618

Moments (Bremen), 585

Monastery of Limburg (Bad Dürkheim), 487

Mondos Arts (Berlin), 119

Money and costs, 664–665

Mont Royal (Traben-Trarbach), 541

Moorish Kiosk (Schloss Linderhof), 358

Moritzbastei (Leipzig), 178

Mosel Valley, 50–51, 535–551

Mosel-Wein-Woche (Cochem), 536

Mosel wines, 536

Mountain climbing, 46

Mozart, Wolfgang Amadeus, 34

Festival

Augsburg, 263

Würzburg, 42, 236

München Tickets, 317

Münchhausen-Erinnerungszimmer (Bodenwerder), 569

Münchhausenplay (Bodenwerder), 569

Münchner Kammerspiele (Munich), 318

Münchner Marionettentheater (Munich), 299

Münchner Moden (Baden-Baden), 405

Münchner Philharmoniker (Munich), 318

Münchner Puppenstuben und Zinnfiguren Kabinette (Munich), 316

Münchner Stadtmuseum (Municipal Museum; Munich), 287, 299

Munich, 48–49, 273–329

accommodations, 323–329

beer gardens, cellars and taverns, 312–313

business hours, 281

currency exchange, 281

dentists and doctors, 281

drugstores, 281

emergencies, 281

entertainment and nightlife, 316–322

exploring, 283–300

Frommer's favorite experiences, 287

getting around, 278, 280

getting there, 274

Internet access, 281

for kids, 299–300

laundry and dry cleaning, 281

layout of, 275, 278

maps and finding addresses, 278

neighborhoods in brief, 278

organized tours, 282–283

outdoor pursuits, 322

post office, 281

restaurants, 300–314

safety, 281

shopping, 314–316

side trips from, 329–330

spectator sports, 322–323

television channels, 282

visitor information, 275

Munich Readery, 314

Münster

St. Georg (Dinkelsbühl), 254

St. Maria und Markus (Reichenau), 376

St. Nikolaus (Überlingen), 378

Ulm, 232–233

Münsterkirch (Hameln), 571

Münsterplatz (Aachen), 507

Museen Behnhaus/Drägerhaus (Lübeck), 633–634

Museen Dahlem (Berlin), 100–101

Museen de Stadt Regensburg, 223

Museum Brandhorst (Munich), 293

Museum der Bildenden Künste (Leipzig), 172

Museum Europäischer Kulturen (Museum of European Culture; Berlin), 101

Museum für Angewandte Kunst

Cologne, 514

Frankfurt, 451

Museum für Asiatische Kunst (Museum for Asian Art; Berlin), 100

Museum für Gegenwart Hamburger Bahnhof (Berlin), 86–87

Museum für Indische Kunst (Museum for Indian Art; Berlin), 100

Museum für Kunsthandwerk (Leipzig), 172

Museum für Moderne Kunst (Frankfurt), 451

Museum für Naturkunde (Berlin), 93–94

Museum für Neue Kunst (Freiburg), 386

Museum für Ostasiatische Kunst (Museum for Far Eastern Art; Berlin), 100

Museum für Völkerkunde (Leipzig), 172

Museum Haus am Checkpoint Charlie (Berlin), 94

Museum Holstentor (Lübeck), 632

Museum im Stadthaus (Triberg), 396

Museum in der Runden Ecke (Leipzig), 172

Museum Kunst Palast (Düsseldorf), 529

Museum Ludwig (Cologne), 514

Museum of Applied Art (Cologne), 514

Museum of Applied Arts (Frankfurt), 451

Museum of Historical Wines (Deidesheim), 487

Museum of Modern Art (Frankfurt), 451

Museum of Technology (Speyer), 482

Museum of the Palatinate (Heidelberg), 415–416

Museums, best, 3–4

Museum Schnütgen (Cologne), 515

Museumsinsel (Museum Island; Berlin), 72, 95–102

Museum Steinau (Steinau an der Strasse), 556

Music, 32–36

Musica Bayreuth, 202

Musical Instruments Museum (Leipzig), 172

Musikalischer Sommer Festival (Baden-Baden), 405

Musikfest Berlin, 43

Musikinstrumentenmuseum (Leipzig), 172

Musiktheater (Bremen), 584

Musik und Kongresshallen Lübeck, 635

MyZeil mall (Frankfurt), 457

N

Nachtcafé (Leipzig), 177

Nachtgalerie (Munich), 319

Napoleon, 16–17

Nasch Markt (Leipzig), 170

Nationaldenkmal Brüder Grimm (Hanau), 554

Naturpark Informationszentrum (Eberbach), 383

Nazism, 283. See also Hitler, Adolf

rise of, 18–19

N. D. R. Symphoniker (Hannover), 577
Neckar Valley, 49
Neckar Valley Cycle Path, 412
Neo (Hamburg), 615
Neubulach, 399
Neue Flora Theater (Hamburg), 615
Neue Nationalgalerie (New National Gallery; Berlin), 87
Neue Pinakothek (New Picture Gallery; Munich), 293
Neue Residenz (New Residence; Bamberg), 208
Neuer Garten (Potsdam), 148
Neues Museum
  Berlin, 97–98
  Weimar, 159
Neues Opernhaus (Leipzig), 176
Neues Palais (Potsdam), 149–150
Neues Rathaus
  Leipzig, 170
  Munich, 283
Neues Schloss (New Palace)
  Bayreuth, 204
  Meersburg, 369
  Stuttgart, 428
Neue Synagoge Berlin-Centrum Judaicum (The New Synagogue; Berlin), 94–95
Neuleiningen, 487
Neumarkt Passage (Leipzig), 176
Neuschwanstein, 267, 268, 270–271
Neustadt, 564
Neustadt-an-der-Weinstrasse, 487–488
Neuwerkkirche (Goslar), 594
New Lighthouse (Lindau), 362
Newton Bar (Berlin), 128
New Year's Day International Ski Jumping (Garmisch-Partenkirchen), 42
Niedersächsisches Landesmuseum Hannover, 573–574
Nieder Sächsische Stadtstheater Hannover GmbH, 577
Niederwald Monument (between Rüdesheim and Assmannshausen), 494
Niederzell, 376
Nietzsche, Friedrich, 503
Nikolaikirche (Church of St. Nicholas)
  Berlin, 97
  Leipzig, 174
Nikolaiviertel (Berlin), 72, 97
Nikolausbrücke (Calw), 399
Nonntal (Berchtesgaden), 334
Nördlingen, 255–257
North Hesse, 51
Nürnberg (Nuremberg), 211–221
  accommodations, 219–221
  exploring, 212–217
  getting there, 212
  nightlife and entertainment, 219
  restaurants, 217–218
  shopping, 218–219
  visitor information, 212
NY Club (Munich), 322
Nymphenbad (Dresden), 188
Nymphenburg, 268
Nymphenburg Palace and Park (Munich), 296, 298

O

Oberammergau, 354–359
Oberhaus Museum (Passau), 227
Obersalzberg, 338–340
Obersee, 338
Oberzell, 376
Obletter's (Munich), 316
The Odeon Club (Frankfurt), 461
Odeonsplatz (Munich), 287–288
Oklahoma (Munich), 319
Oktoberfest (Munich), 43
Old Masters Gallery (Kassel), 563
Oleander Bar (Baden-Baden), 406
Olympia Park (Munich), 296, 322
Olympia-Schwimmhalle (Munich), 322
Olympiasee (Munich), 322
Olympiastadion (Berlin), 80
Olympiaturm (Olympia Tower; Munich), 296
Olympic Ice Stadium (Garmisch-Partenkirchen), 348
Olympischer Berg (Munich), 296
Omnibus (Würzburg), 240
Oper der Stadt Bonn, 503
Oper der Stadt Köln (Cologne), 520
Operettenhaus (Hamburg), 615
Oper Frankfurt, 460
Orangerie (Potsdam), 149
Osho Disco (Hannover), 577
Ottheinrich Building (Heidelberg), 415
Oxymoron (Berlin), 127

P

Päffgen Bräuhaus (Cologne), 520
Pagodenburg (Munich), 298
Painted houses (Mittenwald), 346
Palais (Koblenz), 499
Palais Vischer (Calw), 399
Palast der Republik (Stuttgart), 432
Palastgarten (Palace Gardens; Trier), 547
Palatinate Historical Museum (Speyer), 481
Palmengarten (Frankfurt), 451–452
Palo Palo (Hannover), 577
Pantheon Theater (Bonn), 504
Papa Joe's Biersalon (Cologne), 520
Papa Joe's Jazzlokal (Cologne), 520
Papiertheatermuseum (Hanau), 554
Papyrus Collection (Berlin), 98
Paragliding, 332
Park an der Ilm (Weimar), 156
Park Café (Wiesbaden), 474
Parkwald (Triberg), 396
Partnachklamm, 349
Passau, 226–230
Passports, 665–666
Patio (Schleswig), 642
Paula-Becker-Modersohn Haus (Bremen), 582
Paul Schweitzer (Bonn), 502–503
Pavillon (Stuttgart), 432
Peek & Cloppenburg
  Cologne, 518
  Frankfurt, 458
  Mainz, 491–492
Pentagonal Tower (Nürnberg), 215
Pergamon Altar (Berlin), 98
Pergamonmuseum (Berlin), 98
Perla Zayek (Cologne), 519
Petersgrube (Lübeck), 633
Peterskirche (St. Peter's Church)
  Erfurt, 167
  Lindau, 362
  Munich, 286
Pfalzel, 546
Pfeffermühle (Leipzig), 178
Pforzheim, 400–402
Pharmaceutical Museum (Heidelberg), 415
Philharmonie (Berlin), 99, 123
Philharmonie Baden-Baden, 405
Phillips University (Marburg), 560
Philosophenweg (Philosopher's Way; Heidelberg), 415
Philosopher's Walk (Garmisch-Partenkirchen), 349
Pierre (Konstanz), 374
Pilatushaus (Oberammergau), 355, 356
Pinakothek der Moderne (Munich), 293–294
Plaster-works of the State Museums of Prussia (Berlin), 122
Platanenallee (Tübingen), 436
Police, 666
Pompeiianum (Aschaffenburg), 471
Porcelain Museum (Meissen), 198–199
Porsche Museum (Stuttgart), 430
Porta Nigra (Trier), 546
Porta Praetoria (Regensburg), 223
Porzellan-Manufaktur (Meissen), 198, 199
Porzellan-Manufaktur-Nymphenburg (Munich), 316
Porzellansammlung (Porcelain Collection; Munich), 298
Potsdam, 47, 147–153

Potsdamer Platz (Berlin), 72
Potsdamer Platz Arkaden
(Berlin), 123
Prater Garten (Berlin), 127
Predigerkirche (Erfurt), 167
Prime Club (Cologne), 520
Prinoth (Munich), 314
Print Media Lounge
(Heidelberg), 419
Prinz Eisenherz (Berlin), 119
Prinzknecht (Berlin), 131
Prinzregentenstrasse (Munich),
294–295
Projekttheater Dresden, 194
Pro qm (Frankfurt), 463
Pulverfass (Hamburg), 618
Pupille (Munich), 315
Pusser's New York Bar (Munich),
320

Q

Quasimodo (Berlin), 127
Quedlinburg, 182–184

R

Radio-Sinfonieorchester
Stuttgart, 432
Raschi-Haus Museum (Worms),
485
Rathaus (Town Hall)
Aachen, 507–508
Augsburg, 260
Bremen, 581–582
Dresden, 187
Goslar, 594
Hanau, 554
Hannover, 574
Heilbronn, 425
Höxter, 568
Koblenz, 497
Lübeck, 632
Lüneburg, 588
Marburg, 560
Meersburg, 369
Nördlingen, 256
Passau, 227
Quedlinburg, 182
Rothenburg, 249–250
Stuttgart, 428
Tübingen, 436
Überlingen, 378
Ulm, 232
Ratskeller (Göttingen), 598
Rat und Tat (Bremen), 585
Ravensburg, 379–382
Red Cat (Mainz), 492
Redoute Palace (Bad
Godesberg), 505
Red Wine Festival (Rüdesheim/
Assmannshausen), 43
Reeperbahn (Hamburg), 616–617
The Reformation, 16
Regensburg, 221–226
Regions in brief, 47–51
Reichenau, 375–377
Reichenstrasse (Füssen), 265

Reichsabtei Corvey (Höxter),
568
Reichsburg Cochem, 536
Reichsstadtmuseum
(Rothenburg), 250
Reichstag (Parliament; Berlin),
95
Reingold (Berlin), 129
Renner (Hameln), 571
Residenz
Munich, 288
Würzburg (Schloss und
Gartenverwaltung
Würzburg), 238–239
Residenz Museum (Munich), 288
Residenzschloss (Dresden), 187
Residenztheater im Schloss
(Dresden), 193
Responsible travel, 43–44
Restaurants, best, 10–11
The Rheingau, 494–496
Rheingau- und Weinmuseum
(Rüdesheim), 495
Rheinische Philharmonie
Orchestra (Koblenz), 499
Rheinisches Landesmuseum
(Trier), 548
Rhein-Mosel-Halle (Koblenz),
499
The Rhineland, 50, 479–534
Rieskrater-Museum (Nördlingen),
257
Rittersaal (Knight's Hall)
Füssen, 265
Weikersheim, 245
Riverside (Trier), 550
Rock Am See Festival
(Konstanz), 374
Rock climbing, Baden-Baden,
406
Rödertor (Röder Gate;
Rothenburg), 248
Roland Kleidung (Bremen), 584
Roman Baths (Potsdam), 150
The Romantic Road
(Romantische Strasse), 48,
235–272
bus tours, 235
towns of, 235
Romantik hotels, 658
Römerberg (Frankfurt), 446
Römerplatz (Römerberg Square;
Frankfurt), 449
Römisch-Germanisches Museum
(Roman-Germanic Museum;
Cologne), 515
RosaLinde (Leipzig), 178
Roselius Haus (Bremen), 582
Rothenburger Tor (Dinkelsbühl),
254
Rothenburg ob der Tauber,
247–253
Rübenmarkt (Nördlingen), 256
Rüdesheim, 494, 495–496
Ruprecht-Karl-University
(Heidelberg), 414
Rüstkammer (Armory), Dresden,
189

S

Sababurg, 564, 566–567
Sababurg Castle, 567
Sachsenhausen district
(Frankfurt), 460
Sachsenhausen Gedenkstätte
(Sachsenhausen Memorial &
Museum; Berlin), 101
Safari (Hamburg), 617
Safety, 666
Sage Club (Berlin), 125–126
St. Andreas (Cologne), 516
St. Anne, Chapel of (Füssen),
265
St. Anton, Chapel of
(Partenkirchen), 349
St. Aposteln (Cologne), 516
St. Blaise's Church (Hann.
Münden), 566
St. Castor's (Koblenz), 497
St. Cecilia's Church (Cologne),
516
St. Georg, Münster (Dinkelsbühl),
254
St. Georg (Cologne), 516
St. Georgskirche (Nördlingen),
256
St. Gereon (Cologne), 515
St. Jacobi Kirche (Hamburg),
606
St. Jakobskirche (Church of St.
James; Rothenburg), 250
St. Katarina (Nürnberg), 219
St. Kilian, Dom (Würzburg),
237–238
St. Kilian's (Höxter), 568
St. Killian's Church (Heilbronn),
425
St. Kunibert (Cologne), 516
St.-Lorenz-Kirche (Nürnberg),
216–217
St. Mangkirche (Füssen), 265
St. Maria im Kapitol (Cologne),
515–516
St. Maria Lyskirchen (Cologne),
516
St. Martin, 488
St. Martiner Castell, 488
St. Mary's Church. See
Marienkirche
St. Michael's Fountain
(Bernkastel-Kues), 543
St. Nicholas, side chapel of
(Worms), 485
St. Oswald's, 392
St. Panteleon (Cologne), 515
St. Pauli (Hamburg), 602
St. Pauli district (Reeperbahn;
Hamburg), 616–617
St. Peter's Cathedral (Dom St.
Petri)
Bremen, 581
Schleswig, 640–641
St. Peter's Church (Peterskirche)
Erfurt, 167
Lindau, 362
Munich, 286
St. Petri, Dom (Bremen), 581

St. Petri Kirche (Hamburg), 606
St.-Sebaldus-Kirche (Nürnberg), 217
St. Severi, Church of (Erfurt), 166–167
St. Severin (Cologne), 515
St. Stephen's Cathedral (Passau), 227
St. Thomas Choir (Leipzig), 173
St. Ulrich und St. Afra Kirche (Augsburg), 260, 262
St. Ursula (Cologne), 515
St. Zeno (Bad Reichenhall), 341
Salzbergwerk Berchtesgaden, 336
Sammlung Frieder Burda (Baden-Baden), 403
Sanssouci Palace (Potsdam), 148
S. A. Prüm Winery (Bernkastel-Wehlen), 544
Sausalitos (Munich), 320–321
Saxony, 48
Scala (Regensburg), 225
Schack-Galerie (Munich), 295
Schadow Arcade (Düsseldorf), 531
Schaezlerpalais (Augsburg), 262
Schampanja (Cologne), 521
Schatzkammer (Treasury; Munich), 288–289
Schaubühne am Lehniner Platz (Berlin), 124
Schaubühne Lindenfels (Leipzig), 178–179
Schauinsland, 387
Schauspielhaus
    Cologne, 519
    Dresden, 193
    Düsseldorf, 532
    Leipzig, 177
Scheuenviertel (Berlin), 118
Schillerhaus (Leipzig), 173
Schillerhaus (Weimar), 159
Schillerplatz (Stuttgart), 428
Schillerstrasse (Frankfurt), 457
Schinkel Pavillon (Berlin), 82
Schleswig, 640–642
Schleswig-Holstein, 51, 630–647
Schleswig-Holsteinisches Freilichtmuseum (Kiel), 638
Schleswig-Holstein Music Festival (Lübeck), 632
Schleswig-Holstein Staatsmuseum (Schleswig), 641
Schloss Belvedere (Weimar), 159
Schloss Cecilienhof (Potsdam), 150
Schloss Charlottenburg (Berlin), 80, 82
Schloss Charlottenhof (Potsdam), 150
Schloss Dachau, 330
Schlossfest-Spiele (Heidelberg), 419
Schlossgarten Charlottenburg (Berlin), 82
Schloss Gottorf (Schleswig), 641
Schloss Hambach, 488

Schloss Hohentübingen (Tübingen), 436
Schloss Homburg (Bad Homburg), 476
Schloss Johannisburg (Aschaffenburg), 470–471
Schloss Kassel, 563
Schlosskirche
    Friedrichshafen, 365, 366
    Wittenberg, 181
Schloss Linderhof, 268, 358
Schloss Miltenberg, 242
Schlossmuseum (Weimar), 159–160
Schloss Nymphenburg (Munich), 296, 298, 322
Schlosspark Nymphenburg (Munich), 298
Schloss Philippsruhe & Schlosspark (Hanau), 554
Schlossplatz (Berchtesgaden), 334
Schloss Schönhausen (Berlin), 101
Schloss Steinau (Steinau an der Strasse), 557
Schloss- und Stiftskirche (Castle and Monastery Church; Pforzheim), 400
Schloss Wartburg (Eisenach), 168
Schloss Weikersheim, 245
Schluchsee, 387
Schmidt Theater (Hamburg), 614
Schmidts Tivoli (Hamburg), 614
Schmuckmuseum (Pforzheim), 401
Schnitzschule (Woodcarving School; Oberammergau), 355
Schnoor (Bremen), 582
Schönberg, Arnold, 35–36
Schönbusch Park (Aschaffenburg), 470
Schöneberg Rathaus (Berlin), 87
Schöner Brunnen (Nürnberg), 214
Schötting (Bremen), 580–581
Schrannenhalle (Munich), 317
Schroederstrasse (Lüneburg), 590
Schuhhaus Prange (Hamburg), 613
Schulauer Fährhaus (Hamburg), 607
Schulmuseum (Friedrichshafen), 366
Schumann's Bar am Hofgarten (Munich), 321
Schwabinger Podium (Munich), 319
Schwäbisch Hall, 438–439
Schwalm River, 564
Schwarzfischer (Munich), 283
Schwarzwald (The Black Forest), 49, 383–409
    exploring by car, 383
    traveling to, 383
Schwarzwälder Freilichtmuseum (Triberg), 394

Schwarzwald Hochstrasse, 396
Schwarzwaldhochstrasse, 383
Schwarzwald-Museum Triberg, 393
Schwarzwald Panoramastrasse, 383
Schweigen-Rechtenbach, 488
Schwul Sau (Hannover), 577
SchwuZ (Berlin), 131
Sea Life Berlin, 103
Seamen's Guild House (Lübeck), 633
Seasons, 41
Sebök (Bamberg), 208
Seebuck, 387
Seehotel Off (Meersburg), 370
Seepromenade (Friedrichshafen), 366
Semperoper (Semper Opera House; Dresden), 192–193
Senior travel, 666–667
Shamrock
    Hamburg, 615
    Munich, 321
The Sharon Stonewall Bar (Berlin), 131
Shopkeepers' Bridge (Erfurt), 166
Shopping, best, 12
Siebenbirge (Seven Mountains), 500
Siegessäule (Victory Column; Berlin), 102
Sightseeing Gray Line (Munich), 282
Silver Tower (Frankfurt), 449
Sinfonie an der Regnitz (Bamberg), 208
Singer's Hall (Neuschwanstein), 270
Sinkkasten (Frankfurt), 461
Sinn (Mainz), 492
Skiing, Garmisch-Partenkirchen, 348–349
Ski Stadium (Garmisch-Partenkirchen), 348
Skyper (Frankfurt), 449
Smoking, 667
SO36 (Berlin), 126
Sommernächte (Konstanz), 374
Sonderbar (Heidelberg), 419
Sonia Rykiel (Berlin), 121
Sony Center am Potsdamer Platz (Berlin), 91
Spa hotels, 658
Spandau Zitadelle (Spandau Citadel; Berlin), 102
Spa Park (Bad Homburg), 475
Spas, best, 8–9
Speyer, 479–484
Spiegelsaal (Hall of Mirrors; Meersburg), 370
Spielbank (casino)
    Baden-Baden, 406
    Berlin, 132
    Bremen, 585
    Garmisch-Partenkirchen, 351–352
    Hamburg, 619

Hannover, 577
Lindau, 364
Wiesbaden, 473–474
Spielbank im Kurpark (Bad Homburg), 478
Spielzeit'europa (Berlin), 43
Spielzeugmuseum (Toy Museum)
Munich, 299
Nürnberg, 217
Spiess & Walther (Heidelberg), 418
Spizz (Leipzig), 177–178
Sport Center Buschkrug (Berlin), 133
Sprengel Museum (Hannover), 574
Spring Fairs, 42
Squash Tennis Nord (Berlin), 133
Staatliche Graphische Sammlung (Munich), 293–294
Staatsgalerie (State Gallery of Stuttgart), 430
Staatsgalerie Moderner Kunst (Munich), 293
Staatsoper (State Opera; Stuttgart), 432
Staats Operette (Dresden), 193
Staatstheater
Nürnberg, 219
Stuttgart, 432
Städel Museum (Frankfurt), 448
Stadtgarten (Town Garden; Lindau), 362
Städtische Bühnen/Schauspiel (Frankfurt), 459
Stadtisches Museum (Göttingen), 597
Städtisches Spiel und Festhaus (Worms), 486
Stadtkirche
Pforzheim, 401
Triberg, 396
Wittenberg, 181
Stadtmauer (Überlingen), 378–379
Stadtmuseum
Munich (Münchner Stadtmuseum), 287, 299
Nördlingen, 256
Stadtpark (Hamburg), 608
Stadtschloss (Fulda), 558
Stadttheater
Koblenz, 499
Konstanz, 370, 374
Passau, 228
Stadttheater Company (Passau), 228
Stahwerk (Düsseldorf), 533
Standard (Würzburg), 240
Starkbierzeit (Munich), 317
Starnbergersee (Munich), 322
Steinau an der Strasse, 556–557
Stiftskirche (Abbey Church)
Berchtesgaden, 334
St. George (Reichenau), 376
St. Peter and St. Alexander (Aschaffenburg), 471
St. Peter and St. Paul (Reichenau), 376

St. Servatius (Quedlinburg), 182
Tübingen, 436
The Story of Berlin, 87
Stubu Club (Bremen), 585
Student drinking clubs (Heidelberg), 419
Studentenkarzer (Student Jail; Heidelberg), 416
Studienzentrum Karl-Marx-Haus (Trier), 548
Stuttgart, 49–50, 426–435
Stuttgart Ballet, 432
Stuttgarter Philharmoniker, 432
Südwestdeutsche Philharmonie Konstanz, 374
Suermondt Ludwig Museum (Aachen), 508
Sustainable tourism, 43–44
Swimming
Baden-Baden, 407
Hamburg, 620
Munich, 322
Sylt, 642–647

T

Tacheles (Berlin), 118
Taunus Therme (Bad Homburg), 476
Taxes, 667
Technik-Museum (Speyer), 482
Technisches Museum (Pforzheim), 401
Teddy-Bar (Munich), 322
Teddyland (Rothenburg), 251
Telephones, 667–668
Tennis
Baden-Baden, 407
Frankfurt, 463
Hamburg, 620
Terner (Hannover), 576
Thaliatheater (Hamburg), 614
Theater Aachen, 509
Theater 99 Akut (Aachen), 509
Theater am Goetheplatz
Baden-Baden, 405
Bremen, 584
Theater am Leibnitzplatz (Bremen), 584
Theatercafé (Konstanz), 374
Theater Combinale (Lübeck), 635
Theater der Stadt
Frankfurt, 459
Heidelberg, 418
Theater des Westens (Berlin), 124
Theater im ScharfrichterHaus (Passau), 228
Theater im Schnoor (Bremen), 585
Theater Junge Generation (Dresden), 193
Theater-Kasse (Bonn), 504
Theatinerkirche (Munich), 290
Theatrium (Bremen), 585
Thermen (Berlin), 133
Thick Tower (Heidelberg), 414

Thiersch Antiquitäten (Weimar), 163
Thimble Museum (Creglingen), 246–247
Thomanerchor (Leipzig), 173
Thomas-i-Punkt (Hamburg), 613
Thomaskirche (Leipzig), 173
Thorbräu (Augsburg), 263
Thuringer Wald, 164
Thuringia, 47–48
Thyssen-Haus (Düsseldorf), 528
Tiergarten (Berlin), 72, 102–103, 132
sights and attractions around, 83–87
Tierpark Sababurg, 567
Tigerpalast (Frankfurt), 460
Times Bar (Berlin), 129
Tipping, 668
Titisee, 390–392
Todtnau, 387
Toilets, 668
Tom's Bar (Berlin), 132
Tom's Saloon & Tom's Dancehall (Hamburg), 619
Tonhalle (Düsseldorf), 532
Töpferladen Irene Herold (Bamberg), 208
Topography of Terror (Berlin), 95
Torhalle (Frauenchiemsee), 343
Tourismus Centrale (Hamburg), 614
Tours, 44–46
Town Hall. See Rathaus
Toy Museum (Spielzeugmuseum)
Munich, 299
Nürnberg, 217
Traben-Trarbach, 541–542
Train travel, 650–653
Travel insurance, 662
Treibhaus (Nürnberg), 219
Treykorn (Berlin), 121
Trianon (Frankfurt), 449
Triberg, 392–395
Triebel (Berlin), 121
Trier, 545–551
Trier Cathedral, 547
Trinity Church (Speyer), 482
Trinkhalle (Pump Room; Baden-Baden), 403
Trip-cancellation insurance, 662
Trippen (Berlin), 123
Tritschler (Stuttgart), 432
Tübingen, 49–50, 435–438
TUFA (Trier), 549
Turm Katzenbuckl, 425

U

Überlingen, 377–379
U-Boot 995 (Kiel), 638
Uhland-Passage (Berlin), 117
Ulm, 230–234
Ulmer Museum, 232
Ulm Münster, 232–233
Universität Leipzig, 174
Universität Leipzig Turm, 174
Unter den Linden (Rothenburg), 251

V

Vereinigte Hospitien (Trier), 547
Verkehrszentrum (Transportation Center; Theresienhöhe), 295–296
Veste Oberhaus (Passau), 227
Victoria Bar (Berlin), 129
Victory Column (Siegessäule; Berlin), 102
Viking River Cruises, 482
Villa Grisebach Auktionen (Berlin), 118
Villa rentals, 657
Villeroy & Boch (Nürnberg), 218
Visitor information, 668
Vonderau Museum (Fulda), 558

W

Wagner, Richard, 33, 35, 268
   Bayreuth, 201
   Bayreuther Festspiele, 204
   Festival (Bayreuth), 42
Walderdorffs (Trier), 549–550
Wallanlagen (Bremen), 582
Wallfahrtskirche at Birnau (near Meersburg), 369
Wallfahrtskirche Maria in der Tanne (Triberg), 394
Wallraf-Richartz Museum/ Foundation Corboud (Cologne), 515
Wallringpark (Hamburg), 608
Walpurgis Festivals, 42
Walter Steiger Schuhe (Düsseldorf), 532
Wank, 349
Wannsee (Berlin), 133
Wasserfälle Gutach (Triberg), 393
Watergate Club (Berlin), 126
Weihnachtsland am Zwinger (Dresden), 192
Weihnachtsmarkt (Dresden), 192
Weihnachtswerkstatt (Christmas Workshop; Rothenburg), 251
Weikersheim, 245–246
Weill, Kurt, 33, 36
Weimar, 154–162
Weimar Republic, 17

Weinfest (Cochem), 536
Weingarten, 381–382
Weingarten Basilica, 381–382
Weingut Probsthof (Neustadt-an-der-Weinstrasse), 487–488
Weinhaus (Miltenberg), 243
Wein Museum (Wine Museum; Speyer), 482
Weinstrasse, Deutsche (German Wine Road), 487
Weinstube Löwen (Meersburg), 370
Weinstuben Juliusspital (Würzburg), 240
Weltkulturerbe Rammelsberg (near Goslar), 595
Wempe Juwelier (Düsseldorf), 532
Werkraum (Munich), 318
Werner Scherer (Berlin), 121
Wertheim (Berlin), 120
Weserbergland Festhalle (Hameln), 571
Westerbachstrasse (Höxter), 568
Wheelchair accessibility, 660
White-Trash (Berlin), 126
White-water rafting, 332
Wiesbaden, 472–475
Wieskirche (between Ammer and Lech), 266–267
Wies'n Tracht & Mehr (Munich), 315
Wikinger Museum Haithabu (Schleswig), 641
Wild at Heart (Berlin), 127
Wildenburg Castle (Amorbach), 244
Wilhelmshöhe Park (Kassel), 562–563
Willing Workers on Organic Farms, 44
Willkomm-Höft (Welcome Point; Hamburg), 607
Wine Fair (Mainz), 490
Wines, 39–41
   Deutsche Weinstrasse (German Wine Road), 487–489
   Mosel, 536

Wine Vat Building (Heidelberg), 415
Winter Dom (Hamburg), 43
Wintergarten Varieté (Berlin), 125
Winzerstube zum Becher (Meersburg), 370
Wittumspalais (Weimar), 160–161
Wittwer (Stuttgart), 432
Wochenmarkt (Bonn), 503
Woodcarvings, 355
World War I, 17
World War II, 20
   Berlin art collections and, 78
   Topography of Terror (Berlin), 95
Worms, 484–489
Wunderbar (Regensburg), 224
Wurst (sausage), 38
Würzburg, 236–242

Y

Youth hostels, 658

Z

Zavelstein, 399
Zell an der Mosel, 539–541
Zeltmusik festival (Freiburg), 388
Zeppelinfeld arena (Nürnberg), 211
Zeppelin-Museum (Friedrichshafen), 366
Zollpackhof (Berlin), 128
Zoologischer Garten Berlin (Berlin Zoo-Aquarium), 102, 103
Zoologischer Garten Leipzig, 173
Zugspitze, 349–350
Zum Pitter (Cologne), 521
Zum Roten Ochsen (Heidelberg), 419
Zum Sepp'l (Heidelberg), 419
Zum Wasserweibchen (Bad Homburg), 478
Zwinger (Dresden), 188